Britain

**Bryn Thomas
Tom Smallman
Pat Yale**

LONELY PLANET PUBLICATIONS
Melbourne • Oakland • London • Paris

BRITAIN

SHETLAND ISLANDS

Lerwick

Foula

ORKNEY ISLANDS

Stromness

Thurso

John o'Groats

ORKNEY & SHETLAND ISLANDS
for brilliant birdwatching

100 km

50 miles

Elevation

	1000m (3250 ft)
	500m (1625 ft)
	200m (650 ft)
	100m (325 ft)
	0
	Below Sea Level

DURHAM
fantastic Norman cathedral
on a dramatic site

EDINBURGH
visit in August when the
festival season is at its peak

NORTH SEA

Peterhead

Aberdeen

Montrose

Arbroath

Dundee

St Andrews

Perth

Stirling

Kirkaldy

EDINBURGH

Motherwell

GLASGOW

Kilmarnock

Ayr

Sanquhar

Dumfries

Stranraer

Arran

Firth of Clyde

North Channel

Larne

BELFAST

NORTHERN IRELAND

Derry

Berwick-upon-Tweed

Dunbar

Galashiels

Jedburgh

Cheviot Hills

Carlisle

Lake District

Workington

Whitehaven

Windermere

Newcastle Upon Tyne

Sunderland

Hartlepool

Middlesbrough

Darlington

Durham

Ashington

North York Moors

Pennines

Eden

Tees

SCOTLAND

Elgin

Inverness

Aviemore

Fort William

Oban

Mull

DUNCAN

WEST HIGHLAND RAILWAY
take the train through some of
Scotland's most dramatic scenery

LAKE DISTRICT
largest national park in Britain

Wick

Thurso

Stromness

ORKNEY ISLANDS
See Orkney Islands
inset

Ullapool

Kyle of
Lochalsh

Skye

Rum

Lewis

North Uist

South Uist

St Kilda

OUTER HEBRIDES

INNER HEBRIDES

Coll

Tiree

Colonsay

Jura

Islay

ATLANTIC OCEAN

North Minch

Loch Ness

Moray Firth

Grampian Mountains

North West Highlands

Firth of Forth

Southern Uplands

Solway Firth

58°N

56°N

60°N

59°N

8°W

6°W

4°W

2°W

0°

2°E

1°W

1°W

3°W

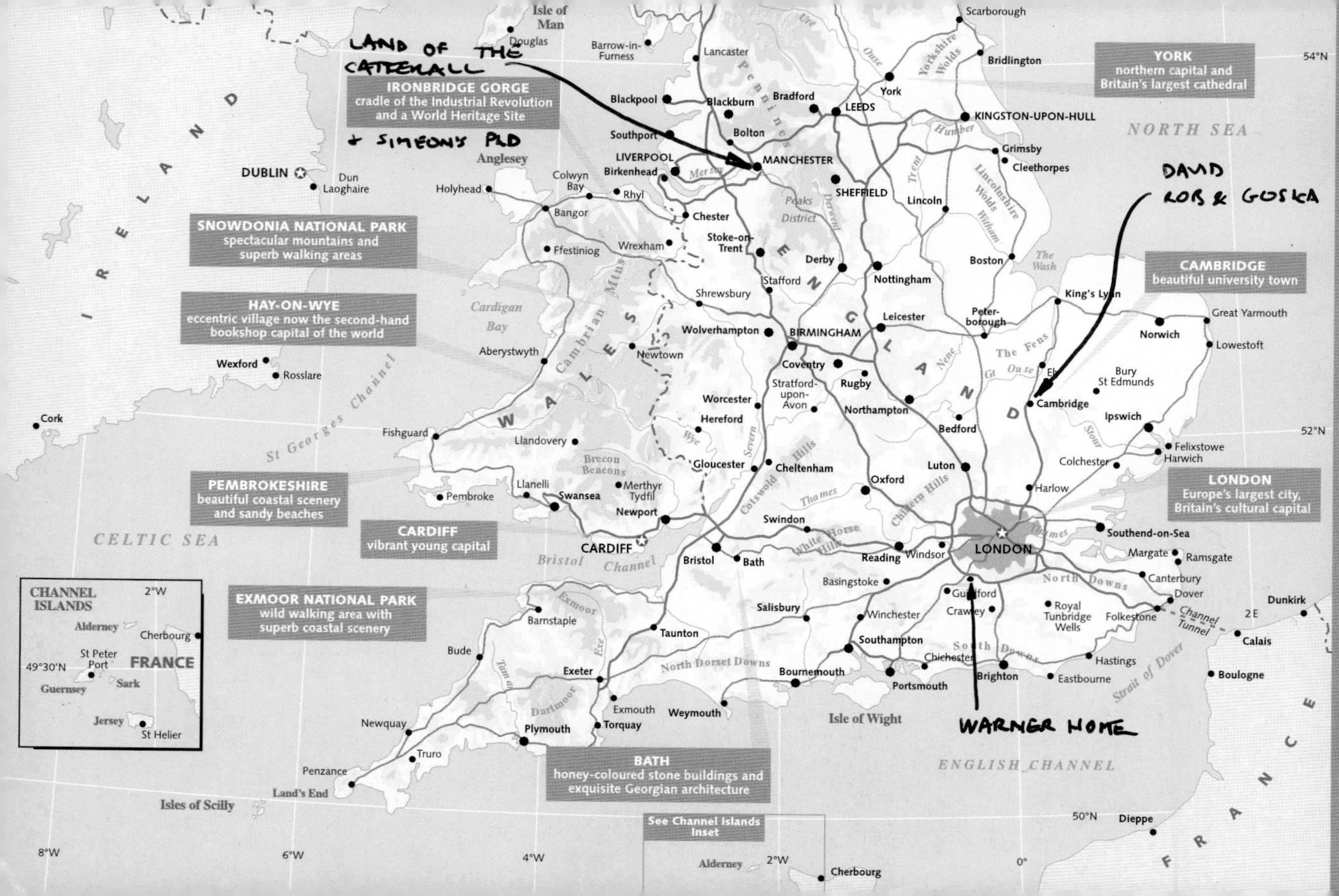

Handwritten annotations:

DAVID LOIS & GOSIA

WARNER HOME

LAND OF THE CATTERVALL + SIMEON'S PAD

Map callout boxes:

YORK
northern capital and Britain's largest cathedral

CAMBRIDGE
beautiful university town

LONDON
Europe's largest city, Britain's cultural capital

IRONBRIDGE GORGE
cradle of the Industrial Revolution and a World Heritage Site

SNOWDONIA NATIONAL PARK
spectacular mountains and superb walking areas

HAY-ON-WYE
eccentric village now the second-hand bookshop capital of the world

PEMBROKESHIRE
beautiful coastal scenery and sandy beaches

CARDIFF
vibrant young capital

EXMOOR NATIONAL PARK
wild walking area with superb coastal scenery

BATH
honey-coloured stone buildings and exquisite Georgian architecture

See Channel Islands inset

CHANNEL ISLANDS
FRANCE
49°30'N
St Peter Port
Alderney   Cherbourg
Sark
Guernsey   Jersey   St Helier
2°W

Seas and water bodies:

NORTH SEA

ENGLISH CHANNEL

CELTIC SEA

St George's Channel

Cardigan Bay

Bristol Channel

Strait of Dover

Channel Tunnel

Regions:

ENGLAND

WALES

IRELAND

FRANCE

Cambrian Mtns

Brecon Beacons

Pennines

Yorkshire Wolds

Lincolnshire Wolds

The Fens

The Wash

Cotswolds

North Wessex Downs

North Downs

South Downs

Chiltern Hills

Peak District

North Dorset Downs

Cities and towns:

Dunkirk, Calais, Boulogne, Dieppe, Cherbourg

York, Scarborough, Bridlington, Kingston-upon-Hull, Grimsby, Cleethorpes, Lincoln, Boston, Leeds, Bradford, Lancaster, Blackpool, Blackburn, Bolton, Southport, Liverpool, Birkenhead, Manchester, Sheffield, Chester, Stoke-on-Trent, Stafford, Shrewsbury, Derby, Nottingham, Leicester, Rugby, Coventry, Birmingham, Wolverhampton, Worcester, Hereford, Gloucester, Stratford-upon-Avon, Cheltenham, Northampton, Bedford, Oxford, Swindon, Reading, Luton, Harlow, Colchester, Ipswich, Bury St Edmunds, Norwich, Great Yarmouth, Lowestoft, King's Lynn, Peterborough, Ely, Cambridge, London, Windsor, Guildford, Crawley, Basingstoke, Winchester, Southampton, Portsmouth, Isle of Wight, Bournemouth, Weymouth, Salisbury, Bath, Bristol, Newport, Cardiff, Swansea, Llanelli, Merthyr Tydfil, Llandovery, Aberystwyth, Newtown, Wrexham, Rhyl, Colwyn Bay, Bangor, Holyhead, Ffestiniog, Fishguard, Pembroke, Anglesey, Isle of Man, Douglas, Barrow-in-Furness, Bradford, Taunton, Exeter, Barnstaple, Bude, Newquay, Truro, Penzance, Land's End, Torquay, Exmouth, Plymouth, Isles of Scilly

Southend-on-Sea, Felixstowe, Harwich, Margate, Ramsgate, Dover, Canterbury, Royal Tunbridge Wells, Hastings, Eastbourne, Brighton, Chichester, Folkestone

Dublin, Dun Laoghaire, Wexford, Rosslare, Cork

Rivers:

Aire, Ouse, Humber, Trent, Derwent, Witham, Nene, Gt Ouse, Stour, Thames, Severn, Wye, Avon, Exe, Tamar, Tame

54°N, 52°N, 50°N

2°E, 0°, 2°W, 4°W, 6°W, 8°W

Britain
3rd edition – April 1999
First published – April 1995

Published by
Lonely Planet Publications Pty Ltd A.C.N. 005 607 983
192 Burwood Rd, Hawthorn, Victoria 3122, Australia

Lonely Planet Offices
Australia PO Box 617, Hawthorn, Victoria 3122
USA 150 Linden St, Oakland, CA 94607
UK 10a Spring Place, London NW5 3BH
France 1 rue du Dahomey, 75011 Paris

Photographs
Many of the images in this guide are available for licensing from
Lonely Planet Images.
email: lpi@lonelyplanet.com.au

Front cover photograph
Late night traffic on the Tower Bridge, London
(Richard I'Anson, Lonely Planet Images)

ISBN 0 86442 578 3

Contents – Text

THE AUTHORS   **11**

THIS BOOK   **13**

FOREWORD   **14**

INTRODUCTION   **17**

REGIONAL FACTS FOR THE VISITOR   18

Highlights 18
Suggested Itineraries 23
Planning 23
Tourist Offices 25
Visas & Documents 26
Embassies & Consulates 29
Customs 30
Money 30
Post & Communications 33
Internet Resources 35
Books 35
Films 36
Media 36

Photography & Video 38
Time 38
Electricity 38
Weights & Measures 38
Laundry 39
Toilets 39
Health 39
Women Travellers 41
Gay & Lesbian Travellers 42
Disabled Travellers 42
Senior Travellers 43
Travel with Children 43
Useful Organisations 44

Dangers & Annoyances 44
Legal Matters 45
Business Hours 46
Public Holidays & Special
Events 46
Courses 47
Work 47
Accommodation 49
Food 54
Drinks 56
Entertainment 57
Spectator Sports 58
Shopping 60

ACTIVITIES   61

Walking 61
Cycling 69
Golf 75
Tracing Your Ancestors 75

Surfing & Swimming 77
Fishing 78
Horse Riding & Pony ....s
Trekking 78

Canal & Waterway Travel 79
Skiing 81
Steam Railways 82

GETTING THERE & AWAY   83

Air 83
Land 90

Sea 93
Departure Taxes 97

Organised Tours 97

GETTING AROUND THE REGION   98

Air 98
Bus 99
Train 102

Car & Motorcycle 110
Bicycle 116
Walking 117

Boat 117
Organised Tours 117
Taxi 117

FACTS ABOUT ENGLAND   121

History 124
Geography 133
Climate 134
Ecology & Environment 134
Flora & Fauna 135

Government & Politics 138
Economy 138
Population & People 140
Education 140
Arts 141

Architecture 144
Society & Conduct 150
Religion 152
Language 153

LONDON   154

History 155
Orientation 155

Information 158
Walking Tour 178

River Tours 180
Canal Tour 182

Bus Routes 182
Bus Tours 182
West End 182
Covent Garden 185
Westminster.........................185
Bloomsbury 191
Holborn & Embankment 193
Marylebone & Regent's
Park 195

The City.........................196
The East End 199
Docklands 200
Chelsea, Kensington &
Earl's Court 202
Hyde Park, Notting Hill &
Bayswater 204
North London 205
Greenwich 206

South London 208
West London 210
Places to Stay 211
Places to Eat 222
Entertainment 233
Spectator Sports 240
Shopping 241
Getting There & Away 245
Getting Around 247

SOUTH-EASTERN ENGLAND   249

Berkshire 251
Windsor & Eton 251
Surrey 256
Kent 257
Canterbury 257
Around Canterbury 265
Margate 265
Broadstairs 265
Ramsgate 266
Sandwich 266
Dover 268
Folkestone 272
Romney Marsh & Around ..272
Ashford 272
Sissinghurst Castle Gardens ..272
Hever 273

Chartwell 273
Knole House 273
Ightham Mote 274
Leeds Castle 274
East Sussex 274
Rye 275
Battle 277
Hastings 278
Beachy Head 282
Charleston Farmhouse 282
Glyndebourne 282
Newhaven 282
Lewes 283
Brighton 286
West Sussex 290
Arundel 291

Chichester 291
Around Chichester 294
Hampshire 294
Winchester 295
Around Winchester 301
Portsmouth 301
Southampton 306
New Forest 306
Isle of Wight 309
Newport & Carisbrooke
Castle 309
Cowes & Osborne House ..309
Ryde to Ventnor 309
Ventnor to Alum Bay 311
The Needles & Alum Bay ..311

SOUTH-WESTERN ENGLAND   313

Dorset 317
Bournemouth & Poole 317
Around Bournemouth &
Poole 318
South-East Dorset 319
Dorchester 322
Around Dorchester 323
Weymouth 324
Weymouth to Lyme Regis ..327
Lyme Regis 328
Around Lyme Regis 329
Sherborne 330
Shaftesbury 331
Wiltshire 331
Salisbury 331
Around Salisbury 338
Stonehenge 338
Around Stonehenge 340
Stourhead 341
Longleat 342

Bradford-on-Avon 343
Chippenham & Around 344
Devizes 346
Avebury 346
Around Avebury 348
Marlborough 349
Malmesbury 349
Bristol & Bath 350
Bristol 350
Bath 357
Around Bath 365
Somerset 365
Wells 366
Mendip Hills 369
Glastonbury 371
Quantock Hills 374
Taunton 375
Montacute House 375
Exmoor National Park 376
Dulverton 378

Dunster 379
Minehead 379
Exford 380
Porlock 380
Lynton & Lynmouth 381
Devon 382
Exeter 382
Around Exeter 388
South Devon Coast 388
Plymouth 390
Around Plymouth 394
North Devon 395
Dartmoor National Park 396
Princetown 400
Postbridge 401
Buckfastleigh 402
Widecombe-in-the-Moor ..402
Moretonhampstead & Steps
Bridge 403
Chagford 403

Castle Drogo 403
Okehampton 403
Lydford 404
Tavistock 405
Cornwall **405**

South-East Cornwall 406
Truro 409
Roseland Peninsula 410
South-West Cornwall 410
Penzance 411

West Cornwall 413
Newquay 419
North Cornwall 421
Isles of Scilly 422

THE MIDLANDS
426

Oxfordshire **427**
Oxford 427
Woodstock & Blenheim
Palace 436
Oxfordshire Cotswolds 437
South of Oxford 438
Henley-on-Thames 439
Around Henley-on-Thames 440
Gloucestershire **440**
North Cotswolds 441
South Cotswolds 446
Cirencester 448
Gloucester 450
Cheltenham 453
Tewkesbury 457
The Forest of Dean 458
Newent 459
Herefordshire &
Worcestershire **459**
Hereford 460
Ross-on-Wye 462
Around Ross-on-Wye 463
Great Malvern 463
Worcester 464
Around Worcester 467
Vale of Evesham 467
Warwickshire & Coventry ..**468**
Coventry 468
Warwick 470

Around Warwick 472
Stratford-upon-Avon 473
Around Stratford-upon-Avon ..478
Birmingham **479**
Around Birmingham 484
Northamptonshire **485**
Northampton 485
Around Northampton 485
Buckinghamshire **486**
Aylesbury 487
Around Aylesbury 487
Chiltern Hills 487
Bedfordshire **488**
Bedford 488
Woburn Abbey & Safari Park ..490
Whipsnade 490
Hertfordshire **490**
St Albans 490
Hatfield House 492
Knebworth House 492
Shaw's Corner 492
Leicestershire **493**
Leicester 493
Around Leicester 496
Shropshire **497**
Shrewsbury 497
Around Shrewsbury 502
Ironbridge Gorge 502
Wenlock Edge 505

The Long Mynd & Church
Stretton 505
Bishop's Castle 506
Clun 506
Ludlow 506
Stokesay Castle 507
Staffordshire **508**
Lichfield 508
Stoke-on-Trent 509
Around Stoke-on-Trent 510
Derbyshire **511**
Derby 511
Around Derby 511
Chesterfield 512
Around Chesterfield 512
Peak District **513**
Bakewell 516
Around Bakewell 518
Eyam 519
Castleton 519
Edale 521
Hayfield 522
Buxton 522
Around Buxton 524
Matlock & Matlock Bath ...524
Nottinghamshire **524**
Nottingham 525
Around Nottingham 529

EASTERN ENGLAND
531

Essex **533**
Colchester 533
Harwich 534
Dedham Vale 534
Thaxted & Saffron Walden ..535
Audley End House 535
Suffolk **535**
Ipswich 535
Stour Valley 536
Lavenham 537
Bury St Edmunds 537

Around Bury St Edmunds ..539
Suffolk Coast 539
Norfolk **540**
Norwich 540
Around Norwich 544
Norfolk Broads 544
Norfolk Coast 545
King's Lynn 546
Around King's Lynn 549
Cambridgeshire **549**
Cambridge 549

Around Cambridge 560
Ely 561
Peterborough 563
Lincolnshire **563**
Lincoln 564
Grantham 568
Stamford 568
Around Stamford 569
Boston 569
Skegness 569

NORTH-WESTERN ENGLAND 571

Cheshire 571
Chester 571
Manchester 578
Merseyside 587
Liverpool 587
Isle of Man 596
Douglas 596
Lancashire 598
Lancaster 598
Blackpool 599
Cumbria 601
Carlisle 601
Cockermouth 605
Lake District National Park ..608
Windermere & Bowness 610
Ambleside 614
Grasmere & Wordsworth
Country 614
Coniston 616
Cumbrian Coast Line 617
Ulverston 617
Keswick 618
Around Keswick 621

NORTH-EASTERN ENGLAND 622

Leeds & Bradford 625
Leeds 625
Harewood House 629
Bradford 630
Haworth 630
Hebden Bridge &
Heptonstall 632
Sheffield & Around 634
Sheffield 634
East Riding of Yorkshire 636
Hull 636
Beverley 637
North Yorkshire 638
York 639
Castle Howard 649
North York Moors NP 650
Helmsley 652
Around Helmsley 654
Thirsk & Around 655
Danby 655
Staithes 656
Whitby 656
Cook Country 661
Robin Hood's Bay 661
Scarborough 662
Pickering 665
North Yorkshire Moors
Railway 665
Yorkshire Dales NP 666
Leeds-Settle-Carlisle Line ..669
Skipton 669
Grassington 670
Settle & Around 670
Kirkby Lonsdale 671
Kirkby Stephen 671
Richmond 672
Fountains Abbey & Studley
Royal Water Garden 674
Harrogate 675
Durham & Around 677
Durham 678
Beamish Open Air Museum ..682
Barnard Castle 682
Around Barnard Castle 683
Newcastle upon Tyne 683
Northumberland 688
Warkworth 688
Alnwick 688
Farne Islands 689
Bamburgh 689
Holy Island (Lindisfarne) 690
Berwick-upon-Tweed 690
Hadrian's Wall 692
Corbridge 694
Hexham 694
Hexham to Haltwhistle 695
Haltwhistle 696
Haltwhistle to Brampton 696
Northumberland NP 697
Bellingham 698

FACTS ABOUT SCOTLAND 701

History 703
Geography & Geology 709
Climate 710
Ecology & Environment 710
Flora & Fauna 711
Government & Politics 712
Economy 713
Population & People 713
Education 714
Arts 714
Sciences 716
Society & Conduct 717
Religion 719
Language 719

FACTS FOR THE VISITOR 720

Planning 720
Tourist Offices 720
Visas & Documents 721
Consulates 721
Money 721
Books 721
Internet Resources 722
Media 723
Useful Organisations 723
Dangers & Annoyances 723
Business Hours 724
Public Holidays 724
Accommodation 724
Food 725
Drinks 727
Entertainment 727
Shopping 728

GETTING THERE & AWAY 730

Air 730
Land 730
Sea 730

GETTING AROUND

73

Passes 732
Air 732
Bus 732
Train 733
Car & Motorcycle 734
Hitching 734
Boat 734

EDINBURGH

735

History 735
Orientation 736
Information 737
Royal Mile 737
South of the Royal Mile 746
Calton Hill 747
New Town 748
West End 749
North of the New Town 749
Bus Tours 750
Special Events 750
Places to Stay 750
Places to Eat 753
Entertainment 755
Getting There & Away 757
Getting Around 757
Around Edinburgh 759

SOUTHERN SCOTLAND

762

Scottish Borders 766
Coldstream 766
Kelso 767
Around Kelso 769
Melrose 769
Around Melrose 770
Galashiels 771
Selkirk 771
Jedburgh 771
Peebles 772
Around Peebles 772
Hermitage Castle 773
Glasgow 773
Around Glasgow 790
Paisley 790
Firth of Clyde 790
Greenock 790
Gourock 790
Lanarkshire 790
Blantyre 791
Lanark & New Lanark 791
Ayrshire 792
North Ayrshire 792
Isle of Arran 792
South Ayrshire 796
Dumfries & Galloway 799
Dumfries 800
Around Dumfries 801
New Galloway & Around ..801
Castle Douglas & Around ..801
Kirkcudbright 802
Gatehouse of Fleet 803
Newton Stewart 803
Wigtown 803
Whithorn 803
Isle of Whithorn 804
Portpatrick 804
Stranraer & Cairnryan 804
Around Stranraer 806

CENTRAL SCOTLAND

807

Argyll & Bute 810
Isle of Bute 811
Loch Lomond 812
Inveraray 813
Kilmartin Glen 814
Kintyre 814
Isle of Islay 815
Isle of Jura 816
Isle of Colonsay 817
Oban & Around 817
Isle of Mull 820
Around Mull 822
Isle of Coll 823
Isle of Tiree 823
Stirling & Around 823
Stirling 824
Around Stirling 829
The Trossachs 829
North Central Region 831
Fife 831
West Fife 832
South Coast 833
Central Fife 833
St Andrews 834
Around St Andrews 839
East Neuk 840
Perthshire & Kinross 841
Kinross & Loch Leven 841
Perth 842
Strathearn 844
Perth to Aviemore 845
West Perthshire 847
Dundee & Angus 847
Dundee 847
Glamis Castle 852
Arbroath 853
Aberdeenshire & Moray 853
Aberdeen 854
Deeside & Donside 860
Inland Aberdeenshire &
Moray 862
Grampian Coast 862

HIGHLANDS & NORTHERN ISLANDS

865

The Cairngorms 869
Aviemore 870
Around Aviemore 873
Grantown-on-Spey 874
Kingussie 874
Kingussie to Fort William ..875
The Great Glen 876
Fort William 876
Fort William to Glen Coe ..880

Glen Coe 880
Fort Willam to Fort
Augustus 882
Fort Augustus 882
Loch Ness 883
Drumnadrochit 883
Inverness 884
Around Inverness 888
East Coast 890
Dingwall to Bonar Bridge ..890
Dornoch 890
Dunrobin Castle 890
Brora & Helmsdale 891
Helmsdale to Latheron 892
Celtic Sites 892
Wick 892
John o'Groats 893
Dunnet Head 894
North & West Coast 894
Thurso & Scrabster 894
Thurso to Durness 896
Durness 896

Durness to Ullapool 897
Ullapool 898
Ullapool to Kyle of
Lochalsh 899
Plockton 900
Kyle of Lochalsh 901
Kyle to the Great Glen 901
Road to the Isles 901
Mallaig 901
The Interior 902
Isle of Skye 902
Portree 903
Kyleakin 904
Kylerhea 904
Armadale 904
Broadford 904
The Cuillins & Minginish
Peninsula 905
North-West Skye 905
Trotternish Peninsula 905
Uig 905
Isle of Raasay 906

Outer Hebrides 906
Lewis 911
Harris 913
North Uist 915
Benbecula 915
South Uist 916
Barra 916
Orkney Islands 916
Kirkwall 918
West & North Mainland 921
East Mainland, Burray &
South Ronaldsay 924
Hoy 925
Northern Islands 926
Shetland Islands 929
Lerwick 932
Around Lerwick 935
South Mainland 935
North Mainland 936
Yell & Unst 936
Other Islands 936

FACTS ABOUT WALES

History 939
Geography 944
Climate 944
Ecology & Environment 944
Flora & Fauna 945

Government & Politics 946
Economy 946
Population & People 947
Education 947
Arts 947

Society & Conduct 948
Religion 949
Language 950

FACTS FOR THE VISITOR

Highlights 951
Suggested Itineraries 951
Planning 951
Responsible Tourism 951
Tourist Offices 951
Visas & Documents 952
Money 952

Internet Resources 952
Books 952
Newspapers & Magazines ..952
Radio & TV 953
Useful Organisations 953
Dangers & Annoyances 954
Business Hours & Public

Holidays 954
Activities 954
Accommodation 955
Food 955
Drinks 956
Entertainment 956
Shopping 957

GETTING THERE & AWAY

Air 958

Land 958

Sea 958

GETTING AROUND

Bus 959
Train 959

Car & Motorcycle 959
Bicycle 960

Hitching 960
Boat 960

SOUTH WALES

South-Eastern Wales 962
Cardiff 963

Around Cardiff 970
Wye Valley 972

Chepstow 973
Swansea 974

Gower Peninsula 978
Carmarthen 979
Laugharne 980
Pembrokeshire Coast
National Park 980

Tenby 984
Around Tenby 985
Pembroke 986
Haverfordwest 987
St Brides Bay 988

St David's 989
St David's to Fishguard 991
Fishguard 992
Newport 993
Around Newport 994

MID WALES 996

Brecon Beacons National
Park 996
Brecon 1001
Brecon to Abergavenny ..1004
Abergavenny 1004
Around Abergavenny 1005

Abergavenny to
Hay-on-Wye 1006
Powys 1009
Llanwrtyd Wells 1009
Llandrindod Wells 1010
Knighton 1010

Welshpool 1010
Machynlleth 1011
Ceredigion 1012
Cardigan 1012
Aberystwyth 1013
Around Aberystwyth 1016

NORTH WALES 1017

North-Eastern Wales 1018
Wrexham 1018
Llangollen 1018
Snowdonia
National Park 1021
Betws-y-Coed 1026
Capel Curig 1027
Llanberis 1027
Beddgelert 1030

Blaenau Ffestiniog 1030
Harlech 1031
Barmouth 1032
Tywyn 1032
Dolgellau 1032
Bala 1033
North-Western Wales 1033
Llandudno 1034
Conwy 1036

Bangor 1038
Around Bangor 1039
Caernarfon 1039
Anglesey (Ynys Môn) 1041
Llŷn Peninsula 1042
Porthmadog 1043
Portmeirion 1044

THE CHANNEL ISLANDS 1047

Jersey 1048
Guernsey 1049

Alderney 1050
Sark 1051

Herm 1051

LANGUAGE 1053

Scottish Gaelic 1053   Welsh 1054

GLOSSARY 1056

GLOSSARY OF RELIGIOUS ARCHITECTURE 1059

ACKNOWLEDGMENTS 1061

INDEX 1071

Text 1071   Boxed Text 1079

MAP LEGEND back page

METRIC CONVERSION inside back cover

Contents – Maps

INTRODUCTION

Britain 17

REGIONAL FACTS FOR THE VISITOR

Britain County Boundaries 20

GETTING AROUND THE REGION

British Railways 103   Motorways, Airports & Seaports..115

FACTS ABOUT ENGLAND

England Chapter Divisions ..121   England 122

LONDON

London Postcodes 156   Colour Maps 161   South Bank Arts Complex ..209

SOUTH-EASTERN ENGLAND

South-Eastern England 250   Rye 276   Winchester..........................295
Windsor & Eton 252   Hastings..............................280   Portsmouth 303
St George's Chapel 254   Lewes 284   New Forest 307
Canterbury...........................259   Brighton...............................287   Isle of Wight 310
Dover...................................269   Chichester 292

SOUTH-WESTERN ENGLAND

South-Western England 314   Avebury 347   Dartmoor National Park 397
Weymouth............................325   Bristol 352   Penzance 412
Lyme Regis 329   Bath....................................359   West Cornwall 414
Salisbury 333   Wells 366   St Ives 417
Stonehenge 339   Glastonbury 371   Newquay 420
Around Stonehenge &   Exmoor National Park 376   Isles of Scilly......................423
Avebury..............................342   Exeter 383
Bradford-on-Avon 343   Plymouth 392

THE MIDLANDS

Oxford.................................429   Stratford-upon-Avon 474   Peak District........................514
The Cotswolds 443   Birmingham 480   Bakewell 517
Gloucester 450   Leicester..............................494   Castleton & Edale 521
Cheltenham 455   Shrewsbury 498   Buxton.................................523
Warwick 471   Ironbridge Gorge 503   Nottingham 526

EASTERN ENGLAND

Eastern England 532   King's Lynn 547   Ely 562
Norwich...............................541   Cambridge 551   Lincoln................................565

NORTH-WESTERN ENGLAND

North-Western England 572   Isle of Man 597   Windermere & Bowness......611
Chester 574   Carlisle................................603   Keswick 619
Manchester 580   Cockermouth 606
Liverpool 588   Lake District National Park ..609

NORTH-EASTERN ENGLAND

North-Eastern England 624
Leeds 626
Haworth 631
Sheffield..............................635
York.....................................640
York Minster 642

North York Moors NP 651
Helmsley 653
Whitby................................657
Scarborough 663
Yorkshire Dales NP 668
Richmond 673

Harrogate 676
Durham 679
Durham Cathedral 680
Newcastle upon Tyne..........684
Berwick-upon-Tweed..........691
Northumberland NP...........697

FACTS ABOUT SCOTLAND

Scotland Chapters 701

Scotland.............................702

EDINBURGH

Central Edinburgh 738

Greater Edinburgh 758-9

SOUTHERN SCOTLAND

Southern Scotland 764
Kelso 768

Glasgow..............................774
Arran 793

Stranraer 805

CENTRAL SCOTLAND

Central Scotland...................808
Islay & Jura 816
Mull, Coll & Tiree................822

Stirling 825
St Andrews 835
Perth 842

Dundee 850
Aberdeen............................855

HIGHLANDS & NORTHERN ISLANDS

Highlands & Northern
Islands 866
The Cairngorms 869
Fort William 877
Inverness 885

Thurso 895
Ullapool 898
Portree................................903
Skye, Small Isles & Outer
Hebrides 907

Orkney Islands....................917
Kirkwall 919
Stromness 922
Shetland Islands..................930
Lerwick 933

FACTS ABOUT WALES

Wales Chapters 939

Wales..................................940

SOUTH WALES

Cardiff 964
Swansea...............................975

Pembrokeshire Coast NP 981
Fishguard............................992

MID WALES

Brecon Beacons NP 998
Brecon 1002

Hay-on-Wye 1008
Aberystwyth 1014

NORTH WALES

Llangollen 1019
Snowdonia NP 1022

Llandudno 1034
Conwy..............................1037

CHANNEL ISLANDS

Channel Islands 1048

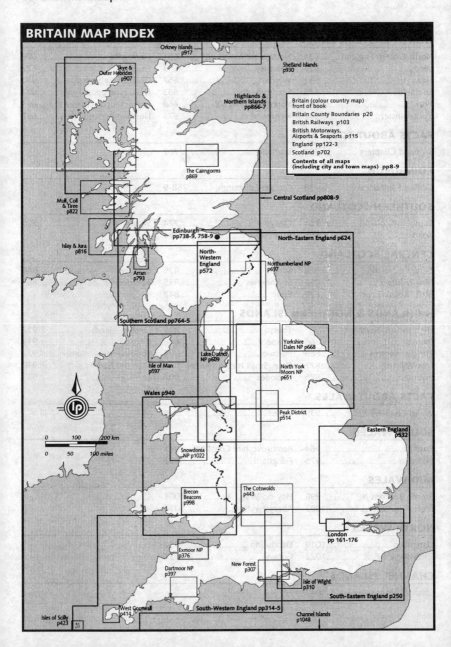

BRITAIN MAP INDEX

Orkney Islands p917

Shetland Islands p930

Skye & Outer Hebrides p907

Highlands & Northern Islands pp866-7

Britain (colour country map) front of book
Britain County Boundaries p20
British Railways p103
British Motorways, Airports & Seaports p115
England pp122-3
Scotland p702
Contents of all maps (including city and town maps) pp8-9

The Cairngorms p869

Mull, Coll & Tiree p822

Central Scotland pp808-9

Islay & Jura p816

Edinburgh pp738-9, 758-9

North-Eastern England p624

North-Western England p572

Northumberland NP p697

Arran p793

Southern Scotland pp764-5

Yorkshire Dales NP p668

Isle of Man p597

Lake District NP p609

North York Moors NP p651

Wales p940

Peak District p514

Eastern England p532

Snowdonia NP p1022

Brecon Beacons p998

The Cotswolds p443

London pp 161-176

Exmoor NP p376

New Forest p307

Dartmoor NP p397

Isle of Wight p310

West Cornwall p414

South-Western England pp314-5

South-Eastern England p250

Isles of Scilly p423

Channel Islands p1048

0   100   200 km
0   50   100 miles

The Authors

Bryn Thomas
Although his roots are in Llanelli, South Wales, Bryn was born in Zimbabwe where he grew up on a farm. During camping holidays by the Indian Ocean in Mozambique he contracted an incurable case of wanderlust. An anthropology degree at Durham University in England earned him a job polishing the leaves of pot plants in London. He has also been a ski-lift operator in Colorado, encyclopaedia seller in South Dakota, and an English teacher in Cairo, Singapore and Tokyo. Travel on six continents has included a 2500km Andean cycling trip and numerous visits to India and Nepal. Bryn's first guide, the Trans-Siberian Handbook, was shortlisted for the Thomas Cook Guidebook of the Year awards. He is also co-author of Lonely Planet's India and has contributed to Walking in Britain, Western Europe and Goa.

Tom Smallman
Tom lives in Melbourne, Australia, and had a number of jobs before joining Lonely Planet as an editor. He now works full time as an author and has worked on Lonely Planet guides to Canada, Ireland, Dublin, Australia, New South Wales, Sydney, Scotland, Edinburgh, Western Europe and Pennsylvania.

Pat Yale
Pat Yale was born and brought up in London where she spent several happy years selling holidays before deciding she'd rather do the travelling herself. Since then she has interspersed her wanderings in Europe, Africa, Asia and Central America with life as a travel writer, working, among other things, on the Lonely Planet guides to Turkey, Ireland and London. These days her home is in Bristol.

FROM THE AUTHORS
Bryn Thomas Thanks to everyone who helped on the three editions of this book. For the first two editions, Anna Jacomb-Hood, Christopher Knowles, Susy Kennard, Pauline Skyrme-Jones, Patricia Thomas, Sue Hall and Trevor Roberts made considerable contributions in research and writing.

For this new edition thanks to Anna Jacomb-Hood for help in unravelling the complexities of the British public transport system, Jane Thomas for help in checking proofs and to everyone at the LP office in London and at World Leisure Marketing for their useful suggestions. In particular I'd like to thank Barney Andrews, Sarah Bennett, Simon Calder, Joanna Clifton, Grant Cornwallis, Jennifer Cox, Dave Cuthbertson, Colin Dart, Liz Filleul, Charlotte Hindle, Sarah Long, Alex Marcovitch, Helen McWilliam, Vicky Wayland and Sara Yorke. Out in the field, thanks again to the patient and helpful staff of TICs in England, Scotland and Wales.

Finally, thanks on behalf of all of the authors to the editors and cartographers who worked on this project – particularly to Jane Fitzpatrick, Helen Yeates, Rachel Black and Jacqui Saunders.

Tom Smallman My gratitude goes to the following people: Sue Graefe for her patience and support; Lindy Mark for her invaluable information, Lyn, Flora and Alex Sharpe and Sue, Jeff and Holly Ross for their hospitality; Marie, Joe and Narelle for their insider tips on Edinburgh; Graeme Cornwallis for risking life and limb in the LP cause; Claire Beaumont for her literary suggestions; the two window cleaners from Peebles who gave me a lift into town; and to all those who patiently answered my questions.

Pat Yale Pat Yale would like to thank everyone in the London office for helping get the ball rolling. Lesley Levene was generous enough to loan me her London home again, while Rick and Alison in Manchester; Tom and Sally in Wolverhampton; the staff of the Embassie hostel in Liverpool; Jonathan Bryant in Henley; and Clare McElwee, Clare Parkinson and Clare Reynolds in London shared some excellent meals and/or conversations with me. As ever, I'd like to thank Bill Scanlon for his wonderful house-sitting services, and Sharon, Tony and Nathan just for being there.

This Book

This is the 3rd edition of LP's Britain guide. Richard Everist, Tony Wheeler and Bryn Thomas wrote the 1st edition. Bryn Thomas, Sean Sheehan and Pat Yale wrote the 2nd edition. Bryn Thomas was coordinating author of this edition. Bryn wrote the Wales, Channel Islands, Eastern England and most of South-Eastern and South-Western England chapters. Pat Yale wrote the London and Midlands chapters and parts of the South-Eastern England, South-Western England, North-Western England and North-Eastern England sections. Tom Smallman updapted the Scotland chapters using Graeme Cornwallis' work on the Lonely Planet Scotland guide for many of the chapters. Tom also updated most of the North-Eastern England chapter.

From the Publisher

This book was edited at the Lonely Planet office in Melbourne by Helen Yeates, with invaluable assistance from Shelley Muir, Craig MacKenzie, Darren Elder, Ron Gallagher, Katie Cody, Anne Mulvaney, Kate Daly, David Burnett, Carolyn Bain, Kirsten John, Martine Lleonart, Sally O'Brien and Jocelyn Harewood. Meg Mundell and Catherine Croft contributed to the architecture section. Quentin Frayne and our phrasebook department produced the language chapter.

A special thank you to Dr Faith Mason of Andover for her expert advice and to Ron Gallagher, Bev Yeates and Jeff Curnow for their research assistance.

Jacqui Saunders coordinated the mapping with help from Piotr Czajkowski, Anthony Phelan, Ann Jeffree, Tony Fankhauser, Adrian Persoglia and Chris Lee Ack. Csanád Csutoros guided the book through layout with assistance from Tim Uden, Rachel Black and Marcel Gaston. Thanks to Matt King for assistance with the illustrations and to artist Kate Nolan for the fantastic new additions. Louise Klep prepared the colourwraps and Margie Jung designed the cover. Thanks to LPI for their image selection.

THANKS
Many thanks to the travellers who used the last edition and wrote to us with helpful hints, advice and interesting anecdotes. Your names appear in the back of this book.

Foreword

ABOUT LONELY PLANET GUIDEBOOKS

The story begins with a classic travel adventure: Tony and Maureen Wheeler's 1972 journey across Europe and Asia to Australia. Useful information about the overland trail did not exist at that time, so Tony and Maureen published the first Lonely Planet guidebook to meet a growing need.

From a kitchen table, then from a tiny office in Melbourne (Australia), Lonely Planet has become the largest independent travel publisher in the world, an international company with offices in Melbourne, Oakland (USA), London (UK) and Paris (France).

Today Lonely Planet guidebooks cover the globe. There is an ever-growing list of books and there's information in a variety of forms and media. Some things haven't changed. The main aim is still to help make it possible for adventurous travellers to get out there – to explore and better understand the world.

At Lonely Planet we believe travellers can make a positive contribution to the countries they visit – if they respect their host communities and spend their money wisely. Since 1986 a percentage of the income from each book has been donated to aid projects and human rights campaigns.

Updates Lonely Planet thoroughly updates each guidebook as often as possible. This usually means there are around two years between editions, although for more unusual or more stable destinations the gap can be longer. Check the imprint page (following the colour map at the beginning of the book) for publication dates.

Between editions up-to-date information is available in two free newsletters – the paper *Planet Talk* and email *Comet* (to subscribe, contact any Lonely Planet office) – and on our Web site at www.lonelyplanet.com. The *Upgrades* section of the Web site covers a number of important and volatile destinations and is regularly updated by Lonely Planet authors. *Scoop* covers news and current affairs relevant to travellers. And, lastly, the *Thorn Tree* bulletin board, and *Postcards* section of the site carry unverified, but fascinating, reports from travellers.

Correspondence The process of creating new editions begins with the letters, postcards and emails received from travellers. This correspondence often includes suggestions, criticisms and comments about the current editions. Interesting excerpts are immediately passed on via newsletters and the Web site, and everything goes to our authors to be verified when they're researching on the road. We're keen to get more feedback from organisations or individuals who represent communities visited by travellers.

> Lonely Planet gathers information for everyone who's curious about the planet – and especially for those who explore it first-hand. Through guidebooks, phrasebooks, activity guides, maps, literature, newsletters, image library, TV series and web site we act as an information exchange for a worldwide community of travellers.

Research Authors aim to gather sufficient practical information to enable travellers to make informed choices and to make the mechanics of a journey run smoothly. They also research historical and cultural background to help enrich the travel experience and allow travellers to understand and respond appropriately to cultural and environmental issues.

Authors don't stay in every hotel because that would mean spending a couple of months in each medium-sized city and, no, they don't eat at every restaurant because that would mean stretching belts beyond capacity. They do visit hotels and restaurants to check standards and prices, but feedback based on readers' direct experiences can be very helpful.

Many of our authors work undercover, others aren't so secretive. None of them accept freebies in exchange for positive write-ups. And none of our guidebooks contain any advertising.

Production Authors submit their raw manuscripts and maps to offices in Australia, USA, UK or France. Editors and cartographers – all experienced travellers themselves – then begin the process of assembling the pieces. When the book finally hits the shops some things are already out of date, we start getting feedback from readers, and the process begins again....

WARNING & REQUEST

Things change – prices go up, schedules change, good places go bad and bad places go bankrupt – nothing stays the same. So, if you find things better or worse, recently opened or long since closed, please tell us and help make the next edition even more accurate and useful. We genuinely value all the feedback we receive. Julie Young coordinates a well-travelled team that reads and acknowledges every letter, postcard and email and ensures that every morsel of information finds its way to the appropriate authors, editors and cartographers for verification.

Everyone who writes to us will find their name in the next edition of the appropriate guidebook. They will also receive the latest issue of *Planet Talk*, our quarterly printed newsletter, or *Comet*, our monthly email newsletter. Subscriptions to both newsletters are free. The very best contributions will be rewarded with a free guidebook.

Excerpts from your correspondence may appear in new editions of Lonely Planet guidebooks, the Lonely Planet Web site, *Planet Talk* or *Comet*, so please let us know if you *don't* want your letter published or your name acknowledged.

Send all correspondence to the Lonely Planet office closest to you:

Australia: PO Box 617, Hawthorn, Victoria 3122
UK: 10A Spring Place, London NW5 3BH
USA: 150 Linden St, Oakland CA 94607
France: 1 rue du Dahomey, Paris 75011

Or email us at: talk2us@lonelyplanet.com.au
For news, views and updates see our web site: www.lonelyplanet.com

HOW TO USE A LONELY PLANET GUIDEBOOK

The best way to use a Lonely Planet guidebook is any way you choose. At Lonely Planet we believe the most memorable travel experiences are often those that are unexpected, and the finest discoveries are those you make yourself. Guidebooks are not intended to be used as if they provide a detailed set of infallible instructions!

Contents All Lonely Planet guidebooks follow the same format. The Facts about the Country chapters or sections give background information ranging from history to weather. Facts for the Visitor gives practical information on issues like visas and health. Getting There & Away gives a brief starting point for researching travel to and from the destination. Getting Around gives an overview of the transport options when you arrive.

The peculiar demands of each destination determine how subsequent chapters are broken up, but some things remain constant. We always start with background, then proceed to sights, places to stay, places to eat, entertainment, getting there and away, and getting around information – in that order.

Heading Hierarchy Lonely Planet headings are used in a strict hierarchical structure that can be visualised as a set of Russian dolls. Each heading (and its following text) is encompassed by any preceding heading that is higher on the hierarchical ladder.

Entry Points We do not assume guidebooks will be read from beginning to end, but that people will dip into them. The traditional entry points are the list of contents and the index. In addition, however, there is a complete list of maps and an index map illustrating map coverage.

There's also a colour map that shows highlights. These highlights are dealt with in greater detail in the Facts for the Visitor chapter, along with planning questions and suggested itineraries. Each chapter covering a geographical region begins with a locator map and another list of highlights. Once you find something of interest in a list of highlights, turn to the index.

Maps Maps play a crucial role in Lonely Planet guidebooks and include a huge amount of information. A legend is printed on the back page. We seek to have complete consistency between maps and text, and to have every important place in the text captured on a map. Map key numbers usually start in the top left corner.

Although inclusion in a guidebook usually implies a recommendation we cannot list every good place. Exclusion does not necessarily imply criticism. In fact there are a number of reasons why we might exclude a place – sometimes it is simply inappropriate to encourage an influx of travellers.

Introduction

At one stage of its history this small island ruled half of the world's population and had a major impact on many of the rest. For those people whose countries once lay in the shadow of its great empire, a visit to Britain may almost be a cliché but it is also essential – a peculiar mixture of home-coming and confrontation.

To the surprise of many, Britain remains one of the most beautiful islands in the world. All the words, paintings and pictures that have been produced are not just romantic, patriotic exaggerations.

In terms of area it is small, but the more you explore the bigger it seems to become. Visitors from the New World are often fooled by this magical expansion and try to do too much too quickly. JB Priestley observed of England, 'She is pretending to be small.' Covering it all in one trip is impossible – and that's before you start thinking of Scotland and Wales.

The United Kingdom comprises Great Britain (England, Scotland and Wales) and Northern Ireland. Its full name is the United Kingdom of Great Britain and Northern Ireland. This book confines itself to the island of Great Britain (the largest of the British Isles), the Isle of Man, the Channel Islands and Scotland's outlying islands – the Hebrides in the west and Orkney and Shetland in the north-east.

Sometimes in summer it seems like the whole world has come to Britain. Don't spend all your time in the big, tourist-ridden towns. Do pick a small area and spend at least a week or so wandering around the country lanes and villages.

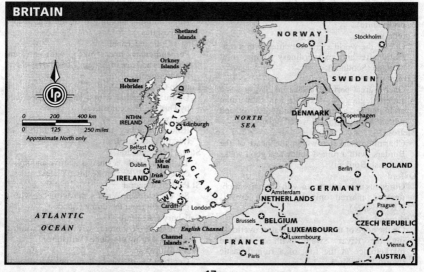

Regional Facts for the Visitor

HIGHLIGHTS

Planning a trip around Britain can be bewildering for the first-timer and is no less straightforward if you live here. The country may be small but its long history as an influential world power has left it with a rich heritage of medieval castles and cathedrals, historic cities and towns, stately homes and elegant gardens. Added to this are the natural attractions, the national parks, beautiful coastal regions, and the spectacular Highlands and islands of Scotland. Britain's highlights are so many that we've broken them down into categories.

Historic Cities & Towns

Bath
  Blessed with superb Georgian architecture, but inundated with tourists (south-west England).
Beverley
  Unspoilt, little-visited market town with two superb medieval churches (East Riding of Yorkshire).
Cambridge
  Famous university town with a compact centre. King's College Chapel is one of Europe's most impressive buildings (Cambridgeshire).
Edinburgh
  One of the world's greatest cities with a dramatic site and extraordinary architectural heritage (Scotland).
Liverpool
  Once a great port and Victorian city, boasts a superb legacy of Victorian and Edwardian architecture, a strong cultural identity and vibrant nightlife (north-west England).
Melrose
  Charming market town in the heart of the Borders, with a ruined abbey and good walks (Scottish Borders).
Oxford
  Gorgeous university town with evocative architecture, marred only by summer crowds (Oxfordshire).
Richmond
  On the edge of the Yorkshire Dales, overlooking the River Swale, with a cobbled marketplace at the foot of a ruined castle (North Yorkshire).

St Andrews
  Old university and golfing town, with ruined castle and harbour, on a headland overlooking a sweeping stretch of sand (Fife, Scotland).
Shrewsbury
  Interesting town with half-timbered architecture and curious medieval streets (Shropshire).
Whitby
  Atmospheric fishing port on magnificent coastline (North Yorkshire).
Winchester
  Ancient English capital, rich in history, with a great cathedral (Hampshire).
York
  Proud city with a spectacular cathedral and medieval walls, and many excellent museums (North Yorkshire).

Cathedrals & Churches

Canterbury Cathedral
  The Church of England's most important cathedral, and crowded with the ghosts of the past (Kent).
Durham Cathedral
  Monolithic Norman cathedral, overwhelming in scale, on a spectacular site overlooking Durham (County Durham).
Ely Cathedral
  Huge building looming over the fens (Cambridgeshire).
King's College Chapel
  Perpendicular masterpiece with brilliant acoustics and one of Britain's best boys' choirs (Cambridge).
Lincoln Cathedral
  Unusual cathedral with a site surpassed only by Durham (Lincolnshire).
Rievaulx Abbey
  Romantic abbey ruins on a beautiful site (North Yorkshire).
St David's Cathedral
  Tucked in a dale, a small, secretive and mystical cathedral (Pembrokeshire, Wales).
St Paul's Cathedral
  Sir Christopher Wren's masterpiece, with a great view from the dome (London).
Salisbury Cathedral
  Stylistically coherent, with Britain's tallest spire, a soaring elegance (Wiltshire).
Wells Cathedral
  Centrepiece of the best medieval cathedral

precinct in Britain, with brilliant west front sculpture (Somerset).

Westminster Abbey
Rich in history – since King Harold, almost every monarch has been crowned here – and with an excellent boys' choir (London).

Winchester Cathedral
Architectural styles from Norman to perpendicular in perfect harmony (Hampshire).

York Minster
Largest medieval church in Britain, incorporating Roman ruins and superb stained glass (North Yorkshire).

Museums & Galleries

British Museum
Great museum with comprehensive coverage of archaeology of ancient civilisations (London).

Burrell Collection
Fascinating moderate-sized art collection made by a wealthy shipowner, housed in a superb museum in parkland (Glasgow).

HMS *Victory* & *Mary Rose*
The world's oldest commissioned warship and Nelson's flagship at the Battle of Trafalgar; and King Henry VIII's flagship rescued from the mud beneath Portsmouth Harbour (Portsmouth).

Ironbridge Gorge
Birthplace of the Industrial Revolution, restored and recreated over a number of sites, including the world's first iron bridge (Shropshire).

National Gallery
National collection of European art from the 15th to the early 20th century (London).

Tate Gallery
Covering British artists from the 16th century, and modern artists (British and foreign) from the Impressionists to the present day (London).

Victoria and Albert Museum
Bewildering array of applied and decorative arts, including furniture, paintings, woodwork, jewellery, textiles and clothing (London).

York Castle Museum
Intriguing museum of everyday life, including reconstructed streets and authentically furnished rooms from the 17th to the 20th century (York).

Historic Houses

Blenheim Palace
Enormous baroque style private house built by Sir John Vanbrugh in 1704, set in parkland (Oxfordshire).

Castle Howard
Another Vanbrugh masterpiece with a dramatic setting in superb landscaped gardens (North Yorkshire).

Charleston Farmhouse
Home to Vanessa Bell, Duncan Grant and David Garnett (of the Bloomsbury Group), decorated with frescoes and postimpressionist art and with a charming garden (East Sussex).

Haddon Hall
Dating from the 12th century and added to for 500 years, one of the most complete surviving medieval manor houses (Derbyshire).

Hampton Court Palace
Begun in 1514 and a royal residence until the 18th century, an enormous, fascinating complex surrounded by beautiful gardens (London).

Ightham Mote
Small moated manor house that has scarcely changed for 500 years (Kent).

Knole House
Enormous house dating from the 15th century and virtually untouched since the 17th century, set in parkland (Kent).

Royal Pavilion
Exotic fantasy, combining Indian, Chinese and Gothic elements, built by George IV in 1815 (Brighton).

Tenement House
Small apartment giving a vivid insight into middle-class life in the late 1800s (Glasgow).

The Queen's House
Inigo Jones masterpiece, built in 1635 (Greenwich).

Traquair
Extraordinary building dating from the 10th century, seemingly untouched by time (Scottish Borders).

Medieval Castles

Alnwick
Dramatic castle begun in the 12th century and converted to a great house without losing its medieval character (Northumberland).

Caerlaverock
Unusual triangular castle, surrounded by a moat (Dumfries & Galloway, Scotland).

Caernarfon
After Windsor, the largest castle in England and Wales (North Wales).

Conwy
One of the most complete of the many fine castles built by Edward I to subdue the Welsh (North Wales).

Dover
Massive fortress begun shortly after the Norman conquest, but encompassing a Roman lighthouse, Saxon church and tunnels last used in WWII (Kent).

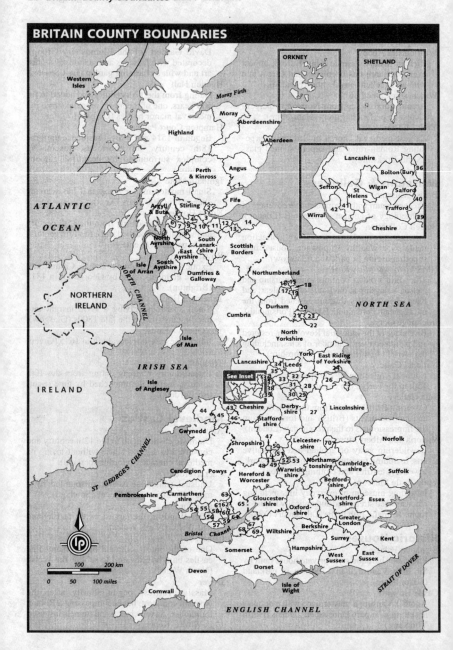

BRITAIN COUNTY BOUNDARIES

1	Dundee	25	North-East Lincolnshire
2	Clackmannanshire	26	North Lincolnshire
3	Falkirk	27	Nottinghamshire
4	East Dunbartonshire	28	Doncaster
5	West Dumbartonshire	29	Rotherham
6	Inverclyde	30	Sheffield
7	Renfrewshire	31	Barnsley
8	East Renfrewshire	32	Wakefield
9	Glasgow	33	Kirklees
10	North Lanarkshire	34	Bradford
11	West Lothian	35	Calderdale
12	Edinburgh	36	Rochdale
13	Mid Lothian	37	Oldham
14	East Lothian	38	Tameside
15	North Tyneside	39	Stockport
16	Newcastle upon Tyne	40	Manchester
17	Gateshead	41	Knowsley
18	South Tyneside	42	Liverpool
19	Sunderland	43	Flintshire
20	Hartlepool	44	Conwy
21	Stockton-on-Tees	45	Denbighshire
22	Middlesbrough	46	Wrexham
23	Redcar & Cleveland	47	Wolverhampton
24	Kingston-upon-Hull	48	Dudley

49	Sandwell
50	Walsall
51	Birmingham
52	Solihull
53	Coventry
54	Swansea
55	Neath & Port Talbot
56	Bridgend
57	Vale of Glamorgan
58	Rhondda Cynon Taff
59	Cardiff
60	Caerphilly
61	Merthyr Tydfil
62	Blaenau Gwent
63	Torfaen
64	Newport
65	Monmouthshire
66	South Gloucestershire
67	Bristol
68	North Somerset
69	Bath & North-East Somerset
70	Rutland
71	Buckinghamshire

Hermitage
  Brutal but romantic castle surrounded by bleakly beautiful countryside (Dumfries & Galloway, Scotland).

Leeds
  Extraordinarily beautiful castle in the middle of a lake, marred by crowds (Kent).

Stirling
  Favoured royal residence of the Stewarts (Central Scotland).

Tower of London
  Begun in 1078, a fortress, royal residence and state prison, now home to the British crown jewels (London).

Windsor
  Royal residence with restored state rooms and the beautiful St George's Chapel (Berkshire).

Coast

Beachy Head
  Spectacular chalk cliffs backed by rolling downland rich in wildflowers (East Sussex).

Brighton
  Tacky but vibrant resort town (East Sussex).

Ilfracombe to Lynton/Lynmouth
  Humpbacked cliffs overlooking the Bristol Channel and backed by the beautiful Exmoor National Park (Devon).

Land's End to St Ives
  Beautiful coast and a landscape littered with historical reminders and relics (Cornwall).

Llandudno
  Old-style seaside resort with great Victorian architecture and a beautiful setting (North Wales).

St David's to Cardigan
  Unspoilt coastline in Pembrokeshire Coast National Park (South Wales).

St Ives
  Picturesque village and artists' haunt with two excellent sandy beaches (Cornwall).

Scarborough
  Classic English seaside resort with a superb location (North Yorkshire).

Scarborough to Saltburn
  Unspoilt coastline with beautiful fishing villages (particularly Staithes and Robin Hood's Bay) and major cliffs, backed by the North York Moors National Park (North Yorkshire).

Scotland
  The Scottish coast ranges from beautiful (Berwick-upon-Tweed to John o'Groats on the east coast, and Gretna to Glasgow on the west) to extraordinary (the north-west). From Oban to John o'Groats it is one of the world's greatest natural spectacles. Some of the most

spectacular cliffs in Britain are to be found in Orkney and Shetland.

Tintagel
Surf-battered headland, topped by a ruined castle, believed to be King Arthur's birthplace (Cornwall).

Islands

Colonsay
Fine sandy beaches, good walks and a mild climate with only half as much rain as on the mainland (Argyll, Scotland).

Farne Islands
Tiny, rocky islands, with amazingly tame nesting seabirds, including puffins and Arctic terns (Northumberland).

Harris
Mountainous and spectacular, with beautiful beaches and isolated crofts (Outer Hebrides, Scotland).

Iona
Very touristy during the day, but spend the night here to experience the magic of this holy island (Argyll, Scotland).

Jura
Wild and remote, with dramatic scenery, superb walks, few people and just one road (Argyll, Scotland).

Orkney
Beautiful beaches, wildflowers and the unique Stone Age ruins at Skara Brae (off north coast of Scotland).

Staffa
Boat trips from Mull to see the incredible rock formations that inspired Felix Mendelssohn's *Hebrides Overture* (Argyll, Scotland).

Gardens

Bodnant Garden
Famed for its rhododendrons and camellias and with fine mountain views – particularly spectacular in spring (North Wales).

Castle Kennedy Gardens
Laid out in the 18th century around castle ruins, with formal gardens and a rhododendron collection (Dumfries & Galloway, Scotland).

Forde Abbey
Former Cistercian abbey with wide lawns, ponds, huge trees and colourful borders (Dorset).

Great Dixter
Series of gardens begun by Sir Edwin Lutyens featuring wildflowers and brilliant spring bulbs (Kent).

Hidcote Manor Gardens
One of Britain's most famous modern gardens (Gloucestershire).

Regents Park
Vast lawns, spectacular Queen Mary's Rose Garden with 60,000 roses, ornamental ponds and a zoo (London).

Royal Botanic Gardens, Kew
Three hundred acres of formal gardens, woods, rock gardens, conservatories and the magnificent Palm House (London).

Sissinghurst
Magical garden created by Vita Sackville-West and Harold Nicholson of the Bloomsbury Group (Kent).

Stourhead & Stourton
Two very different neighbouring gardens. Stourhead comprises superb landscaped parkland designed in the 1740s around a lake. The flower garden of Stourton House is in perfect contrast (Wiltshire).

Stowe Landscape Garden
Enormously influential garden started in the 17th century, now being restored by the National Trust (Buckinghamshire).

Studley Royal & Fountains Abbey
Superb water garden on a grand scale, framing extraordinary monastic ruins (North Yorkshire).

Trelissick Garden
Rhododendrons, magnolias, hydrangeas and sub-tropical plants thrive in this area's mild climate (Cornwall).

Prehistoric Remains

Avebury & Around
More impressive than Stonehenge; extensive remains, including a stone circle and avenue, and nearby Silbury Hill and West Kennet Long Barrow (Wiltshire).

Callanish Standing Stones
Cross-shaped avenue and circle on a dramatic site (Lewis, Scotland).

Castlerigg Stone Circle
Stone circle with a beautiful location near Keswick in the Lake District (Cumbria).

Mousa Broch
Britain's best preserved broch, or defensive tower (Shetland).

Ring of Brodgar
Well-preserved stone circle, part of ceremonial site that includes standing stones and a chambered tomb (Orkney).

Skara Brae
Extraordinarily well-preserved remains of a village inhabited 3000 years ago – including dressers, fireplaces, beds and boxes all made from stone (Orkney).

Stonehenge
Extraordinary monument, but marred by crowds and nearby road (Wiltshire).

Roman Sites

Chedworth Villa
Well-preserved mosaic floors at this remote rural villa (Gloucestershire).

Fishbourne Palace
Britain's only Roman palace, with beautiful mosaics (near Chichester, West Sussex).

Hadrian's Wall
Evocative ruins of a monumental attempt to divide two countries (Northumberland/Cumbria).

Train Journeys

Ffestiniog Line
Most scenic of the 'Great Little Trains' of Wales, runs 14 miles through Snowdonia National Park (North Wales).

Leeds-Settle-Carlisle Line
Spectacular engineering feat running through the beautiful Yorkshire Dales (North Yorkshire).

Snowdon Mountain Railway
Lazy way to the top of Britain's second-highest mountain (Wales).

Tarka Line
From Exeter to Barnstaple through classic Devon countryside (Devon).

Vale of Rheidol
Spectacular 12 mile narrow-gauge steam railway between Aberystwyth and Devil's Bridge (Wales).

West Highland Railway
Scotland's most famous railway line, with particularly dramatic sections crossing Rannoch Moor and from Fort William to Mallaig (Scotland).

SUGGESTED ITINERARIES

Depending on the time at your disposal, you might want to see and do the following:

One week
Visit London, Oxford, the Cotswolds, Bath and Wells.

Two weeks
Visit London, Salisbury, Avebury, Bath, Wells, Oxford or Cambridge, York and Edinburgh.

One month
Visit London, Cambridge, York, Edinburgh, Inverness, Isle of Skye, Fort William, Oban,

Glasgow, the Lake District, Chester, the Cotswolds, Wells, Bath, Avebury, Salisbury, Oxford and Stratford-upon-Avon.

Two months
As for one month, but stay put for a week or so in one place. Explore Snowdonia (North Wales) and perhaps attempt a long-distance walk like the West Highland Way.

PLANNING
When to Go

Anyone who spends any extended period of time in Britain will soon sympathise with the locals' conversational obsession with the weather – although in relative terms the climate is mild and the rainfall not spectacular (see the Climate sections in the Facts About England, Scotland and Wales chapters for more details).

Settled periods of weather – sunny or otherwise – are rare and rain is likely at any time. Even in midsummer you can go for days without seeing the sun, and showers (or worse) should be expected. To enjoy Britain it helps to convince yourself that you *like* the rain – after all, that's what makes it so incredibly green!

The least hospitable months for visitors are November, December, January and February – it's cold, and the days are short (less than eight hours of daylight in December). March is marginal – although there are 12 hours of daylight and daffodils appear in the south, it can still be very cold. October is also marginal – there are nearly 11 hours of daylight, temperatures are reasonable, and weather patterns seem to be unusually stable, which means you can get good spells of sun, or rain.

Temperatures vary around the island but, as you would expect, it's generally true that the further north you go, the colder it gets. There's also quite a difference in the number of daylight hours. In early spring or late autumn, it's probably best to concentrate a visit in the south, especially the mild south-west.

April to September are undoubtedly the best months, and this is when most sights and Tourist Information Centres (TICs) are open, and when most people visit. July and August are the busiest months, and best

Whither the Weather?

It was Dr Johnson who noted that 'when two Englishmen meet, their first talk is of the weather', and two centuries later not much has changed. According to the Meteorological Office, weather reports are the third most watched television broadcasts, and in 1996 a satellite TV channel devoted entirely to the weather started beaming 24-hour forecasts into Britain.

British folklore is rich in ways of second-guessing the weather. If it snows on St Dorothea's day (6 February), we can expect no heavier snowfall. If it rains on St Swithin's day (15 July), brollies should be kept to hand for the next 40 days. The slightest tinge of evening pink and Brits are heard chanting 'A red sky at night is a shepherd's delight, a red sky at morning is a shepherd's warning' like a mantra.

Even so, the weather still manages to defeat us. A few weeks without rain and hosepipe (garden hose) bans are rushed in; one snowflake and the railways grind to a halt. The British Rail spokesperson who attributed a delay to the 'wrong kind of snow' is still trying to live it down.

avoided if possible. The crowds on the coast, at the national parks, in London and in popular towns like Oxford, Bath and York have to be seen to be believed. You're just as likely to get good weather in April, May, June, September and October, although October is getting late for the Scottish Highlands.

What Kind of Trip

Although many people restrict their trip to Britain to a visit to London and a quick whip round the 'milk-run' towns of Oxford, Cambridge, Stratford-upon-Avon, Bath, York, Chester and Edinburgh, you'll get more out of a stay if you take the time to explore some of the less touristy towns (Glasgow, Bristol, Manchester and Leeds

for example) and the wonderful countryside. The remoter parts of Wales and Scotland, in particular, are best appreciated on a longer stay. London is a great city, but it's also very expensive and unrepresentative of Britain as a whole – don't let it absorb all your time.

It's easy enough to get round the country by train or bus, although it's usually much cheaper to travel by bus than by train. Alternatively there are plenty of coach tours either around the whole country from London or around specific areas. There are several hop-on, hop-off coach tours specifically designed for backpackers (see Getting Around for details).

Travellers who are planning to find work and long-term places to live should bear in mind that the peak tourist season generates casual jobs, which are often advertised in May and June. June can be a good time to look for housing as the universities and colleges close for summer and many students move back home; in addition, travellers pack up and move on to the Mediterranean. Everything tightens up in October and November when people return to rebuild their finances and hibernate through winter.

What's in a Name?

England dominates the rest of the UK in all things to such an extent that not only the English but most of the world tend to say 'England' when referring to the UK as a whole. The island of Britain (England, Scotland and Wales) together with Northern Ireland make up the country whose official name is the United Kingdom of Great Britain and Northern Ireland.

It may seem an obvious point but it's important to get the name of the country right. The Scots, the Welsh and the people of Northern Ireland find it deeply insulting if you tell them how much you like being 'here in England' when you're in their part of the UK.

Maps

The best introductory map to Britain is published by the British Tourist Authority (BTA) and is widely available in TICs. If you plan to use the trains, the bad news is that you have to buy the whole hefty timetable just to get the 'free' map that goes with it.

There's not much to distinguish the range of excellent road atlases in terms of accuracy or price (£8-10), but the graphics differ – pick the one you find easiest to read. If you plan to go off the beaten track, you'll need one that shows at least 3 miles to the inch.

The Ordnance Survey (OS) caters to walkers with a wide variety of maps at different scales. The OS Landranger maps at 1:50,000 or about 1¼ inches to the mile are ideal (£4.95). Also look out for the excellent walkers' maps published by Harveys. Unlike the OS equivalents these maps also include tourist information.

What to Bring

Since anything you think of can be bought in British cities (including Vegemite), pack light and pick up extras as you go along. Clothing in particular can be good value in Britain.

A travelpack – a combination of a backpack and shoulder bag – is the most popular item for carrying gear especially if you plan to do any walking – a suitcase will probably force you to use expensive taxis. A travelpack's straps zip away inside the pack when not needed, making it easy to handle in airports and on crowded public transport. Most travelpacks have sophisticated shoulder-strap adjustment systems and can be used comfortably, even for long hikes.

Whether you bring a tent probably depends on how enthusiastic a camper you are; the weather hardly encourages camping and long-distance walks are well served by hostels, camping barns and B&Bs. A sleeping bag is useful in hostels and when visiting friends. A sleeping sheet with pillow cover is necessary for staying in Scottish YHA hostels – if you don't bring one you'll have to hire or purchase one.

A padlock is handy for locking your bag to a train or a bus luggage rack, and may also be needed to secure your hostel locker. A Swiss Army knife (or any pocketknife that includes a bottle opener and strong corkscrew) is useful for all sorts of things. For city sightseeing, a small daypack is harder for snatch thieves to grab than a shoulder bag.

Other possibilities include a compass, an alarm clock, a torch (flashlight), an adaptor plug for electrical appliances, sunglasses and an elastic clothesline.

Use plastic carrier bags to keep things organised, and dry, inside your backpack. Airlines lose bags from time to time, but there's a much better chance of getting them back if they're tagged with your name and address *inside* as well as on the outside.

RESPONSIBLE TOURISM

Except for in its remoter and more mountainous reaches, Britain is a very crowded island even before the peak tourist season brings yet more millions to the streets. Congestion on the roads is a major problem and visitors will do residents – as well as themselves! – a favour if they forgo driving in favour of using public transport.

Mountain bikers should stick to roads or designated bike tracks as considerable damage has been done to mountain paths (eg in Snowdonia) by cyclists. If you're rough camping make sure you ask permission of the landowner first and take care not to damage crops or leave any litter.

If you'd like to know more about the problems caused by tourism, contact Tourism Concern (☎ 0171-753 3330), Stapleton House, 277-281 Holloway Rd, London N7 (tube: Holloway Rd), which has a library of press cuttings and other source materials.

TOURIST OFFICES

The British Tourist Authority stocks masses of information, much of it free. Contact the BTA before you leave home because some discounts are only available to people who book before arriving in Britain. Travellers with special needs (be it disability, diet etc) should also contact the nearest BTA office.

In London the British Travel Centre at 1 Regent St is a good starting point for information collecting.

Local Tourist Offices

Every British town (and many villages) has its own Tourist Information Centre (TIC) where a wide range of information is available, particularly about places within a 50 mile radius. Most also operate a local bed-booking system and a Book-A-Bed-Ahead (BABA) scheme. In addition there are National Park Visitor Information Centres. Local libraries are also good sources of information.

Most TICs are open from 9 am to 5 pm Monday to Friday, although in popular tourist areas they may also open on Saturday and stay open later in the evening. In real honey pots like Stratford and Bath they'll be open seven days a week throughout the year. From October to March smaller TICs are often closed.

Many TICs have 24-hour computer databases that can be accessed even when the office is closed. Others put posters with basic information about accommodation and a town plan in the window.

Tourist Offices Abroad

Overseas, the BTA represents the tourist boards of England, Scotland and Wales. Addresses of some overseas offices are as follows:

Australia
(☎ 02-9377 4400, fax 02-9377 4499)
Level 16, The Gateway, 1 Macquarie Place, Circular Quay, Sydney, NSW 2000
Canada
(☎ 416-925 6326, fax 416-961 2175)
Suite 450, 111 Avenue Rd, Toronto, Ontario M5R 3JD
France
(☎ 01 44 51 56 20)
Tourisme de Grand-Bretagne, Maison de la Grande Bretagne, 19 Rue des Mathurins, 75009 Paris (entrance in les Rues Tronchet et Auber)
Germany
(☎ 069-238 0711)
Taunusstrasse 52-60, 60329 Frankfurt

Ireland
(☎ 01-670 8000)
18-19 College Green, Dublin 2
Netherlands
(☎ 020-685 50 51)
Stadhouderskade 2 (5e), 1054 ES Amsterdam
New Zealand
(☎ 09-303 1446, fax 09-377 6965)
3rd floor, Dilworth Building, corner Queen and Customs Sts, Auckland 1
USA
(☎ 1 800 GO 2 BRITAIN)
625 N Michigan Avenue, Suite 1510, Chicago IL 60611 (personal callers only) 551 Fifth Avenue, Suite 701, New York, NY 10176-0799

There are more than 40 BTA offices worldwide. Addresses are listed on its Web site www.bta.org.uk.

VISAS & DOCUMENTS
Passport

Your most important travel document is a passport, which should remain valid until well after your trip; if it's just about to expire, renew it before you go. This may not be easy to do overseas, and some countries insist your passport remain valid for a specified minimum period (usually three months) after your visit.

Applying for or renewing a passport can be an involved process taking from a few days to several months, so don't leave it till the last minute. Bureaucracy usually grinds faster if you do everything in person rather than relying on the mail or agents. First check what is required: passport photos, birth certificate, population register extract, signed statements, exact payment in cash, whatever.

Australian citizens can apply at post offices, or the passport office in their state capital; Canadians can apply at regional passport offices; New Zealanders can apply at any district office of the Department of Internal Affairs; and US citizens must apply in person (but may usually renew by mail) at a US Passport Agency office or some courthouses and post offices.

Citizens of European countries may not need a passport to travel to Britain. A national identity card can be sufficient, and usually involves less paperwork and processing time. Check with your travel agent or the British embassy.

Visas

A visa is a stamp in your passport permitting you to enter a country for a specified period. Depending on your nationality, the procedure may be a mere formality. Sometimes you can get a visa at borders or airports, but not always – check first with the embassies or consulates of the countries you plan to visit.

There is a variety of visa types, including tourist, transit, business and work visas. Transit visas are usually cheaper than tourist or business visas but only allow a very short stay and can be difficult to extend.

If you're travelling widely, carry plenty of spare passport photos (you'll need up to four every time you apply for a visa).

Access the Lonely Planet Web site on www.lonelyplanet.com.au for more information.

British Visas Visa regulations are always subject to change, so it's essential to check the situation with your local British embassy, high commission or consulate before leaving home.

Currently, if you are a citizen of Australia, Canada, New Zealand, South Africa or the USA, you are given 'leave to enter' Britain at your place of arrival. Tourists from these countries are generally permitted to stay for up to six months, but are prohibited from working. To stay longer you need an entry clearance certificate: apply to the high commission.

Citizens of the European Union (EU) can live and work in Britain free of immigration control – you don't need a visa to enter the country.

The immigration authorities have always been tough and are getting tougher; dress neatly and carry proof that you have sufficient funds to support yourself. A credit card and/or an onward ticket will help. People have been refused entry because they happened to be carrying papers (like references) that suggested they intended to work.

You are most likely to encounter problems in acquiring a British visa if you come from a country whose citizens are perceived as likely to want to stay here (Turkey, for example). It may be grossly unfair but there's little you can do but grin and cough up all the paperwork demanded.

Visa Extensions To extend your stay in the UK contact the Home Office, (☎ 0181-686 0688) Immigration and Nationality Department , Lunar House, Wellesley Rd, Croydon CR9 2BY (East Croydon main line train station) *before* your existing permit expires. You will need to send your passport or ID card with your application.

Photocopies

It's wise to keep photocopies of all important documents (passport, air tickets, insurance policy, travellers cheques serial numbers) in a separate place in case of theft; stash £50 away with the photocopies just in case. Ideally, leave a second set of copies with someone responsible in your home country.

Onward Tickets

Although you don't need an onward ticket to be granted 'leave to enter' on arrival (see Visas), this could help if there's any doubt over whether you have sufficient funds to support yourself and purchase an onward ticket in Britain.

Travel Insurance

A travel insurance policy to cover theft, loss and medical problems is a must. There are all sorts of policies and your travel agent should be able to help. The international student travel policies handled by STA Travel and other student travel organisations are usually good value. Some policies offer lower and higher medical-expense options – go for as much as you can afford, especially if you're also visiting the Channel Islands, the USA, Switzerland, Germany or Scandinavia, where medical costs can be astronomical.

Always read the small print carefully, bearing in mind that:

- Some policies specifically exclude 'dangerous activities' like scuba diving, motorcycling, skiing, mountaineering, even trekking.
- You may prefer a policy that pays doctors or hospitals directly rather than forcing you to pay on the spot and claim the money back later. If you have to claim later, make sure you keep all documentation. Some policies ask you to call back (reverse charges) to a centre in your home country where an immediate assessment of your problem is made.
- Not all policies cover ambulances, helicopter rescue or emergency flights home.
- Most policies exclude cover for pre-existing illnesses, including AIDS.

Driving Licence

Your normal driving licence is legal for 12 months from the date you last entered Britain; you can then apply for a British licence at post offices.

Ask your automobile association for a Card of Introduction. This entitles you to services offered by British sister organisations (touring maps and information, help with breakdowns, technical and legal advice etc), usually free of charge.

Camping Card International

Your local automobile association also issues a Camping Card International, which is basically a camping ground ID. They're also issued by local camping federations, and sometimes on the spot at camp sites. They incorporate third party insurance for damage you may cause, and many camping grounds offer a small discount if you sign in with one. Some hostels and hotels also accept carnets for signing-in purposes, but won't give discounts.

Hostel Card

If you're travelling on a budget, membership of the Youth Hostel Association (YHA)/Hostelling International (HI) is a must (£10 over-18, £5 under-18). There are around 320 hostels in Britain and members are also eligible for all sorts of discounts. See the Accommodation section of this chapter for more information about hostelling in Britain.

Student & Youth Cards

The most useful card is the plastic ID-style International Student Identity Card (ISIC), with your photograph on it. This can perform all sorts of wonders, including producing discounts on many forms of transport. Even if you have your own transport, the card will soon pay for itself through cheap or free admission to attractions, and cheap meals in some student restaurants.

There's a worldwide industry in fake student cards, and many places now stipulate a maximum age for student discounts or, more simply, substitute a 'youth discount' for a 'student discount'. If you're aged under 26 but not a student, you can apply for a Federation of International Youth Travel Organisations (FIYTO) card or a Euro26 Card which give much the same discounts. Your hostelling organisation should be able to help with this.

Both types of card are issued by student unions, hostelling organisations and student travel agencies. They don't automatically entitle you to discounts, but you won't find out until you flash the card.

Seniors' Cards

Discount cards for over 60s are available for rail and bus travel. See Passes & Discounts and Railcards in the Getting Around chapter.

International Health Card & Form E111

You'll only need this yellow booklet if you're travelling onwards through parts of Asia, Africa and South America, where yellow fever is prevalent.

If you're a national of another EU (European Union) country, Form E111 (available from post offices) entitles you to free or reduced-cost medical treatment in Britain.

Other Documents

If you're visiting Britain on a Working Holiday Entry Certificate don't forget to

bring any course certificates or letters of
reference that might help you find a job.

EMBASSIES & CONSULATES

Don't expect too much from your embassy
in Britain, or in any other country for that
matter. They're probably not going to start
worrying about you unless you get into
trouble with the police or inconvenience
them by expiring while on holiday. They
will, however, help you replace a lost passport or offer advice on other emergencies.
They won't hold mail for travellers but will
help someone in your home country get in
touch with you in an emergency.

UK Embassies Abroad

Some UK embassies abroad include:

Australia
  High Commission:
  (☎ 02-6270 6666)
  Commonwealth Ave, Yarralumla, Canberra,
  ACT 2600
Canada
  High Commission:
  (☎ 613-237 1530)
  80 Elgin St, Ottawa K1P 5K7
France
  Consulate:
  (☎ 01 42 66 38 10)
  9 Ave Hoche, 8e, Paris
Germany
  Embassy:
  (☎ 0228-23 40 61)
  Friedrich-Ebert-Allee 77, 53113 Bonn
Ireland
  Embassy:
  (☎ 01-205 3742)
  29 Merrion Rd, Ballsbridge, Dublin 4
Japan
  Embassy:
  (☎ 03-3265 5511)
  1 Ichiban-cho, Chiyoda-ku, Tokyo
Netherlands
  Embassy:
  (☎ 070-427 0427)
  Lange Voorhout 10, 2514 ED, The Hague
New Zealand
  High Commission:
  (☎ 04-472 6049)
  44 Hill St, Wellington 1
South Africa
  High Commission:

(☎ 27-21-461 7220)
91 Parliament St, Cape Town
USA
  Embassy:
  (☎ 202-462 1340)
  3100 Massachusetts Ave NW, Washington DC
  20008

Foreign Embassies in the UK

Countries with diplomatic representation in
the UK include the following:

Australia
  High Commission:
  (☎ 0171-465 8218, tube: Temple)
  Australia House, The Strand, London WC2
Canada
  High Commission:
  (☎ 0171-629 9492, tube: Bond St)
  Macdonald House, 1 Grosvenor Square,
  London W1
France
  Consulate General:
  (☎ 0171-838 2050, tube: South Kensington)
  6A Cromwell Place, London SW7
Germany
  Embassy:
  (☎ 0171-824 1300, tube: Hyde Park Corner)
  23 Belgrave Square, London SW1
Ireland
  Embassy and Consulate:
  (☎ 0171-235 2171, tube: Hyde Park Corner)
  17 Grosvenor Place, London SW1
Japan
  Embassy:
  (☎ 0171-465 6500, tube: Green Park)
  101 Piccadilly, London W1
Netherlands
  Embassy:
  (☎ 0171-584 5040, tube: Gloucester Rd)
  38 Hyde Park Gate, London SW7
New Zealand
  High Commission:
  (☎ 0171-973 0363, tube: Piccadilly Circus)
  New Zealand House, 80 Haymarket, London
  SW1
South Africa
  Embassy:
  (☎ 0171-930 4488, tube: Charing Cross)
  Trafalgar Square, London WC2
US
  Embassy:
  (☎ 0171-499 9000, tube: Bond St)
  5 Upper Grosvenor St, London W1

CUSTOMS

Entering Britain, if you have nothing to declare go through the green channel; if you may have something to declare go through the red channel. For imported goods there's a two-tier system: the first for goods bought duty-free, the second for goods bought in an EU country where tax and duty have been paid.

The second tier is relevant because a number of products (eg alcohol and cigarettes) are much cheaper on the continent. Under single market rules, however, as long as tax and duty have been paid somewhere in the EU there is no prohibition on importing them within the EU, provided they are for personal consumption. The result has been a thriving market for day trips to France where Brits can load up their cars with cheap beer, wine and cigarettes – the savings can more than pay for the trip.

Duty-Free

If you purchase from a duty-free shop, you can import 200 cigarettes or 250 grams of tobacco, two litres of still wine plus one litre of spirits or another two litres of wine (sparkling or otherwise), 60 cc of perfume, 250 cc of toilet water, and other duty-free goods (eg cider and beer) to the value of £145.

Tax & Duty Paid

If you buy from a normal retail outlet, customs will nod through 800 cigarettes or 1kg of tobacco, 10 litres of spirits, 20 litres of fortified wine, 90 litres of wine (not more than 60 sparkling) and 110 litres of beer as legitimate personal imports.

MONEY
Currency

The British currency is the pound sterling (£), with 100 pence (p) to a pound. One and 2p coins are copper; 5p, 10p, 20p and 50p coins are silver; the £1 coin is gold-coloured; and the new £2 coin is gold and silver-coloured. Like its written counterpart the word pence is usually abbreviated and pronounced 'pee'.

Notes (bills) come in £5, £10, £20 and £50 denominations and vary in colour and size. You may also come across notes issued by several Scottish banks, including a £1 note which are legal tender on both sides of the border. If you have any problems getting them accepted in England and Wales, ask a bank to swap them for you.

Exchange Rates

country	unit		pound
Australia	A$1	=	£0.37
Canada	C$1	=	£0.39
euro	€1	=	£0.71
France	FF1	=	£0.10
Germany	DM1	=	£0.35
Ireland	IR£1	=	£0.89
Japan	¥100	=	£0.0050
New Zealand	NZ$1	=	£0.31
USA	US$1	=	£0.60

Exchanging Money

Be careful using *bureaux de change*, especially in London; they may offer good exchange rates but frequently levy outrageous commissions and fees. Make sure you find out in advance. The *bureaux de change* at the international airports are exceptions to the rule. They charge less than most High St banks and cash sterling travellers cheques free of charge. They also guarantee that you can buy up to £500 worth of most major currencies on the spot.

Bank hours vary, but you'll be safe if you visit between 9.30 am and 3.30 pm, Monday to Friday. Friday afternoons get very busy. Some banks are open on Saturday, generally from 9.30 am till noon but increasingly all day in big towns.

The total cost of foreign exchange can vary widely. American Express offices are often cheapest, charging 1% commission, with no minimum charge. NatWest charges 1% commission for sterling travellers cheques, with a £4 minimum charge; Lloyds, Midland and Barclays all charge 1.5% commission, with a minimum charge of £3.

It's difficult to open a bank account, although if you're planning to work it may be essential. Building societies tend to be more welcoming and often have better interest rates. You'll need a (semi) permanent address, and it will smooth the way considerably if you have a reference or introductory letter from your bank manager at home, plus bank statements for the previous year. Owning credit/charge cards also helps.

Personal cheques are still widely used in Britain, but they're validated and guaranteed by a plastic cheque card. Increasingly, retail outlets are linked to the Switch/Delta debit card networks; money is deducted direct from your current account. Look for a current account that pays interest (or at least doesn't charge for ordinary transactions while you're in credit), gives you a cheque book and guarantee card, and offers access to automated teller machines and the Switch/Delta network.

Cash Nothing beats cash for convenience – or risk. It's still wise to travel with some local currency in cash, if only to tide you over until you get to an exchange facility. There's no problem if you arrive at any of the London airports; all have good-value exchange counters open for incoming flights.

If you're travelling in several countries, some extra cash in US dollars is a good idea; it can be easier to change a small amount of cash (when leaving a country, for example) than a cheque.

Banks will rarely accept foreign coins, although some airport foreign exchanges will. Before you leave one country for the next, try to use up your change.

Travellers Cheques The main idea of travellers cheques is to offer some protection from theft. American Express or Thomas Cook travellers cheques are widely accepted and have efficient replacement policies. Keep a record of the cheque numbers and the cheques you've cashed somewhere separate from the cheques themselves.

Although cheques are available in various currencies, there's little point using US$ cheques in Britain (unless you're travelling from the USA), since you'll lose on the exchange rate when you buy them and every time you cash one. Bring pounds sterling to avoid changing currencies twice. In Britain, travellers cheques are rarely accepted outside banks or used for everyday transactions; you need to cash them in advance.

Take most cheques in large denominations to minimise transaction charges. It's only towards the end of a stay that you may want to change a small cheque to make sure you don't get left with too much local currency.

Credit Cards & ATMs If you're not familiar with the options, ask your bank to explain the workings and relative merits of credit, credit/debit, debit and charge cards.

Plastic cards make perfect travelling companions – they're ideal for major purchases and let you withdraw cash from selected banks and automatic telling machines (ATMs – known as cashpoints in Britain). ATMs are usually linked up to international money systems such as Cirrus, Maestro or Plus, so you can shove your card in, punch in a personal identification number (PIN) and get instant cash. But ATMs aren't fail-safe, especially if the card was issued outside Europe, and it's safer to go to a human teller – it can be a headache if an ATM swallows your card.

Credit cards usually aren't hooked up to ATM networks unless you specifically request a PIN number from your bank. You should also ask which ATMs abroad will accept your particular card. Cash cards, that you use at home to withdraw money from your bank account or savings account, are becoming more widely linked internationally – ask your bank at home for advice.

Charge cards like American Express and Diners Club don't have credit limits but may not be accepted in small establishments or off the beaten track. If you have an American Express card, you can cash up to £500 worth of personal cheques at American Express offices in any seven-day period.

Credit and credit/debit cards like Visa and MasterCard (also known as Access in Britain) are more widely accepted. If you have too low a credit limit to cover major expenses like car hire or airline tickets, you can pay money into your account so it's in credit when you leave home.

Visa, MasterCard, Access, American Express and Diners Club cards are widely recognised although some places make a charge for accepting them. B&Bs usually require cash. MasterCard is operated by the same organisation that issues Access and Eurocards and can be used wherever you see one or other of these signs. You can get cash advances using your Visa card at the Midland Bank and Barclays, or using MasterCard at NatWest, Lloyds and Barclays.

If you plan a long stay and have a permanent address, it's usually straightforward to change the billing address for your card.

If you're relying on plastic, go for two different cards – an American Express or Diners Club with a Visa or MasterCard. Better still, combine plastic and travellers cheques so you have something to fall back on if an ATM swallows your card or the local banks don't accept your card.

International Transfers You can instruct your bank back home to send you a draft. Specify the city, the bank and the branch you want your money directed to, or ask your home bank to tell you where a suitable one is, and make sure you get the details right. The whole procedure will be easier if you've authorised someone back home to access your account.

Money sent by telegraphic transfer (usually at a cost of at least £15) should reach you within a week; by mail, allow at least two weeks. When it arrives, it will most likely be converted into local currency – you can take it as it is or buy travellers cheques.

You can also transfer money via American Express or Thomas Cook. Americans can also use Western Union although it has fewer offices in Britain from which to collect.

Security

However you decide to carry your funds, it makes sense to keep most of it out of easy reach of snatch thieves in a money-belt or similar. You might want to stitch an inside

pocket into your skirt or trousers to keep an emergency stash; certainly it makes sense to keep something like £50 apart from the rest of your cash in case of an emergency.

Take particular care in crowded places like the London Underground, and never leave wallets sticking out of trouser pockets or daypacks.

Costs

Britain is extremely expensive and London is horrific. While in London you will need to budget £22 to £30 a day for bare survival. Dormitory accommodation alone will cost from £10 to £22 a night, a one-day travel card is £3.50, and drinks and the most basic sustenance will cost you at least £6, with any sightseeing or nightlife costs on top. There's not much point visiting if you can't enjoy some of the city's life, so if possible add another £15.

Costs will obviously be even higher if you choose to stay in a central hotel and eat restaurant meals. Hotel rates start at around £30 per person and a restaurant meal will be at least £10. Add a couple of pints of beer (£2 each) and entry fees to a tourist attraction or nightclub and you could easily spend £55 per day – without being extravagant.

Once you start moving around the country, particularly if you have a transport pass or are walking or hitching, the costs will drop. Fresh food costs roughly the same as in Australia and the USA. However, without including long-distance transport, and assuming you stay in hostels and an occasional cheap B&B, you'll still need around £25 per day. A country youth hostel will cost from £5.85 to £8.80; add £4 for food, £5 for entry charges and/or local buses, and £4 for miscellaneous items like films, shampoo, books, telephone calls …

If you hire a car or use a transport pass, stay in B&Bs, eat one sit-down meal a day and don't stint on entry fees, you'll need £40 to £50 per day (still not including long-distance transport costs). Most basic B&Bs will be from £15 to £20 per person and dinner will be from £8 to £15 (depending on whether you're eating in a restaurant or a

Pub signs are a distinctive, decorative feature of many British pubs

CHRIS MELLOR

They're changing the guard at Buckingham Palace

RICHARD I'ANSON

View from the Golden Gallery, St Paul's

JON DAVISON

UNDERGROUND

Take the quick and easy route around London

RICHARD I'ANSON

Horse Guard

pub and how much you drink); then add £3 for snacks and drinks, £4 for miscellaneous items and at least £5 for entry fees. If you're travelling by car you'll probably average a further £7 to £12 per day on petrol and parking (not including hire charges); if you travel using some sort of pass you'll probably average a couple of pounds a day on local transport or hiring a bike.

Train fares usually rise by around 5% every January. Bus fares usually increase by a few pence every April and October. Admission fees seem to rise by 50p or £1 a year.

Throughout this book admission costs are given as adult/child.

Tipping & Bargaining

In general, if you eat in a British restaurant you should leave a tip of at least 10% unless the service was unsatisfactory. Waiting staff are often paid derisory wages on the assumption that the money will be supplemented by tips. If the bill already includes a service charge of 10 to 15%, you needn't add a further tip.

Some restaurants have been known to include the service charge in the total cost shown on a credit card voucher, but to leave a blank for a further tip/gratuity. This is a scam – you only have to tip once.

Taxi drivers also expect to be tipped (about 10%), especially in London. It's less usual to tip minicab drivers.

Bargaining is virtually unheard of, even at markets, although it's fine to ask if there are discounts for students, young people, or youth hostel members. Some 'negotiation' is also OK if you're buying an expensive item such as a car or motorcycle.

Taxes & Refunds

Value-Added Tax (VAT) is a 17.5% sales tax that is levied on virtually all goods and services except food and books. Restaurant prices must by law include VAT.

It's sometimes possible to claim a refund of VAT paid on goods – a considerable saving. You're eligible if you've spent *less* than 365 days out of the two years prior to making the purchase living in Britain, and if you're leaving the EU within three months of making the purchase.

Not all shops participate in the VAT refund scheme, and different shops will have different minimum purchase conditions (normally around £40). On request, participating shops will give you a special form/invoice; they will need to see your passport. This form must be presented with the goods and receipts to customs when you depart (VAT-free goods can't be posted or shipped home). After customs has certified the form, it should be returned to the shop for a refund less an administration fee.

Several companies offer a centralised refunding service to shops. Participating shops carry a sign in their window. You can avoid bank charges for cashing a sterling cheque by using a credit card for purchases and asking to have your VAT refund credited to your card account. Cash refunds are sometimes available at major airports.

POST & COMMUNICATIONS
Post

Post office hours can vary, but most are open from 9 am to 5 pm, Monday to Friday, and from 9 am to noon on Saturday. First class mail is quicker and more expensive (26p per letter) than 2nd class mail (20p).

Air-mail letters to other European countries cost 30p, to the Americas and Australasia 43/63p (up to 10/20 grams).

If you don't have a permanent address, mail can be sent to poste restante in the town or city where you are staying. American Express Travel offices will also hold card-holders' mail free of charge.

An air-mail letter generally take less than a week to get to the USA or Canada; around a week to Australia or New Zealand.

Telephone

Although British Telecom (BT) is still the largest telephone operator, with the most public phone booths, there are several competing companies.

The famous red phone booth survives in conservation areas. More usually you'll see two types of glass cubicles, one taking money, the other prepaid plastic debit cards and credit cards.

All phones come with reasonably clear instructions. If you're likely to make several calls (especially international) and don't want to be caught out, buy a BT phonecard. Ranging in value from £2 to £20, they're widely available from all sorts of retailers, including post offices and newsagents.

In this guide telephone area codes are listed at the start of the town entry or, in smaller places, with numbers in the section. Other codes worth knowing about are:

☎ 0345 local call rates apply
☎ 0500 call is free to caller
☎ 0800 call is free to caller
☎ 0891 premium rates apply; 39p cheap rate, 49p at other times
☎ 0990 national call rate applies

Beware of other codes that may indicate you're calling a mobile phone. This is usually considerably more expensive than calling a conventional phone.

Local & National Calls in Britain Local calls are charged by time; national calls are charged by time and distance. Daytime rates are from 8 am to 6 pm, Monday to Friday; the cheap rate is from 6 pm to 8 am, Monday to Friday; the cheap weekend rate from midnight Friday to midnight Sunday. The latter two rates offer substantial savings.

For directory inquiries call ☎ 192. These calls are free from public telephones but will be charged at 25p if you call from a private phone. To get the operator call ☎ 100.

International Calls Dial ☎ 155 for the international operator. To get an international line (for international direct dialling) dial ☎ 00, then the country code, area code (drop the first zero if there is one) and number. Direct dialling is cheaper but budget travellers often prefer operator-connected reverse-charges (collect) calls.

You can also use the Home Country Direct service to make a reverse-charge or credit card call via an operator in your home country which should avoid any language

problems. To find the Home Country Direct number for a particular country, look at the end of the country entry in the phone book.

To call Britain from abroad, dial your country's international access code, then ☎ 44 (Britain's country code), then the local code without the initial zero and the seven-digit phone number.

If you need to get a message overseas urgently, call ☎ 0800-190190.

International Rates For most countries (including Europe, USA and Canada) it's cheaper to phone overseas between 8 pm and 8 am Monday to Friday and at weekends; for Australia and New Zealand, however, it's cheapest from 2.30 to 7.30 pm and from midnight to 7 am every day. The savings are considerable.

The cheapest place to make an international call is often from one of the independent telecom centres. CallShop, in London, for example, offers cheaper international calls than BT. You phone from a metered booth and then settle the bill. It's also possible to undercut BT rates by buying a special phonecard to use from any phone, even a home phone. The most widely available Swiftlink cards are available from newsagents and grocers, but there are several other companies too; to decide which is best you must compare the rate each offers for the particular country you want.

Emergency Dial ☎ 999 (free call) for fire, police or ambulance.

Warning

Changes to Telephone Area Codes
New UK area codes are being introduced from June 1999 in London, Cardiff, Coventry, Portsmouth and Southampton. From 22 April 2000 you must use either the new 8-digit number, or the old number preceded by the old area code, when dialling locally. Check each city for specific details in the regional chapters of this book.

Fax

CallShop etc (see International Calls in the previous section) is the best place for sending or receiving faxes. It costs 25p a page to receive a fax. There's also a BT payfax machine at Victoria Coach Station in London. Shops offering a fax service will probably have a sign on the door.

Email & Internet Access

Modern hotels will be geared up for access and most big towns have at least one cybercafé. Hostels, too, have been keen to offer Internet access to their customers.

INTERNET RESOURCES

Britain is second only to the USA in its number of World Wide Web sites and there are plenty of sites to interest cyber travellers. An increasing number of towns, attractions, even B&Bs, have their own Web sites.

The best place to start is the Lonely Planet Web site (www.lonely planet.com .au) which offers a speedy link to numerous sites of interest to travellers to Britain.

BOOKS

Countless guidebooks explore Britain's every nook and cranny. When you arrive, one of your first stops should be at a good bookshop – there are several excellent possibilities in London (see Bookshops in the London chapter). The YHA Adventure Shop, 14 Southampton Row, Covent Garden, the British Travel Centre and the London Tourist Board's Victoria station centre also stock hundreds of books.

Lonely Planet

Lonely Planet publishes *Walking in Britain*, that outlines all the national trails, long-distance footpaths and interesting walking possibilities throughout Britain.

Lonely Planet's *Scotland, London* and *Edinburgh* also have more detailed information on possibilities for visitors to Britain.

Guidebooks

For history, art and architecture, the excellent *Blue Guide* series offers a wealth of scholarly information on all the important sites, including good maps. They have separate guides to England, Scotland and Wales).

Numerous books list B&Bs, restaurants, hotels, country houses, camping and caravan parks, and self-catering cottages but often their objectivity is questionable as the places they cover pay for the privilege of being included. Those published by the tourist authorities are reliable (if not comprehensive) and widely available in TICs. The *Which?* books produced by the Consumers' Association are good and accurate: no money changes hands for recommendations.

Walkers are very well catered for. The long-distance trails are all covered by the excellent *Countryside Commission National Trail Guide* series published by Aurum Press. For shorter walks, the spiral-bound *Bartholomew Map & Guide* series offers good maps and descriptions; most walks described take two to three hours.

People of literary bent might like to look at the *Oxford Literary Guide to Great Britain and Ireland* that details the many writers who have immortalised the towns and villages.

Travel

Bill Bryson's highly entertaining and perceptive *Notes from a Small Island* is the most recent travelogue covering Britain. Charles Jennings' *Up North – Travels Beyond the Watford Gap* starts promisingly but rapidly becomes monotonous. *The Kingdom by the Sea* by Paul Theroux and Jonathan Raban's *Coasting* were both written in 1982 and so are now a little dated, but they're nonetheless very readable. Older but still readable is John Hillaby's *Journey Through Britain* which describes a walk from Land's End to John o'Groats in 1969, great for measuring the changes that have taken place over the last 30 years.

Dervla Murphy's *Tale of Two Cities*, written in 1987, offers a veteran travel writer's view of life among Britain's ethnic minorities in Bradford/Manningham and Birmingham/Handsworth.

For a look behind the razzamatazz of Cool Britannia, Nick Danziger's *Danziger's*

Britain should be required reading. The picture it paints of late 20th century Britain is thoroughly depressing but this guy has seen the world and if this is how he says it is, then it's hard to argue with him.

History & Politics

A Traveller's History of England by Christopher Daniell offers a quick introduction to English history.

For a left-looking analysis of Britain's position at the close of the 20th century, try either *The State We're In* or *The State to Come,* both by *Observer* editor Will Hutton.

Anyone interested in knowing more about the 1997 election should consult *Were You Still Up For Portillo?* by Brian Cathcart, or *Whatever Happened to the Tories?*, ex-MP Ian Gilmour's examination of Conservatism since 1945.

Natasha Walter has written an upbeat account of the state of late 20th century feminism in Britain in *The New Feminism.* One of the striking things about the 1997 election was the arrival of 100-odd female MPs in a House of Commons previously even more dominated by men. Linda McDougall's *Westminster Women* examines what difference their presence is likely to make.

Windrush – The Irresistible Rise of Multicultural Britain by Mike and Trevor Phillips traces the history of black Britain and the impact of immigrants on British society.

FILMS

The best known film made about Britain recently must be *The Full Monty,* a tale of unemployed Sheffield steelworkers turned male strippers, that went on to become the best-selling British film ever, even outdoing the perennial favourite *Four Weddings and a Funeral* that depicted life at the opposite end of the social spectrum. Less hyped but in some ways an even better film is *Brassed Off,* the sad story of a colliery band attempting to keep going while the South Yorkshire pit on which they depend for work closes down.

A world away from such gritty social realism were the spate of adaptations of Jane Austen novels that hit the screens during the 1990s. *Pride and Prejudice* was made for television but *Emma* and *Sense and Sensibility* were feature-length films. Filming took place all round England; see if you can recognise Montacute in Somerset, Lacock in Wiltshire and Lyme Park in Cheshire.

The French Lieutenant's Woman, based on the John Fowles' novel of the same name, made great play with the landscape around Lyme Regis in Dorset. *Howard's End,* the Merchant-Ivory adaptation of the EM Foster novel, looked as if it was set in the Home Counties but actually strayed as far afield as Ludlow in Shropshire.

NEWSPAPERS & MAGAZINES
Newspapers

Breakfast need never be boring in Britain – there's a very wide range of dailies available.

The bottom end of the British newspaper market is occupied by *The Sun, The Mirror, Daily Star* and *The Sport. The Sun* is a national institution with witty headlines and nasty, mean-spirited contents. After a long period in the doldrums, *The Mirror,* once a decent paper with left-wing sympathies, has started to reposition itself slightly more upmarket. *The Sport* takes bad taste to the ultimate, with a steady diet of semi-naked women of improbable proportions and stories of space invaders.

The middle-market tabloids – the *Daily Mail* and *Daily Express* – are Tory strongholds, thunderously supporting the Conservative government (although even their loyalty faltered in the run-up to the 1997 election) and reserving their spleen for anyone of liberal persuasion. *The European* makes an honourable attempt to make the British feel part of the continent.

The broadsheets can be stuffy and self-important, but are generally stimulating and well written. The *Daily Telegraph,* or 'Torygraph', far outsells its rivals and its readership remains old fogeyish despite efforts to attract a new clientele. *The Times,* once Britain's finest paper, has lost ground under Murdoch's ownership but remains conservative and influential. *The Independent* tries hard to live up to its title but is still struggling to find a settled market. The lively and innovative, if mildly left-wing, *Guardian* is read by the chattering classes.

The Sunday papers are essential to the British way of life. On their day of rest, the British still settle in comfy armchairs and plough their way through endless supplements; *The Sunday Times* must destroy at least one rainforest per issue. Most of the daily papers have a Sunday stablemate that shares their political views. The oldest of the Sundays, *The Observer*, is the seventh day version of *The Guardian*.

You can also buy the *International Herald Tribune* and many foreign-language papers, especially in central London.

Magazines

Walk into any High Street newsagent and you'll realise that Britain boasts a magazine for almost any interest, with whole shelves of computer magazines, trainspotting magazines, heritage magazines, even magazines devoted to such esoteric interests as *feng shui* ... and that's before you raise your eyes to the top shelf!

Most big towns have a listings magazine broadly along the lines of London's *Time Out*. Some are free although the best cost a pound or so and are mentioned in the relevant chapters of this book.

Of the myriad women's magazines *Marie Claire* is probably the most stimulating and original. But in recent years the surprise growth market has been in non-porn magazines for men. Liftoff really came after the launch of *Loaded*, a raunchy magazine aimed at the so-called New Lad culture. Hot on its heels came *FHM*, *GQ* and *Esquire*.

The biweekly satirical *Private Eye* is another British institution that retains its sharp edge even at the risk of regular run-ins with the law.

Time and *Newsweek* are also readily available.

RADIO & TV
Radio

BBC radio caters for most tastes. The main pop music station, Radio 1 (275M/1089kHz and 285M/1053kHz MW; 98.8MHz FM) aims fair and square at a younger audience and has refused to play music by 'dinosaur' bands like Status Quo. They've migrated to Radio 2 (88-90.2MHz FM) to make that channel slightly livelier than it used to be. Radio 3 (247M/1215kHz MW; 91.3MHz FM) spins the classics.

Despite attempts to change its image, Radio 4 (1500M/198kHz LW; 417M/720kHz MW; 93.5MHz FM) still appeals mainly to a more mature audience, offering a mixed bag of drama, news and current affairs; the *Today Programme* (Monday to Saturday, 6 to 9 am) is entertaining. Radio 5 Live (463M/693kHz MW) intersperses sport with current affairs, while the World Service (463M/648kHz MW) offers brilliant news coverage and quirky bits and pieces from around the world. GLR is the Beeb's London station for general listeners.

In the last decade, alternative radio stations have proliferated; wherever you go there's bound to be a local commercial station offering local news alongside the music. Virgin (105.8MHz FM/1215kHz MW) is a commercial pop station: Chris Evans hosts Virgin's popular morning show from 7 to 10 am.

Classic FM (100.9MHz) does classical music with commercials, Kiss FM (100MHz) is the best dance station, whilst the excellent Jazz FM (102.2MHz) caters for jazz and soul buffs. Talk Radio (1053kHz MW) is in the process of changing its image for the umpteenth time since its noisy kickoff with a succession of 'shock jocks' a few years back.

In the London area, other stations include Capital (95.8MHz FM), a commercial version of Radio 1, and Capital Gold (1548kHz MW), that recycles golden oldies.

TV

It's probably true to say that Britain still turns out some of the world's best TV, although the increasing competition as channels proliferate is resulting in standards slipping. Recent years have seen a spate of the sort of fly-on-the-wall documentaries that simply point a camera at the run-of-the-mill (hotels, driving schools, even Tesco's) and leave you amused but none the wiser.

There are currently five regular TV channels – BBC1 and BBC2 are publicly funded by a TV licence and don't carry advertising; ITV and Channels 4 and 5 are commercial stations and do. They're up against competition from Rupert Murdoch's satellite TV, BSkyB, and assorted cable channels. Cable churns out mostly missable rubbish but Sky is slowly monopolising sports coverage and has pioneered pay-per-view screenings of the most popular events.

VIDEO SYSTEMS

With many tourist attractions now selling videos as souvenirs it's worth bearing in mind that British videos are VHS PAL format and not compatible with NTSC or SECAM.

PHOTOGRAPHY & VIDEO
Film & Equipment

Although print film is widely available, slide film can be more elusive; if there's no specialist photographic shop around, Boots, the High St chemist chain, is the likeliest stockist. Print film (36-exposure) costs from £4.30 for ISO 100 to £5 for ISO 400. With slide film it's usually cheapest to go for process-inclusive versions although these will usually need to be developed in Britain: 36-exposure films cost from £7 for ISO 100 to £10.50 for ISO 400.

Technical Tips

With dull, overcast conditions common, high-speed film (ISO 200 or ISO 400) is useful. In summer, the best times of day for photography are usually early in the morning and late in the afternoon when the glare of the sun has passed.

Restrictions

Many tourist attractions either charge for taking photos or prohibit it altogether. Use of flash is frequently forbidden to protect delicate pictures and fabrics. Video cameras

are often disallowed because of the inconvenience they can cause to other visitors.

Airport Security

You will have to put your camera and film through the x-ray machine at all British airports. The machines are supposed to be film-safe, but you may feel happier if you put exposed films in a lead-lined bag to protect them.

TIME

With the millennium looming, all eyes will be on Greenwich in south-east London, the location of the prime meridian that divides the world into eastern and western hemispheres.

Wherever you are in the world, the time on your watch is measured in relation to the time at Greenwich – Greenwich Mean Time (GMT) – although strictly speaking, GMT is used only in air and sea navigation, and is otherwise referred to as Universal Time Coordinated (UTC).

Daylight-saving time (DST) muddies the water so that even Britain itself is ahead of GMT from late March to late October. But to give you an idea, San Francisco is eight hours and New York five hours behind GMT, while Sydney is 10 hours ahead of GMT. Phone the international operator on ☎ 155 to find out the exact difference.

Most public transport timetables use the 24 hour clock.

ELECTRICITY

The standard voltage throughout Britain is 240V AC, 50Hz. Plugs have three square pins and adaptors are widely available.

WEIGHTS & MEASURES

In theory Britain has now moved to metric weights and measures although non-metric equivalents are still used by much of the population. Distances continue to be given in miles except on some Scottish islands where hostel locations are indicated in kilometres. In most cases this book uses miles to indicate distance.

No Kilos Please, We're British

On New Year's Day 2000 not only will the British have to deal with the millennium bug but, worse still, they'll wake up to find that metrication has become compulsory courtesy of a dreaded European Union directive.

No change there then, you might well think. After all, Britain has supposedly been sloughing off imperial measures for the last 30 years.

But oddly enough this is something that seems to have passed Joe Public by. Interrogate a chef and they might well tell you how many ounces of butter to use; ask someone how much they weigh and they'll probably reel off the pounds; question a car salesperson and they'll tell you how fast their products go in miles per hour.

Actually, the car salesperson needn't change their spiel – the EU has ceded a permanent exemption for speed and distance. Pubs will be able to continue pulling pints, milkmen can go on popping a morning pinta on doorsteps.

But the chef? The mind boggles at the prospect of an army of metrication police raiding the nation's kitchens.

Most liquids other than milk and beer are sold in litres. For conversion tables, see the inside back cover.

LAUNDRY

Every High St has its laundrette – with rare exceptions disheartening places to spend much time. The average cost for a single load is £1.60 for washing, and around £1 for drying. Bring soap powder with you; it can be expensive if bought in a laundrette.

TOILETS

Although many conveniences are still pretty grim (graffitied or rendered vandal-proof in solid stainless steel), those at train stations, bus terminals and motorway service stations are generally good, usually with facilities for disabled people and those with young children. At the London rail and coach terminals you usually have to pay 20p to use the facilities but at least they're clean. You also have to pay to use the Tardis-like concrete booths in places like Leicester Square.

In theory it's an offence to urinate in the streets (and men could be arrested for indecent exposure). However, as everywhere, those who've passed the evening in the pub happily make use of underpasses and alleyways, thereby rendering them unpleasant for everyone else.

Many disabled toilets can only be opened with a special key that can be obtained from some tourist offices or by sending a cheque or postal order for £2.50 to RADAR (see Disabled Travellers in this chapter), together with a brief description of your disability.

HEALTH

Travel health largely depends on predeparture preparations, day-to-day health care while travelling and how you handle any medical problem or emergency that does develop.

Dial ☎ 999 for an ambulance or ☎ 0800-665544 for the address of the nearest doctor or hospital.

Predeparture planning

Immunisations No immunisations are necessary.

Health Insurance Make sure you have adequate health insurance. See Travel Insurance under Visas & Documents in this chapter for details.

Other Preparations Make sure you're healthy before you start travelling. If you are going on a long trip make sure your teeth are OK. If you wear glasses take a spare pair and your prescription.

If you require medication take an adequate supply, as it may not be available locally. Take the packaging showing the generic name, rather than the brand, which will make getting replacements easier. It's a good idea to have a legible prescription or letter from your doctor to show that you legally use the medication to avoid any problems.

Basic Rules

Care in what you eat and drink is the most important health rule; stomach upsets are the most likely travel health problem (between 30 and 50% of travellers in a two-week stay experience this) but the majority of these upsets will be relatively minor. Unfortunately, there has been an upsurge in cases of food poisoning in Britain so it doesn't pay to be complacent.

Water Tap water is always safe unless there's a sign to the contrary (eg on trains). Don't drink straight from a stream – you can never be certain there are no people or cattle upstream.

Environmental Hazards

Sunburn Even in Britain, and even when there's cloud cover, it's possible to get sunburnt surprisingly quickly – especially if you're on water, snow or ice. Use 15+ sunscreen, wear a hat and cover up with a long-sleeved shirt and pants.

Heat Exhaustion Dehydration or salt deficiency can cause heat exhaustion. In hot conditions and if you're exerting yourself make sure you get sufficient nonalcoholic liquids. Salt deficiency is characterised by fatigue, lethargy, headaches, giddiness and muscle cramps. Vomiting or diarrhoea can rapidly deplete your liquid and salt levels.

Fungal Infections To prevent fungal infections, wear loose, comfortable clothes, wash frequently and dry carefully. Always wear thongs (flip-flops) in shared bathrooms. If you get an infection, consult a chemist. Try to expose the infected area to air or sunlight as much as possible and wash all towels and underwear in hot water as well as changing them often.

Cold Hypothermia can occur when the body loses heat faster than it can produce it and the body's core temperature falls. It's surprisingly easy to progress from very cold to dangerously cold through a combination of wind, wet clothing, fatigue and hunger, even if the air temperature is above freezing.

Walkers in Britain should always be prepared for difficult conditions. It's best to dress in layers, and a hat is important as a lot of heat is lost through the head. A strong, waterproof outer layer is essential. Carry basic supplies, including food that contains simple sugars to generate heat quickly.

Symptoms of hypothermia are exhaustion, numb skin (particularly toes and fingers), shivering, slurred speech, irrational or violent behaviour, lethargy, stumbling, dizzy spells, muscle cramps and violent bursts of energy.

To treat it, get the person out of wind and rain, remove wet clothing and replace it with dry, warm clothing. Give them hot liquids – not alcohol – and some high-calorie, easily digestible food. This should be enough for the early stages of hypothermia, but if it's gone further, it may be necessary to place victims in warm sleeping bags and get in with them. Don't rub patients, or place them near a fire or remove their wet clothes in the wind. If possible, place a sufferer in a warm (not hot) bath.

Motion Sickness Eating lightly before and during a trip will reduce the chances of motion sickness. If you are prone to motion sickness try to find a place that minimises movement – near the wing on aircraft, close to midships on boats, near the centre on buses. Fresh air usually helps; reading and cigarette smoke don't. Commercial motion-sickness preparations, that can cause drowsiness, have to be taken before the trip commences. Ginger (available in capsule form) and peppermint (including mint-flavoured sweets) are natural preventatives.

Infectious Diseases

Diarrhoea Simple things like a change of water, food or climate can all cause a mild bout of diarrhoea, but a few rushed toilet trips with no other symptoms is not indicative of a major problem.

Dehydration is the main danger with any diarrhoea, particularly in children or the elderly as dehydration can occur quickly. Under all circumstances *fluid replacement* (at least equal to the volume being lost) is the most important thing to remember. Weak black tea with a little sugar, soda water, or soft drinks allowed to go flat and diluted 50% with clean water are all good. With severe diarrhoea a rehydrating solution is preferable to replace minerals and salts lost. Keep drinking small amounts often. Stick to a bland diet as you recover.

HIV & AIDS HIV, the Human Immunodeficiency Virus, develops into AIDS, Acquired Immune Deficiency Syndrome, which is a fatal disease. HIV is a major problem in many countries. Any exposure to blood, blood products or body fluids may put the individual at risk. The disease is often transmitted through sexual contact or dirty needles – vaccinations, acupuncture, tattooing and body piercing can be potentially as dangerous as intravenous drug use. HIV/AIDS can also be spread through infected blood transfusions; but in Britain these are screened and safe.

Sexually Transmitted Diseases Gonorrhoea, herpes and syphilis are among these diseases; sores, blisters or rashes around the genitals, discharges or pain when urinating are common symptoms. In some STDs, such as wart virus or chlamydia, symptoms may be less marked or not observed at all especially in women. Syphilis symptoms eventually disappear completely but the disease continues and can cause severe problems in later years. While abstinence from sexual contact is the only 100% effective prevention, using condoms is also effective. The treatment of gonorrhoea and syphilis is with antibiotics. The different sexually transmitted diseases each require specific antibiotics. There is no cure for herpes or AIDS.

Insect Bites & Stings

Bee and wasp stings are usually painful rather than dangerous. However, in people who are allergic to them severe breathing difficulties may occur and require urgent medical care. Calamine lotion or Stingose spray will give relief and ice packs will reduce the pain and swelling.

Midges – small bloodsucking flies – are a major problem in Scotland during summer. Bring mosquito repellent and some antihistamine if you suffer from allergies.

Women's Health

Antibiotic use, synthetic underwear, sweating and contraceptive pills can lead to fungal vaginal infections. These are characterised by a rash, itch and discharge and can be treated with a vinegar or lemon-juice douche, or with yoghurt. Nystatin, miconazole or clotrimazole pessaries or vaginal cream are the usual treatment.

Sexually transmitted diseases are a major cause of vaginal problems. Symptoms can include painful intercourse, a smelly discharge and sometimes a burning sensation when urinating. Male sexual partners must also be treated. Medical attention should be sought and remember, in addition to these diseases, HIV or hepatitis B can be acquired during exposure. Besides abstinence, it's best to practise safe sex using condoms.

Medical Emergency

Dial ☎ 999 (free) for an ambulance. Not all hospitals have an accident and emergency department; look for red signs with an 'H', followed by 'A&E' (Accident & Emergency).

Pharmacies should have a notice in the window, advising where you'll find the nearest late-night branch.

WOMEN TRAVELLERS
Attitudes Towards Women

The occasional wolf-whistle and groper on the London Underground aside, women will find Britain reasonably enlightened. There's nothing to stop women going into pubs alone, although not everyone likes doing this; pairs or groups of women blend more naturally into the wallpaper. Some restaurants still persist in assigning the table by the toilet to lone female diners, but fortunately such places become fewer by the year.

Safety Precautions

Solo travellers should have few problems, although common-sense caution should be observed in big cities, especially at night. Hitching is always unwise.

While it's certainly not essential, it can help to go on a women's self-defence course before setting out on your travels, if only for the increased feeling of confidence it's likely to give you.

Condoms are increasingly being sold in women's toilets as well as men's. Otherwise, all chemists and many service stations stock them. The contraceptive pill is available only on prescription. So, at the time of writing, was the 'morning-after' pill (actually effective for up to 72 hours after unprotected sexual intercourse), although this could well change. Family planning associations are listed in the phone book.

Useful Organisations

Most big towns have a Well Woman Clinic that can advise on general health issues. Find its address in the local phone book or ask in the library. Should the worst come to the worst, Rape Crisis Centres can offer support after an attack.

If you'd like to stay with women while you're travelling it's worth joining Women Welcome Women, an organisation which exists to put women travellers in touch with potential hostesses. It's at 88 Easton St, High Wycombe, Bucks HP11 1LT (☎/fax 01494-465441).

GAY & LESBIAN TRAVELLERS

In general, Britain is tolerant of homosexuality. Certainly it's possible for people to acknowledge their homosexuality in a way that would have been unthinkable 20 years ago; there are several openly gay MPs in the present parliament. That said, there remain pockets of out-and-out hostility (you only

need read the *Sun*, *Mail* or *Telegraph* to realise the limits of toleration) and overt displays of affection are not necessarily wise away from acknowledged 'gay' venues and districts.

As we go to press MPs have voted to reduce the age of homosexual consent from 18 to 16.

London and Manchester have flourishing gay scenes, and Brighton has long attracted the pink holiday-making pound.

Information & Useful Organisations

The Gay Men's Press has two useful pocket guides: *London Scene* and *Northern Scene*. There are several free listings magazines like *The Pink Paper* and *Boyz*, or the *Gay Times* (£2) which also has listings. They're all available at Gay's The Word (☎ 0171-278 7654), 66 Marchmont St, near Russell Square tube. *Time Out* is also a good source of information, as are other commercial listings magazines outside London.

Another source of information is the 24 hour Lesbian & Gay Switchboard (☎ 0171-837 7324) that can help with most general inquiries. London Lesbian Line (☎ 0171-251 6911) offers similar help but only from 2 to 10 pm, Monday and Friday and from 7 to 10 pm on Tuesday and Thursday.

DISABLED TRAVELLERS

For many disabled travellers, Britain is an odd mix of user-friendliness and unfriendliness. These days few buildings go up that are not accessible to wheelchair users; large, new hotels and modern tourist attractions are therefore usually fine. However, most B&Bs and guesthouses are in hard-to-adapt older buildings. This means that travellers with mobility problems may end up having to pay more for accommodation than their more able-bodied fellows.

It's a similar story with public transport. Newer buses sometimes have steps that lower for easier access, as do trains, but it's always wise to check before setting out. Phone London Transport on ☎ 0171-918 3312 for detailed advice. Tourist attractions sometimes reserve parking spaces near the entrance for disabled drivers.

The 1995 Disability Discrimination Act makes it illegal to discriminate against people with disabilities in employment or the provision of services. Over the next decade barriers to access will have to be removed and the situation for wheelchair users should slowly improve.

Many ticket offices, banks etc are fitted with hearing loops to assist the hearing impaired; look for the symbol of a large ear. Some tourist attractions, cathedrals etc have Braille guides or scented gardens for the visually impaired.

Information & Useful Organisations

If you have a physical disability, get in touch with your national support organisation and ask about the countries you plan to visit. They often have complete libraries devoted to travel, and can put you in touch with travel agents who specialise in tours for the disabled.

The Royal Association for Disability and Rehabilitation (RADAR) publishes a useful guide titled *Holidays and Travel Abroad: A Guide for Disabled People*, that gives a good overview of facilities available in Europe. Its *Access in London* is required reading. Contact RADAR (☎ 0171-250 3222) Unit 12, City Forum, 250 City Rd, London EC1V 8AF.

The Holiday Care Service (☎ 01293-774535), 2nd Floor, Imperial Buildings, Victoria Rd, Horley, Surrey RH6 7PZ, publishes a *Guide to Accessible Accommodation and Travel* for Britain and can offer general advice.

Rail companies in Britain theoretically offer a Disabled Persons' Railcard (£16) but don't make it easy for people to get one. First you must fill out a form published in a booklet which is available from the Railcards Office, TRMC CP 328, 3rd Floor, The Podium, 1 Evershott Rd, London NW1 1DN. You then post it to the Disabled Person's Railcard Office, PO Box York YA1 011FB and wait.

Many TICs have leaflets with accessibility details for their particular area.

SENIOR TRAVELLERS

Senior citizens are entitled to discounts on things like public transport, museum admission fees etc, provided they show proof of their age. Sometimes they need a special pass. The minimum qualifying age is generally 60 to 65 for men, 55 to 65 for women.

Information & Useful Organisations

In your home country, a lower age may entitle you to special travel packages and discounts (on car hire, for instance) through organisations and travel agents that cater to senior travellers. Start hunting at your local senior citizens advice bureau. In Britain, rail companies offer a Senior Citizens Railcard (£16) for people of 60 and over, giving 30% discounts.

TRAVEL WITH CHILDREN

England is notorious as a country whose residents prefer animals to children. Even though having babies is a trendy topic with the media, anyone travelling with children needs to be prepared for hotels that won't accept their offspring and for frosty stares if they bring them into restaurants.

That said, there are some child-friendly oases. Branches of *TGI Friday* lay on crayons and balloons for younger visitors (and, of course, McDonald's tries hard to cultivate future burger-buyers). Many pubs have given up the battle to exclude children and now lay on playgrounds and children's meals.

The *Which? Hotel Guide* identifies a few child-friendly classy hotels, and B&Bs in the big resorts are likely to be fairly welcoming. Modern, purpose-built hotels will almost certainly be able to rustle up a cot.

These days most supermarkets, big train and bus stations, motorway service stations,and major attractions will have toilets with baby-changing facilities. Some rail companies have also launched separate 'family carriages' – they're not all that special but it's a step in the right direction.

Breast feeding in public remains controversial. Women are fighting hard – a brave female MP even tried it in the House of Commons – but it'll be some time before the British feel relaxed about breasts displayed for any purpose other than titillation.

See Lonely Planet's *Travel with Children* by Maureen Wheeler for more information.

(Throughout this book admission costs are given as adult/child.)

USEFUL ORGANISATIONS

Membership of English Heritage (EH) (☎ 0171-973 3434), Portland House, Stag Place, London, SW1E 5EE and the National Trust (NT) (☎ 0171-222 9251), 36 Queen Anne's Gate, London, SW1H 9AS, is worth considering, if you're going to be in Britain for a while and are interested in historical buildings. Both are non-profit organisations dedicated to the preservation of the environment, and both care for hundreds of spectacular sites. Further information is also available from each organisation's Web site: www.english-heritage.org.uk or www.nationaltrust.org.uk.

English Heritage (EH)
 Most EH properties cost nonmembers around £2.30 to enter. Adult membership is £25 and gives free entry to all EH properties, half-price entry to Historic Scotland and Cadw (Wales) properties, and an excellent guidebook and map. You can join at most major sites. Ask about EH open days (usually in September), when properties not usually open to the public can be visited.
National Trust (NT)
 Most NT properties cost nonmembers from £1.50 to £6 to enter. Adult membership is £28; for under 25s it's £14. This gives free entry to all English, Welsh, Scottish and Northern Irish properties, and an excellent guidebook and map. You can join at most major sites. There are reciprocal arrangements with the National Trust organisations in Scotland, Australia, New Zealand, Canada and the USA (the Royal Oak Foundation), all of which are cheaper to join.
Great British Heritage Pass
 This pass gives access to National Trust and English Heritage properties and some of the expensive private properties. A seven-day pass

costs £30, 15 days is £42, one month is £56. It's available overseas (ask your travel agent or contact the nearest Thomas Cook office) or at the British Travel Centre in London.
Australasian Clubs
 The London Walkabout Club (☎ 0171-938 3001), 7 Abingdon Rd W8; Deckers London Club (☎ 0171-244 8641), 35 Earl's Court Rd SW5 9RH; and Drifters (☎ 0171-402 9171), 22A Craven Terrace W2, all offer back-up services like mail holding, local information, discounts on film processing, freight forwarding and equipment purchase, and cheap tours. They're mainly aimed at Aussies and Kiwis, but anyone is welcome. Membership is around £15. The clubs are all associated with tour companies – they hope you'll use them when you come to book tours.

In this book National Trust properties are indicated by the letters NT; English Heritage properties by EH.

Also see Useful Organisations in the Scotland and Wales Facts for the Visitor chapters.

DANGERS & ANNOYANCES
Crime
Britain is a remarkably safe country considering its size and the disparities in wealth. However, city crime is certainly not unknown, so taking caution, especially at night, is necessary. Pickpockets and bag snatchers operate in crowded public places like the London Underground, although this is not a big problem.

Take particular care at night. When travelling by tube in London, choose a carriage containing lots of other people and avoid some of the deserted suburban tube stations; a bus or cab can be a safer choice.

The most important things to guard are your passport, papers, tickets and money. It's always best to carry these items next to your skin or in a sturdy leather pouch on your belt. Carry your own padlock for hostel lockers.

Be careful even in hotels; don't leave valuables lying around in your room. Never leave valuables in a car and remove all luggage overnight. Report thefts to the police and ask for a statement, or your travel insurance company won't pay out; thefts from cars are often excluded anyway.

Touts & Scams

Hotel/hostel touts descend on backpackers at underground and main-line stations like Earl's Court, Liverpool St and Victoria. Treat their claims with scepticism and don't accept an offer of a free lift unless you know precisely where you are going (you could end up miles away).

Never accept the offer of a ride from an unlicensed taxi driver either – they'll drive you round and round in circles, then demand an enormous sum of money. Use a metered black cab, or phone a reputable minicab company for a quote.

Every year foreign men are lured into Soho strip clubs and hostess bars and efficiently separated from their money. It's tempting to say they deserve what they don't get.

Cardsharping – where tourists are lured into playing a game that seems to be going all one way until they join in whereupon the luck changes sides – seems to be on the wane, but in its place have come the mock auctions that operate primarily out of London's Oxford St. You may be handed a flyer advertising an auction of electrical and other goods at unbelievably cheap prices. But watch that word 'unbelievable' because that's just what they are. At the advertised venue you'll see attractive goods on display. However, you'll be asked to bid for goods in black plastic bags that you can't remove until the show's over. When you do remove it, you'll find your wonderful bargain has turned into fool's gold.

Beggars

The big cities, particularly London, have many beggars; if you must give, don't wave a full wallet around – carry some change in a separate pocket. However, it's much better to give to a recognised charity. All the arguments against giving to beggars in developing countries apply in Britain too. Shelter (☎ 0171-253 0202), 88 Old St EC1, is a voluntary organisation that helps the homeless. You could also consider buying *The Big Issue*, an interesting weekly paper available from homeless street vendors who benefit directly from sales.

Racism

Britain is not without racial problems, particularly in some of the deprived inner cities, but in general tolerance prevails. Visitors are unlikely to have problems associated with their skin colour, but please let us know if you find otherwise.

LEGAL MATTERS
Drugs

Although even possession of cannabis is still illegal, drugs of every description are widely available, especially in clubs where Ecstasy is at the heart of the rave scene. Nonetheless, all the usual dangers associated with drugs apply and there have been several high-profile deaths associated with Ecstasy. Possession of small quantities of cannabis usually attracts a small fine (still a criminal conviction) or a warning; other drugs are treated more seriously.

Much of Britain's crime is associated with drug dealing. Don't even think of getting caught up in it, and remember that the dodgiest bits of the cities are usually those associated with dealing.

Driving Offences

The laws against drink-driving are treated more seriously and have become tougher than they used to be. Currently you're allowed to have a blood-alcohol level of 35mg/100ml, but there's talk of reducing the limit to a single drink. The safest approach is not to drink anything at all if you're planning to drive.

The other laws of the road most likely to catch visitors out relate to speeding and parking. The current speed limits are 30mph in built-up areas (indicated by the presence of street lighting), 60mph elsewhere and 70mph on motorways and dual carriageways. Other speed limits will be indicated by signs. Increasingly, speed cameras are being installed to catch boy racers red-handed ... it's hard to argue with the evidence of a film.

Parking in the wrong place may not be a criminal offence but can still cost you a lot of money, especially if your car is clamped and you have to pay to retrieve it from a pound – you won't see much change from £100 if this happens to you. Car park charges may be a pain but they're cheaper than being clamped.

On-the-Spot Fines
In general you rarely have to cough up on-the-spot for your offences. The two main exceptions are trains (including London Underground trains) and buses where people who can't produce a valid ticket for the journey when asked to by an inspector can be fined there and then; at least £5 on the buses, £10 on the trains, no excuses accepted.

BUSINESS HOURS
Offices are generally open from 9 am to 5 pm, Monday to Friday. Shops may be open longer hours, and most are open on Saturday from 9 am to 5 pm. An increasing number of shops also open on Sunday, perhaps from 10 am to 4 pm. In country towns, particularly in Scotland and Wales, shops may have an early-closing day – usually Tuesday, Wednesday or Thursday afternoon. Late-night shopping is usually on Thursday or Friday.

PUBLIC HOLIDAYS & SPECIAL EVENTS
Public Holidays
Most banks, businesses and some museums and other places of interest are closed on public holidays: New Year's Day, 2 January (Bank Holiday in Scotland), Good Friday, Easter Monday (not in Scotland), May Day Bank Holiday (first Monday in May), Spring Bank Holiday (last Monday in May), Summer Bank Holiday (first Monday in August in Scotland, last Monday in August outside Scotland), Christmas Day and Boxing Day. An extra day's holiday has also been announced for the millennium festivities.

Museums and other attractions may well observe the Christmas Day and Boxing Day holidays but generally stay open for the other holidays. Exceptions are those that normally close on Sunday; they're quite likely to close on bank holidays too. Some smaller museums close on Monday and/or Tuesday, and several places, including the British Museum, close on Sunday morning.

Special Events
Countless events are held around the country all year. Even small villages have weekly markets, and many still re-enact traditional customs and ceremonies, some dating back hundreds of years. Useful BTA publications include *Forthcoming Events* and *Arts Festivals*, that list a selection of the year's events and festivals with their dates.

New Year
　Hogmanay – huge street party to greet New Year; Edinburgh
Mid-March
　Crufts Dog Show – premier dog show; Birmingham
　Cheltenham Gold Cup – horse race meeting; Cheltenham
Last week in March
　Oxford/Cambridge University Boat Race – traditional rowing race; River Thames, Putney to Mortlake, London
First Saturday in April
　Grand National – famous horse racing meeting; Aintree, Liverpool
Early May
　FA Cup Final – deciding match in England's premier football knock-out tournament; Wembley, London
　Brighton Festival – arts festival; runs for three weeks
Last week in May
　Chelsea Flower Show – premier flower show; Royal Hospital, London
　Bath International Festival – arts festival; runs for two weeks
First week in June
　Beating Retreat – military bands and marching; Whitehall, London
　Derby Week – horse racing and people watching; Epsom, Surrey
Mid-June
　Trooping the Colour – the Queen's birthday parade with spectacular pageantry; Whitehall, London
　Royal Ascot – more horses and hats; Ascot, Berkshire
Late June
　Lawn Tennis Championships – runs for two weeks; Wimbledon, London

Henley Royal Regatta – premier rowing and social event; Henley-on-Thames, Oxfordshire
Glastonbury Festival – huge open-air festival and hippy happening; Pilton, Somerset
Royal Highland Show – Scotland's national agricultural show; Edinburgh
London Pride – Europe's biggest gay and lesbian march and festival

Early July
Hampton Court Palace International Flower Show – London

Mid-July
Royal Welsh Show – national agricultural show; Llanelwedd, Builth Wells

Late July
Cowes Week – yachting extravaganza; Isle of Wight

Early August
Edinburgh Military Tattoo – pageantry and military displays; runs for three weeks
Royal National Eisteddfod of Wales – Gaelic cultural festival; alternates between sites in North and South Wales

Mid-August
Edinburgh International and Fringe Festivals – premier international arts festivals; run for three weeks

Late August (August Bank Holiday)
Notting Hill Carnival – enormous Caribbean carnival; London
Reading Festival – outdoor rock and roll for three days; Reading, Berkshire

Early September
Braemar Royal Highland Gathering – kilts and cabers; Braemar, Scotland

Mid-September
Farnborough International Aerospace Exhibition and Flying Display – world's largest aerospace exhibition; Farnborough, Surrey

October
Horse of the Year Show – best-known showjumping event in Britain; Wembley, London

5 November
Guy Fawkes Day – commemorating an attempted Catholic coup; bonfires and fireworks around the country

COURSES

No matter whether you want to study sculpture or Sanskrit, circus skills or computing, somewhere in Britain there's going to be a course. Local libraries are often a good starting point for finding information.

Language

Every year thousands of people come to Britain to study English and there are centres offering tuition all round the country. The problem is to identify the reputable ones, which is where the British Council (☎ 0171-930 8466), 10 Spring Gardens, London SW1, comes in. It produces a free list of accredited colleges that meet minimum standards for facilities, qualified staff and pastoral backup. It offers general advice to overseas students on educational opportunities in the UK since many normal colleges and universities now offer courses aimed at students from abroad.

The British Council has offices all round the world that can provide the same beginners information so you don't have to wait until you get to Britain to ask for help in choosing a college. The British Tourist Authority also produces a brochure for people wanting to study in England.

WORK

Despite the fact that large numbers of locals continue to go jobless, if you're prepared to do anything and to work long hours for poor pay, you'll almost certainly find work. The trouble is that without skills, it's difficult to find a job that pays well enough to save money. You should be able to break even, but will probably be better off saving in your home country.

Traditionally, unskilled visitors have worked in pubs and restaurants and as nannies. Both jobs often provide live-in accommodation, but the hours are long, the work exhausting and the pay lousy. If you live in, you'll be lucky to get £125 per week; if you have to find your own accommodation you'll be lucky to get £175. Before you accept a job, make sure you're clear about the terms and conditions, especially how many hours (and what hours) you will be expected to work.

Accountants, nurses, medical personnel, journalists, computer programers, lawyers, teachers and clerical workers with computer experience stand a better chance of finding well-paid work. The job situation is improving as the British economy picks up again.

Even so, you'll probably need some money to tide you over while you search. Don't forget copies of your qualifications, references (which will probably be checked) and a CV.

Teachers should contact London borough councils, that administer separate education departments, although some schools recruit directly. To work as a trained nurse you have to register with the United Kingdom Central Council for Nursing, which can take up to three months; write to the Overseas Registration Department, UKCC, 23 Portland Place W1N 3AF. If you aren't registered you can still work as an auxiliary.

Nationals, who're aged 17 to 27, of Andorra, Bosnia-Herzegovina, Croatia, Cyprus, Czech Republic, The Faroes, Greenland, Hungary, Macedonia, Malta, Monaco, San Marino, Slovak Republic, Slovenia and Switzerland are allowed to work in the UK as au pairs for up to two years. On arrival they must be able to show a letter of invitation from their employers. As well as food and accommodation, au pairs usually get paid around £35 for working five hours a day, five days a week. The Federation of Recruitment & Employment Services (FRES), 36-38 Mortimer Rd, London W1N 7RB (www.fres.co.uk), produces a list of au pair agencies that they'll send on receipt of an international reply coupon.

TNT magazine is a good starting point for jobs and agencies aimed at travellers. For au pair and nanny work buy the quaintly titled *The Lady*. Also check the *Evening Standard*, national newspapers and the government-operated Jobcentres. There's a central branch at 195 Wardour St W1; for others look under Manpower Services Commission in the phone book. Whatever your skills, it's worth registering with several temporary agencies.

For details on all aspects of short-term work consult the excellent *Work Your Way Around the World* (Vacation Work) or *Working Holidays* (Central Bureau for Educational Visits and Exchanges).

Work Permits

EU nationals don't need a work permit, but all other nationalities do to work legally. If the *main* purpose of your visit is to work, you have to be sponsored by a British company.

However, if you're a citizen of a Commonwealth country, aged between 17 and 27 inclusive, you can apply for a Working Holiday Entry Certificate that allows you to spend up to two years in the UK and to take work that is 'incidental' to a holiday. You're not allowed to engage in business, pursue a career, or provide services as a professional sportsperson or entertainer.

You must apply to the nearest UK mission overseas – Working Holiday Entry Certificates are *not* granted on arrival in Britain. It's not possible to switch from being a visitor to a working holiday-maker, nor is it possible to claim back any time spent out of the UK during the two year period. When you apply, you must satisfy the authorities that you have the means to pay for a return or onward journey, and will be able to maintain yourself without recourse to public funds.

If you're a Commonwealth citizen and have a parent born in the UK, you may be eligible for a Certificate of Entitlement to the Right of Abode, which means you can live and work in Britain free of immigration control.

If you're a Commonwealth citizen and have a grandparent born in the UK, or if the grandparent was born before 31 March 1922 in what is now the Republic of Ireland, you may qualify for a UK Ancestry – Employment Certificate, which means you can work full time for up to four years in the UK.

Visiting full-time students from US colleges and universities who're aged at least 18 can get a work permit allowing them to work for six months. It costs US$200 and is available through the Council on International Educational Exchange (☎ 212-822 2600, www.ciee.org), 205 East 42nd St, New York, NY 10017. BUNAC (British Universities North America Club), PO Box 49, South Britain 06487 (☎ 203-264 0901, www.BUNAC.org) can also help you organise a permit and find work.

Tax

As an official employee, you'll find income tax and National Insurance automatically deducted from your weekly pay packet. However, the deductions will be calculated on the assumption that you will work for the entire financial year (which runs from April 6 to April 5).

If you don't work the entire year, you may be eligible for a refund. Contact the tax office, or use one of the agencies that advertise in *TNT* magazine (but check the fee or percentage charge first).

Anyone residing or working in Britain is also required to pay a council tax. Those on extremely low incomes *may* be partially exempt, but otherwise the tax is determined by the council's financial needs and varies only according to the value of your residence. Single householders get 25% discount.

In theory, you're obliged to register with your local council whenever you move into a permanent residence (not including hostels or hotels). In practice, the tax is very difficult to police, particularly in the case of itinerant young travellers.

ACCOMMODATION

This will almost certainly be your single greatest expense. Even camping can be expensive at official sites.

For travel on the cheap, there are two main options: youth hostels and bed & breakfasts (B&Bs), although over the past few years several independent backpackers' hostels have opened and the number is growing, particularly in popular hiking regions.

In the middle range, superior B&Bs are often in beautiful old buildings and some rooms will have private bathrooms with showers or baths. Guesthouses and small hotels are more likely to have private bathrooms, but they also tend to be less personal. If money's no object, there are also some superb hotels, the most interesting in converted castles and mansions.

All these options are promoted by local TICs. Many charge £1 for local bookings for accommodation within the next two nights, although you may also have to pay a 10% deposit which is subtracted from the nightly price.

Most TICs also participate in the Book-A-Bed-Ahead (BABA) scheme that allows you to book accommodation for the next two nights anywhere in Britain. Most charge around £3 and take a 10% deposit. Outside opening hours, most TICs put a notice and map in their window showing which local places have unoccupied beds. These services are particularly handy for big cities and over weekends and the peak summer season.

The national tourist boards operate a classification and grading system; participating hotels, guesthouses and B&Bs have a plaque at the front door. If you want to be confident that your accommodation reaches basic standards of safety and cleanliness, the first classification is 'listed', which denotes clean and comfortable accommodation. One crown means each room will have a washbasin and its own key. Two crowns means washbasins, bedside lights and a TV in a lounge or in bedrooms. Three crowns means at least half the rooms have private bathrooms and that hot evening meals are available. And so on up to five crowns.

In addition there are also gradings ('approved', 'commended', 'highly commended' and 'deluxe') which may actually be more significant since they reflect a judgment on quality.

In practice there's a wide range within each classification and some of the best B&Bs don't participate at all because they have to pay to do so. A high-quality 'listed' B&B can be 20 times nicer than a low-quality 'three crown' hotel. In the end actually seeing the place, even from the outside, will give the best clue as to what to expect. Always ask to look at your room before deciding.

As ever, single rooms are in short supply (see the boxed text 'Is It Just for You, Then?').

The worst value accommodation tends to be in big towns where you often pay more for inferior quality (abrupt service, chaotic

Is It Just for You, Then?

If there's one thing guidebook writers know more about than most people, it's trekking round on their own for weeks on end. And what a disheartening experience that can be in Britain.

You're worn out and hungry, and there's this great little place just up the road. Imagining the warm welcome and even warmer fire inside, you ring the bell. The door opens and your putative host's face falls. 'Is it only for you, then?' they ask accusingly, as if you might have an army of companions lurking out of sight. Then, 'Sorry, we don't have any single rooms' (when they're obviously empty), or 'Come inside' and you're shown to a pokey top-floor room that measures about the size of a prison cell and doubles as the fire escape. For such luxury you're charged a 'single supplement' that doesn't save you from being shown to the table by the swinging kitchen door at breakfast.

Even some of the best places do this and things can only get worse as the chain hotels make flat-rate pricing (so great for couples, so bad if you're alone) the norm. Hoteliers claim it takes the same amount of work to service a room for one as one for two. They also claim, more justifiably, that single rooms take up a disproportionate amount of space.

Of course, there are always the hostels. But just because you're alone it doesn't necessarily mean you want to share a room with half a dozen strangers.

Hats off, then, to those lovely hoteliers who show the same hospitality to their lone visitors as they do to couples. You're heroes, one and all!

décor, ropey fittings). There are rarely any really cheap B&Bs in the city centres which means those without cars are also stuck with bus services that tail off just when they're getting ready to go out in the evening.

Camping

Free camping is rarely possible, except in Scotland. Camp sites vary widely in quality, most have reasonable facilities, but they're usually tricky to get to without your own transport. The RAC's *Camping & Caravanning in Britain* has extensive lists; local TICs also have details.

Those planning to camp extensively, or tour with a van, should join the Camping & Caravanning Club (☎ 01203-694995), Greenfields House, Westwood Way, Coventry CV4 8JH. The world's oldest camping and caravanning club runs many British sites including club-owned sites, certificated sites with minimal facilities taking only five vans, and commercial sites which range from enormous holiday parks to quiet overnight stops for backpackers.

Many sites are open to nonmembers, but 2000 are not, and nonmembers pay higher fees. Members receive a guide to 5000 sites and other useful services (including advice, camping carnets and insurance) for both British and European trips. Membership, which will cover one camp site and all who use it, is £30 – but it will quickly pay for itself.

Camping is possible at some National Trust properties; for a list of addresses send an SAE to the Membership Dept, PO Box 39, Bromley, Kent BR1 3XL (☎ 0181-315 1111). You can also camp in seven Forestry Commission forest parks and in the New Forest; contact the Forestry Commission, Corstorphine Rd, Edinburgh EH12 7AT (☎ 0131-334 0303) for details.

The tourist boards rate caravan and camping grounds with one to five ticks; the more ticks, the higher the standard.

YHA Hostels

Membership of a Youth Hostel Association (YHA) gives you access to a network of hostels throughout England, Wales and Scotland – and you don't have to be young or single to use them.

There are separate local associations for England/Wales and Scotland, and each publishes its own accommodation guide. If you plan to use hostels extensively it's wise to get hold of these as they include the often complicated opening times, as well as exact details of how to reach each place.

All the British associations are affiliated to Hostelling International (HI), which has recently changed its name from International Youth Hostel Federation to move away from the emphasis on 'youth'. Some countries immediately adopted the new name, but Britain is still sticking with YHA and SYHA. It makes no difference – YHA, IYHF or HI, it's all the same thing.

For England and Wales the head office is 8 St Stephen's Hill, St Albans, Herts AL1 2DY (☎ 01727-855215); or try the Web site on www.yha.org.uk. Guides and membership information are available at the YHA Adventure Shop at 14 Southampton St, London WC2E 7HY (tube: Covent Garden), and branches round the country, or you can join in your home country.

For the Scotland YHA the head office is 7 Glebe Crescent, Stirling FK8 2JA (☎ 01786-891400).

National offices include:

Australia
    (☎ 02-9565 1699)
    Each state has its own Youth Hostel Association. The National Administration Office is the Australian Youth Hostels Association, Level 3, 10 Mallett St, Camperdown, NSW 2050
Canada
    (☎ 613-237 7884)
    Hostelling International Canada, 400-205 Catherine St, Ottawa, Ontario K2P 1C3
New Zealand
    (☎ 03-379 9970)
    Youth Hostels Association of New Zealand, PO Box 436, 173 Gloucester St, Christchurch 1
USA
    (☎ 202-783 6161)
    Hostelling International, PO Box 37613, Washington, DC 20013-7613

All hostels have facilities for self-catering and some provide cheap meals. Advance booking is advisable, especially at weekends, bank holidays and at any time over the summer months. Booking policies vary: most hostels accept phone bookings and payment with Visa or Access (MasterCard) cards; some will accept same-day bookings, although they will usually only hold a bed until 6 pm; some participate in the Book-A-Bed-Ahead scheme; some work on a first come, first served basis.

The advantages of hostels are primarily price (although the difference between a cheap B&B and an expensive hostel isn't huge) and the chance to meet other travellers. The disadvantages are that some are still run dictatorially, you're usually locked out between 10 am and 5 pm, the front door is locked at 11 pm, you usually sleep in bunks in a single-sex dormitory, and many are closed during winter. Official youth hostels are rarely in town centres; fine if you're walking the countryside or have your own transport, a pain if you're not.

Overnight prices depend on age: under 18, you pay £4 to £17.90, but mostly around £5.95; adult, you pay £5.85 to £21.30, but mostly around £8.80. By the time you've added £2.95 for breakfast, you can get very close to cheap B&B prices.

Throughout this book, higher hostel prices for adults are given first, followed by the reduced price for juniors.

Independent Hostels

The growing network of independent hostels offers the opportunity to escape curfews and lockouts for a price of around £9 to £12 per night in a basic bunkroom. Like YHA hostels these are great places to meet other travellers, and they tend to be in town centres rather than out in the sticks, which will suit the non-walking fraternity. New places are opening fast so it's worth double-checking with the TIC.

University Accommodation

Many British universities offer their student accommodation to visitors during the holidays: usually for three weeks over Easter and Christmas and from late June to late September. Most such rooms are comfortable, functional single bedrooms but without single supplements. Increasingly, however, there are rooms with private bathroom, twin and family units, self-contained flats and shared houses.

University catering is usually reasonable; full-board, half-board, bed and breakfast and self-catering options are available. Bed and breakfast normally costs from £18 to £25 per person.

For more information contact BUAC (British Universities Accommodation Consortium), Box No 1562E, University Park, Nottingham NG7 2RD (☎ 0115-950 4571, fax 0115-942 2505).

B&Bs & Guesthouses

Bed and breakfasts (B&Bs) are a great British institution and the cheapest private accommodation around. At the bottom end (£12 to £18 per person) you get a bedroom in a private house, a shared bathroom and an enormous cooked breakfast (juice, cereal, bacon, eggs, sausage, baked beans and toast). Small B&Bs may only have one room to let, and you can really feel like a guest of the family – they may not even have a sign.

More upmarket B&Bs have private bathrooms and TVs in each room. Traditionally the British have preferred baths to showers. In many B&Bs and private houses you may find just a bath or a highly complicated contraption that produces a thin trickle of scalding hot or freezing cold water. Get the home-owner to explain how it works if you want a half-decent shower.

Double rooms will often have two single beds (twin beds) rather than a double bed so you don't have to be lovers to share. Many B&Bs have conservative owners so it pays to be a little careful in what you say and how you act.

Some tenants of the National Trust offer B&B in attractive parts of the country. For a complete list of such properties, write to the Membership Dept, PO Box 39, Bromley, Kent BR1 3XL (☎ 0181-315 1111).

British Interior Design

Visitors will gain a vivid insight into modern British interior design if they stay at B&Bs. Most feature do-it-yourself (DIY) renovation and strive for a popular style that has been described as 'cosy, with a country house, cottagey look'!

A classic example of a B&B will have embossed and flowery wallpaper, hung crookedly, and swirly-patterned synthetic carpets, laid badly. The light fittings will be mock candelabras and fussy lamps. The furniture will be covered in orange vinyl, purple velour and lace doilies. There will be a display of porcelain figures and ashtrays, and a collection of souvenirs – including at least one miniature wooden clog and a plastic sombrero. There'll be electric or gas heating and a fake fireplace with plastic logs and orange lights. Finally, there will be at least one print of a kitten in a gilt frame.

Bryn Thomas

Guesthouses, which are often just large converted houses with half a dozen rooms, are an extension of the B&B concept. They range from £12 to £50 a night, depending on the quality of the food and accommodation. In general, they're less personal than B&Bs, and more like small budget hotels.

Hotels

The term hotel covers everything from some local pubs to the grand playgrounds of the hyper-wealthy.

Pubs usually have a bar or two and a lounge where cheap meals are served; sometimes they'll also have a more upmarket restaurant. Increasingly in the countryside they also offer comfortable mid-range accommodation, but they can vary widely in quality. Staying in a pub can be good fun since it places you in the hub of the community, but they can be noisy and aren't always ideal for lone women travellers.

On the coast, and in other tourist-attracting areas, there are often big, old-style, residential hotels. The cheapest have sometimes been taken over by long-term homeless families who are being 'temporarily' housed by local authorities. They're not places for foreign visitors at all … which is one reason why it's wise to stick with tourist board-approved places except in rural areas.

More and more purpose-built chain hotels are appearing along the motorways and in the city centres. Most depend on business trade and offer competitive weekend rates to attract tourists; they also often have a flat rate per room (with twin or double beds and private bathroom), making them relative bargains for couples or small families. Travel Inns (☎ 0800-850950) charge £38 a room except in London. Other such groups are Granada Lodges (☎ 0800-555300), Campanile Hotels (☎ 0181-567 6969), Comfort Inns (☎ 0800-444444), Formule 1 Hotels (☎ 01302-761050), Travel Inns (☎ 01582-4144341) and Ibis (☎ 0181-759 4888).

The very best hotels are magnificent places, often with restaurants to match. If you want to splash out, pick up a copy of the *Which? Hotel Guide* (£14.99) that lists more than 1000 of the country's finest hotels, some of them in converted country-houses and castles. Recommendations are generally trustworthy because hotel owners don't have to pay to appear in the guide.

Rental Accommodation

There has been an upsurge in the number of houses and cottages available for short-term rent. Staying in one place gives you an opportunity to get a real feel for a region and a community. Cottages for four can cost as little as £100 per week; some are even let for three days.

Outside weekends and July/August, it's not essential to book a long way ahead. You may be able to book through TICs, but there are also excellent agencies who supply glossy brochures to help the decision-

making. Most have agents in North America and Australasia. Among them, Country Holidays (☎ 01282-445566), Spring Mill, Earby, Colne, Lancashire BB8 6RN, has been highly recommended. English Country Cottages (☎ 01328-851155), Grove Farm Barns, Sculthorpe, Norfolk, is another large, reliable agency. It's difficult to quote average prices, but expect a week's rent for a two bedroom cottage to cost from £150 in winter, £175 from April to June, and £250 from July to September.

The National Trust also rents out over 240 cottages that tend to be above average in charm, location and price. For a brochure write to the Holiday Booking Office, PO Box 536, Melksham, Wiltshire SN12 8SX (☎ 01225-791133), enclosing £2 towards postage.

The most spectacular possibilities are offered by the Landmark Trust (☎ 01628-825925), Shottesbrooke, Maidenhead, Berkshire SL6 3SW, UK; and in the USA (☎ 802-254 6868) at 28 Birge St, Brattleboro, Vermont 05301. This architectural charity was established to rescue historic buildings and is partly funded by renting the properties after they've been restored. The trust owns 164 unusual buildings, including medieval houses, castles, Napoleonic forts and bizarre 18th century follies (including the wonderful Pineapple near Falkirk, Scotland).

All the properties are advertised in the 280 page *Landmark Handbook* (£8.50, including postage and packing in Britain, US$19.50 including postage and packing in the USA, refundable on booking). Prices vary but average around £200 per week for a two bedroom place in winter, around £250 from April to June, and £300 in midsummer. Four people can stay at the Pineapple, for example, for between £400 and £600 a week.

The tourist boards rate self-catering accommodation with one to five keys; the more keys, the more facilities. One key indicates a property is clean and comfortable, has adequate heating, lighting and seating, a TV, cooker, fridge and crockery and cutlery.

Chain Cuisine

For years British cuisine was famous for little more than greasy fish and chips or steak and kidney pie. Except among the moneyed classes there was really no restaurant culture as in North America; for most people a good night out involved a visit to a pub and a takeaway curry or chop suey on the way home. All that's changed, however, to such an extent that London was recently dubbed the restaurant capital of the world.

Whether it's cruelty-free cosmetics, Italian knitwear or burgers-on-the-move, when a demand in the market becomes obvious the chains move in pronto. In Britain they've expanded spectacularly, getting into everything from Irish theme pubs to French brasseries. At all these places you can be sure that whatever you ate or drank at the branch in Cornwall, for example, will be precisely the same as what you consume in Caithness – even the decor will be identical.

The pub revolution began in 1989 when the Monopolies and Mergers Commission decided that each brewery should not own more than 2000 pubs. Until then most pubs were 'tied', selling just their brewer's products. As the larger breweries sold off their outlets many were bought by new companies that took a fresh look at the industry. Some, such as *JD Wetherspoon* went for value and a more pleasant drinking environment, with quiet smoke-free areas. Others went for the theme pub concept – hence the 'Irish' pubs like *O'Neill's* and *Scruffy Murphy's*, or the Australian *Walkabout Inn* and *Bar Oz*.

The more imaginative companies realised that the British today want more out of a pub than just a pint, and created a whole range of bar-restaurants, continental brasseries, and café bars. The line between the pub and the restaurant has become blurred – you'd be just as likely to visit these places for a cappuccino as for a beer.

Probably most representative of this concept is *All Bar One*. Wooden floors, refectory tables and gilt mirrors create a light and airy atmosphere. The menu is short but interesting (eg Cajun red snapper with Chinese cabbage and new potatoes), with small plates for £4.95 and large plates for £6.95 to £9.95. Wine is not cheap at £2.40 for a small glass, though. Long-running *Browns* is similar but offers a larger menu. The *Slug & Lettuce* has a cosier feel with kilims on the wall and soft sofas. *Edward's* seems to be aimed at a younger crowd with a cheaper menu and all-day breakfasts for £3.95. Other chain bar-restaurants include *Pitcher & Piano*, *Fraternity House* and *Yates's Wine Lodge*.

FOOD

Britain is the nation that brought us mashed potato, mushy peas and the fried Mars Bar, a cuisine so undesirable that there's no English equivalent for the French phrase *bon appétit*.

It's an image that has proved hard to shake off but, fortunately, things are improving fast, especially in the south. The supply of fresh fruit and vegetables has improved immeasurably. In the main towns and cities a cosmopolitan range of cuisines is available. Particularly if you like pizza, pasta and curry, you should be able to get a reasonable

meal pretty well anywhere. Chain restaurants like Café Rouge have also brought 'French' cuisine to most tourist-frequented High Streets for reasonably moderate prices. Indeed, the one thing it may be hard to find (except in pubs) is traditional British cuisine … dishes like roast beef and Yorkshire pudding or steak and kidney pie.

These days you'll come across lots of restaurants serving what is called modern British cookery, originally a term used to cover the mix-and-match use of all sorts of exotic ingredients served into continental-

Chain Cuisine

Chain restaurants have also had phenomenal success in Britain. Stylish, with a French café bar theme is *Café Rouge*. There's a *menu rapide* at lunchtime: three courses for £10, and an à la carte menu served throughout the day (main dishes £6.45-£9.95) but you're just as likely to stop by for a coffee (£1) or a glass of wine (£2). *Dôme* is similar, with rather grander decor.

An Italian version of the above is *Caffé Uno*, bright and cheerful with a Mediterranean feel, and serving standard Italian fare at reasonable prices. Spaghetti alla carbonara is £5.85. You'd be just as welcome for a coffee as for a full-blown meal. *Bella Pasta* is not so stylish but often has special offers that can make eating here very good value.

There are numerous pizzerias including the ubiquitous *Pizza Hut*. The best, however, is *Pizza Express*, with over 150 branches around Britain. Often housed in interesting old buildings, *Pizza Express* is not as expensive as it looks: a regular margarita costs £3.85. Ask is another good pizza chain. For thick crust fans, the *Deep Pan Pizza Co* does what it says at 89 branches around the country, from £4.50 for a regular margarita.

The American diner theme provides the basis for some chain restaurants. *OK Diner* is stuck in the 1950s with jukeboxes, hamburgers, melts, shakes and beers. *Frankie & Benny's* is New York Italian from the same era. Serving both American and British food, long-running but bland *Garfunkel's* is probably best known for its salad bar – all you can eat for £5.95. They're also open for breakfast (£5.50).

As in the US, there are several Mexican chains. *Chiquito* has chimichanga or burritos for £7.95. Nachos are marginally more expensive and have lively bars.

Finally, if all you want is a sandwich, you needn't settle for two bits of limp white bread and a yellow slice of cheddar. For value try the pharmacy chain *Boots*. The department store *Marks & Spencer* will sell you a more superior sandwich, though. Best, however, is *Pret A Manger*. Since they were set up in 1986 to serve passing London yuppies, the stylish, stainless-steel sandwich bars have mushroomed to around 70 outlets. They're a bit more expensive than your average sarnie but far more imaginative. How does oven baked ham in a baguette with mustard cloves and greve cheese sound? Chicken and roasted vegetables in Mediterranean bread is £2.70 as a takeaway, £3.20 if you eat in. Coffee is 99p.

style dishes but now extended to include the 'ironic' serving of staples like bangers and mash with the grease removed and the price inflated accordingly.

Vegetarianism has taken off in a big way. Non-meat-eaters should buy *The Vegetarian Travel Guide*, published annually by the UK Vegetarian Society and covering hundreds of places to eat and stay. Most restaurants have at least a token vegetarian dish, although, as anywhere, vegans will find the going tough. Indian restaurants offer a welcome choice.

Incidentally, curries have overtaken fish and chips as Britain's most popular takeaways.

Takeaways, Cafés & Pubs

Every High Street has its complement of takeaway restaurants, from McDonald's and Pizza Hut to the home-grown and aptly named Wimpy. You may not be able to avoid them because they're relatively cheap. The best of the worst is Burger King (known as Hungry Jack's in Australia), which even serves a vegetarian beanburger.

In the bigger towns, you will also find cafés, usually referred to as caffs or greasy spoons. Although they often look pretty seedy, they're usually warm, friendly, very British places and invariably serve cheap breakfasts (eggs, bacon and baked beans) and English tea (strong, sweet and milky). They also have plain but filling lunches, usually a roast with three veg, or bangers (sausages) and mash (mashed potato).

These days most pubs also do food, although Sunday can be tricky. At the cheap end pub meals are not very different from those in cafés, but at the expensive end they're closer to restaurants. Many pubs embrace both extremes with a cheap bar menu and a more formal restaurant. Chilli con carne or lasagne are often the cheapest offerings on the bar menu. A filling 'ploughman's lunch' of bread, cheese and pickle rarely costs more than £3.50.

On a tight budget it's worth knowing that many supermarkets and department stores have reasonable (and reasonably priced) cafés; as supermarket opening hours lengthen, so do those of their cafés.

Self-Catering

The cheapest way to eat in Britain is to cook for yourself. Hopefully, however, you won't be forced to the extremes of an Australian who was arrested and jailed for attempting to barbecue a Canada goose in Hyde Park! Even if you lack great culinary skills, you can buy good-quality pre-cooked meals from the supermarkets (Marks & Spencer's are the most highly regarded but also tend to be the priciest).

DRINKS

Takeaway alcoholic drinks are sold from neighbourhood off-licences rather than pubs. Opening hours vary, but although some stay open to 9 or 10 pm, seven days a week, many keep ordinary shop hours. Alcohol can also be bought at supermarkets and the diminishing collection of corner shops.

Most restaurants are licensed and their alcoholic drinks, particularly good wines, are always expensive. There are few BYO restaurants (where you can Bring Your Own bottles). Most charge an extortionate sum for 'corkage' – opening your own bottle for you.

Pubs

Given how much pubs epitomise Britain for many visitors, it's odd how unenthusiastic the breweries seem to be about hanging onto them. Not only are the High Streets vanishing beneath a plethora of brewery-owned bars and brasseries but many of the traditional pubs are reinventing themselves as Irish theme bars (O'Neill's etc) or Australian theme bars (Walkabout Inns).

Simultaneously names that have endured sometimes for centuries are being banished in favour of infantile 'brand' names (see the boxed text 'What's In a (Pub) Name?').

Nonalcoholic Drinks

The British national drink is undoubtedly tea, although coffee is now just as popular and it's perfectly easy to get a cappuccino or espresso in southern towns. You can almost measure your geographical position by the strength of the tea in cafés. From a point somewhere around Birmingham the tea gets progressively stronger (and more orange), the sort of brew you can stand your teaspoon up in, or so idiom would have it. Further south you're as likely to be offered Earl Grey or a herbal tea as a traditional Indian or Sri Lankan brew.

Alcoholic Drinks

Beer British pubs generally serve an impressive range of beers – lagers, bitters, ales and stouts. What New Worlders know as beer is actually lager and, much to the distress of local connoisseurs, lagers (including Fosters and Budweiser) now constitute a huge chunk of the market. Fortunately, the traditional British bitter is fighting back, thanks to the Campaign for Real Ale (CAMRA) organisation – look for its endorsement sticker on pub windows.

The wonderfully wide choice of beers ranges from very light (almost like lager) to extremely strong and treacly. They're usually served at room temperature, which

What's In a (Pub) Name?

Wandering around English villages you'll come across hundreds of ancient pubs with workaday names like *The Red Lion*, *The King's Arms* and *The Royal Oak* with attractive signboards to illustrate them.

But what's this in Big Town high street? Yet another pub which manages to mix together some combination of 'rat', 'carrot', 'newt' and 'firkin' in its name. Look closely at the signs and you'll find no trace of the individuality that marked out their predecessors. Instead come cartoon characters which look to have been designed with a kindergarten rather than an adult audience in mind.

Perhaps there's no point in mourning the passing of *The Queen Victoria* and *The Bunch of Grapes*. But many old pub names are as much a part of local history as England's medieval churches.

Take Nottingham's wonderful *Ye Olde Trip to Jerusalem*, a name that commemorates the Crusaders as they assembled for their long journey to the Holy Land. Or *The Nobody Inn* at Doddiscombsleigh, near Exeter, said to recall a mix-up over a coffin. Look harder at that *Royal Oak* sign and you'll see the head of Charles II peeping through the oak leaves – these signs harp back to the story that the king had to hide in an oak tree at Boscobel after his defeat at the Battle of Worcester. Signs for *The Five Alls* regularly show the king who rules over all, the parson who prays for all, the lawyer who pleads for all, the soldier who fights for all, and John Bull who pays for all.

Finally, there's the astonishing *I Am The Only Running Footman*, at 5 Charles St, London W1, a reminder of the 18th century running footmen employed by wealthy men to run in front of their carriages lighting the way and shifting any obstacles.

Who's for the *Slug & Lettuce* then?

---

may come as a shock if you've been raised on lager. But if you think of these 'beers' as something completely new, you'll discover subtle flavours that a cold, chemical lager can't match. Ales and bitters are similar; it's more a regional name difference than anything else. The best are actually hand-pumped from the cask, not carbonated and drawn under pressure. Stout is a dark, rich, foamy drink; Guinness is the most famous brand.

Beers are usually served in pints (from £1.60 to £2.30), but you can also ask for a 'half' (a half pint). The stronger 'special' or 'extra' brews vary in potency from around 2 to 8%. Pubs are allowed to open for any 12 hours a day Monday to Saturday. Most maintain the traditional 11 am to 11 pm hours; the bell for last orders rings out at about 10.45 pm. On Sunday most open from noon to 3 pm and from 7 to 10.30 pm, though some stay open all day.

Wine Good wine is widely available and very reasonably priced (except in pubs and restaurants). In supermarkets an ordinary but drinkable bottle can still be found for around £4.

ENTERTAINMENT

Depending on where you're staying, you'll find a wonderful choice of concert halls, theatres, cinemas and nightclubs to fill your evenings. The world-class venues are mainly in London (see Entertainment in the London chapter) but most of the big towns have at least one good theatre and perhaps an art cinema to supplement the multiplexes. Choice is much more restricted if you're staying in the countryside and here even the one-screen cinemas struggle to survive.

SPECTATOR SPORTS

The Brits love their games and play and watch them with fierce, competitive dedication. They've been responsible for inventing or codifying many of the world's most popular spectator sports: cricket, tennis, football (soccer) and rugby; and the Scots can claim golf. To this list add billiards and snooker, lawn bowls, boxing, darts, hockey, squash and table tennis.

The country also hosts premier events for a number of sports: Wimbledon (tennis), the FA Cup Final (football), the British Open (golf), Test Cricket, Badminton Horse Trials (equestrianism), the British Grand Prix (motor racing), the Isle of Man TT (motorcycle racing), the Derby and the Grand National (horse racing), the Henley Regatta (rowing), the Five Nations Tournament (rugby union), the Super League Final (rugby league) and the Admirals Cup (yachting).

All year round, London hosts major sporting events. If you want to see live action, consult *Time Out* for fixtures, times, venues and ticket prices. Also see Spectator Sports in the London chapter.

Football

Britain's largest spectator sport and one of the most popular participation sports is football, also known as 'soccer' to distinguish it from rugby football.

Since the introduction of the Premier League in 1992, football has become very big business in England. This elite sport, for the top 20 clubs in the country, has had huge cash injections, making the league and its players much better off than before (most players now earn about £10,000 a week). The extra money is mainly generated from television deals signed with Sky, one of the world's largest and richest satellite channels. Unfortunately, few of the smaller and less successful clubs have benefited from these changes. It's a case of the big clubs getting richer and the smaller ones struggling to survive.

This reconstruction has transformed the image of the game. In the 1980s British football was associated with hooliganism and violence. The 90s has seen clubs trying hard to appeal to a wider range of fans, realising the importance of making football more socially acceptable. On the whole, they've succeeded. Britain even has a Minister for Sport who is a keen Chelsea fan. Being broadcast on Sky has made the games more accessible not only to people in England but around the globe. Most football grounds are now suitable places for a family day out.

England boasts some of the best and most expensive footballers in the world. Newcastle United made history in August 1996 when it signed Alan Shearer for £15 million, making him the world's most expensive player.

Many of the bigger clubs have recently been floated on the stock markets and are being run as serious, money-making businesses. It has become so commercial that most clubs make as much money from selling their merchandise as from entry into the games.

The domestic football season lasts from August to May. Most matches are played on Saturday afternoons at 3 pm. Tickets cost from £10 to £35 and are usually very difficult to purchase so try to book them well in advance.

Some of the bigger clubs include Manchester United, Arsenal, Liverpool and Newcastle. Wembley is where the English national team plays its home internationals each season, and also the place where the FA Cup final takes place in May.

Cricket

Sometimes called the English national game, cricket is still a popular participation sport. Every summer weekend, hundreds of teams play on idyllic village greens (and city sports fields), and display all the finest English characteristics – fair play, team spirit and individual excellence (plus maiming the opposing team and abusing the umpire).

Those not familiar with the game will need someone to explain the rules, and may find it slow. But at its best, cricket is exciting, aesthetically pleasing, psychologically involving, and quintessentially English.

Several clubs founded in the 18th century still survive. The most famous and important is Marylebone Cricket Club (MCC), based at Lord's cricket ground in north London.

Every summer, the national side of at least one of the main cricket-playing countries (Australia, India, New Zealand, Pakistan, South Africa, Sri Lanka, West Indies) will tour and play a series of five-day test matches and crowd-pulling one-day matches. Tickets cost from £20 to £40 and tend to go fast. Those for county championship matches are a much more manageable £6 to £12.

The Cricket World Cup (☎ 0870-606 1999) will be held in 21 venues around Britain in May/June 1999. Tickets range from £14 to £100.

Rugby

It was once said that the difference between football and rugby was that football was a gentlemen's game played by hooligans while rugby was a hooligan's game played by gentlemen. Class distinctions may have fallen away, but the hooligan element lives on. A recent report listed rugby as Britain's most dangerous sport, with four times as many serious injuries per player as football.

Rugby (aka rugby football or rugger) takes its name from Rugby school in Warwickshire where the game is supposed to have originated when William Ellis picked up the ball and ran off with it during a football match in 1823.

The professional form of the game, rugby league, is played in the north of England, and differs from the traditionally amateur game of rugby union in that the team has only 13, rather than 15, players. Rules and tactics differ slightly, most notably in that possession changes from one team to the other after five tackles.

Rugby league is primarily a summer game and the Super League final is held at Old Trafford in September. Teams to watch include St Helen's, Wigan and Warrington.

Rugby union is mainly played in the south of England, and in Scotland and Wales. Bath and Leicester are among the better union teams. Union fans will find south-west London the place to be, with a host of good-quality teams (including the Harlequins, Richmond and Wasps). Each year, starting in January, the Five Nations Rugby Union Championship takes place between the four nations of the British Isles and the French. This guarantees two big matches at Twickenham. When Italy joins after the 1999 World Cup, it'll become the Six Nations Rugby Union Championship.

Wales has always been strongly associated with rugby union and hosts the World Cup in 1999. During the 70s the Welsh national team was very successful, winning six out of 10 Five Nations championships. Since then, however, things haven't gone quite so swingingly. Amateur rugby union teams have also been bleeding men and talent to rugby league (although this trend has stopped now that rugby union has become a professional sport too). You can watch most successful club sides like Cardiff, Swansea, Neath and Llanelli, between September and Easter.

Golf

Although games that involve hitting a ball with a stick have been played in Europe since Roman times, it was the Scottish version that caught on. Apparently dating from the 15th century, golf was popularised by the Scottish monarchy and gained popularity in London after James VI of Scotland also became James I of England.

With the Royal and Ancient Golf Club (the recognised authority on the rules) and the famous Old Course both in St Andrews, this small Scottish town is known as the home of golf. London, in contrast, can boast the world's oldest golf club. James VI played on Blackheath in 1608 and London's Royal Blackheath takes the date of its founding from this royal teeing off.

See the Activities chapter for information about playing golf in Britain.

Horse Racing

Even the Queen turns up for Royal Ascot, which takes place for a week in late June. The cheapest tickets cost less than £5 but to be invited into the enclosure you must be well dressed and expect to cough up around £30.

The Derby is run at Epsom on the first Saturday in June. The Grand National steeplechase at Aintree is probably the best known of all Britain's famous horse races. It's run in early April.

SHOPPING

Napoleon once dismissed the British as a nation of shopkeepers but today, as standardised chain stores sweep the High Streets, it would be truer to say they're a nation of shoppers. Shopping is the country's most popular recreational activity.

Multinational capitalism being what it is, there are very few things you can buy that are unique to Britain. On the other hand, if you can't find it for sale in London it probably doesn't exist.

London has some of the world's greatest department stores (Harrods, Fortnum & Mason, Harvey Nichols, Liberty, Marks & Spencer), some of the best bookshops (Borders, Waterstones, Blackwells, Foyles), some of the best fashion (Camden Market, Kensington Market, Covent Garden, Oxford St, Kensington), some of the best music shops (HMV, Virgin, Tower) and specialist shops of every description; see Shopping in the London chapter for details.

Although shop assistants can be unhelpful and few things are cheap, books and clothing can be especially good value.

See Excess Baggage in the Getting There & Away chapter when you realise you've hopelessly exceeded your baggage limit.

Activities

Pursuing a favourite activity or interest is one of the best ways of escaping the beaten track. Becoming part of a country's life, and preferably an active participant, is much more rewarding than remaining an isolated spectator viewing the world through a camera lens or car window.

There's no escaping the fact that Britain is an expensive place to travel, but many activities not only open up some of the most beautiful and fascinating corners of the island, but are also well within the reach of the tightest budget. In fact, those on a shoe-string budget may find themselves hiking or cycling out of necessity. Fortunately, a walk or ride through the countryside will almost certainly be a highlight – as well as the cheapest part – of a British holiday.

At the other end of the scale, those with big budgets may want to try one of the traditional British sports which are still played with enthusiasm. These activities have many variations – most involving horses, hunting, shooting or fishing – but the constant aim is to extract money from fat wallets.

Most activities are well organised and have clubs and associations that can give visitors invaluable information and, sometimes, substantial discounts. Many of these organisations have national or international affiliations, so check with local clubs before leaving home. The British Tourist Authority has brochures on most activities, which can provide a starting point for further research.

Almost every sport, activity and hobby known to humankind has obsessive British devotees. Most are pleased to meet someone who shares their interest, and their response is often generous and hospitable to a fault.

Walking

Every weekend, millions of people take to the parks and countryside. Perhaps because Britain is such a crowded island, a high premium is placed on open space and the chance to find some fresh air. In the cities, ritual weekend expeditions to the shops and markets are very often combined with a stroll in a park, ending somewhere that sells tea or beer. And the countryside is invaded every weekend by people (and dogs) taking short walks – and ending up somewhere that sells tea or beer.

Although modern developments have had a negative impact, a surprising amount of the countryside appears frozen in time, conforming to a picture of rural Britain that every movie-goer, TV-watcher and book-reader is accustomed to.

The infrastructure for walkers is excellent. Every Tourist Information Centre (TIC) has details (free or for a nominal charge) of suggested walks that take in local points of interest. Hundreds of books are available and describe walks ranging from half-hour strolls to week-long expeditions, and these are widely available in TICs, newsagents, book-shops and outdoor-equipment shops.

Every village and town is surrounded by footpaths, so all keen walkers should consider a week based in one interesting spot (perhaps in a self-catering cottage, or a youth hostel or camp site) with a view to exploring the surrounding countryside. Numerous short walks are detailed in this book.

ACCESS

Again, perhaps because Britain is such a crowded island, the rights of people to gain access to land, even privately owned land, are jealously protected. In England and Wales, the countryside is crisscrossed by a network of countless 'rights of way', most of them over private land, that can be used by any member of the public. They may traverse fields, moors, woodlands and even farmhouse yards.

These public footpaths and bridleways (the latter can be used by horse riders and mountain bikers) have existed for centuries, sometimes millennia. They are marked on maps and are often signposted where they intersect with roads. Some also have special markers at strategic points along their length (yellow arrows for footpaths, blue for bridle-ways, or other special markers if they are part of a particular walk). Some, however, are completely unmarked, so a good map, and the ability to use it, can be essential. If a path is overgrown or obstructed in some way, walkers are permitted to remove enough of the obstruction to pass, and to walk carefully through a crop. Discretion is advised – no farmer will appreciate damage to property.

Some rights of way cross land that is owned by the Ministry of Defence (MOD) and used occasionally by the army. When troop manoeuvres or firing are in progress, access is denied and red flags are put up to warn walkers.

There are some areas where walkers can move freely beyond the rights of way, and these are clearly advertised. For instance, the National Trust (NT) is now one of the largest landowners in Britain and some of its properties are open to the public. However, land within national parks does not necessarily fit into this category.

National parks were set up in England and Wales by the Countryside Commission to protect the finest landscapes and to provide opportunities for visitors to enjoy them, but the land remains largely private-ly owned and farmed, and therefore access is restricted. It is almost always necessary to get permission from a landowner before pitching a tent.

Scotland does not have a formal system of registered rights of way, but there is a tra-dition of relatively free access to open country, especially in mountain and moor-land areas (although there may be restrictions during the grouse and deer-hunting seasons). Nor does Scotland have national parks, although development is controlled in a number of areas that have been designated as National Scenic Areas and Nature Reserves.

In England and Wales, Areas of Out-standing Natural Beauty and Heritage Coasts are also legally protected, but again that doesn't guarantee unlimited access.

LONG-DISTANCE WALKS

The energetic, and the impecunious, should definitely consider some long-distance multi-day walks. With the exception of parts of Scotland, civilisation is never far away, so it's easy to put together walks that connect with public transport and link hostels and villages. In most cases, a tent and cooking equipment is not necessary. Warm and waterproof clothing (including a hat and gloves), sturdy footwear, lunch and some high-energy food (for emergencies), a water bottle (with purification tablets), a first-aid kit, a whistle and torch (flashlight), and a map and compass are all you need.

The best areas for long-distance walks include the Cotswolds, the Exmoor Nation-al Park, the Dartmoor National Park, the North York Moors National Park, the York-shire Dales National Park, the Lake District, the Pembrokeshire Coast National Park and the Scottish islands.

There are many superb long-distance walks in Scotland but, in general, the po-tential combination of isolation and severe weather mean they require a reasonably high degree of preparation.

Over the last 30 years, 18 national long-distance paths (LDPs) have been developed by the Countryside Commission (a number of them traverse the national parks) and these offer walkers access to outstanding countryside. They have been created by linking existing public footpaths and bridle-ways and often follow routes that travellers have journeyed for thousands of years.

In addition, there are around 200 LDPs that are regional routes created by county councils and unofficial long-distance routes devised by individuals or groups like the Ramblers' Association. Some are excellent, well organised and have good available in-formation. On the other hand, all you need is a good map and you can plan your own!

Walkers may choose to walk the entire length of a long-distance trail (or *way*, as they are often called), which could be from 30 to

600 miles long but many choose just a section that meets constraints of time and transport. City-bound walkers often manage to walk an entire trail over a series of weekends.

Some of the English long-distance walks, particularly along the coast, and in the Yorkshire Dales and Lake District, can be crowded on weekends and in July/August – advance bookings for accommodation are worthwhile at these times (contact the appropriate TICs).

The countryside can look deceptively gentle, but especially in the hills or on the open moors the weather can turn very nasty very quickly at any time of the year. It is vital if you're walking in upland areas to be well equipped, and to carry (and know how to use) good maps and a compass. Always leave details of your route with someone trustworthy.

Maps, Guides & Information

Lonely Planet's *Walking in Britain* covers not only all the main long-distance walks but also has a good selection of day hikes.

The Countryside Commission, in conjunction with Aurum Press and the Ordnance Survey (OS), publishes excellent guides to each trail, which are widely available. They include detailed track notes, and incorporate the relevant sections from the OS 1:25,000 Pathfinder maps. There are hundreds of other specialist walking guides.

The Ordnance Survey (OS) organisation publishes a wide variety of maps covering the country and they're widely available. For walkers, the Landranger maps at 1:50,000 – about 1¼ inches to the mile, covering about 25 x 25 miles – are usually sufficiently detailed. In some instances, where paths are unclear, the Pathfinder series at 1:25,000 – about 2½ inches to the mile, covering around 12½ x 12½ miles – is useful. There are Pathfinder Walking Guides (covering short walks in popular areas) and Outdoor Leisure maps (covering most national parks), both at 1:25,000. For further information check out the Web site at www.ordsvy.gov.uk.

A useful alternative to OS maps are those published by Harveys. They cover only some of the main walking areas but they also include tourist information. In some cases they may be more up to date than OS maps.

Those intent on a serious walking holiday should contact the Ramblers' Association (☎ 0171-339 8500), 1 Wandsworth Rd, London SW8 2XX. The RA Web site (www.charitynet.org/~Ramblers) has numerous links and information on many walks. Their *Yearbook* is widely available and itemises the information available for each walk and the appropriate maps; it also gives a list of nearby accommodation (hostels, B&Bs and bunkhouses).

South West Coast Path

This is the longest long-distance walk in Britain, officially 594 miles long but actually 613. It follows the coast through four counties, from Minehead in Somerset, around Devon and Cornwall, to Poole in Dorset. The path is also known as the South West Way and the South West Peninsula Coastal Path.

The South West Coast Path is based on the trails used by coastguards to patrol the area in search of smugglers, so it mostly sticks to the edge of the coast and a considerable amount of walking up and down hills is involved.

Few people walk the whole path in one go, since this takes about six to seven weeks. The most scenic and popular part is the route that runs from Padstow to Falmouth around Land's End, a distance of 163 miles entirely within Cornwall. This section is a medium to easy walk and it could easily be done in two weeks. There's plenty to see – secret coves, wrecks, the remains of cliff castles, *barrows* (a heap of earth placed over prehistoric tombs), settlements, disused mines and quarries, a wide range of bird life, seals etc – so a pair of binoculars is a good idea.

This section could be walked as follows: Padstow to Treyarnon Bay (10½ miles); Treyarnon Bay to Newquay (12½ miles); Newquay to Perranporth (11 miles); Perranporth to Portreath (11 miles); Portreath to St Ives (17 miles); St Vies to Pendeen (13 miles); Pendeen to Sennen Cove (9 miles); Sennen Cove to Porthcurno (6 miles);

Porthcurno to Penzance (11 miles); Penzance to Porthleven (13 miles); Porthleven to The Lizard (13 miles); The Lizard to Coverack (11 miles); Coverack to Helford (13 miles); Helford to Falmouth (10 miles).

Accommodation is not a problem, although you should book in advance in summer. There are hostels, camping grounds and B&Bs on or very near the path.

The official Countryside Commission/Aurum Press guides cover Exmouth to Poole, Falmouth to Exmouth, Padstow to Falmouth and Minehead to Padstow. The South West Way Association (☎ 01364-73859) publishes a single-volume guidebook and accommodation list for the whole route.

Cotswold Way

The Cotswold Way follows the western edge of the Cotswold Hills from Chipping Campden, just south of Stratford-upon-Avon, to Bath. The countryside and Cotswold villages are a delight but the way is also a walk through England's history, with numerous prehistoric hillforts and ancient burial barrows. There are Saxon and Civil War battle sites, reminders of the Romans, some fine stately homes, the ruins of a magnificent medieval monastery and many historical markers and monuments. The path itself winds through fields and woods and over hills, and through a patch of England that is at its most affluent. The pretty-as-a-picture postcard villages exude a heady aroma of solid bank accounts and expensive public schools.

The Cotswold Way is about 100 miles long and can be done in five days, although a week is better. A seven day walk could be broken up as follows: Chipping Campden to Broadway (6 miles); Broadway to Winchcombe (12 miles); Winchcombe to Cheltenham (11 miles); Cheltenham to Painswick (19 miles); Painswick to Dursley (16 miles); Dursley to Old Sodbury (20 miles); Old Sodbury to Bath (19 miles).

Mark Richards' *The Cotswold Way* is a step-by-step account of the route with informative hand-drawn maps. The *Cotswold Way Handbook* (The Ramblers' Association,

£2.20 including p&p) is updated annually and has a variety of itinerary suggestions. It is available from the Cotswold Warden Service (☎ 01452-425674), County Planning Department, Gloucestershire County Council, Shire Hall, Gloucester GL1 2TN.

The Cotswold Way is less than ideal for walkers on a tight budget – B&Bs are often pricier than usual, and there are few convenient youth hostels or camping grounds.

Cleveland Way

The 110-mile-long Cleveland Way is the second-oldest National Trail, and unquestionably one of the greatest walks in Britain, showing a cross section of the best scenery in Yorkshire and a region rich in history, geology and wildlife.

It loops around the North York Moors National Park, passing through small Yorkshire villages and farmland, past the ruins of Rievaulx Abbey and over heather-covered moors. It then follows a spectacular coastline through fishing villages and seaside resorts. There is a rich assortment of relics that include Bronze-Age burial sites, Iron-Age forts, Roman signal stations, medieval abbeys and castles, and industrial relics from the 17th and 18th centuries. The region is also closely associated with Captain James Cook and there are monuments and museums commemorating his life.

The full walk is undeniably challenging and takes about a week, although the *way* is never more than a couple of miles from a sealed road, so there are numerous potential cut-out points. There are many options for tackling shorter sections, especially along the coast. Daily sections for the full walk could be as follows: Helmsley to Kilburn (10 miles); Kilburn to Osmotherley (14 miles); Osmotherley to Kildale (20¼ miles); Kildale to Saltburn (14¾ miles); Saltburn to Whitby (20 miles); Whitby to Scarborough (18 miles); and Scarborough to Filey (8 miles).

The best guidebook (as it includes OS maps at 2½ inches to one mile) is *Cleveland Way* by Ian Sampson. The *Cleveland Way* has strip maps at scales between 1¾ inches

Big Ben, one of the popular images of London

Fountain in Trafalgar Square

The gates of Buckingham Palace

Houses of Parliament

Detail of the Houses of Parliament

Covent Garden Market Place

Trafalgar Square

The Thames

Buckingham Palace

and one inch to the mile, plus useful track notes and information about available facilities. The national park authorities publish the *Cleveland Way – Accommodation & Information Guide* (50p), available from visitor centres and local TICs or free if you write to Cleveland Way Project Officer (☎ 01439-770657), North York Moors National Park, The Old Vicarage, Bondgate, Helmsley, York Y06 5BP.

Cumbria Way

The Cumbria Way is a 68 mile walk that traverses the county of Cumbria and the incomparable landscape of the Lake District first popularised for walkers by William Wordsworth and Samuel Taylor Coleridge. Most of the way lies within the Lake District National Park, and most of it follows valleys at relatively low altitudes, so bad weather is not a major issue (although it also traverses several high passes and gives a dramatic taste of the mountains). A number of peaks are within easy reach.

If the weather does remain good (a day or so of rain is virtually inevitable and *cannot* be considered bad weather!), it's impossible to imagine a more beautiful walk. It takes in a full cross section of the best of the Lake District – from the little-visited southern valleys to the shores of Coniston Water, the great peaks of the Langdale Pikes, Derwent Water, the flanks of Skiddaw, and another forgotten backwater between Keswick and Carlisle. As an introduction to the Lake District it's definitely unsurpassed.

It's an easy walk logistically: it travels south-north between Ulverston, on Morecambe Bay, and Carlisle, near Hadrian's Wall. A suggested itinerary is: Ulverston to Coniston (16 miles); Coniston to Dungeon Ghyll (11 miles); Dungeon Ghyll to Keswick (16 miles); Keswick to Caldbeck (14 miles); and Caldbeck to Carlisle (13 miles).

The OS Landranger 1:50,000 series is *almost* detailed enough and covers the walk on three sheets (Nos 85, 90 and 97). A couple of sections are quite tricky to navigate, however, and most people will find the appropriate map from the OS Pathfinder

1:25,000 series useful. The section from Ulverston to Coniston Water is one (Pathfinder No 626), and the section from Skiddaw to Caldbeck is the other (Pathfinder No 576).

Two guidebooks are *The Cumbria Way* by John Trevelyan and the more recently published *Guide to the Cumbria Way* by Philip Dubcock.

Hadrian's Wall

Hadrian's Wall runs for over 70 miles across the north of England from Newcastle upon Tyne to Bowness-on-Solway, west of Carlisle. Much of the wall has disappeared completely or is in ruins but, in theory, the route would make an excellent long-distance trail, and an extra 5 miles would make it a coast-to-coast walk. Currently, however, this involves quite a bit of walking along roads and through towns – the best way to experience the wall is on a series of day hikes, totalling 27 miles. A National Trail is being developed and is due for completion in 2001.

To walk the most interesting sections of the wall you could base yourself in or around Haltwhistle or at Once Brewed, and make use of the good local public transport system. Alternatively, there are places to stay along the route at Greenhead, Gilsland and Brampton. The three day hikes are as follows: Once Brewed to Once Brewed (circular walk; 7½ miles), Once Brewed to Greenhead (7 miles) and Greenhead to Brampton (12½ miles). As well as the wall itself, this route takes in several Roman forts, including Housesteads and Vindolanda, various turrets and temples, and also passes through Northumberland National Park, where the scenery is at its finest.

Hadrian's Wall by Mark Richards is an excellent two-volume guide, one volume describing a route that follows the route of the wall, the other giving detours into the countryside. The OS *Historical Map & Guide – Hadrian's Wall* covers the wall in strip-mat format at scales of 1:25,000 and 1:50,000, and is adequate for finding your way, with the route of the original wall superimposed on the modern information.

The OS Landranger 1:50,000 sheet 86, *Haltwhistle*, goes beyond this strip and covers the walks mentioned here.

The Pennine Way

The 250 mile Pennine Way can claim to be the granddaddy of British long-distance walks as it was first conceived back in 1935, though not 'officially' recognised until the 1960s. It can be one of the toughest walks in Britain if the weather is uncooperative as it follows the mountainous spine of northern England into Scotland, often crossing long stretches of unprotected high country. Careful planning, good equipment and caution are all essential requisites for walking the Pennine Way. Completing the whole walk in two weeks is a real endurance test; allowing three weeks is far more realistic.

The walk starts at Edale, in the north of the Peak District, and immediately makes the tough climb up to the 600m-high Kinder Scout plateau. This 'in the deep end' approach on the first day is followed by a long spell of 'bog hopping' across the exposed moors of the Dark Peak. Continuing north through Brontë country, the route goes right through the Yorkshire Dales National Park then joins Hadrian's Wall for a pleasant jaunt along the most interesting section of this ancient barrier. The final stretch of the walk crosses the full-length of the Northumberland National Park before bringing weary walkers to a well-earned rest at Kirk Yetholm, just over the border in Scotland.

There are numerous books on the Pennine Way, including the two-volume *Pennine Way* by T Hopkins. Classic British walking writer Alfred Wainwright also describes the route in his *Pennine Way Companion* (Michael Joseph). The Pennine Way Council, 29 Springfield Park Avenue, Chelmsford, Essex CM2 6EL, publishes the *Pennine Way Accommodation and Catering Guide* (90p plus 20p p&p). These publications are available from the Peak Park Joint Planning Board, National Park Office, Aldern House, Baslow Road, Bakewell, Derbyshire DE45 1AE.

Peddars Way & Norfolk Coast Path

This is an undemanding 88 mile trail that follows a Roman road across the middle of Norfolk from Knettishall Heath to the beautiful north Norfolk coast at Holme-next-the-Sea. It follows this coastline through a number of attractive, untouched villages like Wells-next-the-Sea and Cromer.

Although the trail ends at Cromer, it's possible to continue for another 40 miles to Great Yarmouth. The start of the trail (Knettishall Heath) is also the end of another path, the Icknield Way, which runs for 105 miles across England from Ivinghoe Beacon. Ivinghoe Beacon also happens to be the end of the Ridgeway (see following section), so these three paths could be linked together into a long march of 284 miles from Avebury to Cromer.

Norfolk Ramblers (☎ 01603-503207), Knight's Cottage, The Old School, Honing NR28 9TR, publishes a guide and accommodation list for £2.36 (including p&p). There are several guidebooks, including *Peddars Way & Norfolk Coast Path* by Bruce Robinson.

The Ridgeway

The remains of a prehistoric track that is Britain's oldest road, the Ridgeway is now a National Trail beginning near Avebury (Wiltshire) and running north-east for 85 miles to Ivinghoe Beacon near Aylesbury (Buckinghamshire). It follows the high open ridge of the chalk downs and then descends to the Thames Valley before finally winding through the Chiltern Hills. The western section (to Streatley) can be used by mountain bikes, horses, farm vehicles and recreational 4WDs. Unfortunately, recreational 4WDs have recently become very fashionable in Britain; for peace and quiet, walk during the week.

The best guide is *The Ridgeway* by Neil Curtis. A range of useful publications, including an excellent *Information and Accommodation Guide* (£1.90 including UK postage), is available from the National Trails Office (☎ 01865-810224), Countryside Service, Department of Leisure & Arts, Holton, Oxford OX33 1QQ.

Friends of the Ridgeway is a voluntary organisation that aims to preserve the trail for quiet recreational use. Contact Nigel Forward (☎ 0171-794 2105), 90 South Hill Park, London NW3 2SN for information.

Thames Path

The path that runs the length of the River Thames, 173 miles from the river's source in Gloucestershire to the Thames Barrier in London, was designated in 1996. This famous waterway rises at Thames Head, south of Cirencester, and flows through a varied landscape that includes quintessentially English villages, peaceful meadow-land and ugly suburban sprawl around the capital.

There are few youth hostels along the route but B&B is available in many towns and villages. For more information contact the Countryside Commission (☎ 01242-521381), John Dower House, Crescent Place, Cheltenham, Gloucestershire GL50 3RA. *The Thames Path & Accommodation Guide* is available from the Ramblers' Association (£3.69 including p&p).

South Downs Way

The South Downs Way National Trail is a bridleway. It covers 100 miles between the coastal resort of Eastbourne and Winchester, a cathedral city and the ancient capital of England.

It's an easy walk, readily accessible from London, so parts can be busy, especially on weekends. It covers a beautiful cross section of classic English landscapes, beginning with spectacular chalk cliffs at Beachy Head, then traversing an open chalk ridge (the Downs) with great views, before entering rolling, wooded country as you approach Winchester.

The chalk downs are among the longest continuously inhabited parts of the island and the way itself follows an ancient ridgeway track that dates back 4000 years. It passes numerous prehistoric remains, and some charming medieval villages. You are never far from a comfortable B&B and a good pub; there are also six youth hostels on or near the way, although they are all in the section between Eastbourne and Arundel.

The way could be walked in a week, although most guides break it up into nine or 10 sections. There are numerous guide-books and some annually produced accommodation guides. The *South Downs Way* by Paul Millmore has route descriptions and maps.

Dales Way

The Dales Way links two of England's greatest national parks – the Yorkshire Dales and Lake District – and although it's not an official National Trail, it is a popular and well-organised route. Some parts aren't sign-posted, however, so you need good maps.

Officially it begins at Ilkley, accessible from Leeds with regular trains, in a densely populated corner of West Yorkshire famous for its mill towns. Alternatively, you could start at Bolton Priory or Grassington (see the Yorkshire Dales National Park in the North-Eastern England chapter), which are both on the way. Much of the walk follows river banks through the Yorkshire Dales, so the walking is easy, although there are some open expanses of moorland between one dale (valley) and the next. The walk ends with a spectacular descent to Bowness on the shores of Lake Windermere, the main town in the Lake District National Park.

The way mostly follows ancient trails, passing through or near many villages, so B&B accommodation isn't a problem (although booking is still advised). There are also some youth hostels along the way (including Grassington), as well as camping barns. It would be an easy seven day walk, or just four or five days from Grassington to Windermere. Distances are: Ilkley to Barden (12 miles); Barden to Grassington (7 miles); Grassington to Buckden (12 miles); Buckden to Dentdale (16 miles); Dentdale to Sedbergh (11 miles); Sedbergh to Burneside (15 miles); and Burneside to Bowness (8 miles).

There are numerous guidebooks, including *The Dales Way* by Colin Speakman, which is supplemented by the *Dales Way Companion* by Paul Hannon, with excellent detailed maps. The TICs at Leeds, Grassington and Windermere are all good sources of information, as is the Ramblers' Association (see Maps, Guides & Information in the Walking section of this chapter), which produces an accommodation brochure, the *Dales Way Handbook*.

Coast-to-Coast Walk

The walk was devised by the creator of superb illustrated walking guides and near-legendary walker, Alfred Wainwright. It's an unofficial trail covering 190 miles from St Bees Head on the west coast to Robin Hood's Bay on the east. It traverses three national parks – the Lake District, Yorkshire Dales and North York Moors – and covers a range of England's most spectacular scenery, from sea cliffs to mountains, dales and moors.

It's a hard walk, since it crosses the grain of the land. It has been divided into 14 daily stages, largely defined by the availability of overnight accommodation: St Bees to Ennerdale Bridge (14 miles); Ennerdale Bridge to Rosthwaite (15 miles); Rosthwaite to Grasmere (10 miles); Grasmere to Patterdale (8 miles); Patterdale to Shap (16 miles); Shap to Kirkby Stephen (20 miles); Kirkby Stephen to Keld (13 miles); Keld to Reeth (11 miles); Reeth to Richmond (11 miles); Richmond to Ingleby Cross (23 miles); Ingleby Cross to Clay Bank Top (12 miles); Clay Bank Top to Blakey (9 miles); Blakey to Grosmont (13 miles); and Grosmont to Robin Hood's Bay (16 miles).

The walk is serviced by the innovative Coast to Coast Packhorse (☎ 01768-371680), who are based at Kirkby Stephen (see Kirkby Stephen in the North-Eastern England chapter). This is a minibus (daily from April to late September) that runs the length of the walk and carries backpacks (and bodies where appropriate). Backpacks are delivered to a pick-up point at the next stop on the walk. Packs cost £3 per stop if unbooked, £3.50 (booked), or £51 (booked) from St Bees to Robin Hood's Bay.

The guidebook to use is *A Coast to Coast Walk* by Alfred Wainwright. There's also Paul Hannon's *A Coast to Coast Walk* which includes maps. An accommodation pamphlet is available (for £2.50 plus a large stamped, self-addressed envelope) from Mrs Whitehead (☎ 01748-886374), Butt House, Keld, Richmond, North Yorkshire DL11 6LJ.

West Highland Way

This 95 mile hike through the Scottish Highlands runs from Milngavie (pronounced mullguy), 7 miles from the centre of Glasgow, north along Loch Lomond to Fort William.

The route passes through a tremendous range of landscape that includes some of the most spectacular scenery in the country. It begins in the Lowlands, but the greater part of this trail is among the mountains, lochs and fast-flowing rivers of the Highlands. In the far north the route crosses wild Rannoch Moor and reaches Fort William via Glen Nevis, in the shadow of Britain's highest peak, Ben Nevis.

The path is easy to follow and it uses the old drove roads along which cattle were herded in the past, the old military road (built by troops to help control the Jacobites in the 18th century) and disused railway lines.

Best walked from south to north, the walk can be done in about six or seven days, in the following sections: Milngavie to Drymen (12 miles); Drymen to Rowardennan (14 miles); Rowardennan to Inverarnan (13 miles); Inverarnan to Tyndrum (12 miles); Tyndrum to Kingshouse (18 miles); Kingshouse to Kinlochleven (9 miles); and Kinlochleven to Fort William (14 miles).

You need to be properly equipped with good boots, maps, a compass, and food and drink for the northern part of the walk. Midge repellent is also worth bringing.

Accommodation shouldn't be too difficult to find, though between Bridge of Orchy and Kinlochleven it's quite limited. In summer you should book B&Bs in advance. There are some youth hostels on and near the path, as well as bunkhouses. It's also possible to camp in some parts.

Harvey's *West Highland Way*, is the most accurate map and also contains tourist information. *The West Highland Way* by Robert Aitken & Roger Smith comes with a 1:50,000 OS route map and is the most comprehensive guide available. *West Highland Way* by Anthony Burton also contains OS maps. A free accommodation list is available from TICs and from the path manager (☎ 01389-758216).

Pembrokeshire Coast Path

This 189 mile cliff-top trail includes some of the finest beaches in Britain and offers the best coastal scenery in Wales.

Lying entirely within the Pembrokeshire Coast National Park in south-west Wales, the coast path passes through tiny fishing villages, skirts secluded coves and crosses some sparsely populated regions. The only towns of any size on the route are Pembroke, Milford Haven and Fishguard but there are, nevertheless, numerous places to stay that are conveniently located along the path.

As well as being renowned for its superb coastal scenery, the area is of particular interest to bird-watchers – only parts of the Scottish coast attract more varied seabird life. Although there are a number of steep climbs and descents along its route, the path is not hard-going if you take it slowly. And there are numerous worthwhile distractions along the way: St David's (the smallest city in Britain, with its fine cathedral), several ruined castles, Iron-Age forts, beaches and nature reserves – not to mention the pubs.

The path is best walked from south to north and you should allow 13 to 15 days. Suggested route divisions are: Amroth to Tenby (7 miles); Tenby to Manorbier (8 miles); Manorbier to Bosherston (13 miles); Bosherston to Angle (15 miles); Angle to Pembroke (11 miles); Pembroke to Milford Haven (10 miles); Milford Haven to Marloes Sands (17 miles); Marloes Sands to Newgale (19 miles); Newgale to Whitesands Bay (18 miles); Whitesands Bay to Trevine (11 miles); Trevine to Fishguard (19 miles); Fishguard to Newport (11 miles); and Newport to St Dogmael's (15 miles).

The Pembrokeshire Coast National Park (☎ 01437-764636) publishes an accommodation guide for the walk. *The Pembrokeshire Coast Path* by Brian John includes OS maps.

Offa's Dyke Path

Offa's Dyke was a grand earthwork project, conceived and executed in the 8th century by the King Offa, to separate his kingdom of Mercia from Wales. The border between England and Wales has been defined roughly by the dyke ever since.

This 177 mile trail runs from Chepstow in the south through the beautiful Wye Valley and Shropshire Hills to end on the north Wales coast at Prestatyn. Rather than sticking religiously to the dyke, which is overgrown in some places and built over in others, the trail makes many detours along quiet valleys and ridges. The route offers a tremendous range of scenery, possibly the most varied of any long-distance trail. Another path, Glyndŵr's Way, leaves Offa's Dyke Path at Knighton, following a 120 mile route west across central Wales to Machynlleth then back to Welshpool.

There are two guidebooks to the walk *Chepstow to Knighton* and *Knighton to Prestatyn* by Ernie & Kathy McKay & Mark Richards. A guide including accommodation and transport details is available (£2.20 including UK p&p) from the Offa's Dyke Association (☎ 01547-528753), Offa's Dyke Centre, West St, Knighton, Powys LD7 1EN.

Cycling

Travelling by bicycle is an excellent way to explore Britain. Away from the motorways and busy main roads there's a vast network of quiet country lanes leading through peaceful villages. Bring your own bike or hire one when you arrive. Cycle routes have been suggested throughout this book.

INFORMATION

The British Tourist Authority publishes a free booklet, *Cycling*, with some suggested routes, lists of cycle holiday companies and other helpful information. Many regional TICs have information on local cycling routes and places where you can hire bikes. They also stock cycling guides and books – look out for the range of route map/guides produced by Ordnance Survey (OS).

The Cyclists' Touring Club (CTC) (☎ 01483-417217, fax 01483-426994), 69 Meadrow, Godalming, Surrey GU7 3HS, is a membership organisation providing comprehensive information (free of charge to members) about cycling in Britain and overseas. It can provide suggested routes (on and off-road), lists of local cycling contacts and clubs, recommended accommodation, organised cycling holidays, a cycle hire directory, and a mail-order service for OS maps and books for cyclists.

Annual membership fees are currently £12.50 for under 18s (or unemployed), £16.50 for senior citizens (over 65s), and £25 for other adults. Some cycling organisations outside Britain have reciprocal membership arrangements with the CTC.

Country Lanes (☎ 01425-655022), 9 Shaftesbury St, Fordingbridge, Hampshire SP6 1JF, is a small company that runs a range of cycling trips in southern England. These range from bicycle hire and self-guided itineraries for those who prefer to travel independently, to five-day group trips. There are numerous other companies offering cycling trips.

Taking Cycles by Air or Train

Air Most airlines will carry a bike free of charge, so long as the bike and panniers don't exceed the per-passenger weight allowance (usually 20kg). Hefty excess baggage charges may be incurred if you do and this applies to internal and international flights. Note that some charter-flight companies do make a charge for the carriage of bikes.

Inform the airline that you will be bringing your bike when you book your ticket. Arrive at the airport in good time to remove panniers and pedals, deflate tyres and turn handlebars around – the minimum dismantling usually required by airlines.

Train Bikes can be taken on most train journeys in Britain. However, the current privatisation of rail services in Britain means that each of the 25 train companies can decide their own policy about bikes on trains.

Generally, bikes can be taken on local services free of charge on a first-come-first-served basis – though some train companies do not carry bikes on certain routes or during peak hours. On most long-distance routes (particularly InterCity services) it is necessary to make a reservation for your bike. Reservations will almost always incur a charge – usually around £3 for a single or day return journey.

To be sure that you can take your bike you should make your reservation (and get your ticket) at least 24 hours before travelling – this is because some trains carry only one or two bikes.

To ensure you have no problems check bike carriage details for the whole of your planned journey at least 24 hours before you travel. You should also check if there are going to be engineering works on the line because bikes cannot be carried on replacement bus services.

Roads, Lanes & Tracks

Bikes are not allowed on motorways, but you can cycle on all other roads (on the left!) unless the road is marked 'private'. A-roads tend to be busy and are best avoided. B-roads are usually quieter and many are pleasant for cycling.

The best roads for the cyclist are the unclassified roads, or 'lanes' as they are called. Linking small villages together, they are not numbered: you simply follow the signposts from village to village. There is a whole network of lanes throughout lowland Britain, meandering via picturesque villages through quiet countryside. Lanes are clearly shown on OS maps.

In England and Wales, cycles can be ridden on any unmade road (track) which is identified as a public right of way on OS maps. A right to cycle does not usually exist on a footpath, however. In Scotland the rules for off-road riding are different, and it's best to inquire locally about whether cyclists can use a particular track. The surface condition of tracks, however, varies considerably: some are very poor and slow going.

WHERE TO CYCLE
South-Eastern England
The south-east corner of England has more traffic than other parts of the country, but with careful route planning you can find quiet roads and tracks and forget how close you are to the busy city of London. Northwest of London, the Chiltern Hills offer scenic cycling. The area to the south and east of London is characterised by the North and South Downs, two ridges of higher land running east-west, and the Weald in between – undulating, often wooded terrain. The landscape is beautiful in places and offers plenty of opportunities for good cycling. The south coast is heavily populated and the main roads here are busy and best avoided by cyclists.

You should also avoid cycling in London if possible; traffic is heavy and road surfaces can be poor. If you must cycle in the city, contact the London Cycling Campaign (☎ 0171-928 7220) for maps and information.

South-Western England
The counties of Somerset, Dorset and Wiltshire have a varied landscape, with a combination of easy valley routes and steeper climbs in the hill ranges. Many parts of this region are popular with cyclists. The ancient woodland and open heath of the New Forest offer easy cycling.

Cornwall and Devon, with their steep country lanes, can be challenging. In the north, the coastline is rugged and sometimes inaccessible. Small roads drop steeply to pretty fishing villages nestling in the coves along the coast. The bleak, upland landscapes of Dartmoor, Bodmin Moor and Exmoor contrast starkly with the seaside towns on the south coast of Devon. The coast enjoys the best of the British climate but suffers its share of tourist traffic during the summer months.

Midlands
The Cotswolds area of Gloucestershire and Oxfordshire is particularly attractive. It's a great place to cycle but there's a shortage of budget accommodation here. The dense network of motorways and heavily trafficked roads serving the industrial centres further north, means that any extensive tour of the region would require careful planning in order to avoid these busy arteries. There are pockets of quiet roads with pretty villages and some forests, lakes and canals worth exploring – Charnwood Forest, for example, and many parts of Hereford and Worcester, and Northamptonshire. The land is relatively low-lying and the cycling is gentler than in the north of England.

The Peak District (Derbyshire) is one of the most popular cycling areas and marks the southern tip of the Pennines. There's challenging terrain, steep hills, rewarding scenery and a fairly good network of quieter roads, plus some excellent cycling/walking tracks along disused railway routes.

Eastern England
This is an excellent area for a first cycle tour and for those seeking an easy-going cycling holiday. East Anglia is generally low-lying and flat, with small areas of gently undulating country and woodland, particularly in Suffolk. Much of the area is characterised by arable farmland dissected by rivers, lakes (broads), marshes (such as the Fens) and many small and picturesque settlements.

Norfolk and Suffolk have a good network of quiet country roads. There are, however, two things to watch out for. First, breezes off the North Sea can sometimes be strong, especially in the Fens. Second, whilst the area is well served with bridges, roads sometimes run parallel to a river or canal and you may have to travel a little further than expected to find a bridge. It pays to have a good map and to plan your route in advance.

Northern England
This region offers superb cycling, much of it strenuous, especially high up in the Pennines where you're exposed to the elements.

There are some exhilarating rides in the wild North York Moors. Take plenty of warm clothes and food for these exposed areas. To the west, the Yorkshire Dales offer tough cycling over the tops of the moors and gentler riding in the valleys. The scenery is superb, there's plenty of interest and some excellent pubs.

The Lake District of Cumbria is best explored by cyclists outside the months of July and August, when its limited network of roads is crammed with tourist traffic. Use the smaller roads where possible and be prepared for some steep, long climbs in this magnificent region of mountains and lakes.

The area around Manchester and Liverpool, built-up and crisscrossed with motorways and other busy roads, is far less attractive to cyclists.

In the far north of England, there are quiet roads and plenty of historical interest in Northumberland. There are some very attractive sections of coastline in this area. Inland, the Cheviot Hills and Kielder Water and Forest offer many rough tracks – great for the off-road rider to explore, but it's easy to get lost. Take good maps and a compass.

Scotland

Cyclists in search of the wild and remote will enjoy north-west Scotland. Its majestic Highlands and mystical islands offer quiet pedalling through breathtaking mountains. There are fewer roads in this part of Scotland and generally less traffic. Roads are well graded, but sometimes very remote, so carry plenty of food with you. Of the isles, Skye has a bridge to the mainland and suffers the worst of seasonal traffic; good ferries between all the islands offer easy escape routes.

For the less intrepid cyclist, the beautiful forests, lochs, glens and hills in the central and southern areas of Scotland are more easily accessible and have a more intimate charm. Cyclists can seek out the smaller roads and tracks to avoid the traffic.

Beware the Scottish midge, prevalent during summer and early autumn, and especially annoying if you're camping.

Wales

The varied landscape of the country and the warm welcome you get from the people make Wales an excellent place to cycle.

In the north, the rugged peaks of Snowdonia National Park rise to over 900m (2952 feet), providing a dramatic backdrop to any cycling trip. During the summer the main roads can get busy with holiday traffic, so it's best to visit this area early or late in the season.

Alternatively, head further east towards the Clwydian and Berwyn hills, where less rugged but more peaceful cycling can be found.

The Cambrian mountains through mid-Wales offer quiet cycling both on and off-road. In south Wales, the scenic Black Mountains and Brecon Beacons National Park are popular cycling areas.

Much of Wales is hilly, and some low gears will be appreciated. For a less strenuous tour, the English/Welsh border is an area of gently undulating hills. The Isle of Anglesey in the far north-west and the Pembrokeshire coast in the far south-west are also popular with cyclists seeking to avoid the hills.

SOME SUGGESTED CYCLING ROUTES

The CTC provides useful touring sheets (free to members) for every cycling region in Britain with accommodation suggestions. It can also help you plan a long-distance cycling trip.

Land's End to John o'Groats

The best-known long-distance route on the island runs from the extreme south-west tip, Land's End, to the north-east corner, John o'Groats. Along quiet roads, this is a distance of some 1000 miles, hopefully with the wind behind you.

The ride is a classic British favourite, but not only with cyclists. Along the route you'll meet such eccentric characters as bed-pushers and three-legged pub-crawlers, all being sponsored per mile, raising money for charitable causes.

Sustrans & the National Cycle Network

Sustrans is a civil-engineering charity whose goal is the creation of a 6500 mile network of cycle paths that will pass through the middle of most major towns and cities in Britain.

When Sustrans announced this objective in 1978 the charity was barely taken seriously but increasingly congested roads have now made the public reconsider the exalted place of the car in modern Britain. The government's massive road building program has been cut back and £42 million has been donated to Sustrans by the Millennium Commission to ensure that 2500 miles of routes will be open by the end of the century. The whole network will be complete by 2005.

Half the network is to be on traffic-free paths (including disused railways and canal-side towpaths), the rest of the system along quiet minor roads. Cyclists will share the traffic-free paths with wheelchair users and walkers. Many useful sections are open now – the 16 mile path between Bath and Bristol, for example, is the ideal way to visit these two places. In 1996 Lôn Las Cymru, the Welsh National Cycle Route stretching north-south across the country, was opened. The Scotland National Cycle Route runs 425 miles from Carlisle to Inverness.

Maps are available from Sustrans covering all the routes (free for the shorter paths, £3.99-£5.99 for map-guides for the national routes). For more information contact Sustrans (☎ 0117-929 0888), 35 King Street, Bristol BS1 4DZ, or visit its Web site: www.sustrans.org.uk.

The route is challenging and goes via the scenic western side of England, crossing to the east once in Scotland. Many cyclists do the ride in two to three weeks, following one of the CTC's recommended routes. The main road route runs via Exeter, Cheddar, Shrewsbury, Carlisle, Dumfries, Fort William and Bonar Bridge. The 14 day youth hostel route follows quiet roads via Exeter, Wells, Leominster, Chester, Slaidburn, Windermere, Dumfries, Glasgow, Loch Lomond, Fort William and Loch Ness. The B&B route also follows quiet roads through North Devon, Cheddar, Ludlow, Slaidburn, Brampton, Peebles, Edinburgh, Crieff, Dunkeld and Inverness.

Furthest East to Furthest West

This is another coast-to-coast challenge through some of the best of Britain's varied scenery. The route starts at Lowestoft Ness in Suffolk and ends at the lighthouse at Ardnamurchan Point, on the west coast of Scotland. It's worth taking two to three weeks for this 700 mile route, although the

CTC has details of a 10 day trip with accommodation in youth hostels.

The route crosses the flat fen lands of Norfolk, passing through the Lincolnshire and Yorkshire Wolds into the beautiful Yorkshire Dales. From here northwards it's low gears as the route climbs high into the Pennines, with spectacular views of the dales below. After a few hairpin bends, the road sweeps down to Barnard Castle, then up again over the moors. Once into Northumberland you pass Kielder Water, then ride through the forest and over the border into Scotland.

Passing through Ettrick Forest and the Moorfoot Hills, you descend to the capital, Edinburgh. From here, follow the cycle path over the Forth Road Bridge and head westwards, passing Lake Menteith. The route goes through the Trossachs beside some of the famous Scottish lochs before heading north into the Grampian range, over breathtaking Rannoch Moor to Glencoe. A short ferry hop across Loch Linnhe and the Ardnamurchan peninsula with its lighthouse is soon in sight. This is an exhilarating ride through some spectacular scenery.

Other Coast-to-Coast Routes

There are many other coast-to-coast variations undertaken by cyclists. You could go from Cumbria to Whitby, staying in youth hostels; from St David's Head (south Wales) to Great Yarmouth (Norfolk); follow the 'Opposite Diagonal' – the opposite route to Land's End-John o'Groats – from Dover (Kent) to Durness and Cape Wrath (north-west Scotland); or ride across Scotland, from Aberdeen to the Isle of Mull and back.

Wye Valley

The River Wye meanders some 130 miles from the Cambrian Mountains in Wales to the Severn estuary. It is usually possible to follow quiet roads near the river. A week to 10 days could easily be spent exploring the area.

The southern part of the Wye Valley is densely wooded and forms the border between the south-east corner of Wales and Gloucestershire in England. Chepstow, situated on the northern reaches of the Severn estuary, is an ideal and accessible starting point. The main road (A466) follows an attractive course alongside the river, but this road can be busy during the tourist season. Climb the steep valley sides onto quieter country roads and enjoy the expansive views out over the Severn estuary. It's undulating terrain, with some steep hills.

A detour east into the Forest of Dean provides opportunities for family cycle rides and day excursions, many of the forest tracks being open to cyclists. Back by the River Wye, Monmouth and Ross-on-Wye are pleasant towns worth visiting.

Yorkshire Dales

A week-long cycle tour through this magnificent national park is an exhilarating experience, and Skipton is a convenient starting point. Cycle northwards to Linton (Wharfedale) and Hubbersholme. Climb north-west over Fleatmoss to Hawes; roads are steep but the scenery is breathtaking. Take quiet roads eastwards along Wensleydale to Askrigg and Aysgarth, then north to Reeth.

For the intrepid, a detour over Tan Hill and back to Keld may be attempted. Alternatively, follow Swaledale westwards, then head north-west to Kirkby Stephen. From here, cycle south to Sedbergh and then through beautiful Dentdale. Head south to Horton-in-Ribblesdale, Stainforth and then east, passing Malham Tarn to Malham and back to Skipton.

This route covers about 130 miles but there are plenty of opportunities for scenic detours.

Hebridean Islands

The Hebridean Islands off the west coast of Scotland, linked by a comprehensive ferry system, provide superb cycling opportunities. You need to allow two to three weeks to give yourself time to enjoy the scenery in this enchanting region. Interesting circular routes are possible on most islands. This route comprises some 280 miles of cycling, and any tour will need to be planned around the timings of the ferry crossings; some are summer only.

Ardrossan, near Ayr, is a good starting point since the ferry to the Isle of Arran leaves from here. On Arran, cycle north to Lochranza for another ferry to the Kintyre peninsula. You can cycle north to Lochgilphead and Oban to catch the ferry to Tobermory on the Isle of Mull.

Mull is worth exploring before taking the ferry across to Kilchoan. Cycle eastwards along the Ardnamurchan peninsula to Salen, then north to Mallaig. Ferries leave from here to Armadale on the Isle of Skye. You can then cycle north to Uig, or follow numerous other routes around the island.

From Uig, take a ferry to Tarbert (Isle of Harris) in the Outer Hebrides. These outer isles are wild and remote places with very quiet lanes to explore. Cycle south to Benbecula and onto South Uist where you can catch the ferry back to Oban.

Golf

Britain, and in particular Scotland, is the home of golf. There are, in fact, more courses per capita in Scotland than in any other country in the world. The game has been played here for centuries and there are currently over 1900 courses in Britain, both private and public.

All courses are tested for their level of difficulty, and most are playable all year round. Some of the private clubs only admit members, friends of members, or golfers who have a handicap certificate or a letter of introduction from their club, but the majority welcome visitors.

Note that most clubs give members priority in booking tee-off times; it's always advisable to book in advance. It should be easier to book a tee-off time on a public course, but weekends on all courses are usually busy. You should also check whether there's a dress code, and whether the course has golf clubs for hire (not all do) if you don't have your own.

INFORMATION

Tourist boards have information leaflets; the BTA has a useful *Golfing Holidays* booklet giving lists of hotels and golfing events. For Scotland, *Golf in Scotland* is a free brochure listing 400 courses and clubs with details of where to stay. Contact the Scottish Tourist Board (☎ 0131-332 2433), 23 Ravelston Terrace, Edinburgh EH4 3EU, for a copy.

The Golf Club of Great Britain (☎ 0181-390 3113) is based at 3 Sage Yard, Douglas Rd, Surbiton, Surrey KT6 7TS.

COSTS

A round of golf on a public course will cost about £6. Private courses are more expensive with green fees ranging from £12 to £20 – and up to £40 on championship courses. However, many clubs offer a daily or weekly ticket. For example, a Golf Pass in Scotland costs between £46 and £70 for five days (Monday to Friday) depending on the area.

A set of golf clubs is about £5 (per round) to hire.

Tracing your Ancestors

Many visitors to Britain have ancestors who once lived in this country. Your trip would be a good chance to find out more about them and their lives; you may even discover relatives you never knew about. There is, however, no one central record office – records for England and Wales are kept in London, and those for Scotland are kept in Edinburgh.

The best place to start a search for your ancestors is the Public Record Office Web site, www.pro.gov.uk, which has comprehensive information for genealogists and a list of useful publications.

ENGLAND & WALES

For records of births, marriages and deaths since 1 July 1837 contact the Family Records Centre (☎ 0181-392 5300), 1 Myddelton St, Islington, London EC1R 1UW. The Public Record Office (PRO, ☎ 0181-876 3444) has records from 1086 (the Domesday Book) to the present day. It's based at Ruskin Ave, Kew, Richmond, Surrey TW9 4DU.

The search rooms are open Monday to Saturday from 10 am to 5 pm (longer hours some days) but are closed for two weeks a year, usually in October. Take your passport or another form of identification if you want to see original records. Remember that documents referring to individuals are closed for 100 years to safeguard personal confidentiality. It is also not possible to see documents or records until the PRO has preserved them, even though they may have been officially released.

For copies of certificates, contact the General Register Office (☎ 0151-471 4800), OPCS, PO Box 2, Southport, Merseyside PR8 2JD.

The PRO has a guide, *The Current Guide*, to help you find your way round the records, but it's quite a complex task. If you'd like someone to complete the search for you (for a fee), the PRO, and the Association of Genealogists & Record Agents

Brass Rubbing

One way to keep the kids amused through a wet afternoon is to take them brass rubbing, a hobby more or less unique to Britain.

From the 12th to the 16th centuries many wealthy individuals were commemorated on brass plaques set into the floor of local churches. Over the centuries many of these plaques have been torn up and melted down (look for the indentations, or matrices, which indicate lost brasses), but a surprising number have survived. Survivals from the 12th century, including four wonderful 1.8m figures of knights in full armour, are very rare, and the quality of the brasses declines markedly from the end of the 15th century.

Some churches will still let you make rubbings of the original brasses, but more often you'll be charged to rub a replica. So popular is this hobby that there are entire brass rubbing centres where you can rub replicas of brasses from all around the country. The most obvious such centres are in the crypt of St Martin-in-the-Fields church overlooking Trafalgar Square in London (☎ 0171-930 1862) and in Westminster Abbey (☎ 0171-222 4589). The end products of your labours make nice wall hangings.

A magnificent example of a brass rubbing showing Sir John Peryent and his wife Joan, Digswell, Oxfordshire 1415

(no ☎), 1 Woodside Close, Stanstead Rd, Caterham, Surrey CR3 6AU, can send you a list of professional record agents and researchers. The association can also supply the name of an agent who will search for living relatives.

SCOTLAND

If your ancestors were Scottish you should first go to the General Register Office (GRO) (☎ 0131-314 4433), New Register House, 3 West Register St, Edinburgh EH1 3YT. This office holds birth, marriage and death records since 1855, the census records and old parochial registers. Contact the GRO for leaflets giving details of its records and fees. The office opens Monday to Friday from 9 am to 4.30 pm. Before you go, contact the office to reserve a search-room seat, particularly if you have limited time in Edinburgh.

Next door is part of the Scottish Record Office (☎ 0131-535 1314), HM General Register House, 2 Princes St, Edinburgh EH1 3YY. There are two search rooms: the historical search room, where you research ancestors (no charge) and the legal search room, where you can see records for legal purposes (a fee is payable). Staff will answer simple inquiries by correspondence if precise details are given. If you want further research to be carried out for you (perhaps before you come) the office can send you a list of professional searchers. All correspondence should be addressed to: The Keeper of the Records of Scotland, Scottish Record Office, and sent to the above address.

BOOKS

Never Been Here Before by Jane Cox and Stella Colwell is a useful guide to the Family Records Centre. *Tracing Your Scottish Ancestors* by Cecil Sinclair is also useful.

Surfing & Swimming

Most overseas visitors do not think of Britain as a place to go for a beach holiday – and there are good reasons for this. The best ones are the climate and the water temperature. You definitely have to be hardy or equipped with a wetsuit to do anything more than take a quick dip. On the other side of the equation, Britain has some truly magnificent coastline and some wonderful sandy beaches. And the British have been taking holidays by the seaside since the 18th century, so there is a fascinating, sometimes bizarre, tradition to explore.

Visiting a British seaside resort should be high on the list of priorities for anyone wishing to gain an insight into British society. The resorts vary from staid retirement enclaves like Eastbourne, to vibrant cultural centres like Brighton and cheerful family resorts like Hastings. And then there's Blackpool, which pretty much defies categorisation. One thing remains common to them all, however, and that is that the fun happens on shore and it's done fully clothed!

Summer water temperatures are roughly equivalent to winter temperatures in southern Australia (approximately 13°C). Winter temperatures are about 5 or 6°C colder, giving a temperature range not dissimilar to that in northern California. So getting in the water, at least in summer, is definitely feasible if you have a wetsuit. A 3mm fullsuit (steamer) plus boots will be sufficient in summer, while winter requires a 5mm suit, plus boots, hood and gloves.

The best beaches, with the best chance of sun and surf and the genuine possibility of luring you into the water, are in Cornwall and Devon. Newquay, on the west Cornish coast five or six hours by road from London, is the capital of a burgeoning British surf scene, and it has a plethora of surf shops and all the appropriate paraphernalia and trappings, from Kombis to bleached hair. The boards and wetsuits sold are good quality and competitively priced in international terms.

Sadly, many British beaches, including those in Cornwall, suffer from pollution, often thanks to local towns draining their storm water and sewage offshore. It's worth checking with a local before taking the plunge.

The most unusual aspect of surfing in Britain is the impact of the tides. The tidal range is huge, which means there are often a completely different set of breaks at low and high tides. As is usually the case, the waves tend to be biggest and best on an incoming tide. Sadly, the waves in spring, autumn and winter tend to be bigger and more consistent than in summer. The conditions in summer are pretty unreliable.

The entire west coast of Cornwall and Devon is exposed to the Atlantic and there is a string of surf spots from Land's End to Ilfracombe. The shallow continental shelf, however, means the waves rarely get over 1.5m. Spring and autumn are the best times. There are a number of good breaks around Newquay, including Fistral, England's premier surfing beach and home to the main surfing contests. There are similar conditions on the Gower Peninsula and the south-west corner of Wales from Tenby to Fishguard.

Northern Scotland has the island's biggest and best surf, and although the outside temperatures are considerably lower than in the south, the water temperatures are only marginally lower. The entire coast has surf but it's the north, particularly around Thurso, that has outstanding world-class possibilities. The west coast is mainly sheltered by islands, and although there are no doubt untapped possibilities on the islands, they are difficult and expensive to get to. Islay is occasionally surfed. The east coast is easily accessible, but the swells are unreliable and short-lived.

There's quite a large surfing community in Thurso, thanks to several famous breaks. There are two breaks, one in front of the harbour wall with lefts and rights, known as Reef, and one at Beach. Thurso East (Castle Reef) is the big one: a huge right that works up to 4½m.

Fishing

Angling, as a sport and pastime, was obviously well established in England by medieval times. A *Treatyse of Fysshnge With an Angle*, published in 1496, described fishing flies which are still in use today. The 17th century saw great improvements in equipment and also brought Izaak Walton's classic book on fishing, *The Compleat Angler*.

Fishing is divided into several distinct categories, topped by dry-fly fishing, considered by its proponents to be the highest form of the sport. An artificial lure, made to imitate a small insect, must be gently dropped on the surface in order to deceive and catch the fish. Fly fishing is used for that most cautious of game fish, the trout. Fish are described as coarse fish or game fish, the latter because they vigorously struggle against capture. Curiously, fishing is an activity with widely differing vocabularies between English and American usage.

Fishing is enormously popular in Britain but also highly regulated. Many prime stretches of river are privately owned, and fishing there can be amazingly expensive. The Environment Agency (☎ 0645-333111) administers licences for rod fishing in England and Wales. A one year licence (valid from 1 April to 31 March) for coarse fishing costs £16 (£8 for those over 65 or for children aged 12 to 16). An eight day licence costs £6 and a one day licence £2. Salmon and sea trout licences cost £55/£27.50 for one year (1 April to 31 March),

£15 for an eight day licence and £5 for a one day licence.

Rod licences are available from every post office in England and Wales, bankside agents and Environment Agency Regional Offices. Contact the Environment Agency (☎ 01454-624400), Rio House, Waterside Drive, Aztec West, Almondsbury, Bristol BS12 4UD for details. Tackle shops are also good places to make fishing inquiries. Before fishing anywhere in England and Wales you must have the correct licence and the permission of the owner or tenants of the fishing rights.

There is a statutory close season (15 March to 15 June) when coarse fishing is banned on all rivers and streams – different rules apply on canals, lakes, ponds and reservoirs. The actual dates for close seasons vary according to the region and need to be checked in advance – the Environment Agency will be able to advise.

The fishing situation in Scotland, where there is a dense thicket of regulations on salmon fishing, is even more complicated. Fishing in Scotland is also amazingly expensive. Purchasing a 'time-share' right to fish a river in Scotland costs about £6000 per year!

Horse Riding & Pony Trekking

Seeing the country from the saddle is highly recommended, even if you're not an experienced rider. There are riding schools catering to all levels of proficiency, many of them in national park areas.

Pony trekking is a popular holiday activity: a half-day should cost around £10, and hard hats are included. Many pony trekkers are novice riders so most rides are at walking speed with the occasional trot. If you're an experienced rider there are numerous riding schools with horses to rent – TICs have details.

For more information contact the British Horse Society (☎ 01926-707795). It publishes *Where to Ride* which lists places throughout the UK and can also send you lists specific to a particular area (eg the Cotswolds).

Canal & Waterway Travel

Britain's surprisingly extensive network of canals and waterways spread rapidly across the country at the same time as the Industrial Revolution transformed the nation. As a method of transporting freight (passengers were always secondary), they were a short-lived wonder, trimmed back by railways and killed off by modern roads. By WWII, much of the waterway system was in terminal decline; the once-bustling canals had become stagnant channels of no economic significance. Today, however, the canals are booming once again as part of the leisure industry.

Exploring Britain by canal can be immensely rewarding. Narrowboats can be rented from numerous operators around Britain and for a family or a group they can provide surprisingly economical transport and accommodation. They also allow you to explore a hidden side of Britain. Travelling the waterways, it's easy to forget that the Britain of motorways and ring roads even exists. Canals lead you to a Britain of idyllic villages, pretty countryside and convenient and colourful waterside pubs. More surprisingly, they can show you a very different side of some otherwise unremarkable cities. Birmingham from its canals is quite different from Birmingham from the ring road.

The canal system is also a wonderful example of the power and vision of the Industrial Revolution's great engineers. No obstacle stood in the way of these visionaries, who threw flights of locks up steep hillsides or flung amazing aqueducts across wide valleys. They built to last as well – the lock equipment which you 'work' as you travel along the canals is often well over a century old.

The canals are not restricted to narrowboat users. The canal towpaths have become popular routes for walkers and cyclists who can enjoy the same hidden perspective as people actually out on the waterways. There are over 3000 miles of navigable canals and rivers in Britain, so there is plenty to explore. Contact TICs for more information.

HISTORY

As the Industrial Revolution swept across Britain, a growing need developed for means of transporting goods ranging from coal and iron to fine Wedgwood pottery. The first serious canals appeared in the 1760s, led by James Brindley's Bridgewater Canal, used for conveying coal to the burgeoning factories in Manchester. The development of canal locks, enabling the canal boats to go up and down hills, facilitated the spread of canals. Thomas Telford pioneered more modern canals, which took the shortest route from A to B, even when it involved multiple locks, tunnels, embankments and other complex engineering work. The Birmingham & Liverpool Junction was an example of this more advanced type of canal.

Some of the most interesting examples of canal engineering include the nearly two-mile-long Blisworth Tunnel near Stoke Bruerne. For particularly long inclines, locks were sometimes arranged in flights, where the top gate of one lock was also the bottom gate of the next. Ingenious attempts were made to design alternatives to canal locks. The inclined plane at Foxton, near Market Harborough, Leicestershire, dating from 1900, moved boats 23 vertical metres (75 feet), the equivalent of a flight of 10 locks. The 1875 Anderton Lift near Northwich, Cheshire, simply floated the boats into a tank which was then lifted 15m (50 feet). When a valley or river intervened, some canal engineers carried their canals right across in aqueducts, the most famous of which is the 307m-long Pontcysyllte Aqueduct in Wales.

For an interesting offshoot of the canals, visit the High Peak Trail in the Peak District. This early railway line has now been recycled to become a walking and bicycle track, but it was originally constructed by canal engineers still thinking in canal terms. Instead of engineering the long gentle inclines so they would be suitable for railway engines, they built the line with short steep rises up which the trains would have to be hauled, a dry-land equivalent of a canal's lock system.

Early canal boats were pulled by horses, walking on the towpaths alongside the canals, but by the mid-1800s steam power was starting to supersede horsepower. Later, diesel power replaced steam. Modern narrowboats for cruising still follow the traditional style but come equipped with all mod cons, from refrigerators to televisions.

Even if you don't get out on the canals, it's fascinating to visit one of the canal museums around Britain. They can be found at Stoke Bruerne near Northampton, at Devizes in Wiltshire, at Ellesmere Port near Chester and right in the centres of Nottingham and Gloucester.

THE WATERWAYS

Britain's boating waterways consist of both natural rivers and lakes and artificial canals. In all there are over 3000 miles of navigable waterways; about half are canals and half of those are 'narrow' canals, where the locks are just over 2m wide.

A narrowboat trip can vary from lazy relaxation to surprisingly hard work. When you're chugging down a wide river with only the occasional lock to be worked, it's the easiest means of transport imaginable. On the other hand, on a steep section of canal where one lock is followed immediately by another, narrowboat travel can be a combination of aerobics (keys to be wound, paddles to be raised and lowered), weight lifting (heavy lock gates to be pushed open and closed) and jogging (the lock crew runs on ahead to prepare the lock before the boat gets there). Canal travel is great if you have children and they're often exhausted by the end of the day!

Locks

A lock enables boats to go up or down a hill. It's a bathtub-shaped chamber with a single door at the top end and a double door at the bottom. *Sluices* in the doors let water

flow into or out of the lock when the *paddles* over the sluices are opened. A winding handle or *key* is used to open or close the paddles and this is one of the essential pieces of equipment for narrowboat travel. The process of going through a lock is known as *working* the lock.

On narrow canals the locks are usually wide enough and long enough for just one boat at a time. On rivers or wider canals they may be large enough for two or more boats. In a wider lock it's essential to keep your boat roped to the side to prevent it yawing around as the water flows in or out of the lock. But don't tie it up tightly – the ropes will need to be shortened or lengthened as the water level changes.

Narrowboats

There are over 200 firms renting narrowboats in Britain. Typically, a narrowboat will be 12 to 21m in length and no more than 2m or so wide. Narrowboats are usually surprisingly comfortable and well equipped with bunks and double beds, kitchen and dining areas, a fridge, cooker, flush toilet, shower and other mod cons. Usually they are rented out by the week, although shorter periods are sometimes available.

As narrowboats usually come so well equipped for everyday living, food supplies are all you need to worry about and there are plenty of shopping opportunities along the waterways. Alternatively, careful planning can see you moored at a riverside pub or restaurant for most meals.

Boats can accommodate from two or three people up to 10 or 12. Costs vary with the size of boat, the standard of equipment and the time of year. At the height of the summer season, a boat for four would vary from around £500 to £1000 per week. Larger boats work out cheaper per person; a boat for eight might cost £1000 per week. This means canal travel can cost not much over £100 per person for a week's transport and accommodation, a terrific travel bargain.

Although there are independent boat operators scattered all over the country, there are also centralised booking agencies who handle bookings for many of the individual companies. One of the biggest is Hoseasons Holidays (☎ 01502-501010), Sunway House, Raglan Rd, Lowestoft, Suffolk NR32 3LW.

If you only want a brief introduction to the canal system, there are over 50 firms operating day trips from various centres. A number of operators offer hotel boat trips where you simply come along for the ride.

Travelling the Waterways

No particular expertise or training is needed, nor is a licence required to operate a narrowboat. You're normally given a quick once-over of the boat and an explanation of how things work, a brief foray out onto the river or canal and then you're on your way. Proceed with caution at first, although you'll soon find yourself working the locks like a veteran. There are a variety of rules and suggestions that will make narrowboat travel easier for you and other waterway users:

Travel at an appropriate speed
 Narrowboats are not made for high-speed travel and if your speed is too fast for the waterway your wake will break along the bank and cause damage. Slow down when passing moored boats.

Keep your narrowboat neat and shipshape
 If you need to quickly tie up by the bank, hammer in a mooring peg, or fend off another boat with a pole, it will be much easier if ropes are neatly coiled, hammer and pegs are kept in the right place and equipment is all to hand.

Don't drop the key into the water!
 Without the key you cannot work the paddles to open and close the locks. A surprising number of keys get dropped into canals so ensure you always have a spare. Fortunately, if you do lose a key a replacement can usually be purchased quite cheaply at a boat yard. Fishing keys out of locks is a popular children's money-raiser, just like fishing golf balls out of water traps.

Get a good guidebook for the waterway you're exploring
 A good guide will point out lunch time pubs, overnight mooring spots and interesting attractions along the way.

Conserve water
 Canals are artificial creations and ensuring a steady supply of water at the top of the system is not always straightforward. Every time you use a lock, thousands of gallons flow downhill. You can help to conserve the water by sharing locks and waiting for oncoming boats if the lock is already set in their direction.

More information on the canal system is available from the Inland Waterways Association (☎ 0171-586 2510), 114 Regent's Park Rd, London NW1 8UQ. It publishes *The Inland Waterways Guide*, a general guide to holiday hire with route descriptions. Approximately two-thirds of the waterways in Britain are operated by the British Waterways Board (☎ 01923-226422), Willow Grange, Church Rd, Watford, Hertfordshire WD1 3QA. It publishes *The Waterways Code for Boaters*, a free, handy booklet packed with useful information and advice. Also available is a complete list of hire-boat and hotel-boat companies. Nicholsons/OS *Guide to the Waterways* is a useful guide that comes in three sections: South, Central and North (for England and Wales only).

Skiing

No one comes to Britain to ski. Indeed, some may be surprised to learn that there are ski resorts here. There are actually five main ski centres, all in Scotland, but the slopes are far less extensive and the weather considerably less reliable than anything you'll find in the Alps. On a sunny day, however, and with good snow, it can be very pleasant.

Scotland offers both alpine (downhill) and nordic (cross-country) skiing as well as other snow-related sports. The high season is from January to April, but it's sometimes possible to ski from as early as November to as late as May. Package holidays are available but it's very easy to make your own arrangements, with all kinds of accommodation on offer in and around the ski centres.

INFORMATION

Contact the Scottish Tourist Board (☎ 0131-332 2433) for its detailed *Ski Scotland* brochure and accommodation list. Alternatively, you can phone the skiing information centre for each area: Nevis Range (☎ 01397-705825); Glencoe (☎ 01855-851226); Glenshee (☎ 013397-41320); The Lecht (☎ 01975-651440); and Cairngorm (☎ 01479-861261). There's an answering machine service for calls outside business hours.

The Ski Hotline weather report service can be useful. Phone ☎ 0891-654 followed by 654 (for all centres); 660 (for Nevis Range); 658 (for Glencoe); 656 (for Glenshee); 657 (for The Lecht); and 655 (for Cairngorm). For nordic skiing the number is ☎ 0891-654659. Alternatively, check the Web site at www.ski.scotland.net which is updated daily during the ski season.

COSTS

It's easy to hire ski equipment and clothes when you arrive but you should book lessons, if you want them, in advance. The prices vary in each centre but on average expect to pay £11 to £13 per day for skis, sticks and boot hire; and £8 to £12 per day for ski clothes.

Lift passes cost £12 to £17 per day, or £65 to £68 for a five day pass (photo required). In a group, ski lessons cost £13 to £20 for a day, and £50 to £65 for five days; private lessons cost around £18 per hour.

Packages including ski hire, tuition and lift pass cost from £90 for three days (midweek). Two, four or five-day, and weekend packages are also available.

Charges are less for juniors – under 18 (Nevis Range and Cairngorm), under 16 (Glencoe, Glenshee, The Lecht).

RESORTS

The biggest ski centres are **Glenshee** (920m, 3019 feet) and **Cairngorm** (1097m, 3600 feet). Glenshee offers the largest network of lifts and selection of runs in Scotland. It also has snow machines for periods when the real thing doesn't appear. Cairngorm has almost 30 runs spread over an extensive area. Aviemore is the main town and there's a ski bus service from here and from the surrounding villages to the slopes.

Glencoe (1108m, 3636 feet) is the oldest of the resorts and opens seven days a week. The **Nevis Range** (1221m, 4006 feet) offers

the highest ski runs, the only gondola in Scotland to take you to the foot of the main skiing area, and a dry (plastic) ski slope. **The Lecht** (792m, 2600 feet) is the most remote centre. However, it's good for beginners and families, as well as for nordic skiers.

Access to the centres is probably easiest by car – there are plenty of car parks. Slopes are graded in the usual way, from green (easy) through blue and red to black (very difficult); and each centre has a ski patrol. You should ensure that your travel insurance covers you for winter sports.

All the ski resorts have facilities for snowboarding. The Lecht is best for beginners and the other four resorts are best for intermediates. They're all OK for advanced snowboarders.

Steam Railways

The invention of the steam engine and the subsequent rapid spread of the railway to almost every corner of Britain transformed life in the 19th century. In 1963 the Beeching Report led to the closure of many rural lines and stations, and in 1968 British Rail stopped using steam trains. For many people these two events brought the first century of rail travel in Britain to a sad end. It wasn't long, however, before rail enthusiasts reopened some of the lines and stations and restored many of the steam locomotives and rolling stock used in the proverbial 'golden age of rail'.

There are now nearly 500 private railways in Britain, many of them narrow gauge, using steam or diesel locomotives from all over the world. The main lines are detailed in the appropriate sections of this book. A useful guide to private steam railways is *Railways Restored* (Ian Allan). The guide is published annually and lists the major preserved railways, museums and preservation centres in the British Isles. It also gives details of opening times and includes a locomotive stock list for most centres.

Getting There & Away

London is one of the most important air transport hubs in the world, and with severe competition between airlines there are plenty of opportunities to find cheap flights.

Forget about shipping, unless by 'shipping' you mean the many ferry services from Europe. Only a handful of ships still carry passengers across the Atlantic; they don't sail often and are expensive, even compared with full-fare air tickets.

Some travellers arrive or leave through Europe, and some head on to Africa, the Middle East and Asia, and what used to be the Soviet Union. The trans-Siberian and Mongolian express trains may begin to carry more people to/from Europe as Russia opens up to tourism.

Whichever way you're travelling, make sure you take out travel insurance. This not only covers you for medical expenses and luggage theft or loss, but also for cancellation of, or delays in, your travel arrangements. Ticket loss is also covered, but make sure you have a separate record of all the details – or better still, a photocopy of the ticket. Buy insurance as early as possible. If you buy it the week before you fly, you may find, for instance, that you're not covered for delays to your flight caused by strikes or other industrial action that may have been in progress before you took out the insurance.

Paying for your ticket with a credit card often provides limited travel accident insurance, and you may be able to reclaim the payment if the operator doesn't deliver. In the UK, credit card providers are required by law to reimburse consumers if a company goes into liquidation and the amount in contention is more than £100. Ask your credit card company what it's prepared to cover.

For travel to/from Europe, buses are the cheapest, most exhausting method of transport, although discount rail tickets are competitive and budget flights (especially stand-by and last-minute offers) can be good value. A small saving on the fare may not compensate you for an agonising two days on a bus that leaves you exhausted for another two days. When making an assessment, don't forget the hidden expenses: getting to and from airports, departure taxes, and food and drink consumed en route.

Rail and bus options to Europe via the Channel Tunnel compete with combined rail/ferry or coach/ferry travel. See Land later in this chapter for information. Of course, it's also possible to get to and from the ferry ports under your own steam and just pay for the ferry itself.

AIR

There are international air links with London, Manchester, Newcastle, Edinburgh

---

Warning

The information in this chapter is particularly vulnerable to change: prices for international travel are volatile, routes are introduced and cancelled, schedules change, special deals come and go, and rules and visa requirements are amended. Airlines and governments seem to take a perverse pleasure in making price structures and regulations as complicated as possible. Check directly with the airline or a travel agent to make sure you understand how a fare (and ticket you may buy) works. In addition, the travel industry is highly competitive and there are many lurks and perks.

The upshot of this is that you should get opinions, quotes and advice from as many airlines and travel agents as possible before you part with your hard-earned money. The details given in this chapter should be regarded as pointers and are no substitute for your own careful, up-to-date research.

and Glasgow, but most cheap flights wind up in one of the five London airports: Heathrow is the largest, followed by Gatwick, Stansted, Luton and London City.

London is Europe's major centre for discounted long-haul airfares. There are countless travel agents, some of dubious reliability; the good ones include Trailfinders and all the main 'student' travel services. You don't have to be a student to use their services, they understand what a tight budget is, and they're competitive and reliable. See Information in the London chapter for details.

The listings magazine *Time Out*, the Sunday papers, and the *Evening Standard* carry ads for cheap fares. Also look out for *TNT Magazine* which you can often pick up free outside main train and tube stations.

All travel agents should be covered by an Air Travel Organisers Licence (ATOL). This scheme is operated by the Civil Aviation Authority (CAA) and means that in the event of either the agent or the airline going bust, you're guaranteed a full refund or, if you're already abroad, to be flown home. It's worth noting that under existing consumer protection legislation, the only way you can lose out is if you book direct from a scheduled airline – even a bucket shop gives you more protection. To be covered by the scheme, however, when you hand over cash you must be given either the ticket or an official ATOL receipt showing the agents number.

Linehaul Express (☎ 01784-421555), Stanwell, offers cheap flights in exchange for carrying documents. The Globetrotters Club (BCM Roving, London WC1N 3XX) publishes a newsletter called *Globe* that can help in finding travelling companions.

North South Travel (☎ 01245-492882, Moulsham Mill Centre, Parkway, Chelmsford, Essex CM2 7PX) is a travel agency that offers competitive fares and gives profits to charities in the developing world, particularly those involved in disadvantaged communities or sustainable tourism.

Buying Tickets

The plane ticket may be the single most expensive item in your budget, and buying it can be an intimidating business. There's a multitude of travel agents hoping to separate you from your money, and it's always worth researching the current state of the market. Start early: some of the cheapest tickets have to be bought months in advance, and some popular flights sell out early.

There's a growing number of low-cost, no-frills airlines operating out of the UK's smaller airports. As long as you book far enough in advance some of their deals are attractive but you need to bear in mind the extra time and expense of getting to and from these regional airports. Check the ads in *Time Out* or in the travel section of Sunday newspapers.

Cheap tickets are available in two distinct categories: official and unofficial. Official ones are advance-purchase tickets, budget fares, Apex, super-Apex, or whatever other brand name airlines care to use.

Unofficial tickets are discounted ones that airlines release through selected travel agents. Airlines can supply information on routes and timetables, and their low-season, student and senior citizens' fares can be competitive, but they don't sell discounted tickets. Remember that normal, full-fare airline tickets sometimes include one or more side trips to Europe free of charge, and/or fly-drive packages, which can make them good value.

Return tickets usually work out cheaper than two one-ways – often *much* cheaper. In some cases, a return ticket can even be cheaper than a one-way. Round-the-World (RTW) tickets can also be great bargains, sometimes cheaper than an ordinary return ticket. RTW prices start at about UK£900, A$2000 or US$1900 depending on the season.

Official RTW tickets are usually put together by two airlines, and permit you to fly anywhere on their route systems so long as you don't backtrack. There may be restrictions on how many stops you are permitted, and on the length of time the ticket remains valid. Travel agents put together unofficial RTW tickets by combining a number of discounted tickets.

Discounted tickets are usually available at prices as low as or lower than the official Apex or budget tickets. When you phone around, find out the fare, the route, the duration of the journey, the stopovers allowed and any restrictions on the ticket (see the Air Travel Glossary in this chapter), and ask about cancellation penalties.

You're likely to discover that the cheapest flights are 'fully booked, but we have another one that costs a bit more'. Or the flight is on an airline notorious for its poor safety standards and liable to leave you confined in the world's least favourite airport for 14 hours in mid-journey. Or the agent claims to have the last two seats available, which they'll hold for you for a maximum of two hours. Don't panic – keep ringing around.

If you're travelling from the USA or South-East Asia, or leaving Britain, you'll probably find that the cheapest flights are advertised by small, obscure agencies. Most are honest and solvent but a few rogue ones will take your money and disappear. If you feel suspicious about a firm, leave a deposit (no more than 20%) and pay the balance when you get the ticket. You could phone the airline direct to check you actually have a booking before collecting the ticket. If the travel agent insists on cash in advance, go somewhere else or be prepared to take a very big risk.

You may decide to pay more than the rock-bottom fare by opting for the safety of a better known travel agent. Firms like STA Travel, which has offices worldwide, Council Travel in the USA, Travel CUTS in Canada and Trailfinders in London offer good prices to most destinations, and are competitive and reliable.

Use the fares quoted in this book as a guide only. They're likely to have changed by the time you read this.

Travellers with Special Needs

If you have special needs – you've broken a leg, you require a special diet, you're taking the baby, or whatever – let the airline people know as soon as possible so that they can make arrangements. Remind them when you reconfirm your booking and again when you check in at the airport.

Children aged under two travel for 10% of the standard fare (or free on some airlines) if they don't occupy a seat, but they don't get a baggage allowance either. 'Skycots', baby food and nappies (diapers) should be provided if requested in advance. Children aged between two and 12 usually get a seat for half to two-thirds of the full fare, and do get a baggage allowance.

Flights within the UK and Europe and on Concorde are smoke free. Smoking is also banned on some flights to South-East Asia and Australia. On other flights non-smokers can ask their agent to request a non-smoking seat in the booking, but there's no guarantee that you'll find one available at check-in unless you have a doctor's note certifying chronic emphysema.

Excess Baggage

Many people, especially those who spend time working while overseas, accumulate considerably more baggage than the 20kg allowed by airlines (note that the routes to/from, or through, the USA often have much more generous allowances than those to the east). The most economic solution is to contact one of the many shipping companies that advertise in *TNT Magazine* or *Traveller Magazine* and arrange to have the surplus either shipped or airfreighted home. This shouldn't be a last-minute decision since companies often need a couple of days notice to arrange, first, the delivery of cartons or tea chests and, second, a pick-up time.

It's also worth giving yourself time to phone around for quotes. Be immediately suspicious of a company that offers rates substantially cheaper than average. Check that the company you choose is either a bonded member of an overseas division of the British Association of Removers, or the Association of International Removers. The shipping business doesn't have standard safeguards for its customers and occasionally companies collapse or disappear. This can mean losing possessions, having bags

Air Travel Glossary

Baggage Allowance This will be written on your ticket and usually includes one 20kg item to go in the hold, plus one item of hand luggage.

Bucket Shops These are unbonded travel agencies specialising in discounted airline tickets.

Bumped Just because you have a confirmed seat doesn't mean you're going to get on the plane (see Overbooking).

Cancellation Penalties If you have to cancel or change a discounted ticket, there are often heavy penalties involved; insurance can sometimes be taken out against these penalties. Some airlines impose penalties on regular tickets as well, particularly against 'no-show' passengers.

Check-In Airlines ask you to check in a certain time ahead of the flight departure (usually one to two hours on international flights). If you fail to check in on time and the flight is overbooked, the airline can cancel your booking and give your seat to somebody else.

Confirmation Having a ticket written out with the flight and date you want doesn't mean you have a seat until the agent has checked with the airline that your status is 'OK' or confirmed. Meanwhile you could just be 'on request'.

Courier Fares Businesses often need to send urgent documents or freight securely and quickly. Courier companies hire people to accompany the package through customs and, in return, offer a discount ticket which is sometimes a phenomenal bargain. In effect, what the companies do is ship their freight as your luggage on regular commercial flights. This is a legitimate operation, but there are two shortcomings - the short turnaround time of the ticket (usually not longer than a month) and the limitation on your luggage allowance. You may have to surrender all your allowance and take only carry-on luggage.

Full Fares Airlines traditionally offer 1st class (coded F), business class (coded J) and economy class (coded Y) tickets. These days there are so many promotional and discounted fares available that few passengers pay full economy fare.

ITX An ITX, or 'independent inclusive tour excursion', is often available on tickets to popular holiday destinations. Officially it's a package deal combined with hotel accommodation, but many agents will sell you one of these for the flight only and give you phoney hotel vouchers in the unlikely event that you're challenged at the airport.

Lost Tickets If you lose your airline ticket an airline will usually treat it like a travellers cheque and, after inquiries, issue you with another one. Legally, however, an airline is entitled to treat it like cash and if you lose it then it's gone forever. Take good care of your tickets.

MCO An MCO, or 'miscellaneous charge order', is a voucher that looks like an airline ticket but carries no destination or date. It can be exchanged through any International Association of Travel Agents (IATA) airline for a ticket on a specific flight. It's a useful alternative to an onward ticket in those countries that demand one, and is more flexible than an ordinary ticket if you're unsure of your route.

No-Shows No-shows are passengers who fail to show up for their flight. Full-fare passengers who fail to turn up are sometimes entitled to travel on a later flight. The rest are penalised (see Cancellation Penalties).

On Request This is an unconfirmed booking for a flight.

Air Travel Glossary

Onward Tickets An entry requirement for many countries is that you have a ticket out of the country. If you're unsure of your next move, the easiest solution is to buy the cheapest onward ticket to a neighbouring country or a ticket from a reliable airline which can later be refunded if you do not use it.

Open Jaw Tickets These are return tickets where you fly out to one place but return from another. If available, this can save you backtracking to your arrival point.

Overbooking Airlines hate to fly empty seats and since every flight has some passengers who fail to show up, airlines often book more passengers than they have seats. Usually excess passengers make up for the no-shows, but occasionally somebody gets bumped. Guess who it is most likely to be? The passengers who check in late.

Point-to-Point Tickets These are discount tickets that can be bought on some routes in return for passengers waiving their rights to a stopover.

Promotional Fares These are officially discounted fares, available from travel agencies or direct from the airline.

Reconfirmation At least 72 hours prior to departure time of an onward or return flight, you must contact the airline and 'reconfirm' that you intend to be on the flight. If you don't do this the airline can delete your name from the passenger list and you could lose your seat.

Restrictions Discounted tickets often have various restrictions on them - such as needing to be paid for in advance and incurring a penalty to be altered. Others are restrictions on the minimum and maximum period you must be away, such as a minimum of 14 days or a maximum of one year.

Round-the-World Tickets RTW tickets give you a limited period (usually a year) in which to circumnavigate the globe. You can go anywhere the carrying airlines go, as long as you don't backtrack. The number of stopovers or total number of separate flights is decided before you set off and they usually cost a bit more than a basic return flight.

Stand-by This is a discounted ticket where you only fly if there is a seat free at the last moment. Stand-by fares are usually available only on domestic routes.

Travel Agencies Travel agencies vary widely and you should choose one that suits your needs. Some simply handle tours, while full-services agencies handle everything from tours and tickets to car rental and hotel bookings. If all you want is a ticket at the lowest possible price, then go to an agency specialising in discounted tickets.

Transferred Tickets Airline tickets cannot be transferred from one person to another. Travellers sometimes try to sell the return half of their ticket, but officials can ask you to prove that you are the person named on the ticket. This is less likely to happen on domestic flights, but on an international flight tickets are compared with passports.

Travel Periods Ticket prices vary with the time of year. There is a low (off-peak) season and a high (peak) season, and often a low-shoulder season and a high-shoulder season as well. Usually the fare depends on your outward flight - if you depart in the high season and return in the low season, you pay the high-season fare.

stuck in Britain, or, if you're lucky, just paying twice!

Shipping is slower and cheaper than airfreight and delivery dates are approximate at best. Most companies quote eight to 12 weeks for shipping to Australasia, but the reality can be 16 to 20 weeks. Airfreight generally takes one to two weeks. For shipping, the charges are based on volume; for airfreight, both weight and volume.

There are generally two other alternatives: door to door, or door to port/airport. Most companies deliver boxes and packing materials and pick up free in London, but you can elect whether you pick up goods from the port or airport at the goods' destination. The additional cost of having a tea chest delivered door to door may add £50 to the charge (providing you live less than 30 miles from the port – more otherwise). But in most cases this is money well spent. It's easy to waste at least a day battling with bureaucracy and there are substantial fees you can't avoid (port and unloading charges, plus customs charges).

Your goods can't be released until they're cleared by customs. Generally, import duty won't be levied if the goods have been privately used for a reasonable period of time, but it's wise to check regulations with your embassy or high commission in advance. If your goods are subject to import duty, make sure you're home before they are so you can provide the appropriate documentation.

If you'll arrive after your goods, make sure a friend or relative can answer Customs inquiries on your behalf. They'll need a photocopy of your passport, the date you left and plan to return, a list of contents and a letter authorising them to obtain the goods. In New Zealand, if a friend or relative clears the goods, import duty will automatically be levied, although you'll be able to claim a refund when you get home.

If you plan to pick your goods up from the port or airport yourself, bear in mind that once the goods arrive you generally have only a couple of days grace before hefty storage charges are levied. Fortunately, most companies store baggage in London (usually for a nominal charge) and ship it on a nominated date.

Insurance is recommended. Check (and that means reading the small print) that it covers loss, theft and breakage of individual items, not just the entire package, that claims can be settled at your destination and that the goods are insured for full replacement value.

The USA & Canada

The North Atlantic is the world's busiest long-haul air corridor and flight options are bewildering. You should be able to fly New York-London return for around US$575. Airhitch (☎ 212-864 2000) is worth contacting for one-way tickets and can get you to London (one way) for around US$350/480 from the east coast/west coast of the USA.

The *New York Times*, the *LA Times*, the *Chicago Tribune*, the *San Francisco Chronicle* and the *San Francisco Examiner* produce weekly travel sections in which you'll find any number of travel agents' ads. Council Travel and STA Travel have offices in major cities nationwide.

In Canada, Travel CUTS has offices in all major cities. Scan the budget travel agents' ads in the *Globe & Mail*, the *Toronto Star* and *Vancouver Sun*. A courier return flight to London or Paris will set you back about C$450 from Toronto or Montreal, around C$495 from Vancouver.

Another option is a courier flight, where you accompany a parcel or freight to be picked up at the other end. A New York-London return can be as little US$150. You can also fly one way. The drawbacks are that your stay in Europe may be limited to one or two weeks, your luggage is usually restricted to hand luggage (the parcel or freight you carry comes out of your luggage allowance), and you may have to be a resident and apply for an interview before they'll take you on (dress conservatively).

Find out more about courier agents and flights from:

International Association of Air Travel Couriers (☎ 561-582 8320, fax 561-582 1381), PO Box 1349, Lake Worth, FL 33460, USA

Worldwide Courier Association (☎ 716-464 0920, fax 716-464 9337), 757 West Main St, Rochester, NY 14611-2332, USA

The *Travel Unlimited* newsletter (PO Box 1058, Allston, MA 02134, USA) publishes monthly details of the cheapest airfares and courier possibilities for destinations all over the world from the USA and other countries, including the UK. It's a treasure-trove of information. A year's subscription is US$25 (US$35 abroad).

Australia & New Zealand

STA Travel and Flight Centres International are major dealers in discounted airfares from Australia and New Zealand. Check the travel agents' ads and ring around.

The Saturday travel sections of the *Sydney Morning Herald* and Melbourne's *The Age* newspapers have ads offering cheap fares to London, but don't be surprised if they happen to be sold out when you contact the agents: they're usually low-season fares on obscure airlines with conditions attached.

Discounted return fares on mainstream airlines through a reputable agent like STA Travel cost between A$1800 (low season) and A$3000 (high season). Flights to/from Perth are a couple of hundred dollars cheaper. A Britannia charter service also operates between Britain and Australia/New Zealand. From November to March, prices can drop as low as £499 return from London to Sydney and £698 return from Sydney to London. Try UK Flight Shop (☎ 02-9247 4833), 7 Macquarie Place, Sydney, or in the UK, Austravel (☎ 0171-838 1011), 152 Brompton Rd, Knightsbridge, London SW3 1HX.

The cheapest fares from New Zealand will probably take the eastbound route via the USA, but a RTW ticket may be cheaper than a return.

Ireland

Dublin is linked by several airlines to cities in Britain including London's major airports. There are also flights to various regional centres in the Republic of Ireland. The standard one-way economy fare from London to Dublin is £100, but advance-purchase fares are available offering return tickets for as low as £70. These must be booked well in advance as seats are often limited.

Regular connections between Belfast and Britain include the British Airways shuttle service (☎ 0345-222111) from London's Heathrow. Costs on the shuttle range from £93 for a regular one-way ticket to £145 for an advance-purchase return. British Midland Airways (☎ 0345-554554) also offer similar fares. Jersey European Airways (☎ 0990-676676) from Gatwick or Stansted and BA Express from Luton have advance-purchase return fares from around £69.

Continental Europe

Excellent discount charter flights are often available to full-time students aged under 30 and all young travellers aged under 26 (you need an ISIC card or an official youth card) and are available through the large student travel agencies.

Low season one-way/return flights from London bucket shops start at: Amsterdam £45/65, Athens £69/99, Frankfurt £55/75, Istanbul £79/129, Madrid £79/99, Paris £40/59 and Rome £69/89. Official tickets with carriers like British Airways can cost a lot more.

Africa

Nairobi, Kenya, is probably the best place in Africa to buy tickets to Britain, thanks to the many bucket shops and the strong competition between them. A typical one-way/return fare to London would be about US$700/900. If you're thinking of flying to London from Cairo, it's often cheaper to fly to Athens and to proceed with a budget bus or train from there.

South Africa Student Travel, Rosebank, Johannesburg (☎ 011-447 5551; Cape Town, ☎ 021-418 6570), is primarily aimed at students and has youth fares to London from R3500 (low season) to R4000 (high season). The Africa Travel Centre (☎ 021-235555), on the corner of Military Rd and

New Church St, Tamboerskloof, Cape Town, also has keen prices.

Asia

Ask the advice of other travellers before buying a ticket. Many of the cheapest fares from South-East Asia to Europe and London are offered by Eastern European carriers. STA Travel has branches in Tokyo, Singapore, Bangkok and Kuala Lumpur.

To/from India, the cheapest flights tend to be with Eastern European carriers like LOT and Aeroflot, or with Middle Eastern airlines such as Syrian Arab Airlines and Iran Air. Mumbai (Bombay) is the air transport hub, with many transit options to/from South-East Asia, but tickets are slightly cheaper in Delhi.

LAND
Overland Route

After the heady 1970s, the Asia overland trail lost much of its popularity – the Islamic regime in Iran made life hard, and the war in Afghanistan effectively closed that country. Now that Iran is rediscovering the merits of tourism, the Asia route is picking up again, though unpredictable instabilities – eg Pakistan – may prevent the trickle of travellers becoming a flood for some time.

A new overland route through what used to be the Soviet Union could become important over the next few years. At this stage the options are more or less confined to the trans- Siberian/Mongolian railway lines to/from Moscow (see Trans-Siberian Trains in this chapter), but other modes of transport are likely to become available beyond the Urals as the newly independent states open up to travellers.

Going to/from Africa involves a Mediterranean ferry crossing (discounting the complicated Middle East route). Unfortunately, due to problems in Africa (trouble in Algeria and Morocco and civil war in Sudan in the east), the most feasible Africa overland routes of the past have all but closed down.

Travelling by private transport beyond Europe requires plenty of paperwork and other preparations, and a detailed description is outside the scope of this book. The following sections tell you what's required within Europe.

Morocco and most of Turkey lie outside Europe, but the rail systems of both countries are still covered by InterRail (though the Youth Pass version for those under 26 isn't valid in Turkey) – see InterRail Pass in the European Rail Passes section in this chapter. If you don't have an InterRail Pass, the price of a cheap return train ticket from London to Morocco compares favourably with equivalent bus fares – it's worth keeping this in mind.

Trans-Siberian Trains To/from central and eastern Asia, a train can work out at about the same price as flying, depending on how much time and money you spend along the way, and it can be lots more fun. There are three routes to/from Moscow across Siberia: the trans-Siberian to/from Vladivostok, and the trans-Mongolian and trans-Manchurian, both to/from Beijing. There's a fourth route south from Moscow and across Kazakhstan, following part of the old Silk Route to/from Beijing. Prices can vary enormously, depending on where you buy the ticket and what is included. For full details see the *Trans-Siberian Handbook* (Trailblazer) by Bryn Thomas.

The trans-Siberian takes just under seven days from Moscow via Khabarovsk to Vladivostok, from where there is a boat to Japan (Niigata) or Hong Kong. The boats only run from May to September.

The trans-Mongolian passes through Mongolia to Beijing and takes about 5½ days. The direction in which you travel and when you go makes a difference in cost and travelling time. A straight Beijing-Moscow economy ticket costs around US$280. If you want to stop off along the way or spend some time in Moscow, you'll need 'visa support' – a letter from a travel agent confirming that they're making your travel/accommodation bookings required in Russia or Mongolia.

Locally based companies that do all-inclusive packages (with visa support) that can be arranged from abroad include the

Travellers Guest House (☎ 0095-971 40 59, fax 280 76 86) in Moscow and Moonsky Star (aka Monkey Business) (☎ 2723 1376, fax 2723 6653) in Hong Kong, with an information centre in Beijing. There are other budget operators.

The trans-Manchurian passes through Manchuria to Beijing and takes six days. The fourth route runs from Moscow via Almaty in Kazakhstan, crosses the border on the line to Ürümqi (north-western China) and follows part of the old Silk Route to Beijing. At present you can't buy through tickets.

There are countless travel options between Moscow and the rest of Europe. Most people opt for a train, usually to/from Berlin, Helsinki, Munich or Vienna.

Bus

Even without using the Tunnel, you can still get to Europe by bus or train – there's just a short ferry/hovercraft ride thrown in as part of the deal. Eurolines (☎ 0990-143219), 52 Grosvenor Gardens, Victoria, London SW1, a division of National Express (the largest UK bus line), has an enormous network of European destinations, including Ireland and Eastern Europe.

You can book through any National Express office, including Victoria coach station, London, which is where coaches depart and arrive, and at many travel agents. It also has agents in Europe, including: Paris (☎ 01-49 72 51 51); Amsterdam (☎ 020-560 8787); Frankfurt (☎ 06979 03240); Madrid (☎ 91-530 7600); Rome (☎ 06-88 40840); and Budapest (☎ 1-1172 562).

Youth fares are available for holders of National Express Discount Coach Cards (see the Getting Around chapter). In fact, the discount is quite disappointing in most cases.

The following single/return prices and journey times are representative: Amsterdam £31/44 (12 hours), Athens £128/207 (56 hours), Frankfurt £52/79 (18½ hours), Madrid £77/138 (27 hours), Paris £31/44 (10 hours) and Rome £88/125 (36 hours).

Eurolines also has some good-value explorer tickets that are valid up to six months and allow travel between a number of major cities. For example, you can visit Amsterdam, Brussels and Paris and return to London for £71.

Busabout (☎ 0181-784 2816) runs coaches along three interlocking circuits. Each circuit costs £109 (£99 for youth and student card-holders) for two weeks, with the add-on from London and Paris an extra £30 return.

You can buy Busabout tickets direct from the company or from suppliers such as Usit Campus or STA Travel.

Train

Trains are a popular mode of transport: they're good meeting places, comfortable, frequent, generally reliable, and rail passes make them affordable.

If you plan to travel extensively by train, consider buying the *Thomas Cook European Timetable*, which gives a complete listing of train schedules (and ferries) and indicates where supplements apply or where reservations are necessary. It's updated monthly and is available from Thomas Cook outlets worldwide. You can also get train times from all over the world on the Internet.

As well as the Channel Tunnel service there are rail/ferry and rail/hovercraft services to/from Europe.

For inquiries concerning European trains contact the following: International Rail Centre (☎ 0171-834 2345) and Wasteels (☎ 0171-834 7066), both at Platform 2, Victoria Station, London SW1; and Rail Europe (☎ 0990 848848), 179 Piccadilly, London W1.

Non-tunnel rail options depend on whether you cross the Channel on a ferry hovercraft, or catamaran or from Harwich, Boulogne/Folkestone or Newhaven. One option is a fare to Paris in 2nd class via Newhaven and the Sealink ferry which costs £39/65 adult single/return and the journey takes nine hours. You can book onward rail connections to anywhere in Europe. London to Amsterdam via Harwich and the Stena high speed catamaran costs £49/75; journey time is about 8¾ hours.

European Rail Passes There are several passes for use on European rail systems but the most important point to note is that they're not valid on Britain's railways!

The Eurail Pass can only be bought by residents of non-European countries. Although it's supposed to be purchased before arriving in Europe, you can buy it within Europe as long as your passport proves you've been there for less than six months. But the outlets where you can do this are limited and it's cheaper to buy the pass outside Europe. Rail Europe (see the Train section earlier) is one such outlet. There's a range of Eurail Passes: a one-month under-26 pass costs £426, for example. Passes for those aged 26 or over are for 1st class travel only, but you can get good discounts if you're travelling with one other person (two other people from April to September).

The Europass is for non-Europeans that gives between five and 15 days of unlimited travel within a two month period. It's a little cheaper than the Eurail Pass because it covers fewer countries.

The InterRail Pass is similar to the Eurail Pass but is available only to residents of European countries. Within the UK, Inter-Rail Passes can be purchased only by people who have been resident for at least six months. There are eight passes each covering a different zone. Zone E, for example, includes France, Belgium, the Netherlands and Luxembourg. A pass for 22 days travel costs £229 (£159 for those under 26). Multi-zone passes are better value and are valid for one month: all eight zones costs £349 (£259).

The Eurodomino Pass (called a Freedom Pass in Britain) is for single countries. It's available for three, five or 10 days. Prices for 10-day passes for under 26/over 26 range from £79/129 (for the Netherlands) to £199/249 (for Spain).

The Carte Vermeil seniors' card is worth investigating for travellers aged over 60.

For the full story on travel in Europe, see Lonely Planet's *Europe* or its other European guides.

Cheap Tickets European rail passes are only worth buying if you plan to do a lot of travelling within a short space of time. When weighing up options, you should consider the cost of other cheap-ticket deals. Travellers aged under 26 can pick up Billet International de Jeunesse (BIJ) tickets that cut fares by up to 50%. Unfortunately, you can't always bank on a substantial reduction. The £162 return from London to Munich represents a £2 saving on the normal fare.

Various agents issue BIJ tickets in London, including Usit Travel (☎ 0171-730 3402), 52 Grosvenor Gardens, London SW1 (tube: Victoria). Options include circular Explorer tickets, allowing a different route for the return trip: London to Madrid, for instance, takes in Barcelona, Paris and numerous other cities. The fare for the Spanish Explorer ticket is £228 (including some accommodation), valid for two months. The International Rail Centre and Wasteels (see the Train section earlier) also sell BIJ tickets.

Channel Tunnel The Channel Tunnel gives Britain a land link with Europe. Two services operate through the Tunnel: Eurotunnel operates a rail shuttle service for motorbikes, cars, buses and freight vehicles, between terminals at Folkestone in the UK and Calais in France; and the railway companies of Britain, France and Belgium operate a high-speed passenger service, known as Eurostar, between London and Paris, and London and Brussels.

Eurotunnel Specially designed shuttle trains run 24 hours a day, departing up to four times an hour in each direction from 6 am to 10 pm and every hour between 10 pm and 6 am.

Eurotunnel terminals are clearly signposted and connected to motorway networks. British and French Customs and Immigration formalities are carried out before you drive on to Eurotunnel. Travel time from motorway to motorway, including loading and unloading, is one hour; the shuttle itself takes 35 minutes. This sounds impressive, but the total time by hovercraft is under two hours, and ferries only take 2½ hours.

A car and all passengers costs £220. You can make an advance reservation (☎ 0990-353535) or pay by cash or credit card at a toll booth.

Eurostar Eurostar (☎ 0990-300003) runs up to 20 trains a day between London and Paris, up to 12 between London and Brussels. There are direct Eurostar services from Glasgow and Manchester to both Paris and Brussels and from Birmingham to Paris. There are onward connections from London to Wales and from Brussels to Germany and the Netherlands. An overnight service offers evening departures from UK stations to give morning arrivals on the continent.

In England, trains arrive at and depart from the international terminal at Waterloo station. Some trains stop at Ashford International station in Kent, and at Frethun (near Calais) or Lille. Immigration formalities are completed on the train, but British Customs are at Waterloo.

London to Paris takes three hours (which will drop to 2½ hours when the high-speed track through Kent is completed). London to Brussels takes two hours 40 minutes (which will drop to two hours 10 minutes).

Get tickets from travel agents and major train stations. The normal single/return fare to Paris is £120/220 but various special offers and advance purchase may reduce this to £99 return in summer and £79 return in winter.

Car & Motorcycle

See the Channel Tunnel section earlier information on the tunnel shuttle arges Sea section later for details on ferpter for for cars. See the Getting Around. information on buying a car

Paperwork & Prep be carried (a ownership should ument for British-Vehicle Registrat driving in Europe. registered cars ational licence and if Also carry

you're on a long overland trip from outside Europe, you may also need an International Driving Permit (IDP) from your motoring organisation. See Visas & Documents in the Regional Facts for the Visitor chapter.

Third party motor insurance is a minimum requirement. Most UK motor insurance policies automatically provide this for European Union (EU) countries and some others. Get your insurer to issue a Green Card (which may cost extra), an internationally recognised proof of insurance, and check that it lists all the countries you intend to visit. You'll need this in the event of an accident outside the country where the vehicle is insured. Also, ask your insurer for a European Accident Statement form.

Taking out a European breakdown assistance policy, such as the AA Five Star Service or the RAC Eurocover Motoring Assistance, is a good investment. Both include a bail bond for Spain, which is also recommended. Ask your motoring organisation for a Card of Introduction, that entitles you to free services offered by affiliated organisations around Europe.

Every vehicle that travels across an international border should display a nationality plate of its country of registration. A warning triangle, to be used in the event of breakdown, is compulsory almost everywhere (although not in Britain). Recommended accessories are a fire extinguisher (compulsory in Greece and Turkey) and a first-aid kit (compulsory in Austria, Slovenia, Croatia, Yugoslavia and Greece). For more information contact the RAC (☎ 0800-550550) or the AA (☎ 0800-444999).

SEA

There's a bewildering array of alternatives between Britain and mainland Europe. This chapter outlines the main alternatives, but doesn't give a complete listing.

Competing companies operate on the main routes, but competition from Eurotunnel (mainly) and airlines has led to mergers (P&O Stena is now the biggest operator), the reduction of prices on some routes and seasonal special offers.

Services are comprehensive but complicated. The same ferry company often has a host of different prices for the same route, depending upon the time of day or year, the validity of the ticket, or the size of a vehicle. Return tickets may be much cheaper than two one-way fares; on some routes a standard five day return is the same as a one-way ticket; and vehicle tickets may also cover a driver and passenger. There are cheap day-return tickets (like Dover-Calais for £11), but they're strictly policed.

It's worth planning (and booking) ahead where possible as there may be special reductions on off-peak crossings. Unless otherwise stated, the prices quoted for cars don't include passengers. The hovercraft/ ferries all carry cars and motorcycles.

Passenger Ships

The days of earning your passage on a freighter to or from Britain have well and truly passed. Even if you have a mariner's ticket, a shipping company is unlikely to want to sign you up for a single trip.

Regular long-distance passenger ships disappeared with the advent of cheap air travel to be replaced by a small number of luxury cruise ships. The grand old lady of them all, Cunard's *Queen Elizabeth II*, sails between New York and Southampton 28 times a year; the trip takes five nights each way, and a return ticket costs from £1690, though there are also one-way and 'fly one way' deals.

The standard reference for passenger ships is the *ABC Cruise & Ferry Guide* published by the OAG Worldwide (☎ 01582-600111), Church St, Dunstable, Bedfordshire LU5 4HB.

A more adventurous (though not necessarily cheaper) alternative is as a paying passenger on a freighter. Freighters are far more numerous than cruise ships and there are many more routes from which to choose. With a bit of homework, you'll be able to sail between Britain and just about anywhere else in the world, with stopovers at exotic ports which you may never have heard of. The previously mentioned *ABC Cruise & Ferry Guide* is a good source of information.

Passenger freighters typically carry six to 12 passengers (more than 12 would require a doctor on board) and, though less luxurious than dedicated cruise ships, give you a real taste of life at sea. Schedules tend to be flexible and costs vary, but seem to hover around US$100 a day; vehicles can often be included for an additional fee.

France

On a clear day, you can see across the Channel from England to France. A true budget traveller would obviously swim – it's only seven hours and forty minutes if you match the record.

Dover/Folkestone/Newhaven The shortest ferry link to Europe is from Dover and Folkestone to Calais and Boulogne.

Dover is the most convenient port for those who plan onward travel (in England) by bus or train. Between Dover and Calais, P&O Stena Line (☎ 0990-980980), a combined company, and Hoverspeed (☎ 0990-240241) operate every one to two hours.

On its 75-minute ferry ride P&O Stena Line charges one-way foot passengers £24; cars and drivers, depending on the date and time, from £60 to £130 including the driver; £68 to £135 for up to nine passengers; motorcycles and riders £39 to £57. However, special offers can make a big difference in cost.

Hoverspeed's hovercraft and catamarans only take 35 minutes to cross the Channel. It charges £25 for a one-way passenger, £47 up to for a car and driver, £55 to £99 for five passengers.

Stena Line also operates seven or eight Dieppe, a day between Newhaven and roughly half hour journey by ferry, at £24 one-way by catamaran. Fares start £139 for a car, a foot passenger, £58 to and one passenger.

Portsmouth P&O (☎ 080555) operates three to four ferries to/from Cherbourg and Le Havre. Day ferries take five to six hours and the night ferries take seven to eight hours. A one-way foot passenger fare costs £15 to £30 and a car costs £70 to £130. Brittany Ferries (☎ 0990-360360) has at least one sailing a day to/from Caen and St Malo. Portsmouth-Caen takes six hours and costs the same as the P&O routes. The Portsmouth-St Malo route costs a little more. (Brittany Ferries also has a ferry from Plymouth to Roscoff.)

Spain

From Plymouth, Brittany Ferries (☎ 0990-360360) operates at least one ferry a week to Santander, on Spain's north coast. The journey time is 24 hours; a single is from £47 to £82 and a vehicle costs from £152 to £275. Brittany also operates a service between Santander and Portsmouth that takes 30 hours. P&O (☎ 0990-980666) operates a service between Portsmouth and Bilbao at similar rates.

Scandinavia

Until you see the ferry possibilities, it's easy to forget how close Scandinavia and Britain are, and why the Vikings found British villages so convenient to pillage.

Aberdeen & Shetland One of the most interesting possibilities is the summer-only link between Shetland, Norway, the Faroes and Iceland. The operator is Smyril Line but the agent is P&O (☎ 01244-572615).

First you have to get to Shetland from Orkney, or from Aberdeen in Scotland. P&O has sailings Monday to Friday from Aberdeen to Lerwick (Shetland). A reclining seat costs £49/55 (one way) depending on whether it's low or high season.

The Smyril Line operates from late May to early September. One-way couchette fares (a couchette is a sleeping berth) vary depending on the season. From Shetland to Norway the trip takes 13½ hours and costs £45/63, to the Faroes (13½ hours, £45/63) and to Iceland (31 hours, £98/139). The journey to Denmark takes 50 hours because it goes via the Faroe Islands and costs £95/135.

Newcastle Norway's Color Line (☎ 0191-296 1313) operates ferries all year to Stavanger, Haugesund and Bergen in Norway. They depart on Saturday, Tuesday and Wednesday from January to April (plus Monday in May) and mid-September to December; and Saturday, Monday and Wednesday from mid-May to mid-September. They're overnight trips, and the high-season fare for a reclining chair is £95; a car and five people costs £315.

Scandinavian Seaways (☎ 0990-333000) operates ferries to Gothenburg (Sweden). They depart Friday from early June to mid-August; it's an overnight journey taking about 22 hours. A return in a four-berth couchette costs £184 to £324 per person; a car costs £70 extra.

Harwich Harwich is the major port linking southern England and Scandinavia. Scandinavian Seaways (☎ 0990-333000) has ferries to Esbjerg (Denmark) and Gothenburg (Sweden).

Ferries to Esbjerg depart Tuesday, Thursday and Saturday for most of the year, plus Friday and Sunday from mid-July to early September; it's an overnight journey taking 20 hours. A return in a four-berth couchette costs £134 to £246 per person; a car costs £70 extra.

Ferries to Gothenburg depart Friday and Sunday for most of the year, but from June to mid-August they leave Sunday and Tuesday; it's also an overnight journey taking 24 hours. A return in a four-berth couchette costs £184 to £324 per person; a car costs £70 extra.

Belgium, the Netherlands & Germany

There are two direct links with Germany but many people prefer to drive to/from the Dutch ferry ports.

Ramsgate Currently the cheapest way to cross the channel is with the new service, Sally Direct (☎ 0845-600 2626), between Ramsgate and Ostend. It's just £5 for a foot passenger and £25 for a car and driver, one way. The drawback is that it's a slow crossing (four hours) and there are not many departures (from Ramsgate at noon and 1 am on weekdays, 8 am at weekends).

Harwich Scandinavian Seaways (☎ 0990-333000) has ferries to Hamburg, Germany every two days for most of the year; the trip takes about 19 hours. A return in a four-berth couchette is £134 to £218 per person; a car costs £70 extra.

Stena Line (☎ 0990-707070) has two ferries a day to the Hook of Holland, the Netherlands; the day ferry takes 7½ hours and the night ferry takes 9½ hours. A single costs £32 to £36, a car plus up to five passengers costs £124 to £218.

Newcastle Scandinavian Seaways has a twice-weekly ferry to Hamburg from late-May to early September, taking 20 hours. The fare and telephone number is the same as from Harwich (see Harwich earlier).

Ireland

There's a great variety of ferry services from Britain to Ireland using modern car ferries. Figures quoted are one-way fares for a single adult, for two adults with a car and for four adults with a car. There are often special deals, return fares and other money savers worth investigating.

Want to travel free? On some routes the cost for a car includes up to four or five passengers at no additional cost. If you can hitch a ride in a less than full car, it costs the driver nothing extra.

From south to north, ferry possibilities include:

Swansea to Cork The 10 hour crossing costs £32/189/189 at peak times but it operates from mid-March to early January only. In Britain, contact Swansea Cork Ferries (☎ 01792-456116), Ferry Port, Kings Dock, Swansea SA1 SRU.

Fishguard and Pembroke to Rosslare This popular short crossing takes 3½ hours (Fishguard) or 4½ hours (Pembroke) and costs as much as £30/149/149 on peak-season weekends. A 99 minute catamaran from Fishguard costs from £36/219/219 down to £27/89/89.

Stena Line (☎ 01233-647047), Charter House, Ashford, Kent TN24 8EX, operates Fishguard-Rosslare. Irish Ferries (☎ 0990-171717), 150 New Bond St, London W1Y 0AQ, operates Pembroke-Rosslare.

Holyhead to Dublin and Dun Laoghaire The 3½ hour crossing between Holyhead and Dublin costs £30/169/169 at peak seasons, down to £20/79/79 in the off season. The regular ferry between Holyhead and Dun Laoghaire takes 3½ hours and costs from £30/169/169 down to £27/104/104. There is also a fast 99 minute service that costs from £36/204/204 down to £27/104/104. Stena Line (☎ 01233-647047), Charter House, Ashford, Kent TN24 8EX, operates Holyhead-Dun Laoghaire. Irish Ferries (☎ 0990-171717), 150 New Bond St, London W1Y 0AQ, operates Holyhead-Dublin.

Liverpool to Belfast The Norse Irish overnight service is not heavily promoted but it's easy to get to Liverpool from London. The trip costs from £105 for a car and up to four passengers, including dinner, breakfast and cabin accommodation. Contact Norse Irish Ferries (☎ 0151-944 1010), North Brocklebank Dock, Bootle, Merseyside L20 1BY, for details.

Stranraer to Belfast The Stena Line and SeaCat high-speed catamaran races across in just 1½ hours at a cost of £27/170/180 at peak times. Call SeaCat (☎ 0345-523523), SeaCat Terminal, West Pier, Stranraer for bookings; subsidiary of Sea Containers Ferries Scotland. Or call Stena Line (☎ 0990-707070).

Stranraer and Cairnryan to Larne There are as many as 15 sailings daily on this route which takes about 2½ hours and costs £27/190/190 at peak times. Stena Line (☎ 01233-647047), Charter House, Ashford, Kent TN24 8EX, operates Stranraer-Larne. P&O (☎ 01581-200276), Cairnryan, Stranraer, Wigtownshire DG9 8RF, operates Cairnryan-Larne.

Liverpool and Heysham via Douglas (Isle of Man) to Dublin It takes 3¾ hours between Heysham and Douglas, 4½ hours between Douglas and Liverpool, and four hours between Dublin and Douglas. Peak time fares to/from the Isle of Man from Belfast, Heysham or Liverpool are £35/209/209. The Isle of Man Steam Packet Company (☎ 01624-661661/645645), PO Box 5, Douglas, Isle of Man IM99 1AF, operates these services.

Campbeltown to Ballycastle The three hour crossing from Campbeltown, Argyll to Ballycastle, County Antrim costs £25/163/179. The Argyll & Antrim Steam Packet Company (☎ 0345-523523), a subsidiary of Sea Containers Ferries Scotland.

DEPARTURE TAXES

People taking flights from Britain have to pay an Air Passenger Duty (built into the price of an air ticket). Those flying to countries in the European Union pay £10; those flying beyond pay £20. There's no departure tax if you leave by sea or the Channel Tunnel.

See Taxes & Refunds in Money in the Regional Facts for the Visitor chapter for details on how to reclaim Value-Added Tax (VAT) when you depart.

ORGANISED TOURS

See your travel agent, check the small ads in newspaper travel pages or contact the British Tourist Authority for the names of tour operators offering general interest or special-interest tours. See Tourist Offices in the Regional Facts for the Visitor chapter.

Getting Around the Region

Public transport in Britain is generally good but it can be expensive. Over the last 20 years, government policy has favoured car ownership, and some local rail and bus services have been reduced. This is bad news for visitors without their own wheels as transport to national parks and small villages is even more poorly serviced.

It's certainly worth considering car rental for at least part of your trip. However, even if you're not driving, with a mix of local buses, the occasional taxi, walking and occasionally hiring a bike, and plenty of time, you can get almost anywhere.

Buses are nearly always the cheapest way to get around. Unfortunately they're also the slowest (sometimes by a considerable margin). With discount passes and tickets bought in advance, trains can be competitive; they're quicker and often take you through beautiful countryside relatively unspoilt by the 20th century.

Ticket types and prices vary considerably. For example, a standard single rail ticket from London to Edinburgh is £72 but a SuperApex return ticket is £35! A standard bus ticket from London to Edinburgh is £14 for a single, but with a small company you might find a return ticket for £22.

See the bus and train fare tables in this chapter to get a full picture of the way the different tickets stack up. If you know how far you're travelling (even if your planned journey is not specifically covered) you can get a *rough* idea of costs by working from the mileage columns.

See the Scotland and Wales Getting Around chapters for information specific to those countries.

AIR

Most regional centres and islands are linked to London. However, unless you're going to the outer reaches of Britain, in particular northern Scotland, planes are only marginally quicker than trains if you include the time it takes to get to/from airports. Note that there is now a £10 airport departure tax added to the price of tickets – check that this is included in the price you're quoted.

All the airlines are now set up to take bookings via their Web sites, and some actively encourage Web bookings with special deals.

Domestic Air Services

The main operators are British Airways (☎ 0345-222111), British Midland (☎ 0345-554554) and KLM UK (☎ 0990-074074). There are several other smaller companies, including easyJet (☎ 01582-445566/08706-000000) and the new British Airways no-frills offshoot, Go (☎ 0845-6054321). You can also check out their respective Web sites at www .british-airways.com, www.iflybritishmidland.com, www.klmuk.com, www.easyjet.com and www.go-fly.com. Most airlines offer a range of tickets including full fare (very expensive but flexible), Apex (for which you must book at least 14 days in advance) and special offers on some services (British Airways calls these Seat Sale fares and also has occasional World Offer fares which may be even cheaper). There are also youth fares (for under 25s) but Apex and special-offer fares are usually cheaper.

Prices vary enormously. For example, a return ticket from London to Edinburgh on BA costs £266 full fare, £140 Apex, £59 to £123 Seat Sale or £59 on World Offer fare. Its cheapest one-way fare is £103. British Midland charges from £59 return but you must stay for one Saturday night and there are restrictions on when you can fly out and back. KLM UK and easyJet offer no-frills flights for £29 one-way between London (Luton/Stansted) and Edinburgh, Glasgow and Aberdeen but easyJet tickets are only sold direct, by phone or on its Web site, not through a travel agent. Tickets are sold on a first-come-first-served basis – when the £29 tickets are sold the price goes up to £39 and so on up to £79. Return flights can be booked.

Examples of other BA Apex/Seat Sale return fares include Inverness for £145/72, Aberdeen for £157/59, Kirkwall (Orkney) for £272/214, and Lerwick (Shetland) for £291/236. One-way tickets are about the same price as Seat Sale fares.

Air Passes

If you're flying into the UK on BA you may be eligible for a UK Airpass. This costs an additional £57 per internal flight between each zone in the country, and must be arranged at least seven days prior to arrival in the UK.

BUS

Road transport in Britain is almost entirely privately owned and run. National Express (☎ 0990-808080) runs the largest national network – it completely dominates the market and is a sister company to Eurolines – but there are often smaller competitors on the main routes. For further info have a look at the National Express Web site at www.nationalexpress.co.uk.

In Britain, long-distance express buses are usually referred to as coaches, and in many towns there are separate terminals for coaches and buses. Over short distances, coaches are more expensive (though quicker) than buses.

A number of counties operate telephone inquiry lines that try to explain the fast-changing and often chaotic situation with timetables; wherever possible, these numbers have been given. Before commencing a journey off the main routes it is wise to phone for the latest information.

Another useful, though somewhat hefty (1000 pages) source of information is the GB Bus Timetable (£11) published three times a year by Southern Vectis (☎ 01983-522456, fax 01983-524961), Nelson Road, Newport, Isle of Wight TO30 1RD. The timetable lists all main bus services in Britain and also gives the best way of reaching places that are not served by rail – the nearest train station

and the frequency of bus services to that particular place are listed.

Unless otherwise stated, prices quoted in this book are for economy single tickets. See the bus fare table on page 106.

Bus Passes & Discounts

The National Express Discount Coach Card allows 30% off standard adult fares. It's available to full-time students, and those aged from 16 to 25 and 50 or over. The cards are available from all National Express agents. They cost £8 and require a passport photo – ISIC cards are accepted as proof of student status, and passports for date of birth.

The National Express Explorer Pass allows unlimited coach travel within a specified period. It's available to all overseas visitors but it must be bought outside Britain. You will be given a travel voucher that can be exchanged for the pass at Heathrow or Gatwick, or at any of the larger National Express agencies around the country. For adults/concessions they cost £59/45 for three days' travel within five consecutive days, £110/80 for seven days in a 21-day period and £170/130 for 14 days in a 30-day period.

Bus Lane to a Fortune

Next time you're hanging about waiting for a Stagecoach bus to come along, you might like to remember that company co-founder Ann Gloag is Britain's second wealthiest woman, pipped at the post only by the Queen!

She and brother Brian Souter were the prime beneficiaries of the deregulation of the bus services in the 1980s. Having spread its tentacles into New Zealand, Portugal and Sweden, Stagecoach has gone into partnership with Virgin Rail to run the West Coast and Cross-Country train services. The trains may or may not run more efficiently but Ann Gloag can probably look forward to a few more million in her bank account.

British Travel Passes

Pass Name	Cost (Prices for adults/ discount card holders)	Bus/train/ferry services offered
National Express Tourist Trail Pass	£49/39 for 3 days; £85/69 for 5 days in a 10-day period; £120/94 for 7 days in a 21-day period; £187/143 for 14 days in a 30-day period	Unlimited travel on all National Express bus services, and Scottish Citylink.
National Express Discount Coach Card (full-time students; under 26; over 50)	£8	30% off adult fares on National Express buses and Scottish Citylink.
National Express Lone Parent/Family Card	£8 (Lone Parent) £15 (Family)	Adults pay the full fare and one child per cardholder travels free on National Express buses and Scottish Citylink.
National Express Explorer Pass (must be bought outside Britain)	£59/45 (adult/youth) for 3 days in a 5-day period; £110/85 for 7 days in a 21-day period; £170/130 for 14 days in a 30-day period; £170/150 for 14 days in a 60-day period	Unlimited travel on all National Express bus services, and Scottish Citylink.
Stray Travel coach)	£119 (Britain)	Hop n, hop off circuit buses (Slow-linking youth hostels.
Explorer	£65 (southern England), £95 (Britain)	Hop on, hop off circuit buses linking youth hostels.
Young Person's or Senior's Railcard	£18 per annum	33% off rail travel throughout Britain.

National Express Tourist Trail Passes are available to UK and overseas citizens. They provide unlimited travel on all services for two days travel within three consecutive days (£49/39 for an adult/discount card-holder), any five days travel within 10 consecutive days (£85/69), any seven days travel within 21 consecutive days (£120/94) and any 14 days travel within 30 consecutive days (£187/143). The passes are available for purchase overseas, or at any National Express agent in the UK.

For more information on prices and what these passes provide, see the British Travel Passes table above.

British Travel Passes

Pass Name	Cost (Prices for adults/ discount card holders)	Bus/train/ferry services offered
BritRail Pass (must be bought outside Britain)	US$259/205 (adult/youth) for 8 days; US$395/318 for 15 days; US$510/410 for 22 days; US$590/475 for 30 days	Unlimited rail travel throughout Britain.
Flexipass (must be bought outside Britain)	US$219/175 for 4 days in a month; US$315/253 for 8 days in a month; US$480 (adult) for 15 days in a month; US$385 (youth) for 15 days in 2 months	Unlimited rail travel throughout Britain.
BritRail/Drive	(Prices for small car) US$264/314 (2 adults/1 adult) for 2 days' car hire plus 3 days' train travel in 2 months Additional day's car hire US$58	Combines Flexipass (above) with Hertz car hire.
BritRail Pass + Ireland (must be bought outside Britain)	US$359 for 5 days in a month; US$511 for 10 days in a month	Unlimited rail travel throughout Britain and Ireland and round-trip ferry between Britain and Ireland.
BritRail Rovers	£260/170 for 7 days; £430/285 for 14 days.	Domestic version of BritRail pass: unlimited train travel in Britain.
Regional Rovers		Train travel in particular regions only.

See also the Disabled Person's Railcard and the Family Railcard described on page 108.

Hop On Hop Off Buses
Stray Travel Network (Slowcoach)
This is an excellent bus service (☎ 0171-373 7737) designed especially for those staying in hostels, but useful for all budget travellers. Buses run on a regular circuit between London, Windsor, Bath, Manchester, Haworth, the Lake District, Glasgow, Stirling, Edinburgh, York, Nottingham, Cambridge and London, and call in at hostels. You can get on and off the bus where you like, and the £119 ticket is valid for the whole circuit for six months. Buses leave London three times a week throughout the year; the price includes some activities and visits en route. Tickets are available

from branches of STA; look in the Yellow Pages for the nearest branch or check out the Web site at www.straytravel.com.

Explorer (☎ 0171-263 5435) operates a similar service, offering two passes: Southern Explorer which includes London, Windsor, Salisbury, Stonehenge, Bath, Oxford, Cambridge, the Cotswolds, Stratford and back to London (£65), or Gold Explorer (£95) which also includes the north of England plus Edinburgh. Buses travel between London and Stratford and from Edinburgh to Manchester on even days of the month (2, 4, 6, etc) and between Stratford and Edinburgh and Manchester to London on odd days. Services operate from mid-April to early October. See Getting Around in the Scotland and Wales chapters for information on other similar operations, and the table in this chapter for price details.

Postbus

Many small places can only be reached by postbus – minibuses that follow postal delivery routes. These are circuitous routes through many of the most beautiful areas of England, Wales and Scotland. For the free *Postbus Guide to England & Wales* contact Postbus Services (☎ 0171-490 2888), Post Office HQ, 130 Old Street, London EC1V 9PQ; for the Scottish postbus timetable contact Postbus Services (☎ 01463-256273) Royal Mail, 7 Strothers Lane, Inverness IV1 1AA.

Sightseeing Buses

Several companies operate bus tours in tourist towns around England. They have regular buses circulating on a fixed route and your one-day ticket lets you get on and off the bus as many times as you like for the day. Guide Friday is the largest company.

TRAIN

Despite the damage wrought by privatisation, Britain still has an impressive rail service – if you're using the rail system as a tourist rather than a commuter, that is. There are several particularly recommended trips on beautiful lines through sparsely

populated country, the most famous being in Wales and Scotland.

Unfortunately, Eurail passes are not recognised in Britain. There are local equivalents but they aren't recognised in the rest of Europe.

Rail Privatisation

Following the privatisation of the railways, instigated by the Conservatives and enthusiastically pursued by the current Labour government, the rail system appears to be becoming less reliable than it was in the days when it was the single nationalised company known as British Rail. Services are now provided by 25 train operating companies (TOCs). A separate company, Railtrack, owns and maintains the track and the stations. For the sake of convenience the British Rail logo and name are still used on direction signs.

The main rail cards are accepted by all the companies and travellers are still able to buy a ticket to any destination from any train station or from authorised travel agents, though travel agents are not able to sell the full range of tickets.

Passengers can travel only on services provided by the company who issued their ticket and each company is able to set whatever fare it chooses. Thus on routes served by more than one operator, passengers can choose to buy a cheaper ticket with a company offering a less frequent/direct service or pay more for a faster (usually InterCity) service. In some cases competing companies use the same route. The era of competition also means that companies often have special offers such as 'two for the price of one' or special reductions for tickets bought in advance.

The main routes are served by excellent InterCity trains that travel at speeds of up to 140 mph and whisk you from London to Edinburgh in just over four hours.

If you do not have one of the passes listed below, the cheapest tickets must be bought at least one week in advance. Phone the general inquiry line ☎ 0345-484950 (open 24 hours) for timetables, fares and the

BRITISH RAILWAYS

numbers to ring for credit card bookings. For short journeys, it's not really necessary to purchase tickets or make seat reservations in advance. Just buy them at the station before you go.

Rail Classes

There are two classes of rail travel: 1st, and what is now officially referred to as standard (although in class-conscious Britain this will always be called 2nd class). First class costs 30 to 50% more than 2nd and,

except on very crowded trains, is not really worth the extra money.

On overnight trains (between London and Exeter, Plymouth and Penzance, and on the routes to Scotland) there are sleeping compartments, with one berth in 1st and two in 2nd. The additional cost for these berths is £30/25 for 1st/2nd class. It's essential to reserve these in advance.

Unless stated otherwise, the prices quoted in this book are for 2nd-class adult single tickets.

Rail Itineraries

The following itineraries include tourist highlights as well as some of the most scenic rail trips. Journey times are approximate. Most of the suggested stops are on InterCity lines so services are fairly frequent. Pick up a copy of the *Guide to InterCity Services*, available at most main train stations, which gives timetables.

Britain (14 Days)

Origin	Destination	Journey Times
London	to York	(two hours)
York	to Durham	(50 minutes)
Durham	to Edinburgh	(1¾ hours)
Edinburgh	to Glasgow	(one hour)
Glasgow	to Windermere	(2½ hours via Oxenholme)
Windermere	to Chester	(3½ hours via Oxenholme and Crewe)
Chester	to Conwy	(1¼ hours)
Conwy	to Cheltenham	(3½ hours via Crewe and Birmingham)
Cheltenham	to Bath	(50 minutes via Bristol)
Bath	to Oxford	(1¼ hours via Didcot)
Oxford	to London	(one hour)

Route

From London's King's Cross, it's only two hours to York. With Roman walls, medieval streets and the largest Gothic cathedral in England, York is high on every visitor's list of priorities. Under an hour north is Durham, tiny in comparison to York but with a magnificent cathedral, rising high above the River Wear.

From Durham, continue north and cross the border to Edinburgh, Scotland's capital, with its famous castle and even more famous festival, the world's largest. Completely different in atmosphere, and with superb galleries and a lively arts scene, Glasgow is under one hour to the west.

To reach the Lake District from Glasgow, you need to change trains in Oxenholme. Stay two nights in Windermere so that you can spend at least one full day taking in the superb scenery that inspired Wordsworth and many other poets and artists. To get to the walled city of Chester, with its black and white Tudor buildings, you need to change trains in Oxenholme and Crewe.

From Chester, follow the north coast of Wales to Conwy to visit one of Edward I's magnificent castles, built to subdue the Welsh. Travel back and change at Chester or Crewe and again at Birmingham for Cheltenham, the grand Regency town on the edge of the Cotswolds. From Cheltenham, move on to the beautiful city of Bath, a 12 minute train journey beyond Bristol.

Bath to Oxford requires a change at Didcot. Spend two nights at Britain's oldest university town, allowing time for an excursion to nearby Blenheim Palace. The trip back to London takes only one hour by train.

Scotland (4 Days)

Origin	Destination	Journey Times
Edinburgh	to Glasgow	(one hour)
Glasgow	to Fort William	(3¾ hours)
Fort William	to Mallaig	(1½ hours)

Rail Itineraries

Scotland Rail Itinerary cont.

Mallaig	to Kyle of Lochalsh	(two hours by boat, summer only)
Kyle of Lochalsh	to Inverness	(2½ hours)
Inverness	to Perth	(2½ hours)
Perth	to Edinburgh	(1½ hours)

Route

This route includes the West Highland Line, arguably the most scenic rail journey in the country, and the Kyle Line across the Highlands from Kyle of Lochalsh to Inverness. The ScotRail Flexi Rover ticket (£64) allows travel on this route for four days out of eight.

It takes less than one hour from Edinburgh to Glasgow's Central station. Nearby, from Queen St station, trains depart on the West Highland Line. The route passes Loch Lomond on the way to Crianlarich, then climbs over wild Rannoch Moor, with views of Ben Nevis, Britain's highest peak. From Fort William, the train crosses the River Lochy. There are superb views of Loch Shiel and, after Glenfinnan station, Loch Eilt. The tracks run through tunnels along the edge of the sea lochs to Arisaig, Britain's most westerly train station, then north to Morar with views across to the islands of Skye, Rhum and Eigg. The line follows the coast from Morar to Mallaig.

In the summer there are ferry services for the two-hour voyage to Kyle of Lochalsh, the terminus of the Kyle Line from Inverness. From Inverness there are frequent departures south to Perth, where it's worth stopping to see Scone Palace before continuing to Edinburgh.

Wales (3 Days)

Origin	Destination	Journey Times
Shrewsbury	to Dovey Junction	(1¾ hours)
Dovey Junction	to Porthmadog	(1½ hours)
Porthmadog	to Blaenau Ffestiniog	(1¼ hours)
Blaenau Ffestiniog	to Llandudno Junction	(1¼ hours)
Llandudno Junction	to Shrewsbury	(two hours via Chester)

Route

Wales is known for its Great Little Trains, narrow-gauge railways passing through some spectacular countryside. This route links several of them with the mainline network to make an enjoyable three day trip around North Wales, starting and ending in Shrewsbury (England). It might just be possible to do the whole journey in one day, but spending a couple of nights in Wales would allow time to appreciate the superb scenery of Snowdonia National Park. The North & Mid Wales Flexi Rover ticket (£25.70) allows travel anywhere on this route for three days out of seven.

From Shrewsbury you travel west to Dovey Junction to join the Cambrian coast railway that follows the coast north. You could stop at Harlech to see the 13th century castle. From Porthmadog, the narrow-gauge Ffestiniog Railway takes you in steam-hauled carriages through Snowdonia to Blaenau Ffestiniog. Another small railway continues through Betws-y-Coed to Llandudno Junction to connect with the coastal railway. Follow the coast east back to England. Connecting trains for Shrewsbury leave from Chester.

Coach/Bus Fares from London

The sample fares below are for single/return travel from London on the National Express coach (bus) system. To qualify for the discount fares you must have a Discount Coach Card (£8 – see Bus in this section for details). The discount is applicable on nonadvance-purchase fares only.

If you're not eligible for a Discount Coach Card, you'll need to buy your ticket at least seven days in advance and avoid travelling on a Friday (or Saturday in July and August) to avoid paying the full fares. If you're just doing a day trip, a day return ticket will be even cheaper than the economy return shown here.

Fares below have been rounded up to the next pound.

From London			Nonadvance Purchase				7-Day Advance	
			Not Fri ✥ (Economy)		Fri (Standard)		Not Fri ✥	Fri
			Adult	Discount	Adult	Discount	Adult	Adult
miles	to	hours	sgl/rtn(£)	sgl/rtn(£)	sgl/rtn(£)	sgl/rtn(£)	rtn(£)	rtn(£)
23	Windsor✱	1	(serviced by other operators – see text)					
51	Brighton	1¾	6/11	5/9	6/11	5/9	–	–
54	Cambridge	2	6/11	5/9	6/11	5/9	–	–
56	Canterbury	2	6/11	5/9	6/11	5/9	–	–
57	Oxford✱	1¾	7/9	6/7	7/9	6/7	–	–
71	Dover	2½	9/14	8/12	9/14	8/12	–	–
83	Salisbury	2¾	13/15	9/11	15/18	11/14	14	17
92	Stratford	2¾	12/15	9/11	14/18	11/13	13	16
106	Bath✱	3	11/19	10/14	18/22	14/16	17	20
110	Birmingham	2½	9/13	9/11	10/14	10/12	–	–
115	Bristol✱	2¼	9/17	8/14	9/17	8/14	–	–
131	Lincoln	4¾	18/22	14/16	22/27	16/20	19	23
150	Shrewsbury	4½	11/16	10/13	12/17	11/14	–	–
155	Cardiff	3¼	19/23	14/17	22/28	16/20	20	23
172	Exeter✱	3¾	21/26	16/19	25/31	19/23	22	27
184	Manchester	4	12/22	12/17	13/24	12/18	18	18
188	York✱	4	18/27	15/20	19/29	17/21	22	22
193	Liverpool	4¼	12/22	12/17	13/24	12/18	18	18
211	Aberystwyth	7¼	18/22	14/16	22/27	16/20	19	23
215	Scarborough	5¾	21/30	19/22	22/31	20/23	26	26
255	Durham	4¾	18/27	15/20	19/29	17/21	22	22
259	Windermere	7	20/30	18/22	21/32	19/24	28	28
280	Penzance	6	30/37	22/27	36/44	26/32	31	37
290	St Ives	7	30/37	22/27	36/44	26/32	31	37
299	Carlisle ✧	5½	17/27	16/25	18/28	17/26	–	–
350	Galashiels	8	30/42	24/31	33/47	22/32	35	35
375	Edinburgh✱ ✧	8	17/27	16/25	18/28	17/26	–	–
397	Glasgow✱ ✧	7	17/27	16/25	18/28	17/26	–	–
434	Dundee	8¼	24/37	22/28	25/39	23/29	29	29
450	Perth	8¼	24/37	22/28	25/39	23/29	29	29
489	Oban	12	39/44	29/33	40/46	30/35	35	35
503	Aberdeen	10½	27/44	25/33	28/46	26/35	35	35
536	Inverness	12	27/43	25/32	28/45	26/34	34	34
590	Ullapool	14	32/47	27/39	33/52	28/53	–	–
652	Thurso	15½	34/49	28/41	35/56	29/46	–	–

✥ Not on Friday or Saturday in July and August.

✱ Other companies also operate this route and are often cheaper. See main text for more information. National Express may have some special EarlyBird fares but they are usually only applicable for the journey into London.

✧ A night service is available but is more expensive than the day service shown here.

Rail Fares from London

Sample fares below are for 2nd-class single/return travel from London and have been rounded up to the next pound. Where two routes are available between London and the destination, the fare for the cheaper route has been listed – but this means that the journey will take longer/be less direct. Destinations to which there is more than one route are marked ❖.

A Eurail pass cannot be used in Britain. You may, however, be eligible for a railcard (see Railcards). If you don't have a BritRail pass and are not eligible for a railcard, you can still save money by buying your ticket in advance, though advance purchase tickets are not available for short journeys.

			Nonadvance Purchase					Advance		
From London			Peak	Saver (Off Peak✱)		SuperSaver ◆		Super-Advance ✪	Apex✚	
			Adult	Adult	Railcard	Adult	Railcard	Adult	Railcard	Adult
miles	to	hours	sgl/rtn(£)	sgl/rtn(£)	sgl/rtn(£)	sgl/rtn(£)	sgl/rtn(£)	sgl/rtn(£)	sgl/rtn(£)	sg/rtn(£)
23	Windsor ❖	½	7/7	6/6	4/4	–	–	–	–	–
51	Brighton ❖	¾	14/15	14/14	9/9	(Awaybreak £18)		(Stayaway £22)		
54	Cambridge	1	15/16	13/14	9/9	(Awaybreak £18)		–		–
56	Canterbury	1½	16/16	14/14	9/9	(Awaybreak £16)		(Stayaway £20)		
57	Oxford ❖	¾	16/28	14/14	9/9	(Awaybreak £18)		–		–
71	Dover	1¼	20/20	18/18	12/12	(Awaybreak £21)		(Stayaway £25)		
83	Salisbury ❖	1¼	22/22	20/25	14/18	(Awaybreak £25)		(Stayaway £30)		
92	Stratford	2¼	18/35	18/22	12/14	(Cheap day return £18)				
106	Bath ❖	1¼	30/61	30/37	20/25	27/27	18/18	17/18	12/12	18/18
110	Birmingham ❖	1½	32/60	32/34	21/23	–	–	17/17	12/12	7/14
115	Bristol ❖	1½	32/63	32/36	21/24	29/29	19/19	17/18	12/12	18/19
131	Lincoln ❖	1¾	35/70	35/42	23/28	35/35	23/23	33/34	22/23	30/31
150	Shrewsbury ❖	2½	40/72	38/39	25/26	34/35	23/23	25/26	17/18	9/17
155	Cardiff ❖	2	39/77	39/43	26/29	34/35	23/24	30/31	20/21	24/24
172	Exeter ❖	2	41/82	41/48	28/32	37/38	25/26	27/28	18/19	20/20
184	Manchester ❖	2½	56/98	46/47	31/32	39/40	26/27	29/30	19/20	10/19
188	York	2	54/108	54/61	36/41	50/51	34/34	43/44	29/30	36/37
193	Liverpool ❖	2½	54/98	46/47	31/32	39/40	26/27	29/30	19/20	10/19
211	Aberystwyth	5¼	53/98	47/48	32/33	38/39	26/27	28/29	19/19	27/27
215	Scarborough	2¾	57/113	57/67	39/45	56/57	38/39	51/52	34/35	44/44
255	Durham	2¾	71/139	71/76	48/51	62/63	42/43	55/56	37/38	41/41
259	Windermere	3¾	66/120	59/60	40/40	53/54	36/37	41/42	28/28	34/35
280	Penzance	5	65/129	54/55	36/37	51/52	34/35	44/45	30/31	30/31
290	St Ives	5½	66/131	55/56	37/38	52/53	35/36	46/47	31/32	30/31
299	Carlisle ❖	3½	68/123	65/66	44/45	58/59	39/40	44/45	30/31	13/25
350	Galashiels	6	77/146	77/83	52/56	72/73	48/49 (bus from Berwick to Galashiels)			
375	Edinburgh ❖	4	72/139	72/76	49/51	65/66	44/45	60/61	40/41	48/49✢
397	Glasgow ❖	5	72/139	72/76	49/51	65/66	44/45	47/48	32/33	15/30✢
434	Dundee	5¾	76/152	76/83	51/56	71/72	48/49	66/66	45/45	57/58
450	Perth	6	76/152	76/83	51/56	71/72	48/49	66/66	45/45	57/58
489	Oban	9½	84/158	84/89	57/60	82/83	55/56	76/77	51/52	63/64
503	Aberdeen	6½	81/161	81/91	55/61	78/79	53/53	74/75	50/51	61/62
536	Inverness	8¼	81/161	81/91	55/61	78/79	53/53	74/75	50/51	61/62
590	Ullapool		(No rail service – bus from Inverness)							
652	Thurso	13	93/185	93/103	63/69	92/93	62/63	86/87	58/59	75/76

✱ You must travel out on an off-peak service and back within one calendar month; on certain routes you can travel back on peak services.

◆ Not valid on Friday after 2.30 pm, Saturday in July and August, Bank Holidays or on following days before 2.30 pm. The return journey must be within one month.

✪ Must be bought before 2 pm on the day prior to travel.

✢ SuperApex fares are available to Edinburgh (£34/35) and Glasgow (£34/35) but these must be bought 14 days in advance.

✚ Also known as Virgin Value. Must be bought before 6pm on the day prior to travel.

BritRail Passes

BritRail passes are the most interesting possibility for visitors, but they are *not available in Britain* and must be bought in your country of origin. Contact the BTA in your country for details. For further information on passes, see the British Transport Passes table on page 105.

Holders of BritRail, Eurail and Euro passes are entitled to discounted fares on Eurostar trains (eg London to Paris/Brussels for $US79/69).

BritRail/Drive

BritRail/Drive combines a Flexipass with the use of a Hertz rental car for side trips. The package is available in various combinations: a three-day Flexipass plus two days car hire in one month costs $US264. For further information, contact the BTA in your country.

Rail Rovers

The domestic version of the passes are BritRail Rovers: a seven-day All Line Rover is £260/170, and 14 days is £430/285. There are also regional Rovers and some Flexi Rovers to Wales, north and mid-Wales, the North Country, the north-west coast and Peaks, the south-west, and Scotland. Details have been given in the appropriate sections.

Railcards

You can get discounts of up to 33% on most off-peak fares (except Apex and SuperApex – see Tickets following) if you're aged 16 to 25, or over 60, or studying full-time, or disabled – but you must first buy the appropriate railcard. There is also a railcard for families.

The cards are valid for one year and most are available from major stations. You'll need two passport photos, and proof of age (birth certificate or passport) or student status.

Young Person's Railcard Costs £18 and gives you 33% off most tickets and some ferry services; you must be aged 16 to 25, or a student of any age studying full-time in the UK.

Senior Railcard Available to anyone over 60, this card costs £18 and gives a 33% discount.

Disabled Person's Railcard Costs £16 and gives a 33% discount to a disabled person and one person accompanying them. Pick up an application form from a station and then send it to Disabled Person's Railcard Office, PO Box 1YT, Newcastle upon Tyne, NE99 1YT. It can take up to three weeks to process this card so you should apply early.

Family Railcard Costs £20 and allows discounts of 33% (20% for some tickets) for up to four adults travelling together, providing a card-holder is a member of the party. Up to four accompanying children pay a flat fare of £2 each. A couple of journeys can pay for the card.

Network Card If you're planning to do a lot of rail travel in the south of England, a Network card may be worth considering. This is valid for the region previously known as Network South East – London and the entire south-east of England, from Dover to Weymouth, Cambridge to Oxford. It costs £20. Discounts of 33% apply to up to four adults travelling together providing a card-holder is a member of the party. Children pay a flat fare of £1. Travel is permitted only after 10 am from Monday to Friday and at any time on the weekend. A couple of journeys can pay for the card.

Tickets

If the various train passes and railcards aren't complicated enough, try making sense of the different tickets.

Children under five travel free; aged between five and 15 they pay half-price for most tickets, and full fare for Apex/SuperApex and Virgin Value tickets. However, when travelling with children it is almost always worth buying a Family Railcard.

See the train fare table for ticket prices.

Single ticket Valid for a single journey at any time on the day specified; expensive.

Day Return ticket Valid for a return journey at any time on the day specified; relatively expensive.

Cheap Day Return ticket Valid for a return journey on the day specified on the ticket, but there are time restrictions and it is usually only available for short journeys; often about the same price as a single. You're not usually allowed to travel on a train that leaves before 9.30 am.

Open Return For outward travel on a stated day and return on any day within a month.

The Brave New World of the Privatised Railways

It's 11.15 am and I'm waiting at Bristol Temple Meads for the train to Birmingham New St. According to the indicator board it's eight minutes late, fair enough, perhaps, on a through-run from Penzance.

The train pulls in and the passengers board. We sit there. And sit there. And sit there. Eventually the Tannoy crackles to life and the conductor announces that they have no driver for the train. What's more, they don't know when they will have a driver. A tad unfortunate, of course, but they'll keep us informed. When we eventually pull out of the station, the train is 33 minutes late.

Still, that was an improvement on the last time I let the train take the strain between Bristol and Birmingham. On that occasion I bowled up to New Street to catch the 19.35. When that was cancelled I consoled myself that another would be coming along at 20.35. Except that that one was 20 minutes late. Journey time from Birmingham to Bristol when the going's good: 1½ hours. Journey time when it's not: 2¾ hours.

Delays, cancellations, incomprehensible fare structures, the newly privatised railways are almost too easy a target. One Wednesday I caught the 10.05 to Hereford via Newport. Return fare: £12.90. The next day I caught the same train but continued to Worcester. Return fare: £12.50. 'Why is it minus 40p to travel from Hereford to Worcester?' I asked the conductor, not expecting much of an answer. Sure enough, there wasn't one.

Stations without staff are a particularly irksome novelty. At unstaffed Kendal I boarded the train to Ulverston. Single fare: £9.60. Changing at Lancaster my eye grazed a board touting an £8.95 all-in train and bus rover ticket. 'Why wasn't I offered that?' I demanded. 'You should have asked for it. We can't know all the possible fares,' the conductor snorted, which begged the question of how anyone boarding at Kendal was supposed to know anything about anything.

Of course, life under the old British Rail was no bed of roses. But at least when something went wrong there was only one authority to sort it out. Now there are 25 competing rail companies, not to mention Railtrack which looks after the stations and track.

It's 17.44 and I'm waiting for the Alphaline train from Newport to Bristol. The platform is occupied by a Great Western Train whose passengers suddenly disembark and vanish down a tunnel. I ask the woman in GWT livery about my train. 'It's probably waiting outside the station,' she tells me.

Then I start to hear mutterings about the closure of the Severn Junction tunnel. 'Won't that affect the 17.44 too?' I ask Ms GWT. She concedes the likelihood but I'm an Alphaline passenger and none of her business.

Outside the station GWT and Alphaline victims jostle for space in a queue for a bus that never comes. It's impossible to hear station announcements from the queue, and no one from GWT or Alphaline sees fit to keep us up to date with developments. At 18.30 the Alphaline trains to Paignton and Portsmouth Harbour are linked together and given the all clear. Passengers rush between the two, unaware that they're both going to the same place now. At 18.35 we slink out of the station. The GWT passengers are still standing in the bus queue but of course no one at Alphaline cares about that.

Pat Yale

Apex One of the cheapest return fares, rivalling National Express prices; for distances of more than 100 miles; you must book at least seven days in advance but seats are limited.

SuperApex The cheapest fare for the most direct route from London to Edinburgh/Glasgow and vice versa; you must book at least 14 days in advance, but seats are limited and not available on all trains so book ASAP.

SuperSaver The cheapest ticket where advance purchase is not necessary; not available in south-eastern England; cannot be used on Friday, Saturdays in July and August, nor in London before 9.30 am or between 4 and 6 pm. The return journey must be within one calendar month.

SuperAdvance Similarly priced to the Super-Saver but fewer time/day restrictions; however tickets must be bought before 2 pm on the day before travel and both the outward and return journey times must be specified; limited availability so book ASAP.

Saver Higher priced than the SuperSaver, but can be used any day and there are fewer time restrictions.

AwayBreak ticket For off-peak travel in the old Network South East region (south-eastern England). Valid for four nights (five days) for journeys over 30 miles, or 40 miles from London.

StayAway ticket As above but valid for one month.

On some return tickets it's possible to stop off at one place on the line with the return portion of the ticket. Check when you buy the ticket.

Telephone Bookings

To make a booking, first phone the 24 hour national rail inquiry line (☎ 0345-484950) to get the time of your train and the price of the ticket. You'll then be given another number for one of the 25 rail companies where you can make a credit card booking for your journey.

Bookings can be paid for with Master-Card (Access), Visa, American Express, Diners Club and Switch. Tickets are sent by post and must be ordered at least five days before travel. Booking lines for some companies are open Monday to Friday from 9 am to 5 pm but others (particularly InterCity) are open daily from 8 am to 10 pm. Some companies accept telephone bookings only for tickets costing more than £10.

CAR & MOTORCYCLE

Travelling by private car or motorcycle enables you to get to remote places, and to travel quickly, independently and flexibly. Unfortunately, the independence you enjoy does tend to isolate you and cars are nearly always inconvenient in city centres.

Despite the traffic density, Britain has the safest roads in the EU. There are five grades of road. Motorways and main A-roads are triple or dual carriageways and deliver you quickly from one end of the country to another but you miss the most interesting countryside. Be careful if you use them in foggy or wet conditions. Minor A-roads are single carriageways and are likely to be clogged with slow-moving trucks.

Life on the road is more relaxed and interesting on the B-roads and minor roads. Fenced by hedgerows, these wind through the countryside from village to village. You can't travel fast, but you won't want to.

If you can, avoid bringing a car into London. Traffic moves slowly and parking is expensive. Traffic wardens and wheel clampers operate with extreme efficiency and if your vehicle is towed away it'll cost you over £100 to get it back.

At around 67p per litre (equivalent to £2.54 for a US gallon), petrol is expensive by American or Australian standards; and diesel is a only few pence cheaper. Distances, however, aren't great.

Road Rules

Anyone using the roads should read the *Highway Code* (often available in TICs). A foreign driving licence is valid in Britain for up to 12 months from the time of your last entry into the country. If you're bringing a car from Europe make sure you're adequately insured.

Briefly, vehicles drive on the left-hand side of the road; front seat belts are compulsory and if belts are fitted in the back they must be worn; the speed limit is 30 mph

(48 kph) in built-up areas, 60 mph (96 kph) on single carriageways, and 70 mph (112 kph) on dual or triple carriageways; you give way to your right at roundabouts (traffic already on the roundabout has the right of way); and motorcyclists must wear helmets.

See Legal Matters in Regional Facts for the Visitor for information on drink-driving rules.

Car Parking

Many places in Britain, big and small, could easily be overrun by cars. As a result, there are often blanket bans on, or at least active discrimination against, bringing cars into the centre. It's a good idea to go along with it even if sometimes you'll have to walk further. The parking will be easier and you'll enjoy a place more if it's not cluttered up with cars – yours and others. This particularly applies in small villages – park in the car parks, not on the street.

In bigger cities there will often be 'short-stay' and 'long-stay' car parks. Prices will often be the same for stays of up to two or three hours, but for lengthier stays the short-stay car parks rapidly become much more expensive. The long-stay car parks may be slightly less convenient but they're much cheaper.

A yellow line painted along the edge of the road indicates there are parking restrictions. The only way to establish the exact restrictions is to find the nearby sign that spells them out. A double line means no parking at any time; a single line means no parking for at least an eight-hour period between 7 am and 7 pm; and a broken line means there are some restrictions. In some cities there are also red lines, which mean no stopping or parking.

Rental

Rates are expensive in the UK; often you will be best off making arrangements in your home country for some sort of package deal. The big international rental companies charge from around £150 a week for a small car (Ford Fiesta, Peugeot 106).

Road Distances (miles)

	Aberystwyth	Birmingham	Bristol	Cambridge	Cardiff	Dover	Edinburgh	Glasgow	Inverness	Lincoln	Liverpool	London	Oban	Oxford	Penzance	Thurso	Windermere	York
Aberystwyth	–																	
Birmingham	113	–																
Bristol	124	85	–															
Cambridge	216	95	146	–														
Cardiff	102	100	45	190	–													
Dover	280	178	187	130	240	–												
Edinburgh	325	295	375	338	390	450	–											
Glasgow	315	295	375	370	390	470	44	–										
Inverness	487	460	545	500	560	610	155	166	–									
Lincoln	195	85	170	90	200	200	260	280	430	–								
Liverpool	107	95	165	170	170	278	219	220	390	120	–							
London	211	110	115	54	155	71	375	397	536	131	193	–						
Oban	415	386	466	460	480	570	123	93	115	373	310	489	–					
Oxford	155	66	75	83	110	130	360	360	519	127	160	57	450	–				
Penzance	315	270	190	360	230	350	560	560	722	365	363	280	650	263	–			
Thurso	626	590	670	630	685	740	290	298	130	555	515	652	250	650	858	–		
Windermere	190	150	230	248	250	350	148	145	310	175	75	259	239	220	415	443	–	
York	206	135	215	150	245	266	195	220	360	75	100	188	312	185	405	480	87	–

Driving Itineraries

If you're only visiting Britain for a short holiday, you can pack in a lot more if you have your own set of wheels and plan your itinerary carefully.

Visitors used to left-hand drive vehicles, and who find the prospect of driving on the 'wrong' side of the road daunting, should avoid driving in the cities.

On the following route around England, you could travel from the airport to London and from London to Cambridge by train or bus, pick up your rental car there, tour round the country and return the car to the airport as you leave, without going back to London.

England (12 Days)

Origin	Destination	Road Distances
London	to Cambridge	(61 miles)
Cambridge	to Lincoln	(94 miles)
Lincoln	to York	(81 miles)
York	to Durham	(75 miles)
Durham	to Windermere	(115 miles)
Windermere	to Chester	(113 miles)
Chester	to Stratford-upon-Avon	(65 miles)
Stratford-upon-Avon	to Bath	(99 miles)
Bath	to Salisbury via Avebury	(59 miles)
Salisbury	to Windsor	(75 miles)
Windsor	to London	(23 miles)

Route

Leave London on the M11, that leads directly to Cambridge. Spend the day in this ancient university town and take a punt out on the river. From Cambridge, take the A604 to Huntingdon to join the A1, stopping at Stamford for a quick look at this unspoilt old town. Continue along the A1, turning off onto the A46 for Lincoln. This old Roman city has a superb Norman cathedral and castle.

Leave Lincoln on the A15, the Roman road known as Ermine St, heading north. Join the M180 for 7 miles, then take the A15 over the Humber Bridge. Immediately after crossing the bridge, take the A63 for 7 miles, then the A1034 to Market Weighton, following signs for York via the A1079. York Minster is the largest Gothic cathedral in England, and York is a fascinating place.

Head west out of York on the A59 to join the A1. Leave the A1(M) and get on the A690 to Durham, an easier route than the A177. Durham is a World Heritage Site with one of the finest cathedrals in the country.

From Durham, take the A691 to Consett, and then the A692 4 miles south-west to join the A68 going north. The A69 leads west through Haydon Bridge to Bardon Mill, where signposts direct you for the 3 mile journey to Housesteads Fort, part of Hadrian's Wall. After stopping to see the fort, continue west along the B6318 to rejoin the A69, following signposts for Carlisle. Two miles east of Carlisle, take the M6 south to the A66, which you follow west for a mile. Turn left onto the scenic A592, which leads into the heart of the Lake District, past Ullswater to Windermere. Stay two nights in Windermere to give yourself time for

Driving Itineraries

a long walk in this beautiful area.

From Windermere take the A591 south-east to join the M6 south, eventually taking the M56 to Chester. Spend the night in Chester before taking the A41 and A442 south to join the M54 near Telford. You may wish to stop at nearby Ironbridge Gorge to see this cradle of the Industrial Revolution and its interesting museums, or at Warwick, south of Birmingham, to see its impressive castle.

Bypass Birmingham on the M6 and join the M40 (watch the signs as this is an easy exit to miss). Take the A3400 to Stratford-upon-Avon for a quick look at Shakespeare's birthplace and to see a play by the Royal Shakespeare Company in the evening.

The following day, visit Blenheim Palace, one of the most impressive stately homes in the country, and drive through Cotswold villages to the beautiful town of Bath. The A3400 and the A44 lead you to Woodstock, and Blenheim stands on the edge of the town.

From Blenheim, take the A4095 to Witney, the A40 to the village of Burford, the B4425 through Bibury to Cirencester, and the A433, then the A46, to Bath.

From Bath, follow the A4 to the prehistoric complex of Avebury, less well known but more atmospheric than Stonehenge. Continue east along the A4 to join the A346 and A338 south to Salisbury, well known for its cathedral.

Leave Salisbury on the A360 north to join the A303 near Stonehenge, continuing east onto the M3. At Basingstoke, take the A33 to join the M4, stopping at Windsor to see the castle. Heathrow airport is only about 10 miles from Windsor, so you could stay the night in the Windsor area and drop off your rental car at the airport as you leave.

Scotland (7 Days)

Origin	Destination	Road Distances
Edinburgh	to St Andrews	(58 miles)
St Andrews	to Aberdeen	(83 miles)
Aberdeen	to Inverness	(106 miles)
Inverness	to Fort William	(65 miles)
Fort William	to Glasgow	(102 miles)
Glasgow	to Stirling	(26 miles)
Stirling	to Edinburgh	(35 miles)

Route

Take the A90 out of Edinburgh over the Forth Road Bridge. The A90 becomes the M90 soon after the bridge, and you should turn onto the A91 north of Kinross, following signs to St Andrews. It's worth spending the night in this interesting seaside town, best known as the home of golf.

From St Andrews, turn off the A91 along the A919 and A92 following signs for Tay Bridge and Dundee. Stop to see Scott's Antarctic research ship *Discovery*, conveniently moored beside the bridge in Dundee. Continue on the A929 and the smaller A928 to Glamis Castle, one of the most famous of Scotland's many castles. From Glamis take the A94 to the affluent granite city of Aberdeen.

You could take one of several routes from Aberdeen to Inverness. The direct route is along

Driving Itineraries

the A96 via Elgin, a distance of 106 miles. Alternatively, and if you have an extra day to spare, consider taking the route through the Grampian Mountains, via the A93, A939, A95 and A9 about 150 miles. Balmoral Castle, the Queen's Scottish residence, which can be visited when the royal family is not at home, is a short distance off this route.

From Inverness, follow Loch Ness on the A92, stopping at Urquhart Castle and the nearby Loch Ness Monster Exhibition. Continue on the A82 to Fort William, leaving yourself time for an evening walk in Glen Nevis. To climb Ben Nevis, Britain's highest peak, you'd need to allow a whole day.

Take the A82 south from Fort William, stopping in Glen Coe and then continuing past Loch Lomond to Glasgow. Spend the following day in this lively city before taking the M80 to Stirling, a drive of under one hour. Look around Stirling's magnificent castle the next day before returning to Edinburgh.

Wales (5 Days)

Origin	Destination	Road Distances
Cardiff	to Brecon	(35 miles)
Brecon	to St David's	(85 miles)
St David's	to Machynlleth	(77 miles)
Machynlleth	to Llanberis	(60 miles)
Llanberis	to Llandudno via Caernarfon	(27 miles)
Llandudno	to Chester	(47 miles)

Route

Cardiff is about 30 miles from the River Severn and the border with England. Spend half a day in the Welsh capital to see the castle or the folk museum before taking the A470 north to Brecon.

After a morning's walk in the Brecon Beacons National Park, drive west on the A40 to St David's. Situated in the heart of the Pembrokeshire Coast National Park, this is Britain's smallest cathedral town.

Follow the coast road, the A487, to the seaside town of Aberystwyth and the village of Machynlleth, on the southern edge of Snowdonia National Park. Located just outside Machynlleth, the Centre for Alternative Technology is an interesting place to visit.

Get an early start the next day and take the quickest route to the foot of Mt Snowdon, the second-highest peak in Britain. From Machynlleth, follow the A487 to Dolgellau, then the A470 and A487, turning off at Penrhyndeudraeth onto the A4085 to Beddgelert. From here take the A498 and the A4086, following signs for Llanberis.

To walk up Snowdon, stop by the youth hostel on the pass before Llanberis; if you're going to cheat and take the mountain railway to the top, continue into Llanberis. There are numerous B&Bs in this area.

From Llanberis it's about 7 miles to Caernarfon, a run-down town dominated by a magnificent castle. Take the A487 and A55 east to Conwy, where there's another interesting castle, and spend the night in Llandudno, 4 miles north. This is a classic British seaside resort with rows of welcoming B&Bs.

To return to England, the A55 provides fast access to Chester, just over an hour's drive east.

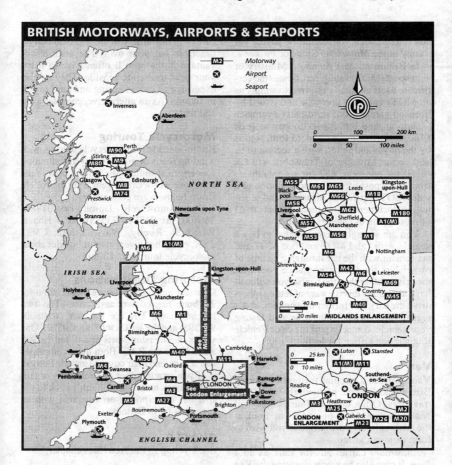

BRITISH MOTORWAYS, AIRPORTS & SEAPORTS

The main companies include Avis (☎ 0990-900500), British Car Rental (☎ 01203-716166), Budget (☎ 0800-181181), Europcar (☎ 0345-222525), National Car Rental (☎ 01895-233300), Hertz (☎ 0990-996699) and Thrifty Car Rental (☎ 01494-442110).

Holiday Autos (☎ 0990-300400) operates through a number of rental companies and can generally offer excellent deals. A week's all-inclusive hire starts at £149 for a very small Fiat. For other cheap operators

check the ads in *TNT Magazine*. TICs have lists of local car-hire companies.

If you're travelling as a couple or a group, a camper van is worth considering. Sunseeker Rentals (☎ 0181-960 5747) has four-berth and two-berth vans from £240 per week.

Purchase

It is possible to buy a reasonable vehicle for around £1000; a reliable van (see the following section) could be up to twice as much. Check *Loot* (every weekday), and

Autotrader (Thursday; includes photos) for ads. To see what you should be paying get a copy of the *Motorists' Guide* or *Parker's*.

In Britain all cars require a Ministry of Transport (MOT) safety certificate (the certificate itself is usually referred to simply as an MOT) valid for one year and issued by licensed garages; full third-party insurance – shop around but expect to pay at least £300; registration – a standard form signed by the buyer and seller, with a section to be sent to the Ministry of Transport; and tax (£150 for one year, £82 for six months) – from main post offices on presentation of a valid MOT certificate, insurance and registration documents. Note that cars that are 25 or more years old are tax exempt.

You are strongly recommended to buy a vehicle with valid MOT and tax. MOT and tax remain with the car through a change of ownership; third-party insurance goes with the driver rather than the car, so you will still have to arrange this (beware of letting others drive the car). For further information about registering, licensing, insuring and testing your vehicle, contact a post office or Vehicle Registration Office for leaflet V100.

Van

Vans provide a popular method of touring Britain and Europe, particularly for budget travellers. Often three or four people will band together to buy or rent a van. Look at the adverts in *TNT Magazine* if you wish to form or join a group.

Autotrader carries ads for vans, as does *Loot*. It may also be worth checking the Van Market in Market Rd, London N7 (near Caledonian Rd tube station). This is a long-running institution where private vendors congregate on a daily basis, but there seems to be less business going on here these days. Some second-hand dealers offer a 'buyback' scheme for when you return from Europe, but buying and reselling privately is better if you have the time.

You will need to spend at least £1000 to £2000 for something reliable enough to get you around Europe. The main advantage of going by van is flexibility: with transport,

eating and sleeping requirements all taken care of in one unit, you are tied to nobody's timetable but your own. The main disadvantage is that you'll often have to leave your gear unattended inside. They're also expensive to buy in spring and hard to sell in autumn. As an alternative, consider a car and tent.

Motorcycle Touring

Britain is made for motorcycle touring, with winding roads of good quality and stunning scenery to stimulate the senses. Just make sure your wet-weather gear is up to scratch. Crash helmets are compulsory.

The Auto-Cycle Union (☎ 01788-566400, fax 01788-573585), ACU House, Wood St, Rugby, Warwickshire, CV21 2YX, publishes a very useful booklet about motorcycle touring in Britain.

Motoring Organisations

Consider joining a motoring organisation for 24 hour breakdown assistance. The two largest in the UK are the AA (☎ 0800-919595) and the RAC (☎ 0800-550550). One year's membership starts at £46 for the AA and £39 for the RAC. Both these companies can also extend their cover to include Europe.

If you're a member of a motoring organisation back home, you should check to see if it has a reciprocal arrangement with an organisation in Britain.

BICYCLE

See Cycling in the Activities chapter.

HITCHING

Hitching is never entirely safe in any country in the world, and we don't recommend it. Travellers who decide to hitch should understand that they are taking a small but potentially serious risk. However, many people do choose to hitch, and the advice that follows should help to make their journeys as fast and safe as possible.

Hitching is reasonably easy in Britain, except around the big cities and built-up areas, where you'll need to use public transport. It's against the law to hitch on motorways or the immediate slip roads; make a sign and use approach roads, nearby roundabouts, or the service stations.

On some of the Scottish islands, where public transport is infrequent, hitching is so much a part of getting around that local drivers may stop and offer you lifts without you even asking.

Although hitching in Britain is probably safer than hitching in many other Western countries, it's obviously not without its dangers, and it's certainly not advisable for a woman to hitch alone. Two women will be reasonably safe but a man and a woman travelling together is probably the best combination.

If you don't like the look of someone who stops for you, don't get in the car. Likewise, if you're a driver, take care over who you pick up. The brother of one of the authors was stabbed by a hitchhiker he stopped for on the M1 motorway.

WALKING

See Walking in the Activities chapter.

BOAT

See the Getting There & Away and Getting Around sections of regional chapters, and Canal & Waterway Travel in the Activities chapter.

ORGANISED TOURS

Since travel is so easy to organise in Britain, there is very little need to consider a tour. Still, if your time is limited and you prefer to travel in a group, there are some interesting possibilities. The BTA has information (see also Hop on Hop off Buses in the Bus section of this chapter).

Outback UK (☎ 01327-704115, fax 01327-703883), The Cottage, Church Green, Badby, Northants, NN11 3AS, offers two to 14-day tours round Britain with departures

every Saturday (from March to November) from London, though it's possible to join at any point. Charges are approximately £35 per day (includes two meals and accommodation in youth hostels) or £18 (travel only).

Other companies with trips pitched at a young crowd include Drifters (☎ 0171-262 1292), Contiki, (☎ 0171-637 0802), Insight (☎ 0990-143433) and Acacia (☎ 01797-344164).

If you don't fit into this category, try Shearings Holidays (☎ 01942-824824), Miry Lane, Wigan, Lancashire, WN3 4AG. It has a very wide range of four to 12-day coach tours covering the whole country. It also offers Club 55 holidays for the more mature holiday-maker – on its West Country tour you can expect resident entertainers, bingo every evening and wrestling one evening per week!

For the over 60s, Saga Holidays (☎ 0800-300500), Saga Building, Middleburg Square, Folkestone, Kent CT20 1AZ, offers holidays ranging from cheap coach tours and resort holidays to luxury cruises around Britain and abroad. Saga also operates in the USA (☎ 617-262 2262) at 222 Berkeley St, Boston, MA 02116, and in Australia (☎ 02-957 4266) at Level 1, 10-14 Paul St, Milsons Point, Sydney 2061.

TAXI

See the London chapter for info on the famous London taxis and their minicab competitors. Outside London and other big cities, taxis are usually reasonably priced. In the country you could expect to pay around £1.40 per mile, which means they are definitely worth considering to get to an out-of-the-way hostel, sight, or the beginning of a walk. A taxi over a short distance will often be very competitive with a local bus, especially if there are three or four people to share the cost.

ENGLAND

Facts about England

England dominates both the political entity that is the United Kingdom and the geographical entity that is the island of Great Britain. Although the Scots and Welsh made an enormous contribution to the British Empire it was, and in some ways remains, an English empire.

England's position on the edge of Continental Europe, removed but in many ways an integral part, has always created unique opportunities and problems. The pendulum has swung from isolation to integration and back again a number of times. In this era of the European Union and the Channel Tunnel, England is probably more European than it has been for 700 years.

Despite this, travellers will find a country where the institutions and symbols that had

ENGLAND CHAPTER DIVISIONS

ATLANTIC OCEAN

SCOTLAND

UNITARY AUTHORITIES
1 York
2 Sefton
3 Liverpool
4 Knowsley
5 St Helens
6 Wigan
7 Bolton
8 Salford
9 Trafford
10 Bury
11 Manchester
12 Rochdale
13 Oldham
14 Tameside
15 Stockport
16 Calderdale
17 Bradford
18 Leeds

Northumberland

Cumbria
NORTH-WESTERN ENGLAND

Durham

NORTH-EASTERN ENGLAND
North Yorkshire

Isle of Man

IRISH SEA

Lancashire

East Riding of Yorkshire

NORTH SEA

Cheshire

Derbyshire

Nottinghamshire

Lincolnshire

Staffordshire

Shropshire

Leicestershire

Norfolk

W A L E S

Hereford & Worcester

Warwickshire

MIDLANDS

Northamptonshire

Cambridgeshire

EASTERN ENGLAND

Suffolk

Gloucestershire

Oxfordshire

Bedfordshire

Buckinghamshire

Hertfordshire

Essex

Berkshire

LONDON

Surrey

Kent

Somerset

Wiltshire

SOUTH-EASTERN ENGLAND

Hampshire

W Sussex

E Sussex

SOUTH-WESTERN ENGLAND

Devon

Dorset

Isle of Wight

Cornwall

19 Kirklees
20 Wakefield
21 Barnsley
22 Sheffield
23 Rotherham
24 Doncaster
25 Kingston-upon-Hull
26 North Lincolnshire
27 North-East Lincolnshire
28 Wolverhampton
29 Walsall
30 Sandwell
31 Birmingham
32 Dudley
33 Solihull
34 Coventry
35 South Gloucestershire
36 Bristol
37 North Somerset
38 Bath & North-East Somerset

ENGLAND .... Chapter
Norfolk .... County

ENGLISH CHANNEL

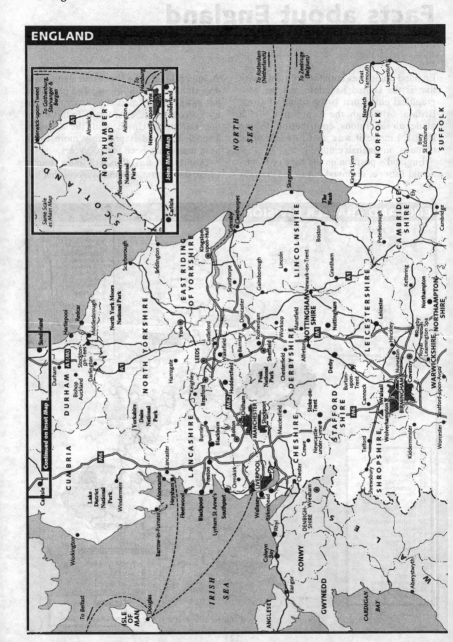

ENGLAND

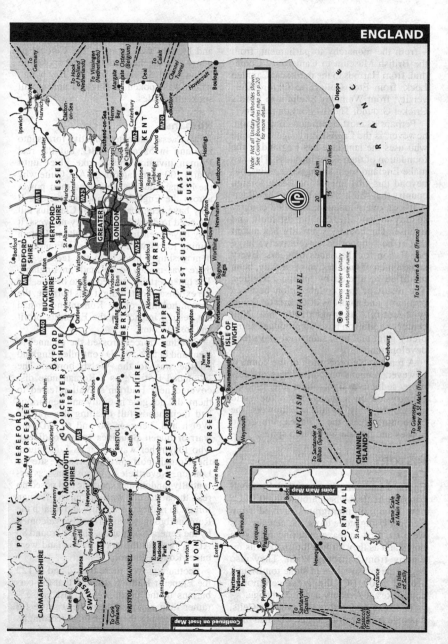

such an enormous role in shaping the modern world remain cherished and intact – from the monarchy to parliament, from the British Museum to Canterbury Cathedral, from Harrods to the market at Camden Lock, from Eton College to Oxford University, from Wembley Stadium to Lord's Cricket Ground. The list goes on and on.

Perhaps its most significant contribution, however, is the English language – anyone who uses the language has England at the foundation of their consciousness. This can make England seem strangely familiar, but beyond this first impression lies a foreign country that still has the ability to bewilder.

It's an overpopulated, crowded country so day-to-day life can be difficult and intense. The country's fertility has meant that it has supported a (relatively) large population for thousands of years. Every square inch of land has, in some way, been modified or altered by human activities. The result of this collaboration between humanity and nature is often breathtakingly beautiful, although 19th and 20th century capitalism has also produced some pretty grim and ugly industrial and urban developments.

A remarkable proportion of the country, however, remains unspoilt. There are few more seductive sights than the English countryside on a sunny day – the vivid greens, the silky air, the wildflowers, the ballooning trees, the villages, the grand houses and the soaring church spires.

HISTORY
Celts
England had long been settled by small bands of hunters when, around 4000 BC, a new group of immigrants arrived from Europe. Using stone tools, the new arrivals were the first to leave enduring marks on the island as they farmed the chalk hills radiating from Salisbury Plain. They also began the construction of stone tombs and, around 3000 BC, the great ceremonial complexes at Avebury and Stonehenge.

The next great influx involved the Celts, a people from central Europe who had mas-

tered the smelting of bronze and, later, of iron. They started arriving around 800 BC and brought two forms of the Celtic language: the Gaelic, which is still spoken in Ireland and Scotland, and the Brythonic, which was spoken in England and is still spoken in Wales.

Romans
Julius Caesar made investigative forays into England in 55 and 54 BC, but the real Roman invasion didn't take place until nearly 100 years later in 43 AD. Quite why the Romans decided to extend their power across the English Channel is unclear. It may have been that Emperor Claudius felt the need to display his military prowess, it may have been fear of the Celts in Britain joining forces with the Gauls in France, or it may simply have been the feeling that there was money to be made in England. The latter certainly turned out to be true, but the expense of obtaining it was horrible; the British holdings of the Romans never had the desired impact on the Empire's profit and loss account.

Claudius' forces crossed the channel to Kent and before 50 AD controlled England all the way to the Welsh border. The 'wretched British', as a Roman note discovered near Hadrian's Wall referred to them, did not give in easily and centurions had their hands full quelling the warlike Welsh and, between 60 and 61 AD, the warrior queen Boudicca (aka Boadicea), who fought her way as far as Londinium, the Roman port on the present site of London. Nevertheless, opposition was essentially random and sporadic and posed no real threat to the well-organised Roman forces. In reality the stability and wealth the Romans brought was probably welcomed by the general population, and by around 80 AD Wales and the north of England were under Roman control.

Scotland proved more tricky, and in 122 the Emperor Hadrian decided that the barbarians to the north were a lost cause – rather than conquer them, he'd settle for simply keeping them at bay. Accordingly, he ordered a wall to be built right across the country; to the south would be civilisation and the Roman Empire, to the north would be the savages. Only 20 years later, the Romans made another attempt at bringing the unruly northerners into line and constructed the Antonine Wall, further north. This was soon abandoned and for nearly 300 years Hadrian's Wall marked the furthermost limit of the Roman Empire. Paved roads radiated from London to important regional centres – Ermine St ran north to Lincoln, York and Hadrian's Wall, and Watling St ran north-west to Chester.

The Romans brought stability and considerable economic advancement to Britain for nearly four centuries. After it was recognised by the Emperor Constantine in 313, they also brought Christianity. By this time the Empire was already in decline but the Romans were not driven out by the British, nor did they withdraw to fight fires closer to home. Britain was simply abandoned. Money stopped coming from Rome and, although the outposts stumbled on for some time, eventually they crumbled and were deserted. The end of Roman power in Britain is generally dated at around 410.

Anglo-Saxons & Viking Invasions

As Roman power faded, England went downhill. The use of money, once supplied by Rome, dwindled – as a result, trade declined, rural areas lost their population, travel became unsafe and local fiefdoms developed. Heathen Angles, Jutes and Saxons – Teutonic tribes originating from north of the Rhine – began to move into the vacuum created by the Roman departure. During the 5th century, these tribes advanced across what had been Roman England, absorbing the Celts so thoroughly that today most place names in England have Anglo-Saxon origins.

By the end of the 6th century, England had split into a number of Anglo-Saxon kingdoms, and by the 7th century these kingdoms had come to think of themselves collectively as English. The Celts, particularly in Ireland, kept Latin and Roman Christian culture alive. Christianity, a fragile late-Roman period import, may have declined at first but the arrival of St Augustine in 597 was followed by the swift spread of Augustinian missions.

As memories of Rome faded and the Celts merged with the Anglo-Saxons, England was divided into three strong kingdoms. In the 7th century, Northumbria was the dominant kingdom, extending its power far across the border into Scotland. In the 8th century, Mercia became stronger and King Offa marked a clear border between England and Wales, delineated by Offa's Dyke. Mercia's power eventually withered, to be replaced by that of King Egbert of Wessex, who was the first to rule all England. At the same time, the fierce northern Vikings inflicted a new round of attacks on the country.

In 865 an occupying Viking army moved in to conquer the Anglo-Saxon kingdoms. The Norwegian Vikings took northern Scotland, Cumbria and Lancashire, while the Danes conquered eastern England, making York their capital. They spread across England until, in 871, they were confronted by Alfred the Great of Wessex.

England was divided between the northern Danelaw and southern Wessex, the old Roman Watling St approximating the border. Alfred's successor, Edward the Elder, ended up controlling both Wessex and the Danelaw, but in subsequent generations control of England seesawed from Saxon (Edgar, king of Mercia and Northumberland) to Dane (Canute and his hopeless sons) and back to Saxon (Edward the Confessor).

Edward the Confessor had been brought up in Normandy – a Viking duchy in France – alongside his cousin Duke William, the future Conqueror. Edward's death left two contenders for the crown: Harold Godwineson, his English brother-in-law, and William, his Norman cousin. Harold eventually gained the throne but ruled less than a year, during which time he marched north to defeat a Viking invasion, then turned south to meet another.

Normans & Plantagenets

The year 1066 is of enormous importance in English history because the Norman invasion in that year capped a millennium of invasions and since then there have been no more. In that year William, soon to be dubbed the Conqueror, landed with 12,000 men and defeated Harold at the Battle of Hastings. The conquest of England by the Normans was completed rapidly; English aristocrats were replaced by French-speaking Normans, dominating castles were built and the feudal system was imposed.

The Normans were efficient administrators; already by 1085-86 the *Domesday Book* had provided a census of the country, its owners, its inhabitants and its potential. William I was followed in 1087 by William II and, when he was killed by a mysterious arrow while hunting in the New Forest, he was succeeded by Henry I. Intermarriage between Normans and Saxons was already becoming common, Henry himself marrying a Saxon princess.

A bitter struggle for the succession followed Henry I's death, and was not finally determined until Henry II (the Count of Anjou and grandson of Henry I) took the throne as the first of the Plantagenet Norman kings in 1154. Henry II had inherited more than half of modern France and his power actually surpassed that of the French king.

Not only was the enduring English habit of squabbling between royalty becoming established, but an almost equally enduring habit of squabbling between royalty and the church was also under way. Henry II blotted his copybook by having Thomas á Becket, that 'turbulent priest', murdered in Canterbury Cathedral in 1170.

Richard I, the Lion-Heart, was too busy crusading around the Holy Land to bother much about governing Britain and by the end of his brother John's reign much of the Norman land in France had been lost, disputes with the church in Rome were never-ending and the powerful barons were so fed up they forced John to sign the Magna Carta in 1215.

This first real bill of human rights may have been intended purely as an agreement between lords and their king but its influence was to spread further afield.

The Magna Carta did not end the power struggle between the king and his barons. In 1265 the barons held both Henry III and Prince Edward, but Edward escaped, defeated the barons and followed Henry III as Edward I in 1272. During his reign English control was extended across the Welsh and Scottish borders.

Edward II ascended the throne in 1307 but his lack of military success (he led his army to an horrendous defeat at the hands of Robert the Bruce of Scotland), his favouring of personal friends over his barons and, it's said, his homosexuality brought his reign to a grisly end when his wife, Isabella, and her lover, Roger Mortimer, had him murdered in Berkeley Castle, Gloucestershire.

Things were scarcely better during Edward III's 50-year reign. His long rule saw the start of the Hundred Years' War with France in 1337 and the arrival of the Black Death in 1349. After a series of return bouts, the plague eventually carried off one and a half million people, more than a third of the country's population. The young Richard II had barely taken the throne before he was confronted with the Peasants' Revolt in 1381. Its brutal suppression led to unrest across an already deeply unsettled country.

As well as this clash between the peasantry and the ruling class, the 14th century saw considerable changes in society, exemplified by the rise of English in place of French, the language of the nobility.

In 1380, John Wycliffe made the first English translation of the Bible, but 150 years later William Tyndale was burnt at the stake for daring to *print* the Bible in English.

Geoffrey Chaucer's *Canterbury Tales*, first published around 1387, was not only one of the first books to be written in English, it was also one of the first printed books.

The struggle to retain English control over territory in France was a prime cause of the Hundred Years' War, and to finance these adventures the Plantagenet kings had to concede a considerable amount of power to parliament, which jealously protected its traditional right to control taxation.

Houses of Lancaster & York

Richard II was an ineffectual king and in 1399 Henry IV seized the throne as the first king of the House of Lancaster. His father, John of Gaunt, one of the younger sons of Edward III, was not only the power behind the throne during Edward III's last years, but had also been the major influence on Richard II.

Henry IV was followed by Henry V, who decided it was time to stir up the dormant Hundred Years' War. He defeated the French at Agincourt and Shakespeare later ensured his position as one of the most popular English kings.

Henry VI ascended the throne as an infant and devoted himself to building works (King's College Chapel in Cambridge and Eton Chapel near Windsor) interspersed with bouts of insanity. When the Hundred Years' War finally ground to a halt in 1453, the English forces returned from France and threw their energies into the Wars of the

Roses (the battle for control of the crown between the houses of Lancaster and York).

Once again it was a question of succession, with Henry VI represented by the red rose of Lancaster and Richard, Duke of York, by the white rose of York. Henry VI may have been helpless, but his wife, Margaret of Anjou, was made of different mettle and in 1460 her forces defeated and killed Richard, only for Richard's son Edward to turn the tables on her and her king a year later.

As Edward IV, he was the first Yorkist king but he now had to contend with Richard Neville, the scheming Earl of Warwick. Labelled 'the kingmaker', the earl teamed up with Margaret of Anjou to bring Henry VI back to the throne and shuttle Edward IV into exile in 1470. Then in 1471 Edward IV came bouncing back to defeat and kill the earl and capture Margaret and Henry. Soon after, Henry was mysteriously dispatched in the Tower of London.

Edward IV was a larger-than-life king but his 12-year-old son Edward V reigned for only two months in 1483 before being murdered, with his younger brother, in the Tower of London. Whether Richard III, their uncle and the next king, was their killer has been the subject of much conjecture, but few tears were shed when he was

Wars - a Hundred Years & the Roses

Wars are rarely what they seem. In recent times, WWI was the 'Great War' until WWII came along to give it a number. The Hundred Years' War was an on-again, off-again affair that effectively lasted for 116 years, from the first English success at Crécy to the final English realisation that they could not hold France as well as England. It's been suggested that the war was as much a French civil war as an Anglo-French conflict but the struggle really resulted from the entangled English and French royal family lines and their conflicting spheres of control. The Black Death, shortage of funds and other 14th century catastrophes combined to provide plentiful interruptions.

The Wars of the Roses were a similarly stop-and-start dispute, which only got their name nearly 400 years later, courtesy of romantic novelist Sir Walter Scott. It's been estimated that over the 30 years from 1455 until Henry VII grabbed the throne, actual 'war' only occupied 60 weeks. Medieval warfare was nothing like later blood-and-death struggles; damaging a rival economically by destroying villages and crops was as likely to be the policy as full-on fighting.

tumbled from the throne by Henry Tudor, first of the Tudor dynasty, in 1485.

Tudors

Henry VII, a Lancastrian descended on his mother's side from John of Gaunt, patched things up with the York side by marrying the daughter of Edward IV and arranged strategic marriages for his own children.

Matrimony may have been a more useful tool than warfare for Henry VII but the multiple marriages of his successor, Henry VIII, were a very different story. Fathering an heir was Henry VIII's immediate problem and the church's unwillingness to cooperate with this quest led to the split with the Catholic church. Parliament made Henry the head of the Church of England and the Bible was translated into English. In 1536 Henry VIII 'dissolved' the smaller monasteries in Britain and Ireland, a blatant takeover of their land and wealth, as much as another stage in the struggle between church and state. The general populace felt little sympathy for the wealthy and often corrupt monasteries, and in 1539-40 another monastic land grab swallowed the larger ones as well. The property was sold or granted to members of the nobility,

Queen Elizabeth I, the virgin Queen

raising money for the king's military campaigns and ensuring the loyalty of his followers.

Nine-year-old Edward VI followed Henry VIII in 1547 but only ruled for six years. During his reign Catholicism declined and Protestantism grew stronger. His devoutly Catholic sister Mary I reversed that pattern, but she too only ruled for five years.

Elizabeth I, the third child of Henry VIII, seemed to have inherited a nasty mess of religious strife and divided loyalties, but her 45-year reign (1558-1603) saw a period of boundless English optimism epitomised by the defeat of the Spanish Armada, the global explorations of English seafarers, the expansion of trade, the literary endeavours of William Shakespeare and the scientific pursuits of Francis Bacon.

Stuarts & the Commonwealth Interlude

The one thing the Virgin Queen failed to provide was an heir, so she was succeeded by James I, first of the inflexible Stuart dynasty. Since he was already James VI of Scotland, he effectively united England, Scotland and Wales into one country. His attempts to smooth relations with the Catholics were set back by the anti-Catholic outcry that followed Guy Fawkes' Gunpowder Plot, an attempt to blow up parliament and king in 1605. The power struggle between monarchy and parliament became even more bitter during Charles I's reign, eventually degenerating into the Civil War which pitched the king's royalists (Cavaliers) against the parliamentarians (Roundheads). Catholics, traditionalist members of the Church of England and the old gentry supported Charles I, whose power base was the north and west. The Protestant Puritans and the new rising merchant class based in London and the towns of the south-east, supported parliament.

The 1644-49 struggle resulted in victory for the parliamentary forces, the execution of Charles I and the establishment of the Commonwealth, ruled by Oliver Cromwell, the brilliant parliamentary military leader. A devastating and cruel rampage around Ireland starting in 1649 failed to exhaust his appetite for mayhem.

By 1653 he had also become fed up with parliament and as the 'Protector' assumed near dictatorial powers. Oliver Cromwell laid the foundation for the British Empire by modernising the army and navy and was followed half-heartedly by his son. But in 1660 parliament decided to re-establish the monarchy as the alternatives were proving far worse.

Charles II (the exiled son of Charles I) proved to be an able, though often utterly ruthless king who brought order out of chaos, and the Restoration foreshadowed a new burst of scientific and cultural activity after the strait-laced Puritan ethics of the Commonwealth. Colonies soon stretched down the American coast and the East India Company established its headquarters in Bombay.

Unfortunately, James II (1685-88) was not so far-sighted and his attempts to ease restrictive laws on Catholics ended with his defeat at the hands of William III, better known as William of Orange (the Dutch husband of Mary II, the Protestant daughter of James II). To take their joint throne, however, William and Mary had to agree to a Bill of Rights, and with the later Act of Settlement Britain was established as a constitutional monarchy with clear limits on the powers of the monarchy and a ban on any Catholic (or anyone married to a Catholic) ascending the throne.

Although William and Mary's Glorious Revolution of 1688 was relatively painless in Britain, the impact on Ireland, where the Protestant ascendancy dates from William's victory over James II at the Battle of the Boyne, laid the seeds for the troubles that have continued until now.

Mary died before William, who was followed by Anne (the second daughter of James II), but the Stuart line died with her in 1714. The throne was then passed to distant (but safely Protestant) German relatives.

Empire & Industry

In the 18th century, the Hanoverian kings increasingly relied on parliament to govern and from 1721 to 1742 Sir Robert Walpole became Britain's first prime minister in all but name. Bonnie Prince Charlie shattered this period of tranquillity in 1745, attempting to seize the throne, but this Jacobite Rebellion ended in disaster for Scotland at the Battle of Culloden.

Stronger English control over the British Isles was mirrored by even greater expansion overseas, where the British Empire absorbed more and more of America, Canada and India, and the first claims were made to Australia after Captain James Cook's epic voyage in 1768.

The Empire's first major reverse came when the American colonies won their independence in 1782. This setback led to a period of isolationism. During this time, Napoleon rose to power in France before naval hero Nelson and military hero Wellington curtailed, then ended, his expansion in 1815.

Meanwhile, at home, Britain was becoming the crucible of the Industrial Revolution. Canals (following the Bridgewater Canal in 1765), steam power (patented by James Watt in 1781), steam trains (launched by George Stephenson in 1830), the development of coal mines and water power transformed the means of production and transport and the rapidly growing towns of the Midlands became the first industrial cities.

Medical advances led to a dramatic increase in the population but the rapid change from an agricultural to an industrial society caused great dislocation. Nevertheless, by the time Queen Victoria took the throne in 1837, Britain was the greatest power in the world. Britain's fleets dominated the seas, linking an enormous empire, and its factories dominated world trade.

Under Prime Ministers Disraeli and Gladstone, the worst excesses of the Industrial Revolution were addressed, education became universal, trade unions were legalised and the right to vote was extended to most men. Women didn't get the vote until after WWI.

Edwardian Era to WWII

Queen Victoria died in 1901 and the ever-expanding Britain of her era died with her. It wasn't immediately evident that a century of relative decline was about to commence when Edward VII, so long the king in waiting, ushered in the relaxed new Edwardian era. In 1914 Britain bumbled into the Great War (WWI), a war of stalemate and horrendous slaughter. It not only added trench warfare to the dictionary but also dug a huge trench between the ruling and working classes as thousands of ordinary men lost their lives at the behest of their commanding officers.

The old order was shattered and by the war's weary end in 1918 one million Britons had died and 15% of the country's accumulated capital had been spent. The euphoria of victory brought with it an extension of the right to vote to all men aged 21 and women aged 30 and over. It wasn't until 1928 that women were granted the same rights as men, despite Winston Churchill's opposition.

Political changes also saw the eclipse of the Liberal Party. It was replaced by the Labour Party which won power, albeit in coalition with the Liberals, for the first time in the 1923 election. James Ramsay MacDonald was the first Labour prime minister. A year later the Conservatives were back in power, but the rankling 'us and them' mistrust which had developed during the war, fertilised by soaring unemployment, flowered in the 1926 General Strike. When over half a million workers hit the streets, the heavy-handed government response included sending in the army which set the stage for the labour unrest which was to plague Britain for the next 50 years.

However, in the mid-1920s, it did look as if Britain had finally solved one centuries-old problem. The war had no sooner ended than Britain was involved in another struggle, the bitter Anglo-Irish War, that commenced in 1919 and ground to a halt in mid-1921, with Ireland finally achieving independence. Unhappily, the decision to divide the island in two was to have long-term repercussions.

The unrest of the 1920s worsened in the 1930s as the world economy slumped, ushering in a decade of misery and political upheaval. Even the royal family took a knock when Edward VIII abdicated in 1936 to marry a woman who was not only twice divorced but also American.

The less-than-charismatic George VI followed his brother Edward, but the scandal hinted at the prolonged trial by media which the royal family would undergo 50 years later.

Britain dithered through the 20s and 30s with mediocre and visionless government failing to confront the country's problems. Meanwhile on the continent, the 30s saw the rise of imperial Germany under Adolf Hitler. By the time Prime Minister Neville Chamberlain returned from Munich in 1938 with a promise of 'peace in our time', the roller coaster was already rattling downhill to disaster. On 1 September 1939, Hitler invaded Poland and two days later Britain declared war.

WWII

German forces swept through France and pushed a British expeditionary force back to the beaches of Dunkirk in May/June 1940. Only an extraordinary flotilla of rescue vessels turned a disaster into a brave defeat. By mid-1940, the other countries of Europe were either ruled by or under the direct influence of the Nazis. Stalin had negotiated a peace agreement, the USA was neutral, and Britain, under Churchill's stirring leadership, was virtually isolated. Neville Chamberlain, reviled for his policy of appeasement, had stood aside to let Churchill lead a wartime national coalition government.

Between July and October 1940, the Royal Air Force withstood the Luftwaffe's bombing raids to win the Battle of Britain. Churchill's extraordinary exhortations inspired the country to resist and Hitler's invasion plans were blocked, although

Kings & Queens

Nobody glancing at England's tempestuous story could ever claim that the country's history was dull. The position of king or queen of England (or perhaps worse, *potential* king or queen) would probably rank with being a drug dealer in a present-day American ghetto as one of history's least safe occupations. They've died in battle (an arrow through the eye for Harold II), been beheaded (Charles I), murdered by a wicked uncle (Edward V at the age of 12) or been knocked off by their queen and her lover (Edward II, for whom a particularly horrible death was concocted as 'punishment' for his homosexuality).

The English monarchs have often been larger-than-life characters: wife abusers of the very worst kind like Henry VIII, sufferers from insanity like George III, even stutterers like George VI. And as for scandal, the current royal family's antics over the past decade is only a fleeting shadow of what their predecessors got up to. Nor has it been left solely to the men. England has been led by some powerful women, from the day Queen Boudicca charged her chariot through the Romans, right down to Maggie Thatcher, who projected herself as a queen even if she wasn't one. The two most successful monarchs in English history were probably Elizabeth I and Victoria, and the hapless Henry VI was lucky to be married to Margaret of Anjou, who seemed to have a private army which she led with much greater aplomb than her husband.

Saxons & Danes
Alfred the Great 871-99
Edward the Martyr 975-79
Ethelred II (the Unready) 979-1016
Canute 1016-35
Edward the Confessor 1042-66
Harold II 1066

Normans
William I (the Conqueror) 1066-87
William II (Rufus) 1087-1100
Henry I 1100-35
Stephen 1135-54

Plantagenet (Angevin)
Henry II 1154-89
Richard I (Lion-Heart) 1189-99
John 1199-1216
Henry III 1216-72
Edward I 1272-1307
Edward II 1307-27
Edward III 1327-77
Richard II 1377-99

Lancaster
Henry IV (Bolingbroke) 1399-1413
Henry V 1413-22
Henry VI 1422-61 & 1470-71

York
Edward IV 1461-70 & 1471-83
Edward V 1483
Richard III 1483-85

Tudor
Henry VII (Tudor) 1485-1509

Henry VIII 1509-47
Edward VI 1547-53
Mary I 1553-58
Elizabeth I 1558-1603

Stuart
James I 1603-25
Charles I 1625-49

Commonwealth & Protectorate
Oliver Cromwell 1649-58
Richard Cromwell 1658-59

Restoration
Charles II 1660-85
James II 1685-88
William III (of Orange) 1689-1702
& Mary II 1689-94
Anne 1702-14

Hanover
George I 1714-27
George II 1727-60
George III 1760-1820
George IV 1820-30
William IV 1830-37
Victoria 1837-1901

Saxe-Coburg-Gotha
Edward VII 1901-10

Windsor
George V 1910-36
Edward VIII 1936
George VI 1936-52
Elizabeth II 1953-

60,000 civilian Britons were killed during the war.

As in WWI a stalemate ensued, although this time the English Channel was the trench between the opposing forces. But, as in WWI, the entry of the USA into the conflict tipped the balance. In December 1941, Japanese forces invaded Malaya and just hours later, bombed the US fleet in Pearl Harbour.

The British colony of Hong Kong fell within days and Singapore fell by February, but in Europe the arrival of American forces and the bitter fighting in Russia, which Hitler had invaded in June 1941, began to change things round. In late 1942, German forces were defeated in North Africa and the 1940-41 raids on England were answered with Allied raids on Germany in 1942-43. Tragically, the Allied forces mirrored the German decision to bomb cities rather than military targets, resulting in huge civilian losses which failed to cripple Hitler's war machine.

By 1944 Germany was in retreat, the Allies had complete command of the skies and the long-awaited D-day invasion took place on the Normandy beaches in June 1944. Meanwhile, the Red Army was pushing back the Nazi forces from the east. In May 1945 it was all over for the Nazis. Hitler was dead, Germany a smoking ruin, and Europe was to suffer new divisions which would last for nearly 50 years. Three months later, two atomic bombs forced the surrender of Japan and ended WWII.

Post-war Reconstruction

Fortunately there was greater post-war wisdom in 1945 than in 1918. The Marshall Plan, which helped rebuild an economically strong Europe, stood in stark contrast to the post-WWI demands for reparations. An electorate hungry for change tumbled Churchill from power and ushered in the Labour Party's Clement Attlee.

In the 1930s the brilliant economist John Maynard Keynes had suggested that government could and should influence the economy, adding the term Keynesian Economics to the dictionary; his ideas on economics were also a factor in the much lower levels of unemployment which followed the war. Nationalisation of key industries, government manipulation of the economy and the institution of the National Health Service were all part of the creation of the post-war welfare state, but rebuilding after the damage of the war was to be a slow process.

The post-war baby boomers experienced rationing and belt-tightening for many years after hostilities ceased. Britain's depleted reserves also had to cope with the retreat from empire as one by one the colonies became independent: India in 1947, Malaya in 1957 and Kenya in 1963. In 1953 Elizabeth II became queen, she is now the world's second-longest reigning monarch.

Post-war Britain was a less powerful nation but the recovery was still sufficiently strong for Prime Minister Harold Macmillan to boast in 1957 that most people in Britain had 'never had it so good'.

Swinging 60s to the Thatcher Years

By the 1960s the wartime recovery was really complete, the last vestiges of the empire had been sloughed off and the Beatles era suddenly made grey old England a livelier place. On the surface the economy also looked stronger and more resilient, but even though Harold Wilson's Labour Party seemed to be doing the right things it was building on shaky foundations. The 1970s brought the oil crisis, inflation and increased international competition, a combination which quickly revealed the British economy's inherent weaknesses.

Everything in Britain eventually comes down to class and the long struggle between a disgruntled working class and an inept ruling class finally boiled over in the 70s.

Neither Labour, under Wilson and Jim Callaghan, nor the Conservatives, under Ted Heath, proved capable of controlling the industrial strife of 1974, and its repercussions later in the decade finally brought drastic change. In the 1979 election the 'Iron Lady', Margaret Thatcher, led the

Conservatives to power and ushered in the tough new era of Thatcherism.

Her solutions were brutal and their consequences are still being debated. British workers and their unions were obstructive and Luddite? She broke them. British companies were inefficient and unimaginative? She drove them to the wall. The post-war nationalised companies were a mistake? Like Henry VIII dissolving the monasteries, she sold them off. To the horror of those who thought a female leader would be more pacific than a man, she led Britain into battle after Argentina invaded the Falkland Islands in 1982.

The new harder working, more competitive Britain was also a polarised Britain, with a new trench dug between the people who prospered from the Thatcher years and the many others who found themselves not only jobless but jobless in a harsher environment. Despite the evident dislike of a large slice of the population, by 1988 Thatcher was the longest serving British prime minister of the 20th century. Her repeated electoral victories were aided by the Labour Party's dark days of destructive internal struggles.

Britain in the 1990s

The unpopular flat-rate poll tax reached even her own party's limits of tolerance, and in 1990 Thatcher was dumped by her party in favour of John Major. Unfortunately for the Labour Party, the immense reserves of suspicion they had managed to bank up were enough to see Major win the 1992 election. But the end came with a vengeance in 1997 when New Labour under Prime Minister Tony Blair rocketed to power with a record parliamentary majority of more than 170 seats.

It's early days to gauge how the new government will fare, although it got off to a flying start with the decisions to bring greater self-government to Scotland and Wales and a tentative peace agreement in Northern Ireland. Left-wingers are disappointed that things aren't moving fast enough and highly suspicious of Blair's talk

of an as yet undetailed 'third way' in politics. But the Conservative defeat was so crushing that Labour looks set to have things its own way for some time to come.

GEOGRAPHY

Covering 50,085 square miles, England is the largest of the three political divisions within the island of Great Britain. Bound by Scotland to the north and Wales to the west, England is no more than 18 miles from France across the narrowest part of the English Channel. However, now that the Channel Tunnel has been completed, it's no longer completely cut off from mainland Europe.

Much of England is flat or low-lying. The highest point (Scafell Pike in Cumbria) is only 978m (3210 feet) above sea level; Scotland and Wales have more mountains and higher peaks.

England can be divided into four main geographic areas. In the north of the country a ridge of limestone hills and valleys, known as the Pennines, stretches from Derbyshire 250 miles north to the border with Scotland. To the west are the Cumbrian Mountains and the Lake District, probably the best known of Britain's national parks.

South of the Pennines is the heavily populated central area known as the Midlands, the industrial heartland since the 19th century. At its centre is Birmingham, Britain's second-largest city after London. The Black Country stretches from north of Birmingham through Staffordshire to Wolverhampton.

The south-west peninsula, known as the West Country and including Cornwall, Devon and parts of Somerset, is a plateau with granite outcrops and a rugged coastline. A high rainfall and rich pastures provide good dairy farming – Devon cream is world-famous. The numerous sheltered coves and beaches, and the mild climate, make the West Country a favourite holiday destination for the British. The wild grass-covered moors of Dartmoor and Exmoor are popular with walkers.

The rest of the country is known geographically as the English Lowlands, which are a mixture of farmland, low hills, an industrial belt and densely populated cities, including the capital. The eastern part of this region, including Lincolnshire and East Anglia (Norfolk, Suffolk and Cambridgeshire), is almost entirely flat and at sea level. The Fens are the rich agricultural lands, once underwater but drained in the 18th century, that extend from Lincoln to Cambridge.

London is in the south-east of the country, on the River Thames. Further south are hills of chalk known as downs. The North Downs stretch from south of London to Dover where the chalk is exposed as the famous white cliffs. The South Downs run across Sussex, parallel to the south coast.

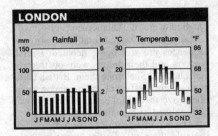

CLIMATE

Climatologists classify England's climate as temperate maritime – read mild and damp.

Despite the country being fairly far north, temperatures in England are moderated by light winds that blow in off seas warmed by the Gulf Stream. In winter, when the sea is warmer than the land, this stops temperatures inland falling very far below 0°C. In summer, when the sea is cooler than the land, it keeps summer temperatures from rising much above 30°C. The average high in London for June to August is 21°C; the average low is 12°C.

Variations in the weather across England are not as great as across Britain. It tends to be colder in the north but not as cold as in Scotland. London, the south-east and the West Country are the warmest regions.

Rainfall is greatest in hilly areas (the Lake District and the Pennines) and in the West Country. Some of these areas can get up to 4500mm of rain a year. The eastern side of England gets the lowest amount of rain in the whole of the UK. Some parts of Essex and Kent have recorded an annual rainfall of less than 600mm.

You can, however, expect some cloudy weather and rain anywhere in Britain at any time. An umbrella or raincoat are recommended. A large plastic cycling cape can be useful even if you're not on a bike, since it can be worn over a backpack. Come prepared and you needn't find the weather as depressing as the locals do – the 50% of Brits who said in a recent survey that they'd emigrate if given the chance cited the climate as the main reason.

ECOLOGY & ENVIRONMENT

In a place as small as Britain, with its long history of human occupation, it's hardly surprising that the way the countryside looks today is largely the result of human interaction with the environment. As the population has grown, so too have the demands made upon the land to yield more food, firewood and building materials. This has led to the extinction of unknown numbers of plant and wildlife species.

Since WWII the pattern of land use in Britain has changed dramatically, with a similarly dramatic effect on wildlife. Modern farming methods have changed the lie of the land in some places from a cosy patchwork of small fields separated by thick hedgerows to vast open cultivated areas. As well as protecting fields from erosion, hedgerows provide habitat for wildlife and shelter for other plant species. Tens of thousands of miles of hedgerows have been destroyed and their destruction continues – since 1984, over 25% of hedgerows have disappeared.

The general reduction in Britain's biodiversity over the last 50 years has numerous other causes, including the increased use of pesticides, blanket planting of conifers (see the Flora section later in this chapter) and huge road-building schemes. For many years government policy favoured road over rail, allocating billions of pounds a year to new roads and encouraging private car ownership. Vehicle numbers have nearly quadrupled over the last 30 years. The tide may finally have turned, however, as congestion on the roads has reduced traffic speeds in cities to what they were in the first half of the century. The problem is so bad that political action groups have been established, dedicated to preventing new road construction and to stopping cars using existing roads.

Tourism is also taking a terrible toll on the environment. Eight million day-trippers a year flock to the New Forest in Hampshire, eroding the soil, churning up meadows and generally disturbing the wildlife. Most come by car and other motorists can't leave the M27 because the slip roads are jammed with forest-goers. It's a similar story in parts of the Lake District and the Peak District, England's most visited national park. Slowly the authorities are realising that better public transport will have to be provided if these problems are to be resolved.

Despite all this bad news, large tracts of the country are also protected as nature reserves, national parks and important natural habitats (Sites of Special Scientific Interest – SSSIs) where development is controlled.

Britain also has hundreds of wildlife and environmental groups. For more information try Greenpeace (☎ 0171-354 5100), Canonbury Villas, London N1 2PN, or Friends of the Earth (☎ 0171-490 1555), 26 Underwood St, London N1 7JQ. To find out more about the problems posed by tourism, contact Tourism Concern (see Responsible Tourism in the Regional Facts for the Visitor chapter).

Wildlife Walks & Holidays

In national parks you can often join nature walks led by park wardens, sometimes free of charge; ask at information centres for details. Seashore rambles can also be an enlightening experience if led by an expert.

Several English companies offer wildlife holidays ranging from weekend breaks to longer residential courses, and include activities ranging from nature rambles to bird-watching, foxes and badgers from special hides. Ask at TICs or try the Countryside Education Trust (☎ 01590-612340), Out of Town Centre, Palace Lane, Beaulieu, Brockhurst SO42 7YG; Wildlife Breaks (☎ 01926-842413), Oaktree Farm, Buttermilk Lane, Yarningale Common, Claverdon, Warwickshire CV35 8HW; or Peak National Park Centre (☎ 01433-620373), Losehill Hall, Castleton, Derbyshire S30 2WB. Also see Flora & Fauna in the Scotland and Wales sections.

If you want to volunteer to work on an environmental project, contact the British Trust for Conservation Volunteers (☎ 01491-839766), 36 St Mary's St, Wallingford OX10 0EU. Organic farms often seek volunteer workers; contact WWOOF (Working Weekends on Organic Farms) in England (☎ 01273-476286), 19 Bradford Rd, Lewes, Sussex BN17 1RB or in Australia (☎ 03-51 550218) at W Tree, Buchan, Victoria 3885 for more information. Earthwatch (☎ 01865-311600), 57 Woodstock Rd, Oxford OX2 6HU, leads scientific expeditions in Britain (as well as worldwide) but you'll probably have to pay at least £500 to join in.

FLORA & FAUNA
Flora

England was once almost entirely covered with woodland, but gradually tree coverage fell until it was the lowest for any other Euro-pean country except Ireland. As long ago as 1919, the Forestry Commission drew up a long-term plan to plant two million hectares of trees by the year 2000, a target already achieved by the early 1980s as a result of substantial grants to landowners. Unfortunately the trees planted were mainly fast-growing conifers instead of indigenous broadleaves. Very little can grow beneath conifers and large areas of ancient peatland were destroyed to create the plantations. These problems have now been recognised and more broadleaf woods are being planted. An ambitious program to create forests on the perimeter of big cities is also well under way.

Apart from the vast stands of conifers (mainly in northern England, Scotland and Wales), other trees common in England include the oak, elm, chestnut, lime (not the citrus variety), ash and beech.

Despite the continued destruction of plant habitat, there's still a wide variety of wildflowers, particularly in spring. Small white snowdrops are the first to flower, sometimes as early as February. Around Easter (late March or early April), parks around the country are bright with daffodils. In woodlands there are purple carpets of bluebells; yellow primroses, buttercups and cowslips are common in meadows. Tall purple foxgloves flower from June to September.

In summer, cultivated fields may be edged with red poppies. You can hardly fail to notice the oilseed rape crop that turns fields brilliant yellow as it flowers.

Gorse bushes, with small yellow flowers and a mass of sharp spines instead of leaves, flourish on heath land and other rough sandy places. Found in the same habitat, broom is very similar, though lacking the prickles. Fern-like bracken is also common.

The moors nurture several varieties of flowering heathers, bracken and whortleberries (also known as bilberries) growing on small shrubs. These tiny blue-black berries are good to eat when they ripen in the summer.

A classic plant identification book is *The Concise British Flora in Colour*, with 1486 beautifully accurate paintings of different species by artist-vicar William Keble Martin.

Fauna

There are 116 protected animal species in Britain but the once common beaver, wolf and reindeer are now extinct.

The red deer is Britain's largest mammal, with herds found on Exmoor and Dartmoor and in the Lake District. Fallow deer, introduced long ago by the Romans, live in small herds of 20 or so animals and can still be seen in the New Forest and Epping Forest. Roe deer are smaller, about the size of a large goat, and are quite common in forest areas where they do con-

siderable damage to young trees. Other species that have been introduced include the Asian muntjac and the Chinese water deer. As Britain's forest cover is spreading, so the number of deer is increasing.

After a period of falling numbers caused by a lethal outbreak of mange, numbers of foxes are rising once again, especially in urban areas. Although nocturnal, the fox can often be seen before dark scavenging around rubbish bins. Badgers are much more shy and although their setts (burrows) may be seen in woods, they only come out at night. Another animal that you're more likely to see as a roadside casualty is the equally nocturnal hedgehog.

The grey squirrel, introduced from North America, is very common and has almost entirely replaced the smaller red squirrel. Having escaped from fur farms, the foreign mink is prospering. Otter numbers are also rising as Britain's rivers are cleaned up; recently otters have been spotted on the outskirts of several big cities. Once very rare, the pine marten is again being seen in some forested regions. Stoats and weasels are rarely encountered.

Rabbits are extremely common; the brown hare, with longer legs and ears, less so. Small species of rodent include the brown rat (originally from Asia), the tiny shrew and harvest mouse (once common in hedgerows) and the water vole (water rat). At dusk, bats sometimes put in an appearance in rural areas.

Two species of seal – the grey seal and the common seal, which is actually less common than the grey – frequent the English coast.

England's only venomous snake is the adder, also known as the viper, which inhabits dry and ferny places on heaths and moors; numbers had fallen from hundreds of thousands to less than 20,000 before it was added to the list of protected species. Other reptiles include the harmless grass snake, the slowworm, the common lizard, and amphibians such as frogs, toads and newts.

Amongst England's various fish species, the salmon and brown trout are best known. See Fishing in the Activities chapter.

Birds Birdwatching is a popular pastime in Britain where the mild climate and varied landscape support a wide variety of species.

While coastal bird species seem to be doing well, the same can't be said for inland species. Several species that were quite common only 25 years ago are rapidly dwindling as their habitats are destroyed. Endangered species now include the tree sparrow, corn bunting, yellow wagtail, turtle dove, bullfinch, song thrush and lapwing. On the other hand, goldfinches, swallows, nuthatches and greater spotted woodpeckers are making a comeback.

England's back gardens harbour the sparrow, the easily recognisable red-breasted robin, thrush, blackbird and blue tit (yellow front, blue/white head). Pigeons are so abundant that they're now considered a pest, particularly in cities (just try eating outside the National Film Theatre in London if you don't believe this). Crows are very common, as is the black and white magpie, another member of the crow family.

Skylarks are becoming less common each year, but you can still them twittering high above open ground. The once common tawny owl recently joined them on the list of endangered birds.

Lakes and inland waterways support all sorts of bird life. The mute swan is Britain's biggest bird. All swans, except for two groups on the River Thames, are said to belong to the monarch. Unfortunately swans have died from lead poisoning after swallowing discarded fishing weights.

The aggressive Canada goose, introduced 300 years ago, has bred so successfully that it's now seen as a menace; large numbers of them can strip fields of crops, and that's not to mention their droppings.

Of the several species of duck, the mallard is most common. The male, with green head and narrow white collar, is easily recognisable.

The pheasant was introduced from Russia over 900 years ago and, while reared on large estates for shooting, now also breeds in the wild. Other game birds include the partridge and grouse.

Raptors are now rare. There are a few heavily protected golden eagles in the Lake District. Kestrels and sparrowhawks are sometimes seen hunting near motorways.

Around the coast are large populations of seagulls, terns, cormorants, gannets, shags, razorbills and guillemots. The tiny, comical puffin, with its clumsy red-and-yellow bill, is a member of the auk family. It comes to land only to breed, which it does in numerous colonies across the length of the British Isles from the Isle of Wight to the Shetland Islands.

Twitchers (or birdwatchers) should contact the Royal Society for the Protection of Birds (☎ 01767-680551), The Lodge, Sandy, Bedfordshire SG19 2BR, which runs over 100 reserves. Membership of the Wildfowl and Wetlands Trust (☎ 01453-890333), Slimbridge, Gloucestershire GL2 7BT, gives free entry to its nine reserves.

Among the shelves of books for birdwatchers, look for the *Where to Watch Birds* regional series published by Christopher Helm.

National Parks

England's national parks – Dartmoor, Exmoor, the Lake District, the Peak District, the Yorkshire Dales, the North York Moors and Northumberland – cover about 7% of the country. The New Forest and the Broads have also been given national park status.

But unlike national parks in some other countries, England's are not wilderness areas where humans have been excluded. Nor are they owned by the nation; most of the land within the national parks is privately owned or belongs to charitable trusts like the National Trust. However, they also include places of outstanding natural beauty that have been given special protection through a 1949 act of parliament.

National park status doesn't guarantee visitors any special rights of access. It does, however, mean that development is controlled through planning committees and that information centres and recreational facilities are provided for visitors.

GOVERNMENT & POLITICS

At present the United Kingdom doesn't have a written constitution but operates under a mixture of parliamentary statutes, common law (a body of legal principles based on precedents dating back to Anglo-Saxon customs) and convention.

The monarch is the titular head of state, but the current Queen is a mere figurehead who acts almost entirely on the advice of 'her' ministers and parliament.

Parliament is made up of three separate elements – the Queen, the House of Commons and the House of Lords. In practice, the supreme body is the House of Commons, which is directly elected every five years. An earlier election can be called at the request of the party in power, or if the party in power loses a vote of confidence.

Voting is not compulsory, and candidates are elected if they win a simple majority in their constituencies (a committee is currently considering whether Britain should change to some form of proportional representation). There are 650 constituencies (seats) – 523 for England, 38 for Wales, 72 for Scotland and 17 for Northern Ireland.

The House of Lords consists of the Lords Spiritual (26 senior bishops of the Church of England) and more than 1100 Lords Temporal (all hereditary and life peers), and the Lords of Appeal (or 'law lords'). None are elected by the general population. The Labour government has announced its intention to abolish life peers during the current parliament. However, it has not yet come up with a clear idea of what should replace them.

The prime minister is the leader of the majority party in the House of Commons and is technically appointed by the Queen. All other ministers are appointed on the recommendation of the prime minister, most of them coming from the House of Commons. Ministers are responsible for government departments. The senior 20 or so ministers make up the Cabinet, which, although answerable to parliament, meets confidentially and in effect manages the government and its policies.

For the last 150 years a predominantly two-party system has operated. Since 1945 either the Conservative Party (also known as the Tory party) or the Labour Party has held power, the Conservatives drawing support mainly from the countryside and suburbia, Labour from urban industrialised areas, Scotland and Wales.

Traditionally, the Conservatives were regarded as right-wing, free-enterprise supporters, while Labour was left-wing in the social-democratic tradition. However, in the 1990s Labour shed much of its socialist credo and accepted many of the arguments of the free-marketers. The New Labour government that was elected in 1997 is shaping up as an odd mix of constitutional radicalism and economic rightism, responsible for the forthcoming Scottish Parliament but ready to partially privatise the air-traffic control system. But Tony Blair's 'third way' in politics looks like a scheme for the long-term which makes it hard to rush to judgement.

Since 1972 Britain has been a member of the European Union (EU), albeit rather grudgingly. The result is that some British legislation now originates in Brussels rather than London. In general British governments have resisted moves to closer integration with Europe. The current Labour government has promised a referendum before Britain will start using the single European currently (the euro) but with an increasing amount of its trade being with Europe, the demise of sterling can't be many years away.

ECONOMY

Britain dominated 19th century world trade but when the 20th century dawned, decline was already under way. Britain had been the pioneering influence in many of the 19th century's leading engineering fields, from railways to ocean liners, but it didn't enjoy the same dominant role when it came to 20th century developments like automobiles and aircraft. Following WWII, much of industry was nationalised as initially railways, gas and electricity services, coal mines, steel manufacturing and shipbuilding, and later even cars, came under

The Decline & Fall of the British Car Industry

In 1968, clutching my degree in engineering, I joined the engineering department of Rootes Cars in Coventry, a company on a one-way street to oblivion. In retrospect it was like being present for the death throes of a dinosaur.

Rootes neatly summed up everything that was wrong with British manufacturing. In the 1950s, Lord Rootes assembled a collection of lesser British automotive brand names like Singer, Sunbeam, Humber and Hillman under the Rootes umbrella. In the early 1960s, Rootes belatedly tried to liven up its staid model line-up with the Hillman Imp, a first-rate automotive disaster. The poor little Imp was actually a delight to drive but every step of the way it was a mistake. When European car manufacturing was moving towards larger and roomier cars, the Imp was a minicar. When smaller manufacturers were realising that high-value niche production was the only way to make money (BMW was the epitome of this discovery) the Imp was a bare-bones economy vehicle. When front-wheel drive was about to become the wave of the future (the Mini pioneered the change in 1958), the Imp was one of the last rear-engined cars like the old VW Beetle. Worse, when Britain was about to establish a solid reputation for building not-yet-production-ready cars, the unfortunate Imp, with its high-tech but underdeveloped die-cast aluminium engine, was a paragon of unreliability.

If all this wasn't bad enough, the British government, intent on decentralising British industry (little realising it was going to self-destruct in the next few decades), persuaded Rootes to build the Imp in Scotland, where the factory was plagued with labour unrest and poor-quality work. Rootes was soon haemorrhaging red ink and in 1967 Chrysler stepped in to take it over. My 1½ years at Rootes/Chrysler saw the US firm try to apply to its British offshoot the same genius that would soon lead them to the brink of disaster in the USA.

The engineering division was full of weirdly archaic British systems, such as the separation of employees into 'works' and 'staff'. Works started and finished 45 minutes earlier than staff. As a result, at the start of the day they had to wait for the staff to arrive and tell them what to do, and at the other end the staff sat around because there was nobody around to do the things that needed doing. Of course, there were plenty of 'works' activities that 'staff' could easily manage themselves (and vice versa) but stepping over rigidly drawn demarcation lines was a recipe for disaster.

In 1970 the car I was working on (later to pop up in Australia as the Chrysler Centura) was dropped and me with it. Soon afterwards Chrysler started to fall through the floor and its European divisions (Simca in France and Rootes in England) were both taken over by the French firm Peugeot. Today, Peugeots are assembled at the old Rootes/Chrysler factory at Ryton-on-Dunsmore. Ramshackle old Rootes did, however, provide some of the inspiration that led me to setting up Lonely Planet. Soon after I joined the company, a Hillman Hunter was entered in the London-Sydney Marathon car rally; remarkably it won. Poring over maps of Afghanistan and Iran used by the team sparked my interest in making the Asia overland trip and led to Lonely Planet's first guidebook.

Tony Wheeler

government control. If anything, public ownership only accelerated the decline until the worldwide upheavals in manufacturing in the 1970s and 80s turned gradual fall into precipitous drop.

Under Margaret Thatcher, the nationalisation process was reversed and many businesses were sold off, sometimes, as in the case of British Airways, with great success.

Meanwhile, many traditional areas of activity, like mining and engineering, simply disappeared and only North Sea oil shielded Britain from a disastrous economic crash. Although manufacturing continues to play an important role (particularly in the Midlands), service industries like banking and finance have grown rapidly, particularly in London and the south-east.

Britain's weak 20th century economy has sometimes been blamed on its strong 19th century one. Investment in Britain has been consistently lower than in competitive nations. For too long Britain lived off its 19th century inheritance, leading to low growth rates and productivity improvements. The elitist education structure led to a shortage of trained technicians and craftspeople, thus compounding the problem. That old British bugbear, the class system, has also played a damaging part.

For too long British business consisted of poorly trained and short-sighted management, locked in semi-permanent conflict with an equally poorly trained workforce. They in turn were dragged back by the large chips on their collective shoulders.

For better or worse Margaret Thatcher changed much of that with her relentless assault on the power of the trade unions and the old-school-tie brigade, but by 1992 Britain's economy was in such poor shape that the government was forced into humiliating withdrawal from the European Exchange Rate Mechanism. Politically this was a disaster, but economically it marked a turning point; exchange rates fell and exporters found business looking up again in the face of a devalued pound.

In 1997 it appeared that the recession was over with the British economy in better shape than many of its European neighbours. Inflation is low and seems to be staying steady but interest rates are now rising and the strong pound had already been making life difficult for exporters before the financial crisis in Asia and Russia began to make itself felt. The first rash of factory closures in the north-east is a grim sign that another recession could well be on its way.

POPULATION & PEOPLE

Britain has a population of around 56 million, or around 600 inhabitants per sq mile, making the island one of the most crowded on the planet. Most of the population is concentrated in England (which has a population of 48 million), in and around London, and in the Midlands around Birmingham, Manchester, Liverpool, Sheffield and Nottingham. To these figures you can factor in an annual influx of nearly 26 million tourists.

The Brits are a diverse bunch, as one would expect given the variety of peoples who have made this island their home. But in general the dominant Anglo-Saxons, as they are sometimes called, are predominantly Germanic/Scandinavian in origin.

Particularly since the Industrial Revolution, England has attracted large numbers of people from Scotland, Wales and Ireland. In the 18th, 19th and 20th centuries there were also significant influxes of refugees, most recently from troubled corners of the globe like Somalia and eastern Turkey.

Since WWII there has also been significant immigration from many ex-colonies, especially the Caribbean, Pakistan and India. Outside London and the big Midlands cities, however, the population is overwhelmingly Anglo-Saxon, although the immigrant influence can be felt in the Chinese and Indian restaurants that can be found in even the smallest of towns. Recently, population growth has been virtually static, even negative, and emigrants have often outnumbered immigrants. See Society & Conduct later in this chapter.

EDUCATION

Schooling is compulsory between ages 5 and 16, and an increasing number of young people stay on at school (or sixth-form college or further education college) until they're 18. Education up to the age of 18 is free. The number of people going on to university (and the number of universities) has also been growing, putting such pressure on funding that the government now expects students to pay their own tuition and living fees by taking out loans.

Despite what should sound a fairly rosy scenario, there's a widely held perception that education standards have been falling, with hotly disputed figures suggesting a rise in the number of people escaping 11 years of compulsory schooling unable to read or write properly. The Labour government has put 'education, education, education' at the top of its list of priorities, with the emphasis on hammering the three Rs firmly into every pupil's head.

ARTS

The greatest artistic contributions of the English have been in theatre, literature and architecture. Although there are notable exceptions, there's not an equivalent tradition of great painters, sculptors or composers.

Perhaps the most distinctive phenomenon is the huge number of extraordinary country houses. Waited-on hand and foot, the elite of a mighty empire, the aristocrats of the 18th and 19th centuries surrounded themselves with treasures in the most beautiful houses and gardens of Europe.

Fortunately, although their successors have often inherited the arrogance intact, inheritance taxes have forced many to open their houses and priceless art collections to the public. England is a treasure house of masterpieces from every age and continent. The architectural heritage is superb but, with a few exceptions, the 20th century has failed to add anything more inspiring than motorways, high-rise housing estates and tawdry suburban development.

British publishers churn out 80,000 new titles a year, and the range and quality of theatre, music, dance and art is outstanding.

Literature

Anyone who has studied 'English' literature will find that the landscapes and people they have read about can still be found to some extent. Travelling in the footsteps of the great English, Scottish and Welsh writers, and their characters, can be one of the high-lights of visiting Britain. A wealth of books capture a moment in time, a landscape, or a group of people. This guide can only make a few suggestions as to where to start.

In the beginning was Chaucer with his *Canterbury Tales* (modern translation by Neville Coghill). This book may have launched a thousand boring lectures, but in its natural environment it gives a vivid insight into medieval society, in particular into the lives of pilgrims on their way to Canterbury.

The next figure to blight schoolchildren's lives was Shakespeare. Nonetheless, many will be tempted to retrace his steps – to Stratford-upon-Avon where he lived and to the new Globe Theatre in London, near the site where his works were originally dramatised.

The most vivid insight into 17th century London life comes courtesy of Samuel Pepys' diary which contains a complete account of the plague and the Great Fire of London.

The popular English novel, as we know it, only appeared in the 18th century with the growth of a literate middle class. If you plan to spend time in the Midlands, read Elizabeth Gaskell's *Mary Barton*, which paints a sympathetic picture of the plight of workers during the Industrial Revolution. This was also the milieu about which Charles Dickens wrote most powerfully. *Hard Times*, set in fictional Coketown, paints a brutal picture of the capitalists who prospered in it.

Jane Austen wrote about the prosperous, provincial middle class. The intrigues and passions boiling away under the stilted constraints of 'propriety' are beautifully portrayed in *Emma* and *Pride and Prejudice*.

If you visit the Lake District, you'll find constant references to William Wordsworth, the romantic poet who lived there for the first half of the 19th century. Modern readers may find him difficult, but at his best he has an exhilarating appreciation of the natural world.

More than most writers, Thomas Hardy depended on a sense of place and on the relationship between place and people. His best work is an evocative picture of Wessex, the region of England centred on Dorchester (Dorset) where he lived. *Tess of the d'Urbervilles* is one of his greatest novels.

Moving into the 20th century, DH Lawrence chronicled life in the Nottinghamshire coal-mining towns in the brilliant *Sons and Lovers*.

Written during the 1930s Depression, George Orwell's *Down and Out in Paris and London* describes the author's destitute existence as a temporary vagrant. Some travellers in the 1990s may find they can identify with him. At about the same time, Graham Greene wrote of the seedy side of Brighton in *Brighton Rock*.

Doris Lessing painted a picture of 1960s London in *The Four-Gated City*, a part of her 'Children of Violence' series. One of the funniest and most vicious portrayals of Britain in the 1990s is by Martin Amis in *London Observed*, a collection of stories set in the capital. In other interesting perspectives, Hanef Kureishi writes about the lives of young Pakistanis in London in *The Black Album*, and Caryl Phillips describes the Caribbean immigrants' experience in *The Final Passage*.

Theatre

London is still one of the world's theatre capitals, with a historical legacy stretching back to Shakespeare and medieval times.

The recession and a succession of penny-pinching governments have combined to make life hard, especially for innovative new theatre. Financial demands and the need for proven reliability explain a depressing growth in the theatrical art of playing safe – whether with Agatha Christie's *Mousetrap*, now in its fifth decade and the longest running play in history, or Andrew Lloyd Webber's *Cats*, now into a second decade.

The National Theatre in London is the nation's flagship theatre and offers a cocktail of revived classics, contemporary plays and appearances by radical young companies. The Barbican in London, and Stratford-upon-Avon are home to the excellent Royal Shakespeare Company. Most regional cities have at least one world-class

company and the facilities to stage major touring productions.

London's many fringe theatre productions offer an eccentric selection of the amazing, the boring, the life-changing and the downright ridiculous. On any night of the year you should also be able to watch performances of plays by great British dramatists like Harold Pinter, John Osborne, Alan Ayckbourn, Alan Bennett, David Hare and Simon Gray. Careful perusal of the schedules in *Time Out* (especially for the Royal National Theatre) may also turn up opportunities to see actors of the calibre of Dame Judi Dench, Daniel Day-Lewis or Vanessa Redgrave strut their stuff. See Entertainment in the London chapter.

Cinema

Film-makers are constantly whingeing that if only there was sufficient funding and support at home, then British directors and actors (Alan Rickman, Tim Roth, Emma Thompson, Mike Figgis ...) wouldn't have to move to Hollywood for work. Even film-makers who mostly work within the country aren't always assured of support. Mike Leigh, who won the 1996 Palme d'Or at the Cannes Film Festival for *Secrets and Lies*, has made several compelling movies about contemporary Britain which were considered too political to be supported.

It's a pity because there is a wealth of talent and tradition associated with film in England. The good news is that Elstree Studios, where the clever bits in *Star Wars* were made, is open again and the BBC has now joined Channel Four (*Four Weddings and a Funeral*) in making movies. The new government has also made encouraging noises about supporting the home film industry, spurred by the success of movies like *The Full Monty*. See Films in the Regional Facts for the Visitor chapter.

Classical Music & Opera

Arguably, London is Europe's classical music capital, and most of the major companies undertake country-wide tours. There are five symphony orchestras, various smaller outfits, a wonderful array of venues, reasonable prices and high standards of performance. The biggest dilemma facing concertgoers is the enviable one of picking from the embarrassment of riches on offer.

Despite this, finding home-grown classical music to listen to can be a struggle. Until this century virtually the only truly major British composer was Henry Purcell (1659-95). But you should be able to track down concerts of music by big 20th century names like Edward Elgar, Ralph Vaughan Williams, Benjamin Britten or William Walton. John Tavener is also riding high on a wave of popularity after his music was played to a worldwide audience at the funeral of Diana, Princess of Wales.

London's flagship opera company, based at the Royal Opera House, is constantly beset by money difficulties but manages to maintain its five-star rating, regularly nabbing opera superstars. The recent popularity of opera in England is partly thanks to Pavarotti's massive hit with Puccini's 'Nessum Dorma'. The English love a good tune.

See Entertainment in the London chapter.

Popular Music

English musicians have had an enormous impact on popular music, much greater, strangely, than their influence on 'serious' music.

We could begin a survey with Gilbert and Sullivan's light operas – but we won't. The swinging 60s produced the Beatles, the Rolling Stones, the Who and the Kinks. The late 60s and the glam years of the early 70s had such stardust-speckled heroes as David Bowie, Marc Bolan and Bryan Ferry, and bands like Fleetwood Mac, Pink Floyd, Deep Purple, Led Zeppelin and Genesis. They were followed by punk's best known spokesmen, the Sex Pistols and the Clash.

The turbulent, ever-changing music scene of the 80s saw the new romantics, left-wing 'agitpop', and the development of a club and rave scene featuring house and techno music. Bands that made it big included the Police, the Eurythmics, Wham, Duran Duran, Dire Straits, UB40 and the Smiths.

In the early 1990s, American grunge dominated rock music. However, the late 90s brought post-grunge music and the renaissance of the quintessentially English indie pop band with the likes of Blur, Elastica, Pulp, Suede and above all Oasis.

Passing in haste over the Spice Girls, the biggest band of the moment is probably The Verve. They, along with hundreds of new bands, confirm the continuing power of British pop to reinvent itself, even if the Britpop bubble has burst and record sales are falling.

All the major cities offer a variety of musical performances. See the Entertainment sections of the relevant entries, especially London.

Visual Arts

William Hogarth (1697-1764) emancipated British art from European influences with a series of paintings and engravings satirising social abuses. The most famous of these is probably A Rake's Progress. The founding president of the Royal Academy, Joshua Reynolds (1723-92), and his rival Thomas Gainsborough (1727-88) raised the artist to a new level of dignity in England; the former through his prodigious output and influence on men of letters such as Dr Samuel Johnson and James Boswell; the latter through his individual genius and the patronage of the Royal Family.

The tradition of landscape painting, which started with Gainsborough, was continued by John Constable (1776-1837) and was the inspiration for a whole generation of French impressionists. Constable's contemporary romantics, William Blake (1757-1827) and JMW Turner (1775-1851) could not have been more different. Blake used personal symbolism to express a mystical philosophy in drawings, prints and poetry – he disliked oils and canvas. Turner on the other hand, was equally at home with oils as he was with watercolours and he increasingly subordinated detail to the effects of light and colour. By the 1830s, with paintings such as Snow Storm: Steam-boat off a Harbour's Mouth, his compositions seemed entirely abstract and were widely vilified.

John Everett Millais *(Christ in the House of His Parents;* 1850*)* and William Holman Hunt *(The Scapegoat;* 1854) attempted to recapture the simplicity of early Italian art. This gave way to the pseudo-medievalism of Dante Gabriel Rossetti *(Beata Beatrix;* 1864) and his followers Edward Burne-Jones *(King Cophetua and the Beggar Maid;* 1862) and William Morris (1834-96). Morris has had a lasting influence in the design of English furniture, tapestry, stained-glass and fabrics, and his emphasis on good workmanship has been the inspiration for generations of small, craft-based workshops in England.

In the 20th century the monumental sculptures of Henry Moore (1898-1986), the contorted, almost surreal, painting of Francis Bacon (1909-92), and David Hockney's stylish, highly representational paintings of friends, swimmers and dachshunds, have ensured the place of British art in the international arena.

Both Paul Nash (1889-1949), who was an official war artist in WWI and WWII and Graham Sutherland (1903-80), followed in the romantic and visionary tradition of Blake, Samuel Palmer, and Turner. Nash introduced surrealism to English painting and incidentally wrote *The Shell Guide to Dorset* (1936). Sutherland is renowned for his paintings (also as an official WWII artist) of ruined buildings. Moore's drawings of people sheltering from air-raids in London's underground (also as an official war artist) consolidated his reputation as one of the most influential English artists of all time.

Richard Hamilton's photomontage *Just what is it that makes today's homes so different, so appealing?* (1956) launched the pop art movement in England. Peter Blake designed the cover of the Beatles' *Sergeant Pepper's Lonely Hearts Club Band* (1967) and heralded an explosion of British popular culture.

In the seventies and eighties conceptual artists and land artists such as Richard Long competed with performance artists such as Gilbert and George. Through the Thatcher era the commercial galleries held sway until in the 1990s a number of prolific young artists working in a variety of media have burst upon the scene: Rachel Whiteread's resin casts of commonplace objects, including an entire East End house, have earned her international acclaim; Damien Hirst's use of animals, both alive and dead, in his work has provoked much debate; Tracey Emin sewed the names of everyone she'd ever slept with inside a tent; and the Chapman brothers' gross figures with misplaced genitals have attracted the attention of censors.

In the year 2000 the Tate Gallery will move its international collection to a new gallery housed in the old Bankside power station next to the newly reconstructed Globe Theatre. The original Tate Gallery at Millbank will then become the Tate Gallery of British Art.

ARCHITECTURE

Britain's architectural heritage reaches back more than 5000 years to the remarkable Stonehenge, and the village of Skara Brae in Orkney. Although the record is sometimes sparse, there are survivors from every period after that.

Roman and Saxon work is rare, which is not so surprising considering the Roman heyday is getting close to 2000 years old. Complete Norman buildings are also rare but there are still many examples of 900-year-old craftsmanship in everyday use especially in the many churches and cathedrals.

Buildings from the 16th and 17th centuries are more common, and more ordinary domestic architecture survives alongside the grand houses. Rural Britain is still home to a number of thatched cob cottages, many of which date back to the 17th century.

Some of the styles that can be seen in churches also appeared in the castles. While church design focused more on decorative or imaginative elements, the design of castles was based largely around their military function. The benefits of living in a large utilitarian pile of stones, however, gradually vanished as times grew more peaceful.

From the 16th century, most of the great architectural innovations were made in houses. Often the English nobility adopted, and adapted, various European styles. Sometimes castles were completely abandoned, or swallowed up by new, improved versions.

One of the most distinctive features of the English countryside and of English culture is the ongoing love affair between the rich and their enormous, and beautiful, country residences. No other country has a comparable number. Like churches, many have evolved over time and incorporate all sorts of architectural styles.

Monumental British architecture has always been outstanding and domestic vernacular architecture was certainly visually appealing up to the Industrial Revolution. But since then the guiding principle for builders and architects has often been to spend as little money as possible; aesthetic considerations were for the wealthy few. Post WWII, much building has shown a lack of regard for the overall fabric of the cities. Prince Charles, for one, has been an outspoken advocate of a more humanistic and aesthetically sensitive architectural approach.

It's not all bad news though, and some fine new buildings do make it past the drawing board, especially in London, where the Lloyd's building is one stunning example.

Fortunately, there's also a strong campaign to protect the island's architectural heritage (thanks in particular to the National Trust and English Heritage). This nostalgic obsession is, however, sometimes carried to extremes and can encourage conservatism in modern British architecture and design.

While distinct architectural styles and periods in Britain are certainly identifiable, the categories were not always rigid: different styles often influenced each other, and certain periods partially overlapped.

The standard works of reference on British architecture are the wonderfully detailed *Buildings of Britain* books by Nikolaus Pevsner. See the architectural glossary at the end of this book for architectural terms.

Church Architecture

As buildings surviving from the middle ages, England's many fine medieval churches provide numerous examples of interesting and unique architecture, and attract a large number of curious visitors.

While this rich collection of churches is of great interest to history and architecture buffs, the terminology can be confusing to outsiders. You're invited to inspect ceilings in chancels, inscriptions in naves, misericords in choirs, monuments in chapels, and tombs in transepts. Furthermore, the church might be Saxon or Norman, Early English or perpendicular, or more likely a combination of two or more of these styles. It may not even be a church after all, but an abbey, chapel, minster or cathedral. What does it all mean?

Basically no matter what the name, they're all places of Christian worship. Technically, a cathedral is the principal church of a diocese and contains the bishop's throne (a diocese is the district for which a bishop is responsible). In practice a cathedral is usually larger and grander than a church, although there are some large churches and some small cathedrals. In contrast, a church is usually a more local affair; the term 'parish church' indicates that local nature. Chapels are even smaller than churches, and are often the 'churches' of Non-Conformist groups like Methodists or Baptists.

An abbey was where a group of monks or nuns lived. The abbey church was a church intended principally for use by the monks or nuns, rather than the general population.

When Henry VIII dissolved the monasteries in the 1530s, many of the abbeys in England and Ireland were destroyed or converted into private homes, although some survived as churches. Thus there are abbey churches which were taken over by the general populace (like Malmesbury Abbey in Wiltshire) and also stately homes which are known as abbeys (like Beaulieu Abbey in Hampshire). A minster (like Wimborne Minster in Dorset) refers to a church at one time connected to a monastery.

English churches are fascinating to wander around, especially once you've learnt something about the various periods, styles and design elements. Very few of them are uniformly of one style. Usually a window from one period has cut into a wall from another. When decay, subsidence or an accident brought part of a church down, the reconstruction was carried out in whatever was the current style; growing congregations or increased wealth often inspired extensions or more magnificent towers or spires, inevitably in the latest style.

Political changes also affected churches and their design. For example, the Reformation of the 16th and 17th centuries saw an attack on imagery in churches and many statues and images were destroyed, particularly during the attack on 'Popish' influence during the reign of Mary I.

Although the great churches were often built using the cutting edge of building technology for their particular time, it wasn't unusual for catastrophic collapses to occur even during construction.

Architectural Styles & Periods

Neolithic & Bronze Ages The communal burial mounds of the agriculturally-based Neolithic people comprise some of the oldest surviving examples of construction in Britain. Dating from around 3500 BC, these 'barrows' are concentrated around the chalky regions of Dorset and Wiltshire.

Stonehenge, arguably Britain's most famous historical landmark, is thought to have been built by a Bronze Age race. Construction on this mysterious monolithic circle began around 3000 BC.

Celtic & Roman The Celtic invaders began to arrive in 700 BC, ushering in the Iron Age and building a number of fortified villages and hilltop forts; Maiden Castle in Dorset is one impressive example.

The Celts were followed about 700 years later by the Roman invaders. The Roman occupation lasted 350 years and left behind an impressive architectural legacy, including the grand Fishbourne Palace in West Sussex (built around 75 AD), and several Roman baths (one of which gave the town of Bath its name).

Anglo-Saxon Following the withdrawal of the Romans, the Vikings were the next invaders to set foot on English soil. England's first churches were built during this Anglo-Saxon era (from around 700 to 1050 AD). Saxon churches were generally small, squat, solid and unembellished, and were characterised by round arches and square towers.

Since most Anglo-Saxon churches were built of wood, few survive. Stone churches have fared better; a notable example is St Laurence in Bradford-on-Avon, Wiltshire. All Saints at Brixworth and All Saints at Earls Barton, both near Northampton, have very clear Anglo-Saxon origins.

Norman After the Norman invasion of 1066, Saxon architecture gave way to Norman; as in Saxon churches, the architectural style was characterised by rounded arches and squat, square towers. The difference in appearance largely comes down to questions of detail and decoration.

The Norman style lasted only about a century, but surviving Norman churches are generally larger than their Saxon predecessors. 'Massive', 'thick' and 'bulky' are all adjectives applied to the Norman style.

There are no purely Norman churches left in England but Norwich, Peterborough and Durham cathedrals are all predominantly Norman.

Gothic The Gothic style developed primarily to serve the needs of the church. The period spanned almost four centuries and is classified into three distinct but related styles. Gothic churches look much lighter and more delicate than their heavier predecessors.

Early English The Early English style was popular from around 1150 to 1280; this period was the first distinct phase of Gothic design, although the Gothic tag itself was not dreamt up until the 17th century. Early English churches are characterised by pointed arches, ribbed vaults and lancet windows (narrow, pointed windows used singly or in groups).

Salisbury Cathedral is the finest example of Early English; Lichfield Cathedral, and Rievaulx Abbey in Yorkshire in Northern England chapter), are also mostly Early English.

Decorated The mid-Gothic or Decorated period followed Early English from 1280 to 1380. As the name indicates, the Decorated period was marked by ornate window tracery and other elaborate design elements.

Examples of the style include the chapter houses of Salisbury Cathedral and Southwell Minster, the naves of Lichfield Cathedral and Exeter Cathedral, the Angel Choir at Lincoln Cathedral and the chapter house of York Minster.

Perpendicular The third Gothic phase thrived between 1380 and 1550 and saw the ornate tracery of the Decorated period give way to more rectilinear designs with an em-phasis on strong vertical lines. The nave of Canterbury Cathedral is a good example.

Engineering developments meant that arches could span further and windows could be much larger and closer together so many of the perpendicular churches are fantastically light and spacious. Stained glass and elaborate fan vaults were also widely featured, notably at King's College Chapel in Cambridge and Henry VII's Chapel in Westminster Abbey.

Many half-timbered houses survive from this time, their great oak beam frames infilled with brick and other materials; examples can be found in Kent, Cheshire, Hereford and Worcestershire.

Elizabethan & Jacobean During the Gothic period most domestic architecture was either very modest or primarily defensive. The terms Early English, Decorated and perpendicular are not very relevant to ruggedly constructed castles. However, by the mid-16th century domestic architecture is much more important.

Reivaulx Abbey in Yorkshire is an example of Early English design and displays typical features of the style.

After the Reformation, church architecture came to a virtual standstill for a century and in more peaceful times, impressing the neighbours was more important than physically fighting them off.

Houses such as Hardwick Hall and Knole combine the perpendicular's large areas of glass with the beginnings of an understanding of classical architecture, both in terms of overall proportions and symmetry and in details such as columns and cornices.

Renaissance In the first half of the 16th century, Henry VIII brought in French, Flemish, and Italian craftsmen to work on the royal palaces, and this imported talent was largely responsible for the introduction of what's sometimes called the Renaissance architectural style. Although Renaissance architecture began in Italy about 1420, pure

classical architecture in Britain had to wait much longer.

Palladianism The course of English architecture was fundamentally altered not once but twice by the work of the Italian architect Andrea Palladio. His famous 'Four Books of Architecture' showing his own austere buildings and his imagined reconstructions of Roman ruins was published in 1570 and the illustrations were closely followed by Inigo Jones who built his masterpieces – the Banqueting Hall (London) and Queen's House (Greenwich) – around 1620.

English Baroque Like the Renaissance style, the baroque originated in Italy. In England it came later (late 17th century to the 1720s) and was less well defined but includes the work of some of the most famous and flamboyant architects. It uses classical

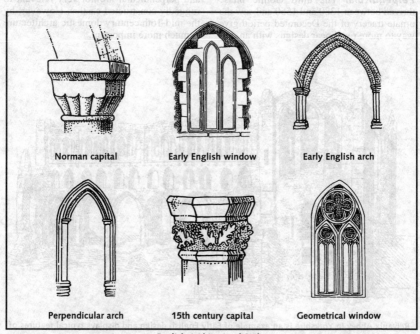

Norman capital   Early English window   Early English arch

Perpendicular arch   15th century capital   Geometrical window

English Architectural Styles

features such as columns, arches and pediments in an exuberant way with dramatic juxtapositions of forms and amazingly elaborate silhouettes.

The greatest and most influential baroque architect was Sir Christopher Wren who, in the aftermath of the Great Fire of 1666, radically changed the appearance of the City of London. His masterpiece is St Paul's Cathedral, but he was responsible for no less than 53 churches. The secular style is most famous in the work of Nicholas Hawksmoor and Sir John Vanbrugh, who collaborated on Castle Howard and Blenheim Palace.

Neo-Palladianism Lord Burlington, an aesthetically minded aristocrat, was responsible for a return to simpler classical forms after the excesses of the baroque period. In the design of his own house at Chiswick (London) he lead the way with strict adherence to rules of proportion and symmetry and soon the accepted form for country houses was a central block with a columned portico and flanking wings. Holkham Hall in Norfolk (by William Kent 1734) and Prior Park, Bath (by John Wood the Elder 1735) are good examples.

The terraced houses of John Wood the Elder and John Wood the Younger in Bath, and Robert Adam in Edinburgh show the same ideals put to different use in a city context.

Neoclassicism The neoclassical style, which flourished between 1760 and 1830 was the result of a more accurate study of classical ruins, not only in Italy but in Greece and Asia Minor. A new generation of architects had a bigger vocabulary of classical motifs and felt free to assemble them as they wished.

Architect Robert Adam was a key proponent of the style, and was known for his decorative interiors; the house at No 20 Portman Square in London, is one famous example of his work.

There was little religious building during the 17th century apart from Sir Christopher Wren's magnificent St Paul's Cathedral (and other London churches), which adopted neoclassical designs copied from the continent.

Gothic & Greek Revivals The Greek Revival countered the more eclectic approach of neoclassicism with an emphasis on accurate recreations of Greek forms and aimed to replicate the heavy massing of Greek prototypes.

The British Museum, designed by Sir Robert Smirke and built between 1823 and 1846, is one notable example of this style which started at the end of the 18th century and carried on until the 1840s.

The first phase of the Gothic Revival (1840s) was based on earnest historic research but this was combined with a passionate belief that a return to Gothic architecture could achieve social reform and that classicism was linked to the urban depravations of industrialism.

Decorated and occasionally Early English Gothic were design sources for churches, schools and vicarages with asymmetric, irregular, plans. High Victorian Gothic used a wider range of sources, including perpendicular, north Italian and French Gothic forms for all types of building. The Houses of Parliament by Augustus Pugin and Sir Charles Barry are an early example of Gothic Revival architecture, while Manchester Town Hall by Alfred Waterhouse 1868, shows how the style had moved on.

Arts and Crafts Heavy-handed Victorian church 'restorations' (often a complete rebuilding) inspired William Morris to found the Society for the Protection of Ancient Buildings in 1877. Morris' ideas, together with the writings of John Ruskin, led to an increased appreciation of craft skills in new building as well as restorations. Many very original buildings as well as new ideas about planning and layout of towns meant that Britain was very influential at this period. Foreign visitors were especially interested in the Garden City Movement of which Letchworth is the first example.

20th Century The rise of Nazism meant that many European modern movement architects fled to Britain in the 1920s and 1930s and had a profound effect. One of the most famous and fun examples of their work is the Penguin Pool at London Zoo by Lubetkin.

Swedish modernism was also influential, evident from the huge number of post-war housing estates and public buildings, replacing bomb damage as well as slum clearance. The tough, sculptural concrete buildings in 1960s brutalist style, such as the National Theatre by Sir Denys Lasdun, are just beginning to be appreciated again.

During the late 1970s and early 1980s, two distinct responses to modernism developed. High-tech architecture celebrated the potential of technology usually with complex lightweight structural skeletons such as Stansted airport by Norman Foster, the Waterloo International train terminal by Nicholas Grimshaw and the Lloyd's Building in London with brilliantly coloured service pipes on the outside.

In contrast postmodern architects returned once more to traditional architectural vocabularies, assembly motifs from many different styles in an ironic way.

In the 1980s the redevelopment of Docklands gave the greatest scope for postmodern architecture, often by American architects, and has been severely criticised. Terry Farrell's buildings on the Thames at Charing Cross and Vauxhall are more popular.

Today the boundaries are harder to define, although many young architects are using restaurant and bar jobs to make a very minimal style fashionable.

Diverse, recent additions to the cityscape include the London Ark by Ralph Erskine and the controversial Millennium Dome, a saucer-shaped building with a distinct space-age feel, in Greenwich.

In addition to London, Oxford and Cambridge are ideal places to see recent architecture as the colleges have commissioned many imaginative projects.

SOCIETY & CONDUCT
Traditional Culture

It's difficult to generalise about the English and their culture but there's no doubt they're a creative, energetic and aggressive people who've had an impact on the world that's entirely out of proportion to their numbers.

Many visitors arrive with strong preconceptions about English characteristics, the most common being that the English are reserved, inhibited and stiflingly polite. The reaction to the death of Princess Diana showed just how outdated this stereotype is. Remember, however, that Britain is one of the planet's most tourist-inundated and crowded countries and that some of the famed reserve is a protective veneer developed to help deal with a constant crush of people. Remember also, that although regional and class differences have shrunk, accents and behaviour still vary widely depending on where you are and who you're mixing it with.

Terms like 'stiff-upper-lip', 'cold' and 'conservative' might apply to some sections of the middle and upper classes, but in general they don't apply to the working class, or to northerners. Visit a nightclub in one of the big cities, a football match, a good local pub, or a country B&B and other terms, like uninhibited, tolerant, exhibitionist, passionate, aggressive, sentimental, hospitable and friendly, might spring to mind more readily.

No country in the world has more obsessive hobbyists, some of whom teeter on the edge of complete madness. Train and bus spotters, twitchers, sports fanatics, fashion victims, royalists, model-makers, egg collectors, ramblers, pet owners, gardeners, they all find a home here.

England is a country of sceptical individualists who deeply resent any intrusion on their privacy or freedom, so it's hardly surprising that their flirtation with state socialism was brief. Change happens slowly, and only after endless consultations, committee meetings, departmental get-togethers and government referrals.

Dianamania

The scenes of mass hysteria that followed the death of the Princess of Wales in 1997 surprised the world almost as much as her death had done. So many flowers were deposited outside Kensington Palace, her London home, that it took three weeks to clear them away.

For almost a year the 'Grief Police' patrolled the British press ensuring that anything Di was treated with absolute reverence. It was like losing a relative and we all needed time to grieve, many said. It was a real tragedy, but a personal tragedy for each of us?

One year on, as the Dianaversary approached, it seemed that the media expected us to do it all again.

But most Britons had had enough. A week before the anniversary a Diana charity walk was organised, with 15,000 people expected. Just 300 turned up. Flowers were once again left by the railings outside Kensington Palace, but nothing like the number that had been brought the previous year.

The British press, however, dared not offend and most papers reported an atmosphere of 'quiet remembrance' as the anniversary approached. It was no holds barred as far as the rest of the world's press was concerned, and some even went as far as *Il Messaggero*, the Italian newspaper, which mocked Diana as 'the embodiment of the spiritual vacuum of our time'.

The debate drags on about how best to commemorate Diana. Althorp, her childhood home where she is buried, can be visited only in July and August and tickets are expensive and must be arranged in advance so it's not really a public memorial to the princess. In Harrods department store, owner Mohammed Fayed has erected a gilt Dodi and Diana shrine that can be visited. Above the crash site in Paris stands the 9m-high replica of the flame from the Statue of Liberty. Given to the French by the American people in 1987, it's been hijacked as a shrine to the princess and is now plastered with messages, flowers and photographs.

There are over 100 applications around Britain to dedicate gardens in Diana's name. Best known is for a special garden in front of Kensington Palace, although it now seems that local residents will block the planning application. There's certainly no shortage of appropriate plants for these gardens; there's already a Princess of Wales rose, a Diana ivy and a Princess of Wales clematis.

Whether it's to be a traditional stone memorial or a garden of remembrance, the sooner a permanent memorial is erected to Diana the better. We can then all let her rest in peace and get on with our own lives.

Bryn Thomas

Dos & Don'ts

Britain being the reasonably tolerant place it is, it's not particularly easy to cause offence without meaning to. That said, it's as well to be aware that most locals would no sooner speak to a stranger in the street than fly to the moon. If you're obviously a tourist battling with directions, there's no problem – but try starting a general conversation at the bus stop and you'll find people staring at you as if you're mad.

Queuing The British are notoriously addicted to queuing, and many comedy sketches depend on the audience accepting that people might actually join a queue without knowing what it's for. The order of the queue is sacrosanct – few things are more calculated to spark an outburst of tutting than an attempt to 'push in' to a queue.

Clothes In some countries what you wear or don't wear in churches can get you into trouble. In general, Britain is as free and easy about this as it is about how you dress in the streets. Bear in mind, however, that if you go into mosques or temples you may be expected to take off your shoes and cover your arms, legs and/or head.

Some classy restaurants and many clubs operate strict dress codes. In restaurants that usually means a jacket and tie for men and no trainers for anyone; in clubs it means whatever the management and their bouncers choose it to mean and can vary from night to night.

Treatment of Animals

The English are widely believed to love their animals more than their children: the Royal Society for the Prevention of Cruelty to Animals was established before the National Society for the Prevention of Cruelty to Children and still rakes in more donations.

Not surprisingly, fox hunting, the ancient sport derided by Oscar Wilde as 'the unspeakable in pursuit of the inedible', has become highly controversial.

Britain's 200-odd hunts are estimated to kill about 20,000 foxes a year (another 40,000 are killed by vehicles and over 100,000 are trapped or shot). Pro-hunt campaigners argue that many foxes actually owe their existence to the hunters since fox-hunting farmers are less likely to dig up the hedgerows and small woods that provide living quarters for their prey.

Nevertheless, most people see hunting as a cruel sport, inappropriate to a 'civilised' society at the end of the 20th century. Anti-hunting sentiment in England runs strong and polls suggest that two-thirds to three-quarters of the population would support a ban, figures mirrored in a recent free vote on the subject in parliament. Unfortunately the pro-hunters are a well-organised and powerful bunch. Their success in rallying thousands of supporters for a Countryside rally in London in 1998 frightened the government off implementing the ban the vote should have made possible.

As often in England, hunting is tied up with class. Hunting is mainly a sport of the upper class or at least the wealthy. The famous attire, starting with a 'pink' (which in fox hunting parlance means red!) jacket, can cost thousands from a London tailor and that's before the fees to join a specific hunt and the cost of the horses.

Recent years have seen high-profile lobbies against factory farming and the export of live animals. Perhaps 10% of the population are vegetarians, or near vegetarians. Most supermarkets stock free-range eggs and meat supposedly from animals who have been allowed to roam free. Don't expect such sops to the conscience to be cheap.

RELIGION

The Church of England, a Christian church that became independent of Rome in the 16th century (see the Tudors under History earlier in this chapter), is the largest, wealthiest and most influential in the land. Like the Church of Scotland, it's an 'established' church, meaning that it's officially the national church, with a close relationship with the state (the queen or king appoints archbishops and bishops on the advice of the prime minister).

Although 70% of the population still claim to be Christian, the latest survey suggests that only 8.2% regularly attend church, a fall of a million people in the last 20 years. It's difficult to generalise about the form of worship that varies from the pomp and ceremony of High church, to the less traditional Low church, which has been more influenced by Protestantism and, more recently by the evangelical movement. Evangelical and charismatic churches are the only ones attracting growing congregations.

Traditionally, the Church of England has been aligned with the ruling classes but some sectors became very critical of the Conservatives in their declining years. In 1994, after many years of agonising, the first women were ordained as priests. The debate has now moved on to the rights and wrongs of gay priests.

Other significant Protestant churches with no connection to the state include Methodists, Baptists, the United Reformed Church and the Salvation Army.

At times since the 16th century, Roman Catholics have been terribly persecuted; one modern legacy is the ongoing problem of Northern Ireland. Today about one in 10 Britons considers themselves a Catholic but over the last 20 years the number attending mass has also slumped.

Recent estimates suggest there are now well over one million Muslims, together with significant numbers of Sikhs and Hindus. Nowadays more English non-Christians visit their places of worship than do Christians.

LANGUAGE

English is probably England's most significant contribution to the modern world. The English, of every class and background, take enormous pleasure in using their language and idiom inventively (nowhere, for instance, are there more crossword fanatics). The language continues to evolve and to be used and exploited to the full. See the glossary at the back of this book for examples.

English English can be incomprehensible to overseas visitors – even to those who assume they've spoken it all their lives. Regional dialects may be disappearing, but significant variations, especially in accent, still flourish and some can be virtually impenetrable to outsiders. It's OK to ask someone to repeat what they've said, but laughing at them is unlikely to go down well.

London

Once the capital of the greatest empire the world has ever known, London is still Europe's largest city and is embedded in the culture, vocabulary and dreams of English speakers worldwide. At times it will be more grand, evocative, beautiful and stimulating than you could have imagined; at others it will be colder, greyer, dirtier and more expensive than you believed possible.

It's a cosmopolitan mixture of Third and First World, of chauffeurs and beggars, of the establishment and the avant-garde, with seven to 12 million inhabitants (depending on where you stop counting), and 26 million visitors a year. As you'll soon discover, many of the visitors are extremely wealthy. Fortunately for the budget traveller however, the majority aren't. You'll know immediately what side of this divide you're on and will discover a London that caters to those who work long hours for lousy wages.

London is a challenge for the budget traveller. Money has a way of mysteriously evaporating every time you move. With limited funds it's necessary to plan, book ahead and prioritise. There's little point in putting up with the crowds, the underground and the pollution if you can't take advantage of at least some of the theatres, exhibitions, shops, pubs and clubs, cafés and restaurants. On a moderate budget, you can find reasonable value. And some of the very best remains free or very cheap.

After the gloom of the early 90s, London is on the up and up. The restaurants are full, the shops are heaving with buyers, the nightlife has never been glitzier. Wherever you look you'll see cranes and scaffolding as a splurge of Lottery-funded renovation work readies the capital for the millennium. Everyone seems agreed that London's the place to be right now. *Newsweek* let the cat out of the bag when it dubbed London the coolest city in the world – but then any Londoner could have told them that!

HIGHLIGHTS

- Battling the crowds at the British Museum
- Taking a quiet Wednesday evening tour of the National Gallery
- Attending an outdoor concert at Kenwood House
- Seeing Shakespeare performed at the new Globe Theatre
- Sailing downriver to Greenwich
- Sailing upriver to Hampton Court
- Gawping at the Blue Whale in the Natural History Museum
- Strolling round Soho on a summer evening
- Eating at one of the 'happening' London restaurants
- Spending Sunday morning at a street market

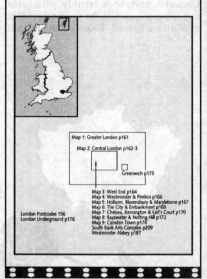

Map 1: Greater London p161
Map 2: Central London p162-3

Greenwich p175

Map 3: West End p164
Map 4: Westminster & Pimlico p166
Map 5: Holborn, Bloomsbury & Marylebone p167
Map 6: The City & Embankment p168
Map 7: Chelsea, Kensington & Earl's Court p170
Map 8: Bayswater & Notting Hill p172
Map 9: Camden Town p174
South Bank Arts Complex p209
Westminster Abbey p187

London Postcodes 156
London Underground p176

HISTORY

Although a Celtic community established itself around a ford across the River Thames, it was the Romans who first developed the square mile now known as the City of London. They built a bridge and an impressive city wall, and made the city an important port and the hub of their road system.

The Romans left, but trade went on. Few traces of Dark Age London can now be found, but the city survived the incursions of the Saxons and Vikings. Fifty years before the Normans arrived, Edward the Confessor built his abbey and palace at Westminster.

William the Conqueror found a city that was, without doubt, the richest and largest in the kingdom. He raised the White Tower (part of the Tower of London) and confirmed the city's independence and right to self-government.

During the reign of Elizabeth I the capital began to expand rapidly. Unfortunately, medieval, Tudor and Jacobean London was virtually destroyed by the Great Fire of 1666. The fire gave Sir Christopher Wren the opportunity to build his famous churches, but did nothing to halt or discipline the city's growth.

By 1720 there were 750,000 people, and London, as the seat of parliament and focal point for a growing empire, was becoming ever richer and more important. Georgian architects replaced the last of medieval London with their imposing symmetrical architecture and residential squares.

As a result of the Industrial Revolution and rapidly expanding commerce, the population jumped from 2.7 million in 1851 to 6.6 million in 1901 and a vast expanse of suburbs developed to accommodate them.

Georgian and Victorian London was devastated by the Luftwaffe in WWII – huge swathes of the centre and the East End were totally flattened. After the war, ugly housing and low-cost developments were thrown up on the bomb sites. The docks never recovered – shipping moved to Tilbury, and the Docklands declined to the point of dereliction, until rediscovery by developers in the 1980s.

Riding on a wave of Thatcherite confidence and deregulation, London boomed in the 1980s. The new wave of property developers proved to be only marginally more discriminating than the Luftwaffe, and most think their buildings only slightly better than the eyesores of the 1950s. What you'll think of the controversial Millennium Dome taking shape at Charlton near Greenwich remains to be seen.

Sometime during the lifetime of this volume, Londoners are going to elect a new citywide mayor. High-profile hopeful candidates include left-wing MP Ken Livingstone, actress-turned-MP Glenda Jackson and maverick novelist Jeffrey Archer.

ORIENTATION

London's main geographical feature is the Thames, a tidal river that enabled an easily defended port to be established far from the dangers of the English Channel. Flowing around wide bends from west to east, it divides the city into northern and southern halves.

London sprawls over an enormous area. Fortunately, the underground system (the 'tube') makes most of it easily accessible, and the ubiquitous (though geographically misleading) underground map is easy to use. Any train heading from left to right on the map is designated as eastbound, any train heading from top to bottom is southbound. Each line has its own colour.

Most important sights, theatres, restaurants and even some cheap places to stay lie within a reasonably compact rectangle formed by the tube's Circle line, just to the north of the river. All the international airports lie some distance from the city centre but transport is easy. See Getting Around later in this chapter for details on airport transport.

London blankets mostly imperceptible hills, but there are good views from Primrose Hill (adjoining Regent's Park), Hampstead Heath (north of Camden), and Greenwich Park (downriver east of central London). Throughout this chapter, the nearest tube station has been given with addresses; the

LONDON POSTCODES

Central London map shows the location of tube stations and the areas covered by the detailed district maps.

Maps

A decent map is vital. Ideally, get a single-sheet map so you can see all of central London at a glance; the British Tourist Authority (BTA) produces a good one or there's the *A-Z Map of London*. The more discreet *A-Z Visitor's Atlas & Guide* is less likely to label you a stranger.

Terminology

'London' is an imprecise term used loosely to describe the over 2000 sq km of Greater London enclosed by the M25 ring road.

London is not administered as a single unit, but divided into widely differing boroughs governed by local governments with significant autonomy.

Boroughs are further subdivided into districts (or suburbs, or precincts if you prefer), which mainly tally with the first group of letters and numbers of the postal code. The letters correspond to compass directions from the centre of London, which according to the post office must lie somewhere not too far from St Paul's Cathedral: EC means East Central, WC means West Central, W means West, NW means North West, and so on. The numbering system after the letters is less helpful: 1 is the centre of the zone, higher numbers relate to the alphabetical order of the postal-district names, which are not always in common use.

Districts and postal codes are often given on street signs, which is obviously vital when names are duplicated (there are 47 Station Roads), or cross through a number of districts. To further confuse visitors, many streets change name – Holland Park Ave becomes Notting Hill Gate, which becomes Bayswater Rd, which becomes Oxford St ... Sometimes they duck and weave like the country lanes they once were. Street numbering can also bewilder: on big streets the numbers on opposite sides can be way out of kilter (315 might be opposite 520) or, for variation, they can go up one side and down the other.

The City & the East

The City refers to the area that was once the Roman and medieval walled city, before the inexorable colonisation of the surrounding towns and villages began. Although it lies in the south-eastern corner of the Circle line, the City is regarded as the centre of London. As you may have guessed, the West End (much more the tourist centre) lies to the west of the City.

The City is one of the world's most important financial centres; full of bankers and dealers during the working week, deserted outside work hours. Here, too, you'll find the Tower of London, St Paul's Cathedral and Petticoat Lane market.

To the east, beyond the Circle line, is the cultural melting pot of the East End which incorporates districts like Shoreditch and Bethnal Green, with some lively corners and relatively cheap rents. In general though it's blighted by traffic and urban decay. Much of the East End was flattened during WWII and it still shows.

Farther east again lie the Docklands. Once part of the busiest port in the world, these thousands of acres of prime real estate fell into disuse after WWII, mirroring the decline of the empire. In the early 1980s, the property developers moved in and they're still hard at work. It's well worth visiting, especially on Sunday when the light railway offers a commentary on the mess of old and new buildings below you.

The West

West of the City, but before the West End proper, are Holborn and Bloomsbury. Holborn (pronounced hoeburn) is Britain's sedate legal heartland, the home of Rumpole and common law. Bloomsbury is still synonymous with the literary and publishing worlds. Besides dozens of specialist shops, this is where you'll find the incomparable British Museum, stuffed to the hilt with loot from every corner of the globe.

The West End proper lies west of Tottenham Court Rd and Covent Garden, which is tourist-ridden but fun, and south of Oxford St, an endless succession of department stores. It includes such magnets as Trafalgar Square, the restaurants and clubs of predominantly gay Soho, the famous West End cinemas and theatres around Piccadilly Circus and Leicester Square, and the elegant shops of Regent and Bond Sts – not forgetting Mayfair, the most valuable property on the Monopoly board.

St James's and Westminster lie to the south-west. This is where you'll find Whitehall, No 10 Downing St, the Houses of Parliament, Big Ben, Westminster Abbey and Buckingham Palace.

To the south of Victoria station lies Pimlico, not a particularly attractive district but with a few cheapish, decent hotels to top up the lure of the Tate Gallery.

Earl's Court, South Kensington and Chelsea are in the south-west corner formed by the Circle line. Earl's Court, once infamous as Kangaroo Valley and home to countless expatriate Australians, now feels more Middle Eastern but still boasts the drawcards of some cheap hotels, several backpackers' hostels and a couple of Australian pubs, plus cheap restaurants and travel agents. It's still a good enough place to start your visit.

South Kensington is much more chic and trendy, with a clutch of world-famous museums (the Victoria and Albert, Science and Natural History). Chelsea is no longer so much bohemian as expensively chic. King's Rd has bid farewell to the punks but remains an interesting place to hunt out youthful fashion.

Farther west you come to some very comfortable residential districts like Richmond, Wimbledon and Chiswick. Sites worth trekking out west for include Hampton Court Palace, Kew Gardens and Syon House.

The North

Notting Hill is a lively, interesting district, with a large West Indian population. It gets trendier by the day, but the Portobello Rd market is still fun and there are pubs, lively bars and interesting shops.

North of Kensington Gardens and Hyde Park, Bayswater and Paddington are virtual tourist ghettos, but there are plenty of hostels, cheap and mid-range hotels, good pubs and interesting restaurants (particularly along Queensway and Westbourne Grove).

From west to east, the band of suburbs to the north of the Central Line include Kilburn, Hampstead, Camden Town, Highgate, Highbury and Islington. Kilburn is London's Irish capital amid bedsit land. Hampstead, with its great views and the marvellous heath, is quiet, civilised and extremely expensive, while Camden Town, although well on its way to gentrification, still nurtures a gaggle of over-populated but enjoyable weekend markets.

In the mid-1990s Islington shot to fame as the home of the Blairs, where some of the strategies which won Labour the election of 1997 were worked out. In Upper St it also boasts one of London's most densely packed arrays of eating places.

The South

Cross the Thames from central London and you could be excused for thinking you've arrived in a different country. This is working-class London and it seems a long way from the elegant, antiseptic streets of Westminster. Much of south London, especially to the east, is still distressingly poor and run-down.

Even short-term visitors are likely to want to take in the cultural oasis of the South Bank Centre, venue for interesting exhibitions and concerts. Beautiful Greenwich is also home to the *Cutty Sark*, and contains superb architecture, open space and the prime meridian – and that's before it takes delivery of the dome which is to play the starring role in the forthcoming Millennium Experience!

If you stay for any length of time, however, there's a fair chance you'll end up living in suburbs like Clapham, Brixton or Camberwell.

Notorious for racial problems in the early 1980s, Brixton is definitely no Harlem, even though unemployment is high and the crumbling buildings and piles of rubbish may look the part. You'll enjoy its tatty market and arcades whatever your skin colour. Most of the district is as safe as anywhere else, but don't wander too far off the main streets until someone locates the 'front line' for you – an area around Railton Rd which is best left to the locals.

INFORMATION

For more detailed information on London, see Lonely Planet's *London* (£9.99). Otherwise, there's no shortage of information on the capital, much of it available free; the problem is wading through it for nuggets relevant to budget travellers.

Time Out magazine (published every Tuesday) is a mind-bogglingly complete listing of everything happening and is recommended for every visitor. The *Time Out Guide to Eating & Drinking in London* (magazine format) lists over 1700 restaurants and bars, although only some are

London's Millennium Attractions

The capital's claim to being the best place to be when the new millennium dawns is based on the fact that the prime meridian, 0 0′ 0″ longitude, the reference for measuring distance and time, runs through Greenwich in East London. It's here that the focus of Britain's millennium celebrations, the Millennium Dome, has been built. Designed by the Richard Rogers Partnership, it's the largest dome ever constructed and covers eight hectares. Inside the Millennium Experience will be a giant human figure, seated yet still 100m high, and a baby. Visitors will follow a series of walkways that will lead right inside these figures and around the 13 zones of the dome, exploring the human mind, the human body, human achievement and the global environment. It's generated an enormous amount of debate – couldn't the £450 million have been better spent on something else than on a building designed to last only 25 years? One thing's for sure, when it opens in December 1999, everyone's going to want to see what all the fuss was about.

Trafalgar Square has always been a traditional focus for New Year's Eve revellers but it's the kind of place you visit once, to be able to say you were there. No official party has yet been organised and there are better ways to spend the New Year than being trapped in a vast mass of bodies trying to go in opposite directions. Local authorities throughout the city will be staging their own open air parties; TICs will have details nearer the time.

You also shouldn't miss the Millennium Wheel, the world's biggest ferris wheel, standing 200m high beside the Thames at Westminster. It'll be operating by August 1999 and will certainly give the best view of the city.

---

cheap. Thursday's *Evening Standard* has its own weekly what's on guide.

Free magazines are also available from pavement bins, especially in Earl's Court, Notting Hill and Bayswater. *TNT Magazine*, *LAM*, *Southern Cross*, *Traveller Magazine* and *SA Times* cover Australian, New Zealand and South African news and sports results, but are mostly invaluable for their entertainment listings, excellent travel sections and useful classifieds covering jobs, cheap tickets, shipping services and accommodation. *TNT Magazine* is the glossiest and most comprehensive; phone ☎ 0171-373 3377 for the nearest distribution point.

Loot is a daily paper made up of classified ads placed free by sellers. You can find everything from kitchen sinks to cars, as well as an extensive selection of flats and house-share ads.

Also worth considering, if you're planning some serious shopping, is the *Time Out Guide to Shopping & Services* (magazine format).

For information on buses, trains and the tube, see Getting There & Away and Getting Around at the end of this chapter; for connections farther afield, see the Getting There & Away and Getting Around chapters at the beginning of this book.

Tourist Offices

London is a major travel centre, so aside from information on London you can also find offices that deal specifically with England, Scotland, Wales, Ireland and most countries round the world.

British Travel Centre The British Travel Centre (☎ 0181-846 9000, 1 Regent St, Piccadilly Circus, tube: Piccadilly Circus) offers comprehensive information on tours, a *bureau de change*, theatre and train tickets, plane and car hire bookings, accommodation bookings, a map and guidebook shop, and yet more info on Wales, Scotland and Ireland. It's open Monday to Friday from 9 am to 6.30 pm, Saturday and Sunday from

10 am to 4 pm (Saturday from 9 am to 5 pm between May and September).

London Tourist Information Centres

There are Tourist Information Centres (TICs) in the four Heathrow terminals, at Gatwick, Luton and Stansted airports, and in the Arrivals Hall at Waterloo International Terminal and Liverpool St underground station. The main centre on the Victoria station forecourt offers services including accommodation bookings, information, and a book and map shop. It's open Monday to Saturday from 8 am to 6 pm, Sunday from 8.30 am to 4 pm, and can be extremely busy. Otherwise, direct inquiries to ☎ 0171-730 3488, 26 Grosvenor Gardens SW1W 0DU.

The City of London Corporation also has an information centre (☎ 0171-332 1456, St Paul's Churchyard, tube: Mansion House), opposite St Paul's Cathedral. From April to September it's open daily from 9.30 am to 5 pm, and closed Saturday afternoon and Sunday for the rest of the year. It doesn't handle accommodation inquiries.

London White Card

Tourist offices sell the London White Card which offers free admission to 15 museums and galleries. It costs £16 for three days or £26 for seven days. Family cards, offering free admission for up to two adults and four children, cost £32 and £50.

Participating museums are Apsley House (Wellington Museum), Barbican Art Gallery, Courtauld Institute, Design Museum, Hayward Gallery, Imperial War Museum, London Transport Museum, Museum of London, Museum of the Moving Image, National Maritime Museum (with Old Royal Observatory and Queen's House), Natural History Museum, Royal Academy, Science Museum, Theatre Museum and Victoria and Albert Museum.

Note that most of London's blockbuster museums, including some of those listed here, offer free admission from 4.30 to 6 pm.

Foreign Consulates

With a few notable exceptions (Iraq, for instance) London is an excellent place to gather information and visas. See the Regional Facts for the Visitor chapter at the beginning of this book.

Money

Whenever possible, avoid using a *bureau de change* to change your money. For more information, see the Regional Facts for the Visitor chapter at the beginning of this book.

There are 24-hour *bureaux de change* in Heathrow Terminals 1, 3 and 4. Terminal 2's bureau is open daily from 6 am to 11 pm. Thomas Cook has branches at Terminals 1, 3 and 4. There are 24-hour bureaux in Gatwick's South and North Terminals and one at Stansted. The airport *bureaux de change* are actually good value; they don't charge commission on sterling travellers cheques, and on other currencies it's 1.5% with a £3 minimum.

At Victoria train station near the tourist office, Thomas Cook has a *bureau de change* that's open daily from 6 am to 11 pm.

The main American Express office (☎ 0171-930 4411, 6 Haymarket, tube: Piccadilly) is open for currency exchange Monday to Friday from 9 am to 5.30 pm, Saturday from 9 am to 6 pm, and Sunday from 10 am to 5 pm. Other services are available weekdays from 9 am to 5 pm and Saturday from 9 am to noon.

The main Thomas Cook office (☎ 0171-499 4000, 45 Berkeley St, tube: Green Park) is open from 9 am (10 am on Thursday) to 5.30 pm Monday to Friday, and from 9 am to 4 pm on Saturday. There are branches scattered around the centre of London.

Post & Communications

Poste Restante Unless otherwise specified, poste restante mail is sent to London Chief Office (☎ 0171-239 5047, King Edward Building, King Edward St ECI, tube: St Paul's). It's open from 9 am to 6.30 pm, Monday to Friday. It's more convenient to have your mail sent to Poste Restante, Trafalgar Square Branch Office, London WC2N 4DL (actual address: 24-28 William IV St, tube: Charing Cross). Mail will be held for four weeks; ID is required.

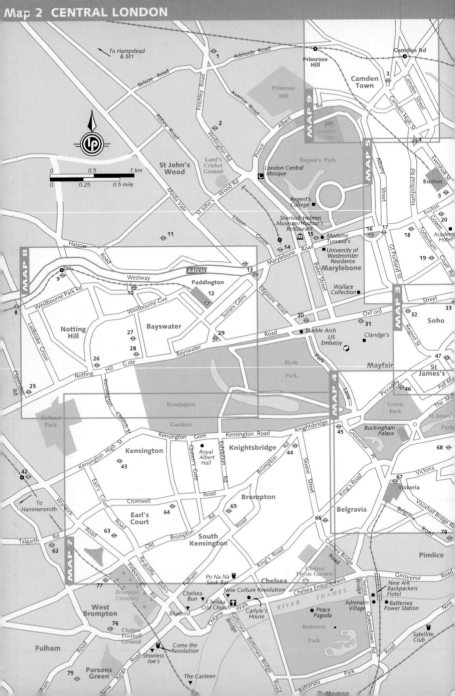

Map 2 CENTRAL LONDON

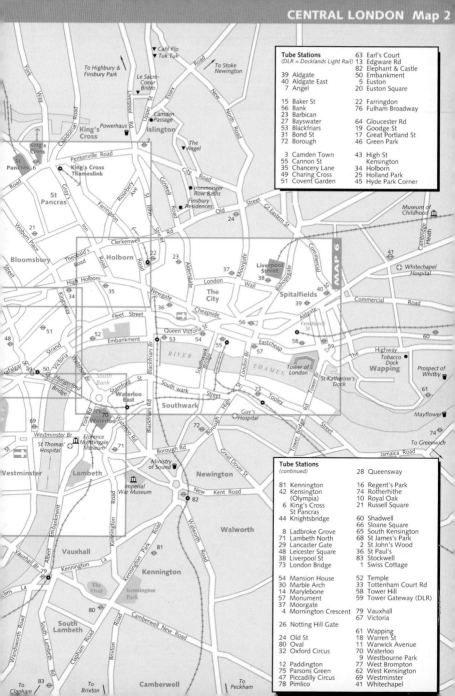

Map 3 WEST END

WEST END

PLACES TO STAY
8 Oxford St Youth Hostel
16 Hazlitt's
27 High Holborn
53 Fielding Hotel
61 Regent Palace Hotel
81 The Hampshire
96 One Aldwych
97 Strand Palace Hotel
118 Ritz Hotel

PLACES TO EAT
7 Yo Sushi
10 Pizza Express
11 Nusa Dua
12 Websnack
13 Dell'Ugo
17 Mildred's
18 Gay Hussar
24 Neal's Yard
25 Food for Thought
26 Belgo Centraal
28 Diana's Diner
31 Wagamama
32 The Sugar Club
33 Melati
35 Freedom Café Bar
36 Mezzo
37 French House Pub & Dining Room
38 Patisserie Valerie
40 Chiang Mai
41 The Blue Room
42 Bar Italia
43 Old Compton St Café
44 Pollo & Stockpot
46 Bunjies
47 The Ivy
48 Café Pacifico
51 Café des Amis du Vin
59 Atlantic Bar & Grill
60 New Piccadilly
64 The Criterion
68 Wong Kei

71 Planet Hollywood & Fashion Café
72 Chuen Cheng Ku
73 Poons
77 Gaby's Continental Bar
82 Sofra
83 Café Pelican
90 Chez Gerard
98 Joe Allen
100 La Perla del Pacifico Bar
101 Rules
107 The Wren at St James's
109 Football, Football
110 Sports Café
117 Quaglino's

PUBS & CLUBS
2 100 Club
4 Hanover Grand
5 Flamingo Bar
14 Dog & Duck
15 Riki Tik
19 Astoria
20 Velvet Underground
21 Borderline
23 Freud
30 Emporium
34 Village Soho & The 'O' Bar
39 Ronnie Scott's
45 Coach & Horses
49 Lamb & Flag
54 Sun
57 Legends
66 Rainforest Café
67 Bar Rumba
69 Café de Paris
74 Polar Bear
76 Hippodrome
78 Cork & Bottle
79 All Bar One
86 Rock Garden; Gardening Club
88 Walkabout Inn
114 Heaven
115 Gordon's Wine Bar

OTHER
1 HMV Records
3 Virgin Megastore
6 Liberty
9 Black Market Records
22 Foyle's Bookshop
29 Hamley's
50 Stanfords
52 Royal Opera House (Closed for Rebuilding)
55 Peacock Theatre
56 Royal Arcade
58 Royal Academy of Arts
62 British Travel Centre
63 Tower Records
65 Rock Circus
70 Pepsi Trocadero
75 Prince Charles Cinema
80 Half-Price Ticket Booth
84 English National Opera
85 The Africa Centre; Calabash Restaurant
87 St Paul's Church
89 Covent Garden Market
91 Theatre Museum
92 London Transport Museum
93 India House
94 Australia House
95 Courtauld Institute; Somerset House
99 YHA Adventure Shop; Campus Travel
102 Trafalgar Square Post Office
103 St Martin-in-the-Fields; Café in Crypt
104 National Portrait Gallery
105 National Gallery
106 American Express
108 Fortnum & Mason
111 Canada House
112 Nelson's Column
113 South Africa House
116 New Zealand House
119 ICA

Soho

RICHARD I'ANSON

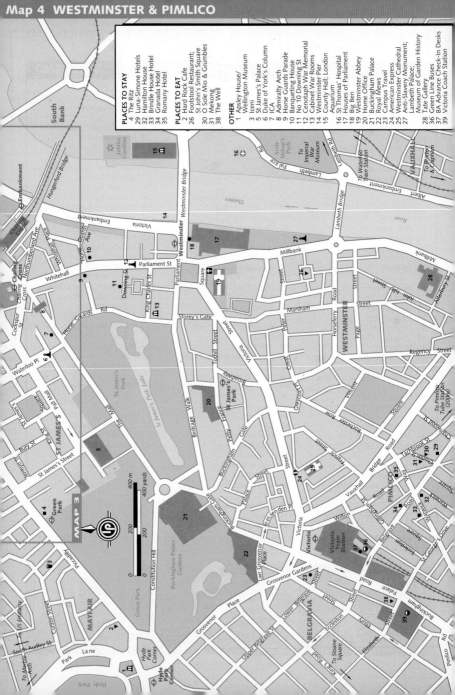

Map 4 WESTMINSTER & PIMLICO

PLACES TO STAY
4 The Ritz
29 Luna-Simone Hotels
32 Hamilton House Hotel
33 Brindle House Hotel
34 Granada Hotel
35 Romany Hotel

PLACES TO EAT
2 Hard Rock Cafe
26 Footstool Restaurant;
   St John's Smith Square
30 O Sole Mio & Grumbles
31 Mekong
38 The Well

OTHER
1 Apsley House/
   Wellington Museum
3 Iceni
5 St James's Palace
6 Duke of York's Column
7 ICA
8 Admiralty Arch
9 Horse Guards Parade
10 Banqueting House
11 No 10 Downing St
12 Cenotaph War Memorial
13 Cabinet War Rooms
14 Westminster Pier
15 County Hall; London
   Aquarium
16 St Thomas's Hospital
17 Houses of Parliament
18 Big Ben
19 Westminster Abbey
20 Home Office
21 Buckingham Palace
22 Royal Mews
23 Campus Travel
24 American Express
25 Westminster Cathedral
27 Anti-Slavery Monument;
   Lambeth Palace;
   Museum of Garden History
28 Tate Gallery
36 Green Line Buses
37 BA Advance Check-In Desks
39 Victoria Coach Station

PLACES TO EAT
2   Ravi Shankar
12 Ravi Shankar
20 North Sea Fish
    Restaurant
26 October Gallery Café
27 Mille Pini
34 The Greenhouse
42 Cyberia Cyber Café
45 Wagamama
46 Coffee Gallery

PUBS & CLUBS
1   Central Station
    Nightclub
23 Lamb
28 Queen's Larder
43 100 Club
47 Truckle's
48 The Princess Louise
49 Leisure Lounge

OTHER
4   Royal Free Hospital
5   King's Cross Travel Shop
9   British Library
14 UCL Hospital
15 University College London
21 Gay's The Word Bookshop
22 STA Travel
24 Charles Dickens' House
25 Gray's Inn Court
33 British Museum
37 Dillons the Bookstore
39 BT Tower
40 BBC Experience
41 Middlesex Hospital
50 Sir John Soane's Museum
51 Lincoln's Inn Court

PLACES TO STAY
3   Rosebery Avenue Hall
6   Alhambra Hotel
7   Desmond Dere Hotel
8   St Pancras International
    Youth Hostel
10 Euston Hotel
11 Ibis Euston
13 International
    Students House
16 John Adams Hall
17 Passfield Hall
18 Jenkin's Hotel
19 Crescent Hotel
29 St Margaret's Hotel
30 Repton Hotel
31 Ruskin Hotel
32 Museum Inn
35 Hotel Haverstock
36 Arran House Hotel
38 Carr Saunders Hall
44 YMCA (Central Club)

Map 6 CITY & EMBANKMENT

THE CITY & EMBANKMENT

PLACES TO STAY
5 Barbican YMCA
6 London City YMCA
45 City of London
    Youth Hostel
57 St Christopher's Hostel

PLACES TO EAT
14 Fatboy's Diner
16 Aladin; Nazrul
44 Sweeting's
52 Le Pont de la Tour
54 The Apprentice

PUBS & CLUBS
4 Turnmill's; Café Gaudi
10 The Cock Tavern
13 Hamilton Hall
26 Ye Olde Cheshire Cheese
55 George Inn

OTHER
1 Gray's Inn Fields
2 Gray's Inn
3 CallShop etc

7 Barbican Centre
8 St Bartholomew-the-Great
9 Smithfield Market
11 St Bartholomew's Hospital
12 Museum of London
15 Spitalfields Market;
    Spitz Café
17 Brick Lane Market
18 Whitechapel Art Gallery &
    Café
19 Petticoat Lane Market
20 NatWest Tower
21 Stock Exchange
22 Bank of England
23 Guildhall
24 GPO
25 Central Criminal Court/
    Old Bailey
27 Dr Johnson's House
28 Lincoln's Inn
29 Royal Courts of Justice
30 Australia House
31 St Clement Danes
32 Temple Church
33 St Bride's

34 St Paul's Cathedral
35 St Mary-le-Bow; Place Below
    Café
36 Mansion House
37 Royal Exchange
38 Leadenhall Market
39 Lloyd's of London
40 World Trade Centre
41 Tower of London
42 All Hallows by the Tower;
    Brass Rubbing Centre
43 The Monument
46 Gabriel's Wharf; Gourmet
    Pizza Company
47 Oxo Tower & Restaurant
48 Shakespeare Globe Centre;
    Restaurant & Theatre
49 Southwark Cathedral
50 Hay's Galleria
51 HMS Belfast
53 Design Museum; Blue Print
    Café
56 Guy's Hospital
58 King's Campus Vacation
    Bureau

RICHARD I'ANSON

Tower Bridge

Map 7 CHELSEA, KENSINGTON & EARL'S COURT

CHELSEA, KENSINGTON & EARL'S COURT

PLACES TO STAY
1 Vicarage Private Hotel; Abbey House
8 Holland House Youth Hostel
14 The Gore
16 Imperial College of Science & Technology Residence
21 Basil St Hotel
25 London Lodge Hotel
26 Amber Hotel
31 Court Hotels
33 Merlyn Court Hotel
34 Curzon House Hotel
35 St Simeon
37 Five Sumner Place
38 Hotel Number Sixteen
44 Annandale House Hotel
48 Magnolia Hotel
49 Blakes Hotel
50 Hotel 167
51 Swiss House Hotel
52 Earl's Court Youth Hostel
54 London Town Hotel
55 Regency Court Hotel; Windsor House
56 Chelsea Hotel

57 Philbeach Hotel; Wilde About Oscar Restaurant
58 York House Hotel
60 Boka Hotel
61 Court Hotels

PLACES TO EAT
12 Wodka
19 Patisserie Valerie
29 Benjy's
32 Nando's
39 Spago
40 Daquise
41 Bibendum/Michelin Building
42 Daphne's
43 Oriel
45 Chelsea Kitchen
46 Chelsea Farmers' Market
47 Henry J Bean's
53 Mr Wing
63 Krungtap
65 Troubadour

PUBS & CLUBS
30 Prince of Teck
62 Blanco's

64 Coleherne

OTHER
2 Kensington Palace
3 Serpentine Art Gallery
4 Albert Memorial
5 Hyper-Hyper
6 YHA Shop; Campus Travel
7 Trailfinders (Main Office)
9 Commonwealth Institute
10 Trailfinders
11 Kensington Market
13 Royal Geographical Society
15 Imperial College of Science & Technology
17 Harvey Nichols; Fifth Floor Café
18 Harrods
20 Brompton Oratory
22 Victoria and Albert Museum
23 Science Museum
24 Natural History Museum
27 Airbus, Route A1, Stop 6
28 Top Deck Travel
36 STA Travel
59 Earl's Court Exhibition Centre

Piccadilly Circus

NEIL SETCHFIELD

Map 8 BAYSWATER & NOTTING HILL

BAYSWATER & NOTTING HILL

PLACES TO STAY
9   Norfolk Court; St David's Hotel
10 Gresham Hotel
11 Europa House Hotel
12 Balmoral House Hotel
16 Garden Court Hotel
18 Leinster Inn
24 Portobello Gold Hotel
26 Portobello Hotel
27 The Gate Hotel
30 Hillgate Hotel
31 Manor Court Hotel
32 Palace Hotel
33 Quest Hotel; Royal Hotel
34 Oxford Hotel; Sass House
41 Holland Park Hotel
44 London Independent Hostel

PLACES TO EAT
3   Café Grove
5   All Saints
14 Khan's
17 L'accento
19 Inaho
20 Veronica's
21 The Mandola
25 Spider Café
28 Prost
29 Modhubon
36 Novelli W8
37 Kensington Place
38 Geales
39 Costa's Grill
42 Pharmacy Restaurant & Bar
43 Nachos

PUBS & CLUBS
1   Subterania
4   Market Bar
6   The Westbourne
22 Beach Blanket Babylon
45 Windsor Castle

OTHER
2   Portobello Rd Market
7   Jason's Boats
8   Waterbus
13 Portchester Spa
15 Whiteley's Shopping Centre
23 Travel Bookshop
35 Statue of Peter Pan
40 Airbus, Route A2, Stop 14
46 Kensington Palace

Speaker's Corner

NEIL SETCHFIELD

Lloyd's Building

NEIL SETCHFIELD

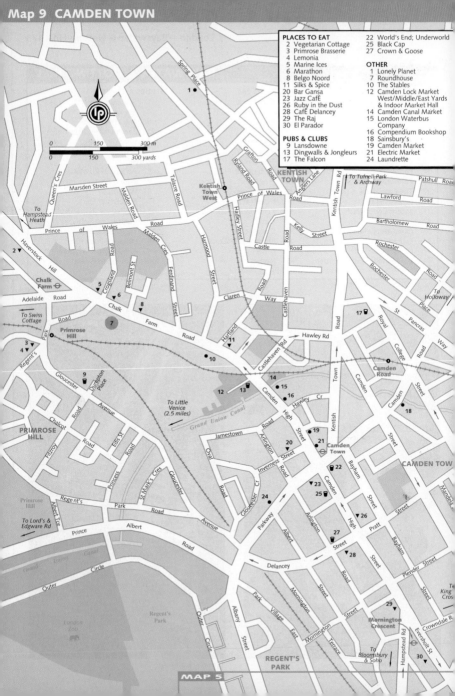

Map 9 CAMDEN TOWN

PLACES TO EAT
- 2 Vegetarian Cottage
- 3 Primrose Brasserie
- 4 Lemonia
- 5 Marine Ices
- 6 Marathon
- 8 Belgo Noord
- 11 Silks & Spice
- 20 Bar Gansa
- 23 Jazz Café
- 26 Ruby in the Dust
- 28 Café Delancey
- 29 The Raj
- 30 El Parador

PUBS & CLUBS
- 9 Lansdowne
- 13 Dingwalls & Jongleurs
- 17 The Falcon
- 22 World's End; Underworld
- 25 Black Cap
- 27 Crown & Goose

OTHER
- 1 Lonely Planet
- 7 Roundhouse
- 10 The Stables
- 12 Camden Lock Market West/Middle/East Yards & Indoor Market Hall
- 14 Camden Canal Market
- 15 London Waterbus Company
- 16 Compendium Bookshop
- 18 Sainsbury's
- 19 Camden Market
- 21 Electric Market
- 24 Laundrette

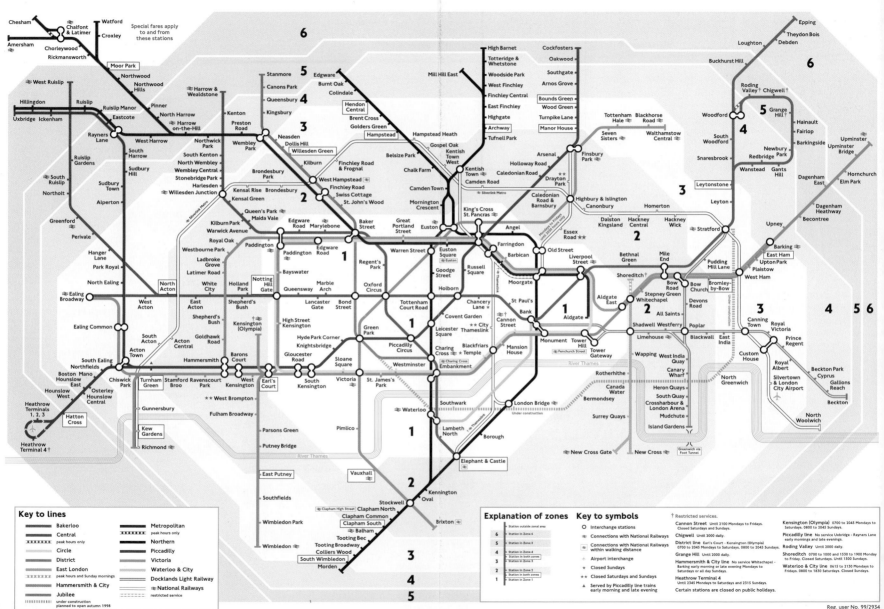

Map 10 GREENWICH

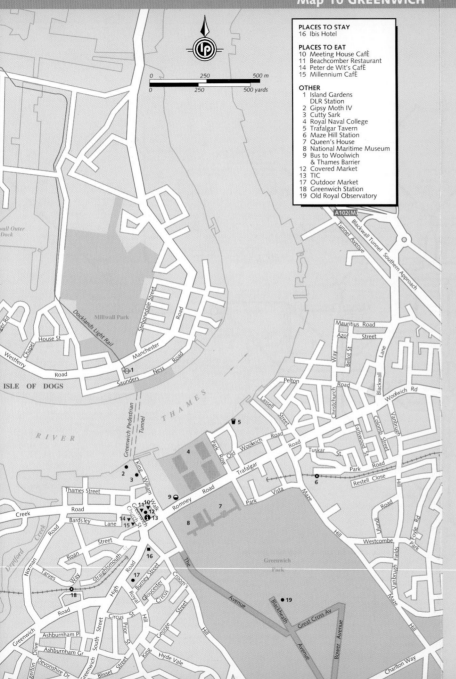

PLACES TO STAY
16 Ibis Hotel

PLACES TO EAT
10 Meeting House Cafè
11 Beachcomber Restaurant
14 Peter de Wit's Cafè
15 Millennium Cafè

OTHER
1 Island Gardens
   DLR Station
2 Gipsy Moth IV
3 Cutty Sark
4 Royal Naval College
5 Trafalgar Tavern
6 Maze Hill Station
7 Queen's House
8 National Maritime Museum
9 Bus to Woolwich
   & Thames Barrier
12 Covered Market
13 TIC
17 Outdoor Market
18 Greenwich Station
19 Old Royal Observatory

BOUNDARIES

- International
- State
- Suburb

HYDROGRAPHY

- Coastline
- River
- Creek
- Lake
- Intermittent Lake
- Canal
- Spring, Rapids
- Waterfalls

ROUTES & TRANSPORT

- Freeway
- Highway
- Major Road
- Unsealed Road
- City Highway
- City Road
- City Lane
- Pedestrian Mall
- Tunnel
- Train Route & Station
- Metro & Station
- Tramway
- Cable Car or Chairlift
- Walking Track
- Walking Tour
- Ferry Route

AREA FEATURES

- Building
- Park, Gardens
- Cemetery
- Market
- Beach
- Urban Area

MAP SYMBOLS

- ✪ CAPITAL ....National Capital
- ⊙ CAPITAL ....State Capital
- ● CITY ....City
- ● Town ....Town
- ● Village ....Village
- ○ ....Point of Interest
- ....Place to Stay
- ⛺ ....Camping Ground
- ....Caravan Park
- ....Hut or Chalet
- ▼ ....Place to Eat
- ....Pub or Bar

- ✈ ....Airport
- ....ATM, Bank
- ....Beach
- 🚲 ....Bike Rental
- ....Castle or Fort
- ....Church
- ....Cliff or Escarpment
- ....Embassy
- ....Hospital
- ....Monument
- ....Mosque
- ▲ ....Mountain or Hill
- 🏛 ....Museum
- ....National Park

- → ....One Way Street
- P ....Parking
- ....Petrol
- ★ ....Police Station
- ....Post Office
- ❖ ....Shopping Centre
- 🏠 ....Stately Home
- ....Swimming Pool
- ....Synagogue
- ☎ ....Telephone
- ....Toilet
- ℹ ....Tourist Information
- ....Transport
- ....Zoo

Note: not all symbols displayed above appear in this book

See London Underground Map Overleaf

Telephone & Fax London telephone numbers currently have two codes (☎ 0171 for central London or ☎ 0181 for outer London) before a seven-digit number but, as of Easter Saturday 2000, the area code will change to ☎ 020. Subscribers will have to put a 7 in front of numbers that used to have an 0171 code and 8 in front those with an old 0181 code.

CallShop etc (☎ 0171-390 4549, 181a Earl's Court Rd and ☎ 0171-837 7788, 88 Farringdon Rd) offers cheaper rates than British Telecom for international calls, and it's also one of the best places to send or receive faxes. Both branches are open until midnight.

Email & Internet Access These days, getting your mail sent to Poste Restante is beginning to seem a bit old hat. If you're one of the keen users of the Internet, you may find that your hotel has a terminal you can use. If not, there are many Internet cafés dotted about town to keep the most mouse-happy person satisfied.

The Cyberia Cyber Café (☎ 0171-209 0983, 39 Whitfield St, tube: Goodge St) was London's first Internet café. There are 10 terminals in the café (£2.50 for half an hour) and 12 in the training room. Weekday training costs £30 for two hours and must be booked in advance. The food's good with specials from £4 to £5.

Webshack (☎ 0171-439 8000, 15 Dean St W1, tube: Piccadilly Circus) is the most central of the Internet cafés.

Spider Café (☎ 0171-229 2990, 195 Portobello Rd W11, tube: Notting Hill Gate) has computers upstairs and down, and serves food and milk shakes. Access costs £2.50 a half-hour. Tuition is £5.95 for half an hour or £35 for a two-hour session.

Portobello Gold (☎ 0171-460 4910, 95 Portobello Rd W11, tube: Notting Hill Gate) is a classy hotel/restaurant whose upstairs bar has terminals available for customer use.

The Bean (☎ 0171-739 7829, 126 Curtain Rd) is a Hackney coffee shop cum Internet access point.

Check out Lonely Planet's award-winning Web site: www.lonelyplanet.com.au for travel information.

Travel Agencies
London has always been a cheap travel centre. Refer to the Sunday papers (especially the *Sunday Times), TNT Magazine* and *Time Out* for listings of cheap flights, and watch out for sharks.

Long-standing, reliable firms include:

Trailfinders
    (☎ 0171-938 3939, 194 Kensington High St W8, tube: High St Kensington), a complete travel service, including a bookshop, information centre, visa service and immunisation centre). There are also branches at 215 Kensington High Street and 42-50 Earl's Court Road, Kensington W8.
STA Travel
    (☎ 0171-361 6262, 74 Old Brompton Rd SW7, tube: South Kensington), the largest worldwide student/budget travel agency. There is another branch at 40 Bernard St WC1, tube: Russell Square, that stocks equipment sold by the Nomad Travellers Store and has a *bureau de change.*
Campus Travel
    (☎ 0171-730 8111, 52 Grosvenor Gardens SW1, tube: Victoria), also offices in large YHA Adventure Shops.
Council Travel
    (☎ 0171-437 7767, 28A Poland St W1, tube: Oxford Circus), the USA's largest student and budget travel agency.

Another agency to consider is the King's Cross Travel Shop (☎ 0171-837 8599, 292 Pentonville Rd, tube: King's Cross), which sells tickets and guidebooks but also offers a message board and a chance to meet other travellers.

Bookshops
All the major chains are good sources for guidebooks and maps, but there are also several specialist travel bookshops.

Stanfords
    (☎ 0171-836 1321, 12 Long Acre WC2, tube: Covent Garden) has one of the best selections of maps and guides in the world.

Travel Bookshop
    (☎ 0171-229 5260, 13 Blenheim Crescent, Notting Hill W11, tube: Ladbroke Grove) has all the new guides, plus a selection of out of print and antiquarian gems.
Daunt Books
    (☎ 0171-224 2295, 83 Marylebone High St W1, tube: Baker St) has a wide selection of travel guides in a beautiful old shop.
Borders Books, Music & Café
    (☎ 0171-292 1600, 203 Oxford St, tube: Oxford Circus) is a new mega-bookshop with a café and bar. It's open long hours, from 8 am to 11 pm, Monday to Saturday and from noon to 6 pm on Sunday.

Laundry

You will find a laundrette on every High St. Try Forco, 60 Parkway in Camden Town; Bendix, 395 King's Rd in Chelsea or Notting Hill Laundrette, 12 Notting Hill Gate.

Medical Services

Reciprocal arrangements within the European Union (EU) and with Australia and New Zealand mean that citizens of these countries don't pay for emergency medical treatment. Non-EU residents do have to pay if admitted to a hospital ward. Regardless of nationality, anyone should receive free emergency treatment if it's a simple matter like bandaging a cut.

The following hospitals have 24 hour accident and emergency (A&E) departments:

Guy's Hospital
    St Thomas St SE1 (☎ 0171-955 5000, tube: London Bridge)
University College Hospital (UCL)
    Grafton Way WC1 (☎ 0171-387 9300, tube: Euston Square)
Charing Cross Hospital
    Fulham Palace Rd W6 (☎ 0181-846 1234, tube: Hammersmith)
Royal Free Hospital
    Pond St NW3 (☎ 0171-794 0500, tube: Belsize Park)

To find an emergency dentist phone the Dental Emergency Care Service on ☎ 0171-955 2186; or call into Eastman Dental Hospital (☎ 0171-837 3646, 256 Gray's Inn Rd WC1, tube: Chancery Lane).

Several companies offer visa and immunisation services and some advertise in *TNT Magazine*. Charges can differ widely. Trailfinders (☎ 0171-938 3999) at 194 Kensington High St W8 has both a visa service and an immunisation centre. The International Medical Centre (☎ 0171-486 3063) has two branches, including one at the Top Deck (Deckers) headquarters, 131 Earl's Court Rd SW5. Top Deck also hosts the Rapid Visa Service (☎ 0171-373 3026). Nomad (☎ 0171-889 7014) at 3 Turnpike Lane, N8 sells travel equipment and medical kits, and gives immunisations (Saturday only).

Drop-in doctor services have opened in several main-line train terminals, including Victoria, but their charges are more suited to high-earning commuters than backpackers.

Emergency

Dial ☎ 999 (free) for fire, police or ambulance. Pharmacies should have a notice in the window, advising where you'll find the nearest late-night branch.

WALKING TOUR

As always, walking is the best way to discover a new city. Central London is easy to explore on foot. The following tour could be covered in a day but doesn't allow you the chance to explore any of the individual sights in detail. It will, however, introduce you to the West End and Westminster. See the separate sections later in this chapter for details on the individual sights.

Start at **St Paul's Cathedral**, Wren's masterpiece that was completed in 1710, and climb to the top of the Golden Gallery for one of the best views of London. Then, unless you're feeling very energetic, catch a tube from St Paul's station to Covent Garden (west on the Central line to Holborn, then west on the Piccadilly line).

Once London's fruit and vegetable market, **Covent Garden** has been restored to a bustling piazza. It's one of the few places in London where pedestrians rule, and you can watch the buskers for a few coins and the tourists for free. The opera house (under redevelopment wraps for the time being) is on the north-east corner, the main YHA Adventure Shop in Southampton St off the south side.

Return to the tube station and turn left into Long Acre (look for Stanfords bookshop on your left) and continue across Charing Cross Rd to **Leicester Square** with its cinemas and fast food outlets. Note the Leicester Square Half-Price Ticket Booth, which sells cheap theatre tickets on the day of performance.

Continue along Coventry St, past the Pepsi Trocadero and the Rock Circus, until you get to **Piccadilly Circus**, with Tower Records, one of London's best music shops. Shaftesbury Ave enters the circus at the north-eastern corner, marked by cheap kebab/pizza counters. This famous street of theatres runs back into Soho, with its myriad restaurants and vibrant nightlife. Regent St curves out of the north-west corner up to Oxford Circus.

Continue west along Piccadilly to St James church and the Royal Academy. Detour into the extraordinary **Burlington Arcade**, just after the academy; beware the arcade Burties (private 'police') who, among other things, are supposed to stop you whistling.

Return to Piccadilly and continue until you get to St James's St on your left (south). This takes you down to **St James's Palace**, the royal home from 1660 to 1837 until it was judged insufficiently impressive. Skirt around its east side and you come onto The Mall.

Trafalgar Square is to the east (left), **Buckingham Palace** to the west. Cross back into St James's Park, London's most beautiful open space, and follow the lake to its east end. Turn right onto Horse Guards Rd. This takes you past the **Cabinet War Rooms**, which give an extraordinary insight into the dark days of WWII.

Continue south along Horse Guards Rd, then turn left on Great George St, which takes you through to Parliament Square with beautiful Westminster Abbey, the Houses of Parliament and Westminster Bridge. **Westminster Abbey** is so rich in history you need half a day to do it justice.

St Stephen's Tower better known as Big Ben

The coronation chair where all but two monarchs since 1066 have been crowned, is behind the altar, and many greats – from Darwin to Chaucer – have been buried here.

The **Houses of Parliament** and St Stephen's Tower, better known by the name of its famous bell, **Big Ben**, were actually built in the 19th century in mock medieval style. The best way to get into the building is to attend the Commons or Lords visitors' galleries during a parliamentary debate.

Walking away from Westminster Bridge, turn right into Whitehall (Parliament St). On your left, **No 10 Downing St** offers temporary accommodation to British prime ministers. Farther along on the right is the Inigo Jones-designed Banqueting House, outside which Charles I was beheaded. Continue past the Horse Guards, where you can see a less crowded version of the Buckingham Palace changing of the guard ceremony.

Finally, you reach **Trafalgar Square** and Nelson's Column. The National Gallery and National Portrait Gallery are on the north side.

OTHER WALKS

Although central London is blighted by heavy traffic, there are still plenty of places to escape.

You can, for example, follow the Grand Union Canal from Little Venice to the River Thames 8 miles away. Start at Blomfield Rd, near Warwick Ave tube station. Except for a few breaks where it disappears underground, the canal runs around Regent's Park, through Camden Lock Market, and past grubby but interesting warehouses and industrial areas. Eventually it enters the river at Limehouse in the East End. From there you can catch the Docklands Light Railway (DLR) back to Tower Gateway, which links with the Tower Hill tube station. See Canal Tour later in this chapter if you want to catch a boat part of the way.

Try and make the most of London's glorious parks. A long walk starting at St James's and continuing through Green, Hyde, Kensington and Holland parks will banish any urban blues.

Original London Walks (☎ 0171-624 3978) has daily two-hour guided walks for £4 that begin and end outside underground stations.

RIVER TOUR – EAST

If walking doesn't seem a good idea, consider catching a boat downriver from Westminster Pier (beside Westminster Bridge) to Greenwich (every half-hour from 10 am, single/return £5.30/6.30). You pass the site of Shakespeare's Globe Theatre, stop at the Tower of London, and continue under Tower Bridge and past many famous docks.

Greenwich can absorb the best part of a day. Start with the **Cutty Sark**, the only surviving tea and wool clipper and one of the most beautiful ships ever built. Wander around the Greenwich market, then visit the **Queen's House**, a masterpiece designed in 1616 by Inigo Jones. If you're interested in boats and naval history, continue to the **National Maritime Museum**. The **Royal Naval College**, beside the river, was designed by Wren.

Climb the hill behind the museum to the **Old Royal Observatory**. A brass strip in the observatory courtyard marks the prime meridian that divides the world into eastern and western hemispheres. There are great views over Docklands – with the massive Canary Wharf development just over the river – and back to central London.

Walk back down the hill and through the Greenwich foot tunnel (near the *Cutty Sark)* to Island Gardens. From the other side of the river there's a superb view of the Naval College and the Queen's House. The Docklands Light Railway whizzes above ground from Island Gardens back to Tower Gateway offering fine views of the Docklands developments. On Sunday there's even a commentary. Zone 1 & 2 Travelcards are valid all the way out here.

RIVER TOUR – WEST

River boats also run west from Westminster Pier, an enjoyable excursion, although it takes considerably longer and is not as dramatic or interesting as the trip east. The two possible destinations – Kew Gardens and Hampton Court Palace – are highlights of a London visit.

Kew Gardens, the Royal Botanic Gardens, make a glorious refuge from the outside world. Ferries sail from Westminster Pier every 30 minutes from 10.15 am to 2.30 pm (from the Monday before Easter through September). They take 1½ hours and a single/return costs £6/10. It's possible to return by tube (tube: Kew Gardens, Zone 3). Admission to the gardens is £4.50/3.

London in a Hurry

If you've only got a few days to 'do' London, the following suggestions would ensure you cover the highlights.

Two Days

With only a couple of days to spare, you might want to use one of the hop-on-hop-off sightseeing buses (see the Bus Tours section in this chapter) to get round with minimum delay. Make sure you see Trafalgar Square, Buckingham Palace (Changing of the Guard), Big Ben, the Houses of Parliament and Westminster Abbey. Then head for Tower Bridge and the Tower of London (for the Crown Jewels) or St Paul's Cathedral (climb to the top of the dome for a superb view of the City).

Explore the West End, particularly Covent Garden and Piccadilly Circus, and pop in to Harrods department store. If you've still got time, visit the British Museum. In the evening take in a show at the new Globe Theatre on the South Bank, and visit one of London's many pubs.

Four Days

Add on a cruise from Charing Cross Pier to Greenwich to visit the Royal Observatory, the Royal Naval College, the Queen's House and the *Cutty Sark* (allow at least an afternoon).

Explore one of the weekend markets in Camden, Portobello Rd or the East End. Take a canal cruise from Little Venice to Camden Lock (for the market) or Regent's Park (for the zoo). Squeeze in a picnic in Hyde Park (try to get to Speaker's Corner on a Sunday) or St James's Park.

Spend an evening strolling the streets of Soho, taking in some of the trendy bars and cafés.

Wind up your stay with a trip to Hampton Court Palace (stopping off at Kew Gardens provided you don't take the slow boat to get there), or to Windsor Castle and Eton College in Berkshire (see the South-Eastern England chapter for details).

One Week

With more time to spare you should be able to explore more of the galleries and museums, particularly the National Gallery, the Tate, the Museum of London and the South Kensington museums.

To see how modern London is shaping up, walk along the South Bank from Hungerford Bridge to London Bridge and then take a ride on the Docklands Light Rail.

Go for a walk on Hampstead Heath and stay for an outdoor concert at Kenwood House.

Hampton Court Palace is England's grandest Tudor mansion. Built by Cardinal Thomas Wolsey in 1514 and 'adopted' by Henry VIII, the palace is a beautiful mixture of particular architectural styles – from Henry's splendid Great Hall to the State Apartments built for William III and Mary II by Wren. The superb grounds on the banks of the River Thames enclose a famous 300-year-old maze. Ferries leave from Westminster Pier from April to October at 10.30 and 11.15 am and noon (3½ hours, £12/8). There are also trains every half-hour from Waterloo station (Zone 6, £3.90 return). Admission to the palace is £9.25/7.

CANAL TOUR

The London Waterbus Company (☎ 0171-482 2550) runs 90-minute trips between Camden Lock and Little Venice, via London Zoo and Regent's Park. From April through October, boats depart from the locks at Camden and Little Venice every hour between 10 am and 5 pm; the last return trip departs at 3 pm, the last one-way trip at 3.45 pm. There's a weekend service from November to March. One-way tickets are £3.70/2.30, return tickets £4.80/2.90.

BUS ROUTES

One of the cheapest ways to explore London is to buy a Travelcard and jump on one of the double-decker buses. Travelling north to south, or vice versa, the No 24 is good. Beginning in Hampstead, it travels through Camden and along Gower St (passing London University) to Tottenham Court Rd. From Tottenham Court Rd it travels along Charing Cross Rd, past Leicester Square to Trafalgar Square, then along Whitehall, and past the House of Commons, Westminster Abbey and Westminster Cathedral. From Victoria station it carries on to Pimlico, which is handy for the Tate Gallery.

From east to west, take the No 8 'routemaster' bus (red, open-backed and with a conductor) which comes from Bethnal Green Market. It passes or runs close to the Whitechapel Art Gallery, Petticoat Lane Market, Liverpool St station, the City, the Guildhall and the Old Bailey. It then crosses Holborn and travels along Oxford St, passing Bond St, Selfridges and the largest Marks & Spencer store. Get off at Hyde Park Corner for Hyde Park.

BUS TOURS

The Original London Sightseeing Tour (☎ 0181-877 1722), the Big Bus Company (☎ 0181-944 7810) and London Pride Sightseeing (☎ 01708-631122) offer tours of the main sights in double-decker buses which allow you to either go straight round without getting off, or hop on and off along the way. They're all expensive (around £12) and probably only worth considering if you're only going to be in London for a day or two. Most companies can sell you advance tickets to the biggest attractions to save wasting time in queues.

Convenient starting points are in Trafalgar Square in front of the National Gallery, in front of the Trocadero on Coventry St between Leicester Square and Piccadilly Circus, and in Wilton Gardens opposite Victoria station.

London Pride Sightseeing includes Docklands and Greenwich in one tour, while the Original London Sightseeing Tour has an express tour for those with limited time.

WEST END

London's West End is a heady mixture of crass consumerism and high culture. Several outstanding museums and galleries rub shoulders with tacky tourist traps, while world-famous places and monuments share the streets with some of the capital's best shopping and entertainment possibilities.

Trafalgar Square (Map 3)

Trafalgar Square (tube: Charing Cross) is the closest you'll get to the heart of the city. This is where great marches and rallies take place, and where the New Year is seen in by thousands of crushed, drunken revellers.

The square was designed by John Nash in the early 19th century, and executed by Sir Charles Barry, who also worked on the Houses of Parliament. The 50m-tall **Nelson's Column** commemorates Napoleon's defeat at sea in 1805. The four bronze lions round its foot were designed by Landseer and attract tourists and pigeons in equal numbers.

Although the crowds and the traffic swirling past make it difficult to get much sense of perspective, the Square is virtually ringed with imposing buildings. To the north stands the National Gallery, with the church of St Martin-in-the-Fields to the north-east. Directly to the east stands **South Africa House** (1933), while to the south the square opens out and you catch glimpses down Whitehall. To the south-west stands **Admiralty Arch**, with The Mall leading to

Buckingham Palace beyond it. To the west is **Canada House** (1824-7).

Hopefully by the time you read this, work will have commenced on closing the north side of the square to traffic.

National Gallery The porticoed front of the National Gallery (☎ 0171-839 3321) extends along the north side of the square. With over 2000 paintings on display it's one of the world's finest art galleries ... and the fact that admission is still free means you'll be able to visit more than once if you want to.

The Sainsbury Wing on the west side was only added after considerable controversy during the course of which Prince Charles put paid to one possible modernist design by describing it as like 'a carbuncle on the face of a much-loved friend'.

To make life easier for visitors, the paintings in the National Gallery are hung in a continuous time line from 1260 to 1920. Highlights include *The Annunciation* by Filippino Lippi, Raphael's *Pope Julius*, Jan van Eyck's *Arnolfini Wedding*, Titian's *The Killing of Actaeon*, Diego Velásquez's *Rokeby Venus* and *The Bathers* by Paul Cézanne. That's without mentioning priceless works by Leonardo da Vinci, Hans Holbein, Hieronymus Bosch, Peter Breughel, Nicolas Poussin, Jan Vermeer, and Georges Seurat.

Look out for free guided tours which introduce you to a manageable half-dozen paintings at a time. The gallery is open Monday to Saturday from 10 am to 6 pm (8 pm on Wednesday), and Sunday from 2 to 6 pm.

National Portrait Gallery You visit the National Portrait Gallery (☎ 0171-306 0055), opposite St Martin's church, not so much for the quality of its paintings but to put the faces to the famous and not-so-famous names in British history. It's open the same hours as the National Gallery.

St Martin-in-the-Fields An influential early 18th century masterpiece by James Gibbs, this well-known church (☎ 0171-930 0089) occupies a prime site at the north-eastern corner of Trafalgar Square. The wedding-cake spire is offset by the splendid visual harmony of white stone linking St Martin's and the National Gallery. When floodlit this becomes one of London's greatest vistas.

St Martin's has a long tradition of tending to the poor and homeless. It also runs the adjoining craft market, and a brass rubbing centre, bookshop and café in the crypt. There are also regular lunch time and evening concerts.

It's open Monday to Saturday from 10 am to 6 pm, Sunday from noon to 6 pm.

Leicester Square (Map 3)

Despite efforts to smarten it up, and the presence of four huge cinemas, various nightclubs, pubs and restaurants ringing it, Leicester (pronounced lester) Square still feels more like a transit point between Covent Garden and Piccadilly Circus. You're bound to pass through at some point but it's hard to imagine a time when artists Joshua Reynolds and William Hogarth actually chose to live here.

Piccadilly Circus (Map 3)

Piccadilly Circus is the world-famous, neon-lit home of the statue Eros. Once the hub of London, a place where flower girls flogged their wares and people arranged to meet, it's now fume-choked and pretty uninteresting. Eros itself is one of those monuments every tourist feels obliged to visit and photograph just to prove they've done so. But behind this statue of the Greek god of Love lies the romantic story of the Earl of Shaftesbury, a Victorian philanthropist who struggled to prevent women and children working in coal mines and whose memorial this is. At least no one need risk life or limb to inspect the statue now that it's been moved out of the middle of the road.

Rock Circus The Rock Circus (☎ 0171-734 8025, London Pavilion, Piccadilly Circus, tube: Piccadilly Circus) is one of the capital's most popular attractions, despite the fact that virtually none of those immortalised in wax would be known to the younger generation.

It won't take long to eye up the images of rock stars and absorb the few snatches of their greatest hits relayed to you through crackly headsets. Then you may have to queue for up to 15 minutes to see a show which whips you back to rock's cotton-picking origins so fast you barely have time to take in what's happening, after which you're treated to a succession of animated models who fail to lip-sync to their music while jerking their limbs around like puppets. The triumphant finale is Springsteen warbling *Born in the USA*. Britpop might never have happened.

It's open daily from 10 am to 10 pm from late June to early September, otherwise Monday, Wednesday, Thursday and Sunday from 11 am to 9 pm; Tuesday from noon to 9 pm; Friday and Saturday to 10 pm; £7.95/6.90.

Pepsi Trocadero The Pepsi Trocadero (☎ 0171-439 1791, Piccadilly Circus W1, tube: Piccadilly Circus) is an indoor entertainment complex with several hi-tech attractions, anchored by the Segaworld indoor theme park. It's a good place to take youngsters who can't be sold on London's more educational attractions, but don't expect a cheap night out. It's open from 10 am until midnight daily (until 1 am Friday and Saturday).

Royal Academy of Arts (Map 3)

The Royal Academy (☎ 0171-439 7438, Burlington House, Piccadilly W1, tube: Green Park) tends to play second fiddle to the Hayward Gallery (see South Bank later in this chapter), with international exhibitions that aren't quite as sexy or high profile (although the recent *Sensation* exhibition was an in-your-face attempt to change its image once and for all). Anyone can enter the popular annual Summer Exhibition. The quality can be mixed but on the right day, amid the glorious setting of one of London's few remaining 18th century mansions, nobody seems to care.

The RA is open daily from 10 am to 6 pm. Admission prices depend on what's on but expect to pay around £5. For blockbuster exhibitions tickets are sold on a timed basis to prevent too many people crowding in.

Burlington & Royal Arcades (Map 3)

Built in 1819, Burlington Arcade, off Piccadilly (tube: Piccadilly Circus), recalls a bygone age and sells the kinds of things that only the very rich could want. Watch out for the beadles, the uniformed guards who patrol the arcade, with a brief to prevent high spirits, whistling and the inelegant popping of gum.

The Gothic-style Royal Arcade is a covered thoroughfare built in 1879 and lined with extremely expensive shops selling hunting jackets, pipe tobacco, cashmere jumpers and golfing knickerbockers. It runs off Old Bond St.

Wallace Collection (Map 2)

The Wallace Collection (☎ 0171-935 0687, Hertford House, Manchester Square W1, tube: Bond St) is London's finest small gallery in a splendidly Italianate mansion. It has a treasure-trove of high-quality paintings from the 17th and 18th centuries, including Frans Hals' *Laughing Cavalier* and Rembrandt's *Titus*, excellent porcelain and a collection of armour. It tends to be a well-kept secret, the kind of gallery you might overlook – which would be a mistake.

It's open, free, Monday to Saturday from 10 am to 5 pm, Sunday from 2 to 5 pm.

BBC Experience (Map 5)

In Langham Place, off Oxford Circus, the BBC Experience (☎ 0171-580 4468) gives you a chance to descend into the bowels of Broadcasting House and learn about the history of radio. You can also listen to clips of particularly famous scripts and take part in a 'recording' of the famous Radio 4 soap *The Archers*. Expect long queues in summer.

It's open daily from 9.30 am to 5.30 pm for £5.75/4.

COVENT GARDEN (MAP 3)

In the 1630s, the architect Inigo Jones (1573-1652) converted something that had started life as a vegetable field attached to Westminster Abbey into the elegant Covent Garden piazza. In time it became the haunt of writers like Samuel Pepys, Henry Fielding and James Boswell in search of shady nightlife, but by Victorian times the fruit and vegetable market immortalised in the film *My Fair Lady* (the screen adaptation of George Bernard Shaw's play *Pygmalion*) had been established. When the fruit and veg moved out to Nine Elms in Battersea in the 1980s, the old market was transformed into one of central London's liveliest hubs, with glitzy shops built into the old arcades.

Covent Garden (tube: Covent Garden) gets horribly overcrowded in summer, but there's always a corner of relative peace where you can watch the world, and the licensed buskers, go by. Unfortunately there are signs of a gradual slither downmarket, as Pizza Hut and Dunkin' Donuts outlets open on the fringes.

Where stallholders once flogged fresh produce, they now sell antiques, clothes and overpriced bric-a-brac. At the junction of the piazza and Southampton St, the covered Jubilee Market sells cheap clothes and jewellery from Tuesday to Friday but becomes a more upmarket crafts fair at the weekend.

Tucked away in the basement of the piazza is the **Cabaret Mechanical Theatre** (☎ 0171-379 7961), a treasure-trove of automata with buttons to push and handles to turn, guaranteed to bring out the child in all of us. Overlooking the piazza on the western side is the porticoed rear of **St Paul's Church**. Designed by Inigo Jones in the 1630s, it's little more than a stone rectangle with a pitched roof … 'the handsomest barn in England'. In the square in front, where Pepys watched England's first Punch and Judy show in 1662, you can still see buskers perform. For a quiet escape, head down King St or Henrietta St and look for the entrances into the peaceful churchyard.

On the opposite side of the piazza stands the Victorian **Floral Hall**, currently under restoration as part of ambitious plans to redevelop and expand the adjoining **Royal Opera House**.

Beyond the piazza are lively streets of clothes shops and bars, restaurants and designer gift shops. **Neal St**, a narrow lane leading from Long Acre to Shaftesbury Ave, is particularly worth exploring (See Places to Eat later in this chapter for details on Neal's Yard).

For all things African, turn left down King St after leaving St Paul's for the Africa Centre (☎ 0171-836 1973, 38 King St WC2). There are often African bands here as well as an excellent, moderately priced African restaurant.

A block farther north is **Floral St**, where swanky designer clothing outlets include Paul Smith, Jigsaw, Jones and Agnès B. Another block north and you're in Long Acre which boasts Emporio Armani, Woodhouse, The Gap, and Flip (a thrift shop selling 50s American clothing) as well as Stanfords for guidebooks and maps.

Tucked into the corner of Covent Garden between the Jubilee Market and Tutton's restaurant, the **London Transport Museum** (☎ 0171-379 6344) tells how London made the transition from streets choked with horse-drawn carriages to the arrival of the Docklands Light Railway, a more interesting story than you might imagine. It's open daily from 10 am to 5.15 pm (from 11 am on Friday) for £4.95/2.95.

The **Theatre Museum** (☎ 0171-836 7891), round the corner in Russell St, displays costumes and artefacts relating to the history of the theatre, including memorabilia of great actors and actresses like David Garrick, Edmund Kean, Henry Irving and Ellen Terry. It's open Tuesday to Sunday from 11 am to 6.30 pm for £3.50/2.

WESTMINSTER (MAP 4)

Since a British city is defined as a town with a cathedral, London actually consists of two cities: Westminster and London, with Westminster Cathedral and St Paul's Cathedral respectively. It's the City of London that is known simply as 'the City' but Westminster is the centre of political power and most of its places of interest are defined by their association with royal and/or parliamentary power.

Westminster Abbey

Westminster Abbey (☎ 0171-222 7110, Dean's Yard SW1, tube: St James's Park or Westminster) is one of the most visited churches in the Christian world. It's played an important role in the history of the English church and since 1066 every sovereign apart from Edward V and Edward VIII has been crowned here.

It's world-famous as the resting place of monarchs and the venue for other great pageants, most notably in recent years as the setting for the funeral of Diana, Princess of Wales. Also within its walls is Britain's largest collection of tombs and monuments to the famous.

One of the best ways to visit the abbey is to come to a service, preferably evensong when the atmosphere and acoustics will send shivers down your spine. Evensong lasts less than an hour; Monday, Tuesday, Thursday and Friday at 5 pm; Saturday and Sunday at 3 pm.

The main entry is at the west door, above which are two towers built by Wren and his baroque pupil Nicholas Hawksmoor. Entering the nave you'll see the **Tomb to the Unknown Warrior**, brought back from the battlefields of WWI, in the centre of the floor, surrounded by poppies. Nearby is a memorial to Sir Winston Churchill.

At the east end of the nave is the **screen** separating it from the choir. Against it are monuments to Sir Isaac Newton and Lord Stanhope, by Rysbrack. Above the screen is the magnificent organ, dating from 1730. Look skyward to the beautiful stone vaulted ceiling in the nave, and the fan-vaulted aisles.

To the right is the **musicians' aisle**, with memorials commemorating musicians who served the abbey. Appropriately sited, at the

second pillar on the right after the organ pipes, is the memorial to **Henry Purcell**, once organist at the abbey.

Make your way eastwards to the Lantern, the heart of the abbey, where coronations take place. The **ornate altar**, designed by Sir Gilbert Scott in 1897, depicts the last supper.

Turn around to admire the stunning gold, blue and red Victorian Gothic **choir** created in the mid-19th century by Edward Blore. It's here that 20 boys from the Choir School and 12 lay vicars sing the daily services.

The **north transept** commemorates statesmen and many politicians. William Gladstone and Benjamin Disraeli, both prime ministers but of opposing opinions, are ironically close. Robert Peel, the creator of the police force, stands near. Above them the rose window, designed by Sir James Thornhill, depicts the 12 disciples with Judas Iscariot omitted.

On your left as you continue eastwards are three wonderful medieval **tombs**, one of them that of Edmund Crouchback, founder of the House of Lancaster.

Beyond the chapels, up the steps and to your left is the **Queen Elizabeth Chapel** where Elizabeth I and her half-sister Mary I share an elaborate tomb. In life, they didn't get on, which may be why there's no effigy of Mary.

The most easterly part of the abbey is **Henry VII's Chapel**, an outstanding example of late perpendicular architecture added in 1503. The magnificently carved wooden stalls, reserved for the Knights of the Order of the Bath, feature a colourful headpiece. Recent members of the order include former US President Ronald Reagan and General Norman Schwarzkopf.

Behind the altar is the black-marble **sarcophagus** of Henry VII and his queen, Elizabeth of York, housed under an amazing fan-vaulted Tudor ceiling. Beyond this is the **Battle of Britain stained-glass window**. At its entrance a **plaque** marks the spot where Oliver Cromwell's body lay until the Restoration, whereupon it was disinterred, hanged at Tyburn and beheaded.

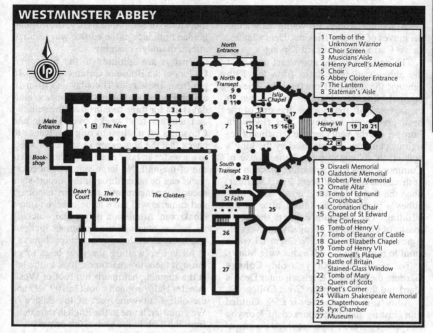

WESTMINSTER ABBEY

1 Tomb of the
   Unknown Warrior
2 Choir Screen
3 Musicians' Aisle
4 Henry Purcell's Memorial
5 Choir
6 Abbey Cloister Entrance
7 The Lantern
8 Statesman's Aisle

9 Disraeli Memorial
10 Gladstone Memorial
11 Robert Peel Memorial
12 Ornate Altar
13 Tomb of Edmund
   Crouchback
14 Coronation Chair
15 Chapel of St Edward
   the Confessor
16 Tomb of Henry V
17 Tomb of Eleanor of Castile
18 Queen Elizabeth Chapel
19 Tomb of Henry VII
20 Cromwell's Plaque
21 Battle of Britain
   Stained-Glass Window
22 Tomb of Mary
   Queen of Scots
23 Poet's Corner
24 William Shakespeare Memorial
25 Chapterhouse
26 Pyx Chamber
27 Museum

In the south aisle is the **tomb of Mary Queen of Scots** (beheaded on her cousin's orders) and the breathtaking **tomb of Lady Margaret Beaufort**, the mother of Henry VII.

Across the bridge, **Henry V's tomb** lies at the entrance to the **Chapel of St Edward the Confessor**, the most sacred spot in the abbey, behind the high altar. St Edward was the founder of the abbey and the original building was consecrated a few days before his death. The original tomb was destroyed during the Reformation.

Edward is surrounded by five kings and four queens, including the wife of Edward I, **Eleanor of Castile**. She lies in one of the oldest and most beautiful surviving bronze tombs beside Henry II who was responsible for rebuilding the abbey.

The **Coronation Chair** faces Edward's tomb and sits in front of an amazing stone screen portraying scenes from his life. The chair dates from around 1300 and is made of oak. Below its seat used to lie the Stone of Scone (pronounced skoon) – the Scottish coronation stone pilfered in 1297 by Edward. The stone was finally moved back to Edinburgh Castle in 1996.

In the **south transept** is **Poet's Corner**, where several of England's finest writers are buried, a precedent that was established with Geoffrey Chaucer, although he was actually buried here because he had been Clerk of Works to the Palace of Westminster, not because he had written *The Canterbury Tales*.

In front of two medieval wall paintings on the south wall stands the **memorial to William Shakespeare**, who, like TS Eliot, George Byron, Alfred Lord Tennyson, William Blake and various other luminaries, is not actually buried here. There are memorials to Georg Friedrich Händel, holding a score of the *Messiah*, Edmund Spenser, Lord Tennyson and Robert Browning, as well as the graves of Charles Dickens, Henry James, Lewis Carroll and Rudyard Kipling.

The entrance in the north-east corner of the abbey's cloister dates from the 13th century, the rest of it from the 14th. The octagonal **Chapter House**, east down a passageway off the cloister, has one of the best preserved medieval tile floors in Europe. On the walls are the remains of religious paintings. It was used by the king's council as its chamber, and the House of Commons used it as a meeting place in the 16th century. The adjacent **Pyx Chamber**, once the Royal Treasury, now displays the abbey's plate and the oldest altar in the building. The **museum** exhibits the death masks of generations of royalty and wax effigies of Charles II and William III (on a stool to make him as tall as his wife Mary).

To reach the 900-year-old **College Garden**, the oldest in England, enter Dean's Yard and the Cloisters on Great College St.

Admission to the abbey is £5/2. Guided tours lasting about 1½ hours cost £7, or you can take a portable tape-recorded commentary to stop and start at your leisure for £6.

The nave is open daily from 8 am to 6 pm, to 7.45 pm on Wednesday and between services on Sunday. The royal chapels and transepts are open Monday to Friday from 9 am to 4 pm, reopening from 6 to 7.45 pm on Wednesday, and Saturday from 9 am to 2 pm and 3.45 to 5 pm.

The Chapter House, Pyx Chamber and Abbey Museum (☎ 0171-222 5897, EH) are open from 10.30 am to 5.30 pm daily from April through October, closing at 4 pm between November and March, for £2.50/1.90. The College Garden is open from April to September, Tuesday and Thursday from 10 am to 6 pm (Tuesday and Thursday from 10 am to 4 pm in winter).

Houses of Parliament

The Houses of Parliament (☎ 0171-219 4272, Parliament Square SW1, tube: Westminster) include the House of Commons and House of Lords. Jointly built by Sir Charles Barry and Augustus Pugin during the Victorian neogothic frenzy, the original golden brilliance of the edifice was restored after a thorough cleaning.

Visitors are admitted to the Strangers' Gallery of the House of Commons after 4.15 pm from Tuesday to Thursday and from 10 am on Friday. Parliamentary recesses (holidays) last for three months over the summer and another few weeks over Easter and Christmas, so it's best to ring in advance to check that the houses are in session. Expect to queue for an hour even when the debate is run-of-the-mill. No large suitcases or backpacks can be taken through the airport-style security arrangements, and even handbags and cameras will have to be checked into a cloakroom. Admission is free and watching the arcane rituals of the Commons makes a good way to while away a wet few hours.

As you're waiting for your bags to go through the x-ray machines, look to the left at the stunning hammerbeam roof of **Westminster Hall**, originally built in 1097-99 and the oldest surviving part of the Palace of Westminster, home to the English monarchy from the 11th to the early 16th century.

Whitehall

This wide avenue leads from Trafalgar Square to Parliament Square. The flanking buildings house government offices including the Admiralty and the Ministry of Defence at the north end, Downing St in the middle and The Treasury to the south.

The only exceptional edifice is Inigo Jones' splendid Banqueting House. Opposite is Horse Guards Parade where the mounted guard is changed twice daily, offering a more accessible version of the ceremony than the one held outside Buckingham Palace. The Cenotaph, near the Parliament Square end of Whitehall, commemorates those who died in WWI and II.

Downing St Sir George Downing was a Dublin diplomat who was supposedly the second man ever to graduate from Harvard. After his glory years in the American colonies, Downing came to London and built a row of sturdy-looking houses off Whitehall, of which four remain.

Since 1732, when George II made a gift of No 10 to Robert Walpole, it has been the official residence of Britain's prime minister. The chancellor of the exchequer (the country's senior economic and financial minister) lives next door at No 11. The other two houses are used for government offices.

Banqueting House Built in 1622, the imposing Banqueting House (☎ 0171-930 4179, Whitehall SW1, tube: Westminster) is the only surviving part of the old Whitehall Palace which once stretched most of the way along Whitehall but burnt down in 1698.

Inspired by what Palladio had done with porticoes and pilasters, Inigo Jones returned from a visit to Italy to build England's first Renaissance building. Although it was designed as a venue for banquets and masques, the Banqueting House's greatest claim to fame is that it was on a scaffold built against a 1st floor window that Charles I was executed on 30 January 1649.

Despite the resumption of its original role on the Restoration of Charles II, once the palace burnt down the Banqueting House fell from favour. It's still occasionally used for state banquets, concerts and other events, and can sometimes be closed to the public.

It's open Monday to Saturday from 10 am to 5 pm for £3.25/2.50.

Cabinet War Rooms
During WWII the British Government took refuge underground, conducting its business from beneath 3m of solid concrete. It was from the Cabinet War Rooms (☎ 0171-930 6961, Clive Steps, King Charles St SW1, tube: Westminster) that Churchill made some of his most stirring speeches, and you can hear extracts from some of them here. Restored to its 1940s condition, the bunker is a fascinating place to visit although its narrow corridors become uncomfortably crowded in summer. The 40 minute recorded commentary helps make

sense of the maze of tunnels and doors. Even people who're not much interested in military matters will find this a fascinating glimpse at a hidden world.

The War Rooms are open daily from 9.30 am to 6 pm (from 10 am October to March). Admission costs £4.60/2.30.

Institute for Contemporary Arts
The Institute for Contemporary Arts (☎ 0171-930 3647, The Mall SW1, tube: Charing Cross) is an innovative complex incorporating a small bookshop, an art gallery, cinema, bar, café and theatre. There's always something worthwhile to see, the bar and restaurant are good value, and it attracts a relaxed young crowd.

St James's Park & Green Park
St James's Park (☎ 0171-930 1793, The Mall SW1, tube: St James's Park) is the neatest and most royal of London's royal parks, with the best vistas – of Westminster, Buckingham Palace, St James's Palace, Carlton Terrace and Horse Guards Parade. The flower beds are sumptuous and colourful, some of them newly replanted to mix shrubs, flowers and trees. But what makes St James's so particularly special is its large lake and the collection of waterfowl that live on it, including a group of pelicans, descendants of birds who've been here since the reign of Charles II. Come here in early evening and you'll see Londoners whose lives revolve around the birds, summoning them with imitation tweets and whistles.

St James's Palace is not open to the public. The striking Tudor gatehouse, only survivor of a building initiated by the palace-hungry Henry VIII in 1530, is best approached from St James's St. It's never been much used, although foreign ambassadors are still accredited to the court of St James.

Green Park adjoins St James's just across The Mall, and is a less fussy, more naturally rolling park, with a mix of trees and open space. Once a duelling ground and, like Hyde Park, a vegetable field during WWII,

Green Park tends to be less crowded than its illustrious neighbour.

The parks are open daily from 6 am to midnight.

Buckingham Palace

Buckingham Palace (☎ 0171-930 4832, SW1, tube: Victoria) is located at the end of The Mall, where St James's Park and Green Park meet at a giant traffic (partially pedestrianised) roundabout.

It's easy to be sniffy about the palace, especially given that neither exuberant white and gold decoration nor flock wallpaper are flavour of the decade. But, hell, we wouldn't really expect the Queen's front room to look like our own, would we? Anyway, all but the most hardened anti-monarchist should get a kick out of seeing what lies behind that expressionless façade. If nothing else it's fun to discover that such a familiar landmark does have other faces – and the view from the garden is much better than that from the front.

Most people will enjoy seeing the Throne Room, with his and hers thrones lined up under something like a theatre arch; the State Dining Room with a portrait of George III looking extremely fetching in furs; and the Blue Drawing Room with a gorgeous fluted ceiling by Nash. The paintings on display in the Long Gallery are also very fine, with several impressive Rembrandts, a Vermeer and a pair of Van Dyck portraits of Charles I.

The palace is open daily from 9.30 am to 4.30 pm from early August to September. Admission costs £9.50/5. Tickets are sold from a booth in Green Park but you can also book by credit card on ☎ 0171-321 2233.

Royal Mews The Royal Mews (☎ 0171-930 4832) is tucked away in Buckingham Palace Rd SW1, behind the palace. What started life as a home for falcons now houses all the flashy vehicles the royals use for getting around on ceremonial occasions, including the stunning Gold State Coach of 1761 used for every coronation since George IV's and the Glass Coach of 1910

which is used for royal weddings. Don't forget to look at the stables where the royal horses munch their oats in stalls designed by Nash in the 1820s.

The Royal Mews is open from Easter to October, Tuesday to Thursday, from noon to 4 pm; the rest of the year open Wednesday only. Admission costs £4/2.

Changing the Guard This is one of those quintessentially English events visitors to London must see, although you'll probably go away wondering what all the fuss was about. The old guard comes off duty to be replaced by the new guard in the forecourt of Buckingham Palace, giving tourists a chance to gawp at the bright red uniforms and bearskin hats (synthetic alternatives are being sought). If you arrive early, grab a prime spot by the railings; more likely than not, however, you'll be 10 rows back and hardly see a thing. A similar ceremony takes place at Horse Guards in Whitehall.

Buckingham Palace
  Early April through July daily at 11.30 am;
  August to early April alternate days at 11.30 am.
Whitehall
  Monday to Saturday at 11 am, Sunday at 10 am.

Westminster Cathedral

Completed in 1903, Westminster Cathedral (☎ 0171-798 9064, Ashley Place SW1, tube: Victoria) is the headquarters of the Catholic Church in Britain, and the only good example of neo-Byzantine architecture in the city. Its distinctively striped red-brick and white-stone tower features prominently on the west London skyline, although remarkably few people think to look inside. For £2 you can take a lift up the tower for panoramic views of London from 9 am to 5 pm daily (closed Monday to Wednesday from December to March).

The interior is part splendid marble and mosaic and part bare brick – the money ran out although there are now plans to complete it. The highly regarded stone carvings of the 14 Stations of the Cross by controversial sculptor Eric Gill and the marvellously sombre atmosphere, especially in early evening when the mosaics glitter in the dark, make this a cherished haven from the traffic outside.

Tate Gallery

The Tate Gallery (☎ 0171-887 8000, Millbank SW1, tube: Pimlico) is custodian to both the nation's international modern art collection and its archive of British art. A bright, modern gallery, it only has hanging space for a quarter of its treasures at any one time, and these are displayed in chronological order. Director Nicholas Serota gets round this problem by rehanging the pictures once a year, which means you can't be sure any one particular painting will be on display without calling first to check. Nevertheless, you can be sure that high-quality works by Pablo Picasso, Henri Matisse, Cézanne, Gwen and Augutus John, Mark Rothko and Jackson Pollock will be on display – alongside stuffy Victorian paintings of thoroughbred racehorses and the sort of contemporary art that brings the Establishment out in a sweat. Likely highlights include the mystical paintings by William Blake in rooms 6 and 7, the Hogarths in room 2 and the Constables in room 8.

The adjacent **Clore Gallery**, James Stirling's quirky stab at acceptable, post-modern architecture, houses the JMW Turner paintings. He is perhaps the only British artist who would consistently be counted among the all-time greats. For most people, the Clore, like the main gallery, will be a must-see.

An extension to the Tate is currently under construction in the old Bankside power station across the river. It's unlikely to open before the year 2000 but when it does there's likely to be some rationalisation of the collections at the National Gallery and the two Tates; all the pre-1900 pictures (apart from the Turners) are likely to wind up at the National, with the newer pictures in the Tates.

The Tate is open, free, Monday to Saturday from 10 am to 5.50 pm, Sunday from 2 to 5.50 pm. Special exhibitions attract a variable admission fee. The enormously popular basement café, with a mural by Rex

Whistler, offers a wide range of reasonably priced hot and cold food.

BLOOMSBURY (MAP 5)

East of Tottenham Court Rd and north of Holborn, elegant Bloomsbury is an area of fine Georgian squares and neat Victorian terraces, home to the British Museum and London University.

Between the world wars these pleasant streets were colonised by the group of artists and intellectuals known as the Bloomsbury Group who spawned an entire industry of collections of letters, memoirs and biographies. The novelists Virginia Woolf and EM Forster, who lived in Tavistock Square and Brunswick Square respectively, and the economist John Maynard Keynes are perhaps the best known Bloomsbury Group members. Others included the biographer Lytton Strachey; the art critic Roger Fry, who organised the first-ever London show of the French Impressionists and has been rather dubiously credited with coining the movement's name; Vanessa Bell, sister of Virginia Woolf; and Duncan Grant, who painted mediocre pictures.

The heart of literary Bloomsbury was **Gordon Square** where, at various times, Strachey lived at No 51, Vanessa and Clive Bell at No 37, and Keynes and the Woolf family at No 46. Strachey, Dora Carrington and Lydia Lopokova (later the wife of Keynes) all took turns living at No 41.

British Museum

The British Museum (☎ 0171-636 1555, Great Russell St WC1, tube: Tottenham Court Rd or Russell Square) is Britain's largest museum and one of the oldest in the world. It's also London's most visited tourist attraction. Six million people can't be wrong so make sure you don't miss it.

The collection is vast, diverse and amazing; so vast, diverse and amazing in fact that it can seem pretty daunting, especially on a stuffy summer's day when it seems that all six million have chosen the same day to visit. To make the most of the

Whose Marbles Are They Anyway?

Wonderful though it is, the British Museum can sometimes feel like one vast repository for stolen booty. Much of what you're looking at wasn't just 'picked up' along the way by Victorian travellers and explorers, but stolen, or purchased under dubious circumstances.

During the 1990s restive foreign governments occasionally popped their heads over the parapet to demand the return of 'their' property. The loudest voice was that of the Greeks calling for the return of the so-called Elgin Marbles to their original home on the Parthenon in Athens, but almost the first act of the incoming Labour government in 1977 was to announce that they would be staying put.

Elgin marbles: one of Selene's chariot horses.

Other particularly contentious exhibits are the Benin Bronzes gracing the main stairs and the Nereid Monument removed from Xanthos in Turkey. Strangely enough the Egyptians seem reasonably phlegmatic about the loss of the Rosetta Stone which was used to translate the hieroglyphic alphabet.

museum don't plan on seeing too much in one day; admission is still free so you can come back several times and appreciate things at your leisure.

There are two entrances: the imposing, Smirke-designed, porticoed main entrance off Great Russell St, and the sneaky back entrance off Montague Place which tends to be less congested. Assuming you come in with the masses through the front entrance, head straight for the information desk at the back of the main hall and ask for a list of the free hour-long Eye Opener tours of individual galleries. These take place between 11 am and 3 pm Monday to Saturday and between 3.30 and 4.30 pm on Sunday. The museum's own 90-minute tours of the highlights cost £6 and can get booked up.

If you don't want to be shown around, the most obvious strategy is to home straight in on the highlights, bearing in mind that most people will do the same thing. If you don't like crowds, head for the less visited galleries housing Japanese arts, Chinese and South-East Asian arts or the antiquities of Western Asia.

With limited time, fix upon a few 'must see' exhibits, such as the weird Assyrian treasures and Egyptian mummies, the Elgin Marbles, the Rosetta Stone, the Magna Carta, the Sutton Hoo treasure, the exquisite pre-Christian Portland Vase and the 2000-year-old corpse found in a Cheshire Bog, fondly known as Lindow Man. Then make time for some personal fancies, be it Saxon weaponry, Hindu sculptures, or Japanese teahouses.

At the heart of the museum, the grand **British Library Reading Room** is where Shaw and Mahatma Gandhi studied and where Karl Marx wrote *Das Kapital*. The British Library has now moved to its new home at St Pancras and work has started on modernising the museum to ease congestion in the main hall. Eventually the ethnographical collections which used to be housed in the Museum of Mankind will be displayed in new galleries here.

Note that work on the new Great Court may cause disturbance to the usual exhibitions. If you can't find something, ask. A new café has opened but is rather pricey. Better head off along Museum St in search of sustenance.

The museum is open Monday to Saturday, from 10 am to 5 pm and on Sunday from 2.30 to 6 pm. Admission is free (£2 donations requested). Information for visitors with disabilities is available by phoning ☎ 0171-637 7384.

Dickens' House (Map 5)

Charles Dickens' House (☎ 0171-405 2127, 49 Doughty St WC1, tube: Russell Square) is the only surviving residence of the many the great Victorian novelist occupied before moving to Kent. Here he wrote *Pickwick Papers*, *Nicholas Nickleby* and *Oliver Twist*, between bouts of anxiety over various debts, deaths and the burden of an ever-growing family.

Inside this standard Victorian terraced house, two desks illustrate Dickens' rags-to-riches story. The rough-hewn wooden table where he worked as a 15-year-old Gray's Inn lawyer's clerk for 13s 6d could hardly stand in sharper contrast to the velvet-topped desk he later used on reading tours of England and America.

It's open Monday to Saturday from 10 am to 5 pm, £3.50/2.50.

HOLBORN & EMBANKMENT

Of the millions of tourists who flood London every year, relatively few find the select places of interest – a beautiful church, museum and art gallery – in the Holborn and Embankment area. This most interesting corner of London is also the lair of lawyers.

Inns of Court (Map 5)

There are four Inns of Court all clustered near to Holborn and Fleet St: **Lincoln's Inn** (☎ 0171-405 1393, Lincoln's Inn Fields WC2, tube: Holborn), **Gray's Inn** (☎ 0171-

405 8164, Gray's Inn Rd WC1, tube: Holborn or Chancery Lane), **Inner Temple** (☎ 0171-797 8250, King's Bench Walk EC4, tube: Temple), and **Middle Temple** (☎ 0171-353 4355, Middle Temple Lane EC4, tube: Temple).

All London barristers are attached to one of the inns which can boast a roll call of former members ranging from Cromwell to Mahatma Gandhi, from Dickens to Margaret Thatcher. Anyone who believes Britain is becoming a classless society should drop by one of these oases to have their illusions shattered; the aloof air of complacency and permanence that you see here suggests that not much has changed after all.

It would take a lifetime spent working here to grasp all the intricacies and subtleties of the inns' arcane protocols – they're a lot like the Freemasons (both organisations date back to the 13th century) and, needless to say, lots of barristers are indeed Freemasons.

Despite being rather inaccessible to outsiders, both Gray's Inn and Lincoln's Inn have peaceful, picturesque lawns and quadrangles. These make for a delightful walk, especially early on weekday mornings before the legal machine has cranked into action, and the hordes of self-important barristers in funny gowns and wigs have started to rush around.

All four inns were badly damaged during the war. Lincoln's Inn is relatively intact, with original 15th century buildings, including the Tudor Chancery Lane Gatehouse – although the archway leading from the adjoining park, Lincoln's Inn Fields, is a copy. Inigo Jones helped plan Lincoln's Inn chapel, which was built in 1621 and remains pretty well preserved.

Not far from the inns, at the bottom of the Strand, are the Royal Courts of Justice, an extraordinary Gothic Revival confection of arches, turrets and spires. This is where many landmark cases wind up and the High Court often forms the backdrop to television news coverage of important cases. Visits are possible although you can't take a camera inside the building.

The Lincoln's Inn grounds are open Monday to Friday from 9 am to 5 pm, and Lincoln's Inn Chapel is open Monday to Friday from 12.30 to 2.30 pm. Gray's Inn and the Inner Temple and Middle Temple are open Monday to Friday from 10 am to 4 pm.

Temple Church (Map 6)

Temple Church (☎ 0171-353 1736, Inner Temple, King's Bench Walk EC4, tube: Temple, or Blackfriars on Sunday) was originally planned and built by the secretive Knights Templar between 1161 and 1185. They modelled it on the Church of the Holy Sepulchre in Jerusalem, and the core of the building is one of only four round churches in Britain (the only one left in London).

Although the Knights Templar were eventually suppressed for being too powerful, stone effigies of notable 13th century knights still adorn the floors of the circular nave.

The church was badly damaged during the last war, but has since been sensitively restored. It's open Wednesday to Saturday from 10 am to 4 pm, and Sunday from 12.45 to 4 pm. Westminster Abbey and St Paul's Cathedral aside, this is London's most architecturally important church. Don't miss it.

Sir John Soane's Museum (Map 5)

Sir John Soane's Museum (☎ 0171-405 2107, 13 Lincoln's Inn Fields, WC2, tube: Holborn) is partly a beautiful, if quirky, house and partly a diverse collection of interesting objects.

Sir John Soane was a leading early 19th century architect (he also designed the Bank of England) who married into a fortune which he spent on customising two houses in Lincoln's Inn Fields, close to the Inns of Court. The end result is a curiosity, with a glass dome bringing light to the basement, a lantern room filled with statuary, and a picture gallery where each painting folds away if pressed to reveal another one behind. Nothing is quite how it seems, which, along with the ragbag collection, is its charm.

Soane's Egyptiana predated the Victorian flirtation with all things pharaonic. Here too, you'll find the original *Rake's Progress* paintings, William Hogarth's cartoon burlesques of late 18th century London lowlife. The museum is open, free, Tuesday to Saturday from 10 am to 5 pm.

Courtauld Institute (Map 3)

Housed in the Strand Block of the splendid Palladian Somerset House, the Courtauld Gallery (☎ 0171-873 2526, Strand WC2, tube: Covent Garden) displays some of the Courtauld Institute's marvellous collection of paintings. Exhibits include work by Peter Paul Rubens, Velásquez and Sandro Botticelli. However, for many visitors the most memorable display is of the Impressionist and post-Impressionist art by Vincent Van Gogh, Cézanne, Édouard Manet, Camille Pissarro, Alfred Sisley, Henri Rousseau, Henri Toulouse-Lautrec, Paul Gauguin, Pierre Auguste Renoir, Edgar Degas and Claude Monet shown on the top floor. Rarely have so many world-famous paintings been gathered together in one beautifully lit, undivided room.

By the time you read this the gallery should have reopened after a National Lottery-funded overhaul. It should be open Monday to Saturday from 10 am to 6 pm, Sunday from 2 to 6 pm but the admission fee is yet to be decided.

Fleet Street (Map 6)

Fleet St used to be known as the Street of Shame, where clapped-out printing presses and equally clapped-out journalists padded out the nation's newspapers with gossip, speculation and lies.

Since Caxton's day, people round here had had ink on their fingers. But the mid-1980s brought Rupert Murdoch, new technology and the Docklands redevelopment. Now that the action has moved east only ghosts linger on: El Vino's, the journos' number one watering hole, the glamorous former *Daily Telegraph* building (1930) now occupied by assorted banks, and the former *Daily Express* building (1932), London's first modernist glass-box high-rise (the 'Black Lubianka') designed by Sir Owen Williams.

St Bride's Church (Map 6)

St Bride's (☎ 0171-353 1301, Fleet St EC4, tube: Blackfriars) is a small but perfect church, the fifth on the site and designed by Wren between 1670 and 1675. The add-on spire of 1701-03 may have inspired the design of the traditional English wedding cake. The church was hit by bombs in 1940 and the interior layout reflects a modern rethink when the time came to rebuild.

In the 16th century, Wynkyn de Worde moved Caxton's printing press from Westminster to beside St Bride's, thus starting an association with the printing trade that has continued ever since; a chapel in the north aisle honours journalists who have died in the course of their work.

Be sure to descend to the crypt which contains a small museum of the printing trade amid the foundations of previous churches and Roman remains found during post-war renovations.

St Bride's is open Monday to Friday from 8 am to 4.45 pm, Saturday from 9 am to 4.45 pm, and Sunday from 9 am to 12.30 pm and 5.30 to 7.30 pm.

Dr Johnson's House (Map 6)

Dr Johnson's House (☎ 0171-353 3745, 17 Gough Square EC4, tube: Blackfriars) is the well-preserved Georgian town house where Johnson lived from 1748 to 1759. Johnson was a lexicographer who, along with six full-time assistants working in the attic upstairs, compiled the first English dictionary.

Johnson is also famous for his witty, scathing aphorisms, all written down by his amanuensis and fellow Scot, James Boswell. It was Johnson who claimed that 'when a man is tired of London he is tired of life; for there is in London all that life can afford'.

The house is full of pictures of Johnson's friends and intimates, including his black manservant Francis Barber to whom he was surprisingly generous in his will. But the house is of rather specialist interest if you're short of time.

It's open from May to September, Monday to Saturday from 11 am to 5.30 pm,

closing at 5 pm for the rest of the year. Admission costs £3/1.

MARYLEBONE & REGENT'S PARK

Marylebone Rd is north of Oxford St and home to the capital's number one tourist trap, Madame Tussaud's. Fortunately, it is also close to Regent's Park which provides a haven of peace as well as being near the hustle of Camden Town which lies just to the east.

Madame Tussaud's & the Planetarium (Map 2)

Madame Tussaud's (☎ 0171-935 6861, Marylebone Rd NW1, tube: Baker St) is one of London's most visited sights and, in summer at least, one of its most hideously overcrowded: expect long queues.

Much of the ground space is devoted to the Garden Party exhibition where you can have your picture taken alongside sporting greats like Muhammad Ali and comedians like Lenny Henry. The Grand Hall is where you'll find models of world leaders past and present, and of the Royal Family, now minus Fergie, the disgraced Duchess of York, and with the departed Princess Diana on the sidelines.

In the **Spirit of London** time ride you sit in a mock-up of a black taxi cab and are whipped through a five minute summary of London's history. Tucked away in the basement and certainly not for very young children or anyone particularly squeamish is the revamped **Chamber of Horrors** where models of contemporary prisoners like Denis Nilson ('the Muswell Hill Murderer') sit uneasily alongside tacky, not to say tasteless, representations of historic horrors – the mutilated corpse of one of Jack the Ripper's victims is particularly unpleasant.

The **Planetarium** presents 30-minute spectaculars on the stars and planets livened up with special effects which, sadly, can't match those you'd find at the Staffordshire theme park, Alton Towers.

Madame Tussaud's is open May through September daily from 9 am to 5.30 pm; and October through April, Monday to Friday from 10 am to 5.30 pm, Saturday and Sunday from 9.30 am to 5.30 pm. An all-inclusive ticket costs £11.50/7.55. Madame Tussaud's only is £9.95/6.10, the Planetarium only £5.85/3.85.

Regent's Park (Map 2)

Regent's Park (tube: Baker St or Regent's Park), north of Marylebone Rd and west of Camden, was once a royal hunting ground, subsequently farmed and then revived as a place for fun during the 18th century.

Soon after, Nash was employed by the Prince Regent to create something more grand. Nash's architectural blueprint was the closest London has ever come to a grand plan, with Regent St carving its way from the park all the way down to the Mall. Most of Regent St was torn down by the Victorians, but Nash's immaculate, stuccoed terraces around the perimeter of Regent's Park still survive.

With its **mosque**, the **London Zoo**, the **canal** at the northern end, an **open-air theatre** where Shakespeare is performed during the summer months (☎ 0171-486 2431), ponds and colourful flowerbeds, football pitches and summer softball games, Regent's Park is a lively haven in the city centre. The **Queen Mary Rose Gardens**, which lie at the heart of the park, are particularly spectacular.

To the north-east of Regent's Park, across Prince Albert Rd, is **Primrose Hill**, which, besides being less touristy and conventionally pretty, also has a spectacular view over London.

London Zoo (Map 9) One of the world's oldest zoos, London Zoo (☎ 0171-722 3333, Regent's Park NW1, tube: Camden Town) is, like the underground, a victim of its great age, saddled with many historically interesting buildings that no longer meet the expectations of animal-rights-minded modern visitors.

However, the emphasis is now firmly on conservation and education, with fewer species kept, wherever possible in breeding groups. Don't miss the elegant and cheerful

Penguin Pool, one of London's foremost modernist structures designed by Berthold Lubetkin in 1934.

The zoo is open March through September daily from 10 am to 5.30 pm, and October to February daily from 10 am to 4 pm. Admission is £8.50/6. A visit can easily be combined with a canal boat ride to Little Venice, or a walk along the canal to Camden Lock Market.

THE CITY (MAP 6)

This is where the Romans built a walled community 2000 years ago and the boundaries of today's City of London haven't changed much. There's plenty to see and do and a quiet Sunday stroll offers a unique chance to appreciate the architectural richness of the area's many famous buildings.

St Paul's Cathedral

St Paul's Cathedral (☎ 0171-236 4128, tube: St Paul's or Mansion House) was built by Wren between 1675 and 1710 on the site of two previous cathedrals, the first of which dated back to 604.

St Paul's was one of the 50 commissions given to Wren after the Great Fire of London. Plans for alterations had already been made, but the fire gave him the opportunity to build from scratch.

Despite being surrounded by some less-than-pleasant architecture (due for demolition), the dome still dominates the City and is only exceeded in size by St Peter's in Rome. The pictures of the cathedral miraculously extant amid the devastation of WWII bombing are well known; fortunately, the dome survived virtually unharmed, although the windows were blown out (hence the quantity of clear glass) and various other parts damaged.

In 1981 the cathedral featured in acres of newsprint as the venue for the ill-fated wedding of Prince Charles and Lady Diana Spencer. Charles picked the cathedral because its acoustics were judged to be better than those in Westminster Abbey. Time your visit to coincide with a service and judge for yourself.

Visitors who enter the west door are greeted by attendants waiting for admission fees, but things improve once you negotiate this obstacle. Proceed up the nave until you reach the dome; 30m above is the **Whispering Gallery** (the lower part of a triple dome), so called because if you talk close to the wall it carries your words around to the other side.

This gallery, and the **Stone** and **Golden** galleries, can be reached by a staircase in the south transept, but give them a miss if you suffer from claustrophobia or vertigo. All in all there are 530 narrow steps as you ascend and 543 narrow steps when you descend. The reward is a stunning view from the Stone Gallery – one of the best views of London. You can continue up to the Golden Gallery, if you feel like climbing farther.

When you get back down, inspect the ornately carved **choir stalls** by Grinling Gibbons, and the **iron screens** by Jean Tijou. Walk around the altar, with its outrageous canopy, to the **American Chapel**, a memorial to Americans killed during WWII.

At the west side of the south transept, close to a memorial to the painter JMW Turner, a staircase leads down to the **Crypt** and the **Treasury**. The Crypt has memorials to a number of military demigods including Wellington, Kitchener and Nelson, who is below the dome in a black sarcophagus. There are also battered effigies rescued from the previous cathedral and a niche that exhibits Wren's controversial plans and his 'great' model.

The most poignant memorial of all is Wren's, adorned with his son's famous epitaph: *Lector, si monumentum requiris, circumspice* – Reader, if you seek his monument, look around you.

The cathedral is open year-round Monday to Saturday from 8.30 am to 4 pm. Admission is £4/2, or £7.50/5.50 if you want to visit the galleries. Forty-five minute recorded tours cost £2.50. Guided 90 minute tours leave at 11 and 11.30 am, and 1.30 and 2 pm.

The Museum of London

Despite its unprepossessing setting amid the concrete walkways of the Barbican, the Museum of London (☎ 0171-600 3699, 150 London Wall EC2, tube: Barbican) is one of the city's finest museums, showing how it has evolved from the Ice Age to the mobile-phone age. The sections on Roman Britain and Roman Londinium make use of the nearby ruins of a Roman fort discovered during road construction. Otherwise, the displays work steadily through the centuries, using audiovisuals to show major events like the Great Fire of London.

The focus is on people as much as on the buildings and streets; the days of Dickensian London, of mass prostitution, sweatshop labour, unionisation and suffragettes make particularly poignant stories. The London Now gallery brings the story right up to date (or at least as far as the watershed of the last election).

The museum is open Tuesday to Saturday from 10 am to 5.50 pm and Sunday from noon to 5.50 pm, and costs £4/2 (free from 4.30 to 6 pm). Tickets are valid for three months, so you might want to come here at the start of your stay and then again just before you leave.

Barbican

Tucked into a corner of the City of London where there was once a watchtower (or 'barbican'), the Barbican (☎ 0171-638 8891, Silk St EC2, tube: Barbican or Moorgate) is a vast urban development built on a large bomb site left over from WWII. The original ambitious plan was to create a terribly smart, modern complex for offices, housing and the arts. Perhaps inevitably, the result was a forbidding series of wind tunnels with a dearth of shops, plenty of expensive high-rise apartments and an enormous cultural centre lost in the middle.

Here you'll find the London homes of the Royal Shakespeare Company (RSC), the London Symphony Orchestra and the London Classical Orchestra. There are also two cinemas, smaller theatrical auditoria, and ample gallery space, with possibly the best photographic shows in London. But be warned – even Londoners get here early to make sure of finding their way to the right spot at the right time.

For details of the theatres, cinemas and concert halls, see Entertainment later in this chapter.

St Bartholomew-the-Great

One of London's oldest churches, adjoining one of London's oldest hospitals, St Bartholomew-the-Great (☎ 0171-606 5171, West Smithfield EC1, tube: Barbican) is a stone's throw from the Barbican and well worth a visit. The Norman arches and details lend this holy space a kind of rustic calm.

The approach from nearby Smithfield's Market through the restored 13th century archway is like walking into history. Film buffs might note that the climactic wedding scene from *Four Weddings & A Funeral* was filmed in St Bart's.

From mid-February to mid-November it's open Monday to Friday from 8.30 am to 5 pm, Saturday from 10.30 am to 1.30 pm and Sunday from 8 am to 8 pm.

Smithfield Market

Smithfield Market (West Smithfield EC1, tube: Farringdon) is central London's last-surviving produce market; Billingsgate (fish) and Covent Garden (fruit and vegetables) have long since moved out. Supposedly Europe's largest wholesale meat market, this is no place for faint hearts or vegetarians.

They stopped selling livestock here a century ago, around the same time that the main buildings were erected by Horace Jones, the man responsible for Leadenhall Market. Early weekday mornings Smithfield is a hive of activity. Many of the local pubs open from the middle of the night to cater for the stall-holders' unsociable work hours; assuming you can pass yourself off as a cockney meat seller, there's always the chance of an early morning pint with your fried breakfast. It's open Monday to Friday from 5 am to 10.30 am.

Tower of London

The Tower of London (☎ 0171-709 0765, Tower Hill EC3, tube: Tower Hill) is a beau-

tifully preserved monument to cruelty. This may seem an odd description, but from 1078, when William the Conqueror laid the first stone of the White Tower, until well into this century, the Tower of London has been much more than an ancient tourist attraction.

When Rudolf Hess' 1941 peace mission turned into a fiasco, it was at the Tower that he commenced his long years of incarceration. No visitor will forget the Bloody Tower, where the young princes, sons and heirs of Edward IV, were allegedly slaughtered by their wicked uncle Richard III in the 15th century. Thomas More, Anne Boleyn, Lady Jane Grey and Walter Raleigh are also among the notable ex-residents. Other bloodcurdling attractions include Traitor's Gate, the river entrance through which condemned prisoners arrived to face their death, and the Martin Tower with its display of torture implements.

Historically, the tower has served as both castle and palace. Though never the royal seat, which has either been in Winchester or Westminster, it was where all of Henry VIII's wives set up home, even before it turned into a prison for a couple of them prior to their execution. There are some remnants of royal residence from long ago, the most impressive being the Chapel of St John, with its beautiful stone Romanesque arches and magical golden light.

Dwarfed as it is by the high-rise blocks of the nearby City business district, and spic and span thanks to years of restoration, it is rather difficult to take the Tower seriously as a fortress. The ramparts and battlements look like a movie set for Camelot. Nevertheless, in its time the 27m-high White Tower was the tallest building in London, in a prime position to see off any invading forces that sailed up the River Thames, and well situated to keep an eye on the notoriously restive populace of the city.

Start with a quick peek at the famous **ravens** on the green. Their wings are clipped as legend says the day they desert the Tower, London will fall to its enemies. Next, who could resist a snapshot of the famous beefeater guards? Of the many towers, don't miss the **Bloody Tower** where the Princes in the Tower were probably murdered. The **White Tower** has been undergoing extensive restoration but should have reopened to display an array of weapons and torture racks by the time you read this.

The Crown Jewels are housed in the **Waterloo Barracks**, a neogothic building facing the White Tower. Queues in summer are so long that the lines are provided with entertainment boards and videos. When you do finally make it through the massive steel doors to the inner sanctum a moving pavement will whisk you past the jewels in next to no time.

The Tower is open March through October Monday to Saturday from 9 am to 5 pm, Sunday from 10 am to 5 pm; and November through February daily from 9 am to 4 pm, opening at 10 am on Sunday and Monday. Admission is £9/6.80. Several readers have written to say they don't think it's worth so much. To get the most out of a trip, visit out of peak periods, and allow the best part of a day for looking round.

Tower Bridge

Tower Bridge (☎ 0171-407 0922) was built in 1894 when London was still a thriving port. Until then London Bridge was the most easterly crossing point and congestion was so bad that ship owners were forced to agree to a new bridge equipped with an ingenious mechanism which can clear the way to oncoming ships in under two minutes.

Now that London's port days are over you rarely see the bridge do its stuff but its walkways afford excellent views across the City and Docklands. A lift takes you up into the north tower where the building's story is recounted. The basement engine room and engineers' gallery are worth visiting, although the re-enactment of the royal opening of the bridge is missable. Rumour has it that some naughty visitors have rebelled against the tour and made off on their own to see the views.

The Bridge (tube: Tower Hill) is open April through October daily from 10 am to 6.30 pm; and November through March

daily from 9.30 am to 6 pm. Museum entry is £5.95/3.95.

Leadenhall Market

There's been a market on this site in Whittington Ave (Gracechurch St EC1, tube: Bank) since the year dot. It began life as a Roman forum, and in the 15th century Richard Whittington, the Lord Mayor of London, made it an official food market. Nowadays the Leadenhall arcades serve food and drink to hard-working City folk. Naturally, the prices aren't cheap but the selection is excellent, and the Victorian glass-and-iron structure is an architectural treat. It's open Monday to Friday from 7 am to 3 pm.

Guildhall

The Guildhall (☎ 0171-606 3030, off Gresham St EC2, tube: Bank) has been the City's seat of government for nearly 800 years. The present building dates from the early 15th century and the walls have survived both the Great Fire of 1666 and the Blitz of 1940, although surrounding development makes it hard to appreciate them from the outside.

Visitors can see the Great Hall where the mayor and sheriffs are still elected, a vast empty space with church-style monuments and the banners of the 12 great livery companies of London lining the walls. The impressive wooden roof is a post-war reconstruction by Sir Giles Gilbert Scott. The minstrels gallery at the west end carries statues of the legendary giants Gog and Magog, modern replacements for 18th century figures destroyed in the Blitz.

Meetings are still held in the hall every third Thursday of each month (except August) and the Guildhall hosts an annual flower show and various ceremonial banquets including that for the Booker Prize, the leading British literary prize.

The Guildhall is open (free) daily from 9 am to 5 pm.

THE EAST END

Although the East End districts of Spitalfields and Whitechapel may lie within walking distance of the City, the change of pace and style is quite extraordinary. Traditionally, this was working-class London, an area settled by wave upon wave of immigrants, giving it a curiously mixed Irish, Huguenot, Bangladeshi and Jewish culture. Run-down and neglected in the early 1980s, the East End is starting to look up in places, especially where it rubs up against the City in Spitalfields. Here Georgian houses have been snapped up by city suits with a few grand to spare.

But the tarting up coexists with appalling squalor and deprivation which should make anyone pause for thought.

For anyone interested in modern, multicultural London, it's well worth venturing a look at the East End. Attractions include some interesting small museums and some excellent-value Asian cuisine.

Geffrye Museum

The Geffrye Museum (☎ 0171-739 9893, Kingsland Rd, Dalston E2, tube: Old St, leave by exit 2 and take bus No 243) was originally built to provide homes for the elderly poor by Robert Geffrye, a late 16th century mayor of London who had made a fortune from the slave trade.

When the occupants were moved to healthier surroundings outside London, the house became a school for carpenters and artisans. It's now a museum of domestic interiors, with each room furnished to show how homes would have looked from Elizabethan times through to the present day. The original chapel also survives.

It's open (free) Tuesday to Saturday from 10 am to 5 pm, and Sunday from 2 to 5 pm.

Bethnal Green Museum of Childhood (Map 2)

The Bethnal Green Museum of Childhood (☎ 0181-983 5200, Cambridge Heath Rd E2, tube: Bethnal Green) is guaranteed to bring memories of childhood rushing back. Set in a rather grungy 19th century building, it's packed with dolls, dolls' houses, train sets, model cars, children's clothes, old board games, children's books, toy theatres

and puppets. The upstairs gallery provides a context for the toys by tracing the stages of childhood from babyhood to leaving home.

It's open Monday to Thursday and Saturday from 10 am to 5.50 pm, and Sunday from 2.30 to 5.50 pm (closed Friday). Admission is free.

DOCKLANDS (MAPS 2 & 6)

The Port of London was once the greatest port in the world, the hub of the British Empire and its enormous worldwide trade. In the 16th century there had been 20 cargo quays to the east of London. By the 18th century these were hard-pressed to cope with the quantity of cargo flowing through and in the 19th century new docks were opened. Even these proved inadequate as goods from the empire poured in and out and a new wave of dock building kicked off in the late 19th century. Finally, the King George Dock VI was built in 1921.

However, in 1940 25,000 bombs fell on the area over 57 consecutive nights. Already reeling, the docks were in no state to cope with the post-war technological and political changes as the empire evaporated, and enormous new bulk carriers and container ships demanded deep-water ports and new loading and unloading techniques. From the mid-1960s dock closures followed each other as fast as the openings had in the 19th century. The number of jobs available slumped from around 50,000 in 1960 to just 3000 by 1980. Almost one-eighth of the land area of London slowly succumbed to dereliction.

This was the area Mrs Thatcher saw as ripe for development. The builders moved in, the Docklands Light Rail (DLR) was constructed to link it to the rest of London, and yuppification proceeded apace. In a rush of activity, offices were built and toytown houses were thrown up beside new marinas. It was all very controversial, with complaints that very little of the money spent filtered down to the local population.

The recession of the early 1990s burst the bubble. The offices stood empty, the yuppies lost their jobs, their apartments wouldn't sell, and the trendy shops hung up

For Sale signs. Over it all towered the flagship development of Canary Wharf which had already come a financial cropper before the IRA bomb of 1996 devastated the area immediately around it. Now, however, things are moving along nicely again and Canary Wharf is home to the *Telegraph* and *Independent* newspapers.

Getting around was always the Docklands' Achilles heel. In the Thatcherite 80s, it was thought philosophically unsound for government to underwrite development by providing decent transport infrastructure. However, the DLR has got over its teething problems and now provides an excellent way of seeing what's going on from on high. Things will get even better when the Jubilee Line is eventually extended to Canary Wharf and beyond.

Walking Tour

The obvious starting point for a tour of Docklands is Tower Hill, where the underground connects with the DLR at the aptly named Tower Gateway. Just behind Tower Hill is **St Katherine's Dock**, the first of the rejuvenated docks, once the vanguard of change and a symbol of Docklands optimism. Of all the dockland developments this is the one of most interest to tourists. Cafés and shops ring the waterside where several old ships have been given a new home. The Dickens pub was also restored with an eye as much to the tourists as to the workers from the nearby World Trade Centre.

If you head east along the river from St Katherine's Dock you'll come to **Wapping** and Wapping High St, home to Murdoch's media empire and the scene of pitched battles between police and printers in the mid-1980s. The ancient Prospect of Whitby (☎ 0171-481 1095, 57 Wapping Wall) is a popular riverside pub. At nearby Shadwell station you can catch the DLR across to the Isle of Dogs.

The next DLR station is at Limehouse Basin, the centre of London's Chinatown in the last century. The only reminders are street names like Ming and Mandarin Sts. It's easy to forget the long history of the Docklands, especially when it is buried by enormous developments like Canary Wharf, three stops farther on. **Canary Wharf** (DLR: Canary Wharf) is dominated by Cesar Pelli's tower – a square prism with a pyramidal top. When building stopped, one quarter of London's unlet office space was in Canary Wharf. But the Cassandras who forecast disaster and thought their prophecies had come true when the developers went bust in 1992, are having to eat their words as the floors fill up and the surrounding areas come to life. Fashionable chef Marco Pierre White has opened MPW, the first of a planned string of franchise brasseries, here which just about says it all.

Continue on the DLR to Island Gardens, across the river from Greenwich. Alternatively, change at West India Quay station for a northbound DLR train to All Saints station. At 240 East India Dock Rd E14 (DLR: All Saints), you'll see a building that amply illustrates the ups and downs of life in Docklands. A brilliant Nicholas Grimshaw creation of metal and glass, it originally housed the **Financial Times Print Works**. Now, however, the newspaper has moved on and the building stands empty, awaiting the arrival of a new, wealthier owner.

Farther east is the **Thames Flood Barrier**, built to protect London from the great tidal river. The massive floodgates are supported by a row of concrete piers capped with gleaming metal, like an extraordinary sculpture. The Victoria, Royal Albert and George VI docks close by were the largest and last docks to be built and the last to capitulate. Here you'll find **London City airport**, built to cater for businessfolk from the City but now a good starting point for trips to north European cities.

London Docklands Visitor Centre

London Docklands Visitor Centre (☎ 0171-512 1111, 3 Limeharbour, Isle of Dogs E14, DLR: Crossharbour) is the best place to find out what went on here in the past and what is likely to happen in the future. Inevitably its ownership ensures a rosy presentation which concentrates on the good works of the London Docklands Development Centre in providing new health centres, water-sports facilities etc. Still, in the past the Docklands development has been so widely slated that it's interesting to listen to people trumpeting the one bit of London which certainly can't be accused of pandering to the heritage industry.

It's open (free) Monday to Friday from 8 am to 6 pm and at weekends from 9.30 am to 5 pm.

CHELSEA, KENSINGTON & EARL'S COURT

Chelsea still cashes in on its avant-garde fashion image even though the last punks moved on aeons ago. The best shops are a little to the north in Kensington where there's also a cluster of topnotch museums that will do less damage to your budget than department stores like Harrods or Harvey Nichols.

Carlyle's House (Map 2)

Carlyle's House (☎ 0171-352 7087, NT, 24 Cheyne Row SW3, tube: Sloane Square) is the Queen Anne residence where the great essayist and historian Thomas Carlyle came to live in 1834. Here he wrote, among many other things, his famous history of the French Revolution. Legend has it that when the manuscript was complete, a maid mistakenly threw it on the fire, whereupon the good and diligent Thomas duly wrote it all again.

This is a charming house and it's not hard to see how it became an artists' hang-out, attracting the likes of John Stuart Mill, William Thackeray and Dickens. Frédéric Chopin often played the piano that's here, and the easy-going staff will permit you to sit at it by yourself.

It's open from April through October, Wednesday to Sunday from 11 am to 5 pm, and admission costs £3.20/1.60.

Chelsea Royal Hospital (Map 7)

Well known as the site of Chelsea's annual Flower Show, the Royal Hospital (☎ 0171-730 5282, Royal Hospital Rd SW3, tube: Sloane Square) is a superb building de-

signed by Wren during the reign of Charles II. It's home to 420 Chelsea Pensioners who you may spot around town in their striking scarlet (summer) or blue (winter) jackets and black pillbox hats.

You can visit the elegantly simple Chapel and the Great Hall (which is really, in spite of the flags and royal portraits, a glorified canteen prone to smelling of fish). Visible across the river are the four white chimneys of the old Battersea Power Station, due to become a giant multiplex cinema.

It's open Monday to Saturday from 10 am to noon and 2 to 4 pm (Sunday afternoon only). Admission is free.

South Kensington Museums (Map 7)

Victoria and Albert Museum The Victoria and Albert Museum (☎ 0171-938 8500, Cromwell Rd SW7, tube: South Kensington) is a vast, rambling, wonderful museum of decorative art and design, part of Prince Albert's legacy to Londoners in the aftermath of the successful Great Exhibition of 1851.

Here you can see a mixed bag of ancient Chinese ceramics and modernist architectural drawings, Korean bronze and Japanese swords, samples from William Morris' 19th century Arts and Crafts movement, cartoons by Raphael and Asian watercolours, Rodin sculptures, gowns from the Elizabethan era and dresses straight from this year's Paris fashion shows, ancient jewellery, a 1930s wireless set, an all-wooden Frank Lloyd Wright study, and a pair of Doc Martens.

Like the British Museum, this is one that needs careful planning if you're to get the most out of your visit. Sadly, the fact that you must pay to enter makes repeat trips a less practical option unless you invest in a London White Card (see Information earlier in this chapter). As soon as you're through the turnstile look at the floor plan and decide what you're most interested in; then stick to that plan unless you want to find the time has flown by and you're still inspecting the plaster casts of classical statues!

Alternatively, take one of the free introductory guided tours.

The museum is open Monday from noon to 5.45 pm, and Tuesday to Sunday from 10 am to 5.45 pm. Admission costs £5/3.

Science Museum The Science Museum (☎ 0171-938 8008, Exhibition Rd, South Kensington SW7, tube: South Kensington) has had a complete make-over since the days when it was a rather dreary place for machine boffins and reluctant school children.

The ground floor looks at the history of the Industrial Revolution via examples of its machinery, and forward to the exploration of space. There are enough old trains ('Puffing Billy' among them) and cars to keep the kids well and truly happy.

Up a floor and you can find out about the impact of science on food, up another one and you're into the world of computers.

The 3rd floor is the place to come for the old aeroplanes, among them the ones in which John Alcock and Arthur Brown first flew across the Atlantic in 1919 and in which Amy Johnson flew to Australia in 1930. Finally on the 4th and 5th floors you'll find exhibits relating to the history of medicine.

The museum is open daily from 10 am to 6 pm. Admission costs £5.95/3.20.

Natural History Museum The Natural History Museum (☎ 0171-938 9123, Cromwell Rd, South Kensington SW7, tube: South Kensington) is one of London's finest Gothic Revival buildings, with a cathedral-like main entrance, gleaming brick and terracotta frontage, thin columns and articulated arches, and detailed stone carvings of plants and animals.

In recent years the museum has changed out of all recognition, not least because it has absorbed the old Geological Museum in Exhibition Rd; the two collections are now divided between the adjoining Life and Earth Galleries. Where once there were dreary glass cases you'll now find wonderful interactive displays on themes like human biology and creepy crawlies, alongside the crowd-attracting exhibition on dinosaurs and mammals.

In term-time the Life Galleries tend to be overrun with screaming school kids. Luckily they flock to see the dinosaurs, leaving more space on the wondrous mammal balcony, at the blue whale exhibit, or in the spooky ecology gallery.

But the Earth Galleries are even more staggering. Enter from Exhibition Rd and you'll find yourself facing an escalator which slithers up and into a hollowed-out sphere. Upstairs the Power Within and the Restless Surface exhibits explain how wind, water, ice, gravity and life itself impact on the earth. The Power Within includes an extraordinary mock-up of what happened to one shop during the Kobe earthquake in Japan in 1995 which killed 6000 people.

The museum is open Monday to Saturday from 10 am to 5.50 pm, and Sunday from 11 am to 5.50 pm. Admission costs £6/3. To avoid the crowds, visit early in the morning or late in the afternoon.

Kensington State Apartments & Gardens (Map 7)

Sometime home to Princess Margaret and the late Princess Diana, Kensington Palace (☎ 0171-937 9561, Kensington Gardens W8, tube: High St Kensington) dates back to 1605. Queen Victoria was born here in 1819 and one room is preserved as a memorial to her.

Hour-long tours of the palace take you round the small, wood-panelled State Apartments dating back to the Stuart period and the much grander, more spacious apartments of the Georgian period.

The **Sunken Garden** near the palace is at its prettiest in summer. Also nearby is **The Orangery**, designed by Hawksmoor and Sir John Vanbrugh and with carvings by Grinling Gibbons. Tea here is a pricey treat.

The State Apartments are open May to October from 10 am to 6 pm Monday to Saturday and from 11 am on Sunday. Admission costs £7/3.50.

Holland Park (Map 7)

West of Notting Hill and High St Kensington, Holland Park is a residential district with elegant pastel-painted town houses. The park itself was once the grounds of Holland House which was destroyed during WWII. Here you'll find a youth hostel, playground and restaurant, and some delightful formal gardens.

Nearby **Leighton House** (☎ 0171-602 3316, 12 Holland Park Rd W14, tube: High St Kensington) is a jewel of a house, once home to Lord Leighton, a 19th century Pre-Raphaelite painter who decked out his house Arab-style, with mosaic floors, Islamic tiles, carved wooden screens and a small fountain. This lovely house contains some notable Pre-Raphaelite paintings. It's open Monday to Saturday from 11 am to 5.30 pm; admission is free.

HYDE PARK, NOTTING HILL & BAYSWATER

The growing popularity of the Notting Hill Carnival (in late August) reflects the multicultural appeal of this area of West London. Notting Hill became a focus for immigrants from Trinidad in the 1950s. Today it's a thriving, vibrant corner of London separated from the West End by the expanse of Hyde Park.

Hyde Park (Maps 7 & 8)

Hyde Park is central London's largest royal park. Acquired from the church by Henry VIII, it was a hunting ground of kings and aristocrats, and then a venue for duels, executions, horse racing, the 1851 Great Exhibition, an enormous wartime potato field and, more recently, music concerts by the likes of Queen, the Rolling Stones and Pavarotti. It's a riot of colour during spring, and full of lazy sunbathers in summer. Boating on the Serpentine Lake is an option for the energetic.

Besides sculptures by Henry Moore and Jacob Epstein, Hyde Park boasts its own permanent art gallery. The **Serpentine Art Gallery** (☎ 0171-402 6075), south of the lake and west of the main road that cuts through the park, specialises in contemporary art (admission is free from 10 am to 6 pm).

Speaker's Corner, at the Marble Arch corner of the park, started life in 1872 as a response to serious riots. Every Sunday anyone with a soapbox can hold forth on whatever subject takes their fancy. It's still an entertaining experience provided you don't go along expecting Churchillian oratory.

On the southern edge of the park, the **Albert Memorial** is an over-the-top monument to Queen Victoria's German husband. Until recently the monument was slowly crumbling. Work to restore it is now under way and is unlikely to finish before the summer of 1999. While the monument itself is under wraps you can explore a visitors centre which explains Albert's role in the development of South Kensington ('Albertopolis').

Like all big-city parks, Hyde Park/Kensington Gardens is best avoided once darkness falls.

Apsley House (Wellington Museum, Map 4)

After Buckingham Palace, London's most prestigious address would surely be No 1 London, although to most people this striking 18th century mansion overlooking the nightmarish Hyde Park Corner roundabout is better known as Apsley House or the Wellington Museum (☎ 0171-499 5676, tube: Hyde Park Corner). Apsley House was designed by Robert Adam between 1771 and 1778 for Baron Apsley but was eventually sold to the first Duke of Wellington, victor at the Battle of Waterloo and later prime minister. Unlike most 18th century London town houses, Apsley House retains most of its furnishings and collections.

The stairwell is dominated by Antonio Canova's staggering 3.26m statue of Napoleon, naked but for the obligatory fig leaf – try not to laugh when you see the portrait of the un-Adonis-like real man on the landing. But the most striking exhibit is the 1000 piece Portuguese silver-gilt table centrepiece on display in the dining room. This used to be brought out for the annual Waterloo Banquets to commemorate the victory of 1815.

The house is open Tuesday to Sunday from 11 am to 5 pm. Admission is £4.50/3.

NORTH LONDON

From the Gothic splendour of St Pancras station one can walk past the British Library, along to Euston station and up Eversholt St to Camden Town, a tourist mecca that is especially lively at weekends (for Camden Market, see Shopping later in this chapter). Twenty years ago Camden Town was home to a large Irish community, but yuppiefication has changed all that and nowadays parts of it blend harmoniously into the sedate middle-class suburb of Hampstead farther north.

St Pancras Station (Map 5)

Together with Barry and Pugin's Houses of Parliament, St Pancras station is the pinnacle of the Victorian Gothic Revival. Whether you go for the style or not, beautifully restored St Pancras is something special: there's a dramatic glass-and-iron train shed at the back, engineered by the great Brunel, and a fantastically pinnacled hotel designed by Sir George Gilbert Scott at the front.

Though the train station is still active, the hotel has been disused for years. Next door is the new **British Library** (☎ 0171-412 7000, tube: St Pancras) building, its stark, prison-like, red-brick architecture in blatant contrast to the station. After 15 years and £500 million, the library (the largest public building to be erected in England in the 20th century) has finally opened to readers, taking over from the British Museum as London's copyright library.

Hampstead & Highgate

Perched on a hill 4 miles north of the City, Hampstead is an exclusive suburb attached to an enormous, rambling heath which just about gets away with calling itself a village. You can lose yourself on Hampstead Heath and forget that you're in one of the world's largest, noisiest cities – something harder to

forget when walking up Hampstead High St, or Heath St, both inundated with pricey shops and bumper-to-bumper traffic.

Nonetheless, Hampstead still keeps its charm and character – part left-wing intelligentsia, part arty bohemia. Ex-Labour Party leader Michael Foot lives here and Hampstead's MP is Glenda Jackson, the actress-turned-politician. Famous people have been making their home here since the 18th century, among them Samuel Taylor Coleridge, John Keats and Alexander Pope; Charles II's mistress, Nell Gwyn; General de Gaulle; Sigmund Freud; and John Constable and William Hogarth. More recently Oasis songwriter Noel Gallagher took up residence in a house called Supernova Heights in Belsize Park on the southern edge of Hampstead.

Architecturally, Hampstead is a harmonious balance of Georgian and early Victorian, speckled with a few notable examples of modernist architecture. The excellent *Hampstead Town Trail,* available from second-hand bookshops in Flask Walk and in Keats House, will take you along the prettier backstreets. You'll soon realise why there was an uproar when McDonald's announced plans to open a branch in Hampstead. It got its way, of course, but the golden arches had to be cut down to a little logo on a black fascia.

The heath boasts woods, meadows, hills, bathing ponds and, most important of all, space. Also you'll find **Kenwood House** (☎ 0181-348 1286, EH, Hampstead Lane, tube: Hampstead), a magnificent house rejigged by Adam in the middle of the 17th century and stuffed with paintings by the likes of Rembrandt, Vermeer and Anthony Van Dyck.

Keats House This house (☎ 0171-435 2062, Keats Grove, Hampstead NW3, tube: Hampstead) was home to the golden boy of the Romantic poets who was persuaded to take refuge here from 1816 to 1821. Under a plum tree in the back garden, John Keats wrote his most celebrated poem, *Ode to a Nightingale*.

Apart from many preserved mementos, plenty of original Keats manuscripts, and his collection of Shakespeare and Chaucer, the visitor can take a peek at some of his love letters.

It's open April to October, Monday to Friday from 10 am to 1 pm and 2 to 6 pm, Saturday from 10 am to 1 pm and 2 to 5 pm, Sunday from 2 to 5 pm; and November to March, Monday to Friday from 1 to 5 pm, Saturday from 10 am to 1 pm and 2 to 5 pm, Sunday from 2 to 5 pm. Admission is free.

Freud's House Sigmund Freud lived at 20 Maresfield Gardens NW3 (☎ 0171-435 2002, 20 Maresfield Gardens, tube: Finchley Rd) for the last 18 months of his life after it became clear in 1938 that it was no longer safe for him to stay in Nazi-occupied Vienna. Here you can see the original psychiatrist's chair from which sprang all later models, together with all his Greek and oriental artefacts and, of course, his books. A photo shows how carefully he attempted to reproduce his Viennese home in the unfamiliar surroundings of London.

Later the house was occupied by Freud's daughter, Anna, a child psychologist of note in her own right; one room upstairs has mementos of her, including a loom which is still in use.

It's open Wednesday to Sunday from noon to 5 pm. Admission costs £3/1.50.

Highgate Cemetery This is the final resting place for Karl Marx, the novelist George Eliot and of other ordinary mortals who lie within eccentric and extraordinary tombs. Highgate Cemetery (☎ 0181-340 1834, Swain's Lane N6, tube: Highgate) has wild, hectic acres of absurdly overdecorated Victorian tombs, catacombs, family plots linked in a ring and based on ancient Egyptian burial sites, all topped off by spooky cypresses.

It's divided into two parts. The only way to see the western section is by tour (£3), possible on Saturday and Sunday all year on the hour from 11 am to 4 pm; or Monday to Friday from March to November at noon and 2 and 4 pm.

Marx's tomb can be found in the comparatively uninteresting eastern part, which is open daily from 10 am to 4 pm (to 5 pm from April to October). Admission is another £1.

GREENWICH (MAP 10)

Packed with beautiful architecture, Greenwich (pronounced grenitch) has strong connections with royalty, the sea and science. It lies to the south-east of central London, where the River Thames widens and deepens, and has a sense of space rare in the big city.

Quaint and villagey, and boasting the magnificent *Cutty Sark*, delightful Greenwich is a UNESCO World Heritage List site. A trip there will be a highlight of any visit to London, and you should certainly allow at least a day to do it justice, particularly if you want to head on down the river to the Thames Barrier and the site of the Millennium Dome in Charlton.

Greenwich is home to an extraordinary interrelated cluster of buildings; all the great architects of the Enlightenment made their mark here, thanks to royal patronage. Henry VIII and his daughters Mary I and Elizabeth I were born here. Charles II was particularly fond of the area and had Wren build the Royal Observatory and part of the Royal Naval College, which Vanbrugh then completed in the early 17th century.

A 371m pedestrian tunnel under the River Thames connects Greenwich with the Isle of Dogs, where new office developments, yuppie housing and inner-city squalor rub shoulders uneasily. The entrance to the tunnel offers exquisite views of the Greenwich skyline.

It's worth timing your visit for Friday, Saturday or Sunday when the arts and crafts and antiques markets will be in full swing.

There's a TIC (☎ 0181-858 6376) at 46 Greenwich Church St. A passport ticket for £5/2.50 covers admission to the National Maritime Museum, Queen's House and the Royal Observatory.

Cutty Sark

The *Cutty Sark* (☎ 0181-858 3445) is in King William Walk, right beside Greenwich Pier. It was once the fastest ship that had ever sailed the seven seas and remains one of the most beautiful ever built.

Launched in 1869, it's the sole surviving example of the clippers which dominated mid-19th century trade in tea and wool across both the Pacific and Atlantic. The *Cutty Sark* sailed its last journey in 1938 and retired to Greenwich in the 50s. You can stroll on the decks and peep inside the refitted cabins, then read up on the history below deck and inspect the world's largest collection of ship's figureheads in the hold.

It's open April through September, Monday to Saturday from 10 am to 6 pm, opening at noon on Sunday, and closing an hour earlier from October to March. Admission costs £3.50/2.50.

Gipsy Moth IV

Nearby, the *Gipsy Moth IV* (☎ 0181-853 3589) was the boat Francis Chichester used to complete the first solo circumnavigation of the world by an Englishman in 1966-67. Chichester was 64 at the time and endured 226 days in this pokey, bath-sized craft. Later he was given a knighthood and various civic plaudits.

Royal Naval College

If you walk straight ahead from the *Cutty Sark* you'll come to the entrance to the Royal Naval College (☎ 0181-858 2154), off King William Walk on the left. Despite its splendour, this Wren masterpiece is largely off-limits to the public and its future is uncertain.

The Naval College was built on the site of the old Greenwich palace between 1696 and 1701 as a thank you to the British navy from William III and Queen Mary for the naval victory over the French at La Hogue in 1692. It was intended to provide a retirement home for navy veterans in the same way that the Chelsea Royal Hospital provided one for army veterans.

You can visit the chapel, which was completed 20 years after Wren's death, only to be gutted by fire in 1779. It was redecorated in a lighter rococo style. The east end of the chapel is dominated by a painting by the 18th century American artist Benjamin West showing *The Preservation of St Paul After Shipwreck at Malta*.

Even more wonderful is the Painted Hall. As soon as you step inside, your eye will be drawn ceilingwards to marvel at the paintings by James Thornhill. These show William and Mary enthroned amid symbols of the Virtues. Beneath William's feet, you can see the defeated French king Louis XIV grovelling.

Up a few steps is the Upper Hall where George I is depicted with his family on the west wall. At the bottom right Thornhill drew himself into the picture too.

The Pepys Buildings currently house the **New Millennium Experience Visitors' Centre** (☎ 0181-305 3456), open Monday to Friday from 11 am to 7 pm, from 10 am to 6 pm on weekends. Come here to find out what may or may not be in the Millennium Dome when it's finally completed. (The dome itself is shaping up downriver at Charlton.)

The college is open (free) daily from 2.30 to 4.45 pm.

National Maritime Museum

Farther along King William Walk you'll come to the National Maritime Museum (☎ 0181-858 4422, Romney Rd SE10), a collection of boats, maps, charts and uniforms designed to tell the long history of Britain as a seafaring nation. Some galleries are likely to be closed while they're given an overhaul for the millennium, but the exhibition on 20th century sea power should be open; look out for its bland account of the controversial sinking of the Argentinian ship, the *Belgrano*, during the Falklands conflict.

Upstairs, the Nelson Gallery is interesting enough to grab the imagination even of those not much interested in naval history. Otherwise, the best thing about the museum is the building itself. Designed by Inigo

Jones and completed by Wren, it slots in behind the Naval College, and from its colonnaded walkways you'll get fine views up One Tree Hill to the Royal Observatory.

The museum is open from 10 am to 5 pm daily.

Queen's House

The Palladian-style Queen's House (☎ 0181-858 4422) is a continuation of the National Maritime Museum on the eastern side. Jones started work on the house for Anne of Denmark, wife of James I, in 1616 but it wasn't completed until 1635 when it became the home of Charles I and his wife, Henrietta Maria.

Rooms open off a Great Hall which originally had a ceiling painted by Orazio Gentileschi and his daughter Artemisia, one of the few early women artists to achieve much celebrity. Sadly what you see now are just laser photographs. Most of the original furniture has also been lost, so the rooms are perhaps not as exciting as you might expect.

It's open daily from 10 am to 5 pm.

Greenwich Park & Old Royal Observatory

Greenwich Park is one of London's loveliest parks, with a grand avenue, wide open spaces, a rose garden and rambling, picturesque walks. It's partly the work of André Le Nôtre, who landscaped the gardens at Versailles.

In 1675 Charles II had the **Old Royal Observatory** (☎ 0181-858 4422) built in the middle of the park, intending that astronomy be used to establish longitude at sea. The Octagon Room, designed by Wren, is where John Flansteed, the first astronomer royal, made his observations and calculations, and where he was visited by Tsar Peter the Great of Russia. This is one of the few Wren interiors known to have survived intact.

Thereafter Greenwich became accepted as Prime Meridian, or zero hour, and from 1884 the whole world has accepted Greenwich Mean Time (GMT) as the universal measurement of standard time. Here the globe divides between east and west and you can

place one foot either side of the meridian line and straddle the two hemispheres. A machine generates a certificate confirming that you've done just that. Nearby a clock accurate to one-millionth of a second is counting down time towards the millennium.

The observatory is open daily from 10 am to 5 pm.

Getting There & Away

The best way to get to/from Greenwich is by boat. The boats drop you off at Greenwich Pier close to both the *Cutty Sark* and *Gipsy Moth IV*. They leave from Westminster Pier (beside Westminster Bridge) every half-hour from 10 am to 4 pm; singles cost £5.50/3, returns £6.70/3.50. Last boats return from Greenwich at 5 or 6 pm, depending on demand.

Alternatively, there are trains from Charing Cross station to Greenwich station, which are quicker and cheaper, or you can catch the DLR from Tower Gateway to Island Gardens and walk through the pedestrian tunnel to the south side of the river. There can be longish gaps between trains at weekends and you should check the time of the last train if planning a late return.

SOUTH LONDON

Just 10 years ago, the southern part of central London was the city's forgotten underside; run-down, neglected and offering little for foreign visitors once they'd visited the South Bank arts venues. Recently, however, all that has changed and parts of London immediately south of the river can seem as exciting as anywhere farther north. The new Globe Theatre has already opened to considerable acclaim and the new Tate Gallery at Bankside should be up and running for the millennium. A rash of small museums and exhibitions have opened in and around Southwark, and the success of the new, top floor restaurant in the old Oxo Tower has served to consolidate the area's popularity.

Imperial War Museum (Map 2)

The Imperial War Museum (☎ 0171-416 5000, Lambeth Rd SE1, tube: Lambeth

North) is one of London's most popular museums. Try to go early in the morning or late afternoon to dodge the inevitable crowds.

Although there's still plenty of military hardware on show and the core of the museum is a chronological exhibition on the two world wars, these days the Imperial War Museum places more emphasis on the social cost of war. Particularly popular exhibits are the Trench Experience that depicts the grim day-to-day existence of a WWI foot soldier, and the Blitz Experience that lets visitors sit inside a mock-up bomb shelter during an air raid and then stroll a set of the ravaged streets of the East End. Also popular is the Secret History exhibition that takes a look at the work of the secret services, with video footage of the siege of the Iranian embassy in Knightsbridge in 1980, brought to a dramatic end by balaclava-clad SAS commandos.

It's open daily from 10 am to 6 pm; admission is £4.70/3.70.

Shakespeare Globe Centre & Theatre (Map 6)

The Shakespeare Globe Centre (☎ 0171-928 6406, Bear Gardens, Bankside SE1, tube: London Bridge) consists of the Globe Theatre and an exhibition in the shell of a 17th century Inigo Jones theatre. A visit to the exhibition includes a guided tour of the Globe Theatre itself. The exhibition is open daily from 10 am to 5 pm for £5/3.

The original Globe (Shakespeare's 'wooden O') was built from 1598 to 1599, burnt down in 1613 and was immediately rebuilt. Brainchild of Canadian producer Sam Wanamaker, the new Globe opened in 1997 to great acclaim. Unlike other venues for Shakespearean plays, it has been designed to resemble the original as closely as possible – even if that means leaving the arena open to the skies and expecting the 500 'groundlings' to stand.

For ticket details, see Theatre in the Entertainment section later in this chapter.

HMS *Belfast* (Map 6)

HMS *Belfast* (☎ 0171-407 6434, Morgan's Lane, Tooley St SE1, tube: Tower Hill or

London Bridge), a cruiser that fought in WWII and was involved in the sinking of the *Scharnhorst* in 1943, is now moored peacefully in the River Thames. It probably helps to be keen on military manoeuvres, but the *Belfast* is surprisingly interesting anyway for what it shows of the way of life on board a cruiser.

It's open March through October, from 10 am to 6 pm daily, closing an hour earlier in winter. Admission costs £4.40/3.30.

South Bank

Across the River Thames from Embankment, the South Bank is a labyrinth of arts venues strung out on rain-stained concrete walkways between Hungerford Bridge and Waterloo Bridge (tube: Waterloo). Almost no one has a good word to say about the concrete slopes and buttresses which host a motley assortment of art lovers, skateboarders and homeless people.

The **Royal Festival Hall**, built in 1951 for the Festival of Britain, now hosts classical, opera, jazz and choral music. Free recitals take place in the foyer most evenings. The

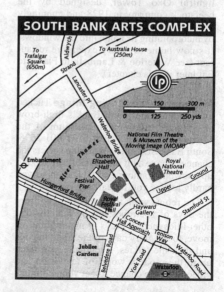

SOUTH BANK ARTS COMPLEX

smaller **Queen Elizabeth Hall** and **Purcell Room** host similar concerts.

Tucked almost out of sight is the **National Film Theatre (NFT)**. A second-hand book and print market takes place right in front of the NFT on the river side.

The **Hayward Gallery** (☎ 0171-928 3144), built in the mid-1960s, caters for blockbuster modern art exhibitions. Finally, the **Royal National Theatre**, a love-it-or-hate-it complex of three theatres, is the nation's flagship theatre. Dismissed by Prince Charles as resembling a 'disused power station', the National was designed in 1976 by the modernist architect Denys Lasdun, a great fan of concrete and horizontal lines.

A short walk east along the South Bank is **Gabriel's Wharf**, a cluster of craft shops which forms part of the local residents' successful attempt to resist further large-scale development in the area. From the South Bank Walkway you look across the river to stunning views of St Paul's, Lloyds, Canary Wharf and so on – a veritable Manhattan-on-Thames.

Just east of Gabriel's Wharf is the delightful **Oxo Tower**, designed by the beefstock company in 1928 and cunningly circumventing a ban on outdoor advertising by incorporating its name into the windows. It's now home to a very expensive restaurant (see Waterloo & Lambeth in Places to Eat later in this chapter).

Museum of the Moving Image Tucked away among the South Bank's high-brow arts venues, the popular Museum of the Moving Image (MOMI, ☎ 0171-401 2636, South Bank SE1, tube: Waterloo) offers the chance to have a bit of fun, skilfully mixing up showbiz glamour and education so you hardly realise you're learning.

The rooms work their way through from the days of zoetropes, magic lanterns and other idiosyncratic ways of making images move, to the glory days of the silent movies and then the talkies. Eventually you fetch up in the modern world of television and video, with the chance to get yourself interviewed with TV film critic Barry Norman and to rewatch your favourite TV ads.

MOMI is open daily from 10 am to 6 pm. Admission costs £6.25/4.40.

London Aquarium (Map 4)

Odd that County Hall, once the seat of London's local government, should have ended up housing an aquarium beneath a Chinese restaurant and a chain hotel! The London Aquarium (☎ 0171-967 8000, tube: Westminster) is a state-of-the-art 'zoo' for all manner of fish but lacks the colour and airiness of more purpose-built structures. At £7/5 admission it's also pretty expensive. Walk across Westminster Bridge to get here.

WEST LONDON

If you make one short foray into London's hinterland, it should really be to Hampton Court, but Kew Gardens runs a close second and nearby Syon House isn't far behind this.

Kew Gardens

Kew Gardens, or the Royal Botanic Gardens (☎ 0181-940 1171, Kew Rd, Kew, Surrey, tube: Kew Gardens) is one of the most visited sights on the tourist itinerary, which means it can get very crowded during summer, especially on weekends. Spring is probably the best time to visit, but at any time of year this expansive array of lawns, formal gardens and botanical greenhouses has delights to offer. As well as being a park, Kew is an important botanical research centre and it maintains its reputation for having the most exhaustive botanical collection in the world.

Two soaring glass-and-iron Victorian conservatories, the Palm House and the Temperate House, house a variety of exotic plant life, while the Princess of Wales Conservatory houses plants from 10 different climate zones.

Red-brick **Kew Palace** was once a royal residence dating from the early 1600s, and very popular with George III and his family (his wife Charlotte died here in 1818); it's furnished as it might have been when they lived there. The gardens surrounding the palace are especially pretty.

The gardens are open from 9.30 am to dusk daily for £4.50/3. Kew Palace is usually open April to September daily from 11 am to 5.30 pm for £1.60/80p.

As an alternative to the tube to Kew Gardens station (Zone 3), ferries sail from Westminster Pier every 30 minutes from 10.15 am to 2.30 pm (from the Monday before Easter until the end of September). They take 1½ hours. A single/return costs £6/10.

For the pleasant riverside pubs at **Strand-on-the-Green**, cross Kew Bridge and turn right along the river bank.

Richmond

Nearby Richmond is a pleasant riverside village, and **Richmond Park** is the largest and most rural of the royal parks. It can be reached on foot from Kew by following the river towards Twickenham. There are good places to eat and drink in Richmond, including the White Swan pub-restaurant adjoining Richmond Theatre, where you can go before taking the tube back to central London.

Syon House

Syon House (☎ 0181-560 0881, Syon Park, Brentford, Middlesex, tube: Gunnersbury, station: Syon Lane) is a superb example of the English stately home. The house where Lady Jane Grey ascended to the throne for her nine day monarchy in 1554 was remodelled by Adam in the 18th century, and possesses plenty of Adam furniture and oak panelling. The interior was designed along gender-specific lines, with pastel pinks and purples for the ladies' gallery, and mock Roman sculptures for the men's dining room. The gardens, including an artificial lake, were landscaped by Capability Brown.

Syon House can be reached easily from Kew. It's open April through September, Wednesday to Sunday from 11 am to 5 pm, closing at 4 pm on Friday and Saturday. Admission costs £5.50/4.

Hampton Court Palace

Hampton Court Palace (☎ 0181-781 9500, East Molesey, Surrey, station: Hampton Court), by the River Thames, is England's largest and grandest Tudor structure, knee deep in historical circumstance, close to London and yet very much removed, with superb gardens, and a famous 300-year-old maze.

In 1515 Cardinal Wolsey, Lord Chancellor of England, decided to build himself a palace. Unfortunately he was unable to persuade the pope to grant Henry VIII a divorce from Catherine of Aragon and relations between king and chancellor turned sour. Given that background, you only need to take one look at Hampton Court Palace to realise why Wolsey felt obliged to present it to Henry, a monarch not too fond of anyone trying to muscle in on his mastery of all he surveyed. The hapless Wolsey was charged with high treason in 1530 but died before he could come to trial.

Henry expanded the palace, adding the Great Hall, the Chapel and the sprawling kitchens. In the late 17th century, William and Mary employed Wren to build extensions, the result being a beautiful blend of Tudor and neoclassical architecture.

It's open April through October, Monday from 10.15 am to 6 pm, Tuesday to Sunday from 9.30 am to 6 pm; and November through March, Monday from 10.15 am to 4.30 pm, Tuesday to Sunday from 9.30 am to 4.30 pm; admission is £9.25/6.10.

There are trains every half-hour from Waterloo station (£3.90 return, Zone 6), or the palace can be reached by boat from Westminster Pier. Ferries depart from April through October at 10.30 and 11.15 am and noon; they take 3½ hours and cost £8/4. Allow the best part of a day for the excursion.

PLACES TO STAY

Whichever way you cut it, accommodation is going to make a big hole in your budget. Most of the letters of complaint that Lonely Planet receives about London relate also to accommodation, especially the budget end of the market. The problem comes down to demand outstripping supply in a situation where exorbitant property prices make it hard for anyone to open a B&B and charge less than through the nose for it – none of which excuses the dodgy décor, crummy fittings and pokey rooms you may be offered.

If you're on a budget, you're probably stuck with the hostels. Moving up a price bracket it's worth considering staying in one of the new-look chain hotels run by companies like Travel Lodge or Ibis. Loath though we would usually be to recommend such accommodation, at least you can be sure that everything will be new and the colour scheme restrained, which might make up for lack of personality. At the top end, of course, you get to pick from some of Britain's best and jazziest hotels.

Hostel dormitory accommodation will cost from £10 to £22. Expect to pay £25/30 for very basic singles/doubles without bathroom, £28/40 with. You'll be lucky to find anything really pleasant for much less than £35/50. If you have enough money for the odd splurge, wait until you get into the countryside, where you'll get much better value for your money.

Good-quality hotels are scattered around, but there are some excellent places in Notting Hill, Marble Arch, the West End and Bloomsbury.

Some of the best bargains are in the steadily growing chain of Travel Inns where rooms cost a flat £49.50 a night; phone central reservations on ☎ 01582-414341 for an update on the latest openings. Ibis Hotels offers similar flat-rate rooms and has branches at Heathrow (☎ 0181-759 4888) and Gatwick (☎ 01239-611762) airports.

Accommodation Bookings

It's well worth prebooking a night or two's accommodation, especially in July and August. You can make same-day accommodation bookings at the TICs at Victoria and Heathrow, although they charge £5 for a hotel or B&B booking and £1.50 for hostels; ☎ 0171-824 8844 for bookings.

Alternatively, the British Hotel Reservation Centre (☎ 0800-726298) has a booking office on the main Victoria station concourse. It charges £3 per hotel/hostel booking, but some readers have been less than happy with the service.

Thomas Cook also operates a hostel and hotel reservation service, charging £5 per booking. There are kiosks at Paddington (☎ 0171-723 0184), Charing Cross (☎ 0171-976 1171), Euston (☎ 0171-388 7435), King's Cross (☎ 0171-837 5681) and Victoria (☎ 0171-828 4646) train stations; at Earl's Court (☎ 0171-244 0908) and South Kensington (☎ 0171-581 9766) tube stations; and at Gatwick airport (☎ 01293-529372) train station.

The YHA operates a central reservations system (☎ 0171-248 6547, fax 0171-236 7681) to help match people with beds. You still pay the hostel directly, but staff will know what beds are available where. You can also send email to YHALondonReservations@compuserve.com or write to YHA Central Reservations at 36 Carter Lane, London EC4V 5AB.

Advance bookings (minimum three days) for some private B&Bs can be made free through London Homestead Services (☎ 0181-949 4455, 24 hours, Coombe Wood Rd, Kingston-upon-Thames, Surrey KT2 7JY). Bed & Breakfast (GB, ☎ 01491-578803, PO Box 66, Henley-on-Thames RG9 1XS) specialises in central London. Primrose Hill B&B (☎ 0171-722 6869, 14 Edis St NW1 8LG) is a small agency with select properties in or near Hampstead. Guests get their own latchkeys and rates are between £20 and £30. You could also try the BTA or local TICs.

PLACES TO STAY – BUDGET
Camping

Tent City (☎ *0181-743 5708, Old Oak Common Lane W3, tube: East Acton*) is London's cheapest option, short of sleeping rough. Beds in dormitory-style tents cost £6. It's open from June through August and booking is advisable. It also has tent sites but doesn't take caravans or camper vans.

A second *Tent City* (☎ *0181-985 7656, Millfields Rd, Hackney, station: Clapton*), north-east London, has space for tents or vans for £5.

Lee Valley Park (☎ *0181-345 6666, Picketts Lock Sport & Leisure Centre, Picketts Lock Lane, Edmonton N9, tube: Tottenham Hale, then bus No 363)* has 200 pitches for tents or caravans. It's open all year and the nightly charge is £5/2.10 (adult/junior) per person plus £2.20 for electricity.

YHA/HI Hostels

Central London's seven YHA/HI hostels get very crowded in summer. An eighth is out in Epping Forest. At a push you could even try the Windsor hostel. All take advance bookings by phone if you pay by Visa or MasterCard. They also hold some beds for those who wander in on the day, but come early and be prepared to queue. All but Epping Forest offer 24 hour access and all have a *bureau de change*. Most have facilities for self-catering and some offer cheap meals.

The excellent *City of London Hostel* (☎ *0171-236 4965, 36 Carter Lane EC4, tube: St Paul's)* is virtually next door to St Paul's Cathedral in a pleasantly restored building which was the cathedral choir's school. Rooms are mainly four, three or two beds and only two are *en suite*. There's a licensed cafeteria but no kitchen. Beds cost £21.30/17.90. This part of town is pretty quiet outside working hours.

Earl's Court Hostel (☎ *0171-373 7083, 38 Bolton Gardens SW5, tube: Earl's Court)* is a Victorian town house in a tacky, though lively, part of town. Rooms are mainly 10-bed dorms with communal showers, although there's one triple and five family rooms. It's not the best equipped of hostels but there's a café and kitchen. Rates are £18.70/16.45.

Hampstead Heath Hostel (☎ *0181-458 9054, 4 Wellgarth Rd NW11, tube: Golders Green)* is in a beautiful setting with a well-kept garden, although it's rather isolated. The dorms are comfortable, and each room has a washbasin. There's a rather average, though licensed, café and a kitchen. Rates are £15.60/13.35.

Holland House Hostel (☎ *0171-937 0748, Holland Walk, Kensington W8, tube: High St Kensington)* has a great location built around the remains of a Jacobean mansion in the middle of Holland Park. It's large, very busy and rather institutional, but the position can't be beaten. There's a café and kitchen. Rates are £18.70/16.45.

Right in the town centre, *Oxford St Hostel* (☎ *0171-734 1618, 3rd floor, 14-18 Noel St W1, tube: Oxford Circus)* is the most basic of the London hostels, with a large kitchen but no meals. Rates are £18.70/15.25. There are only 75 beds so book ahead.

St Pancras International (☎ *0171-248 6547, Euston Rd N1, tube: King's Cross or St Pancras)* is London's newest hostel. The area isn't great, although it's certainly convenient if you want to head east or north afterwards. The hostel itself is a state-of-the-art affair, with kitchen, restaurant, lockers, cycle shed and lounge. Rates are £21.30/17.90.

Rotherhithe (☎ *0171-232 2114, Salter Rd SE16, tube: Rotherhithe)* is a highly recommended purpose-built hostel. Unfortunately, it's a bit far out and the area isn't great, although transport is reasonable. Rooms are mainly six-bed, with some fours and a few doubles; all have attached bathroom. There's a licensed restaurant as well as kitchen facilities. B&B rates are £21.30/17.90. Six rooms are specially adapted for disabled visitors.

Epping Forest (☎ *0181-508 5161, High Beach, Loughton, Essex, tube: Loughton)* is over 10 miles from central London and a good 2 mile walk from the nearest tube station, so it's only worth considering if all else is full. Rates are £8/5.40 (but allow for the tube fares).

Even farther out but still worth remembering is the hostel at Windsor (see Places to Stay in Windsor & Eton in the South-Eastern England chapter).

University Accommodation

University halls of residence are let to non-students during the holidays, usually from the end of June to mid-September. They're somewhat more expensive than the youth hostels, but you usually get a single room (there are a small number of doubles) with shared facilities, plus breakfast. Bookings are coordinated by the British Universities Accommodation Consortium (BUAC, ☎ 0115-950 4571, Box 653, University Park, Nottingham NG7 2RD), although you can also contact the colleges direct.

The London School of Economics (Room B508, LSE, Houghton St WC2A 2AE) lets several of its halls at Easter and during summer for £21 (£25 with private bath). *Carr-Saunders Hall* (☎ 0171-323 9712, 18-24 Fitzroy St W1, tube: Warren St) is not in the greatest part of town, but is near Oxford St and so fairly central. Self-catering flats of different sizes are also available on a weekly basis in summer only, ranging from £238 for a two person flat to £539 for five people. There are more rooms at the central *High Holborn* (☎ 0171-379 5589, 178 High Holborn WC1, tube: Holborn); at *Passfield Hall* (☎ 0171-387 3584, Endsleigh Place WC1, tube: Euston), in the heart of Bloomsbury; and at *Rosebery Avenue Hall* (☎ 0171-278 3251, 90 Rosebery Ave EC1, tube: Angel).

The *Imperial College of Science & Technology* (☎ 0171-594 9507, Prince's Gardens SW7, tube: South Kensington) is brilliantly positioned near the South Kensington museums and offers B&B for £28/45 a single/double.

Regent's College (☎ 0171-487 7483, Inner Circle, Regent's Park NW1, tube: Baker St) is a converted Regency manor right in the middle of beautiful Regent's Park, convenient for Camden and central London, and costs £26/37.

John Adams Hall (☎ 0171-387 4086, 15-23 Endsleigh St WC1, tube: Euston) is a row of Georgian houses with its own swimming pool. B&B costs from £20/34.

King's Campus Vacation Bureau (☎ 0171-928 3777, 127 Stamford St SE1, tube: Waterloo) administers bookings for several central King's College residence halls. The *Hampstead Campus* (☎ 0171-435 3564, Kidderpore Ave NW3, tube: Finchley Rd) has 392 beds from £12.80/22.30.

Finsbury Residences (☎ 0171-477 8811, Bastwick St EC1, tube: Angel/Old Street) comprises two modern halls belonging to City University. Bed and continental breakfast is £21 a head.

University of Westminster (☎ 0171-911 5000, 35 Marylebone Rd NW1, tube: Baker St) has beds for £19.50 without breakfast or £22.50 with breakfast.

YMCAs

The National Council for YMCAs (☎ 0181-520 5599) can supply a list of all its London hostels, where rooms cost from £20/35 a single/double. The main ones to know about are the *Barbican* (☎ 0171-628 0697, 2 Fann St EC2, tube: Barbican); the *London City Hostel* (☎ 0171-628 8832, 8 Errol St EC1, tube: Barbican); and the *Central Club* (☎ 0171-636 7512, 16 Great Russell St WC1, tube: Tottenham Court Rd).

Private Hostels

London's various private hostels seem to operate on the principle that if you squash six people in a room and charge them £10 each you make more profit than if you have a couple at £20 per person. They're certainly not suitable for fastidious, antisocial claustrophobics.

In terms of facilities, the hostels don't vary much. Most have three or four small bunk beds jammed into a room, a small kitchen and some kind of lounge room. Some have budget restaurants and a few even have a bar. They're cheaper and much more relaxed than the official YHA hostels, but the standards are more hit and miss. Problems with theft are relatively unusual, but be careful with your possessions and deposit your valuables in the office safe. Some hostels are pretty casual about fire safety – check that the fire escapes are accessible.

Apart from noise levels, safety and cleanliness, the most important variable is the atmosphere. This can change by the week, as to a large extent it depends on who happens to be staying.

Most private hostels are in Earl's Court (SW5), which consequently has the biggest backpacker scene, but there are also some in Bayswater (W2), Notting Hill and Holland Park (W11), Bloomsbury (WC1), Victoria (SW1) and Chelsea (SW8). With the possible exceptions of Notting Hill and Bloomsbury, all these areas are pretty seedy. Notting Hill is a great part of London but Bayswater is also pretty central, while the Chelsea hostel has the advantage of novelty.

Notting Hill The pleasant, conveniently located *Palace Hotel* (☎ *0171-221 5628, 31 Palace Court W2, tube: Notting Hill Gate)* has dorm beds for £15 to £18 and isn't quite as run-down and manic as some places.

Bayswater The friendly *Quest Hotel* (☎ *0171-229 7782, 45 Queensborough Terrace W2, tube: Bayswater)* is just round the corner from the Queensway action but gets pretty crowded. There are kitchen facilities and a pool table. Dorm beds cost £11.50 or £12.50; a few are available on a weekly basis for about £2 a night less.

Owned by the same Astor group that runs the Quest is the *Leinster Inn* (☎ *0171-229 9641, 7-12 Leinster Square W2)*. Dorm beds cost £12.50 to £15, or there are singles/doubles for £22/36.

Earl's Court The relaxed, friendly *Curzon House Hotel* (☎ *0171-581 2116, 58 Courtfield Gardens SW5, tube: Gloucester Rd)* is one of the better private hostels. Dorms are £13 per person, singles/doubles with facilities are £23/36.

The *Chelsea Hotel* (☎ *0171-244 6892, 33 Earl's Court Square SW5, tube: Earl's Court)* is a classic hostel, with hundreds of cheery backpackers wandering around. There are some good-value rooms from £25/35 as well as dorm beds for £12. Some readers have complained that the staff were less than welcoming though.

At the *Windsor House* (☎ *0171-373 9087, 12 Penywern Rd SW5, tube: Earl's Court)* a dorm bed is £10, a single £28, a double £38 and a triple £48, all including breakfast.

The *Court Hotels* (☎ *0171-373 0027, 194-196 Earl's Court Rd SW5 and ☎ 0171-373 2174, fax 0171-912 9500, 17-19 Kempsford Gardens, tube: Earl's Court)* are under Australasian management and have well-equipped kitchens and a TV in most rooms. Dorm beds cost £11, and rooms are £21/24. Weekly rates are also available.

Victoria A relative newcomer on the scene is the *Granada Hotel* (☎ *0171-821 7611, 73 Belgrave Rd SW1, tube: Victoria)*, which is handy if you're arriving late or leaving early from Victoria station. Beds in rooms with private baths cost £15 a night (£65 a week). A kitchen and TV lounge are also available.

Bloomsbury The slightly shambolic *Museum Inn* (☎ *0171-580 5360, 27 Montague St WC1, tube: Russell Square or Tottenham Court Rd)* has an excellent position opposite the British Museum. It has a small kitchen and lounge, and a few rooms have colour TVs. A basic breakfast is included in the price: £17 per person in the one twin; £15 in a four bed dorm; £14 in a 10 bed dorm.

The *International Students House* (☎ *0171-631 8300, 229 Great Portland St W1, tube: Great Portland St)* is more like a university residential college and has its own cybercafé. The single and double rooms – you don't have to be a student to rent them – are ordinary but clean. B&B ranges from £9.99 for a dorm to £28 for a single. It's very busy so book in advance.

Southwark *St Christopher's Inn* (☎ *0171-407 1856, 121 Borough High St SE1, tube: London Bridge)* is conveniently positioned if you want to explore up-and-coming south London, but attracts a lot of long-stay tenants; you'll need to book ahead in summer. Beds in eight-bed dorms cost £10 including continental breakfast; they're £14 in a three bed dorm. St Christopher's is attached to a pub and claims to be run by 'travellers who know how to party'.

Chelsea The *New Ark Backpackers Flotel (☎ 0171-720 9496, Adrenalin Village, Queenstown Rd SW8, tube: Sloane Square)* comes recommended as 'a very funky place' and is certainly different. A converted barge sleeps up to 40 people in four-bunk cabins with each bunk costing just £12 a night. There's a 24 hour bar and quayside barbecues. What's more, you're within heart-stopping distance of the Chelsea Wharf Tower with its bungee-jumping opportunities. But the cabins are small and cramped, without proper doors, so they won't suit anyone wanting peace and quiet.

B&Bs & Hotels

Bloomsbury (WC1), Bayswater (W2), Paddington (W2), Pimlico (SW1) and Earl's Court (SW5) are prime centres for budget hotels. Each area has advantages and disadvantages, but the prices remain pretty consistent. If you want an attached bathroom you will be lucky to find anything for less than £28, even in winter.

Outside the high season, prices are nearly always negotiable; don't be afraid to ask for the 'best' price and for a discount if you are either staying more than a couple of nights or don't want a cooked breakfast. In July, August and September prices can jump by 25% or even more, and it is definitely worth phoning ahead. Many of the cheapies don't take credit cards.

B&Bs in private houses can be good value; double rooms range from £16 to £32 per person per night. At £16 you would be some distance out and sharing a bathroom, at £18 a little closer, at £20 you should be in a central location like Bloomsbury, and from £28 to £32 in a central area with private bathroom.

Paddington Paddington is a pretty seedy area, and although there are lots of cheap hotels, single women in particular will probably feel more comfortable elsewhere.

Nevertheless, it's convenient and there are a few decent places at decent prices.

Right in the centre of the action, *Norfolk Court & St David's Hotel (☎ 0171-723 4963, 16 Norfolk Square W2, tube: Paddington)* is a clean, comfortable, friendly place with the usual out-of-control décor. Basic singles/doubles have washbasin, colour TV and telephone and cost £30/46. With shower and toilet, prices jump to £56 for a double. A big plus in summer is Norfolk Square itself, just outside and a small oasis of greenery. The *Camelot Hotel (☎ 0171-723 9118)* at No 45 is another good choice but slightly more expensive. Should these be full, the square is ringed with similar places.

Bayswater Bayswater is extremely convenient and, as a result, some parts feel as if they are under constant invasion. Some of the streets immediately to the west of Queensway – which has an excellent selection of restaurants – are depressingly run-down.

Sass House Hotel (☎ 0171-262 2325, 11 Craven Terrace W2, tube: Lancaster Gate) is fairly threadbare but rooms with continental breakfast cost from £23/30.

One of Bayswater's best options is the *Garden Court Hotel (☎ 0171-229 2553, 30 Kensington Gardens Square W2, tube: Bayswater)*. It's a well-run, well-maintained family hotel, with well-equipped rooms with telephone and TV. Rooms without bathroom are £32/48, with bathroom £46/72. You can save a couple of pounds by forgoing breakfast, although this is actually good value.

Manor Court Hotel (☎ 0171-729 3361, 7 Clanricarde Gardens W2, tube: Queensway) is off Bayswater Rd. It's not spectacular, but you could do worse for the money. Rooms with private showers are from £30/45.

Earl's Court Earl's Court has been a hangout for refugees from the far-flung corners of the empire for decades but these days Australians are less conspicuous than Africans, Arabs and Indians. Most people seem to be in transit, and it shows in the grubby, unloved streets (although some smartening up of the side streets could see things improve). It's not really within walking distance of many places you'll want to be, but Earl's Court tube is a busy interchange, so getting around is a cinch.

The *St Simeon* (☎ *0171-373 0505, 38 Harrington Gardens SW7, tube: Gloucester Rd*) is within walking distance of the South Kensington museums and has dorms as well as singles and doubles. Prices start at around £18 per person but seem to be negotiable.

Guests at the relaxed *Boka Hotel* (☎ *0171-370 1388, 33 Eardley Crescent SW5, tube: Earl's Court*) have use of a kitchen. Rooms start at £25/40 (mostly without bathroom) and there's also a dorm with beds from £16.

Pimlico & Victoria
This may not be the most attractive part of London, but you'll be very close to the action and, despite the large transient population, the quality of the hotels is reasonably good. In general, the cheap hotels (around £30 per person) are better value than their Earl's Court counterparts.

The adjoining *Luna & Simone Hotels* (☎ *0171-834 5897, 47 Belgrave Rd SW1, tube: Victoria*) are run by affable Maltese brothers and offer clean, comfortable rooms within easy reach of the train and coach stations. Rooms without bathroom but with full English breakfast are from £28/50; a double with bathroom is £65. You can usually leave bags here while you go travelling.

The *Brindle House Hotel* (☎ *0171-828 0057, 1 Warwick Place North SW1, tube: Victoria*) is in an old building off the main thoroughfares. Although the décor won't impress everyone, the light, clean rooms are more pleasant than the foyer suggests. Singles are £30 (shared facilities), doubles are £42/38 (with/without facilities).

The *Romany Hotel* (☎ *0171-834 5553, 35 Longmoore St SW1, tube: Victoria*) is in a quiet street and pleasingly old-fashioned. You'll share a bathroom but breakfasts are good and rooms cost from £25/35.

Bloomsbury
Bloomsbury is very convenient, especially for the West End. In general, it's a little more expensive than the other areas, but the hotels also tend to be a little better, making it worth consideration.

In Gower St, the *Hotel Cavendish* (☎ *0171-636 9079, No 75, tube: Goodge St*) and the *Jesmond Hotel* (☎ *0171-636 3199, No 63, tube Goodge St*) are both fairly basic but clean and entirely adequate. They have rooms for £28/38, including breakfast. You share bathrooms, although all rooms have basins.

The *Repton Hotel* (☎ *0171-436 4922, 31 Bedford Place WC1, tube: Russell Square*) is pretty good value considering that Bedford Place isn't nearly as busy as Gower St. Rooms with TV and telephone are £48/63. It also has one dorm with six beds at £15 a head.

The family-run *St Margaret's Hotel* (☎ *0171-636 4277, 26 Bedford Place WC1, tube: Russell Square*) is in a classic Bloomsbury town house. It's not particularly inspiring but it's clean and all rooms have TV and telephone and cost £42.50/54.50.

King's Cross
Readers have recommended the welcome and the breakfast at the *Alhambra Hotel* (☎ *0171-837 9575, 17 Argyle St, tube; King's Cross*), which has rooms for £25/34. The nearby *Jesmond Dene Hotel* (☎ *0171-837 4654, 27 Argyle St, tube: King's Cross*) charges £28/38/51 a single/double/triple.

Kensington
Real cheapies are at a premium in this expensive area which is especially convenient for museum visits and shopping.

The *Magnolia Hotel* (☎ *0171-352 0187, 104-5 Oakley St SW3, tube: South Kensington*) has a good position and is remarkably good value. The rooms, all with colour TV, are pleasant, but try and get one at the back, away from traffic noise. Singles are from £35, doubles from £45 without bathroom and £60 with bathroom. Triples are £60. The only drawback is the hike to the tube.

PLACES TO STAY – MID-RANGE
Notting Hill
Notting Hill is one of the most interesting and convenient parts of London. It has become increasingly trendy and expensive over the last few years, but it's still home to a wide variety of Londoners and a large West Indian community.

Holland Park Hotel (☎ 0171-792 0216, *6 Ladbroke Terrace W11, tube: Notting Hill Gate)* has a great position on a quiet street near Holland Park and Notting Hill. The pleasant rooms are particularly good value, with singles/doubles without bathroom for £42/55 and with bathroom for £55/73.

At the start of Portobello Rd, the *Gate Hotel* (☎ 0171-221 2403, *6 Portobello Rd W11, tube: Notting Hill Gate)* is an old town house with frilly English décor. Well-equipped rooms with bathroom cost from £38/70.

Paddington
Sussex Gardens is lined with small hotels, but unfortunately it's also a major traffic route. Most places aren't inspiring, but there are some gems among the dross. *Balmoral House* (☎ 0171-723 7445, *156 Sussex Gardens W2, tube: Paddington)* is immaculate and very comfortable, with singles with/without bathroom for £40/35, and doubles with facilities for £60 (breakfast extra).

All rooms at the clean, quiet *Europa House* (☎ 0171-723 7343, *151 Sussex Gardens W2, tube: Paddington)* have bathrooms, TVs and telephones and cost £45/60.

The *Gresham Hotel* (☎ 0171-402 2920, *116 Sussex Gardens W2, tube: Paddington)* is a stylish, small hotel, with well-equipped rooms. Expect to pay £60/75.

Bayswater
The *Oxford Hotel* (☎ 0171-402 6860, *13 Craven Terrace W2, tube: Lancaster Gate)* offers reasonable value. Rooms with TV cost £65 which reduces to £50 if you rent for eight days.

Earl's Court
The *Philbeach Hotel* (☎ 0171-373 1244, *30 Philbeach Gardens SW5, tube: Earl's Court)* is a pleasant, well-decorated hotel, popular with a gay and lesbian clientele. There's a decent restaurant and bar and a nice garden. Rooms without a bathroom are £45/55; with bathroom they're £50/70.

The *York House Hotel* (☎ 0171-373 7519, *27 Philbeach Gardens SW5, tube: Earl's Court)*, just down the street from the Philbeach, is relatively cheap, although the rooms are pretty basic. Rooms without bath are £28/45; rooms with bath are £62/75.

London Town Hotel (☎ 0171-370 4356, *15 Penywern Rd SW5, tube: Earl's Court)* is a pleasant hotel. Rooms with bathroom are from £38/62. At No 14 the newly renovated *Regency Court Hotel* (☎ 0171-244 6615) charges from £30/40/55.

The *Merlyn Court Hotel* (☎ 0171-370 1640, *2 Barkston Gardens SW5, tube: Earl's Court)* has a good atmosphere. Clean, small rooms with bathroom cost £50/55; without, they're £25/35. Triples and quads with/without bathrooms are £65/70.

Victoria
The *Hamilton House* (☎ 0171-821 7113, *60 Warwick Way SW1, tube: Victoria)* has rooms with private bathrooms, TV and telephones for £48/58. At No 142, the *Windermere Hotel* (☎ 0171-834 5163) is another good choice with small, clean rooms from £51/64 and its own restaurant.

Westminster
One of the best-value deals in London at the moment must be the new 313 room *Travel Inn Capital* (☎ 01582-414341, *tube: Westminster)* in County Hall across Westminster Bridge from Big Ben. Clean, modern rooms cost £49.50 – and you'd be well advised to book ahead.

Bloomsbury
Tucked away in a crescent around a leafy garden to the north of Russell Square are a few of London's most comfortable, attrac-

tive and best-value hotels, all within walking distance of the West End. Although they're not the cheapest places, they're certainly worth it if you have the money to spend.

Jenkin's Hotel (☎ 0171-387 2067, *45 Cartwright Gardens WC1, tube: Russell Square*) has stylish, comfortable rooms. All have basins, TVs, telephones and fridges and prices include English breakfasts. Rooms are from £45/55. Guests can use the tennis courts in the gardens across the road.

The bigger *Crescent Hotel* (☎ 0171-387 1515, *49 Cartwright Gardens WC1, tube: Russell Square*) is a high-quality family-owned operation charging from £38/71. The *Euro* (☎ 0171-387 4321) and *George* (☎ 0171-387 8777) hotels, in the same street, are also good and cost around the same price.

A row of places along Gower St are also pretty fair value but not all of them have double-glazing on the front windows, which is essential if you're sensitive to traffic noise. Insist on one of the back rooms overlooking the garden, which are the nicest anyway.

The *Arran House Hotel* (☎ 0171-636 2186, *77 Gower St WC1, tube: Goodge St*) is a friendly, welcoming place with a great garden. Singles range from £32 to £42 (with shower and toilet), doubles from £47 to £62, and there are also triples and quads. The front rooms are soundproofed, and all have colour TV and telephones. There are also laundry facilities.

The *Ruskin Hotel* (☎ 0171-636 7388, *23 Montague St WC1B, tube: Holborn*) and its sister hotel, *Haddon Hall Hotel* (☎ 0171-636 2474, *39 Bedford Place WC1B, tube: Holborn*), are both fairly basic places with ordinary décor, but they have good locations and are entirely adequate (many rooms have private bathroom). Doubles with bathroom are £67; singles/doubles without are £39/55.

Sloane Square, Chelsea & Kensington

The *Swiss House Hotel* (☎ 0171-373 2769, *171 Old Brompton Rd W8, tube: Earl's Court*) is a clean, good-value hotel, nudging Earl's Court. Rooms without shower and toilet are £36/68; doubles with shower are £68, which is a bit steep since you only get continental breakfast. Still, rooms do have TV and direct-dial phones.

The *Vicarage Private Hotel* (☎ 0171-229 4030, *10 Vicarage Gate W8, tube: High St Kensington*) is well placed near Hyde Park, and between Notting Hill and Kensington. It's pleasant and well kept, with good showers and some charm and costs £38/60. It's recommended in several guidebooks so you need to book ahead.

Abbey House (☎ 0171-727 2594, *11 Vicarage Gate W8, tube: High St Kensington*) is a good-value small hotel that modestly describes itself as a B&B. The décor is decent and the welcome warm. Rooms are £38/60. Booking is recommended.

Midway between Kensington and Earl's Court, the *Amber Hotel* (☎ 0171-373 8666, *101 Lexham Gardens W8, tube: Earl's Court*) is pretty good value with fully equipped rooms from £75/95. Across the road, the *London Lodge Hotel* (☎ 0171-244 8444, *134 Lexham Gardens W8, tube: Earl's Court*) has fully equipped rooms for £75/85, and excellent breakfasts.

Annandale House Hotel (☎ 0171-730 5051, *fax 0171-730 2727, 39 Sloane Gardens, Sloane Square SW1, tube: Sloane Square*) is a discreet, traditional small hotel in a fashionable part of London – expect real linen napkins and tablecloths. Rooms with phone and TV cost from £40/75.

West End

Ideally, it would be great to stay in the West End, in the heart of the action, but few of the hotels hereabouts can be afforded by other than the best-heeled.

Glynne Court Hotel (☎ 0171-262 4344, *41 Great Cumberland Place W1, tube: Marble Arch*) is fairly typical. Rooms are from £45/50, but you only get a continental breakfast which one reader thought ungraciously served.

Ripe for a make-over but pretty cheap for its position right beside Piccadilly Circus, is the *Regent Palace Hotel* (☎ *0171-734 7000, tube: Piccadilly Circus)*, where rooms without bath or breakfast start at £50/75.

Hampstead

La Gaffe (☎ *0171-794 7526, fax 0171-794 7592, 107 Heath St NW3, tube: Hampstead)* is a small, rather eccentric, but nonetheless comfortable hotel in an 18th century cottage. The Italian restaurant here has been going forever. Rooms with bathroom are from £50/75.

Euston

If you're going to be travelling north from King's Cross or Euston it's worth knowing about the new *Euston Hotel* (☎ *01582-414341, tube: Euston)* in Euston Rd run by Travel Inns. Its garish blue exterior won't suit everyone but the rooms, at a flat £49.50, are a bargain and likely to be snapped up quickly; phone for a reservation.

The nearby *Ibis Euston* (☎ *0171-388 7777, Melton St, tube: Euston)* offers similar modern rooms for a flat £58.

PLACES TO STAY – TOP END

At the top end of the range you're choosing from some truly excellent hotels.

Notting Hill

Hillgate Hotel (☎ *0171-221 3433, fax 229 4808, 6 Pembridge Gardens W2, tube: Notting Hill Gate)* has a great position and all the facilities you'd expect in a good hotel. Rooms are £70/94.

The *Portobello* (☎ *0171-727 2777, fax 792 9641, 22 Stanley Gardens W11, tube: Notting Hill Gate)* is a beautifully appointed place in a great location. It's not cheap but most people consider the £80/140 well spent.

Knightsbridge, Chelsea & Kensington

Hotel 167 (☎ *0171-373 0672, fax 0171-373 3360, 167 Old Brompton Rd SW5, tube: Gloucester Rd)* is small, stylish and immaculately kept, with an unusually uncluttered and attractive décor. All rooms have private

bathroom. Singles are from £65, doubles range from £82 to £90.

For stylish luxury you could hardly do better than *Blakes* (☎ *0171-370 6701, fax 0171-373 0442, 33 Roland Gardens SW7, tube: Gloucester Rd)*, five Victorian houses knocked into one and decked out with four-posters and antiques on stripped floorboards. Such comfort doesn't come cheap; you're looking at from £150/175.

In Kensington proper, two excellent places on Sumner Place fail to hang out signs. There's not much to distinguish them but *Five Sumner Place* (☎ *0171-584 7586, fax 0171-823 9962, 5 Sumner Place SW7, tube: South Kensington)* has won several awards and is the cheaper. The rooms are comfortable and well equipped (all have bathroom, TV, phone, and drinks cabinet) and there's an attractive conservatory and garden. Singles range from £81 to £92, doubles are £116.

Hotel Number Sixteen (☎ *0171-589 5232, fax 0171-584 8615, 16 Sumner Place)* shares all the attributes of No 5. Singles range from £80 to £105, doubles from £140 to £170, but ask about weekend specials from £50 per person.

Lovers of Victoriana might want to try the *Gore* (☎ *0171-584 6601, fax 0171-589 8127, 189 Queen's Gate SW7, tube: Gloucester Rd)* where aspidistras run wild amid thousands of fading prints and Turkish carpets. Some will love the antique-style bathrooms, but not all have actual baths. Rooms cost from £111/156.

Right in Knightsbridge, *Basil Street Hotel* (☎ *0171-581 3311, fax 0171-581 3693, tube: Knightsbridge)* is a surprisingly unpretentious, antique-stuffed hideaway, perfectly placed for carrying back the shopping parcels. Rooms start at £70/110 but a few still lack bathrooms.

West End

Right in the heart of town, *Hazlitt's* (☎ *0171-434 1771, fax 0171-439 1524, 6 Frith St, Soho Square W1, tube: Tottenham Court Rd)* is one of London's finest hotels with efficient, personal service. Built in 1718, it comprises three linked Georgian houses. All 23 rooms have names and are individually decorated with antique furniture and prints. They cost from £135/174 and booking is advisable.

The *Fielding Hotel* (*☎/fax 0171-836 8305, 4 Broad Court, Bow St WC2, tube: Covent Garden*) is remarkably good value considering that it's in a pedestrian walk, almost opposite the Royal Opera House. The hotel looks like an old pub, but the rooms are clean and well run. Most have private bathroom, TVs and telephones and cost £65/85.

Wigmore Court Hotel (*☎ 0171-935 0928, fax 0171-487 4254, 23 Gloucester Place, Portman Square W1, tube: Marble Arch*) has pretty horrible décor, although someone must love it. On the other hand, it's a well-organised place whose guests have access to a kitchen and self-service laundry. Well-equipped rooms with bath are £45/79 in the peak season, and about 10% cheaper out of season.

The small, comfortable *Edward Lear Hotel* (*☎ 0171-402 5401, fax 0171-706 3766, 30 Seymour St W1, tube: Marble Arch*) was formerly home to Victorian painter and poet Edward Lear. All rooms have TV, tea and coffee facilities and telephone. Singles/doubles without bathroom cost from £39.50/54.50, with bathroom £70/84.50.

Just behind the Wallace Collection and excellently placed for shopping, the luxurious *Durrants Hotel* (*☎ 0171-935 8131, fax 0171-487 3510, George St W1, tube: Marble Arch*) is a large hotel that, amazingly, was once a country inn and still retains something of the feel of a gentleman's club. Comfortable rooms with bathroom start at £93/115, but breakfast is extra.

Bryanston Court (*☎ 0171-262 3141, fax 0171-262 7248, 55 Great Cumberland Place W1, tube: Marble Arch*) also has something of a club atmosphere, with leather armchairs and a formal style. It's particularly aimed at businesspeople, and all rooms have private bathroom, TV and phone. They cost from £73/90.

Handy for Oxford St and the British Museum, the *Academy Hotel* (*☎ 0171-631 4115, fax 0171-636 3442, 21 Gower St, tube: Goodge St*) is in a busy street, although double-glazing keeps the noise down. Rooms are pale and pretty and there's a pleasant back garden; they cost from £90/130.

The big *Strand Palace* (*☎ 0171-836 8080, fax 0171-836 2077, Strand WC2, tube: Charing Cross*) went through a bad patch but has had some work done to improve things. Its position, close to Covent Garden, is excellent but the price tag (from £94/121 without breakfast) is still pretty steep. Look out for a package deal.

You can't get more central than *The Hampshire* (*☎ 0171-839 9399, fax 0171-930 8122, Leicester Square, tube: Leicester Square*). It's part of the Radisson Edwardian group, which has several luxury hotels scattered around London, all of them aimed at people for whom money is no object. The Hampshire tends to be full of rich, retired Americans and top-flight businesspeople. Rooms are £230/265.

Claridges (*☎ 0171-629 8860, fax 0171-499 2210, Brook St W1*) is one of the greatest of London's five-star hotels. It's from a bygone era where you could easily bump into people you last saw in *Hello* magazine. The Art Deco suites were designed in 1929 and have log fires in winter. Expect to pay £258/348.

The *Ritz* (*☎ 0171-493 8181, fax 0171-493 2687, 150 Piccadilly W1, tube: Green Park*) is the most famous of London's hotels, and has a spectacular position overlooking Green Park. Rooms cost a staggering £253/306 for which you get all the luxury you would quite rightly expect.

You can hardly get more central than *One Aldwych* (*☎ 0171-300 1000, tube: Charing Cross*), London's latest place for a splurge. It's midway along The Strand, facing Waterloo Bridge and around the corner from Covent Garden. There's an on-site cinema and a choice of restaurants; comfortable, modern rooms start at £275 a double.

Short-Term Rental

Prices for rental accommodation are high and standards are low. At the bottom end of the market, expect to pay £60 to £120 per week for a bedsit (a single furnished room, usually with a shared bathroom and kitchen, although some have basic cooking facilities). The next step up is a studio, which normally has a separate bathroom and kitchen for between £85 and £150. One bedroom flats average between £100 and £150. Shared houses and flats are the best value, with a bedroom for between £50 and £75 plus bills. Most landlords demand one month's rent as a security deposit, plus a month's rent in advance.

For help in finding a flat, phone ☎ 0171-388 5153 or call into the foyer of Capital Radio at 29/30 Leicester Square WC2 and pick up its flatshare list; new lists appear at 4 pm every Friday and the best places go fast. *The Guide* which comes with Saturday's *Guardian* newspaper reproduces this list. Rooms and flats are also advertised at the *New Zealand News UK* office in the Royal Opera Arcade behind New Zealand House, in *TNT*, *Time Out*, the *Evening Standard* and *Loot*. When you inspect a flat it's wise to take someone else with you, both for safety reasons and for help in spotting any snags.

If you decide to use an agency, check that it doesn't charge fees to tenants; Jenny Jones (☎ 0171-493 4381) and Derek Collins (☎ 0171-930 2773) are free.

PLACES TO EAT

It's difficult but not impossible to eat out in London at a reasonable price. In general, restaurant-going is the province of the moneyed classes; you'll be lucky to get a decent meal and glass of wine for less than £10 per head, except in pubs where the food is not always that great. If you want to keep costs down, resist the temptation of alcohol, which is always ridiculously expensive, or bottled water, which can come as a nasty shock.

Indian restaurants are consistently good value; unfortunately they often tone down their spices for the English palate. The endless pasta and pizza places can also be good, especially if they're run by Italians (which many aren't). It's probably hardest to find good-quality English cuisine at a reasonable price although the restaurants serving Modern British food are very much at the heart of London's currently trendy image.

Of guides to London restaurants, the best is the *Time Out Eating & Drinking in London Guide* (£8.50), but it doesn't have much for budget travellers and is difficult to wade through. Harden's *Good Cheap Eats* (£5.95) is an annual guide to budget establishments.

There are several happy hunting grounds in the West End (W1): around Covent Garden, especially north-east between Endell St and St Martin's Lane; around Soho, especially north-west of the intersection of Charing Cross Rd and Shaftesbury Ave (including Old Compton St and Frith St) and north of Leicester Square on Lisle and Gerrard Sts (Chinatown with obligatory Chinese street furniture). For something more hippyish, head for Neal's Yard in Covent Garden, a flower-bedecked courtyard surrounded by cheap vegetarian eateries.

Camden Town (NW1) has a cosmopolitan range of restaurants and cafés that become very crowded over weekends. For a good selection, start at Mornington Crescent and wander north-west along Camden High St and its continuation, Chalk Farm Rd.

The hotel zone around Bayswater (W2) boasts many moderately priced restaurants along Queensway and Westbourne Grove. There are other interesting possibilities around Notting Hill – a couple of places at the southern end of Pembridge Rd and on Hillgate St across Notting Hill Gate, and around Blenheim Crescent and its intersection with Portobello Rd.

The budget eateries along Earl's Court Rd and the streets opposite the tube station are generally pretty uninspiring. You're better off eating elsewhere.

Of the places to look for Indian food, Brick Lane (E1) in the East End has lots of cheap, good Bangladeshi restaurants, while Drummond St (NW1) is good for South Indian menus which often suit vegetarians.

In this section, cafés and restaurants listed as budget conscious are those where you should be able to eat for less than £10 a head, sometimes for considerably less. At those listed as moderately priced, the bill is likely to fall between £10 and £20 a head. The splash-out places are those where you're looking at more than £20 a head.

West End & Soho

Soho is London's gastronomic centre, with numerous restaurants and numerous cuisines to choose from. Interesting cafés also spill out onto the street, especially around the corner of Frith and Old Compton Sts.

Two veritable institutions are *Bar Italia* (☎ 0171-437 4520, 22 Frith St W1), which is crowded and boisterous and the home of London's first decent coffee; and *Patisserie Valerie* (☎ 0171-823 9971, 44 Old Compton St W1), which is famous for its artistic and calorie-busting cakes. Get to both from Tottenham Court Rd tube.

Tiny *Poons* (☎ 0171-437 4549, 27 Lisle St WC2, tube: Leicester Square) is where the upmarket Poons empire started. It offers exceptional food at very good prices and specialises in superb wind-dried meats. The dried duck is heavenly, the steamed chicken equally sensational. If you're hungry, start with soup and order perhaps two dishes and rice – you'll pay around £10 per person. Be prepared to queue at busy times, and to be hustled out again pretty quickly.

Wong Kei (☎ 0171-437 6833, 41 Wardour St W1, tube: Leicester Square) is famous for the rudeness of its waiters. Some find this adds to the experience, but even if you don't you might be tempted by the cheap and good Cantonese food. A set menu starts at £5.80 for a minimum of two people.

Nusa Dua (☎ 0171-437 3559, 11 Dean St W1, tube: Tottenham Court Rd) is a rather garish Indonesian restaurant, but the prices are fair, with noodle specials for £3.95 and set lunches for £5.95. The tofu and tempeh are excellent and there are plenty of other vegetarian offerings.

Pizza Express (☎ 0171-439 8722, 10 Dean St W1, tube: Tottenham Court Rd) is part of a long-standing chain which serves unusually good pizzas. This branch is also known for its excellent jazz accompani-

---

Time for Tea?

Given the vital role that tea plays in their culture, it should be no surprise that going out for 'afternoon tea' is something dear to the souls of the English. But forget stewed tea and a Rich Tea biscuit – a traditional tea comes with a selection of delicate sandwiches (cucumber and smoked salmon are favourites), gooey cakes and scones with cream and jam. Oh, and lashings of tea too.

The two most famous venues are Fortnum & Mason and the Ritz. Fortnum's Fountain (☎ 0171-734 8040, 181 Piccadilly W1, tube: Piccadilly Circus) has afternoon tea from £6.95, and a champagne tea for £15.75. These are served between 3 and 6 pm (not Sunday). The Ritz (☎ 0171-493 8181, Piccadilly W1, tube: Piccadilly Circus) has afternoon tea between 2 and 6 pm for a bargain £21 per person. Booking is essential and a strict dress code applies.

In comparison, tea in the splendid setting of The Orangery (☎ 0171-376 0239, Kensington Gardens, tube: High St Kensington) is a positive snip at £7.50.

---

ments (phone to find out what's on and the admission fee). There's a jazz-free branch round the corner at 20 Greek St.

Pollo (☎ 0171-734 5917, 20 Old Compton St W1, tube: Leicester Square) attracts an art-student crowd with numerous pastas for around £3.50. It can be very busy.

Stockpot, next door at No 18, also has a long list of dishes for under £5.

Stepping into the *New Piccadilly* (☎ 0171-437 8530, 8 Denman St, tube: Piccadilly Circus) is like stepping into a time warp – nothing, except the prices, has changed since it first opened in the 1950s. Even the prices haven't changed as much as you would expect: pastas and pizzas are around £3.50, and chicken and steaks weigh in at around £4.75.

Melati (☎ 0171-437 2745, 21 Great Windmill St W1, tube: Piccadilly Circus) is an acclaimed Indonesian, Malaysian and Singaporean restaurant with excellent food and a good range of vegetarian options. Various noodle and rice dishes are around £6. You'll probably spend around £10 without wine.

Mildred's (☎ 0171-494 1634, 58 Greek St W1, tube: Tottenham Court Rd) is small and popular, so you may have to share a table. The chaos is worth it, however, because the vegetarian food is both good and well priced. Expect to pay around £5 for a substantial main meal.

Yo Sushi (☎ 0171-287 0443, 52 Poland St W1, tube: Oxford Circus) is one of London's livelier sushi bars where the drinks trolley moves by itself on magnetic rails. Dishes cost from £1.30 to £3.50; you should be able to get away with around £10 a head.

The *Blue Room* (Bateman St between Frith and Greek Sts W1, tube: Tottenham Court Rd) is a trendsetting coffee shop, favoured by the young and the hip of Soho but not at all intimidating. There are comfortable sofas at the back, with newspapers for browsing over a sandwich.

Bunjies (☎ 0171-240 1796, 27 Litchfield St WC2, tube: Leicester Square) is a folk club tucked away off Charing Cross Rd where you can also get cheap, reasonable vegetarian food. Main dishes are around £4. There's also a fish menu.

Wagamama (☎ 0171-292 0990, 10A Lexington St W1, tube: Piccadilly Circus) is not the place for a quiet dinner. It's loud and fun with great Japanese food but you have to share tables and may have to queue. Main dishes range from £4 to £7. There's another branch (☎ 0171-323 9223, 4 Streatham St WC1, tube: Tottenham Court Rd).

Diana's Diner (☎ 0171-240 0272, 39 Endell St, tube: Covent Garden) is very basic but also very cheap. While not inspiring, the food is OK. Spaghetti costs from £3.75 and you'll find a range of grills and roasts for around £4.60.

Sofra (☎ 0171-930 6090, 17 Charing Cross Rd, tube: Leicester Square) is one of a chain of Turkish restaurants and cafés.

Other branches are at 18 Shepherd St, Mayfair W1 (☎ 0171-493 3320) and 36 Tavistock St WC2 (☎ 0171-240 3972). Particularly worth sampling is the set £9.95 array of mezes. Turkish cuisine is generally thought of as unmitigatedly meaty but Sofra does a surprisingly good job of catering for vegetarians too.

Across the road, *Gaby's Continental Bar* (☎ 0171-836 4233, 30 Charing Cross Rd, tube: Leicester Square) is a wonderful snack bar right beside Wyndham's theatre. It's been there forever and attracts queues for staples like hummus and felafel for £3.20 and couscous royale for £7.50. Juices are pricey at £1.70 but generally this is a great-value place.

Café in the Crypt (☎ 0171-839 4342, St Martin-in-the-Fields Church, Trafalgar Square, tube: Charing Cross) is in an atmospheric crypt under the church. The food is good, with plenty of offerings for vegetarians. Main dishes usually cost around £5 to £6. Dinner is served daily from 5 to 7.30 pm.

Cheap food to go is available from pizza counters on the north-eastern corner of Leicester Square. You should be able to get a slice of pizza and salad for around £2.

A particularly good way to sample the best of Chinese cuisine is to try a Cantonese *dim sum* lunch: numerous small dishes with relaxing jasmine tea. The *Chuen Cheng Ku* (☎ 0171-437 1398, 17 Wardour St W1, tube: Leicester Square) is open daily from 11 am to 11.45 pm. All the dishes – dumplings, rice paper-wrapped prawns and numerous other delicacies – are trundled around on heavily laden trolleys. Nibbles start at £1.50 and soon mount up.

Café Pelican (☎ 0171-379 0309, 45 St Martin's Lane WC2, tube: Leicester Square) functions as a restaurant, brasserie and café bar. Its location, close to the English National Opera, is fantastic and it's a great people-watching spot, particularly in fine weather. There are reasonably priced snacks in the brasserie. More substantial French dishes are available from the restaurant where *confit de canard* (duck confit), for example, is £9.25.

Taking the elevator down to the basement and walking through the kitchens is all part of the fun at *Belgo Centraal (☎ 0171-813 2233, 50 Earlham St WC2, tube: Covent Garden)*, where the waiters dress up as monks. Moules and spit-roasts are the inevitable specialities and there's a choice of 100 different flavoured lagers including banana, peach and cherry. The set lunch menu costs £5 but from Monday to Friday from 5.30 to 8 pm you can try their 'Beat the Clock' menu – the time you sit down decides the price you pay for your main dish (sit down at 6.15 pm and pay £6.15; minimum charge £6). There's another branch called *Belgo Noord (☎ 0171-267 0718, 72 Chalk Farm Rd NW1, tube: Chalk Farm)*.

The *French House Dining Room (☎ 0171-437 2477, 49 Dean St W1, tube: Tottenham Court Rd)* is on the 1st floor of a typically old-fashioned Soho pub. Upstairs is a tiny, high-ceilinged room with a convivial atmosphere. The short, ever-changing menu offers robust English food. Typical examples are duck confit (£5.50) and roast guinea fowl (£11.50). Booking is advised.

The *Atlantic Bar & Grill (☎ 0171-734 4888, 20 Glasshouse St W1, tube: Piccadilly Circus)* is one of *the* places to dine. High ceilings, a large floor area and two bars make this a very buzzy and atmospheric place but food is expensive (£30 for the average dinner) and you must book at the weekend. A cheaper bar menu is available until 2 am.

Right on Piccadilly Circus, *The Criterion (☎ 0171-930 0488, tube: Piccadilly Circus)* has a spectacular interior, all chandeliers, mirrors and marble, and quite an atmosphere; you won't feel comfortable unless you dress accordingly. The menu offers Marco Pierre White's fashionable Mediterranean-style food (eg sauteed goat's cheese and roasted peppers), but there are also some British classics like fish and chips. Although this is a pricey place where you won't have much change from £30 for dinner, set two-course lunches cost £14.95 and three-course lunches £17.95. Portions tend to *cuisine minceur* dimensions.

Chiang Mai (☎ 0171-437 7444, 48 Frith St W1, tube: Tottenham Court Rd) is a top-class Thai restaurant with a separate vegetarian menu and a wide range of soups. Set menus cost £46.50 or £55.65 for two.

Dell'Ugo (☎ 0171-734 8300, 56 Frith St W1, tube: Tottenham Court Rd) gets variable reports on its food, but the atmosphere appeals to many customers. It is on three floors: a café and bar on the ground floor, a bistro on the 2nd floor and a restaurant on the 3rd floor. Expect to pay around £25 for a meal in the restaurant, although a set bistro lunch is just £10.

Now into its fifth decade, *The Gay Hussar (☎ 0171-437 0973, 2 Greek St W1, tube: Tottenham Court Rd)* sticks to a familiar format, offering a wide range of Hungarian dishes. Firm favourites include veal goulash which costs £14.75. The extras (like vegetables!) could make this an expensive trip, but it's a one-off experience within a rich and decorous setting.

Mezzo (☎ 0171-314 4000, 100 Wardour St W1, tube: Piccadilly Circus) is one of restaurant-entrepreneur Terence Conran's successful ventures which attracts London's media crowd and those with aspirations. Nevertheless, it's a fun place to eat. Come between 6 and 7 pm to take advantage of two courses for £7.95. On weekends it often does over 1000 covers per evening.

With its liveried doorman, *The Ivy (☎ 0171-836 4751, 1 West St WC2, tube: Leicester Square)* is a showbizzy event in itself and you need to book ahead. A modern British menu lists dishes like steak tartare, Cumberland sausages, onions and mash. Fillet of sea trout is £16.75, eggs benedict £5. It's a pricey outing (expect to pay £30 per person) but perfect for a special occasion.

Tucked away behind Regent St, *The Sugar Club (☎ 0171-437 7776, 21 Warwick St W1, tube: Oxford Circus)* serves up chef Peter Gordon's 'Pacific rim cookery' which mixes and matches culinary traditions of east and west. Since it moved, the restaurant has attracted more mixed reviews than when it was famous as the place that turned away Madonna.

Covent Garden

There's a cluster of enjoyable New Age cafés in Neal's Yard. The **Beach Café, World Food Café, Neal's Yard Salad Bar** and **Paprika** all offer a similar diet of wholesome dishes like cheese breads and home-made noodles in pleasing surroundings, but space fills up quickly. Neal's Yard is off Short's Gardens and Monmouth St and is signposted from Neal St. Lunch in any of these places should cost less than £5 if you choose carefully.

Food for Thought (☎ 0171-836 0239, 31 Neal St WC2, tube: Covent Garden) is a small, reliable vegetarian place. The menu features dishes like spinach and mushroom South Indian bake for £2.90, stir-fried vegetables for £2.70. It's nonsmoking, but you can bring your own bottle.

For Mexican food in a cheerful atmosphere try **Café Pacifico** (☎ 0171-379 7728, 5 Langley St WC2, tube: Covent Garden), which manages a daily lunch special for £3.75. If you're hooked you can always move on to **La Perla del Pacifico Bar** (☎ 0171-240 7400, 28 Maiden Lane WC2, tube: Covent Garden), which is owned by the same people and boasts healthy lunches and not quite so healthy rare and premium tequilas.

Calabash (☎ 0171-836 1976, Africa Centre, 38 King St WC2, tube: Covent Garden) serves food from all over Africa. The menu describes dishes to the uninitiated; a typical dish is Senegalese yassa (£6.50), chicken marinated with lemon juice and peppers. There are beers from all over Africa and wines from Algeria, Zimbabwe and South Africa. A typical meal costs £15.

Chez Gerard (☎ 0171-379 0666, The Market, The Piazza WC2, tube: Covent Garden) offers traditional French fare such as steak frites. It has a balcony overlooking the opera house but tables can't be reserved. Main dishes range from £9 to £15.

Café des Amis du Vin (☎ 0171-379 3444, 11-14 Hanover Place WC2, tube: Covent Garden) is very handy for meals before or after the theatre. Each of its three floors has a different price range. The ground floor brasserie is reliable and offers all the favourites: steak frites, quiches and omelettes cost between £6 and £9. Upstairs, in the more expensive eatery, a lunch or dinner set meal is £17.95.

Joe Allen (☎ 0171-836 0651, 13 Exeter St WC2, tube: Covent Garden) is a star-spotter's paradise. Theatre posters adorn the walls and the tables are covered by gingham at lunch time and white tablecloths and candles at night. There's a jolly buzz to this place and it gets pretty crowded. The menus are pretty standard US fare: clam chowders and pecan pie. A three course lunch costs £15.50.

Rules (☎ 0171-836 5314, 35 Maiden Lane WC2, tube: Covent Garden) is very British; there's an Edwardian interior and the waiters proudly wear starched white aprons. The menu is very meat-oriented but freshwater fish is also available. Puddings are traditional: trifles, pies and an abundance of custard. The quality and feel of the place make up for the steep prices (main courses average around £15).

Westminster & St James's

The **Wren at St James's** (☎ 0171-437 9419, 35 Jermyn St SW3, tube: Piccadilly Circus) is the perfect escape from the West End but is only open during the day. It adjoins St James's Church (which often has free lunch time concerts) and in summer it spills out into the shady churchyard. There are plenty of vegetarian dishes for around £3.60, and excellent home-made cakes.

A stone's throw from Westminster Abbey and the Houses of Parliament, the **Footstool Restaurant** (☎ 0171-222 2779, tube: Westminster) is housed in the crypt of 18th century St John's, Smith Square, now a concert hall. Choose between a buffet with soups for £3 and casseroles for £6.50 and a more formal restaurant for à la carte lunches and post-concert set dinners (£10 for two courses).

Pimlico & Victoria

O Sole Mio (☎ 0171-976 6887, 39 Churton St SW1, tube: Victoria) is a standard, decent-value Italian restaurant with pizzas and pastas under £6. Next door but one,

Grumbles is a pleasant wine bar with, among other things, stuffed aubergine for £6.45 and kebabs for £7.25.

If you're waiting for a coach at Victoria, don't hang about the coach station but head across Eccleston Place to *The Well* (☎ 0171-730 7303, tube: Victoria), a church-run enterprise which has been dispensing tea and cakes, as well as soups and light meals, to travellers since time immemorial. It's open until 6 pm on weekdays and 5 pm on Saturday (closed Sunday).

Mekong (☎ 0171-834 6896, 46 Churton St SW1, tube: Victoria) is reputed to be one of London's best Vietnamese restaurants. It's a bit beyond a budget budget but does offer a set meal for £12 (minimum two persons) and house wine at a reasonable £1.80.

The City

In the crypt below St Mary-le-Bow (the cockney church) you'll find *The Place Below* (☎ 0171-329 0789, tube: St Paul's or Mansion House), a pleasant vegetarian restaurant, open from 7.30 am to 2.30 pm; come between 11.30 am and noon and you'll get a £2 discount on most main dishes. Salads cost £6.95, spicy lentil soup £2.95.

For those who like their burgers served American-style, *Fatboy's Diner* (☎ 0171-375 2763, 296 Bishopsgate EC2, tube: Liverpool St) will come as a real treat. Burgers, hot dogs, eggs, bacon and hash browns are all served up here, with a quality to make McDonald's weep. Expect to spend between £3.50 and £5 on a main course.

Sweeting's Oyster Bar (☎ 0171-248 3062, 39 Queen Victoria St EC4, tube: Mansion House) is a wonderfully old-fashioned place, with a mosaic floor and waiters in white aprons serving up traditional delights. Something like wild smoked salmon costs £9, so you're likely to run up a bill of around £15 to £20.

East End & Docklands

There are many cheap Bangladeshi restaurants on Brick Lane, including *Aladin* (☎ 0171-247 8210) at No 132 and *Nazrul* (☎ 0171-246 2505) at No 130 (tube: Aldgate

East). Both are unlicensed, but you should eat for around £7. Many people believe this is London's best subcontinental food.

Brick Lane Beigel Bake (☎ 0171-729 0616, 159 Brick Lane E1, tube: Whitechapel) is open 24 hours at the Bethnal Green Rd end of Brick Lane. You won't find bagels better, fresher or cheaper; the salmon and cream cheese version for 90p is just heavenly.

The Spitz (☎ 0171-247 9747, 109 Commercial St EC1, tube: Aldgate East) is at the east side of Spitalfields Market and makes a great place to stop for a quick snack while shopping at the Sunday market (although it's open the rest of the week, too).

The café upstairs in *Whitechapel Art Gallery* (☎ 0171-522 7878, 80-82 Whitechapel High St E1, tube: Aldgate East) serves dishes like carrot filo strudel and salad for £4.65. It's open from 11 am to 5 pm Tuesday to Sunday (8 pm on Wednesday).

Camden & Islington

At the quiet *El Parador* (☎ 0171-387 2789, 245 Eversholt St, tube: Camden Town), good vegetarian selections include *empanadillas de espinacas y queso* (pasties with spinach and cheese) for £3.50, with meat and fish dishes just a little more expensive.

Ruby in the Dust (☎ 0171-485 2744, 102 Camden High St, tube: Camden Town) is an atmospheric café bar worth a trek across town. There isn't a huge menu, but it's interesting: Mexican snacks, soup for £2.90 and mains like bangers and mash for £6.45.

The Raj (☎ 0171-388 6663, 19 Camden High St, tube: Camden Town) is a small Indian place with all-you-can-eat lunch and dinner buffets for £3.50 and £3.75 respectively.

Silks & Spice (☎ 0171-267 2718, 28 Chalk Farm Rd NW1, tube: Camden Town) is a Thai/Malay restaurant doing express lunches for £4.95.

Bar Gansa (☎ 0171-267 8909, 2 Inverness St NW1, tube: Camden Town) is an arty but fun tapas bar with dishes around £3. Service is good and the staff friendly. Breakfast costs £3.95.

As the name suggests, *Marine Ices* (☎ *0171-485 3132, 8 Haverstock Hill NW3, tube: Chalk Farm*) started out as a Sicilian ice-cream parlour but these days it does some savoury dishes as well. Whether you indulge in a meal or not it's imperative to try one of the amazing ice creams; sundaes start at £2.40. The nearby *Marathon* (☎ *0171-485 3814*) is a source of late-night kebabs and beer.

Primrose Brasserie (☎ *0171-483 3765, 101 Regents Park Rd NW1, tube: Chalk Farm*) serves good-value Eastern European food, such as salt beef. Starters cost from £2.50, main dishes from £5.50, and it's BYO.

Close to Primrose Hill, *Lemonia* (☎ *0171-586 7454, 89 Regent's Park Rd NW1, tube: Chalk Farm*) is often busy so it's wise to book. It offers good-value food and a lively atmosphere. Meze cost £12.25 per person and both the vegetarian and meat moussakas for £7.50 are particularly tasty.

Heading into Upper St, Islington N1, *Tuk Tuk* (☎ *0171-226 0837, tube: Angel*) at No 330 offers reliable Thai food for not too outrageous prices; a bowl of noodles with peanuts, prawns, egg and bean sprouts costs £4.95. Singha beer is available.

At No 331, *Café Flo* (☎ *0171-226 7916*) offers reliable French food like Alsatian hotpot for £8.50, plus an area for coffee and cakes and watching the world go by.

At No 324 the *Upper St Fish Shop* (☎ *0171-359 1401*) doles out classy fish and seafood, like half a dozen Irish oysters for £5.90. Even cod and chips costs £7. Still, if you're keen on seafood this is a good place to come.

Ravi Shankar (☎ *0171-833 5849, 422 St John St EC1, tube: Angel*) is a small but inexpensive restaurant favoured by vegetarians – the all-you-can-eat lunch time buffets for £4.50 are extremely popular. There's another branch (*133 Drummond St NW1, tube: Warren St or Euston Square*).

Café Delancey (☎ *0171-387 1985, 3 Delancey St NW1, tube: Camden Town*) offers the chance to get a decent cup of coffee with a snack or a full meal in a large, relaxed European-style brasserie complete

with newspapers. Main dishes are from £7 to £13 and wine starts at £6.50 for a half-bottle. The cramped toilets seem suitably Parisian too.

The award-winning *Le Montmartre* (☎ *0171-359 3996, 26 Liverpool Rd N1, tube: Angel*) is a minuscule and very popular French bistro whose reasonable prices attract the crowds; booking is advisable. A big bowl of fish soup followed by salmon, mushroom and chive pasta washed down with wine will set you back about £15.

Part of the same chain, the *Sacre Coeur* (☎ *0171-354 2618, 18 Theberton St N1, tube: Angel*) offers similarly reliable French food in similarly cramped surroundings. The *moules et frites* for £4.95 are excellent value but the overall bill will still top £10.

Vegetarian Cottage (☎ *0171-586 1257, 91 Haverstock Hill NW3, tube: Chalk Farm*) is a good-quality vegetarian restaurant. The delicious cottage special combines mushrooms, Buddha's cushion fungus, lotus roots, nuts and vegetables wrapped in a lotus leaf. Expect to pay around £15 for a full meal.

Bloomsbury & Holborn

If you're visiting the British Museum it's worth knowing that Museum St (tube: Tottenham Court Rd) is packed with places to eat where you'll get better value for your money than in the museum café. *Ruskin's Coffee Shop* at No 41 does soup for £1.80 and filled jacket potatoes from £2.85. *Uncle Sam's Deli* does felafel feasts for £2.80. The tiny *Garden Café* at No 32 has cakes to kill for. Best of all is the tremendously popular *Coffee Gallery* (☎ *0171-436 0455*) at No 23 where dishes like grilled sardines and salad can be savoured in a bright, cheerful room with modern paintings on the walls.

The busy *Greenhouse* (☎ *0171-637 8038, below the Drill Hall, 16 Chenies St WC1, tube: Goodge St*) serves excellent vegetarian food, with main courses for £3.95. You'll probably have to share a table.

The *North Sea Fish Restaurant* (☎ *0171-387 5892, 7 Leigh St WC1, tube: Russell Square*) sets itself the simple task of serving fresh fish and potatoes well. The fish (deep-fried or grilled) and a huge serving of chips will set you back from £6 to £7.50.

Mille Pini (☎ *0171-242 2434, 33 Boswell St WC1, tube: Holborn*) is a true Italian restaurant with reasonable prices. You'll waddle out but only spend about £10 for two courses and coffee.

The *October Gallery Café* (☎ *0171-242 7367, 24 Old Gloucester St WC1, tube: Russell Square*) is inside a small art gallery with a courtyard but only opens for lunch. Meals are around £6.

The *Museum Street Café* (☎ *0171-405 3211, 47 Museum St WC1, tube: Tottenham Court Rd*) is packed at lunch times but is less busy in the evening. The food, like the interior, is straightforward. Freshly cooked ingredients combine to offer char-grilled fish and snappy salsas. Lunch set meals are cheaper but a three course meal in the evening will cost £22.50. You can BYO for a £5 corkage charge.

Chelsea & South Kensington

King's Rd (tube: Sloane Square or South Kensington) has all sorts of eating possibilities. If the weather is decent make for the Chelsea Farmers' Market just off King's Rd in Sydney St where several small stalls spill out into a pleasant outdoor area. Among them, the *Market Place Restaurant-Bar* does soup (£3) inspired by what was on sale at the market that morning, and a big hang-over breakfast including steak and eggs for £6.50. *Il Cappuccino* has coffee for £1, while *La Delicia* does pizzas from £5.20. The *Chelsea Deli* does filled baguettes from £1.80 and vegetarian ravioli for £4.

The *Chelsea Kitchen* (☎ *0171-589 1330, 98 King's Rd SW3, tube: Sloane Square*) has some of the cheapest food in London although the surroundings are pretty spartan. Minestrone is 80p, spaghetti is £2.40 and apple crumble is 99p.

New Culture Revolution (☎ *0171-352 9281, 5 King's Rd, tube: Sloane Square*) is a trendy but good-value dumpling and noodle bar. Top to bottom windows at the front mean that the restaurant is bright –

you eat in full view of passers-by. Main dishes cost around £6.

Popular *Henry J Bean's* (☎ *0171-352 9255, 195 King's Rd SW3, tube: Sloane Square*) is an American bar and restaurant, one of the few London places to have a garden. Music and a happy hour give it a fun atmosphere. Main dishes are from £5 to £7.

A British version of the American diner, the *Chelsea Bun* (☎ *0171-352 3635, Limerston St SW10, tube: Earl's Court*) is brilliant value. Breakfast is served all day, and there's seating on an upstairs veranda. Main dishes cost between £4 and £7.

Spago (☎ *0171-225 2407, 6 Glendower Place SW7, tube: South Kensington*) is the best-value restaurant in the vicinity with pastas and pizzas from £4, hence the queues.

Shabby-looking *Daquise* (☎ *0171-589 6117, 20 Thurloe St SW7, tube: South Kensington*) is a Polish place very close to the museums with a good range of vodkas and reasonable food. A set lunch is £6.80.

Wodka (☎ *0171-937 6513, 12 St Albans Grove W8, tube: High St Kensington*) is a new Polish restaurant in a quiet residential area away from the hustle and bustle of High St Kensington. Be warned that too much sampling of the large array of vodkas can push the bill up more than you might anticipate.

With its wicker chairs and mirrors, *Oriel* (☎ *0171-730 2804, 50 Sloane Square SW1, tube: Sloane Square*) makes a perfect place to meet before shopping in King's Rd. The brasserie has tables overlooking the square. Main dishes cost from £5 to £11.

Bluebird (☎ *0171-559 1000, 350 King's Rd SW3, tube: Fulham Broadway*) is another Conran venture, where a vast restaurant and bar sit above an upmarket food market and the smaller *Café Bluebird*.

The Canteen (☎ *0171-351 7330, Chelsea Harbour SW10, tube: Fulham Broadway*) is Michael Caine's well-known restaurant in the uninspiring Harbour Yard shopping centre. A good traditional British and French menu averages out at £25 but the décor – based on a playing card theme – may not be to everyone's taste.

In a pretty setting in the heart of South Kensington, *Daphne's* (☎ *0171-589 4257, 110-112 Draycott Ave, tube: South Kensington)* is small enough to be cosy but not claustrophobic. It serves delicious Mediterranean-style food, with main courses from around £12. It's very popular with the who's who crowd and booking is a must.

In what must be one of London's finest settings, *Bibendum* (☎ *0171-581 5817, 81 Fulham Rd SW3, tube: South Kensington)* is Conran's superb restaurant in a former Michelin factory. The ground floor accommodates a popular oyster bar where you really feel at the heart of the Art Deco finery. Upstairs it's all much lighter and brighter, and at weekends you'll need to have booked two weeks ahead to stand much chance of getting a table. The food is Modern British, with dishes like breast of guinea fowl costing £10.

Knightsbridge

There's a definite continental feel to *Patisserie Valerie* (☎ *0171-823 9971, 215 Brompton Rd SW5, tube: Knightsbridge),* a wonderful place to stop for a coffee and pastry or light snack after a trip to the V&A. Breakfast is popular at the weekend and newspapers are provided.

Pizza on the Park (☎ *0171-235 5273, 11 Knightsbridge SW5, tube: Hyde Park Corner)* is popular for its pizzas and jazz in the basement. There's also a spacious restaurant upstairs and, if you're lucky, a few tables overlooking Hyde Park. Pizzas average £6.50.

The Fifth Floor at Harvey Nichols (☎ *0171-235 5250, Knightsbridge SW1, tube: Knightsbridge)* is the perfect place to drop after you've shopped. It's expensive – a set lunch for £19.50.

Earl's Court

The *Troubadour* (☎ *0171-370 1434, 265 Old Brompton Rd, tube: Earl's Court)* has an illustrious history as a coffee shop and folk venue. Among others it has hosted Dylan, Donovan and John Lennon. These days it still occasionally has bands plus good-value food. Service is slow, but the wait is worthwhile. Vegetable soup is £2.10, pasta £4.

Although it's really nothing more than a traditional café, *Benjys* (*157 Earl's Court Rd SW5, tube: Earl's Court)* is always busy. The food is nothing to write home about, but cheap and filling. Serious breakfasts with as much tea or coffee as you can drink are around £3.50, 50p less for vegetarians.

Nando's (☎ *0171-259 2544, 204 Earl's Court Rd SW5, tube: Earl's Court)* serves Portuguese-style cooking concentrating on flame-grilled chicken dishes. A meal with a drink costs around £5.

Krungtap (☎ *0171-259 2314, 227 Old Brompton Rd SW10, tube: Earl's Court)* is a busy, friendly Thai and generally oriental restaurant. Most dishes are in the £3 to £4 range. Portions are generous although beer is expensive.

Mr Wing (☎ *0171-370 4450, 242-244 Old Brompton Rd, tube: Earl's Court)* is one of London's best Thai and Chinese restaurants. Make sure you get a seat in the jungle-style basement. The food is expensive but very good.

Notting Hill & Bayswater

Portobello has plenty of trendy bars and restaurants; *Café Grove (tube: Ladbroke Grove)* at the Ladbroke Grove end of Portobello, with a veranda overlooking the action, has cheap vegetarian food at around £5.

Costa's Grill (☎ *0171-229 3794, 14 Hillgate St W8, tube: Notting Hill Gate)* is a reliable Greek place, with dips at £1.50 and mains like souvlaki for £4.50.

Prost (☎ *0171-727 9620, 35 Pembridge Rd W11, tube: Notting Hill Gate)* is a small one-up, one-down restaurant serving traditional German cuisine. Main courses are under £10; venison in red wine with blueberry sauce, for example, is £8.25 but between 5.30 and 11 pm any two courses are £8.95. Dinner is served daily but it's only open for lunch on weekends.

Modhubon (☎ *0171-243 1778, 29 Pembridge Rd W11, tube: Notting Hill Gate)* serves good, inexpensive Indian food. Main dishes are under £5 and a set lunch is £3.90.

Geales (☎ *0171-727 7969, 2 Farmer St W8, tube: Notting Hill Gate*) is a very popular fish restaurant where fish and chips average out at about £7 a person – a lot more than you'd pay in the local chippie, but worth it. It's closed on Sunday.

For something more unusual, try *The Mandola* (☎ *0171-229 4734, 139 Westbourne Grove W2, tube: Bayswater*), which offers vegetarian Sudanese dishes like *tamiya*, a kind of felafel, for £4 and meat dishes for £7. The portions are small so it's better value if a couple share dishes.

Khan's (☎ *0171-727 5420, 13 Westbourne Grove W2, tube: Bayswater*) is a vast and popular Indian restaurant where diners eat amid pillars and palms. There are vegetarian dishes and a selection of meat curries for around £4.

All Saints (☎ *0171-243 2808, 12 All Saints Rd W11, tube: Westbourne Park*) is a funky place which is especially popular on Saturday during the Portobello Rd Market. If you can make yourself think over the pounding music you'll realise you're in another of those Modern British places where a meal is likely to cost you around £20.

Stylish *L'accento* (☎ *0171-243 2201, 16 Garway Rd W2, tube: Bayswater*) offers a two course set menu for £11.50 which could include mussel stew in white wine and fresh herbs, followed by grilled pork chop filled with sun-dried tomatoes and leeks. Once you step away from this menu it becomes more expensive.

Veronica's (☎ *0171-229 5079, 3 Hereford Rd W2, tube: Bayswater*) is trying to establish that England does have a culinary heritage while, promoting healthy eating. There are some fascinating dishes and the restaurant has won many awards. A three course set menu is £16.50 and you'll have fun studying the annotated menu.

Latest of the fashionable places where the eating is almost incidental to the being there is the *Pharmacy Restaurant & Bar* (☎ *0171-221 2442, 150 Notting Hill Gate W11,* *tube: Notting Hill*), with décor based on chemistry by the art world's *enfant terrible* Damien Hirst. Initial reports on the food are good so it might be worth trying to get there for the set two course lunch for £12.50.

Kensington Place (☎ *0171-727 3184, 201 Kensington Church St W8, tube: Notting Hill Gate*) has an impressive glass front and a design-conscious interior, which has made it the perfect place for publicly settling business deals. Starters cost from £4 and main courses from £9.

Novelli W8 (☎ *0171-229 4024, 122 Palace Gardens Terrace W8, tube: Notting Hill*) serves good-quality French food, with main courses for around £20 in a romantic hideaway restaurant. Booking is recommended. There's another branch on Clerkenwell Green (☎ *0171-251 6606*).

Inaho (☎ *0171-221 8495, 4 Hereford Rd W2, tube: Bayswater*) is a tiny Japanese restaurant where a tempura set dinner of an appetiser, soup, mixed salad, yakitori, sashimi, tempura, rice and seasonal fruits costs £20. A teriyaki equivalent is £22.

Hammersmith & Fulham

Deals (☎ *0181-563 1001, The Broadway Centre W6, tube: Hammersmith Broadway*) offers good-value food (£8 for a main dish) and a menu for everyone. There's some seating outside, a cocktail bar upstairs and a happy hour in the early evening.

The super-trendy *River Café* (☎ *0171-381 8824, Thames Wharf, Rainville Rd W6, tube: Hammersmith*) has a fabulous location on the River Thames, and serves what is probably the best nouvelle Italian cuisine in London. It's not cheap – you're unlikely to have much change from £40 if you go for a pudding as well.

Bermondsey

The Apprentice (☎ *0171-234 0254, 31 Shad Thames SE7, tube: Tower Hill*) is so named because trainee chefs practise here. Prices are lower than at the neighbouring Conran restaurants, with a set lunch for £9.50 and a set dinner for £17.50. It closes at 8.30 pm (6 pm on weekends).

Conran, who set up the Design Museum in Docklands, also located some excellent, expensive restaurants nearby. These include the stylish *Blue Print Café* (☎ *0171-378 7031*), which is actually on top of the Design Museum with spectacular river views. Modern British cooking is the order of the day and you won't see much change from £35 for dinner with wine.

Alternatively you could try *Le Pont de la Tour* (☎ *0171-403 8403, Butlers Wharf Building, 36D Shad Thames SE1, tube: Tower Hill*), which has more spectacular river views, a Frenchish menu and a 30 page wine list. Expect dinner to cost around £25 a head.

Waterloo & Lambeth

It may not look much but the *Gourmet Pizza Company* (☎ *0171-928 3188, Gabriel's Wharf SE1, tube: Waterloo*) usually has queues for its pizzas, which come with such outlandish toppings as Thai chicken (£7.50) and Italian sausage (£6.60). Standard cheese and tomato pizzas kick in at £4.70.

A branch of *Four Regions* (☎ *0171-928 0988, Westminster Bridge Rd SE1, tube: Waterloo or Lambeth North*) is now ensconced inside the old County Hall alongside the London Aquarium. The food here is said to be garnered from the four main cuisines of China (Peking, Cantonese, Szechuan and Shanghai) and made without resort to MSG, but it fetches rather mixed reviews. No one is going to quibble over one of the finest river views in London.

The immensely popular *Fire Station* (☎ *0171-401 3267, 150 Waterloo Rd SE1, tube: Waterloo*) is in a part of town that was once a culinary desert. The bar is pleasant enough to make the wait for a table enjoyable and there's a varied menu with reasonable prices (£7 to £10 for main courses).

For a quieter, more intimate atmosphere try *Bar Central* (☎ *0171-928 5086, 131 Waterloo Rd E1, tube: Waterloo*). Despite the name, this is actually a restaurant with a small bar. Main courses cost around £7.

The big news in eating out recently has been the conversion of the old Oxo Tower on the South Bank into housing with a restaurant at the top. The *restaurant* (☎ *0171-803 3888, Barge House St SE1, tube: Waterloo*) is owned by the Harvey Nichols department store and its venue and river views have ensured it a popularity that means five-week waits for a dinner table. A set lunch costs £24.50, dinner more like £40 a head. If you can't get into the restaurant, there's a cheaper brasserie, with a bistro, downstairs.

The new *Shakespeare's Globe Restaurant* (☎ *0171-928 9444, New Globe Walk SE1, tube: London Bridge*) is attached to the theatre and offers yet more splendid views as you tuck into Modern British cuisine at around £30 a head.

Hampstead

Coffee Cup (☎ *0171-435 7565, 74 Hampstead High St NW3, tube: Hampstead*) is a popular café with a wide-ranging menu from bacon and eggs to pasta.

The *Everyman Café* (☎ *0171-431 2123, Holly Bush Vale NW3, tube: Hampstead*) is attached to the cinema of the same name. If you're looking for a quiet place to eat in Hampstead, with reasonable food, this is a good choice. The three course set menu is £7.

Greenwich

Church St has a couple of decent cheap cafés, and there's a branch of *Café Rouge* attached to the Ibis Hotel at the end of the road. The *Millennium Café* will do you a Cornish pasty for £3.50, while *Peter de Wit's Café* serves cream teas for £3.80 in what it describes as its tiny courtyard.

In the covered market the *Meeting House Cafe* does ploughman's lunches for £3.50 and milk shakes for £1.30. There's a minimum £2 charge at weekends when it closes promptly at 5 pm.

The *Beachcomber Restaurant* (☎ *0181-853 1155*) does set two-course lunches for £5.90 and there are a few rather cramped outdoor tables.

ENTERTAINMENT

The essential tool is *Time Out*, which is published every Tuesday and covers a week of events. There's so much happening that there's a danger of being paralysed by indecision.

The biggest problem is transport. The last underground trains leave between 11.30 pm and 12.30 am, so you either have to figure out the night buses or pay for a minicab. The second biggest problem is that most pubs close at 11 pm. Fortunately, there are clubs where you can continue partying, although you'll have to pay to enter (£5 to £10), and the drinks are always expensive.

Late-night venues often choose to have a 'club' licence, which means you have to be a member to enter. In practice, they usually include the membership fee as part of the admission price. Many venues have clubs that only operate one night a week, and have a particular angle, whether it's the style of music they play or the kind of people they aim to attract.

Venues can change with bewildering speed – and they sometimes use the membership requirement to exclude people they don't think will fit in. In some places you'll be excluded if you wear jeans, runners and a T-shirt, in others you'll be excluded if you don't. It's not a bad idea to phone in advance to get an idea of cost and membership policy.

Pubs & Bars

Pubs are probably the most distinctive contribution the English have made to urban life and nothing really compares to a good one. Traditionally, the 'local' has been at the hub of the community and in some parts of London this tradition is still very much alive, with people treating pubs as virtual extensions of their homes. The 'regulars' become members of an extended gregarious family, although, curiously, relationships don't always extend beyond the door of the pub. Finding a local where you feel comfortable is the first step to being a real Londoner.

These days traditional pubs are thin on the ground. If you're after something authentic, steer clear of pubs with the words 'slug', 'lettuce', 'rat', 'carrot', 'firkin', 'newt', 'parrot' or any combination of the above in their name. It's not that there's necessarily anything wrong with them, just that they're the ones most likely to come with antipodean bar staff and noisy 'fruit' machines competing with a TV and a jukebox. Most will sell a good range of beers, and cheap and filling bar food; the more traditional the pub, the more limited the range of food is likely to be.

Bars are starting to outnumber pubs in some parts of London. You pay more for a drink (beer may not be on tap) and the fridges are full of imported designer drinks. However, the stylish décor, late opening hours and more upmarket atmosphere attract women and upwardly mobile 20 to 35 year olds. Some bars have a DJ at weekends and make a door charge. *Pitcher & Piano* and *All Bar One* are fast-growing chains. *Dôme* and *Café Rouge* are more like continental brasseries where you can just drink, have a snack or eat a decent meal.

If you're the sort of person who likes pubs but doesn't like the noise or the smoky atmosphere, it's worth knowing about the *Wetherspoon* chain, which has been trying to lure back drinkers who've drifted away by offering nonsmoking areas, decent food and even some pubs without jukeboxes. A clue is the word 'moon' in the name, as in *JJ Moon's, The Moon and Stars* and so on.

West End & Soho

Coach & Horses (29 Greek St W1, tube: Leicester Square), small, busy pub with regular clientele, but nonetheless hospitable to visitors.

Dog & Duck (18 Bateman St W1, tube: Tottenham Court Rd), tiny, but retains much of its old character and has loyal locals.

Riki Tik (23 Bateman St W1, tube: Leicester Square), famous for its flavoured vodka shots and half-price jugs of cocktails before 8 pm during the week.

The French House (49 Dean St W1, tube: Leicester Square), very popular bar serving only halves, which is strange, but with an enjoyable atmosphere.

The Flamingo Bar (Hanover St W1, tube: Oxford Circus), Latin American theme bar. Often has live sets. Good for pre-Hanover Grand drinks (see Clubs later in this chapter).

The '0' Bar (83-85 Wardour St W1, tube: Piccadilly Circus), two main drinking floors with a DJ downstairs at the weekend (£5 cover charge). Best during the week for half-price pitchers of cocktails before 8 pm.

All Bar One (Leicester Square, tube: Leicester Square), unmissable vast bar with good food, facing the square.

Cork & Bottle (44 Cranbourn St, tube: Leicester Square), long-lived basement bar with atmosphere and excellent food.

Covent Garden

Lamb & Flag (33 Rose St WC2, tube: Covent Garden), pleasantly unchanged pub tucked down a narrow alley between Garrick and Floral Sts; food available.

Walkabout Inn (11 Henrietta St, tube: Covent Garden), popular Australiana-theme bar with live music and cheap midweek drink specials; packed to the hilt from Thursday to Sunday.

The Polar Bear (30 Lisle St WC2, tube: Leicester Square), West End pub popular with Australasians.

Gordon's (47 Villiers St WC2, tube: Embankment), old wine bar in ancient vaults beneath the street, but spilling out into the Embankment Gardens in summer; good food.

Freud (198 Shaftesbury Ave, tube: Covent Garden), small, arty basement bar with pricey beers but great atmosphere.

Chelsea & Fulham

Po Na Na Souk Bar (316 King's Rd SW3, tube: Sloane Square), African-style fun bar where you drink in tented alcoves, seated on leopard skin sofas or chairs, playing backgammon. Even the cigarette machine has zebra stripes.

Come The Revolution (541 King's Rd SW6, tube: Fulham Broadway), Italianate interior with murals and wrought-iron tables and chairs; this bar is large but can get very crowded, though there's also a garden.

Bloomsbury & Holborn

Lamb (94 Conduit St WC1, tube: Russell Square), well-preserved Victorian interior of mirrors, old wood and 'snob screens'.

The Queen's Larder (1 Queen's Square WC1, tube: Russell Square), handy retreat on the corner of the square, with outside benches and pub grub.

Princess Louise (208 High Holborn WC1, tube: Holborn), delightful and eternally popular

example of Victorian pub décor with fine tiles, etched mirrors etc.

Truckle's (Pied Bull Yard WC1, tube: Tottenham Court Rd), lively pub with courtyard, handy for British Museum.

Notting Hill & Earl's Court

Beach Blanket Babylon (45 Ledbury Rd W11, tube: Notting Hill Gate), extraordinary Gaudiesque décor, and a great place for watching Notting Hill trendies; expensive food.

Market Bar (240A Portobello Rd W11, tube: Ladbroke Grove), interesting décor, interesting crowd and relaxed atmosphere.

Windsor Castle (114 Camden Hill Rd W11, tube: Notting Hill Gate), pleasant garden and good pub food: half a dozen oysters and a half-bottle of champagne for £15.

The Westbourne (101 Westbourne Park Villas W2, tube: Westbourne Park), trendy pub where the Notting Hill crowd congregates; large forecourt is great in summer; good-value bar food.

Prince of Teck (161 Earl's Court Rd SW5, tube: Earl's Court), infamous Australasian pub.

Blanco's (314 Earl's Court Rd SW5, tube: Earl's Court), lively, authentic Spanish tapas bar serving Spanish beer. Open until midnight.

Camden & Islington

Crown & Goose (100 Arlington Rd NW1, tube: Camden Town), new-style pub attracting a youngish crowd with good, no-nonsense food.

Lansdowne (90 Gloucester Ave NW1, tube: Chalk Farm), new-style pub with bohemian style. On Sunday there's a pricey set lunch but it's very popular, so book if you feel inclined to spoil yourself.

Cuba Libre (92 Upper St, tube: Angel), lively bar with good cocktails at rear of 'Cuban' restaurant.

The Engineer (65 Gloucester Ave NW1, tube: Chalk Farm), pretty Victorian pub which attracts the trendy north London set.

Hampstead

Flask (14 Flask Walk NW3, tube: Hampstead), friendly local, handy for the tube, with real ale and good food.

Holly Bush (22 Holly Mount NW3, tube: Hampstead), idyllic pub with a good selection of beers; ordinary food.

Spaniards Inn (Spaniards Rd NW3, tube: Hampstead), dating from 1585; in winter you can warm up around an open fire, in summer you can enjoy the garden.

Gay & Lesbian London

Gay London boasts a livelier, more eclectic scene than most other European cities – so much so that you could easily feel overwhelmed by the choice of places to visit.

The best starting points for research are the free listings magazines, *The Pink Paper* and *Boyz*, available from most gay clubs, bars and cafés. Magazines like *Gay Times* (£2) and the lesbian *Diva* (£2) also include listings. As ever, *Time Out* is a great source of info. There's also the Gay & Lesbian Hotline (☎ 0891-141120) to call for details on everything from bars to the Gay & Lesbian Film Festival. It's a premium-rated line, though, so check the price before dialling.

London's bars and clubs cater for every predilection, but there's a growing trend towards mixed gay/straight clubs. There are also some men or women-only nights; check the press for details.

In the 'gay village' of Soho, bars and cafés are thick on the ground. Walk down Old Compton St from Charing Cross Rd. On your right at No 34 is the friendly, sometimes frantic, 24 hour Old Compton St Café. Balaans at No 60 is a moderately priced, popular, continental-style café. Farther up the street are numerous gay-owned bars, shops and eateries. Farther into Soho you'll find the hyper-trendy Freedom Café (60 Wardour St) serving food and drink to a mixed clientele. At 57 Rupert St, The Yard has a pleasant courtyard for eating and drinking.

Near Tottenham Court Rd tube, the long-established, friendly First Out (52 St Giles High St) is a mixed lesbian-gay café serving vegetarian food and hosting periodic exhibitions.

Café de Paris (3 Coventry St, tube: Leicester Square) is an intimate club playing mainly house and garage. Just beyond Long Acre is Europe's largest gay bar, The Base (167 Drury Lane, tube: Covent Garden). There's also the Gardening Club (4 The Piazza, tube: Covent Garden), where the most popular nights are Club for Life (Saturday) and Queer Nation (Sunday).

The farther you move from the West End, the more local the clientele. The Black Cap (171 Camden High St, tube: Camden Town) is a late-night bar with a good drag reputation. Farther out on Hampstead Heath, a popular cruising area, the King William IV (75 Heath St, station: Hampstead Heath) is a friendly pub with sofas and log fires. In north London, the Central Station (37 Wharfedale Rd, tube: King's Cross) has a bar with special one-nighters, including a women-only night called the Clit Club.

Earl's Court also has a few places of interest including the excellent Wilde About Oscar restaurant (Philbeach Hotel, 31 Philbeach Gardens) and the long-lived Coleherne (261 Old Brompton Rd).

Love Muscle at The Fridge (1 Town Hall Parade, Brixton Hill, tube: Brixton) attracts a mixed crowd for dance music on Saturday nights. Heaven (Villiers St, tube: Embankment), in the West End, is London's most famous gay club with three dance floors. Every night has a different slant, so check the press for details.

Turnmills (55B Clerkenwell Rd EC1, tube: Farringdon), has three gay nights. From 10 pm to 3 am on Saturday it's Pumpin Curls, a women's club. From 3 am onwards it's Trade, which goes on until 12.30 pm on Sunday; breakfast is served at 6 am. On Sunday at the same venue ff pumps out techno and trance music until 8 am on Monday.

Before hitting the clubs it's worth combing the bars for advertising fliers offering reduced entry prices. Any saving is worthwhile, because clubbing can be expensive. Places tend to be packed at the weekends but you can party nonstop from Friday into Monday.

If the club scene's not for you, you can also make new friends at the myriad social, sport and dance groups and classes. *Time Out* and the gay press have details.

Hammersmith

Dove (19 Upper Mall W6, tube: Ravenscourt Park), small 17th century building close to the River Thames; good food and fine ales.

Bootsy Brogans (1 Fulham Broadway SW6, tube: Fulham Broadway), newly renovated Irish pub favoured by travellers.

Chiswick

The City Barge and *Bull's Head* (Strand on the Green, Chiswick W4, tube: Kew Gardens), great places to retreat to after visiting Kew Gardens.

Richmond

White Cross Hotel (Water Lane Riverside TW9, tube: Richmond), popular thanks to riverside location, good food and fine ales.

City

Eagle (159 Farringdon Rd EC1, tube: Farringdon), busy pub with delicious food and good range of beers.

Ye Olde Cheshire Cheese (Wine Office Court EC4, tube: Blackfriars), picturesque wood-panelled pub favoured by literary greats of the past.

Hamilton Hall (Bishopsgate, tube: Liverpool St), vast pub in converted ballroom; handy for drinks before catching the train.

The Cock Tavern (The Poultry Market, Smithfield Market EC1, tube: Farringdon), local for Smithfield meat market workers; open from 5.30 am for breakfast.

Southwark

George Inn (77 Borough High St SE1, tube: London Bridge), London's only surviving galleried coaching inn surrounding a courtyard; beautiful but busy after-work drinking hole.

Docklands

Mayflower (117 Rotherhithe St SE16, tube: Rotherhithe), surprising survival amid the Docklands developments.

Prospect of Whitby (57 Wapping Wall E1, tube: Wapping), one of London's oldest surviving drinking houses; on tourist trail, but good terrace overlooking the River Thames.

Greenwich

Trafalgar Tavern (tube: Greenwich), on the waterfront just past Royal Naval College with lovely water views; whitebait for £3.75 a portion.

Guess the Theme?

The 1990s saw a rash of theme restaurants open in central London, most of them serving international burger-style fare for reasonable – if not rock-bottom – prices, in interesting surroundings. Granddaddy of them all is the original *Hard Rock Café* (☎ 0171-629 0382, 150 Old Park Lane W1, tube: Hyde Park Corner), now over 25 years old but as popular as ever.

Arnie, Bruce and Sly's venture into the restaurant world has been an international success. Be prepared to queue at *Planet Hollywood* (☎ 0171-287 1000, 13 Coventry St W1, tube: Piccadilly Circus) for standard American fare at Beverly Hills prices. Nearby at 5-6 Coventry St, super-models Naomi Campbell, Claudia Schiffer, Christy Turlington and Elle MacPherson are doing their bit for the girls at the *Fashion Café* (☎ 0171-287 5888).

No prizes for guessing the theme at the 330 seat *Football Football* (☎ 0171-930 9970, 57-60 Haymarket, tube: Piccadilly Circus). Be prepared to fork out around £10 for a burger followed by ice cream and coffee, but the videos etc come free.

Fans of other sports should continue down the road to *The Sports Café* (☎ 0171-839 8300) at No 80, which boasts a dance floor, ski simulator, basketball court and acres of memorabilia. There's no escaping sport here: table-side TVs keep you occupied with favourite memories while you await burger and chips for around £8.

The Rainforest Café (☎ 0171-434 3111, 20 Shaftesbury Ave, tube: Piccadilly Circus) is an even more extraordinary Disney-meets-McDonald's venture, where waiters have been transformed into safari guides, you peer at the menu through dense foliage, and animatronic (ie moving) model animals keep you company while you dine.

Popular Music

London offers an enormous variety of music, whether it be megastars raking in the cash at Wembley, Earl's Court and similar hangar-sized venues, or hot new bands at the Astoria in Charing Cross Rd and Subterania in Notting Hill.

There's new and happening jazz at Ronnie Scott's and the Camden Jazz Café, or folk and country & western at Harlesden's Mean Fiddler.

Capital FM radio station has a useful ticket hotline (☎ 0171-420 0958). i-D is a lifestyle/fashion magazine with good coverage of the hot and the hip.

Major venues for live, contemporary music include:

Astoria (☎ 0171-434 0403, 157 Charing Cross Rd WC2, tube: Tottenham Court Rd), dark, sweaty and atmospheric, with good views of the stage. Cheap gay nights on Monday and Thursday.
Brixton Academy (☎ 0171-924 9999, 211 Stockwell Rd SW9, tube: Brixton), enormous venue with good atmosphere.
Hackney Empire (☎ 0181-985 2424, 291 Mare St E8, tube: Bethnal Green), superb Edwardian theatre; an excellent venue.
Shepherd's Bush Empire (☎ 0181-740 7474, Shepherd's Bush Green W12, tube: Shepherd's Bush), one of London's best venues.
The Forum (☎ 0171-344 0040, 9-17 Highgate Rd NW5, tube: Kentish Town), formerly the Town and Country Club, and still an excellent roomy venue.
The Grand (☎ 0171-738 9000, St John's Hill SW11, station: Clapham Junction), converted cinema with balcony.
Royal Albert Hall (☎ 0171-589 8212, Kensington Gore SW7, tube: South Kensington), huge historic auditorium which attracts big-name performers for one-off spectaculars.
Wembley Arena (☎ 0181-900 1234, Empire Way, Middlesex, tube: Wembley Park), huge venue with little to recommend it.

Smaller places with a more 'club-like' atmosphere that are worth checking for interesting bands include:

Barfly at the Falcon (☎ 0171-485 3834, 234 Royal College St NW1, tube: Camden Town), small club where Oasis played its first London gig, still giving a succession of small-time artists their big break.
Borderline (☎ 0171-734 2095, Orange Yard, off Manette St WC2, tube: Tottenham Court Rd), small relaxed venue, with a reputation for big-name bands playing under pseudonyms.
Rock Garden (☎ 0171-240 3961, The Piazza WC2, tube: Covent Garden), small basement venue, often packed with tourists, but also hosting good bands.
Subterania (☎ 0181-960 4590, 12 Acklam Rd W10, tube: Ladbroke Grove), atmospheric and showcasing up-and-comers.
Underworld (☎ 0171-482 1932, 174 Camden High St NW1, tube: Camden Town), beneath the World's End pub, a small venue hosting more up-and-coming bands.

Jazz Historically, London has always had a thriving jazz scene and, with its recent resurgence thanks to acid-jazz, hip-hop, funk and swing, it's stronger than ever:

Jazz Café (☎ 0171-344 0044, 5 Parkway NW1, tube: Camden Town), trendy restaurant/venue; best to book a table.
Pizza Express (☎ 0171-437 9595, 10 Dean St W1, tube: Leicester Square), small basement venue beneath the main restaurant.
Ronnie Scott's (☎ 0171-439 0747, 47 Frith St W1, tube: Leicester Square), operating since 1959; seedy and enjoyable but £15 admission fee for nonmembers.
100 Club (☎ 0171-636 0933, 100 Oxford St W1, tube: Oxford Circus), legendary London venue, once showcasing the Stones and at the centre of the punk revolution, now concentrating on jazz.

Blues & Folk Three places worth checking out are:

Biddy Mulligans (☎ 0171-624 2066, 205 Kilburn High Rd NW6, tube: Kilburn), traditional Irish pub with live music on weekends.
Bunjies (☎ 0171-240 1796, 27 Litchfield St WC2, tube: Leicester Square), legendary folk club with good-value restaurant.
Mean Fiddler (☎ 0171-961 5490, 24 High St, Harlesden NW10, tube: Willesden Junction), top-quality acoustic folk.

Clubs

It's not uncommon for a London club to be remembered more for the evening it hosts than for the venue. Clubs can change from night to night, depending on the DJ. If you want to know where the happening places are, comb through *Time Out* or *Mixmag*. Alternatively, some of the record shops around Soho have flyers and details of events. Many clubs host gay nights (see the boxed text 'Gay & Lesbian London' in this chapter).

Most clubs charge from £10 to £15 for entry, plus about £3 for each alcoholic drink. The most hip clubs don't kick off until midnight and usually stay open until 4 or 5 am. Dress codes are all-important. Some places are smart (no suits but no trainers either), others casual, but the more outrageous you look the better chance you have of getting in!

Bagleys (☎ 0171-278 4300, off York Way N1, tube: King's Cross), huge converted warehouse with five dance floors, four bars and an outside area for summer. The music varies from room to room; atmosphere can get heavy at weekends.

Bar Rumba (☎ 0171-287 2715, 36 Shaftesbury Ave W1, tube: Piccadilly Circus), varied nights including salsa and jungle. Small but very popular club; Thai food served all night.

Blue Note (☎ 0171-729 8440, 1 Hoxton Square N1, tube: Old St), relaxed club with live sets, funk, jazz and soul.

Browns (☎ 0171-831 0802, 4 Great Queen's St WC2, tube: Holborn), the stars' after-party hang-out. Slightly pretentious but a lively, fun club – if you can get in.

Café de Paris (☎ 0171-734 7700, 3 Coventry St W1, tube: Piccadilly), completely revamped as a dining bar. If you'd rather be a spectator, a galleried restaurant overlooks the dance floor.

Cloud 9 (☎ 0171-735 5590, 67 Albert Embankment SE1, tube: Vauxhall), brash, noisy club under railway arches, good for a Saturday night.

The Cross (☎ 0171-837 0828, Goods Way Depot, off York Way N1, tube: King's Cross), one of London's leading venues, hidden under the arches. Brilliant DJs and great ambience guarantee a good night.

Dingwalls (☎ 0171-267 0545, East Yard, Camden Lock NW1, tube: Camden Town), comedy acts at weekends, music during the week and club nights every night. Upstairs terrace bar gives aerial view of the lock and the market.

Emporium (☎ 0171-734 3190, 62 Kingly St W1, tube: Oxford Circus), very popular with the beautiful set, Emporium is one of the trendiest clubs in town.

The End (☎ 0171-379 4770, 16A West Central St WC1, tube: Holborn), modern industrial décor; free water fountain. For serious clubbers who like their music underground.

The Fridge (☎ 0171-326 5100, Town Hall Parade SW2, tube: Brixton), wide variety of club nights in excellent venue which is neither too big, nor too small. Saturday is gay night.

Gardening Club (☎ 0171-497 3154, 4 The Piazza WC2, tube: Covent Garden), cave-like club which tends to attract fun-loving out-of-towners.

Hanover Grand (☎ 0171-499 7977, 6 Hanover St W1, tube: Oxford Circus), two very different floors. You may have to queue but it's definitely worth it.

Heaven (☎ 0171-930 2020, Craven St WC2, tube: Embankment), long-lived, popular gay nightclub.

Hippodrome (☎ 0171-437 4311, Hippodrome Corner WC2, tube: Leicester Square), notorious for its glitzy dance floors and bright lights. Expensive and popular with tourists. Hardly cutting edge.

HQ's (☎ 0171-485 6044, West Yard, Camden Lock NW1, tube: Camden Town), soul and funk on Friday night, salsa on Saturday night and club nights during the week.

Iceni (☎ 0171-495 5333, 11 White Horse St, off Curzon St W1, tube: Green Park), three floors of contrasting music and friendly atmosphere make this one of the more accessible clubs.

Legends (☎ 0171-437 9933, 29 Old Burlington St W1, tube: Green Park), place for dressing up to suit the lavish décor.

Madame Jo Jo's (☎ 0171-734 2473, 8 Brewer St W1, tube: Piccadilly Circus), beautiful transvestite waiting staff in keeping with Soho's old image but there's nothing sleazy about this place.

Ministry of Sound (☎ 0171-378 6528, 103 Gaunt St SE1, tube: Elephant & Castle), internationally renowned, cavernous club attracting hard-core clubbers as well as people who just want to chill out. Open until 9 am.

Turnmills (☎ 0171-250 3409, 63 Clerkenwell Rd EC1, tube: Farringdon), wonderful sound system and varied club nights in hyper-trendy corner of London.

Velvet Underground (☎ 0171-439 4655, 143 Charing Cross Rd, WC2, tube: Tottenham Court Rd), intimate, friendly club swathed in red velvet.

Classical Music & Opera

London is Europe's classical music capital with five symphony orchestras, various smaller outfits, a brilliant array of venues, reasonable pricing and high standards of performance.

The biggest dilemma is likely to be how to pick from the riches on offer. On any night of the year the choice will range from traditional crowd-pleasers to new music and 'difficult' composers.

Venues include *Wigmore Hall* (☎ *0171-935 2141, 35 Wigmore St W1, tube: Bond St)*, which offers intimacy, variety and particularly good Sunday-morning recitals. The South Bank provides innovation and diversity in its three main auditoria, the *Royal Festival Hall, Queen Elizabeth Hall* and *Purcell Room*. Tickets cost from £5 to £50 (☎ *0171-960 4242*). The *Royal Albert Hall* (☎ *0171-589 8212, Kensington Gore SW7, tube: South Kensington)* is a splendid old concert hall that, from mid-July to mid-September, plays host to the Proms – one of the biggest and most democratic classical-music festivals in the world. Tickets cost from £5 to £32.

Opera tends to be more of a problem because it's costly to produce and so costly to attend. Fortunately the Covent Garden *Royal Opera House* (ROH) is likely to be closed through much of the life of this book, so you're unlikely to be tempted to take out a mortgage to see a performance. The *London Coliseum* (☎ *0171-632 8300, St Martin's Lane WC2, tube: Leicester Square)*, home of the English National Opera, is more reasonably priced, if rather variable in its quality and programming. From 10 am on the day of performance, balcony seats go on sale for £5. Expect a long queue.

On Hampstead Heath, *Kenwood House* (☎ *0171-413 1443)* holds evening musical recitals during the summer. People sit on the grass, eat strawberries, drink chilled white wine and listen to classical music – a highlight of summer in the city.

Theatre

Despite all the stories of gloom and doom, London theatre continues to thrive. Few cities in the world can offer comparable variety and quality or such reasonable prices.

The *National Theatre* (☎ *0171-928 2252)*, the nation's theatre flagship, has three auditoria in the South Bank complex (the Olivier, Lyttleton and Cottesloe) and uses them effectively to stage classics, contemporary plays and guest appearances by the best young companies from around the world. Good tickets for matinees start at £8 and there are cheaper student stand-by tickets.

The *Barbican* (☎ *0171-638 8891, Silk St EC2, tube: Barbican or Moorgate)* is the London home of the Royal Shakespeare Company; it's undoubted excellence can sometimes be disappointingly conservative. Midweek matinee tickets start at £6, and there are cheap student stand-by tickets.

The *Royal Court* (☎ *0171-730 1745)*, operating out of two other theatres until its own Sloane Square theatre has been rebuilt, tends to favour the anti-establishment and the new – various *enfants terribles* from John Osborne to Caryl Churchill got their first break here.

The *Globe Theatre* (☎ *0171-401 9919, tube: London Bridge)*, a replica of Shakespeare's 'wooden O', now dominates Bankside. Although there are wooden bench seats in tiers around the stage, you can emulate the 17th century 'groundlings' who stood in front of the stage, moving around as the mood took them. You should wrap up warmly and bring a flask, although no umbrellas are allowed. Performances are staged from May to September only. Tickets for seats cost from £10 to £20. The 500 standing spaces per performance cost £5 each and can be booked, although you may find a few unsold on the day.

There are also 50-odd West End theatres, which every summer stage a new crop of plays. If this isn't enough, at any time of the year, London's many off-West End and fringe-theatre productions offer a selection of the amazing, the life-changing, the boring and the downright ridiculous. The many theatre agencies will sell you tickets, especially for popular 'sold-out' performances like *Cats*. Most charge a hefty commission so it's always worth checking with the theatre first to see if you can get a ticket for the original price. Some have student stand-bys available anyway.

The Leicester Square Half-Price Ticket Booth, on the south side of Leicester Square, sells half-price tickets (plus £2 commission) for West End productions on the day of performance. It opens daily from noon to 6.30 pm. Beware of booths nearby, like the one opposite the Hippodrome on Cranbourn St, which advertise half-price tickets but fail to mention the hefty commission added to the original price.

Ballet & Dance

London is home to five major dance companies and a host of small experimental companies. Unfortunately, the *Royal Ballet* shares the Royal Opera House in Covent Garden, and so will be itinerating around temporary venues during the life of this book while its home is rebuilt.

Sadler's Wells (Rosebery Ave, tube: Angel) is a wonderfully refurbished venue for visiting ballet companies. More accessible is the *Peacock Theatre (☎ 0171-314 8800, Portugal St WC2, tube: Holborn)*, which hosts the London Contemporary Dance Theatre and London City Ballet.

The *Riverside Studios (☎ 0181-741 2255, Crisp Rd W6, tube: Hammersmith)* and the *ICA (☎ 0171-930 3647, The Mall SW1, tube: Charing Cross)* are important venues for small experimental companies.

Cinema

The 1990s have seen a boom in the development of vast multi-screen cinema complexes but this isn't altogether good news: the new places are expensive and thrive on mainstream American fare. Full-price tickets cost around £7.50, but afternoon shows are usually cheaper, and on Monday some places offer half-price tickets all day.

You can see an awful lot of movies in London. The last bastions of diversity and creative programming include Hampstead's *Everyman (☎ 0171-435 1525, Holly Bush Vale NW3, tube: Hampstead)*, and the more

modern *National Film Theatre (☎ 0171-928 3232, South Bank, tube: Embankment)*. Every November, it hosts the London Film Festival (☎ 0171-420 1122), a cornucopia of less regularly screened gems.

The *Notting Hill Coronet (☎ 0171-727 6705, Notting Hill Gate W11, tube: Notting Hill Gate)* is an attractive old theatre which still lets people smoke in the auditorium.

The *Prince Charles Cinema (☎ 0171-437 8181, Leicester Place WC2, tube: Leicester Square)* is London's cheapest cinema, with tickets for new-release films from only £1.35. It screens several different films each day so check the program carefully.

SPECTATOR SPORTS

All year round London plays host to a myriad of events. As always *Time Out* is the best source of information on fixtures, times, venues and ticket prices. Many pubs have large-screen TVs showing Sky coverage of major events.

Football

Wembley (☎ 0181-902 8833) is where the English national football team plays international matches and where the FA Cup final takes place in mid-May. A tour of Wembley stadium includes the opportunity to walk down the players' tunnel onto the pitch, as well as going up to receive the Cup to the (taped) roar of the crowd. Tours take place daily (☎ 0181-902 8833) between 10 am and 4 pm (3 pm in winter) and cost £6.95/4.75.

There are a dozen league teams in London. Big teams like Tottenham (☎ 0171-365 5000) and Arsenal (☎ 0171-704 4040) play in the top-flight Premier League, meaning that any weekend of the season (August to April) good-quality football is just a tube ride away. Hooliganism isn't much of a problem these days. Since the Hillsborough stadium tragedy in 1989 most have gone all-seating, and the mood at most matches has cooled accordingly. The only thing that holds people back now is the exorbitant prices (from £15 upwards), although you'll pay considerably less if you patronise the less well-known teams.

Cricket

Cricket continues to flourish, despite the dismal fortunes of the England team. Test matches take place at Lord's (☎ 0171-432 1066) and the Oval (☎ 0171-582 6660) cricket grounds. Sadly, tickets cost a fortune and tend to go fast. You're better off looking out for a county fixture: Middlesex plays at Lord's, Surrey at the Oval.

Daily tours (☎ 0171-432 1033) of Lord's take in the famous Long Room, at noon and 2 pm, as well as at 10 am on county match days (no tours when major matches are on). Tours cost £5.80/4.20.

Rugby Union

For rugby union fans, south-west London is the place to see a host of good-quality teams like Harlequins, Richmond and Wasps. Each year, starting in January, the Five Nations Rugby Union Championship pitches the four nations of the British Isles, and the French against each other, guaranteeing two big matches at Twickenham (☎ 0181-892 8161), the shrine of English union football.

The Museum of Rugby at Twickenham (☎ 0181-892 2000) sometimes includes a tour of the stadium. It's £4/2.50 for the museum and tour, £2.50/1.50 just for the museum. Advance booking is essential.

Rugby League

Rugby league fans would be advised to get on a train and head for the north of England, or settle for watching the London Broncos, southern England's only rugby league side. In May, the Challenge Cup final is held at Wembley.

Tennis

Tennis and Wimbledon (☎ 0181-946 2244) are synonymous, but queues, exorbitant prices, limited ticket availability and cramped conditions can turn a Wimbledon dream into a nightmare. Wimbledon has sold its soul (and most of its seating) to cor-porate entertainers; the rest of the world has to make do with the leftovers.

If you haven't got a show court ticket and you don't want to camp out all night, go along in the late afternoon and take your chances on buying a returned ticket for £5. Otherwise you might try the tournament at Queen's (☎ 0171-385 3421) before Wimbledon that attracts many of the top male players.

Athletics

Athletics meetings take place regularly throughout the summer at Crystal Palace (☎ 0181-778 0131), attracting major inter-national and domestic stars. Tickets are from £10.

Racing

If you're looking for a cheap and thrilling night out, consider going to 'The Dogs'. Greyhounds run at Walthamstow, Wimble-don, Wembley and Catford and entry is as little as £3 for a 12 race meeting. A few small bets guarantee excitement, and you'll rub shoulders with a gregarious, and more than slightly shady London subculture.

Alternatively, there's horse racing with plenty of top-quality courses a train ride south of the city. Ascot in June can be nice, if rather posh; Epsom on Derby Day can be a crush-ing experience in more ways than one.

SHOPPING

Napoleon famously described the British as a nation of shopkeepers. These days it would be equally true to describe them as a nation of shoppers. Either way, London is the UK's shopping mecca; if you can't find it here you probably can't find it at all.

Some London shops are more or less tourist attractions in their own right. Few visitors come away without popping into Harrods, even if only to gawp. Since *Absolutely Fabulous* brought Edina and Patsy steaming onto our screens, Harvey Nichols ('Harvey Nicks') has become another must-see attraction.

Carnaby Street still reeks of the 60s al-though it's had something of a revival since the 'Cool Britannia' kick brought Union Jack dresses back into fashion. The last punks have long since slunk away from Chelsea's King's Rd but there are still plenty of interesting shops slotted in amid the high-street chains.

The shops and stalls inside the old Covent Garden market building tend to be pricey and tourist-oriented, while the streets running off it remain a happy hunting ground for shoppers, with Neal St and Neal's Yard in particular offering a range of interesting one-off shops.

Oxford St and classier Regent St come into their own in the six weeks running up to Christmas when they're festooned with lights. At other times of the year Oxford St can be a great disappointment. Selfridge's is up there with Harrods as a place to visit and the flagship Marks & Spencers at the Marble Arch end has its fans, but the farther east you go the tackier and less interesting it becomes.

Although most things can be bought in most parts of town, there are also streets with their own specialities; Tottenham Court Rd, for example, is one long electrical goods shop (watch out for rip-offs though), while Charing Cross Rd is still the place to come for offbeat books.

Many tourist attractions have excellent shops selling good-quality souvenirs like mugs, pens, pencils, stationery and T-shirts, often with themes to match their content (war books and videos at the Imperial War Museum). By buying from these shops you help contribute towards the building's maintenance, especially important in the cases of those without entry charges.

Department Stores

Harrods This famous store (☎ 0171-730 1234, Brompton Rd SW1, tube: Knightsbridge) is a real one-off. The toilets are fab, the food hall enough to make you swoon, and if they haven't got what you want, it probably doesn't exist. No other store has such a sense of sheer, outrageous abundance. Don't miss it, although you may be wise to leave your credit cards somewhere safe. It's open Monday, Tuesday and Satur-

day from 10 am to 6 pm, Wednesday to Friday to 7 pm. Backpacks are not allowed.

Harvey Nichols Harvey Nichols (☎ 0171-235 5000, 109-125 Knightsbridge SW1, tube: Knightsbridge) boasts a great food hall, an extravagant perfume department and jewellery to save up for. But with all the big names from Miyake to Lauren, Hamnett to Calvin Klein and a whole floor of up-to-the-minute menswear, it's fashion that Harvey Nichols does better than the rest. The selection is unrivalled and the prices high, although the sales offer some great bargains, and the store's own clothing line is reasonable. It's open Monday, Tuesday, Thursday and Friday from 10 am to 7 pm, Wednesday to 8 pm, and Sunday from 2 to 5 pm.

Fortnum & Mason Fortnum & Mason (☎ 0171-734 8040, 181 Piccadilly W1, tube: Piccadilly Circus) is noted for its exotic, old-world food hall where all kinds of strange foodstuffs can be purchased, along with the famous food hampers that cost an arm and a leg. This is where Scott of the Antarctic stocked up before heading off to the wilderness. These days you'd be better advised to buy your travel provisions elsewhere and settle for a small, gift-wrapped box of chocolates for a show-off present. It's open Monday to Saturday from 9.30 am to 6 pm.

Liberty Almost as amazing as Harrods, Liberty (☎ 0171-734 1234, Regent St W1, tube: Oxford Circus) stocks high fashion, great modern furniture, wonderful luxurious fabrics and those inimitable silk scarves. It was born out of the influential Arts and Crafts movement – in Italy Art Nouveau was called Liberty Style after the store. It's open Monday to Wednesday, Friday and Saturday from 10 am to 6.30 pm, and Thursday to 7.30 pm.

Markets

One of the great pleasures of a sunny Sunday morning is to visit one of London's many markets and then have lunch in a nearby restaurant. The markets are widely spread out around the capital and each has its own individual character. Many also take place on Friday and Saturday.

Berwick St Market Tucked away between Oxford and Old Compton Sts, Berwick St Market (tube: Oxford Circus) is a fruit and vegetable market which has somehow managed to hang onto its prime location, even though the stallholders' sales patter has to compete with a babble of sounds from the surrounding record shops. This is a great place to put together a picnic to eat in one of the parks.

Portobello Rd Market Camden Market aside, Portobello Rd (tube: Notting Hill Gate, Ladbroke Grove or Westbourne Park) is London's most famous (and crowded) weekend street market. Starting near the Sun in Splendour pub in Notting Hill, it wends its way northwards to the Westway flyover in Ladbroke Grove.

As you head north along Portobello Rd what you'll find on sale slowly changes, with the antiques, handmade jewellery, paintings and ethnic stuff concentrated at the Notting Hill Gate end. Later the stalls dip downmarket and you'll find more fruit and veg, second-hand clothing, cheap household goods and bric-a-brac. Beneath the Westway a vast tent covers yet more stalls selling cheap clothes, shoes and CDs, while the Portobello Green Arcade is home to some cutting-edge clothes designers. On Friday and Saturday bric-a-brac goes on sale here too.

Portobello certainly has character and colour but it's too well known for there to be much chance of a bargain other than on cheap T-shirts. Nonetheless it's a fun place to while away a few hours, especially if you get there early before people-gridlock sets in.

Since most people walk up Portobello Rd from Notting Hill Gate, the Ladbroke Grove and Westbourne Park tube stations are likely to be much less congested.

Petticoat Lane Market Petticoat Lane (tube: Aldgate, Aldgate East or Liverpool

St) is east London's celebrated Sunday morning market on Middlesex St, which borders the City and Whitechapel. These days, it's all pretty run-of-the-mill with faintly bemused tourists struggling to get past locals sifting through the stalls of cheap T-shirts and underwear. By 2 pm it's all over.

Brick Lane Market A few streets east of Petticoat Lane, Brick Lane Market (tube: Aldgate East) is more fun although it, too, is probably past its prime. Activity kicks off at around 5 am on Sunday and spreads out along Bethnal Green Rd to the north, and the many side streets. Once again, by 2 pm it's all over. A mix of stalls sell clothes, fruit and veg, household goods and paintings, but you'll also see people picking through piles of dirt-cheap shoes, and for whom finding a bargain is more a necessity than a bit of fun.

The big plus of heading out here is that you can round off a visit with lunch in one of the many curry houses or with a bagel in one of the bakeries (see East End under Places to Eat earlier in this chapter).

Spitalfields Market More interesting than Brick Lane itself is Spitalfields undercover market off Commercial St (tube: Liverpool St). Not only is this market weatherproof but there's a great mix of arts and crafts, organic fruit and veg, stylish and retro clothes, and second-hand books, with genuinely interesting ethnic shops ringing the central area and a football pitch and children's model railway (50p) to keep nonshoppers entertained.

It's open on Sunday from 8 am to 5 pm. Unfortunately developers have their beady eyes on this piece of prime London territory; the market's future was uncertain at the time of writing.

Columbia Rd Market Although visitors may have little need of geraniums or pelargoniums, a stroll up to Columbia Rd Flower Market (tube: Old St) is an excellent way to round off the Sunday morning market experience. To get there walk north along Brick Lane and then along Virginia Rd. Turn right when you emerge on Columbia Rd and the market is about 100m along the road past a tower block. The action takes place between 8 am and 2 pm and, as well as the flower stalls, a couple of basic cafés and several arty shops throw open their doors.

Camden Market These days Camden Market stretches most of the way from Camden Town tube station north to Chalk Farm tube station. To see it at its most lively, time your visit for a weekend, although most days there'll be some stalls up and running.

First off as you head north from Camden Town station is the Electric Market in an old ballroom. A busy student club on Friday and Saturday nights, it's transformed into a market on Sunday. Sometimes there are record sales, but 60s clothes usually dominate. Opposite is a covered area with stalls selling a mishmash of leather goods, army-surplus stuff and a café. Next up is Camden Market (open from Thursday to Sunday), which houses stalls for fashion, clothing and jewellery.

Continue north, past the bootleg music sellers and hair plaiters, and over the bridge. On the right is the Camden Canal Market, with bric-a-brac from around the world. On the left, and beyond the comparatively new indoor market, is the small section where the market originated. This area, right next to the canal lock, houses a diverse range of food, ceramics, furniture, oriental rugs, musical instruments, designer clothes and so on.

From here you can walk along the Railway Arches, inspecting second-hand furniture as you go. A slow meander eventually leads to The Stables, the northernmost part of the market, where it's possible to snap up antiques, eastern artefacts, rugs and carpets, pine furniture, and 50s and 60s clothing. If you want to get straight to The Stables there's an entrance on Chalk Farm Rd.

Greenwich Market Every Friday, Saturday and Sunday, from 9.30 am to 5.30 pm,

Greenwich (station: Greenwich) hosts an undercover arts and crafts market, squeezed in between King William Walk and Greenwich Church St. It's not necessarily the place to come to find a bargain, but if you need to buy a present, this is an excellent place to look for decorated glass, rugs, prints etc.

Covent Garden While the shops in Covent Garden Piazza (tube: Covent Garden) are open every day, several markets also take place in the Jubilee Hall: Monday is for antiques and a flea market which kicks off at 5 am; and from Tuesday to Friday a general market offers clothes, records, books, sweets, you name it. On weekends a craft market migrates into the piazza itself – nice things but you won't be able to afford many of them.

Brixton Market Brixton Market (tube: Brixton) is a cosmopolitan mix of everything from The Body Shop and reggae music to slick Muslim preachers, halal meat, and fruit and exotic veg. In Electric Ave and the covered Granville Arcade you can buy wigs, unusual foods like tilapia fish and Ghanian eggs (really vegetables), weird spices and homeopathic root cures, rare records and dreadful end-of-the-line furnishings.

It's open Monday to Saturday from 8.30 am to 5.30 pm, closing at 1 pm on Wednesday. To find it, exit Brixton station and turn left, and then take the first left again for Electric Ave.

Camden Passage At the junction of Upper St and Essex Rd, near Islington Green (tube: Angel), you'll find this Aladdin's cave of antique shops and stalls, selling pretty well anything to which the label 'antique' could reasonably be attached. The stallholders know their stuff, so real bargains are few and far between, but it's still a fun place to browse. Wednesday is the busiest day when the action kicks off at 7 am and is all over by 2 pm. On Saturday it's worth coming along until 4 pm. Thursday sees a second-hand book market in full swing from 7 am to 4 pm.

Bermondsey Market This market in Bermondsey Square (tube: Borough) is the place to come if you're after old opera glasses, bowling balls, costume jewellery or anything else that could loosely be described as an antique. The main market takes place outdoors in Bermondsey Square although adjacent warehouses shelter the more vulnerable furnishings. For a bargain you need to be up with the larks; the market kicks off at around 4.30 am on Friday; by lunch time it's more or less over.

Clothes Shops

Behind Oxford Circus tube station, Carnaby St is experiencing something of a revival on the back of the Cool Britannia mood. If you still think it too tacky, near Carnaby St is more salubrious west Soho, with plenty of groovy outlets for hip designers like Pam Hogg and the Duffer of St George.

It's easy to believe that only the most trendy fashion victims will be made welcome at London's indoor fashion markets. However, designers at Hyper-Hyper (☎ 0171-938 4343, 26-40 Kensington High St W8, tube: High St Kensington) and the Garage (☎ 0171-352 8653, 181 King's Rd SW3, tube: Sloane Square) are mostly struggling types, more than a little keen to offload their imaginative glad rags.

Three storey Kensington Market (☎ 0171-938 4343, 49-53 Kensington High St W8, tube: High St Kensington) is something of a dinosaur, and a hot, sticky shambles in summer, but it's a lot of fun. It's more leather and patchouli oil than high fashion – the place to come for second-hand Levis, chain-mail bikinis and handmade jewellery.

For more traditional apparel head for Burberry (☎ 0171-930 3343, 18-22 Haymarket SW1, tube: Piccadilly Circus) or Aquascutum (☎ 0171-734 6090, 100 Regent St W1, tube: Piccadilly Circus), both famed for its macs.

GETTING THERE & AWAY

London is the major gateway to Britain, so transport information is in the Getting There & Away and Getting Around chapters. Look up your proposed British destination for prices and possibilities to/from London; in particular see the tables in the Getting Around chapter.

Airports

Heathrow Heathrow is one of the world's largest and busiest airports. It now has four terminals, with a fifth on the drawing board.

Although the place appears chaotic and it's hard to find anywhere pleasant for a farewell drink, it's actually well organised. Duty-free facilities are not impressive (they're particularly weak on photographic and electronic equipment) but each terminal has good information counters, excellent, competitive currency-exchange facilities, and accommodation booking desks.

The large 'international' hotels nearby are served by the Heathrow Hoppa buses; you may need to consider them if you're leaving or arriving at a peculiar time, but none are cheap or particularly noteworthy. Even if the tube and main-line trains aren't running, those on a budget will do better to take a minicab into central London for cheaper accommodation. Earl's Court is a good bet because it's on the right side of town.

Baggage Hold has left-luggage facilities in Terminal 1 (☎ 0181-745 5301) and Terminal 4 (☎ 0181-745 7460) from 6 am to 11 pm. The charge is £2.50 per item up to 12 hours and £3 per item up to 24 hours. Excess Baggage (☎ 0181-759 3344) offers a similar service in terminals 2 and 3. Both companies also have a baggage forwarding service.

For general inquiries and flight information (except British Airways) phone ☎ 0181-759 4321. For British Airways ring ☎ 0181-759 2525. Other useful numbers are:

Car Park Information ☎ 0800-844844
London Underground ☎ 0171-222 1234
Hotel Reservation Service ☎ 0181-759 2719

Note that theft can be a problem at Heathrow.

Getting There & Away The airport is accessible by bus, underground (between 5 am and 11 pm) and main-line train.

The new Heathrow Express rail link whisks passengers from Paddington station to Heathrow in just 20 minutes. Tickets cost a hefty £10 each way. Trains leave every 15 minutes from 5.10 am to 11.40 pm.

The underground station for Terminals 1, 2 and 3 is directly linked to the terminus buildings; there's a separate station for Terminal 4. Check which terminal your flight uses when you reconfirm. The adult single fare is £3.30, or you can use an All Zone Travelcard which is £4.30. The journey time from central London is about 50 minutes – allow an hour.

The Airbus (☎ 0171-897 2688) services are also useful. There are two routes: the A1, which runs along Cromwell Rd to Victoria; and the A2, which runs along Notting Hill Gate and Bayswater Rd to Russell Square. Buses run every half-hour and cost £6. A metered black cab to or from central London will cost around £42.

Gatwick Although large, Gatwick is a much smaller airport than Heathrow and in many ways easier and more pleasant to use. Its only drawback is the relative expense of the rail link to Victoria.

The north and south terminals are linked by an efficient monorail service; check which terminal you will use when you reconfirm your ticket. There are all the predictable stores, and several eating and drinking areas.

Accommodation options close to the airport are expensive and unremarkable. If you need more information phone Thomas Cook (☎ 01293-529372), which can deal with hotel reservations.

Excess Baggage (☎ 01293-5699900), in both the North and South terminals, has left-baggage facilities available daily from 6 am to 10 pm. The charge is £2.50 per item up to 12 hours and £3 per item up to 24 hours. It also has a baggage forwarding service.

Getting There & Away The Gatwick Express runs nonstop between the main terminal and Victoria station from 4.30 am to 11 pm. Singles are £9.50 and the journey takes 30 minutes. The Connex SouthCentral service takes a little longer but costs a little less. British Airways customers can check in advance at Victoria station.

A metered black cab to central London would cost around £80.

London City Airport A shuttle bus connects this pleasant small airport with Liverpool St station (£4 single) and Canary Wharf (£2 single) between 6 am and 9 pm. Services are every 15 minutes from Monday to Friday, every 30 minutes on Saturday and every 20 minutes on Sunday, and the journey takes 25 minutes from Liverpool St and eight minutes from Canary Wharf. There are flights from LCA (☎ 0171-474 5555) to some 20 European destinations, including Paris, Dublin and Edinburgh.

Stansted A direct train (£10.40) takes 40 minutes to run from Liverpool St to Norman Foster's impressive new terminal. Trains run every half-hour and you can change at Tottenham Hale for the West End and other Victoria line stations, including Victoria. There's one phone number (☎ 01279-680500) for all general inquiries, hotel reservations and rail information.

Luton Luton is mainly used for charter flights although easyJet (☎ 08706-000000) also operates cheap flights out of this airport. Catch the airport-to-station Luton Flyer bus outside the arrivals hall for a 15 minute trip to the train station, then take the train for King's Cross or St Pancras (another 45 minutes); the all-in price is £9.90. There are regular services approximately every 20 minutes, starting early and finishing late.

Bus

Bus travellers arrive and depart from Victoria coach station, Buckingham Palace Rd, about 10 minutes walk south of the Victoria train and tube station. There's also a connecting bus if you've got lots of luggage.

Train

There are 10 main-line rail terminals in London, and all are connected by tube. For those with combined rail/ferry tickets, if your train goes via south-east England (to/from France, Belgium, Spain or Italy), Victoria is the station; to/from Harwich or Felixstowe (for Germany, the Netherlands and Scandinavia), it's Liverpool St; and to/from Newcastle (for Scandinavia), it's King's Cross. There's a superb international terminal at Waterloo from which all Channel Tunnel services depart.

All the main stations have information centres. One inquiry number covers all rail destinations in Britain: ☎ 0345-484950.

GETTING AROUND
Bus & Underground

London Regional Transport is responsible for the buses and the tube. It has several information centres where you can get free maps, tickets and information on night buses. Among others, there are centres in each Heathrow terminal, and at Victoria, Piccadilly and King's Cross stations; or phone ☎ 0171-222 1234. See Underground map on page 176.

Buses are more interesting and pleasant to use than the tube, although they can be frustratingly slow. There are four types of tickets: one-journey bus tickets sold on the bus (minimum 60p), daily and weekly bus passes, single or return tube tickets (sold at stations, sometimes from vending machines, minimum £3.10), and Travelcards.

Travelcards are the easiest and cheapest option, and they can be used on all forms of transport (Network SouthEast trains in London, buses and tubes) after 9.30 am. London is divided into concentric rings, or zones, and the Travelcard you need will depend on how many zones you cross. Most visitors will find that a Zone 1 & 2 card will be sufficient (£3.50). Weekly Travelcards are also available; they require an ID card with a passport photo (Zone 1 & 2 costs £16.60). If you plan to start moving before 9.30 am you can buy a Zone 1 & 2 LT (London Transport) Card for £4.50.

Times of the last tube trains vary from 11.30 pm to 12.30 am, depending on the station and line. A reasonably comprehensive network of night buses runs from or through Trafalgar Square. London Regional Transport's free *Buses for Night Owls* lists all the services. One-day Travelcards can't be used on night buses, but weekly Travelcards can.

When riding escalators at tube stations, always stand to the right – especially during rush hour. This allows those in a hurry to pass on your left.

Train

Several rail companies now run passenger trains in London; most lines interchange with the tube. Travelcards can be used.

Taxi

London's famous black cabs (☎ 0171-272 0272) are excellent, but not cheap. A cab is available for hire when the yellow sign is lit. Fares are metered and a 10% tip is expected. They can carry five people.

Minicabs are cheap, freelance competitors to the black cabs; anyone with a car can work, but they can only be hired by phone. Some have a very limited idea of how to get around efficiently and safely. They don't have meters, so it's essential to get a quote before you start. They can carry four people. Women are advised to use black cabs.

Small minicab companies are based in particular areas – ask a local for the name of a reputable company or phone one of the large 24-hour operations (☎ 0171-272 2612, ☎ 0181-340 2450 or ☎ 0181-567 1111). Women could phone Lady Cabs (☎ 0171-272 3019). Gays and lesbians can choose Freedom Cars (☎ 0171-734 1313).

Car & Motorcycle

You're strongly advised not to drive in London – you really don't need the aggro – but if you're blessed/cursed with private transport, avoid peak hours (7.30 to 9.30 am, 4.30 to 7 pm), and plan ahead if you need to park in the centre. Cars parked illegally will end up with a clamp locked on a wheel. To get the clamp removed you have to travel across town, pay an enormous fine, then wait most of the day for someone to come and release you. Phone National Car Parks (☎ 0171-499 7050) for car park addresses; rates vary.

Bicycle

Cycling around London is one way of cutting transport costs, but it can be a grim business, with heavy traffic and fumes detracting from any possible pleasure. The London Cycling Campaign (☎ 0171-928 7220) is working to improve conditions, not least by campaigning to establish the London Cycle Network which is up and running in some parts of the capital; by 2000 there should be 1200 miles of bike route throughout the capital. It produces a pack including a map showing established cycle routes and advisory cycle routes, as well as green routes where cycling is actually fun (£4.95).

At Bikepark 14 (☎ 0171-430 0083, 1/2 Stukeley St WC2) the minimum rental charge is £4 for four hours, £10 for the first day, £5 the second day and £3 for subsequent days.

Boat

There are all sorts of services on the River Thames. See the Greenwich, Kew Gardens and Hampton Court Palace sections earlier in this chapter for two popular trips. The main starting points are Westminster Bridge and Charing Cross. For information on downriver trips (towards Greenwich) phone ☎ 0171-930 1616; for information on upriver trips (towards Kew) phone ☎ 0171-930 4721.

South-Eastern England

While many of the towns and villages of Berkshire, Surrey, Kent, East and West Sussex and Hampshire are virtual dormitories for London workers, this is still a region exceptionally rich in beauty and history. The south-east has always been Britain's front line – it's a mere 22 miles from the French coast – and names like Hastings, Dover and Portsmouth inevitably evoke images of invasion and war.

From a visitor's point of view, this region's proximity to London is both its strength and its weakness. On one hand, parts are very beautiful, very English and very convenient. There are few areas more densely packed with sights. On the other hand, crowds of tourists can be difficult to evade.

Whatever images you have of England, you can find them in this region: picturesque villages and towns with welcoming old pubs (Chilham, Sandwich, Rye, Lewes and Winchester, among many others), spectacular coastline (the famous white cliffs of Dover and Beachy Head), impressive castles (Dover, Hever, Leeds, Bodiam and Ightham Mote), great houses (Chartwell, Knole, Penshurst and Petworth), gardens (Sissinghurst), great cathedrals (Canterbury and Winchester) and, finally, the kitsch and vibrant seaside resort of Brighton.

ORIENTATION & INFORMATION

The main roads and railway lines radiate from London like spokes in a wheel, linking the south-coast ports and resorts with the capital. Chalk country runs through the region along two hilly east-west ridges, or downs.

The North Downs curve from Guildford towards Rochester, then to Dover where they become the famous white cliffs. The South Downs run from north of Portsmouth to end spectacularly at Beachy Head near Eastbourne. Lying between the two is the Weald, once an enormous stretch of forest, now orchards and market gardens.

HIGHLIGHTS

- Royal Pavilion and the pier, Brighton
- Ye Olde Englishe Towne of Rye
- Ightham Mote
- HMS *Victory* & the Historic Ships, Portsmouth
- Sissinghurst Castle Garden
- Winchester Cathedral

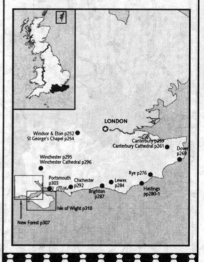

PLACES TO STAY

There are youth hostels in the main towns and several on the Isle of Wight. Some local Tourist Information Centres charge a B&B reservation fee of up to £4 if they book for you; others do so free of charge.

GETTING AROUND
Bus

Fast, regular buses follow the spokes out from London, but it is very difficult to

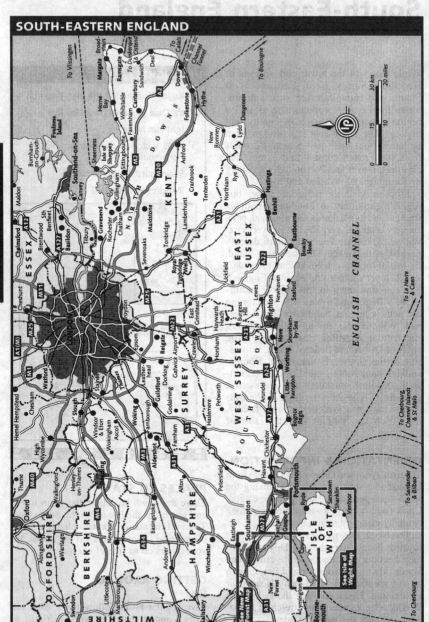

SOUTH-EASTERN ENGLAND

travel east-west by bus without resorting to the slow, local buses. For information on all public transport options in Kent, ring ☎ 0345-696996; for West Sussex, ring ☎ 01243-777556; for East Sussex, ring ☎ 01273-474747; and for Hampshire, ring ☎ 01962-868944.

Most services in Kent, Sussex and Hampshire accept Explorer tickets, which give unlimited travel and cost £5.40/3.20 for adults/children. These can be bought from the bus drivers or from bus stations, and are nearly always the best value option if you are travelling extensively.

Train

It is possible to do an interesting rail loop from London via Canterbury East, Dover, Ashford, Rye, Hastings, Battle (via Hastings), Brighton, Littlehampton, Arundel, Portsmouth, Southampton and Winchester. If you are considering this kind of extensive rail travel, a Network SouthEast Card (£20, allowing 33% off) is essential. For rail information call ☎ 0345-484950.

Berkshire

Pretty Windsor has long been Berkshire's greatest tourist draw, but these days people make the trek out from London as much to visit Legoland as to see the famous castle and nearby Eton.

WINDSOR & ETON
• pop 31,000   ☎ 01753
Windsor Castle is one of Britain's premier tourist attractions and since it's only 20 miles from central London, and easily accessible by rail and road, it crawls with tourists. If possible, avoid weekends, especially in summer.

Orientation & Information

Windsor Castle overlooks the town of Windsor spreading out to the west and the River Thames. Eton is essentially a small village, linked to Windsor by a pedestrian bridge over the Thames.

The TIC (☎ 743900), 24 High St, is open daily from 9.30 am to 5 pm, closing at 6.30 pm in July and August. The Town & Gown Exhibition upstairs whips through local history but barely justifies the £1/50p admission fee. Both the post office in Peascod St and the TIC have *bureaux de change*.

Windsor Castle

Standing on chalk bluffs overlooking the Thames, Windsor Castle (☎ 831118) has been home to British royalty for over 900 years and is one of the greatest surviving medieval castles. It started life as a wooden motte and bailey in 1070 but was rebuilt in stone in 1165 and then successively extended and rebuilt right through to the 19th century.

Castle areas to which the public are admitted are generally open March through October from 10 am to 5 pm (last entry 4 pm), closing an hour earlier the rest of the year. In summer, weather and other events permitting, the changing of the guard takes place at 11 am (not on Sunday). The State Apartments are closed when the royal family is in residence, the most regular occasion being during the annual Ascot horse racing meeting in June. The Union Jack flying over the castle doesn't mean the Queen's at home; instead watch out for the Royal Standard flying from the Round Tower.

Entry to the castle is £9.80/5.60, except on Sunday when entry is £7.70/4.60 because St George's Chapel and the Albert Memorial Chapel are closed.

St George's Chapel One of Britain's finest examples of Gothic architecture, the chapel was commenced by Edward IV in 1475 but not completed until 1528.

The nave is a superb example of perpendicular architecture with beautiful fan vaulting arching out from the pillars. The chapel is packed with the **tombs of royalty** including George V (ruled 1910-36) and Queen Mary, George VI (1936-52), and Edward IV (1461-83). The **wooden oriel window** was built for Catherine of Aragon by Henry VIII. The **garter stalls** dating back to 1478-85 are the chapel's equivalent of

WINDSOR & ETON

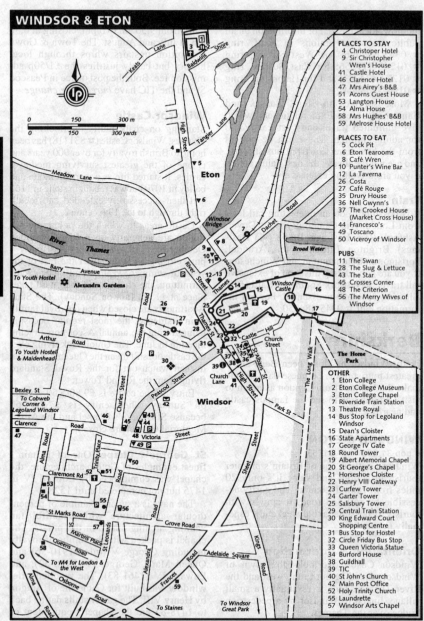

PLACES TO STAY
4 Christoper Hotel
9 Sir Christopher Wren's House
41 Castle Hotel
46 Clarence Hotel
47 Mrs Airey's B&B
51 Acorns Guest House
53 Langton House
54 Alma House
58 Mrs Hughes' B&B
59 Melrose House Hotel

PLACES TO EAT
5 Cock Pit
6 Eton Tearooms
8 Café Wren
10 Punter's Wine Bar
12 La Taverna
26 Costa
27 Café Rouge
35 Drury House
36 Nell Gwynn's
37 The Crooked House (Market Cross House)
44 Francesco's
49 Toscano
50 Viceroy of Windsor

PUBS
11 The Swan
28 The Slug & Lettuce
43 The Star
45 Crosses Corner
48 The Criterion
56 The Merry Wives of Windsor

OTHER
1 Eton College
2 Eton College Museum
3 Eton College Chapel
7 Riverside Train Station
13 Theatre Royal
14 Bus Stop for Legoland Windsor
15 Dean's Cloister
16 State Apartments
17 George IV Gate
18 Round Tower
19 Albert Memorial Chapel
20 St George's Chapel
21 Horseshoe Cloister
22 Henry VIII Gateway
23 Curfew Tower
24 Garter Tower
25 Salisbury Tower
29 Central Train Station
30 King Edward Court Shopping Centre
31 Bus Stop for Hostel
32 Circle Friday Bus Stop
33 Queen Victoria Statue
34 Burford House
38 Guildhall
39 TIC
40 St John's Church
42 Main Post Office
52 Holy Trinity Church
55 Laundrette
57 Windsor Arts Chapel

SOUTH-EASTERN ENGLAND

choir stalls. The banner, helm and crest above each stall indicate the current occupant. Plates carry the names of knights who occupied the stalls right back to the 14th century.

In between the garter stalls, the **Royal Vault** is the burial place of George III (1760-1820), George IV (1820-30) and William IV (1830-37). Another **vault** between the stalls contains Henry VIII (1509-47), his favourite wife Jane Seymour, and Charles I (1625-49), reunited with his head which was chopped off after the Civil War. Whenever the Knights of the Garter meet here they're joined by the Queen and the Prince of Wales. The gigantic **battle sword** of Edward III, founder of the Order of the Garter, hangs on the wall near the **tombs** of Henry VI (1422-61 and 1470) and Edward VII (1901-10) and Queen Alexandra.

Albert Memorial Chapel After leaving St George's Chapel, don't miss the fantastically elaborate Albert Memorial Chapel next door. It was built in 1240 and became the original chapel of the Order of the Garter in 1350, falling into disuse when St George's Chapel was built. It was completely restored after the death of Prince Albert in 1861. There's a monument to the prince, although he's actually buried with Queen Victoria in the Frogmore Royal Mausoleum in the castle grounds.

State Apartments The State Apartments are a combination of formal rooms and museum-style exhibits. In 1992 a disastrous fire destroyed St George's Hall and the adjacent Grand Reception Room. Restoration work has now been completed and a rather cramped **exhibition** describes the decision-making process behind the reconstruction and how the work was carried out.

Like other parts of the castle, the State Apartments have gone through successive reconstructions and expansions, most notably under Charles II (ruled 1660-85) who added lavishly painted ceilings by Antonio Verrio and delicate wood carvings by Grinling Gibbons. Further extensive modifications were made under George IV and William IV in the 1820s and 30s.

Access to the State Apartments is via the North Terrace, which offers a splendid view out towards Eton. The Grand Staircase and Grand Vestibule, decorated with suits of armour and weaponry, lead to the Ante Throne Room and to the Waterloo Chamber, created to commemorate the Battle of Waterloo and still used for formal banquets. The walls display Sir Thomas Lawrence's portraits of the men who defeated Napoleon.

The first set of State Apartments you reach belonged to the king. The King's Drawing Room was once known as the Rubens Room, after the three paintings hanging there. The King's Bed Chamber has paintings by Giovanni Canaletto and Thomas Gainsborough. Charles II actually slept in the adjacent King's Dressing Room, and some of Windsor's finest paintings hang here, including Sir Anthony Van Dyck's magnificent *Triple Portrait of Charles I* and works by Hans Holbein, Rembrandt, Peter Paul Rubens and Albrecht Dürer. The King's Closet was used by Charles II as a study and has works by Canaletto, Sir Joshua Reynolds and William Hogarth.

From here you pass through the Queen's Drawing Room into the King's Dining Room, with a fine ceiling painting by Verrio – one of only three to survive – and woodcarvings by Grinling Gibbons. The Queen's Ballroom has a remarkable collection of Van Dyck paintings, including one of Charles I's children, while the Queen's Audience Chamber boasts another ceiling by Verrio. More Gobelins tapestries and another Verrio ceiling adorn the Queen's Presence Chamber.

The Queen's Guard Chamber leads through to the restored St George's Hall, currently a bit too squeaky new to have much atmosphere. The hammerbeam roof is painted with the arms of the Knights of the Garter. A new Lantern Lobby stands on the site of the chapel where the fire originally started and is used to display silver gilt plate. A corridor leads to the magnificent plush-and-gold Crimson Drawing Room,

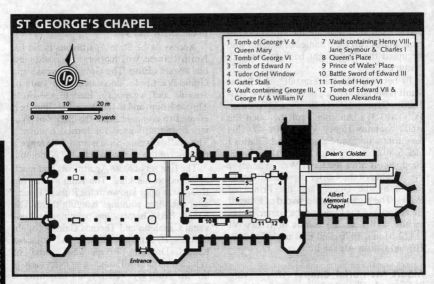

ST GEORGE'S CHAPEL

1 Tomb of George V & Queen Mary
2 Tomb of George VI
3 Tomb of Edward IV
4 Tudor Oriel Window
5 Garter Stalls
6 Vault containing George III, George IV & William IV
7 Vault containing Henry VIII, Jane Seymour & Charles I
8 Queen's Place
9 Prince of Wales' Place
10 Battle Sword of Edward III
11 Tomb of Henry VI
12 Tomb of Edward VII & Queen Alexandra

Dean's Cloister

Albert Memorial Chapel

Entrance

with the smaller Green Drawing Room visible through a door on the right. Both these rooms were designed for George IV and were restored as part of the post-1992 refit. The State Dining Room and Octagon Dining Room also had to be thoroughly restored.

The ceiling of the French-style Grand Reception Room caved in 1992 but has now been replaced and leads through to the Garter Throne Room, used for investing new Knights of the Order of the Garter.

The State Apartment circuit eventually winds up back in the Waterloo Chamber. Note that some of the smaller rooms are not always open to the public at busy times – an excellent reason for visiting out of season!

Queen Mary's Dolls' House The work of architect Sir Edwin Lutyens, the dolls' house was built in 1923 on a 1:12 scale. It's complete in every detail down to running water to the bathrooms. Entry to Queen Mary's Dolls' House is via the North Terrace.

Windsor Great Park Stretching behind Windsor Castle almost all the way to Ascot is the 1940 hectare Windsor Great Park, with wonderful stands of trees and areas of formal gardens. These include the Savill Garden (☎ 860222), which is open daily from March through October from 10 am to 6 pm, closing at 4 pm in winter.

Around Town

Windsor's fine **Guildhall** stands on High St beside Castle Hill. It was built between 1687 and 1689, the construction completed under the supervision of Sir Christopher Wren. The council insisted that central columns were required to support the 1st floor even though Wren thought them unnecessary. The few centimetres of clear air proved him right.

Some of the oldest parts of Windsor are found along the cobbled streets behind the Guildhall. The visibly leaning **Market Cross House** of 1768 is right next to the Guildhall. Charles II kept Nell Gwyn, his favourite mistress, in **Burford House** on Church St.

Eton College

Cross the Thames by the pedestrian Windsor Bridge to arrive at another enduring symbol of Britain's class system: Eton College, a famous public (meaning private) school that has educated no fewer than 18 prime ministers and now counts Princes William and Harry among its pupils. Several buildings date from the mid-15th century when the school was founded by Henry VI.

The college (☎ 671177) is open to visitors from Easter through September, from 2 to 4.30 pm during term, or from 10.30 am during the holidays. Entry is £2.50/2. Guided tours at 2.15 and 3.30 pm cost £3.50/3. Thinking of sending your offspring to join the 1200 to 1300 pupils at Eton? Set aside around £13,000 per year for the basic fees; you can shop for the top hat and tails uniform as you walk back along High St to Windsor.

Legoland Windsor

Visitors with children are unlikely to escape from Windsor without a trip to this fantasia mix of model masterpieces and pink-knuckle rides. The formula is much the same as at the Danish forerunner – family fun with the emphasis on the 2 to 12 age group. But it's pricey fun, with adult tickets costing £16, or £13 for children aged 3 to 15.

Buses (£2/1) run from Thames St from 10 am to 6.15 pm. South West Trains have tickets which include admission to Legoland.

It's open daily from mid-March through October from 10 am to 6 pm (8 pm mid-July through August). Advance booking (☎ 0990-040404) saves queuing or the risk of being turned away if the park is full.

Places to Stay

Since Legoland opened, accommodation in Windsor has come under great pressure. If possible, book well ahead of your visit.

Hostel *Windsor Youth Hostel* (☎ 861710) is a mile west of the Riverside train station at Edgworth House, Mill Lane. Either catch bus No 50A/B from outside Barclays Bank in Thames St or follow Arthur Rd or Barry Ave from the centre; you can walk along the riverbank. It's open from 2 January to 23 December and the nightly cost is £9.75/6.55 for adults/juniors.

B&Bs & Hotels The Windsor TIC charges £2.50 to make accommodation bookings. Cheaper, but centrally located, B&Bs include *Mrs Hughes'* (☎ 866036, 62 Queens Rd), where beds cost from £20 per person. Nearby are *Langton House* (☎ 858299, 46 Alma Rd), with doubles for £40 to £50, and the similarly priced *Alma House* (☎ 862983) at No 56.

Melrose House Hotel (☎ 865328, 53 Frances Rd), has rooms from £45/55 for singles/doubles. *Suffolk Lodge* (☎ 864186, 4 Bolton Ave), charges £30/54 for rooms with bathroom. In Clarence Rd *Mrs Airey's* (☎ 855062) at No 48 does B&B for £42 to £48, *Cobweb Corner* (☎ 852372) at No 115 costs from £20 per person, and *Clarence Hotel* (☎ 864436) at No 9 charges from £33/39. *Acorns Guest House* (☎ 840692) is right by Holy Trinity Church at 14 Trinity Place.

Prominently positioned at 10 High St, the *Castle Hotel* (☎ 852359) has rooms from £79/130. On Thames St, just south of Windsor Bridge, *Sir Christopher Wren's House* (☎ 861354) was built by Wren in 1676 and costs from £94 to £153, less if it's quiet. Across the river at 10 High St, Eton, the *Christopher Hotel* (☎ 852359) dating from 1511 has rooms from £87/104.

Places to Eat

With such a steady flow of visitors it's hardly surprising that Windsor is chock-a-block with eateries, many of them upping their prices for a captive clientele. The cobbled streets of Old Windsor, particularly Church St and Church Lane, harbour lots of possibilities. At 4 Church St *Drury House* (☎ 863734) does cream teas for £3.75, while *Nell Gwynn's* (☎ 850929) next door has themed set teas; Tudor teas cost £1.95, a Charles II tea £6.75.

Right next to the Guildhall on High St *The Crooked House*, in the precarious-looking Market Cross House, charges over the odds for sandwiches but dishes like mushroom and nut fettucine are more sensibly priced (£5.35).

Prices are generally more reasonable along pedestrianised Peascod St and its extension St Leonards Rd. *Francesco's* (☎ 777093, 53 Peascod St) specialises in pizzas and pastas for around £6. *Crosses Corner* (☎ 862867, 73 Peascod St) does reasonable, if unimaginative, pub grub. Just past the Victoria St junction at 5 St Leonards Rd, *Toscano* (☎ 857600) has a set lunch menu for £8.75, dinner £11.75. Further along, the *Viceroy of Windsor* (☎ 858005) is a flashy tandoori restaurant serving Sunday buffet lunches for £8.50.

At the popular *La Taverna* (☎ 863020, 2 River St) an Italian meal will cost about £10 a head. *Punter's Wine Bar* (☎ 865565, Thames St) near the bridge to Eton is good for lunches and light meals; a pre-theatre dinner costs £12.50. Across the street *Café Wren* doles out soup and a roll for £2.95 in cheery surrounds.

Along Eton High St places to eat jostle shoulders with antique shops. The rickety *Cock Pit* dates back to around 1420 and has the stocks outside to prove it. You can eat Italian here any day except Monday. More unassuming are the *Eton Tearooms*, which still dish up such staples as mixed grills for down-to-earth prices.

There are branches of *Costa* and *Café Rouge* in the Central train station concourse.

Entertainment

Popular pubs include the *Merry Wives of Windsor* on St Leonards Rd, *Crosses Corner* and the *Criterion* on the Peascod St/Victoria St corners and the *Star*, further up Peascod St towards the castle. In the lee of the castle in Thames St the *Slug & Lettuce* is one of the new-generation bars, all stripped floorboards and kilims on the wall. Also in Thames St, near the Windsor Bridge to Eton, the *Swan* is an altogether noisier and more crowded hang-out.

The *Windsor Arts Centre* (☎ 859336) on the corner of St Leonards Rd and St Marks Rd contains a bar, theatre and live music venue and attracts a young crowd. The *Theatre Royal* (☎ 853888, Thames St) is the town's main theatre.

Getting There & Away

Windsor is 20 miles by road or rail from central London and only about 15 minutes by car from Heathrow airport. See also the fares tables in the Getting Around chapter.

Bus Bus Nos 700 or 702 depart for Windsor from London's Victoria coach station about every hour. No 192 (Monday to Saturday) or No 190/191 (Sunday) connects Windsor with Heathrow airport. For further details phone ☎ 524144.

Train There are two Windsor and Eton train stations – Central station on Thames St, directly opposite the Windsor Castle entrance gate, and Riverside station near the bridge to Eton.

From London, trains run to the Riverside station from Waterloo every half hour (hourly on Sunday) and take 50 minutes. Services from Paddington to Central require a change at Slough, five minutes from Windsor, but take about the same time. The fare is £5.50 one way, £5.70 day return, on either route.

If you are travelling further west to Bath (£20.50) or Oxford (£10.30), go to Slough to pick up the main westbound trains.

Getting Around

Guide Friday open-top double-decker bus tours of the town cost £6.50/2. From Easter to October, French Brothers (☎ 851900) operate 35-minute riverboat trips from Windsor. Tickets cost £3.20/1.60. Rowing and motorboats are also available for hire.

Surrey

It's said that if Kent is the 'Garden of England' then Surrey is the patio. But among the sprawling dormitory towns for London

Peak National Park, Derbyshire

White cliffs, south coast

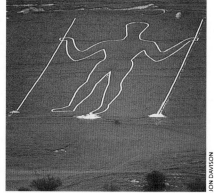

Coat of arms, Winchester Museum

The Long Man of Wilmington, West Sussex

CHRIS MELLOR

The Market Cross, Chichester

CHRIS MELLOR

Statue of King Alfred, Winchester

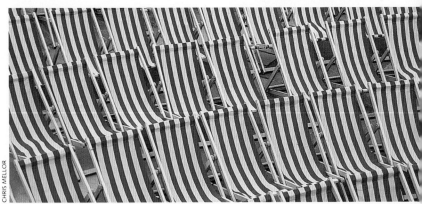

CHRIS MELLOR

Waiting for the sun to shine!

commuters this much-derided county has some lovely corners that are easy to reach on a day out from the capital.

The administrative centre is **Guildford**, an affluent town with an attractive cobbled High St, an excellent range of shops, the ruins of a Norman castle and an ugly modern cathedral.

Five miles north of Guildford, just off the A3 London road, are the Royal Horticultural Society's **Wisley Gardens** (☎ 01483-224234) – members only on Sunday. On the eastern outskirts of Guildford, **Clandon Park** (☎ 01483-222482, NT) is a Palladian-style house (designed by a Venetian architect) built about 1730.

Epsom Downs Racecourse, near Epsom, has operated since the days of James I and is home to the Derby, one of Britain's premier races.

Box Hill, on the North Downs 2½ miles north of Dorking, was famous as a beauty spot long before Jane Austen's Emma came here for her disastrous picnic. For everyone else Box Hill is an excellent place for a long walk, with 20 mile views from the top of the hill. Pick up a trail leaflet at the Box Hill National Trust office (☎ 01306-885502). The two pubs in Mickleham are both good for lunch. This is also a good area to come for mountain biking. There are regular trains between London Victoria and Box Hill and Westhumble station (45 minutes, £5.70).

Five miles north-west of Dorking off the A246, **Polesden Lacey** (☎ 01372-458203, NT) is a Regency villa with an attractive garden and good views.

Kent

Kent can be divided between the coastal towns and ports, and the dreamy, fertile hills of the hinterland. The history of the coastal towns is long and interesting, but most were wrecked by the arrival of the railway and mass tourism in the 19th century.

The inland area, however, has some of the country's loveliest countryside and most attractive villages. Between the North and South Downs lies an area known as the Weald, much of it designated an Area of Outstanding Natural Beauty.

The fertile rolling hills are now home to hop gardens (and the distinctive cone-shaped roofs of oast houses used for drying hops), orchards and well-off London commuters. It is still possible to see woods that are being managed with traditional coppicing techniques, and the area is still leafy and beautiful.

GETTING AROUND

Reflecting the fact that it is both densely populated and home to many London commuters, Kent has a good network of public transport. The county council has a public transport information line (☎ 0345-696996).

Bus

Stagecoach East Kent (☎ 01227-472082) has a good network around the region. Its Kent Compass 100 bus runs hourly (less frequently on Sunday) on a circuit taking in Canterbury, Dover, Deal, Sandwich, Ramsgate, Broadstairs, Margate, Herne Bay, Whitstable and back to Canterbury. The 200 bus does the same circuit in the opposite direction.

Explorer Tickets (£5.40/3.20 for adults/children) are accepted by all the main companies in the south-east.

Bicycle

It is possible to follow an interesting cycle route between Dover, Deal, Sandwich and Canterbury. The countryside is mostly flat and there are plenty of quiet country lanes. Depending on how circuitous the route, it is approximately a 35 mile ride. TICs stock the *Cycling in East Kent* pack, which details several routes.

CANTERBURY
• pop 36,000   ☎ 01227

Canterbury's greatest treasure is its magnificent cathedral, the successor to the church St Augustine built after he began converting the English to Christianity in 597. After the martyrdom of Archbishop Thomas à Becket in 1170, the cathedral became the centre of one of the most important medieval pilgrimages in Europe, immortalised by Geoffrey Chaucer in *The Canterbury Tales*.

The Archbishop of Canterbury is the head of the Church of England and the leader of the worldwide Anglican Communion (including Episcopalians). He plays an important symbolic and leadership role but, unlike the pope, has little direct authority. Although it is not the most beautiful, it is certainly one of the most impressive and evocative of cathedrals – the ghosts of saints, soldiers and pilgrims seem to crowd around. Not even baying packs of children can completely destroy the atmosphere although, if you can, you should go late in the day to avoid school groups.

The city of Canterbury was severely damaged by bombing during WWII and parts, especially to the south of the cathedral, have been rebuilt insensitively. However, there's still plenty to see and the bustling centre is atmospheric. The town crawls with tourists, but that simply means all is well with the world – they've been coming for a very long time.

Canterbury can easily be visited on a day trip from London and it makes an ideal stopover on the way to or from Dover. There are interesting places nearby (particularly Chilham and Sandwich), but it's too far north and east to use as a base for more than a night or two.

History

The first settlement on the site of Canterbury dates to the 1st century BC when there was a Celtic community on either side of the River Stour. It became an important place under the Romans, and after they left the Jutes (from southern Scandinavia) resettled the city. In 597 St Augustine arrived, beginning his mission at the court of Ethelbert, whose wife Bertha was already Christian. Augustine (and Bertha?) successfully converted the king and many of his subjects.

Augustine founded a Benedictine monastery and abbey, and the city was established as the centre of the English church. It thrived, both under the Anglo-Saxons and those great cathedral builders, the Normans. The cathedral's fame, however, did not eclipse that of St Augustine's Abbey until after the murder of Archbishop Becket.

In 12th century England the natural tension between church and state reached breaking point when Henry II refused to accept the independence of the Roman church and the authority of a foreign pope.

Before Henry made him archbishop, Becket had been a loyal and worldly courtier, a close friend of the king famed for his brilliance and luxurious lifestyle. Henry thought Becket would be an ally in his battle against the pope – but he was wrong. From the time he became archbishop in 1162, Becket completely renounced his old lifestyle and his friend the king. In 1170 the personal and political conflict reached a tragic culmination when four of Henry's knights, apparently without the king's knowledge, cut down and killed the archbishop in the cathedral.

Within hours of the murder rumours of miracles spread and a few years after his death Becket was made a saint. His jewel-encrusted shrine became the most important place of pilgrimage in England and was famous throughout Europe. As Chaucer observed, however, for many the pilgrimage quickly became an excuse for a holiday and Canterbury's merchants thrived on the pilgrim/tourist trade.

Becket again became a victim of the battle between church and state when Henry VIII acted to dissolve the increasingly corrupt monasteries. In 1538 St Augustine's Abbey was demolished and St Thomas' shrine, remains and relics were totally destroyed.

Orientation

The centre of Canterbury is enclosed by a medieval city wall and a modern ring road. The centre is easy to get around on foot, virtually impossible to get around by car.

Information

The Canterbury Visitor Information Centre (☎ 766567), 34 St Margaret's St, is open daily from 9.30 am to 5 pm (5.30 pm in

SOUTH-EASTERN ENGLAND

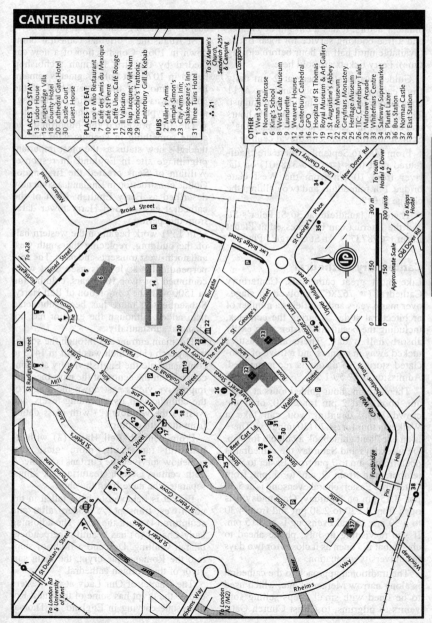

CANTERBURY

PLACES TO STAY
13 Tudor House
15 Kingsbridge Villa
18 County Hotel
20 Cathedral Gate Hotel
30 Castle Court
Guest House

PLACES TO EAT
4 Tuo e Mio Restaurant
7 Café des Amis du Mexique
10 Café St Pierre
11 Caffè Uno; Café Rouge
27 Il Vaticano
28 Flap Jacques; Viêt Nam
29 Pinocchio's Trattoria;
Canterbury Grill & Kebab

PUBS
2 Miller's Arms
3 Simple Simon's
23 City Arms Inn;
Shakespeare's Inn
31 Three Tuns Hotel

OTHER
1 West Station
5 Norman Staircase
6 King's School
8 West Gate & Museum
9 Laundrette
12 Weavers' Houses
14 Canterbury Cathedral
16 GPO
17 Hospital of St Thomas
19 Royal Museum & Art Gallery
21 St Augustine's Abbey
22 Roman Museum
24 Greyfriars Monastery
25 Heritage Museum
26 TIC; Canterbury Tales
32 Marlowe Arcade
33 Whitefriars Centre
34 Planet Lazer
35 Safeway Supermarket
36 Bus Station
37 Norman Castle
38 East Station

summer). Staffed by a helpful group of amateur actors, it has a *bureau de change* and a free booking service for local B&Bs (available until half an hour before closing time). Ferry tickets are sold here.

Guided walks start here at 2 pm daily from early April to October and also at 11 am Monday to Saturday in July and August. The cost is £3.50. The walks take 1½ hours and explore the cathedral precincts, King's School and the town's medieval centre.

From May to September there are chauffeured punt trips (☎ 0585-318301) on the river from 10 am from the West Gate bridge. For four adults and two children the charge is £18.

There's a laundrette at 36 St Peter's St, and the Internet can be accessed at Planet Lazer (☎ 787377), 41 St George's Place.

Canterbury Cathedral

Like most great cathedrals, Canterbury Cathedral (☎ 762862) evolved in stages over many years and it reflects a number of architectural styles. Touring the complex, including the beautiful cloisters, can easily absorb half a day. There are treasures tucked away in corners and a trove of associated stories, so a tour is recommended. Admission is £2.50/1.50.

There are one hour guided tours at 10.30 am, noon, and 2 pm for £2.80, or if the crowd looks daunting you can take a Walkman tour for £2.70 (30 minutes). There is an excellent guidebook available for 95p. On weekdays and Saturday the cathedral is open from 9 am to 7 pm from Easter to September, and from 9 am to 5 pm from October to Easter; choral evensong is at 5.30 pm, 3.15 pm on Saturday. On Sunday it is open from 12.30 to 2.30 pm and from 4.30 to 5.30 pm; choral evensong is at 3.15 pm. If you're visiting in July, phone ahead to check that it's open as it closes for two days for university graduation.

The traditional approach to the cathedral is along narrow Mercery Lane, which used to be lined with small shops selling souvenirs to pilgrims, to Christ Church Gate.

Once inside the gate, turn right and walk east for 50m, to get an overall picture.

St Augustine's original cathedral burnt down in 1067. Construction of a new cathedral by the first Norman archbishop began in 1070 but only fragments remain. In 1174 most of the eastern half of the building was destroyed by fire but the magnificent crypt beneath the choir survived.

The fire presented the opportunity to create something in keeping with the cathedral's new status as the most important pilgrimage site in England. In response, William of Sens created the first major Gothic construction in England, a style now described as Early English. Most of the cathedral east of Bell Harry tower dates from this period.

In 1391 work began on the western half of the building, replacing the south-west and north-west transepts and nave. The new perpendicular style was used, and work continued for over 100 years, culminating in 1500 with the completion of Bell Harry. Subsequently, more has been subtracted than added, although the exterior has not changed substantially.

The main entrance is through the **southwest porch** (1), which was built in 1415 to commemorate the English victory at Agincourt. From the centre of the nave there are impressive views east down the length of the church, with its ascending levels, and west to the **window** (2) with glass dating from the 12th century.

From beneath **Bell Harry** (3) with its beautiful fan vault, more glass that somehow survived the Puritans is visible. A 15th century screen, featuring six kings, separates the nave from the choir.

Becket is believed to have fallen in the north-west transept. A modern **altar and sculpture** (4) mark the spot. The adjoining **Lady Chapel** (5) has beautiful perpendicular fan vaulting. Descend a flight of steps into the Romanesque crypt, the main survivor of the Norman cathedral.

The Chapel of Our Lady at the western end of the crypt has some of the finest Romanesque carving in England. St Thomas

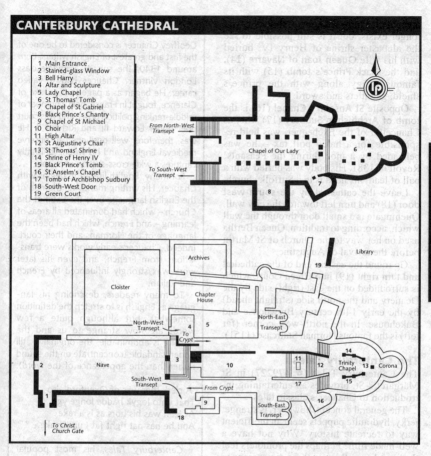

CANTERBURY CATHEDRAL

1 Main Entrance
2 Stained-glass Window
3 Bell Harry
4 Altar and Sculpture
5 Lady Chapel
6 St Thomas' Tomb
7 Chapel of St Gabriel
8 Black Prince's Chantry
9 Chapel of St Michael
10 Choir
11 High Altar
12 St Augustine's Chair
13 St Thomas' Shrine
14 Shrine of Henry IV
15 Black Prince's Tomb
16 St Anselm's Chapel
17 Tomb of Archbishop Sudbury
18 South-West Door
19 Green Court

was entombed in the Early English eastern end (6) until 1220. This is where Henry was whipped for Becket's murder and is reputed to be the site of many miracles. The **Chapel of St Gabriel** (7) features 12th century paintings, and the **Black Prince's Chantry** (8) is a beautiful perpendicular chapel, donated by the prince in 1363 and now used by Huguenots (French Protestants).

Exit the crypt to the south-west transept. The **Chapel of St Michael** (9) includes a wealth of tombs, including that of Arch-

bishop Stephen Langton, one of the chief architects of the Magna Carta. The superb **12th century choir** (10) rises in stages to the **High Altar** (11) and Trinity Chapel. The screen around the choir stalls was erected in 1305 and evensong has been sung in this inspiring space every day for 800 years. **St Augustine's Chair** (12), dating from the 13th century, is used to enthrone archbishops.

The stained glass in Trinity Chapel is mostly from the 13th century and celebrates the life of St Thomas and the miracles attributed to him. **St Thomas' shrine** (13) no longer exists, but it is still possible to see the alabaster shrine of Henry IV, buried with his wife **Queen Joan of Navarre** (14), and the **Black Prince's tomb** (15) with its famous effigy along with the prince's shield, gauntlets and sword.

Opposite **St Anselm's Chapel** (16) is the **tomb of Archbishop Sudbury** (17) who, as Chancellor of the Exchequer, was held responsible for a hated poll tax – he was beheaded by a mob during the Peasants' Revolt of 1381. His body was buried with a ball of lead; his head is in a Suffolk church.

Leave the cathedral by the **south-west door** (18) and turn left towards the city wall. Queningate is a small door through the wall which, according to tradition, Queen Bertha used on her way to the Church of St Martin before the arrival of Augustine.

Go round the eastern end of the cathedral and turn right (19) into Green Court, which is surrounded on the east (right) side by the Deanery and the north side (straight ahead) by the early 14th century Brewhouse and Bakehouse. In the north-west corner (far left) is the famous Norman Staircase (1151).

The Canterbury Tales

The Canterbury Tales (☎ 479227) in St Margaret's St, provides an entertaining introduction to Chaucer's classic tales.

The general concept, however, is strange: jerky, hydraulic puppets seem an inefficient way to recreate history. Why not have a well-made film? Perhaps the promoters feel they need something in three dimensions to justify the £4.95/3.95 ticket. The centre is open all year from 9.30 am to 5.30 pm (4.30 pm November to February).

Museums

The **Royal Museum & Art Gallery**, on the High St, has military memorabilia and works by local artists; entry is free. The city's three other museums can all be visited with one passport ticket for £3.90/1.95. Individual entry charges are given below.

West Gate & Museum, dating from the 14th century, is the only remaining city

Chaucer's Canterbury Tales

Geoffrey Chaucer is considered to be one of the first and greatest of English writers. Born around 1340, the son of a middle-class London vintner, Chaucer had a varied career. He began as a page to the Duke of Clarence, fought in France, held a number of middle-ranking political posts, and was court poet under Edward III and Richard II. He was, therefore, well positioned to observe medieval England and his writing brilliantly captures a wide cross-section of people.

For many, English literature begins with Chaucer. His writing marks the triumph of the English language over the Latin of the Church – which had dominated all areas of learning – and French, which had been the language of the Normans and their court. Indeed, Chaucer's early works were translations from French, and even his later work was strongly influenced by French and Italian.

To many readers, describing his language as English is to stretch the definition somewhat, but although quite a few words are now strange to us and the spelling is abominable, the original is still understandable (concentrate on the sound rather than the appearance of the word):

'A clerk ther was of Oxenford also
That unto logyk hadde longe ygo
As leen was his hors as is a rake
And he nas nat right fat I undertake...'

Canterbury Tales, his most popular work, consists of a collection of some 24 stories told by a party of pilgrims on their journey to the shrine of Becket at Canterbury. Chaucer paints a lively, ironic picture of the pilgrims and although the world has changed, the personalities he describes are still easily recognisable. Most 20th century readers will find a modern translation a good deal more enjoyable to deal with than the original, however. The Canterbury Tales recreation in St Margaret's St also provides an entertaining introduction.

gate. It survived because it was used as a prison; it is now a small museum featuring arms and armour. It's open all year, Monday to Saturday, from 11 am to 12.30 pm and from 1.30 to 3.30 pm; 90p/45p.

Canterbury Heritage Museum (☎ 452747), Stour St, in a converted 14th century building, gives good though rather dry coverage of the city's history and local characters – who include Rupert Bear and Joseph Conrad. The building, once the Poor Priests' Hospital, is worth visiting in its own right. It's open all year from 10.30 am to 5 pm, but Sunday only from June to October and then only from 1.30 to 5 pm; £2.20/1.10.

At the interesting **Roman Museum** (built underground around the remains of a Roman town house in Butchery House, opposite Shakespeare's Inn) you get to visit the marketplace, smell the odours of a Roman kitchen, handle artefacts and take a computer-generated tour of the town house.

It's open all year, Monday to Saturday, from 10 am to 5 pm, and on Sunday from June through of October from 1.30 to 5 pm; £2.20/1.10.

St Augustine's Abbey

Henry VIII acted with thoroughness when St Augustine's Abbey (☎ 767345, EH) was demolished in 1538 – only foundations remain. Admission is £2.50/1.30; there's a new museum and a worthwhile audio tour.

St Martin's Church

Believed to be the oldest parish church in England, St Martin's predates St Augustine and is possibly Roman in origin. To reach the church, continue 250m past St Augustine's Abbey and take the first road left; the church is on the right after 100m.

Greyfriars Monastery

This was the first Franciscan (the Grey Friars) monastery in England, founded in 1267. The picturesque building spans a small branch of the River Stour, and includes an upstairs chapel that is open to the public from mid-May to September, Monday to Saturday from 2 to 4 pm. Eucharist is celebrated every Wednesday at 12.30 pm.

Places to Stay

Camping *Canterbury Caravan and Camping Site* (☎ 463216, *Bekesbourne Lane*), off the A257, is just under 2 miles from the centre and charges from £9 to £10 for two people and a tent.

Hostels The *Youth Hostel* (☎ 462911, *54 New Dover Rd*) is half a mile or so from the East train station. Continue out St George's St (the continuation of High St), which eventually becomes New Dover Rd. The hostel is in an old Victorian villa and is closed from late December to the end of January; the nightly charge is £9.75.

Kipps (☎ 786121, *40 Nunnery Fields, off Old Dover Rd*) is an independent hostel with dorm beds from £9.95 and single/twin/family rooms for £14/13/10.95 per person. There's a self-catering kitchen and a laundrette.

The *University of Kent* (☎ 828000, *Tanglewood*) is a 20 minute walk from the centre and open only when students are away (in April and from July to September). B&B is from £14.50 per person.

B&Bs & Hotels Most Canterbury accommodation is quite expensive, particularly in July and August. In some cases prices almost double; ring ahead to avoid nasty surprises.

You can stay in the heart of the city at the *Cathedral Gate Hotel* (☎ 462800, *36 Burgate*), which has comfortable singles/doubles from £22/40 to £50/75. Although the walls are on the thin side and some of the floors slope alarmingly, the rooms are comfortable and the views of the cathedral are magnificent. It's a fantastic location, but cars have to be parked about 500m away.

Kingsbridge Villa (☎ 766415, *15 Best Lane*), also in the centre of town, just off High St, is a comfortable B&B with TVs in rooms, some of which have their own bathrooms. Singles are £22, doubles from £35 to £45. Parking is available.

Also central, *Tudor House* (☎ *765650, 6 Best Lane*) is good. In addition to the usual facilities, it has canoes and boats for guests to hire. Singles/doubles start from £18/34.

Castle Court Guest House (☎ *463441, 8 Castle St*) is a clean, straightforward B&B. There is a mixture of singles, doubles and twins for around £17 per person.

Still within walking distance of the centre, but not in the heart of the old city, *Ann's House* (☎ *768767, 63 London Rd*) is an attractive, well run B&B. With bath, rooms are around £26/44. Across the road is *Yorke Lodge* (☎ *451243, 50 London Rd*), similarly priced and also recommended. Nearby the *Derwent Guest House* (☎ *769369, 62 London Rd*) has three rooms (shared bathrooms) at £40, or £36 if you just want a light breakfast.

There are others closer to the St Dunstan's St intersection (and therefore town), including the *London Guest House* (☎ *765860, 14 London Rd*) with rooms for around £19 per person, and *Courtney Guest House* (☎ *769668, 4 London Rd*) with rooms from £25/32, or £30/38 with shower.

The more upmarket hotels mainly cluster on New Dover Rd; there are a number with doubles for around £55. The *Canterbury Hotel* (☎ *450551, 71 New Dover Rd*) has rooms from £45/58 and a very good restaurant. The *Ersham Lodge Hotel* (☎ *463174, 12 New Dover Rd*), nearer town, is a bit cheaper; prices are from £34/47.

If money's no object, the centrally located *County Hotel* (☎ *766266*) with rooms from £90/110 is recommended.

Four miles away, the *Thruxted Oast* (☎ *730080, Mystole, Chartham*) is an excellent B&B in converted oast houses (where hops were dried). The buildings have loads of character. Rates are £78 for luxurious twin accommodation. Book in advance, because there are only three rooms.

Places to Eat

The crowds of pilgrims and students ensure that there's a good range of reasonably priced eating places in Canterbury. If you want to do some menu window-shopping

start in St Margaret's St and then walk down High St to West Gate. Bookings are recommended, especially on Friday and Saturday nights.

For self-catering there's a big Safeway supermarket on the corner of New Dover Rd and Lower Chantry Rd, on the way to the youth hostel.

For a snack or a light meal, *Café St Pierre* (☎ *456791, 41 St Peter's St*) is an excellent French bakery and café. There's usually an exotic baguette of the day (eg Merguez spicy Arabic sausage, £2.10) and good coffee. A few doors down on St Peter's St are branches of *Café Rouge* and *Caffé Uno* (pizzas from £4.95 and live jazz on Thursday).

Flap Jacques (☎ *781000, 71 Castle St*) is an inexpensive French bistro serving traditional Breton (buckwheat) pancakes. Close by is the new *Viêt Nam*, with an interesting menu. Spicy grilled pork on vermicelli is £5.95.

Also on Castle St is the Italian *Pinocchio's Trattoria* (☎ *457538*) at No 64. A few doors down is *Canterbury Grill & Kebab* where for £1.20 you can sample that wonderful British contribution to world cuisine, the chip buttie (French fries sandwich).

Il Vaticano (☎ *765333, 35 St Margaret's St*) has good Italian food, in particular a wide range of pastas from £4.50. The *Three Tuns Hotel*, at the end of St Margaret's St, stands on the site of a Roman theatre and itself dates from the 16th century. It serves good-value pub meals from around £4.

Very popular with local students is *Café des Amis du Mexique* (☎ *464390*) just beyond the West Gate. It serves authentic Mexican cuisine – which is very different from the usual repetitive mix of beans, cheese and chilli. There's a cheerful atmosphere and the prices are reasonable. Enchiladas are £5.95.

There's an excellent restaurant at the *Canterbury Hotel* (☎ *450551, 71 New Dover Rd*) mainly serving traditional French cuisine. Two courses are £12.95, three courses are £15.95.

Entertainment

What & Where When, a free leaflet to what's on in Canterbury, is available from the TIC.

There are quite a few lively pubs. Two on St Radigund's St worth checking out are **Simple Simon's**, which has a beer garden and usually features folk music in the evening, and the **Miller's Arms**, which is a classic student hang-out.

Other possibilities are the **City Arms Inn** and **Shakespeare's Inn**, close to the main gate to the cathedral on Butchery Lane.

Getting There & Away

Canterbury is 58 miles from London and approximately 15 miles from Margate, Ramsgate, Sandwich, Dover, Folkestone and Ashford. See also the fares tables in the Getting Around chapter.

Bus The bus station is just within the city walls at the east end of High St.

National Express (☎ 0990-808080) sells London-Victoria tickets for as little as £5, or £8 for a day return. Stagecoach East Kent (☎ 472082) has a good network around the region (see Getting Around at the start of the Kent section). Canterbury to Dover costs £2 and takes 30 minutes.

Train There are two train stations: East (for the youth hostel), accessible from London Victoria; and West, accessible from London's Charing Cross and Waterloo. The journey takes about 1¾ hours and costs £13.90 for a day return. There are regular trains between Canterbury East and Dover Priory (45 minutes, £4.10).

Getting Around

Taxi Try Longport Taxis (☎ 458885).

Bicycle Downland Cycles (☎ 479643) is based at Canterbury West station. Mountain bikes are £10 per day or £50 per week. You can save about £2 with its combined cycle hire and return train ticket from London, if that deal is still running.

AROUND CANTERBURY

Four miles south-west of Canterbury on the A252, **Chilham** is a medieval village built in true feudal fashion around a square at the gate of a castle. There are several Tudor and Jacobean timber-framed and thatched houses and a couple of friendly pubs. Chilham lies on the North Downs Way and would make a pleasant walk from Canterbury.

MARGATE

Margate was one of the earliest and most popular seaside resorts in England, with Londoners travelling down by boat.

There are now hundreds of B&Bs and hotels as well as a number of tacky entertainment centres, including Dreamland Funpark, said to be one of the biggest attractions in this part of Kent. If you'd like to experience Margate's charms, a well-run **youth hostel (☎ 01843-221616, The Beachcomber, 3-4 Royal Esplanade)** has opened in a converted hotel. The charge is £9.75/6.55 for adults/juniors.

There's a TIC (☎ 01843-220241) on Marine Drive, four doors down from the sex shop.

BROADSTAIRS

• pop 21,600   ☎ 01843

Broadstairs developed later than Margate, in late Regency/early Victorian times. It has remained much smaller and still has the peculiar fascination of a real English resort that has not gone completely to seed.

It's probably best known for its links with Charles Dickens, who had a series of holiday homes here. There's an annual week-long Dickens Festival in June, which culminates in a ball in Victorian dress.

Between 1837 and 1859 Dickens spent much of his time here, and wrote parts of *Bleak House* and *David Copperfield* in the house on top of the cliff above the pier. It's now a museum, **Bleak House** (☎ 862224). Privately run by its enthusiastic owners, the museum is well worth a visit. There are several rooms arranged as they would have been in Dickens' time, a display on local wrecks and, in the cellars, an entertaining display about local smuggling. If the Kentish Giant looked anything like his mannequin here he must have been absolutely terrifying. The museum is open from March to November, daily from 10 am to 6 pm (9 pm in summer) and entry is £2.80/1.50.

The **Dickens House Museum** (☎ 862853), 2 Victoria Pde, wasn't actually his house but the home of Mary Pearson Strong, on whom he based Betsey Trotwood. Dickensiana on display includes personal possessions and letters; open daily from 2 to 5 pm; £1/50p.

The TIC (☎ 862242) is on High St.

Places to Stay & Eat

The *Broadstairs Youth Hostel* (☎ 604121, *Thistle Lodge, 3 Osborne Rd*) is run by a helpful couple; the overnight charge is £8.80/5.95 for adults/juniors. From the station, turn right under the railway and continue for 30 yards to a crossroads with traffic lights, then turn left into The Broadway leading to Osborne Rd. Ferry tickets are on sale.

There are plenty of B&Bs, including some quality places, all with sea views, on the Eastern Esplanade. The *East Horndon Private Hotel* (☎ 868306, *4 Eastern Esplanade*), *Gull Cottage Hotel* (☎ 861936) at No 5, and *Bay Tree Hotel* (☎ 862502) at No 12, charge around £22 per person.

There's a wide range of places to eat. The *York Gate Café & Milk Bar*, near the beach, is a wonderful traditional seaside café. Local plaice and chips is £2.95. A cream tea costs £1.95.

Getting There & Away

The Stagecoach 100/200 service runs hourly to Ramsgate, Sandwich, Dover and Canterbury.

There are regular trains to/from London Victoria (via Chatham), Canterbury West, and Dover Priory.

RAMSGATE
• pop 38,000   ☎ 01843

Ramsgate was a fashionable Victorian resort, but it has been hit by recession and the decline in English seaside holidays.

The harbour is attractive and overlooked by some impressive Regency crescents. There are interesting narrow streets with unusual buildings further behind. Near the marina is a **Maritime Museum** (☎ 587765) that charts the seafaring history of Ramsgate back to Roman times. Across the harbour, the **Motor Museum** (☎ 581948) is also worth a visit.

The TIC (☎ 583333) is on Harbour St and is open Monday to Saturday (and Sunday mornings in summer).

Sally Lines ferries to Ostend and Dunkirk were recently suspended. Check to see if they've started running again.

SANDWICH
• pop 4500   ☎ 01304

Sandwich is literally a backwater. Once a thriving Cinque Port on the sheltered Wantsum Channel, it has been deserted by the sea and pretty much forgotten by the world. Because it is 2 miles inland it has escaped the horrible fate of most Cinque Ports, which were 'developed' as seaside resorts in the 19th century. More remarkably, the town has avoided being turned into Ye Cute Olde Englishe Village in the 20th.

Modern day interest has centred on the three golf courses on the sand dunes east of the town. The Royal St George, perhaps the finest course in England, is sometimes host to the British Open.

Orientation & Information

The town is on the south bank of the River Stour and is still mostly surrounded by an earthen embankment dating from the 14th century. Everything is within easy walking distance.

The TIC (☎ 613565), on the New St side of the Guildhall, is open from May through September, daily from 11 am to 3 pm. The TIC sells an interesting town trail leaflet for 60p, and has information on some pleasant short walks in the surrounding countryside.

Things to See & Do

Sandwich is not renowned so much for outstanding individual buildings as for the

Cinque Ports

Kent juts into the Channel – it's a mere 17 miles between Dover and Cap Gris Nez – so it's not surprising its past is a mixed story of war and trade. The Romans had important ports at Regulbium (Reculver), Rutupiae (Richborough), Dubrae (Dover) and Anderida (Pevensey), and a naval fleet and chain of forts defending what they called the Saxon Shore against German raiders.

When the German raiders (the Jutes, Angles and Saxons, otherwise known as the Anglo-Saxons) succeeded the Romans they exploited the region's natural advantages by trading and fishing. In the absence of a professional army and navy, however, their thriving east-coast towns were the front line against Viking raids and invasions and were frequently called upon to defend themselves, and the kingdom, at land and sea.

In 1278, King Edward I formalised this already ancient arrangement by legally defining the Confederation of Cinque (pronounced sink) Ports. The five Head Ports – Sandwich, Dover, Hythe, Romney (now New Romney) and Hastings – were granted numerous privileges in exchange for providing the king with ships.

As the ports became more powerful and the demands of trade and defence increased, the confederation expanded to include Rye and Winchelsea, and each Head Port incorporated Limbs, or supporting towns and villages. At times there were up to 30 Limbs of the confederation, in addition to the Head Ports.

By the end of the 15th century most of the Cinque Ports' harbours had become largely unusable thanks to the shifting coastline, and a professional navy was based at Portsmouth. Only Dover now remains an important port.

As is often the case in Britain, while real importance and power has evaporated, the pomp and ceremony remains. The Lord Warden of the Cinque Ports is a prestigious post now given to faithful servants of the crown – they get an apartment at Walmer Castle and a chance to wear funny clothes and a big, gold chain. The current warden is the Queen Mother, but among the previous incumbents was Sir Robert Menzies, the Prime Minister of Australia from 1939 to 1941 and from 1949 to 1966. Sir Robert earned his reward with uninhibited grovelling, including his famous speech to Elizabeth II where he quoted a medieval poet:

'I did but see her passing by
and yet I love her 'til I die'

overall impact of its unspoilt medieval street-scapes. **Strand St** is said to have more half-timbered houses than any other in England. Elsewhere, a number of buildings have Dutch or Flemish characteristics (note the stepped gables in some buildings), the legacy of Protestant Flemish refugees who settled in the town in the 16th century. The impressive **Barbican** is a toll gate dating from the 16th century. The exterior of the **Guildhall** (☎ 617197) was substantially altered in 1910 but the interior is little changed since the 16th century.

The **Church of St Clement** has one of the finest surviving Norman towers in England – designed for defensive. The **Prince's Golf Club** (☎ 611118) is recommended for visiting golfers.

Places to Stay & Eat

The range of places to stay is quite limited, but Sandwich is an easy day trip from Canterbury or Dover.

The *Sandwich Leisure Park* (☎ 612681, *Woodnesborough Rd*) is open from March

Britain's First Fast Food

Despite the name, Sandwich town takes no responsibility for the invention of the sandwich. This has, in fact, been attributed to John Montague, the Fourth Earl of Sandwich, in the 18th century. Rather than leave the gambling table for meals, the earl ordered cold beef which he placed between slices of bread so as not to get grease on the cards.

As with many a great British invention, the basic idea was developed abroad - as the hot dog, the burger and the open sandwich. In Victorian times it became fashionable to serve dainty cucumber sandwiches with afternoon tea.

In recent years the humble sandwich has undergone something of a renaissance in Britain with sales rising nearly 50% over the last five years. For an interesting range of breads and fillings try Marks & Spencer or the sandwich chain Pret A Manger.

through October; £5.50 for one person and a tent.

There are very few cheap B&Bs, but you could try **Mrs Rogers** (☎ 612772, 57 St George's Rd), who charges £16 per person. The **New Inn** (☎ 612335, Harnet St), near the Guildhall, has rooms with private shower for £25 per person.

The **Bell Hotel** (☎ 613388, The Quay), overlooking the river, is the town's posh hotel with rooms for £70/95; **Magnums** is a café belonging to the hotel and has a wide range of meals for around £5. A cream tea is £2.80 at the **Little Cottage Tearooms** nearby. For a splurge, visit the **Fisherman's Wharf** (☎ 613636) near the Barbican. A whole Dover sole is £16.50.

Getting There & Away

Sandwich is about 15 miles from Canterbury and about 10 from Dover. Stagecoach East Kent's 100/200 hourly service connects Sandwich to Dover (45 minutes, £3.50 day return), Canterbury and Ramsgate.

Sandwich is on the train line between Margate, Dover Priory and Folkestone Central; there are regular trains.

DOVER

- **pop 37,000   ☎ 01304**

Europhobic Brits view Dover as the 'Gateway to Europe'. The place has just two things going for it: the world's busiest passenger harbour and a spectacular medieval castle.

Dover is sited along the River Dour, a safe harbour on a stretch of coast dominated by the famous white cliffs. There is evidence of an Iron Age settlement, and the Romans identified the strategic importance of the site. Dubrae, as Dover was known, was a fortified port in the chain of defences along the Saxon shore.

The Normans, needless to say, immediately built a castle. The existing building dates to 1181 and was known as the Key of England. It has played an important military role, most recently in WWII.

The foreshore of Dover is basically an enormous, complicated (though well-signposted) and unattractive vehicle ramp for the ferries. The town itself was badly damaged during WWII and today, under siege from heavy traffic, has no charm. The feeling that everyone is en route to somewhere much more interesting – as quickly as possible – doesn't help.

Orientation & Information

Dover is dominated by the profile of the castle to the east. The town itself runs back from the sea along a valley formed by the unimpressive River Dour (in Roman times, this formed a navigable estuary).

The TIC (☎ 205108) is on Townwall St near the seafront and is open daily from 9 am to 6 pm. It has an accommodation and ferry-booking service.

The Mangle, on Worthington St, is a convenient laundrette just near the Riveria Coffee House. It's open daily from 8 am to 8 pm.

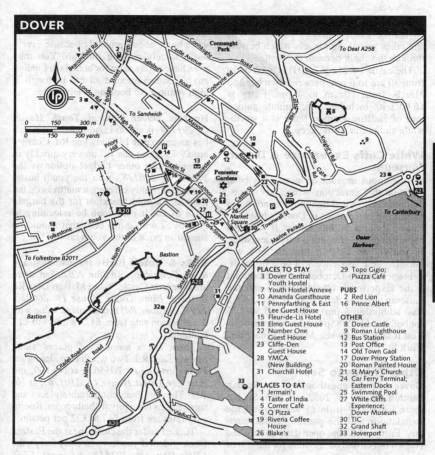

DOVER

To Deal A258

Connaught Park

Castle Avenue

To Canterbury

To Sandwich

To Folkestone B2011

Bastion

Bastion

Outer Harbour

The Viaduct

Hoverport

PLACES TO STAY
3 Dover Central Youth Hostel
7 Youth Hostel Annexe
10 Amanda Guesthouse
11 Pennyfarthing & East Lee Guest House
15 Fleur-de-Lis Hotel
18 Elmo Guest House
22 Number One Guest House
23 Cliffe-Den Guest House
28 YMCA (New Building)
31 Churchill Hotel

PLACES TO EAT
1 Jermain's
4 Taste of India
5 Corner Café
6 Q Pizza
19 Riviera Coffee House
26 Blake's

29 Topo Gigio; Piazza Café

PUBS
2 Red Lion
16 Prince Albert

OTHER
8 Dover Castle
9 Roman Lighthouse
12 Bus Station
13 Post Office
14 Old Town Gaol
17 Dover Priory Station
20 Roman Painted House
21 St Mary's Church
24 Car Ferry Terminal; Eastern Docks
25 Swimming Pool
27 White Cliffs Experience; Dover Museum
30 TIC
32 Grand Shaft
33 Hoverport

Dover Castle

Dover's main attraction is a well-preserved medieval fortress with a beautiful location and spectacular views across the Channel. To add to its fascination, there are the remains of a Roman lighthouse or Pharos within the fortifications, as well as a restored Saxon church.

The **Pharos** is possibly the oldest standing building in England (dating from 50 AD), and certainly one of the most intriguing. The Romans built the lighthouse to guide ships into the estuary of the Dour below.

The **keep** was built on the orders of Henry II between 1181 and 1187 and its walls are seven metres thick in places. The castle survived sieges from rebellious barons in 1216 and the French in 1295, was captured by the Parliamentarians in 1642, was the headquarters for operations against German submarines in WWI, and served as the command post for the evacuation of Dunkirk in 1940.

The excellent tour of **Hellfire Corner** covers the castle's history during WWII, and takes you along tunnels which burrow through the chalk beneath the castle.

The castle (☎ 211067, EH) is open daily from 10 am to 6 pm; between October and March, from 10 am to 4 pm. Entry is £6.60/3.30, including a 55 minute guided tour of Hellfire Corner; there is a worthwhile audio tour of the keep.

White Cliffs Experience & Dover Museum

An enormous amount of money has been spent on this attraction, which has robots, dioramas, actors and light-and-sound shows presenting two periods in Dover's history – Roman times and 1940s Dover. If you are a history buff, the museum is very interesting. If you've got kids in tow and it's wet outside, the Experience will be a lifesaver.

From April to October the electronic bit – the Experience (☎ 210101) – and the museum are open daily from 10 am to 6 pm (last admission 5 pm); entry is £5.50/3.75 for both, or £1.65/85p for the museum only. You'll find it between Market Square and York St.

Other Things to See

Dover's oldest guesthouse is the **Roman Painted House** (☎ 203279), New St, but there's actually little to see beyond the foundations and the painting is fragmentary. Entry is £2/80p; open daily in July and August but closed on Monday for the rest of the year.

There are hour-long guided tours of the cells and Victorian court room at the **Old Town Gaol** in the town hall. It's closed on Sunday morning and on Monday.

Beginning at Snargate St, there's a 43m triple staircase, the **Grand Shaft**, which was cut into the white cliffs as a short cut to town for troops stationed on the Western Heights during the Napoleonic Wars. According to tradition, one staircase was for officers and their ladies, the second for the NCOs and their wives, and the third for soldiers and their women!

Places to Stay

Accommodation in Dover is nothing to write home about, probably because everyone's merely passing through. You may even have to pay extra for breakfast. Finding any accommodation at all can be tough in high summer, so booking is advisable.

Hostels *Dover Central Youth Hostel* (☎ 201314) is at 306 London Rd, but it also has an annexe at 14 Godwyne Rd. Charges are £9.75 and it can fill up very quickly in summer. The other budget option is the *YMCA* (☎ 206138), near the youth hostel annexe, currently offering a mattress on the floor and a light breakfast for the bargain price of £6. It may soon be relocating to Princes St with dorm beds that should be similar in price to the youth hostel.

B&Bs & Hotels B&Bs are mainly strung along Folkestone Rd (the A20), but there are others on Castle St and Maison Dieu Rd in town. *Elmo Guest House* (☎ 206236, 120 Folkestone Rd) is reasonable value with a per-person rate from £12 (winter) to £17 (summer).

There are a number of places along Maison Dieu Rd. Two worth considering are *Pennyfarthing* (☎ 205563), at No 109, and *East Lee Guest House* (☎ 210176), at No 108. They are both comfortable places and some rooms have private bathrooms. Room-only rates are from £17 to £22 per person.

Tucked under the castle, near the Eastern Docks (ideal if you have an early ferry), the *Cliffe-Den* (☎ 202418, 63 East Cliff, Marine Parade) is quiet and pleasant with a per-person rate from £14 to £18. Rooms at *Amanda Guest House* (☎ 201711, Harold St) range from £16/28 in winter to £20/34 in summer.

Fleur-de-Lis Hotel (☎ 240224, 9 Effingham Crescent) is centrally located. There are a couple of attic singles for £13, and rooms for £18/30, or £26/38 with bath. Breakfast is another £3.50.

Number One Guest House (☎ 202007, 1 Castle St) is a popular place charging £45 for double rooms with showers. Breakfast is served in your room. There's a lock-up garage.

Blakes (☎ *202194, 52 Castle St*) charges £47.50 for each of six suites. They're very well equipped, not only with bathrooms but also with kitchen/diners and sitting rooms.

Down on the waterfront is the refurbished **Churchill Hotel** (☎ *203633)*. It's a comfortable place popular with business travellers. Charges range from £37.50 to £50.50 per person.

Places to Eat

There's not a lot of joy for gourmets in Dover, despite (or because of?) the proximity of Calais. There are a number of restaurants and fast-food outlets around Market Square, but you will probably do best with a pub meal.

For a cheap breakfast try the **Corner Café** on the High St. The **Riveria Coffee House** on Pencester Rd does what it says – and well. Light meals are also available – baked potatoes from £1.60.

Convenient to the hostel, **Jermain's** (☎ *205956, Beaconsfield Rd)* is a clean, efficient place with a range of good value traditional lunches like roast beef for £3.55 – followed by spotted dick (£1) for pud.

The **Red Lion**, just off Frith Rd, has excellent, filling meals for around £4.50; and the **Prince Albert** on Biggin St is also recommended for pub grub. With pizzas from £3.60, the most popular pizzeria is **Q Pizza** on the High St. The **Taste of India**, also on the High St, offers a daily buffet for £6.50.

There are several places in and around Market Square. **Topo Gigio** is an Italian place with pasta from £3.30 and pizzas from £4.10. Opposite, **Piazza Café** has a range of interesting snacks (eg ciabatta sandwiches from £1.85) as well as more substantial fare. **Blakes** (☎ *202194)* is a wine lodge at 52 Castle St. It has an early evening dinner special with wine for £10.80.

Getting There & Away

Dover is 75 miles from London and 15 from Canterbury. See the fares tables in the Getting Around chapter.

Ferry departures are from the Eastern Docks (accessible by bus) below the castle, but the Hoverport is below the Western Heights. The train station is a short walk to the west of the town centre. The bus station is in the centre of town.

Bus National Express has numerous buses between Dover and London, and most stop at Canterbury. Dover to Canterbury costs £2.50. Stagecoach East Kent (☎ 240024) has an office on Pencester Rd. There's a bus hourly to Brighton which costs £5 and takes an interminable five hours, stopping everywhere in between.

Train There are over 40 trains a day from London Victoria and Charing Cross stations to Dover Priory.

There's an enjoyable hourly service that runs across the rich Romney Marsh farmlands from Ashford to Rye and Hastings. Ashford to Hastings takes 45 minutes and costs £6.60. There are hourly trains from Hastings to Battle (15 minutes, £2.20). Hastings to Brighton is another hour and costs £8.20.

Boat For information on ferries to/from Dover see the introductory Getting There & Away chapter.

Getting Around

Bus Fortunately, the ferry companies run complimentary buses between the docks and train station as they're a long walk apart, especially if you've got some heavy bags. There are infrequent East Kent buses to the Eastern Docks from the Pencester Rd bus station.

Taxi Central (☎ 240441) and Britannia (☎ 204420) have 24-hour services. One way to Folkestone or Deal would cost about £7.50. Local trips start at £1.40 plus 80p per mile.

Bicycle You can hire a range of bicycles from Andy's Cycle Shop (☎ 204401), 156 London Rd. Charges are £8 per day.

SOUTH-EASTERN ENGLAND

FOLKESTONE

- **pop 46,280**   ☎ 01303

'Trifle not, thy time is short', reads the inscription on the old church tower near The Leas in Folkestone. That's apt for Folkestone as there's little to see here, although the **Russian submarine** (☎ 240400) moored in the harbour is interesting to visit.

Folkestone is basically a ferry port with SeaCat services to Boulogne. The Channel Tunnel begins (or ends) just outside Folkestone: Eurotunnel's car-carrying rail services (no foot passengers) use the terminal 2 miles north-west of the town.

The TIC (☎ 258594), Harbour St, near the inner harbour, is open daily from 9 am to 5.30 pm.

Folkestone is a more pleasant place to stay than Dover. The Leas is a garden promenade lined by substantial Victorian hotels with great views. Near The Leas, the *Salisbury Hotel* (☎ 252102, *30 Clifton Gardens*) has rooms with bathrooms, some with sea views, from £24.75 per person. The *Westward Ho! Hotel* (☎ 221515, *13 Clifton Crescent*) has views and is only £16.50 for a single or £24/38 with bath. The pleasant *Rhodesia Hotel* (☎ 253712, *2 Clifton Crescent*) doesn't have the views so is only £15.

For information on ferries to/from Folkestone, see the introductory Getting There & Away chapter.

ROMNEY MARSH & AROUND

Romney Marsh is a flat and fertile plain reclaimed from the sea, drained by meandering ditches and now protected by an impressive and ugly sea wall. It's nevertheless appealing, particularly around the hilly rim. It is, somehow, a landscape in microcosm, which makes it an appropriate location for the world's smallest public railway, the **Romney, Hythe & Dymchurch Railway** (☎ 01797-362353), which runs from Hythe to Dungeness.

Hythe is a low-key seaside resort with an attractive old town. In the crypt of St Leonard's Church is a ghoulish attraction – 8000 thigh bones and 2000 skulls, some arranged on shelves like pots of jam in a supermarket.

Dungeness is a low shingle spit, the largest in Europe, dominated by a nuclear power station. There's a strange magic here that for many people transcends the apocalyptic bleakness. The shingle supports an unusual community of plants and is host to the largest seabird colony in the south-east. There's an RSPB Nature Reserve visitor centre (☎ 01797-320588). The area is also popular with writers and artists, best known of whom was the late film director Derek Jarman, whose cottage garden (not open to the public) has become something of a pilgrimage site for his fans.

ASHFORD

Ashford is of interest solely for its train station, the only passenger boarding point between London and the Continent for trains using the Channel Tunnel. See the introductory Getting There & Away chapter for information.

The TIC (☎ 01233-629165), 18 The Churchyard, is open Monday to Saturday from 10 am to 5 pm and to 5.30 pm in summer. Ashford is 70 miles from London, 15 from Canterbury, 7 from Dover, and about 25 from Rye and Tenterden.

SISSINGHURST CASTLE GARDENS

Sissinghurst (☎ 01580-715330, NT), off the A262 between Biddenden and Cranbrook, is an enchanted place. Vita Sackville-West and her husband Harold Nicholson (of the infamous Bloomsbury Group) discovered a ruined Elizabethan mansion in 1930 and created a superb series of gardens in and around the surviving buildings. The castle and gardens are surrounded by a moat and rolling wooded countryside. All the elements come together to create an exquisite, dreamlike English beauty. Anyone who doubts the rich seductiveness of the English landscape has not been to Sissinghurst in spring or summer.

The gardens are open from 1 April to 15 October – Tuesday to Friday from 1 to 6.30

pm, and on Saturday and Sunday from 10 am to 5.30 pm; they're closed on Monday. The ticket office opens at noon from Tuesday to Friday. Admission is £6/3.

It's possible to stay in the substantial estate manager's house, 100m from Sissinghurst Castle. Every room (including the bathroom) has stunning views over the famous gardens and surrounding countryside. *Sissinghurst Castle Farm* (☎ 01580-712885) is deservedly popular and costs from £24 per person; booking is advised.

Getting There & Away

The nearest train station is Staplehurst on the line between Tonbridge and Ashford. Maidstone & District's Maidstone to Hastings bus service (No 4/5) passes the station and Sissinghurst.

HEVER

Idyllic Hever Castle (☎ 01732-861702) near Edenbridge, a few miles west of Tonbridge, was the childhood home of Anne Boleyn, mistress to Henry VIII and then his doomed queen. The moated castle was built in the 13th and 15th centuries and restored in the early 1900s by William Waldorf Astor. The exterior is unchanged from Tudor times, but the interior now has superb Edwardian woodwork. The castle is surrounded by a garden, again the creation of the Astors, that incorporates a number of different styles, including a formal Italian garden with classical sculpture. As well as a traditional yew hedge maze there's also a new water maze.

It's open from March to late November daily from noon to 6 pm; admission to the castle and gardens is £7/3.80, to the gardens only £5.50/3.60. The nearest train station is Hever on the Uckfield line, a mile from the castle itself (£6.20 from London Victoria).

CHARTWELL

Chartwell (☎ 01732-868381) is the large country house just north of Edenbridge that Winston Churchill bought in 1922 and which remained the family home until his death.

Filled with memorabilia and the statesman's paintings, the house is open April through October, Wednesday to Sunday from 11 am to 4.30 pm. In July and August it's also open on Tuesday and there are plans for limited opening in March (phone for details). Entry is £5.20/2.60.

The Chartwell Explorer bus (☎ 0345-696996) runs between Sevenoaks train/bus stations and Chartwell at weekends, and Wednesday to Friday in July and August. The £3 ticket includes a pot of tea at Chartwell. A combined ticket including entry, bus and return rail travel to London costs £12.

KNOLE HOUSE

In a country that is full of extraordinary country houses, Knole (☎ 01732-450608, NT), just south of Sevenoaks, is outstanding. It may be exceeded in size by Blenheim, but its graceful Elizabethan/Jacobean simplicity is more beautiful. Substantially dating from 1456, it is not as old as some of the great houses that incorporate medieval fortresses, but it is more coherent in style.

It seems as if *nothing* substantial has been changed since early in the 17th century, including the furniture. It is the Sackville family, owners of the house since 1566, who can take credit for somehow resisting the temptation to rebuild and redecorate according to 'modern' fashions. After all, there are some things that just cannot be improved.

Vita Sackville-West, co-creator of Sissinghurst, was born in the house in 1892, and her friend Virginia Woolf based the novel *Orlando* on the history of the house and family.

The house is vast, with seven courtyards, 52 staircases and 365 rooms, so the excellent guidebook is recommended. There is public access from April through October; Wednesday, Friday, Saturday and Sunday from 11 am to 5 pm, Thursday from 2 to 5 pm; admission is £5 and last entry is at 4 pm. Parking is £2.50 (free for NT members). The grounds are open all year.

Places to Stay

Nearby Sevenoaks is not particularly exciting, but there are plenty of B&Bs. The TIC (☎ 01732-450305) is on Buckhurst Lane, just to the east of High St. *Mrs Lloyd* (☎ *01732-453236*) and *Beech Combe* (☎ *01732-741643, Holly Bush Lane*) are both central and both have rooms for around £20/36.

Getting There & Away

Knole is to the south of Sevenoaks, east of the A225. The town's train station, which is on the line from London's Charing Cross to Tonbridge, is a 1½ mile walk from the house.

IGHTHAM MOTE

For six and a half centuries Ightham (pronounced eye-tam) Mote has lain hidden in a narrow, wooded valley in the Weald. Not only has it survived, it has grown more beautiful – as the stone mellowed, a wing was added here, a room converted there …

It has survived wars, storms, changes in ownership, and generation after generation of occupants. This is all the more remarkable since it is not an aristocratic mansion full of priceless treasures, just a small medieval manor house surrounded by a moat.

Although parts date from around 1340, the building today is an architectural jigsaw puzzle, and you need a detailed guide to unravel which bit belongs to what century. Some of the additions and alterations seem haphazard, but the materials (wood, stone, clay), the building's scale and the frame of water create a harmonious whole.

The location is picturesque, the building is extraordinary and, with the first phase of the National Trust's £4 million restoration now complete, it's well worth a visit. Ightham Mote (☎ 01732-810378, NT) is 6 miles east of Sevenoaks off the A25, 2½ miles south of Ightham off the A227. It's open from April through October, daily except Tuesday and Saturday, from 11 am to 5.30 pm; £4.50/2.25.

LEEDS CASTLE

Just east of Maidstone, Leeds Castle (☎ 01622-765400) is justly famous as one of the world's most beautiful castles. Like something from a fairy tale, it stands on two small islands in a lake surrounded by rolling wooded hills. The building dates from the 9th century, but Henry VIII transformed it from a fortress into a palace. It is overrun by families, especially at the weekend, and, stunning though the surroundings are, the atmosphere is more hysterical than historical. Weekday afternoons are least busy.

It's open daily from March to October from 10 am to 5 pm, and from November to February from 10 am to 3 pm; admission is £8.80. National Express (☎ 0990-808080) has one bus a day direct from Victoria coach station (leaving at 9 am); it must be pre-booked and combined admission/travel is £12.50. The nearest train station is Bearsted on the Kent Coast Line to Ashford. There's a combined admission/ travel ticket for £16.90.

East Sussex

East Sussex has some of the most spectacular coastal scenery in Britain, superb countryside along the spine of the South Downs, and a variety of towns and sights – all within easy reach of London.

Although they are touristy, Rye and Battle have a certain magic. Lewes is as historically interesting but seems to be bypassed by the crowds.

Hastings and Brighton are two of England's largest and most entertaining seaside towns, but with its extraordinary mix of class and tackiness Brighton is in a category of its own.

GETTING AROUND

East Sussex has a good network of public transport, and rail is particularly good from a traveller's point of view. The county council operates a very helpful public transport information line (☎ 01273-474747), Monday to Friday, from 9 am to 4 pm.

Bus

There's quite an overlap between Kent and East Sussex bus operators. In particular,

Stagecoach East Kent Buses (☎ 01227-472082) helps operate several routes. In Sussex itself, the major operators are East-bourne Buses (☎ 01323-416416), Stage-coach South Coast Buses (☎ 01424-433711) – who cover Hastings and South-down as well – Brighton & Hove Buses (☎ 01273-886200), and Stagecoach Coast-line Buses (☎ 01903-237661).

Explorer Tickets (£5.40/3.20 for adults/ children) are accepted by all the main com-panies in the south-east.

Train

Most people without their own transport will find that rail will serve them best in East and West Sussex. There are fast regular services from London to Hastings, Brighton and Chichester on the coast, and a line that runs the length of the Sussex coast linking these three main towns and many smaller ones.

RYE

- pop 5400   ☎ 01797

Rye, once a Cinque Port, is a picturesque medieval town with half-timbered build-ings, winding cobbled streets and a number of literary associations.

Rye is sometimes claimed to be the most beautiful town in Britain and, as a result, is full of tea shops and tourists. Because it is so popular and so perfectly meets expecta-tions for Ye Olde Englishe Towne, it can seem strangely unreal – as if all you see is a façade and real life has long since fled. If you do visit – and the town would make a good base – avoid summer weekends.

Orientation & Information

Rye is only small, so it can easily be covered on foot. The Rye Heritage Centre and TIC (☎ 226696), Strand Quay, is south-west of the train station on the River Tillingham. The TIC is open daily, in summer from 9 am to 5.30 pm, in winter from 10 am to 4 pm.

Things to See & Do

The best place to start is the TIC's **Rye Town Model Sound & Light Show**, which

gives a theatrical half-hour introduction to the town's history (open daily, £2/1).

From the TIC, walk up cobbled **Mermaid St**, one of the most famous streets in England, with timber-framed houses dating from the 15th century. The Mermaid Inn was a notorious smugglers' haunt and in the 18th century the Hawkhurst Gang, one of the most feared gangs in the country, used the pub to openly celebrate successful runs.

Turn right at the T-junction for **Lamb House** (☎ 224982, NT), West St, mostly dating from 1722 and Georgian in style. It was the home of the American writer Henry James from 1898 to 1916. It's open from April to October, on Wednesday and Satur-day from 2 to 5.30 pm; £2.50.

Continue round the dogleg until you come out at Church Square, which is sur-rounded by a variety of attractive houses, including the Friars of the Sack on the south side at No 40, which was part of a 13th century friary. The **Church of St Mary the Virgin** is on the highest point in Rye and in-corporates a mixture of ecclesiastical styles. The turret clock is the oldest in England (1561), still working with its original mech-anism; the two gilded cherubs, known as the Quarter Boys, strike bells on the quarter hour only. There are great views from the church tower (£1.50).

Turn right at the eastern corner of the square for **Ypres Tower** (pronounced wipers), which is part of the 13th century town fort that survived French raids. It now houses a small local museum which may soon be re-located to East St. Admission is £1.50/50p.

The **Rye Treasury of Mechanical Music** (☎ 223345) is at 20 Cinque Ports St. The en-thusiastic owner gives interesting demon-strations of the workings of some of his phonographs, pianolas and other instruments daily from 10 am to 5 pm. Entry is £3/1.50.

Walks

The 1066 Country Walk links Rye to Pevensey. It's 3 miles to the village of Winchelsea, which is almost as attractive as Rye yet without the tourists. The path is an excellent way to reach Battle (15 miles).

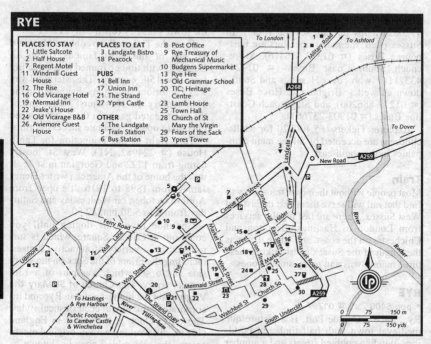

RYE

PLACES TO STAY
1 Little Saltcote
2 Half House
7 Regent Motel
11 Windmill Guest House
12 The Rise
16 Old Vicarage Hotel
19 Mermaid Inn
22 Jeake's House
24 Old Vicarage B&B
26 Aviemore Guest House

PLACES TO EAT
3 Landgate Bistro
18 Peacock

PUBS
14 Bell Inn
17 Union Inn
21 The Strand
27 Ypres Castle

OTHER
4 The Landgate
5 Train Station
6 Bus Station
8 Post Office
9 Rye Treasury of Mechanical Music
10 Budgens Supermarket
13 Rye Hire
15 Old Grammar School
20 TIC; Heritage Centre
23 Lamb House
25 Town Hall
28 Church of St Mary the Virgin
29 Friars of the Sack
30 Ypres Tower

See the boxed text 'The 1066 Country Walk' in this chapter.

Another good walk from Rye is to Camber Castle (1½ miles).

Places to Stay

This is one place where it's really worth spending a bit more and staying somewhere special. The obvious choice, if you can afford it, is the historic *Mermaid Inn* (☎ 223065, *Mermaid St*). Visited by royalty and proud of its resident ghost, the hotel charges from £54 per person for bed and breakfast. For £136 you could have Dr Syn's Bedchamber for a night – which was where the Queen Mum slept when she visited.

Somewhat cheaper but still highly recommended are the *Old Vicarage* (☎ 222119, *66 Church Square*) – not to be confused with the Old Vicarage Hotel – and *Jeake's House* (☎ 222828, *Mermaid St*). They're both at-

mospheric old houses with comfortable, attractive rooms, most with bathroom and rates from £22.50 to £43.50 per person. At weekends there's a minimum two-night stay.

Among the cheaper places to stay, *The Rise* (☎ 222285, *82 Udimore Rd*) is comfortable and welcoming. It's £20 to £25 per person in double or twin rooms, all with bath.

The *Windmill Guest House* (☎ 224027, *Mill Lane*) off Ferry Rd is also recommended. The rooms are in the extension by the windmill. A double with bath is around £20 per person.

Little Saltcote (☎ 223210, *Military Rd*) and *Half House* (☎ 223404) are still within walking distance of the town; prices are from £17 to £22 per person.

The *Aviemore Guest House* (☎ 223052, *28 Fishmarket Rd*) is close to the town centre and has rooms from £16 to £20 per person, some with bathroom.

The *Regent Motel* (☎ 225884, 42 Cinque Ports St) is conveniently situated and has private parking and rooms with bathroom for £20/32 (without breakfast).

The *Old Vicarage Hotel & Restaurant* (☎ 225131, East St) is a Queen Anne house with spacious and attractive rooms, some with four-poster beds, all with bathroom; from £35 to £42 per person.

Places to Eat

There's a surprisingly diverse range of eateries for a small English town.

The best pub grub is at *The Strand*, near the TIC on the street of the same name. Garlic mussels are £5.95, a salmon steak is £6.95. The *Union Inn* on East St also has some interesting dishes – roast partridge for £7.50 or squirrel pie at £5.45. The *Bell Inn* in The Mint and the *Ypres Castle* in Gun Gardens have nice outdoor areas.

There are numerous teashops. For the ultimate in decadence try the chocolate fudge cake – three huge layers for £3.25 – at the *Peacock* in Lion St. Full meals are also available here.

For a splurge, the three-course set lunches (£16) at the *Mermaid Inn* (see Places to Stay) are very good, and the setting couldn't be more atmospheric. However, the top restaurant in town is the *Landgate Bistro* (☎ 222829, 5/6 Landgate), which specialises in local ingredients. Open evenings only from Thursday to Tuesday, there's a set menu for £15.90 (three courses and coffee). It's popular at weekends, so book if possible.

If you're self-catering there's a *Budgens supermarket* near the train station.

Getting There & Away

Rye is only 1½ hours from London's Charing Cross, via Ashford. Trains leave Ashford hourly from Monday to Saturday and there are five services on Sunday. The service continues to Hastings. See the Dover Getting There & Away section.

Stagecoach East Kent runs an hourly bus service (No 711) between Dover and Brighton via Hythe, Rye and Hastings. Local Rider No 344/345 links Rye with Hastings. Many sights are close, so a shared taxi (about £13 to Hastings) is worth considering.

Try Rye Motors Taxis (☎ 223176) or Rother (☎ 224554). Alternatively, you could rent bikes – from around £8 per day from Rye Hire (☎ 223033), Cyprus Place.

BATTLE

- pop 5000   ☎ 01424

1066 and all that … Battle, 6 miles north of Hastings, is built on the site where Duke William of Normandy defeated Harold II in the last successful invasion of Britain. The town is surprisingly unspoilt and attractive considering the number of visitors it attracts. The highlight of any visit is the 1½ mile walk around the battlefield.

Orientation & Information

The train station is a short walk to the southeast of High St, but is well signposted. There's an excellent TIC (☎ 773721) on High St, open daily during summer from 10 am to 6 pm and during winter from 10 am to 4 pm.

Battlefield & Battle Abbey

It is known that Harold's army arrived first on the scene of the Battle of Hastings and occupied a strong defensive position. There were around 7000 infantry and archers, making one of the most formidable armies of the time.

On 14 October, hearing of Harold's arrival, William marched north from Hastings and took up a position about 400m south of the English. His army was also around 7000 men, but included 2000 to 3000 cavalry.

William's forces made several unsuccessful uphill attacks against the English shield wall; then the knights feigned retreat, drawing many English after them. Volleys of arrows caused more English casualties and, finally, Harold was struck in or near the eye. While he tried to pull the arrow from his head he was struck down by Norman knights. At the news of his death the last of the English resistance collapsed.

Construction of the abbey began in 1070 and it was occupied by Benedictines until the Dissolution in 1539. Only foundations of the church can now be seen and the altar's position is marked by a plaque, but quite a few monastic buildings survive. In the gatehouse there's an interesting audio-visual display and museum relating to the daily life of a monastery.

Battle Abbey and Battlefield (☎ 773792, EH) is open daily, from 10 am to 6 pm (4 pm November through March). Entry, including the abbey, is £3/1 plus £1 for the audio tour. An excellent guidebook is available.

Places to Stay & Eat

There are not many cheap places to stay within easy walking distance, so it may be preferable to use Hastings as a base.

The *Old School Cottage* (☎ 773825, 66A High St) is a delightful place to stay but there's just one bedroom, with a four-poster bed and bathroom, for £20 per person. *High Hedges* (☎ 774140, 28 North Trade Rd) is about a 10 minute walk from the TIC and has rooms for £18/32.

Two miles north-west of Battle at Netherfield (on the B2096), *Netherfield Hall* (☎ 774450), opposite the church and a mile from the village inn, has comfortable double rooms; £30 to £40.

Senlac Park (☎ 773969, Main Rd, Cats-field) is a camp site within sight of the abbey; tents or vans are £7.50 a night.

Getting There & Away

Battle is on the main train line between London's Charing Cross and Hastings; there are numerous services. A cheap day return from London is £13.90. The National Express London to Hastings service (No 067) passes through Battle.

From Battle you can reach Pevensey (45 minutes) and Bodiam (20 minutes) on East-bourne Buses' irregular No 19 service. Local Rider service No 4/5 runs hourly to Hastings and Maidstone.

HASTINGS

• **pop 82,000   ☎ 01424**

When people think of English seaside towns, Hastings is unlikely to spring to mind

---

The 1066 Country Walk

Britain's newest footpath, the 1066 Country Walk, opened in late 1997. Walking the 31 mile path is an excellent way to get the history of this area into per-spective.

The path begins (or ends) in Pevensey, at the castle. It's then a seven mile walk to Herstmonceux Castle, and a further eight miles to Battle. A further 15 miles brings you to Rye, but halfway along this section is a side route down to Hastings.

A leaflet showing the route and listing places to stay along the way is available free from TICs.

---

in the same way that places like Brighton, Eastbourne and Blackpool do, but it is nonetheless a classic. It still attracts 3½ million people a year – so there *must* be something going for it. It's a very English place, a down-to-earth family resort with lots of touristy things to do and, perhaps what is most surprising, a peculiar charm. There's also a thriving community of artists, writers and various 'fringe dwellers'.

It can seem a contradictory place, partly because several different Hastings from several historical periods survive cheek by jowl. Along the coast there's a long stretch of tackiness – mostly run-down Regency/ Victorian guesthouses, the inevitable fun parks and a pier. At the eastern end of town, below the castle, you'll find an atmospheric Old Town and the Stade, a beach that is tangled with nets, winches and working fishing boats.

Orientation & Information

In response to the new fad for the seaside, St Leonards was founded to the west of Hastings in 1827. It's a planned resort, with some impressive, if crumbling, architecture. Moving eastwards, there's a pier, the town centre with the train station and main bus stops, West Hill, with the ruined castle, the

Old Town and the Stade and, finally, East Hill, with good walks in the Country Park.

Hastings Information Centre (☎ 781111), beside the town hall at Priory Meadow, is open daily from 9.30 am to 5 pm (from 10 am on Sunday). There's another branch on the foreshore near the Stade.

There's a laundrette on High St opposite the Museum of Local History, and a Marks & Spencer food store in the Priory Meadow shopping centre.

The Stade

The bustling activity on the Stade creates one of the most memorable sights on the south coast. Fishing has increasingly become a high-tech industry requiring ocean-going vessels, so a large fleet of small boats is a rarity. There have been several failed attempts to build a harbour, so the fishermen must still haul their luggers onto the Stade. Winches, housed in small shacks, now do the hard work.

Farther behind the Stade are the unique three-storey, wood-and-tar sheds known as net shops. Dating from the 16th century, although most are now modern constructions, they were built high to minimise the ground rent the fishermen had to pay. There are now a number of shops selling fresh fish and crabs and along Rock-A-Nore Rd, places offering traditional delicacies like jellied eels (£1.50, and something you'll probably want to try only once), cockles, whelks and mussels.

The Fishermen's Museum (☎ 461446), Rock-A-Nore Rd, is housed in what was the fishermen's chapel, built in 1854. Open daily from 10 am to 5 pm, entry is free. Nearby attractions are a Sea Life Centre (☎ 718776) and the Shipwreck Heritage Centre (☎ 437452).

The East Hill Lift (cliff railway) is one of the steepest in Britain and runs from near the Fishermen's Museum to the Country Park. It's open all year except January, from 10 am to 5.30 pm (shorter hours in winter); 70p/40p.

West Hill

It is believed William erected a prefabricated wooden castle here before the Battle of Hastings. The surviving fragmentary remains of Hastings Castle date from after the battle, but there are good views and an audiovisual presentation, the 1066 Story.

The castle is open all year, from Easter to September, 10 am to 5 pm, and from October to April, 11 am to 3.30 pm; £2.90/1.90. Combined entry to the tunnels and caves of the entertaining Smuggler's Adventure attraction is £6.25/3.80.

The West Hill Lift (cliff railway) gives easy access (70p/40p).

The Pier

Hastings Pier is an honest, unpretentious pier and, electric fruit machines and laser games aside, it hasn't made much effort to keep up with the 20th century.

Places to Stay

Camping Shearbarn Holiday Park (☎ 423583) has a great location in the hills to the east of town, about 1½ miles from the Old Town. It's a large park and the summer charge for two backpackers and a tent is £8.

Hostel There's a youth hostel (☎ 812373), but it's definitely not located with convenience in mind. It's on the west side of the main road (A259) to Rye, north of the White Hart pub at Guestling Hill; the nightly charge is £8.80/5.95 for adults/juniors and camping is £4 per person. Stagecoach South Coast bus No 711 from Dover to Brighton via Hastings passes it; it stops at Hastings train station.

B&B & Hotels Pissarro's (☎ 421363, 9 South Terrace) is convenient for the train station and has a good bar and restaurant attached. A basic single costs £16.50. With shower, rooms are £19.50/38. Breakfast is included and there's also a 10% discount off the à la carte menu in the restaurant.

For a sea view, try the Marina Lodge Guest House (☎ 715067, 123 Marina St, St Leonards) – although it's about a mile west of the pier. It's a small, pleasant place with B&B from £16 per person, or £20 with bathroom.

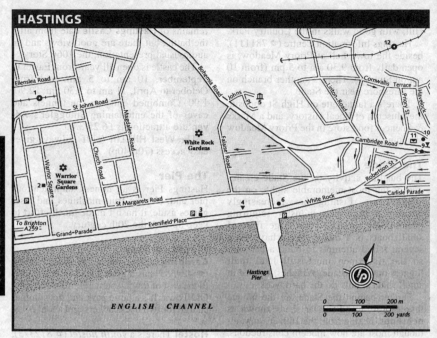

HASTINGS

Ellenslea Road

St Johns Road

Magdalen Road

Warrior Square Gardens

Church Road

St Margarets Road

To Brighton A259

Grand-Parade

Eversfield Place

Bohemia Road

Johns

White Rock Gardens

Falaise Road

White Rock

Hastings Pier

ENGLISH CHANNEL

Cornwallis Terrace

Linton Road

Priory St

Havelock

Cambridge Road

Robertson St

Carlisle Parade

0   100   200 m
0   100   200 yards

Charging £13 to £15 per person, **Tudor Guest House** (☎ 424485, 191 Bexhill Rd) is good value but far from the centre on the west side of town.

Warrior Square Gardens, with its bandstand, is the formal centrepiece of St Leonards. It's surrounded by hotels, including the **Windsor Hotel** (☎ 422709), with singles/doubles for £19/38 (£43 for a double with bathroom).

Nearer to town, the **Mayfair Hotel** (☎ 434061, 9 Eversfield Place, St Leonards) is a traditional B&B; some rooms have bathrooms; rates range from £18 to £25 per person. Similar rates apply at the **Waldorf** (☎ 423771) and the **Gainsborough** (☎ 434010), both on Carlisle Parade.

There are several guesthouses and hotels tucked away in the Old Town. Dating from the 16th century, **Lavender & Lace** (☎ 716290, 106 All Saints St) is an attractive

place with three rooms from £18 per person. **Jenny Lind Hotel** (☎ 421392, 69 High St) has double rooms with a bath for £20 per person. **Lionsdown House** (☎ 420802, 116 High St) has three rooms from £20.50 per person. It's a medieval building with exposed beams and inglenook fireplaces.

Places to Eat

Fresh seafood is the most appropriate choice, and there are plenty of places selling fish and chips, particularly in the Old Town and along towards Rock-A-Nore Rd.

There are a number of interesting old pubs on George St in the Old Town: the 400-year-old **Anchor Inn** has live music in the evening and **Ye Olde Pump House** is also an atmospheric old place. **The First In Last Out**, on High St, is known as the Filo; it brews its own beer and serves interesting

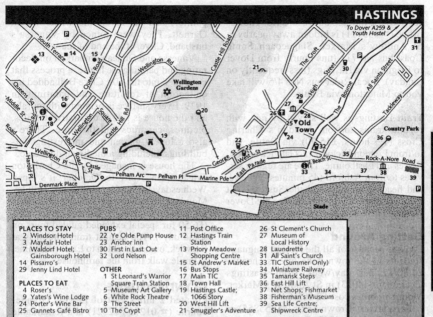

HASTINGS

PLACES TO STAY
- 2 Windsor Hotel
- 3 Mayfair Hotel
- 7 Waldorf Hotel; Gainsborough Hotel
- Pissarro's
- 29 Jenny Lind Hotel

PLACES TO EAT
- 4 Roser's
- 9 Yates's Wine Lodge
- 24 Porter's Wine Bar
- 25 Gannets Café Bistro

PUBS
- 22 Ye Olde Pump House
- 23 Anchor Inn
- 30 First in Last Out
- 32 Lord Nelson

OTHER
- 1 St Leonard's Warrior Square Train Station
- 5 Museum; Art Gallery
- 6 White Rock Theatre
- 8 The Street
- 10 The Crypt
- 11 Post Office
- 12 Hastings Train Station
- 13 Priory Meadow Shopping Centre
- 15 St Andrew's Market
- 16 Bus Stops
- 17 Main TIC
- 18 Town Hall
- 19 Hastings Castle; 1066 Story
- 20 West Hill Lift
- 21 Smuggler's Adventure
- 26 St Clement's Church
- 27 Museum of Local History
- 31 All Saint's Church
- 33 TIC (Summer Only)
- 34 Miniature Railway
- 35 Tamarisk Steps
- 36 East Hill Lift
- 37 Net Shops; Fishmarket
- 38 Fisherman's Museum
- 39 Sea Life Centre; Shipwreck Centre

lunches. Near the Stade, the **Lord Nelson** is a convenient pub with outside seating.

Bar meals at **Pissarro's** (see Places to Stay) are good value – £4.95 for spicy Mexican beef or mushroom tagliatelle. There's live jazz/blues here most weeks from Thursday to Sunday.

There are a few restaurants along George St and on High St. **Porters Wine Bar** (☎ 427000, 56 High St) has reasonably priced meals; main courses are around £5. **Gannets Café Bistro** (☎ 439678), at No 53, is good value and open for breakfast (£3). At 69 High St, the **Jenny Lind Hotel** has bar food and a restaurant serving good fish dishes. Back in the centre of town, on Cambridge Rd, there's a branch of **Yates's Wine Lodge**.

The top place to eat is **Roser's** (☎ 712218, 64 Eversfield Place), near the pier. Home-smoked meats (eg wild boar) and fish feature on the menu and there are three-course set

lunches (£18.95) and dinners (£21.95), Tuesday to Friday; à la carte only on Saturday. It's closed Sunday and Monday.

Entertainment

There's plenty of live music in Hastings. **The Crypt** club (☎ 444675, Havelock Rd) has interesting music nearly every night. **The Street** (☎ 424458, 53 Robertson St) has live jazz on Tuesday evening and a varied mix the rest of the week.

Getting There & Away

The countryside east to Rye is attractive and the coast has some dramatic cliffs. To the west it's basically a flat and continuously developed strip of beach without much interest.

Bus There's no bus station, so when you buy your ticket you need to check where your bus will stop. Most National Express services use the stop on Queens Rd. The bus office (☎ 433711) is hidden away nearby in St Andrew's Market. Stagecoach South Coast bus No 711 runs hourly from Dover to Brighton via Hastings (less frequently on Sunday). Local Rider bus Nos 4/5 will take you to Maidstone via Battle.

Train Hastings is well served by rail, with regular trains to/from London's Charing Cross (1½ hours, £15.90) via Battle, and to/from London Victoria via Gatwick airport, Lewes and Eastbourne. There are regular services to/from Ashford (45 minutes) via Rye, and heading west around the Sussex coast from Hastings to Portsmouth. See the Dover Getting There & Away section.

Getting Around

Perhaps because of all the foreign language students in the town, bike hire is cheap – £1.80/12 per day/week from Hastings Cycles (☎ 444013) in St Andrew's Market. Mountain bikes cost £2.50/16.80.

For a taxi try Crown Taxis (☎ 855855) or Thomas Taxis (☎ 424216).

BEACHY HEAD

The chalk cliffs at Beachy Head are the southern end of the South Downs. Completely sheer, 175m-high coastal cliffs would be awe-inspiring enough in themselves, but when they are chalk white and backed by emerald green turf they are breathtaking.

There's a countryside centre (☎ 01323-737273), car park and restaurant above Beachy Head. Better than coming by car, you could walk the 3 miles along the South Downs Way from the engagingly geriatric seaside town of Eastbourne.

CHARLESTON FARMHOUSE

Charleston (☎ 01323-811265) is a fascinating memorial to the Bloomsbury Group. It's a Tudor/Georgian farmhouse at the foot of the South Downs, just south of the A27 between Lewes and Eastbourne. Vanessa Bell (Virginia Woolf's sister, and an important painter) moved into the farmhouse in

1916 with her lover Duncan Grant (another painter) and his lover, the writer David Garnett. They were joined by Vanessa's husband, Clive, at the end of the war.

Vanessa and Duncan embarked on decorating and painting the house, a process that continued into the 60s. Clive Bell added his collection of furniture and paintings in 1939. Every surface is painted with murals, and the house is full of decorative textiles, pictures, ceramics and furniture. There's also a lovely garden and interesting outbuildings, including a medieval dovecote.

The house is managed by the Charleston Trust; from April to October it's open Wednesday to Sunday (and Bank Holiday Mondays) from 2 to 5 pm but ring in advance as schedules change. Admission is £5/3 (£6.50 for special extended guided tours on some days). The nearest train station is at Berwick, on the Brighton to Eastbourne line, a 2 mile walk from the farmhouse.

GLYNDEBOURNE

Located 2 miles east of Lewes, Glyndebourne (☎ 01273-812321) is a remarkable English phenomenon. In 1934, John Christie, a science teacher from Eton, inherited a large Tudor mansion and indulged both his, and his opera singer wife's, love of opera by building an opera house – in the middle of nowhere. It is now internationally famous; seats range from £21 to £118 in summer, or £10 if you're happy to stand. In the autumn it's just £3 to stand, and seats are from £10 to £50.

The season runs from May until October, with performances beginning around 6 pm. There is a long supper interval when patrons have champagne picnics on the lawns (bring your own, or there is a buffet). Private transport is essential.

NEWHAVEN

Most British ferry ports are unpleasant, depressing places and Newhaven has the unfortunate distinction of being one of the worst. Since it is linked by train to London (58 miles, 1¼ hours), by boat to Dieppe, France (65 miles, four hours), and by bus to

Smuggling on the South Coast

Smuggling in England has a long history, presumably beginning in the 13th century when Edward I first imposed duties on exported wool and imported wine. His motives were straightforward – he wanted the money. Enterprising sailor/merchants, especially those placed close to the coast of France in Kent and Sussex, immediately seized the opportunity to make profits by avoiding the Crown's tax.

A system of enforcing the customs laws was not established until 1680, when sloops were introduced to patrol the coast. The customs officers were, however, poorly paid, especially in comparison to the fortunes being earned by smugglers, so there was soon widespread corruption.

The general public was inclined to look on smugglers at worst as honest thieves, at best as romantic heroes who provided struggling folk with cheap goods. They called the smugglers *owlers*, since they often used imitation owl calls to communicate at night. Whole communities cooperated by building tunnels to link cellars and trapdoors to join attics so that contraband could be whisked from one end of a village to the other under the noses of the law.

In Elizabethan times, wool and guns from the Wealden fields and foundries were smuggled out and wine was smuggled in. As the taxes broadened, so did the smugglers' shopping lists, until they finally included spirits, tobacco, tea, coffee, chocolate and silk. From 1614 to 1825 the export of wool was actually forbidden altogether, which was a great boost to the smugglers' business.

They used small swift craft to transport their goods and to outpace the law. In East Kent, Deal Galleys (powered by oarsmen) were famous for their speed. Such was Prime Minister William Pitt's frustration that in 1784 – and again in 1812 – he ordered all Deal Galleys to be burnt.

Large-scale, community-sanctioned smuggling dwindled after 1832 when a new and more efficient coastguard was established and the newfangled idea of free trade led to reduced duties. It is difficult to say what the current situation is. Certainly, the bales of marijuana that occasionally wash up on the coast are not figments of anyone's imagination. The demand is there, and if someone has a boat and the right contacts, so is the ability.

Corruption, at least in some countries, is rife. And among a fairly wide section of society the smuggler is likely to be seen, at worst, as an honest thief…

'Them that asks no questions isn't told a lie,
Watch the wall, my darling, while the Gentlemen go by'

SOUTH-EASTERN ENGLAND

Brighton (8 miles, service No 712), there is absolutely no need to eat there, let alone stay.

See the introductory Getting There & Away chapter for information on ferries to/from Newhaven.

LEWES
- **pop 15,376**   ☎ 01273

Lewes, an attractive old town that occupies a ridge above the River Ouse, is the administrative capital of East Sussex. An important Norman castle was constructed soon after the invasion, but it fell into disuse in the mid-14th century.

From 1768 to 1774, Thomas Paine, the author of *The Rights of Man* and *The Age of Reason*, lived in The Bull on High St (now Bull House, opposite St Michael's) and for a time he was married to the daughter of the publican. Paine was eventually sacked from his job as an excise officer, his marriage collapsed and he went to America. His books advocated universal voter franchise, a progressive income tax, old age pensions, family allowances and a national system of education!

Much of the town is Georgian, but there are also much older styles (sometimes hidden behind Georgian façades). A large variety of materials have been used – timber beams, brick, flint, stone, weatherboards and wooden tiles – creating an absorbing architectural mosaic.

Orientation & Information

Lewes was an important river port and there are still warehouses (and Harvey's, the brewery) along the river. The town is built on a steep ridge between the river and the castle ruins, with High St climbing the spine and a number of *twittens* (steep streets and passages) running off it.

The TIC (☎ 483448), 187 High St, is open Monday to Friday from 9 am to 5 pm, Saturday from 10 am to 5 pm and Sunday from 10 am to 2 pm; there are reduced hours in winter. Pick up the free *Town Guide*, which includes a walking tour.

There's a Safeway supermarket near Phoenix Causeway, and an interesting collection of craft shops in the Old Needlemakers, West St.

Lewes Castle & Museum

The ruins of the castle date back to the 12th century. There isn't much left, but the views make a visit memorable. The adjacent museum portrays the impact on the region of various invaders and has a collection of prehistoric, Roman, Saxon and medieval objects. Don't miss the **Lewes Living History Model**, an entertaining 22 minute audiovisual introduction to the town and its history.

The complex (☎ 486290) is open all year, Monday to Saturday from 10 am to 5.30

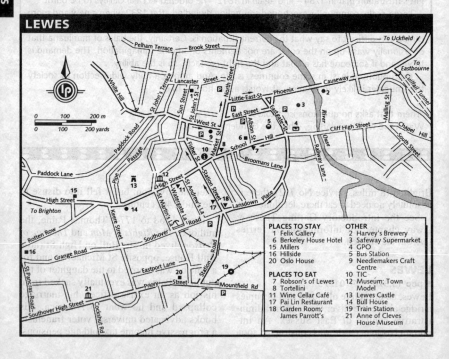

LEWES

To Uckfield
To Eastbourne

Pelham Terrace — Brook Street
Lancaster Street
White Hill
St John's Terrace
St John's St
Sun Street
North Street
Little East St
Phoenix
Causeway
Guilfail Tunnel
Malling St
River Ouse
Cliff High Street
Chapel Hill
South Street
West St
East Street
East St
Albion St
Market St
High St
School Hill
Broomans Lane
Railway Lane
Paddock Road
Pipe Passage
Fisher St
Station Street
St Andrew's La
Paddock Lane
High Street
St Waterate La
Lansdown Place
Keere Street
St Martin's La
Road
To Brighton
Rotten Row
Grange Road
Southover
Eastport Lane
Priory Street
Mountfield Rd
Southover High Street
Cockshut Rd
St Pancras Road

0   100   200 m
0   100   200 yards

PLACES TO STAY
1 Felix Gallery
6 Berkeley House Hotel
15 Millers
16 Hillside
20 Oslo House

PLACES TO EAT
7 Robson's of Lewes
8 Tortellini
11 Wine Cellar Café
17 Pai Lin Restaurant
18 Garden Room;
   James Parrott's

OTHER
2 Harvey's Brewery
3 Safeway Supermarket
4 GPO
5 Bus Station
9 Needlemakers Craft
   Centre
10 TIC
12 Museum; Town
   Model
13 Lewes Castle
14 Bull House
19 Train Station
21 Anne of Cleves
   House Museum

pm, Sunday from 11 am to 5.30 pm; £3.40/1.80. It is possible to buy a combined ticket that includes Anne of Cleves House Museum for £4.50/2.50.

Anne of Cleves House Museum

Anne of Cleves House (☎ 474610), Southover High St, dates back at least to the early 16th century; it was given to Anne of Cleves by Henry VIII as part of the settlement for their divorce.

It now houses a folk museum that includes all sorts of amazing things. At the prosaic end of the spectrum there's furniture, toys, musical instruments, odds and ends, and an extensive collection relating to the Sussex iron industry. At the fantastical end, there's a witch's effigy (complete with pins) and an ancient marble tabletop which miraculously prevented Archbishop Becket's murderers eating from it.

Both the house and the museum are highly recommended; entry is £2.20/1.10, or £4.50/2.50 including Lewes Castle. Anne of Cleves House is open from March through November, Monday to Saturday from 10 am to 5 pm, Sunday from noon to 5 pm.

Places to Stay

Reflecting Lewes' status as a tourist backwater, there is not a huge range of choice, and what there is isn't cheap. At *Felix Gallery* (☎ 472668, 2 Sun St) there's one single (£26) and one twin room (£40). *Oslo House* (☎ 473263, 15 Priory St) has just one twin room (£44). *Bailiwick* (☎ 474377, 15 Cranedown St) and *Hillside* (☎ 473120, Rotten Row) charge £19 to £25 per person.

The choice is more interesting if you can afford to pay a little more. The *Berkeley House Hotel* (☎ 476057, 2 Albion St) is a carefully restored Georgian town house; singles/doubles are £47/55. *Millers* (☎ 475631, 134 High St) is a 16th century timber-framed town house with two doubles with bathrooms (£50, non-smoking).

Places to Eat

Robson's of Lewes (☎ 480654, 22A High St, School Hill)* is a good coffee shop that

---

Bonfire Night

On 5 November 1605 Guy Fawkes was caught attempting to blow up the Houses of Parliament in order to replace the Protestant king with a Catholic monarch. In celebration of this narrow escape, bonfires are lit each year on this day all over the country and effigies of Guy Fawkes consigned to the flames to the popular chant of:

Remember, remember the fifth of November
The Gunpowder Treason and Plot
I see no reason why Gunpowder Treason should ever be forgot.
Guy Fawkes, Guy Fawkes 'twas his intent
To blow up the King and the Parliament
Three score barrels were laid below to prove old England's overthrow.
By God's mercy he was catched
With a dark lantern and burning match
Holler boys, holler boys, let the bells ring.
   Holler boys, holler boys, God save the King.

Lewes has long had a reputation for putting on a far more impressive show than any other town in the country. There are six Bonfire Societies which compete to put on the best show, with processions in fancy dress, flaming tar barrel races and firework displays. If 5 November falls on a Sunday the event takes place a day early; otherwise it's always on 5 November. A pamphlet issued by Lewes District Council helpfully advises that you 'do not wear easily inflammable clothing'!

---

also serves snacks and ice cream. For baguettes with interesting fillings (eg Cajun chicken and lime, £2.79) try *Wine Cellar Café* on the High St.

Tortellini (☎ 487766, 197 High St) is a stylish Italian place with good-value set meals. The express lunch is £2.95; there are pizzas from £5.50.

There are several places to eat on Station St. At No 20 is the Thai *Pai Lin Restaurant* (☎ 473906). At No 14 is *The Garden Room Café-Gallery* (☎ 478636), a relaxed place for coffee and light meals. *James Parrott's Continental Cafe* (☎ 472223) is next door and similar. A ciabatta sandwich here is £2.20.

Getting There & Away
Lewes is 50 miles from London, 9 from Brighton and 16 from Eastbourne.

Bus South Coast buses (☎ 474747) has a frequent service to Brighton (No 28) for £2.40 return. The No 729 runs hourly between Brighton and Royal Tunbridge Wells via Lewes.

Train Lewes is well served by rail, being on the main line between London Victoria (55 minutes, £13.20) and Eastbourne (20 minutes, £4.20) and on the coastal link between Eastbourne and Brighton (15 minutes, £2.50).

BRIGHTON
* pop 180,000 ☎ 01273

'How did England ever produce a town with the fizz and craziness of Brighton? It is a marvellous mystery – like a family of duffers producing a babe of Mozartian genius', says author Nigel Richardson in his very readable *Breakfast in Brighton – Adventures on the Edge of Britain.*

Brighton is deservedly Britain's number one seaside town – a fascinating mixture of seediness and sophistication. Londoners have been travelling here since the 1750s, when a shrewd doctor suggested that bathing in, and drinking, the local sea water was good for them. It's still fine to swim here, though a little on the cool side and the pebble beach comes as a bit of a shock if you're used to fine, Caribbean sand. Drinking the sea water, however, is definitely not recommended.

The essential flavour of the town dates from the 1780s when the dissolute, music-loving Prince Regent (later George IV) built his outrageous summer palace for lavish parties by the sea. Brighton still has some of the hottest clubs and venues outside London, including the largest gay club on the south coast, a vibrant population of students, excellent shopping, a thriving arts scene and countless restaurants, pubs and cafés.

Orientation & Information
Brighton train station is a 15 minute walk north of the beach. When you leave the station, go straight down the hill along Queen's Rd. The interesting part of Brighton lies to the left. When you reach the major intersection at the clock tower, turn left into North St, which will take you down towards the Royal Pavilion. To get to the briny and unmistakable Palace Pier, continue down North St and turn right into Old Steine (it's a road and it's pronounced steen).

West of Brighton, and now part of the same administrative unit, is slightly snobbish Hove. It's jokingly referred to as 'Hove Actually' in Brighton because most Hove residents when asked where they live will reply, 'Hove, actually', to emphasise that they don't live in Brighton!

The tiny bus station is tucked in a small square sandwiched between the beach and Palace Pier (south) and the main traffic roundabout (north) formed by Old Steine. There's an information/booking office for buses on Old Steine. The TIC (☎ 292599), 10 Bartholomew Square, is open Monday to Friday from 9 am to 5 pm, Saturday from 10 am to 5 pm and, in summer, on Sunday from 10 am to 4 pm. Copies of Brighton's listings magazine, *The Latest*, are available.

For information on Brighton's thriving gay scene, visit Pure Café Bar (☎ 692457), 50 George St.

There's a branch of American Express at 82 North St (☎ 321242). Bubbles Laundrette is at 75 Preston St and there's a Safeway on St James St. To collect your email, try Cybar (☎ 384282), 9 Middle St, or Surfers@Paradise (☎ 684184), 18A Bond St.

To park in the central part of Brighton (£1 per hour) you need to buy vouchers – sold in many shops.

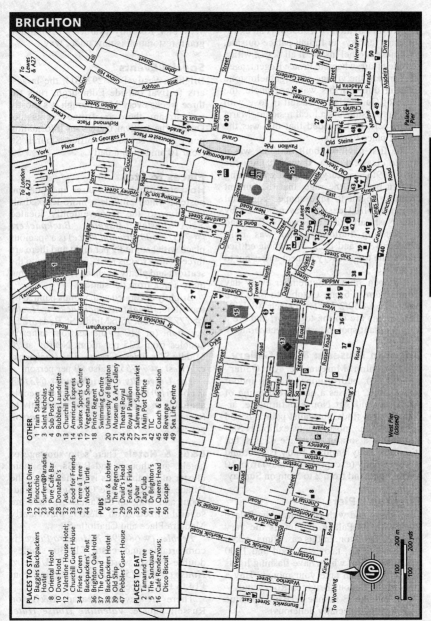

BRIGHTON

SOUTH-EASTERN ENGLAND

PLACES TO STAY
7 Baggies Backpackers Hostel
8 Oriental Hotel
10 Dove Hotel
12 Valentine House Hotel; Churchill Guest House
34 Friese Green Backpackers' Rest
36 Brighton Oak Hotel
37 The Grand
38 Backpackers Hostel
39 Old Ship
47 Pebbles Guest House

PLACES TO EAT
2 Tamarind Tree
5 The Sanctuary
16 Café Rendezvous; Disco Biscuit
19 Market Diner
22 Pinocchio
23 Surfers@Paradise
26 Pure Café Bar
28 Donatello's
32 Ask
33 Food for Friends
43 Terre à Terre
44 Mock Turtle

PUBS
6 Lion & Lobster
11 The Regency
29 Druid's Head
30 Font & Firkin
35 Cybar
40 Zap Club
41 Dr Brighton's
46 Queens Head
50 Escape

OTHER
1 Train Station
3 Saint Nicholas
4 Sub Post Office
9 Bubbles Laundrette
13 Churchill Square
14 American Express
15 Sussex Sports Centre
17 Vegetarian Shoes
18 Prince Regent Swimming Centre
20 University of Brighton
21 Museum & Art Gallery
24 Theatre Royal
25 Royal Pavilion
27 Safeway Supermarket
31 Main Post Office
42 TIC
45 Coach & Bus Station
48 Revenge
49 Sea Life Centre

Royal Pavilion

The Royal Pavilion (☎ 290900) is an extraordinary fantasy; an Indian palace outside, a Chinese brothel inside. It all began with a seaside affair, when the Prince Regent, aged 21, came to the village of Brighthelmstone to hang out with his wayward uncle, the Duke of Cumberland. He fell in love with both the seaside and a local resident, Maria Fitzherbert, and decided that this was the perfect place to party.

The first pavilion, built in 1787, was a simple classical villa. It wasn't until the early 19th century, when everything Eastern became the rage, that the current creation began to take shape. The final Indian-inspired design was produced by John Nash, architect of Regent's Park and its flanking buildings, and was built between 1815 and 1822. The whole edifice is over the top in every respect and is not to be missed.

It's open June to September every day from 10 am to 6 pm, October to May to 5 pm; price £4.50/2.75. The Queen Adelaide Tea Rooms are on the top floor, and are a very pleasant spot to rest and recuperate.

Brighton Museum & Art Gallery

The Brighton Museum & Art Gallery (☎ 290900), built originally as an indoor tennis court, houses a quirky collection of Art Deco and Art Nouveau furniture, archaeological finds, surrealist paintings and costumes. The most famous exhibit is Salvador Dali's sofa in the shape of lips, but it's often away on loan. Entry is free, and it's open daily (except Wednesday) from 10 am to 5 pm, and from 2 to 5 pm on Sunday.

Brighton's Piers

Open daily and with free entry, the **Palace Pier**, with its Palace of Fun, is the very image of Brighton. In this case, fun is taken to mean funfair, takeaway food and 1000 machines, all of which have flashing lights and all of which take your money. Buy a stick of the famous Brighton Rock candy – check out the E numbers (Brilliant Blue FCF sounds especially delicious).

Farther along the beach is the derelict West Pier. Recently awarded a £20 million grant, restoration is now under way.

Special Events

Brighton Festival (☎ 292961), the largest arts festival outside Edinburgh, runs for three weeks every May; though it's mostly mainstream, there are fringe events too. During the festival there's an information point at the Dome box office, Church St, from 10 am to 6 pm daily.

Places to Stay

Hostels Brighton has three independent hostels, which provide a more relaxed alternative to the inconveniently located YHA hostel. *Baggies Backpackers* (☎ 733740, 33 Oriental Place) is a spacious place with beds at £9 per night and there are three double rooms for £25. It's close to the seafront and plenty of cheap restaurants, but quite a trek from the station.

Brightly decorated with murals painted by travellers, *Brighton Backpackers Hostel* (☎ 777717) is at 75-6 Middle St. Beds are £9 per night (or £10 in the seafront annexe), doubles from £25 per room. Nearby at 20 Middle St is *Friese Green – The Backpacker's Rest* (☎ 747551), also £9 per person.

The *University of Brighton* (☎ 643167, fax 642610) has flats for two to eight people available in various locations from July to September. Prices start at £55 per person per week.

B&Bs & Hotels There's no shortage of hotels, guesthouses and B&Bs. The main cluster of cheap B&Bs is to the east of the Palace Pier. Cross the Old Steine roundabout and walk up St James St; there are several streets with B&Bs, particularly Madeira Place and Charlotte St.

Pebbles (☎ 684898, 8 Madeira Place) is comfortable and costs £18/30 singles/doubles. Also worth trying is *Madeira House* (☎ 681115), at No 14, charging from £14 to £18 per person.

There are several pleasant B&Bs on Russell Square. *Valentine House Hotel*

Looe harbour and village, Cornwall

Cornish pasties

St Michael's Mount, Cornwall

Pulteney Bridge over the River Avon in the beautiful Georgian city of Bath

Pretty Polperro fishing village, Cornwall

Abbey Spire and archway, Bath

Smugglers Cottage

A cottage doorway in summer, Cornwall

(☎ 700800), at No 38, charges £17.50 to £22.50 per person for rooms with a bath. At No 44, **Churchill Guest House** (☎ 700777) is similarly priced.

Decorated with tall mirrors, terracotta pots and stylish furniture, the **Oriental Hotel** (☎ 205050, 9 Oriental Place) is certainly not your average hotel. During the week singles/doubles go for £25/47.50. At weekends it's £25/57.50.

The **Dove Hotel** (☎ 779222, 18 Regency Square) is close to restaurant-filled Preston St and the West Pier. All bedrooms have a bathroom and cost from £35/49.

Centrally located, the **Brighton Oak Hotel** (☎ 220033, West St) was built in the 1930s in Art Deco style and has rooms for £54/64.

The elegant **Grand** (☎ 321188, Kings Rd) was built in the 1860s and completely refurbished following the IRA bombing during the Tory party conference of October 1984. Prices are hefty, with rooms from £145/180. Special offers are available.

The immense and slightly shabby **Old Ship** (☎ 329001) also on Kings Rd, is the doyen of Brighton's hotels. In the 1830s, Thackeray stayed there whilst writing *Vanity Fair*. It costs from £33/66 (minimum of two nights stay in July and August).

Places to Eat

You'll eat well in Brighton and the range and individuality of the city's restaurants has, so far, kept out most of the chain restaurants. Wander around the Lanes or head down to Preston St, which runs back from the seafront near West Pier, and you'll turn up all sorts of interesting, affordable possibilities. If you can't afford to eat well for around £7, buy a hot dog at the pier or throw yourself off the end.

For tea and stickies, the **Mock Turtle** is near the bus station in Pool Valley. The window is piled high with appetising cakes and it's good value. Also recommended are the **Queen Adelaide Tea Rooms** at the Brighton Pavilion.

There are three excellent vegetarian restaurants. Long-running **Food for Friends** (☎ 736236) is at 17 Prince Albert St. The taster plate at £5.20 gives you a portion of all the main dishes and is highly recommended. The **Sanctuary** (☎ 770002, 51 Brunswick St East) is five blocks west of Baggies Backpackers, hardly central, but it's an excellent place to hang out. There's a good vegetarian menu and a cosy bar/music venue downstairs. The top veg restaurant, **Terre à Terre** (☎ 729051), Pool Valley, is so popular you're unlikely to get in without a reservation. It's quite expensive, with main dishes around £8 and the puds ain't cheap (£4.25), but it's certainly recommended.

On Queens Rd, the **Café Rendezvous** may not be very plush but it's excellent value and run by a friendly family. All day breakfasts are £2.60, veg couscous is £4.50 and there are sandwiches for £1. In comparison, **Disco Biscuit** next door seems self-consciously stylish. Milk shakes, snacks and sandwiches are served at comfy sofas.

The **Tamarind Tree** (☎ 298816, 48 Queens Rd) is a cool Caribbean café where the food and the service are absolutely authentic.

There are numerous pizza/pasta places. **Donatello's** (☎ 775477, 1 Brighton Place) is good value, offering a starter and a pizza for £5.95. **Ask** (☎ 710030, 58 Ship St) is smart yet not expensive, with many main courses under £6. **Pinocchio** (☎ 677676, 22 New Rd), near the theatre and the Pavilion, offers a full range of Italian fare at reasonable prices – a three-course dinner is £9.95.

Black Chapati (☎ 699011, 12 Circus Pde, New England Rd) is in an unpleasant part of town about a mile north of the centre, but the food is deservedly famous – a brilliant blend of Asian cuisines. Starters are from £5 and main meals are £9.50 to £11.50.

Surfers@Paradise (☎ 684184, 18A Bond St) is a stylish cybercafé open daily from 10 am to 6 pm and for dinner on Friday and Saturday. There's an open plan kitchen, the music's funky and the food's Pacific Rim – and delicious. The other cybercafé, **Cybar** (☎ 384282, 9 Middle St), is as the name suggests more of a bar than a restaurant; it does good sandwiches, though.

Market Diner, on Circus St, is open 24 hours.

Pubs No pub could be more Brighton than *The Regency*, just off Russell Square. Very plain outside, inside it's pure Regency, like an extension of the Pavilion with its striped green wallpaper and painted cameos. The lunches are very good value.

The *Font & Firkin*, Union St, is a popular pub in the Lanes. It's in a converted church dating from 1688. The *Druid's Head*, Brighton Place, decorated with skulls and votive offerings, is also recommended.

The *Greys* (☎ 680734, 105 Southover St) between Richmond Terrace and Queen's Park Rd due east of the station, is a very pleasant pub with a studenty feel. There's live music on some nights. The *Lion & Lobster*, Sillwood St, is another good pub with live music.

Gay pubs include *Dr Brighton's*, King's Rd, and the *Queen's Head*, on the small side street off Marine Parade. Recognise the bloke on the pub sign here?

Entertainment

Brighton is literally jumping with pubs, bars and clubs, but as always fashion is fickle – check *The Latest* and bar and café walls for places of the moment. All are open until at least 2 am, some as late as 5 am. Entry charges range from £4 to £8.

Some of the long-standing clubs worth investigating include *Zap* (☎ 821588, Kings Rd Arches) midway between the two piers; *Escape* (☎ 606906, 10 Marine Pde); and the more laid-back *Jazz Place* and the studenty *Enigma*, both at 10 Ship St.

Revenge (☎ 606064, 32 Old Steine St) is a gay club with a big sound system, two dance floors, two bars and lots of cabaret.

Things to Buy

Just south of North St (and north of the TIC) you'll find **The Lanes**, a maze of narrow alleyways crammed with jewellery, antique and fashionable clothes shops. Some of the best restaurants and bars are around here, too.

But for trendier, cheaper shops, good cafés and a slightly less touristy feel, explore **North Laine**, a series of streets north of North St, including Bond, Gardner, Kensington and Sydney Sts. On Gardner St visit Vegetarian Shoes for animal-friendly footwear. Check out the flea market on Upper Gardner St on Saturday mornings.

Getting There & Away

Transport to and from Brighton is fast and frequent. See the fares tables in the introductory Getting Around chapter. London is 53 miles away.

Bus National Express has numerous buses from London (£6), and there's a coast link west to Cornwall.

Local bus companies include Brighton & Hove (☎ 886200) and Stagecoach Coastline (☎ 01903-237661).

Train There are over 40 fast trains a day from London Victoria and King's Cross stations (one hour). There are plenty of trains between Brighton and Portsmouth (1½ hours, £11). There are also frequent services to Eastbourne, Hastings, Canterbury and Dover.

Getting Around

Taxi Try Brighton & Hove Radio Cabs (☎ 204060), Southern Taxis (☎ 324555) or Hove Streamline (☎ 202020); rates are £2 for the first mile, £1.20 to 1.40 thereafter.

Bicycle You can hire from Sunrise Cycles (☎ 748881) by West Pier, or Alpine Cycles (☎ 625647), 7 Beaconsfield Rd. Rates start at £10 a day.

West Sussex

West Sussex is not as densely packed with castles and great houses as East Sussex and Kent, but it has some superb countryside and some lovely small villages. Chichester makes a good base for exploring the rolling hills and the small villages that are tucked away within them.

GETTING AROUND

Bus

The major bus operators are National Express (☎ 0990-808080), Brighton & Hove (☎ 01273-886200), Stagecoach Hampshire Bus (☎ 01256-464501), Stagecoach Coastline (☎ 01903-237661) and Stagecoach South Coast (☎ 01273-474747).

Explorer Tickets are accepted by all the main companies in the South East.

Train

Chichester is served by the main line from London Victoria to Portsmouth (via Gatwick airport). Chichester is also on the Sussex coast line that runs west from Hastings to Portsmouth.

ARUNDEL

Arundel is a pleasant little tourist trap at the foot of a romantic-looking castle. Despite its ancient appearance and history, however, most of the town dates from Victorian times. Although neither the town nor the castle are particularly interesting, the town does make a good base (best avoided on summer weekends). The countryside north along the Arun valley and west along the South Downs is among the most beautiful in England.

The TIC (☎ 01903-882268), 61 High St, is open daily in summer. There are numerous B&Bs and hotels. *Arundel Youth Hostel* (☎ *01903-882214*) is 1½ miles from the town.

Rail is definitely the efficient way of getting to/from Arundel; it's 55 miles from London, 20 from Brighton and 11 from Chichester.

CHICHESTER

- **pop 28,000   ☎ 01243**

Chichester is the thriving administrative centre for West Sussex and has been an important town since the time of the Romans. It lies on the flat meadows between the South Downs and the sea and was once a port.

East, West, North and South Sts were laid out by the Romans for their town, Noviomagus, and the foundations for an enormous Roman villa and its beautiful mosaics, survive at Fishbourne on the town outskirts. The Norman castle has long disappeared but the cathedral survives. The City Cross at the centre of town dates from 1501 (built by Bishop Story for the 'comfort of the poore people there') and is one of the finest in the country. A substantial part of the town centre is dominated by classic Georgian architecture.

Orientation & Information

Chichester is a busy shopping town, so it has had to come to grips with a traffic problem – which it has done well. There's a bypass and an inner ring road outside the old city walls with a number of long-stay parking areas along it, all of which are within easy walking distance of the town centre.

The TIC (☎ 775888), 29A South St, is open Monday to Saturday, from 9.15 am to 5.15 pm and, from April to September also on Sunday from 10 am to 4 pm.

There's a Waitrose supermarket near the train station.

Chichester Cathedral

The Chichester Cathedral of today has evolved over 900 years, but it remains substantially Norman, or Romanesque, and is more harmonious in appearance than most other churches of similar antiquity. It is also smaller than some of the more famous cathedrals, but though it is less awe-inspiring, it is also more intimate.

Work began in 1075 and continued for over 100 years – the nave survives; at the beginning of the 13th century the inside of the clerestory, the retrochoir, sacristy and porches were built in the Early English Gothic style; the side chapels and Lady Chapel date from the beginning of the 14th century and are in the Decorated style; and, finally, the cloisters, bell tower and unique detached belfry were built in perpendicular style around the turn of the 15th century.

There are a number of treasures on display in the cathedral and the building's story is best revealed by an expert: guided tours operate from Easter to October, Monday to Saturday at 11 am and 2.15 pm. In particular, don't miss the 16th century

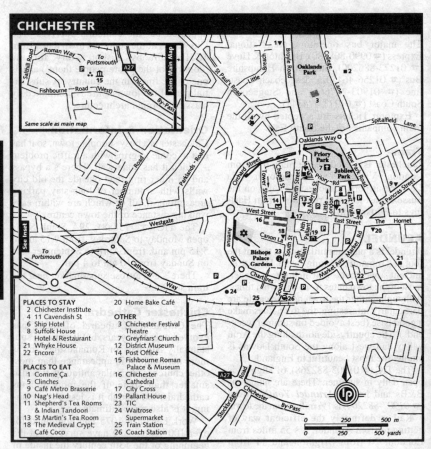

CHICHESTER

PLACES TO STAY
2　Chichester Institute
4　11 Cavendish St
6　Ship Hotel
8　Suffolk House
　　Hotel & Restaurant
21　Whyke House
22　Encore

PLACES TO EAT
1　Comme Ça
5　Clinches
9　Café Metro Brasserie
10　Nag's Head
11　Shepherd's Tea Rooms
　　& Indian Tandoori
13　St Martin's Tea Room
18　The Medieval Crypt;
　　Café Coco

20　Home Bake Café

OTHER
3　Chichester Festival
　　Theatre
7　Greyfriars' Church
12　District Museum
14　Post Office
15　Fishbourne Roman
　　Palace & Museum
16　Chichester
　　Cathedral
17　City Cross
19　Pallant House
23　TIC
24　Waitrose
　　Supermarket
25　Train Station
26　Coach Station

---

paintings by Lambert Barnard, the exquisite 12th century stone carvings, said to be among the finest masterpieces of Romanesque sculpture, the shrine of St Richard, the window designed by Marc Chagall, and the poignant tomb of the Earl of Arundel and his countess. The two are shown holding hands, with their feet resting on their pet dogs (this in 1376) – which inspired Philip Larkin to write *An Arundel Tomb*, but also shows the English have been peculiar about dogs for a long time.

Chichester Cathedral (☎ 782595) is open daily from 7.30 am until 7 pm. It has a fine choir, which sings daily at evensong. Evensong is at 5.30 pm from Monday to Saturday, 3.30 pm on Sunday. Admission to the cathedral is free but there is a suggested donation of £2.

Pallant House

Of the many fine Georgian houses in the town, Pallant House (☎ 774557), 9 North Pallant, is outstanding. It was built by a wealthy wine merchant who spared no expense. It has been carefully restored and now houses an excellent collection of mainly modern, mainly British art. It's open all year, Tuesday to Saturday, from 10 am to 5.30 pm, and afternoons only on Sunday in summer; £2.80/1.70.

Church of the Greyfriars

The Franciscans established a church here in 1269 on the old site of the castle – now Priory Park, in the eastern corner of the town. The simple, but quite beautiful, building which remains was their choir and now overlooks the local cricket pitch. After dissolution in 1538 the building became the guildhall and later a court of law, where William Blake was tried for sedition in 1804.

Special Events

Chichester's Festival Theatre (☎ 781312), built in 1962, is a striking modern building in parkland to the north of the ring road. Sir Laurence Olivier was the theatre's first director and it is now at the centre of an important arts festival, the Chichester Festivities (☎ 780192), held every July.

Places to Stay

From July to September you can stay at the **Chichester Institute** (☎ 816070, College Lane) from £18 per person. There are 100 single rooms, 90 doubles and 20 triples.

For B&B, **Encore** (☎ 528271, 11 Clydesdale Ave) is a short walk from the centre. The rate is from £18 to £21 per person. **11 Cavendish St** (☎ 527387) is a non-smoking B&B, with one double and one single at £17 per person.

Whyke House (☎ 788767, 13 Whyke Lane) is run by a helpful couple who live next door to the guesthouse, which means you can use the fully equipped kitchen if you choose. There is one single room, one double, two twins and a family room, and continental breakfasts are served. The charge is £20 per person with discounts if you stay more than one night.

The Ship (☎ 778000, North St), an attractive hotel dating from the 18th century,

is convenient for the theatre. There are singles/doubles from £52.50/81, and a good restaurant.

Suffolk House Hotel & Restaurant (☎ 778899, 3 East Row) is a Georgian house in the heart of the city with a range of comfortable rooms from £56/84.

Places to Eat

Chichester is well endowed with good restaurants, but it's worth booking at any time during the Chichester Festivities and if you wish to eat after theatre performances.

The best place for a cheap feed is **Home Bake Café**, The Hornet. Its yorkie (Yorkshire pudding), sausage, mash and beans is great value at £3.35 and excellent teas and cakes are also served. **Clinchs Coffee Shop & Restaurant** (☎ 789915, 4 Guildhall St) is a good-value place close to the theatre. Main courses are around £5.50 to £7.95.

If it's a French snack you're after, try **Café Coco** on South St. The coffee's very good here and tasty baguettes – Cajun chicken in a baguette served with chips and salad for £4.95 – are also available. Nearby is **The Medieval Crypt** (☎ 537033), a brasserie/bar in an interesting old building. A steak sandwich is £4.95, roast poussin £6.95.

For tea and cakes in comfortable surroundings there's **St Martin's Tea Room** (☎ 786715, 3 St Martin's St) and **Shepherd's Tea Rooms** (☎ 774761, 35 Little London).

French run **Café Metro Brasserie** (☎ 788771, St Pancras St) does set lunches for £4.50 and there's live jazz on Tuesday evening. The best curry house in town is the **Little London Indian Tandoori** (☎ 537550, 38 Little London). Main dishes are around £4.95. A veg thali is £9.95.

The top restaurant is **Comme Ça** (☎ 788724, 67 Broyle Rd) near the theatre. Cooking is French and main dishes are around £11.50 (eg fillet of beef with a Noilly Prat and Roquefort cream sauce). It's open Tuesday to Saturday and for Sunday lunch (three courses for £16.75).

For a pub meal try the bar in the **Nag's Head** on St Pancras St.

Getting There & Away

Chichester is 60 miles from London, 11 from Arundel and 18 from Portsmouth.

Bus Chichester is served by the Coastline Express (No 700/701) which runs between Brighton (two hours, £3.25) and Portsmouth (one hour), from Monday to Saturday every half-hour; on Sunday every hour.

Train Chichester can be reached easily from London Victoria (1¾ hours, £15.70) on an hourly service via Gatwick airport and Arundel. It's also on the Sussex coast line between Brighton (one hour, twice as fast as the bus; £7.30) and Portsmouth (30 minutes, £4.40).

AROUND CHICHESTER

To the south of Chichester lies the popular Chichester Harbour, with a huge marina and several attractive fishing villages such as Bosham. To the north lie the beautiful South Downs, and several more unspoilt villages – like East and West Dean and Charlton (which is 6 miles from Chichester). *The Fox Goes Free* and *Woodstock House* in Charlton and the *Hurdlemakers* in East Dean are pubs worth looking for.

Fishbourne Roman Palace & Museum

Discovered in 1960, the palace at Fishbourne (☎ 01243-785859), Salthill Rd, is believed to have been built for a local king who allied himself to the Romans. The palace was built and altered in several stages, but the main construction began around 75 AD. It was spectacular in size and luxury – its bathing facilities would still put most contemporary British arrangements to shame. Although all that survives are foundations and some extraordinary mosaic floors, the ruins still convey a vision of 'modern' style and comfort.

The pavilion that shelters the site is an ugly creation, but there are some excellent reconstructions and the garden has been replanted as it would have been in the 1st century. The museum is open all year, with variable hours – May to September from 10 am to 5 pm (to 6 pm in August); admission is £4/2.20.

Getting There & Away The museum is just west of Chichester, north of the A259, off Salthill Rd, signed from Fishbourne village. Regular buses (No 11/700, hourly from Monday to Saturday, No 56 on Sunday) leave from outside the cathedral and stop at the bottom of Salthill Rd (a five minute walk away). The museum is a 10 minute walk from Fishbourne train station, on the line between Chichester and Portsmouth.

Petworth House & Park

Twelve miles north-east of Chichester, Petworth House dates primarily from 1688. The architecture is impressive (especially the west front), but the art collection is extraordinary. JMW Turner was a regular visitor and the house is still home to the largest collection (20) of his paintings outside the Tate Gallery. There are also many paintings by Van Dyck, Reynolds, Gainsborough, Titian and Blake. Petworth is, however, most famous for its park, which is regarded as the supreme achievement of Lancelot (Capability) Brown's natural landscape theory.

The house (☎ 01798-342207, NT) is open April to October, daily except Thursday and Friday, from 1 to 5.30 pm; £5/2.50. The car park and Pleasure Ground, a part of the landscaped grounds that features a number of classical follies, are open from noon to 6 pm. The park is open daily throughout the year from 8 am to sunset; entry is free.

Petworth is 6 miles from the train station at Pulborough. There is a limited bus service (No 1/1A) from the station to Petworth Square, Monday to Saturday.

Hampshire

Hampshire has plenty to slow down visitors on their way to the West Country. First there's Winchester with its important cathedral; then, the important maritime centres of Portsmouth and Southampton; and finally, the beautiful New Forest – the largest remaining relict (ie still original) area of forest in England.

For bus information in Hampshire ring ☎ 01962-868944. The *Public Transport Map of Hampshire* is very useful and stocked by TICs.

WINCHESTER
• pop 37,000   ☎ 01962

Winchester is a beautiful cathedral city with a lovely river and water meadows surrounded by rolling chalk downland. If one place lies at the centre of English history and embodies the romantic vision of the English heartland, it is Winchester. Despite this it seems to have escaped inundation by tourists – certainly by comparison with nearby Salisbury and with theme parks like Bath and Oxford.

An Iron Age hill fort overlooks the city. The Romans built Venta Bulgarum on the present-day site; part of their defensive wall can still be seen incorporated into a later

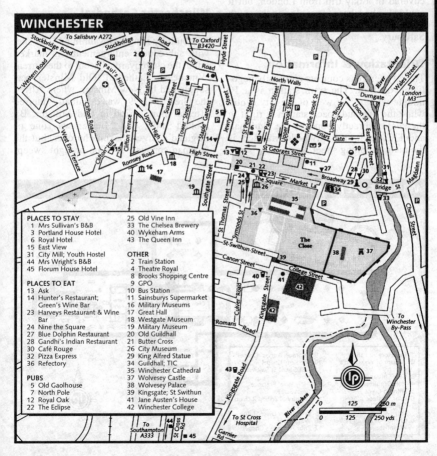

WINCHESTER

PLACES TO STAY
1 Mrs Sullivan's B&B
3 Portland House Hotel
6 Royal Hotel
15 East View
31 City Mill; Youth Hostel
44 Mrs Wright's B&B
45 Florum House Hotel

PLACES TO EAT
13 Ask
14 Hunter's Restaurant;
    Green's Wine Bar
23 Harveys Restaurant & Wine
    Bar
24 Nine the Square
27 Blue Dolphin Restaurant
28 Gandhi's Indian Restaurant
30 Café Rouge
32 Pizza Express
36 Refectory

PUBS
5 Old Gaolhouse
7 North Pole
12 Royal Oak
22 The Eclipse

25 Old Vine Inn
33 The Chelsea Brewery
40 Wykeham Arms
43 The Queen Inn

OTHER
2 Train Station
4 Theatre Royal
8 Brooks Shopping Centre
9 GPO
10 Bus Station
11 Sainsburys Supermarket
16 Military Museums
17 Great Hall
18 Westgate Museum
19 Military Museum
20 Old Guildhall
21 Butter Cross
26 City Museum
29 King Alfred Statue
34 Guildhall; TIC
35 Winchester Cathedral
37 Wolvesey Castle
38 Wolvesey Palace
39 Kingsgate; St Swithun
41 Jane Austen's House
42 Winchester College

medieval defence. Alfred the Great and many of his successors, including Canute and the Danish kings, made Winchester their capital, and William the Conqueror came to the city to claim the crown of England. The Domesday Book was also written here. However, much of the present-day city dates from the 18th century, by which time history had passed Winchester by and the town had settled down as a prosperous market centre.

There are lots of good walks in the surrounding countryside. Winchester can be covered in a day trip from London, but it could also be a base for exploring the south coast or the country farther west towards Salisbury.

Orientation & Information

The city centre is compact and easily negotiated on foot. The train station is a 10 minute walk to the west of the city centre while the bus and coach station is right in the centre, directly opposite the Guildhall and TIC. High St, partly pedestrianised, is the main shopping street.

The TIC (☎ 840500), the Guildhall, Broadway, is open Monday to Saturday, from 10 am to 6 pm and Sunday from 11 am to 2 pm during the June to September peak season. It produces the excellent *Winchester Visitor's Guide* that includes info on sights and places to stay and eat. Regular guided walking tours (£3/50p) operate from April to October, and on Saturday only between November and March.

Motorists are advised to use the park-and-ride car parks (£1.50).

Winchester Cathedral

Winchester's first church, the Old Minster, was built by King Kenwalh in 648. Its site, with subsequent enlargements, is marked out in the churchyard adjacent to the current Winchester Cathedral. Old Minster was supplanted by New Minster, where Alfred the Great (871-99) was eventually interred after a short period in Old Minster. By around 1000, Old Minster was one of England's largest Saxon churches, but the Norman conquest in 1066 brought sweep-

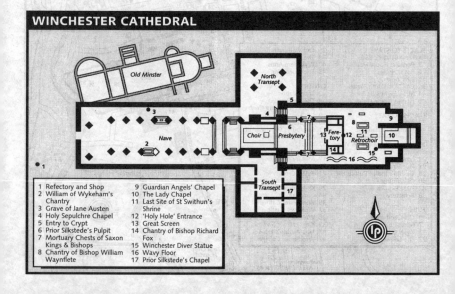

WINCHESTER CATHEDRAL

Old Minster

North Transept

Nave

Choir

Presbytery

Fere-tory

Retrochoir

South Transept

1 Refectory and Shop
2 William of Wykeham's Chantry
3 Grave of Jane Austen
4 Holy Sepulchre Chapel
5 Entry to Crypt
6 Prior Silkstede's Pulpit
7 Mortuary Chests of Saxon Kings & Bishops
8 Chantry of Bishop William Waynflete
9 Guardian Angels' Chapel
10 The Lady Chapel
11 Last Site of St Swithun's Shrine
12 'Holy Hole' Entrance
13 Great Screen
14 Chantry of Bishop Richard Fox
15 Winchester Diver Statue
16 Wavy Floor
17 Prior Silkstede's Chapel

ing changes and the foundations for a new cathedral were laid in 1079.

By 1093 the cathedral was nearly complete; the remains of St Swithun, whose name was attached to the associated monastery, were transferred to the new building and the very next day demolition orders were served on the Old Minster. The New Minster was also demolished, around 1110. The completed cathedral was the longest in Britain at the time but it faced problems, in part due to the soggy ground upon which its inadequate foundations were laid. Plans for towers at the transept ends were soon abandoned and in 1107 the central tower collapsed.

In the 13th century the east end of the cathedral was enlarged and extended in the Early English style to make the retrochoir. The central choir and presbytery were next rebuilt and from the mid-14th century the Norman nave, suffering from severe subsidence, was completely rebuilt in the perpendicular style. The Priory of St Swithun was demolished at the time of the dissolution of the monasteries and the cathedral suffered some damage during the Civil War, but there have subsequently been no major changes.

The cathedral is entered from the west end into the towering nave, which has been described as 'fudged Gothic'. In the north aisle is the **grave of Jane Austen**, who died a stone's throw from the cathedral in 1817. There's a memorial window to her above. The transepts are the most original part of the cathedral and the **Holy Sepulchre Chapel** has wall paintings dating from 1120 and 1240.

Crypt tours normally commence from the north transept but are often suspended if the crypt is flooded. They take place Easter to September, Monday to Saturday, at 10.30 am and 2.30 pm. As an alternative, try the **door** which gives access to the first part of the crypt where a modern statue is displayed.

The choir features amusingly carved wooden choir stalls, the work of William Lyngwode from 1307. King William Rufus was originally buried in the choir but the presence of the unpopular king's tomb was

cited as a reason for the collapse of the tower in 1107. His bones are now believed to be in one of the mortuary chests. The **pulpit** was provided by Prior Silkstede around 1520 and the carved folds of silk are a visual pun on his name!

At the end of the presbytery is the magnificent 15th century **Great Screen**. At the Reformation the figures in the screen were removed and broken up. The current figures are 1890 replacements, which is how Queen Victoria (2nd level, 3rd row from right of minor figures) has managed to sneak in among the Saxon royalty. **Mortuary chests**, high up under the arches on both sides of the presbytery, contain the bones of Saxon royalty (including King Canute) and bishops.

The retrochoir has a number of **chantry chapels**, small chapels each devoted to one person such as Bishop William Waynflete,

Winchester Cathedral

Chancellor of England and founder of Magdalen College, Oxford. The particularly original **Guardian Angels Chapel** has wall paintings dating from 1240. Later paintings can be seen in the **Lady Chapel**, and just outside this chapel is a small **statue** to the memory of William Walker, the diver who spent five years shoring up the submerged cathedral footings early this century. The **wavy floor** each side of the retrochoir is a reminder of the subsidence problems the cathedral faced at this end.

In the middle of the retrochoir is the last **site of St Swithun's shrine**. After his rainy arrival the saint toured around the cathedral in subsequent centuries before Henry VIII's Commission for the Destruction of Shrines got rid of him in 1538. From 1150 to 1476 St Swithun's shrine featured a **Holy Hole**, a tunnel beneath the shrine for keen pilgrims to crawl through. The entrance can still be seen. The **chantry of Bishop Richard Fox** has a skeletal effigy.

In the south transept, **Prior Silkstede's Chapel** has the grave of Izaak Walton (1593-1683) and a window dedicated to this patron saint of the pastime of fishing and author of *The Compleat Angler*. The south transept Library and Triforium Gallery house a display of cathedral treasures including damaged figures from the Great Screen and the illuminated 12th century Winchester Bible. Opening hours are somewhat variable; entry is £1/50p. In the south aisle of the nave is the **chantry of Bishop William of Wykeham**, founder of New College, Oxford, and of Winchester College and also responsible for the nave, although he died in 1404 when it was still under construction.

Tours of the cathedral are run by enthusiastic local volunteers at 11 am and 2 pm daily except Sunday. It's worth going to evensong at 5.30 pm Monday to Saturday or 3.30 pm on Sunday. There are tower tours on Wednesday at 2.15 pm, Saturday at 11.30 am and 2.15 pm (£1.50), and crypt tours at 10.30 am and 2 pm daily except Sunday. The cathedral (☎ 853137) is open daily, from 7.30 am to 6.30 pm and a £2.50 donation is requested.

City Mill

The first bridge across the Itchen at the end of Broadway is credited to St Swithun. Right over the river the City Mill (☎ 870057, NT), which once ground grain for the local bakers, was rebuilt in 1743 although a mill had stood here in medieval times. The mill is open weekends only in March, and April to October, Wednesday to Sunday, from 11 am to 4.45 pm; £1/50p. The building is shared by the youth hostel; check out the old print of the hostel bathing facilities in 1938.

City Museum

The museum (☎ 863064) on The Square has interesting displays on Roman ruins on the top floor, a collection of Winchester shopfronts on the middle floor, and the story of Saxon and Norman Winchester on the ground floor. It's open April to September, Monday to Saturday, from 10 am to 5 pm (closed from 1 to 2 pm on Saturday), and Sunday from 2 to 5 pm. The rest of the year it closes on Monday. Entry is free.

Westgate & Great Hall

The Westgate Museum (☎ 869864) on High St is in the old medieval gateway, at one time a debtors' prison. The displays include a macabre set of gibbeting irons, last used to display the body of an executed criminal in 1777. It's open April to September, Monday to Saturday, from 10 am to 5 pm (closed between 1 and 2 pm on Saturday) and Sunday from 2 to 5 pm. The rest of the year, apart from November to January when it's closed all week, it closes on Monday. Entry is 30p.

Little remains of Winchester Castle, which was begun by William the Conqueror and was the site of many dramatic moments in English history, including the trial of Sir Walter Raleigh in 1603. The Great Hall (☎ 845610) was the only part Oliver Cromwell did not destroy and it houses King Arthur's Round Table, now known to be a fake at 'only' 600 years old. It's open all year, daily from 10 am to 5 pm and to 4 pm at weekends in winter; free.

Rain, Floods & Divers

IN HONOUR
OF
WILLIAM
WALKER
THE DIVER
WHO SAVED
THIS
CATHEDRAL
WITH HIS
TWO HANDS
1906-1912

'William Walker'

Winchester Cathedral is a curiously waterlogged place; to this day the church's crypts are prone to flooding and the subterranean tours are liable to be suspended due to water seeping in after a heavy rainfall. According to legend, St Swithun is the cause of the problem. He insisted that he be buried outside the Old Minster but on 15 July 971, 109 years after his death, his request was forgotten and his remains were moved inside. The deceased saint showed his displeasure with an awesome rainstorm and ever since he has been reputed to have special powers over the English weather. If it rains on 15 July, so the legend goes, it will continue to rain for the next 40 days.

All this rainfall led to serious problems with the cathedral's foundations, which had not been properly seated at the east end. By the early 1900s it was clear there were major problems and it was feared the walls could actually collapse. Since it was impossible to drain out the foundations or to shore them up underwater, it was decided to bring in a deep-sea diver who would dig out the beech-log foundations and repack the area with sacks of cement. From 1906 to 1911 William Walker worked away at rebuilding the waterlogged foundations and the success of his labours is commemorated with a small statue of a diver by the Lady Chapel at the east end. The figure is not of Walker, however. Due to a mix up in the photographs the sculptor produced a likeness of the project's engineer, Francis Fox, rather than the diver!

Wolvesey Castle & Palace

Wolvesey Castle's (☎ 854766, EH) name, so the story goes, comes from a Saxon king's demand for an annual payment of 300 wolves' heads. Commenced in 1107, the castle was completed by Henry de Blois, grandson of William the Conqueror, over half a century later. In the medieval era it was the residence of the Bishop of Winchester when this was the richest bishopric in England. It was largely demolished in

the 1680s and today the bishop lives in the adjacent Wolvesey Palace; £1.80/90p.

A beautiful walk runs alongside the River Itchen to Wolvesey Castle with attractive flower-decked gardens backing the houses on the other side of the river.

Winchester College

Winchester College (☎ 621217) on College St was founded in 1382 by Bishop Wykeham and students are still known as

Wykehamists. It was the model for the great public (meaning private) schools of England. The chapel and cloisters are open to visitors from 10 am to 1 pm and from 2 to 5 pm (except Sunday morning). From April to September, one-hour guided tours leave at 11 am (except Sunday) and 2 and 3.15 pm (£2.50/2).

Water Meadow Walk & St Cross Hospital

From the college there's a beautiful one mile walk to the Hospital of St Cross (☎ 851375), which was founded in 1136. The hospital is the oldest charitable institution in the country and is open April to October, Monday to Saturday from 9.30 am to 5 pm; the rest of the year the hours are from 10.30 am to 3.30 pm. Entry is £2/50p, which entitles you to the Wayfarer's Dole (a crust of bread and horn of ale), sustenance doled out to any itinerant passer-by. St Catherine's Hill, topped by an Iron Age hill-fort site, looks across to the hospital over the bypass and river.

Places to Stay

Camping The *Morn Hill Caravan Club Site* (☎ 869877, *Morn Hill*) is 3 miles east of the city centre off the A31. There are tent sites for £2.50, plus £3.90 per person.

Hostel The *Youth Hostel* (☎ 853723, *City Mill, 1 Water Lane*) is in a beautiful 18th century, restored water mill. From the centre of town walk down High St, which becomes The Broadway, cross the River Itchen and take the first left into Water Lane. The nightly cost is £8.80/5.95 for adults/juniors.

B&Bs & Hotels There are plenty of small B&Bs, most with only one or two rooms. St Cross Rd and parallel Christchurch Rd are good hunting grounds.

Mrs B Sullivan (☎ 862027, *29 Stockbridge Rd*), near the train station, has singles/doubles from £16/28. *Mrs R Wright* (☎ 855067, *56 St Cross Rd*) charges from £18/36. Across the road at No 47 is *Florum*

House Hotel (☎ 840427) with rooms for £42/59 with a bathroom.

Conveniently located, *East View* (☎ 862986, *16 Clifton Hill*) is a small B&B with three comfortable rooms from £35/45. Each room has its own bathroom.

Portland House Hotel (☎ 865195) is centrally located at 63 Tower St and has rooms with bathrooms from £38/48. The *Wykeham Arms* (☎ 853834, *75 Kingsgate St*), near the college, has some fine rooms at £69.50/79.50.

The *Royal Hotel* (☎ 840840, *St Peter St*) is right in the heart of the city, down a quiet side street. There's an attractive garden. Rooms are from £85/98 to £91/124. Outside the summer there are special weekend deals at £87 to £113 per person for two days including dinner, bed and breakfast.

Places to Eat

To make up a picnic, there are several supermarkets in the centre of the town. The best is *Sainsbury's*, on Middle Brook St, a short walk from the cathedral.

For a good cheap meal, the *Refectory*, near the entrance to the cathedral, is recommended. It does teas and lunches (eg fresh sardines with tomatoes, £3.65). Sandwiches are from £1.70 and a cream tea costs £3.45. Alternatively, you can get fish and chips and a cup of tea for £5 at the *Blue Dolphin Restaurant* on Broadway. *Gandhi Indian Restaurant & Takeaway* (☎ 863940) is at 163 High St opposite the Guildhall.

Harveys Restaurant & Wine Bar (☎ 843438, *31B The Square*) has tables by the pavement in summer and a menu that includes bar snacks (eg baguettes £5) as well as more substantial meals from £8.50 to £15. The summer pudding (£5) served with clotted cream is a classic.

Nearby, *Nine the Square* (☎ 864004, *9 Great Minster St*) is also a wine bar but a touch more formal. There's excellent homemade pasta for £5.85 and interesting dishes such as roast guinea fowl with garlic and rosemary for £12.95.

There are several places to eat on Jewry St. At No 4 is *Green's Wine Bar*, a good place for a light meal. *Hunter's Restaurant* (☎ 860006) is next door.

There are branches of several chains in Winchester. *Café Rouge* is by the roundabout at the top of Broadway, *Pizza Express* is nearby at the foot of Magdalen Hill, and *Ask* (also pizza) is on the High St.

Pubs The *Wykeham Arms* (75 Kingsgate St) looks authentically old English with school desks as tables and tankards hanging from the ceiling. This is an excellent place to eat, with restaurant dishes from £9 to £13 and a cheaper bar menu; but no food is served on Sunday. The *Queen Inn*, nearby on Kingsgate Rd, serves food every day.

The *Chelsea Brewery*, Bridge St, has a pleasant outside sitting area above the river. The *Old Gaolhouse* on Jewry St is a Wetherspoons pub with good-value pints and cheap pub grub.

The *Royal Oak* on High St is yet another claimant for the title of oldest bar in England. Close to the City Museum there's the minute but atmospheric *Eclipse* and the popular *Old Vine*. The *North Pole*, Parchment St, is a bar/venue that's popular with students.

Getting There & Away
Winchester is 65 miles from London by the M3 and only 15 miles from Southampton.

Bus There are regular National Express buses to London via Heathrow (1½ hours, £8.50), and less frequent ones to Oxford.

Solent Blue Line (☎ 01703-618233) runs buses every half hour to Southampton (30 minutes, £1.80).

Stagecoach/Hampshire Bus (☎ 01256-464501) has a good network of local buses linking Salisbury, Southampton, Portsmouth and Brighton. Its Explorer ticket (£5.40) is also good on most Wilts & Dorset buses, which serve the region farther to the west.

Train There are fast links with London's Waterloo station, the south coast and the Midlands. There are two or more departures most hours to London, taking less than 1½ hours and costing £15.90 one way. The fare

to Southampton is £3.40, to Portsmouth it's £6.40.

AROUND WINCHESTER
Chawton
In this small village north-west of Winchester, a mile from Alton, is the **Jane Austen House** (☎ 01420-83262), where the author lived from 1809 until her death in 1817, although she actually died in Winchester. The house has a variety of Austen memorabilia and is open March through December daily from 11 am to 4.30 pm, and at weekends for the rest of the year; £2.50/50p.

Bishop Waltham Palace
Constructed from the 12th century to the 14th century, and ruined in the Civil War, Bishop Waltham Palace (☎ 01489-892460, EH) was another imposing residence of the powerful Bishop of Winchester. The palace is between Winchester and Portsmouth and you can get there on a Winchester-Southsea bus No 69 (hourly; two hourly on Sunday). Admission is £2/1.

PORTSMOUTH
• **pop 183,000   ☎ 01705**
For much of British history, Portsmouth has been the home of the Royal Navy and it is littered with reminders that this was, for hundreds of years, a force that shaped the world. Portsmouth's major attractions are the historic ships in the Naval Heritage Area but it is still a busy naval base and the

---

Warning

The telephone area code 01705 is changing to code 023. Local 6-digit numbers in the 01705 area are being prefixed with 92 to make local 8-digit numbers.

Numbers 01705-XXXXXX will become 023-92XX XXXX. From 22 April 2000 you must use either the new 8-digit number or the old number preceded by the old area code, when dialling locally.

SOUTH-EASTERN ENGLAND

sleek, grey killing machines of the 20th century are also very much in evidence.

Largely due to bombing during WWII, the city is not a particularly attractive place; but Old Portsmouth, around the Camber, has some interesting spots, and the adjoining suburb of Southsea is a lively seaside resort.

A major millennium restoration project for the Portsmouth harbour area is currently under way.

Orientation

The bus station, Portsmouth Harbour train station, the harbour, and the passenger ferry terminal for the Isle of Wight are conveniently grouped together, a stone's throw from the Naval Heritage Area and the TIC. The quay is known as The Hard.

Southsea, where most accommodation and restaurants are concentrated, is about a mile south of Portsmouth Harbour. The Isle of Wight vehicle ferry and Old Portsmouth are both on the old harbour known as the Camber, midway between Portsmouth Harbour and Southsea.

Information

The TIC (☎ 826722) on The Hard provides guided tours, an accommodation service and plenty of brochures. In summer the office is open daily from 9.30 am to 5.45 pm. There are also TIC offices at 102 Commercial Rd (☎ 838382) and, in summer, at Southsea (☎ 832464).

There's a Mace mini supermarket on the High St.

Flagship Portsmouth (Naval Heritage Area)

The Naval Heritage Area (☎ 861512) has three classic ships and several other maritime attractions which you can visit together or one at a time. The Royal Navy has often shown a fairly flexible attitude in its fund-raising techniques, so at the end of a day in Portsmouth you should not be surprised to find you have been separated from many gold coins. Entry is £5.75/4.25 for each ship or £11.50/8.50 for an All-Ships ticket that in-cludes the three ships plus the Royal Naval

Museum (separately £3/2). You don't have to see everything on the same day as the ticket is valid for two years. A Passport ticket (£14/10) includes all the above plus the Dockyard Apprentice exhibition and a War-ships by Water harbour tour.

The area is open March to October, daily from 10 am to 5.30 pm, and November to February, daily from 10 am to 5 pm.

The Ships HMS *Victory* was Lord Nelson's flagship at the Battle of Trafalgar in 1805; Nelson died on board the ship during the battle. Commissioned in 1765, the *Victory* was already 40 years old at the time of its great battle and it was still afloat, though in tatty condition, when it was converted to museum use in 1922.

Exploring HMS *Victory*, and walking in the footsteps of Lord Nelson and his multi-cultural crew of ruffians and gentlemen, is about as close as you can get to time travel – an extraordinary experience. However, this is a popular tourist attraction, and entry is by 45 minute guided tour with a timed entry ticket. The tours are conducted at high speed although with considerable humour. Even the gruesome story that the ship's surgeon amputated 54 limbs during the course of the battle is recounted with a grin.

Adjacent to the *Victory* are the carefully conserved remains of the hull of Henry VIII's favourite ship, the *Mary Rose*. Built in 1509, the 700 tonne *Mary Rose* sank off Portsmouth in 1545. Its time-capsule contents were raised to the surface in 1982, after 437 years underwater. Finds from the ship are displayed in the Mary Rose Exhibition Centre, which also recounts the discovery and salvage of the ship.

Dating from 1860, and at the cutting edge of the technology of the time, HMS *Warrior* was a transition ship, as wood was forsaken for iron and sail for steam. The ship illustrates life in the navy in the Victorian era.

Royal Naval Museum The museum, housed in five separate galleries, has an extensive collection of ship models, dioramas

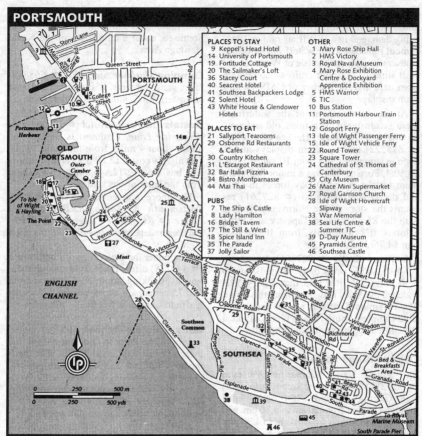

PORTSMOUTH

PLACES TO STAY
9 Keppel's Head Hotel
14 University of Portsmouth
19 Fortitude Cottage
20 The Sailmaker's Loft
36 Stacey Court
40 Seacrest Hotel
41 Southsea Backpackers Lodge
42 Solent Hotel
43 White House & Glendower Hotels

PLACES TO EAT
21 Sallyport Tearooms
29 Osborne Rd Restaurants & Cafés
30 Country Kitchen
31 L'Escargot Restaurant
32 Bar Italia Pizzeria
34 Bistro Montparnasse
44 Mai Thai

PUBS
7 The Ship & Castle
8 Lady Hamilton
16 Bridge Tavern
17 The Still & West
18 Spice Island Inn
35 The Parade
37 Jolly Sailor

OTHER
1 Mary Rose Ship Hall
2 HMS Victory
3 Royal Naval Museum
4 Mary Rose Exhibition Centre & Dockyard Apprentice Exhibition
5 HMS Warrior
6 TIC
10 Bus Station
11 Portsmouth Harbour Train Station
12 Gosport Ferry
13 Isle of Wight Passenger Ferry
15 Isle of Wight Vehicle Ferry
22 Round Tower
23 Square Tower
24 Cathedral of St Thomas of Canterbury
25 City Museum
26 Mace Mini Supermarket
27 Royal Garrison Church
28 Isle of Wight Hovercraft Slipway
33 War Memorial
38 Sea Life Centre & Summer TIC
39 D-Day Museum
45 Pyramids Centre
46 Southsea Castle

of naval battles, displays relating to Lord Nelson and a mass of other equipment, plus exhibits on the history of the Royal Navy (for times and costs see Flagship Portsmouth earlier in this chapter).

Old Portsmouth to Southsea

On a sunny day it's very pleasant to sit at **The Point**, beside the cobbled streets of Old Portsmouth, and sip a pint from one of the pubs while watching the car ferries and navy ships enter or depart the harbour.

Only fragments of the **Cathedral of St Thomas of Canterbury** in Old Portsmouth date back to its foundation in 1180. The nave and tower were rebuilt around 1690 and more additions and extensions were made in 1703 and 1938-39. Immediately south of Old Portsmouth is the **Round Tower**, originally built by Henry V, a stretch of old fort walls and the **Square Tower** of 1494.

Continue south to the ruins of the **Royal Garrison Church**, which started life in 1212, was closed in 1540, then reopened in its new role and restored in 1866-68 before being damaged in a WWII air raid in 1941. A **moat** runs beside the waterfront before an amusement park and the Isle of Wight hovercraft slipway. Harbour cruises also operate from here and the anchor of HMS *Victory* is on display.

At the Southsea end of the waterfront there's a cluster of attractions, old and new, on Clarence Esplanade. The **Sea Life Centre** (☎ 875222) has aquarium displays and is open in summer, daily from 10 am to 5 pm; £5.50/4. Portsmouth was a major departure point for the Allied D-Day forces in 1944 and the **D-Day Museum** (☎ 827261) recounts the story of the Normandy landing with the 83m Overlord Tapestry and other exhibits. It's open daily, from 10 am to 5 pm; £4.75/2.85.

Southsea Castle (☎ 827261) dates from 1544-45 and is open daily, from 10 am to 5.30 pm; £2/1. It's said that Henry VIII watched the *Mary Rose* sink from this point. The **Pyramids Centre** is a pool and waterslide complex. **South Parade Pier** is a typical British seaside pier with amusements.

Other Things to See

The **Royal Navy Submarine Museum** (☎ 529217) is across the water in Gosport (see Getting Around). It's open April through October from 10 am to 5.30 pm, and November to March from 10 am to 4.30 pm. Entry is £3.75/2.50. A joint ticket for the **Royal Marines Museum** (☎ 819385) on Barracks Rd (back in Portsmouth) costs £7.50/5.

The 'Story of Portsmouth' is recounted in the **City Museum** (☎ 827261) on Museum Rd. It's open daily from 10 am to 5.30 pm; free.

Charles Dickens Birthplace (☎ 827261) is at 393 Old Commercial Rd. It's furnished in a style appropriate to 1812, the year of his birth, but the only genuine piece of Dickens' furniture is the couch on which he died in 1870! The house is open April to October, daily from 10 am to 5.30 pm; entry is £2/1.

Places to Stay

The main concentration of B&Bs is in Southsea, about a mile south of the Naval Heritage Area.

Camping *Harbour Side Site* (☎ 663867) takes vans and tents. It's on the waterfront at Eastern Rd, 2 miles east of the town.

Hostels The *Youth Hostel* (☎ 375661, *Old Wymering Lane, Cosham*) is well to the north, about 4 miles from the main sights. The nightly cost is £8.80/5.95 adults/juniors and bus Nos 12/12A operate to Cosham from the harbour bus station.

Far more convenient is the friendly *Portsmouth & Southsea Backpackers Lodge* (☎ 832495, *4 Florence Rd, Southsea*), an independent hostel charging £9 a night.

In summer the *University of Portsmouth* (☎ 843178) offers B&B-style accommodation overlooking Southsea Common from £16.75 per person, or six-person flats at the Nuffield Centre, St Michael's Rd.

B&Bs & Hotels The most pleasant area to stay in is The Point in Old Portsmouth, but there are just two small B&Bs. *The Sailmaker's Loft* (☎ 823045, *5 Bath Square*) charges £20/40 single/double with views across the water. Around the corner is *Fortitude Cottage* (☎ 823748, *51 Broad St*), with doubles only and similarly priced.

Right by the bus station and Naval Heritage Area is the *Lady Hamilton* (☎ 870505, *21 The Hard*) offering B&B at £18 to £25 per single, £32 to £50 per double. Also on The Hard, the *Keppel's Head Hotel* (☎ 833231) charges £49/69 for rooms with a bathroom.

The main accommodation area, however, is to the south in Southsea where there are a great many B&Bs with cheaper places costing from £14 to £19 per person. Close to South Parade Pier, there are numerous places along Waverley Rd, Granada Rd, St Ronan's, Malvern Rd and Beach Rd. See the map for this B&B happy hunting ground. It's easy just to wander around checking vacancy signs but a few names to start with are the **Quetta Guest House** (☎ 734414) at 53 St Ronan's Rd (rooms from £14/28), and the **Albatross Guest House** (☎ 828325) at 51 Waverley Rd, with navy-inspired rooms from £16 per person.

The hotels nearby, fronting Southsea Common, have rooms with sea views and more upmarket prices. The **Stacey Court** (☎ 826827, 42 Clarence Pde) has rooms from £17.50/35 to £22.50/45. The **White House Hotel** (☎ 823709, 26 South Pde) is similarly priced.

The **Seacrest Hotel** (☎ 875666, 12 South Pde), **Solent Hotel** (☎ 875566, 14-17 South Pde) and **Glendower** (☎ 827169, 22 South Pde) charge £25 to £50 per person.

Places to Eat

You can get pub grub at the **Ship & Castle** and the **Lady Hamilton** on The Hard. At The Point in Old Portsmouth there are several popular pubs (see Entertainment) and the **Sallyport Tearooms** on Broad St does cream teas and snacks such as jacket potatoes (£2.95) and even toast and marmite (£1.15).

Osborne Rd in Southsea is the restaurant centre with a variety of cafés, pubs and restaurants, including Thai, Indian and Chinese places. The **Osborne** is popular for pub food while **Fatty Arbuckle's** (☎ 739179) at No 61 has burgers and steak. **Barnaby's Bistro** (☎ 821089) at No 56 is a glossier restaurant with main courses at £5 to £9.

On nearby Palmerston Rd is **Bar Italia Pizzeria**. You can get a filled baguette and a soft drink here for £2.99. At 59A Marmion Rd, **Country Kitchen** is a wholefood restaurant, open Monday to Saturday from 9.30 am to 5 pm.

Also close to Osborne Rd is the **Bistro Montparnasse** (☎ 816754) at 103 Palmerston Rd. Main dishes are £11.50 to £15.50, or there are set menus – two courses for £12.50, three for £14.90. At **L'Escargot** (☎ 812761, 7 Stanley St) a six course feast is £20.

Just off South Parade is **Mai Thai** (☎ 732322, 27A Burgoyne Rd), a good Thai restaurant where a four course meal is £11.

Chicken coconut curry costs £4.95. It's open daily until midnight.

Entertainment

Pubs On a warm summer's evening there can be no better place for a drink than outside the **Still & West** or the **Spice Island Inn** on the harbour side at The Point. The **Bridge Tavern**, overlooking the Camber, is also popular.

Along Clarence Pde in Southsea there's a variety of discos, clubs and pubs like the **Parade** and **Jolly Sailor**.

Getting There & Away

Portsmouth is 75 miles south-west of London and is well connected to the rest of the country.

Bus National Express has a daily service between Brighton and Portsmouth (£6.25). There are numerous buses to London, some via Heathrow airport (three hours, £9.25). One bus a day heads west as far as Penzance in Cornwall (11 hours, £28). The bus station is right on The Hard by the Portsmouth Harbour train station.

Train There are over 40 trains a day from London Victoria and Waterloo station (faster from Waterloo, 1½ hours; £17.80). There are plenty of trains between Brighton and Portsmouth (1½ hours, £11), and trains about every hour to Winchester for £6.40.

For the ships at Flagship Portsmouth get off at the final stop, Portsmouth Harbour.

Boat There are a number of ways of getting to the Isle of Wight from Portsmouth. See the Isle of Wight later in this chapter for more information.

Channel Hoppers (☎ 01534-639111) has a daily catamaran service to Jersey. This service also stops at Guernsey, except on Sunday when it visits Sark.

See the introductory Getting There & Away chapter for information on services to France. The Continental Ferryport is north of Flagship Portsmouth.

Getting Around

Bus A No 6 bus operates between the Portsmouth Harbour bus station, right beside the train station, and South Parade Pier in Southsea. Bus No 17 or 6 will take you from the station to Old Portsmouth.

Boat Ferries shuttle back and forth between The Hard and Gosport (£1.40 return). Bicycles travel free.

There are harbour cruises to see the navy ships in port from The Hard. Typical costs are around £3 for a 45 minute voyage.

SOUTHAMPTON
- **pop 211,000** ☎ **01703**

Southampton is a fairly large city and port of only mild interest. It developed as a major medieval trading centre with important connections to France and other European countries. Its trading role gradually declined but Southampton took up a new life as an important shipbuilding and then aircraft manufacturing centre.

These pursuits were its downfall in WWII when over two nights in late 1940 over 30,000 bombs rained down on the city. There's a surprising amount of the medieval city remaining, despite the wartime destruction, and a well-signposted circuit walk round the walls.

The TIC (☎ 221106) is on Civic Centre Rd (at the northern end of the pedestrian stretch of Above Bar St) and is open Monday to Saturday, from 9 am to 5 pm.

Warning

The telephone area code 01703 is changing to 023. Local 6-digit numbers in the 01703 area are being prefixed with 80 to make local 8-digit numbers.

Numbers 01703-XXXXXX will become 023-80XX XXXX. From 22 April 2000 you must use either the new 8-digit number or the old number preceded by the old area code, when dialling locally.

Getting There & Away

National Express (☎ 0990-808080) has bus services to major centres all over Britain including Heathrow and London. From Southampton Central station services to London's Waterloo (80 minutes) operate twice-hourly for much of the day.

Red Funnel (☎ 334010) has frequent ferries to the Isle of Wight from Southampton. See the introductory Getting There & Away chapter for details of other ferries.

NEW FOREST

The New Forest is not a national park, but outside the Highlands of Scotland this is the largest area of relatively natural vegetation in Britain. It's been that way since 1079 when William the Conqueror gave the area its name.

A variety of ancient traditions survive in the New Forest. The wild ponies for which the forest is famed are each owned by a *commoner*; it's one of the New Forest rights for commoners to graze their stock on the Open Forest. The forest is managed by 10 *verderers* who meet six times a year at the Verderers' Court in Lyndhurst.

The New Forest covers 145 sq miles, of which 105 sq miles is forest and woodland; the rest is occupied by villages and farmland. It's a pretty area to drive through but even better when you get off the roads and onto the cycling and walking tracks.

Information

The Lyndhurst Visitor Centre (☎ 01703-282269) is open daily from 10 am to 5 pm and has a wide variety of information on the New Forest. It also sells the Ordnance Survey (OS) map (No 22, £5.95) which covers the area in greatest detail. There's also a useful pack of cycling maps (£3.50).

Visitors are requested not to feed the ponies; they are wild animals and feeding will attract them onto the roads.

Walks

There are signposted walks at Bolderwood, Rhinefield and Ober Water. Contact the tourist office for details of guided walks.

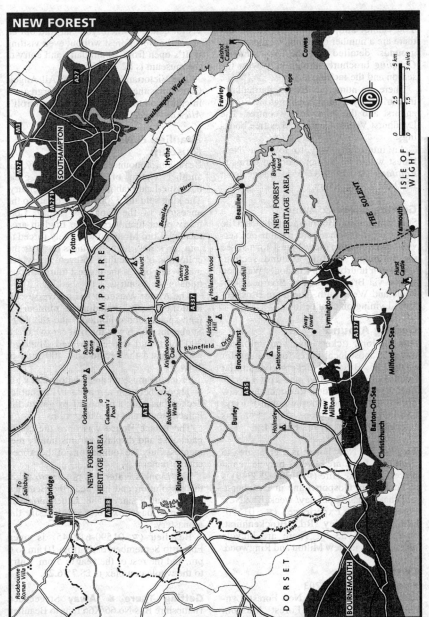

NEW FOREST

SOUTH-EASTERN ENGLAND

Cowes

Calshot Castle

Lepe

Fawley

ISLE OF WIGHT

Southampton Water

SOUTHAMPTON

Hythe

Buckler's Hard

NEW FOREST HERITAGE AREA

Beaulieu

THE SOLENT

Yarmouth

Beaulieu River

Totton

Hurst Castle

HAMPSHIRE

Ashurst

Matley

Denny Wood

Hollands Wood

Roundhill

Lymington

Sway Tower

Rufus Stone

Minstead

Lyndhurst

Knightwood Oak

Aldridge Hill

Rhinefield Drive

Brockenhurst

Setthorns

Milford-On-Sea

Ocknell/Longbeach

Cadman's Pool

Bolderwood Walk

Burley

Holmsley

New Milton

Barton-On-Sea

To Salisbury

NEW FOREST HERITAGE AREA

Fordingbridge

Ringwood

Christchurch

Rockbourne Roman Villa

Avon River

DORSET

BOURNEMOUTH

5 km
3 miles
0   2.5
0   1.5

Places to Stay

You cannot simply camp anywhere, but there are a number of commercial camping grounds detailed in the *New Forest Camping* brochure. Prices vary with the season and the facilities.

There are numerous B&Bs, particularly in Burley, Lyndhurst, Lymington, Brockenhurst and the other forest centres. The Lyndhurst Visitor Centre makes free bookings.

An interesting way to tour the New Forest would be by horse-drawn caravan. *Equitana* (☎ 01489-877551) charge from £500 for a week's hire.

Getting There & Away

Southampton and Bournemouth bracket the New Forest and there are regular bus services from both to New Forest towns; see the following Getting Around section. Trains run hourly from London's Waterloo station via Brockenhurst to Bournemouth, Poole and Weymouth. There are Brockenhurst-Lymington connections.

Getting Around

Bus Explorer tickets give you unlimited travel on most local buses for one day for £4.60/2.35. Busabout tickets give similar freedom for seven days and cost £19/10. The X1 service goes through the New Forest taking the Bournemouth-Burley-Lyndhurst-Southampton route. For bus information call ☎ 01962-846924.

Bicycle The New Forest is a great area to cycle and there are several bicycle rental places. AA Bike Hire (☎ 01703-283349) is at Fern Glen, Gosport Lane in Lyndhurst, and charges £8/42 per day/ week. The New Forest Cycle Experience (☎ 01590-624204), Brookley Rd, Brockenhurst, charges £9.50/53.20. There are bicycle rental outlets in New Milton and Ringwood.

Lyndhurst

• pop 3000   ☎ 01703

Right in the centre of the New Forest, Lyndhurst has the New Forest Museum (☎ 283914) – in the same building as the visitor centre – where you can find out all about the New Forest without even visiting it. It's open from 10 am daily and entry to the museum is £2.75/1.75.

The Victorian St Michael & All Angels Church has the grave of Alice Hargreaves, in childhood the model for Lewis Carroll's *Alice in Wonderland.*

Beaulieu & National Motor Museum

Beaulieu (pronounced bew-lee) Abbey was another victim of Henry VIII's great monastic-land grab in the mid-16th century. The king sold the 3200 hectare estate to the ancestors of the Montagu family. Like many other members of the English aristocracy, Lord Montagu was lately forced to join the stately home business but it is the collection of more than 250 vehicles which makes this one of the biggest tourist attractions in the country.

The **Motor Museum** has a diverse collection of cars including a number of land-speed record-holders, like the 1927 Sunbeam, which was the first car to exceed 200 mph, and the jet-powered Bluebird, which raised the record past 400 mph in 1964.

From the museum area visitors can walk or choose between a replica 1912 double-decker bus and a monorail to get to the Palace House and the Abbey ruins.

The **Palace House** was once the abbey gatehouse and displays various family mementos. Only the foundations of the Abbey church remain.

The **Monk's Frater** was not destroyed at the dissolution and has been the Beaulieu parish church since 1538. Other monastic buildings have exhibits on life in the monastery.

Beaulieu (☎ 01590-612345) is open Easter to September, daily from 10 am to 6 pm, and the rest of the year to 5 pm. Entry to the whole complex is £8.75/6.25.

Getting There & Away

Stagecoach Hampshire Bus No 66/X66 runs to Beaulieu

from Winchester via Lyndhurst. You can also get here from Southampton by taking a ferry to Hythe and catching bus Nos 112 or X9.

Isle of Wight

- **pop 124,000** ☎ **01983**

Since the time of George III, British royalty has been fond of the seaside; the Isle of Wight's resort status was confirmed when Queen Victoria shifted her beach allegiance there from Brighton.

Lying only a couple of miles off the Hampshire coast, the Isle of Wight makes a popular day trip from the mainland (try to avoid summer weekends) although there's enough of interest to justify a longer stay.

The relatively uncrowded roads, particularly along the south coast, are an attraction for cyclists and a 62 mile cycleway round the island was recently opened. There are also 500 miles of walking paths.

ORIENTATION & INFORMATION

The island covers 147 sq miles, stretching 23 miles long by 13 miles wide and is shaped like a parallelogram with north-east, north-west, south-west and south-east sides. Newport, in the middle of the island, is the main town. Other towns are mainly along the north-east and south-east coasts; the south-west coast is less developed. Isle of Wight Tourism (☎ 813800) is at Quay House, Town Quay, Newport; it also has information centres at Cowes, Sandown Ryde, Shanklin, Ventnor and Yarmouth.

NEWPORT & CARISBROOKE CASTLE

The island's major town is Newport, with a Roman villa (☎ 529720) on Cypress Rd and nearby Carisbrooke Castle (☎ 522107, EH). The ridge-top castle is 2 miles south-west of Newport and dates from Norman times although the site is Saxon. Charles I was imprisoned here in 1647-8 before his trial and execution in London. The window in which he got stuck while trying to escape

can still be seen. It's open daily from 10 am to 6 pm (4 pm in winter) and entry is £4/2.

COWES & OSBORNE HOUSE

Located at the northern tip of the island, Cowes is a major yachting centre and the late-July/early August Cowes Week is an important international yachting event. Naturally, the town has a Maritime Museum.

Since its appearance in the film *Mrs Brown*, **Osborne House** (☎ 200022, EH) in East Cowes has become English Heritage's most visited attraction.

The house was built from 1845-51 and Queen Victoria died here in 1901. The rooms she was using at that time were left virtually untouched from her death until 1954 when the house was opened to the public. The Indian-inspired Durbar room is of particular interest.

It's open daily from mid-March through October, 10 am to 5 pm. From November to mid-December and from February until mid-March it's open on Sunday, Monday, Wednesday and Thursday from 10 am to 2.30 pm but only for guided tours. Admission to the house is £6.50/3.30.

Osborne House has an antipodean connection: Victoria's Government House in Melbourne's Botanic Gardens is a copy, built in 1872.

RYDE TO VENTNOR

Ryde, Sandown, Shanklin and Ventnor, on the eastern side of the island, are typical English seaside resorts. **Ryde** is the most important entry point to the island and the busiest of these resort towns.

Quarr Abbey at Binstead near Ryde was founded in 1132 and destroyed in 1536. A Benedictine monastery was built here in 1908. Steam trains operate on Havenstreet Railway (☎ 884343), starting just south of Ryde.

Brading has a Roman villa (☎ 406223) with fine mosaic floors. It's open from April to September, Monday to Saturday, from 9.30 am to 5 pm, and Sunday from 10.30 am to 5 pm; £2.50/1.25. The town also has two interesting old houses – Morton Manor and

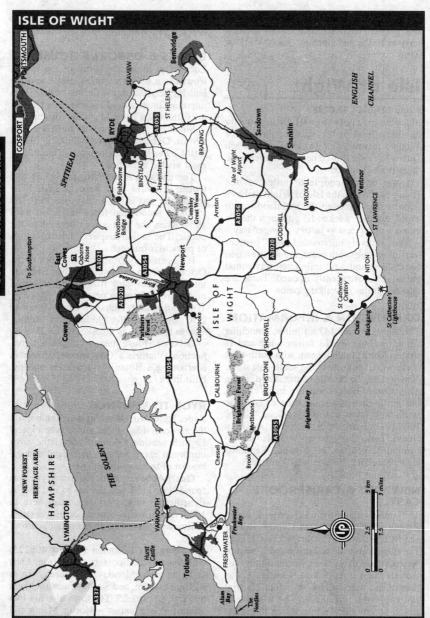

ISLE OF WIGHT

Nunwell House – and a wax museum (yes, there's a chamber of horrors).

At the easternmost tip of the island is **Bembridge**, which has a Shipwreck Centre & Maritime Museum (☎ 872223), open from March to October, daily from 10 am to 5 pm; £2.35/1.35. The only windmill on the island (☎ 873945, NT), dating from 1700, can also be seen here. It's open from April to October, Sunday to Friday, from 10 am to 5 pm, and Saturday in July and August only; £1.20/60p. A fine 5 mile coastal walk leads from Bembridge to Sandown.

VENTNOR TO ALUM BAY

The south coast from Ventnor to Alum Bay is the quietest stretch of the island circuit. The southern point of the island is marked by **St Catherine's Lighthouse**, which was built in 1837-40 and is usually open to the public from Easter to mid-September, Monday to Saturday, from 1 to 6 pm. The Buddle Inn (☎ 730243) is a popular pub at Niton Undercliff .

Looking like a stone rocket ship, **St Catherine's Oratory** is a lighthouse dating from 1314 and marks the highest point on the island. It's perched on a hilltop overlooking Blackgang Chine. The Clarendon Hotel & Wight Mouse Inn (☎ 730431) at Chale is a good place for a pub meal and has comfortable double rooms from £50.

The **Tennyson Trail** runs across High Down Ridge, past Tennyson's Monument to the Needles, from Freshwater Bay; Lord Tennyson, son of the poet, lived near here.

THE NEEDLES & ALUM BAY

The **Needles**, at the western tip of the island, are three towering rocks which rise out of the sea to form the postcard symbol of the island. A lighthouse, topped by an ugly helicopter landing pad, stands at the end of the final rock. At one time there was another rock, a 37m-high spire, which really was needle-like, but it collapsed into the sea in 1764.

The road and bus service to this end of the island ends at **Alum Bay**, famed for its coloured sands. There's an unappealing

melange of amusement park rides and souvenir shops at Alum Bay and a chairlift to take you down to the beach. From Alum Bay a walking path leads a mile (buses every hour, every half hour in peak season) to the **Needles Old Battery** (☎ 754772, EH), a fort established in 1862 and used as a lookout during WWII. The fort directly overlooks the Needles and there's a café where you can sip tea and enjoy the view. The fort is open from late March to October, Sunday to Thursday, from 10.30 am to 5 pm; during July and August it opens daily; £2.40/1.20.

PLACES TO STAY

There are two youth hostels on the island – *Sandown Youth Hostel* (☎ 402651) on the eastern end (£8.80/5.95 adults/juniors) and *Totland Bay Youth Hostel* (☎ 752165) on the western end (£9.75/6.55).

There are numerous camping grounds and a brochure is available from Isle of Wight Tourism. Charges for a tent and two people £5 to £16 in the high season, £4 to £8 in the low.

There's a huge range of B&B and hotel accommodation and the tourist information centres will make bookings. Self-catering accommodation and farm holidays are also popular.

GETTING THERE & AWAY

There is a wide variety of passenger or car-and-passenger ferry services from the mainland, although if you're bringing a car it's wise to book ahead at busy times of year. Standard fares are listed but there are all sorts of special deals available.

Portsmouth to Ryde & Fishbourne

Wightlink (☎ 0990-827744) operates a passenger catamaran ferry from The Hard to Ryde (15 minutes) and a car ferry (35 minutes) to Fishbourne. The day return fare is £6.75/3.40 to Ryde, standard return is £7.90/4 to Fishbourne. A host of car fares are quoted, starting from £36.90 for the cheapest summer return.

Hovertravel (☎ 01705-811000) hover-crafts zoom back and forth between Southsea (near Portsmouth) and Ryde. The 10 minute crossing costs £8.20/4.10 for a day return. Connecting buses operate between the Portsmouth & Southsea train station and the terminal.

Southampton to Cowes

Red Funnel (☎ 01703-334010) operates car ferries from Southampton to East Cowes (£7.80, day return £6.50; car £55 return) and high-speed passenger ferries from Southampton to West Cowes (£11.50, day return £9.50). Children travel for half-price.

Lymington to Yarmouth

The passenger day return on the Wightlink (☎ 0990-827744) car ferry is £6.40/3.20. A day return ticket for car and passengers costs £36.90. The trip takes 30 minutes.

GETTING AROUND

Bus & Train

Southern Vectis (☎ 827005) operates a comprehensive bus service around the island. There's a short railway line from Ryde to Shanklin with a steam railway line branching off from Havenstreet. Rover Tickets give you unlimited use of bus and trains for £6.25/3.50 for a day, £9.95/5 for two days, or £25.50/12.75 for a week.

Bicycle

Bicycles can be rented in Cowes, Freshwater Bay, Ryde, Sandown, Shanklin, Ventnor and Yarmouth. Offshore Sports (☎ 866269), 19 Orchard Leigh Rd, Shanklin, charges £5 for five hours, £9 for a day; there are branches in Cowes (☎ 290514) and Sandown (☎ 401515). Wavells (☎ 760219) in The Square, Yarmouth, charges £10 for a day.

South-Western England

The counties of Dorset, Wiltshire, Somerset, Devon and Cornwall include some of the most beautiful countryside and spectacular coastline in Britain. They are littered with the evidence of successive cultures and kingdoms that have been swept away by one invader after another.

The region can be divided between Devon and Cornwall, out on a limb to the far west, and Wiltshire, Dorset and Somerset in the east, which are more central and so more easily accessible.

Devon and particularly Cornwall were once Britain's Wild West and rife with smuggling. Cornwall even had its own language although the last Cornish speaker died in the 1770s. The weather in this part of England is milder than elsewhere and some of the beaches boast golden sand and surfable surf. Despite the competition from cheap holidays abroad, the 'English Riviera' still seethes with sunburnt suburbanites every summer. It's wise to steer clear of the coastal towns in July and August, not least because the narrow streets are choked with traffic.

Some people find Cornwall disappointing. You'll certainly feel cheated if you expect the extreme south-western tip of the island to be full of untouched, undiscovered hideaways. Thanks to thoughtless development, Land's End – a veritable icon – has been reduced to a commercially minded tourist trap, and inland much of the peninsula has been devastated by generations of tin and china-clay mining. However, many of the coastal villages retain their charm, especially if you visit out of season.

The South West Coast Path, a long-distance walking route, follows the coastline from Minehead in Somerset, around the peninsula to Poole, near Bournemouth in Dorset, giving spectacular access to the best and most untouched sections of the coast-

HIGHLIGHTS

- Walking the streets of Georgian Bath
- Exploring Avebury and the surrounding prehistoric monuments
- Wells Cathedral choir by candlelight
- The Tate Gallery at St Ives
- The Coast Path in West Cornwall
- Watching a play in the Minack Theatre
- Day tripping to Lundy Island
- Walking on Dartmoor
- Tresco Abbey Gardens, Isles of Scilly

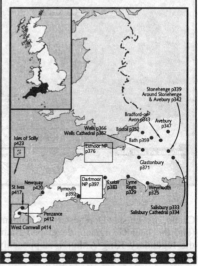

SOUTH-WESTERN ENGLAND

line. The Dartmoor and Exmoor national parks are equally popular with walkers.

Further east, some truly great monuments flag up the story of English civilisation: the Stone Age left Stonehenge and spellbinding Avebury; Iron Age Britons created Maiden

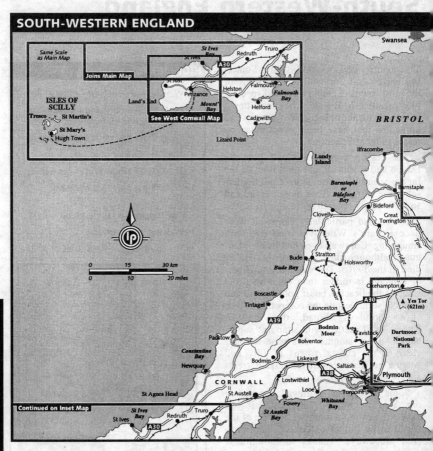

Castle, just outside Dorchester; the Romans (and the later Georgians) developed Bath; the legendary King Arthur is supposedly buried at Glastonbury; the Middle Ages left the great cathedrals at Exeter, Salisbury and Wells; and the 16th and 17th century landed gentry left great houses like Montacute and Wilton. The east is densely packed with things to see, and the countryside, though varied, is a classic English patchwork of hedgerows, stone churches, thatched cottages, great estates and emerald green fields.

Towns like Bath and Salisbury are honey pot tourist attractions on every first-time visitor's hit list. The charms of Dorset, Somerset and North Devon are more low-key, and you can happily wander around without too many plans and without stumbling over too many people.

ORIENTATION & INFORMATION
The chalk downs centred on Salisbury Plain run across Wiltshire and down through central Dorset to the coast. Granitic Dartmoor and

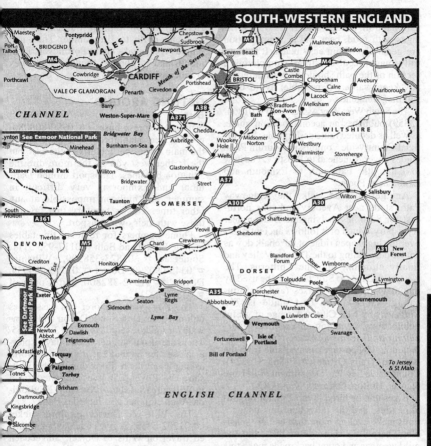

SOUTH-WESTERN ENGLAND

Exmoor dominate the Devon landscape. The railways converge on Exeter, the west's most important city, then run round the coast, skirting the granite *tors* (outcrops) of Dartmoor, to Truro, Cornwall's uninspiring administrative centre, and Penzance. Bristol and Salisbury are other important transport hubs.

There are several YHA youth hostels in the Dartmoor and Exmoor national parks, and at Salisbury, Bath, Bristol, Exeter, Plymouth, Penzance, Land's End, Tintagel and Ilfracombe.

WALKS & CYCLE ROUTES

The south-west has plenty of beautiful countryside, but walks in the Dartmoor and Exmoor national parks, and round the coastline, are the best known. The barren, open wilderness of Dartmoor can be an acquired taste, but Exmoor covers some of the most beautiful countryside in England, and the coastal stretch from Ilfracombe to Minehead is particularly spectacular. See the sections on Dartmoor and Exmoor later in this chapter for more information.

The South West Coast Path, the longest national trail, is not a wilderness walk – villages with food, beer and accommodation are generally within easy reach. It follows truly magnificent coastline. Completing a section of the path should be considered by any keen walker; if possible, avoid busy summer weekends.

The South West Way Association (☎ 01364-73859) publishes an accommodation guide, as well as detailed route descriptions. The official Countryside Commission/Aurum Press guides cover Minehead to Padstow, Padstow to Falmouth, Falmouth to Exmouth and Exmouth to Poole.

Another famous walk, the Ridgeway Path, starts near Avebury and runs northeast for 85 miles to Ivinghoe Beacon near Aylesbury. Much of it follows ancient roads over the high, open ridge of the chalk downs before descending to the Thames Valley and finally climbing into the Chilterns. The western section (to Streatley) can be used by mountain bikes and horses (and, unfortunately, 4WDs). The best guide is *The Ridgeway* by Neil Curtis. A range of useful publications, including an excellent *Information and Accommodation Guide* (£1.90 including UK postage), is available from the National Trails Office (☎ 01865-810224), Countryside Service, Department of Leisure & Arts, Holton, Oxford OX33 1QQ.

Bikes can be hired in most major regional centres, and the infrequent bus connections make cycling more than usually sensible. There's no shortage of hills, but the mild weather and quiet backroads make this great cycling country. The West Country Way, recently opened by Sustrans (see Cycling in the Activities chapter), runs from Padstow in Cornwall to Bristol, via Bodmin Moor and Exmoor. It follows disused railway tracks and quiet back roads.

OTHER ACTIVITIES
Surfing
The capital of British surfing is Newquay on the west Cornish coast which comes complete with surf shops, bleached hair, Kombis and neon-coloured clothing. The surfable coast runs from Porthleven (near Helston) in Cornwall, west around Land's End and north to Ilfracombe. The most famous reef breaks are at Porthleven, Lynmouth and Millbrook; though good, they are inconsistent.

GETTING AROUND
Bus
National Express buses (☎ 0990-808080) provide reasonable connections between the main towns, particularly in the east, but the farther west you go the more dire the situation becomes. Transport around Dartmoor and Exmoor is very difficult in summer, and nigh on impossible at any other time. This is territory that favours those with their own transport.

Phone numbers for regional timetables include Bristol and Bath ☎ 0117-955 5111, Somerset ☎ 01823-358299, Wiltshire ☎ 0345-090899, Dorset ☎ 01305-224535, Devon ☎ 01392-382800 and Cornwall ☎ 01872-322142.

The Key West Explorer bus pass gives unlimited travel in South Devon and Cornwall for three/seven days for £13.40/22.65. There are also a number of one-day Explorer passes for around £5; it's always worth asking about them. For example, the Wiltshire Day Rover (£5) gives unlimited travel in Wiltshire (Salisbury, Avebury, Bradford-on-Avon etc), but also includes Bath.

The Wilts & Dorset Explorer ticket (☎ 01202-673555) gives one day's unlimited travel on Wilts & Dorset, Stagecoach Hampshire Bus, Damory Coaches, and Solent Blue Line buses for £4.60/2.30. This pass will take you from Portsmouth, Winchester or Southampton in the east all the way through the New Forest to Dorchester and Weymouth in the west. From the south coast, it will take you north through Salisbury to Bath, Devizes, Swindon or Newbury. A seven day Busabout pass costs £22.20/11; one passport photo is required.

Train
Train services in the east are reasonably comprehensive, linking Bristol, Bath, Salis-

bury, Weymouth and Exeter. Beyond Exeter, a single line follows the south coast as far as Penzance, with spurs to Barnstaple, Gunnislake, Looe, Falmouth, St Ives and Newquay. The line from Exeter to Penzance is one of Britain's most beautiful. For more information phone ☎ 0345-484950.

Several regional rail passes are available, including the Freedom of the SouthWest Rover which, over 15 days, allows eight days unlimited travel west of a line drawn through (and including) Salisbury, Bath, Bristol and Weymouth (£69 in summer, £59 in winter).

Dorset

Despite its natural beauty and attractive towns and villages, most of Dorset manages to avoid inundation by tourists. The impressively varied coast includes the large resort towns of Bournemouth and Weymouth, as well as Lyme Regis, a particularly attractive spot with famous literary connections. The Dorset Coast Path, part of the longer 613 mile South West Coast Path, runs for most of the length of the coast.

Inland is Dorchester, the heart of Thomas Hardy's fictional Wessex. Dorset also boasts famous earthworks (Maiden Castle), castles (Corfe Castle), stately homes (particularly Kingston Lacy), a string of Lawrence of Arabia connections, some fine churches (Christchurch Priory, Wimborne Minster and Sherborne Abbey) and one of England's best known chalk hill figures (the Cerne Giant).

ORIENTATION & INFORMATION

Dorchester makes a good base for exploring the best of Dorset, but Lyme Regis, Bridport or Weymouth will suit those who prefer the coast. One of the reasons for Dorset's backwater status is that no major transport routes cross it. A rail loop runs west from Southampton to Dorchester, then north to Yeovil, and the main westbound InterCity trains stop at Axminster (East Devon).

BOURNEMOUTH & POOLE
• pop 265,000 ☎ 01202

Technically two separate towns, Bournemouth and Poole are virtually continuous.

With 7 miles of clean sand, Bournemouth has been a popular beach resort since the mid-19th century and continues to exude an air of Victorian seaside prosperity, yet it also attracts a younger crowd with nightlife to rival Brighton's.

In a recent survey by a well-known condom manufacturer, Bournemouth beach was voted the most popular place in Britain for open-air sex.

The medieval port of Poole is now a container dock and yachting centre.

Orientation & Information

Bournemouth's TIC (☎ 451700) is on Westover Rd. Poole's TIC (☎ 253253) is at the Quay.

Things to See

Bournemouth is noted for its beautiful *chines* (sharp-sided valleys running down to the sea). The wonderful **Russell-Cotes Art Gallery & Museum** (☎ 451800) looks out to sea from Russell-Cotes Rd in Bournemouth and has a varied collection, much of it garnered from its namesake's travels. Currently closed for refurbishment, the museum should fully reopen in late 1999.

In Shelley Park, Beechwood Ave, in Boscombe, the **Shelley Rooms** (☎ 303571) house a collection of Shelley memorabilia. They're open Tuesday to Sunday from 2 to 5 pm, and entry is free. *Frankenstein* author Mary Shelley is buried at St Peters.

Compton Acres (☎ 700778) is a cluster of gardens in a sheltered cliff chine. They're open March to October, daily from 10 am to 5.15 pm. Entry is £4.75/1. Bus Nos 150 and 151 go there from the centre.

Poole Old Town has attractive 18th century buildings, including a wonderful Customs House. The **Waterfront Museum** (☎ 683138) recounts the town's history, including the prosperity brought by its Newfoundland fishing trade. It's open Monday to Saturday from 10 am to 5 pm, and Sunday from noon to 5 pm. Entry is £1.75/1.20, except in August when the £3.50/2.50 charge also includes nearby **Scaplen's Court Museum**. Open for the rest of the year to school parties only, this museum is in a medieval merchant's house.

Brownsea Island is a NT nature reserve at the mouth of Poole Harbour where the first Boy Scout camp was held in 1907. From April to October boats from Sandbanks (on the peninsula between Bournemouth and Poole) cost £2.50/1.80 return, plus a landing fee of £2.40/1.20. During winter the RSPB operates sporadic Birdboats to watch the harbour bird life; phone ☎ 666226 for boat information.

Places to Stay & Eat

Bournemouth and Poole are full of places to stay and the TICs make free bookings. There are also plenty of camping grounds around the towns.

In Bournemouth, *Cartrefle Guest House* (☎ 297856, 45 St Michael's Rd) and *Denbry Hotel* (☎ 558700, 179 Holdenhurst Rd) both offer B&B for around £17 per person in midsummer. *Parklands Hotel* (☎ 552529, 4 Rushton Crescent) has rooms for £25/44 for singles/doubles, or £28/50 with a four-poster bed.

Amid the fish and chip shops are more interesting, if pricier, places to eat. Try *Sala Pepe* (☎ 291019, 43 Charminster Rd, Bournemouth) where fresh fish dishes include monkfish with crabmeat and prawns for £13.95. *Corkers* (☎ 681393, 1 High St, The Quay, Poole) is open as a café bar all day, and as a restaurant for lunch and dinner.

Entertainment

For clubbing in Bournemouth, the best-known places are the *Cage* and the *Zoo* both in the same building (☎ 311178) on Firvale Rd. They're both open Monday, Wednesday, Friday and Saturday from 9 pm to 2 am; entry charges range from £2 to £6.

Getting There & Away

Trains take about two hours from London Waterloo. There are also regular bus connections, including National Express (☎ 0990-808080). A ferry shuttles across from Sandbanks to Studland (pedestrians 90p, car and passengers £2.20). This is a short cut from Poole to Swanage, Wareham and the west Dorset coast, but summer queues can be horrendous.

AROUND BOURNEMOUTH & POOLE
Christchurch
- **pop 30,000   ☎ 01202**

Five miles east of Bournemouth is Christchurch, an attractive small town that might make a pleasant alternative base to Bournemouth. The TIC (☎ 471780) is at 23 High St.

The magnificent **Christchurch Priory** (☎ 485804) stands between the Avon and Stour rivers. The Norman nave had a new choir added to it in the 15th century, when the tower was also built. Among the wonderful misericords in the choir, look for a carving of Richard III and another of a fox 'friar' preaching to a flock of geese. In summer you can climb the tower for views and learn about priory life in the **St Michael's Loft Museum**. Visitors are asked for a £1 donation.

Opposite the Priory is the **Red House Museum & Gardens** (☎ 482860), a workhouse now accommodating a local history museum. It's open Tuesday to Saturday from 10 am to 5 pm and Sunday from 2 to 5 pm. Admission costs £1/60p.

Wimborne
- **pop 14,000   ☎ 01202**

The attractive small town of Wimborne is centred around its interesting old church, or minster. The TIC (☎ 886116) is on High St, near the minster.

Wimborne Minster Founded around 1050, the minster was considerably enlarged in Decorated style in the 14th century and became the parish church in 1537 when Henry VIII began attacking monasteries. It's notable for its twin towers and for the varied colours of its stonework. The mid-15th century perpendicular-style west tower was added when there were fears for the strength of the simpler Norman-style 12th century central tower. Those fears were realised when the crossing spire fell in 1600.

Inside, the nave columns, the piers of the central tower and the north and south transepts are the main Norman survivors. Traces of 13th to 15th century painted murals can be seen in a Norman altar recess in the north transept. In the presbytery is a 1440 brass of King Ethelred who was killed in battle in 871, the only brass commemorating a king in England.

In Holy Trinity Chapel is the tomb of Ettricke, the 'man in the wall'. A local eccentric (but obviously one with some influence), he refused to be buried in the church or in the village and was interred in the church wall. Confidently expecting to die in 1693, Ettricke also had his memorial engraved. When he survived his prediction by 10 years, the 1693 was rechiselled to 1703.

Above the choir vestry is a **chained library** established in 1686.

Priest's House Museum Near the minster is the 16th century Priest's House Museum (☎ 882533), an interesting local history museum with a series of reconstructed period rooms. It's open April to October, Monday to Saturday from 10.30 am to 5 pm, and June to September on Sunday from 2 to 5 pm. Entry is £2/90p.

Kingston Lacy
Two miles north of Wimborne is Kingston Lacy (☎ 01202-883402, NT), a fine 17th century house with 18th century landscaped gardens. It's unusual in that it didn't decline into genteel poverty and then have to be completely refurnished. The last occupant lived in the house until 1981 without selling a thing, so the house is dense with furniture and art, much of it collected by William Bankes, who was responsible for major renovations in the 1830s.

The house is open April to October, Saturday to Wednesday from noon to 5.30 pm. Entry is £6/3; grounds only £2.50/1.25.

SOUTH-EAST DORSET
The south-eastern corner of Dorset – the Purbeck peninsula – is crowded with pretty thatched villages and crumbling ruins. The Dorset Coast Path, part of the 613 mile South West Coast Path, runs through wonderful scenery along this stretch. There are plenty of camping grounds around and B&Bs in almost every village.

Tolpuddle
Tolpuddle, on the A35, played a historic role in the development of trade unions. In 1833, a group of farm workers met to discuss a cut in their wages and were promptly arrested, convicted of holding an illegal meeting (striking was not illegal) and sentenced to transportation to Australia. Public support for the 'Tolpuddle Martyrs' resulted in their pardon in 1836.

A memorial stands by a tree under which they probably gathered. A small museum on the western outskirts recounts the tale. It's open daily except Monday; entry is free.

Wareham
• pop 2800   ☎ 01929
The pretty village of Wareham forms a neat square, bounded by the River Frome on its southern side and by a remarkably intact Saxon wall on the other three sides. To complete the pattern, North, East, South and West Sts run in the four cardinal directions from The Cross in the centre. The village was badly damaged by a succession of fires, most disastrously in 1762, after which thatched buildings were banned. Purbeck TIC (☎ 552740), in Holy Trinity Church, South St, stocks an excellent guide and walking-tour map (free).

The recently refurbished **Wareham Museum** (☎ 553448), on East St, adjacent to the town hall, is open Easter to mid-October, daily from 11 am to 1 pm and 2 to 4 pm. A Lawrence of Arabia collection supplements the usual local items.

You can rent rowing boats from **Abbots Quay**, once a busy port on the River Frome. The sturdy **earth banks** around the town were built after a Viking attack in

Lawrence of Arabia

The green fields and pretty villages of Dorset are a long way from the sandy wastes of Arabia but there are numerous Lawrence connections to this area. The TIC in Wareham even produces *The Lawrence of Arabia Trail* leaflet.

Born in 1888 in Wales, TE Lawrence was the son of Sir Thomas Chapman, who had abandoned his first wife and their daughters in Ireland to run off with the girls' governess. As Mr and Mrs Lawrence they had five boys; Thomas Edward was the second. Lawrence studied history at Oxford University, specialising in the Middle East. He travelled extensively in the region between 1909 and 1914, and his expertise led to a Cairo army posting at the outbreak of WWI.

Turkey, still known as the Ottoman Empire at the time, was allied with Germany and, as Arab unrest began to develop, Lawrence led a brilliant guerrilla campaign against the Ottoman forces, culminating in the capture of Aqaba in mid-1917. After the war, he was disgusted to find his Arab visions discarded at the bargaining table as the old Ottoman Empire was carved up between Britain and France. Refusing military honours, he spent several years shuttling between Europe and the Middle East, while at the same time revelations of his dramatic exploits earned him the epithet 'Lawrence of Arabia'.

Lawrence was always an enigmatic character and in 1922 he clandestinely joined the Royal Air Force as a low-ranking enlisted man under the assumed name of John Hume Ross. At the same time he published, in a very limited edition, his immense work *Seven Pillars of Wisdom*. Newspapers soon broke the story of his RAF hideaway but a year later he joined the army as Private TE Shaw, a name he later assumed legally. He was stationed at Bovington Camp in Dorset and bought Clouds Hill, a nearby cottage. In 1925 he transferred to the RAF and spent the next 10 years in India and England before his discharge in 1935. Retiring to Clouds Hill at the age of 46, he was killed two months later in a motorbike accident.

Lawrence connections in Dorset include Bovington Camp, where the tank museum has a small Lawrence display. He died at Bovington Military Hospital six days after his accident, which took place between the camp and Clouds Hill, only a mile away. His grave is in the cemetery of St Nicholas Church, Moreton. The Wareham Museum houses more Lawrence memorabilia, and the small Saxon church in Wareham has a stone effigy of Lawrence.

876. A stretch on the West Wall is known as Bloody Bank, after Monmouth rebels were executed here in 1685 following the Bloody Assizes (see the boxed text 'The Bloody Assizes' in the Dorchester section of this chapter).

Standing on the wall beside North St is Saxon **St Martin's Church**, which dates from about 1020. Although the porch and bell tower are later additions, and larger windows have been added over the centuries, the basic structure is unchanged.

Inside, there's a 12th century wall painting on the northern wall and a marble effigy of Lawrence of Arabia.

Places to Stay & Eat Several camping grounds can be found around Wareham. Convenient B&Bs include *Belle Vue* (☎ 552056, *West St*) right on top of West Wall, which costs £20 a head. The *Black Bear Hotel* (☎ 553339, 14 South St) is fronted by a life-size figure of a bear. Rooms with bathroom cost from £25/40 for singles/doubles. The picturesque *Old Granary* (☎ 552010, The Quay) charges £20 to £42.50 per person and has a good restaurant.

Bovington Camp Tank Museum

Six miles from Wareham, the Tank Museum (☎ 01929-405096) houses an extensive collection from the earliest WWI prototypes, through to WWII tanks from both sides, and on to examples from Cold War days. From more recent times, there's also a collection of Iraqi tanks from the Gulf War. It's open daily from 10 am to 5 pm, and entry is £6/4. Lawrence of Arabia was stationed here in 1923 and there's a small museum in the shop.

Clouds Hill

Lawrence of Arabia's former home (☎ 01929-405616, NT) is open April through October, Wednesday to Friday and Sunday from noon to 5 pm. Entry to the tiny house is £2.30.

Corfe Castle

Corfe Castle's magnificent ruins tower above the pretty stone village, offering wonderful views over the surrounding countryside. Even by English standards, the 1000-year-old castle had a dramatic history. In 978, 17-year-old King Edward was greeted at the castle gate by his stepmother, Queen Elfrida, proffering a glass of poisoned wine; even before the poison could take effect he was stabbed to death. His half-brother, Ethelred the Unready, succeeded him, as the wicked queen had

planned, but the martyred boy king was canonised as St Edward in 1001.

The castle (☎ 01929-481294, NT) was besieged twice during the Civil War, being reduced to the present picturesque ruin after the second assault, in 1646. It's now open February to October, daily from 10 am to 5.30 pm (4.30 pm in March), and from 11 am to 3.30 pm the rest of the year. Entry is £3.80/2.

Places to Stay & Eat The village has several pubs and B&Bs, and there are camping grounds nearby. The *Greyhound* is a good pub by the castle moat, with a pleasant garden.

Swanage

In Victorian times local quarryman John Mowlem made a fortune supplying stone from Swanage for the huge rebuilding projects in booming London. The firm bearing his name is still a major building contractor. He also judiciously chose buildings in London which were due for demolition and shipped material back to Swanage. As a result, there are City of London bollards dotted around town, the town hall has a grandiose stone front removed from the Wren-influenced Cheapside Mercers Company building and the Wellington Clock Tower was rescued from London Bridge and stands on the pier.

The TIC (☎ 01929-422885) is on Shore Rd. There's the centrally located *Youth Hostel* (☎ 01929-422113, Cluny Crescent) and lots of B&Bs to confirm Swanage's popularity as a beach resort.

Lulworth Cove & the Coast

The lovely Dorset coast is at its most spectacular (and crowded) between Lulworth Cove and Durdle Door. Lulworth Cove is almost perfectly circular and nearly enclosed by towering cliffs. Durdle Door has a fine beach, a dramatic cove and an impressive natural archway. It's about a mile west of Lulworth Cove with fine cliff-top walks in both directions.

Places to Stay The *Durdle Door Caravan Park* (☎ 01929-400200) on the fields above the cliffs has tent sites. There are a number of places to stay at Lulworth Cove, and more just back from the coast in West Lulworth. *Lulworth Cove Youth Hostel* (☎ 01929-400564, School Lane, West Lulworth) costs £8.80/5.95 for adults/juniors.

DORCHESTER
• pop 14,000   ☎ 01305

Despite its fame as the home of novelist Thomas Hardy, Dorset's administrative centre is a sleepy place and brash Weymouth or pretty Cerne Abbas would make equally good bases for exploring the local attractions.

Orientation & Information

Most of Dorchester's action takes place along South St which runs into pedestrianised Cornhill and then emerges in the High St, divided into East and West parts at St Peter's church. The TIC (☎ 267992) is in Trinity St alongside the Antelope Walk shopping arcade. It sells the *Historical Guide – Dorchester* with interesting walks around town, and lots of Hardy literature including a set of leaflets which retrace the scenes of individual novels.

Things to See & Do

Dorset County Museum (☎ 262735), on High West St, houses the study where Hardy did his writing. There are also sections on the archaeological excavations at Maiden Castle, fossil finds from Lyme Regis and a rural craft collection. It's open Monday to Saturday from 10 am to 5 pm (in July and August on Sunday too) and entry is £3/1.50.

The **Tutankhamun Exhibit** (☎ 269571) in High West St may seem out of place in Dorset but it's nevertheless an interesting place to visit. The discovery of the tomb and its contents have been recreated in montages complete with sounds and smells. It's open daily from 9.30 am to 5.30 pm; entry is £3.50/2.25.

The **Keep Military Museum** (☎ 264066), beyond the Bridport Rd roundabout, traces

---

The Bloody Assizes

In 1685 the Duke of Monmouth, illegitimate son of Charles II, landed at Lyme Regis intending to overthrow James II and become king. His rebellion ended in defeat at the Battle of Sedgemoor in Somerset, and the duke was beheaded in the Tower of London – it took four swings of the axe to sever his head. Judge Jeffreys, the chief justice, tried the rebels in Dorchester in a barbaric trial known as the Bloody Assizes. Over 300 rebels were hanged and their gruesome drawn-and-quartered remains were displayed in towns and villages all over the region. Nearly 1000 more rebels were transported to Barbados and many more were imprisoned, fined or flogged.

Dorset military valour overseas. There's also a small **Dinosaur Museum** (☎ 269880), Icen Way.

The **Barclay's Bank building** at No 10 South St provided the fictional home for Hardy's *Mayor of Casterbridge*. Hardy himself worked for a time at an architect's office at No 62. A **statue** of Hardy watches the traffic from a seat by the West Gate roundabout.

Places to Stay

The cheaper B&Bs in Dorchester have only a few rooms. *Hillfort View* (☎ 268476, 10 Hillfort Close) has a single for £15 and a double for £30. *Maumbury Cottage* (☎ 266726, 9 Maumbury Rd) is convenient for the stations and charges from £16. *Mountain Ash* (☎ 264811, 30 Mountain Ash Rd) charges £20/36 for a single/double.

Casterbridge Hotel (☎ 264043, 49 High East St) is a luxurious small hotel where B&B costs £38/68 in summer. In High St West the *Westwood House Hotel* (☎ 268018) at No 29 and *Wessex Royale Hotel* (☎ 262660) at No 32 are fine Georgian hotels charging around £40/60.

Places to Eat

An atmospheric place to take tea or a bigger meal, provided you're not squeamish about the gruesome historical associations, is the half-timbered *Judge Jeffreys' Lodgings* (☎ *264369, 6 High West St*). Main dishes are £7.25 to £10.50.

Allow around £21 a head for a three course meal at the *Mock Turtle* (☎ *264011, High West St*). *The Old Tea House* across the road serves cream teas and light meals.

The *Kings Arms* (☎ *265353, High East St*) has associations with Hardy's *Mayor of Casterbridge*. There's good pub grub and a coffee shop. The *Royal Oak (High West St)* and the nearby *Old Ship Inn* (the oldest pub in town) are also recommended.

Getting There & Away

There are two train stations, Dorchester South and unstaffed Dorchester West, both south-west of the town centre. Dorchester South is linked seven times daily to London's Waterloo (three hours, £30.30) via Bournemouth (£6.80) and Southampton (£13.60). There are numerous services to Weymouth (10 minutes, £2.30). Dorchester West has connections to Bath (two hours, £9.80) and Bristol.

Bus connections tend to be much slower – buses from London take four hours. Local bus operators include Southern National (☎ 783645) for Lyme Regis and Taunton, Wilts & Dorset (☎ 01202-673555) for Salisbury, and Dorchester Coachways (☎ 262992) for Weymouth (£1.20 return).

Getting Around

Dorchester Cycles (☎ 268787), at 31B Great Western Rd, rents bikes for £10 a day (discounts for weekly rental).

AROUND DORCHESTER
Maiden Castle

One and a half miles south-west of Dorchester, the earthwork ramparts of Maiden Castle stretch for 3 miles and enclose nearly 20 hectares. The site has been inhabited since Neolithic times but the first fort was built here around 800 BC. It was subse-

---

Charlieville

Taking shape on Dorchester's western outskirts is Poundbury, a model town designed to immortalise Prince Charles' conservative ideals, and known locally as Charlieville. The estate will eventually house 5000 people, although only 135 houses have been built so far. They're all based on traditional designs but with modern conveniences such as double glazing and central heating.

Central to the Prince's concept of a modern town is that different social groups should be mixed, living on the same street, rather than separated onto different parts of the estate. Another idea was to make the town as pedestrian-friendly as possible. Planning controls are strict, however. Window surrounds may only be painted white, and telephone wires, TV aerials and satellite dishes must be kept out of sight.

Although the project has had many critics, it's quite obviously a success. Houses are sold as quickly as they are put up and property prices have increased dramatically.

---

quently abandoned, then rebuilt around 500 BC. The earth walls were later extended and enlarged in 250 and 150 BC. Despite the addition of more defences, the Romans still captured it in 43 AD, finally abandoning it in the 4th century. The sheer size of the walls and ditches and the area they enclose is stunning, and there are wonderful views. Dorset County Museum displays finds from the site.

Hardy's Cottage

The cottage where Thomas Hardy was born and where he wrote *Far from the Madding Crowd* is at Higher Bockhampton, about 3 miles north-east of Dorchester and reached by a 10 minute walk from the car park. Despite the absence of Hardy memorabilia, the cottage is a popular attraction. Entry is

£2.60 and it's open April to October, Sunday to Thursday from 11 am to 5 pm.

Cerne Abbas & the Cerne Giant

Eight miles north of Dorchester, delightful little Cerne Abbas has several fine 16th century houses and a medieval church. The much rebuilt abbey house is now a private residence, although the ruins behind the house can be visited. The Abbot's Porch (1509) was once the entrance to the whole complex.

Just north of the village is the Cerne Giant, one of Britain's best-known chalk figures. The giant stands 55m tall and wields a 37m-long club. He's estimated to be anything between a few hundred and a couple of thousand years old. One thing is obvious – this old man has no need of Viagra!

With several B&Bs, Cerne Abbas would make a good alternative to staying in Dorchester (20 minutes by bus). There's good pub food at the **Red Lion** and **Royal Oak**, both on Long St.

WEYMOUTH
- pop 40,000   ☎ 01305

Only 8 miles south of Dorchester, this bustling seaside resort makes a good alternative to Dorchester as a base for exploring Hardy country – Weymouth was 'Budmouth' in the novels.

It was George III's experimental dip in Weymouth waters in 1789 that sparked the British passion for the seaside. Despite the shock of emerging from his 'bathing machine' to hear a band strike up in his honour, the king revisited Weymouth 13 times.

Orientation & Information

The main part of Weymouth, between the beach and the Inner Harbour, is only a few blocks wide. The Esplanade is the main walk along the beach, but each block of the road has a different secondary name. St Mary St is the pedestrianised shopping centre but Hope Square, on the far side of the pretty Old Harbour, is more inviting. The TIC (☎ 785747) is on The Esplanade.

Esplanade & Old Harbour

Weymouth is a fine example of the archetypal English seaside resort and a summer walk along The Esplanade will reveal garish beach-equipment stands, deck chairs for hire, donkey rides and Punch & Judy shows. Look for the brightly painted Jubilee Memorial Clock of 1888 and the equally vivid statue of King George III, patron saint of Weymouth tourism.

The less brash Old Harbour inlet is lined with attractive old buildings used as shops, restaurants and pubs, and packed with fishing trawlers and fancy yachts from around the world.

Deep Sea Adventure

The Deep Sea Adventure (☎ 760690), in an old grainstore at 9 Custom House Quay, traces the history of diving, with exhibits on local shipwrecks, the *Titanic* and the £40 million gold recovery from HMS *Edinburgh*, sunk while part of a convoy from Russia. William Walker, the Winchester Cathedral diver (see Winchester in the South-Eastern England chapter) plays his part, as does the intriguing story of John Lethbridge and his pioneering 'diving engine' of 1715. The exhibit is open daily from 9.30 am to 7 pm (8 pm in July and August). Last entry is 1½ hours before closing time. Tickets are £3.50/2.50.

Brewer's Quay & the Timewalk

Brewer's Quay on Hope Square has a shopping centre and plentiful attractions, including the Timewalk (☎ 777622) that takes you through the town's early history as a trading port, the disaster of the Black Death plague years, the drama of the Spanish Armada and its development as a resort. You even see a figure of the portly George III emerging from his famous bathing machine. This excellent Timewalk tour ends with the story of the Devenish brewery, in which it is housed. It's open daily from 10 am to 5.30 pm (8 pm in July and August). Entry is £3.75/2.50.

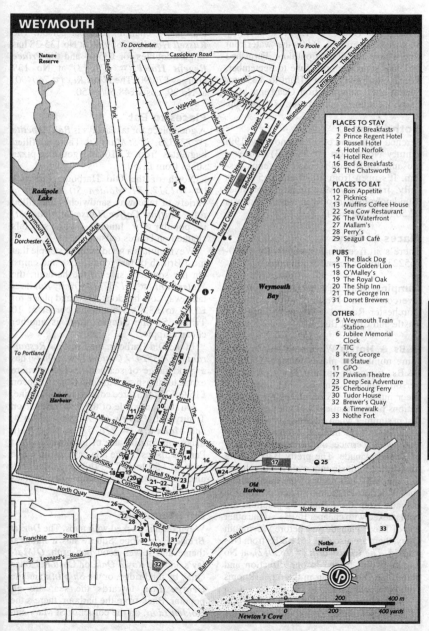

WEYMOUTH

PLACES TO STAY
1 Bed & Breakfasts
2 Prince Regent Hotel
3 Russell Hotel
4 Hotel Norfolk
14 Hotel Rex
16 Bed & Breakfasts
24 The Chatsworth

PLACES TO EAT
10 Bon Appetite
12 Picknics
13 Muffins Coffee House
22 Sea Cow Restaurant
26 The Waterfront
27 Mallam's
28 Perry's
29 Seagull Café

PUBS
9 The Black Dog
15 The Golden Lion
18 O'Malley's
19 The Royal Oak
20 The Ship Inn
21 The George Inn
31 Dorset Brewers

OTHER
5 Weymouth Train Station
6 Jubilee Memorial Clock
7 TIC
8 King George III Statue
11 GPO
17 Pavilion Theatre
23 Deep Sea Adventure
25 Cherbourg Ferry
30 Tudor House
32 Brewer's Quay & Timewalk
33 Nothe Fort

SOUTH-WESTERN ENGLAND

Tudor House

When Tudor House (☎ 812341) at 3 Trinity St was built around 1600, the waterfront would have lapped the front door. Furnished in Tudor style, it's open June to September, Tuesday to Friday from 11 am to 3.45 pm; Sunday afternoons only from October to May. Entry, including a guided tour, is £1.50/50p.

Nothe Fort

Perched on the end of the promontory, 19th century Nothe Fort (☎ 787243) houses a museum on Britain's coastal defence system. It's open from 10.30 am to 5.30 pm daily, from early May to late September (Sunday from 2 pm only in winter). Entry is £2.50 (children free).

Places to Stay

There's a freephone number (☎ 0800-765223) for accommodation bookings.

Camping There are caravan parks between Overcombe and Preston, north along the Dorchester Rd and south near Sandsfoot Castle and Chesil Beach.

B&Bs & Hotels Weymouth has an awesome number of places to stay. Cheaper B&Bs, typically costing £14 to £18 per person, can be found all over town. The sheer number of B&Bs makes recommendations pretty pointless, but good places fill fast in summer when owners may also prefer long lets. Good hunting grounds include Brunswick Terrace, on the northern stretch of The Esplanade. The pretty B&Bs along this stretch look straight over the beach.

Lennox St, just north of the train station, and Waterloo Place, the stretch of The Esplanade from the Lennox St junction, are both packed with cheaper B&Bs. At the other end of The Esplanade, just before Weymouth Quay, there are also ranks of B&Bs from Nos 1 to 34. *The Chatsworth (☎ 785012)*, at No 14, looks out to sea in one direction and across the Old Harbour in the other. Rooms with bathroom are £25 to £32 per person.

Most of the places along the central part of The Esplanade are expensive but the *Hotel Norfolk (☎ 786734)* at No 125-26 is reasonable, charging £26 per person. The *Russell Hotel (☎ 786059)* at No 135-38 has singles/doubles for £35/64 and the *Prince Regent Hotel (☎ 771313)* at No 139 charges £70/90. The *Hotel Rex (☎ 760400)* at No 29, costs £48.50/84.50.

Places to Eat

A good place for takeaways is *Bon Appetite (☎ 777375, 32 St Mary St)*. There are filled baguettes from £2.10 and gourmet pizza slices from £1.50.

North of the Old Harbour, *Picknics (☎ 761317, 31 Maiden St)* prepares a variety of takeaway sandwiches and filled rolls. *Muffins Coffee House (St Albans St)* is popular for lunches, with specials chalked on boards outside.

Weymouth is a good place to sample that most British of fast foods – fish and chips. On the southern side of the harbour, the *Waterfront (☎ 781237, 14 Trinity Rd)* does takeaway cod, haddock, skate and plaice for £2.60 to £3.80. Round the corner at 10 Trinity St, the *Seagull Café* is another cheap chippie.

In the Old Harbour, the *Sea Cow Restaurant (☎ 783524, 7 Custom House Quay)* has a good range of seafood, including more exotic local fish such as John Dory. Count on £15 to £25 for a three course meal with wine.

On the south side of the Old Harbour on Trinity Rd, *Perry's (☎ 785799)* at No 4, and *Mallam's (☎ 776757)* at No 5 both make imaginative use of local seafood. At Perry's dishes on the à la carte menu range from £12.50 to £22.50 (lobster). Mallam's also has a fixed price menu – two courses for £17.90.

Entertainment

Weymouth is packed with pubs. The *Dorset Brewers* on Hope Square has a nautical theme and serves good pub grub. *O'Malley's* and the *Royal Oak*, on Custom House Quay by the bridge, or the *Ship Inn* and the *George Inn*, towards the sea, are all popular. Back from the harbour, there's the *Golden Lion*, on the corner of St Mary and

St Edmund Sts. The **Black Dog**, on pedestrianised St Mary St, is said to be the oldest pub in town, and is named after the first black Labrador brought into England on a ship from Newfoundland.

Weymouth Pavilion (☎ *783225*), on the quay, has a busy schedule of events year-round. It's pretty highbrow stuff – recent extravaganzas have included Australian male strippers and Ronnie Corbett.

Getting There & Away

Bus Buses stop along the Esplanade. Phone ☎ 224535 for local bus information. Dorchester Coachways (☎ 262992) has daily buses to London for £14. Wilts & Dorset operates to Dorchester, Salisbury, Lyme Regis, Taunton, and Poole and Bournemouth.

Train Weymouth station is conveniently located at the junction of Ranelagh Rd and King St. There are hourly services to London (3½ hours, £32) via Bournemouth (£8.30) and Southampton. Services to other centres in the south-west include nearby Dorchester (12 minutes, £2.30).

Boat Condor (☎ 761551) high-speed catamaran car ferries whiz across to Cherbourg in France in 4¼ hours. A day trip costs £29.90 return. Condor also runs ferries to Guernsey.

WEYMOUTH TO LYME REGIS
Portland

South of Weymouth, Portland is joined to the mainland by the long sweep of Chesil Beach. Many famous buildings have been made from locally quarried Portland stone. **Portland Castle** (☎ 820539, EH) is one of the finest examples of the defensive castles constructed during Henry VIII's castle-building spree, spurred by fear of an attack from France. Entry costs £2.30/1.20.

There are superb views from the lighthouse, which houses the TIC (☎ 01305-861233), at the end of **Portland Bill**. It's £1.50 to climb the 41m-high tower. An earlier, smaller lighthouse now acts as a bird observatory.

Chesil Beach

Chesil Beach is a long curving sandbank (except that it's made of pebbles rather than sand) stretching along the coast for 10 miles from Portland to Abbotsbury. The bank encloses the slightly stagnant waters of the Fleet Lagoon, a haven for water birds, including the famed Abbotsbury swans. The stones vary from pebble size at Abbotsbury in the west to around 15cm in diameter at Portland in the east; local fishermen can supposedly tell their position along the bank by gauging the size of the stones. In places, the stone bank reaches 15m high. Although winter storms can wash right over the top, it has never been broken up. The bank is accessible at the Portland end and from just west of Abbotsbury.

Abbotsbury

Pretty little Abbotsbury boasts several attractions. The huge **tithe barn**, at one time a communal storage site for farm produce, is 83m long and was used for a harvest supper scene in Polanski's *Far from the Madding Crowd*. It houses an interesting country museum and is open April to October, daily from 10 am to 6 pm, Sunday only the rest of the year. Entry is £2.50/1.

On the coast, and offering fine views of the Fleet Lagoon, is **Abbotsbury Swannery** (☎ 01305-871130). Swans have been nesting here for 600 years and the colony can number up to 600, plus cygnets. The walk through the swannery and reed beds will tell you all you ever wanted to know about swans. Come in May for the nests, in late May and June for the cygnets. It's open daily from 10 am to 6 pm (to dusk in winter), and entry is £5.20/2.50.

The swannery was founded by Abbotsbury's Benedictine monastery, which was destroyed in 1541. Traces of the monastery remain by the tithe barn. The energetic can walk up to 14th century **St Catherine's Chapel**, overlooking the swannery, the village and Chesil Beach.

Places to Stay & Eat Abbotsbury has several B&Bs and places to eat. The old

SOUTH-WESTERN ENGLAND

SOUTH-WESTERN ENGLAND

Ilchester Arms (☎ 871243), right in the village, has interesting pub food (eg Dorset sausage baguette, £2.60) and a restaurant. You can also stay here; double rooms are £42.95, and £30.95 at weekends.

LYME REGIS

- **pop 4600**   ☎ **01297**

The attractive seaside town of Lyme Regis marks the end of Dorset – Devon begins just beyond the pier known as the Cobb. The Cobb is a famous literary spot: not only did Louisa Musgrove's accident in Jane Austen's novel *Persuasion* take place here, but it was also where *The French Lieutenant's Woman* stood and stared out to sea in John Fowles' novel (and where Meryl Streep stood in the film version).

The town's other claim to fame is prehistoric. The limestone cliffs on either side of town are some of Britain's richest sources of fossils, and the first dinosaur skeletons were discovered here.

In 1685, the Duke of Monmouth landed on Monmouth Beach, west of the town, to start his abortive rebellion against James II. See the boxed text 'The Bloody Assizes' in the Dorchester section.

Orientation & Information

The A3052 drops precipitously into Lyme Regis from one side and climbs equally steeply out on the other. From Bridge St, where the A3052 meets the coast, Marine Parade runs west to the harbour. The TIC (☎ 442138) is situated where Bridge St becomes Church St.

Museums

Lyme Regis Philpot Museum (☎ 443370), in Bridge St, has displays of fossils and local history. The cliffs west of the harbour and Monmouth Beach are still prone to fossil-exposing landslips; the museum has details of the Dowlands Landslip on Christmas Day 1839, when a stretch of cliff top three quarters of a mile long slid away, taking with it farms and houses. It's open daily from 10 am to 5 pm (closed from noon to 2.30 pm on Sunday); entry is £1/40p.

Dinosaurland (☎ 443541), on Coombe St, is an eclectic mix of science, fossils and local folklore. It's open Easter to November, daily from 10 am to 5 pm; entry is £3.20/1.90.

The Cobb

The Cobb is a 183m-long stone jetty-cum-breakwater. The small **Marine Aquarium** (☎ 443678) has interesting displays of local marine life. It's open April to October, daily from 10 am to 5 pm (later in mid-season). Entry is £1.30/80p.

From Cobb Gate towards East Cliff runs **Gun Cliff Walk**. The superstructure ingeniously conceals the town's sewage system.

Places to Stay

Lyme Regis has plenty of hotels, guesthouses and B&Bs. Two people with a tent can camp at **Uplyme Touring Park** (☎ 442801, *Hook Farm, Uplyme*) for £7.50 in summer. To get there, walk up Silver St/Uplyme Rd (towards Exeter) for about 15 minutes.

Lym Guest House (☎ 442164, 1 Mill Green), at the junction of Hill Rd and Sherborne Lane, has B&B from £17 per person. *Coombe House* (☎ 443849, 41 Coombe St) costs £16 for rooms with bathroom.

On Cobb Rd, up from the harbour, there's *Harbour View* (☎ 443910) charging £13.50 (bed only, no breakfast), and *Cliff Cottage* (☎ 443334) with doubles for £33, or £37 with bath. Both have great views.

St Michael's Hotel (☎ 442503, Pound St) has nice views and costs £21 to £25 per person for rooms with bathroom. Nearby is the *Alexandra Hotel* (☎ 442010), one of the town's finest hotels, which charges £50/84 for singles/doubles.

Round the corner on Pound Rd, the *Kersbrook Hotel* (☎ 442596) costs £41.25 per person. The *Bay Hotel* (☎ 442059, Marine Parade) costs from £34 to £39 per person.

Places to Eat

For fish and chips try *Lyme's Fish Bar (34 Sherborne Lane)* or the *Cobb Gate Fish Bar* on the waterfront.

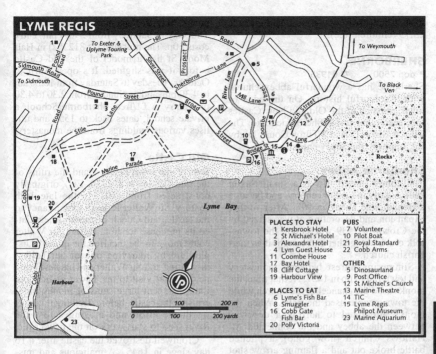

LYME REGIS

To Exeter &
Uplyme Touring
Park

To Sidmouth

To Weymouth

To Black
Ven

Lyme Bay

Rocks

Harbour

The Cobb

0   100   200 m

0   100   200 yards

PLACES TO STAY
1 Kersbrook Hotel
2 St Michael's Hotel
3 Alexandra Hotel
4 Lym Guest House
11 Coombe House
17 Bay Hotel
18 Cliff Cottage
19 Harbour View

PLACES TO EAT
6 Lyme's Fish Bar
8 Smuggler
16 Cobb Gate
Fish Bar
20 Polly Victoria

PUBS
7 Volunteer
10 Pilot Boat
21 Royal Standard
22 Cobb Arms

OTHER
5 Dinosaurland
9 Post Office
12 St Michael's Church
13 Marine Theatre
14 TIC
15 Lyme Regis
Philpot Museum
23 Marine Aquarium

SOUTH-WESTERN ENGLAND

Polly Victoria (☎ *442886*), at the Cobb end of Marine Parade, has steaks for £9.70, duck for £9.90 and fillets of plaice for £7.95. The *Smuggler (Broad St)* does all-day breakfasts, lunches, cream teas, and early suppers, closing at 8 pm.

Many of the pubs do food – try the *Cobb Arms* or the *Royal Standard*, both on Marine Parade by the Cobb. Other possibilities include the *Volunteer (Broad St)* and the *Pilot Boat (Bridge St)*. Crab sandwiches at the Pilot Boat are £2.95.

Getting There & Away

Lyme Regis makes a convenient midway point between Dorchester or Weymouth and Exeter. National Express buses connect with Exeter, a 1¾ hour trip. Southern National Bus No 31 links Lyme Regis to Taunton and Weymouth via Axminster.

AROUND LYME REGIS
Parnham

Parnham (☎ 01308-862204) is both a home and a showroom for owner John Makepeace's contemporary furniture. You might pick up a chair for £600 but most pieces are in the £3000 to £10,000 range. It's near Beaminster, 5 miles north of Bridport, and is open April to October, Tuesday to Thursday and Sunday from 10 am to 5 pm. Entry is £5/2.

Forde Abbey

Set in 12 hectares of magnificent gardens, Forde Abbey (☎ 01460-220231) is a monastery converted into a private home. It's 6 miles north-east of Axminster, and is open April to October, Wednesday and Sunday from 1 to 4.30 pm. Entry is £5 (children free), which includes admission to the gardens. The gardens are open from 10 am to 4.30 pm, daily year-round, and entry is £3.75 (children free).

SHERBORNE
- **pop 7500**   ☎ 01935

Sherborne has a wonderful abbey church with a colourful history. On the edge of town, remains of the Old and New Castles face each other across Sherborne Lake. The TIC (☎ 815341) is at 3 Tilton Court, Digby Rd, opposite the abbey entrance.

Sherborne Abbey
The abbey started life as a small Saxon church early in the 8th century, and became a Benedictine abbey in 998. After further expansion and decoration, it was seized by the Crown in 1539 whereupon the townsfolk clubbed together and bought it as their parish church.

Simmering unrest between monastery and town flared up in 1437. At that time, the monks used the chancel of the church while the townspeople used the nave. When the monks attempted to narrow a doorway between the abbey and the connected All Hallows Church (now gone), a pitched battle broke out and a flaming arrow shot across the church from town end to monastery end and set the roof alight.

The abbey is entered via a Norman porch built in 1180. Immediately on the left is the Norman door, built in 1140, which was the cause of the 1437 riots and fire. The remains of All Hallows are to the west of the Saxon wall; a Saxon doorway from 1050 survives. The superb fan vault above the choir dates from the early 15th century and is the oldest ceiling of this type and size in the country. The similar vault over the nave is from later in the century. Solid Saxon-Norman piers support the abbey's soaring central tower.

The monk's choir stalls also date from the mid-15th century and are carved with amusing figures.

Other Abbey Sights The abbey has a cathedral-like close where you'll find the 1437 St John's Almshouses, open to the

public May to September on Tuesday and Thursday to Saturday from 2 to 4 pm; entry costs 50p. The **museum** (☎ 812252) in Half Moon St has a model of the Old Castle before it was slighted. It's open April to October, Tuesday to Saturday from 10.30 am to 4.30 pm, and on Sunday from 2.30 to 4.30 pm; entry is £1/free. **Sherborne School**, a private school, dates back to 1550 and utilises various buildings from the monastery.

Old Castle
East of the town centre stand the ruins of the Old Castle (☎ 812730, EH), originally constructed from 1107. In the late 16th century, Sir Walter Raleigh took a fancy to the castle, and Queen Elizabeth I negotiated its purchase for him. Before Sir Walter could move in, he incurred the queen's displeasure by marrying one of her ladies-in-waiting and Sir Walter and his new bride paid a short visit to the Tower of London. Later he spent large sums of money modernising the castle, before deciding it wasn't worth the effort and moving across the River Yeo to start work on the new castle.

Cromwell destroyed the castle after a 16 day siege in 1645. 'A malicious and mischievous castle, like its owner', (the Earl of Bristol) he thundered. Admission costs £1.60/80p.

Sherborne Castle
Sir Walter Raleigh commenced his New Castle (☎ 813182) in 1594 but by 1608 he was back in prison, this time at the hands of James I. The king first gave the castle away, then took it back, and in 1617 sold it to Sir John Digby, the Earl of Bristol. It's been the Digby family residence ever since. The castle is open Easter through September on Thursday, Saturday and Sunday from 1.30 to 4.30 pm; entry is £4.80/2.40.

Places to Stay
There are few budget B&B places in Sherborne. The *Britannia Inn* (☎ 813300, Westbury St) costs £18.50/34 for a single/double. *Clatcombe Grange* (☎ 814355,

Bristol Rd) has comfortable accommodation in a converted barn, from £21 per person.

The *Antelope Hotel* (☎ 812077, Greenhill) costs from £22.50 to £30 per person.

In Milborne Port, 2 miles from Sherborne, is *The Old Vicarage* (☎ 01963-251117, Sherborne Rd). B&B costs from £28 to £45 per person, depending on the room. There are weekend breaks also including dinner, from £43 to £58 per person. It's a listed building in an attractive country setting.

Places to Eat

For light meals try the *Three Wishes Coffee Shop & Restaurant* (78 Cheap St). The *Cross Keys Hotel* (☎ 812492), at the junction of Cheap and Long Sts, right by the abbey, has an extensive pub-food menu. Also near the abbey is the *Digby Tap*, a pub offering a wide range of ales and good-sized portions of traditional fare – ham and eggs for £3.25, or a ploughman's lunch from around £3.

SHAFTESBURY

- **pop 4900**   ☎ 01747

Situated on a 240m-high ridge, **Shaftesbury Abbey** (☎ 852910) was founded in 888 by Alfred the Great and was at one time England's richest nunnery. Today, only scant signs of the foundations remain, situated off Park Walk with fine views over the surrounding countryside. St Edward (see Corfe Castle in the South-East Dorset section earlier in this chapter) was said to have been buried here, and King Canute died at the abbey in 1035. It's open from April to October, daily from 10 am to 6 pm and entry is £1/40p.

The picturesquely steep cobbled street known as **Gold Hill** tumbles down the ridge from beside the abbey ruins. **Shaftesbury Museum** (☎ 852157) at the top of the hill is open from Easter to September, daily from 11 am to 5 pm; entry is £1/free.

The TIC (☎ 853514) at 8 Bell St has a board outside listing local B&Bs and other accommodation. The *Ship Inn* and *King's Arms*, by the central car park, have pub food, or try *The Salt Cellar*, a cosy café at the top of Gold Hill.

Wiltshire

Wiltshire boasts wonderful rolling chalk downs, Britain's most important prehistoric sites at Stonehenge and Avebury, a fine cathedral at Salisbury and a number of the stateliest of stately homes at Wilton, Stourhead and Longleat. The Ridgeway Path, taking walkers along a crest of the downs, has its western end in Wiltshire.

ACTIVITIES

The **Wiltshire Cycleway** comprises six circular routes ranging from 70 to 160 miles. TICs stock the *Wiltshire Cycleway* brochure that details the routes and lists cycle shops and rental outlets. *Wiltshire Cycleway Campsites* lists camping grounds along the routes.

Stretching from Bristol to Reading, the 87-mile-long **Kennet & Avon Canal** was reopened in 1990 after standing derelict for 40 years. Built by the brilliant engineer John Rennie between 1794 and 1810, it's now used by narrowboats and has some fine stretches of towpath. The stretch from Bath to Bradford-on-Avon passes a notable aqueduct. The flight of 29 locks just outside Devizes is an engineering marvel. The Kennet & Avon Canal Museum (☎ 01380-721279) on the wharf in Devizes has information on the canal.

SALISBURY

- **pop 37,000**   ☎ 01722

Salisbury is justly famous for its cathedral and its close, but it's still very much a bustling market town, not just a tourist trap. Markets have been held in the town centre twice weekly for over 600 years and the jumble of stalls still draws a cheery crowd. The town's architecture mixes every style since the Middle Ages and includes some beautiful, half-timbered, black-and-white buildings.

Salisbury makes a good base for visiting attractions throughout Wiltshire and for excursions to the coast.

SOUTH-WESTERN ENGLAND

Chalk Figures

Wiltshire's rolling fields are a green cloak over a chalk substructure, and the practice of cutting pictures into the hillsides has a long history. The technique is simple: mark out your picture and

cut away the green grass and topsoil to reveal the white chalk below. The picture will need periodic maintenance, but not much – some of the chalk figures may date back to prehistoric times, although the history of the oldest figures is uncertain. Although Wiltshire has more chalk figures than any other county, the best are probably the 55m-tall Cerne Giant (with his even more notable 12m penis) in Dorset and the 110m-long Uffington White Horse in Oxfordshire (which really requires a helicopter or hot-air balloon for proper inspection).

Chalk figure in Wiltshire – the Cherhill Horse

Horses were particularly popular subjects for chalk figures in the 18th century and noteworthy ones can be seen in Wiltshire at Cherhill near Calne, Alton Barnes and Hackpen, and at Osmington near Weymouth in Dorset.

During WWI a series of regimental badges were cut into a hillside outside Fovant in Wiltshire. A New Zealand WWI regiment left a gigantic kiwi on a hillside at Bulford, near Amesbury in Wiltshire. Get a copy of Kate Bergamar's *Discovering Hill Figures* (Shire Publications) for the complete lowdown on England's chalk figures.

Orientation & Information

The town centre is a 10 minute walk to the east of the train station or just a couple of minutes down Endless St from the bus station. Everything is within easy walking distance of Market Square, the town centre, with its impressive guildhall.

Directly behind the guildhall, on Fish Row, the TIC (☎ 334956) is open Monday to Saturday from 9.30 am to 5 pm, and on Sunday in summer. It sells *Seeing Salisbury*, a useful pamphlet which outlines walks around the town and across the water meadows for classic views of the cathedral.

Excellent one hour walking tours of Salisbury (£2/1) leave from the TIC from May to September, daily at 11 am and 6 pm. On Friday the 6 pm tour is replaced by a ghost walk at 8 pm.

Salisbury Cathedral

The Cathedral Church of the Blessed Virgin Mary (☎ 555100) is one of the most beau-

tiful and cohesive in Britain, an inspiration to the artist John Constable who painted it from across the water meadows. It was built in uniform Early English (or early pointed) Gothic, a style characterised by the first pointed arches and flying buttresses and a feeling of austerity. The uniformity is a result of the speed with which the cathedral was built between 1220 and 1258 and that it has not subsequently undergone major rebuilding. The sole exception is the magnificent spire, at 123m the highest in Britain, an afterthought added between 1285 and 1315.

Salisbury cathedral had its origins 2 miles further north with a Norman cathedral at Old Sarum (see Old Sarum later in this chapter). In 1217, Bishop Poore petitioned the pope for permission to move the cathedral to a better location, complaining that the water supply on the hilltop was inadequate, the wind drowned out the singing, the weather gave the monks rheumatism,

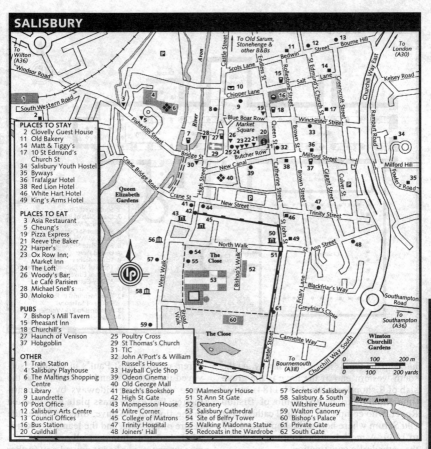

SALISBURY

PLACES TO STAY
2 Clovelly Guest House
11 Old Bakery
14 Matt & Tiggy's
17 10 St Edmund's
   Church St
34 Salisbury Youth Hostel
35 Byways
36 Trafalgar Hotel
38 Red Lion Hotel
46 White Hart Hotel
49 King's Arms Hotel

PLACES TO EAT
3 Asia Restaurant
5 Cheung's
19 Pizza Express
21 Reeve the Baker
22 Harper's
23 Ox Row Inn;
   Market Square
24 The Loft
26 Woody's Bar;
   Le Café Parisien
28 Michael Snell's
30 Moloko

PUBS
7 Bishop's Mill Tavern
15 Pheasant Inn
18 Churchill's
27 Haunch of Venison
37 Hobgoblin

OTHER
1 Train Station
4 Salisbury Playhouse
6 The Maltings Shopping
   Centre
8 Library
9 Laundrette
10 Post Office
12 Salisbury Arts Centre
13 Council Offices
16 Bus Station
20 Guildhall
25 Poultry Cross
29 St Thomas's Church
31 TIC
32 John A'Port's & William
   Russel's Houses
33 Hayball Cycle Shop
39 Odeon Cinema
40 Old George Mall
41 Beach's Bookshop
42 High St Gate
43 Mompesson House
44 Mitre Corner
45 College of Matrons
47 Trinity Hospital
48 Joiners' Hall
50 Malmesbury House
51 St Ann St Gate
52 Deanery
53 Salisbury Cathedral
54 Site of Belfry Tower
55 Walking Madonna Statue
56 Redcoats in the Wardrobe
57 Secrets of Salisbury
58 Salisbury & South
   Wiltshire Museum
59 Walton Canonry
60 Bishop's Palace
61 Private Gate
62 South Gate

the crowded site meant the housing was inadequate and, worst of all, the soldiers were rude. His request was granted and in 1220 a new cathedral was constructed on the plains, conveniently close to three rivers.

Starting at the eastern end, **Trinity Chapel** was completed by 1225, the main part of the church by 1258 and the whole thing by 1266. The cloisters were added at about the same time and a few years later it was decided to add the magnificent tower and spire. Because this had not featured in the original plans the four central piers of the building were expected to carry an unexpected extra 6400 tons. Some fast thinking was required to enable them to do this.

The highly decorative West Screen was the last part of the cathedral to be completed and provides a fine view from across the close. The cathedral is entered via the cloister passage and the **south-west door**. The 70m-long nave, with its beautiful Purbeck marble piers, was 'tidied up' by James Wyatt in 1789-92; among other things he

SALISBURY CATHEDRAL

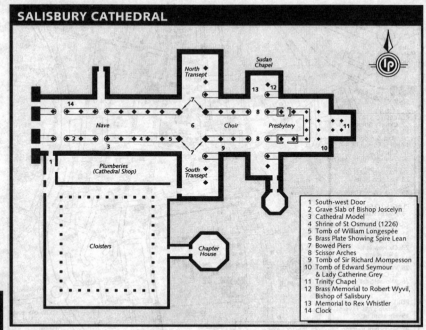

1 South-west Door
2 Grave Slab of Bishop Joscelyn
3 Cathedral Model
4 Shrine of St Osmund (1226)
5 Tomb of William Longespée
6 Brass Plate Showing Spire Lean
7 Bowed Piers
8 Scissor Arches
9 Tomb of Sir Richard Mompesson
10 Tomb of Edward Seymour
   & Lady Catherine Grey
11 Trinity Chapel
12 Brass Memorial to Robert Wyvil,
   Bishop of Salisbury
13 Memorial to Rex Whistler
14 Clock

lined up the tombs in the nave neatly. At the south-western end of the nave is the **grave slab of Bishop Joscelyn** (1141-1184), at one time thought to be the tomb of Bishop Roger, who completed the final cathedral at Old Sarum where he was bishop from 1107 to 1139. A **model** in the south aisle shows the cathedral's construction.

The **Shrine of St Osmund** was installed the in 1226, a year after Trinity Chapel was completed. St Osmund had completed the original cathedral at Old Sarum in 1092 and was canonised in 1457. His actual grave remains in the Trinity Chapel. The **Tomb of William Longespée** was the first new tomb in the cathedral, following his death in 1226. A son of Henry II, he was present at the signing of the Magna Carta and also laid one of the cathedral's foundation stones.

The soaring spire is the cathedral's most impressive feature. In 1668, Sir Christopher

Wren, creator of St Paul's in London, surveyed the cathedral and calculated that the spire was leaning sideways by 75 centimetres. In 1737, a **brass plate** was inserted in the floor of the nave, directly under the centre of the spire, and the lean was recorded. It had not shifted at all since Wren's measurement, nor had it moved any further when re-recorded in 1951 and 1970.

Other parts of the cathedral clearly show the strain, however. The tower and spire are supported by four **piers**, each nearly 2m square, but the additional weight has bent these massive stone columns. If you look up from the bottom, the curve is quite visible, particularly on the eastern piers. Flying buttresses were later added to the outside of the building to support the four corners of the original tower. More buttresses were added internally and the openings to the eastern transepts were reinforced with **scissor** arches as in Wells cathedral. Reinforcement work on the notoriously 'wonky spire' continues to this day.

Not everything in the cathedral requires looking upwards. The **tomb of Sir Richard Mompesson**, who died in 1627, and his wife Catherine, is a brilliantly colourful work. The grandiose **tomb of Edward Seymour** (1539-1621) and **Lady Catherine Grey**, sister of Lady Jane Grey, is at the east end of the ambulatory. The first part of the cathedral to be built, **Trinity Chapel**, at the eastern end, has fine Purbeck marble pillars; the vivid blue *Prisoners of Conscience* stained-glass window was installed in 1980.

The Sudan chapel contains a magnificent 14th century **memorial brass** to Bishop Robert Wyvil showing him praying in Sherborne castle, and a **prism memorial** to artist Rex Whistler who lived in the close. The **clock** displayed in the north aisle is the oldest in England and one of the oldest in the world. It was certainly in existence in 1386 when funds were provided for maintenance of a 'clocke'. Restored in 1956, it continues to operate, maintaining the 600-year-old tradition of having a clock in this position.

The cloisters lead to the beautiful Gothic **Chapter House** of 1263-84 which houses one of the four surviving original versions of the **Magna Carta**, the agreement made between King John and his barons in 1215. The delicate fan-vaulted ceiling is supported by a single central column. A frieze around the room recounts Old Testament tales.

The cathedral is open daily from 8 am to 6.30 pm; a donation of £2.50/50p is requested. The Chapter House (30p) is open Monday to Saturday from 9.30 am to 4.45 pm, and Sunday from 1 to 4.45 pm. On Monday to Saturday there are roof tours (£1) up to four times daily and tower tours to the base of the spire (£2) at 11 am and 2 pm. Both offer unique opportunities to come to grips with medieval building practices and are highly recommended.

Cathedral Close

Salisbury cathedral has England's largest, and arguably most beautiful, cathedral close. Many of the buildings were constructed at the same time as the cathedral although it owes most of its present appearance to Wyatt's late 18th century clean-up of the cathedral. The Close was actually walled in, physically separating it from the town, in 1333, using the old cathedral at Old Sarum as a source of building material. To this day it remains an elite enclave, with the gates in the wall still locked every night. Residents have their own gate keys. The most famous current resident is former prime minister Edward Heath.

Wyatt also cleared the close grounds of gravestones and demolished the late 13th century external belfry, by then in a ruinous condition. Striding across the close lawns on the western side of the cathedral is Elizabeth Frink's **Walking Madonna** (1981).

The close has several museums and houses open for inspection, most of them with café facilities. The **Salisbury & South Wiltshire Museum** (☎ 332151) in the King's House has exhibits on local prehistory, including Stonehenge and Old Sarum. It's open daily, Monday to Saturday from 10 am to 5 pm. In July and August, it's also open on Sunday from 2 to 5 pm. Entry is £3/75p. A half-hour audiovisual performance, **'Secrets of Salisbury'**, is on show in the Medieval Hall (☎ 412472) which is open daily from 10 am to 5.30 pm, for £1.50/1. The **Redcoats in the Wardrobe** exhibit (☎ 414536) is open April to October, daily from 10 am to 4.30 pm and shows military paraphernalia. In November, February and March, it's open only on weekdays. Entry is £2/50p.

Built in 1701, **Mompesson House** (☎ 335659, NT) is a fine Queen Anne house with a walled garden. It's open April to October, Saturday to Wednesday from noon to 5.30 pm. Entry is £3.40/1.70.

Malmesbury House (☎ 327027) was originally a 13th century canonry and later the residence of the Earls of Malmesbury. It can be visited by guided tour (£5). Phone ahead for times.

From High St, the close is entered by the narrow High St Gate. Just inside is the

College of Matrons, founded in 1682 for widows and unmarried daughters of clergymen. South of the cathedral is the **Bishop's Palace**, now the Cathedral School, parts of which date back to 1220. The **Deanery** on Bishop's Walk mainly dates from the 13th century. Izaak Walton, patron saint of fishermen (see Winchester Cathedral in the South-Eastern England chapter), lived for a time in the **Walton Canonry**, and no doubt dropped a line in the nearby Avon.

St Thomas's Church

Were it not for Salisbury cathedral, splendid St Thomas's Church would attract much more attention. The light, airy edifice you see today dates mainly from the 15th century and its principal drawcard is the superb 'doom', or judgement day, painting which spreads up and over the chancel arch. Painted around 1475, it was whitewashed over during the Reformation and uncovered again in 1881. In the centre, Christ sits in judgment astride a rainbow with scenes of heaven on the left and hell on the right; hell is supervised by a hairy devil whose foot pokes out onto the chancel arch. On the hell side look out for a bishop and two kings, naked except for their mitre and crowns, and for a miser with his moneybags and a female alehouse owner, the only person allowed to hang on to her clothes.

Market Square

Markets were first held here in 1219 and since 1361 have been held every Tuesday and Saturday. The market once spread much further than the present car-park area and street names like Oatmeal Row, Fish Row or Silver St indicate their medieval specialities. The square is dominated by the late 18th century guildhall.

Facing the guildhall are two **medieval houses**: John A'Port's of around 1425 and William Russel's of 1306. Russel's looks newer because of a false front, but inside its age is revealed. The present shop owners, Watson's of Salisbury, are used to sightseers and produce a leaflet about what is probably the town's oldest house.

Immediately behind Market Square look out for Fish Row, with some fine old houses, and for the 15th century **Poultry Cross**.

Places to Stay

Hostels The *youth hostel (☎ 327572, Milford Hill)* is an attractive old building in large gardens, an easy 10 minute walk along Milford St from the centre of Salisbury, just beyond the ring road. Nightly cost is £9.75/6.55 for an adult/junior.

Close to the bus station, *Matt & Tiggy's (☎ 327443, 51 Salt Lane)* is an independent hostel-like guesthouse with simple dorm rooms and no curfew. It's a pleasant old house with a café attached. A bed costs £9.50, breakfast another £2.

Camping The *Coombe Nurseries Park (☎ 328451)* is about 3 miles west of Salisbury at Netherhampton. A tent site for two costs £8. There are other sites in the vicinity.

B&Bs & Hotels Castle Rd, the A345 continuation of Castle St north from Salisbury, has a wide choice of B&Bs between the ring road and Old Sarum. *Leena's Guesthouse (☎ 335419)* at No 50 has six singles/doubles from £22.50/37. *Castlewood (☎ 421494)* at No 45 is similarly priced. The *Edwardian Lodge (☎ 413329)* at No 59 charges £29.50/42 for rooms with bath.

Follow Milford St out of the centre and, just beyond the ring road and the youth hostel, turn right to *Byways (☎ 328364, 31 Fowlers Rd)*. Rooms cost from £25/39, almost all of them with bathroom. This is a pleasantly quiet area but only a short walk from the centre of town.

On the other side of the centre, near the train station, *Clovelly Hotel (☎ 322055, 17-19 Mill Rd)* has rooms for £26/50, most with bathroom.

The *Old Bakery (☎ 320100, 35 Bedwin St)* is a small B&B in a 16th century house with rooms from £18/34. It's an 'extremely interesting structure', enthused one reader. Another B&B that has been recommended is 17th century *10 St Edmunds Church St (☎ 328259)*, a small comfortable place where even the bread is home-baked. There are just two doubles at £36; outside the peak season single occupancy costs £26.

The *Red Lion Hotel* (☎ *323334, Milford St*), with rooms from £79.50/99.50, is very comfortable and of great historical interest. Dating from 1230, it's said to be the oldest purpose-built hotel in Britain. The *King's Arms Hotel* (☎ *327629, 9-11 St John's St*) has rooms from £50/78. Five hundred years old, the *Trafalgar Hotel* (☎ *338686, 33 Milford St*) has 18 rooms, all with bathroom, costing £45/55 (breakfast is extra).

Concealed behind a grand portico near the cathedral close is Salisbury's top hotel, the *White Hart Hotel* (☎ *327476, 1 St John's St*). There are 68 rooms at £90/107; breakfast is extra. Cheaper B&B deals are available at weekends.

Places to Eat

Restaurants Upstairs on Market Square, *Harper's* (☎ *333118*) has set lunches for £5.50/6.90/8.50 for one/two/three courses. Also open for dinner, the à la carte menu includes dishes such as roast Barbary duck with plum and ginger sauce (£11.50) and salmon with fennel (£8.90). Also looking out on the square is *The Loft* (☎ *328923*), which offers breakfasts, light meals, soups and filled baguettes, and French-run *Le Café Parisien* (☎ *412356, Oatmeal Row*).

Also very centrally located is a branch of *Pizza Express* (☎ *415191, 50 Blue Boar Row*). Pizzas range from £3.85 for a Margherita to £6.20 for a Capricciosa.

Fisherton St, between the centre and the station, features a choice of reasonably priced ethnic restaurants. *Cheung's* (☎ *327375*), at No 60-64, is a popular Chinese restaurant, while the *Asia Restaurant* (☎ *327628*) at No 90 is good for spicy Indian food.

Cafés & Pubs In Market Square in the centre, *Reeve the Baker* has an upstairs tearoom, popular for lunch and snacks. *Michael Snell's*, near St Thomas's Church, does light lunches and teas.

The *Haunch of Venison* (☎ *322024, 1-5 Minster St*) is an atmospheric old pub with panelled walls and oak beams. There's an interesting range of pub food, including venison pie for £4.50, and over 100 malt whiskies on offer. Eat your meal *before* asking to see the 200-year-old mummified hand of the card player.

The *Pheasant Inn* (☎ *327069*), an old pub on the corner of Salt Lane and Rollestone St, attracts a young crowd and serves lunches from around £5. There's a good vegetarian menu.

Entertainment

There is often interesting live entertainment including high-quality contemporary music and performances in the *Salisbury Arts Centre* (☎ *321744*), a converted church in Bedwin St. It's open Tuesday to Saturday from 10 am to 4 pm.

The *Salisbury Playhouse* (☎ *320333*) is on Malthouse Lane. The *Odeon Cinema* on New Canal must be one of the few cinemas in the world with a medieval foyer.

Moloko (☎ *507050, 5 Bridge St*) and *Woody's Bar*, (*12 Minster St*) are both lively hang-outs. *Churchill's*, on Endless St, just north of Market Square, features live music while *Hobgoblin (Milford St)* is a noisy, smoky pub with a young clientele. The *Ox Row Inn* and the *Market Inn* are dead central on Market Square, while *Bishop's Mill Tavern* has an outdoor area with river views.

Getting There & Away

See the fares tables in the Getting Around chapter at the start of the book. Salisbury is 88 miles west of London, 52 miles east of Bristol and 24 miles from Southampton.

There are excellent walking and cycling routes to and from Salisbury; Hayball Cycle Shop (see Getting Around) has the useful *Cycling Around Salisbury* (free). The Clarendon Way is a 26 mile walking route to Winchester.

Bus Three National Express (☎ *0990-808080*) buses a day run from London via Heathrow to Salisbury (three hours, £10.25). National Express has a daily Portsmouth-

Salisbury-Bath-Bristol service, but it's more expensive than local operators Wilts & Dorset (☎ 336855). Salisbury-Bath costs £5.70 with National Express, £4.60 with the local operator. There are roughly hourly services to Bath via Wilton and Bradford-on-Avon (X4, two hours), to Bournemouth and Poole (X3, 1½ hours) and to Southampton (X7, 1¼ hours).

Wilts & Dorset operates bus No 3 to Stonehenge; Nos 5 (Monday to Saturday) and 6 (Sunday only) to Avebury, Marlborough and Swindon; and Nos 184 and 185 (and X84 in summer) to Dorchester. Hampshire Bus operates No 68 to Winchester.

Train Salisbury is linked by rail to Portsmouth (1¼ hours, numerous, £10.80), Bath (two hours, numerous, £9.40) and Exeter (two hours, 10 per day, £19.50). There are 30 trains a day from London's Waterloo station (1½ hours, £20.20). To get to Winchester (£9.10) requires a change at Basingstoke or Southampton.

Getting Around
Bikes can be hired from Hayball Cycle Shop (☎ 411378) on Winchester St for £9 per day.

AROUND SALISBURY
Old Sarum
Once an Iron-Age hillfort, Old Sarum (☎ 01722-335398, EH) became a town with its own cathedral in the Middle Ages. Today, the 22 hectare site consists of impressive earthworks offering fine views of Salisbury, with ruins of the Norman fortifications and the foundations of the old cathedral nestling inside.

Bishop Osmund completed the first 53m-long cathedral in 1092 but it was immediately struck by lightning and badly damaged. Around 1130, it was rebuilt and extended but this cathedral was abandoned with the shift to Salisbury and finally demolished in 1331 to provide building material for the walls of the cathedral close.

By 1540 the last house had disappeared but Old Sarum continued to elect two

members to parliament until 1833 – a classic example of the sort of 'rotten borough' the 1832 Reform Act was designed to abolish.

Old Sarum is 2 miles north of Salisbury, and from Monday to Saturday there are up to four buses an hour. Entry costs £2/1.

Wilton House
Henry VIII gave Wilton House (☎ 01722-746720) to William Herbert in 1541. Herbert became the Earl of Pembroke in 1551, a title the colourful family has held since. After a fire destroyed most of the house it was redesigned by Inigo Jones and completed when the fifth Earl took over. The present Earl of Pembroke is the seventeenth.

A visit to Wilton House and its 8 hectares of grounds starts with a video, followed by a tour of the kitchen and laundry. The hall has a statue of Shakespeare, who dedicated the first folio edition of his plays to the third Earl. Inigo Jones was responsible for the Single and Double Cube Rooms, with their magnificent painted ceilings, elaborate plaster work and paintings by Van Dyck.

Wilton House is 2½ miles west of Salisbury on the A30 and buses depart up to six times hourly. It's open April to October from 11 am to 6 pm (last admission 5 pm). Admission to the house is £6.75/4.

While in Wilton you might also visit the **Wilton Carpet Factory** (☎ 01722-744919) in King St which is open all year round (except 10 days over Christmas and the New Year) Monday to Saturday from 9 am to 5 pm and Sunday from 11 am to 5 pm. Entry costs £4/2.

Old Wardour Castle
Just north of the A30 between Salisbury and Shaftesbury, the Old Castle (☎ 01747-870487, EH) was built around 1393 and suffered severe damage during the Civil War. Entry to the picturesquely sited ruins is £1.70/90p.

STONEHENGE
Stonehenge (☎ 01980-624715, EH/NT) is Europe's most famous prehistoric site. It

consists of a ring of enormous stones (some of which were brought from Wales), built in stages beginning 5000 years ago. Reactions vary, some feeling that the car park, gift shop and crowds of tourists swamp the monument, and that the two roads surging past rob it of atmosphere. Avebury, 19 miles to the north, is more isolated and recommended for those who would like to commune with the ley lines in relative peace (see Avebury later in this chapter).

The Site

Stonehenge was built and rebuilt over a 1500 year period. Construction started around 3000 BC when the outer circular bank and ditch were constructed. An inner circle of granite stones, known as bluestones from their original colouring, was erected 1000 years later. The stones weighed up to 4 tons each and were brought from the Preseli Mountains in South Wales, nearly 250 miles away.

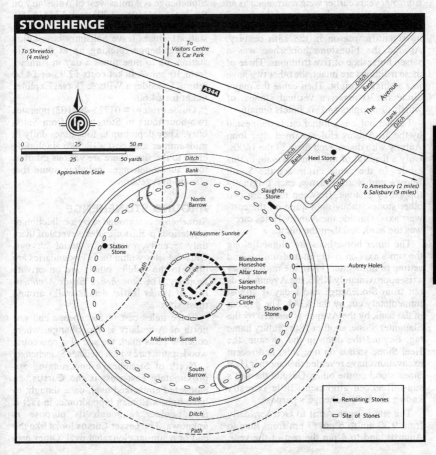

STONEHENGE

To Shrewton (4 miles)

To Visitors Centre & Car Park

A344

The Avenue

Ditch Bank

Bank Ditch

Heel Stone

To Amesbury (2 miles) & Salisbury (9 miles)

Ditch
Bank
Approximate Scale
0   25   50 m
0   25   50 yards

Ditch
Bank

Slaughter Stone

North Barrow

Midsummer Sunrise

Station Stone

Path

Bluestone Horseshoe
Altar Stone
Sarsen Horseshoe
Sarsen Circle

Aubrey Holes

Station Stone

Midwinter Sunset

South Barrow

Bank

Ditch

Path

■ Remaining Stones
□ Site of Stones

SOUTH-WESTERN ENGLAND

Around 1500 BC, the huge stones which make Stonehenge instantly recognisable were dragged to the site, erected in a circle and topped by equally massive lintels to make the sarsen (the type of sandstone) trilithons (the formation of vertical and horizontal stones). The sarsens were cut from an extremely hard rock found on the Marlborough Downs about 20 miles from the site. It's estimated that dragging one of these 50-ton stones across the countryside to Stonehenge would require about 600 people.

Also around this time, the bluestones from 500 years earlier were rearranged as an inner horseshoe. In the centre of this horseshoe went the altar stone, a name given for no scientific reason in the 18th century. Around the bluestone horseshoe was a sarsen horseshoe of five trilithons. Three of these trilithons are intact, the other two have just a single upright. Then came the major circle of 30 massive vertical stones, of which 17 uprights and six lintels remain.

Further out was another circle delineated by the 58 Aubrey Holes, named after John Aubrey who discovered them in the 1600s. Only a handful of the stones remain in this circle. In the same circle are the South Barrow and North Barrow, each originally topped by a stone. Between them are two other stones, though not quite on the east-west axis. Outside the Aubrey Holes circle was the bank and then the ditch.

The inner horseshoes are aligned along the sun's axis on rising in midsummer and setting in midwinter. From the midsummer axis, approximately NNE, the Avenue leads out from Stonehenge and today is almost immediately cut by the A344. The gap cut in the bank by the Avenue is marked by the Slaughter Stone, another 18th century name tag. Beyond the ditch in the Avenue, the Heel Stone stands on one side, and recent excavations have revealed that another Heel Stone stood on the other. Despite the site's sun-influenced alignment, little is really known about Stonehenge's purpose.

The site is open April to October, daily from 9.30 am to 6 pm (7 pm from June to August), and to 4 pm the rest of the year.

Entry is £3.90/2, including audio tour. Some feel that it is unnecessary to pay the entry fee because you can get a good view from the road, and even if you do enter you are kept at some distance from the stones. If you can afford it the most atmospheric way to see the stones is with an hour-long private view outside the standard opening hours. This must be arranged well in advance and a pass (£12/6) obtained from English Heritage (☎ 01980-623108).

Getting There & Away

Stonehenge is 2 miles west of Amesbury on the junction of the A303 and A344/A360. It's 9 miles from Salisbury (the nearest train station). Buses leave Salisbury bus station for Stonehenge, picking up at the train station, up to nine times a day in summer from 10 am. A ticket costs £2.95 or £4.60 return. Consider a Wilts & Dorset Explorer ticket for £4.60.

Guide Friday (☎ 01225-444102) operates two-hour tours to Stonehenge from Salisbury. They depart up to four times daily in midsummer and cost £12.50/6, including entry to the site. There are various minibus tours to Stonehenge, including some that also go to Avebury.

AROUND STONEHENGE

Stonehenge is surrounded by a collection of mysterious prehistoric sites, several of them only recently revealed by aerial surveys. Only the sites within the NT boundaries are open to the public; others are on private property. The *Stonehenge Estate Archaeological Walks* leaflet details walks around these sites.

Three miles east of Stonehenge and just north of Amesbury is **Woodhenge**, where concrete posts mark the site of a concentric wooden structure which predates Stonehenge.

North of Stonehenge and running approximately east-west is the **Cursus**, an elongated embanked oval, once thought to have been a Roman hippodrome; in fact it is far older, although its purpose is unknown. The **Lesser Cursus** looks like the end of a similar elongated oval. Other pre-

The Battle for Stonehenge

Despite its World Heritage Site status, the 20th century hasn't been kind to Stonehenge, which is hemmed in by the busy A303 to the south and the A344 to the north. Instead of being encouraged to let their imaginations rip, visitors have to put up with being funnelled through a tunnel under the A344 and then staring at the stones from behind a barbed-wire barricade with a constant backdrop of roaring traffic.

For a relatively small site, Stonehenge has always received a daunting number of visitors ... over 700,000 at the last count. To make matters worse, in the 1980s latter-day Druids and New Age travellers began to descend on Stonehenge for the summer solstice en masse, often lingering for weeks afterwards. Archaeologists claimed that they would damage not just the stone circle but the lesser monuments in the surrounding fields as well. The ensuing police clampdown on solstice visits turned into an annual stand-off, culminating in the infamous Battle of the Beanfield when television viewers were treated to pictures of women and children being tipped out of a motley assortment of ancient vehicles in a none too gentle fashion. The barbed wire is one legacy of the clash; the 1994 Criminal Justice and Public Order Act, aimed at making it harder for convoys to assemble, is another.

'A national disgrace' is how the Public Accounts Committee of the House of Commons described the situation at Stonehenge back in 1992. But what hope for a brighter future? Ideally English Heritage and the National Trust would like to see both roads moved back from the site, and the A303 rerouted through a tunnel – at a cost of £300 million.

The NT and EH are pressing on with plans for a Stonehenge Millennium Park which would at least see the A344 closed and the visitor centre repositioned a mile away to give the site back some of its mystique by the year 2000. In 1998, however, Stonehenge failed to attract a £20 million Millennium Fund grant for the project.

It's still not clear where the money's coming from but Culture Secretary Chris Smith recently announced that Stonehenge would be restored to its natural setting before the next election.

historic sites around Stonehenge include a number of burial mounds, like the **New King Barrows**, and **Vespasian's Camp**, an Iron-Age hillfort.

STOURHEAD

Stourhead (☎ 01747-841152, NT) is another of England's fine stately homes, but here the house is merely an adjunct to the stunning garden. If you have to choose between house and garden, opt for the outdoors.

Wealthy banker Henry Hoare built the house between 1721 and 1725, while his son, Henry Hoare II, created the garden in the valley beside the house. Subsequent Hoares enlarged and enriched the house: traveller and

AROUND STONEHENGE & AVEBURY

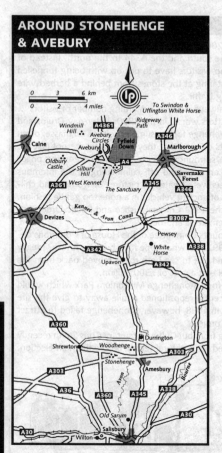

0 3 6 km
0 2 4 miles

To Swindon &
Uffington White Horse

Windmill
Hill
A4361
Avebury
Circles
Avebury
Fyfield
Down
Ridgeway
Path
A346
Calne
A4
Marlborough
Oldbury
Castle
Silbury
Hill
A361 West Kennet
The Sanctuary
Savernake
Forest
A345 A346
Devizes
Kennet & Avon Canal
B3087
Pewsey
A342
White
Horse
A338
Upavon
A342
A360
Shrewton
Woodhenge
Stonehenge
Durrington
A303
Amesbury
A303
A36
A360 A345 A338
Old Sarum
A30
A30
Salisbury
Wilton

county historian Sir Richard Colt Hoare added wings between 1790 and 1804, and the house was rebuilt after a fire in 1902. Landscapes by Claude and Gaspard Poussin betray the inspiration for the Stourhead gardens.

A 2 mile circuit takes you around a garden and a lake created by Henry Hoare II out of a series of medieval fish ponds. From the house, the walk leads by an **ice house**, where winter ice would be stored for summer use. At the **Temple of Flora** it continues around the lake edge, through a **grotto** and past a

Gothic cottage to the **Pantheon**. There's a climb up to the **Temple of Apollo**, copied from a temple at Baalbek in Lebanon, which has fine views down the length of the lake. From the temple, you descend to the 15th century **Bristol Cross**, acquired from the city of Bristol in 1765, past **St Peter's Church** and the **Spread Eagle Inn** back to the starting point. From near the Pantheon, a 3½ mile side trip can be made to **King Alfred's Tower**, a 50m-high folly overlooking Wiltshire, Somerset and Dorset.

The garden is open daily from 9 am to 7 pm (or sunset). The house is open April to October, Saturday to Wednesday from noon to 5.30 pm. Entry costs £4.40/2.40 to the house, and another £4.40/2.40 to the garden (£3.30/1.50 in winter). A combined house and garden ticket costs £7.90/3.70. King Alfred's Tower is another £1.50/ 70p.

LONGLEAT

Longleat (☎ 01985-844400) is the English stately home turned circus act. Following Henry VIII's monastic land grab, Sir John Thynne picked up the priory ruins and Longleat's 360 hectares for the princely sum of £53 in 1541. Having acquired the 13th century Augustinian priory, he turned 16th century architecture on its head to produce a house that looked out onto its magnificent park rather than in towards its courtyards. It was still under construction when he died in 1580 but although its external appearance hasn't changed since, there have been many internal alterations. The rooms are sumptuously furnished and feature seven libraries with 40,000 books. Capability Brown landscaped the surrounding park in 1757-62, planting woods and creating the Half Mile Pond.

After WWII, taxation started to nibble away at the English nobility's fortunes, just as maintenance costs skyrocketed and servants became scarce and expensive. The sixth Marquess of Bath responded by pioneering the stately home business at Longleat, going on to add new, less serious attractions in the grounds. These days Longleat boasts a pub, a narrow-gauge railway, a Dr Who exhibit, a pets' corner, a butterfly garden and a safari park with lions, as well as the magnificent old house. The eccentric seventh Marquess has even added a series of murals, some depicting his numerous 'wifelets', in his private apartments.

Longleat House is open daily from 10 am to 4 pm (6 pm from Easter to September). The safari park is open mid-March through October from 10 am to 5 pm; the other attractions open an hour later. Entry to the grounds costs £2/1, to the house £5/4, to the safari park £5.50/4.50, and there are entry charges to 13 other features. An all-inclusive ticket costs £12/10. Buses run to the safari park's entrance gate, a 2½ mile walk from Longleat House through marvellous grounds.

BRADFORD-ON-AVON
• pop 9000   ☎ 01225

Bradford-on-Avon is a beautiful old town with fine stone houses and factories rising like a series of terraced paddy fields from the river. Bath, with a much wider range of accommodation and eating options, is only 8 miles away, making a day trip a good alternative to staying here. Unfortunately the recent extension of the Bath bypass has had the effect of displacing unwanted excess traffic onto Bradford.

Orientation & Information
The Town Bridge is Bradford's most important landmark. The crowded buildings rise up from the river on the northern side. The TIC (☎ 865797) is across the bridge from the train station. The Kennet and Avon Canal passes through Bradford-on-Avon, and there's a pleasant 1½ mile walk or cycle ride along it to neighbouring Avoncliff, with its impressive Victorian aqueduct.

Around Town
Although Bradford-on-Avon dates back to Saxon times, it reached its peak as a weaving centre in the 17th and 18th centuries. The magnificent factories and imposing houses were the showpieces of the town's wealthy clothing entrepreneurs. The soothing honey colour of the solid

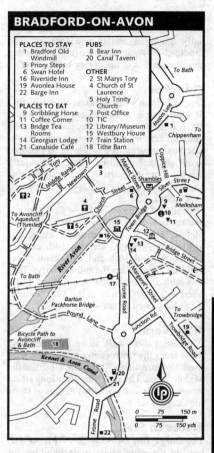

BRADFORD-ON-AVON

PLACES TO STAY	PUBS
1 Bradford Old Windmill	8 Bear Inn 20 Canal Tavern
3 Priory Steps	
6 Swan Hotel	**OTHER**
16 Riverside Inn	2 St Marys Tory
19 Avonlea House	4 Church of St
22 Barge Inn	Laurence
	5 Holy Trinity
PLACES TO EAT	Church
9 Scribbling Horse	7 Post Office
11 Coffee Corner	10 TIC
13 Bridge Tea	12 Library/Museum
Rooms	15 Westbury House
14 Georgian Lodge	17 Train Station
21 Canalside Café	18 Tithe Barn

stone buildings encourages wandering. Start at the **Shambles**, the original marketplace, inspect adjacent **Coppice Hill** and wander up Market St to the terrace houses of **Middle Rank** and **Tory**, a name probably derived from the Anglo-Saxon word 'tor', meaning a high hill. Across the river, by the **Town Bridge**, is **Westbury House**, where a riot against the introduction of factory machinery in 1791 led to three deaths.

The first bridge across the Avon at the Town Bridge site was constructed around the

12th century but the current bridge dates from 1610. The small room jutting out was originally a chapel and then a **lock-up**. The **Bradford-on-Avon Museum** (closed Monday and Tuesday) is in the library by the river.

Churches

One of Britain's finest Saxon churches, tiny **St Laurence** probably dates from around 1001. Later it was put to secular use and by the 19th century was no longer even recognised as a church. It has now been restored to its original condition; note particularly the lofty walls, narrow arches and stone angels above the chancel arch. It's open all year round.

Bradford quickly outgrew St Laurence and the new **Holy Trinity Church** was completed in 1150. The original church is virtually submerged beneath 14th century extensions and 15th and 19th century rebuilding. Higher up the hill **St Marys Tory** was built as a hermitage chapel about 1480. Used as a cloth factory in the 18th century, it has now been restored.

Tithe Barn

A pleasant short walk along the river bank leads from the town centre to the tithe barn used to store tithes (taxes in kind) in the Middle Ages. The imposing 50m-long structure was built in 1341 with 100 tons of stone tiles to roof it.

Places to Stay

The *Barge Inn* (☎ 863403, 17 Frome Rd) beyond the canal, has singles/doubles for £22.50/35. *Avonlea House* (☎ 868324, 93 Trowbridge Rd) costs from £20 per person.

If you can afford more, this is a good town for a splurge. *Priory Steps* (☎ 862230) at Newtown, is only a few minutes walk from the town centre but has wonderful views from its hillside position. Rooms, all with a bathroom, are from £50/66. The *Bradford Old Windmill* (☎ 866842, 4 Masons Lane) is a beautifully converted old windmill overlooking the town with rooms from £65/75.

The *Swan Hotel* (☎ 868686, 1 Church St), right in the town centre, has singles

from £40 to £60, doubles from £53 to £70. Close to the bridge, the *Riverside Inn* (☎ 863526, 49 St Margarets St) has a pleasant riverside setting and simple rooms with a bathroom for £25/42. The *Georgian Lodge* (☎ 862268) across Frome Rd has rooms with bath for £40/58.

Places to Eat

The olde-worlde *Bridge Tea Rooms* beside the Town Bridge serves excellent lunches and teas: stilton and celery soup with a roll for £2.95, cream tea for £4.45. Other possibilities for lunch or tea include the tiny *Coffee Corner* behind the TIC and the *Scribbling Horse* beside it. The *Canalside Café* in the Lock Inn Cottage, near where Frome Rd crosses the canal, does things like corned beef hash for £3.15.

The *Swan Hotel* in the centre does bar food for £3 to £5 and has a restaurant with set meals. Other pub food possibilities include the *Bear Inn (26 Silver St)* and the *Canal Tavern (49 Frome Rd)*. The *Georgian Lodge* beside the Town Bridge is definitely flashier with dishes like oak smoked salmon with capers and lime for £9.

Getting There & Away

A day return by train from Bath costs £3.30 but there are also hourly buses (No X4). Once a week there are also buses to Devizes; phone ☎ 0345-090899 for details.

Getting Around

Bicycles can be hired for £9 a day from the Lock Inn Cottage (☎ 868068), at 48 Frome Rd by the canal. Canoes can also be hired here.

CHIPPENHAM & AROUND
• pop 22,000   ☎ 01249

Chippenham is an unexceptional market town with a newly pedestrianised centre which makes a touring base for several nearby attractions.

The TIC (☎ 657733) stocks a town trail map and can advise on accommodation costing from £15 a head. The museum in the 15th century **Yelde Hall** is open March to October from 10 am to 12.30 pm and from 2 to 4.30 pm (closed Sunday). While you're waiting for a bus you could pop into the delightfully old-fashioned **Waverley Restaurant**, opposite the Bear Hotel, for a cup of tea at just 40p.

Castle Combe

A Cotswold village that's strayed, Castle Combe is as close to the dream English village as you can get. There's a 13th century market cross and a packbridge with weavers' cottages reflected in a pool, and the main street is lined with flower-covered stone cottages, pubs and tasteful shops. Pretty medieval St Andrew's Church also contains a remarkable 13th century monument of Sir Walter de Dunstananville.

Gates Tea Shop (☎ 782111), by the market cross, has two double rooms costing £45 or £50 depending on the bed. During the day you can get a cream tea here too. At the opposite end of the price spectrum, the cheapest bed at the grand *Manor House Inn* (☎ 782206) is £67.50. Both the *Castle Inn* and the *White Hart* do pub lunches.

One bus a day (7 am) leaves Chippenham train station for Castle Combe – you really need a car.

Corsham Court

An Elizabethan mansion dating from 1582, Corsham Court (☎ 01249-701610) was enlarged and renovated in the 18th century to house an art collection accumulated by Paul Methuen and his descendants. The house is 3 miles south-west of Chippenham and is open Easter through October, Tuesday to Sunday from 11 am to 5.30 pm; shorter hours and days the rest of the year. Entry is £4.50/2.50.

Lacock
☎ 01249

Pretty little Lacock lays claim to being the birthplace of photography and has many buildings from an extensive medieval monastic complex. The village dates back to the Saxon era, well before the foundation of Lacock Abbey. Many of the buildings date

from medieval times and are owned by the NT; few were built after the 18th century.

The NT's free *Lacock Village* leaflet plots a route round the most interesting buildings. King John's **Hunting Lodge** dates in part from the 13th century, while the adjacent **St Cyriac's Church** is mainly late 15th century; note the brass in the south transept to Robert and Elizabeth Baynard and their 18 children (1501). The **At the Sign of the Angel** hotel dates from 1480. WH Fox Talbot of Lacock Abbey founded the village **primary school** in High St in 1824. His **grave** is in the village cemetery. Note also the 14th century **tithe barn & lock-up.**

Lacock provided the setting for many scenes in the BBC's acclaimed production of *Pride and Prejudice*.

Lacock Abbey & The Fox Talbot Museum of Photography Lacock Abbey (☎ 730227) was established as a nunnery in 1232, then sold to Sir William Sharington by Henry VIII in 1539. Sharington converted the nunnery into a home, demolished the church, tacked a tower onto the corner of the abbey building and added a brewery, while retaining the abbey cloister and other medieval features. Despite his three marriages he died childless and the house passed to the Talbot family, who bequeathed the whole village to the NT in 1944.

In the early 19th century, William Henry Fox Talbot, a prolific inventor, conducted crucial experiments in the development of photography here. Inside the entrance to the abbey a museum (☎ 730459) details his pioneering photographic work in the 1830s, when Louis Daguerre was also working in France. Fox Talbot's particular contribution was the photographic negative, from which further positive images could be produced. Before that a photograph was a one time, one image process. A picture of the abbey's oriel window may be the first photograph ever taken.

The abbey is open April to October, Wednesday to Monday, from 1 to 5.30 pm; the grounds open at noon, the museum at

11 am. Entry is £5.50/3, although if you just want to see the cloister, museum and grounds it's £3.50/2.

Places to Stay & Eat Lacock makes a wonderful place to stay although accommodation is both limited and relatively pricey. *King John's Hunting Lodge* (☎ 730313, 21 Church St) has two lovely rooms with exposed beams costing £45/55 a single/double for B&B. It also houses a weekend and summer-season tearoom. At 1 The Tanyard, *Lacock Pottery* (☎ 730266) offers beds from £20 a head, with good healthy breakfasts and the chance to sign up for a pottery course thrown in. Pricier but highly atmospheric are rooms in the 15th century *At the Sign of the Angel* (☎ 730230); beds beneath exposed beams cost from £55/80.

All three village pubs do food. At *At the Sign of the Angel* a dinner costs £22.50 a head. The *George* is cheaper and hugely popular. The *Carpenters Arms* is the most reasonably priced and spacious. In season teas are served in *The Stables* opposite the abbey.

Getting There & Away Monday to Saturday bus Nos 234/237 operate a roughly hourly service from Chippenham (10 minutes).

DEVIZES
- **pop 12,500   ☎ 01380**

An attractive market town, Devizes was once an important coaching stop and several old coaching inns survive in the market square. The TIC (☎ 729408) is at 39 St John's St, right by the square. Interesting buildings nearby include the **Corn Exchange**, topped by a figure of Ceres, goddess of agriculture, and the **Old Town Hall** of 1750-52.

Just beyond the TIC, **St John's Alley** has a wonderful collection of Elizabethan houses, their upper storeys cantilevered over the street. The new **town hall**, dating from 1806, is at this end of St John's St.

St John's Church displays elements of its original Norman construction, particularly

in the solid crossing tower. **Devizes Museum** (☎ 727369) at 41 Long St, has interesting displays on the development of Avebury and Stonehenge, a section on Roman history and an upstairs social history room. It's open Monday to Saturday from 10 am to 5 pm (closed on Saturday from 1 to 2 pm). Entry is £2/1.50 (free on Monday).

The **Kennet & Avon Canal Exhibition** (☎ 729489) in The Wharf just north of the town centre, is open Easter to Christmas, daily from 10 am to 5 pm (4 pm in winter); entry is £1/free. The **Caen Hill** flight of 29 successive locks raises the water level 72m in 2½ miles on the western outskirts of Devizes.

Places to Stay & Eat
There are camping grounds charging between £6 and £7 at *Lakeside* (☎ 722767) in nearby Rowde and at *Lower Foxhangers Farm* (☎ 828254).

Pinecroft (☎ 721433, Potterne Rd) has single/double rooms for £30/40. In Market Place, the 17th century *Bear Hotel* (☎ 722444) charges £54/80, while the 18th century *Black Swan Hotel* (☎ 723259) costs £40/60. The *Castle Hotel* (☎ 729300, New Park St) has rooms for £45/65.

The popular *Wiltshire Kitchen* (☎ 724840, 11/12 St John's St) does light lunches. A cellar restaurant also opens on Tuesday to Saturday from 7 pm. Otherwise the pubs around Market Place are your best bet for reasonably priced fare, especially on market days.

Getting There & Away
Bus Nos 33/X33 run a service from Chippenham except on Sundays.

AVEBURY
☎ 01672

Avebury stone circle stands at the hub of a prehistoric complex of ceremonial sites, ancient avenues and burial chambers. It's a bigger site and less visited than Stonehenge and you may find it more atmospheric. The impact of Neolithic people on the environment is so dramatic you can almost feel them breathing down your neck. Avebury itself is a pretty village where even the church walls are thatched. Silbury Hill and West Kennet Long Barrow are close by, and the Ridgeway Path ends here.

Orientation & Information

The Avebury stones encircle much of the village, but don't drive into it as the car park on the A4361 is only a short stroll from the circle. The TIC (☎ 539425) is in the late 17th century Great Barn.

Stone Circle

The stone circle dates from around 2600 to 2100 BC, between the first and second phase of construction at Stonehenge. With a diameter of about 348m, it's one of the largest stone circles in Britain. The site originally consisted of an outer circle of 98 standing stones from three to six metres in length, many weighing up to 20 tons. These had been

selected for their size and shape, but had not been worked to shape like those at Stonehenge. The stones were surrounded by another circle formed by a 5½m-high earth bank and a six to 9m-deep ditch. Inside were smaller stone circles to the north (27 stones) and south (29 stones).

The circles remained largely intact through the Roman period. A Saxon settlement grew up inside the circle from around 600 but in medieval times, when the church's power was strong and fear of paganism even stronger, many of the stones were deliberately buried. As the village expanded in the late 17th and early 18th century, the stones were broken up for building material. Fortunately, William Stukeley (1687-1765) surveyed the site around this time so some record survives of what had existed.

In 1934, Alexander Keiller supervised the re-erection of the buried stones and the

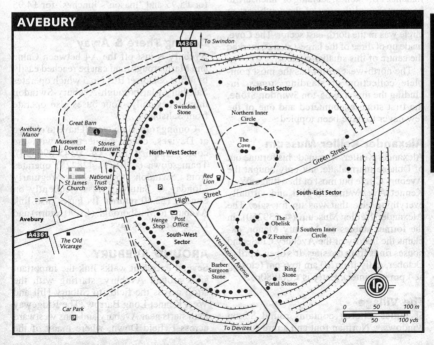

AVEBURY

placing of markers to indicate those that had disappeared. The wealthy Keiller eventually bought Avebury in order to restore 'the outstanding archaeological disgrace of Britain'.

Modern roads into Avebury neatly dissect the circle into four sectors. Start from High St, near the Henge Shop, and walk round the circle in a counter-clockwise direction. There are 12 standing stones in the south-west sector, one of them known as the **Barber Surgeon Stone**, after the skeleton of a man found under it; the equipment buried with him suggested he was a medieval travelling barber-surgeon, killed when a stone accidentally fell on him.

The south-east sector starts with the huge **portal stones** marking the entry to the circle from West Kennet Ave. The **southern inner circle** stood in this sector and within this circle was the **Obelisk** and a group of stones known as the **Z Feature**. Just outside this smaller circle, only the base of the **Ring Stone** remains. Few stones, standing or fallen, are to be seen around the rest of the south-east or north-east sectors. Most of the northern inner circle was in the north-east sector. The **Cove**, made up of three of the largest stones, marked the centre of this smaller circle.

The north-west sector has the most complete collection of standing stones, including the massive 65-ton **Swindon Stone**, the first stone encountered and one of the few never to have been toppled.

Alexander Keiller Museum

Alexander Keiller, who made his fortune out of Dundee marmalade, not only bought the Avebury Circle but most of the village, West Kennet Ave, Windmill Hill and virtually everything else that was up for sale. The Alexander Keiller Museum (☎ 539250), in the former stables of Avebury Manor, explains the history of the Avebury Circle and houses finds from the sites. It's open April to October, daily from 10 am to 6 pm (closing at 4 pm in winter). Entry is £1.60/80p.

The Village

St James Church contains round Saxon windows, a Norman font and a rare surviv-

ing rood (cross) loft. Plans exist to develop a new museum in the thatched **Great Barn**. It will exhibit information on the local landscape and the rediscovery of the stone circle. Note the 16th century circular **dovecot** close by.

Graceful **Avebury Manor** (☎ 539388, NT) dates back to the 16th century but was altered in the early 18th century. It's open from April through October, Tuesday, Wednesday and Sunday from 2 to 5.30 pm. Admission costs £3/1.50. The gardens are open daily except Monday and Thursday from 11 am to 5.30 pm.

Places to Stay & Eat

B&B is available at *The Old Vicarage* (☎ 539362) for £21 a head, or at *The Red Lion* (☎ 539240) where doubles cost from £40.

Beside the Great Barn, the popular *Stones Restaurant* offers 'megaliths' (hot dishes) for £5.95 and 'mason's lunches' for £4.95 (weekends only November through March).

Getting There & Away

Avebury is just off the A4 between Calne and Marlborough, and can be reached easily by Wilts & Dorset Bus No 5 which operates Salisbury-Marlborough-Avebury-Swindon three times daily. Tour buses also operate from Salisbury.

Coming from Bath, you'll have to change at Devizes; check connections with the county inquiry line (☎ 0345-090899). Thamesdown (☎ 01793-428428) operates from Swindon to Avebury regularly Monday to Saturday, less frequently on Sunday (£2.40 return). Its buses also link Avebury to Marlborough (£1.90 return) and Devizes on weekdays.

AROUND AVEBURY

Several excellent walks link the important sites around Avebury, starting with the stroll across the fields to Silbury Hill and West Kennet Long Barrow. The Ridgeway Path starts near Avebury and runs westward across Fyfield Down, where many of the sarsen stones at Avebury (and Stonehenge) were collected.

Windmill Hill

The earliest site around Avebury, Windmill Hill was a Neolithic enclosure or 'camp' dating from about 3700 BC. Ditches confirm its shape.

The Avenue & Sanctuary

The 1½ mile-long West Kennet Ave, lined by 100 pairs of stones, connects the Sanctuary with the Avebury Circle. Today, the B4003 road follows the same route and at its southern end the A4 virtually overrides the avenue. The stone shapes along the avenue alternate between column-like stones and triangular-shaped ones; Keiller thought they might have been intended to signify male and female.

Only the site of the Sanctuary remains, although the post and stone holes indicate there was a wooden building surrounded by a stone circle. The possible route of Beckhampton Ave, a similar 'avenue' into Avebury from the south-west, is mainly guesswork.

Silbury Hill

Rising abruptly from the surrounding fields, Silbury Hill is one of the largest artificial hills in Europe, similar in size to the smaller Egyptian pyramids. Like a truncated cone, its 40m-high summit ends in a flat top measuring 30m across. It was constructed in stages from around 2500 BC but its purpose is a mystery. Certainly no one seems to have been buried here.

West Kennet Long Barrow

Across the fields south of Silbury Hill stands West Kennet Long Barrow, England's finest burial mound, dating from around 3500 BC and measuring 104m by 23m. Its entrance is guarded by huge sarsens, massive stones like those at Stonehenge, and its roof is constructed of gigantic overlapping capstones. About 50 skeletons were found when it was excavated. The finds are displayed in Devizes Museum.

MARLBOROUGH
- **pop 5400** ☎ 01672

Marlborough started life as a Saxon settlement at The Green, and the main street extended westward from there to an 18m-high prehistoric mound where the Normans later erected a motte and bailey fortification. To make more room for a market as the town grew, the houses along High St were pushed back until the road reached its present extraordinary width.

Today's High St makes an interesting stroll, particularly on Wednesday and Saturday, which are market days. The 17th century **Merchant's House** at No 132 (☎ 511491) is scheduled to become a museum. The exclusive Marlborough College now occupies the site of the **old Norman castle**. Just to the west is a small white horse cut into the hillside by schoolboys in 1804.

The TIC (☎ 513989) is in George Lane car park off High St. There's plenty of accommodation along High St and George Lane. Pubs with good food along High St include the **Green Dragon**, the 15th century **Sun Inn** and the **Wellington Arms**. **Options** behind the Ivy House Hotel has some vegetarian dishes on its menu. Best of the teashops is **Harpers**, across the road from St Peter's church, although service may be quicker at the **Tudor** and **Polly Tea Rooms** in the High St.

MALMESBURY
- **pop 4300** ☎ 01666

Perched on top of a hill, Malmesbury has a superb semi-ruined abbey church, a late 15th century market cross and several pleasant pubs and restaurants. The well-stocked TIC (☎ 823748) in the town hall on Market Lane has a good *Town Trail* (10p). It's round the corner from the small **Athelstan Museum** and car park.

Malmesbury Abbey

Malmesbury Abbey is a wonderful mix of ruin and living church. The church was begun in the 12th century and by the 14th was a massive construction 100m long with a tower at the western end and a tower and spire at the crossing. In 1479, a storm brought the tower and spire crashing down; its fall destroyed the crossing and the eastern end of the church.

When the monastery was suppressed in 1539, the abbey was sold to a local clothier who initially moved looms into the nave. Later he changed his mind and gave it to the town to replace the ruinous parish church of St Paul's. In about 1662, the west tower fell, destroying three of the west bays of the nave. Today's church consists of the remaining six bays – about a third of the original church – framed by ruins at either end.

The church is entered via the magnificent south porch, its doorway a Norman work with stone sculpture illustrating Bible stories. The huge carved Apostles on each side of the porch are some of the finest Romanesque carvings in Britain. Looking out over the nave from the south side is a watching loft whose purpose is obscure. In the north-eastern corner of the church is a medieval cenotaph (empty tomb) commemorating Athelstan, king of England from 925 to 939 and grandson of Alfred the Great.

Steps lead up to the parvise, a small room above the porch (£1 requested), which contains a collection of books, including a four-volume illuminated manuscript Bible of 1407. A window at the western end of the church shows Elmer the Flying Monk. In 1010, he strapped on wings and jumped from the tower. Remarkably, he survived, and blamed his crash-landing on aerodynamic problems.

In the churchyard, the 14th century steeple of St Paul's, the original parish church, now serves as the belfry. Towards the south-eastern corner of the churchyard is the **gravestone of Hannah Twynnoy** who died in 1703, aged 33. Her headstone reads: 'For tyger fierce, Took life away, And here she lies, In a bed of clay'. The tiger belonged to a visiting circus and she was killed in the White Lion pub where she was a serving maid.

The abbey is open from 10 am to 4 pm daily. A £1 donation is requested.

Places to Stay & Eat

Burton Hill Camping Park (☎ 822585) is a 10 minute walk along the river and has sites for £7.

The *King's Arms Hotel* (☎ 823383, High St) is an old coaching inn with rooms from £27.50 per person. *Bremilham House* (☎ 822680, Bremilham Rd) is an easy walk from the town centre and costs £18.50/32 for singles/doubles. The historic *Old Bell Inn* (☎ 822344, Abbey Row) by the abbey, charges from £75/90 for luxurious rooms.

The cheerful *Whole Hog* (☎ 825845) wine bar is right behind the market cross. A hogburger costs £4.35 (vegetarian version available), a pigwitch sandwich from £2.95.

Bristol & Bath

Just 12 miles apart, Bath and Bristol are the Edinburgh and Glasgow of England. Bath, with its gorgeous honey-coloured Georgian architecture, is one of the great 'must see' cities of Britain. Far fewer tourists make it to Bristol, but those that do sometimes enjoy it more just because it has to make fewer concessions to outsiders.

BRISTOL
- **pop 414,000   ☎ 0117**

Home to Portishead, Tricky, Massive Attack, and Wallace and Gromit, Bristol is south-western England's largest city. Unfortunately WWII bombing raids destroyed much of the centre, which was rebuilt with scant regard for aesthetics in the 1950s and 60s. The city does, however, have pockets of magnificent architecture, docks and warehouses that have been rescued from ruin, and plenty of pubs and restaurants.

Although it's 6 miles from the Severn estuary, Bristol is most famous as a port. However, by the late 19th century changing trading needs had rendered the docks obsolete and they were relocated from the city centre to nearby Avonmouth and Portishead. Work has finally started on restoring the last pocket of dereliction around the old Floating Harbour. It's unlikely to be completed much before the millennium.

The mainly Afro-Caribbean suburb of St Paul's, just north-east of the centre, remains a run-down, occasionally tense part of town with a heavy drug scene, best not visited alone at night.

Bristol is an important transport hub, with connections north to the Cotswolds and the Midlands, south-west to Devon and Cornwall, and east to Bath (an easy day trip). South Wales is linked to Bristol across the Severn Bridge and the unimaginatively named Second Severn Crossing.

History

Little is known about Bristol until the 10th century, but in the Middle Ages a town grew up around a castle near what is now Bristol Bridge. The centre of town was then around Wine, High, Broad and Corn Sts.

Several religious houses were established on high ground above the marshes, commemorated in the name of Temple Meads station. The importance of choosing high ground is shown by a look at Bristol's own leaning tower, attached to Temple Church in Victoria St.

Soon Bristol's wealth was dependent on the triangular trade in slaves, cocoa, sugar, tobacco and manufactured goods with Africa and the New World. William Canynges, a wealthy merchant, paid for the original church on the site of St Mary Redcliffe and it was from Bristol that John Cabot sailed to discover Newfoundland in 1497.

By the 18th century, the city was suffering from competition from Liverpool in particular, and the Avon Gorge made it hard for large ships to reach the city-centre docks. By the 1870s, when new docks were opened at Avonmouth and Portishead, Britain's economic focus had shifted northwards.

Orientation

The city centre, to the north of the Floating Harbour, is easy to get around on foot but very hilly. Clifton lies to the north-west, accessible by bus from the centre. Bristol's main shopping centre is the undercover Galleries shopping mall in Broadmead, but the shops lining Park St, Queens Rd and

Whiteladies Rd, and those in Clifton, are more interesting.

The main train station is Bristol Temple Meads, a mile south-east of the centre and linked to it by regular buses. Some trains use Bristol Parkway, 5 miles to the north, just off the M4 and accessible from the centre by bus and train. A taxi will cost about £8.

The bus station in Marlborough St to the north of the city centre serves National Express coaches and Badgerline buses to surrounding towns and villages.

Information

The TIC (☎ 926 0767) is housed in St Nicholas Church, St Nicholas St, which has a magnificent 18th century altarpiece by William Hogarth. The comprehensive *Visitors Guide* is worth buying, as are the booklets describing the *Bristol Heritage Trail* and the *Slave Trade Trail*.

The fortnightly listings magazine *Venue* gives details of what's happening in Bristol. Bristol Books (☎ 924 5458), 180B Cheltenham Rd, is excellent for second-hand books.

Bristol Cathedral

Originally founded as the church of an Augustinian monastery in 1140, Bristol Cathedral (☎ 926 4879) on College Green gained cathedral status in 1542. One of its most striking features is its Norman chapter house. The choir dates back to the 14th century but much of the nave and the west towers were designed by George Street in 1868. The south transept shelters a rare Saxon carving of the 'Harrowing of Hell'.

Museums

The **City Museum & Art Gallery** (☎ 922 3571) at the top of Park St, houses a mixed bag of exhibits, ranging from Egyptian mummies through natural history and local history to fine art. It's open daily from 10 am to 5 pm; admission is free.

Those interested in Bristol's links with the aerospace industry should head for the **Industrial Museum** (☎ 925 1470) at Princes Wharf in the docks. It's open April to

BRISTOL

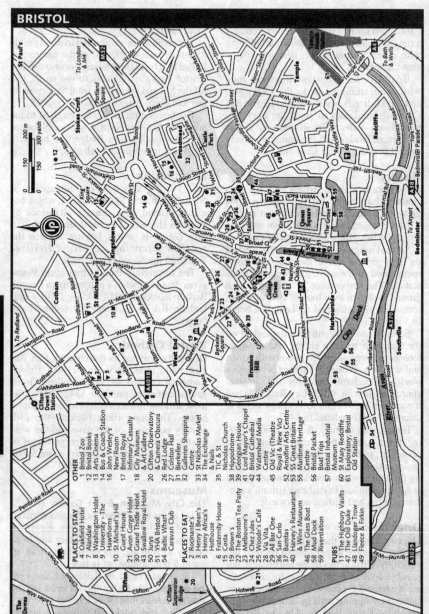

PLACES TO STAY
4 Oakfield Hotel
7 Alandale
8 Washington Hotel
9 University - The Hawthorns
10 St Michael's Hill Guest House
21 Avon Gorge Hotel
30 Grand Thistle Hotel
43 Swallow Royal Hotel
50 Jurys
51 YHA Bristol
54 Baltic Wharf Caravan Club

PLACES TO EAT
2 Rocinante's
3 Henry J Bean's
5 Henry Africa's Hothouse
6 Fraternity House
15 Costa
19 Brown's
22 The Boston Tea Party
23 Melbourne's
24 Chez Jules
25 Woode's Café
28 Via Vita
29 All Bar One
37 Banistas
40 Harvey's Restaurant & Wine Museum
46 The Glass Boat
58 Mud Dock
59 Riverstation

PUBS
11 The Highbury Vaults
47 The Old Duke
48 Llandoger Trow
49 Fleece & Firkin

OTHER
1 Bristol Zoo
12 Bristol Books
13 Arts Cinema
14 Bus & Coach Station
16 John Wesley's New Room
17 Bristol Royal Infirmary Casualty
18 City Museum & Art Gallery
20 Clifton Observatory & Camera Obscura
26 Red Lodge
27 Colston Hall
31 Bierkeller
32 Galleries Shopping
33 St Nicholas Market
34 The Exchange & Nails
35 TIC & St Nicholas Church
38 Hippodrome
39 Georgian House
41 Lord Mayor's Chapel
42 Bristol Cathedral
44 Watershed Media Centre
45 Old Vic (Theatre Royal & New Vic)
52 Arnolfini Arts Centre
53 SS Great Britains
55 Maritime Heritage Centre
56 Bristol Packet Boat Trips
57 Bristol Industrial Museum
60 St Mary Redcliffe
61 Exploratory: Bristol Old Station

October, Saturday to Wednesday from 10 am to 5 pm (weekends only in winter), admission free.

SS *Great Britain*

Bristol was home to the Victorian engineering genius Isambard Kingdom Brunel (1806-59), best known for the Clifton Suspension Bridge. In 1843, he designed the first ocean-going iron ship, the SS *Great Britain*, the first large ship to be driven by a screw propeller.

For 43 years the ship served as a cargo vessel and a liner, carrying passengers as far as Australia. Then in 1886 it was badly damaged passing Cape Horn. The cost of repairs was judged too high, so it was sold for storage. In 1970, it was returned to Bristol and since then has been undergoing restoration in the dry dock where it was originally built.

The ship (☎ 926 0680) is off City Dock and is open daily from April through October from 10 am to 5.30 pm (4.30 pm in winter); tickets are £3.90/2.70.

Entrance is via the **Maritime Heritage Centre**, which celebrates Bristol's shipbuilding past (same opening hours as the ship; admission free).

Clifton & the Suspension Bridge

The northern suburb of Clifton boasts some splendid Georgian architecture, including the Cornwallis and Royal York crescents, as well as some of Bristol's most attractive shopping streets. Bus Nos 8/9 and 508/9 run to Clifton from the city centre.

The spectacular 75m-high **Clifton Suspension Bridge**, designed by Brunel, spans a dramatic stretch of the Avon Gorge. Work on the bridge began in 1836 but wasn't completed until 1864, after Brunel's death. The bridge is an inevitable magnet for stunt artists. More poignantly, it's also a favoured suicide spot. A famous story relates how Sarah Ann Hedley jumped from the bridge in 1885 after a lovers' tiff. Her voluminous petticoats parachuted her safely to earth and she lived to be 85. A new visitors centre is open daily from 10 am to 6 pm for £1/80p.

On Durdham Downs, overlooking the bridge, an **observatory** houses a fascinating camera obscura (75p/50p). Nearby is **Bristol Zoo Gardens** (☎ 970 6176), open daily from 9 am to 5.30 pm (4.30 pm in winter). Admission costs £6.50/3.50.

Georgian House & Red Lodge

The Georgian House (☎ 921 1362) at 7 Great George St was home to 18th century sugar merchant John Pinney, and retains complete period fixtures and fittings.

The Elizabethan Red Lodge (☎ 921 1360) with walled garden in Perry Rd, was much altered in the 18th century. One room is preserved as a memorial to Mary Carpenter who set up the first women's reformatory here in 1854.

Both are open Saturday to Wednesday from 10 am to 5 pm. Admission is free.

Bristol Old Station

Before rushing for their train, visitors to Temple Meads station should pause to look at what is the oldest surviving major railway terminus in the world, built to yet another Brunel design in 1839-40. The original terminus stands to the left of the modern one; the Great Train Shed, with its mock hammerbeam roof, last saw a train in 1966 – try the door of the **Brunel Centre** and you may be able to look round.

At the time of writing, parts of the old station housed the **Exploratory** (☎ 907 9000), Bristol's hands-on science exhibition. It's open daily from 10 am to 5 pm and costs £5/3.50 but may close during the life of this book.

Churches & Chapels

Described as 'the fairest, goodliest and most famous parish church in England' by Queen Elizabeth I in 1574, **St Mary Redcliffe** (☎ 929 1487) is a stunning piece of perpendicular architecture with a grand hexagonal porch which easily outdoes the cathedral in splendour. It's open daily from 8 am to 8 pm, closing at 5.30 pm in winter.

Once the chapel of St Mark's Hospital, the **Lord Mayor's Chapel** (☎ 929 4350) in

Park St is a medieval gem squeezed in between shops opposite the cathedral and packed with stained-glass windows, medieval monuments and ancient tiles. The church-loving poet John Betjeman dubbed it 'for its size one of the very best churches in England ... '. It's open daily except Monday, from 10 am to noon and 1 to 4 pm.

Tucked away in Broadmead Shopping Centre, the **New Room** (☎ 926 4740) was the world's first Methodist chapel when it opened in 1739. John Wesley, whose equestrian statue stands in the courtyard, preached from its double-decker pulpit. Upstairs, visit the old living quarters, with rooms for John and Charles Wesley and Francis Asbury.

Entry to the chapel (☎ 926 4740) is free and it's open from 10 am to 1 pm and from 2 to 4 pm daily except Sunday (and Wednesdays in winter).

Blaise Castle House Museum

In the northern suburb of Henbury lies Blaise Castle (☎ 950 6789), a late 18th century house which contains a fine museum of West Country rural and urban life. Admission is free and it's open Saturday to Wednesday, from 10 am to 5 pm.

On a hill stands a mock castle, in grounds laid out by Humphrey Repton. Across the road is **Blaise Hamlet**, a cluster of thatched cottages designed for estate servants in 1811 by John Nash; with its neatly-kept green and flower-filled gardens, it's everyone's fantasy of a 'medieval' English village.

Bus Nos 1/501 pass this way from the city centre.

Organised Tours

From June to the end of September, hop-on, hop-off open-top bus tours circle 14 points in Bristol every day except Saturday. Tickets (£5/3) can be bought on board the bus or from the TIC. Pick up the bus in St Augustine's Parade, outside the Hippodrome.

Special Events

St Paul's Carnival, a smaller version of London's Notting Hill Carnival, livens up the first Saturday of each July. There's a regatta in the harbour in July, and not-to-be-missed hot-air balloon and kite festivals in Ashton Court, across Clifton Suspension Bridge, in August and September.

Places to Stay

Camping The *Baltic Wharf Caravan Club* site (☎ 926 8030, Cumberland Rd), 1½ miles from the centre, charges £10.50 for a tent space for two people. It's near the A370, A369, A4 and A3029 junctions. Advance booking is essential, especially at weekends.

Hostels Bristol has very little cheap accommodation, but the 129-bed *Bristol Youth Hostel (☎ 922 1659, 14 Narrow Quay St)* in a converted warehouse, five minutes from the town centre, is an excellent place to stay. The nightly charge is £11.65/8 for adults/juniors.

Outside term times, the university also lets out rooms, most centrally in *The Hawthorns (☎ 923 8366, Woodland Rd, Clifton)* which charges £20/32 a single/double.

B&Bs & Hotels *St Michael's Hill Guest House (☎ 973 0037, 145 St Michael's Hill)* is well situated and good value, for £15/20 without breakfast, £17/24 with. The *Lawns Guest House (☎ 973 8459, 91 Hampton Rd)* in the leafy suburb of Redland, offers singles/doubles for £24/40.

Most of the other cheap B&Bs tend to be a fair distance from the centre. Clifton, 1½ miles from the centre, is a very attractive suburb and a good place to stay, but most of the B&Bs here cost £20 to £25 per person. On Oakfield Rd (off Whiteladies Rd), the *Oakfield Hotel (☎ 973 5556)* has rooms for £27/37. In Tyndalls Park Rd the *Alandale (☎ 973 5407)* charges from £30/45.

The *Washington Hotel (☎ 973 3980, St Paul's Rd)* is midway between the city centre and Clifton Suspension Bridge. During the week, rooms are £45/62 with a bathroom, £36/46 without. At weekends, dinner and bed and breakfast costs £38 a head.

About a mile north of the centre, *Courtlands Hotel (☎ 942 4432, 1 Redland Court*

Rd, Redland) is a family-run place with a bar and restaurant. There are 25 rooms, most with bathroom, for £46/56.

Most of the city centre hotels rake in the loot from their business clientele midweek and then slash prices at weekends. A good bet is the *Avon Gorge Hotel* (☎ 973 8955, *Sion Hill, Clifton*) which has a terrace overlooking the suspension bridge. It's expensive during the week, but prices drop to £38 a head for B&B, or £53 for half-board, provided you stay two nights, at the weekend.

The *Grand Thistle Hotel* (☎ 929 1645, *Broad St*) is a Victorian hotel in the heart of the city. During the week, rooms are £100/110, without breakfast. At weekends, B&B costs £42 a head.

Jurys (☎ 923 0333, *Prince St*) has a splendid position overlooking the Floating Harbour but charges £128 for a room midweek, falling to £64 at weekends.

Flashiest of all is the 19th century *Swallow Royal Hotel* (☎ 925 5100, *College Green*) beside the cathedral. Swish B&B costs £120/125 during the week, £60/95 at weekends.

Places to Eat

If you're dining on a shoestring, one of the cheapest places to eat in the city centre is inside *St Nicholas Market* where sausage sandwiches can be had for £1.30 and cups of tea for 50p. The food hall on the top floor of the Galleries shopping centre offers the chance of mixing and matching all sorts of reasonably priced fast foods.

Other popular lunch spots include the café bars in the *Watershed* (☎ 921 4135) and the *Arnolfini* (☎ 937 9191), both overlooking the waterfront; quick, tasty meals in either cost around £5. Not far away the *Mud Dock* (☎ 934 9734, 40 The Grove) above a bike shop, is a bit pricier but very popular, with more water views. The nearby *River-station* (☎ 914 4434) has excellent food (scrumptious desserts) that costs less downstairs than upstairs.

Coffee houses are springing up around the centre; try *Baristas* at the junction of Baldwin and Clare Sts, or *Costa* in the Broadmead arcade.

Heading towards Clifton, Park St is lined with reasonably priced pizzerias: try *Pastificio* or *Vincenzo's*. *Woode's Café*, at the bottom of Park St, sells excellent sandwiches, while *Chez Jules* (☎ 929 7298) at No 64 doles out reasonably priced French food and wine. Hottest spot of all is *The Boston Tea Party* (☎ 929 8601) at No 75 which does such tasty lunches that you'll be lucky to get a seat between 1 and 2 pm. There's a larger branch in Lewins Mead.

Melbourne's (☎ 922 6996, 74 Park St) keeps prices down with a bring-your-own-bottle policy. *Brown's* (☎ 930 4777, 38 Queens Rd), serves excellent pasta from £6.55 in the classy surroundings of the neo-Venetian ex-university refectory.

A 20 minute walk from the centre and running off Queens Rd, Whiteladies Rd now boasts so many flashy café bars that it's been dubbed 'The Strip'. See and be seen at *Henry J Bean's* American diner (☎ 974 3794) at No 95, at *Henry Africa's Hothouse* (☎ 923 8300) at No 65, or at the vast *Fraternity House* at No 59 where £5 meals are on offer from 4 to 7 pm Monday to Friday.

Rocinante's (☎ 973 4482) at No 85 is a lively tapas bar with good choices for vegetarians.

Recently the grand old bank buildings along Corn St have been given new life as pubs, café bars and restaurants. There are branches of *All Bar One* and *Via Vita*, while *San Carlo* does pizzas from £4.80.

For a splurge, the place to go is *Harvey's Restaurant* (☎ 927 5034, 12 Denmark St) above Harvey's Wine Museum; four-course dinners cost £29. In a prettier setting is *The Glass Boat* (☎ 929 0704), a converted barge on Welsh Back, where dinner will cost around £20.

Entertainment

Venue magazine gives details of theatre, music, gigs – the works.

Pubs & Clubs Most pubs in and around St Augustine's Parade (the city centre) are best

SOUTH-WESTERN ENGLAND

avoided, especially at weekends. Instead, head down King St to the *Llandoger Trow* or the *Old Duke* which hosts nightly jazz sessions. Popular student hang-outs include *The Albion*, in Boyces Ave, Clifton, and the *Highbury Vaults* on St Michael's Hill, which has a courtyard for alfresco tippling. Cider-lovers shouldn't miss *The Coronation Tap* in Sion Place, Clifton. The rash of Irish pubs between Baldwin St and Corn St are cheerful enough but no more 'Irish' than those with fewer shamrocks on display.

The *Fleece & Firkin* (☎ 927 7150, St Thomas St) hosts world-music sessions and live bands, as does the legendary *Bierkeller* (☎ 926 8514, All Saints St) that has played host to plenty of rock luminaries; entry costs from £1 to £12 depending on the night of the week and who's playing.

Trendy nightspots come and go with alarming frequency. The popular *Lakota* (☎ 942 6208, 2 Upper York St) stays open until 4 or 6 am, whereupon you can move on to *Club Loco* (☎ 942 6208, Hepburn Rd) off Stokes Croft, which has a 24-hour licence. *Yum Yum* on Saturday night at Club Leo (☎ 929 2420, St Nicholas St) is the place for gay clubbers.

Theatre, Cinema & Concerts Of the theatres, the *Hippodrome* (☎ 929 9444, St Augustine's Parade) hosts ballet, musicals and pantomimes, while the *Old Vic* (☎ 926 4388, King St) sticks with straight drama. The *Colston Hall* (☎ 922 3686, Colston St) stages everything from wrestling bouts to concerts.

Most interesting cinema programs tend to be at the *Watershed Media Centre* (☎ 925 3845), the *Arnolfini Centre* (☎ 929 9191) and the King's Square *Arts Cinema* (☎ 942 0195).

Getting There & Away
See the fares tables in the Getting Around chapter. Bristol is 115 miles from London, 75 from Exeter and 50 from Cardiff.

Air Bristol International Airport (☎ 01275-474444) is 8 miles south-west of town, off the A38. There are buses to the airport from Marlborough St bus station and less frequently from Temple Meads train station.

Bus Every 1½ hours National Express (☎ 0990-808080) has services to Heathrow airport (2½ hours, £23) and Gatwick airport (three hours, £26). Services into central London are equally regular (2½ hours, £9). Bakers Dolphin (☎ 961 4000) also sells tickets to London at £8.95/15.95 a single/return. Tickets are sold in Bakers Dolphin travel agencies around town.

National Express has frequent buses to Cardiff (1¼ hours, £4). There are a couple of buses a day to Barnstaple (2¾ hours, £14) and regular buses south to Truro in Cornwall (4½ hours, £24), Exeter in Devon (1¾ hours, £9.10), Oxford (2½ hours, £11.75) and Stratford-upon-Avon (2½ hours, £11.75).

Local Badgerline buses (☎ 955 3231) also operate out of Marlborough St bus station. There are frequent services to Bath, Wells and Glastonbury. Hourly buses to Bath can also be picked up outside Temple Meads train station. There are also services to Salisbury and north to Gloucester. Day Rambler tickets (£4.95) let you use Badgerline and City Line buses all day.

Train Bristol is an important rail hub, with regular connections to London Paddington (1½ hours). Most trains (except those to the south) use both the Temple Meads and Parkway stations.

Only 20 minutes away, Bath makes an easy day trip (£4.30 day return). There are frequent links to Cardiff (¾ hour, £6.10), Exeter (one hour, £13.90), Fishguard (3½ hours, £19.40), Oxford (1½ hours, £18) and Birmingham (1½ hours, £12).

Boat Between July and October you can travel by boat along the Bristol Channel from Bristol to Clevedon, Penarth, Ilfracombe, Barry and Lundy Island. Sailings are on the SS *Balmoral* or the SS *Waverley*, the world's last seagoing paddle steamer. Prices start at £5.95 to Clevedon. Full details from Waverley Excursions on ☎ 01446-720656.

Getting Around

Bus City Line (☎ 955 3231) bus fares aren't cheap, but Dayrider tickets available on the bus after 9 am from Monday to Friday and at any time at the weekend, let you make six journeys for £2.80.

Clifton is a long walk from the town centre. Catch bus Nos 8/9 (508/509 at weekends) from bus stop 'Cu' on Colston Ave, or from Temple Meads train station. In summer, half-hourly bus No 511 loops from Baltic Wharf to Broadmead, through Clifton Triangle and Hotwells, and back to Baltic Wharf, linking many of the major attractions and shopping centres.

Taxi The taxi rank on St Augustine's Parade is central but not a good place to hang around late at night. To call a cab free, ring 1A Premier Cabs on ☎ 0800-716777. A taxi to the airport costs around £13.

Boat The nicest way to get around is to use the ferry which, from April to September, plies the Floating Harbour, stopping at the SS *Great Britain*, Hotwells, the Baltic Wharf, the Centre, Bristol Bridge (for Broadmead Shopping Centre) and Castle Park. The ferry (☎ 927 3416) runs every 40 minutes. A short hop is 80p/50p, a complete circuit £2.50/1.50.

BATH

- **pop 84,400**　☎ **01225**

Beautiful Bath is one of the 'must sees' on any first-time visitor's list. For more than 2000 years, the city's fortune has revolved around its hot springs and the tourism linked to it. It was the Romans who first developed a complex of baths and a temple to the goddess Sulis-Minerva on the site of what they called Aquae Sulis. Today, however, Bath is just as famous for its glorious Georgian architecture that has won it World Heritage Site status from UNESCO.

Throughout the 18th century, Bath was the fashionable haunt of English society. Aristocrats flocked here to gossip, gamble and flirt. Fortunately, they had the good sense and fortune to employ the brilliant architects who designed the Palladian terraced housing, the circles, crescents and squares, that dominate the city.

Like Florence in Italy, Bath is an architectural gem. It too has a shop-lined, much-photographed bridge. Like Florence, it can also seem at times like little more than an upmarket shopping mall for wealthy tourists. However, when sunlight brightens the honey-coloured stone, and buskers and strollers fill the streets and line the river, only the most churlish would deny its charm. Head up some of the steep hills and you can even find pockets of Georgiana that only the residents seem to appreciate.

Bath looks wealthier than Bristol, in part because its beauty attracts moneyed residents, in part because the sheer crush of visitors ensures the good life to those involved in tourism. The best known sites in and around Abbey Courtyard receive too many visitors for their own good. Away from the centre, however, smaller museums fight for the droppings from their more famous neighbours' tables and are genuinely pleased to see those who trouble to seek them out. Inevitably, Bath also has its share of residents for whom affluence is somebody else's success story. For all the glitzy shops, you'll still see beggars on the streets.

The big news in Bath is that at long last the city looks set to have a spa again. A grant from the Millennium Fund is to finance the restoration of the old Hot and Cross Baths and the building of a brand-new spa complex designed by Nicholas Grimshaw, the architect behind the Eurostar Terminal at Waterloo. Work began in August 1998 and is due for completion in the year 2000.

History

Prehistoric camps on the hills around Bath indicate settlement before the Romans arrived, and legend records King Bladud founding the town after being cured of leprosy by a bath in the muddy swamps. The Romans established the town of Aquae Sulis (named after the Celtic goddess Sul) in 44 AD and it was already a spa, with an extensive baths complex, by the reign of Agricola (78-84).

When the Romans left, the town declined and was captured by the Anglo-Saxons in 577. In 944, a monastery was set up on the site of the present abbey and there are still traces of the medieval town wall in Borough Walls St. Throughout the Middle Ages, Bath served as an ecclesiastical centre and a wool trading town. However, it wasn't until the 18th century that it really came into its own, when the idea of taking spa water as a cure for assorted ailments led to the creation of the beautiful city visitors see today. Those were the days when Ralph Allen developed the quarries at Coombe Down and employed the two John Woods (father and son) to create the glorious crescents and terraces; when Doctor William Oliver established the Bath General Hospital for the poor and gave his name to the Bath Oliver biscuit; and when the gambler Richard 'Beau' Nash became the arbiter of fashionable taste.

By the mid-19th century, sea bathing had become more popular than spa visiting and Bath fell out of fashion. Curiously, even in the 1960s few people appreciated its architecture and many houses were pulled down to make way for modern replacements before legislation was introduced to protect what remains.

Orientation

Although hemmed in by seven hills, Bath still manages to sprawl quite a way (as you'll discover if you stay at the youth hostel). Fortunately, the centre is compact and easy to get around on foot.

The train and bus stations are both south of the TIC at the end of Manvers St. The most obvious landmark is the abbey, across from the Roman Baths and Pump Room. Guided tours and open-top bus tours leave from Terrace Walk nearby.

Information

From mid-June to mid-September, the TIC (☎ 462831), Abbey Chambers, Abbey Churchyard, is open until 7 pm from Monday to Saturday, and until 6 pm on Sunday. For the rest of the year, it closes at 5 pm, and 4 pm on Sunday. Free walking tours (highly recommended) leave from the Abbey Churchyard at 10.30 am (except Saturday). Bath's hilly terrain makes life difficult for disabled visitors but the TIC supplies a free guide with helpful information.

Bath has a bad traffic problem and parking space is hard to find. In the city centre, you must display a parking disc in your windscreen. It will cost you 50p for quarter of an hour and can be bought from local shops.

From mid-May to early June the Bath Festival is in full swing with events in all the town's venues, including the abbey. *Venue*, the Bristol and Bath listings magazine, publishes full program details, although popular events are booked up well in advance. Details are available from the Festival Box Office (☎ 462231), Linley House, 1 Pierrepont Place, from February each year. Accommodation is likely to be particularly hard to find during the festival.

Much of the city centre, including the maze of passageways just north of Abbey Churchyard and Shire's Yard off Milsom St, is given over to shops of the pricey 'novelty' kind, but the Saturday and Sunday morning flea market (antiques and clothes) in Walcot St, near the YMCA, is popular with bargain hunters. The covered Guildhall Market in High St has excellent second-hand bookstalls.

Walking Tour

Bath was designed for leisurely exploration – you need at least a day to take in the highlights.

The best starting point is the **abbey**, conveniently situated across from the **Roman Baths** and **Pump Room**. Ahead of it, you'll see a colonnade – walk under it and turn left into Stall St. On the right, Bath St has convenient arcading so bathers could walk between the town's three sets of baths without getting wet.

Walk down Bath St. At the end stands the **Cross Bath** where Mary of Modena, wife of

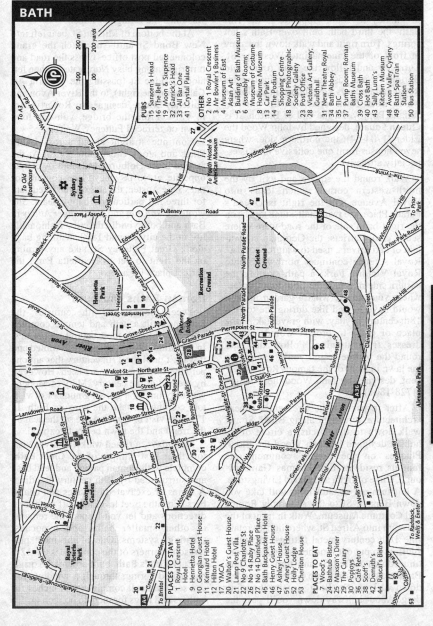

BATH

PUBS
15 Saracen's Head
16 The Bell
19 Moon & Sixpence
32 Garrick's Head
33 All Bar One
41 Crystal Palace

OTHER
2 No 1 Royal Crescent
3 Mr Bowler's Business
4 Museum of East
  Asian Art
5 Building of Bath Museum
6 Assembly Rooms;
  Museum of Costume
8 Holburne Museum
13 Car Park
14 The Podium
18 Shopping Centre
23 Post Office
28 Royal Photographic
  Society Gallery
31 Victoria Art Gallery;
  Guildhall
34 New Theatre Royal
35 Bath Abbey
37 TIC
39 Pump Room; Roman
  Baths Museum
40 Cross Bath
43 Hot Bath
44 Sally Lunn's
  Kitchen Museum
48 Avon Valley Cyclery
49 Bath Spa Train
  Station
50 Bus Station

PLACES TO STAY
1 Royal Crescent
  Hotel
9 Henrietta Hotel
10 Georgian Guest House
11 Kennard Hotel
12 Hilton Hotel
17 YMCA
20 Walton's Guest House
21 Lamp Post Villa
26 No 9 Charlotte St
27 No 14 Dunsford Place
45 Bath Backpackers Hotel
46 Henry Guest House
47 Ashley House
51 Arney Guest House
52 Holly Lodge
53 Cheriton House

PLACES TO EAT
7 Wood's
24 Bathtub Bistro
25 Maxson's Diner
29 The Canary
30 Popjoys
36 Café Retro
38 Scoff's
42 Demuth's
44 Rascal's Bistro

James II, erected a cross in gratitude for her pregnancy in 1688. Opposite is the **Hot Bath**, the third bath built over Bath's hot springs. Turn right and walk down the alley in front of the cinema into Westgate St. Turn left and follow the road round into Barton St and past the Georgian **Theatre Royal** and **Popjoys Restaurant**, in the house where Beau Nash lived with his mistress Juliana Popjoy. At the end of Barton St is **Queen Square**, designed by John Wood the Elder (1704-54); the northern side, where seven houses form one cohesive unit, is especially attractive.

Walk round the square and exit by the north-western corner which leads into Royal Avenue. On the right is Queen's Parade Place; the two small, stone kiosks on the right-hand side of the road were where sedan chair carriers, the Georgian equivalent of taxi drivers, used to wait for custom. Royal Avenue continues northwards into Royal Victoria Park; a path skirting the eastern side runs past the **Georgian Garden**, where you can see what a garden in Bath would have looked like during the town's 18th century heyday, with gravel taking the place of grass to protect women's long dresses from staining. Follow the path round the perimeter and you'll emerge on the lawn in front of the famous **Royal Crescent**, designed by John Wood the Younger (1728-1801).

After inspecting the Crescent's superb architecture, turn right along Brock St and walk down to the **Circus**, a circle of 30 houses designed by John Wood the Elder. Plaques on the houses commemorate famous residents like Thomas Gainsborough, Clive of India and David Livingstone. A left turn out of the Circus will take you down Bennett St to the **Assembly Rooms** and **Costume Museum**. Walk in front of the museum into Alfred St, where houses retain fine 18th century metal fittings, including snuffers to put out footmen's torches. Continue down Alfred St and turn right into Bartlett St, then right into George St and left down Milsom St, Bath's main shopping drag. About halfway down you'll pass the

Royal Photographic Society Gallery in what was once the Octagon Chapel.

At the bottom of Milsom St, bear left into New Bond St until you reach the grand colonnaded post office. Cross the road and turn right along busy Northgate St, then left along Bridge St (passing the **Victoria Art Gallery** on the right), to the River Avon and **Pulteney Bridge**, designed by Robert Adam in 1774. From the bridge, you can look down on terraced Pulteney Weir.

Continue straight ahead across Laura Place and along Great Pulteney St. At the far end is the **Holburne Museum**. A plaque opposite, at No 4 Sydney Place, commemorates Jane Austen, the author who lived here for three not particularly happy years. She wrote *Persuasion* and *Northanger Abbey* in Bath and both vividly describe fashionable life in the city around 1800. Walking back along Great Pulteney St, take any turning on the right to get to Henrietta Park, the perfect place for a rest.

Roman Baths Museum

Between the 1st and 4th centuries, the Romans built a bath and temple complex over one of Bath's three natural hot springs. In the Middle Ages, the baths crumbled and it wasn't until the 17th century that anyone paid the spring much more heed. However, by the end of the century, Mary of Modena was only one of a growing number of visitors coming to 'take the cure' in Bath. In 1702 the visit of Queen Anne set the seal on the trend and the town began to expand.

Nowadays, a raised walkway gives visitors their first glimpse of the **Great Bath**, complete with Roman paving and lead base and surrounded by 19th century arcading. A series of excavated passages and chambers beneath street level lead off in several directions and let you inspect the remains of other smaller baths and hypocaust (heating) systems. One of the most picturesque corners of the complex is the 12th century **King's Bath**, built around the original sacred spring; through a window you can see the pool, complete with niches for bathers and rings for them to hold on to; 1.5

million litres of hot water still pour into the pool every day. The museum outlines the history of the baths and exhibits finds made during excavations, including the fine gorgon head found on the site of the temple of Sul and the gilt bronze head from the cult statue.

The Roman Baths (☎ 477000), Abbey Courtyard, are one of England's most popular attractions and can be uncomfortably congested in summer, when the museum's enclosed corridors can also feel very claustrophobic. Visit early on a midweek morning and you'll probably have a much better time. The baths are open daily from 9 am to 6 pm (5 pm in winter and on Sunday) and you should allow an hour to get round. Tickets are £6.30/3.80, but a combined ticket giving entry to the Costume Museum as well costs £8.40/5.

Pump Room

The elegant 18th century Pump Room is attached to the Roman Baths Museum and a fountain from the King's Bath dispenses tepid spa water which is on sale in the classy restaurant. Since Georgian times, diners have been serenaded by a Palm Court trio, a tradition that continues today. Pictures on the wall depict Georgian luminaries, including Sir Robert Walpole and Ralph Allen, whose quarries at Coombe Down provided much of the Bath stone used to build the town's squares and crescents. There's also a statue of Richard 'Beau' Nash (1674-1761), the uncrowned 'king' of Georgian Bath, a gambler who laid down the rules of etiquette for the town's fashionable visitors. The Pump Room is open for stylish dining from 9.30 am to 5 pm (4.30 pm in winter).

Bath Abbey

Edgar, the first king of united England, was crowned in a church in Abbey Courtyard in 973, but the present abbey, more glass than stone, was built between 1499 and 1616, making it the last great medieval church raised in England. The nave's wonderful fan vaulting was erected in the 19th century.

The most striking feature of the abbey's exterior is the west façade, where angels climb up and down stone ladders, commemorating a dream of the founder Bishop Oliver King. The abbey boasts 640 wall monuments, the second-largest collection after Westminster Abbey; among those buried here are the Reverend Thomas Malthus, the Victorian philosopher famous for his views on population control; Sir Isaac Pitman, who devised the Pitman method of shorthand; and Beau Nash, who is buried at the eastern end of the south aisle.

Bath Abbey (☎ 422462) is open Monday to Saturday from 9 am to 6 pm (4.30 pm in winter) and Sunday afternoon only; a donation of £2 is requested.

On the abbey's southern side, steps lead down to a vault in which a small **museum** describes the abbey's history and its links with the baths and fashionable Georgian society. It's open Monday to Saturday from 10 am to 4 pm; entry is £2/free.

Assembly Rooms & Museum of Costume

In the 18th century fashionable Bath visitors gathered to play cards, dance and listen to music in the Assembly Rooms in Bennett St. Nowadays, the basement museum displays costumes worn from the 16th to late 20th centuries, including alarming crinolines that would have forced women to approach doorways side on.

The museum (☎ 461111) is open daily from 10 am to 5 pm (opening at 11 am on Sunday); tickets are £3.80/2.70. Combined tickets with the Roman Baths Museum are cheaper.

No 1 Royal Crescent

Superbly restored to the minutest detail of its 1770 magnificence, this grand Palladian town house (☎ 428126) in the Royal Crescent is well worth visiting to see how people lived during Bath's glory days.

It's open from March to October, Tuesday to Sunday from 10.30 am to 5 pm (4 pm in November). Tickets cost £3.80/3.

Building of Bath Museum

Housed in the 18th century chapel of the Countess of Huntingdon in the Paragon, the Building of Bath Museum (☎ 333895) details how Bath's Georgian splendour came into being, a more interesting story than you might imagine. It's open March through November, Tuesday to Sunday from 10.30 am to 5 pm; entry is £3/1.50.

Holburne Museum

The fine 18th century Holburne Museum in Sydney Street (☎ 466669) was originally designed as the Sydney Hotel. It now houses a collection of porcelain, antiques, and paintings by great 18th century artists like Gainsborough and Stubbs. It's open from Easter to mid-December, Monday to Saturday from 11 am to 5 pm, and on Sunday from 2.30 to 5.30 pm. Tickets are £3.50/1.50.

Mr Bowler's Business

Tucked away in Julian Rd, Mr Bowler's Business (☎ 318348) is Bath's industrial heritage centre housed in what was originally an 18th century 'real' tennis court. Most of the fittings belonged to Jonathan Burdett Bowler's 19th and 20th century mineral-water bottling plant and brass foundry. It's open daily from 10 am to 5 pm (weekends only November to Easter); entry is £3.50/2.50.

Sally Lunn's Kitchen Museum

Round the corner from the abbey in North Parade Passage, Sally Lunn's Kitchen Museum (☎ 461634) consists mainly of exposed foundation stones, but a commentary describes how Sally Lunn, a 17th century Huguenot refugee, used to bake brioche. Similar brioche are still on sale in the café upstairs. It's open Monday to Saturday from 10 am to 6 pm and on Sunday from noon to 6 pm. Entry costs 30p.

Victoria Art Gallery

Opposite Pulteney Bridge, the Victoria Art Gallery (☎ 477772) contains two Thomas Rowlandson cartoons belonging to a series entitled *The Comforts of Bath*. It also has paintings by Walter Sickert who lived nearby. Admission is free, and it's open daily from 10 am to 5.30 pm, closing at 5 pm on Saturday and opening at 2 pm on Sunday.

Royal Photographic Society Gallery

In Milsom St, the Royal Photographic Society Gallery (☎ 462841) contains exhibits illustrating the history of photography, a bookshop and the excellent In Focus café. It's open daily from 9.30 am to 5.30 pm; entry is £2.50/free.

Museum of East Asian Art

The Museum of East Asian Art (☎ 464640), 12 Bennett St, contains more than 500 jade, bamboo, porcelain and bronze objects from China, Korea, Cambodia, Thailand and Japan. It's open daily from 10 am to 6 pm (5 pm on Sunday; shorter hours in winter). Entry is £3.50/2.50.

Organised Tours

Free two-hour walking tours of Bath leave from outside the Pump Room daily (except Saturday in winter); phone ☎ 477786 for details.

Guide Friday (☎ 444102) runs open-top, hop-on, hop-off bus tours daily from 9.25 am to 5 pm, Easter to October; shorter hours for the rest of the year. The buses pass Terrace Walk behind the abbey, and Bath bus station. Tickets cost £6.50/2.

Two-hour ghost walks (☎ 463618) depart from the Nash Bar in the Garrick's Head pub, off Saw Close, at 8 pm Monday to Friday, May to October; Friday only in winter (£3). Bizarre Bath comedy walks (☎ 335124) leave nightly from the Huntsman Inn in North Parade Passage at 8 pm (£3).

Places to Stay

Finding somewhere to stay during busy periods can be tough and you might want to pay the TIC's £2.50 booking fee for its help. Bath Visitor Call can fax you an accommodation list; call ☎ 0891-194601 (calls cost at least 45p a minute).

Camping About 3 miles west of Bath, at Newton St Loe, the *Newton Mill Touring Centre (☎ 333909)* charges £8.50 for a tent and two people. It's open year-round. To reach it, take the B3310 off the A4.

Hostels The wonderfully decorated, 52-bed *Bath Backpackers Hotel (☎ 446787, 13 Pierrepont St)* is Bath's most convenient budget accommodation, less than 10 minutes walk from the bus and train stations. B&B in non-smoking dorm rooms with up to eight beds costs £10. There's a lounge, cooking facilities and Internet hook-up.

Also central, the *YMCA International House (☎ 460471)* takes men and women and has no curfew, but is often full, especially in summer. Approaching from the south along Walcot St, look out for an archway and steps on the left about 180m past the post office. Singles/doubles with continental breakfast are £12.50/23, dorm beds £10.

The 117-bed *Bath Youth Hostel (☎ 465674, Bathwick Hill)* is out towards the University of Bath, a good 25 minute walk, or catch Badgerline bus No 18 (75p return) from the bus station. There are compensatory views and the building is magnificent. It's open all day, all year, and charges £9.75/6.55 for adults/juniors.

B&Bs & Hotels Staying in Bath doesn't come cheap. In summer, most places charge at least £17/35 for singles/doubles. The main areas are along Newbridge Rd to the west, Wells Rd to the south, and around Pulteney Rd in the east. Bath is a popular place to spend the weekend and prices reflect this.

Considering its location, just a few minutes walk from the bus and train stations, *Henry Guest House (☎ 424052, 6 Henry St)* is a bargain at £17 per person. The eight rooms all have shared baths. *No 9 Charlotte St (☎ 424193)* is also dead central, and good value from £30 for a double.

There are numerous B&Bs on and around Pulteney Rd. *Ashley House (☎ 425027, 8 Pulteney Gardens)*, has eight rooms, some with a shower, from £20 to £25 per person. Non-smoking *No 14 Raby Place (☎ 465120)* off Bathwick Hill just after you turn off Pulteney Rd, charges £18 to £20 per person. Continue along Bathwick Hill over the canal to *No 14 Dunsford Place (☎ 464134)*, a two-room B&B charging from £15 per person (no singles).

There are several places along Henrietta St, near Henrietta Park. At No 34, the *Georgian Guest House (☎ 424103)* has a range of rooms from £20/35 a single/double. *Henrietta Hotel (☎ 447779)*, next door, charges from £25/35; at weekends, the price rises to £35/55. Across the road, the *Kennard Hotel (☎ 310472)* at No 11, has rooms with baths from £38/54.

In an idyllic location beside the River Avon, the *Old Boathouse (☎ 466407, Forester Rd)* is an Edwardian boating station within walking distance of the centre. Comfortable non-smoking rooms with bathrooms cost from £20 per person (no singles).

The B&Bs west of the centre along Upper Bristol Rd (A4) mostly cost at least £20 a head, more if you're travelling alone. On Crescent Gardens, try *Lamp Post Villa (☎ 331221)* at No 3, or *Walton's Guest House (☎ 426528)* at No 17.

Wells Rd (A367) also harbours B&Bs. At No 99, *Arney Guest House (☎ 310020)* has three rooms and charges from £20/35 with shared bath. There are numerous other places nearby.

Holly Lodge (☎ 424042, 8 Upper Oldfield), a 10 minute walk from the centre Park, has views over the city. Rooms in this non-smoking award-winning hotel are from £48/75. Readers have also recommended *Cheriton House (☎ 429862)*, across the road, that has big rooms from £35/48.

Bath's top place to stay is on the grandest of grand crescents. The *Royal Crescent Hotel (☎ 739955, 15-16 Royal Crescent)* has 46 rooms in the two central houses. There's a garden behind the hotel and an excellent restaurant. Decorated with period furnishings, rooms are officially from £105/140, but if it's low season and mid-week you can negotiate a lower price.

If you can afford prices like that and have a car it's worth considering staying outside Bath at **Ston Easton Park** (☎ 01761-241631), a stunning Georgian mansion in landscaped grounds with wonderful rooms for £145/175. The village of Ston Easton is 10 miles south-west of Bath.

Places to Eat

To put together a picnic head straight for the market next to the Guildhall. Otherwise, Bath is packed with pleasant places to eat and drink.

In Union Passage, **Ben's Cookies** does home-made soups with a roll for £1.40.

Near the abbey, trendy **Café Retro** (☎ 339347, York St) does three-course meals for around £10, although you can snack for much less. There's also a popular branch of **All Bar One** in the High St.

Demuth's (☎ 446059, North Parade Passage) serves delicious vegetarian/vegan meals from £4.50. Vegetarians might also like to try the branch of **Scoff's** in the Arts Café in the Hotbath Gallery where hot dishes start at £2.55. Good cakes are on offer in the **In Focus** café in the Royal Photographic Society Gallery.

In Argyle St is **Maxson's Diner** (☎ 444440), a small, cosy diner featuring Cajun and North American dishes. Nearby, at 2 Grove St, the good-value **Bathtub Bistro** (☎ 460593) serves interesting dishes like spinach, lentil and apricot filo parcel for £6.75. **Rascals Bistro** (☎ 330201, 8 Pierrepont St) is a basement restaurant serving three-course lunches for £6.95. The scenery is more inviting at **Wood's** (☎ 314812, 9 Alfred St) where prices for two-course lunches start at around £5.

Right in the centre of town, on Walcot Rd, there are several restaurants upstairs in the modern Podium shopping complex; choose from Tex-Mex at **Footlights** (☎ 480366) or Italian at **Caffe Piazza** (☎ 429299). There's also a very popular branch of **Carwardine's Coffee House**.

In an attractive cobbled street, **The Canary** (☎ 424846, 3 Queen St) has an interesting menu with a range of main dishes for around £5.95; cream teas cost £3.95. The real place for cream teas, however, is the **Pump Room**. Here one sips one's tea and heaps one's scones with jam and cream while being serenaded by the Pump Room Trio. At £5.75, it's hardly cheap but is very much part of the Bath experience. Alternatively, pop into **Sally Lunn's** which has been baking brioche for over 300 years.

The Crystal Palace (☎ 423944, Abbey Green) south of Abbey Churchyard, has a beer garden, traditional ale and meals like lasagne and salad for £4.75. The pleasant **Moon & Sixpence** (☎ 460962, 6 Broad St) offers two-course eat-all-you-can lunches for £5. Pubs will probably be your best bet for cheap evening meals, too.

Entertainment

Pubs Bath has lots of atmospheric pubs. As well as those mentioned in Places to Eat, you could also try the intimate **Coeur de Lion** (17 Northumberland Place), off the High St, the **Bell** (Walcot St) or the **Saracen's Head**, the city's oldest pub, on Broad St. To work up a thirst, follow the canal north-east 1½ miles out of Bath to the village of Bathampton, where the **George** is beside the towpath.

Theatre The sumptuous **Theatre Royal** (☎ 448844, Barton St) often features shows on their pre-London run. **Bath Abbey** has a regular program of lunch time recitals; tickets cost £2 on the door. There's also a **Puppet Theatre** under Pulteney Bridge.

Getting There & Away

See the fares tables in the Getting Around chapter. Bath is 106 miles from London, 19 miles from Wells and only 12 from Bristol.

Bus There are National Express (☎ 0990-808080) buses every two hours from London (three hours, £10.50) but Bakers Dolphin (☎ 0117-961 4000) usually sells the cheapest tickets – currently £9.50/15.95 a single/return.

There's one bus a day between Bristol and Portsmouth via Bath and Salisbury (see the Salisbury section for details). There's also a link with Oxford (two hours, £9.10), and Stratford-upon-Avon via Bristol (2½ hours, £13).

Some excellent map-timetables are available from the bus station (☎ 464446). The Badgerline Day Rambler (£4.95) gives you access to a good network of buses in Bristol, Somerset (Wells, Glastonbury), Gloucestershire (Gloucester) and Wiltshire (Lacock, Bradford-on-Avon, Salisbury).

Train There are numerous trains from London Paddington (1½ hours, £29.50). There are also plenty of trains to Bristol for onward travel to Cardiff, Exeter or the north. Hourly trains link Portsmouth and Bristol via Salisbury and Bath. A single ticket from Bath to Salisbury is £9.40; Bath to Portsmouth is £20.20. A day return to Bristol is £4.30.

Getting Around

Bicycle Bikes can be hired from Avon Valley Cyclery (☎ 461880), behind the train station, from £9 per day. Cyclists can use the 12 mile Bristol and Bath Railway Path that follows a disused railway line.

Boat Hourly passenger boats sail from beneath Pulteney Bridge to Bathampton from April to October. Alternatively, you can hire canoes, punts or rowing boats to propel yourself along the Avon from £4 an hour; try Bath Boating station (☎ 466407) in Forester Rd.

AROUND BATH
Prior Park

This recently restored, beautiful 18th century park (☎ 833422, NT) with spectacular views of Bath was created for Ralph Allen by Capability Brown. It's in Ralph Allen Drive, accessible only by bus No 2, 4 or 733, or on foot. Admission is £3.80/1.90 (£1 refund if you show your bus ticket) and

is open daily except Tuesday from noon to 5.30 pm.

American Museum

Three miles south-east of Bath, Claverton Manor (☎ 460503) is an 1820s mansion housing re-created 17th to 19th century American home interiors, a collection of quilts and other American memorabilia.

Bus No 18 to the university drops you half a mile from the entrance (75p return). The house is open daily except Monday from March through October, from 2 to 5 pm, the grounds from 1 to 6 pm. Tickets cost £5/2.50, although you can buy a grounds-only ticket for £2/1.

Dyrham Park

Eight miles north of Bath on the A46, Dyrham Park is a 105 hectare deer park surrounding the fine 17th century house of William Blathwayt, secretary of state to William III.

The house (☎ 891364, NT) is open April through October, Friday to Tuesday from noon to 5.30 pm; tickets cost £5.40/2.70. The park can be visited daily year-round, from noon to 5.30 pm; entry is £1.70/80p. On Friday and Saturday Ryans Coaches connect Dyrham with Bath; phone ☎ 424157 for times.

Somerset

A largely agricultural county, Somerset is known for its cider-making, cricket club and Cheddar cheese. The most interesting towns are Wells, with its superb cathedral, and mystical Glastonbury, a magnet for druids and New Age hippies.

Somerset offers good walking country. The Mendip Hills are cut by gorges where caves were inhabited from prehistoric times. The Quantocks to the west are less cultivated, while to the far west of the county, the wilder Exmoor National Park (see Exmoor National Park in this chapter) spans the border with Devon.

GETTING AROUND

The Somerset transport inquiry line is ☎ 01823-358299 but you can also phone the bus companies direct: the region is roughly split between Badgerline (☎ 0117-955 3231) north of Bridgwater, and Southern National (☎ 01823-272033) to the south.

The 613 mile South West Coast Path begins in Minehead and follows the West Country coast round to Poole in Dorset. See the Activities chapter for information. TICs stock the free *Cycle Round South Somerset* describing an 80 mile cycle route, and *The Somerset Cycle Guide*.

WELLS

- pop 9400   ☎ 01749

Taking its name from three springs that emerged near the medieval Bishop's Palace, Wells is England's smallest cathedral city. It has managed to hang on to much of its medieval character and the cathedral is one of England's most beautiful, with one of the best surviving examples of a full cathedral complex.

Wells is 22 miles south-west of Bath, on the edge of the Mendip Hills. As well as being a good base for touring the Mendip Hills, it's within easy reach of Cheddar, Wookey Hole and Glastonbury.

Orientation & Information

The city centre is compact and easy to get around. The TIC (☎ 672552) is in the town hall in picturesque Market Place near the cathedral. Bike City (☎ 671711), 91 Broad St, has bikes for hire from £7.95 per day, and there are lots of interesting walking and cycling routes nearby; the TIC has details. Markets are held in Market Place on Wednesday and Saturday.

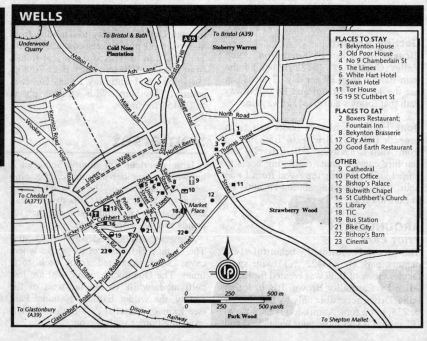

WELLS

PLACES TO STAY
1 Bekynton House
3 Old Poor House
4 No 9 Chamberlain St
5 The Limes
6 White Hart Hotel
7 Swan Hotel
11 Tor House
16 19 St Cuthbert St

PLACES TO EAT
2 Boxers Restaurant;
   Fountain Inn
8 Bekynton Brasserie
17 City Arms
20 Good Earth Restaurant

OTHER
9 Cathedral
10 Post Office
12 Bishop's Palace
13 Bubwith Chapel
14 St Cuthbert's Church
15 Library
18 TIC
19 Bus Station
21 Bike City
22 Bishop's Barn
23 Cinema

SOUTH-WESTERN ENGLAND

Wells Cathedral

The cathedral was built in stages from 1180 to 1508 and incorporates several Gothic styles. Its most famous feature is the wonderful **west front**, an immense sculpture gallery with over 300 figures, that was built between 1230 and 1250 and restored to its original splendour in 1986. Apart from the figure of Christ, installed in 1985 in the uppermost niche, all the other figures are original.

Inside, the most striking feature is the pair of **scissor arches**, separating the nave from the choir, a brilliant solution to the problem posed by the subsidence of the central tower; they were added in the 14th century, shortly after the tower's completion. Just before the hour, make sure you're standing in front of the intriguing **mechanical clock** in the north transept.

Among other things to look out for in the cathedral are the elegant **Lady Chapel** at the eastern end; the seven **effigies** of Anglo-Saxon bishops ringing the choir; and the **chained library** upstairs from the south

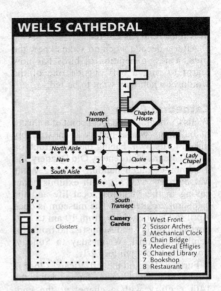

WELLS CATHEDRAL

North Transept
Chapter House
North Aisle
Nave
South Aisle
Quire
Lady Chapel
South Transept
Camery Garden
Cloisters

1 West Front
2 Scissor Arches
3 Mechanical Clock
4 Chain Bridge
5 Medieval Effigies
6 Chained Library
7 Bookshop
8 Restaurant

Wells Cathedral Clock

High up in the north transept is a wonderful mechanical clock dating from 1392, the second oldest surviving in England after the one in Salisbury cathedral.

The complex-looking dial shows the hours in two sets of 12 on the outer circle, with the sun rotating round the earth to mark the hours. The minutes are shown on the inner circle, each indicated by a rotating star.

The clock also shows the position of the planets and the phases of the moon, but it's the entertaining cabaret act performed above it by jousting knights on horseback that draws a small crowd on the hour (the quarter-hour in summer).

Quarterjacks in the shape of 15th century knights use poleaxes to hit a bell to mark the time on the clock's exterior face.

transept. The library is open from April to October, Tuesday to Saturday from 2.30 to 4.30 pm; entry is 50p.

Reached by worn steps leading off the north transept is the glorious mid-13th century **Chapter House**, the ceiling ribs of which sprout like a palm from a central column.

Externally, look out for the **Chain Bridge** built from the northern side of the cathedral to Vicars' Close to enable clerics to reach the cathedral without getting their robes wet. The **cloisters** on the southern side surround a pretty courtyard.

The cathedral (☎ 674483) is open daily from 7 am to 7 pm (8.30 pm in July and August); visitors are asked to donate £3/1. Guided tours are free, photography permits cost £1.

Bishop's Palace

Beyond the cathedral is the moated Bishop's Palace (☎ 678691), a private residence dating back to the 13th century that has beautiful gardens. It's open Tuesday to Friday and bank holidays from 11 am to

6 pm; Sunday from 2 am to 6 pm; and daily in August; entry is £3/free.

After a decade when no swans knew the trick, a new generation of birds has now learnt to ring a bell outside one of the windows when they want to be fed.

Cathedral Close

Wells Cathedral is the focal point of a cluster of buildings whose history is inextricably linked to its own. Facing the west front, on the left are the 15th century **Old Deanery** and a salmon-coloured building housing **Wells Museum** (☎ 673477), with exhibits about caving in the Mendips, local life and the cathedral architecture. The museum is open April to October, daily, from 10 am to 5.30 pm (8 pm in July and August); and from November to April, Wednesday to Sunday, from 11 am to 4 pm for £2/1.

Further along on the left, **Vicars' Close** is a cobbled street of houses dating back to the 14th century with a chapel at the end; members of the cathedral choir still live here. Passing under the Chain Bridge, inspect the outside of the Lady Chapel and a lovely medieval house called **The Rib**, before emerging at a main road called The Liberty. In the Middle Ages, this marked the boundary of the cathedral precincts within which a refugee could take sanctuary.

St Cuthbert's Church

Wells Cathedral is such a major draw that many visitors never venture beyond its beautiful close. However, it's worth dropping by stately **St Cuthbert's Church** in Cuthbert St, to admire its splendid 15th century perpendicular tower and brilliantly coloured nave roof. Look out for the boss of a sow suckling five piglets in the south porch.

Places to Stay

There are plenty of B&Bs but most have only a few rooms so advance booking is advised. *9 Chamberlain St* (☎ 672270) is very central and charges £18 per person. At 29 Chamberlain St is *The Limes* (☎ 675716), with two rooms. For the four-poster bed, B&B costs £20 per person; in the twin room

it's £18. There's a £2 reduction if you'd prefer a continental breakfast.

The B&B at *19 St Cuthbert St* (☎ 673166) overlooks the cathedral in a quiet part of town and charges from £16 a bed. The *Old Poor House* (☎ 675052, 7A St Andrew St) is a comfortable 14th century cottage just outside the cathedral precincts. The nightly charge is £18 per person. Slightly further out, at 7 St Thomas St, *Bekynton House* (☎ 672222) is £22 per person, or £24.50 for a room with a bathroom. *Tor House* (☎ 672322, 20 Tor St) charges from £24 to £38 per person.

There's a cluster of hotels in Sadler St near the cathedral. The *White Hart Hotel* (☎ 672056) has single/double rooms for £50/70 with bathrooms. The *Swan Hotel* (☎ 678877) is a fine 15th century inn with some four-poster beds; some of the rooms look straight onto the cathedral's west front. Room prices are £72.50/89.50 for singles/doubles but ask about special deals.

Places to Eat

The most atmospheric place to eat is the *Refectory* in the cathedral cloisters where you can lunch on soup and a roll for £1.95, overlooked by 18th century monuments; it's open Monday to Saturday from 10 am to 5 pm, and Sunday from 12.30 to 5 pm.

Katie's Tea Room, opposite the White Hart Hotel, does a good cream tea for £2.95. Near the bus station is the *Good Earth Restaurant* (☎ 678600, 4 Priory Rd) an excellent vegetarian restaurant. The courgette and stilton lasagne (£2.75) is recommended. The *Bekynton Brasserie (Sadler St)* is a good place for lunch. Cottage pie costs £4.95. The *City Arms* (☎ 673916, 69 High St) serves good pub grub and also has a restaurant open in the evening. Part of the pub used to be a jail in Tudor times.

The town's best restaurant is probably *Boxers* (☎ 672317, 1 St Thomas St) upstairs in the Fountain Inn, where you'll pay about £16 for a three-course meal.

Entertainment

A year-round program of lunch time recitals and evening concerts offers the chance to hear the historic cathedral choir in full voice. For details, phone ☎ 674483.

Getting There & Away

Badgerline (☎ 0117-955 3231) operates hourly buses from Bristol and Bath. No 163 runs from Wells to Glastonbury and Street. Bus Nos 161/2 travel via Shepton Mallet to Frome. Heading for the coast, bus Nos 126 and 826 travel to Weston-Super-Mare via Cheddar, while the No 170 service heads for Burnham-on-Sea. There's no train station in Wells; the nearest is 15 miles away at Castle Cary, linked to Wells by bus No 168.

MENDIP HILLS

The Mendip Hills are a ridge of limestone hills about 25 miles long and 5 miles wide in northern Somerset. These are not lofty hills – their highest point is Black Down (326m) to the north-west – but they stand out in an area that is otherwise very flat, giving way in the south to the Somerset Levels where roads often run on causeways above flood level.

Nowadays, the Mendip Hills form a densely cultivated agricultural area, but in the past they were more famous for coal mining, traces of which can be seen round Radstock and Midsomer Norton to the east. The Romans are known to have mined for lead around Charterhouse and Priddy; lead mining continued throughout the Middle Ages and right up until 1900. Pubs that seem to be in the middle of nowhere are survivors from a time when mining brought plenty of thirsty drinkers. You can see the remains of St Cuthbert's lead mines near Priddy, and scruffy hollows around Charterhouse mark the sites of shallow mine workings. Quarrying for stone is an important (and controversial) industry to this day.

The A371 skirts the southern side of the Mendip Hills and any of the towns along it – Axbridge, Cheddar, Wells or Shepton Mallet – would make good touring bases, though Wells is probably best.

Getting There & Away

Badgerline buses (☎ 0117-955 3231) serve this area, although don't expect services to be very frequent off the major roads. Apart from the buses to Wells and Glastonbury, Nos 126/826 run between Wells, Cheddar and Axbridge. Nos 160/162 regularly link Wells with Shepton Mallet, while No 173 runs between Bath, Radstock, Midsomer Norton and Wells.

Coming by car, the Mendip Hills are squeezed in between the A38 Bristol to Burnham-on-Sea and A37 Bristol to Wells roads.

Wookey Hole

Wookey Hole, the site of a sequence of caves carved out by the River Axe, one of them containing a striking lake, is just 2 miles east of Wells. The striking shape of one particular stalagmite gave rise to the legend of the Witch of Wookey. Nowadays, the caves are the focal point of a series of other attractions, including an ancient hand-made paper mill, an Edwardian fairground, a maze of mirrors and an arcade of vintage amusement machines.

The Wookey Hole (☎ 01749-672243) attractions are open daily April through September from 10 am to 5 pm (10.30 am to 4.30 pm in winter); entry is £6.70/3.60. Bus No 171 offers an hourly service between Wells and Wookey Hole (10 minutes, 95p). A 3 mile walk to Wookey is signposted from New St in Wells.

Cheddar Gorge

The Mendips' most dramatic scenery can be found along its southern side where the Cheddar Gorge cuts a mile swathe through the landscape, exposing great sweeps of 138m-high grey stone cliff. Approaching on foot from the north or walking along the cliff-top paths, it's possible to imagine how wild and spectacular Cheddar must have been before the stalactite and stalagmite-filled Cox's and Gough's caves started to suck in the crowds; however, the area immediately around the caves can be very off-putting in summer when the place heaves with visitors. It's probably best to visit out of season, bearing in mind that most of the teashops and fish and chip shops only open over winter weekends.

The **Cheddar Showcaves** (☎ 01934-742343) are open daily from Easter to September, from 10 am to 5 pm; and from October to Easter, from 10.30 am to 4.30 pm. Entry is £6.90/4 which covers entry to the heritage centre, lookout tower and cliff-top walk.

The TIC (☎ 01934-744071) in the gorge is open daily from Easter through October, and Sunday only for the rest of the year.

Cheddar village, to the south-west of the gorge, has an elegant church and an ancient market cross but is otherwise disappointing. *Cheddar Youth Hostel* (☎ 01934-742494) is a mile from the caves on Hillfield, a road off The Hayes on the western side of the village. The nightly charge is £8.80/5.95.

Cheddar Cheese

The country's most famous cheese only began to become widely known when people started visiting Cheddar Gorge and taking home some of the local cheese. Cheddar was just one of many Somerset villages that produced this type of cheese.

Over the years, and with mass production not only all over Britain but in several other countries as well, Cheddar has become a generic name for any pale yellow, medium-hard cheese. The name covers a wide range of qualities, from soapy supermarket Cheddar to the delicious farmhouse variety, which is mature and tangy.

If you're interested in the process of making genuine Cheddar Cheese, the Cheddar Gorge Cheese Company (☎ 01934-742810) is open daily. You can watch the cheese-maker at work and on the hour there's a short talk. It's part of the Rural Village (just off the B3135) that also includes demonstrations of lace-making, pottery, fudge-making and spinning. Entry to the village is £1.95/1.25.

Badgerline bus Nos 126/826 run between Wells (9 miles) and Weston-Super-Mare via Cheddar (20 minutes, £2), hourly from Monday to Saturday and every two hours on Sunday.

Axbridge
☎ 01934

Just 1½ miles from Cheddar, the pretty village of Axbridge is light years away from Cheddar's tackiness and makes a much nicer, albeit pricier, place to stay. One corner of the central square is dominated by the striking half-timbered **King John's Hunting Lodge** (☎ 732012, NT), a Tudor merchant's house now housing the local museum. It's open daily from 2 to 5 pm from Easter to 30 September. Another corner is occupied by the huge late Gothic church of St John with a 17th century plaster ceiling. The rest of the square is ringed with hotels and restaurants.

For somewhere to stay, try *The Lamb* (☎ 732253) where doubles cost £50 with bath, or *The Oak House* (☎ 732444) where it's £48/68 for a single/double. To eat, choose between the *Spinning Wheel Restaurant* (☎ 732476) where a three-course dinner midweek costs £15.95 or the 15th century *Almshouse Bistro* (☎ 732493).

You can walk or cycle to Axbridge from Cheddar. Badgerline bus No 126 from Cheddar to Burnham-on-Sea also passes through the centre.

Mendip Villages
The Mendip villages are not renowned for particularly striking buildings, although you might be interested in the 19th century **Downside Abbey**, established by English monks driven from France by the French Revolution. Downside is now a famous Roman Catholic boys' school.

Otherwise, many of the villages are pretty, in a low-key way, and several have fine perpendicular church towers. Especially impressive is that at **Chewton Mendip** (on the A37 from Bristol to Wells), where there's an attractive medieval churchyard cross. The village of **Compton Martin** has a Norman church with a 15th century tower.

A mile to the east, **West Harptree** is a prettier village with two 17th century former manor houses. Near **East Harptree** are the remains of Norman Richmont Castle, captured from supporters of Matilda by those of King Stephen in 12th century skirmishing.

GLASTONBURY
- **pop 6900**   ☎ **01458**

Although it's little more than a large village, Glastonbury is England's unofficial New Age capital – the place to come if you want your runes read, if you want to find out about English paganism or to buy crystals, candles or made-to-measure shoes.

Myths and legends about Glastonbury abound. One story tells how Jesus came here with his great-uncle Joseph of Arimathea, while another reports Joseph bringing the chalice from the Last Supper with him. Later legends also made Glastonbury the burial place of King Arthur and Queen Guinevere, and the tor (the nearby hill), the Isle of Avalon. Finally, the tor was thought to guard a gateway to the underworld. Over time, these different tales became entangled with each other in a potent mixture that has left Glastonbury important to Christians and atheists alike, as a glimpse at the various bookshops confirms.

Whatever you choose to believe, Glastonbury has the ruins of a 14th century abbey, a couple of museums, mystic springs and superb views from the tor to make it well worth a day of your time.

Orientation & Information

The main bus stop is opposite the town hall in Magdalene St, within sight of the market cross and the abbey ruins.

The TIC (☎ 832954), in the Tribunal, 9 High St, stocks free maps and accommodation lists, and sells leaflets describing local walks and village trails. From Easter to October you can hire bikes for £7/30 a day/week at Pedalers (☎ 831117), opposite the abbey entrance. There's a market on Tuesday.

You can pick up your email at Café Galatea (see Places to Eat).

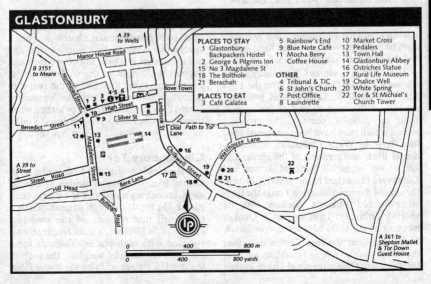

GLASTONBURY

PLACES TO STAY
1 Glastonbury Backpackers Hostel
2 George & Pilgrims Inn
15 No 3 Magdalene St
18 The Bolthole
21 Berachah

PLACES TO EAT
3 Café Galatea

5 Rainbow's End
9 Blue Note Café
11 Mocha Berry Coffee House

OTHER
4 Tribunal & TIC
6 St John's Church
7 Post Office
8 Laundrette

10 Market Cross
12 Pedalers
13 Town Hall
14 Glastonbury Abbey
16 Ostriches Statue
17 Rural Life Museum
19 Chalice Well
20 White Spring
22 Tor & St Michael's Church Tower

Glastonbury Abbey

Legend suggests that there has been a church on this site since the 1st century, but the first definite traces date back to the 7th century when King Ine gave a charter to a monastery here. The first abbey church seems to have reached the height of its importance under the abbacy of St Dunstan, later an archbishop of Canterbury. During his time in office, King Edgar, the first king of a united England, died and was buried at Glastonbury.

In 1184, the old church was destroyed by fire; reconstruction began in the reign of Henry II. In 1191, monks claimed to have had visions confirming hints in old manuscripts that the 6th century warrior-king Arthur and his wife Guinevere were buried in the grounds. Excavations to the south of the old church uncovered what was said to be their tomb, and a lead cross recording that fact, which has since disappeared. The couple were reinterred in front of the high altar of the new church in 1278 and the tomb survived until 1539 when Henry VIII dissolved the monasteries.

The last abbot was hanged, drawn and quartered on the tor. After that, the abbey complex gradually collapsed, its component parts scavenged to provide building materials. It wasn't until the 19th century that Romanticism brought renewed interest in King Arthur and the sites associated with him.

The ruins you see at Glastonbury today are mainly of the church built after the 1184 fire. They include a **Lady Chapel**, built, unusually, at the western end of the church; some nave walls; parts of the crossing arches which may have been scissor-shaped like those in Wells Cathedral; some **medieval tiles**; and remains of the choir. The site of the supposed **tomb of Arthur and Guinevere** is marked in the grass. A little to the side of the main site, don't miss the flagstone-floored **Abbot's Kitchen** with its soaring chimney; later use as a Quaker meeting house allowed it to survive intact.

An excellent **Visitors Centre** describes the history of the site and contains a model showing what the ruins would have looked like in their heyday. Behind it, and easy to overlook, are tiny **St Patrick's Chapel** and a **thorn tree** supposedly grown from the original which sprouted on Wearyall Hill when Joseph of Arimathea stuck his staff into the ground. It flowers in spring and at Christmas.

The site (☎ 832267) is open daily from 9.30 am (9 am from June to August) to 6 pm or dusk; entry is £2.50/1. There's a small car park (60p) at the site.

Lake Village Museum

A small museum devoted to the prehistoric village that flourished near Glastonbury when the surrounding lowlands had not yet been drained is upstairs in the Tribunal, the medieval courthouse which dates back to 1400 and now houses the TIC. Wet conditions have allowed an unusually large quantity of wooden artefacts to survive – even a dugout canoe (in a separate room at the back). The museum (☎ 832949, EH) is open from April to September, Sunday to Thursday from 10 am to 5 pm (5.30 pm on Friday and Saturday; 4.30 pm from October to March). Admission costs £1.50/75p.

St John's Church

Set back from the High St is this stunning open-plan perpendicular church that has a spectacular 15th century wooden roof and pillars so thin it's hard to believe they can support the weight of the walls. Look out for the egg-timer attached to the pulpit to guard against overlong sermons. Vandalism means the church must be kept locked when there's no one to supervise visitors. You're most likely to find it open on market day.

Glastonbury Tor

Tor is a Celtic word used to describe a hill shaped like a triangular wedge of cheese, and Glastonbury tor is open to walkers year-round. On the 160m-high summit stands a tower, all that remains of the medieval church of St Michael, a saint frequently associated with high places. You can see a carving of St Michael weighing the souls of the dead in a giant scale on the tower front.

It takes three-quarters of an hour to walk up and down the tor and there are short-stay car parks at the bottom of both paths. From May to September a Tor Bus runs to the tor every 20 minutes from Magdalene St (50p).

White Spring

This spring flows out into a cave at the foot of the tor in Wellhouse Lane, and has been dressed up with a café and mock medieval and Tudor house façades; atmospheric or Disneyfied depending on your mood and the number of other visitors.

Chalice Well

The Chalice Well has become entwined in Glastonbury myths and legends, even though its name probably relates to its site in Chilkwell St rather than to real links with the Holy Grail. The well has a long association with traditions of healing and you can drink from it as the water pours out through a lion's head spout. It then runs through brick channels into the gardens below, eventually cascading down a series of ceramic dishes into two interlocking basins surrounded by flowers. It's a beautiful, peaceful spot to spend a few hours and is open daily March to October from 10 am to 6 pm, November to February from noon to 4 pm; entry is £1/75p.

Rural Life Museum

Partially housed in a fine late 14th century tithe barn, the Rural Life Museum in Bere Lane exhibits artefacts associated with farming, cider-making, cheese-making and other aspects of country life in Somerset. In the grounds, you can see rare breeds of sheep and chicken, and apple trees. Upstairs, don't miss the three-seater toilet, with holes for Mum, Dad and Junior.

The barn has fine carvings on the gables and porch and an impressive timber roof; it now houses a collection of old agricultural machinery. The museum (☎ 831197) is open from Easter to October, weekdays except Monday from 10 am to 5 pm, weekends from 2 pm to 6 pm; for the rest of the year it's open Tuesday through Saturday, from 10 am to 3 pm. Entry is £2.20/50p.

Glastonbury Festival

The Glastonbury Festival, a three-day summer extravaganza of music, theatre, circus, mime, natural healing etc, is a massive affair with over 1000 acts, which doesn't always go down too well with the locals. It takes place at Worthy Farm, Pilton, 8 miles from Glastonbury. Admission is by advance ticket only (around £80 for the whole festival). Phone ☎ 832020 for details.

Places to Stay

Glastonbury Backpackers Hostel (☎ *833353, 4 Market Place*) is at the Crown Hotel. Dorm beds are £9 and there are also a few doubles, and even a bridal suite (£30). There's a kitchen, TV room and café (open from 8 am to 8 pm) downstairs.

The nearest HI hostel is *Street Youth Hostel* (☎ *442961*), about 3 miles south. Beds cost £8/5.50 for adults/children. Bus No 376 from Glastonbury stops at Marshalls Elm, from where the hostel is a 500m walk.

There are several camping grounds in and around Glastonbury. *Isle of Avalon* (☎ *833618*) is a 10 minute walk from the centre, off the B3151. A tent site costs from £4.80, plus £1.85 per person.

Glastonbury has B&Bs from around £15 a night and many establishments offer aromatherapy, muesli breakfasts, vegetarian meals, etc. The TIC has a complete list.

Non-smoking *Tor Down Guest House* (☎ *832287, No 5 Ashwell Lane*) has rooms from £15/30 for singles/doubles. *The Bolthole* (☎ *832800, 32 Chilkwell St*) is near the foot of the tor, and has two doubles and a twin, for £16 per person. There are a couple of similar B&Bs nearby in the same street.

Berachah (☎ *834214, Well House Lane*) is convenient for the tor and the wells, and has beds from £17.

The *George & Pilgrims Inn* (☎ *831146, 1 High St*) has a history dating back to the reign of Edward III. Rooms cost from £65/75 for singles/doubles but two-night special breaks including dinner are better value.

Travellers may be interested in peaceful *No 3 Magdalene St* (☎ *832129*) whose owners have seen a bit of the world themselves, hence the Indian fabrics and wall hangings. Comfortable rooms with private bathrooms cost £50/70.

Places to Eat

If you've ever considered becoming a vegetarian, Glastonbury would be an ideal place to start since it's one of the few places in England where nut roasts are more common than pot roasts.

A good place for a coffee is the *Mocha Berry Coffee House*, near the Market Cross. The *Blue Note Café (4A High St)* has tables in a courtyard; soup and bread costs £1.70, garlic mushrooms are £3.40. Across the street, at 5A, *Café Galatea* does salads for £3.95 and main dishes from £5.75. It's also a sculpture gallery and cybercafé (£3 for half an hour on the Internet).

Rainbow's End (17A High St) has delicious leek and mushroom pie (£3) and huge chunks of chocolate cake (£1.20). It's in an alley with shops selling second-hand books and shoes and is open from 10 am to 4 pm.

A three-course lunch at the *George & Pilgrims Inn* (☎ *831146, 1 High St*) costs £9.50.

Getting There & Away

There's a daily National Express bus to London (4¼ hours, £16.25), and also to Bath. Badgerline runs buses from Bristol (No 376) to Wells, Glastonbury and Street. Glastonbury is only 6 miles from Wells – a 15 minute bus journey (every half hour, £1.70). Bus No 376 continues to Ilchester and Yeovil.

QUANTOCK HILLS

The Quantocks, in western Somerset, are a ridge of red sandstone hills, 12 miles long, not much more than 3 miles wide and running down to the sea at Quantoxhead. Like the Mendips, these are lowly hills – just 385m high at their highest point – but they're less cultivated and can look much more

bleak. The narrow country lanes and woody dells make this enjoyable walking country.

Some of the most attractive country is owned by the NT, including the Beacon and Bicknoller hills that offer views of the Bristol Channel and Exmoor to the northwest. In 1861, red deer were introduced to these hills from Exmoor and there's a thriving local tradition of stag hunting.

A road runs across the bleaker part of the Quantocks from Over Stowey to Crowcombe, and there's a walkers' track as well. At Broomfield, 6 miles north of Taunton, Fyne Court houses a visitors centre (☎ 01823-451587), open daily from 9 am to 6 pm, where you can pick up information.

Bridgwater or Taunton would make passable bases for exploring the Quantocks, but it's more atmospheric to stay in one of the villages.

Getting There & Away

To appreciate the lanes and woods of the Quantocks at their peaceful best, aim to arrive on a weekday when the Bridgwater and Taunton weekend visitors are back at their desks. Coming by car, the M5 linking Bristol and Exeter skirts the eastern edge of the Quantocks. The A358 then runs along the western side of the hills, linking Taunton to Williton in the north.

Trains from Bristol, Bath and Exeter call at Taunton and Bridgwater, and infrequent Southern National (☎ 01823-272033) buses serve the main roads. Its No 28 bus runs along the southern edge from Minehead to Taunton. Southern National also has one bus a day (No 23) between Taunton and Nether Stowey. No 15 runs between Minehead and Bridgwater. No 29A from Bristol continues to Bridgwater and Taunton after Wells and Glastonbury on Sunday and bank holidays only.

Nether Stowey & Holford

One of the Quantocks' most famous residents was the poet Samuel Taylor Coleridge, who lived in **Nether Stowey** from 1769 to 1796. You can visit **Coleridge Cottage** (☎ 01278-732662, NT) where he wrote *The*

Rime of the Ancient Mariner; it's open April to October, Tuesday to Thursday and Sunday from 2 to 5 pm; entry is £1.70/80p. Some of the rooms have been recently restored to their original bright colours.

Coleridge's friend William Wordsworth, and Wordsworth's sister Dorothy, also spent 1797 at nearby Alfoxden House in **Holford** – a pretty village near a wooded valley. *Lyrical Ballads*, published in 1798, was the joint product of Coleridge's and Wordsworth's stays.

Two miles west of Holford is the *Quantock Hills Youth Hostel* (☎ *01278-741224*) set in a wooded area. It's open daily in July and August, and daily except Sunday from April through June; the nightly charge is £7.20/4.95 for adults/juniors. Southern National bus No 15 from Bridgwater gets you to Nether Stowey, No 28 from Taunton or Minehead will drop you at Williton; in either case it's then a 3½ mile walk.

West Somerset Railway

Trains on Britain's longest privately run railway steam between Bishops Lydeard and Minehead, a seaside town 20 miles away. There are stops along the line at Crowcombe, Doniford Beach, Stogumber, Williton, Watchet, Washford, Blue Anchor and Dunster.

Trains run daily from June to September, and at winter weekends. A ticket from Bishops Lydeard to Minehead costs £5.70/8.60 for an adult single/return; children are half-price. Phone ☎ 01643-707650 for 24-hour talking timetables, ☎ 01643-704996 for other information.

Southern National bus Nos 28 and 28A from Taunton and Minehead pass through Bishops Lydeard.

Crowcombe

One of the prettiest Quantock villages, Crowcombe still has cottages built of stone and cob (a mixture of mud and straw), many with thatched roofs. There's a pleasant church with 16th century bench ends, and part of its spire still in the churchyard where it fell when struck by lightning in 1725. The 16th century Church House has mullioned windows and a Tudor door. Crowcombe Court is a fine Georgian house.

Crowcombe Heathfield Youth Hostel (☎ *01984-667249, Denzel House*) is 2 miles from the village and half a mile from Crowcombe station on the West Somerset Railway. It's a 7 mile hike over the Quantocks from the hostel in Holford. You can also get here on bus No 28C from Taunton station, getting off at Triscombe Cross and walking about three-quarters of a mile. The hostel is open daily from April through August (but closed on Thursday in May and June). Beds cost £7.20/4.95 for adults/juniors.

TAUNTON

- **pop 35,000**   ☎ **01823**

Coming to the Quantocks by bus or train you're likely to arrive in Taunton, Somerset's disappointing administrative centre. The TIC (☎ 336344) is by the library in Paul St.

Somerset County Museum (☎ 255504) in part of the castle, is open Tuesday to Saturday from 10 am to 5 pm; £2.20/50p. The **Church of St Mary Magdalene** has one of Somerset's finest towers, and an impressive oak Tudor roof in the nave.

Taunton is on a main National Express coach route, with services to London (3½ hours, £10), Bristol (1¾ hours, £4.50), Bridgwater (20 minutes) and Exeter. It's also on the main West Country rail line.

MONTACUTE HOUSE

Twenty-two miles south-east of Taunton, and 4 miles west of the market town of Yeovil, Montacute House (☎ 01935-823289, NT) is an impressive Elizabethan mansion built in the 1590s for Sir Edward Phelips, a Speaker of the House of Commons. The Long Gallery displays Tudor and Jacobean portraits on loan from London's National Portrait Gallery. Formal gardens and a landscaped park surround the house.

It's open from April to October, daily except Tuesday from noon to 5 pm; £5.20/2.60.

Exmoor National Park

Covering parts of West Somerset and North Devon, Exmoor is a small national park (265 sq miles) enclosing a wide variety of beautiful landscapes. Along the coast, the scenery is particularly breathtaking with humpbacked headlands giving superb views across the Bristol Channel. Exmoor's cliffs are the highest in England, rising in places to 366m.

A high plateau rises steeply behind the coast, but is cut by steep, fast-flowing streams. The bare hills of heather and grass run parallel to the coast; the highest point is Dunkery Beacon at 519m. On the southern side the two main rivers, the Exe and Barle, wind their way along wooded valleys.

Horned sheep, Exmoor ponies (descended from ancient hill stock) and England's last wild red deer still roam the moors. The symbol of the park is the antlered head of a stag, and depending on the season you may see people hunting. Although the sport is supported by local farmers, who see the deer as a pest, it's equally strongly opposed by others, including the National Trust, causing conflict in the hunting season.

There are several particularly attractive villages: Lynton and Lynmouth, joined by a water-operated railway; Porlock, on the edge of the moor in a beautiful valley; Dunster, dominated by its partly-medieval castle; and Selworthy, with traditional thatched cottages.

Arguably the most dramatic section of the South West Coast Path is between Minehead in the park to Padstow in Cornwall.

ORIENTATION

From west to east the park measures only about 21 miles and north to south just 12 miles. It's accessible from the west through Barnstaple, from the south through Tiverton, and from the east through Minehead.

Within the park boundaries, the main centres are Dulverton on the southern edge; Exford in the centre; Dunster in the east; and Porlock, Lynton and Lynmouth on the coast.

There are over 600 miles of public footpaths and bridleways (a path that can be

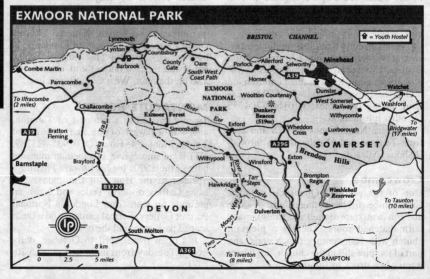

EXMOOR NATIONAL PARK

used by walkers, horse riders and cyclists), most of them waymarked.

INFORMATION

The National Park Authority (NPA) has five information centres in and around the park, but it's also possible to get information in the TICs at Barnstaple, Ilfracombe, Lynton and Minehead. The NPA centres at Dunster (☎ 01643-821835), Lynmouth (☎ 01598-752509), County Gate (☎ 01598-741321), and Combe Martin (☎ 01271-883319) are open daily from the end of March to October. For the rest of the year, some of these offices are closed or operate limited opening hours. The main visitors centre and the Exmoor NPA headquarters (☎ 01398-323841) in Dulverton is open all year but for limited hours in winter.

The *Exmoor Visitor* is a free newspaper listing useful addresses, accommodation and a program of guided walks and bike rides from the villages offered by the NPA and local organisations. Most walks are in the summer but there are some throughout the year.

The visitors centres and TICs stock a wide range of walking guides and Ordnance Survey maps.

WALKS

Although over 70% of Exmoor is privately owned, there are numerous waymarked paths. The best known routes are the Somerset and North Devon Coast Path (part of the South West Coast Path) and the Exmoor section of the Two Moors Way, which starts in Lynmouth and follows the River Barle through Withypool and on to Dartmoor.

Part of the 180 mile Tarka Trail (based on the countryside that inspired Henry Williamson's *Tarka the Otter*) is in the park. Join it in Combe Martin and walk to Lynton/Lynmouth, and then inland to Brayford and Barnstaple.

Exmoor's main walking centres are Lynton, Porlock, County Gate, Oare, Horner, Exford, Simonsbath, Withypool and Dulverton. The *Exmoor & West Somerset Public Transport Guide*, free from TICs, also in-

cludes detailed route descriptions of a dozen walks that are accessible by public transport.

CYCLE ROUTES

Cyclists are not allowed on public footpaths or the open moor, and horse riders and walkers have priority on public bridleways and roads used as public paths. The visitors centres will be able to advise on where you can go.

Official places for cyclists include a coastal route – along the old Barnstaple railway line, parts of the Tarka Trail, the Brendon Hills and Crown Estate woodland. The West Country Way runs through Exmoor from Padstow to Bristol.

OTHER ACTIVITIES
Pony Trekking & Horse Riding

Exmoor is popular riding country and stables scattered round the park offer ponies and horses for all abilities for rides from a few hours to a full day. Wet weather gear is recommended – it can turn cold and rainy very quickly. Charges are from about £7 per hour.

Contact Pine Lodge Riding & Holidays (☎ 01398-323559), Higher Chilcott Farm, Dulverton; or Burrowhayes Farm (☎ 01643-862463), West Luccombe, Porlock.

Red Deer Tracking

Several companies offer Exmoor safaris – tracking wild red deer. Moorland Wildlife Safaris (bookings phone ☎ 01398-323465) charge £10 per person for three-hour excursions.

Fishing

To fish for salmon and trout, you need a licence, usually obtainable from the main shop or village post office. Sea fishing is possible from the harbour walls, and boats can be hired in the larger coastal villages.

PLACES TO STAY & EAT

There are youth hostels in Minehead and Ilfracombe (outside the park) and Lynton and Exford in the park. Camping is allowed with the landowner's permission; local shops will usually know who owns the surrounding land. Along the coast, there are regular camping grounds with all the usual facilities.

There are also camping barns (£3.50 per night: bring your own sleeping bag) at Woodadvent Farm, Roadwater, and Northcombe, a mile from Dulverton. For bookings phone ☎ 01271-24420.

There's no shortage of B&Bs and hotels in this holiday area. There are plenty of places to eat in Exmoor – old country pubs with low beams to hit your head on and log fires in the winter, little shops serving cream teas, as well as more upmarket restaurants.

GETTING THERE & AWAY
Bus
National Express coaches go from London to Barnstaple (5 hours) and Ilfracombe (5½ hours) daily. There are also buses from Plymouth and Bristol to Barnstaple.

Red Bus (☎ 01271-345444) and Southern National (☎ 01823-272033) run services from Minehead, Barnstaple, Ilfracombe, Dunster and Williton. You could also do part of this journey on the privately run West Somerset Railway (see Somerset earlier in this chapter). W Ridler (☎ 01398-323398) has a daily bus from Dulverton to Taunton and back.

Train
From London Paddington, InterCity services stop at Taunton (2¼ hours), Tiverton Parkway (2½ hours) and Exeter (2¾ hours). These places can also be reached from Bristol (on the Bristol-Plymouth line). From Exeter, the scenic Tarka Line runs to Barnstaple; the journey takes about 1½ hours and there are about four trains a day.

GETTING AROUND
It's easiest to get around with your own transport, on foot or horseback, because bus services are limited. Some services are based on school runs, some are operated by volunteer drivers, most are seasonal and few operate on Sunday. On the other hand, the narrow streets of Exmoor villages

quickly clog up in peak season and parking can be tricky.

Bus
The *Exmoor & West Somerset Public Transport Guide*, free from TICs, is invaluable. It also includes information on day hikes.

The Exmoor Bus Service's three-day ticket costs £9.50/6.50 and gives unlimited travel on Red Bus and Southern National services for three days.

Bicycle
Tarka Trail Cycle Hire (☎ 01271-324202), Train Station, Barnstaple, has all kinds of bikes for hire. Charges start from £6 per day for tourers, £8 for mountain bikes.

DULVERTON
* **pop 1300**   ☎ **01398**
This attractive village, south of the moor in the Barle Valley, is the local 'capital' and home to the park's head office. The Exmoor National Park Visitors Centre (☎ 323841) is at 7-9 Fore St.

Dulverton's narrow streets get choked with traffic in summer so try to visit out of season.

Walks
The four-hour circular walk along the river from Dulverton to Tarr Steps – an ancient stone clapper bridge across the River Barle – is recommended. Add another three or four hours to the walk by continuing from Tarr Steps up Winsford Hill for distant views over Devon.

Places to Stay & Eat
There's a camping barn (£3.50 per night) at Northcombe, a mile from Dulverton. Phone ☎ 01271-24420 for bookings.

You get breakfast in bed at *Town Mills* (☎ *323124*) for £18.50 per person. The driveway is just off the High St.

Springfields Farm (☎ *323722*) is 4 miles from Dulverton on the Exford road; and just 1½ miles from Tarr Steps. B&B costs £19 per person, or £22 in rooms with a bath. Evening meals (£12.50) are served but only from mid-May, when the lambing season is over.

Right on the edge of the moor, *Higher-combe Farm* (*☎ 323616*), is 2 miles north of Dulverton at the end of a no-through road. B&B in rooms with a bathroom costs from £20.

Crispins Restaurant (*☎ 323397, 26 High St*) serves decent vegetarian food and also has a few non-veg choices. *The Lion Hotel* in Bank Square has generous servings of good bar food.

Getting There & Away

Red Bus runs the DevonBus 290 Exe Valley Link from Exeter to Minehead via Dulverton. There are three buses a day from Monday to Friday and one on Saturday. The Devon Bus 295 Heart of Exmoor Link runs three times a day in each direction between Dulverton and Lynton (1½ hours).

DUNSTER
• pop 800   ☎ 01643

Possibly the most attractive Exmoor village, Dunster can be packed with people in summer. The main attraction is the castle but there's also St George's Church, a working water mill, an old packhorse bridge, the nearby beach and the 17th century octagonal Yarn Market – a relic of a time when the people of Dunster made their living from weaving, rather than tourism.

An Exmoor National Park Visitors Centre (☎ 821835) is on Dunster Steep.

Dunster Castle

Heavily restored to the Victorian ideal of how castles should look – turrets, crenellations etc – Dunster Castle (☎ 821314, NT) dates back to Norman times, although only the 13th century gateway of the original structure survives. Inside are Tudor furnishings and portraits of the Luttrell family, including a bizarre 16th century portrait of Sir John skinny-dipping.

It's open from April to October, Saturday to Wednesday, from 11 am to 5 pm (4 pm in October). Entry is £5.20/2.70. The surrounding garden and park are open most of the year. It's a short, steep walk up from the village.

Places to Stay

The nearest youth hostel is 2 miles away at Minehead (see Minehead later in this section).

Woodville House (*☎ 821228, West St*) charges £18 for B&B. *The Old Priory* (*☎ 821540*) is a medieval house in walled gardens opposite the dovecote. It's open all year and charges from £22.50 per person for B&B (£50 for a room with a four-poster bed).

Dollons House (*☎ 821880, Church St*) does luxury B&B from £25 in non-smoking rooms, all with bathroom. *Exmoor House Hotel* (*☎ 821268, 12 West St*) is a very comfortable, non-smoking hotel which charges from £32.50 per person for B&B in rooms with a bathroom.

Places to Eat

The *café* (*☎ 821759*) at Dunster Watermill, Mill Lane, is a good place to go for lunch or tea in summer; for £1.80/90p you can watch flour being ground in the mill.

The Tea Shoppe (*☎ 821304, 3 High St*) does morning coffee, lunches and cream teas in its 15th century tearooms. If it's full there are several other places along the High St.

The Luttrell Arms (*☎ 821555*) opposite the Yarn Market does good bar snacks including filled baguettes from £3.50; and main dishes for around £5.

Getting There & Away

Southern National runs an hourly service (No 34) between Minehead and Dunster. On Sundays and public holidays there are just four buses. You can also get here on the West Somerset Railway (see Somerset section).

MINEHEAD
• pop 8500   ☎ 01643

Somerset's largest seaside resort is just outside the park's eastern border. During summer, it's packed with British holidaymakers, many of them escapees from Somerstworld, a vast holiday camp. Visit in May, however, and the town still enacts medieval May Day ceremonies with a Hobby Horse performing a fertility dance through the streets.

The TIC (☎ 702624) at 17 Friday St has a list of B&Bs if you want to stay. Two miles south of Minehead, in a secluded spot, is *Minehead Youth Hostel* (☎ 702595) at Alcombe Combe. It's open daily in July and August;, daily except Monday from April to June; and daily except Monday and Tuesday in September and October. The nightly charge is £8.80/5.95 for adults/juniors.

Red Bus runs the DevonBus 290 service between Minehead and Exeter (three per day, two hours). From Minehead, Southern National operates service No 28 to Taunton (hourly, 1¼ hours), No 34 to Dunster, No 37 to Wheddon Cross, No 38 to Porlock Weir and No 300 to Lynton. Minehead is the northern terminus for the West Somerset Railway.

EXFORD
☎ 01643

This tiny village in the centre of the park makes a good base for walks, especially to Dunkery Beacon, the highest point on Exmoor, 4 miles from Exford.

Places to Stay & Eat

Exford Youth Hostel (☎ 831288) is in a Victorian house by the River Exe in the village centre. A bed costs £8.80/5.95 for adults/juniors, and the hostel is open daily in July and August; daily except Sunday in April, May and June. Phone for other opening hours.

Just outside Exford, off the Porlock road, *Wester Mill Farm Campsite* (☎ 831238) is open from April to October and charges £3.50 per person. There are also cottages to rent.

Exmoor House Hotel (☎ 831304, *Chapel St*) does B&B from £18/40 for a single/double.

The *White Horse Inn* (☎ 831229), a 16th century inn right by the bridge, does B&B from £49 per person for rooms with a bathroom. There are cheaper deals for mini-breaks. There's bar food during the week and a carvery on Sunday.

Getting There & Away

Over the moor, it's a 7 mile walk to Exford from Porlock, 10 from Minehead Youth Hostel, 12 from Dunster and 15 from Lynton. DevonBus 295 runs between Dulverton and Lynton via Exford. Exmoor Bus 285 (☎ 01823-358232) links Porlock, Minehead and Exford.

PORLOCK
• pop 1500   ☎ 01643

This attractive village of thatched cottages lies in a deep valley, reached by a steep lane. Two miles farther west is the charming harbour, Porlock Weir.

The picturesque NT-owned village of **Selworthy** is 2½ miles east of Porlock. Its cream-painted cob and thatch cottages make this a popular movie location; Thomas Hardy's *The Return of the Native* was filmed here.

Places to Stay & Eat

Well-signposted and in the centre of Porlock is *Sparkhayes Farm Campsite* (☎ 862470). Charges are £3.50 per person.

Most places to stay are on the High St. For B&B, cosy, thatched *Myrtle Cottage* (☎ 862978) charges from £25 per person for rooms with a bath. It's open all year.

The *Lorna Doone Hotel* (☎ 862404) charges £25/48 for a single/double with bathroom, with reductions for stays of three or more days.

The Ship Inn (☎ 862507) is a 13th century thatched hostelry mentioned in *Lorna Doone*. B&B is £25 per person and the pub serves meals. Try the inn's country wines – damson is good.

Open every evening, *Piggy in the Middle* (☎ 862647) does good steak and seafood. A salmon steak is £8.25; the seafood platter (lobster, prawns etc) costs £19.95. There are several tearooms in the High St which serve lunch as well.

Getting There & Away

Southern National (☎ 01823-272033) runs service No 300 along the coast from Barnstaple through Lynton and Porlock to Minehead and Bridgwater.

LYNTON & LYNMOUTH
- **pop 2075** ☎ **01598**

A water-operated cliff railway links the village of Lynton with Lynmouth, 185m below it. The picturesque, steeply wooded gorge of the West Lyn River, which meets the sea at Lynmouth, can be delightful out of season. This is a good base for walks along the coast and in the northern part of the park.

In 1952, storms caused the East and West Lyn rivers to flood, destroying 98 houses and claiming the lives of 34 people. The disaster is recorded at the **Lyn and Exmoor Museum** (☎ 752317), in haunted St Vincent's Cottage, Market St, Lynton. From late March to late October, the museum is open daily (afternoon only on Sunday) but closes from 12.30 to 2 pm for lunch.

The **cliff railway** is a simple piece of environmentally friendly Victorian engineering. Two cars linked by a steel cable descend or ascend the slope according to the amount of water in their tanks. For 50p it's the best way to get between the two villages between Easter and November.

There's a TIC (☎ 752225) in Lynton Town Hall and a National Park Visitors Centre (☎ 752509) by Lynmouth harbour.

Walks
Lynton TIC and Lynmouth Visitors Centre have information about the many local walks. The South West Coast Path and the Tarka Trail pass through the villages, and the Two Moors Way, linking Exmoor with Dartmoor, starts in Lynmouth.

As you leave Lynmouth you'll see signs to **Glen Lyn Gorge** which is open year-round and has a small exhibition centre, open in summer only. It costs £2/1 to walk along the gorge.

The **Valley of the Rocks**, which is believed to be where the River Lyn originally flowed, was described by the poet Robert Southey as 'rock reeling upon rock, stone piled upon stone, a huge terrifying reeling mass'. It's just over a mile west of Lynton and makes a pleasant walk along the coastal footpath. East of Lynmouth, the lighthouse at **Foreland Point** is another good focus for a walk.

Watersmeet, 2 miles along the river from Lynmouth, makes another popular hike. The old hunting lodge houses a NT teashop.

Places to Stay & Eat
Lynton Youth Hostel (☎ 753237) is at Lynbridge, roughly a mile outside Lynton. It's a Victorian house in the gorge, open daily in July and August; phone for other times. The nightly charge is £8.80/5.95 for adults/juniors.

The Retreat (☎ 753526, 1 Park Gardens, Lydiate Lane, Lynton) has B&B for £15 per person. Lydiate Lane is parallel to the main street. *Orchard House Hotel* (☎ 753247, Watersmeet Rd, Lynmouth) charges from £18, as does *Oakleigh* (☎ 752220, 4 Tors Rd, Lynmouth). In Lynbridge Rd, *Valley House* (☎ 752285) charges £24 per person in summer.

The *Rising Sun* (☎ 753223) is a 14th century inn beside Lynmouth harbour. The poet Shelley brought his 16-year-old bride here for their honeymoon, and you can stay in their rose-clad cottage for £70/140 (singles/doubles). Cheaper rooms cost from £49 per person, and there are also two-night packages including dinner available. This is an excellent place for a pub lunch or evening meal.

Getting There & Away
Red Bus (☎ 01271-345444) service No 310 runs five times a day between Barnstaple and Lynton (one hour, £2.10), Monday to Saturday. No 295 links Lynton with Dulverton.

Southern National's service No 300 runs through Lynton on its way from Williton to Ilfracombe.

Lyn Valley Bus (☎ 01598-752225) runs an infrequent service twice a week from Lynton to Taunton.

Driving from Porlock, note that Porlock Hill is notoriously steep; look out for the old AA box at the top where motorists could phone to report overheated radiators. There are two alternative toll roads (£1), both of them scenic and both of them less steep.

Devon

Devon's tourist attractions are no secret. For the British, the county has long been a popular place for a traditional family holiday by the seaside and the coastal resorts are still crowded in summer. The county's history is inextricably bound up with the sea; from Plymouth, Drake set out to fight the Spanish Armada and the Pilgrim Fathers sailed to America. Exeter Cathedral has the longest stretch of Gothic vaulting in the world. Little country lanes lead to idyllic villages of thatched cottages; tearooms serve traditional cream teas and you can buy rough cider from local farms. Inland, there's superb walking country in two national parks – wild Dartmoor in the centre and Exmoor in the north, which extends into Somerset (see Dartmoor National Park later in this chapter, and Somerset and Exmoor National Park earlier in this chapter).

GETTING AROUND

Contact the Devon County Public Transport Help Line (☎ 01392-382800) weekdays from 9 am to 5 pm for information. They can send you the invaluable *Devon Public Transport Map* and the useful *Dartmoor Bus Services Timetable*.

Devon's rail network skirts along the south coast through Exeter and Plymouth to Cornwall. There are some picturesque stretches where the line travels right beside the sea. Two branch lines run north – the 39 mile Tarka Line from Exeter to Barnstaple, and the 15 mile Tamar Valley Line from Plymouth to Gunnislake.

Away from the main roads, Devon is good cycling country. TICs have the absurdly named free leaflet, *Now You're Really Cycling*, which gives details of the main routes. Sustrans' West Country Way route crosses North Devon through Barnstaple and continues via Taunton to Bristol.

EXETER
- **pop 89,000**   ☎ 01392

The West Country's largest city, with one of the finest medieval cathedrals in the region, Exeter is the main transport hub for Devon and Cornwall, and a good starting point for Dartmoor.

Many of the older buildings were destroyed in the air raids of WWII and much of Exeter is modern and architecturally uninspiring. It is, however, a thoroughly livable university city with a thriving nightlife.

Until the 19th century, Exeter was an important port, and the waterfront is slowly being restored. Unfortunately the Maritime Museum has now closed.

History

Exeter was founded by the Romans in about 50 AD to serve as the administrative capital for the Dumnonii of Devon and Cornwall. There was, however, a settlement on the banks of the River Exe long before the arrival of the Romans.

By the 3rd century, the city was surrounded by a thick wall, parts of which can still be seen although most of it has either been buried or incorporated into buildings.

The fortifications were battered by Danish invaders and then by the Normans in the 11th century. In 1068, William the Conqueror took 18 days to break through the walls. He appointed a Norman seigneur (feudal lord) to construct a castle, the ruins of which can still be seen in Rougemont Park.

Exeter was a major trading port until Isabel, Countess of Devon built a weir across the river, halting river traffic. It was not until 1563, when the first ship canal in Britain was dug to bypass the weir, that the city began to re-establish itself as a trading centre.

Exeter has been closely involved in many of England's greatest battles. Three of the ships sent to face the Spanish Armada were built here and some of the greatest sea captains of the time, Drake, Raleigh and Frobisher, lived in the area for part of their lives. In 1942 heavy air raids reduced large areas of Exeter to rubble.

EXETER

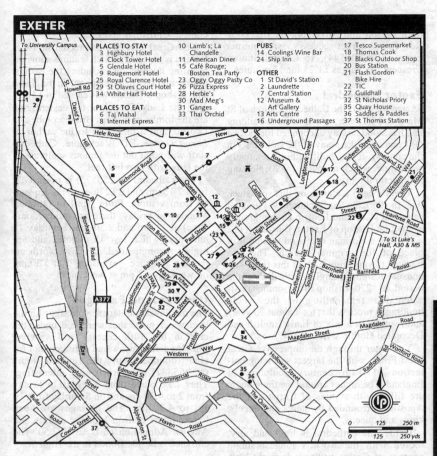

PLACES TO STAY
3 Highbury Hotel
4 Clock Tower Hotel
5 Glendale Hotel
9 Rougemont Hotel
25 Royal Clarence Hotel
29 St Olaves Court Hotel
34 White Hart Hotel

PLACES TO EAT
6 Taj Mahal
8 Internet Express

10 Lamb's; La
   Chandelle
11 American Diner
15 Café Rouge;
   Boston Tea Party
23 Oggy Oggy Pasty Co
26 Pizza Express
28 Herbie's
30 Mad Meg's
31 Ganges
33 Thai Orchid

PUBS
14 Coolings Wine Bar
24 Ship Inn

OTHER
1 St David's Station
2 Laundrette
7 Central Station
12 Museum &
   Art Gallery
13 Arts Centre
16 Underground Passages

17 Tesco Supermarket
18 Thomas Cook
19 Blacks Outdoor Shop
20 Bus Station
21 Flash Gordon
   Bike Hire
22 TIC
27 Guildhall
32 St Nicholas Priory
35 Quay House
36 Saddles & Paddles
37 St Thomas Station

SOUTH-WESTERN ENGLAND

Orientation

The old Roman walls enclose a hill in a bend of the River Exe, and the cathedral's great square towers dominate the skyline. Most of the sights are accessible on foot; long-stay car parks are well signposted. There are two main train stations (Central and St David's); most InterCity trains use St David's, a 20 minute walk west of the city centre.

Information

The TIC (☎ 265700), Civic Centre, Paris St, is just across the road from the bus station.

It's open Monday to Saturday from 9 am to 5 pm, and also on Sunday from 10 am to 4 pm from May to September.

Free guided tours led by the volunteer Exeter 'Redcoats' are well worth joining. They last 1½ to two hours and cover a range of subjects, from a standard walking tour (daily) to a ghost walk (Tuesday, 7 pm). Tours leave from outside the Royal Clarence Hotel or from Quay House. Ask at the TIC for details.

There are several supermarkets, including Tescos, on Sidwell St. Convenient laundrettes include Soaps beside St David's train station and Silverspin on Blackboy Rd. For Internet access visit Internet Express (☎ 201544), 1b Central Station Crescent. It charges £1.25 for 15 minutes.

Exeter Cathedral

Exeter's jewel is the Cathedral Church of St Mary and St Peter, a magnificent building that has stood largely unchanged for the last 600 years. Unlike many of the cathedrals in the country, it was built within a relatively short time, which accounts for its pleasing architectural unity.

There's been a church on this spot since 932. In 1050, the Saxon church was granted cathedral status and Leofric was enthroned as the first Bishop of Exeter. Between 1112 and 1133, a Norman cathedral was built in place of the original church. The two transept towers were built at this time – an unusual design for English cathedrals of the period. In 1270, Bishop Bronescombe instigated the remodelling of the whole building, a process that took about 90 years and resulted in a mix of Early English and Decorated Gothic styles.

You enter through the impressive Great West Front, with the largest surviving collection of 14th century sculpture in England. The niches around the three doors are filled with statues of Christ and the Apostles surrounded by saints and angels, kings and queens.

Inside, the cathedral is light and airy, roofed with the world's longest single expanse of Gothic vaulting. It might have been even brighter if a controversial plan to clean all the stonework and repaint the ceiling bosses in their original bright colours hadn't been stopped. Looking up, you can see where restoration was brought to a halt by those who thought the scheme over the top even though much of the medieval cathedral would have been brightly painted.

Walking clockwise around the building, you pass the **astronomical clock** in the north tower, which shows the phases of the moon as well as the time. The dial dates from the 15th century but the works are modern. Op-

posite is the **minstrels' gallery**, used by the choir at Christmas and Easter.

The **Great Screen** was erected in 1325. Behind is the choir, which features some interesting misericords including the earliest representation of an elephant in England. The **Bishop's Throne** was carved in 1312.

In the Lady Chapel, at the eastern end, are the **tombs** of bishops Bronescombe and Leofric, and a memorial to the author of *Lorna Doone*, RD Blackmore. Cathedral staff will point out the famous sculpture of the **lady with two left feet**.

The cathedral (☎ 255573) is open daily from 7.15 am and a £2 donation is requested from visitors. From April to October, Monday to Friday, there are guided tours (free) at 11 am and 2.30 pm (Saturday 11 am only) which last 45 minutes and are highly recommended. It's also worth attending a service – evensong is at 5.30 pm on weekdays, 3 pm at weekends.

Underground Passages

The medieval maintenance passages for the lead water pipes that were laid under the city in the 14th century still survive. They're dark, narrow and definitely not for claustrophobes but the guided tours (☎ 265887) are surprisingly interesting. They take place from Tuesday to Friday from 2 to 4.30 pm and on Saturday from 10 am to 4.30 pm. The passages are open longer hours and on Monday in July and August. Admission costs £3.50/2.50. The entrance is beside Boot's in the High St.

Royal Albert Memorial Museum & Art Gallery

Most of the galleries in this large museum (☎ 265858) are laid out in classic Victorian style, with crowded display cases and lots of dusty hunting trophies. The history of the city is covered in a series of exhibitions from prehistory, through Roman Exeter to modern times. The gallery upstairs includes works by Devon artists from the 18th and 19th centuries. It's open Monday to Saturday from 10 am to 5 pm; free entry. The café is good value, too.

Guildhall

Parts of the Guildhall (☎ 265500) date from 1160, making it the oldest municipal building in the country that is still in use. It was, however, mainly built in the 14th century and the impressive portico that extends over the pavement was added at the end of the 16th century. Inside, the city's silver and regalia are on display. It's open (as long as there are no functions) Monday to Friday, from 10 am to 1 pm and from 2 to 4 pm; morning only on Saturday. There's no entry charge.

St Nicholas Priory

Originally built as accommodation for overnight visitors to the Benedictine priory, St Nicholas Priory (☎ 265858), off Fore St, became the house of a wealthy Elizabethan merchant. It's now preserved, with period furniture and plaster ceilings, as it might have looked when lived in by the merchant and his family. It's open Easter to October, Monday, Wednesday and Saturday from 3 to 4.30 pm; free entry.

Quay House Interpretation Centre

Down by the river, this display and audio-visual presentation offers a painless resumé of the city's history and its commercial reliance on the river. There's no charge, and it's open daily Easter to October from 10 am to 5 pm.

Walks & Cycle Routes

The 11 mile walk to the *Steps Bridge Youth Hostel* on Dartmoor follows country lanes through Shillingford St George and Doddiscombleigh (stop at the *Nobody Inn*, one of the south-west's best pubs). A 30 mile cycle tour of Dartmoor takes you from Exeter through Doddiscombleigh and Bovey Tracey to Widecombe-in-the-Moor and back to Exeter.

Places to Stay

Hostels In a large house overlooking the River Exe, *Exeter Youth Hostel* (☎ 873329, 47 Countess Wear Rd) is 2 miles south-east of the city towards Topsham. It's open year-round and the nightly charge is £9.75/6.55 for adults/juniors. From High St, catch minibuses J, K or T (10 minutes) and ask for Countess Wear post office. Bus No 57 will get you there from the bus station.

The best value accommodation in Exeter is the university's *St Luke's Hall* (☎ 211500) – just £12.95 per person including breakfast. The catch is that it's available only in March, April, July, August and September (college holidays).

B&Bs & Hotels The cheapest B&Bs are on the outskirts of the city. The *Old Mill* (☎ 259977, Mill Lane, Alphington) is in a quiet residential suburb and has B&B for £12.50 (£10 for stays of seven nights or more). It's easy to reach by bus.

Most B&Bs and cheaper hotels lie in the area east of St David's station and north of Central station. There are several reasonable B&Bs on St David's Hill. The *Highbury* (☎ 434737, 85 St David's Hill) is good value from £15/25, or £19/30 with a bath. *Glendale Hotel* (☎ 274350) at No 8, has rooms from £18 per head, some with showers.

The *Clock Tower Hotel* (☎ 424545, 16 New North Rd) has a few singles from £15, doubles from £35 or £25/38 with a bathroom. There are several other places along this road and more on Blackall Rd and Howell Rd. *Rhona's* (☎ 277791, 15 Blackall Rd) has rooms from £13/26 each. *Raffles Hotel* (☎ 270200, 11 Blackall Rd) is more upmarket; all rooms have a bathroom and charges are £32/46.

The *Claremont* (☎ 274699) is a comfortable B&B for non-smokers at 36 Wonford Rd, quite a drive out on the eastern side of the city. Rooms are £28/38 with bathrooms.

The *White Hart Hotel* (☎ 279897, South St) is an old coaching inn, and the cobbled courtyard through which the coachmen drove their horses is still the focal point. It's an interesting place to stay, with rooms with a bath from £49/64 at weekends, £61/94 during the week.

The centrally located *St Olaves Court Hotel* (☎ 217736, Mary Arches St) has 15 comfortable rooms each with a bathroom.

SOUTH-WESTERN ENGLAND

Prices are from £60/70 at the weekend, £73/88 during the week. Some rooms come with a jacuzzi.

The *Rougemont Hotel* (☎ *254982, Queen St*) is opposite Central train station and part of the Thistle group. Popular with businesspeople, rooms are £89/99. At the weekend the price drops to £86 for a double room for two nights.

Dating back to the 14th century, the *Royal Clarence Hotel* (☎ *319955*) has the best location of all, right in Cathedral Yard. Its weekend B&B deals are good value at £96 a head for two nights; pay the extra £10 for a front room with a superb view of the cathedral. During the week, these rooms cost £95/120; breakfast is extra. Former guests include Tsar Nicholas I and Lord Nelson.

Places to Eat
On Queen St, just along the road from Central station, *The American Diner* (☎ *493095*) plays the part with Mom's meatloaf on its menu for £5.50. There are also hot cakes, hoagies and delicious ice creams with a shot of liquor (£2.75). Nearby on Queen St is the *Oggy Oggy Pasty Co* with a great range of pasties from 99p (vegetarian) to £1.35 (beef and stilton). Across the road is a branch of *Café Rouge*.

In the alley off Queen St is *The Boston Tea Party* open daily from 8 am and in the evenings from Thursday to Saturday. All meals are under £5; a bagel with cream cheese is £1.50.

In Cathedral Close there are several places to choose from. *St Martin's Café Bar* (☎ *310130*) has a jolly menu that includes a British Buttie (soda bun with bacon, fried egg and lashings of House of Commons HP Sauce) for £3.95. There are also salads, pasta, pizzas and steaks. Also in Cathedral Close is a branch of *Pizza Express,* and *Hanson's Restaurant* for a cream tea or traditional lunch.

Nearby, on the other side of the cathedral green is *Thai Orchid* (☎ *214215*), which does good set lunches for £8.50 and is also open for dinner.

There are several bistro-style places around Gandy St. *Coolings Wine Bar* (☎ *434184*) at No 11, has a good range of main dishes (from £4.25) and an extensive wine list.

Herbies (☎ *258473, 15 North St*) is an excellent vegetarian restaurant. Its home-made soups, chilli dishes and apple pie are highly recommended. Garlic mushrooms with granary bread are £2.95.

The *Ganges* (☎ *272630, Fore St*) is reputed to be the best of the Indian restaurants, but the *Taj Mahal* (☎ *258129, 50 Queen St*) is good value and does an all-you-can-eat Sunday buffet for £6.95.

Said to have terrorised the kitchens of the Sheriff of Exeter, Mad Meg now lends her name to a Middle Ages theme restaurant with long wooden tables and bare flagstones. *Mad Meg's* (☎ *221225, Fore St*) serves English baronial fare steaks – ribs, pheasant, rabbit etc. Main courses range from £5.95 to £15.85, but students get a discount on Monday.

The city's top restaurants include *Lamb's* (☎ *254269, 15 Lower North St*) under the old iron bridge. The three course set dinner costs £19. A couple of doors down is *La Chandelle* (☎ *435953*) where the set menu is £14.90. The restaurant at *St Olaves Court Hotel* is also recommended: two courses cost £11.50, three courses are £14.50.

Sir Francis Drake's favourite local is said to have been the *Ship Inn* (☎ *270891*) in Martin's Lane – the alley between the High St and the cathedral. The place trades heavily on its famous customer, but it's convenient and the food's good value. The *Tap Bar* at the White Hart Hotel feels more authentic with sawdust on the floor and jugs of real ale.

The *Double Locks* (☎ *256947*) is a popular pub right beside the Exeter Shipping Canal, with good food, great puddings and daily barbecues in summer. It's a 20 minute walk south along the canal from the The Quay.

Entertainment
The *Arts Centre* (☎ *421111, Gandy St*) stages dance, theatre, film and music events and is open daily except Sunday. It's cur-

rently under renovation. There are two theatres: the **Northcott** (☎ 493493), on the university campus, and the smaller **Barnfield** (☎ 71808, Barnfield Rd), that features programs from touring companies and local groups.

There's live music each night in the subterranean **Cavern** (☎ 495370, 83 Queen St). Entry is free on Saturday but there are charges for gigs on other nights.

Nightclubs come and go. Down on The Quay are **Volts**, **Boxes** and **Warehouse**, popular with students.

Getting There & Away

See the fares tables in the Getting Around chapter. Exeter is 172 miles from London, 75 from Bristol, 45 from Plymouth and 120 from Land's End. If you're driving down from London, follow the M3 and then the A303, not the congested A30. It's even faster to take the M4 to Bristol and then the M5 south to Exeter.

Air Scheduled services run between Exeter airport (☎ 367433) and Ireland, Birmingham, the Channel Islands and the Isles of Scilly.

Bus The booking office at the bus station is open daily from 7.45 am to 6.30 pm.

National Express runs coaches between Exeter and numerous towns in Britain, including London (four hours, £21) via Heathrow airport (three hours), Bath (2¾ hours, £11.35), Bristol (1½ hours, £9.10), Salisbury (two hours, £15.60) and Penzance (five hours, £15).

There's a daily south-coast service between Brighton and Penzance (via Portsmouth, Weymouth, Dorchester, Bridport, Exeter and Plymouth) departing Exeter for Brighton (seven hours, £21 if you don't travel on Friday) at 12.25 pm (and 2.25 pm in summer).

Stagecoach Devon (☎ 427711) runs the hourly No X38 to Plymouth (1¼ hours, £4.50). Western National (☎ 01752-222666) has buses to Okehampton (one hour, £3.90) and Torquay.

Stagecoach Devon produces a useful *Smugglers' Trail* leaflet with details of walks accessible by bus. The area includes Sidmouth, Exeter, Torquay and Dartmouth. An Explorer ticket costs £5.50 for a day's unlimited bus travel.

Train The fastest trains between London and Exeter use London Paddington and take 2½ to three hours (hourly, £37). Trains from London's Waterloo also leave hourly but take three hours, following a more scenic route via Salisbury.

Exeter is at the hub of lines running from Bristol (1½ hours, £15.20), Salisbury (two hours, £19.70) and Penzance (three hours, £18.10).

The 39 mile branch line to Barnstaple (1½ hours, £9.40) is promoted as the Tarka Line, following the river valleys of the Yeo and Taw and giving good views of traditional Devon countryside with its characteristic, deep-sunken lanes. There are 11 trains a day, Monday to Friday, nine on Saturday and four on Sunday. A reduced service operates during the winter. Most InterCity trains use St David's station.

Getting Around

Bus Exeter is well served by public transport. A one-day Freedom ticket on the Exeter bus system costs £2.60. Bus N links St David's station with Central station and passes near the coach station.

Taxi There are taxi ranks outside the train stations. Alternatively, try Capital Taxis (☎ 433433).

Bicycles & Canoes At 15 Clifton Rd, Flash Gordon (☎ 424246), rents bicycles (as well as camping equipment and canoes). Three-speeds cost £5/20 a day/week, mountain bikes cost £12 and a tandem £25.

Saddles & Paddles (☎ 424241), on The Quay, rents bikes and Canadian canoes (from £6 per hour or £20 per day). It also organises nightly paddling parties, with a barbecue at the Double Locks Hotel.

AROUND EXETER
Powderham Castle
The castle (☎ 01626-890243) is on the estuary of the River Exe, 8 miles from Exeter. It dates from the 14th century but was considerably altered in the 18th and 19th centuries. The home of the Courtenay family, it contains collections of French china and Stuart and Regency furniture and features some garish rococo ceilings. It's open from April to September, daily except Saturday, from 10 am to 5.30 pm; entry is £4.95/2.85.

A la Ronde
Jane and Mary Parminter planned to combine the magnificence of the Church of San Vitale, which they'd visited in Ravenna, with the homeliness of a country cottage, to create the perfect dwelling place. The result is an intriguing 16-sided house (☎ 01395-265514, NT) whose bizarre interior decor includes a shell-encrusted room, a frieze of feathers and sand and seaweed collages.

It's open April to October, Sunday to Thursday, from 11 am to 5.30 pm; entry is £3.20/1.60. It's 2 miles north of Exmouth on the A376; Stagecoach Devon bus No 57 runs close by en route to Exeter.

SOUTH DEVON COAST
Devon's south coast is dotted with traditional seaside resorts, which are crowded in summer. They are linked by the South West Coast Path which follows the length of the coast.

Sidmouth
- pop 11,000   ☎ 01395

A busy fishing port in the Middle Ages, Sidmouth became a fashionable holiday resort when the future Queen Victoria visited with her parents in 1819. The town still retains a certain grandeur, with many gracious Regency buildings. To the east, a steep path climbs Salcombe Hill, with superb views from the top.

Sidmouth is best known for its folk festival which has grown from a small gathering to a major event on the international folk scene. The festival takes over the town for a week in late July or early August. Tickets for all the events cost £120/60, plus £27/9 to camp for adults/juniors; a day's ticket is £25 plus £5 if you're camping. Phone ☎ 01296-393293 for information.

The TIC (☎ 516441) shares a home with the public swimming pool in Ham Lane.

The nearest hostel is the **Beer Youth Hostel** (☎ *01297-20296, Bovey Combe, Townsend*) in a large house half a mile west of the village of Beer. It's open daily in July and August; and daily except Sunday from April to June, September and October. The nightly charge in summer is £8.80/5.95.

There are two buses an hour from Exeter (45 minutes, £2.95) to Sidmouth. Axe Valley (☎ 01297-625959) runs to Beer village.

Torbay Resorts
The three towns set around Torbay – Torquay, Paignton and Brixham – describe themselves as the English Riviera, but while it's true that the climate here is one of the most equable in the country, if you're expecting Cannes, forget it.

Torquay, with a population of over 60,000, is the largest and brashest of the three. There's a long seaside promenade, hung with coloured lights at night, and streets of hotels and cheap B&Bs, all trying to vanquish the ghost of *Fawlty Towers* that took Torquay as its location. The TIC (☎ 01803-297428) is on Vaughan Parade, near the harbour.

Agatha Christie was born here and **Torquay Museum** (☎ 293975), 529 Babbacombe Rd, has a display on the author. In summer it's open Monday to Saturday from 10 am to 4.45 pm, and on Sunday from 1.30 pm; weekdays only in winter. Entry is £2/1.25. **Torre Abbey** (☎ 293593), in the park set back from the beach, was a monastery converted into a country house. It now houses a collection of furniture, glassware and more Agatha Christie mementos. It's open April to October, daily from 9.30 am to 5 pm. Entry is £2.75/1.50.

Torquay Backpackers (☎ *299924, 119 Abbey Rd*) charges £7 per night and is near the town centre and the beach.

To the south around the bay, Torquay merges into **Paignton**, that promotes itself as a seaside resort for the family. Roundham Head separates the two main beaches. The TIC (☎ 01803-558383) is on the Esplanade.

Riviera Backpackers (☎ 01803-550160, 6 Manor Rd, Preston Sands) is a short walk from the beach. Dorm beds are £7.50. Call from the train station and they'll meet you.

Brixham is a fishing town crowded round a small harbour. In the middle of the 19th century, this was the country's busiest fishing port and is still the place to come for a fishing expedition. Kiosks line the harbour touting boat trips. It costs around £18 to fish for conger, ling and coalfish around the wrecks in the bay, less to fish for mackerel. Before parting with your money, it's worth asking whether there are any mackerel shoals about. To arrange a trip, contact the skippers directly – *Sea Spray* (☎ 851328), *Boy Richard* (☎ 521986), *Calypso/Gemini* (☎ 851766) or *Our Jenny* (☎ 854444). The TIC (☎ 01803-852861) is on the quay.

Four miles from Brixham and across the water from Dartmouth, the attractively located *Maypool Youth Hostel (☎ 01803-842444)* is a mile south-west of Galmpton. Beds are £8/5.40 for adults/juniors and it's open every day from April to August. Stagecoach Devon bus No 12 stops at Churston Pottery, a mile away beside Churston train station.

Getting There & Away The No X46 bus service runs hourly from Exeter to Torquay (one hour, £3.90). Service No 100 operates every 12 minutes along the coast from Torquay to Paignton (15 minutes, £1.25) and Brixham (25 minutes, £1.85).

A branch rail line runs from Newton Abbot, via Torquay to Paignton. The Paignton & Dartmouth Steam Railway (☎ 01803-555872) runs from Paignton along the coast on the scenic 7 mile trip to Kingswear on the River Dart, linked by ferry (six minutes) to Dartmouth. A combined rail/ferry ticket to Dartmouth costs £5.30/3.50 for an adult/child, one way; £7/4.60 return.

Dartmouth
- **pop 5300**   ☎ 01803

On the River Dart estuary, Dartmouth is an attractive port with a long history. The deep natural harbour has sheltered trading vessels since Norman times, fishing boats for many more centuries, the Pilgrim Fathers in 1620 on their way to Plymouth, and D-day landing craft bound for France in 1944. Today, it's filled with yachts, but naval associations continue with the Royal Navy's officers' training college located on the edge of town.

Narrow streets wind through the town. In the centre, the Butterwalk is a row of timber-framed houses built in the 17th century, with a museum featuring a large collection of model boats. **Dartmouth Castle** (☎ 833588), three-quarters of a mile outside the town, dates from the 15th century and was designed so that a chain could be placed to the companion castle at Kingswear to block off the estuary. The castle is open daily in summer; entry is £2.50/1.30. There's a ferry across to the castle from the town every 15 minutes (90p).

The TIC (☎ 834224) is on Mayor's Ave.

Places to Stay The youth hostel (see Brixham) is across the river at Maypool, about 5 miles away.

There are cheap B&Bs along Victoria Rd. *Pickwick (☎ 833415)* at No 75 charges £15 per person. Near the waterfront is the *Captain's House (☎ 832133, 18 Clarence St)* with rooms from £35/55, all with bathrooms. *Galleons Reach (☎ 834339)* at No 77 costs £16 per person, or £18 in a room with a bath.

Places to Eat *Dartmouth Castle Tea Rooms*, at the castle, do cream teas and light lunches, and there are excellent views over the water from here.

The town has something of a reputation for gourmet dining. The *Royal Castle Hotel*

(☎ 833033) on The Quay, has a popular restaurant, but better known is the **Carved Angel** *(☎ 832465)* on South Embankment, where a memorable feast will cost £48 for three courses. Run by the same people but with a cheaper menu, the **Carved Angel Café** *(☎ 834842, 7 Foss St)* offers bistro-style main courses from £3.50; fish is a speciality.

The **Cherub** *(☎ 832571)*, also in Higher St, claims to be the town's oldest building and is a good place for a pint or a bar meal.

Getting There & Away The best way to approach Dartmouth is by boat, either on the ferries across from Kingswear (six minutes, £2 for a car and four people, 50p for a foot passenger) or downstream from Totnes (1¼ hours, £4.50/£6 single/return). River Dart Cruises *(☎ 832109)* is one operator. From Exeter, take a train to Totnes and a boat from there.

Totnes
* **pop 7500**   ☎ **01803**

Nine miles inland from Torquay and 10 miles upriver from Dartmouth, Totnes was once one of the most prosperous towns in Britain, a centre for the tin and wool industry. It's now a trendy market town ('the Glastonbury of the west') with a thriving arts community.

This is a pleasant place to wander around, with interesting shops, numerous Elizabethan buildings and a busy quay. There are cruises on the river with frequent departures to Dartmouth in summer.

Totnes Museum, is in a Tudor building on Fore St. It's open Monday to Saturday. A £3 ticket also covers the **Guildhall** and the **Museum of Period Costume**. **Totnes Castle** *(☎ 864406, EH)* is open daily in summer; entry is £1.60/80p.

The TIC *(☎ 863168)* is in The Plains. Its *Town Trail Guide* is recommended.

Places to Stay & Eat *Dartington Youth Hostel (☎ 862303)*, Lownard, is 2 miles from Totnes off the A385 near Week. It's open daily in July and August, daily except Monday from April to June, and daily except Monday and Tuesday in September

and October; the nightly charge is £8/5.40 for adults/juniors. Western National bus No X80 from Torquay to Plymouth via Totnes passes close by.

Five minutes walk from the Totnes train station, there's non-smoking B&B at **Mrs Park's** *(☎ 862555, 1 Castle View)* for £16/32 for singles/doubles, or **Mrs Allen's** *(☎ 862638, 7 Antrim Terrace)* from £16 per person.

At 3 Plymouth Rd, off the High St, **Alison Fenwick** *(☎ 866917)* offers B&B for around £15 per person, and can arrange private tours of Dartmoor.

The 600-year-old **Old Forge** *(☎ 862174, Seymour Place)* is more atmospheric and even has its own old lock-up. Rooms cost £42/52.

Totnes High St is lined with interesting places to eat. **Willow Vegetarian Restaurant** *(☎ 862605, 87 High St)* does main dishes from £3.60 and has a nice garden. **Tolivers Vegetarian Bistro** *(65 Fore St)* is more expensive but has live music on Thursday, Friday and Saturday evenings. How does chickpea and peanut balls with a hot sweet chilli sauce served with poppy seed noodles and a pineapple and avocado salad (£6.95) sound?

At **Rumour** *(☎ 864682, 30 High St)* you can order anything from a cappuccino to a full meal.

Getting There & Away Buses run only a few times a week to Exeter, but National Express coaches stop here. There are frequent rail connections to Exeter (45 minutes, £6.60) and Plymouth (25 minutes, £5.10). The train station is a 15 minute walk from the town centre.

A short walk from Totnes mainline train station, the private South Devon Railway *(☎ 01364-642338)* runs to Buckfastleigh (25 minutes, £5.90/3.90 return; £5.40/3.40 if you book at the TIC) on the edge of Dartmoor.

PLYMOUTH
* **pop 239,000**   ☎ **01752**

Plymouth was renowned as a maritime centre long before Drake's famous game of bowls on Plymouth Hoe in 1588, but this history is difficult to appreciate as you approach through the extensive modern suburbs of Devon's largest city. Devastated by WWII bombing raids, most of Plymouth has been rebuilt, although the Barbican (the old quarter by the harbour where the Pilgrim Fathers set sail for the New World) has been preserved.

History

Plymouth really began to expand in the 15th century, with the development of larger ships; the Plymouth Sound provided a perfect anchorage for warships.

The seafarer most commonly associated with Plymouth is Sir Francis Drake who achieved his knighthood through an epic voyage around the world; setting out from Plymouth in 1577 in the *Golden Hind*, he returned three years later.

In 1588, Drake played a prominent part in the defeat of the Spanish Armada, the fleet sent to invade England by Philip II who wanted to restore Catholicism to this country. On the way home from a Caribbean raid in 1586, Drake had taunted the Spanish king with an attack on some ships in Cadiz harbour.

Whether Drake really was playing bowls on the Hoe at the time is debatable, but the English fleet certainly did set sail from here. Drake was vice admiral and John Hawkins (who had sailed with him on the 1586 raid) was rear admiral. The Armada was chased up the English Channel to Calais, where the troops they were supposed to collect for the planned invasion of Britain failed to arrive. The English then attacked the fleet with fire ships. Many of the Spanish vessels escaped but were blown off course and wrecked off Scotland. Losses were England nil, Spain 51.

Thirty-two years later, the Pilgrim Fathers' two ships, the *Mayflower* and the *Speedwell*, put into Plymouth. Because the second ship was badly damaged, only the *Mayflower* set sail for America on 16 September 1620. Some of the 102 passengers and crew spent their last night on English soil in Island House, now the TIC. Another famous Plymouth mariner is Captain James

Cook, who set out from the Barbican in 1768 in search of a southern continent.

The royal dockyard was established at Devonport beside the River Tamar in 1690, and there's still a large naval base here.

Orientation & Information

The train station is about a mile north of Plymouth Hoe, the grassy park overlooking the sea. Between them is the pedestrianised city centre, with shopping streets branching off Armada Way, and the bus station. To the east of the Hoe is the Barbican, the interesting old quarter, by Sutton Harbour.

The TIC (☎ 264849) is in Island House, 9 The Barbican. It's closed on Sunday in winter. If you're driving into Plymouth there's another TIC (☎ 266030) next to the Sainsbury's supermarket at Marshall's roundabout (off A38).

Plymouth Boat Cruises (☎ 822797) offers a number of boat trips ranging from an hour-long harbour cruise (£4/2) to a four hour cruise up the Tamar (£6/3). The cruise to Calstock can be combined with a rail trip on the Tamar Line. Boats leave from Phoenix Wharf, along the Barbican (below the citadel).

There's a laundrette, open daily from 8 am to 8 pm, on Pier St.

Plymouth Hoe

This famous promenade gives wonderful, breezy views over Plymouth Sound. In one corner there's even a bowling green; the one on which Drake finished his game was probably where his statue now stands.

The Hoe's most obvious landmark is the red-and-white-striped **Smeaton's Tower**, originally the Eddystone Lighthouse but rebuilt here in 1882. This may look like just another lighthouse but it's actually the first scientifically-designed jointed masonry lighthouse in the world. Open in summer, it costs 75p to climb the 93 steps.

The **Plymouth Dome** (☎ 603300), below Smeaton's Tower, details Plymouth's history through high-tech audiovisual shows. There's also a Tudor street with rowdy locals to liven things up, and a

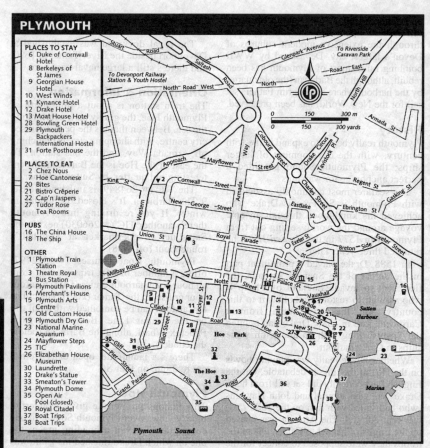

PLYMOUTH

PLACES TO STAY
6 Duke of Cornwall Hotel
8 Berkeleys of St James
9 Georgian House Hotel
10 West Winds
11 Kynance Hotel
12 Drake Hotel
13 Moat House Hotel
28 Bowling Green Hotel
29 Plymouth Backpackers International Hostel
31 Forte Posthouse

PLACES TO EAT
2 Chez Nous
7 Hoe Cantonese
20 Bites
21 Bistro Crêperie
22 Cap'n Jaspers
27 Tudor Rose Tea Rooms

PUBS
16 The China House
18 The Ship

OTHER
1 Plymouth Train Station
3 Theatre Royal
4 Bus Station
5 Plymouth Pavilions
14 Merchant's House
15 Plymouth Arts Centre
17 Old Custom House
19 Plymouth Dry Gin
23 National Marine Aquarium
24 Mayflower Steps
25 TIC
26 Elizabethan House Museum
30 Laundrette
32 Drake's Statue
33 Smeaton's Tower
34 Plymouth Dome
35 Open Air Pool (closed)
36 Royal Citadel
37 Boat Trips
38 Boat Trips

harbour observation deck with interactive computers and radar. It's open daily from 9 am to 7.30 pm (5.30 pm in winter); entry is £3.95/2.50. Last admission is at 6 pm.

East of the Hoe is the **Royal Citadel**, built by Charles II in 1670 and still in military use. There are guided tours of parts of the fortress including the chapel from May to September, daily at 2 and 3.30 pm. Tickets (£3/2) can be purchased at Plymouth Dome or at the TIC.

The Barbican

To get an idea of what Plymouth was like before the Luftwaffe redesigned it, visit the Barbican with its Tudor and Jacobean buildings and busy Victorian fish market. Americans will want to make a pilgrimage to the **Mayflower Steps** where a sign listing the passengers marks the spot.

The narrow streets harbour interesting galleries and craft shops. One famous local artist to look out for is Beryl Cook, whose naughty, plump figures fetch high prices.

The Barbican Gallery (☎ 661052), 15 The Parade, sells prints of her work.

The **Elizabethan House** (☎ 253871), 32 New St, is the former residence of an Elizabethan sea captain. It's open April to October, Wednesday to Sunday, from 10 am to 5 pm; entry is £1/50p.

At 60 Southside St, **Plymouth Dry Gin** (☎ 667062) has daily tours of the distillery from April to December, daily except Sunday from 10.30 am to 4 pm; tickets are £2.75/2.25.

Between the Barbican and the city centre is the **Merchant's House** (☎ 264878), 33 St Andrews St, a museum of social history, open the same times as the Elizabethan House; entry is 90p/30.

National Marine Aquarium

Opened in 1998 in an impressive building opposite the Barbican, the aquarium is a non-profit making venture designed to educate as well as amuse. Following a route along ramps winding through the building, visitors can examine aquatic life in a range of habitats – moorland stream, river estuary, shore and shallow sea, and deep reef. There's also the mandatory shark pool but Jaws gets good press here. You're more likely to die from a coconut dropping on your head than from being savaged by a shark, we're told.

The aquarium (☎ 220084) is well worth visiting. It's open daily from 10 am to 6 pm; entry is £5.99/3.99, and if you get a stamp on the way out you can visit again the same day.

Places to Stay

Camping The nearest camping ground is *Riverside Caravan Park* (☎ 344122), which is 4 miles from the centre on Longbridge Rd (off Plympton Rd). It costs £9.50 for a tent and two people in summer.

Hostels Two miles from the centre, *Plymouth Youth Hostel* (☎ 562189, *Belmont Place, Stoke*) is in a Grecian-style mansion. In summer, beds cost £9.75/6.55 for adults/juniors. The hostel is open daily from January to Christmas. Western National bus

Nos 15 and 81 and Citybus Nos 33/4 pass this way from the city centre. Devonport train station is a quarter of a mile from the hostel.

Plymouth Backpackers International Hostel (☎ 225158) is a friendly place at 172 Citadel Rd, the Hoe. There are beds in dorms from £7.50 a night, with cheaper weekly rates. There are also some double rooms. Showers are free (baths cost £1.50) and there's a laundry service.

B&Bs & Hotels B&Bs and hotels cluster round the north-western corner of the Hoe. Citadel Rd is lined with places to stay. *West Winds* (☎ 601777, 99 Citadel Rd) charges £18/28 for singles/doubles; the doubles have showers.

The large, friendly *Kynance Hotel* (☎ 266821, 107 Citadel Rd) has rooms from £25/38 with a bath. A continental breakfast is provided if you're leaving early on the ferry. Slightly more upmarket is the *Georgian House Hotel* (☎ 663237, 51 Citadel Rd) where rooms with a bath cost from £26/38. In winter prices drop to £20/32.

Berkeleys of St James (☎ 221654, 4 St James Place East) is a comfortable, non-smoking guesthouse charging from £25/40 for rooms with a bath.

Bowling Green Hotel (☎ 667485, 9 Osborne Place, Lockyer St) is, as the name suggests, located right beside the Hoe bowling green. It's a small, comfortable place run by friendly people. Rooms with a shower cost from £35/46. Also on Lockyer St is the *Drake Hotel* (☎ 229730, 1 Windsor Villas) with rooms for £42/52 with a bathroom, £29/44 without. Nearby is the *Imperial Hotel* (☎ 227311) with rooms from £34/48.

The *Forte Posthouse* (☎ 662828), the Hoe, charges £90 for a double at weekends. It has good views over Plymouth Sound. The *Plymouth Hoe Moat House* (☎ 639988, Armada Way) charges £82 for a double at weekends.

The *Duke of Cornwall* (☎ 266256, Millbay Rd) is an impressive Victorian Gothic hotel situated between the Hoe and

SOUTH-WESTERN ENGLAND

the ferry terminal. B&B costs from £74.50/89.50.

Places to Eat

The Barbican area makes the best hunting ground for interesting places to eat, especially along Southside St and New St behind the TIC. The *Tudor Rose Tea Rooms* (☎ 255502, New St) have a pleasant garden at the back where teas and lunches are available. Beef and Guinness pie is £4.25.

For a takeaway sandwich visit *Bites* on Quay Rd. A filled baguette costs £2.20. Nearby is *Bistro Crêperie* with a range of crêpes from £1.60 to £3.15. *Cap'n Jasper's* is a popular snack stand that does breakfasts and burgers near the Mayflower Steps. Half a yard of hot dog costs £2.95. *The Ship* (☎ 667604), beside the marina in the Barbican, offers good value carvery meals.

There's a good restaurant by the *National Aquarium* where light lunches include a baked potato filled with tuna (£2.75) – dolphin friendly, of course.

There are few restaurants in the Lockyer and Citadel Rds area but *Hoe Cantonese* (Elliott St) is an exception – and it stays open late.

The city's top restaurant is the predominantly French *Chez Nous* (☎ 266793, 13 Frankfort Gate), a short walk from the Theatre Royal. Seafood is a speciality, and main courses are around £18; a three course set lunch or dinner is £29.50. Booking is advisable.

Entertainment

Plymouth's *Theatre Royal* (☎ 267222, Royal Parade) attracts surprisingly big names for a regional theatre. *Plymouth Arts Centre* (☎ 206114, 38 Looe St) has a cinema, art galleries and a vegetarian restaurant. The *Pavilions* (☎ 229922, Millbay Rd) hosts everything from Tom Jones to the Bolshoi Ballet.

The Barbican is a good place to drink in the evening; the *Dolphin*, on Southside St, and the *Ship*, on the Barbican, are both popular. The *China House* (☎ 260930, Marrowbone Slip, off Exeter Rd), overlooking Sutton Harbour, is a popular pub in a converted warehouse. There's live jazz on Sunday at lunch time and bands on Friday and Saturday evening.

Getting There & Away

Plymouth is 211 miles from London, 90 from Land's End and 46 from Exeter.

Bus First Western National (☎ 01752-222666) runs three buses an hour to Yelverton (35 minutes), with an hourly service on Sunday or bank holidays. Explorer tickets for one/three/seven days cost £5.50/13.40/22.65.

National Express (☎ 0990-808080) has direct connections to numerous cities including London (4½ hours, £28) and Bristol (2½ hours, £17.50). Stagecoach runs the cheapest buses to/from Exeter (¾ hour, £4.55).

Train The fastest way to get to London is by train (3½ hours, £42). There are also direct services to Bristol (1½ hours, £25) and Penzance (two hours, £10).

There's a scenic route to Exeter (one hour, £10.10) – the line follows the River Exe estuary, running beside the sea for part of the way. The Tamar Valley Line, through Bere Ferrers, Bere Alston and Calstock to Gunnislake, is another scenic route. In summer, it's possible to travel to Calstock by train (£3.80) and return by boat (see Orientation & Information under Plymouth earlier).

Boat Brittany Ferries (☎ 0990-360360) sails from Millbay Docks to Roscoff in France (six hours, up to three departures a day in summer, £13 to £29 return) and Santander in Spain (24 hours, Monday and Wednesday in summer, £47 to £149 return).

AROUND PLYMOUTH
Mount Edgcumbe

The 400-year-old home of the Earls of Mount Edgcumbe lies across the water in Cornwall. Although the house is open to the public and filled with 18th century furniture, it's the French, Italian and English gardens that draw visitors. The gardens are open daily and admission is free. You get to them from Plymouth on the Cremyll foot ferry.

Buckland Abbey

Eleven miles north of Plymouth, Buckland Abbey (☎ 01822-853607, NT) was a Cistercian monastery, transformed into a family residence by Sir Richard Grenville and bought in 1581 by Sir Francis Drake. Among the memorabilia is Drake's Drum, used to summon sailors onto the deck of the *Revenge* before battle with the Armada. When Britain is in danger of being invaded, the drum is said to beat by itself.

It's open April to October, daily except Thursday from 10.30 am to 5.30 pm; and from 2 to 5 pm at weekends in winter; entry is £4.30/2.10. Bus Nos 83/84 from Plymouth connect with the No 55 from Yelverton.

NORTH DEVON
Barnstaple
• pop 24,500   ☎ 01271

Barnstaple is a large town and transport hub – a good starting point for North Devon and Exmoor (see Exmoor National Park in this chapter). **The Museum of North Devon** (☎ 346747) in The Square aside, there's little reason to stay. Contact the TIC (☎ 388583), 36 Boutport St, for B&Bs. The nearest youth hostel is 6 miles away at Instow.

Barnstaple is at the north-western end of the Tarka Line from Exeter and connects with a number of bus services around the coast. Red Bus (☎ 01271-345444) No 310 runs every two hours to Lynton, but the most interesting option is the excellent No 300 scenic service that crosses Exmoor from Barnstaple, through Lynton to Minehead and Bridgwater.

Mountain bikes are available from Tarka Trail (☎ 324202) at the train station from £6 per day.

Ilfracombe
• pop 10,471   ☎ 01271

Rising above its little harbour, Ilfracombe is North Devon's largest seaside resort, al-

though the best beaches are 5 miles west at Woolacombe, and at Croyde Bay, 2 miles beyond. Both are popular with surfers.

In 1998, the striking Ilfracombe Pavilion opened, comprising the 500-seat Landmark Theatre and a circular ballroom. They're housed in two white brick cones that look a bit like enormous lampshades.

The TIC (☎ 863001) is on the Promenade, and the town is packed with B&Bs. *Ilfracombe Youth Hostel (☎ 865337, 1 Hillsborough Terrace)* stands above the town, overlooking the harbour. The nightly charge is £8.80/5.95 for adults/juniors, and it's open from April to September, daily except Sunday (every day in July and August).

Red Bus operates frequent services between Ilfracombe and Barnstaple (35 minutes, £1.80).

Lundy Island

Ten miles out in the Bristol Channel, Lundy is a granite mass, 3 miles long, half a mile wide and up to 122m high. There's a resident population of just 19 people, one pub (the *Marisco Tavern*), one church and no roads.

People come to climb the cliffs, watch the birds, dive in the marine nature reserve or escape from the world in one of the 23 holiday homes.

Interesting properties that can be rented include the lighthouse and the castle but they need to be reserved months in advance. You can also camp from £3 per person. For information, phone ☎ 01237-431831.

Otherwise you can day trip from Ilfracombe or Bideford (two hours, £25/12.50 for adults/juniors). There are between two and five sailings a week from these ports, possibly more when the new deep water jetty is completed in 1999. For bookings, phone ☎ 01237-470422.

Bideford
• pop 14,000   ☎ 01237

Charles Kingsley based his epic novel *Westward Ho!* on the town of Bideford, not on the nearby seaside resort of the same name – that was actually named after the

SOUTH-WESTERN ENGLAND

Puffin Pence

Martin Harman, owner of Lundy Island from 1925 to 1954, was a typical English eccentric. Not satisfied with owning the remote island, he was determined to make it independent from the rest of the UK, closing the post office and issuing his own stamps. Given that Lundy took its name from the old Norse word for puffin, the stamps were denominated in 'puffinage' instead of sterling.

The stamps were ignored but in 1930 Harman carried things a step further and issued a Lundy coinage, with his own head in place of the king's and a puffin on the reverse. These, too, were denominated in 'puffins' instead of shillings and pence. Such defiance couldn't be overlooked and Harman was duly convicted of counterfeiting under the 1870 Coinage Act.

Sadly, Lundy's once-common puffins are now a thoroughly endangered species; you'll be lucky to see any at all.

book. Bideford's a pleasant enough place but there's no need to stay here. Several useful bus services pass through the town, though, and the boat to Lundy Island leaves from the quay.

The TIC (☎ 477676) is by Victoria Park. Bicycles can be hired from Bideford Bicycle Hire (☎ 424123), Torrington St, from £7.50 a day.

There are frequent buses to Barnstaple (30 minutes). Service No 2A runs to Appledore (15 minutes).

Appledore

This attractive little town with its narrow streets and olde-worlde charm is the complete antithesis of tacky Westward Ho! nearby. Appledore was long associated with boat-building, but the industry declined in the early part of this century. Revived in 1963, it has managed to continue through the recession. The North Devon Maritime

Museum (☎ 01237-422064) tells the story of local boat-building, shipwrecks and smuggling.

The *Seagate Hotel* (☎ *01237-472589*) is a friendly waterside pub that does B&B for £25 per person.

Foot passengers can cross to Instow on the ferry (£1.25) in summer; half a mile east is *Instow Youth Hostel* (☎ *01271-860394, Worlington House, New Rd*). Beds are £8.25/5.55 for adults/juniors; it's open daily from April through September; phone ahead for other opening days. It's close to the Tarka Trail and accessible by bus No 301 from Barnstaple followed by a three-quarters of a mile walk.

Clovelly
☎ 01237

Clinging to a steep slope above a picturesque harbour, Clovelly must be Devon's most photographed village. It's now so popular with visitors that it has built itself a visitors centre (☎ 431781) and you now have to pay £2 to get in from the car park above. From Easter to October, Land Rovers ferry visitors up the slope between 9.30 am and 5.30 pm.

The tiny village, with its one cobbled street (flat shoes advisable), is certainly attractive and the best way to appreciate it is to stay here. Several places do B&B. Try *Temple Bar* (☎ *431438*) which charges £17.50 per person, or *Mrs Golding's* (☎ *431565, 104 High St*) for £15 per person. Right by the harbour, the *Red Lion Hotel* (☎ *431237*) charges £83 for a double.

There are several departures a day on Red Bus (☎ 01271-345444) service No 319 to Bideford (40 minutes). There are three departures per day.

Dartmoor National Park

Although the park is only about 365 square miles in area, it encloses some of the wildest, bleakest country in England – suitable terrain for the Hound of the Baskervilles (one of Sherlock Holmes' more famous opponents). The landscape and weather (mist, rain and snow) can make this an eerie place to be.

Dartmoor lies within the county of Devon and is named after the River Dart, which has its source here; the West and East Dart rivers merge at Dartmeet. The park covers a granite plateau punctuated by distinctive tors (high rocks), which can look uncannily like ruined castles, and is cut by deep valleys, or combes, and fast-flowing

rivers and streams. Some tors, such as Vixen Tor, are almost 30m high. The moorland is covered by gorse and heather, and is grazed by sheep, cattle and semi-wild Dartmoor ponies. The countryside in the south-east is more conventionally beautiful, with wooded valleys and thatched villages.

There are plenty of prehistoric remains – Grimspound is possibly the most complete Bronze Age village site in England and the many cairns and tumuli mark the burial places of ancient chieftains.

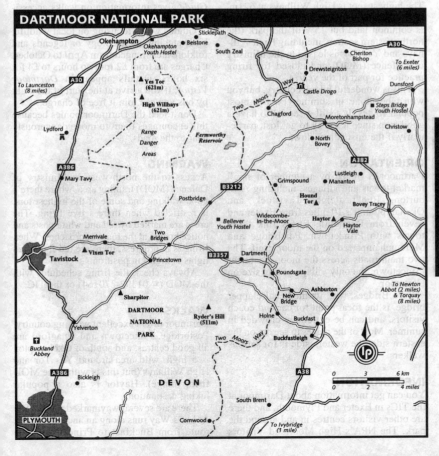

DARTMOOR NATIONAL PARK

The area was once rich in minerals such as tin, copper, silver, lead and china clay and the remains of old mines and quarries are scattered about. Most of Dartmoor's prehistoric monuments are built of rough grey local granite. The quarries at Haytor produced stone for Nelson's Column, London Bridge and many other monuments. The wealth generated by these enterprises has left the moor's small communities with attractive churches and buildings. Dartmoor's best known building, however, is the high-security prison at Princetown.

Most of the park is around 600m high. The highest spot is High Willhays at 621m, near Okehampton. About 40% of Dartmoor is common land but 15% of the park (the north-western section, including High Willhays and Yes Tor) is leased to the Ministry of Defence (MOD) and closed for firing practice for part of the year.

This is wonderful hiking country, but you won't be alone in summer on the most popular routes. It's still essential to have a good map since it's easy to get lost, particularly if the mist comes down.

ORIENTATION

Dartmoor is ringed by a number of small market towns and villages, including Ashburton, Buckfastleigh, Tavistock and Okehampton. It's 10 miles from Exeter and seven from Plymouth. Buses link these towns with Princetown, Postbridge and Moretonhampstead on the moor itself. The two main roads across the moor meet near Princetown, the only village of any size on Dartmoor.

Two Bridges, with its medieval clapper bridge, is the focal point for car and coach visitors, and can be extremely crowded in summer. Most of the places to see are on the eastern side; the western side is for serious walkers.

INFORMATION

You can get information about Dartmoor at the TICs in Exeter and Plymouth, and there are other visitors centres in and around the park. The NPA's High Moorland Visitors Centre (☎ 01822-890414), Old Duchy Hotel, Princetown, is open daily all year.

The other visitors centres are generally open from April to October, daily from 10 am to 5 pm, and are at Haytor (☎ 01364-661520); Postbridge (☎ 01822-880272); New Bridge (☎ 01364-631303); Okehampton (☎ 01837-53020); Ivybridge (☎ 01752-897035); and Tavistock (☎ 01822-612938).

These information centres have useful publications, including the *Dartmoor Visitor*, free and updated annually. They also stock walking guides and Ordnance Survey maps. The *Dartmoor Public Transport Guide* gives information on walks accessible by bus.

Guided walks focusing on local wildlife, birdwatching, archaeology or legends and folklore are arranged from April to October. Charges are from £2 for two hours to £4 for six hours. Details appear in *Dartmoor Visitor*. If you arrive at the start of the walk by bus you can join it free of charge.

Don't feed the Dartmoor ponies because this encourages them to move dangerously near to the roads.

WARNING

Access to the north-western Ministry of Defence (MOD) training area, where there's good walking and some of the highest tors, is restricted when there's live firing. The areas are marked by red and white posts and notice boards at the main approaches. When firing is in progress, there are red flags (red lights at night) in position.

Always check the firing schedules with the MOD (☎ 01392-270164) or the TIC.

WALKS

Dartmoor offers excellent walking country. Postbridge, Princetown and Chagford are all good centres, and south of Okehampton is a high, wild area around Yes Tor and High Willhays (but this is within the MOD firing range). Haytor is also a popular hiking destination.

There are several waymarked routes. The Abbot's Way runs along an ancient 14 mile route from Buckfast to Princetown. The

West Devon Way is a 14 mile walk between Tavistock and Okehampton along old tracks and through pretty villages on the western edge of Dartmoor. You can always take a bus for part of this route since the walk runs parallel to the No 187 bus route.

Youth hostels are conveniently placed a day's walk apart across the moor, so a five-day circuit from Exeter is possible.

The Templer Way is an 18 mile hike from Teignmouth (on the south coast) to Haytor, following the route originally designed to transport Dartmoor granite down to the docks.

The Two Moors Way runs from Ivybridge, on the southern edge of the moor, 103 miles north to Lynmouth in Exmoor. The *Two Moors Way* (£3 plus 70p UK p&p) is available from the Ramblers' Association (☎ 0171-339 8500), 1 Wandsworth Rd, London SW8 2XX.

The Tarka Trail (see Exmoor National Park earlier in this chapter) circles north Devon and links with Dartmoor, south of Okehampton.

It's always wise to carry a map, compass and rain gear since the weather can change very quickly and not all walks are waymarked. The Ordnance Survey's *Dartmoor Map* shows the park boundaries as well as the MOD firing range areas.

CYCLE ROUTES

Cycling is only allowed on public roads, byways open to all traffic, public bridlepaths and Forestry Commission roads.

Plym Valley Cycle Way follows the disused Great Western Railway between Plymouth and Yelverton, on the edge of the moor. Other cycle routes include a 3 mile stretch of forest tracks from Bellever; the 26 mile West Devon Tavistock Cycle Route, along country lanes; and the 30 mile Sticklepath Cycle Route, also on lanes.

Bikes can be hired in Exeter (see the Getting Around section in Exeter earlier in this chapter), and also from Tavistock Cycles (☎ 01822-617630), Paddons Row, Brook St, Tavistock and Mountain Bike Hire (☎ 01364-631505) beside the pub in Poundsgate.

OTHER ACTIVITIES
Pony Trekking & Horse Riding
There are riding stables all over the park. Lydford House Riding Stables (☎ 01822-820321), Lydford House Hotel, Lydford, charges from £9.50/17 for one/two hours.

Near Widecombe-in-the-Moor, Babery Farm Stables (☎ 01364-631296) offers half-day rides and pub rides (three hours riding, one hour in the pub) from £20.

Climbing
Rock climbing can only be done where there is a right of access – on private land you must ask the owner's permission first. Popular climbing areas are at Haytor, owned by the NPA, and Dewerstone, owned by the NT. Groups need to book in advance. Ask at a visitors centre or TIC for details.

Fishing
You can fish on certain stretches of the Rivers East and West Dart (with a Duchy of Cornwall permit), on the Rivers Tavy, Walkham, Plym, Meavy and Teign, as well as on seven reservoirs in the park. A permit is usually needed; phone the Environment Agency (☎ 01392-444000, ext 2052) for information.

PLACES TO STAY & EAT
If you're backpacking, the authorities and owners of unenclosed moorland don't usually object to campers who keep to a simple code: don't camp on moorland enclosed by walls or within sight of roads or houses; don't stay on one site for more than two nights; don't light fires; and leave the site as you found it. With large tents, however, you can only camp in designated camping grounds. There are several camping and caravan parks around the area, many on farms.

There are youth hostels at Postbridge, bang in the middle of the moor, and at Steps Bridge, near Dunsford (between Moretonhampstead and Exeter), as well as at Okehampton, Exeter, Plymouth and Dartington.

There are youth hostel camping barns at Manaton (Great Houndtor), Postbridge (Runnage), Sticklepath (Sticklepath Halt), Cornwood (Watercombe), Bridestowe (Fox & Hounds), and Lopwell (Lopwell Dam). These are 'stone tents' which sleep up to about 15 people. Cooking and shower facilities and a wood burner are provided. You sleep on the floor or on a bunk bed; bring your own bedding. Charges are £3.50 per person. For more information and central bookings, phone ☎ 01271-324420. There are also some independent barns and bunkhouses.

The larger towns on the edge of the park (like Okehampton and Tavistock) all have plentiful supplies of B&B and hotel accommodation. Within the park itself, accommodation is sometimes limited, so you need to book ahead in summer. There are also several comfortable country-house hotels in the park.

The Dartmoor Tourist Association (☎ 01822-890567) produces an accommodation guide; there's a service charge of £2.75 if you book rooms through any of the National Park Visitors Centres. TICs have details of farm B&Bs.

The old pubs and inns provide a focus for local communities and are sometimes the only places you can get anything to eat in small villages.

GETTING THERE & AWAY

Exeter or Plymouth are the best starting points for the park, but Exeter has the better transport connections to the rest of the country. Totnes, Exeter, Newton Abbot and Plymouth all have InterCity train services to London, Bristol and the Midlands. National Express has coach services between London and Exeter, Newton Abbot, Okehampton and Plymouth.

In 1997 Okehampton train station was reopened and there's now a Sunday service six times a day to Exeter (40 minutes). The only other train stations near the park are at Ivybridge and South Brent on the Exeter/

Plymouth line. Ivybridge is useful for people who want to walk the Two Moors Way. The return fare from Exeter is £9.20 (40 minutes).

The most useful bus that actually crosses Dartmoor is DevonBus No 82, the Transmoor Link, running between Exeter and Plymouth via Steps Bridge, Moretonhampstead, Warren House Inn, Postbridge, Princetown, Sharpitor and Yelverton. It runs daily in summer (late May to late September), but there are only three buses each way. For more information phone ☎ 01752-222666.

DevonBus No 359 follows a circular route from Exeter through Steps Bridge, Moretonhampstead and Chagford to Drewsteignton, and then back to Exeter (Monday to Saturday, three times a day each way). The No X39 (operated by Stagecoach Devon) goes along the A38 between Plymouth and Exeter, stopping at Buckfastleigh and Ashburton. First Western National Nos 83/84 operates from Plymouth via Yelverton to Tavistock every 20 minutes.

The summer-only Dartmoor Sunday Rover ticket (£5.50) entitles you to unlimited travel on most bus routes within the area and to rail travel on the Tamar Valley Line from Plymouth to Gunnislake.

On summer Sundays, DevonBus No 187 loops round from Plymouth, through Gunnislake, Tavistock, Mary Tavy, Lydford, Okehampton and Sticklepath, on its way to Exeter; you could do part of this journey on the Tamar Valley Line or even by boat (see Plymouth earlier in this chapter).

Since buses are infrequent and subject to change, it's best to work out what you want to do, then contact the Devon County Public Transport Help Line (☎ 01392-382800) weekdays from 8.30 am to 5 pm. They will send you the *Dartmoor Public Transport Guide* with suggestions for walks connected to bus routes.

PRINCETOWN
☎ 01822

At 420m, Princetown is England's highest settlement and Dartmoor's largest community. With the infamous prison located here, it's not Dartmoor's most beautiful town but is close to excellent walking country.

The town was created in the late 18th century by Thomas Tyrwhitt, who wanted to convert large areas of the moorland into arable farmland. When this failed, he came up with another plan to create employment for the people who had moved into the area, suggesting that a prison be built to house prisoners of war. In the first half of the 19th century, the prison housed both French and American POWs. When hostilities with those countries ceased, British prisoners were transferred here. There are now about 600 inmates in the maximum-security prison.

The High Moorland Visitors Centre (☎ 890414) was once the Duchy Hotel. It has displays on Dartmoor and an information centre which stocks maps.

Places to Stay & Eat

The *Plume of Feathers Inn* (☎ 890240), Princetown's oldest building, is a pub near the visitors centre, with all sorts of cheap accommodation. The camping ground (from £2.50 per person) is open year-round, the stone tent costs from £3.50 and there's bunkhouse accommodation from £5.50 (including rooms for two and four people). You need to book well in advance. There's also B&B from £15.50 per person.

The *Railway Inn* (☎ 890232, Two Bridges Rd), across from the visitors centre, is a pub offering B&B from £12.50 per person.

Getting There & Away

DevonBus No 82 (Transmoor Link) runs here from either Exeter or Plymouth (both 50 minutes). The service operates daily between July and late September, and on Saturday, Sunday and bank holidays between May and June. A £5.50 Sunday Rover ticket allows a day's travel on the system. The No 170 links Princetown with Tavistock and Newton Abbot.

POSTBRIDGE
☎ 01822

Right in the middle of the park, Postbridge makes a popular starting point for local walks. It's known for its granite clapper bridge which crosses the East Dart River. Clapper bridges date from the 13th century and are made of large slabs of granite supported at each end by short, stone pillars.

Local legend tells of the landlady of an 18th century temperance house who took to serving alcohol – much to the horror of her husband who poured it into the river. A dog which paused to quench its thirst was driven mad by the potent mixture and died. Its tormented spirit is still said to haunt Dartmoor, one version of the story that gave Conan Doyle the idea for *The Hound of the Baskervilles*.

From April to October, there's a NPA Visitors Centre in the car park. There's also a post office and shop in the village.

Places to Stay & Eat

Bellever Youth Hostel (☎ 880207) is a mile south-east of Postbridge on the western bank of the river. It's open daily in July and August, daily except Sunday from April to June, and also except Monday in September and October. A bed costs £8.80/5.95 for adults/juniors.

Runnage Farm (☎ 880222) has a camping barn – the nightly charge is £4 per person. To reach the farm, take the small road off the B3212 just before you reach Postbridge coming from the Moretonhampstead side.

East Dart Hotel (☎ 880213) is 100m from the clapper bridge and has rooms for £26/49. The *Lydgate House Hotel* (☎ 880209) is a quarter of a mile from the village centre in an attractive, sheltered valley. It's an excellent place to stay with beds from £28; a good three course dinner for £16 is also available.

Two miles north-east of Postbridge, along the B3212 towards Moretonhampstead, is the *Warren House Inn* (☎ 880208). It's a good place to come after a walk, and you can warm yourself by a fire they claim has been burning continuously since 1845. There's real ale, and pub food including home-made rabbit pie (£6).

Headland Warren Farm (☎ 880206) is a farm on the moor, 5 miles from Postbridge.

SOUTH-WESTERN ENGLAND

B&B is from £20 per person and it's convenient for walkers since it's by the Two Moors Way.

Getting There & Away

The Transmoor Link (DevonBus No 82) runs through Postbridge between Plymouth and Exeter.

BUCKFASTLEIGH
☎ 01364

On the park's south-eastern edge, Buckfastleigh is an old market town near the Upper Dart Valley. Nearby is Buckfast Abbey, Britain's last working monastery.

For centuries, Buckfastleigh was a centre for the manufacture of woollen cloth. Above the town is the parish church, and in the graveyard in a heavy tomb built by villagers to ensure he could not come back to life, lies Sir Richard Cabell, the most hated man in Dartmoor. When this evil landowner died in the 17th century, it's said that black phantom hounds were seen speeding across the moor to howl beside his grave.

Buckfast Abbey

Buckfast Abbey, 2 miles north of Buckfastleigh, was founded in 1016 and flourished in the Middle Ages through its involvement in the wool trade. With the Dissolution, it was abandoned in 1539. In 1806, the ruins were levelled and a mock-Gothic mansion erected; the house was purchased in 1882 by a group of exiled French Benedictine monks. The abbey church was built between 1906 and 1932 by the monks, and an impressive, modern stained-glass figure of Christ dominates the eastern end chapel.

The abbey (☎ 642519) is a popular tourist attraction. Entry is free. The monks augment their income by keeping bees and making tonic wine.

Places to Stay & Eat

About 3 miles north-west of Buckfastleigh, in Holne, there's budget accommodation in a stone barn at **Holne Court Farm** (☎ 631271) from £3.50 per person.

The **Furzeleigh Mill Hotel** (☎ 643476, *Old Ashburton Rd, Dartbridge*) has rooms for £32/58 singles/doubles. The **Dartbridge Inn** (☎ 642214, *Totnes Rd*) offers B&B from £63 for a double with a bath.

The restaurant and tearooms at **Buckfast Abbey** are good for lunch or tea.

Getting There & Away

First Western National No X88 runs between Plymouth and Buckfastleigh three times a day, Monday to Saturday (one hour). It continues to Newton Abbot (30 minutes). Bus No X39 runs from Buckfastleigh to Exeter (one hour).

The South Devon Railway (☎ 01364-642336) links Totnes and Buckfastleigh (25 minutes, every 1½ hours, £5.90/3.90 return) with a 7 mile journey beside the River Dart on a steam-operated country branch line. The service operates daily from mid-May to September. In April and October, trains run on Wednesday, Saturday and Sunday, and in May every day except Monday, Thursday and Friday.

WIDECOMBE-IN-THE-MOOR
☎ 01364

Uncle Tom Cobbleigh and all still flock to this popular little Dartmoor village, and not just on the second Tuesday of September when the fair, commemorated in the famous folk song, takes place. The fine 14th century granite church, known as the Cathedral in the Moor, was funded by prosperous tin miners and has a 37m-high tower.

There's a Visitor Information Point at Sexton's Cottage, adjacent to the Church House. Built in 1537 as a brewhouse, the Church House is now the village hall.

Five miles from Ashburton is **Cockingford Farm Campsite** (☎ 621258), 1½ miles south of Widecombe. It costs £2 per person to camp here. On the edge of Widecombe, there's B&B at **Sheena Tower** (☎ 621308) for £16 per person, £17 in a room with a bath.

MORETONHAMPSTEAD & STEPS BRIDGE

Moretonhampstead, a market town at the junction of the B3212 and the A382, is on the Transmoor Link bus route, 14 miles from Princetown.

Just inside the park's north-eastern border, 4½ miles east of Moretonhampstead, along the B3212, is *Steps Bridge Youth Hostel* (☎ *01647-252435*). Beds cost £7.20/4.95 for adults/juniors and it's open daily from April to September. It's a 10 mile walk from here to the hostel in Exeter.

You can camp at *Clifford Bridge Park* (☎ *01647-24226, Clifford*) from Easter to September, from £3.75 a person and tent. The site is by the River Teign, 3 miles west of Steps Bridge, and there's even a heated swimming pool.

CHAGFORD

- **pop 1500**   ☎ **01647**

This delightful country town by the River Teign makes a more attractive base for the park's north-eastern area than nearby Moretonhampstead. In the 14th century, it was a Stannary town where the tin mined on the moor was weighed and checked, and the taxes paid. It's an excellent walking and riding centre.

Places to Stay & Eat

Glendarah House (☎ *432404*) has rooms for £30/54 for singles/ doubles, with a bath. There are price reductions for stays of two nights or more. *Lawn House* (☎ *433329, Mill St*) offers B&B from £18 per person.

Opposite the church, the pretty *Three Crowns Hotel* (☎ *433444, High St*), dates from the 13th century. Beds here cost from £25.

Evelyn Waugh stayed at *Easton Court Hotel* (☎ *433469*) while writing *Brideshead Revisited*. It's a lovely thatched 15th century building, just off the A382 at Easton, on the opposite side from the turning to Chagford. B&B is from £45 per person.

Getting There & Away

From Exeter (one hour, £2.40), Red Bus No 359 goes via Moretonhampstead. From Okehampton, there are buses daily except Monday and Thursday.

CASTLE DROGO

Just over a mile from Chagford is **Castle Drogo** (☎ 01647-433306, NT), a medieval-looking granite fortification that was designed by Sir Edwin Lutyens, and constructed between 1910 and 1930 for a wealthy businessman, Julius Drewe, who died shortly after moving in. It overlooks the wooded gorge of the River Teign with fine views of Dartmoor.

Once you've been round what must be the most comfortable castle in the kingdom, you can rent croquet sets for a game on the lawn. It's open from April to October, daily except Friday, from 11 am to 5.30 pm; entry is £5.20/2.60.

OKEHAMPTON

- **pop 4200**   ☎ **01837**

The A30, the main route to Cornwall, divides bustling Okehampton from Dartmoor. Some of the wildest walking on the moor lies south of Okehampton, but since it's within the MOD's firing area, you should phone in advance to check that it's open. The part of the park that is south of Belstone is also good, and is outside the MOD zone.

Okehampton has several attractions to delay hikers. The ruined **castle** (☎ 52844, EH) above the town charges £2.30/1.20 for admission. The **Museum of Dartmoor Life** (☎ 52295), West St, has interactive exhibits, displays and photographs about the moor and its inhabitants. It's open daily from June to September, from 10 am to 5 pm; phone for other opening times; entry is £1.90/90p.

It's a pleasant three to four-hour walk along part of the Tarka Trail from Okehampton to Sticklepath, where the Finch Foundry (☎ 840046, NT) has three working water wheels. It's open April to October, daily except Tuesday, from 11 am to 5 pm;

SOUTH-WESTERN ENGLAND

entry is £2.50. The *Two Museums Walk* leaflet has information on this hike. Bus No 629 (daily) links Sticklepath with Oke-hampton.

The TIC (☎ 53020) is at 3 West St, by the museum.

Places to Stay & Eat

Okehampton Youth Hostel (☎ 53916) is in a newly-converted goods shed at the train station. It has 64 beds in small dormitories and the nightly charge is £9.75/6.55 for adults/ juniors. There's also a kitchen and laundry.

Yeritz Caravan & Camping Park (☎ 52281) is three-quarters of a mile east of Okehampton on the B3260. The charge is £4 for one person and a tent in summer.

Olditch Caravan & Camping Park (☎ 840734) is on the edge of Sticklepath, 4 miles east of Okehampton.

The *Fountain Hotel (☎ 53900, Fore St)* charges £16 per person for rooms with shared bathrooms. *Heathfield House (☎ 54211, Klondyke Rd)* does B&B with a bathroom from £20 per person.

The *Coffee Pot (14 St James St)* does teas and lunches. It's open daily from 7.30 am to 6 pm.

Getting There & Away

Okehampton is 23 miles west of Exeter, 29 miles north of Plymouth. There's a daily National Express bus from London via Heathrow.

First Western National Bus Nos X9 and X10 run hourly between Exeter and Oke-hampton (one hour). There are only four buses on Sunday. Bus No 86 runs every two hours between Plymouth and Okehampton (1½ hours).

In 1997, Okehampton train station was reopened and there's now a Sunday service six times a day to Exeter (40 minutes). The service may be extended to other days in 1999.

The Tarka Trail passes through Oke-hampton and Sticklepath on a 180 mile route through north Devon.

LYDFORD
* pop 1800   ☎ 01822

This picturesque village on the western edge of the moor is best known for the 1½ mile **Lydford Gorge**.

An attractive but strenuous riverside walk leads to the 28m-high White Lady waterfall and past a series of bubbling whirlpools, including the Devil's Cauldron. It's owned by the NT and is open daily from April through October, from 10 am to 5.30 pm; entry is £3.20.

There's evidence of both Celtic and Saxon settlements here, and the ruins of a Norman castle. Lydford was the adminis-trative centre for the Stannary towns (see Chagford). Courts trying recalcitrant tin workers were particularly harsh; it was said that perpetrators of offences punishable by death would be hanged in the morning and tried in the afternoon.

Places to Stay & Eat

The 16th century *Castle Inn (☎ 820242)* was featured in *The Hound of the Baskervilles* and is right beside the castle and 150m from Lydford Gorge.

It's a good place to stay, as well as an at-mospheric place for a pint and an excellent place to eat, offering interesting dishes such as venison and juniper berry pie (£6.50) and wild boar. The B&B charge is £34.50/62 with a bathroom.

By the main entrance to the White Lady waterfall, *Manor Farm Tea Rooms* serves cream teas and light lunches.

Lydford House Hotel (☎ 820347), on the edge of the village, offers B&B from £36 per person. There's a riding stable in the grounds (£9.50 per hour, or two hours from £17).

Getting There & Away

First Western National DevonBus No 86 crosses Devon from Barnstaple to Plymouth via Lydford, every two hours, Monday to Saturday. Service No 187 operates between Exeter and Tavistock via Lydford six times a day on Sunday in the summer.

Letterboxing

If you see a walker acting furtively and slipping an old Tupperware box into a tree stump or under a rock, you may be witnessing someone in the act of letterboxing. This wacky pastime has more than 10,000 addicts and involves a never-ending treasure hunt for several thousand 'letterboxes' hidden all over Dartmoor.

In 1844 the railway line reached Exeter, and Dartmoor started to receive visitors, for whom this was a chance to imagine themselves as great explorers. One guide for these intrepid Victorian gentlefolk was James Perrott of Chagford. In 1854, he had the idea of getting them to leave their calling cards in a glass jar at Cranmere Pool – the most remote part of the moor accessible at that time. It was not until 1938 that the second 'box' was established, and the idea really took off after WWII. Originally, people left their card with a stamped addressed envelope in a box and if someone else found it they would send it back.

There are now about 4000 boxes, each with a visitors' book for you to sign and a stamp and ink pad (if they haven't been stolen) to stamp your record book. Although it's technically illegal to leave a 'letterbox' because in effect you're leaving rubbish on the moor without the landowner's permission, as long as the boxes are unobtrusive, most landowners tolerate them. Now there are even German, French, Belgian and American boxes, not to mention 'mobile boxes', odd characters who wander the moors waiting for a fellow letterboxer to approach them with the words 'Are you a travelling stamp?'!

Once you've collected 100 stamps, you can apply to join the '100 Club' whereupon you'll be sent a clue book with map references for other boxes. Contact Godfrey Swinscow (☎ 015488-21325), Cross Farm, Diptford, Totnes, Devon TQ9 7NU, for more information.

Inevitably, as more people go letterboxing, a downside (other than general nerdiness) has been identified. A code of conduct now prohibits letterboxers from disturbing rocks, vegetation or archaeological sites in their zeal. Even so there have been mutterings about the disturbance caused to nesting golden plovers and ring ouzels ...

TAVISTOCK

• **pop 8700**   ☎ **01822**

Tavistock's glory days were in the late 19th century, when it was one of the world's largest copper producers. Until the Dissolution, Tavistock Abbey controlled huge areas of Devon and Cornwall; only slight ruins remain.

On the outskirts of town is a statue of **Sir Francis Drake**, who was born in Crowndale, just over a mile from Tavistock. **Buckland Abbey**, the mansion he bought after circumnavigating the globe, can be visited (see Around Plymouth earlier in this chapter).

There's a TIC (☎ 612938) underneath the town hall. Bikes can be rented from Tavistock Cycles (☎ 617630), Paddons Row,

opposite Goodes Café, Brook St, for £12 for the first day, £8 for further days.

First Western National Nos 83, 84 and 86 run up to three times an hour, between Tavistock and Plymouth (50 minutes). The Sunday No 187/8 service links Exeter and Tavistock with Gunnislake train station for Plymouth.

Cornwall

At the country's extreme south-western tip, Cornwall has been described as a beautiful frame around a plain picture. The metaphor is a good one, for the coastline is wonderful – a mix of high, jagged cliffs and pretty inlets sheltering little fishing villages. The interior, however, is much less attractive, even desolate in places.

Cornwall likes to emphasise its separateness from the rest of the country and the county's cultural roots are indeed different, for this was the Celts' last bastion in England after they were driven back by the Saxons. The Cornish language survived until the late 19th century. Efforts are being made to revive it, but Cornish mainly lives on in place names – every other village name seems to be prefixed with *tre-* (meaning settlement).

In the 18th and 19th centuries Cornwall dominated the world's tin and copper markets. Most of the mines have now closed but the industrial past has left scars on the landscape. China clay is still mined around St Austell but tourism has largely replaced the mining industry. Unfortunately though, it offers mainly low-paid, seasonal work and Cornwall is now one of the poorest parts of Britain.

In summer, Cornwall's seaside resorts are packed but don't let this put you off, since the holiday-makers tend to congregate around the larger resorts of Bude, Newquay, Falmouth, Penzance and St Ives, and even at the height of the season some of these towns are still worth a visit. Newquay is Britain's surfing capital, and you can't fail to be impressed by beautiful St Ives.

Cornish churches lack the splendour of those in Devon and Somerset and even Truro cathedral is a relative newcomer. However, the names of the churches speak loudly of Cornwall's separateness. Where else would you cross paths with St Non, St Cleer, St Keyne and the many others whose lives are detailed in *The Cornish Saints* by Peter Berresford Ellis?

If you're planning to visit around 11 August 1999 you'll need to book months in advance. The total eclipse of the sun visible from Cornwall on that day means that the county will be packed around this time. The central line of the eclipse crosses Cornwall just north of Land's End and leaves over Falmouth Bay.

WALKS & CYCLE ROUTES

The Cornwall Coast Path is the most scenic section of the long-distance South West Coast Path. The Saints' Way is a 26 mile waymarked trail that runs from Fowey across the centre of the county to Padstow on the northern coast. It was used in the 6th century as a route for Celtic missionaries between Brittany (France) and Wales or Ireland, saving a long sea trip around Land's End.

Youth hostels are well placed along the coast for stops on a walk or cycle route around Cornwall. In the north, the 17 mile Camel Trail follows an old railway line from just outside Padstow through Bodmin and along the River Camel. You can rent bikes from Bridge Bike Hire (☎ 01208-813050) in Wadebridge.

GETTING AROUND

For information about buses, there's an efficient helpline (☎ 01872-322142). The main bus operator is First Western National (☎ 01209-719988); an Explorer ticket gives a day's travel on its system for £5.50/2.75 and there are several other passes.

For rail information, phone ☎ 0345-484950. The main rail route from London terminates in Penzance, but there are branch lines to St Ives, Falmouth, Newquay and Looe. A Cornish Regional Rover ticket costs £39 for eight days travel in a 15-day period, or £24.50 for three days in seven. Plymouth is included in this ticket.

The TICs stock the county council's annual *Public Transport Timetable* (with a map), listing all the air, bus, rail and ferry options in Cornwall.

SOUTH-EAST CORNWALL

Southern Cornwall is very different in character to the wild north and central parts of the county. This is a more gentle area of farms, wooded inlets and pretty fishing villages – some overrun by tourists in the summer but worth visiting at quieter times.

The mild climate favours many plants that thrive nowhere else in Britain and there are several gardens worth visiting, with rhododendron trees growing almost as tall as in their natural Himalayan habitat. TICs stock the free *Gardens of Cornwall* map and guide with full details.

The best gardens in the area are **Heligan** (☎ 01726-845100), 4 miles south of St Austell, and **Trelissick Garden** (☎ 01872-862090, NT), 4 miles south of Truro, beside King Harry's Ferry. Entry is £4/2. The **Eden Project** (see the boxed text 'The Garden of Eden' in this chapter) is a new garden opening in 2000.

Cotehele

Seven miles south-west of Tavistock, on the west bank of the Tamar, the river that forms the boundary between Devon and Cornwall, the Cotehele estate comprises a small stately home with splendid garden, a quay with a museum, and a working water mill.

One of Britain's finest Tudor manor houses, Cotehele has been the Edgcumbe family home for centuries. The hall is particularly impressive, and many rooms are hung with great tapestries; because of their fragility, there's no electric lighting. Visitor numbers are limited, so you may have to wait. Pick up a timed ticket when you arrive.

Cotehele Quay is part of the National Maritime Museum and has a small museum with displays on local boat-building and river trade. The *Shamrock*, the last surviving River Tamar barge, is moored nearby.

Cotehele Mill is a 15 minute walk away and can be seen in operation; there's also an adjoining cider press.

The estate (☎ 01579-351346, NT) is open April to October, daily except Friday from 11 am to 5.30 pm; entry is £5.60/2.80; £2.80/1.40 for the garden and mill only. You can get here by bus from Tavistock to Calstock, a mile from Cotehele, on Western National bus No 99.

East & West Looe
☎ 01503

A bridge connects these twin towns, on either side of the river. They make up the county's second largest fishing port, the place to come if you're into shark fishing. Contact the Tackle Shop (☎ 262189) for day trips (£25).

East Looe is the main part of the town, with narrow streets and little cottages; the wide, sandy beach is to the east. There are boat trips from the quay to tiny Looe Island, a nature reserve, and to Fowey and Polperro. The TIC (☎ 262072) is in the Guildhall on Fore St.

Trains travel the scenic Looe Valley Line from Liskeard (30 minutes, £2.20), on the main London-Penzance line, at least six times a day.

Walk An excellent 5 mile walk links Looe to the nearby village of Polperro via beaches, cliffs and the old smuggling village of Talland. You should allow around two hours; buses connect the villages every day in summer.

Polperro

Much prettier than Looe, Polperro is an ancient fishing village around a tiny harbour, best approached along the coastal path from Looe or Talland. Unfortunately, it's very popular with day-trippers so you should try to visit in the evening or during low season.

The village is a picturesque jumble of narrow lanes and fishing cottages, and was once heavily involved in pilchard fishing by day and smuggling by night – there's a small smugglers' museum in the centre. There's no TIC.

Fowey
• pop 2600   ☎ 01726

Pronounced foy, unspoilt Fowey lies on the estuary of the same name. The town has a long maritime history and in the 14th century conducted its own raids on coastal towns in France and Spain. This led to the Spanish launching an attack on Fowey in 1380. The town later prospered by shipping Cornish china clay, which it still does, although yachts mainly fill its harbour today. Although there are no specific sights (apart

When did Cornish Die?

A Celtic language akin to Welsh, Cornish was spoken west of the Tamar until the 19th century. Written evidence indicates that it was still widely spoken at the time of the Reformation, but after a Cornish rising against the English in 1548, the language was suppressed. By the 17th century only a few people living in the peninsula's remote western reaches still spoke nothing but Cornish.

Towards the end of the 18th century linguistic scholars foresaw the death of Cornish and fanned out round the peninsula in search of people who still spoke it. One such scholar, Daines Barrington, visited Mousehole in 1768 and recorded an elderly woman called Dolly Pentreath abusing him in Cornish for presuming she couldn't speak her own language.

Dolly died in 1769 and has gone down in history as the last native speaker of Cornish. However, Barrington knew of other people who continued to speak it into the 1790s, and an 1891 tombstone in Zennor commemorates one John Davey as 'the last to possess any traditional considerable knowledge of the Cornish language'.

Recently efforts have been made to revive the language. Unfortunately there are now three conflicting varieties of 'Cornish' – Unified, Phonemic and Traditional – and no sign that it can regain its former importance.

SOUTH-WESTERN ENGLAND

from a small museum and aquarium), Fowey is a good base for walks around the estuary. The TIC (☎ 833616) is in the post office, 4 Custom House Hill.

Walk Fowey is at the southern end of the Saints' Way (see Walks & Cycle Routes under Cornwall earlier in this chapter). Ferries operate across the river to Bodinnick (50p a foot passenger, £1.40 for a car)

to access the 4 mile Hall Walk to Polruan. You can catch a ferry from Polruan back to Fowey.

Places to Stay & Eat *Golant Youth Hostel* (☎ 833507, Penquite House) is 4 miles north of Fowey in Golant. It's open daily from February through September and daily except Friday from October to early November. The nightly charge is £9.75/6.55 for adults/juniors. Western National's bus No 24 from St Austell to Fowey stops in Castle Dore, 1½ miles from the hostel.

The delightful *Marina Hotel* (☎ 833315) is right on the waterfront on the Esplanade. Rooms with sea view and a bath are £66. It also has an excellent restaurant.

The Old Ferry Inn is near the slipway at Bodinnick. There are rooms with river views and bathrooms; charges range from £20 to £35 per person for B&B. Other recommended pubs in Fowey include the big *King of Prussia*, on the quay, and the *Ship* and the *Lugger*, back from the water on Lostwithiel St.

Getting There & Away There are frequent departures from St Austell (50 minutes) on First Western National's service No 24, which also passes Par, the closest train station to Fowey.

Lanhydrock House

Amid parkland above the Fowey River, 2½ miles south-east of Bodmin, this grand country house (☎ 01208-73320, NT) was rebuilt after a fire in 1881. The impressive gallery, with its fine plaster ceiling, survived the fire, but the house is mainly of interest for its portrayal of the 'Upstairs Downstairs' divisions of life in Victorian England. The kitchens are particularly interesting, complete with all the gadgets that were mod cons 100 years ago.

The house is open April to October, daily except Monday from 11 am to 5.30 pm. Entry is £6.20; £3.10 for the gardens only. The garden is open year-round and entry is free in winter. Bodmin Parkway train station is 1¾ miles from the house.

Charlestown

Despite its size, St Austell is not particularly exciting and most people will pass straight through. However, it's worth making a detour south to visit the port of Charlestown, a marvellously picturesque village and harbour built by Charles Rashleigh between 1790 and 1815. On the best days the harbour will be filled with magnificent square-rig ships. However, these are sometimes away taking part in worldwide film assignments. The film of Daphne du Maurier's *Frenchman's Creek* was partly shot here in 1998.

The **Shipwreck and Heritage Centre** (☎ 01726-69897) has exhibits on many aspects of Cornish sea life, with animated models illustrating 19th century village life. It's open March to October from 10 am to 5 pm (6 pm in high summer) and costs £3.95. The attached *Bosun's Bistro* does teas, coffees and lunches.

If you'd like to stay, *T'Gallants* (☎ 01726-70203) is a fine Georgian house doing B&B for £25/38. Alternatively, the *Pier House Hotel* (☎ 01726-67955) right on the quayside charges £35/57.

TRURO

• pop 18,000   ☎ 01872

Truro was once the distribution centre for Cornwall's tin mines and its prosperity dates from this time. Lemon St has some fine Georgian architecture, and the cathedral is worth a visit if you're passing through, even though it only dates back to the late 19th century. Built in neo-Gothic style, it was the first new cathedral to be built in Britain since St Paul's in London.

The TIC (☎ 274555) is in the municipal buildings on Boscawen St, near the covered market. The **Royal Cornwall Museum** (☎ 272205) in River St has exhibits on Cornish history, archaeology and mineralogy. It's open every day except Sunday from 10 am to 5 pm.

Places to Stay & Eat

There's no hostel but cheap B&Bs near the train station can be found on Treyew Rd.

The Fieldings (☎ 262783) at No 35, charges £20/32 for singles/doubles. There are more B&Bs on Tregolls Rd, including *Karenza* (☎ 274497) at No 72, which charges £17 per person.

The *Royal Hotel* (☎ 270345, Lemon St) is a fine Georgian building convenient for the cathedral. Beds cost from £52/70.

The *Old Ale House* is a recommended pub on Quay St. In this age of themed chain pubs it's a relief to find a traditional place like this. Pub grub includes generous sized sandwiches and main dishes served in small/large helpings from £3.50/3.95.

Getting There & Away

Truro is 246 miles from London, 26 from St Ives and 18 from Newquay.

National Express (☎ 0990-808080) has buses to numerous destinations, sometimes

SOUTH-WESTERN ENGLAND

The Garden of Eden

Construction is under way in a disused china clay pit near St Austell to create the most spectacular botanical gardens of the next millennium. The Eden Project is a scientific foundation which aims to educate visitors about the human race's dependency on plant life.

Masterminded by Tim Smit, the man responsible for the gardens at Heligan, the project will comprise a vast geodesic dome structure 1km long and 60m high. This will be heated to 35°C and filled with 10,000 species of plants from around the world. The structure is designed by Nicholas Grimshaw, architect of the Eurostar terminal at Waterloo. Trees such as teak and mahogany will have enough space to grow to their full size, although this will take up to 50 years.

Project Eden should be open to the public in April 2000, and although the plants may not have had time to grow much by then, the structure is sure to impress.

requiring a change at Plymouth. There are four direct daily services to London (6½ hours, £28.75), St Ives (one hour, £2.85) and Penzance (1½ hours, £3.15). First Western National (☎ 01209-719988) covers many local bus routes.

Truro is on the main rail line between London Paddington (4¾ hours, £50) and Penzance (45 minutes, £6.10). There's a branch line from here to Falmouth (20 minutes, £2.20) and to St Ives (£5.80, change trains at St Erth).

ROSELAND PENINSULA

South-west of Truro, the Roseland peninsula gets its intriguing name not from flowers (although there are plenty of them) but from the Cornish word *ros*, meaning promontory. Villages worth visiting include **Portloe**, a wreckers' hang-out on the Coastal Path, **Veryan** which is awash with daffodils in spring, **St Mawes** with a castle (☎ 01326-270526, EH) built by Henry VIII to guard the Fal estuary, and **St Just-in-Roseland** that boasts what must be one of the most beautiful churchyards in the country, full of flowers and tumbling down to a creek with boats and wading birds.

SOUTH-WEST CORNWALL
Falmouth
• pop 18,000   ☎ 01326

Falmouth is not Cornwall's most exciting town, but has an interesting castle with a youth hostel in its grounds. There are also several worthwhile boat trips from the pier.

The port came to prominence in the 17th century as the terminal for the Post Office Packet boats which took mail to America. The dockyard is still important for ship repairs and building.

Pendennis Castle (☎ 316594, EH), on the end of the promontory, is Cornwall's largest fort, worth visiting for the displays inside and the superb views from the ramparts. It was an operations centre in WWII. Entry costs £3/1.50.

The TIC (☎ 312300) is at 28 Killigrew St, by the bus station in the town centre. From the Prince of Wales pier, there are ferries to St Mawes. In summer, boat trips travel to Truro (£5 return) and there are excursions to a 500-year-old Smuggler's Cottage upriver. For information, contact Enterprise Boats (☎ 374241) or St Mawes Ferries (☎ 313201).

Places to Stay & Eat *Pendennis Castle Youth Hostel* (☎ 311435) is at the castle, three-quarters of a mile from Falmouth train station. It's open daily from mid-February through September, and daily except Sunday and Monday in October and November; a bed costs £8.80/5.95 for adults/juniors.

There are B&Bs and small hotels lining Melvill Rd, convenient for the train station. Try *Ivanhoe* (☎ 319083) at No 7, or *Tudor Court Hotel* (☎ 312807) at No 55, both offering beds from around £19 per person.

Bon Ton Roulet (☎ 319290), in pretty cobbled Church St is a good place for a meal, with pasta from £6.95 and more exotic dishes such as king prawns for £9.60. There's pub food in the *Kings Head*, also on Church St.

Getting There & Away National Express has buses from Falmouth to numerous destinations, including London (6¼ hours, £31.50). There are two-hourly buses to Penzance (one hour, £2.20). For St Ives, you must change at Penzance or Truro; this also applies to Newquay (except on Sunday).

Falmouth is at the end of the branch line from Truro (20 minutes, £2.20). In summer, you can also travel by boat to Truro (one hour, £2.50); at low tide, when boats can only get as far as Malpas, there's a bus service to Truro.

The Lizard

The Lizard peninsula is Britain's most southerly point and good walking country since much of the coastline is owned by the National Trust. The mild climate guarantees that several rare plant species flourish, and there are stretches of unusual red-green serpentine rock.

In 1901 Marconi transmitted the first transatlantic radio signals from Poldhu. The

Lizard is still associated with telecommunications and the centre is dominated by the white satellite dishes of the Goonhilly Earth Station.

Across the north of the Lizard is the beautiful **Helford River**, lined with ancient oak trees and hidden inlets – the perfect smugglers' hideaway. Daphne du Maurier's Frenchman's Cove can be reached on foot from the car park in **Helford** village.

On the northern bank of the river is **Trebah Garden** (☎ 01326-250448), dramatically situated in a steep ravine filled with giant rhododendrons, huge Brazilian rhubarb plants and Monterey pines. It's open daily from 10.30 am to 5 pm; entry is £3.20/1. Near Gweek, at the western end of the river, is the **Cornish Seal Sanctuary** (☎ 01326-221361), which treats injured marine animals and is open to visitors every day from 9 am to 5.30 pm; entry is £5.95/3.75.

Cadgwith is the quintessential Cornish fishing village, with thatched, whitewashed cottages and a small harbour. *Cadgwith Cove Inn* usually serves delicious crab sandwiches. Lizard Point is a 3½ mile walk along the coast path from here. It's about 8 miles in the opposite direction to *Coverack Youth Hostel* (☎ 01326-280687) which is open from April through October.

The Lizard's transportation hub is Helston which is served by Truronian buses (☎ 01872-273453). Bus No T1 runs from Truro via Helston to the village of Lizard (1¾ hours); there are four buses daily, Monday to Saturday. It's just under a mile from the village to Lizard Point.

St Michael's Mount

In 1070 St Michael's Mount was granted to the same monks who built Mont St Michel off Normandy. Though not in such a dramatic location as the French model, St Michael's Mount is still impressive. High tide cuts the island off from the mainland, and the priory buildings (☎ 01736-710507, NT) rise loftily above the crags.

St Michael's Mount was an important place of medieval pilgrimage. Since 1659

the St Aubyn family has lived in the ex-priory buildings.

At low tide, you can walk across from Marazion, but at high tide in summer a ferry (☎ 01736-710265; 40p one way) lets you save your legs for the stiff climb up to the house. The best way to appreciate the house is to use the Walkman tour (£1.50). The house is open from April to October, Monday to Friday from 10.30 am to 5.30 pm; entry is £3.90. Phone for other opening times.

First Western National's bus Nos 2 and 2A pass Marazion from Penzance and continue to Falmouth.

PENZANCE
- **pop 19,000 ☎ 01736**

At the end of the line from London, Penzance is a very pleasant small town in which to linger (and shop) with a curious mix of seaside holiday-makers, locals, artists and New Age hippies. Newlyn, on the western edge of Penzance, was the centre of a community of artists in the late 19th century; some of their handiwork can be inspected in **Newlyn Museum and Art Gallery**, New Rd.

Orientation & Information

The harbour spreads along Mount's Bay, with the ferry terminal to the east, the train and bus stations just to the north and the main beach to the south. The town itself spreads uphill towards the domed Lloyds Bank building with a statue of local man, Humphrey Davy, inventor of the miner's lamp, in front. Part of the bank now houses craft shops.

The TIC (☎ 362207) is in the car park by the train and bus stations. There's a laundrette opposite the train station.

Things to See

Penzance has some attractive Georgian and Regency houses in the older part of town around Chapel St, where you'll also find the exuberant early 19th century **Egyptian House**. Farther down towards the harbour is the **Maritime Museum** by the Georgian House Hotel.

National Lighthouse Centre (☎ 360077), Wharf Rd, relates the history of the lighthouses that have helped keep ships off this dangerous coast. It's open daily from March to October, from 10.30 am to 4.30 pm; entry is £2.50/1. Some examples of the Newlyn school of painting are exhibited in the **Penzance Museum & Art Gallery** (☎ 363625), on Morrab Rd. It's open daily except Sunday. Entry is £2 (free on Saturday).

Walks

The 25 mile section of the Coast Path around Land's End to/from St Ives is one of the most scenic parts of the whole route. It can be broken at the youth hostel at St Just (near Land's End), and there are plenty of other cheap farm B&Bs along the way. See Lonely Planet's *Walking in Britain* for more information.

Places to Stay

Penzance Youth Hostel (☎ 362666, *Castle Horneck, Alverton*) is an 18th century mansion on the outskirts of town. Bus Nos 5B, 6B or 10B run from the train station to the Pirate Inn, from where it's a 500m walk. The nightly charge is £9.75/6.55 for adults /juniors.

Friendly *Blue Dolphin Penzance Backpackers* (☎ 363836, *Alexander Rd*) has 30 bunk beds for £8 each, and there are two doubles at £18. You can use the kitchen and washing machine (£3). It's all spotlessly clean – 'the bed sheets smell great', wrote one reader!

Penzance has lots of B&Bs and hotels, especially along the Promenade, Alexandra Rd and Morrab Rd. *Pendennis Hotel* (☎ 363823, *Alexandra Rd*) and *Kimberley House* (☎ 362727, *10 Morrab Rd*) both charge around £15 per person. Friendly

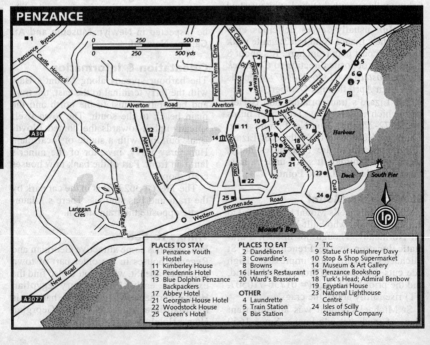

PENZANCE

PLACES TO STAY	PLACES TO EAT	7 TIC
1 Penzance Youth Hostel	2 Dandelions	9 Statue of Humphrey Davy
11 Kimberley House	3 Cowardine's	10 Stop & Shop Supermarket
12 Pendennis Hotel	8 Browns	14 Museum & Art Gallery
13 Blue Dolphin Penzance Backpackers	16 Harris's Restaurant	15 Penzance Bookshop
	20 Ward's Brasserie	18 Turk's Head; Admiral Benbow
17 Abbey Hotel	**OTHER**	19 Egyptian House
21 Georgian House Hotel	4 Laundrette	23 National Lighthouse Centre
22 Woodstock House	5 Train Station	24 Isles of Scilly
25 Queen's Hotel	6 Bus Station	Steamship Company

SOUTH-WESTERN ENGLAND

Woodstock House (☎ *369049, 29 Morrab Rd*) charges from £20 to £25 a head for rooms with a shower or bath.

In the older part of Penzance, the *Georgian House Hotel* (☎ *365664, 20 Chapel St*) has beds from £21 with a bathroom, from £18 without. The *Queen's Hotel* (☎ *362371*) on the Promenade charges £47 per person.

The *Abbey Hotel* (☎ *366906, Abbey St*) is owned by 60s supermodel Jean Shrimpton, and is the top place to stay. Singles/doubles cost £70/90-135. Alternatively you could rent a floor of the *Egyptian House* (see Things to See) from the Landmark Trust (☎ *01628-825925*). Costs range from around £152 for a four-day winter break to £449 for a week in summer.

There's excellent farmhouse accommodation at *Ennys* (☎ *740262, St Hilary*) about 5 miles east of Penzance, near Marazion. Rooms have a bath or shower and B&B costs from £30 to £40 per person. There's a heated swimming-pool.

Places to Eat

Cowardine's, 10 Causeway Head, has a range of speciality teas and coffees, and does good value meals. A crispy bacon and melted cheese baguette is £3.15; cod and chips costs £3.95. Full breakfasts are served until noon and it's open daily from 9 am to 11 pm (from 10 am to 4 pm on Sunday).

Dandelions, nearby at 39A Causeway Head, is a small vegetarian café and takeaway. *Browns* in Bread St is similar, and also has a gallery attached.

Chapel St has several cheap places to eat as well as two well known pubs: the kitschy *Admiral Benbow* (☎ *363448*), and the *Turk's Head* (☎ *363093*) with a good reputation for its food. Across the road is *Wards Brasserie* (☎ *363540*), open daily except Sunday, from 10 am to 3 pm and from 7 pm for dinner. Main dishes are well priced – £5.75 to 7.25 for lunch, £7.95 to £11.50 for dinner.

For a splurge, head for *Harris's Restaurant* (☎ *364408*) at 46 New St, a narrow, cobbled street opposite Lloyds Bank.

Smoked salmon cornets with fresh crab are £7.50, venison costs £14.95.

For self-caterers, Stop and Shop in Queen St is a small supermarket that's open late.

Getting There & Away

See the fares tables in the Getting Around chapter. Penzance is 281 miles from London, nine from Land's End and eight from St Ives.

There are five buses a day from Penzance to London (five hours, £29.50 if you book a week ahead) and Heathrow airport, one direct bus a day to Exeter (five hours, £15) and three buses a day to Bristol via Truro and Plymouth. To St Ives (20 minutes, £2.25) there are at least two services an hour. There are daily First Western National services to Land's End (one hour), hourly during the week, less frequent at weekends.

The train offers an enjoyable if pricey way to get to Penzance from London. There are five trains a day from London Paddington (five hours, £30 if you buy your ticket a week in advance and travel via Slough). There are frequent trains from Penzance to St Ives between 7 am and 8 pm (20 minutes, £2.80).

For ferries to the Scilly Isles, see the Isles of Scilly later in this chapter.

WEST CORNWALL
Mousehole

Mousehole (pronounced mowsel) is another idyllic fishing village that's well worth seeing outside the height of the season. It was once a pilchard fishing port, and tiny cottages cluster round the edge of the harbour. Like St Ives, the village attracts artists and there are several interesting craft shops.

The excellent *Ship* (☎ *01736-731234*) does good seafood and fresh fish; beds cost £25 per person. The *Lobster Pot* (☎ *01736-731251*) is more upmarket and charges £39.95 for lobster for two people; rooms overlooking the harbour cost £54 per person, but there are cheaper rooms from £24 per person. *Annie's Eating House* serves cream tea for £2.95.

Infrequent buses run the 20 minute journey to Penzance.

Minack Theatre

Probably the world's most spectacularly located open-air theatre, Minack perches on the edge of the cliffs overlooking the bay. It was built by Rowena Cade, an indomitable local woman who did much of the construction herself, until her death in 1983. The idea came to her when her family provided the local theatre group with an open-air venue for a production of *The Tempest*. The place was so well suited that annual performances were instituted.

There are performances at the theatre (☎ 01736-810181) from late May to late September; tickets cost £6/3. Seats are hard, so bring a cushion or hire one here. There's also an exhibition centre open daily from Easter to September, from 9.30 am to 5.30 pm (sometimes closed when there's a performance taking place); tickets are £2/free.

The theatre is below the village of Porthcurno, 3 miles from Land's End and 9 miles from Penzance. First Western National's bus No 1 from Penzance to Land's End stops at Porthcurno, Monday to Saturday.

Land's End
☎ 01736

The coast on either side of Land's End is some of the most spectacular in Britain, but the theme park development (☎ 01736-871501) is a Thatcherite monument to the elevation of commerce over all else. Peter de Savary was the man who outbid the National Trust to inflict this monstrosity on Britain's most westerly point. He's long since cashed in and moved on but the damage is done.

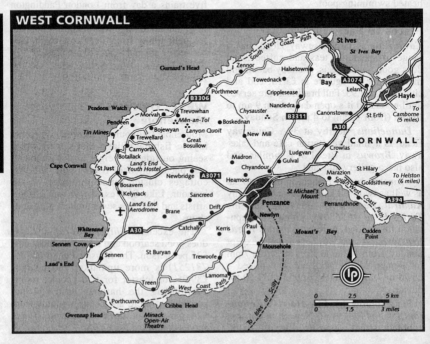

WEST CORNWALL

That said, the Spirit of Cornwall exhibit (£7.95/4.95) is quite interesting, and the complex does provide 250 jobs in an unemployment black spot. If you walk from Sennen Cove, less than half an hour away, you escape the car-parking charge (£3).

In summer, the place is extremely crowded, with stands selling everything from burgers to strawberry and clotted cream crêpes. To have your picture taken by the signboard listing your home town and its distance from this famous spot costs £5.

Places to Stay & Eat *Land's End Youth Hostel* is at St Just, 5 miles from Land's End.

The comfortable *Land's End Hotel* (☎ 871844), the 'first and last hotel in England', is part of the complex and is the only place to stay right at Land's End. Staying the night gives you the chance to stroll around the headland in the evening after the crowds have gone. B&B costs from £39.50 per person. You can eat here too, in the *Atlantic Restaurant* or in the bar.

Just over a mile north of Land's End, Sennen Cove boasts a beautiful, sandy beach. There are good pub lunches at the *Old Success Inn* (☎ 871232), where you can also stay from £22 per person (£36 in rooms with a bath). *Myrtle Cottage* (☎ 871698) serves cream teas and light lunches. You can stay for £15 per person, and there's also a fish and chip shop.

Getting There & Away Land's End is 3147 miles from New York, 886 miles from John o'Groats and 9 miles from Penzance. There are buses along the coast to St Ives from Sunday to Friday; and daily buses to Penzance.

Westward Airways (☎ 788771) offers flights over Land's End in Cessnas; a seven minute hop costs £17/15.

St Just-in-Penwith

Although there are no specific sights in remote St Just, it makes a good base for walks west to Cape Cornwall or south along the Coast Path to Land's End.

In Victorian times St Just was a centre for local tin and copper mining. **Geevor Tin Mine** (☎ 01736-788662), at Pendeen, north of St Just, finally closed in 1990 and is now open to visitors daily from 10.30 am to 5.30 pm. Entry is £5/2.50.

Alongside the abandoned engine houses from old tin and copper mines, the area between St Just and St Ives is littered with standing stones and other mysterious ancient remains. If prehistory's your thing, it's worth tracking down **Lanyon Quoit**, the **Mên-an-Tol** and **Chysauster Iron Age Village**.

Land's End St Just Youth Hostel (☎ 01736-788437) is about half a mile south of the village at Letcha Vean. It's open daily from April through October; phone for other times. The nightly charge is £8.80/5.95 for adults/juniors. You can also stay at the independent *Whitesands Lodge* (☎ 01736-871776) backpackers hostel in Sennen village; dorm beds cost £9 (£12 with breakfast). There's also B&B for £17.50.

At *Kelynack Caravan & Camping Park* (☎ 01736-787633), a mile south of St Just, a bed in the bunk barn costs £6, camping is £2.50 per person.

At Botallack, there's comfortable farmhouse accommodation at *Manor Farm* (☎ 01736-788525). B&B is £23 per person.

Zennor

There's a superb four hour walk along the coast path from St Ives to the little village of Zennor, where DH Lawrence wrote part of *Women in Love*. The interesting church has a mermaid carved on one of its bench ends, and there's a small museum.

There are beds for £9 at *Old Chapel Backpackers Hostel* (☎ 01736-798307), and breakfasts from £2. The *Tinners Arms* serves good food and cream teas.

At least four buses a day run to Zennor from St Ives.

End to End Records

The craze for covering the route between the two extremities of Britain in as short a time as possible was started in 1875 by an American, Eliuh Burritt, who walked from John o'Groats to Land's End in 'several weeks'. Times are now measured a little more accurately and the walking record for the 886⅓ miles is currently held by Malcolm Barnish, who did it in 12 days, three hours and 45 minutes. The cycling record is held by Andy Wilkinson, who in 1990 covered an 847 mile route in a mere one day, 21 hours, two minutes and 19 seconds.

Recently, people have been devising ever more offbeat ways of doing the End to End. It's been done with a wheelbarrow in 30 days, in a battery-powered Sinclair C5 in 80 hours, on a tricycle in 5½ days and on roller skates in 9½ days. In 1990, it was run in 26 days and seven hours by Arvind Pandya – no great record in itself, apart from the fact that he was running backwards!

ST IVES
- pop 9500   ☎ 01736

St Ives is an exceptionally beautiful little town. The omnipresent sea, the extraordinary brightness of the light, the harbour, the beautiful sandy beaches, the narrow alleyways, steep slopes and hidden corners are all captivating. Artists have been coming here since Turner visited in 1811, and in 1993 a branch of London's Tate Gallery opened here. These days countless galleries and craft shops line its narrow streets.

Unfortunately in summer St Ives is unbelievably crowded – avoid July and August weekends.

Orientation

The area above St Ives' harbour is very built up and merges into Carbis Bay. Fore St, the main shopping street, is set back from the wharf and crammed with eating places. The north-facing section of the town, overlooking Porthmeor Beach, comprises the Tate Gallery and many guesthouses. The train station is by Porthminster Beach, with the bus station nearby, up Station Hill.

Information

The TIC (☎ 796297) is in the Guildhall in Street-an-Pol.

In summer, a Park & Ride service operates from the Park Avenue car park above the town. Windansea on Fore St, rents wet suits, seven-foot boards (£5 per day) and mountain bikes (£10 per day).

St Ives Tate

Opened in 1993 in a £3 million building designed by Evans and Shalev (architects of the award-winning Truro Law Courts), the Tate is a showcase for the St Ives school of art. The impressive building (☎ 796226) replaced an old gasworks, and has wide central windows framing the surfing scene on Porthmeor Beach below. The collection is small and exclusive, with works by Ben Nicholson, Barbara Hepworth, Naum Gabo, Terry Frost and other local artists.

The gallery is open daily, April to September from 11 am to 7 pm (to 5 pm on Sunday); October to March, Tuesday to Sunday from 11 am to 5 pm. Entry is £3.50; a £5.50 ticket includes admission to the Barbara Hepworth Museum. The café on the roof is almost as popular as the gallery itself.

Barbara Hepworth Museum

Barbara Hepworth was one of the 20th century's greatest sculptors. In the 1930s, with Henry Moore and Ben Nicholson (her then husband), she was part of the leading group of artists with an interest in abstraction. While Moore's sculpture remains close to the human form, Hepworth avoided representational works.

She moved to Cornwall in 1939 and lived here from 1949 until her death in a fire in 1975. The beautiful garden forms a perfect

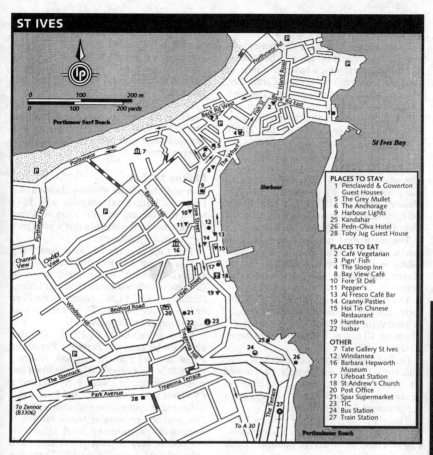

ST IVES

Porthmeor Surf Beach

St Ives Bay

Porthmeor

Harbour

Channel View

Clodgy View

Windsor Hill

Bedford Road

Park Avenue

To Zennor (B3306)

The Stennack

Tregenna Terrace

The Terrace

To A 30

Porthminster Beach

PLACES TO STAY
1 Penclawdd & Gowerton Guest Houses
5 The Grey Mullet
6 The Anchorage
9 Harbour Lights
25 Kandahar
26 Pedn-Olva Hotel
28 Toby Jug Guest House

PLACES TO EAT
2 Café Vegetarian
3 Pign' Fish
4 The Sloop Inn
8 Bay View Café
10 Fore St Deli
11 Pepper's
13 Al Fresco Café Bar
14 Granny Pasties
15 Hoi Tin Chinese Restaurant
19 Hunters
22 Isobar

OTHER
7 Tate Gallery St Ives
12 Windansea
16 Barbara Hepworth Museum
17 Lifeboat Station
18 St Andrew's Church
20 Post Office
21 Spar Supermarket
23 TIC
24 Bus Station
27 Train Station

SOUTH-WESTERN ENGLAND

backdrop for some of her larger works. The museum (☎ 796226) is on Ayr Lane, across town from the Tate, and is open the same times.

Leach Pottery

Bernard Leach travelled to Japan in 1909 to teach etching, but soon discovered a talent for pottery. When he returned in 1920, his Japanese-inspired work had a profound influence on British ceramics. He died in 1979 but the pottery he established is still used by several craftspeople, (including his wife, Janet Leach, until her death in 1997). The showroom (☎ 796398) is open from 10 am to 5 pm on weekdays and on Saturday in summer. It's along the road to Zennor, on the outskirts of St Ives.

Beaches

There are several excellent, clean beaches in the area. **Porthmeor** is the surfing beach to the north of the town, below the Tate.

Just east is the tiny, sandy cove of **Porthgwidden**, with a car park nearby.

There are sandy areas in the sheltered St Ives Harbour, but most families head south to **Porthminster**, which has half a mile of sand and a convenient car park. **Carbis Bay**, to the south-west, is also good for children. **Porthkidney Sands**, the next beach along, is only safe for swimming between the flags. It's dangerous to swim in the Hayle estuary.

Places to Stay

The nearest hostel is in Zennor. There's no camping ground by the beach, but *Ayr Holiday Park* (☎ 795855) is only half a mile above the town in Higher Ayr. It costs from £6.65 for one person and a tent.

The main road into St Ives from Penzance, above Carbis Bay, is lined with B&Bs in the £15 to £18 bracket, but the closer you are to the town centre the better.

The *Toby Jug Guest House* (☎ 794250), convenient for the bus station at 1 Park Ave, is good value with B&B for £15 per person. There are 10 rooms, each with a toby jug as a teapot.

On Sea View Place, in an excellent location right by the sea, there's *Penclawdd* (☎ 796869) at No 1, charging £18 per person in summer; and *Gowerton* (☎ 796805) at No 6, for around £17 per person.

There's B&B at the *Sloop Inn* (☎ 796584) by the harbour, although this location could be noisy in summer. B&B costs from £25.

The Grey Mullet (☎ 796635, 2 Bunkers Hill) is an excellent guesthouse in the old part of town, close to the harbour. Rooms cost from £20 to £24 per person, with a bath. Opposite is an attractive cottage called the *Anchorage* (☎ 797135) with B&B prices slightly lower than at the Grey Mullet.

Harbour Lights (☎ 795525, Court Cocking) is right in the centre. B&B costs around £19 per person in summer.

Kandahar (☎ 796183, 11 The Warren) is right on the rocks by the water. It charges £19 to £24 per person It's ideally located for the bus and train stations. Nearby is the more upmarket *Pedn-Olva Hotel* (☎ 0796222, Porthminster Beach) which has a similar waterside location. Beds cost from £40 to £49 and there's a small swimming pool and sun deck.

To the south, overlooking Porthminster Beach, is the comfortable *Longships Hotel* (☎ 798180, Talland Rd) where rooms with sea views and bathrooms cost from £23 to £26 per person.

Places to Eat

Fish and chips is an obvious choice and a favourite with local seagulls who have learnt to divebomb anyone eating outdoors. It's fun to watch – less fun if it's your grub they're making off with.

The *Café Vegetarian* is a small veg restaurant just off Back Rd East. *Granny Pasties*, Fore St, has a good range of Cornish pasties with some unusual fillings (Indian chicken, £1.80). Nearby is the *Fore St Deli* for self caterers. There's also a *Spar supermarket* on Tregenna Hill.

For a pizza (£4.45 to £5.75, 10% discount on takeaways), *Pepper's Pasta and Pizza* just off Fore St is good. *Hunters* (☎ 797074, St Andrews St) is a seafood and game restaurant. Nearby is *Wilbur's* (☎ 796663) serving lobster and local fish.

Best of the pubs is the 14th century *Sloop Inn* next to the harbour where the bar is hung with paintings by local artists. Its seafood is very popular; fresh fish (cod, sole, plaice) costs £6 to £9. There are several other places to eat along the Wharf, including *Hoi Tin Chinese Restaurant* and the *Bay View Café*.

Places to be seen in St Ives include the Italian *Alfresco Café Bar* (☎ 793737) on the Wharf, offering a Mediterranean-style menu, and *Isobar* on Tregenna Hill. Isobar is a café bar with a nightclub open until 1 am. This is about as happening as St Ives gets.

The top place to eat is the *Pig'n'Fish* (☎ 794204, Norway Lane) which is renowned for its seafood. Main dishes range from about £11 to £17, with turbot, monkfish, bass, red mullet and mussels usually featuring on the menu. Prior notice needs to be given for vegetarian meals.

Getting There & Away

See the fares tables in the Getting Around chapter. St Ives is 277 miles from London and eight from Penzance. National Express (☎ 0990-808080) has three buses a day to London (7½ hours, £29.50). There are also buses to Newquay (1¼ hours, £3.85), Truro (one hour, £2.85) and Plymouth (three hours). For Exeter, you must change at Plymouth.

There's a bus service from St Ives to Land's End via Zennor, St Just-in-Penwith and Sennen Cove every day in summer. There are three buses a day, and an Explorer ticket allowing a day's travel on the route is £5.50. In winter, you must go via Penzance.

St Ives is easily accessible by train from Penzance and London via St Erth.

NEWQUAY
• pop 14,000   ☎ 01637

This is a brash and tacky tourist town – a schizophrenic cross between a 1970s surf town and a traditional beach resort. Until they moved to Seignosse in France in 1998, the World Surfing Championships were held here each summer.

Little that predates the 19th century survives in Newquay, but on the cliff north of Towan Beach stands the whitewashed **Huer's House**, where a watch was kept for approaching pilchard shoals. Every Cornish fishing village had a watchtower like this and the netting operation was directed by the huer. Until they were fished out early in this century, these shoals were enormous – one St Ives catch of 1868 netted a record 16.5 million fish.

Orientation & Information

The TIC (☎ 871345) is on Marcus Hill near the bus station in the town centre.

The surf shops all hire fibreglass boards and wet suits for around £5 each per day. Try Fistral Surf Co on Beacon Rd, or Tunnel Vision Surf Shop opposite the Somerfield supermarket on Alma Place. If you don't know how to surf, contact Offshore Surfing (☎ 877083), on Tolcarne Beach, for an all-inclusive, half-day beginner's lesson (around £20). The Sunset Surf Shop (☎ 877624) at 106 Fore St also runs in-shop 'soft' tuition.

If you don't have a tattoo, at least get yourself a temporary one before hitting the beach. Cut Snake on Fore St have a range (£3 to £20) and they'll last for up to four weeks.

Beaches

Fistral Beach, to the west of the town round Towan Head, is the most famous British surfing beach. There are fast hollow waves, particularly at low tide, and good tubing sections when there's a south-easterly wind.

Watergate Bay is a 2 mile-long sandy beach on the east side of Newquay Bay. At low tide it's a good place to learn to surf. A mile south of Newquay, **Crantock** is a small north-west-facing sheltered beach, where the waves are best at mid to high tide.

Places to Stay

Hostels Several independent hostels cater for surfers in particular. The nearest to Fistral Beach is *Fistral Backpackers* (☎ 873146, 18 Headland Rd). Dorm beds range from £5 to £8 (depending on the season) and there are doubles for £18.

In an excellent central position, *Newquay Cornwall Backpackers* (☎ 874668, Beachfield Ave), overlooks Towan Beach and has dormitory beds for £7 a night or £39 per week.

Newquay International Backpackers (☎ 879366, 69 Tower Rd) charges £10 in peak season for a dorm bed. *Rick's* (☎ 851143, 8 Springfield Rd) only does weekly rents in summer (£60 in August). Outside the peak season it's £5 per night or £35 per week. *Matt's Surf Lodge* (☎ 874651, 110 Mount Wise) has dorm beds for £8 to £10 including continental breakfast.

Camping There are several large caravan parks/camping grounds in the area. *Trenance Caravan & Chalet Park* (☎ 873447)

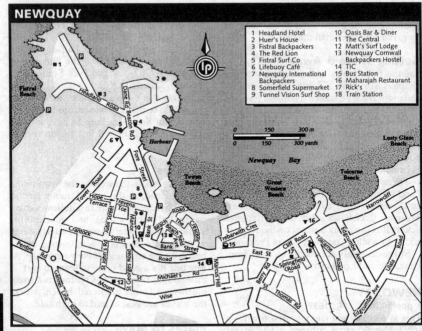

NEWQUAY

1 Headland Hotel
2 Huer's House
3 Fistral Backpackers
4 The Red Lion
5 Fistral Surf Co
6 Lifebuoy Café
7 Newquay International
   Backpackers
8 Somerfield Supermarket
9 Tunnel Vision Surf Shop
10 Oasis Bar & Diner
11 The Central
12 Matt's Surf Lodge
13 Newquay Cornwall
   Backpackers Hostel
14 TIC
15 Bus Station
16 Maharajah Restaurant
17 Rick's
18 Train Station

SOUTH-WESTERN ENGLAND

at the southern end of Edgcumbe Ave charges £5 per person.

B&Bs & Hotels Newquay is so crammed with cheap B&Bs that it makes little sense to recommend some above others. Bear in mind that you still need to book ahead in July and August. Prices vary greatly according to season, particularly at the larger hotels. Trebarwith Crescent, Mount Wise, Dane Rd, Tower Rd, Cliff Rd and Narrowcliffe are all packed with places to stay and the TIC has full details.

The eyesore *Headland Hotel* (☎ 872211) is the best located of Newquay's large hotels. As the name suggests it's out on the headland above Fistral Beach. Rooms cost from £47 to £62 per person.

Places to Eat

Lifebuoy Café, at the junction of Fore St

and Beacon Rd, does good cheap meals. Steak pie and chips is £2. *Oasis Bar & Diner*, Fore St, does all-day breakfasts and burgers. The top Indian place is *Maharajah* (☎ 877377, 39 Cliff Rd). *The Central* is a busy bar on Central Square. At the junction of Fore St, Tower Rd and Beacon Rd is the *Red Lion* pub, a surfers' hang out. Head there to find out what's going on.

Getting There & Away

Newquay is 252 miles from London and 32 from St Ives. National Express provides connections through Plymouth to most places in Britain and has two direct buses daily to London (six hours, £28.50). There are four buses to Plymouth (1¼ hours) and one direct service to Exeter.

There are four trains a day between Par and Newquay on the main London to Penzance line.

NORTH CORNWALL

Some of Britain's best beaches face the Atlantic along the North Cornwall coast but getting around this area without your own transport can be tricky. From Newquay, the coastal road passes **Bedruthan Steps**, a series of rock stacks along a sandy beach. There's a NT teashop here. At **Constantine Bay**, there's a wide, sandy beach, good for surfing.

Padstow

• pop 2300   ☎ 01841

On the Camel River estuary, Padstow is an attractive fishing village best known for its **May Day Hobby Horse**, a man dressed up in an enormous tent-like dress and mask. As he dances through the streets, he is taunted by the local women; if he catches one, he pulls her under the tent, and pinches her – to ensure future motherhood, of course.

The poet John Betjeman is buried at St Enodoc Church, across the water and north of Rock. Above the village is **Prideaux Place** (☎ 532411), built in 1592 by the Prideaux-Brune family. It's open from Easter to September, Sunday to Thursday, from 1.30 to 5 pm; entry is £4/1.

The TIC (☎ 533449) is on the North Quay.

Padstow has one restaurant worth a detour. Television chef Rick Stein's *Seafood Restaurant* (☎ 532485) on the harbour front serves all manner of fish dishes; expect to pay at least £28 a head. When it's closed on Sunday you can eat bistro-style at 4 New St, *St Petroc's House* (same telephone number). Rick Stein is now so well known in Britain that you'll need to book months in advance.

Tintagel & Boscastle

• pop 1750   ☎ 01840

Tintagel has sold its soul to the great god Tourist for whom innumerable car parks and tacky teashops have been provided. That said, even the summer crowds and the grossly commercialised village can't entirely destroy the surf-battered grandeur of Tintagel Head. The scanty ruins are not King Arthur's castle, since they mainly date

from the 13th century; but there's no reason to disbelieve the theory that he was born here in the late 5th century. The ruins (☎ 770328, EH) are open from April to October, daily from 10 am to 6 pm (4 pm in winter); entry costs £2.80/1.40. There are exhilarating walks along the cliffs.

Back in the village, **Tintagel Old Post Office** (☎ 770024s, NT) is a higgledy-piggledy 14th century house turned post office. It's open from April to October, daily from 11 am to 5.30 pm; entry is £2.20/1.10.

A couple of miles along the coast, **Boscastle** can also get overcrowded but is still absurdly picturesque. In particular, hunt out Minster church in a wonderful wooded valley. There's a well-stocked visitors centre in the car park (☎ 250010).

Places to Stay *Tintagel Youth Hostel* (☎ 770334) is in a spectacular setting on the Coast Path, three-quarters of a mile west of the village. It's open daily from April through September; beds cost £8.80/5.95 for adults/juniors. Alternatively, *Boscastle Harbour Youth Hostel* (☎ 250287) is open from mid-May to mid-September (phone for other opening days) for the same price. It's perfectly positioned right on the edge of the harbour.

The *Cornishman Inn* (☎ 770238) in the centre of Tintagel charges from £22.50 a head in rooms with bath. With a car, you might prefer to follow the signs to Trebarwith to stay in the *Old Millfloor* (☎ 770234), a B&B in a delightful setting charging from £18 per person. Or there's *Sunnyside* (☎ 250453) right beside Boscastle harbour, with beds from £15 without bath.

Getting There & Away First Western National's Nos 52/B run from Bodmin Parkway, and the X4 comes from Bude. There are occasional buses from Plymouth.

Bodmin Moor

Cornwall's 'roof' is a high heath pockmarked with bogs and with giant tors like those on Dartmoor rising above the wild

The Daphne du Maurier Trail

Daphne du Maurier, author of a number of best-selling thriller romances set in Cornwall, has probably done more to publicise the county than anyone else. For many years she lived on the Fowey estuary, originally in Ferryside (a house in Bodinnick) and later in Menabilly.

Her first big success was *Jamaica Inn*, an entertaining tale of a smuggling ring based at the famous inn. The idea for the story is said to have come when she and a friend got lost in the mists of Bodmin Moor, eventually stumbling upon the inn. The local vicar entertained them with gripping yarns of Cornish smugglers. Jamaica Inn has a small display about the author. The vicar was from nearby Altarnun, where the church receives a steady flow of du Maurier fans.

The author's next book was *Rebecca*, written in 1938. Manderley, the house in the book, was based on Menabilly, where the author lived – it's not open to the public. *Frenchman's Creek* was set around the inlet of the same name on the Helford River. Lanhydrock House and Falmouth's Pendennis Castle both feature in *The King's General*.

The West Country Tourist Board produce a useful *Daphne du Maurier in Cornwall* leaflet. The Daphne du Maurier Festival of Arts & Literature (☎ 01726-74324) takes place in May.

landscape – Brown Willy (419m) and Rough Tor (400m) are the highest.

The A30 cuts across the centre of the moor from **Launceston**, which has a castle perched above it like the cherry on a cake (☎ 01566-772365, EH) and a granite church completely covered in carvings. At **Bolventor** is *Jamaica Inn* (☎ *01566-86250*), made famous by Daphne du Maurier's novel of the same name. Stop for a drink on a misty winter's night and the place still feels atmospheric. In summer, it's full of day-trippers queuing to view the author's desk and the bizarre Mr Potter's **Museum of Curiosity**, a collection of stuffed kittens and rabbits in the best of Victorian bad taste. Bolventor is a good base for walks on Bodmin. About a mile to the south is **Dozmary Pool**, said to have been where Arthur's sword, Excalibur, was thrown after his death. It's a 4 mile walk north of Jamaica Inn to Brown Willy.

Bude
* **pop 2700**   ☎ **01288**
Five miles from Devon, Bude is another resort that attracts both families and surfers. Crooklets Beach is the main surfing area, just north of the town. Nearby Sandymouth is good for beginners, and Duckpool is also popular. Summerleaze Beach, in the centre of Bude, is a family beach.

The Bude Visitors Centre (☎ 354240) on the Crescent has lists of B&Bs.

Bude is well served by buses, including a daily National Express coach to London (6½ hours, £31).

ISLES OF SCILLY
* **pop 2000**   ☎ **01720**
Twenty-eight miles south-west of Land's End, the Scilly Isles comprise a group of 140 rocky islands with an extremely mild climate caused by the warm Gulf Stream that allows plants and trees that grow nowhere else in Britain to flourish. One of the main objectives for visitors is the subtropical garden at Tresco Abbey. Growing flowers for the mainland is an important industry.

St Mary's, Tresco, St Martin's, St Agnes and Bryher are inhabited. St Mary's is the largest (3 miles by two) and has most of the population. Most of the islands have white, sandy beaches and gin-clear water that attracts divers. The pace of life is slow and gentle – forget any idea of a wild nightlife.

Information
The Isles of Scilly Tourist Board (☎ 422536) is in the Wesleyan Chapel, St Mary's.

Accommodation should be booked in advance, particularly in summer, and tends to be more expensive than on the mainland. Many places close between November and March.

All the islands except Tresco have camping grounds that charge from £2.75 to £5.50 per person. The TIC will send you an accommodation list.

Every Friday evening, and on some Wednesdays in summer, you can watch gig racing – traditional six-oar boats (some over 100 years old) originally used to race out to wrecked ships.

St Mary's

The capital is Hugh Town, on an isthmus that separates the Garrison area from the main part of the town, where boats from the mainland dock. The TIC and most of the places to stay are here.

There are several enjoyable walks on St Mary's. The hour-long Garrison Walk offers good views of the other islands and you pass Star Castle, once an Elizabethan fort, now a hotel. There's a two hour walk to Peninnis headland, where numerous ships have been wrecked, and a three hour Telegraph Walk via assorted ancient historical sites and burial chambers. The TIC has details.

The *camping ground* (☎ 422670) is at Garrison Farm. Cheaper B&Bs in Hugh Town include *Lyonnesse Guest House* (☎ 422458), which costs around £22, and *The Wheelhouse* (☎ 422719) from £26.

The *Atlantic Hotel* (☎ 422417) is right by the water in Hugh Town, and has a good restaurant. It costs from £55 to £76 per person for B&B and dinner.

The top place to stay on St Mary's is the *Star Castle Hotel* (☎ 422317). Luxuries include a heated swimming pool and four-poster beds. Rooms are from £65 per person for B&B and dinner.

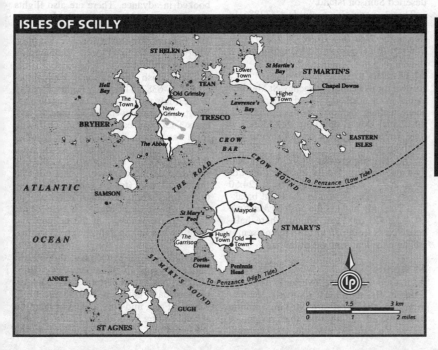

ISLES OF SCILLY

Tresco

The second largest island is best known for the Abbey Garden, laid out in 1834 on the site of a 10th century Benedictine abbey. There are more than 5000 subtropical plants and a display of figureheads from the many ships that have been wrecked off these islands.

There's no camping ground or budget accommodation on the island, just the *New Inn* (☎ 422844), which charges £55 to £78 per person including dinner, and the up-market *Island Hotel* (☎ 422883), from £95 to £155 per person. There's a heated swimming-pool.

Bryher

The smallest of the inhabited islands is wild and rugged; Hell Bay in an Atlantic gale is a powerful sight. There are good views over the islands from the top of Watch Hill. From the quay, occasional boats cross to deserted Samson Island.

There's a *camping ground* (☎ 422886) in Jenford, and very comfortable accommodation at the *Hell Bay Hotel* (☎ 422947) for £54 to £76 per person including dinner.

St Martin's

Known for its beautiful beaches, St Martin's is the most northerly island. There's cliff scenery along the north shore, a good walk on Chapel Downs up to the Day Mark and long stretches of sand on both north and south coasts.

The *camping ground* (☎ 422888) is near Lawrence's Bay. B&Bs include *Polreath* (☎ 422046), which has rooms from £24.50 to £41 per person, dinner, bed and breakfast. The only hotel is the posh *St Martin's* (☎ 422092) on Tean Sound where half-board costs from £75 to £135 per person. It has an excellent seafood restaurant.

St Agnes

A disused lighthouse overlooks the bulb fields of Britain's most southerly community. To the west are striking granite outcrops, including one that resembles Queen Victoria. At low tide, you can walk across the sand to the neighbouring island of Gugh.

The *camping ground* (☎ 422360) is near the beach at Troy Town Farm. There's B&B and evening meals at *Covean Cottage* (☎ 422620) for £32 to £35 per person.

Getting There & Away

There's no transport to or from the Scillies on a Sunday.

Air Isles of Scilly Skybus (☎ 0345-105555) is the islands' airline. It has frequent flights in summer (daily except Sunday) between Land's End aerodrome and St Mary's. The flight takes 15 minutes and for an adult/child costs £44/22 one way (£36/18 stand-by), £56/28 for a day return and £60/30 for a short break of one to three nights. There's a free car park at the Land's End aerodrome, or a free shuttle bus from Penzance train station, which should be booked in advance. There are also flights from Exeter and Newquay (both Monday to Saturday), Plymouth (Monday, Wednesday and Friday), Bristol (Monday, Tuesday, Thursday and Friday) and Southampton (Monday and Friday).

The British International Helicopters (☎ 01736-63871) has daily flights, Monday to Saturday, year-round, from Penzance heliport. The journey takes 20 minutes and costs £46/23 in each direction, £61/30.50 for a day return, £65/32.50 for a five-day excursion and £58/29 for a late saver return for a one to three-night stay (you can book only one day in advance). There are also flights to Tresco (for the gardens), Monday to Saturday, from Penzance; prices are the same as those for St Mary's. It costs £2 per day to leave your car at the heliport and there's a bus link to Penzance train station.

Boat From April to October, the Isles of Scilly Steamship Company (☎ 0345-105555) has one departure a day, Monday to Saturday, between Penzance and St Mary's. From mid-July to August there's a second sailing on Saturday. The trip takes 2¾ hours and costs £70/35 in high season for an adult/child return ticket. One to three-night breaks cost £49/24.50 return. In Penzance, the reservations office is by the south pier.

Getting Around

There are regular departures to the other four islands from St Mary's harbour. A return trip to any island costs £5. Daily boat trips to see the seals and sea birds cost £5.

On St Mary's, you can hire bikes from Buccabu Hire (☎ 422289), near the TIC, from £4.50 per day. There's also an infrequent circular bus service, and tours of St Mary's by minibus.

The Midlands

The heart of England is a mixture of large and small counties that exemplify the best and worst of England. The worst can be found in a wide corridor either side of the M1 motorway, getting worse as you head farther to the north-west around Coventry, Birmingham and Stoke-on-Trent. Even the areas close to the capital can seem pretty dire. However, although Hertfordshire, Bedfordshire and Buckinghamshire are between them a graveyard for modern town planning (see, for example, Milton Keynes), there are still occasional gems like Hatfield House.

To the south-west, however, it's a different story. Despite the usual modern suburban problems, Oxford is still extremely beautiful. The south-west Chilterns remain largely unspoilt and accessible to walkers of the Ridgeway, the 85 mile trail that starts in Avebury and runs north-east to Ivinghoe Beacon, near Aylesbury.

The Cotswolds embody the popular image of the English countryside. The prettiness can seem artificial, and few of the villages are strangers to mass tourism, but there will be moments when you'll be transfixed by the combination of golden stone, flower-draped cottages, church spires, towering chestnuts and oaks, rolling hills and emerald green fields.

The Cotswolds Way follows the western escarpment overlooking the Bristol Channel for 100 miles from Chipping Campden to Bath, but it's quite feasible to tackle a smaller section.

In the south-west the Bristol Channel and the wide Severn Valley form a natural border with agricultural Herefordshire, Worcestershire and the region known as the Welsh Marches. The Wye Valley (see also the Southern Wales chapter) is a famous beauty spot, popularised by the 18th century Romantic poets.

The southern Midlands boasts some of England's most popular tourist sites includ-

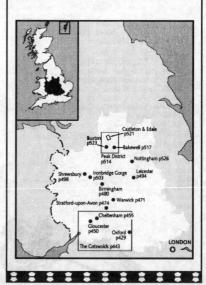

ing Blenheim Palace, Warwick Castle, Stratford-upon-Avon and Oxford.

In contrast the northern Midlands is often dismissed as England's industrial backyard. The dense motorway network gives forewarning of the claustrophobic development and the continuing economic importance of the region, despite the decline of some traditional industries. In a very real sense this is England's working-class heartland, with a wide gap in living standards between these northern cities and those south of Birmingham.

There are, nonetheless, some places well worth visiting, including attractive Shrewsbury and the fascinating Iron Gorge Bridge Museum. Shropshire offers some beautiful, little visited countryside, while in the centre there's the wonderful Peak District National Park. Those keen on fine bone china will also want to brave the wastes of Stoke-on-Trent in search of the big-name suppliers.

Oxfordshire

Oxfordshire is famous worldwide for the university town of Oxford, a mecca for tourists who come to admire the lovely honey-coloured colleges and riverside views.

The surrounding countryside has the gentle, unspectacular charm of middle England. Major features are the River Thames, which flows through the centre and south of the county; the chalk Chilterns, a wooded ridge running across the southeastern corner of the county; and the limestone Cotswolds, extending from the west across Gloucestershire.

As well as the colleges, museums and gardens of Britain's oldest university, no one should miss Blenheim Palace, the spectacular birthplace of Sir Winston Churchill. There are good walks in the hills, and many pretty villages whose character stems from the use of local building materials.

WALKS & CYCLE ROUTES

Oxfordshire is crossed by three long-distance paths. The ancient ridge track known

as the Ridgeway runs along the county's southern border. If you want to walk it look out for either the *Ridgeway National Trail Information & Accommodation* leaflet or for the Countryside Commission official guide.

The Oxfordshire Way is a 65 mile waymarked trail connecting the Cotswolds with the Chilterns and runs from Bourton-on-the-Water to Henley-on-Thames. The leaflet *Oxfordshire Way* divides the route into 16 walks of between 2 and 8 miles in length.

The Thames Path follows the river from its mouth near the Thames' Barrier in London, 175 miles west across the centre of Oxfordshire to its source at Thames Head in Gloucestershire. Look out for the *Thames Path National Trail Information & Accommodation* leaflet or for the Countryside Commission official guide.

Oxfordshire is also good cycling country. There are few extreme gradients and Oxford offers cheap bike hire. The *Oxfordshire Cycleway* map covers Woodstock, Burford and Henley.

GETTING AROUND

Oxfordshire has a reasonable rail network, with Oxford and Banbury the main stations. There are InterCity services on the Cotswolds and Malvern line between London Paddington and Hereford, and between London Euston and Birmingham.

Oxford is the hub of a fairly comprehensive bus service. Tourist Information Centres (TICs) stock a useful free *Bus & Rail Map* showing routes and giving contact numbers for each operator. The main companies are Stagecoach (☎ 01865-772250) and Oxford Bus Company (☎ 01865-785400).

OXFORD

• **pop 115,000   ☎ 01865**

The poet Matthew Arnold described Oxford as 'that sweet city with her dreaming spires', a phrase that still has some resonance today provided you're up the tower of St Mary's looking down rather than strolling across the abomination which is Gloucester Green or battling to cross the road between the solid wedges of buses.

MIDLANDS

For some, Oxford University is synonymous with academic excellence, for others it's an elitist club whose members unfairly dominate many aspects of British life. That sense of elitism is taking on new life as the colleges, sinking under the weight of mass tourism, increasingly close themselves off from would-be sightseers.

These days the dreaming spires coexist with a flourishing commercial city that has some typical Midlands social problems. But for visitors the superb architecture and unique atmosphere of the colleges, courtyards and gardens remain major drawcards.

History

Oxford is strategically located at the point where the River Cherwell meets the Thames. Already an important town in Saxon times, it was fortified by Alfred the Great in the battle against the Danes.

Oxford's importance as a centre of academia grew out of a 12th century political quarrel between the Anglo-Normans and the French which prevented Anglo-Normans from studying at the then centre of European scholastic life, the Sorbonne in Paris.

Students came to study at the Augustinian abbey in Oxford, which soon became known for theological debate among different religious orders. When such debates were conducted in an academic setting all was well, but discussions among students occasionally spilled over into violence. Eventually universities at Oxford and Cambridge were given royal approval, so that future student rebellions would take place far from London. To help the authorities keep an eye on student activity, the university was broken up into colleges, each of which developed its own traditions.

The first colleges, built in the 13th century, were Balliol, Merton and University. At least three new colleges were built in each of the following three centuries. More followed, though at a slower rate and some of the older colleges were redesigned in baroque or neoclassical style. New colleges, like Keble, were added in the later 19th and 20th centuries to cater for a growing student population. There are now about 14,500 undergraduates and 36 colleges. Lady Margaret's Hall, built in 1878, was the first to admit women but they weren't awarded degrees until 1920. These days the colleges are open to everyone and almost half the students are female.

During the Civil War, Oxford was the Royalist headquarters, and the city was split between the Royalist university and the town, which supported the Parliamentarians.

In 1790 Oxford was linked by canal to the Midlands industrial centres, but the city's real industrial boom came when William Morris began producing cars here in 1912. The Bullnose Morris and the Morris Minor were both produced in the Cowley factories.

These days Oxford depends more on the service industries, but its congested centre and sprawling suburbs and housing estates are the legacy of its manufacturing past.

Orientation

The city centre is surrounded by rivers and streams to the south, east and west and can easily be covered on foot. Carfax Tower, at the intersection of Queen and Cornmarket/St Aldates Sts, makes a useful central landmark.

The train station to the west has frequent buses to Carfax Tower. Alternatively, turn left into Park End St and it's a 15 minute walk. The bus station is nearer the centre, off greenless Gloucester Green.

University buildings are scattered throughout the city, with the most important and architecturally interesting at its centre. You need more than a day to do justice to them all but if pushed for time, make sure you visit Christ Church, New and Magdalen colleges.

Information

The TIC (☎ 726871) in Gloucester Green can be pretty hectic in summer. It's open Monday to Saturday from 9.30 am to 5 pm, and on summer Sundays from 10 am to 3.30 pm.

College opening hours are increasingly restrictive; some don't open at all, some only accept guided groups, many close in the morning and others charge for admission.

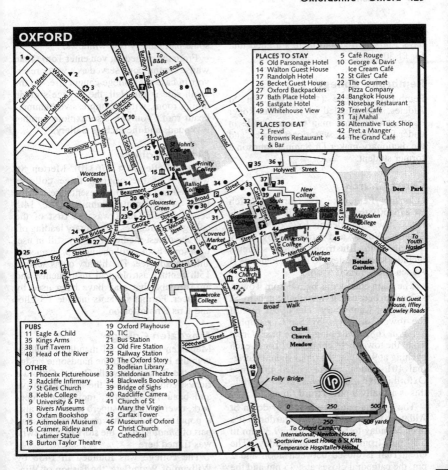

OXFORD

PLACES TO STAY
6 Old Parsonage Hotel
14 Walton Guest House
17 Randolph Hotel
26 Becket Guest House
27 Oxford Backpackers
37 Bath Place Hotel
45 Eastgate Hotel
49 Whitehouse View

PLACES TO EAT
2 Frevd
4 Browns Restaurant & Bar
5 Café Rouge
10 George & Davis' Ice Cream Café
12 St Giles' Café
22 The Gourmet Pizza Company
24 Bangkok House
28 Nosebag Restaurant
29 Travel Café
31 Taj Mahal
36 Alternative Tuck Shop
42 Pret a Manger
44 The Grand Café

PUBS
11 Eagle & Child
35 Kings Arms
38 Turf Tavern
48 Head of the River

OTHER
1 Phoenix Picturehouse
3 Radcliffe Infirmary
7 St Giles Church
8 Keble College
9 University & Pitt Rivers Museums
13 Oxfam Bookshop
15 Ashmolean Museum
16 Cramer, Ridley and Latimer Statue
18 Burton Taylor Theatre
19 Oxford Playhouse
20 TIC
21 Bus Station
23 Old Fire Station
25 Railway Station
30 The Oxford Story
32 Bodleian Library
33 Sheldonian Theatre
34 Blackwells Bookshop
39 Bridge of Sighs
40 Radcliffe Camera
41 Church of St Mary the Virgin
43 Carfax Tower
46 Museum of Oxford
47 Christ Church Cathedral

The TIC stocks the *Welcome to Oxford* brochure, which has a walking tour with college opening times. Two-hour guided walking tours of the colleges leave the TIC at 11 am and 1 and 2 pm; they cost £4/2.50. Inspector Morse tours, around sites associated with the fictional detective, also leave the TIC every Saturday at 1.30 pm (£4.50/3).

Carfax Tower

At the top of St Aldates street in the city centre, Carfax Tower, with its quarterjacks

(figures who hammer out the quarter hours on bells), is the sole reminder of medieval St Martin's Church. There's a fine view from the top of the tower which is good for orientating yourself. It's open daily from Easter through October from 10 am to 5.30 pm, closing at 3.30 pm in winter. Admission is £1.20/60p.

Museum of Oxford

This museum (☎ 815559), St Aldates, introduces the city's history. It's open Tuesday to

Friday, from 10 am to 4 pm (5 pm on Saturday). Entry is free, but there's a good tour for £1.50.

Pembroke College

Pembroke College (☎ 276444) in St Aldates, was founded in 1624. Sir Roger Bannister, the first man to run a mile in under four minutes, was a past master, and the dictionary-maker Dr Samuel Johnson a former student.

Christ Church

Opposite Pembroke is Christ Church (☎ 276150), the grandest of all Oxford colleges. It was founded in 1525 by Cardinal Thomas Wolsey and refounded by Henry VIII in 1546. Illustrious former students include John Wesley, William Penn, WH Auden and Lewis Carroll.

The main entrance is below Tom Tower, so called because it was dedicated to St Thomas of Canterbury. The upper part of the tower, designed by Sir Christopher Wren in 1682, rests on a Tudor base. Great Tom, the tower bell, chimes 101 times each evening at 9.05 pm, the time when the original 101 students were called in. Since Oxford is five minutes west of Greenwich, this is actually 9 pm Oxford time.

The visitors entrance is farther down St Aldates, via the Memorial Gardens. It's open Monday to Saturday from 9.30 am to 5.30 pm (from 11.30 am on Sunday). The Great Hall is closed between noon and 2 pm, the cathedral closes at 4.45 pm and the Chapterhouse at 5 pm. There's an admission charge of £3/2.

The cloisters lead to **Christ Church Cathedral**, the smallest cathedral in the country, which has been the city's Anglican cathedral since the reign of Henry VIII. It was founded on the site of the nunnery of St Frideswide, whose shrine was a focus of pilgrimage until it was partly destroyed on Henry VIII's orders. The shrine was reconstructed in the 19th century. Beside it is a **Watching Loft** for the guard, who made sure no one walked off with the saint's relics. The Lady and Latin chapels boast some particularly fine windows.

From the cathedral, you enter **Tom Quad** whose central pond served as a water reservoir in case the college caught fire. To the south side is the **Hall**, the college's grand dining room, with an impressive hammerbeam roof. You can also explore another two quads and the **Picture Gallery**.

Merton College

Merton College (☎ 276310), Merton St, was one of the original three colleges founded in 1264 and represents the earliest form of collegiate planning. The 14th century **Mob Quad** was the first of the college quadrangles. The **library** leading off it is the oldest medieval library still in use, with some books still chained up, an ancient anti-theft device. The library owns several 15th century astrological instruments, and an astrolabe that may have been used by Chaucer. Former students include TS Eliot and Kris Kristofferson.

Magdalen College

Magdalen (pronounced maudlen) College is in the High St, near the handsome bridge over the River Cherwell. One of Oxford's richest colleges, it has the most extensive and beautiful grounds, including a deer park, river walk and superb lawns. It's also a popular location for movie-makers and part of *Shadowlands*, the story of CS Lewis, was filmed here.

The college was founded in 1458 by William of Waynflete, the Bishop of Winchester. The chapel with its 43m-high bell tower dates from the late 15th century. At 6 am each year, the college choir ushers in May Day by singing a hymn from the top of the tower to the crowds below. Pubs open before breakfast, ensuring that this is a well-supported tradition.

Former Magdalen students include Oscar Wilde, Sir John Betjeman and Dudley Moore. The college (☎ 276000) is open Monday to Friday from noon to 6 pm and at weekends from 2 pm. There's an entry charge of £2/1 from April to September.

Botanic Gardens

Opposite Magdalen is the Botanic Gardens (☎ 276920), founded in 1621 by Henry Danvers for the study of medicinal plants. It's open daily from 9 am to 5 pm and there's a £1.50 entry charge from mid-June to September.

St Edmund Hall

St Edmund Hall (☎ 279000), Queen's Lane, is where the Mohawk chief, Oronhyatekha, studied in 1862. Its small chapel was decorated by William Morris and Edward Burne-Jones.

Queen's College

Queen's College (☎ 279121), High St, was founded in 1341 but the current buildings are all in classical style. Like most colleges, Queen's preserves some idiosyncratic traditions: students are summoned to meals with a trumpet call and at Christmas a boar's head is served to commemorate a time when a scholar fought off an attacking boar by thrusting a volume of Aristotle down its throat! How appropriate, then, that Rowan Atkinson (aka Mr Bean) once studied here. To visit the college, you must join an official tour.

University College

University College (☎ 276602), High St, has acquired new fame as the college where Bill Clinton didn't inhale noxious substances. Despite claims for King Alfred as a founder, the college actually started life in 1249. A romantic memorial commemorates the poet Percy Bysshe Shelley, who was sent down (ie expelled) for publishing *The Necessity of Atheism* in 1811. You need a private invitation to visit the college.

All Souls College

All Souls College (☎ 279379), High St, was founded in 1438, the souls in question being those of soldiers who died in the Hundred Years' War. The 100 years theme is repeated in the tradition of 'All Souls Mallard', which will be re-enacted on 14 January 2000 when the warden will lead a procession to look for a mythical duck that appeared when the college foundations were being dug. No undergraduates are admitted to All Souls, a small college of just 70 fellows. The college chapel, open weekdays from 2 to 4.30 pm, is worth seeing.

Church of St Mary the Virgin

At the junction of High and Catte Sts, the Church of St Mary the Virgin has a 14th century tower offering splendid views (£1.50/75p). It's open daily from 9 am to 7 pm in July and August (5 pm for the rest of the year).

Radcliffe Camera

The Radcliffe Camera is a spectacular circular library ('camera' means room) built in 1748 in the Palladian style. It's not open to the public.

Brasenose College

Dating from the 16th century, Brasenose College (☎ 277830) is entered from Radcliffe Square and takes its name from an 11th century snout-like door knocker that now graces the dining room. It's open daily from 10 to 11.30 am and 2 to 4.30 pm.

New College

To reach New College (☎ 279555), turn down New College Lane under the **Bridge of Sighs**, a 1914 copy of the famous bridge in Venice. New College was founded in 1379 by William of Wykeham, Bishop of Winchester, and its buildings are fine examples of the perpendicular style. Don't miss the chapel, which has superb stained glass, much of it from the 14th century. The west window is a design by Sir Joshua Reynolds, and Sir Jacob Epstein's disturbing statue of Lazarus is also here. The gardens contain a section of Oxford's medieval wall.

A former college warden was William Spooner, whose habit of transposing the first consonants of words made his name part of the English language. It's claimed that he once reprimanded a student with the words, 'You have deliberately tasted two

MIDLANDS

worms and can leave Oxford by the town drain'. The college is open daily from Easter to October from 11 am to 5 pm (2 to 4 pm in winter). Entry costs £1.

Sheldonian Theatre

In Broad St stands the Sheldonian Theatre, the university's main public building. Commissioned by Gilbert Sheldon, Archbishop of Canterbury, it was Wren's first major work and was built in 1667 when he was Professor of Astronomy. It's open Monday to Saturday from 10 am to 12.30 pm and 2 to 4.30 pm (3.30 pm in winter). Admission costs £1.50/1.

Bodleian Library

Britain's second most important copyright library, the Bodleian Library, is off the Jacobean-period Old Schools Quadrangle. Library tours (☎ 277000) take place at 10.30 and 11.30 am, and 2 and 3 pm daily (mornings only on Saturday) and show off Duke Humfrey's library (1488). They book up fast and cost £3.50 (no children under 14). Also not to be missed is the Divinity School, with its superb vaulted ceiling. Renowned as a masterpiece of 15th century English Gothic architecture, it's open weekdays from 9 am to 5 pm and on Saturday until 12.30 pm.

Trinity College

Trinity College (☎ 279900), Broad St, was founded in 1555, but the existing buildings mostly date from the 17th century. It's open daily from 10.30 am to noon and 2 to 4 pm.

Balliol College

Balliol College (☎ 277777), Broad St, was founded in 1263, but most of the buildings date from the 19th century. The wooden doors between the inner and outer quadrangles still bear scorch marks from when Protestant martyrs were burnt at the stake in the mid-16th century. It's open daily from 2 to 5 pm.

The Oxford Story

Across Broad St from Balliol is The Oxford Story (☎ 790055), a much-publicised and reasonably entertaining 40 minute ride through the university's history in carriages designed to look like old college desks. It's open April through October from 9.30 am to 5 pm (9 am to 6 pm in July and August), and from 10 am to 4.30 pm for the rest of the year. Tickets cost £4.95/3.95.

Ashmolean Museum

Established in 1683, the Ashmolean is the country's oldest museum, based on the collections of the gardening Tradescant family and Dr Elias Ashmole who presented their possessions to the university.

The Beaumont St building is one of Britain's best examples of neo-Grecian architecture, and dates from 1845. It houses extensive displays of European art (including works by Raphael and Michelangelo) and Middle Eastern antiquities. Other exhibits include a unique Saxon enamel portrait of Alfred the Great and Guy Fawkes' lantern.

The museum (☎ 278000) is open Tuesday through Saturday from 10 am to 4 pm, Sunday from 2 to 4 pm, and bank holiday Mondays. There's no entry charge, but a £2 donation is requested.

University & Pitt Rivers Museums

Housed in a superb Victorian Gothic building on Parks Rd, the University Museum is devoted to natural science. The dinosaur skeletons are perfectly suited to the surroundings, the patterns of their bones echoed in the delicate ironwork and glass above. The dodo relics, along the wall to the left as you enter the museum, are particularly popular.

You can reach the Pitt Rivers Museum (☎ 270949) through the University Museum. The glass cases at the Pitt Rivers are crammed to overflowing with everything from a sailing boat to a gory collection of shrunken South American heads. There are said to be over one million items, and some (mainly musical instruments) have been moved to an annexe, the Balfour Building, on Banbury Rd.

Both museums are open Monday to Saturday, the University from noon to 5 pm, the Pitt Rivers from 1 to 4.30 pm. They're free but a £2 donation is requested.

Punting

There's no better way to soak up Oxford's atmosphere than to take to the river in a punt. The secret to propelling these flat-bottomed boats is to push gently on the pole to get the punt moving and then to use it as a rudder to keep on course.

Punts are available from Easter to September and hold five people, including the punter. Both the Thames and the Cherwell are shallow enough for punts, but the best advice is to bring a picnic and head upstream along the Cherwell. You can rent a punt from C Howard & Sons (☎ 761586, £7 per hour, £20 deposit) by Magdalen Bridge, or from the Cherwell Boat House (☎ 515978, £6 per hour, £30 deposit, £8 and £40 at weekends) farther upstream at the end of Bardwell Rd.

Alternatively, follow the Cherwell downstream from Magdalen Bridge for views of the colleges across the Botanic Gardens and Christ Church Meadow.

Organised Tours

Guide Friday (☎ 790522) runs a hop-on, hop-off city bus tour every 10 minutes from 9.30 am to 6 pm in summer, less frequently in winter. It leaves from the train station and tickets cost £8/2.50.

Cotswold Roaming (☎ 250640) runs guided bus tours to several places around Oxford, including Blenheim Palace, Bath and the Cotswolds.

Places to Stay

Finding a place to stay in summer can be difficult; arrange things in advance or join the queues in the TIC and pay £2.75 for help.

Camping *Oxford Camping International* (☎ 246551, 426 Abingdon Rd) is conveniently located by the Park & Ride car park 1½ miles south of the centre. Charges are

£2.50 for a small tent, plus £1.50 per person and £2.50 for a car.

Hostels The most convenient hostel is *Oxford Backpackers* (☎ 721761, 9A Hythe Bridge St), which is less than a five minute walk from the train station. There are 80 beds, mostly in dorms, and good cooking facilities. From April to September you need to book a week in advance and leave a deposit. Beds in dorms cost £10 each.

Oxford Youth Hostel (☎ 762997, 32 Jack Straw's Lane) gets booked up quickly in summer although it's hardly central. Get there on bus No 14 or 14A from outside the post office just down the hill from the TIC. It's open all year and beds cost £9.75/6.55 for adults/juniors.

Readers have also recommended the unregistered *St Kitts Temperance Hospitallers hostel* (☎ 433225, 84 Ridgefield Rd) where beds cost just £7. Get there on Blackbird Leys Bus No 1.

University Accommodation Over the Easter and the summer holidays you can sometimes find a room in empty student accommodation.

From July to September, St Edmund Hall turns into the *Isis Guest House* (☎ 248894, 45-53 Iffley Rd), offering student digs as superior B&B accommodation. The 37 single/double rooms cost £30/50 with a bathroom, £20/40 without.

Otherwise you could try *Canterbury Road House* (☎ 554642, 12 Canterbury Rd), which lets rooms from £15/26 over Easter and from late June through September or *Old Mitre Rooms* (☎ 279821, 4B Turl St), which lets rooms from £19/37 in July and August only.

B&Bs & Hotels – Central In the peak season you're looking at around £20 per person for a room in a B&B. The main areas are on Abingdon Rd to the south, Cowley and Iffley Rds to the east, and Banbury Rd to the north. All are on bus routes, but Cowley Rd has the best selection of places to eat.

The fairly basic *Becket Guest House* (☎ 724675, 5 Becket St) is just a short walk from the train station and has singles/doubles from £25/36. West of the station, the small *River Hotel* (☎ 243475, 17 Botley Rd) by Osney Bridge is a popular business hotel with rooms from £45/68. The *Westgate Hotel* (☎ 726721, 1 Botley Rd) charges £30/42 for a room, or £39/56 with a bath.

St Michael's Guest House (☎ 242101, 26 St Michael's St) just off Cornmarket St couldn't be more central. Rooms with shared bath are £25/45, but you need to book weeks in advance. The closest B&B to the bus station is the basic *Walton Guest House* (☎ 52137, 169 Walton St) with bathless rooms for £18 per person.

Oxford's choicest accommodation is also centrally located. Forte's *Randolph Hotel* (☎ 247481, Beaumont St), opposite the Ashmolean Museum, was built in 1864 in neogothic style; rooms cost from £99/161 but there are reductions at weekends. The delightful *Old Parsonage Hotel* (☎ 310210, 1 Banbury Rd) has well-equipped rooms for £120/160.

Bath Place Hotel (☎ 791812, 4 & 5 Bath Place) is a luxurious 10 room retreat in which all the rooms have different decorating styles, and some have four-poster beds. Rooms cost from £75/90 with continental breakfast. Similarly priced is the *Eastgate Hotel* (☎ 248244, High St).

B&Bs & Hotels – East East of the centre there are several B&Bs in the student area on Cowley Rd and numerous ones along Iffley Rd to the south. Another cluster lies to the north, along Headington Rd.

Farther out, the *Bravalla Guest House* (☎ 241326, 242 Iffley Rd) charges from £18 per person. Some rooms have a bath. *Brenal Guest House* (☎ 721561, 307 Iffley Rd) has singles/doubles from £25/40. The *Athena Guest House* (☎ 243124, 253 Cowley Rd) is within walking distance of shops and restaurants and has beds for £18 a head. A bit farther out, the comfortable *Earlmont* (☎ 240236) has rooms from £25/36.

B&Bs & Hotels – North There are several B&Bs along Banbury Rd, north of the centre. *Cotswold House* (☎ 310558, 363 Banbury Rd) is very comfortable; rooms with bathroom cost from £39/57. *Burren Guest House* (☎ 513513, 374 Banbury Rd) is more basic and offers B&B from £20 a head.

B&Bs & Hotels – South Closest to the city centre is the good-value *Whitehouse View* (☎ 721626, 9 Whitehouse Rd) on a side road off Abingdon Rd, with rooms from £18/34.

There are numerous other places along Abingdon Rd. *Newton House* (☎ 240561, 82 Abingdon Rd) is quite large, with rooms from £22/30. The *Sportsview Guest House* (☎ 244268, 106 Abingdon Rd) has rooms, mostly with bath, from £23/34.

Places to Eat

Many Oxford eateries are aimed at the wallets of wealthy parents and tourists. To eat cheaply you need to track down the places that get the student trade.

Self-caterers should visit the *covered market*, on the north side of High St at the Carfax Tower end, for snacks, fruit and vegetables. Among the stalls, *Palm's Delicatessen* offers a good range of patés and cheeses. *Brown's Café* will do you sausage and beans for £1.95. Otherwise, the *Alternative Tuck Shop* (Holywell St), does excellent filled rolls and sandwiches at lunch time. A popular place for snacky meals is *St Giles' Café* (St Giles') where fry-ups cost around £3.95 and toasted sandwiches from £1.60. The popular *George & Davis' Ice Cream Café* (Little Clarendon St) serves light meals (bagels from £1) as well as delicious home-made ice cream. It's open until midnight.

The nonsmoking *Nosebag Restaurant* (☎ 721033, St Michael's St) does good soups for £2.70 and has a fine selection of cakes. Light lunches, teas and coffees are available in the *Convocation Coffee House* attached to the Church of St Mary the Virgin; soup and a roll costs £2.30, a meat pie £2.65. If you're at the TIC around lunch time the adjoining *Old School* pub does snack meals like filled baguettes at reasonable prices. Gloucester Green is also ringed with eateries, most of them uninviting, although *The Gourmet Pizza Company* (☎ *793146*) is worth trying for its unusual toppings, including Chinese duck (£8.35).

Slap bang in the middle of the High St, *The Grand Café* (☎ *204463*) offers luxury sandwiches and salads in suitably grand surroundings, amid pillars and mirrors. Just as inviting is *Frevd* (☎ *311171, Walton St*), a café bar inside an old church. There's Latin dancing here on Sunday from 7 to 11 pm. There's also a pleasant café in the *Old Fire Station* (see Theatres & Cinema under Entertainment). Stylish *Browns Restaurant & Bar* (☎ *511995, 5 Woodstock Rd*) looks more expensive than it is. Starters include toasted olive bread with sun-dried tomatoes (£1.85); main dishes range from mushroom stroganoff (£6.95) to fillet steak (£14.95).

The *Taj Mahal* (☎ *243783, 16 Turl St*) is a particularly good Indian restaurant; typically, mushroom biryani costs £5.95. Near the station, the *Bangkok House* (☎ *200705, 42a Hythe Bridge St*) does set Thai meals for £15.50, assuming two diners.

The city's topnotch hotels boast equally topnotch restaurants. The *Bath Place Hotel* (☎ *791812*) does two-course set lunches for £14.50, although dinner is likely to weigh in at closer to £40. A bistro-style dinner at the *Old Parsonage Hotel* (☎ *310210*) should come closer to the £25 mark.

An interesting new venture is the *Travel Café* (☎ *727737, 1-5 Broad St*), a kind of travel agency-cum-café where you can book a flight, buy a guidebook and organise your jabs while ordering a meal and a drink. If it works, expect to see clones springing up around the country before you can say *ciabatta*. *Café Rouge* is in Little Clarendon St and *Pret A Manger* is in Cornmarket St.

Entertainment

Pubs Oxford has some excellent city centre pubs as well as others within walking distance along the Thames.

The *Head of the River*, ideally situated by Folly Bridge, is very popular. Less prominent is the tiny *Turf Tavern,* which is hidden down a city centre alley (Bath Place) and featured in the *Inspector Morse* TV series based on Colin Dexter's books.

Academics loosen up in the 17th century *Eagle & Child*, St Giles', where JRR Tolkein and CS Lewis used to meet for readings from *The Hobbit* and the chronicles of Narnia.

The *Kings Arms* is a crowded student pub in the heart of the city, opposite the Sheldonian Theatre. Most weekends find Irish bands playing at the *Bullingdon Arms* (*162 Cowley Rd*), a lively Irish local with live jazz/blues on Wednesday evening.

The *Isis Tavern*, a 1½ mile walk along the towpath from Folly Bridge, is the perfect place to go on a sunny day provided you don't mind the crowds. The thatch-roofed *Perch* by the river in Binsey is a 25 minute walk from the city centre; from Walton St, take Walton Well Rd and cross Port Meadow.

Theatre & Cinema The *Oxford Playhouse* (☎ *798600, Beaumont St*) puts on a mixed bag of theatre, music and dance. The *Old Fire Station* (☎ *794490, George St*) stages mainly classical plays while *Burton Taylor Theatre* (☎ *798600, Gloucester St*) goes for more offbeat productions.

The most interesting films tend to be shown at the *Phoenix Picturehouse* (☎ *554909, Walton St*).

Getting There & Away

Oxford is 57 miles from London, 74 miles from Bristol and 33 miles from Cheltenham. Driving, the M40 provides fast access from London but Oxford has a serious traffic problem and finding anywhere to park can be difficult. It's best to use the Park & Ride system; as you approach the city follow the signs for the four car parks. Parking is free but the buses to the city centre cost £1 return. They leave every 10 minutes throughout the day,

MIDLANDS

Monday to Saturday. For fares see the tables in the Getting Around chapter.

Bus Several bus lines compete for business on the route to London. The Oxford Tube (☎ 772250) goes to Victoria coach station but also stops at Marble Arch, Notting Hill Gate and Shepherd's Bush. An overnight return to Victoria costs £7; the journey takes around 1½ hours and the service operates 24 hours a day. The Oxford Tube also stops on St Clements St, near Cowley Rd.

National Express (☎ 0990-808080) has numerous buses to central London and Heathrow airport. There are three buses a day to Cambridge (three hours, £12.50), two or three services to/from Bath (two hours, £8.75) and Bristol (2¼ hours, £11.50), and two to/from Gloucester (1½ hours, £7.25) and Cheltenham (one hour, £7).

The Oxford Bus Company (☎ 785400) is the third major operator with frequent departures to London, Heathrow, Gatwick, Birmingham and Stratford-upon-Avon.

Train Oxford has a snazzy modern station with frequent services to London Paddington (1½ hours, £12 single).

There are regular trains north to Coventry and Birmingham, the main hub for transport farther north, and north-west to Worcester and Hereford via Moreton-in-Marsh (for the Cotswolds).

To connect with trains to the south-west you have to change at Didcot Parkway (15 minutes). There are plenty of connections to Bath (1½ hours). Change at Swindon for another line running into the Cotswolds (Kemble, Stroud and Gloucester).

Getting Around

Bus Oxford was among the world's first cities to introduce battery-operated electric buses. They run every 12 minutes from the train station into the city centre Monday to Saturday from 8 am to 6.24 pm for a flat fare of 30p.

The city has fallen victim to the worst excesses of bus deregulation, with so many competing buses plying Cornmarket St that

it can be difficult to cross the road. The biggest companies are Citylink (☎ 785410) and Stagecoach (☎ 772250). Citylink bus No 4A serves Iffley Rd and Nos 11A and 52 serve Cowley Rd. The information office in the bus station has full details.

Car For car hire, Budget (☎ 724884) is near the station on Hythe Bridge St.

Taxi There are taxis outside the train station and near the bus station. A taxi to Blenheim Palace will cost around £15.

Bicycle Students have always espoused pedal power and there are cycle lanes along several streets. The *Cycle into Oxford* map shows all the local cycle routes.

Pennyfarthing (☎ 249368), 5 George St, near the bus station, offers mountain bikes for £10/25 a week.

Boat Salter Bros (☎ 243421) offers several interesting boat trips from Folly Bridge between May and September, including a two hour trip to Abingdon. See also Punting earlier in the Oxford section.

WOODSTOCK & BLENHEIM PALACE

The nearby village of Woodstock owes its fame and prosperity to glove-making and the Churchill family. Although people usually come here en route to Blenheim Palace, there's also a fine collection of 17th and 18th century buildings, particularly the Bear Hotel and the town hall, built at the Duke of Marlborough's expense in 1766. The church has an 18th century tower tacked onto a medieval interior. Opposite the church, Fletcher's House accommodates **Oxfordshire County Museum** (closed on Monday).

The TIC (☎ 01993-811038) is on Hensington Rd.

Blenheim Palace

One of Europe's largest palaces, Blenheim was a gift to John Churchill from Queen Anne and the parliament as a reward for his role in defeating Louis XIV. A vast baroque fantasy, it was built by Sir John Vanbrugh and Nicholas Hawksmoor between 1704 and 1722. It's now a UNESCO World Heritage List site.

You enter the house through the great hall where 20m above the ceiling is decorated with a painting by Sir James Thornhill showing the Duke of Marlborough presenting Britannia with his plan for the Battle of Blenheim. West of the great hall, apartments once used by the domestic chaplain now house the Churchill Exhibition; in the room where Winston was born you can view the great prime minister's slippers and a lock of his hair.

The windows of the sumptuous state dining room offer a glimpse of the tower of Bladon Church where Churchill and his parents are buried. Between the saloon and library are three state rooms, hung with tapestries commemorating Marlborough's campaigns.

You can also visit the chapel and grounds, which cover over 800 hectares, some of it parkland landscaped by Capability Brown. Blenheim Park railway leads to the herb garden, the butterfly house, a large maze, bouncy castles etc. A separate ticket lets you look round the current duke and duchess's private apartments.

Blenheim Palace (☎ 811325) is open from mid-March through October from 10.30 am to 5 pm and entry is £8/4. The park is open from 9 am every day, all year.

Places to Stay & Eat
Mrs McCabe's (☎ *812051, 14 Hensington Rd*) charges £17 a head, or there's *Plane Tree House* (☎ *813075, 15 High St*) at £38 a double. The best place in town is the *Feathers Hotel* (☎ *812291, Market St*), with luxurious rooms for £88/105. There are numerous tearooms and pubs. Bar food at the popular *Black Prince* includes Mexican dishes and pizzas.

Getting There & Away
To get to Woodstock from Oxford, catch Stagecoach bus No 20/A/B/C from Oxford bus station (30 minutes, £2.70 return).

Cotswold Roaming (☎ 308300) offers organised excursions to Blenheim from Oxford.

OXFORDSHIRE COTSWOLDS
Although most of the Cotswolds lie in Gloucestershire, about one-fifth strays across the border into Oxfordshire.

Burford
☎ 01993
One of the loveliest Cotswold villages, Burford has one long street of handsome stone houses and attracts crowds of tourists in summer. Once an important coaching town, it boasts fine 14th to 16th century houses and a medieval bridge over the River Windrush. The TIC (☎ 823558) is by the Lamb Inn on Sheep St.

The 16th century **Tolsey** (Toll House), in the High St, houses a small summer-only museum (50p).

Just outside Burford is the **Cotswold Wildlife Park** (☎ 823006), a long-established zoo in the grounds of a Gothic mansion. It's open daily from 10 am to 5 pm (4 pm in winter). Admission costs £5.50/3.50.

Places to Stay & Eat Burford is no place for those on a tight budget; most cheaper accommodation is 4 miles north-east at Leafield. In Burford, *Chevrons* (☎ *823416, near the corner of Swan Lane and High St*) has singles/doubles with bathroom from £25/35. *Byways* (☎ *823609, Witney St*) has one double with a bathroom for £40, one without for £30.

Burford's oldest pub, the 15th century *Lamb Inn* (☎ *823155, Sheep St*) is now a very comfy place to stay, with beamed ceilings and creaking stairs. Rooms with bathroom cost from £58/90 during the week, more at weekends.

Burford has several other good pubs. On the High St, the *Mermaid* and the *Golden Pheasant* do bar snacks and full meals. In Witney St, the *Angel* is popular not only for its real ale but also for its award-winning food. The restaurant is pricey but something like a four cheese platter costs £5.95 in the bar.

The High St has several tearooms; at *Huffkins* a Cotswold breakfast with kippers costs £3.65, but service may be better at the *Priory Tea Rooms* across the road.

Getting There & Away From Oxford, Swanbrook (☎ 01452-712386) runs four buses a day (two on Sunday) to Burford via Witney.

Witney

• pop 19,000   ☎ 01993

Ten miles west of Oxford, Witney is a gateway to the Cotswolds. Since 1669, the town has specialised in the production of blankets. Sheep on the Cotswolds and the local downs provided the wool, while the River Windrush provided the water. High-quality blankets continue to be made and the Queen still orders hers from Early's of Witney.

Although the town has grown to absorb the demands of Oxford commuters and light industry, the centre retains some character. In the High St, blankets were formerly weighed and measured in the 18th century baroque-style Blanket Hall. In Market Place stands the 17th century Buttercross, originally a covered market.

The TIC (☎ 775802) is in the 18th century town hall in Market Square.

There are numerous daily buses from Oxford.

Cogges Manor Farm Museum

Clearly signposted in the suburbs of Witney is Cogges Museum (☎ 772602), where domestic farm animals roam the grounds of a 13th century manor house, which was drastically altered in the 17th and 18th centuries. Here you can sample cakes and scones freshly baked on the old range. It's open from late March through October, Tuesday to Friday from 10.30 am to 5.30 pm (from noon at weekends). Admission is £3.25/1.75. The Witney Weaver bus from Oxford to Witney drops you within walking distance.

SOUTH OF OXFORD
Abingdon

• pop 30,000   ☎ 01235

Pretty Abingdon is a market town 6 miles south of Oxford. The impressive **County Hall** building was designed in 1678 by Christopher Kempster, who worked on St Paul's Cathedral in London. It now houses a local museum. Wider than it is long, **St Helen's Church** is a fine example of perpendicular architecture. The TIC (☎ 522711) is in Abbey Close, near the river.

On St Helens Wharf, overlooking the Thames, is the *Old Anchor*, a friendly pub that also serves meals.

The nicest way to reach Abingdon from Oxford is by boat (see the Oxford section). Alternatively, Stagecoach bus No 31 links Abingdon with Oxford and Wantage.

Dorchester-on-Thames

A street of old coaching inns and a magnificent medieval church are more or less all there is of Dorchester-on-Thames, although in Saxon times there was a cathedral here. In the 12th century an abbey was founded on the site. Following the Reformation it became the parish church of Saints Peter and Paul, and it's worth stepping inside to see the rare Norman lead font with figures of the apostles; a wonderful Jesse window with carved figures and stained glass tracing Christ's ancestry; and a 13th century monument of a knight. There's a small museum and café in the Abbey Guest House, which also dates back to the Middle Ages.

Stagecoach bus No X39 connects Dorchester with Oxford and Abingdon.

Wantage

• pop 9700   ☎ 01235

Wantage lies at the foot of the Downs, 15 miles south-west of Oxford. Alfred the Great was born here in 849, and his statue dominates the main square. The Ridgeway is less than 3 miles to the south.

The **Vale & Downland Museum Centre** (☎ 771447), in a converted 16th century cloth merchant's house in Church St, has information about King Alfred and life around the Ridgeway. It's open Tuesday to Saturday from 10.30 am to 4.30 pm (2.30 to 5 pm on Sunday) and is free. The TIC (☎ 760176) in the museum keeps the same hours.

Places to Stay & Eat About 2 miles south of Wantage, the *Ridgeway Youth Hostel* (☎ 760253, Court Hill) was created out of several old barns set round a courtyard. It's open daily from May to early September, but not on Sunday from mid-March through April and early September through November. The nightly charge is £8/5.40.

The Chalet (☎ 769262, 21 Challow Rd) has beds from £15. The *Bell Inn* (☎ 763718, Market Square) is pricier at £45 a double. You can get bar meals in *The Shears (Mill St)*. The *Flying Teapot*, beside the church, does snacks like jacket potatoes for £2.30.

Getting There & Away Stagecoach (☎ 01604-20077) operates regular buses to Didcot and Swindon. A Sunday Rover ticket lets you travel throughout the area for £5.

The White Horse

About 6 miles west of Wantage, a stylised image of a horse cut into the hillside is probably the most famous chalk figure in Europe. Why this mysterious figure (114m long and 49m wide) was carved into the turf about 2000 years ago is unclear. How the artist managed to get the lines and perspective exact when the whole horse can only be seen from a distance is a mystery.

Above the chalk figure are the grass-covered earthworks of Uffington Castle. From the Ridgeway Youth Hostel, near Wantage, a wonderful 5 mile walk leads along the Ridgeway to the White Horse.

Thomas Hughes, author of *Tom Brown's Schooldays*, was born in Uffington village. His house is now a museum. *The Craven* (☎ 01367-820449) is a thatched farmhouse offering B&B for around £20.

HENLEY-ON-THAMES
• pop 11,000   ☎ 01491

Henley is world famous for its rowing regatta, one of those awfully English occa-sions of boaters and blazers, strawberries and cream, which these days tend to be commandeered by the high ranks of the corporate entertainers.

The stately High St is dominated by St Mary's Church, which dates back to the 13th century. Above the arches of Henley Bridge, built in 1786, are sculptures of Isis and Father Thames. Two fine coaching inns, the Red Lion and the Angel, stand sentinel at the High St end of the bridge. Both predate their 18th century heyday, and have played host to many eminent people, from the Duke of Wellington to James Boswell.

The TIC (☎ 578034) is in the basement of the town hall on Market Place. In summer there's also a booth in Mill Meadows.

Henley Royal Regatta

In 1829, the first Oxford and Cambridge boat race took place between Hambledon Lock and Henley Bridge. Ten years later the regatta was developed to enhance Henley's growing reputation.

Each year, in the first week of July, the regatta still plays host to the beau monde. Despite its peculiar mix of pomposity and eccentricity, it's a serious event that attracts rowers of the highest calibre.

There are two main areas for spectators – the stewards' enclosure and the public enclosure – although most people appear to take little interest in what's happening on the water. Epicurean picnics are consumed, large quantities of Pimm's (an alcoholic fruit cup) and champagne are drunk, and it's still a vital fixture in the social calendar. Those with contacts in the rowing or corporate worlds can get tickets to the stewards' enclosure; others pay £5 for a day ticket to the public enclosure on Wednesday, Thursday or Friday, £6 at weekends.

River & Rowing Museum

Henley recently acquired a purpose-built museum designed by minimalist architect David Chipperfield in which to display paintings and artefacts associated with the history of Henley and with the River Thames and rowing. Like all the best modern museums,

MIDLANDS

the River & Rowing Museum (☎ 415600) harnesses modern technology to liven up its story. The views from the building are lovely, and there is, of course, a café and shop.

It's open daily from 10 am to 5 pm (from 11 am on Sunday) and admission costs £4.95/3.75. The museum is in Mill Meadows, with its own car park.

Places to Stay

If you want to stay anywhere near Henley during the regatta you need to book weeks in advance. Even at quiet times B&Bs are relatively pricey.

Camping The *Swiss Farm International Camping* (☎ 573419) site is a quarter of a mile out of Henley on the Marlow Rd. Pitching a tent costs £8.

B&Bs and Guesthouses *No 4 Riverside* (☎ 571133, 4 River Terrace) has rooms facing the river from £35. Or try *Alftrudis* (☎ 573099, 8 Norman Ave), a friendly B&B about a five minute walk from the centre; doubles cost from £40 to £50 with bath. *Avalon* (☎ 577829, 36 Queen St) charges from £20 per person.

Lenwade (☎ 573468, 3 Western Rd) has three double rooms from £40 (from £20 for single occupancy). *Abbotsleigh* (☎ 572982, 107 St Marks Rd) has doubles with a bath for £48.

Places to Eat

Several pubs offer reasonably priced food. Near the TIC, the *Three Tuns* (5 Market Place) does good bar meals, including Sunday lunch for £5.25. Alternatively, there are branches of *Café Rouge* (☎ 411733) and *Caffe Uno* (☎ 411099) facing each other in the High St, and nearby is a *Pizza Express* (35 Market Place). *Henley Tea Rooms* faces onto the river on River Terrace, and you can get high tea with all the trimmings for £4.70 at the *Old Rope Walk* (High St).

Getting There & Away

Henley is 21 miles south-east of Oxford on the A423 and 40 miles west of London.

Stagecoach bus No X39 (☎ 01565-772250) links Henley with Oxford and Abingdon.

To get from Henley to Oxford by train you must change in Twyford or Reading. Henley to London Paddington takes about one hour and costs £6.70.

Getting Around

Henley is the perfect place to indulge in a bit of messing about on the river, and plenty of boat companies near the bridge are ready to help you enjoy yourself. On summer Sundays the *New Orleans* (☎ 572035) organises cruises from £14 a head. Shorter trips to Hambledon Lock and back cost £3.85/2.85. To hire a five seater rowing boat costs £9.50 an hour.

AROUND HENLEY-ON-THAMES
Stonor Park

Stonor Park (☎ 01491-638587) has been occupied by the Stonor family, an unrepentant Catholic family that has suffered much indignity since the Reformation, for over 800 years. The house has a fine collection of paintings, including works by Tintoretto and Caracci.

Stonor Park is 5 miles north of Henley. You need your own transport to get here. It's open on Sunday in April, Wednesday and Sunday from May to September, plus Thursday in July and August, and Saturday in August. Opening hours are 2 to 5.30 pm; entry is £4.50.

Gloucestershire

Straddling the River Severn to the west, Gloucestershire is the source of the traditional picture of rustic, rosy-cheeked England typified by the Cotswolds, the limestone escarpment overlooking the Severn Vale between Bath and Chipping Campden. It's a region of stunningly pretty, honey-coloured stone villages and remarkable views. Some of the villages are extremely popular; the best way to escape the commercialism is to explore on foot or by bike.

Accommodation can be pricey, with few hostels or camping grounds.

The Severn Vale nurtures Cheltenham (Britain's best preserved Regency town), Tewkesbury (with a beautiful abbey) and Gloucester (the capital, with a historic cathedral) as well as Berkeley Castle and Slimbridge Wildfowl Trust. To the west, and geographically part of Wales, are the Forest of Dean, and, bordering Wales, the beautiful Wye Valley (see the South Wales chapter).

WALKS & CYCLE ROUTES

Gloucestershire and the Cotswolds are perfect for walking and cycling, with plenty of quiet roads, mild but rewarding gradients and fine pubs.

The 100 mile Cotswold Way (see Walking in the Activities chapter) runs from Bath to Chipping Campden. TICs stock walking guides and a useful pack of *Cycle Touring Routes in Gloucestershire*. Bartholomew's *Cycling in the Cotswolds* (£8.99) gives full details. The Cotswold Cycling Company (☎ 01242-250642) organises mountain-bike tours of the region, starting from Cheltenham, while Cotswold Country Cycles (☎ 01386-438706) rents out bikes for £10 a day from Chipping Campden.

Several companies offer guided or unguided walking tours; try Cotswold Walking Holidays (☎ 01242-254353), 10 Royal Parade, Bayshill Rd, Cheltenham.

GETTING AROUND

Some TICs stock local bus timetables, or you can phone the Gloucestershire public transport inquiry line for details (☎ 01452-425543). Limited as it is, the Cotswolds bus service is still more comprehensive than the rail network, which skims the northern and southern borders.

NORTH COTSWOLDS

The northern Cotswolds are characterised by charming villages of soft, mellow stone built in folds between the rolling wolds. Although they owed their being to the medieval wool industry, most now rely on tourism for a living. A handful have been overwhelmed, but even these repay a look.

Northleach
- **pop 1000**   ☎ **01451**

Off the A40 from Oxford, Northleach clusters around a market square. The village is a marvellous mixture of architectural styles and evocative names and is home to perhaps the finest of the wool churches, a masterpiece of the Cotswold perpendicular style, with an unrivalled collection of medieval memorial brasses. Near the square is Oak House, a 17th century wool house that contains **Keith Harding's World of Mechanical Music** (☎ 860181), a collection of clocks and musical boxes; admission costs £5/2.50. Just as interesting is the **Cotswold Countryside Collection** in the old Northleach House of Correction on the Fosse Way, once a model 19th century prison. It's open April to October from Monday to Saturday from 10 am to 5 pm (Sunday from 2 pm) for £2.50/80p. The TIC (☎ 860715) is housed in the prison.

About 4 miles south-west of Northleach is **Chedworth Roman Villa** (☎ 01242-890256, NT) in a peaceful setting. Built around 120 AD for a wealthy landowner, it contains some wonderful mosaics illustrating the seasons. Most of the year it's open daily (except Monday) from 10 am to 5 pm (4 pm in winter). Admission costs £3.20.

Market House (☎ 860557, *Market Square*) offers B&B for £21/36 a single/double. *Bank Villas Guest House* (☎ 860464, *West End*) has rooms for £20/36. The *Sherborne Arms*, *Red Lion* and *Wheatsheaf*, all around the main square, are the readiest sources of sustenance.

Northleach is 9 miles from Burford (Oxfordshire) and 13 miles from Cheltenham. Swanbrook (☎ 01452-712386) runs several buses a day between Cheltenham and Oxford via Northleach.

Bibury
- **pop 500**   ☎ **01285**

Described by William Morris as 'the most beautiful village in England', Bibury is a

MIDLANDS

delightful place that manages to retain some dignity despite the hordes of visitors.

The River Coln flows alongside the road and is filled with trout, which you can pay to fatten at the local trout farm. There are some lovely houses, most notably **Arlington Row**, a line of National Trust (NT) owned weavers' cottages. Opposite is Rack Isle, where cloth was once dried after weaving and fulling (compressing) in the 17th century **Arlington Mill**, now a folk museum (☎ 740368). The mill is open from Easter to October from 10 am to 6 pm (5 pm in winter); admission costs £2/1.40.

If you want to splash out, try *Bibury Court* (☎ 740337) where singles/doubles cost £50/76. *Jenny Wren's Tearoom* offers afternoon tea so filling you won't need dinner.

Bourton-on-the-Water
- pop 2600   ☎ 01451

Bourton is certainly attractive, with the River Windrush passing beneath a series of low bridges in the village centre and an array of handsome houses in Cotswold stone, but why it's become such a honey pot is a mystery.

To justify the large area set aside for coaches and cars, a number of specific attractions (model railway and village, perfume exhibition, maze) have opened in the village. A serious bird conservation project, **Birdland** (☎ 820480), started after the owner purchased two islands in the Falklands to save the local penguin colonies. It's open daily from 10 am to 6 pm and costs £4/2.

Tearooms and restaurants line the main street. The best times to see Bourton are summer evenings after the coaches have left, or winter.

The Slaughters

Along with Bourton-on-the-Water, the Slaughters, Upper and Lower, are the most famously picturesque villages of the Cotswolds. Their repellent name is actually a corruption of a Saxon word meaning 'place of sloe trees'.

The best way to enjoy the Slaughters is to spend an hour walking to them from Bourton. Following part of the Warden's

Way will take you across the Fosse Way from Bourton, over a meadow and along a path into Lower Slaughter. Continuing past the Victorian flour mill, the route crosses meadows and goes behind the Manor House into Upper Slaughter. The mill is open daily from March through October from 10 am to 6 pm; admission is £1.50/75p.

Stow-on-the-Wold
- pop 2000   ☎ 01451

At almost 240m, Stow-on-the-Wold is the highest town in the Cotswolds, the windswept meeting point of eight routes and the site of the last Civil War battle. The pretty main square resembles an Italian piazza. The Royalist Hotel claims to be England's oldest inn; some of its timbers have been carbon dated to the 10th century.

The TIC (☎ 831082), Hollis House, is on the square.

Places to Stay *Stow-on-the-Wold Youth Hostel* (☎ 830497, east side of Market Square) charges £8/5.40 per night for adults/juniors, and is open daily from April to early September. Phone for other opening times.

Otherwise cheap accommodation is thin on the ground. The *White Hart Inn* (☎ 830674, The Square) has singles/doubles for £20/32, while the attractive *Gate Lodge* (☎ 832103, Stow Hill), half a mile out of the centre, charges £20/34 for rooms. Another possibility, also charging from £34 a double, is *The Limes* (☎ 830034, Evesham Rd).

Getting There & Away Pulhams Coaches (☎ 01451-820369) operates a daily service linking Stow with Moreton-in-Marsh (15 minutes), and a Monday to Saturday service to Cheltenham (45 minutes).

The nearest train stations are 4 miles away at Kingham and Moreton-in-Marsh.

Moreton-in-Marsh
- pop 2600   ☎ 01608

Straddling the Fosse Way, Moreton may not be the most attractive Cotswold town, but has some of the best transport connections.

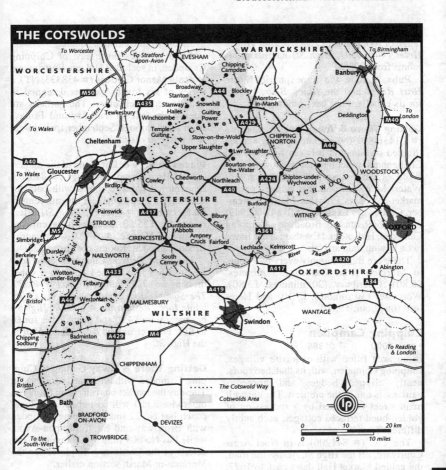

THE COTSWOLDS

The Cotswold Way

Cotswolds Area

0   10   20 km

0   5   10 miles

It's nowhere near a marsh (a corruption of March, meaning boundary) and grew first as a staging post and then as a railway town. Its Tuesday market, an old-fashioned affair with over 200 stalls, is worth a look.

About 2 miles from Moreton is spectacular, Moghul-style **Sezincote House**, built in 1805 by Charles Cockerell of the East India Company and thought to have inspired Brighton Pavilion. There are tours of the house on Thursday and Friday afternoons in May, June, July and September. Entry is £4.50 for the house and garden, £3/1 for the garden only. The garden is open from 2 to 6 pm on the same days from January to November.

Places to Stay & Eat The nearest hostel is in Stow-on-the-Wold, 4 miles south. B&Bs in Moreton include *Treetops* (☎ 651036, *London Rd*), which has singles/doubles with bathroom for £30/42. About a mile from the centre, *Rest Harrow* (☎ 650653, *Evenlode Rd*) does B&B for £16/28. **Moreton House**

(☎ *650747, High St)* has a restaurant and a range of rooms from £22/42. *Manor House Hotel (☎ 650501, High St)* has luxurious rooms from £65/90.

Pubs include the atmospheric *White Hart Royal* and the *Black Bear*, known for its excellent hot beef sandwiches.

Getting There & Away Pulhams Coaches (☎ 01451-820369) operates a daily service (limited on Sunday) between Moreton and Cheltenham (one hour) via Stow-on-the-Wold (15 minutes) and Bourton-on-the-Water. Many surrounding villages put on market-day buses. From late May to September, Castleways Explorer (☎ 01242-602949) bus No 569 runs to Broadway, Chipping Campden, Hidcote and Evesham and is timed to tie in with train arrivals.

There are trains roughly every two hours to Moreton from Oxford (35 minutes, £6.80), Charlbury (20 minutes, £3.80), Worcester (30 minutes, £7.10) and Hereford (one hour, £9.80).

Chipping Campden
• pop 2000   ☎ 01386

In an area filled with exquisite villages, Chipping Campden, with its thatched roofs, neatly clipped hedges and gorgeous gardens, is one of the prettiest. The unspoilt main street is flanked by a succession of golden-hued terraced cottages, each subtly different from the next.

The TIC (☎ 841206) is in Noel Arms Courtyard, off the High St. Across the road, the gabled Market Hall dates back to 1627. At the west end is **St James**, one of the finest Cotswold wool churches with some splendid 17th century monuments. Nearby are the Jacobean lodges and gateways of the vanished manor house, and opposite is a remarkable row of **almshouses**.

Above the town, **Dover's Hill** is named after Robert Dover, who instigated the 17th century Cotswold Olimpick Games, recently reinstated. The games take place on Spring Bank Holiday and include sports such as slippery pole climbing and welly wanging, culminating in a torch-lit proces-

sion and dancing in the square. Transport is available from Campden square.

About 4 miles north-east of Chipping Campden, in secluded Hidcote Bartrim, are **Hidcote Manor Gardens** (☎ 438333, NT), a series of six lovely gardens designed to complement each other. The gardens are open daily (except Tuesday and Friday) from April through September from 11 am to 7 pm; entry is £5.50.

Places to Stay & Eat None of the numerous B&Bs is cheap. *Sparlings (☎ 840505, Leysbourne)* has two rooms with bath for £27/46.50 a single/double. Fifteenth century *Badgers Hall (☎ 840839, High St)* offers rooms for £35/50. Readers have enjoyed staying at *Marnic (☎ 840014)* in nearby Broad Campden. Rooms cost from £25/40.

The *Eight Bells* in Church St does delicious dishes like braised lamb in a caper dressing for £7.50. *Badger Bistro (☎ 840520, The Square)* does Sunday lunch for £5.75, while *Joel's Restaurant (☎ 840598, High St)* has pasta from £4.95 and main dishes for £6 to £13. For a cream tea try *Badgers Hall* in the High St.

Getting There & Away Getting to Chipping Campden without a car is tricky. On Tuesday the market bus runs from Moreton, otherwise a taxi will cost about £8. Stagecoach bus No 22 links Chipping Campden with Broadway and Stratford-upon-Avon, while bus No 608 runs to Cheltenham. For details of the Castleways Explorer see the Moreton-in-Marsh section earlier.

Getting Around You can hire a bike from Cotswold Country Cycles (☎ 438706), Longlands Farm Cottage, for £10 a day or £60 a week.

Broadway
• pop 2000   ☎ 01386

Just over the border in Worcestershire, this well-known and much visited village is strung out along two sides of a broad street, beneath the crest of an escarpment. Undeniably handsome, and largely unspoilt despite its fame, it has inspired artists and writers from JM Barrie to Edward Elgar. A new bypass has brought some relief from through traffic although coaches still manage to cause maximum chaos in high summer.

The most striking house is the Lygon Arms, now a famous hotel. The unspoilt medieval **Church of St Eadburgha** is signposted from the town, a 30 minute walk away. For a longer walk, take the footpath opposite the church which leads up to **Broadway Tower** (☎ 852390), a crenellated 18th century folly that stands above the town with a small William Morris exhibition on one floor. On a clear day you can see 12 counties from the top. Entry is £3/2.20.

The TIC (☎ 852937) is at 1 Cotswold Court, alongside some interesting shops.

Places to Stay & Eat Broadway has lots of high-quality accommodation but the luxury is inevitably pricey. The excellent *Cinnibar Cottage* (☎ 858623, 45 Bury End) is about half a mile from the centre and charges £25/36 for a single/double. The *Olive Branch Guest House* (☎ 853440, 78 High St) has rooms from £19.50/48.

The best place to stay is the *Lygon Arms* (☎ 852255, High St) – if your gold card will stretch to £98/155. Its restaurant, *Olivers*, does dishes like fish cakes in sorrel sauce for £8.75. For cheaper meals try *Roberto's Coffee House*, one of the few places open on Sunday.

Getting There & Away Broadway is 6 miles from Evesham (see the Herefordshire & Worcestershire section later in this chapter) and 9 miles from Moreton-in-Marsh. Castleways (☎ 01242-602949) runs buses to Cheltenham via Hailes and Winchcombe (one hour, £1.45) and Evesham (25 minutes, £1.05).

Snowshill
About 3 miles south of Broadway, **Snowshill Manor** (☎ 01386-852410, NT) is furnished with an extraordinarily eclectic collection of items, from Japanese armour to Victorian perambulators gathered by the eccentric

Charles Paget Wade. The walled gardens are particularly delightful and the restaurant has wonderful views. It's open daily (except Tuesday) from April through October from 1 to 5 pm (timed tickets are issued for the cramped house); entry is £5.50. It's an uphill walk to get here from Broadway.

Hailes
About 3 miles north-east of Winchcombe along the Cotswold Way, this former Cistercian abbey, now a romantic ruin, was once an important place of pilgrimage; people came from all over Europe to see the phial of Christ's blood kept here. After the dissolution of the monasteries, the blood was exposed as a mixture of honey and saffron. **Hailes Abbey** (☎ 01242-602398, EH) is open daily from Easter through October, but weekends only for the rest of the year; entry is £2.50/1.90.

The small neighbouring **church**, with medieval stained glass, murals and heraldic tiles, is delightful. A short walk away are the organic Hayles Fruit Farm (good cider) and Orchard Tea Room.

Winchcombe
• pop 5000   ☎ 01242
Saxon Winchcombe was the capital of its own county and the seat of Mercian royalty. Its Benedictine abbey was one of the country's main pilgrimage centres.

These days its main attraction is **Sudeley Castle** (☎ 604357), where the chapel houses the tomb of Catherine Parr, Henry VIII's last wife. Parts of the original building have been left in ruins, but the rest was restored in the 19th century. It's open daily from Easter to October from 11 am to 5.30 pm; admission is £5.50/3. The gardens are especially beautiful.

In the village proper, splendid **St Peter's Church** is noted for its fine gargoyles, including one that looks like Lewis Carroll's Mad Hatter.

An excellent 2½ mile hike along the Cotswold Way leads to **Belas Knap**, a false-entrance burial chamber built about 5000 years ago. The TIC (☎ 602925), in the High St, has information about other local walks.

MIDLANDS

Places to Stay & Eat The *Courtyard House* (☎ 602441, *High St*) has two double rooms for £35 each, while half-timbered *Wesley House* (☎ 602366, *High St*) charges £48/60 for a single/double (dinner in the excellent restaurant is £21.50). Farther out, *Blair House* (☎ 603626, *41 Gretton Rd*) has beds from £17.50. *Almsbury Farm* (☎ 602405, *by the entrance to Sudeley Castle*), about a mile from the centre, charges £25/44.

Wincelcumbe Tearooms (☎ 603578, *7 Hailes St*) does soup with tasty rosemary and raisin bread for £2.25 and a cream tea for £2.70.

Poachers Restaurant (☎ 604566, *6 North St*), round the corner from the TIC, has main dishes from £8 to £11. The *Shepherd English Restaurant* (☎ 604434, *High St*) does traditional three-course dinners for £11.95.

The *Old White Lion* in North St is an inviting 15th century pub. The *Plaisterers Arms*, near the church, does good meals and real ales.

Getting There & Away Castleways Coaches (☎ 602949) runs buses almost hourly, Monday to Saturday, from Winchcombe to Cheltenham (30 minutes), Broadway (30 minutes) and Evesham.

Guiting Power & Temple Guiting

The Guitings lie about 4 miles east of Winchcombe. Set around a green, Guiting Power is particularly attractive, with a shop, post office and two pubs. It even has its own music festival in July, and a remarkable Norman doorway to its church. Nearby, the **Cotswold Farm Park** (☎ 01451-850307) preserves endangered species of farm animals like the Gloucester old spot pig. It's open daily from April through October from 10 am to 5 pm (6 pm on Sunday) and costs £3.50/1.80.

SOUTH COTSWOLDS

The southern Cotswolds are quite different in character to the northern area: the stone is more soberly coloured, the valleys are steeper and the area is less reliant on tourism. If you want to get away from the Cotswold honey pots, it's worth exploring some of these villages.

Painswick

• pop 2800   ☎ 01452

Sometimes called the 'Queen of the Cotswolds', Painswick is a picture-perfect Cotswold village. **St Mary's Church** is particularly interesting, its graveyard bristling with the table-top tombs of rich wool merchants who made the town prosperous from the 17th century. The yew trees are said to be uncountable but certainly number no more than 99; if the 100th should grow, legend claims the devil will shrivel it. The church tower still has Civil War cannonball scars.

The streets behind the church are lined with handsome merchants' houses. Bisley St, with several 14th century houses, was the original thoroughfare, while New St is a medieval addition. Rare iron spectacle stocks stand in the street just south of the church.

Painswick Rococo Garden The gardens of Painswick House (☎ 813204), half a mile north of the town, are open from mid-January through November from Wednesday to Sunday from 11 am to 5 pm. They're best visited in February or March for the spectacular snowdrop displays. Admission costs £3/1.60.

Places to Stay & Eat The pleasant *Hambutts Mynd* (☎ 812352, *Edge Rd*) caters especially for Cotswold Way walkers, with singles/doubles for £21/40. Inquire at Rudge House about camping beside Edge Rd at *Hambutt's Field* (☎ 812495) for £2.

Centrally positioned, *Cardynham House* (☎ 814006, *The Cross*) has rooms from £36/46; it dates back to the 15th century. Sixteenth century *Thorne* (☎ 812476, *Friday St*) has two doubles for £50. *Painswick Hotel* (☎ 812160, *Kemps Lane*) is the best hotel, with luxurious rooms from £80/105, many with views over the valley.

The *Royal Oak* (☎ 813129, *St Mary's St*) is a popular local. The *Country Elephant*

(☎ *813564, New St*) does great food but you're looking at £25 per head for dinner. *Bertram's Café-Bistro*, opposite the church, is more hopeful, with ploughman's lunches for £4.50.

Getting There & Away Bus No 46 connects Cheltenham with Painswick fairly frequently. The No 23 from Gloucester is far more hit and miss.

Stroud

• pop 37,800   ☎ 01453

The narrow, steep-sided Stroud Valley stands out from the rest of the southern Cotswolds and was the scene of the Cotswold wool industry's final fling.

Stroud is built around a spur above the River Frome. Very little cloth is produced today although Stroudwater scarlet used to be famous throughout the world. Many of the old mill buildings remain, though most now have new uses. A walk around Stroud's hilly streets should take in the old Shambles market (Wednesday, Friday and Saturday), the Tudor town hall and, if it has reopened, the Stroud Museum. The Stroud Subscription Rooms on George St house the TIC (☎ 765768).

Places to Stay & Eat The *London Hotel* (☎ *759992, opposite the town centre car park*) does B&B from £27.50 a head. *Fern Rock House* (☎ *757307, 72 Middle St*) charges £16/30 for singles/doubles, while the nonsmoking *Deben House* (☎ *766573, off the London Rd*) charges from £19.50/38.

In Union St, the *Pelican* serves pub lunches, or there are several cafés in the pedestrianised High St, behind the TIC. Try *Woodruff's Organic Café*, where filled potatoes cost from £1.50, or *Mills Café*, which is down an alley and has a few outdoor tables.

Getting There & Away Stagecoach Stroud Valleys (☎ 763421) is the main local operator; No 46 runs every two hours to Painswick (10 minutes, 96p) and Chel-

tenham (40 minutes, £1.50). No 93 operates hourly to Gloucester (45 minutes, £1.40).

Slimbridge

Eleven miles south-west of Gloucester, the **Slimbridge Wildfowl & Wetlands Trust** (☎ 01453-890065) was established in 1946 by the late Sir Peter Scott as a breeding ground for wildfowl, notably geese and swans. Open daily from 9.30 am to 5.30 pm, the centre is as interesting in winter (closes at 4.30 pm), when Arctic 'visitors' arrive, as it is in summer. Entry is £5.25/3, and is discounted if you stay the night before at *Slimbridge Youth Hostel* (☎ *01453-890275*), half a mile south across the Sharpness Canal. The hostel is open from March through August; phone to check other times. The nightly charge is £9.75/6.55 for adults/juniors.

Badgerline's (☎ 0117-955 3231) No 308 service links Bristol with Gloucester and passes by the Slimbridge crossroads, 2 miles from the centre. On Sunday, Stagecoach operates one bus to and from the sanctuary; phone ☎ 01452-527516 for exact times.

Berkeley

☎ 01453

This quiet Georgian town is best known as the place where Edward II met his grisly end in **Berkeley Castle** (☎ 810332). His last days must have been as awful as his death (supposedly impaled on a red-hot poker); the ventilation shaft in the murder room was connected to a pit in which the rotting carcasses of dead animals were kept.

The beautiful medieval castle is set in terraced Elizabethan gardens surrounded by lawns. It's open from June through September from Tuesday to Saturday from 11 am to 5 pm (from 1 pm on Sunday); at other times of the year opening hours are more restricted. Entry is £4.95/2, or £1.75/90p just for the grounds. The **Butterfly Farm** across the car park opens one hour after the castle. Admission is £1.75/85p.

A path winds through **St Mary's** churchyard, with its unusual detached bell tower, to the **Jenner Museum** (☎ 810631), in the house where Edward Jenner performed the first smallpox vaccination in 1796. Opening hours are virtually the same as the castle's. Entry is £2/75p.

Berkeley is 6 miles south-west of Slimbridge. Badgerline's No 308 bus from Bristol to Gloucester passes this way.

Tetbury
- **pop 4500**   ☎ **01666**

East of Wotton, on the A433, Tetbury has an interesting 18th century Gothic church with a graceful spire and wonderful interior. The 17th century Market House was used for wool trading. The TIC (☎ 503552) is at Old Court House in Long St.

Westonbirt (☎ 880220) is a huge arboretum with a magnificent selection of temperate trees, is 2½ miles south-west of Tetbury. Walks through the trees are particularly stunning in spring and autumn. It's open daily from 10 am to 8 pm (or sunset). Admission costs £3.50/1.

Lechlade
☎ **01367**

At the highest navigable point of the River Thames, Lechlade is graced by the spire of St Lawrence's Church, described as an 'aerial pile' by Shelley in 1815 in his poem *A Summer Evening Churchyard, Lechlade, Gloucestershire*. A wool church, it was rededicated to the Spanish saint by Catherine of Aragon, who held the manor in the 16th century.

About 3 miles east of Lechlade off the Faringdon road, **Kelmscott Manor** (☎ 252486) was home to William Morris, the poet, artist and founder of the Arts and Crafts movement. It's open from April to September on Wednesday only from 11 am to 1 pm and 2 to 5 pm; entry is £6/3. The Memorial Cottages nearby feature a beautiful carving of Morris seated under a tree.

Fairford

Fairford's claim to fame is **St Mary's Church**, which houses Britain's only complete set of medieval stained-glass windows. The gift of wealthy wool merchant John Tame, who also rebuilt the church, the windows are thought to be by Barnard Flower, master glass painter to Henry VII. Tiddles, the church cat, is buried in the churchyard. The High St largely consists of graceful 18th century houses.

CIRENCESTER
- **pop 13,500**   ☎ **01285**

Cirencester is about 12 miles south of Cheltenham. Founded as a military base at the junction of the Roman Akeman St, Fosse Way and Ermin Way, it started life as Corinium, the second largest Roman town after London. Eventually it was one of the principal towns of north-west Europe. The 2nd century amphitheatre, on Cotswold Ave, is mostly grassed over, but was one of the largest in the country. The Saxons destroyed the town in the 6th century and built smaller settlements outside the walls, renaming it Cirencester. It only really regained its status in the Middle Ages when it became the most important Cotswold wool town.

These days it's an affluent medium-sized town with several worthwhile sights. Weekly markets still take place every Monday and Friday.

The centre clusters round the parish church on the Market Square, where you'll also find the TIC (☎ 654180), in the Corn Hall.

Church of St John the Baptist

One of England's largest churches, St John's seems more like a cathedral. It has a magnificent perpendicular-style tower, built with the reward given by Henry IV to a group of earls who foiled a rebellion. The highlight of the exterior, however, is the three storey south porch, which faces the square. Built as an office by late 15th century abbots, it subsequently became the medieval town hall.

Inside the church several memorial brasses record the matrimonial histories of important wool merchants. A 15th century painted stone pulpit comes complete with hourglass and the east window contains fine medieval stained glass. A wall safe displays the Boleyn Cup, made for Anne Boleyn,

New Forest, Hampshire

Cityscape of the High Street, Oxford

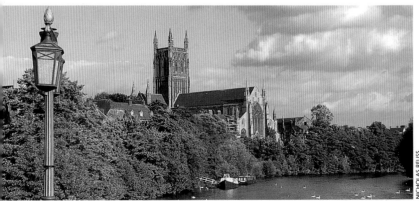

Worcester Cathedral on the River Severn, Worcester

National Tramway Museum, Derbyshire

Town crier, Manchester

Hanchurch Woods, Staffordshire

The Radcliffe Camera, Oxford

Cock Pheasant

second wife of Henry VIII, in 1535. The church is also notable for the oldest 12-bell peal in the country and continues to observe the ringing of the 'pancake bell' on Shrove Tuesday and the celebration of the Restoration on 29 May.

Corinium Museum

This museum (☎ 655611) in Park St shows local Roman finds in tableaux complete with impressive mosaics. It's open daily Monday to Saturday from 10 am to 5 pm (2 to 5 pm on Sunday); it's closed on Monday in winter. Entry is £2.50/80p.

Cirencester Park

On the western edge of town, this park features magnificent geometrical landscaping, designed with the help of the poet Alexander Pope. The Broad Ride makes an excellent short walk.

The was house built by the First Earl Bathurst between 1714 and 1718 and hides behind one of the world's highest yew hedges. It's not open to the public.

Places to Stay

Camping If you're prepared to swap lack of facilities for a cheap stay, there's camping space for £2 at *Abbey Home Farm* (☎ 652808), an organic farm a mile north of Cirencester on the Northleach road.

Hostel *Duntisbourne Abbots Youth Hostel* (☎ 821682) is 5 miles north-west of Cirencester in a Victorian vicarage. It's open daily (except Sunday) from April through October. The nightly charge is £8/5.40 for adults/juniors, and the hostel is renowned for its good food. You need your own transport to get here.

B&Bs & Hotels Victoria Rd has several B&Bs and guesthouses. *Apsley Villa Guest House* (☎ 653489, 16 Victoria Rd) has five rooms from £20/35 for a single/double. *26 Victoria Rd* (☎ 656440) has just three rooms, for £15/25. *Wimborne House* (☎ 653890, 91 Victoria Rd), which is nonsmoking, has rooms with bath from £25/35.

The *White Lion Inn* (☎ 654053, 8 Gloucester St) is a 17th century coaching inn five minutes walk from the town centre. Rooms with bath are from £35/45. The *Golden Cross* (☎ 652137, Black Jack St) has rooms from £18/30.

The comfortable *Kings Head Hotel* (☎ 653322, Market Place) is opposite the church. Rooms cost £63/80, less for two days or more.

During college holidays, rooms are available at the *Royal Agricultural College* (☎ 652531), on the northern outskirts. Beds cost from £21.50 a head.

Places to Eat

Cirencester has plenty of good places to eat, especially in Castle St where *Pizza Provencale* (☎ 650092) makes tasty pizzas from £5.30, the *Rajdoot Tandoori* (☎ 652651) has Sunday eat-as-much-as-you-want lunches for £6.95 (£4.95 vegetarian), and *Tatyans* (☎ 653529) does the sort of Chinese that makes the pages of the good food guides.

For lighter lunches try *The Café-Bar (Brewers Courtyard)*, off Cricklade St, which has a range of filled baguettes and ciabatta rolls from £1.95. There's another *café* inside the Brewery Arts Centre (☎ 657181) opposite, but both are closed on Sunday.

Keith's Coffee Shop and the *Black Jack Coffee House* in Black Jack St are good places to pause for refreshment, while the *Swan Yard Café (6 Swan Yard)* does mouthwatering cakes.

For putting together a picnic you could hardly better *Jeroboams*, beside the church, where they claim to 'build' sandwiches rather than make them. The filled pastries are pretty scrummy too.

There's a branch of the *Slug & Lettuce* near Market Place, while *The Mad Hatter Wine Bar* in Castle St serves pub-style lunches. There's real ale at the otherwise dingy *Courtyard Bar* down the alley under the Kings Head, and good pub food at *The Black Horse* in Castle St.

Getting There & Away

National Express buses run from Cirencester to London (2¼ hours, £9.75).

Stagecoach (☎ 01242-522021) bus No 51 runs to Cheltenham every two hours (30 minutes, £1.45). The less frequent No 52 runs to Gloucester.

GLOUCESTER

- **pop 106,600   ☎ 01452**

The county capital (pronounced gloster) sits in the vale beneath the Cotswold escarpment and beside the River Severn. The city has suffered greatly from WWII bombing and unsympathetic urban planning but is still worth visiting, particularly for its wonderful Gothic cathedral and the cluster of museums in the restored docks. It also has some of the cheapest accommodation around, making it a good base for exploring the surrounding area.

History

To the Romans, Gloucester was Glevum, an important military stronghold against the Welsh tribesmen. It remained important to the Saxons as a garrison town at the junction of the kingdoms of Mercia and Wessex and grew to become a major monastic centre.

When Ethelred, Alfred the Great's brother, was buried in the Saxon royal palace near the cathedral, Gloucester equalled Winchester in importance and it remained so to the Normans.

In 1216, Henry III's coronation took place in St Peter's Abbey. After murdered Edward II was buried here, Gloucester became an important place of pilgrimage, which helped develop its commercial importance.

During the Civil War, the city was a Puritan stronghold and withstood a 26 day siege. In the 18th century Gloucester flour-

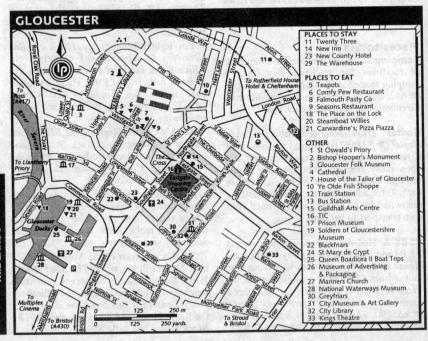

GLOUCESTER

PLACES TO STAY
11 Twenty Three
14 New Inn
23 New County Hotel
29 The Warehouse

PLACES TO EAT
5 Teapots
6 Comfy Pew Restaurant
8 Falmouth Pasty Co
9 Seasons Restaurant
18 The Place on the Lock
20 Steamboat Willies
21 Carwardine's; Pizza Piazza

OTHER
1 St Oswald's Priory
2 Bishop Hooper's Monument
3 Gloucester Folk Museum
4 Cathedral
7 House of the Tailor of Gloucester
10 Ye Olde Fish Shoppe
12 Train Station
13 Bus Station
15 Guildhall Arts Centre
16 TIC
17 Prison Museum
19 Soldiers of Gloucestershire Museum
22 Blackfriars
24 St Mary de Crypt
25 Queen Boadicea II Boat Trips
26 Museum of Advertising & Packaging
27 Mariners Church
28 National Waterways Museum
30 Greyfriars
31 City Museum & Art Gallery
32 City Library
33 Kings Theatre

Surfing the Severn Bore

A 'bore' is a tidal phenomenon that occurs when flood-tides pour into the wide mouth of an estuary in greater volume than can easily flow along the normal channel of the river. The incoming tide then sweeps over the slower river flow and pushes upstream, flooding the riverbanks as it goes.

In Britain the most striking bore occurs on the River Severn, the country's longest river. At its deepest point the Severn Bore can be 2.75m deep, although in October 1966 a bore measuring 2.82m and travelling at 13 miles an hour was recorded.

In recent years a new sport of bore-surfing has developed, with surfers, body-boarders and canoeists lining up to catch the wave. If they time it right they can ride for 1½ miles upriver, much to the irritation of traditionalists who think they're spoiling a great natural phenomenon.

The best places to see the Severn Bore are between Awre, where the estuary narrows, and Gloucester. Gloucester TIC will be able to tell you the dates to go bore-watching. Wear wellies, as the water floods the surrounding roads.

ished on the back of the Forest of Dean's iron, coal and timber industries. Throughout the 20th century it has been an industrial centre, producing at various times railway rolling stock, aircraft and motorcycles.

Orientation & Information

The city centre is based around Northgate, Southgate, Eastgate and Westgate Sts, which all converge on The Cross. The TIC (☎ 421188), in St Michael's Tower at The Cross, sells the *Via Sacra* town trail and a leaflet outlining the route of the 26 mile Glevum Way round the city outskirts. On Sunday, information is available from the tourist information point in the National Waterways Museum, Gloucester Docks.

Gloucester Cathedral

The city's focal point is still the gorgeous Gothic cathedral, one of the earliest examples of the English perpendicular style. Built as part of St Peter's Abbey, the cathedral's foundation stone was laid in 1089. When the abbey was dissolved in 1541, the church became the centre of the new Gloucester diocese. The nave has some wonderful Norman arcading, with the last two bays at the western end rebuilt in perpendicular style in 1420. Note how the south wall of the south aisle leans out of true because of the defensive ditch of the Roman town beneath.

The magnificent 69m-high tower was constructed from 1450 to replace the 13th century spire.

The newly restored east window, made in 1349 to commemorate local participation in the Battle of Crecy, is the largest in England, while the wooden choir stalls date from 1350. Above them soars wonderfully elaborate lierne vaulting. The late 15th century Lady Chapel represents the final flowering of the perpendicular style.

In the south ambulatory is an effigy of Robert, William the Conqueror's eldest son. Edward II's magnificent tomb, surmounted by an alabaster effigy, is in the north ambulatory.

The north transept, containing a 13th century reliquary, leads into the treasury and also gives access to the tribune gallery, with an exhibition on the cathedral's history (summer only). In the north aisle is a memorial to John Stafford Smith, a Gloucester composer who wrote the tune for the US national anthem.

At the west end stands a statue of Edward Jenner (1749-1823), who discovered how to vaccinate people against smallpox at nearby Berkeley.

The Great Cloister has the country's oldest fan vaulting, dating from the 14th century. Don't miss the stone basin for the monks to wash at, with niches for their towels across the way.

The cathedral (☎ 528095) is open daily from 8 am to 6 pm. Donations of £3 are requested. There are guided tours Monday to Saturday from 10.30 am to 12.30 pm.

Every third year Gloucester Cathedral hosts the Three Choirs Festival. It will be Gloucester's turn next in 2001.

Gloucester Docks

The present quay was first recorded in 1390. Direct trade with foreign ports started in 1580 and by 1780 some 600 ships a year were docking at Gloucester, although large ships generally got only as far as Bristol. The 15 warehouses in the dock area were built for the 19th century corn trade. Now redundant, they've been refurbished and most house museums, offices and restaurants.

Llanthony, the largest warehouse, houses the excellent **National Waterways Museum** (☎ 318054), which has a varied collection of historic vessels and imaginative displays. In summer it's open daily from 10 am to 6 pm (5 pm in winter); entry is £4.50/3.50.

The Albert Warehouse, part of the Victoria Dock, which specialised in salt transhipment, houses the **Museum of Advertising & Packaging** (☎ 302309), Robert Opie's nostalgia-provoking collection of packaging ephemera. It's open daily from 10 am to 5 pm. Entry is £2.95/95p.

In the old Custom House, the **Soldiers of Gloucestershire Museum** (☎ 522682) is livelier than most military museums. It's open Tuesday to Sunday from 10 am to 5 pm, and also on summer Mondays; entry is £3.50/1.90.

In Hempsted Lane, across Llanthony Bridge from the dock area, are the remains of **Llanthony Priory**, one of the richest Augustinian houses in England when it was dissolved in 1538.

Other Things to See

The **Gloucester Folk Museum** (☎ 526467), 99 Westgate St, is in a 16th century former clothier's house. Displays include a dairy, an ironmonger's shop and a Victorian schoolroom. It's open Monday to Saturday from 10 am to 5 pm (4 pm on Sunday from July through September only); entry is free. St Nicholas House, next door, was the

---

The Tailor of Gloucester

Beatrix Potter's own favourite story was apparently *The Tailor of Gloucester*, the famous children's story she wrote and illustrated in 1901 as a Christmas present for a friend.

While visiting cousins at Harescombe Grange, near Stroud, she heard a story about a real-life tailor, John Prichard of Gloucester. As in her tale, he'd been asked to make a waistcoat for the city's mayor. So busy was he that the Saturday before the Monday when the garment was due, he'd only reached the cutting stage. But when he returned to the shop on Monday, he found it complete, bar a single buttonhole. A note pinned to it read, 'No more twist'.

Mystified (but commercially minded), he placed an advert in his window imploring people to come to Prichard's where the 'waistcoats are made at night by the fairies'. Later it transpired that the tailor's assistants had finished the waistcoat after sleeping in the shop because they'd stayed out too late to get home.

John Prichard died in 1934 and his tombstone at Haresfield records that he was the Tailor of Gloucester. In Potter's version, the young tailor became an old one, the fairies became mice. She spent hours sketching on the streets of Gloucester and in local cottages. The house in Gloucester's College Court, which she chose as the tailor's fictional premises, is now a gift shop-cum-museum.

---

family home of the Whittingtons of pantomime fame, and one of those places where Elizabeth I slept. Nearby are the remains of St Oswald's Priory and St Mary de Lode, Gloucester's oldest church.

At 5 Southgate St, an Edwardian shop boasts a curious mechanical clock, with figures to represent the four countries making up the United Kingdom. **Blackfriars**,

Ladybellgate St, is Britain's finest surviving example of a Dominican friary. Entry is free and it's open daily.

Along Eastgate St are 15th century St Michael's Tower; Eastgate Market (pop inside to inspect the Beatrix Potter clock); and the remains of the East Gate itself. The **City Museum & Art Gallery** (☎ 524131), on Brunswick Rd, is open Monday to Saturday from 10 am to 5 pm. Entry is free and it's worth dropping by to see the beautiful Birdlip Mirror dating back to the 1st century AD.

Fans of the books will want to visit the recently renovated **Beatrix Potter Gift Shop** (☎ 422856), in the house that inspired the story of *The Tailor of Gloucester*.

In Barrack Square the **Prison Museum** (☎ 529551) opens from Easter through September from Monday to Saturday from 10 am to 4 pm. Admission costs £1/50p.

Places to Stay

Gloucester has a tiny independent hostel, the *Twenty Three* (☎ 418152, 23 Alvin St). Beds cost £8.50 each, but you should ring ahead to check if any are available. If it's full, *The Bunk House* (☎ 302351) in The Warehouse climbing centre in Parliament St has 12 beds in a very basic bunkroom for £3.50 each; there's a café bar downstairs. Phone ahead in case climbers have bagged all the beds.

Many people prefer to day-trip from nearby Cheltenham but *Westville Guesthouse* (☎ 301228, 255 Stroud Rd) does B&B from £16. Along London Rd are more B&Bs, including *Glenmore Guest House* (☎ 528840, 73 London Rd), less than a mile from the centre, which charges £14.

Rotherfield House Hotel (☎ 410500, 5 Horton Rd) has doubles from £46. At the time of writing the impressively galleried *New Inn* (☎ 522177, Northgate St) was closed for lack of an owner. It's worth checking whether it's reopened, as the rooms used to be perfectly presentable.

The *New County Hotel* (☎ 307000, Southgate St), a four minute walk from the centre, has doubles with showers or baths from £50.

Places to Eat

The cathedral *Undercroft*, in part of the former monastery great hall, is a good place for lunch or tea. Also near the cathedral are the *Comfy Pew Restaurant* (☎ 415648) and *Teapots* (☎ 306302), which both do teas, coffees and lunches. Opposite the Beatrix Potter shop try the *Seasons Restaurant* (☎ 307060) which does a two course lunch for £5.95. For fish and chips, go to *Ye Olde Fish Shoppe* (☎ 522502, Hare Lane), just east of the cathedral; prices are on the steep side but the nosh is thoroughly superior. The *Falmouth Pasty Co* rustles up fresh pasties from £1.

Gloucester Docks has several good places to eat. *The Place on the Lock* (☎ 330253), on the 1st floor of the Gloucester Docks Antiques Centre, is cheaper than you might fear (tea and scones for £2). The Kimberley Warehouse houses *Steamboat Willies* (☎ 300990) with Tex Mex dishes and pasta from £5.95. *Pizza Piazza* (☎ 311951), overlooking the water in Merchants Quay shopping centre, does pizzas from £3.95. There's also a *Carwardine's* coffee shop here.

Getting There & Away

Gloucester is 105 miles from London, 49 miles from Oxford, 45 miles from Bath and 16 miles from Cirencester. National Express has all the usual connections, and buses every two hours to London (3½ hours, £9.25). Stagecoach operates most local bus services; phone ☎ 01242-522021 for details. An Explorer ticket to use the Gloucestershire bus network for a day costs £3.50. There are buses every 15 minutes to Cheltenham (30 minutes, £1.20) but the quickest way to get there is by train (10 minutes, £3.20).

CHELTENHAM
- **pop 88,000**   ☎ **01242**

Cheltenham is probably best known for its racecourse and its public school, Cheltenham Ladies' College. The planners haven't been quite as kind to what is essentially a Regency town as they have to Bath, with which Cheltenham is often compared. The town's handsome squares, colourful public gardens and elegant early 19th century architecture are interspersed with dreary shopping areas. Whoever gave planning permission for the hideous Eagle Star office block defacing Bath Rd should probably consider another career.

With plenty of restaurants and accommodation, Cheltenham makes an ideal base for exploring the western Cotswolds. It's also the scene of four important festivals: the National Hunt Meeting in March, during which the Cheltenham Gold Cup is run; the Music and Cricket festivals in July; and the Literature Festival in October. At these times, places to stay are like gold dust.

History

As a village midway between Gloucester and Tewkesbury, and on the road to Winchcombe and Oxford, Cheltenham received its market charter in 1226, when it was little more than a row of houses each side of the current High St. It remained important after the Civil War when the area of the south Cotswolds became associated, briefly, with tobacco production but really started to flourish after 1788, when George III visited to take the waters.

In 1716, pigeons pecking in a field under what is now the Ladies' College turned out to be eating salt crystals from a spring. Following fashion, the owner's son-in-law built a substantial pump room and opened it to the public. The king's visit sealed the spa's future and several new wells were built, as well as houses to accommodate the hordes of visitors, among them Handel and Jane Austen.

Modern visitors usually find the architecture more interesting than the waters. The elegant Regency style is evident around town in beautifully proportioned terraces, mostly creamy white and decorated with wrought-iron balconies and railings.

Orientation

Cheltenham train station is out on a limb to the west; bus F or G will run you to the centre for 65p. The bus station is more conveniently positioned immediately behind The Promenade in the town centre.

Central Cheltenham is eminently walkable. The High St runs roughly east-west and south from it is The Promenade, the most elegant shopping area ('the Bond St of the West'). The Promenade extends into Montpellier, a 19th century shopping precinct, beyond which lie Suffolk Square and Lansdown Crescent. Pittville Park and the old Pump Room are a mile north of the High St.

Information

The helpful TIC (☎ 522878) is on The Promenade and sells all sorts of Cotswold walking and cycling guides, as well as *The Romantic Road*, a guide to a 30 mile circular driving tour of the south Cotswolds (£1.50). It also stocks a leaflet listing public transport options to the most popular tourist destinations around Cheltenham.

The Promenade

The Promenade is the heart of Cheltenham and is at its best in summer, when its hanging baskets are full of flowers.

The **Municipal Offices**, built as private residences in 1825, are one of the best features of one of Britain's most beautiful thoroughfares. In front of the offices stands a **statue of Edward Wilson** (1872-1912), a Cheltenham man who went on Captain Scott's ill-fated second expedition (1910-12) to the South Pole and died in Antarctica.

Following The Promenade towards Montpellier, you come to the **Imperial Gardens**, originally built to service the Imperial Spa but covered by the Winter Gardens in 1902. The iron-and-glass structure was dismantled during WWII in case its reflection attracted German bombers.

Pittville Pump Room

Set in a delightful area of villas and park a mile from the town centre, the Pump Room is the town's finest Regency-style building. Built between 1825 and 1830, it was constructed as a spa and social centre for Joseph Pitt's new estate. Upstairs, in the former

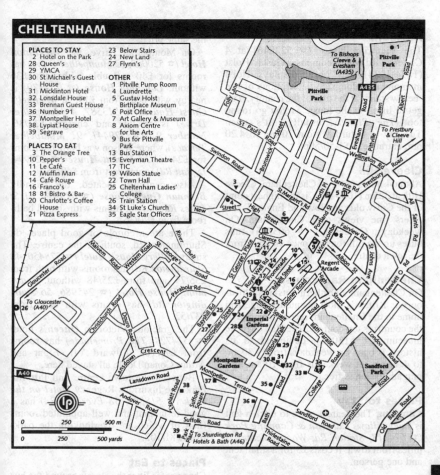

CHELTENHAM

PLACES TO STAY
2 Hotel on the Park
28 Queen's
29 YMCA
30 St Michael's Guest House
31 Micklinton Hotel
32 Lonsdale House
33 Brennan Guest House
36 Number 91
37 Montpellier Hotel
38 Lypiat House
39 Segrave

PLACES TO EAT
3 The Orange Tree
10 Pepper's
11 Le Café
12 Muffin Man
14 Café Rouge
16 Franco's
18 81 Bistro & Bar
20 Charlotte's Coffee House
21 Pizza Express

23 Below Stairs
24 New Land
27 Flynn's

OTHER
1 Pitville Pump Room
4 Laundrette
5 Gustav Holst Birthplace Museum
6 Post Office
7 Art Gallery & Museum
8 Axiom Centre for the Arts
9 Bus for Pittville Park
13 Bus Station
15 Everyman Theatre
17 TIC
19 Wilson Statue
22 Town Hall
25 Cheltenham Ladies' College
26 Train Station
34 St Luke's Church
35 Eagle Star Offices

library and billiard rooms, the Pittville Pump Room Museum (☎ 523852) displays historical costumes but looks rather sad since thieves made off with its fine jewellery collection. It's open daily (except Tuesday) from 10 am to 4.30 pm (11 am to 4 pm from October through April). Admission costs £1.50/50p. Downstairs (where you can still try the spa water), the former ballroom is used for concerts. The park itself is also used for concerts ('Pittville on Sunday') throughout the summer.

Art Gallery & Museum

Cheltenham's history is imaginatively displayed at the Art Gallery & Museum (☎ 237431) in Clarence St, which has excellent sections covering Edward Wislon, William Morris and the Arts and Crafts movement and Dutch and British art. There's a temporary exhibition gallery on the ground floor and a café on the first floor. The gallery and museum is open Monday through Saturday from 10 am to 5.20 pm; entry is free.

MIDLANDS

Gustav Holst Birthplace Museum

The Victorian house (☎ 524846) at 4 Clarence Rd where composer Gustav Holst (1874-1934) was born, displays Holst memorabilia alongside descriptions of life 'below stairs' at the turn of the century. You get to listen to the music as you go round too (*The Planets*, usually). It's open Tuesday to Saturday from 10 am to 4.20 pm; entrance is £1.50/50p.

Cleeve Hill

About 4 miles north of Cheltenham, Cleeve Hill, at 325m (1066 feet), is the highest point of the Cotswolds and lowland England, and offers fine views over Cheltenham. On weekdays, Castleways (☎ 603715) runs buses up the hill roughly once an hour from the town centre.

Cheltenham Racecourse

On Cheltenham's northern outskirts, Prestbury is Britain's most haunted village and home to the Cheltenham racecourse, one of the country's top courses. The Hall of Fame museum (☎ 513014), dedicated to its history, is open on weekdays from 9.30 am to 4.30 pm, at weekends from 10 am to 2 pm; admission is free.

Places to Stay

Camping The nearest place to pitch a tent is *Longwillows Caravan & Camping Park* (☎ 674113, Station Rd, Woodmancote), 3 miles from town. It costs £3 for a small tent and one person.

Hostels The YMCA (☎ 524024, 6 Vittoria Walk) has some singles for £13.50, but is often fully booked. Over the Easter and the summer holidays *Cheltenham and Gloucester College* (☎ 532774) also lets rooms at its three sites; a single costs from £18.

B&Bs & Hotels There are several places in the Montpellier area, just south-west of the centre. *Segrave* (☎ 523606, 7 Park Place) is a small B&B charging £16/30 a single/double. Along the same road, *32*

Park Place (☎ 582889) has two rooms for the same price.

On Montpellier Drive, the *Micklinton Hotel* (☎ 520000, 12 Montpellier Drive) has rooms for £40 a double with bath, £36 without. *Lonsdale House* (☎ 232379) is nearby with beds from £19. *St Michael's Guest House* (☎ 513587, 4 Montpellier Drive) is smaller and charges £23/36. *Number 91* (☎ 579441, 91 Montpellier Terrace)*, where Wilson was born, has rooms for £24/46. At *Lypiatt House* (☎ 224994, Lypiatt Rd) rooms cost from £49/55.

Also centrally located, the friendly *Brennan Guest House* (☎ 525904, 21 St Lukes Rd) has six rooms with shared bathroom from £20/36.

There are a couple of good places on Shurdington Rd, south of the centre. The smart *Hallery House Hotel* (☎ 578450, 48 Shurdington Rd) has rooms with bath from £55/75, and from £25/48 without. *Beaumont House Hotel* (☎ 245986, 56 Shurdington Rd) has rooms with bath from £37/52.

The gracious Victorian *Queen's* hotel (☎ 514724, The Promenade) has rooms from £90/105. Edward VII, Elgar and Arthur Conan Doyle all stayed here.

Between the town centre and Pittville Park, the luxurious Regency *Hotel on the Park* (☎ 518898, 38 Evesham Rd) has a good restaurant and well-appointed rooms (half of which are overlooking the park) from £81/102.

Places to Eat

Cheap cafés litter the streets around the bus station; try *Muffin Man* (3 Crescent Terrace) or *Le Café* (1 Royal Well Rd). For a good, reasonably priced lunch in a central position try *Café Museum* in the Clarence St art gallery; soup, a roll and a cake will cost less than £4. The *Orange Tree* (☎ 234232, 317 High St) is an inviting vegetarian restaurant where a mushroom and nut rissole costs less than £5. *Axiom Centre for the Arts* (☎ 253183, 57 Winchcombe St) has a vegetarian café serving veggie shepherd's pie for £2.50.

Below Stairs (☎ 234599, 103 The Promenade) is a popular bistro specialising in seafood; main courses are between £10 and £16. The *New Land* (☎ 525346, 119 The Promenade) Vietnamese restaurant has a set dinner for £12.

The excellent *Indus* (☎ 516676, 226 Bath Rd) is possibly the best of the town's Indian restaurants.

Franco's (☎ 224880, 49 Rodney Rd) is a traditional Italian restaurant where three courses will cost about £15. *Pizza Express* (☎ 253896, Imperial Square), inside Belgrave House, has live jazz on Wednesday evenings. *Pepper's* (☎ 573488, Regent St) is a brasserie serving dishes like spiced lamb kebab (£5.75) in trendy surroundings.

One of Cheltenham's top restaurants, *81 Bistro & Bar* (☎ 222466, 81 The Promenade) offers starters from £2.95 and main courses from £6.50, but a three course meal is likely to add up to about £30.

There are branches of *Café Rouge* and *Costa* for coffee.

Entertainment

The *Everyman* theatre (☎ 572573, Regent St) stages everything from comedy and panto to Shakespeare. *Pittville Pump Room* often hosts classical music concerts, while the *Town Hall* (☎ 227979, Imperial Square) goes for the more popular stuff. The *Axiom Centre for the Arts* (☎ 690243, 57 Winchcombe St) also has a regular program of less mainstream musical and theatrical events.

Getting There & Away

Cheltenham is 100 miles from London, 43 miles from Oxford, 40 miles from Bristol and 9 miles from Gloucester.

Bus National Express (☎ 0990-808080) runs buses between Cheltenham and London (2¾ hours, £9.25), Oxford (1¼ hours, £7) and all other places on the National Express network. Swanbrook Coaches (☎ 01452-712386) also has buses to Oxford (1½ hours, £4).

Stagecoach (☎ 522021) runs buses every 10 minutes to Gloucester (30 minutes,

£1.20). Monday to Saturday it has buses every two hours to Cirencester (30 minutes, £1.50).

Pulhams Coaches (☎ 01451-820369) runs daily buses to Moreton (one hour, £1.20) via Bourton and Stow. Castleways Coaches (☎ 602949) operates about nine buses a day, Monday to Saturday, between Cheltenham and Broadway (45 minutes, £1.45) via Winchcombe. Monday to Saturday it also operates one bus a day to Warwick Castle.

Train Cheltenham is on the Bristol to Birmingham line, with hourly trains to London (2½ hours, £31), Bristol (45 minutes, £6.80) and Bath (30 minutes, £10.70), and frequent departures for Gloucester (10 minutes, £2.30).

Getting Around

Bicycle Crabtrees (☎ 515291), 50 Winchcombe St, rents mountain bikes for £8/35 a day/week.

TEWKESBURY
- pop 9500   ☎ 01684

About 8 miles north-west of Cheltenham, Tewkesbury is a delightful small town liberally endowed with timber-framed buildings and dominated by its magnificent partly Norman abbey church. It's well worth wandering in and out of the narrow alleys and courts, down one of which you'll find an old Baptist chapel in a building dating back to the 15th century. Church St, Mill St and Mill Bank are particularly worth exploring. During the summer, daily cruises (☎ 294088) along the Severn and Avon rivers depart from Riverside Walk.

The TIC (☎ 295027) is in the museum (50p) on Barton St. The **John Moore Countryside Museum** (☎ 297174), 41 Church St, is open April through October from Tuesday to Saturday, from 10 am to 1 pm and 2 to 5 pm; admission is £1/50p.

Tewkesbury Abbey

The town's focal point is the church of the former Benedictine abbey, the last of the

monasteries to be dissolved by Henry VIII.
Stone to build it was brought by sea and
river from Normandy in the 12th century.
Tewkesbury's fortunes depended on the
wool industry because the abbey owned
land and sheep all over the Cotswolds.
When the abbey was dissolved, the church
survived because the townspeople bought it.

One of Britain's largest churches, with a
40m-high tower, it has some spectacular
Norman pillars lining the nave, 14th
century stained glass above the choir and an
organ dating from 1631. Don't miss the
tombs of Edward, Baron Le Despenser,
who fought at Poitiers in 1356 and John
Wakeman, the last abbot, who is shown as
a vermin-ridden skeleton.

A new visitors centre by the gate houses
the Abbey Refectory, which does tea,
coffee and lunches. Abbey visitors are
asked for donations of £1.50.

Places to Stay

The nicest places to stay are all near the
abbey in Church St. The **Crescent Guest
House** (☎ 293395, 30 Church St) charges
£25/36 for singles/doubles with bath, while
the **Abbey Hotel** (☎ 294247, 67 Church St)
charges from £36/48. Opposite the abbey
entrance the **Bell Hotel** (☎ 293293) has
rooms with bath for £85 a double. The attractive **Jessop House Hotel** (☎ 292017, 65
Church St) charges £55/75.

There are a couple of cheaper places in
Barton Rd, east of the TIC. The **Bali Hai**
(☎ 292049, 5 Barton Rd) charges £20/28
and **Hanbury House** (☎ 299911, Barton
Rd) from £32 to £40 a double, but the
setting is less inviting.

Places to Eat

My Great Grandfather's (☎ 292687, 85
Church St) is a homely restaurant and
tearoom. Cream teas are £2.70, soup £2.30,
and there's roast beef, pork or lamb for
weekday lunches for £4.75. The **Hen &
Chickens Eating House** (☎ 292703, 73
Church St) does dishes like smoked fish and
seafood crumble for £7.50. Nearby, the

Abbey Tea Rooms (☎ 292215, 59 Church
St) does roasts for £4.50.

Le Bistrot André (☎ 290357, 78 Church
St) is a reasonably priced French restaurant.
Starters are around £3; main dishes range
from £8 to £13.

The **Royal Hop Pole** (Church St), mentioned in Dickens' *Pickwick Papers*, is a
popular pub, restaurant and hotel. Alternatively, try the **Berkeley Arms** (Church St)
for a drink.

Getting There & Away

The easiest way to get to Tewkesbury is on
Stagecoach's hourly bus No 41 from
Clarence St in Cheltenham (20 minutes,
£1.30, not Sunday). Stagecoach also has
weekday bus services to Tewkesbury from
Gloucester and Worcester; phone ☎ 01242-
522021 for details.

You can also get from Cheltenham to
Tewkesbury by train (Ashchurch station, £3
day return). On arrival you'll either have to
wait for a bus (50p) or trudge along the
main road for 25 minutes to get to the town
centre. Ashchurch station is unstaffed. Best
stick with the bus!

THE FOREST OF DEAN

Formerly a royal hunting ground, the Forest
of Dean occupies a triangular plateau
between Gloucester, Ross and Chepstow,
and comprises an area of 42 sq miles (including 28 sq miles of woodland) subject to
ancient forest law.

Few tourists make it to the forest even
though it's an excellent area for walking or
cycling. The main TIC (☎ 01594-836307)
in Coleford's High St stocks walking and
cycling guides. Impressive moated *St Briavels Castle Youth Hostel* (☎ 530272,
Lydney) was once a hunting lodge used by
King John. It's west of the forest above the
Wye Valley and charges £9.75/6.55 for
adults/juniors.

The **Clearwell Caves** (☎ 832535), near
Coleford, have been mined for iron since the
Iron Age, and you can wander through nine
dank, spooky caves and inspect the paraphernalia of the mine workings alongside

Miners of the Forest of Dean

From before Roman times the Forest of Dean was an important source of timber, iron and stone. A coal seam covering thousands of acres also runs under the Forest. By a curious anomaly, for the past 700 years a select band of Foresters from St Briavels have retained the right to mine this coal, a right won by their forefathers as a reward for their skill in tunnelling under castle fortifications. Although many men could still lay theoretical claim to this right after working for a year and a day in a mine, only two full-time 'free mines' are still in operation and they are one-man operations.

pools and rock formations. Every Halloween something akin to an underground rave takes place in Barbecue Churn, the largest cave; you need to book ahead to get in. The caves are open daily from March to October from 10 am to 5 pm. Admission costs £3/2. The *Tudor Farmhouse* (☎ 833046) in Clearwell village has excellent double rooms with bath for £57.

Less than 3 miles away is the pretty village of **Newland**, dominated by All Saints, the so-called 'Cathedral of the Forest'. In the Greyndour Chantry look for the brass depicting a free miner with a *nelly*, or tallow candle, in his mouth, a pick in his hand and a *billy*, or backpack, on his back. *Scatterford Farm* (☎ 836562) and *Cherry Orchard Farm* (☎ 832212) have reasonably priced rooms.

At the Beechenhurst Enclosure near Cinderford (parking £1.50) you can follow the easy Forest of Dean **sculpture trail**.

The **Dean Heritage Centre** (☎ 822170), in an old mill at Soudley, near Cinderford, recounts the history of the forest and the free miners. It's open daily February through October, from 10 am to 6 pm; it closes at 5 pm in February, March and October. Admission costs £3.30/2. The *Dean Heritage Kitchen* does lunches and teas.

Getting There & Away

Buses run from Gloucester and Monmouth to Coleford and the smaller villages. Trains also run to Lydney Junction. From April to September you can take the Dean Forest Railway from Lydney to Norchard (£3.50). For details phone ☎ 01594-845840.

NEWENT
* pop 5160   ☎ 01531

The unspoilt small town of Newent has some attractive architecture and the **Shambles Museum of Victorian Life** (☎ 822144), with assorted Victorian-style shopfronts around a tearoom. It's open from Easter to December, Tuesday to Sunday from 10 am to 6 pm. Admission is £3.25/1.95.

At the **National Birds of Prey Centre** (☎ 820286), on the outskirts of Newent, you can watch hawks and owls in free flight during daily displays. It's open February through November from 10.30 am to 5.30 pm; entry costs £4.75/2.75.

The TIC (☎ 822468) is at 7 Church St, almost opposite the museum. Good food with English wine can be sampled at the *restaurant* at the Three Choirs Vineyard (☎ 890223), where self-guided tours are available for £2.50.

Stagecoach bus No 32 runs here from Gloucester.

Herefordshire & Worcestershire

Bounded by the Malverns in the east and Wales to the west, Herefordshire is a sleepy county of fields and hedgerows, virtually untainted by tourism. Worcestershire comprises the flattish plains of the Severn Vale and the Vale of Evesham, but is surrounded by hills, with the Malverns to the west and the Cotswolds to the south. The rivers Wye, Severn and Avon flow through, and the county has many attractive market towns.

WALKS
Two long-distance paths pass through this area. Offa's Dyke Path runs along the

MIDLANDS

western border with Wales; the 107 mile Wye Valley Walk begins in Chepstow (Wales) and follows the river's course upstream into England through Herefordshire and Worcestershire and back into Wales to Rhayader.

GETTING AROUND

Midland Red West (☎ 01905-763888) is the region's biggest bus company. Its Day Rover pass costs £4.30 and allows travel anywhere on its system. For general bus information, phone ☎ 0345-125436. There are rail links to Hereford and Worcester.

HEREFORD

• pop 48,400   ☎ 01432

Hereford is a quiet market town that rewards quiet rambling along the mainly pedestrianised streets around the cathedral; Church St is particularly enjoyable.

Hereford owes its importance to its position on the River Wye on the border of Wales, where it became a garrison protecting the Saxons from the Welsh tribes. It was the capital of the Saxon kingdom of Mercia, and has been a cathedral city since the beginning of the 8th century. The main local industry is cider production.

Orientation & Information

The High Town shopping centre is the heart of the city on the north bank of the River Wye, with the cathedral a few blocks south along Church St. The bus station lies to the north-east, off Commercial Rd, with the train station a little farther out, behind the Safeway supermarket.

The TIC (☎ 268430) is at 1 King St, near the cathedral. There are guided walking tours (☎ 266867) Monday to Saturday from June to September at 10.30 am and on Sunday at 2.30 pm (£1/50p).

Hereford Cathedral

The purple-red cathedral (☎ 359880) is less aesthetically satisfying than many of the great English cathedrals, partly because of the reconstruction after the west tower collapsed into the nave in 1786 and partly because the stonework is a bit too frilly.

Although parts of the cathedral date back to the 11th century and the 50m-high central sandstone tower was built in the 14th century, the west front is less than 100 years old. Inside the cathedral, much of the Norman nave, with its arches, remains. In the choir is the 14th century Bishop's throne and King Stephen's chair, said to have been used by the king himself. In the north transept is the shrine of St Thomas Cantilupe, a 13th century Hereford bishop whose tomb became an object of veneration and pilgrimage. The south transept contains three tapestries showing the Tree of Life designed by John Piper in 1976.

The cathedral is best known for two ancient treasures: the 13th century Mappa Mundi and the chained library of 1500 volumes, some of them dating back to the 8th century. To house them, an impressive 'high tech medieval building' has been erected to the south-west side of the cathedral. It's open Monday to Saturday from 10 am to 4.15 pm and Sunday from 11 am to 3.15 pm (11 am to 3.15 pm daily except Sunday in winter). Admission costs £4/3.

The cathedral will host the Three Choirs Festival in 2000.

Old House

Stranded in pedestrianised High Town, the Old House (☎ 364598) is a marvellous black and white three storey wooden house built in 1621 and fitted with 17th century wooden furnishings. Note the murals of the Muses on the 1st floor. It's free and open Tuesday to Saturday from 10 am to 5 pm; to 4 pm on Sunday and bank holiday Mondays from April to September.

Other Things to See

Near the cathedral, the **Bishop's Palace** contains one of England's oldest timber halls. East of the cathedral is the ancient Cathedral School and Castle Green, site of a castle that was pulled down in 1652. Narrow streets and alleys lead from Cathedral Close to the shopping area.

The **Museum & Art Gallery** (☎ 364691), above the Broad St library, contains Roman antiquities, English watercolours and traditional farming implements. It's open Tuesday to Saturday from 10 am to 5 pm. In the High St, **All Saints Church** has a slightly bent 65m-high tower surmounted by England's largest weathercock. More unusually, it also contains a medieval carving of a man mooning and exposing himself; it's on a beam immediately above the café.

At the time of writing the **Churchill House Museum**, on the outskirts of town, beyond the train station, was closed and not expected to reopen. Ask at the TIC for an update.

Cider Factory Tours

Just off the A438 to Brecon, the **Cider Museum & King Offa Distillery** (☎ 354207) is in Pomona Place in a former cider works. In 1984 production of cider brandy recommenced after a 250 year gap. The museum and distillery are open daily from April through October from 10 am to 5.30 pm, and Tuesday to Sunday from 11 am to 3 pm in winter; entry is £2.20/1.70.

Bulmers Cider Mill (☎ 352000) offers two-hour factory tours (£2.95/1.95) from Monday to Friday. You're meant to book in advance by writing to: Visitor Centre, HP Bulmer Ltd, The Cider Mills, Plough Lane, Hereford HR4 0LE, although it may still be worth phoning to see if there's space left on a tour if you haven't planned ahead.

Places to Stay

Tenby Guest House (☎ 274783, 8 St Nicholas St), just north of the Wye Bridge, has a good range of rooms from £15 to £20 per person. Nearby, *Bowes Guest House* (☎ 267202, 23 St Martin's St) has singles/doubles from £18.50/34. At the nonsmoking *Collins House* (☎ 272416, 19 St Owen's St), opposite the grandiose town hall, rooms with continental breakfast cost £29.50/39.

Merton Hotel (☎ 265925, Commercial Rd), convenient for the station, charges £45/60 at weekends, £55/70 during the week. Just off the main street, across from the train station, the comfortable *Aylestone Court Hotel* (☎ 341891, Aylestone Hill) has rooms with a bathroom from £36/48.

Castle Pool Hotel (☎ 356321, Church St), close to the cathedral, was once the bishop's residence and has large well-equipped rooms with baths for £50/82, or smaller ones for £40/55. At the *Green Dragon* (☎ 272506, Broad St) you'll pay from £71/97 for a room with the usual city centre comforts.

Places to Eat

The most atmospheric place to eat is *Café@All Saints* at the west end of beautiful All Saints Church. Chickpea and sage soup is £1.80; courgette, fetta and filo pie is £4.85. Dinner on Friday evening is £16 a head.

If you're after a cream tea, you can tuck in amid genuine antiques at the *Antique Tea Shop* (5A St Peter's St) for £3.40. Alternatively, for a good cup of coffee, try the *Coffee Bean Co* (St Owen's St), which does light lunches (toasties, jacket potatoes etc) and is open Monday to Saturday, until 8 pm in the peak season.

Tiny *Nutters* (☎ 277447, Capuchin Yard, Church St) is a good vegetarian restaurant with set specials like nut roast and two salads for £4.45.

Cherries (2 Bridge St) offers a wide selection of breakfasts starting at 99p. The vast *Marches* (Union St) is worth a try if you're after standard burger-style meals.

To put together a picnic, head straight for the covered *Butter Market,* which dates back to 1860, in the High Town.

Entertainment

Hereford's most prominent nightclub is *The Crystal Rooms* (☎ 267378, Bridge St) where you're advised to dress to kill. Of town centre pubs, you could try the *Spread Eagle* or *The Orange Tree* in King St. Both do food for when the cider gets too much.

By the time you read this the new *Courtyard Centre for the Arts* (☎ 268785, off Edgar St), should have opened with a

MIDLANDS

theatre, two cinemas, a gallery and the usual bar and café.

Getting There & Away

Hereford is 140 miles from London, 25 miles from Worcester and 38 miles from Brecon in Wales.

Bus National Express (☎ 0990-808080) operates three services a day from London (four hours, £13) via Heathrow, Cirencester, Cheltenham, Gloucester, Newent and Ross-on-Wye.

Midland Red West connects Hereford to Worcester (1¼ hours, £2.60) and Ludlow (£2.80). There are also buses to Brecon via Hay-on-Wye, Monday to Saturday, five times a day; phone ☎ 0345-125436 for details.

Train Hereford is linked by hourly train to London (three hours, £30), usually via Newport or Worcester. From Hereford, there are also rail services to Worcester (one hour, £4.60).

Getting Around

You can rent bikes from Coombes Cycles (☎ 354373), 94 Widemarsh St, for £3.75 a day for standard bikes or £10.35 for mountain bikes.

ROSS-ON-WYE

- pop 8300   ☎ 01989

Winding through a landscape of woods and meadows past Ross-on-Wye, Symonds Yat and then along the border with Wales, the River Wye empties into the Bristol Channel beneath the Severn Bridge. Built on a red-sandstone bluff, Ross makes a good base for exploring the **Wye Valley**, the most scenic part of the river.

There are fine views of the valley and ruined Wilton Castle from the **Prospect**, a cliff-top public garden designed by 17th century town planner John Kyrle, the 'Man of Ross', who also laid out some of the streets. His philanthropic works were much praised by Pope in *Of the Use of Riches*. Kyrle is buried in the parish church, where

the Plague Cross records the burial of 315 victims of the 1637 plague.

The **Lost St Museum** (☎ 562752) is upstairs at 27 Brookend St. Usually open Monday to Saturday, it re-creates a street of shops and a pub as they would have been between 1885 and 1935. A small **Heritage Centre** is on the 1st floor of the stilted Market House.

The TIC (☎ 562768) is in Edde Cross St. Bikes can be rented from Revolutions (☎ 562639), 48 Broad St, from £10 a day.

Places to Stay

The nearest hostel is 6 miles south of Ross at Welsh Bicknor (see Goodrich in the Around Ross-on-Wye section).

In Ross, the Georgian *Vaga House* (☎ 563024, Wye St) is in a pretty street near the TIC and does B&B from £18 per person. The nonsmoking *Linden House* (☎ 565373, 14 Church St), opposite the church, charges £25/44 a single/double, while the *Rectory* (☎ 562175, Church St) has beds for £17 a head.

The smartest place to stay is the beautifully positioned *Royal* (☎ 565105, Palace Pound), where rooms cost £52/95. *Rosswyn Hotel* (☎ 562733, 17 High St) has rooms with bath from £25. The comfortable *King's Head Hotel* (☎ 763174, 8 High St) charges from £35 per person.

Places to Eat

Ross' High St is full of tea shops, the most interesting being the *Antique Teashop* (40 High St), where a cream tea taken on antique chairs costs £3.65. The *Priory Coffee House* (45 High St) serves toasties from £1.80, while *Poppy's Bistro* (9 High St) does hot dishes of the day for £4.95.

Oat Cuisine (☎ 566271, 47 Broad St) does vegetarian lunch dishes for £2.25, while the *Canberra Restaurant* (12 Gloucester Rd) does roasts for £4.20.

For a night out, *Pheasants Restaurant* (☎ 565751, 52 Edde Cross St) does fine English cuisine from Tuesday to Saturday; main courses cost around £12. Alternatively head for *Meaders* (☎ 562803, 1 Copse Cross

St), where a Hungarian meal for two, with wine, costs £27. Opposite, *Cloisters* wine bar (☎ *567717)* has hot dishes for £7.95.

Getting There & Away

Ross is 14 miles from Hereford and 16 miles from Gloucester, with bus links to London via Cheltenham and Cirencester. Stagecoach (☎ 485118) operates a daily bus service between Hereford and Gloucester via Ross, and a Monday to Saturday Ross-Monmouth bus (for Goodrich and Symonds Yat).

AROUND ROSS-ON-WYE

Goodrich

Goodrich Castle (☎ 01600-890538, EH) is a red-sandstone castle dating back to the 12th century. A Royalist stronghold during the Civil War, it fell to the Roundheads after a siege lasting 4½ months and was destroyed by Cromwell. Admission costs £2.95/1.50.

Just under 2 miles from Goodrich is *Welsh Bicknor Youth Hostel (☎ 01594-860300)*, a Victorian rectory standing in 10-hectare grounds by the river. Beds for adults/juniors cost £8.80/5.95. It's open daily from April through October; phone for other times.

Symonds Yat

Symonds Yat, 2½ miles south of Goodrich, is a popular beauty spot overlooking the Wye. It's crowded in summer but worth visiting at quieter times. There are good views from Yat Rock (Symonds Yat East), and rare peregrine falcons nest in the rockface. Telescopes enable you to watch them from April to August. Parking costs £1.50 (50p after 5 pm).

GREAT MALVERN

- **pop 30,000** ☎ 01684

Great Malvern is the biggest and best known of a cluster of settlements in the Malvern Hills, which rise suddenly from the vale in a long, humpy line. Famous for mineral water, a summer music festival (late May), a public school and Morgan motorcars, Great Malvern looks a bit like

one of the Mid Welsh spa towns with a mini version of Gloucester Cathedral and lots of cedars, pines and monkey puzzle trees. Turner was inspired to paint it, before the grand Victorian piles started to straddle the hills, of course! Be warned that the steep main drag can be a daunting prospect if you're carrying a heavy bag.

The TIC (☎ 892289), 21 Church St, sells an access guide for disabled visitors (£1), although just getting up the hill to buy it could be a problem. It also stocks a leaflet describing six cycle routes round the Malvern Hills.

The newly restored Malvern Festival Theatre (☎ 892277) is based in the Winter Gardens Complex in Grange Rd.

Great Malvern Priory

The Priory Church, with Norman pillars lining the nave, is famous for its stained glass and tiles. Of particular note are the 15th century west window, the clerestory

---

On the Elgar Trail

Sir Edward Elgar, composer of Britain's almost-national anthem *Land of Hope and Glory*, was born in Broadheath, three miles west of Worcester, in 1857 and died in Worcester in 1934. He lived in Hereford for eight years and drew much of the inspiration for music like the *Pomp and Circumstance* marches and the *Enigma Variations* from the nearby Malvern Hills. The Hereford, Worcester and Malvern TICs stock a leaflet detailing a signposted 'Elgar Route' that takes you through places associated with his life. He is buried in St Wulstan's church in Little Malvern, just south of Great Malvern.

Elgar Birthplace Museum (☎ 01905-66224) in Lower Broadheath is open Thursday to Tuesday, May to September from 10.30 am to 6 pm; 1.30 to 4.30 pm during most of winter and is closed from 16 January to 15 February.

windows of the choir, and the window in the Jesus Chapel in the north transept, which shows the Joys of Mary. The choir is decorated with 1200 medieval tiles, the oldest and finest such collection in the country.

Walks in the Malvern Hills

Cut up St Ann's Rd for a short, steep walk to the summit of Worcestershire Beacon (419m, 1374 feet), offering tremendous views. Herefordshire Beacon (334m, 1095 feet), south of Great Malvern, is the site of the British Camp, an Iron Age fort. There's a superb walk along the path that meanders across the summits of the Malverns.

The Malvern Hills provided Elgar with the inspiration for his *Enigma Variations* and the *Pomp & Circumstance* marches (see the boxed text 'On the Elgar Trail').

The TIC stocks *Malvern Map Sets*, three maps covering the chain of hills.

Places to Stay & Eat

Although there's plenty of accommodation, much of it very pleasant, this is an upmarket area with prices to match. *Malvern Hills Youth Hostel* (☎ 569131, 18 Peachfield Rd) is in Malvern Wells, 1½ miles south of Great Malvern (bus No 675 to British Camp). It's open from mid-February to October and costs £8/5.40 for adults/juniors.

Goodrich Cottage (☎ 573237), on the hill a mile outside Great Malvern, offers bargain B&B for £16 a head. *Spa Guest House* (☎ 561178, 16 Manby Rd) charges £35 a double.

Great Malvern Hotel (☎ 563411, 7 Graham Rd) is very central, with singles/doubles with baths for £45/60. The *Cottage in the Wood* (☎ 575859, Holywell Rd), 3 miles away near Malvern Wells, boasts views to kill for. Rooms cost from £70/89.50. Dinner in its excellent restaurant costs around £26.

Church St hosts frilly *Victorias*, where you can get tea or a jacket potato from £2.10. Round the corner from the TIC the

Blue Bird Tearooms serves cream teas for £2.40.

Lady Foley's Tearoom (☎ 893033, Imperial Rd) serves lunches and teas in the splendid Victorian train station. On Friday and Saturday night from 7 to 9 pm the station also hosts *Passionata*, serving more elaborate dishes like gruyere pancakes for £7.95.

The Indian *Anupam Restaurant* (☎ 573814, 85 Church St), above Boots, has tasty thali meals from £11.90.

Getting There & Away

Great Malvern is 8 miles from Worcester and 15 miles from Hereford. The quickest way to get there is by train from Worcester (£2.40 day return) or Hereford (£4 day return). There are connections to London and Birmingham. National Express has a daily bus between Great Malvern and London (four hours, £12.50) via Worcester and Pershore.

WORCESTER
- pop 75,500 ☎ 01905

World famous for its bone china, Worcester (pronounced 'wooster') also has an impressive cathedral where King John of Magna Carta fame is buried. It's a disjointed town, not always immediately inviting, but some streets boast the half-timbered buildings more usually associated with Stratford-upon-Avon.

Orientation & Information

The main part of the city lies on the east bank of the River Severn, with the cathedral rising above it. The High St, just to the north, runs through a bewildering number of name changes as it heads north: The Cross, The Foregate, Foregate and The Tything.

The TIC (☎ 726311) is in the Guildhall, in the High St. Walking tours (£3/1.50) leave from here at 11 am and 2.30 pm on summer Wednesdays.

Worcester Cathedral

The present cathedral was begun in 1084 by Bishop – later saint – Wulfstan and the atmospheric crypt dates back to this period.

The choir and Lady Chapel were built in 13th century Early English style, while the Norman nave was given a make-over in 14th century Decorated style. Take a look at the carvings in the ambulatory and transepts and you'll see scenes of judgement and hell as well as of the nativity.

Wicked King John, whose treachery towards brother Richard left the country in turmoil at his death, is buried in the choir. Knowing he stood only a slim chance of making it past the Pearly Gates, the dying king is said to have asked to be buried disguised as a monk. When the tomb was opened in 1797, shreds of a monk's cowl were found over his skull.

An ornate chantry chapel south of the high altar commemorates Prince Arthur, Henry VIII's elder brother, who died while honeymooning with Catherine of Aragon.

The cathedral (☎ 28854) is open daily from 7.30 am to 6 pm. A £2 donation is requested. The cathedral choir sings evensong at 5.30 pm daily, except Thursday, and at 4 pm on Sunday.

Commandery Civil War Centre

Beside Sidbury Lock, south-east of the cathedral, the Commandery (☎ 355071) is in a splendid Tudor building used as Charles II's headquarters during the Battle of Worcester. This brought the Civil War to an end in 1651 and the centre details the ins and outs of this and many other battles that raged in 17th century England. It's open Monday to Saturday from 10 am to 5 pm, and Sunday from 1.30 to 5.30 pm. Entry is £3.40/2.30.

Royal Worcester Porcelain Works

Worcester has been manufacturing ornate bone china since 1751, the longest continuous production of any British porcelain company. In 1789, the company was granted a royal warrant, and Worcester remains the Queen's preferred crockery.

The Royal Worcester Porcelain Works (☎ 21247) was moved to its current Severn St site in 1840. It now boasts an entire visitors complex, with shops, restaurant and museum, which is open Monday to Saturday from 9 am to 5.30 pm and Sunday from 11 am to 5 pm.

Conducted **factory tours** lasting one hour run from Monday to Friday. They cost £3.50/3 and should be booked in advance. The **Manufactory** (£1/75p) lets you see what a turn-of-the-century potter's life was like, while a **film** (£1/75p) tells the story of the pottery. You can see the film and visit the Manufactory for £1.50/1.

The **gift shop** sells everything from a 23 piece 'best' dinner service for £891 to single seconds for just a few pounds.

The newly updated **Museum of Worcester Porcelain** tells the factory's story and houses the world's largest collection of Worcester porcelain, including some of the first pieces. It's open Monday to Saturday from 9.30 am to 5 pm (from 10 am on Saturday). Entry is £1.50/1.

Other Things to See

The splendid **Guildhall**, in the High St, is a Queen Anne building of 1722, designed by a pupil of Wren.

Half-timbered **Trinity House** (on The Trinity, just off The Cross) once belonged to the Guild of the Holy Trinity. After the Battle of Worcester Charles II is supposed to have hidden in what was later named **King Charles House**, 29 New St, which is now a restaurant.

Friar St is lined with fine Tudor and Elizabethan buildings. Built in 1480, **The Greyfriars** (☎ 23571, NT) has been painstakingly restored and is full of textiles and furnishings. It's open from Easter through October on Wednesday, Thursday and bank holiday Mondays from 2 to 5 pm. Entry is £2.40. The **Museum of Local Life** (☎ 722349) evokes Worcester's past with reconstructed Victorian shops, displays of toys and costumes, and details of daily life during WWII. It's open daily, except Thursday and Sunday, for £1.50/75p, less if you buy a combined ticket for the Commandery as well.

Worcester City Museum and Art Gallery (☎ 25371), Foregate St, has exhibits about the River Severn and is open daily, except Thursday and Sunday, from 9.30 am to 6 pm (5 pm on Saturday). Entry is free.

Places to Stay

The nearest hostel is in Malvern Wells, 8 miles away. In summer, you can camp at *Worcester Racecourse* (☎ 23936) for £4.50 a head. About 3 miles north of Worcester is the *Mill House Caravan & Camping Site* (☎ 451283), which charges from £5.50.

Barbourne Rd, north of the centre, has several B&Bs. The *Shrubbery Guest House* (☎ 24871, 38 Barbourne Rd) charges from £16 per person and has some rooms with private bath. The *Barbourne* (☎ 27507, 42 Barbourne Rd) charges from £17 a head. There's another cluster of B&Bs at the north end of The Tything.

Park House Hotel (☎ 21816, 12 Droitwich Rd) has singles/doubles with bath from £24/36. *Loch Ryan Hotel* (☎ 351143, 119 Sidbury), near the cathedral, has rooms from £40/50.

The huge *Fownes Hotel* (☎ 613151, City Walls Rd), in a converted warehouse, is a popular business hotel. Midweek prices of £85/100 a room drop to £40 a head at weekends.

Places to Eat

You could do worse than lunch in the Guildhall's elaborate *Assembly Room Restaurant*, which is open Monday to Saturday from 10 am to 5 pm. *Peppers Café-Bar* (☎ 723035, The Cross) also has a splendid location in the converted St Nicholas Church; a seafood combo plate will cost you £5.75. Otherwise head for New St and its extension into Friar St for the best choice of eateries.

The 16th century *King Charles House* (☎ 22449, 29 New St) offers traditional three-course lunches for £9.95. Next door is the picturesquely named, reasonably priced *Swan with Two Nicks* (☎ 28190). *Saffrons Bistro* (☎ 610505, 15 New St) offers everything from Thai to modern British. Nearby *Chesters Café-Restaurant* (☎ 611638, 51

New St) concentrates on Mexican, but also has jacket potatoes from £1.95.

The *Lemon Tree* (☎ 27770, 12 Friar St) offers more Modern British cooking in attractive surroundings: things like courgette, Shropshire blue cheese and broccoli bake for £5.95. *Heroes Restaurant* (☎ 25451, 26 Friar St) does two-course lunches for £6.95; the lengthy menu includes chilli, chicken and burgers.

Il Pescatore (☎ 21444, 34 Sidbury), near the cathedral, is a popular Italian restaurant offering light lunch dishes for £4.90. *Thyme After Thyme* (☎ 611786, 27 College St) serves up garlic prawns and rice for £4.75. Handy for the porcelain works and the cathedral, the *Shepherd's Purse* (7 Severn St) does soup and a sandwich for £2.95.

Entertainment

The popular *Farrier's Arms* (Fish St), near the cathedral, has some outdoor seating, while Worcester's oldest pub, the *Cardinal's Hat* (Friar St) has open fires in winter. *Heroes* (Friar St) has live jazz on Tuesday.

Music by Elgar is always a highlight of the Three Choirs Festival, hosted by Worcester Cathedral (☎ 616211) every third year. It will be Worcester's turn in 1999.

Getting There & Away

Worcester is 113 miles from London, 57 miles from Oxford, 26 miles from Stratford-upon-Avon and 25 miles from Hereford.

Bus National Express (☎ 0990-808080) runs at least one coach a day between Worcester, Heathrow and London (3½ hours, £11.25). Another service links Aberdare and Great Yarmouth via Worcester, Great Malvern and Hereford. Worcester to Great Malvern takes just 20 minutes.

Midland Red West (☎ 763888) operates services to Hereford, Tewkesbury and Evesham. A Day Rover ticket costs £4.30/2.70.

Cambridge Coach Services (☎ 01223-423900) has a weekday service linking Worcester with Cambridge (£15) via Stratford-upon-Avon (£4) and Warwick (£5).

Train Worcester Foregate station (for trains to Birmingham and Hereford) is more central than Worcester Shrub Hill, which offers regular trains to London Paddington (2¼ hours, £22.50). Shrub Hill is a dismal 15 minute walk from the centre. Bus 30 passes nearby or a taxi is about £2.30.

Getting Around

Bickerline (☎ 670679) operates 45-minute cruises along the river (£3/1.50). Alternatively, you could consider taking to the skies with Worcester Balloons (☎ 650737). Peddlers (☎ 24238), 46 Barbourne Rd, hires out bicycles for £8/30 for a day/week, and mountain bikes for £15.60.

AROUND WORCESTER
Elgar's Birthplace Museum

About 3 miles west of Worcester is Broadheath, birthplace of Sir Edward Elgar (1857-1934). The cottage (☎ 01905-333224) is now a museum of Elgar memo- rabilia, open Thursday to Tuesday from May to September from 10.30 am to 6 pm; 1.30 to 4.30 pm during most of winter and is closed from 16 January to 15 February. Entry is £3/50p and the 10 minute bus ride to Broadheath costs £1.45.

Severn Valley Railway

A 20 minute ride from Worcester Forest Hill to Kidderminster lets you link in with the Severn Valley Railway (☎ 01299-403816), which offers a scenic steam-powered journey from Kidderminster to Bridgnorth (Shropshire), via the pretty village of Bewdley. A return ticket costs £9.20/3.

VALE OF EVESHAM

Worcestershire's south-eastern corner looks particularly splendid in spring when its myriad fruit trees are in blossom. The Vale's two principal towns are Evesham itself and Pershore.

Evesham

• pop 15,000   ☎ 01386

A quiet market town on the River Avon, Evesham was the scene of the battle where Prince Edward, son of Henry III, defeated Simon de Montfort in 1265. The TIC (☎ 446944), in the picturesque Almonry Centre on the south side of town, houses a small heritage centre; admission costs £2 (children free).

The river flows close to the 16th century bell tower of the lost Benedictine abbey, which makes a fine grouping with the twin medieval churches of All Saints and St Lawrence. Look out for the beautiful fan vaulting of the Lichfield Chantry in All Saints.

Places to Stay & Eat *Berryfield House* (☎ 48214, *172 Pershore Rd, Hampton*) does B&B from £15 for nonsmokers only. *Park View Hotel* (☎ 442639, *Waterside*) has singles/doubles from £19.50/36. The Georgian *Croft* (☎ 446035, *54 Green Hill*) is 180m from the train station and has rooms from £30/38. Readers have enjoyed staying at *Brookside Guest House* (☎ 443116, *Mill St*), which is three-quarters of a mile along the river from the centre in Hampton, with rooms from £16/30.

Comfortable *Evesham Hotel* (☎ 765566, *Cooper's Lane*) has rooms for £66/88.

The best place for a snack is the *Gateway Cake Shop*, beside the abbey, which does soup and a roll for £1.25.

The *Vine Wine Bar* (☎ 446799, *16 Vine St*) offers delicacies like swordfish steak for £9.45.

Getting There & Away The hourly Midland Red West (☎ 01788-535555) 550 service operates to Pershore (25 minutes, £2.10) and Worcester (one hour, £2.60), Monday to Saturday. Bus No 218 runs to Stratford-upon-Avon (one hour, £2.10), Monday to Saturday.

There are frequent trains to Worcester (20 minutes), and to London (two hours) via Oxford (one hour).

Pershore

• pop 6900   ☎ 01386

A backwater town of graceful Georgian houses, Pershore is chiefly noted for its abbey, which was founded in 689. The TIC (☎ 554262) is inside a travel agency at 19 High St.

Pershore Abbey When Henry VIII's henchmen moved in to dissolve Pershore Abbey the townsfolk bought the austere Early English choir to serve as their parish church. That, and the earlier south transept, parts of which may predate the Norman Conquest, are all that now remain.

About 8 miles from Worcester, and 7 miles from Evesham, Pershore is best reached by bus from either place. The train station is 1½ miles north of town.

Warwickshire & Coventry

Warwickshire is home to two of England's biggest tourist attractions: Stratford-upon-Avon, with its Shakespearian connections, and Warwick, with its popular castle. The ruined castle at Kenilworth is also worth a look, as is the modern cathedral in Coventry. Elsewhere the county has plenty of museums, castles, market towns, canals and pleasant countryside.

For bus information throughout the area phone ☎ 01926-414140.

COVENTRY
• **pop 318,800 ☎ 01203**

Coventry is easy to get to from Birmingham or Stratford-upon-Avon and fans of modern architecture will want to drop by to see the new cathedral built beside the bombed-out ruins of the medieval one.

But away from the area immediately around the cathedral a combination of damage inflicted by WWII bombs and by architects and town planners in the 1950s and 60s make for a dismal cityscape of car parks, ring roads and windswept shopping precincts.

Medieval Coventry was a thriving wool and cloth manufacturing centre; by the 14th century it was one of the four largest towns in England outside London. Then decline

set in and Coventry was still essentially a medieval town when the Industrial Revolution hit it in the 19th century.

Coventry was one of the most inventive of the Victorian industrial centres and claims to be the birthplace of the modern bicycle.

The first car made in Britain was a Daimler built in Coventry in 1896, and in the early years of the 20th century Coventry was Britain's motor manufacturing capital as well as a major aircraft manufacturing centre. But steady growth switched to headlong decline in the 1970s and 80s as Sunbeam, Hillman, Singer, Humber and Triumph cars and Triumph motorcycles all disappeared. Now only Jaguar cars remain of the home-grown models, although French Peugeots are also assembled in Coventry.

Orientation & Information
Central Coventry is encircled by a ring road with most points of interest tucked inside. Much of the centre is dominated by the bleak Precinct, one of the first pedestrian-only shopping centres to rise from WWII destruction.

Medieval Spon St features several half-timbered buildings relocated from elsewhere in the city.

The TIC (☎ 832303), in Bayley Lane beside the University of Coventry and facing the two cathedrals, sells the informative *Coventry City Centre Trail* (£1).

Cathedrals
Founded in the 12th century and rebuilt from 1373, St Michael's was one of England's largest parish churches when it became a cathedral in 1918, its spire topped only by those of Salisbury and Norwich cathedrals. Then on 14 November 1940, a Luftwaffe raid gutted the cathedral, leaving only the outer walls and the spire standing amid the smoking ruins.

After the war, the ruins were left as a reminder. The new St Michael's Cathedral (☎ 227597) was built beside it. Designed by Sir Basil Spence and built between 1955 and 1962, the cathedral is one of the few examples of post-war British architecture to inspire popular affection. It's noted for the soaring etched glass screen wall at the west end, for the Graham Sutherland tapestry above the altar, for Piper's lovely stained glass and for Epstein's sculpture of St Michael subduing the devil beside the entrance steps.

The visitors centre screens an audiovisual presentation on the destruction of the old cathedral and the birth of its replacement for £1.25/75p (not Sunday). Visitors to the new cathedral are asked for a £2 donation. The old cathedral spire still looks down on the ruins and its 180 steps lead up to magnificent views. Entry is £1/50p.

Museum of British Road Transport

The museum (☎ 832425), in Hales St, has a huge collection of bicycles, motorcycles, racing cars, rally cars and even Thrust 2, the fastest wheeled 'thing' ever to hurtle across a salt flat, alongside plain, ordinary British family cars. It's open daily from 10 am to 5 pm; entry is free.

Other Things to See

The statue of Lady Godiva at the edge of the Precinct is a Coventry meeting spot handily overlooked by the Coventry Clock. A figure of the naked lady parades from the clock each hour, while Peeping Tom peers out from above. Godiva appears again, this time with husband Leofric, on the fairy-tale façade of the Council House in High St.

The Herbert Art Gallery & Museum (☎ 832386), in Jordan Well, provides a quick run through Coventry's history. The upstairs art gallery has paintings of the Lady Godiva legend and the original sketches for Sutherland's cathedral tapestry. It's free and open Monday to Saturday from 10 am to 5.30 pm (noon to 5 pm on Sunday).

Places to Stay & Eat

Many visitors just want to check out the cathedral and the museums and then head on again. If you do want to stay the TIC makes bookings free of charge (☎ 0800-243748), although many places are uncomfortably close to the noisy ring road.

There's no hostel, but in July and August the *Priory Halls of Residence* (☎ 838445, Priory St) at Coventry University offer accommodation for £18 per person.

Friars Rd is a reasonably quiet residential enclave within easy walking distance of the centre. *Avalon Guest House* (☎ 251839, 28 Friars Rd) has beds from £15 to £19 per person. Across the road, the *Crest Guest House* (☎ 227822, 39 Friars Rd) charges £20 to £30 a head.

Immediately opposite the bus station, *Fishy Moore's (10-12 Fairfax St)* serves a complete cod meal for £3.75. The Museum of British Road Transport, the Herbert Museum and the cathedral all have *cafés*.

Near the cathedral, pedestrianised Hay Lane has a branch of *Pizza Express* and *Bunty's*, a pleasant tearoom serving filled bagels (£2.65) and excellent hot chocolate.

Old-world Spon St has several eateries including cosy *Ostler's* (☎ 226603, 166 Spon St), which serves various home-cooked dishes including some suitable for vegetarians, and *Tête à Tête* (☎ 550938, Spon St), which scoops the afternoon tea trade. Nearby, the excellent *Cottage in the Town* (☎ 223642, 1-3 Ryley St), off Hill St, has a bistro serving dishes like gammon steak for £6.95 and a pricier upstairs restaurant (closed Sunday evening).

Of the café bars creeping into the city centre, most striking is *Browns* (☎ 221100, Earl St), which has a lengthy menu of cooked dishes for £4.50 each.

Entertainment

Pubs With two universities, Coventry has a thriving nightlife. The *Golden Cross*, in the shadow of the cathedrals in Hay Lane, is a popular student hang-out and one of Coventry's oldest pubs (though much restored). Next to it is the equally popular, though centuries newer, *Newt & Cucumber*.

Spon St offers the pleasantly quiet *Old Windmill*, the popular *Rising Sun*, the psychedelic *Flares* and the *Shakespeare*.

Theatre & Cinema The University of Warwick, 4 miles south of the city, has the largest *Arts Centre* (☎ 524524) outside London, with a regular program of events and a popular cinema. *Belgrade Theatre* (☎ 553055) is in Corporation St.

Getting There & Away
Birmingham international airport (☎ 0121-767 5511) is actually closer to Coventry than Birmingham.

The train station is just across the ring road, south of the centre. Coventry is on the main rail route to London (less than 1½ hours, £21.90). Birmingham is £2.60 by rail.

Pool Meadow bus station is in Fairfax St. West Midlands bus services are coordinated by Centro (☎ 559559). One-way National Express tickets cost £6 to London, £7.25 to Oxford and £12.25 to Bath. Foxhound offers hourly buses to Leicester (one hour, £3).

Stagecoach (☎ 01788-535555) has Explorer tickets for £4.50/2.50, allowing a day's bus travel to Birmingham, Evesham, Kenilworth, Leamington, Northampton, Oxford, Stratford and Warwick.

Getting Around
Phone ☎ 559559 for local bus service information; a £3.95 Daytripper ticket gives you a day's use of local bus and train services.

WARWICK
- **pop 22,000   ☎ 01926**

Warwickshire's pleasantly quiet county town is home to Warwick Castle, one of England's major tourist attractions. It's also a handy base for visits to Stratford-upon-Avon.

Orientation & Information
Warwick is simple to navigate; the A429 runs right through the centre with Westgate at one end and Eastgate at the other. The old town centre lies just north of this axis, the castle just south. The TIC (☎ 492212) is in Jury St, near the junction with Castle St.

Warwick Castle
Warwick Castle, one of England's finest medieval castles, is owned by Madame

Tussaud's and could easily take up half a day of your time.

Warwick was first fortified in Saxon times, but the first real castle was constructed on the banks of the River Avon in 1068, soon after the Norman Conquest. The castle's external appearance principally dates from the 14th and 15th centuries, but the interiors are from the late 17th to late 19th centuries, when the castle changed from a military stronghold to a grand residence. Capability Brown landscaped the magnificent grounds in 1753.

You enter the castle through a gatehouse beside the armoury and the dungeon and torture chamber. Just inside, a sign points to the 'Kingmaker' exhibition. The most powerful of all the castle's powerful owners was Warwick the Kingmaker, Richard Neville, the 16th Earl (1428-71). Having replaced the ineffectual Henry VI with the king's son Edward IV in 1461, Neville then fell out with Edward IV and brought Henry VI back in 1470, only to be defeated and killed by Edward IV less than a year later. At one time, he had Henry VI under lock and key in the Tower of London while Edward IV was his prisoner at Warwick. The 'Kingmaker' exhibit uses models to show preparations for one of his many battles.

The Tussaud influence is most strongly felt in the private apartments which are furnished as they would have been in 1898, with a series of waxwork figures attending a weekend house party. As you walk round you bump into various members of the nobility, their servants and attendants as well as historic figures like the young Churchill and the Prince of Wales, later Edward VII.

The castle is open daily from 10 am to 6 pm, closing an hour earlier in winter. Entry is £8.95/5.95. Phone ☎ 406600 for details of medieval banquets in the castle.

Collegiate Church of St Mary
Originally built in 1123, this church (☎ 400771) was badly damaged by a fire in 1694, and rebuilt in a mishmash of styles. The remarkable perpendicular Beauchamp Chapel was built between 1442 and 1460 at

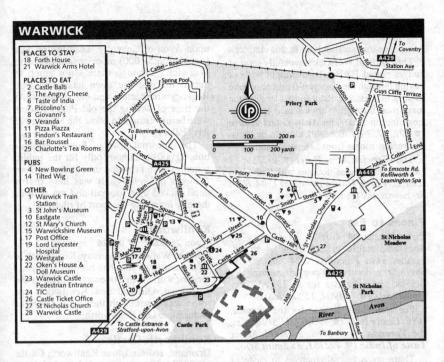

WARWICK

PLACES TO STAY
18 Forth House
21 Warwick Arms Hotel

PLACES TO EAT
2 Castle Balti
5 The Angry Cheese
7 Taste of India
7 Piccolino's
8 Giovanni's
9 Veranda
11 Pizza Piazza
13 Findon's Restaurant
16 Bar Roussel
25 Charlotte's Tea Rooms

PUBS
4 New Bowling Green
14 Tilted Wig

OTHER
1 Warwick Train Station
3 St John's Museum
10 Eastgate
12 St Mary's Church
15 Warwickshire Museum
17 Post Office
19 Lord Leycester Hospital
20 Westgate
22 Oken's House & Doll Museum
23 Warwick Castle Pedestrian Entrance
24 TIC
26 Castle Ticket Office
27 St Nicholas Church
28 Warwick Castle

a cost of £2400, a huge sum for the time. Luckily it survived the fire.

The gilded bronze effigy of Richard Beauchamp, 13th Earl of Warwick, sits in the centre of the chapel; Richard Neville is the sinister-looking figure on the corner of the tomb.

The church is open daily from 10 am to 6 pm (November to March to 4 pm). Don't miss the 12th century crypt with remnants of a medieval ducking stool, used to drench scolding wives.

Lord Leycester Hospital

At the Westgate end of the town, the road cuts through a sandstone cliff. In 1571 Robert Dudley, Earl of Leicester, founded the impressive Lord Leycester Hospital (☎ 491422) above it as an almshouse.

It has a beautiful courtyard, a 14th century chapel and a guildhall built by Neville containing a military museum. The hospital is open Tuesday to Sunday from April to October from 10 am to 5 pm (4 pm in winter). Entry costs £2.50/1.25.

Museums

Warwickshire Museum (☎ 412500) in the 17th century market building has displays on natural history and archaeology. The museum is open Monday to Saturday, from 10 am to 5.30 pm; from May to September it's also open Sunday, from 2.30 to 5 pm. Admission is free.

In Castle St, the **Doll Museum** (☎ 412500), in the half-timbered medieval Oken's House, is open from Easter to September. **St John's House** (☎ 410410), a Jacobean mansion on St John's, has exhibits on the county's social history. It's closed on Monday, and on Sunday in winter.

MIDLANDS

Places to Stay

The nearest hostel is in Stratford-upon-Avon (see that section later in this chapter).

The centre of Warwick is woefully short of budget-priced B&Bs. To overnight without paying through the nose you'll probably have to stay in Emscote Rd, the east end of the main road through Warwick as it heads for Leamington Spa. The *Avon Guest House* (☎ *491367, 7 Emscote Rd*), close to the town centre, has rooms from £18 per person.

The *Warwick Arms Hotel* (☎ *492759, 17 High St*) has singles/doubles with bath from £35/50. *Forth House* (☎ *401512, 44 High St*) has rooms for £40/46.

Places to Eat

Pizza Piazza (☎ *491641, 33-35 Jury St*) does reasonable pizzas from £4 to £8. Farther east, *Piccolino's* (☎ *491020, 31 Smith St*) is deservedly popular, serving delicious seafood pasta for £6.45. Also try *Giovanni's* (☎ *494904, 15 Smith St*).

For something Indian, try the popular, BYO *Castle Balti* (☎ *493007, 11 St John's*), the *Veranda* (☎ *491736, 24 Smith St*) or *Taste of India* (☎ *492151, 35 Smith St*).

There are a few alternatives to pasta or curry. The *Angry Cheese* (☎ *400411, St Nicholas Church St*) is a wine bar-cum-bistro specialising in Mexican food. The *Tilted Wig* (☎ *410466, 11 Market Place*) has a lengthy bar menu. *Charlotte's Tea Rooms* (6 *Jury St*) does toad-in-the-hole lunches for £6.25 and is open Thursday, Friday and Saturday night too.

Across the road from St Mary's, *Findon's Restaurant* (☎ *411755*) does romantic candlelight two-course dinners for £15.95.

Getting There & Away

Trains operate to Birmingham, Stratford-upon-Avon and London, but there are more connections from nearby Leamington Spa. Stagecoach buses (☎ *01788-535555*) stop in Market Place; a bus to Coventry is £2.25 (one hour). National Express buses operate from Old Square.

AROUND WARWICK

Warwick is an easy day trip from Stratford-upon-Avon or Coventry. **Leamington Spa** (population 57,000) more or less runs into Warwick. Although there's not much to detain tourists, the town has some fine Regency architecture and classy shops. At the time of writing the old Pump Rooms were being restored to house the Museum & Art Gallery.

The industrial town of **Rugby** (population 60,000) is famous only for the public school, which provided the setting for *Tom Brown's Schooldays*. It was here that a pupil picked up a football and ran with it, thereby inventing the sport of rugby.

Kenilworth

- **pop 21,000   ☎ 01926**

Close to Warwick University, Kenilworth is a pleasant town that has become a dormitory for workers in Coventry, 4 miles to the north-east. Old and new Kenilworth are some way apart, with the castle closer to picturesque Old Kenilworth.

Kenilworth Castle

Dramatic, red-sandstone Kenilworth Castle (☎ 52078, EH) was founded around 1120 and enlarged in the 14th and 16th centuries. Edward II was briefly imprisoned here before being transferred to Berkeley Castle and murdered. In 1563, Elizabeth I granted the castle to her favourite, Robert Dudley, Earl of Leicester. Between 1565 and 1575 she visited him at Kenilworth on four occasions and the theatrical pageants he arranged for her in 1575 were immortalised in Sir Walter Scott's 1821 work *Kenilworth*. The castle was deliberately ruined in 1644, after the Civil War. Admission costs £2.75/1.40.

Places to Stay & Eat

Abbey Guest House (☎ *512707, 41 Station Rd*) has singles/doubles for £21/36, while *Priory Guest House* (☎ *856173, 58 Priory Rd*) charges £20/36. *Nightingales Hotel* (☎ *853514, 95 Warwick Rd*) charges £18/34 and is attached to *La Cicata Restaurant*. Opposite the castle on Castle Hill the

Clarendon Arms is renowned for serving good food. More or less next door, *Harringtons* (☎ 52074) serves such delicacies as mustard and onion crusted sirloin in wine sauce for £11.95. Next to that is *Time for Tea*, where soup and a roll costs £2.10.

Getting There & Away

To get to Kenilworth take bus No X18 from Coventry (£1.40) or from Warwick (£1.60).

STRATFORD-UPON-AVON

• pop 22,000 ☎ 01789

The freak chance of being the birthplace of the world famous Elizabethan playwright William Shakespeare (1564-1616) has elevated Stratford from an also-ran Midlands market town into one of the busiest tourist attractions outside London. Its position beyond the northern edge of the Cotswolds makes Stratford a handy stopover en route to or from the north. It's a good base for visiting the castles at Warwick and Kenilworth.

Orientation & Information

Arriving by coach or train, you'll find yourself within walking distance of the town centre, which is easy to explore on foot. Transport is only really essential for visiting Mary Arden's House.

The TIC (☎ 293127), close to the river on Bridgefoot, has plenty of information but gets frantically busy in summer. It's open Monday to Saturday from 9 am to 6 pm and Sunday from 11 am to 5 pm; from November to March it closes an hour earlier and all day on Sunday.

Every Thursday and Saturday two-hour guided walks (☎ 412602) depart from outside the Swan Theatre at 10.30 am. Tickets cost £5/4.

The Shakespeare Properties

The Shakespeare Birthplace Trust (☎ 204016) looks after five buildings associated with Shakespeare. In summer the crowds can be horrendous and none of the houses was designed to accommodate such a squash; visit out of season if you possibly can. Note that wheelchair access to the properties is very restricted.

Three of the houses are centrally located, one is a short bus ride away, and the fifth a drive or bike ride out. A £10/5 ticket lets you into all five properties, or you can pay £7/3.50 for the three town houses. To pay for each place individually would cost nearly twice as much. From late March to mid-October the properties are open Monday to Saturday from 9 or 9.30 am to 5 pm, and Sunday from 9.30 or 10 am. In winter, they open Monday to Saturday from 9.30 or 10 am to 4 pm, and Sunday from either 10 or 10.30 am. More information is available from the trust's Web site at www.shakespeare.org.uk.

Shakespeare's Birthplace The number one Shakespeare attraction, in Henley St, has been so extensively rebuilt over the centuries that Will might have trouble recognising it despite having been born here. It's been a tourist attraction for three centuries; you'll see the evidence of famous 19th century visitor-vandals who scratched their names on one of the windows. A ticket costing £4.50/2 includes admission to the adjacent Shakespeare Centre, which has the lowdown on its famous son.

Across the road the **Shakespeare Bookshop** (☎ 292176) sells the complete works in a multitude of formats.

New Place & Nash's House In retirement, the wealthy Shakespeare bought a fine home at New Place on the corner of Chapel St and Chapel Lane; the house was demolished in 1759 and only the site and grounds remain. An Elizabethan knot garden has been laid out on part of the New Place grounds. The adjacent Nash's House, where his granddaughter lived, tells the town's history and contains an interesting picture of what the house looked like in 1876 and after a complete face-lift in 1911. Entry is £3/1.50.

Hall's Croft Shakespeare's daughter Susanna married the eminent doctor John

STRATFORD-UPON-AVON

PLACES TO STAY
3 Dukes
4 Payton Hotel
10 Alcester Rd B&Bs
30 Falcon Hotel
33 The Shakespeare
39 Swan's Nest Hotel
42 Arden Thistle Hotel
48 Main B&B Centre

PLACES TO EAT
5 Greek Connection
11 Lalbagh Balti Restaurant
12 Raj Tandoori Balti
13 Wholefood Café
18 Costa
29 Absolutely Fatty's
34 Vintner Wine Bar
35 Lambs
36 Opposition
37 Glory Hole
38 Boathouse Bar & Restaurant

PUBS
19 Slug & Lettuce
20 The Pen & Parchment
26 Garrick Inn
43 The Dirty Duck
47 Windmill Inn

OTHER
1 Bus Station
2 Stratford Leisure & Visitor Centre
6 The Shakespeare Centre
7 Shakespeare Bookshop
8 Cinema
9 Train Station
14 American Fountain
15 Bus to Anne Hathaway's Cottage
16 Shakespeare's Birthplace
17 Post Office
21 Guide Friday Bus Stop
22 TIC
23 Gower Memorial

OTHER (Continued)
24 Taxi Rank
25 Harvard House
27 Midland Bank Building
28 Police Station
31 New Place & Knott Garden
32 Nash's House
40 Royal Shakespeare Theatre
41 Swan Theatre
44 Guild Chapel
45 King Edward VI School
46 Almshouses
49 The Other Place
50 Hall's Croft
51 Sparklean Laundrette
52 Holy Trinity Church

Hall, and their fine Elizabethan town house stands near Holy Trinity Church. Displays explain medical practice in Shakespeare's time. Entry is £3/1.50. There's a café right next door.

Anne Hathaway's Cottage Before their marriage, Shakespeare's wife lived in Shottery, a mile west of Stratford, in a pretty thatched farmhouse with a garden and orchard. The nearby Tree Garden has samples of all the trees mentioned in Shake-

speare's plays. A footpath (no bikes allowed) leads to Shottery from Evesham Place, or catch a bus from Wood St (£1.20 return). Entry is £3.50/1.50.

Mary Arden's House The home of William's mother now houses the Shakespeare Countryside Museum with exhibits tracing local country life over the last four centuries. Since there's also a collection of rare farm animals and a turn-of-the-century farmhouse here, you'll probably need more

MIDLANDS

The Old Bard, William Shakespeare

Probably the greatest dramatist of all time, William Shakespeare was born in Stratford-upon-Avon in 1564, the son of a local glove maker. At the age of 18 he married Anne Hathaway, eight years his senior, and their first daughter, Susanna, was born about six months later. Boy and girl twins, Hamnet and Judith, followed two years later, but the son died at the age of 11.

Around the time of the twins' birth, Shakespeare moved to London and began to write for the Lord Chamberlain's Company. This successful company enjoyed the finest theatre (the Globe) and the best actors. It wasn't until the 1590s that Shakespeare's name appeared on his plays. Before that, the company's name was regarded as more important than the dramatist's.

Shakespeare's 37 plays made novel and inventive use of the English language, but also boasted superb plot structures and

William Shakespeare's house

deep insights into human nature – characteristics that have ensured not only their survival over the centuries but also their popularity in other languages. His earliest writings included comedies like *Comedy of Errors*, historical accounts like *Henry VI* and *Richard III* and the tragedy *Romeo and Juliet*. The new century saw his great tragedies, first *Hamlet* and then *Othello*, *King Lear* and *Macbeth*.

Around 1610 he retired, moved back to Stratford-upon-Avon, and lived in comfortable circumstances until his death in 1616. He was buried in the parish church. His wife outlived him by seven years.

Despite Shakespeare's prodigious output of plays, no letters or other personal writing have survived and the little that is known about him and his family has been pieced together from birth, death and marriage files and other official records (including the will in which he left his wife his 'second-best bed'!). This paucity of information has bred wild theories that Shakespeare didn't actually write the plays. Since none have survived in manuscript form, there's no handwriting evidence to prove they're his. Nonbelievers speculate that Shakespeare's origins and education were too humble to have provided the background, experience and knowledge to write the plays. Their favourites for the 'real' Shakespeare are the Earl of Derby or the Earl of Oxford who, they claim, may have had reasons for wanting to remain anonymous.

MIDLANDS

time here than at the other properties. Entry is £4/2.

Mary Arden's House is at Wilmcote, 3 miles west of Stratford. If you cycle there via Anne Hathaway's Cottage, follow the Stratford-upon-Avon Canal towpath to Wilmcote rather than retracing your route or riding back along the busy A3400.

Holy Trinity Church

Holy Trinity Church (☎ 266316) has transepts from the mid-13th century, when it was greatly enlarged. It has had frequent later additions; the spire dates from 1763. In the chancel, there are photocopies of Shakespeare's baptism and burial records, his grave and that of his wife, and a bust that was erected seven years after Shakespeare's death but before his wife's and thus assumed to be a good likeness. An off-putting barrier across the choir makes it hard to wriggle out of paying the 60p donation 'requested' to see these mementos. In summer, the church is open Monday to Saturday from 8.30 am to 6 pm and Sunday from 2 to 5 pm.

Harvard House

Exuberantly carved Harvard House, in High St, was home to the mother of John Harvard, who founded Harvard University in the USA in the late 16th century. It now houses a collection of pewter. It's free and open Tuesday to Saturday from May to late October from 10 am to 4 pm (Sunday from 10.30 am).

Next door is the Garrick Inn, while across the road the Midland Bank Building has reliefs illustrating scenes from Shakespeare's plays.

Other Things to See

Erected in 1881, the Gower Memorial features a statue of Shakespeare surrounded by four of his characters – Falstaff, Hamlet, Lady Macbeth and Prince Hal. It overlooks the canal basin, where the Stratford-upon-Avon Canal meets the Avon River, a popular place to watch narrowboats 'working the lock'.

The Guild Chapel, at the junction of Chapel Lane and Church St, dates from 1269, although it was rebuilt in the 15th century. Next door is King Edward VI School, which Shakespeare probably attended; it was originally the Guildhall.

The Royal Shakespeare Company Gallery (☎ 412602) inside the Swan Theatre exhibits the RSC's collection of props, costumes and theatrical paraphernalia. It's open Monday to Saturday from 9.30 am to 5 pm and Sunday from noon to 4.30 pm (11 am to 3.30 pm on winter Sundays); entry costs £1.50/1. Theatre tours operate Monday to Friday from 1.30 and 5.30 pm (except matinee days) and Sunday at 12.30, 1.45, 2.45 and 3.45 pm (one hour earlier in winter). Tours plus entry to the RSC collection cost £4/3.

Places to Stay

Hostel The *youth hostel (☎ 297093, Hemmingford House, Alveston)* is 1½ miles from the town centre. From the TIC, walk across Clopton Bridge and turn left (north-east) along Tiddington Rd (B4086). Bus No 18 runs to Alveston from Bridge St. The hostel is open from early January to mid-December and charges £13.45/10.05 for adults/juniors.

Camping There are two camping grounds on Stratford's western outskirts. *Dodwell Park (☎ 204957, Evesham Rd)* charges from £6 to £9 for a tent for two. From Easter to September two people can camp at *Stratford Racecourse (☎ 267949, Luddington Rd)* for £4.

B&Bs B&Bs can be ridiculously expensive – and hard to find – during summer. Prime hunting grounds for cheaper places are Evesham Place, Grove Rd and Broad Walk, only a couple of minutes walk from the town centre. If you're stuck, the TIC charges £3 plus a 10% deposit to help you find something. South Warwickshire Tourism also has a booking hotline (☎ 415061) for credit card bookings. It operates Monday to Friday from 9.30 am to 4 pm.

Possibilities in Evesham Place that will cost between £15 and £20 a head include the cheerful *Grosvenor Villa (☎ 266192, 9 Evesham Place)*; the *Dylan Guest House*

(☎ 204819, 10 Evesham Place); the good-value, nonsmoking **Clomendy** (☎ 266957, 157 Evesham Place); and the **Arrandale** (☎ 267112, 208 Evesham Place). Others along Grove Rd include **Woodstock Guest House** (☎ 299881, 30 Grove Rd), or the **Ambleside Guest House** (☎ 297239, 41 Grove Rd).

Along Evesham Place slightly pricier B&Bs (£20 to £25 a head) with private bathroom include the cosy **Virginia Lodge** (☎ 292157, 12 Evesham Place) and **Aberfoyle** (☎ 295703, 3 Evesham Place). Some rooms at the otherwise good **Carlton Guest House** (☎ 293548, 22 Evesham Place) lack private bathrooms. Up a price bracket but decidedly snazzy is **Twelfth Night** (☎ 414595, 13 Evesham Place), with singles/doubles from £35/44.

There are several places on Alcester Rd, near the train station. **Hunters Moon Guest House** (☎ 292888, 150 Alcester Rd) has beds from £19 to £26 a head, while the **Moonlight Bed & Breakfast** (☎ 298213, 144 Alcester Rd) charges from £15 to £17 per person. Rooms with baths at **Moonraker House** (☎ 299346, 40 Alcester Rd) cost from £35/46.

Hotels Numerous pricey hotels cater to international package tours. Theatre-goers could hardly do better than stay at the **Arden Thistle Hotel** (☎ 294949), immediately across the road from the Swan Theatre, but rooms start at £92/100. In Chapel St, **The Shakespeare** (☎ 294771), with its beautiful historic buildings, has rooms from £106/136 while the **Falcon Hotel** (☎ 279953) has rooms from £80/105.

Smaller, more reasonably priced hotels include **Dukes** (☎ 269300, Payton St), which backs onto the canal and has rooms with bath from £50/70.

The much smaller **Payton Hotel** (☎ 266442, 6 John St), across the road, charges from £38/56.

Places to Eat

Sheep St is wall-to-wall restaurants. The **Glory Hole** (☎ 293546, 21 Sheep St) offers steaks for £8.95. The **Opposition** (☎ 269980, 13 Sheep St) has pasta from £5.95. **Lambs** (☎ 292554, 12 Sheep St) does dishes like hot satay chicken for £6.95, while the **Vintner Wine Bar** (☎ 297259, 5 Sheep St) does vegetarian gnocchi for £6.50.

At **Absolutely Fatty's** (☎ 267069, 9 Chapel St) you can expect to pay around £8.50 for a meal in stylish surrounds. The **Greek Connection** (☎ 292214, corner of Birmingham Rd and Shakespeare St) is the place to go for plate-smashing fun; moussaka costs £9.25.

Asian restaurants include **Lalbagh Balti Restaurant** (☎ 293563, 3 Greenhill St) and the **Raj Tandoori Balti** (☎ 267067, 7 Greenhill St). Nearby, the **Wholefood Café** does pleasant soups (£2) and salads from 11.45 am to 2.15 pm.

The **Boathouse Bar & Restaurant** is pleasantly positioned by Clopton Bridge, allowing river views to go with sizeable portions of food.

If you're just after a coffee go to **Costa** (corner of Union and Henley Sts).

Entertainment

Pubs A pint at the **Dirty Duck** (aka the Black Swan), close to the river in Waterside, is an essential Stratford experience because of its theatrical connections. The popular **Slug & Lettuce** (38 Guild St) also does food. The **Windmill Inn** (Church St) is reputed to be the oldest pub in town, although the **Falcon Hotel** (Chapel St) has been licensed for the longest continuous period.

Theatre Seeing a Royal Shakespeare Company production (☎ 295623) is a must. Performances take place in the main **Royal Shakespeare Theatre**, the adjacent **Swan Theatre** or, nearby, **The Other Place**. Tickets cost from £8 to £37 and the box office in the Royal Shakespeare Theatre is open Monday to Saturday from 9.30 am to 8 pm. Stand-by tickets are available to students, under-19s and over-60s on the day of the performance (£11 or £14); over-60s also qualify for £12 tickets for weekday matinees and Wednesday evening shows, provided they book 24 hours in advance. Standing room tickets may be available up to the last moment for £5.

Getting There & Away

Stratford is 93 miles from London, 40 miles from Oxford and 8 miles from Warwick.

Bus National Express (☎ 0990-808080) buses link Birmingham, Stratford, Warwick, Oxford, Heathrow and London several times a day. Singles from Stratford include Birmingham (£4.65) and Heathrow/Victoria (£11.50). The National Express stop is on Bridge St, opposite McDonald's.

Stagecoach Midland Red (☎ 01788-535555) operates to Warwick (20 minutes, £2.50), Coventry (1¼ hours, £2.50), Birmingham (one hour, £2.60) and Oxford (1½ hours, £3.90). The useful Cotswold Shuttle offers three daily services (except Sunday) to Broadway, Moreton-in-Marsh, Stow-on-the-Wold and Bourton-on-the-Water. With a £4.50 Day Explorer ticket you could stop off at Broadway and then continue on the same day to one of the other Cotswold towns. There's also a weekday service to Chipping Campden.

Train Stratford station is on Station Rd, a few minutes walk west of the centre. There are several daily services direct from London Paddington (2½ hours, £17.50).

Coming from the north, it's sometimes easier to transfer at Leamington Spa, sometimes at Birmingham. Services from Birmingham depart from Moor St station (50 minutes, £3.30).

Getting Around

Call Busline (☎ 01788-535555) for local bus information. Bus No 18 operates via the Alveston hostel to Warwick and Leamington Spa, hourly from Monday to Saturday.

Guide Friday (☎ 294466) operates open-top buses that do circuits past the five Shakespeare properties every 15 minutes during peak summer months for £7.50/2. You can pick them up outside the TIC.

Stratford is small enough to explore on

foot, but a bicycle is good for getting out to the surrounding country or the rural Shakespeare properties. The canal towpath offers a fine route to Wilmcote. Punts, canoes and rowing boats are available from the boat-house by Clopton Bridge for £4 an hour.

AROUND STRATFORD-UPON-AVON

Stratford-upon-Avon is ringed by pretty villages, atmospheric pubs and stately homes. The popular Cotswold villages of Chipping Campden and Broadway are only a short distance south, and Warwick, Coventry and Birmingham are within day-tripping distance. You could even walk or cycle to Birmingham along the Stratford-upon-Avon Canal towpath.

Charlecote Park

Sir Thomas Lucy is said to have caught the young Shakespeare poaching deer in the grounds of Charlecote Park (☎ 01789-470277, NT), around 5 miles east of Stratford-upon-Avon. The park, which was landscaped by Capability Brown, still has deer. The house was built in the 1550s and rebuilt in the 1830s. It's open Friday to Tuesday from April through October from 11 am to 5 pm. Entry is £4.80. Bus Nos 19/X18 go there from Stratford-upon-Avon (25 minutes, £2.30 return).

Ragley Hall

Ragley Hall (☎ 01789-762090) is a Palladian house a couple of miles south-west of Alcester. The house was built between 1679 and 1683, but the over-the-top plaster ceilings and huge portico were added later. The intriguing South Staircase Hall with its murals and ceiling painting was painted between 1968 and 1982. The house is open Thursday to Sunday from April through September, from 11 am to 5 pm (guided tours are at 11 am and noon); the park also opens daily in July and August from 10 am to 6 pm. Entry is £5/3.50.

Birmingham

• pop 1,014,000 ☎ 0121

Birmingham is Britain's second largest city and it's a great shame that most visitors arrive either at New St train station or at Digbeth coach station and so get the worst possible introduction. Birmingham remains a major manufacturing centre, a city of fierce pride and boundless vitality. Although there are no essential sights and the city centre is chopped to pieces by ring roads, there are still some interesting corners, especially in Brindleyplace, the award-winning waterfront development around the old canal network.

The city was one of the great centres of the Industrial Revolution, home to inventors like steam pioneers James Watt (1736-1819) and Matthew Boulton (1728-1809), gas lighting whiz kid William Murdock (1754-1839), printer John Baskerville (1706-75) and chemist Joseph Priestley (1733-1804). But by the mid-19th century, the 'workshop of the world' exemplified everything that was bad about industrial development. Under enlightened mayors like Joseph Chamberlain (1869-1940), father of the unfortunate Neville, the city became a trendsetter in civic development, but WWII air raids undid their good work; post-war town planners completed the vandalism by designing the ring roads and motorways that virtually obliterated the old city centre. The connection between the M5, M6 and M42 is such a mess that it's commonly known as Spaghetti Junction.

The Birmingham accent is consistently rated England's most unattractive. Locally, the city is known as Brum, the inhabitants as Brummies and the dialect as Brummie.

Orientation

The endless ring roads and roundabouts make Birmingham a confusing city to find your way around, particularly if you're driving. Make life easier for yourself and leave your car at home.

The city centre is the pedestrian precinct in front of the huge Council House. Head west from here to Centenary Square, the Convention Centre and Symphony Hall, and the Gas St Basin/Brindleyplace development. Head north-west for the Jewellery Quarter.

South-east of the Council House most of Birmingham's shops can be found along pedestrianised New St and in the modern City Plaza, Pallasades, Pavilions and Bull Ring shopping centres; the latter is overlooked by the landmark Rotunda office block.

After dark the underpasses linking New St station to Digbeth coach station can seem very alarming especially for lone women. The good news is that plans in the pipeline will see the whole ghastly Bull Ring mess razed to the ground.

Information

The most useful TIC (☎ 693 6300) is the one at 130 Colmore Row, on Victoria Square. There's another TIC at 2 City Arcade (☎ 643 2514) and a third in the National Exhibition Centre (☎ 780 4321), roughly midway between Birmingham and Coventry and near Birmingham airport.

Town Centre

The central pedestrian precinct of Victoria and Chamberlain squares features a statue of Queen Victoria, a fountain, a memorial to Joseph Chamberlain and some of Birmingham's most eye-catching architecture. The imposing **Council House** forms the north-east face for the precinct and houses the Museum & Art Gallery, which is connected by a bridge to the Gas Hall building topped by the Big Brum clock tower. The precinct's north-west corner is formed by the modernist Central Library, an inverted ziggurat with the Paradise Forum shop and café complex next to it.

To the south stands the **Town Hall**, designed by Joseph Hansom (creator of the Hansom Cab) in 1834 to look like the Temple of Castor and Pollux in Rome. For those who won't make it to Gateshead to see Antony Gormley's 'Angel of the North' statue, his wingless 'Iron Man' of 1993 should give you the general idea.

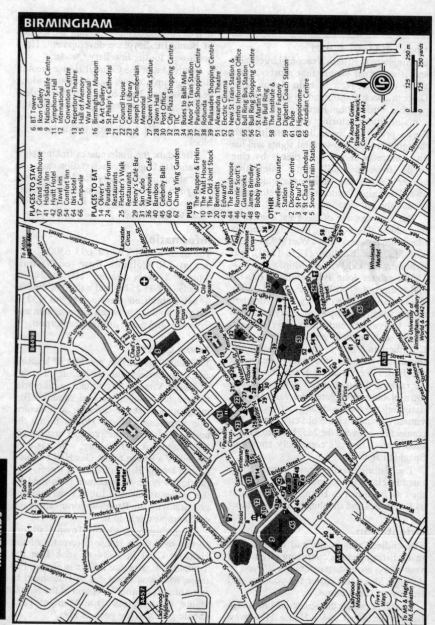

BIRMINGHAM

PLACES TO STAY
17 Grand Moathouse
41 Holiday Inn
42 Hyatt Hotel
50 Travel Inn
54 Comfort Inn
64 Ibis Hotel
66 Campanile

PLACES TO EAT
14 Oliver's
24 Paradise Forum
   Restaurants
25 Fletcher's Walk
29 Henry's Café Bar
31 San Carlo
36 Warehouse Café
45 Bambos
45 Celebrity Balti
60 Circo
62 Chung Ying Garden

PUBS
7 The Flapper & Firkin
10 The Mad House
19 The Old Joint Stock
20 Bennetts
43 Edward's
44 The Brasshouse
47 Ronnie Scott's
   Glassworks
48 James Brindley
49 Bobby Brown's

6 BT Tower
8 Ikon Gallery
9 National Sealife Centre
11 Symphony Hall
12 International
   Convention Centre
13 Repertory Theatre
15 Hall of Memory
   War Memorial
16 Birmingham Museum
   & Art Gallery
18 St Philip's Cathedral
21 TIC
22 Council House
23 Central Library
26 Joseph Chamberlain
   Memorial
27 Queen Victoria Statue
28 Town Hall
30 Post Office
32 City Plaza Shopping Centre
33 TIC
34 Buses to Balti Mile
35 Moor St Train Station
37 Pavilions Shopping Centre
38 Rotunda
39 Palisades Shopping Centre
51 Alexandra Theatre
52 Electric Cinema
53 New St Train Station &
   Centro Information Office
55 Bull Ring Bus Station
56 Bull Ring Shopping Centre
57 St Martin's in
   the Bull Ring
58 The Institute &
   Dance Factory
59 Digbeth Coach Station
61 Pulse
63 Hippodrome
65 Arcadian Centre

OTHER
1 Jewellery Quarter
   Station
2 Discovery Centre
3 St Paul's
4 St Chad's Cathedral
5 Snow Hill Train Station

King's College pinnacles, Cambridge

King's College Chapel

Lavenham, Suffolk

Tudor style house, Lavenham

Christ's College gate, Cambridge

A donkey ride along the beach at Blackpool, Lancashire

South-west of the precinct, Centenary Square is another pedestrian square closed off at the east end by the International Convention Centre and the Symphony Hall, and overlooked by the Repertory Theatre. In the centre is the Hall of Memory War Memorial and a curious modern statue ('Forward') depicting a cluster of Brummies.

Canal System

Birmingham sits on the hub of England's canal network, and visiting narrowboats can moor in the Gas St Basin right in the heart of the city.

During the 1990s the creation of Brindleyplace, a waterfront development of trendy cafés and bars alongside the National Indoor Arena and the National Sealife Centre, has turned this into the most vibrant, attractive part of the city, a must for visitors. If you follow the towpath north-east along the Birmingham and Fazeley Canal you'll see just what a wonder has been worked – the farther out you walk, the grimmer and more run-down the surroundings become.

The state-of-the-art **National Sealife Centre** (☎ 633 4700) is open daily from 10 am to 5 pm for £6.50/4.50.

St Philip's Cathedral

In Colmore Row, St Philip's was built in neoclassical style between 1709 and 1715 and became a cathedral in 1905. The 19th century Pre-Raphaelite artist Edward Burne-Jones was responsible for the magnificent stained-glass windows: the Last Judgement at the west end, the Nativity, Crucifixion and Ascension at the east end.

Birmingham Museum & Art Gallery

In Chamberlain Square, the newly restored museum (☎ 235 2834) boasts displays on archaeology, local and natural history, but pride of place goes to the art collection, particularly the Pre-Raphaelite paintings. Until the Museum of Science and Industry finds a new home in the planned Millennium Point development, people keen on science will have to make do with the Light on Science Gallery here. The museum is open Monday to Saturday from 10 am to 5 pm and on Sunday from 12.30 to 5.30 pm. Entry is free.

Jewellery Quarter

Birmingham is a major jewellery manufacturing centre and the Jewellery Quarter is

---

The Pre-Raphaelites and the Arts and Crafts Movement

The Pre-Raphaelite Brotherhood was formed in 1848 by three young British artists: Dante Gabriel Rossetti, William Holman Hunt and John Everett Millais. Four other artists soon joined them in their rejection of contemporary English art and reverence, in favour of the directness of art prior to the High Renaissance, especially the work of Raphael.

Often unashamedly romantic in its view of the past, their work was characterised by almost photographic attention to detail, a combination of hyper-realism and brilliant colours that ensured the movement's popularity to this day.

Birmingham Museum & Art Gallery has one of the best collections of works by the Pre-Raphaelites. If you get the bug, there are more fine paintings in the Lady Lever Art Gallery at Port Sunlight near Liverpool.

The Arts and Crafts movement followed Pre-Raphaelitism in its rejection of contemporary standards and its yearning for an earlier, purer and more naturalistic style. The socialist William Morris, the movement's leading light, had worked with Rossetti and projected the same ideals into tapestries, jewellery, stained glass and textile prints. Cheltenham Art Gallery & Museum has a fine display of Arts and Crafts furniture, as does Arlington Mill in Bibury, Gloucestershire.

MIDLANDS

packed with manufacturers and showrooms. The *Jewellery Quarter Magazine* has an interesting walking tour map taking you past the 1903 Chamberlain Clock and various other sights.

The Discovery Centre (☎ 554 3598), 75-79 Vyse St, shows you the Smith & Pepper jewellery factory, as it was on the day it closed in 1981 after 80 years of operation. It's open Monday to Friday from 10 am to 4 pm and Saturday from 11 am to 5 pm. Entry is £2/1.50.

You can walk to the Jewellery Quarter in 15 minutes or take a train from Moor St to Jewellery Quarter station.

Soho House

The industrialist Matthew Boulton lived in Soho House (☎ 554 9122), Soho Ave, Handsworth, which has been restored to let visitors see what such a house would have looked like in the 18th century. It's open Tuesday to Saturday from 10 am to 5 pm and on Sunday from noon. Admission costs £2/1.50. You could walk here from the Jewellery Quarter, or bus Nos 70, 74, 78 and 79 pass by.

Aston Hall

Built between 1618 and 1635, this Jacobean mansion (☎ 327 0062) with a fine long gallery is in Aston Park on Trinity Rd, Aston, about 3 miles north of the city centre. It's open from Easter through October, daily from 2 to 5 pm and entry is free. Get there on bus No 65 or 104 or take a train to Aston station.

Other Galleries

The small collection of old masters at the **Barber Institute of Fine Arts** (☎ 472 0962) is at the University of Birmingham, 2½ miles south of the city centre (get off at University station). The **Ikon Gallery** (☎ 248 0708), Oozells Square, Brindleyplace, features changing exhibitions of modern art.

Organised Tours

From May to September Guide Friday operates seven daily 90-minute bus tours for £7/2 a head. Phone the TIC (☎ 693 6300) for details of ghost and graveyard tours (£4.50/4) as well as more conventional walking tours of the city centre.

Canal boat trips can be arranged from the Gas St Basin or the Convention Centre quay (☎ 507 0477) for around £3/2 a head.

Places to Stay

Birmingham has no YHA hostel. Most accommodation in the centre is aimed at business visitors, and over weekends or during summer it may be worth asking at the TIC in case there are special deals to fill surplus beds. Otherwise, since the B&Bs are out in the suburbs and a day is enough to see the sights, you could consider staying farther out and day-tripping into Birmingham. Stratford-upon-Avon is a short train ride away.

Although one reader recommended the 92 room *YWCA* (☎ 726110, *Alexandra House, 27 Norfolk Rd, Edgbaston*), which has dorm beds for £8 a night, the hostel is clear that 'our priority is to provide accommodation for those people without homes'.

Popular areas for B&Bs include Edgbaston (to the south-west) and Acocks Green (to the south-east). The friendly *Ashdale House Hotel* (☎ 706 3598, *39 Broad Rd, Acocks Green*) has six singles from £20, and three doubles from £30; some rooms have a bathroom. Vegetarian breakfasts can be arranged.

Birmingham has a full set of mid-range chain hotels – perfectly comfortable although lacking in character. Closest to New St station is the *Comfort Inn* (☎ 643 1134, *Station St*), with singles/doubles for £45/65. The centrally located *Ibis Hotel* (☎ 622 6010, *Arcadian Centre, Ladywell Walk*) has double rooms at £44 (breakfast is £5.25 extra). The *Travel Inn* (☎ 644 5266, *230 Broad St*) is ideally placed for exploring the Brindleyplace nightlife. Rooms cost a flat £49.95.

Just beyond the ring road, the *Campanile* (☎ 622 4925, *55 Irving St*) offers motel-style accommodation. Doubles with bath are £36.50 (£29.95 on Friday and Saturday); breakfast is £4.50 per person.

Nicest of the posh places is the *Grand Moathouse* (☎ *607 9988, Colmore Row*), overlooking the cathedral, but a single/double would set you back £110/130.

Places to Eat

Birmingham's contribution to world cuisine is the Balti, a uniquely Midlands version of Indian food. England is now engulfed with Balti houses, but Birmingham remains their homeland. The most down-to-earth prices are in the Birmingham Balti Mile of Sparkbrook, Sparkhill and Balsall Heath, 2 miles south of the centre, where 54 restaurants are squeezed into just three streets. Pick up a complete listings leaflet in the TIC and head out on bus No 4, 5 or 6 from Corporation St.

Luckily there are also a few goodies in the city centre. The *Celebrity Balti* (☎ *632 6074, 44 Broad St*) is much glossier than average, but the food is delicious. Baltis range from £6.25 to £8.95.

Off Chamberlain Square, *Paradise Forum* has a variety of fast-food outlets (a vast *McDonald's*) and cafés (*Starbucks*). Fletcher's Walk, Paradise Place, immediately to the south, boasts *Ciao Bella* (☎ *233 2484*), a good Italian restaurant, and *Casa Paco* (☎ *233 1533*), with decent Spanish grub.

Dine in classier surroundings in the *Edwardian Tea Room* in the Museum & Art Gallery; fish pie costs £4.25 or there are sandwiches and cakes.

Big, busy *Henry's Café Bar* (☎ *631 3827, Hill St*) serves everything from burgers to cashew nut paella for £5.95. *Bambos* (☎ *643 5621, 113 John Bright St*) features Greek food and live music.

In the same building as Friends of the Earth, the *Warehouse Café* (☎ *633 0261, 54 Allison St, Digbeth*) specialises in vegan food and is open Monday to Saturday until 9 pm.

In the Arcadian Centre in Hurst St the *Green Room* serves a popular pre-theatre menu to Hippodrome punters; specials are around £4.95. Excellent Cantonese cuisine can be had nearby at *Chung Ying Garden* (☎ *666 6622, 17 Thorpe St*), which wheels out 70 varieties of dim sum and chicken dishes from £6.80. *Circo* (☎ *643 1400, 6 Holloway Circus*) is a popular tapas bar offering a £5 lunch time special of 1kg of mussels, French fries, salad and mayonnaise.

San Carlo (☎ *633 0251, 4 Temple St*) has a lengthy Italian menu, well worth sampling. *Olivier's* (☎ *644 6464*), the Repertory Theatre's restaurant, comes in for plenty of praise; try the pre-theatre menu for £9.50 or go à la carte and pay more like £15 – the Balti duck is said to be delicious. Press on to Brindleyplace and you'll find wall-to-wall eateries, with many of the big chains represented. More one-off is *Tin Tin* (☎ *633 0888*), a classy Chinese restaurant where fish dishes are particularly good.

Entertainment

What's On (free at the TIC, otherwise 80p) is a fortnightly listings guide to entertainment in and around Birmingham.

Pubs & Clubs Pleasant canal-side pubs include the *James Brindley (Gas St Basin)*, which is named after the canal pioneer, and the trendy *Glassworks (Gas St Basin)*. Facing each other across the canal in Broad St are the *Brasshouse* and *Edward's*, while the *Flapper & Firkin*, a little farther along at Cambrian Wharf, is decorated in canal style. The *Malt House* has a great position near the National Indoor Arena.

Birmingham has several impressive banks turned bars. *Bennetts* (☎ *643 9293, Bennetts Hill*) serves up tasty food (garlic and ginger creole prawns for £4.25) to accompany the drinks in grand surroundings. Alternatively, try *The Old Joint Stock (Temple Row)*, facing the cathedral.

The *Institute & Dance Factory* (☎ *643 7788, Digbeth High St*) is a large nightclub that often has live music. The busy *Steering Wheel* (☎ *622 3385, Wrottesley St, Chinatown*) has three dance floors, or there's *Pulse* (☎ *643 4715, Hurst St*), which serves up something different every night of the week.

The **Glee Club** (☎ 693 2248, Hurst St) hosts stand-up comedians four nights a week.

Theatre & Cinema The Victoria Square TIC has a ticket shop (☎ 643 2514) where, from 11 am daily, you can buy half-price theatre tickets (75p booking fee). Theatres include the **Hippodrome** (☎ 622 7486), home of the Birmingham Royal Ballet; the **Alexandra Theatre** (☎ 643 1231); and the **Repertory Theatre** (☎ 236 4455).

The fantastically decorated **Electric Cinema** (☎ 643 7277, Station Rd) sometimes has double bills for £2.70.

Music **Ronnie Scott's** famous jazz club (☎ 643 4525, Broad St) charges £11 to £16 entry depending on the night. The City of Birmingham Symphony Orchestra plays in the ultramodern **Symphony Hall** (☎ 212 3333). Big rock acts appear at the **National Exhibition Centre** (☎ 780 4133).

Getting There & Away
Birmingham is a major train and coach interchange; see the fares tables in the Getting Around chapter. It also boasts an increasingly busy international airport (☎ 767 7000) with flights to numerous European destinations and to New York.

Train New St station, one of England's busiest rail interchanges, is underneath the Pallasades shopping centre, which in turn is linked with the Bull Ring bus station and Bull Ring shopping centre. For the National Exhibition Centre or Birmingham airport get off at Birmingham International station.

Bus National Express (☎ 0990-808080) has links to most parts of Britain from dreary Digbeth coach station. A single ticket to London costs £9 (3½ hours). Local buses operate from the Bull Ring bus station. Bus No X93 goes to Kidderminster for the Severn Valley Railway.

Getting Around
For rail and bus services in and around Birmingham, the Centro phone number is ☎ 200 2700. A Daytripper ticket (£3.70) gives all-day travel on buses and trains after 9.30 am. Local trains, including the Stratford-upon-Avon service, operate from Moor St station, which is only a few minutes walk from New St – follow the red line on the pavement. Other handy stations are at Snow Hill and the Jewellery Quarter.

AROUND BIRMINGHAM
Cadbury World & Bournville Village
Chocoholics should make a beeline for Cadbury World, where you can find out the story behind a crème egg and visit the chocolate packaging plant where around 800 bars a minute are wrapped and dispatched. Not surprisingly this place is packed over weekends and school holidays when it's best to book ahead by phoning ☎ 0121-451 4159. Opening hours vary throughout the year but are generally daily from 10 am to 5.30 pm. Entry is £6.25/4.50.

To get to Cadbury World take a train to Bournville station from Birmingham New St (15 minutes, £1.55 return). In summer Guide Friday tours drop off at Cadbury World.

Before returning, follow the signs to pretty Bournville village, designed for early 20th century factory workers by the Cadbury family with large houses set round a green. It's also well worth visiting **Selly Manor** (☎ 0121-472 0199), the sort of half-timbered medieval-cum-Elizabethan house you see in Stratford but without the crowds. It's open Tuesday to Friday from 10 am to 5 pm. Entry costs £1.50/50p. The manor also stocks the excellent *Bournville Trail Guide*.

Black Country Museum
The area stretching west of Birmingham and out to Wolverhampton was traditionally known as the Black Country because of the smoke and dust generated by the local coal and iron industries. The 10.5 hectare Black Country Museum (☎ 0121-557 9463) fea-

tures a re-created coal mine, village and fairground on the banks of the Dudley Canal at Tipton in Dudley. It's a great place for a day out, with a full program of mine trips, Charlie Chaplin films and chances to watch glass cutters and sweet makers in action.

From March through October you can also take a 40 minute boat ride through the Dudley Canal Tunnel to explore assorted caverns (£2.50/2).

The museum is open daily from March through October from 10 am to 5.30 pm, and Wednesday to Sunday from 10 am to 4 pm in winter. Admission costs £6.95/4.50. The **Stables Restaurant** offers pretty mundane on-site meals, or there's the excellent re-created **fish and chip shop** (£2 a portion). The **Bottle & Glass Inn** serves a limited range of beverages.

To get there from Birmingham city centre, take the No 126 bus from Corporation Rd and ask to be put off at Tipton Rd. It's a 10 minute walk along Tipton Rd to the museum, or you can catch bus No 311 or 313. A £2.30 day ticket will cover the entire journey.

Northamptonshire

Northampton itself has just a handful of buildings of interest, but the surrounding area boasts two of England's finest surviving Saxon churches, a fine canal museum, Britain's most important motor racing circuit and the shrine to the late Princess Diana in the grounds of Althorp House.

For local bus information phone ☎ 01604-620077.

NORTHAMPTON
• pop 154,000 ☎ 01604

Although nothing significant remains of it, Thomas à Becket was tried for fraud in Northampton Castle in 1164. A fire in 1675 left few other reminders of medieval Northampton. The Industrial Revolution made the town a shoe-manufacturing centre and the **Central Museum & Art Gallery** (☎ 39415), Guildhall St, has a collection of shoes to make foot fetishists drool. That

aside, there's little to linger for, although **Holy Sepulchre Church** has curiosity value as one of only four round churches in the country. The TIC (☎ 22677) is at 10 Giles Square, directly across from the Guildhall, and has information about surrounding attractions.

AROUND NORTHAMPTON
Althorp

With the late Diana, Princess of Wales, generating as much newspaper footage in death as she did in life, you can be certain that thousands of people will throng to visit the memorial and museum in the grounds of her ancestral home, Althorp Park, off the A428 north-west of Northampton. But the park is only open in July and August and tickets cost a hefty £9.50/5 (profits go to her Memorial Fund). The limited number of tickets must be booked in advance (☎ 01604-592020), making it unlikely that many tourists will stand a chance of getting past the gates. Incidentally, Althorp should be pronounced altrup!

Stoke Bruerne Canal Museum

On a pretty stretch of the Grand Union Canal at Stoke Bruerne, 8 miles south of Northampton, the excellent Canal Museum (☎ 01604-862229) explains the development of English canals and displays models of pioneering canal engineering. Entry costs £2.90/1.90 – the £1.20 car park fee will be refunded with the ticket. It's open daily from Easter to September from 10 am to 6 pm; and Tuesday to Sunday from 10 am to 4 pm in winter.

There are several pleasant pubs serving food on the banks of the canal, as well as the stylish **Old Chapel** restaurant (☎ 863284), which stays open until 9 pm. **Wharf Cottage** (☎ 862174) offers B&B overlooking the canal.

Silverstone

The British Grand Prix motor race is held in July at Silverstone (☎ 01327-857271), just south of the A43. It's still one of the fastest racing circuits in Europe, with a lap record of more than 140 mph, despite the extra corners added in to slow cars down.

All Saints, Brixworth

About 8 miles north of Northampton off the A508, All Saints (☎ 01604-880286) is England's largest relatively intact Saxon church. Built on a basilica plan around 680, it incorporates Roman tiles from an earlier building. The tower and stair turret were

Saxon Tower of Earls Barton church

added after 9th century Viking raids, the spire around 1350. It's usually open from 10 am to 5 pm (4 pm in winter). Stagecoach bus Nos X60 and 62 come here from Northampton.

All Saints, Earls Barton

About 8 miles east of Northampton, the church at Earls Barton is notable for its solid Saxon tower with patterns seemingly imitating earlier wooden models. It was probably built during the reign of Edgar the Peaceful (959-95) and the 1st floor door may have offered access to the tower during Viking raids. Around 1100, the Norman nave was added to the original tower; other features were added in subsequent centuries. Stagecoach bus Nos 45, 46 and 47 come here from Northampton.

Buckinghamshire

Buckinghamshire is uneventful commuter country, a pleasant mix of urban and rural landscapes. To the south the M40 motorway bypasses the gentrified dormitory towns of Beaconsfield and High Wycombe en route to Oxford and Birmingham. To the north, beside the M1, is Milton Keynes, England's most famous, if dull, planned new town and home to more than a quarter of Buckinghamshire's population. The county town of Aylesbury is centrally located.

Among the many commuters drawn here were the influential Rothschilds, who constructed several impressive houses around Aylesbury. In 1852 they built Mentmore Towers (now headquarters to the Transcendental Meditation organisation), enlarged Ascott House and created an imitation French chateau at Waddesdon. Other well-known figures who have lived in Buckinghamshire include the poets John Milton (in Chalfont St Giles, where his cottage is open to the public), TS Eliot and Shelley (Marlow), and Robert Frost (Beaconsfield).

Stretching across the south of Buckinghamshire, the Chilterns are a range of chalk hills famous for their beech woods. The countryside is particularly attractive in autumn.

WALKS

The 85 mile Ridgeway follows the Chilterns to Ivinghoe Beacon in the east of the county. There are forest trails in the Chilterns and along the Grand Union Canal, which cuts across the county's north-eastern edge on its way from London to Birmingham.

GETTING AROUND

For Buckinghamshire bus information, phone the weekday inquiry line (☎ 01296-382000).

AYLESBURY

• pop 52,000   ☎ 01296

Affluent Aylesbury has been the county town since 1725. Yet apart from being a transport hub with frequent trains to London Marylebone (one hour, £8.60), it has little to offer visitors. However, the TIC (☎ 330559), 8 Bourbon St, can provide general Buckinghamshire information.

AROUND AYLESBURY
Waddesdon Manor

Designed by a French architect for Baron Ferdinand de Rothschild, Waddesdon Manor (☎ 01296-651226, NT) was completed in 1889 in Renaissance style to house the baron's art collection, Sèvres porcelain and French furniture.

Several million pounds have been spent on restoring the house. It's open Thursday to Sunday from April through October from 11 am to 4 pm; also on Wednesday in July and August. Entry is £6. The grounds are open Wednesday to Sunday from March to mid-December from 10 am to 5 pm; entry costs £3/1.50. Entry is by timed ticket. You can book in advance but must pay a £2.50 booking fee.

The chateau is 6 miles north-west of Aylesbury. From Aylesbury bus station, take Aylesbury Bus No 16 (☎ 84919, 15 minutes).

Claydon House

The decoration of Claydon's grand rooms is said to be England's finest example of the light, decorative rococo style that developed from the more ponderous baroque in early 18th century France. Florence Nightingale lived here for several years and a museum houses mementos of her Crimean stay.

Claydon House (☎ 01296-730349, NT) is open Saturday to Wednesday from April through October from 1 to 5 pm; entry is £4. It's 13 miles north-west of Aylesbury; buses drop you in Middle Claydon, 2 miles from the house.

Stowe Landscape Gardens

About 4 miles north of the pleasant county town of Buckingham, Stowe is the sort of private school so exclusive its driveway is half a mile long. The greatest British landscape gardeners, Charles Bridgeman, William Kent and Capability Brown, all worked on the grounds.

The gardens (☎ 01280-822850, NT) are known for their 32 temples, created in the 18th century by the wealthy owner Sir Richard Temple, whose family motto was *Templa Quam Delecta* (How Delightful are your Temples). Among them, the Temple of British Worthies displays busts of Shakespeare and others.

The gardens are open to the public during school holidays. From early July through September they're open daily from 10 am to 5 pm for £4.20. For another £2 you can also look round parts of the house.

CHILTERN HILLS

The nearest range of hills to London, the Chilterns stretch from the outskirts of Reading (Berkshire) 40 miles north-east across southern Buckinghamshire. There are good though undramatic views and this is a popular walking area.

Wendover

An attractive small town on the Ridgeway, Wendover makes a good base for several walks. The TIC (☎ 01296-696759) is in the clock tower in the High St.

At 260m (853 feet), **Coombe Hill**, 1½ miles west of Wendover, is the highest point in the Chilterns, with lovely views from its summit and a network of footpaths. Chequers, the British prime minister's country seat, is to the west near Kimble.

There are frequent trains to Wendover from London Marylebone (45 minutes, £7.50). Aylesbury Bus runs a regular daily service between Aylesbury and Wendover.

Ivinghoe Beacon

This bare hill, marking the end of the Ridgeway, can be crowded with walkers over summer weekends. If you've just finished the Ridgeway walk, you can step out again along the 105 mile Icknield Way, which crosses Bedfordshire to join the Peddars Way at Knettishall Heath (Suffolk).

Standing 230m above sea level, Ivinghoe was the site of one of the many beacons set up to summon men to arms if the Spanish invaded. Half a mile to the south is Pitstone Windmill, the country's oldest windmill, built in 1627.

Places to Stay *Ivinghoe Youth Hostel* (☎ 01296-668251) is in a Georgian mansion half a mile from the windmill and a mile from Ivinghoe Beacon. From July to mid-September it's open daily, closing on Sunday from April through June, and on Sunday and Monday from mid-September through October. Phone for other opening times. Beds cost £8/5.40 for adults/juniors.

Getting There & Away The nearest train station is Tring, 2½ miles to the south-west, on the line from London Euston to Milton Keynes. From London, it's 40 minutes (£7.30) by rail. Aylesbury Bus (☎ 01296-84919) has buses from Aylesbury to Ivinghoe via Tring hourly from Monday to Saturday and every two hours on Sunday. On Sunday and public holidays from mid-May to late September the Chiltern Ramblers bus (☎ 01582-574191) runs to Ivinghoe and Tring from Hemel Hempstead (Hertfordshire).

Jordans

About 2 miles east of Beaconsfield, **Jordans Quaker Meeting House** was built in 1688,

its simple style reflecting the tenets of the Christian sect founded in 1650. One of its best known followers was William Penn, founder of Pennsylvania, who is buried in the graveyard here. Nearby is the **Mayflower Barn**, possibly constructed from the timbers of the ship that took the Pilgrim Fathers to America.

Half a mile away is *Jordans Youth Hostel* (☎ *01494-873135*), open daily in July and August, and daily (except Thursday) from March through October. Phone for other times. The nightly charge is £7.20/4.95 for adults/juniors.

The closest train station and bus stop are at Seer Green, just under a mile from the hostel.

Bedfordshire

Bedfordshire is compact, peaceful and largely agricultural. The River Great Ouse winds across the fields of the north and through Bedford; the M1 motorway roars across the uninteresting semi-industrial south.

The county town of Bedford is best known to tourists as the home of John Bunyan (1628-88), the 17th century Nonconformist preacher and author of *Pilgrim's Progress*. South-east of Bedford lies the much publicised stately home of Woburn Abbey.

GETTING AROUND

For information on buses around the county, phone the inquiry line (☎ 01234-228337). Stagecoach (☎ 01604-620077), the main regional bus company, has an Explorer ticket allowing a day's travel anywhere on its routes for £5/3.50.

BEDFORD

• **pop 77,000**   ☎ 012343

Most places with links to John Bunyan are in and around Bedford, a pleasant riverside town with a high-class art gallery.

Information

The TIC (☎ 215226) is just off the High St at 10 St Paul's Square. It stocks *John*

Bunyan's Bedford, a free guide to places with a Bunyan connection.

The Bunyan Meeting

The **Bunyan Meeting** (☎ 358870), Mill St, was built in 1849 on the site of the barn where Bunyan preached from 1671 to 1678. The church's bronze doors, inspired by Ghiberti's doors for the Baptistry in Florence, show scenes from *Pilgrim's Progress*. One famous stained-glass window shows Bunyan in jail. From April to October the church is open to visitors Tuesday to Saturday from 10 am to 4 pm. At the time of writing the small museum of Bunyan memorabilia was open afternoons only but once a new visitors centre is completed the opening hours should be extended so more people can admire some 169 editions of *Pilgrim's Progress* from around the world. Admission costs 50/30p.

Cecil Higgins Art Gallery

The **Cecil Higgins Art Gallery** (☎ 353323), Castle Close, houses a splendid collection of glass, porcelain and colourful Victorian furniture. **Bedford Museum**, with archaeological and historical exhibits, is next door. Both are open from Tuesday to Saturday from 11 am to 5 pm, and on Sunday from 2 to 5 pm; entry is free.

Places to Stay & Eat

Bedford makes an easy day trip from London, but if you want to stay overnight there are several hotels and B&Bs along leafy De Pary's Ave, which leads north from the High St to Bedford Park. *Bedford Park House* (☎ 215100, 59 De Pary's Ave) has singles/doubles for £18/30. *De Pary's Guest House* (☎ 261982, 48 De Pary's Ave) has nine singles and six doubles. Rooms cost from £18 a head. The historic *Swan Hotel* (☎ 346565), right beside the river, does two-night weekend breaks including half-board for £39.50 per head.

The *Bunyan Meeting* serves tea and coffee in its foyer or in summer you can snack alfresco on filled potatoes or sandwiches in the *Piazza* immediately behind St

Paul's Church. Pub meals are available at the *Saracen's Head* (*St Paul's Square*), *The Hogshead* (*High St*) or *Pitcher's Sports Bar* (*High St*). *Polly's Tea Rooms* (*13 High St*), upstairs in Polly Flinder's, does soup and a roll for £1.95 or filled potatoes for £3.25.

Getting There & Away

Bedford is 50 miles north of London and 30 miles west of Cambridge. There are frequent trains from King's Cross Thameslink (one hour, £13.20 day return) to Midland station, a well-signposted 10 minute walk west of High St.

National Express has direct links between Bedford and London, Cambridge and

---

John Bunyan & *Pilgrim's Progress*

The son of a tinker, John Bunyan was born in 1628 at Elstow, near Bedford. He joined a Nonconformist church and became an accomplished preacher. In 1660, when the monarchy was restored, the government tried to restrain Nonconformist sects by forbidding preaching. Bunyan was arrested and spent the next 12 years in jail.

The allegorical work he started in prison, The Pilgrim's Progress from this world to that which is to come, became one of the most widely read books ever written.

An immediate success when it was published in 1678, its popularity stems from the fact that it's a gripping adventure story as well as a religious text. The pilgrim Christian, with his knapsack full of sins, embarks on a journey to paradise, via the Slough of Despond and Hill of Difficulty. On the way he is tempted by Vanity Fair and imprisoned in a giant's castle, but triumphing over these difficulties, he finally reaches the Celestial City.

Pilgrim's Progress has been translated into over 200 languages. The TIC produces a leaflet listing places associated with Bunyan in and around Bedford.

MIDLANDS

Coventry. The bus station is half a mile west of High St.

WOBURN ABBEY & SAFARI PARK

Not an abbey but a grand stately home built on the site of a Cistercian abbey, **Woburn Abbey** (☎ 01525-290666) has been the seat of the dukes of Bedford for the last 350 years. The house dates mainly from the 18th century, when it was enlarged and re-modelled into a vast country mansion. Although half the building was demolished in 1950 because of dry rot, it remains well worth visiting and is stuffed with furniture, porcelain and paintings.

The 1200 hectare park is home to the largest breeding herd of Père David's deer, extinct in their native China for a century (although a small herd was returned to Beijing in 1985).

It's open daily from late March to October from 11 am to 4 pm; weekends only from January to March and in October. Entry is £7.50/3 (free to under-12s). Although it's easily accessible by car off the M1 motorway, trains from King's Cross Thameslink only run to Flitwick, leaving you to take a taxi for the last 5 miles to the abbey.

A mile from the house is **Woburn Safari Park** (☎ 01525-290407), the country's largest drive-through animal reserve. It's open daily from late March to October; weekends only in winter. Entry is £10.50/7. If you visit the abbey first you qualify for a 50% discount.

WHIPSNADE

Whipsnade Wild Animal Park This park (☎ 01582-872171) is an offshoot of London Zoo that was originally established to breed endangered species in captivity; it claims to release 50 animals into the wild for every one captured. The 2500 animals in the 240 hectare site can be viewed by car, on the park's railway, or on foot. It's open daily all year from 10 am to 6 pm (4 pm from November to March); entry is £8.50/6, plus £7 for a car if you want to drive round.

In summer you can get to Whipsnade by Green Line bus from Buckingham Palace Rd near Victoria coach station (☎ 0181-668 7261, £6.50 day return).

Hertfordshire

Hertfordshire is a mixture of commuter-belt housing estates in the south and rolling farmland in the north. The M25 London orbital motorway sweeps round the south-ern border of the county while the busy M1 and A1(M) whisk traffic north.

Lively, interesting St Albans dates back to Roman times and has an abbey dedicat-ed to Britain's first Christian martyr. About 6 miles east of St Albans is Hatfield House, one of Britain's most important stately homes and Hertfordshire's top attraction.

GETTING AROUND

Bus and rail timetables are available from TICs; the *Central Area Travel Guide* is the most useful. Phone ☎ 01992-556765 for public transport information.

ST ALBANS
• **pop 77,000   ☎ 01727**

Just 25 minutes train ride to the north, the cathedral city of St Albans makes a pleas-ant day trip from London. To the Romans, St Albans was Verulamium, and their theatre and parts of the ancient wall can still be seen to the south-west of the city.

Orientation & Information

The town centre is St Peter's St, a 10 minute walk (or S2 bus ride) west of St Albans train station. St Peter's becomes Chequer St and then Holywell Hill as it heads south. The cathedral lies to the west, off High St, with the ruins of Verulamium even farther to the west.

The TIC (☎ 864511) is in the grand Town Hall on Market Place and sells the useful *Discover St Albans* town trail (95p).

St Albans Cathedral

In 209, a Roman citizen named Alban was beheaded for his Christian beliefs, becom-ing Britain's first Christian martyr. In the 8th century King Offa of Mercia founded an abbey on the site of his martyrdom. The Norman abbey church was built in 1077, incorporating parts of the Saxon building and many Roman bricks, conspicuously in the central tower. After the dissolution of the monasteries in 1538 the abbey church became the parish church. Considerable restoration took place in 1877 when it was redesignated a cathedral.

In the heart of the cathedral is St Alban's shrine, immediately behind the presbytery and overlooked by a wooden watcher's loft, where monks would stand guard to ensure pilgrims didn't pilfer relics. Look out for a particularly fine 14th century mural of St William of York on a nearby column.

The Norman nave columns are decorated with 13th and 14th century murals, mainly of crucifixion scenes.

In the south aisle you can watch an audiovisual account of the cathedral's history. From Monday to Friday there are screenings from 11 am to 4 pm, with the last showing at 3.30 pm on Saturday (2 to 5 pm on Sunday). The cost is £1.50/1.

Verulamium Museum & Roman Ruins

Britain's best museum (☎ 819339) of everyday life under the Romans, in St Michael's St, displays wonderful mosaic pavements and murals. It's open daily from 10 am to 5.30 pm (2 to 5.30 pm on Sunday) for £2.80/1.10.

In adjacent **Verulamium Park** you can inspect remains of a basilica, bathhouse and parts of the city wall. Across the busy A4174 are the remains of a **Roman theatre**. They're open daily from 10 am to 4 pm for £1.50/50p, but they're probably only worth it if you're seriously keen on the Romans.

Gardens of the Rose

With about 30,000 specimens, the Gardens of the Rose (☎ 850461), 3 miles south-west of St Albans, contain the world's largest rose collection. They're open from mid-June to mid-October for £4 (children free).

Other Things to See & Do

The **Museum of St Albans** (☎ 819340), Hatfield Rd, gives a quick rundown of the city's history since Roman times. It's open Monday to Saturday from 10 am to 5 pm and on Sunday from 2 to 5 pm; admission is free.

The Elizabethan **Kingsbury Water Mill**, St Michael's St, is open Tuesday to Saturday from 11 am to 6 pm, opening at noon on Sunday. Admission is £1.10/60p.

Places to Stay

B&Bs convenient to the train station include *Mrs Jameson's (☎ 865498, 7 Marlborough Gate)*, off Upper Lattimore Rd, which charges £15/30 for a single/double with shared bathroom; and *Mrs Matheson-Tilt's (☎ 766764, 3 Upper Lattimore Rd)*, where rooms cost from £22/34. *Care Inns (☎ 867310, 29 Alma Rd)* has rooms with bath for £25/40.

The *Black Lion Inn (☎ 851786, 198 Fishpool St)* is on the quiet, pretty west side of town near Verulamium Park. Doubles are £45 on Friday and Saturday, £60 during the week. St Albans' best is *The Manor (☎ 864444, Fishpool St)*, with lovely views from the garden terrace. Rooms start at a whopping £95/120.

Places to Eat

St Albans has no shortage of places to eat, not least in the popular *Abbey Refectory*, where the hot dish of the day costs £3.95. *Upstairs Downstairs (☎ 854843)*, along the alley opposite the 15th century clock tower, has a three course set menu for £13.75 (£16.25 on Saturday). The Village Arcade nurtures *Abigail's Tearooms* for tea and sandwiches, while the *Pasta Bowl (High St)* does reliable Italian food, with pasta from £4.85. In stylish surroundings, the *Café des Amis (☎ 853569, 31 Market Place)* specialises in fish and seafood.

In George St, west of the High St, the *Tudor Rooms Restaurant (☎ 853233)* is part of the lively *Tudor Tavern* and offers a bowl of mussels for £6.95. Farther down George St, the *Bottom Drawer Tea Rooms* does cheaper lunches.

MIDLANDS

In St Michael's St the *Waffle House* (☎ 853202), attached to Kingsbury Water Mill, has picturesque surroundings and serves waffles from £1.40. But for atmosphere you could hardly beat the wonderful *Ye Olde Fighting Cocks*, in a converted 15th century pigeon house at the end of Abbey Mill Lane, near the abbey; chicken curry is £5.15 or there are excellent toasted sandwiches.

Getting There & Away

There are eight trains an hour from King's Cross Thameslink to St Albans (£5.40). For London's Victoria coach station, take a bus to Bricket Wood and change.

The main bus company serving this area is Sovereign Buses (☎ 854732). There are several buses an hour to Hatfield train station forecourt (20 minutes), Hatfield House, and at least one bus an hour for Wheathampstead (15 minutes) and Shaw's Corner.

HATFIELD HOUSE

Only 25 minutes north of London by train, Hatfield House (☎ 01707-262823) is England's most impressive Jacobean house, a graceful red-brick and stone mansion full of treasures, built between 1607 and 1611 for Robert Cecil, 1st Earl of Salisbury and secretary of state to both Elizabeth I and James I. Modelled on an earlier Tudor palace where Elizabeth I spent much of her childhood, only the restored great hall and one wing converted into stables survive.

Inside, the house is extremely grand with a wonderful Marble Hall and famous portraits of Elizabeth and numerous English kings. The oak Grand Staircase is decorated with carved figures, including one of John Tradescant, the 17th century botanist responsible for the gardens.

Five-course Elizabethan banquets, complete with minstrels and court jesters, are held in the great hall at 7.30 pm on Tuesday, Friday and Saturday, and also on Thursday from April to September. Phone ☎ 01707-262055 for tickets (around £30 depending on the day) and information.

Hatfield House is 21 miles from London and 8 miles from St Albans. It's open Tuesday to Saturday from noon to 4 pm, Sunday from 1 pm; admission is £5.70/3.40. The entrance is opposite Hatfield train station, and there are numerous trains from London King's Cross station (25 minutes, £5.40 day return).

KNEBWORTH HOUSE

Home to the Lytton family since 1490, Knebworth House (☎ 01438-812661) is a Tudor house sheathed in Victorian Gothic stucco – a fantasy of battlements, towers and turrets. Most of the alterations were made by Edward Bulwer-Lytton, Victorian statesman and author. The Tudor great hall survives and the house contains 17th and 18th century furniture and paintings, and an exhibition on the British Raj. The 100 hectare grounds boast a herd of deer and an adventure playground. In summer, when the grounds play host to huge rock concerts, the house may be closed.

Frequent trains from London King's Cross station run to Stevenage (30 minutes), a mile north of Knebworth, or you can take the No 300 bus from St Albans. In summer the house is open daily from 11 am to 5.30 pm (Monday from noon to 5 pm), and on weekends only in spring and autumn; entry is £5/4.50.

SHAW'S CORNER

The Victorian villa in Ayot St Lawrence where the Anglo-Irish playwright George Bernard Shaw died in 1950 is preserved much as he left it. In the garden is the revolving summerhouse (revolving to catch the sun) where he wrote several works including *Pygmalion*, the play on which the film *My Fair Lady* was based.

Shaw's Corner (☎ 01438-820307, NT) is open April through October, Wednesday to Saturday and bank holiday Mondays, from 1 to 5 pm; entry is £3.20.

Bus No 304 from St Albans drops you at Gustardwood, 1¼ miles from Ayot St Lawrence.

Leicestershire

At first glance just another grey Midlands county, Leicestershire has several interesting towns and historic sites. For general bus information phone ☎ 0116-251 1411.

LEICESTER

• **pop 320,000 ☎ 0116**

Leicester (pronounced lester) is another Midlands town that has suffered the triple disasters of wartime damage, uninspired post-war development and catastrophic industrial decline. The modern town has a large and vibrant Asian community and there are Hindu, Moslem, Jain and Sikh temples as well as some excellent Indian, Bangladeshi and Pakistani restaurants. Many of the city's most interesting events are staged around festivals like Holi, Diwali and Eid-ul-Fitr.

The city's history dates back to Roman times. Later, it was one of the five Danelaw towns and was the traditional home of Shakespeare's tragic King Lear and his daughters. In 1239 Simon de Montfort, Earl of Leicester, captured the castle. Medieval Leicester became a centre for manufacturing stockings but remained a small town until the rapid industrial growth of the 19th century. Leicester bequeathed the word 'Luddite' to the language, after apprentice Nedd Ludd smashed stocking frames in a protest against modern production methods. The Luddite riots took place from 1811 to 1816.

Orientation & Information

Leicester is initially difficult to navigate as there are few landmarks. For those on wheels, it's plagued by the usual maze of one-way streets and forbidden turns.

The friendly TIC (☎ 265 0555) is at 7-9 Every St, Town Hall Square. There's another office (☎ 251 1301) in St Margaret's bus station in the summer.

The centre of the Asian community, Belgrave Rd ('the Golden Mile'), is about a mile north-east of the centre. Castle Park, with many of the historic attractions, lies immediately west of the centre, beside De Montfort University.

Jewry Wall & Museums

All Leicester's museums are open free, Monday to Saturday, from 10 am to 5.30 pm, and on Sunday from 2 to 5.30 pm.

On St Nicholas Circle, by the Holiday Inn, the **Museum of Leicestershire Archaeology** (☎ 247 3021) is next to the remains of a Roman bath and **Jewry Wall**. Despite its name, this wall is one of Britain's largest Roman civil structures and has nothing to do with Judaism. Despite its grim external appearance the museum contains some wonderful Roman mosaics and frescoes.

The **Leicestershire Museum & Art Gallery** (☎ 255 4100) in New Walk houses a mixed bag of Egyptian mummies, stuffed animals and fine paintings. The **Newarke Houses Museum** (☎ 247 3222) is in buildings dating from the early 16th and 17th centuries. There are some reconstructed period shops, and information on two of Leicester's best known citizens: Daniel Lambert (see the boxed text 'Leicester's Weightiest Citizen') and Thomas Cook, the package holiday pioneer.

In the late 14th century **Guildhall** (☎ 253 2569), next to the cathedral, you can peep into old police cells and inspect a copy of the last gibbet used to expose the body of an executed murderer. Nearby **Wygston's House** (☎ 247 3056) houses a small museum of costume.

Temples

Materials were shipped in from India to convert a disused church into a **Jain Centre** (☎ 254 3091), on the corner of Oxford St and York Rd. The building is faced with marble and inside, the temple (the first outside the subcontinent) boasts a forest of beautifully carved pillars. Jainism evolved in India at around the same time as Buddhism. The temple is open to visitors Monday to Friday, from 2 to 5 pm.

There are several Hindu temples in the Belgrave Rd area. The **Sri Jalaram Temple** (☎ 254 0117), Narborough Rd, is dedicated

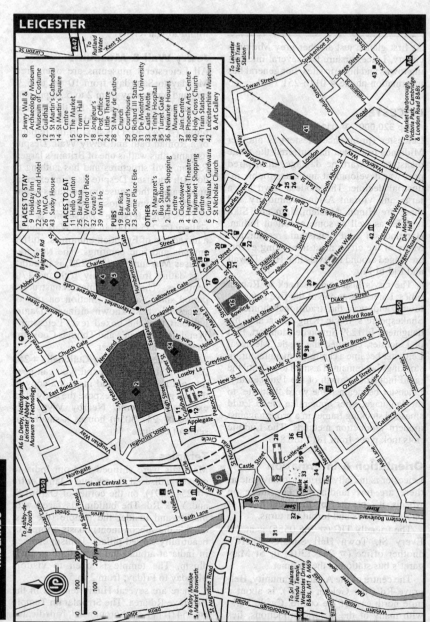

LEICESTER

PLACES TO STAY
9 Holiday Inn
22 Jarvis Grand Hotel
26 YMCA
43 Saxby House

PLACES TO EAT
11 Hello Canton
25 Bar Nasa
27 Welford Place
32 Covati's
39 Man Ho

PUBS
19 Bar Risa
20 Edward's
23 Some Place Else

OTHER
1 St Margaret's Bus Station
2 The Shires Shopping Centre
3 Clocktower
4 Haymarket Theatre
5 Haymarket Shopping Centre
6 Guru Nanak Gurdwara
7 St Nicholas Church
8 Jewry Wall & Archaeology Museum
10 Museum of Costume
12 Guildhall
13 St Martin's Cathedral
14 St Martin's Square Centre
15 The Market
16 Town Hall
17 TIC
18 Jongleur's
21 Post Office
24 Little Theatre
28 St Mary de Castro Church
29 Courthouse
30 Richard III Statue
31 De Montfort University
33 Castle Motte
34 Trinity Hospital
35 Turret Gate
36 Newarke Houses Museum
37 Jain Centre
38 Phoenix Arts Centre
40 Holy Cross Church
41 Train Station
42 Leicestershire Museum & Art Gallery

to the Hindu saint Pujya Bapa. Marble carvings depict his life and there are colourful murals of Vedic scriptures.

Close to the Jewry Wall is the Sikh **Guru Nanak Gurdwara** (☎ 262 8606), at 9 Holybones. The small museum contains an impressive model of the Golden Temple in Amritsar. It's open on Thursday only, from 1 to 4 pm.

Great Central Railway

The Great Central Railway (☎ 01509-230726) operates steam locomotives between Leicester North and Loughborough Central. The 8 mile trip runs every weekend and daily from May to August. The round trip costs £7/4.70.

Places to Stay

The TIC charges £2 to make bookings but apart from expensive hotels there's little in the centre.

The *Copt Oak Youth Hostel* (☎ 01530-242661, Whitwick Rd, Copt Oak) is 8 miles north-west of the centre, near junction 22 on the M1. In July and August it's open daily. From November through March it's closed.

Leicester's Weightiest Citizen

Born in 1770, Daniel Lambert, the onetime keeper of Leicester Gaol, started life as a normal baby but soon began to tip the scales at ever more alarming totals. Despite eating only one meal a day, by age 23 he weighed 32 stone and by 39 an astounding 52 stone 11 lb, making him, as the Dictionary of National Biography puts it, 'the most corpulent man of whom authentic record exists'.

When he died in Stamford in 1809 one wall of the house had to be dismantled to remove the coffin, and 20 pallbearers were needed to carry it to the graveyard. A whole room in Leicester's Newarke Houses Museum is devoted to Lambert's memory.

At other times of year it closes on Tuesday. Beds cost £6.50/4.45 for adults/juniors.

Dodgy Dick's Backpackers Hostel (☎ 267 3107) is 3 miles north of the centre, just off the A6 at 157 Wanlip Lane. Book ahead as space is very limited. The nightly cost is £8, plus £3 for tent space or (if you have a sleeping bag) in the chalet.

The *YMCA* (☎ 255 6507, 7 East St) is just across from the train station and has a few single rooms at £11 (£43 a week). There are some cheap places on Saxby St, off London Rd just south of the train station, although this may not be the best area for lone women. Friendly but basic *Saxby House* (☎ 254 0504) at No 24 is just £12 per person, and there are other cheapies nearby.

Try Westcotes Drive off Narborough Rd for B&Bs. The *Scotia Hotel* (☎ 254 9200) at No 10 has singles from £21 to £27, and doubles from £38 to £42, some with a bath. The *Cumbria Guest House* (☎ 254 8459) at No 16 and the *Beaumaris* (☎ 254 0621) at No 18 are slightly cheaper with rooms from £15/28.

The centrally located *Jarvis Grand Hotel* (☎ 255 5599, Granby St) has rooms from £84/94 during the week, £46.50/65 at weekends. Rooms at the *Holiday Inn* (☎ 253 1161, St Nicholas Circle) drop from £110 during the week to £69 at weekends.

Places to Eat

The Belgrave Rd area, to the north of the centre (55p by bus), is noted for its fine Indian cuisine and excellent vegetarian food. The award-winning but budget-priced *Friends Tandoori* (☎ 266 8809, 41-43 Belgrave Rd) serves North Indian food. Other popular vegetarian choices include *Sayonara* (☎ 266 5888) at No 49, *Sharmilee* (☎ 261 0503) at No 71-73, where a thali costs £7.50 and *Bobby's* (☎ 266 0106) at No 154.

Lovely *Welford Place* (☎ 247 0758, 9 Welford Place) is open for breakfast, lunch and dinner. It's not as expensive as its appearance might indicate, especially if you stick with the bistro-style daily menu. A little

MIDLANDS

down Newarke St there's a pleasant *café* upstairs in the Phoenix Arts Centre.

Bar Nasa (☎ *255 4667, 153 Granby St*) does pizzas or pasta for £5. But for stylish Italian dining, head straight for *Covati's* (☎ *251 8251, Westbridge Place*), a purpose-designed restaurant accessible by footbridge from Castle Gardens and with main courses from £6.

Man Ho (☎ *537700, New Walk*) does Chinese business lunches for a round £5. In Guildhall Lane, the big *Hello Canton* (☎ *629029*) offers set meals from £11.50.

There's a plethora of café bars along Granby St, including *Bar Risa*, *Edward's* and *Some Place Else*.

Entertainment

The *Phoenix Arts Centre* (☎ *255 4854, Newarke St*) hosts films, plays and dance events. Plays are also staged at the *Little Theatre* (☎ *255 1302, Dover St*) and sometimes at the *Haymarket Theatre* (☎ *253 9797*).

Classical concerts are performed at the *De Montfort Hall* (☎ *233 3111, Granville Rd*).

The *Jongleurs Comedy Club* (☎ *0800-783 9933, 30 Granby St*) hosts comedians on Thursday, Friday and Saturday at 7.15 pm.

Getting There & Away

Leicester is 105 miles from London, 40 miles from Birmingham, and 25 miles from Coventry and Nottingham.

Bus National Express (☎ 0990-808080) operates from St Margaret's bus station in Gravel St, north of the centre, which has left-luggage facilities. There are hourly services to London. The Stagecoach Express service 757 runs to Nottingham hourly (one hour, £2). The Busline (☎ 251 1411) offers general bus information.

Train A statue of Thomas Cook stands outside the train station on London Rd, south-east of the centre. Trains from London St Pancras operate every half-hour; the fastest take just over one hour. There are hourly services between Birmingham and Cambridge or Norwich via Leicester.

AROUND LEICESTER
Bosworth Battlefield

South-west of Leicester at Sutton Cheny, 2 miles from Market Bosworth, Richard III was defeated by the future Henry VII in 1485, ending the Wars of the Roses. 'A horse … a horse … my kingdom for a horse', was his famous death cry. The visitors centre (☎ 01455-290429) is open April through October, daily from 1 to 5 pm. Admission costs £2.30/1.50, plus 50p parking charge.

Ashby-del-la-Zouch

Driving from Leicester to Derby it's easy to divert via this pleasant little town with its castle (☎ 01530-413343, EH). Built in Norman times, and owned by the Zouch family until 1399, it was extended in the 14th and 15th centuries and then reduced to its present picturesque ruined state in 1648 after the Civil War. Bring a torch (flashlight) to explore the underground passageway which connects the tower with the kitchen. Admission costs £2.30/1.20.

Donington Park

The Donington Park motor racing circuit at Castle Donington, 20 miles north-west of Leicester, hosts the annual British Motorcycle Grand Prix. It also features the Donington Collection (☎ 01332-811027) of racing cars (including probably the world's best collection of Formula 1 racing cars) and motorcycles, open daily, from 10 am to 4 pm; entry is £7/2.50.

Belvoir Castle

North-east of Leicester, Belvoir (pronounced beever) Castle (☎ 01476-870262) is 6 miles from Grantham, off the A1. This baroque and Gothic fantasy was rebuilt in the 19th century after suffering serious damage during the Civil War. It's open April to September on Tuesday, Wednesday, Thursday, Saturday and Sunday from 11 am to 5 pm. In October it opens only on Sunday; entry is £5/3.

Shropshire

Covering the rolling hills between Birmingham and the Welsh border, Shropshire is a large county with a relatively small population centred on the attractive regional capital of Shrewsbury and the new town of Telford. Just outside Telford is Ironbridge, where a series of remarkable museums commemorate the birthplace of the Industrial Revolution.

Shropshire is bisected by the River Severn, which flows west to east through Shrewsbury. To the north the countryside is largely flat and uninteresting, but to the south lie the Shropshire Hills, the 'blue remembered hills' of local poet AE Housman, author of *A Shropshire Lad*. The best known of a series of ridges are Wenlock Edge, the Long Mynd and the Stiperstones. Mostly below 518m, this is excellent walking country that sees relatively few hikers.

CYCLE ROUTE

Starting from Shrewsbury, a good 100 mile five or six-day cycle route takes you round the most scenic parts of Shropshire. You can rent bikes in Church Stretton and Ludlow. Delamere Cycle Hire in Telford (☎ 0500-333575) can also deliver a bike to Ironbridge.

The route goes from Shrewsbury via Wroxeter to Ironbridge (14 miles), Ironbridge to Much Wenlock (only 5 miles but there's a lot to see in Ironbridge), Much Wenlock to Ludlow (20 miles), Ludlow to Clun (an easy 17 mile ride), Clun to Church Stretton (15 miles), and Church Stretton to Shrewsbury (16 miles, along side roads parallel to the busy A49).

GETTING AROUND

Public transport between Shropshire's main towns isn't bad, with railway lines and most bus routes radiating from Shrewsbury. Getting to country areas without a car is less easy but the county council has a useful phone line (☎ 0345-056785) for bus and rail information. The invaluable *Shropshire Bus & Train Map*, available free from TICs, shows all the bus routes.

SHREWSBURY

- pop 60,000 ☎ 01743

When Charles Dickens was staying at the Lion Hotel in Shrewsbury, he wrote, 'I am lodged in the strangest little rooms, the ceilings of which I can touch with my hands. From the windows I can look all downhill and slantwise at the crookedest black and white houses, all of many shapes except straight shapes'.

The county's capital can still claim to be the finest Tudor town in Britain, famous for its higgledy-piggledy half-timbered buildings and winding medieval streets. There are no vitally important sights here, which has saved Shrewsbury from inundation by tourists, but it makes a good base for exploring Shropshire and a convenient stop en route to Wales.

History

Strategically positioned within a defensible loop of the River Severn, Shrewsbury has been important since the 5th century; the Saxon town of Scrobbesbryrig was established on the two hills here. After the Norman Conquest, the town came under the control of Roger de Montgomery, who built the castle. The Benedictine abbey was founded in 1083.

For many centuries Shrewsbury played an important part in the control of the Welsh, and in 1283 the Welsh prince David III was executed here after a parliament convened in the abbey chapterhouse. Despite problems with its unruly neighbours, the town prospered from the wool trade with the Welsh hill farmers. Many of the beautiful Tudor buildings were built by wealthy wool merchants.

The town's best known former resident, Charles Darwin, was born here in 1809 and educated at Shrewsbury's famous public school. His statue stands outside the library. The town has also done him the questionable honour of naming the shopping mall after him.

Orientation & Information

Housman described Shrewsbury as 'islanded in Severn stream'. The train station now lies across the narrow land bridge formed by the loop of the River Severn, a five minute walk north of the town centre. The bus station is central and the whole town is well signposted. Many of the old winding streets still have names that reflect the occupations of their former inhabitants – Butcher Row, Fish St, Milk St.

The TIC (☎ 350761) in The Square is open Monday to Saturday from 9.30 am to 5 pm, and on Sunday until 4 pm from May to September. From May to October guided 1½ hour walking tours (£2/1) leave the TIC at 2.30 pm daily and at 11 am on Sunday.

Combined tickets for the castle, Rowley's House and Clive House cost £6/2.50.

Walking Tour

Start from the TIC, which is in the old **Music Hall** of 1839. Opposite, in the square, is the **Market Hall**, an open-sided building erected in 1595. Until the mid-19th century trade was carried on in this square and, on

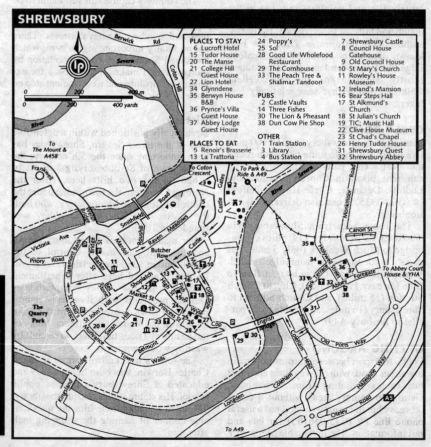

SHREWSBURY

PLACES TO STAY
6 Lucroft Hotel
15 Tudor House
20 The Manse
21 College Hill Guest House
27 Lion Hotel
34 Glynndene
35 Berwyn House B&B
36 Prynce's Villa Guest House
37 Abbey Lodge Guest House

PLACES TO EAT
5 Renoir's Brasserie
13 La Trattoria

24 Poppy's
25 Sol
28 Good Life Wholefood Restaurant
29 The Cornhouse
33 The Peach Tree & Shalimar Tandoori

PUBS
2 Castle Vaults
14 Three Fishes
30 The Lion & Pheasant
38 Dun Cow Pie Shop

OTHER
1 Train Station
3 Library
4 Bus Station

7 Shrewsbury Castle
8 Council House Gatehouse
9 Old Council House
10 St Mary's Church
11 Rowley's House Museum
12 Ireland's Mansion
16 Bear Steps Hall
17 St Alkmund's Church
18 St Julian's Church
19 TIC; Music Hall
22 Clive House Museum
23 St Chad's Chapel
26 Henry Tudor House
31 Shrewsbury Quest
32 Shrewsbury Abbey

MIDLANDS

the insides of the pillars at the northern end, you can still see holes for the markers used to record the numbers of fleeces sold.

Walk across the square into the High St and you'll find a statue to Robert Clive, who laid the foundations for British control of India and was mayor of Shrewsbury in 1762. On your left is the 16th century **Ireland's Mansion**, most impressive of the town's timber-framed buildings.

Retrace your steps along the High St and turn left into narrow Grope Lane with its overhanging buildings. Cross Fish St and go up the steps into St Alkmund's Place, the original town square. The medieval tower aside, **St Alkmund's Church** was completely remodelled at the end of the 18th century. You can look round the restored 14th century **Bear Steps Hall** between 10 am and 4 pm. Nearby St Julian's Church now houses a craft centre. There are several black and white houses along **Butcher Row**, including the Abbot's House, built in 1450.

The 'cathedral' of the Churches Conservation Trust, magnificent **St Mary's Church** is no longer used for worship but is worth visiting for its beautiful 15th century angel roof and stained glass. Best of all is the great Jesse window made from rare mid-14th century English glass. The spire collapsed in 1894 – because the townsfolk were planning a memorial to Darwin (according to the vicar).

Opposite the north side of the church, past 17th century **St Mary's Cottage**, St Mary's Water Lane leads back down into Castle St. At the far end of the street is **Shrewsbury Castle** which houses the **Shropshire Regimental Museum**, open Tuesday to Saturday from 10 am to 4.30 pm, and summer Sundays. Entry costs £3/1 but you're free to walk round the grounds without charge. The entrance gate is Norman but much of the castle was remodelled by Edward I. The Scottish engineer Thomas Telford added Laura's Tower in 1780.

Down the alley near the entrance to the castle is the Jacobean-style **Council House Gatehouse** dating from 1620. Beyond it is the **Old Council House** where the Council

of the Welsh Marches used to meet to administer the area.

Across the road from the castle is the library with a **statue of Charles Darwin** outside. Retrace your steps to St Mary's St and follow it down Dogpole. At the end of Dogpole, turn right onto Wyle Cop, which is Welsh for 'hilltop'. The **Lion Hotel** was where Dickens stayed on his visit to Shrewsbury; a 200-year-old gilded lion marks its entrance. Henry VII is said to have stayed in the **Henry Tudor House**, on the other side of Barracks Passage, before the Battle of Bosworth.

Walk right down Wyle Cop and bear left for the graceful 18th century **English Bridge**, widened and reconstructed in 1927 and offering magnificent views of the Shrewsbury skyline.

Retrace your steps up Wyle Cop and turn left along Barracks Passage. Then turn right up Belmont Bank to **St Chad's Chapel**, all that remains of the medieval church. Turn right again into College Hill for the **Clive House Museum** (☎ 354811) where Clive lived when he was mayor. There's not much about Clive but the house contains interesting displays on social and domestic life in 18th and 19th century Shrewsbury, plus a fine collection of porcelain. The museum is open Tuesday to Saturday from 10 am to 4 pm, and on Sunday from mid-May through September; entry is £2/1. It's a short walk back to the TIC.

Rowley's House Museum

Shrewsbury's main museum (☎ 361196), on Barker St, is housed in a restored 16th century timber-framed building and an adjoining 17th century mansion built by a wealthy merchant.

The museum displays some of the finds from the nearby Roman town of Wroxeter (including a particularly beautiful mirror) and has a good section on medieval Shrewsbury, as well as exhibits on costume and local wildlife. It's open Tuesday to Saturday from 10 am to 5 pm, and until 4 pm on Sunday, from mid-May to September; entry is £3/1.

MIDLANDS

Shrewsbury Abbey

This huge red-sandstone church in Abbey Foregate is virtually all that remains of the Benedictine monastery founded by Roger de Montgomery in 1083. Inside, the architecture is part pure Norman and part Victorian copy. In the vestry don't miss the photo of men rowing in the choir after a flood! The churchyard contains a memorial to Wilfred Owen, one of the best known of the WWI poets, killed just a week before the war ended. In the car park opposite, a stranded stone pulpit also survives from the abbey.

Shrewsbury Quest

Across the street from the abbey, the Shrewsbury Quest (☎ 243324) stands on the site of some of the old abbey buildings. It was inspired by the Brother Cadfael medieval detective stories. Visitors look for clues to solve a medieval murder as they wander round displays relating to 12th century monastery life and a pleasant herb garden. Fans of the Ellis Peters books will love it. Open daily from 10 am to 6.30 pm (5.30 pm November to March). Admission costs £3.95/2.95. There's a good café on-site.

Places to Stay

Hostel *Shrewsbury Youth Hostel* (☎ 360179, *Abbey Foregate*) is a mile from the train and bus stations, just off the roundabout by Lord Hill's Column. From November to Christmas it only opens on Friday and Saturday and in January it closes altogether. It's a great place to stay for £8/5.40 for adults/juniors.

Camping Four miles north of Shrewsbury, at Montford Bridge on the B4380, *Severn House* (☎ 850229) has a riverside site where you can camp for £5 a tent.

B&Bs & Hotels While most hotels are in the town centre (some of them in appropriately historic timber-framed buildings), B&Bs are mainly concentrated in and around Abbey Foregate, to the north up Coton Hill, and to the west along the A458

and A488. As ever, there's a shortage of decent single rooms.

In the Abbey Foregate area, *Glynndene* (☎ 352488), overlooking the abbey in Park Terrace, has rooms from around £15 per person. Nearby is *Berwyn House* (☎ 354858, *14 Holywell St*), a comfortable family house with B&B from £15/34 a single/double. *Prynce's Villa Guest House* (☎ 356217, *15 Monkmoor Rd, off Abbey Foregate*) has beds from £13.50 a head.

Abbey Court House (☎ 364416, *134 Abbey Foregate*) is comfortable and has rooms with bathroom from £17 per person. Farther along, *Abbey Lodge Guest House* (☎ 235832) at No 68 charges from £16 a head. About a 10 minute walk north of the train station, the Coton Hill area harbours another group of B&Bs and hotels. In Coton Crescent, *Bancroft Guest House* (☎ 231746) at No 17, and *The Stiperstones Guest House* (☎ 246720) at No 18 offer B&B from around £15 per person.

Lucroft Hotel (☎ 362421, *Castle Gates*), on the way into town from the train station, has clean if unexciting rooms from £20/34.

The excellent *Manse* (☎ 242659, *16 Swan Hill*) is a beautiful Georgian town house, offering superior B&B from £18 per person. *College Hill Guest House* (☎ 365744, *11 College Hill*) has six rooms, with similar prices to the Manse.

Dating from 1460, quaint *Tudor House* (☎ 351735, *2 Fish St*) is centrally located on a quiet medieval street. Beds in pretty beamed rooms with no straight lines cost from around £20 per person.

The *Lion Hotel* (☎ 353107, *Wyle Cop*) is a Forte Heritage hotel with well-appointed rooms from £45/60. Two-night bed, breakfast and dinner deals offer better value from £48 a head. Rooms at the luxurious *Prince Rupert Hotel* (☎ 499955, *Butcher Row*) cost £70/80.

Places to Eat

Shrewsbury has plenty of reasonably priced places to eat during the day but in the evening most of the cheaper places close.

On a tight budget, you'll be best off heading for a pub.

Right beside the TIC, *Oscar's Café & Bistro* (☎ 358057) will do you half a pizza and a baked potato for £4.25. *Poppy's* (☎ 232307, 8 Milk St) serves salads for £4.50.

Owens Café-Bar (☎ 363633, Butcher Row) has a wide range of wines, bottled and draught beers and interesting dishes like mixed tapas for £4.25. Opposite in the 14th century timber-framed *Henry's Restaurant* (☎ 353117), most main dishes cost over £10; bar meals are much cheaper. Round the corner in Fish Row, *La Trattoria* (☎ 249490) not only serves moderately priced Italian food but stays open in the evening, too.

The popular restaurant at *Cromwell's Hotel* (☎ 361440, 11 Dogpole) offers main dishes from £8.95 plus excellent bar food.

The *Good Life Wholefood Restaurant* (☎ 350455), in restaurant-lined Barracks Passage off Wyle Cop, does good-value lunches until 3.30 pm and teas until 4.30 pm. If it's closed the *Old Lion Tap* (☎ 270330) across the alley has a big pub/restaurant in a restored timber-framed building.

Sol (☎ 340560, 82 Wyle Cop) is a splash-out option where three-course meals costing £25 a head are served in classy, colourful surroundings. At the bottom of the hill, *The Cornhouse* (☎ 231991) serves beautifully presented Modern British cuisine between 6.30 and 10 pm; dishes like brie and spinach strudel cost around £6.45.

The *Peach Tree* (☎ 355055, 21 Abbey Foregate) also specialises in good Modern British cuisine. Expect to pay around £15 a head. A meal at the *Shalimar Tandoori* (☎ 344440), two doors down the road, is likely to be cheaper.

Renoir's Brasserie (☎ 350006, School Gardens) is tucked down an alley off Castle St. Lunches cost around £5 but in the evening you're looking at roughly twice that.

Entertainment

City centre pubs worth trying include the *Castle Vaults* (Castle St), the *Lion & Pheasant* near the English Bridge and the nonsmoking *Three Fishes* (Fish St).

Farther out in Abbey Foregate the *Dun Cow Pie Shop* is full of clutter but manages to be extremely cosy.

In the old Music Hall that houses the TIC, a small *cinema* (☎ 244255) shows recent releases, classics and foreign films to small audiences. The small *theatre* has the same booking office.

Getting There & Away

See the fares tables in the Getting Around chapter. Shrewsbury is 150 miles from London, 68 miles from Manchester, 43 miles from Chester and 27 miles from Ludlow.

Bus National Express (☎ 0990-808080) has three buses a day to and from London (five hours) via Telford and Birmingham.

For information on transport in Shropshire, call the county help line (☎ 0345-056785). Williamsons (☎ 231010) X96 Wrekin Rambler runs between Shrewsbury and Telford via Ironbridge roughly every two hours, daily except on Sunday; on Saturday it continues to Birmingham. Arriva (☎ 01543-466123) runs Shropshire Link bus No 435 to Ludlow via Church Stretton and Craven Arms (for Stokesay Castle).

Train Two fascinating small railways terminate at Shrewsbury, in addition to plenty of main-line connections. It's possible to do an excellent rail loop from Shrewsbury around north Wales to Chester. Although you can do it in a day if you don't miss any of the connections, it's much better to allow a couple of days as there are plenty of interesting places to visit along the way. The North & Mid-Wales Flexi Rover ticket, allowing travel on three days out of seven, is the most economical way of covering this route (£25.70/12.80).

From Shrewsbury you head due west across Wales to Dovey Junction (1¾ hours), to connect with the Cambrian Coast Line, which hugs the beautiful coast on its way north to Porthmadog (1½ hours). Here you can pick up the Ffestiniog Railway, a superbly restored narrow-gauge steam train that winds up into Snowdonia National Park to the slate-mining town of Blaenau Ffestiniog (1¼ hours). From Blaenau another small railway carves its way through the mountains and down the beautiful Conwy Valley to Llandudno (1¼ hours) and Conwy. From there it's a short trip to Chester.

Another famous line, promoted as the Heart of Wales Line (☎ 0345-023641), runs south-west to Swansea (four hours), connecting with the main line from Cardiff to Fishguard.

There's one direct train a day to and from London Euston (three hours, £26.90), and regular links to Chester (one hour, £4.80). There are also regular trains from Cardiff to Manchester via Bristol, Ludlow and Shrewsbury. A train to Telford Central costs £2.80.

AROUND SHREWSBURY
Attingham Park

This elegant late 18th century neoclassical house (☎ 01743-709203, NT) is 4 miles south-east of Shrewsbury on the B4380. Set in a 92 hectare deer park, it's the grandest of Shropshire's stately homes. It features magnificent state rooms with decorated ceilings, a 300 piece collection of Regency silver, and a picture gallery designed by John Nash.

Attingham Park is open from late March through October, Saturday to Wednesday from 1.30 to 5 pm; the grounds are open daily in daylight hours. Entry to house and park costs £4/2. Bus No X96 stops in Atcham at the end of the lengthy drive (£1.80 return).

Wroxeter Roman City

In Roman times Wroxeter was the fourth largest British city, after London, Colchester and Verulamium (St Albans). Much of the site lies under farmland but visitors can explore the extensive remains of the baths. Admission to the ruins (☎ 01743-761330, EH) costs £2.75/1.40.

A short walk along a country lane leads to **Wroxeter church** where a huge font was created out of a column from the Roman site. The church has some fine 17th and 18th century woodwork and 17th century monuments.

Bus No X96 runs to Wroxeter (£2.40 return).

Hawkstone Historic Park & Follies

This restored 40 hectare park (☎ 01939-200611) is an 18th century fantasia of follies, caves and cliffs, mostly artificially created. A 2½ hour walking tour takes you up the White Tower (from which a dozen counties are said to be visible), over the Swiss Bridge, into the Hermit's Cave and rhododendron jungle, and through a rocky chasm. Bizarre as it is, fans of Disneyland will probably find it tame.

Hawkstone Park is about 10 miles north of Shrewsbury off the A49, and you need your own transport to get here. It's open daily from April through October; entry is £4.50/2.50.

IRONBRIDGE GORGE
☎ 01952

Blessed not just with a beautiful setting but with a wealth of important industrial relics, Ironbridge, near Telford, is a UNESCO World Heritage List site and a monument to the Industrial Revolution. In 1709 it was here that Abraham Darby pioneered the technique of smelting iron ore with coke that led to the production of the first iron wheels, the first iron rails, the first steam locomotive and the first iron bridge. Readily accessible deposits of iron ore and coal and easy transportation on the River Severn soon made Ironbridge the Silicon Valley of the 18th century, but by 1810 its glory days were already behind it.

The Ironbridge Gorge Museum is Britain's best industrial archaeology complex, with seven museums and several smaller sites spread over 6 sq miles around the beautiful old iron bridge. It's well worth visiting even if industrial archaeology isn't usually your thing.

Orientation & Information

Ideally you need your own transport since the museum sites are so spread out and

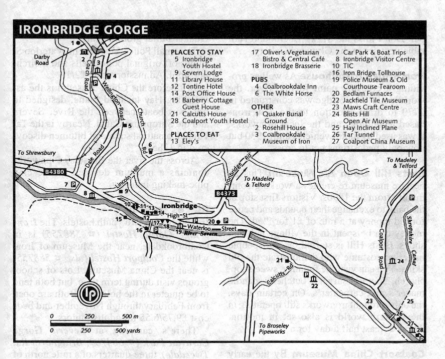

IRONBRIDGE GORGE

PLACES TO STAY
5 Ironbridge
   Youth Hostel
9 Severn Lodge
11 Library House
12 Tontine Hotel
14 Post Office House
15 Barberry Cottage
   Guest House
21 Calcutts House
28 Coalport Youth Hostel

PLACES TO EAT
13 Eley's

17 Oliver's Vegatarian
   Bistro & Central Café
18 Ironbridge Brasserie

PUBS
4 Coalbrookdale Inn
6 The White Horse

OTHER
1 Quaker Burial
   Ground
2 Rosehill House
3 Coalbrookdale
   Museum of Iron

7 Car Park & Boat Trips
8 Ironbridge Visitor Centre
10 TIC
16 Iron Bridge Tollhouse
19 Police Museum & Old
   Courthouse Tearoom
20 Bedlam Furnaces
22 Jackfield Tile Museum
23 Maws Craft Centre
24 Blists Hill
   Open Air Museum
25 Hay Inclined Plane
26 Tar Tunnel
27 Coalport China Museum

buses are very infrequent. It's 3 miles from Blists Hill to the Museum of Iron.

It's best to start your trip at the visitors centre to the west of the centre, where a video provides a good introduction to the site and to the Industrial Revolution in general.

The TIC (☎ 432166) near the bridge is the only place in Ironbridge where you can change money. For details of boat trips along the river phone ☎ 418844. Delamere Cycle Hire will deliver mountain bikes from Telford if you phone ☎ 0500-333515. They cost £10 a day.

Ironbridge Gorge Museum

The Ironbridge Gorge Museum (☎ 433522) is open daily from 10 am to 5 pm (6 pm in summer). Some of the minor sites (Rosehill House, Tollhouse, Broseley Pipeworks, Tar Tunnel) close from November through March. A passport ticket (valid indefinitely

until you've visited all the sites) allowing entrance to all the museums costs £9.50/5.50. Separate tickets to the individual museums cost from £1 (Tar Tunnel and visitors centre) to £6.80 (Blists Hill); the combined ticket saves you around £15. To see everything properly you really need a good two days.

Ironbridge Visitor Centre An interesting video sets the museum in its historic context but otherwise the centre mainly focuses on the environmental consequences of industrialisation. A useful model shows the gorge in its late 18th century heyday when the River Severn was choked with sailing boats.

Coalbrookdale Museum of Iron On the site where Abraham Darby first succeeded in smelting iron ore with coke, the ruined furnace is lovingly preserved. The museum shows all the uses to which iron has been put. Don't miss the 812kg Deerhound Hall table upstairs in the Glynwed Gallery.

Iron Bridge & Tollhouse As well as providing a crossing point for the river, the world's first iron bridge was constructed in 1779 to draw attention to the new iron-based technology and the local ironworks. It was used by motor vehicles until 1930 but now only pedestrians get to cross.

Blists Hill Open Air Museum This 20 hectare museum re-creates a working community from the 1890s. Visitors first stop at the bank to exchange their pounds and pence for old money at a rate of £1 for 2½d. The money can be spent in the village pub and shops. Blists Hill is staffed by craftspeople in period costume who demonstrate the old skills. You can visit the foundry, sweetshop, church, doctor's surgery, butcher's, candle maker's and carpenter's. On certain days, the only wrought ironworks still operating in the western world is also set in motion. Allow at least half a day for a visit.

Coalport China Museum By the early 19th century, iron-making skills had spread to other parts of the world and Ironbridge went into a steep decline, slowed only by the development of the porcelain and decorative tile industries around Coalport and Jackfield. Fine Coalport china was made here until the company moved to Staffordshire in 1926. The museum exhibits all sorts of elaborate pottery but also describes the life of the factory workers and how they carried out their tasks.

Jackfield Tile Museum A footbridge leads across the river to an abandoned factory where you can see displays of the decorative tiles produced here until the 1960s.

Other Things to See About 90m up the hill from the Museum of Iron, 18th century **Rosehill House** was built by the Darbys but is maintained as it was when it was home to

an early 19th century ironmaster. There's a **Quaker burial ground** nearby.

The small **Police Museum** in Waterloo St shows off original police cells and a birching stool. Admission costs £2/1.

Just before the China Museum is the astonishing **Hay Inclined Plane**, designed to transport boats between the River Severn and the Shropshire Canal. Nearby is the **Tar Tunnel**, a natural source of bitumen discovered in 1785.

Across the river the **Broseley Pipeworks** contains a museum devoted to the clay pipe-making industry.

Places to Stay

Ironbridge has two youth hostels. The *Ironbridge Gorge Hostel* (☎ 588755) is in Coalbrookdale, near the Museum of Iron, while the *Coalport Hostel* (also ☎ 588755) is near the China Museum. Lots of school groups visit during term time, but both tend to be quieter in the holidays. Both are open from February through November and beds cost £9.75/6.55 for adults/juniors.

There's camping at *Severn Gorge Caravan Park* (☎ 684789, Bridgnorth Rd, Tweedale), three-quarters of a mile north of Blists Hill. The charge is £5 for two people and a tent.

Overlooking the famous bridge, *Post Office House* (☎ 433201, 6 The Square) has three rooms, one with a bathroom, costing from £17.50 per person. The historic *Tontine Hotel* (☎ 432127), also on the square, has singles/doubles for £20/38 without bathroom or £34/52 with bathroom.

Across the river is the comfortable, friendly *Barberry Cottage Guest House* (☎ 882110, 71 Bower Yard) with rooms for £22/38. Also over here is *Calcutts House* (☎ 882631), a Georgian ironmaster's house, with rooms from £29/39.

Other accommodation in Ironbridge tends to be pricey. The snazzy Georgian *Library House* (☎ 432299, 11 Severn Bank), right in the centre of Ironbridge, has rooms for £40/50. A short walk above the river is the delightful *Severn Lodge* (☎ 432148), an attractive Georgian house with a secluded garden. There are two doubles and a twin room, all with bath, for £52.

Places to Eat

There are *cafés* at the Museum of Iron, the China Museum, Blists Hill (a pub, too) and Rosehill House, as well as in the Maws Craft Centre. The other places to eat all huddle round the centre of Ironbridge. For a snack or a picnic, *Eley's* on the square does an excellent, really porky pork pie (95p), among other pies and pasties.

Oliver's Vegetarian Bistro (☎ *433086, 33 High St)* opens for lunch and dinner from Tuesday to Saturday; starters cost £2.45, main courses £5.95. Upstairs at the *Coracle Restaurant* (☎ *433913)* main dishes tend to cost more like £8.50.

Nearby, the cheap and cheerful *Central Café* serves everything with chips, while the *Ironbridge Brasserie* (☎ *432716)* goes for modern British cuisine with prices and décor to match. *The Old Courthouse* (☎ *433838)* above the Police Museum in Waterloo St, is the most interesting of the *tea shops*, where you sip your drink in what was a Victorian courtroom. An American cream tea for £5.50 includes beef and horseradish sandwiches and lemon cake.

One reader wrote to rate the *Coalbrookdale Inn* (☎ *433953)* near the Ironbridge youth hostel the best pub in the world. It would take some research to verify that claim but the real ale and pub grub (not Sunday) certainly go down a treat.

Getting There & Away

Ironbridge is 14 miles from Shrewsbury. If you're driving from the other direction it's well signposted off the M54. See Getting There & Away under Shrewsbury earlier in this chapter for buses. The nearest train station is at Telford and there are fairly frequent buses (85p) to Ironbridge from there. On Saturday the Williamsons X96 runs to Ironbridge from Birmingham.

WENLOCK EDGE

There are great walks along this steep escarpment that stretches 15 miles from Ironbridge Gorge to Craven Arms, with superb views across to the Long Mynd to the west. It's geologically famous, in particular for its ancient coral reef exposures. Wenlock limestone was formed 400 million years ago when this area was under the sea.

Wilderhope Manor Youth Hostel (☎ *01694-771363)*, 7 miles south of Much Wenlock, is open February through October for £8.80/5.95 for adults/juniors. There are several trails, including one west along the top of Wenlock Edge. There are infrequent buses from Ludlow; you really need your own transport.

THE LONG MYND & CHURCH STRETTON
☎ 01694

The Long Mynd is probably the best known of Shropshire's hills – an excellent area for walking. Mynd is an abbreviation of the Welsh *mynydd* (mountain) but since these hills are below 550m they can hardly be called mountains. Nevertheless, there are superb views from the top of the ridges. **The Portway** is an ancient track that runs the full length of the Long Mynd.

The village of Church Stretton makes a good base for walks on the Long Mynd. The Victorians called the area Little Switzerland, bottled the local spring water and promoted Church Stretton as a health resort.

From Easter to September, Monday to Saturday, you can get walking information and leaflets from the Shropshire Hills Information Centre (☎ 723133), beside the library in Church Stretton. At other times, inquire in the library itself. Mountain bikes and tandems can be rented from Terry in All Stretton; phone ☎ 01694-723302 to arrange pick-up or delivery.

Walks

Just a 10 minute walk from Church Stretton Market Place, the **Carding Mill Valley** trail leads up to the 517m-high (1695 foot) summit of the Long Mynd, with views of the Stiperstones to the east. You can drive part of the way and in summer a National Trust information centre and tea shop opens in the valley. On the other side of the A49, the walk up **Caer Caradoc** to an ancient fort is less busy. The 5 mile trip should take about 2½ hours.

Places to Stay

Bridges Long Mynd Youth Hostel (☎ 01588-650656) is 5 miles from Church Stretton in an old village school at Ratling-hope, in the valley between the Long Mynd and the Stiperstones. It's open all year (but book ahead in winter). Beds cost £7.20/4.95 for adults/juniors. The walk from Church Stretton train station takes a couple of hours.

Just inside the grounds of the Long Mynd, *Dalesford* (☎ 723228) has blissfully quiet rooms for £18/34 a single/double. At *Woodbank House* (☎ 723454, *Watling St South*), there's B&B from £15 per person. *Brookfields Guest House* (☎ 722314, *Watling St North*), charges £28 per person for very comfortable rooms with a bathroom.

The excellent 16th century *Jinlye Guest House* (☎ 723243) is on Castle Hill on the Long Mynd, just outside All Stretton and 2 miles north of Church Stretton. Rooms with views and showers cost from £23 per person.

Longmynd Hotel (☎ 722244, *Cunnery Rd*) stands above Church Stretton and boasts a heated swimming pool, sauna and solarium. Rooms are from £50/90.

Getting There & Away

Shropshire Link bus No 435 takes 45 minutes from Shrewsbury, or 35 minutes from Ludlow. Trains are more than twice as fast but Church Stretton station is unstaffed.

BISHOP'S CASTLE

The main reason for visiting Bishop's Castle in the south-west corner of Shropshire is not the castle (which no longer exists) but the Three Tuns (☎ 01588-638797) in Salop St, a pub that still brews its own beer.

Tourist information is available from Old Time (☎ 01588-638467) at 29 High St. There are good local walks. Eight miles to the north, the **Stiperstones** are an inhospitable group of ridges topped with rough rocks. When the mist comes down and

Satan settles into The Devil's Chair, it can seem a pretty sinister place.

CLUN
☎ 01588

About 6 miles south of Bishop's Castle is the village of Clun, with a wonderful ruined castle and more good walking country; it's just a few miles east of Offa's Dyke. Despite the current shortage of trees, this area is known as Clun Forest because it was once a royal hunting ground.

Beds at *Clun Mill Youth Hostel* (☎ 640582), in an old water mill on the outskirts of the village, cost £7.20/4.95 for adults/juniors. It's open daily from mid-July through August. Phone to confirm other opening times. *Clun Farm* (☎ 640432, *High St*) does B&B for £15 per person.

Midland Red West service No 742/5 runs this way from Ludlow.

LUDLOW
• pop 7500 ☎ 01584

Ludlow is less knocked about than most British towns and its centre, especially along Broad St, boasts fine Georgian town houses interspersed with occasional half-timbered black and white buildings. A rambling ruined castle rises above the River Teme.

Ludlow developed around its 11th century castle. Involved in the medieval wool trade, it prospered from the sale of fleeces and the manufacture of woollen cloth. The town was also an important administrative centre and until 1689 the Council of the Welsh Marches was based here.

The TIC (☎ 875053) is in the 19th century Assembly Rooms in Castle St, with a small museum attached (£1/50p). Guided tours leave from outside the castle entrance at 2.30 pm on summer weekends.

Pearce Engineering (☎ 876016), Fishmore Rd, three-quarters of a mile north-east of the centre, rents out mountain bikes.

Ludlow Castle

Built around 1090 by Roger de Lacy to control the Welsh, this impressive castle consists of a huge fortification with a large outer courtyard where the townspeople could shelter if attacked, and a solid keep of generous proportions. Note the unusual ruins of a 12th century circular chapel. In the 14th century the castle was turned into a palace by Roger Mortimer, whose mistress was Queen Isabella, wife of Edward II. In the 16th century the Judges' Lodgings were added to accommodate the March administrators.

The castle (☎ 873355) is open daily from May through September from 10 am to 5 pm, closing at 4 pm in winter. Admission costs £2.50/1.50. In late June and early July it doubles as an open-air theatre for Shakespearean plays during the Ludlow Festival. Phone ☎ 872150 for full details.

Other Things to See

The large, mainly Early English and Decorated-style Church of St Laurence has some fine medieval misericords including one showing a mermaid admiring herself in a mirror. On the outside wall by the north entrance is a simple memorial to Housman. Note the unusual hexagonal porch.

Near the castle, the partially half-timbered Castle Lodge dates back to the 14th century although most of what you'll see inside is Tudor or later. There's some particularly fine plasterwork – and it seems astonishing that the threat to replace it with an office block has only just been lifted! Ring the bell for admission (£2).

The waymarked 30 mile Mortimer's Trail to Knighton starts just outside the castle entrance. Phone ☎ 797052 for details.

Places to Stay & Eat

Ludlow Youth Hostel (☎ 872472, Ludford Lodge) faces the town across Ludford Bridge, just south of town. It costs £7.20/4.95 for adults/juniors and is open mid-February through August daily except Sunday, and September and October daily except Sunday and Monday.

Ludlow's B&Bs tend to be expensive but about a mile from the centre, Cecil Guest House (☎ 872442, Sheet Rd) has 10 rooms from £19 per person.

If you can afford it, you should stay at the timber-framed Jacobean Feathers Hotel (☎ 875261, Bull Ring). Some rooms have four-poster beds and staying in this beautiful building is a delight. Singles/doubles normally cost from £60/80 but it's worth asking about cheaper leisure breaks. Right beside the castle the Georgian Dinham Mill Hotel (☎ 876464) is equally pricey, at £65/95. The restaurant here is well thought of.

For teas and coffees, head for the old-fashioned De Grey's Café (Broad St). For anything more substantial the classy Ego Café-Bar (Quality Square), off Castle Square, does tasty food (soups and crostini for £1.95) in attractive surrounds. Bacchus (☎ 878488, Broad St) offers moussaka for £6.50.

Getting There & Away

Ludlow is 29 miles from Shrewsbury and 24 miles from Hereford. From Ludlow train station there are direct services to Shrewsbury (30 minutes, £6.40), Church Stretton (15 minutes, £3.50), Hereford (25 minutes, £5), Cardiff, Liverpool and Manchester.

For information on Midland Red buses to Hereford, Birmingham, Kidderminster and Shrewsbury phone ☎ 01905-763888.

STOKESAY CASTLE

Seven miles north-west of Ludlow, Stokesay Castle (☎ 01588-672544, EH) is one of the most picturesque 13th century fortified manor houses in England. The grouping of stout stone walls, half-timbered 17th century gateway and church tower is one to set a thousand camera shutters clicking – as it does on sunny summer days.

Shropshire Link bus No 435 runs to Stokesay from Shrewsbury and Ludlow; drivers will drop you at the bottom of the lane leading to the castle. It's often quicker to take a train to Craven Arms and walk a mile south to the site. Teas and light lunches are available in Pottery Cottage beside the car park; or there's food and accommodation back in Craven Arms.

Staffordshire

Most visitors pass straight through Staffordshire, which stretches from the northern edge of Birmingham nearly to the southern fringes of Manchester. It's worth a pause to see Lichfield's wonderful cathedral, to sample the beer in Burton-upon-Trent or to scare yourself silly at Alton Towers. Lovers of fine porcelain will also want to break their journey in Stoke-on-Trent, heart of the famous Potteries district. To the north-east the Staffordshire moorlands blend into the Peak District National Park.

For information on Staffordshire buses, call the Busline on ☎ 01782-206608.

LICHFIELD
* pop 25,000   ☎ 01543

Lichfield is a small, easily assimilated market town with a famous cathedral. It was also home to the famous 18th century diarist and wit Samuel Johnson.

The TIC (☎ 252109), on Market Square, organises guided city walks throughout the summer (£1.50/1.25).

Lichfield Cathedral

The fine red-brick cathedral is famous for its three spires although it also boasts a fine west front adorned with statues of the kings of England from Edgar through to Henry I. Most of what you see dates from the various rebuildings of the Norman cathedral during the Middle Ages. St Chad, the first Bishop of Lichfield, was laid to rest in each building in turn. His gold-leafed skull was once kept in St Chad's Head Chapel, just to the west of the south transept.

The Lichfield Gospels, a superb illuminated manuscript from 730, are displayed in the beautifully vaulted mid-13th century chapterhouse. Don't miss the effigy of George Augustus Selwyn, first Bishop of New Zealand in 1841, in the Lady Chapel, or the poignant memorial to the two daughters of a cathedral prebendary at the east end of the south aisle. A donation of £3 is requested.

When you've finished in the cathedral, it's worth walking round the **cathedral** close which is ringed with fine 17th and 18th century houses.

Other Things To See & Do

Samuel Johnson was born here in 1709. His pioneering dictionary together with the biography written by his close friend James Boswell (*The Life of Samuel Johnson*) established him as one of the great scholars, critics and wits of the English language but, like so many modern media superstars, Johnson was mainly famous simply for being famous. Statues of Johnson and Boswell adorn the Market Square. The **Samuel Johnson Birthplace Museum**, on the square, is open daily from 10.30 am to 4.30 pm; entry is £1.40/80p. You can inspect the famous diary on computer in the bookshop in the lobby.

The **Heritage & Treasury Exhibition**, also on the square, is open from 10 am to 5 pm daily; entry is £1.50/80p. You can climb the tower for fine views of the city (£1/80p).

By the time you read this, a new **museum** commemorating the doctor Erasmus Darwin, grandfather of the more famous Charles, should have opened in the house where he lived from 1756 to 1781 in Beacon St.

Places to Stay & Eat

There are several B&Bs charging £16 to £18 a head in Beacon St, round the corner from the cathedral close. For a few pounds more you can stay on the Close; there's one double room at *No 8* (☎ 418483) for £34 to £38, and one family room at *No 23* (☎ 263337) for £38. The *Angel Croft Hotel* (☎ 258737, *Beacon St*) has comfortable rooms for £44/54.50 a single/double at weekends.

The visitors centre opposite the cathedral does soup and sandwich lunches for around £3.50. For a splash-out, try *Colleys Yard* (☎ 416606, 26 Bird St) where a modern British dinner costs from £15 to £20.

Getting There & Away

Lichfield is an easy half-hour's ride from Birmingham New St station and trains leave every 15 minutes (£3 day return).

STOKE-ON-TRENT
☎ 01782

Gentrification has yet to hit ugly Stoke-on-Trent which is, nevertheless, *the* place to come if you're interested in porcelain. Many famous names have factories here, the most famous of all being probably Wedgwood. Factory tours generally need to be booked in advance and don't run during factory holiday periods, but you can always visit the Wedgwood, Spode and Royal Doulton visitors centres, as well as the Gladstone and The Potteries museums where you can look without being tempted to buy.

Arnold Bennett left memorable descriptions of the area in its industrial heyday in his novels *Clayhangar* and *Anna of the Five Towns* – something of a misnomer since Stoke actually consists of six towns!

Orientation & Information
Stoke-on-Trent is made up of Tunstall, Burslem, Hanley, Stoke, Fenton and Longton – which, together, are often called The Potteries. Hanley is the official 'city centre'. Stoke-on-Trent train station is south-west of the city centre, but buses from outside the main entrance will run you there in minutes. The bus station is right in the city centre.

The various visitors centres, factories and showrooms are widely scattered about but the TIC (☎ 236000) in Quadrant Rd, Hanley, stocks maps with their locations.

Royal Doulton Visitor Centre
The Royal Doulton Visitor Centre (☎ 292434), in Nile St, Burslem, is open Monday to Saturday from 9.30 am to 5 pm, and on Sunday from 11 am; entry is £2.50/2. Factory tours take place Monday to Friday at 10.30 am and 1.15 and 2.45 pm.

Spode Museum & Visitor Centre
The Spode Museum & Visitor Centre (☎ 744011) is conveniently situated near the train station in Church St, Stoke. It's open Monday to Saturday from 9 am to 5 pm, Sunday from 10 am to 4 pm; entry is £2.50/1.50. Factory tours take place Monday

to Thursday at 10 am and 1.30 pm, and on Friday at 10 am.

Wedgwood Visitor Centre
Wedgwood Visitor Centre (☎ 204218), in Barlaston, is open daily from 9 am to 5 pm, opening at 10 am at weekends and closing

Josiah Wedgwood

Born in 1730, Josiah Wedgwood was the twelfth child of parents who were already turning out pots. When he was nine his father died and Josiah went to work in the family business inherited by his older brother Thomas. After a lengthy apprenticeship, he jumped ship and went into partnership with Thomas Whieldon who had a pottery in Fenton. It was there that he started the experiments that eventually led to his own distinctive wares.

Although Wedgwood is best known for his blue and white jasper, and black basalt wares, his first success was in creating a green glaze which could be used to finish off the then fashionable pots and jugs in the shape of vegetables.

Five years after joining Whieldon, Wedgwood was confident enough to branch out on his own, opening the Ivy House Works in Burslem. In 1765 he was allowed to name his distinctive cream-coloured pottery Queen's Ware after Queen Charlotte, wife of George III. Five years later he completed an order for Catherine II of Russia.

Wedgwood perfected his technique for producing black basalt pottery in 1768 but the distinctive blue and white jasper ware didn't put in an appearance until 1775.

Wedgwood was more than just a master potter. A supporter of the French and American Revolutions, he also worked for the abolition of slavery, finding time to devise new machinery for his business at the same time. When he died in 1795, he left a business well on its way to the international success it enjoys today.

MIDLANDS

at 4 pm on Sunday; entry is £3.25/1.60. Factory tours take place Monday to Thursday at 10 am and 1.30 pm.

Potteries Museum

This large museum and art gallery (☎ 232323), in Bethesda St, Hanley, is open daily from 10 am to 5 pm, opening at 2 pm on Sunday; entry is free. Come here to discover the history of The Potteries and to inspect a miscellaneous collection of ceramics.

Gladstone Pottery Museum

Constructed around Stoke's last remaining bottle kiln and its yard, this wonderful museum (☎ 319232), Uttoxeter Rd, Longton, is great on evoking the hot, unhappy working life of those who worked in The Potteries until the Clean Air Acts of the 1950s changed everything beyond recognition. Particularly fun is the gallery devoted to Victorian sanitaryware – toilet bowls more flowery than you would think possible. It's open daily from 10 am to 5 pm; entry is £3.75/2.25. Make sure you try a Staffordshire oatcake (actually a pancake) in the pleasant café.

Etruria Industrial Museum

On the site of the original canal-side Wedgwood factory, Stoke's newest museum (☎ 287557), Lower Bedford St, Etruria, incorporates a steam-powered bone and flint mill and a blacksmith's forge, as well as a visitors centre. It's open Wednesday to Sunday from 10 am to 4 pm; entry is free.

Places to Stay & Eat

It takes more than a day to see all Stoke's sights properly which is a shame, since decent accommodation is thin on the ground. Two places in Leek Rd convenient for the train station are *L. Beez Guest House* (☎ 846727) and *Rhodes Hotel* (☎ 416320); to find them, come out of the station, turn right and walk along Station Rd to the junction with Leek Rd, where you'll see them on the left, past a couple of pubs. Both offer B&B from £16; L. Beez is more welcoming to single travellers.

Café bar culture has yet to hit Stoke. Gourmet cuisine is extremely scarce. You're probably best off eating at the cafés attached to the museums and visitors centres, although food at the *North Stafford Hotel* (☎ 744477), opposite the station, is reputedly good.

Getting There & Away

There are regular trains to Stoke-on-Trent from Birmingham New St and from Manchester Piccadilly. National Express (☎ 0990-808080) buses do day returns from London to The Potteries for £12, if you think you can squeeze everything in in six hours.

Getting Around

The Wedgwood Express offers a four-times-a-day bus service linking most of the main sites for £4/2. Since the times are not all that convenient you can use the same ticket on PMT local buses (☎ 747000) too – not that all the drivers necessarily know that!

AROUND STOKE-ON-TRENT
Biddulph Gardens

The National Trust has recently restored these gorgeous Victorian gardens (☎ 01782-517999), with their Chinese and Egyptian corners. Seven miles north of Stoke, they're open from April through October daily, except Monday and Tuesday, from noon to 6 pm, opening at 11 am at weekends. Admission costs £4/2 but if you also visit Little Moreton Hall, 6 miles to the east, a joint ticket costs £6/3.

Little Moreton Hall

Off the A34 south of Congleton, Little Moreton Hall (☎ 01260-272018, NT) is England's most spectacular black and white timber-framed house, dating back to the 15th century. It's open from late March through October daily, except Monday and Tuesday, from noon to 5.30 pm (from 11 am in August) for £4/2.

Burton-upon-Trent

Burton-upon-Trent has been a brewing centre for centuries and the **Bass Museum & Visitor Centre** (☎ 01283-511000) tells the full story. Founded in 1777, Bass is now Britain's biggest brewer. The centre is open daily, from 10.30 am to 5 pm, and the £3.75 entry fee includes an end-of-visit Bass beer if you're of drinking age.

Alton Towers

With over 100 rides and an entrance fee of £18.50/14.50, Alton Towers (☎ 0990-204060) is Britain's most popular theme park. Between Stoke-on-Trent and Ashbourne, it's open from mid-March through October from 9.30 am to 7 pm. A family room at the on-site *hotel* costs £98 to £118.

Derbyshire

Derbyshire has the industrial town of Derby and some wonderful stately homes but its major attraction is the Peak District, most of which falls within the county boundaries (see the Peak District section later in this chapter). For general bus information phone ☎ 01332-292200.

DERBY

• pop 220,000 ☎ 01332

The Industrial Revolution transformed sleepy Derby (pronounced darby) first into a pioneering silk production centre, then into a major railway centre. In this century it became famous as the home of Rolls-Royce aircraft engines. Although there are no major tourist attractions, the town makes a peaceful base for exploring the surrounding area.

Derby's 18th century **cathedral** boasts a 64m tower and some magnificent ironwork. Look out for the tomb of Bess of Hardwick (see Hardwick Hall in the Around Chesterfield section later in this chapter) in the south aisle.

A short walk from the cathedral, in Full St, **Derby Industrial Museum** (☎ 255308) recounts Derby's industrial history with pride of place going, of course, to Rolls-

Royce aircraft engines. Other possibilities include the **Museum & Art Gallery** (☎ 716659) in The Strand, and **Pickford's House Museum** (☎ 255363), 41 Friar Gate, a museum of Georgian life. All these museums are free and open daily (from 2 to 5 pm only on Sunday).

Tours of the **Royal Crown Derby** china factory at 194 Osmaston Rd take place from Monday to Friday at 10.30 am and 1.45 pm. Phone ☎ 712841 for more information.

The TIC (☎ 255802) is in the Assembly Rooms in the Market Place.

Places to Stay & Eat

Crompton St is central and has a number of standard B&Bs like the *Wayfarer* (☎ 348350) at No 27, with singles/doubles for £17/26 and *Chuckles* (☎ 367193) at No 48 where they cost £13/27.

The large, modern *International Hotel* (☎ 369321, 288 Burton Rd) just south of the centre charges £35 to £70 for a room.

Huge *Arkwright's* is a popular café bar on the square by the TIC; a New York burger will cost you £4.15 but the menu is extensive. By the time you read this a new *Pizza Express* should have opened in Irongate, opposite a branch of *PJ Pepper's*. For good Indian food, head south down Normanton Rd, where there's a large Asian community.

Getting There & Away

Derby is 130 miles from London, 60 miles from Manchester, 40 miles from Birmingham and 30 miles from Leicester.

The dismal bus station is close to the centre. The TransPeak TP service operates from Manchester through the Peak District to Derby, taking just 30 minutes to continue to Nottingham (compared with the Barton R5 series which take over an hour).

InterCity trains link Derby with London in just under two hours.

AROUND DERBY
Kedleston Hall

Construction of this superb neoclassical mansion (☎ 01332-842191, NT) with its

Palladian front was started in 1758 by a trio of architects. The Curzon family has lived at Kedleston since the 12th century and Sir Nathaniel Curzon tore down an earlier house in order to construct this stunning masterpiece. He also moved Kedleston village a mile down the road so it wouldn't interfere with the landscaping! Only the medieval village church beside the house remains.

The entrance to the Marble Hall with its statues of Greek and Roman deities is breathtaking. The 20 alabaster columns were originally plain but from 1776 to 1777 it was decided that the room was too austere and fluting was chiselled into the columns *in situ*. The circular saloon with its domed roof was modelled on the Pantheon in Rome.

The whole house is lavishly decorated and includes the Indian Museum, displaying a later Lord Curzon's oriental collection. From 1898 to 1905 he was the viceroy of India – a century earlier, Government House in Calcutta (now Raj Bhavan) was modelled on Kedleston Hall. The adjacent church houses a collection of family memorials, their increasing magnificence indicating the Curzons' escalating fortunes.

Kedleston Hall is 5 miles north-west of Derby. It is open from Easter through October daily, except Thursday and Friday, from 1 to 5.30 pm. Entry costs £4.70/2.40.

Calke Abbey

Ten miles south of Derby in Ticknall is Calke Abbey (☎ 01332-863822, NT), which was built between 1701 and 1703 but had been left untouched since the last baronet died in 1924. It contains a varied collection ranging from natural history to a caricature room. Entry is by timed ticket; at busy periods it's wise to phone ahead and check that you'll be able to get in.

The house is open from April through October daily, except Thursday and Friday, from 12.45 to 5.30 pm; entry is £4.90/2.45.

CHESTERFIELD
- **pop 70,000 ☎ 01246**

Located on the eastern edge of the Peak District, Chesterfield is famous for the twisted spire of **St Mary's & All Saints Church** in Church Way. The 68m-high spire leans nearly 3m to one side and performs a painful-looking twist, the result of heavy lead tiles over a poorly seasoned timber frame. You can climb it on bank holiday Mondays for £2.50/1.

The TIC (☎ 207777) is on Low Pavement. The **Museum & Art Gallery** in St Mary's Gate is open daily, except Wednesday and Sunday, from 10 am to 4 pm. A market is held on Monday, Friday and Saturday. You can get to Chesterfield by bus from Sheffield.

AROUND CHESTERFIELD
Hardwick Hall

Hardwick Hall (☎ 01246-850430, NT) was Bess of Hardwick's crowning achievement and the ES initials on the walls loudly trumpet her ownership as Elizabeth, Countess of Shrewsbury. Separated from her fourth husband, the Earl of Shrewsbury, Bess moved to Hardwick after buying it from her bankrupt brother in 1583. Lacking the means to build a home commensurate with her high opinion of herself, she initially settled for rebuilding Hardwick Old Hall. But as soon as her husband died in 1590, and she got her hands on his fortune, work started on Hardwick Hall.

The house features the very best of late 16th century design including vast amounts of glass, a considerable status symbol at the time. It's notable for its many late 16th to early 17th century tapestries and for a remarkably thorough inventory taken in 1601; many items from that inventory still exist. Over the centuries the house managed to escape both modernisation and neglect so it retains a wonderfully ancient feel. Despite its airy appearance – 'more glass than wall' – it remains rather austere.

The house is open from April through October on Wednesday, Thursday, Saturday and Sunday from 12.30 to 5 pm (or sunset if earlier) for £6/3. The adjacent ruins of Hardwick Old Hall are watched over by English Heritage (EH) and are open from 10 am to 6 pm for £2.30/1.70 (a joint ticket to both properties is £7.70/4.20). Hardwick Hall is about 10 miles south-east of Chesterfield, just off the M1 between junctions 28 and 29.

Peak District

Although the Peak District is principally in Derbyshire it spills over into five adjoining counties. It's a remarkable region – smack in the middle of one of the most densely populated, and at times greyest and dullest, parts of England in one of the country's best loved national parks. Dotted with pretty villages, historic sites and fascinating limestone caves, the Peak District also encompasses some of England's most wild and beautiful scenery.

ORIENTATION

Although it's squeezed between Manchester and Sheffield, with the industrial towns of Yorkshire to the north and the southern Midlands to the south, there are no large towns within the Peak District National Park.

Nor are there any actual peaks in the Peak District; the name comes from the ancient people who once inhabited the region. The 555 sq miles of the national park are divided into two areas: the harsher, wilder Dark Peak to the north, and the more pastoral, 'prettier' White Peak to the south. Both areas are limestone but the higher Dark Peak moorlands are on coarse gritstone, while the green fields of the White Peak are patterned with dry-stone walls, much like Ireland, and divided by deep-cut dales.

INFORMATION

There are TICs or National Park Information Offices in Bakewell, Castleton, Edale and other locations. Information for disabled visitors is available by calling ☎ 01629-816200. The Ordnance Survey (OS) *Peak District* map (1:63,360) will be adequate for most users, but there are also separate maps of the White and Dark Peaks.

Pick up a copy of the free *Peakland Post* from TICs. It lists all sorts of walks guided by National Park rangers.

WALKS & CYCLE ROUTES

The Pennine Way has its southern end at Edale in the Peak District. See the Activities chapter for more information on this classic British long-distance walk and for essential preparations and precautions. There are many other shorter walks within the park but those intending to explore the Dark Peak or engage in the local practice of 'bog trotting' should be prepared for the often viciously changeable weather; a map and compass, wet weather gear and emergency food supplies are essential. TICs stock the handy *Walks Around ...* and *Walks About ...* guides.

The High Peak and Tissington trails are equally popular with walkers and cyclists. There are several Peak Cycle Hire centres, including the Parsley Hay centre near the junction of the Tissington and High Peak trails. A leaflet details the centres, their opening times and rental charges (£8/5.50 for one day, 10% discount for YHA members).

TICs also stock the *Peak Park Cycle Route* booklets produced by the national park authorities.

Limestone Way

The 26 mile Limestone Way winds through the White Peak from Castleton to Matlock via Peak Forest, Miller's Dale, Taddington, Flagg, Monyash, Youlgreave, Winster and Bonsall. There are youth hostels at both ends and at Ravenstor (near Miller's Dale), Youlgreave and Elton (near Winster). Camping barns and camping grounds are dotted about, and there are B&Bs in most of the villages as well as an ample supply of pubs. The walk is signposted with fingerposts, yellow arrows and the walk's Derbyshire Ram logo. TICs and the Bakewell national park office have a detailed walk leaflet.

High Peak & Tissington Trails

The 17½ mile High Peak Trail follows the pioneering High Peak & Cromford Railway line. This was originally envisaged as a canal but when the engineering problems proved insurmountable the developers

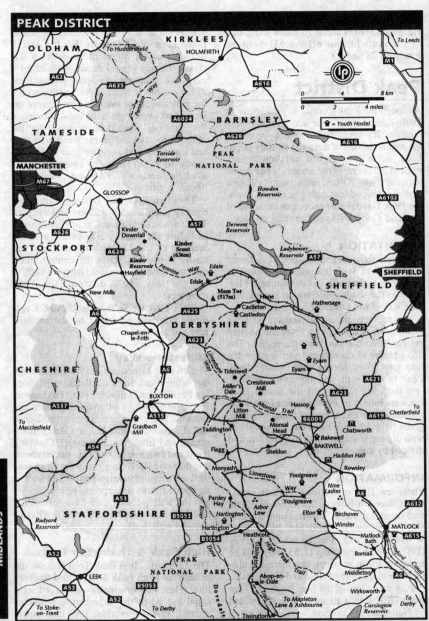

PEAK DISTRICT

0   4   8 km
0   2   4 miles

🏠 = Youth Hostel

OLDHAM

KIRKLEES

To Huddersfield

HOLMFIRTH

To Leeds

A62

A635

M1

A6024

BARNSLEY

TAMESIDE

Pennine Way

A628

PEAK

A616

MANCHESTER

Torside Reservoir

NATIONAL PARK

A616

M67

Howden Reservoir

A6102

GLOSSOP

A57

Derwent Reservoir

A626

Kinder Downfall

Kinder Scout (636m)

Ladybower Reservoir

A57

STOCKPORT

A624

Kinder Reservoir Hayfield

Pennine Way

Edale

SHEFFIELD

New Mills

Edale

SHEFFIELD

A6

Mam Tor (517m)

Hope

Hathersage

Castleton

Castleton

A625

DERBYSHIRE

Bradwell

Chapel-en-le-Frith

A623

River

A625

CHESHIRE

A6

Limestone Way

Tideswell

Eyam

A621

Eyam

A537

Cressbrook Mill

A623

To Chesterfield

Miller's Dale

Hassop

Derwent

A619

BUXTON

A515

Litton Mill

Monsal Trail

B6001

Gradbach Mill

Monsal Head

Chatsworth

A54

Taddington

Bakewell

Flagg

Sheldon

BAKEWELL

Haddon Hall

To Macclesfield

Monyash

Limestone

Rowsley

STAFFORDSHIRE

B5053

Youlgreave

Nine Ladies

A6

Way

Rudyard Reservoir

Parsley Hay

Youlgreave

A632

A53

Hartington

Arbor Low

Elton

Birchover

MATLOCK

Hartington

Winster

Matlock Bath

A615

Heathcote

Bonsall

A52

High Peak Trail

Cromford Canal

LEEK

B5054

PEAK

Alsop-en-Dale

Middleton

A6

A53

B5053

NATIONAL PARK

Tissington Trail

Wirksworth

To Stoke-on-Trent

A52

To Derby

Dovedale

To Mapleton Lane & Ashbourne

Carsington Reservoir

To Derby

Tissington

decided to build a railway line instead. They applied canal thinking to the new technology, labelling the stations as wharfs and ending up with a line which surmounted hills by going up them steeply, like a flight of canal locks. As a result the line never worked very well; railway engineers soon discovered that trains worked best on long, gentle inclines rather than short, steep ones. Opened in 1830, the line actually predated the general use of steam locomotives and at first the carriages were hauled by horses and pulled up the steep inclines by stationary engines installed at the tops of the hills.

When the line finally closed in 1967 the tracks were torn up and it was made into a walking and cycling track. The wide, well-surfaced trail is ideal for cycling and makes a pleasant day out in rolling White Peak country. The 1-in-14 Hopton Incline was the steepest gradient worked by locomotives in the British Isles. At Middleton Top the 1829 steam winding engine which used to haul trains up the 1-in-8¾ Middleton Incline is still in working order and jolts into action on summer Sundays. The Sheep Pasture Incline also required winding engines to haul the trains up. At the High Peak Junction at the southern end of the trail, near Matlock Bath, the former railway workshop is now used as a visitors centre and museum. Goods were transferred to boats on the Cromford Canal at this point. Later it took trains up to seven hours to cover the distance a cyclist can ride in just a couple.

The 13 mile Tissington Trail was a much later line, opened in 1899, but it never proved economically feasible and like the High Peak Trail, was closed in 1967. The two trails meet just south of Parsley Hay and continue farther north, although not all the way to Buxton.

Bicycles can be hired on the trails at Parsley Hay (☎ 01298-84493), at Middleton Top, towards the southern end of the High Peak Trail, or at Mapleton Lane, at the southern end of the Tissington Trail. If you've got time it's a pleasant 40 mile round trip from Parsley Hay down the High Peak Trail and up the Tissington Trail, linking the two trails by the B5053 from Matlock Bath to Ashbourne. The B5053 section undulates a lot so make sure you allow plenty of time.

Monsal Trail

Like the High Peak and Tissington trails, the Monsal Trail, along the deep valley of the River Wye, follows a disused railway line. It's used by walkers more than cyclists (unlike the other two).

The 8½ mile trail starts from the Coombs Rd Viaduct, just east of Bakewell, but there's no view of the viaduct from the trail. You can also walk from Rowsley on the A6 to the beginning of the trail. The old train station at Hassop near Bakewell has been converted into the Country Bookstore. At Monsal Head there's a pub, B&B and a superb view of the **Monsal Viaduct**, a man-made wonder of the Peak District and the subject of considerable controversy when it was first built. **Cressbrook Mill** opened as a water-powered cotton mill in 1783 and continued in operation, powered by steam, from 1890 until 1965. **Litton Mill** opened in 1782 and was infamous for its owner's exploitation of child labourers. Walking west, the final tunnel requires what can be a very muddy, slippery and wet detour. The trail ends at Blackwell Mill Junction, a short walk from the A6, 3 miles east of Buxton.

Other Walks

The Peak District is crisscrossed with good walks and the TICs are packed with information. Castleton and Bakewell in the White Peak make particularly good centres for short walks. From Edale you can walk in either direction: north to the Dark Peak and nearby Kinder Scout, or south towards Castleton. Hayfield is another good starting point for walks into the Dark Peak.

OTHER ACTIVITIES

The Peak District limestone is riddled with caves including 'showcaves' open to the public in Castleton, Buxton and Matlock Bath. For information on caving trips and courses contact Pennine National Caving

MIDLANDS

(☎ 01831-44919). *The Caves of Derbyshire* by TD Ford has extensive information on the county's caves.

The Peak District has been a training ground for some of Britain's best known mountaineers, and cliff faces like High Tor, overlooking Matlock Bath, are still popular. Jumping off the cliff faces on hang-gliders is becoming equally popular. Fishing on most Peak District rivers is private.

PLACES TO STAY

Walkers may appreciate the *camping barns* (☎ 01629-825850) that offer a roof over your head for a nightly cost of £3 per person. A leaflet shows the locations of the barns and explains how to book a place. Another brochure details camping grounds in and around the Peak District.

GETTING THERE & AWAY

The Peak District authorities are trying hard to wean visitors off their cars, and TICs stock the excellent *Peak District Timetable* covering all local bus and train services.

There are train services from Derby to Matlock, at the southern edge of the Peak District, or from Sheffield across the northern part of the district through Edale to New Mills and on to Manchester. There's also a Manchester-New Mills-Buxton service.

The convenient TransPeak TP bus operates right across the Peak District, linking Nottingham, Derby, Matlock, Bakewell, Buxton, New Mills and Manchester (3½ hours); Matlock to Buxton takes about an hour. Yorkshire Traction has services from Barnsley into the district from the north and down to Castleton and Buxton.

A Derbyshire Wayfarer ticket costs £7.25 (including one child or dog) for one day's unlimited travel on most train and bus services into and around the Peak District. An Explorer ticket also gives you all-day travel on Trent and Barton buses including the TransPeak TP service. It costs £4.95 and includes one child. The Busline information service can be contacted on ☎ 01298-23098.

BAKEWELL
- **pop 3900   ☎ 01629**

This pretty village is the largest population centre within the Peak National Park boundaries and a notorious traffic bottleneck on summer weekends. The village found its way into the cookbooks as a result of the accidental invention of the Bakewell pudding.

Information

The TIC (☎ 813227), in the 17th century Market Hall on Bridge St, has an informative display about the national park. There's a market on Mondays.

Things to See

All Saints Church has Norman features and a fine octagonal tower/spire. There's a Saxon cross from around 800 in the graveyard. The **Old House Museum** in Cunningham Place

---

Which Bakewell Pudding?

Bakewell blundered into the cookbooks around 1860 when a cook at the Rutland Arms Hotel misread the strawberry tart recipe and spread the egg mixture on top of the jam instead of stirring it into the pastry, thus creating the Bakewell pudding (*pudding* mark you, not *tart*). It features regularly on local dessert menus and is certainly worth sampling.

Bakewell establishments are locked in battle over whose is the original recipe, a dispute so serious it may finally be settled by the European Court in Brussels. Bloomers (☎ 813724), Water St, insists it created 'the first and only Bakewell puddings' and swiftly converted its name to a registered trademark. But the Old Original Bakewell Pudding Shop (☎ 812193) is adamant that its recipe is older, and it pulls more trade thanks to its position on the main thoroughfare.

In a blind tasting, this author preferred Bloomers' version. The pastry was thicker, and the egg mixture less heavy. It also cost 65p as opposed to 99p.

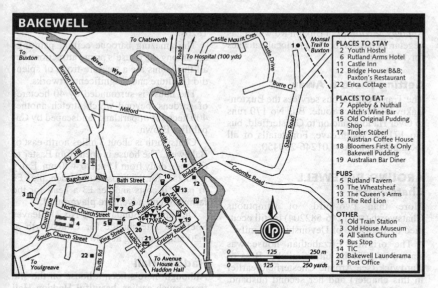

BAKEWELL

PLACES TO STAY
2 Youth Hostel
6 Rutland Arms Hotel
11 Castle Inn
12 Bridge House B&B;
   Paxton's Restaurant
22 Erica Cottage

PLACES TO EAT
7 Appleby & Nuthall
8 Aitch's Wine Bar
15 Old Original Pudding
   Shop
17 Tiroler Stüberl
   Austrian Coffee House
18 Bloomers First & Only
   Bakewell Pudding
19 Australian Bar Diner

PUBS
5 Rutland Tavern
10 The Wheatsheaf
13 The Queen's Arms
16 The Red Lion

OTHER
1 Old Train Station
3 Old House Museum
4 All Saints Church
9 Bus Stop
14 TIC
20 Bakewell Launderama
21 Post Office

near the church has a local collection housed in a 1534 building but is only open on summer afternoons (£2/1).

The pretty five-arched **bridge** over the River Wye dates from medieval times. The popular **Monsal Trail** walking and cycling track starts just outside Bakewell but there are many other good walking routes around the village including trails to Magpie Mine, Haddon Hall and Chatsworth House.

Places to Stay

Hostel The *youth hostel* (☎ 812313), on Fly Hill, costs £7.20/4.95 for adults/juniors. It's open daily except Sunday from April through October; only on Friday and Saturday for the rest of the year.

B&Bs & Hotels *Erica Cottage* (☎ 813241, *Butts Rd)* charges £15 per person but phone to check it's open.

The *Castle Inn* (☎ 812103, *Bridge St)* charges £36.50 for rooms accommodating up to four people. *Bridge House* (☎ 812867, *Bridge St)* charges from £15 a head for a room and continental breakfast, from £18.50 with full English breakfast.

The accidentally gastronomically pioneering (see the boxed text 'Which Bakewell Pudding?') *Rutland Arms Hotel* (☎ 812812) is a fine establishment right on the main square in town, with singles/doubles for £45/64. Front rooms can be a bit noisy.

Places to Eat

Bakewell has lots of tea and coffee shops. The most imaginative is the *Tiroler Stüberl Coffee House* attached to Bloomers First & Only Bakewell Pudding shop.

Most of the pubs – the *Red Lion*, the *Queen's Arms*, the *Wheatsheaf* and the *Rutland Tavern* – also serve food; the food at the *Castle* is especially good.

There are also a few restaurants. In Granby Rd, the *Australian Bar Diner* has set meals for £2.95 and all sorts of meaty options. *Aitch's Wine Bar* (☎ 813895, *Rutland St)* has the most imaginative menu, and at weekends *Paxtons* (☎ 814336, *Bridge St)* by the river swaps from a tearoom to a more romantic restaurant.

MIDLANDS

For a picnic it's worth dropping in on *Appleby & Nuthall* in Buxton Rd which has vegetarian pasties for 70p and local oatcakes for 15p each.

Getting There & Away

The TransPeak TP bus services the Buxton-Bakewell-Matlock route. Bus No 170 runs to Over Haddon and on to Chesterfield, bus No 171 to Youlgreave. For details of all local buses phone ☎ 01246-250450.

AROUND BAKEWELL
Chatsworth

More than two-thirds of sumptuous Chatsworth (☎ 01246-582204) is still occupied by the Duke of Devonshire's family.

The original Elizabethan house was started in 1551 by the inimitable Bess of Hardwick (see Around Chesterfield earlier in this chapter) and her second husband. Mary Queen of Scots was imprisoned here several times between 1570 and 1581 at the behest of her cousin Elizabeth I. Mary's jailer, the Earl of Shrewsbury, was Bess' fourth husband but her suspicion that the 'knave, fool and beast' was rather more than just a jailer led to their separation. The house was extensively altered between

---

The Return of Rutland

The latest of a string of rearrangements of the county boundaries has seen the reinstatement of Rutland, England's smallest, blink-and-you'll-miss-it county, squeezed in between Leicestershire, Northamptonshire and Lincolnshire.

Not that a Rutland tourist officer would be run off their feet promoting the territory. There's the county town of Oakham, a smattering of villages with a strong hunting tradition, gently rolling hills and that's about it.

Was it really worth all those changes to stationery, one asks oneself?

1686 and 1707 and then enlarged in the 1820s.

The amazing baroque ceiling paintings are among the house's prime attractions but all the rooms are a treasure-trove of splendid furniture and magnificent artworks.

The house is surrounded by 40 hectares of gardens, beyond which stretch another 400 hectares of parkland landscaped by Capability Brown.

Chatsworth is about 3 miles north-east of Bakewell. The house is open from Easter to October, daily from 11 am to 4.30 pm. Entry is £6.25/3 for the house and garden, plus £1 to park. It costs another £3 a head for the **farmyard and adventure playground**.

On summer Sundays bus No 210 leaves Sheffield Interchange for Chatsworth at 9.20 am, returning at 5.40 pm.

Haddon Hall

Although there's been a house on the site from much earlier, beautiful Haddon Hall (☎ 01629-812855) dates mainly from Tudor times. The site was originally owned by William Peveril (see Castleton later in this chapter). The house was abandoned right through the 18th and 19th centuries, hence the minor changes in that period. Highlights include the 14th century chapel and the medieval kitchens and great hall.

Outside, terraced gardens step down to the River Wye near an old stone packhorse bridge. The house is 2 miles south of Bakewell on the A6 and is open daily, April through September, from 11 am to 5 pm. Entry costs £5.50/3.

Dovedale

The steep-sided valley of the **River Dove** is one of the most beautiful – and so most crowded – of the Derbyshire Dales. The river flows beneath natural features like Thorpe Cloud, Dovedale Castle, Lovers' Leap, the Twelve Apostles, Tissington Spires, Reynard's Kitchen and Ilam Rock. **Beresford Dale**, upstream from Dovedale, was a favourite haunt of Izaak Walton, author of *The Compleat Angler*. The 17th century Fishing Temple is a memorial to him.

Tideswell

☎ 01298

The huge church at Tideswell is sometimes described as the 'cathedral of the Peaks' and is worth visiting to see its brasses, woodwork and fine ceilings.

Poppies (☎ 871083, Bank Square) is an excellent small restaurant (closed Wednesday) which also does B&B from £16. The *George Hotel (☎ 871382)* beside the church does good pub food and has rooms from £23.95 per person.

With your own car, you might want to stay in the delightful, partially medieval *Hall (☎ 871175)* in nearby Great Hucklow, with beds for £20 a head.

EYAM

- pop 900   ☎ 01433

The small village of Eyam (pronounced ee-em) is famous for a dreadful incident in 1665, when a consignment of cloth from London delivered to a local tailor brought with it the Black Death. As the dreaded disease spread through Eyam, the village rector, William Mompesson, convinced the villagers that rather than risk spreading it to other villages Eyam should quarantine itself. By the time the plague burnt itself out in late 1666, more than 250 of the village's 350-strong population were dead, including the rector's wife. The *Eyam History Trail* details all the sites associated with the plague.

The **Church of St Lawrence** dates from Saxon times and has many reminders of the events of 1665 and 1666, including a cupboard said to have been made from the wooden box which carried the infected cloth to Eyam. The plague register records the names of those who died during the outbreak. The church also has a leaflet describing some of the monuments and headstones in the churchyard, which has an 8th century **Celtic cross**, one of the finest in the country. Many of the plague victims were buried in the churchyard but apart from that of Catherine Mompesson, the rector's wife, only one other headstone relating to the plague has survived. Other victims were buried around the village

– at the Riley graves, Mrs Hancock buried all seven members of her family one by one.

Next to Eyam's church are the **plague cottages** where the tailor lived. A walk up Water Lane from the village square, or a drive towards Grindleford from Hawkhill Rd, will bring you to **Mompesson's Well**. Food and other supplies were left here by friends from other villages. Back in Eyam, the 17th century **Eyam Hall** (☎ 631976) is open from Easter through October on Wednesday, Thursday and Sunday from 11 am to 4.30 pm; entry is £3.50/3.

Places to Stay & Eat

The *youth hostel (☎ 630335, Hawkhill Rd)* charges £8/5.40 for adults/juniors. *Delf View House (☎ 631533, Church St)* offers comfortable B&B in a Georgian house from £20 per person. The *Miner's Arms* on the square, which dates from 1630, turns out good sandwiches.

Getting There & Away

There are daily buses from Tideswell to Eyam. On Monday bus No 175 also runs from Bakewell to Eyam.

CASTLETON

- pop 900   ☎ 01433

Overlooked by 517m-high (1696 foot) Mam Tor, this tiny village is a popular base for exploring the Peaks and features caves and a castle. It's also the northern terminus of the Limestone Way. Mam Tor is the boundary between the limestone of the White Peak and the gritstone of the Dark Peak.

Orientation & Information

Castleton nestles at the western end of the Hope Valley. Mam Tor's unstable condition undermined the A625 road through Castleton and it's now bypassed by the spectacular Winnats Pass road which goes through a steep-sided dale. Castle St is home to the church, pubs, B&Bs and the youth hostel.

The National Park Information Centre (☎ 620679) in Castle St is open daily from Easter to October, weekends only in winter.

MIDLANDS

Peveril Castle

Castleton is overlooked by the ruins of Peveril Castle (☎ 620613, EH), built by William Peveril, son of William the Conqueror. The keep, which is about all that remains, was added by Henry II in 1176. The castle sits more or less on top of Peak Cavern. From it there are superb views north to Mam Tor and the Dark Peak and south over pretty Cave Dale, directly behind the castle. Entry costs £1.75/1.30.

Walks

Start the 26 mile Limestone Way by taking the narrow, rocky entrance into beautiful Cave Dale behind the castle. There are many other excellent walks around Castleton. A fine day walk (see the Castleton & Edale map) of about 7 miles can be taken by going south along the Cave Dale track to a road where you turn right, and right again to pass by Rowter Farm and meet the Buxton Rd just beyond Winnats Pass. The route then climbs up to Mam Tor where ditches marking a pre-Roman fort can be distinguished on the top. The trail follows the ridge to Back Tor, but just before reaching that high point there's a path down from the ridge directly into Castleton along Hollowford Lane and Mill Bridge. Another pleasant day walk makes a 7 mile round trip via Edale, starting point of the Pennine Way.

Caves

The area around Castleton is riddled with caves, four of which are commercially operated and open to the public. Although most of them are natural, the area has also been extensively mined for Blue John, a reddish-pink form of fluorspar, as well as lead, silver and other minerals. Miners often broke into natural chambers during the course of their excavations.

The **Peak Cavern** (☎ 620285), popularly known as the Devil's Arse, is reached by a pretty stream-side walk from the village centre. Unfortunately the ugly wall erected to stop you sneaking a free peek into the yawning 18 by 30m chasm detracts from

the natural beauty. Rope was made here until 1974 and rope-makers' houses used to stand just inside the cave entrance. The cave is open daily from Easter through October from 10 am to 5 pm. Entry costs £4.50/2.50.

The small, stalactite-filled **Treak Cliff Cavern** (☎ 620571) is open all year from 9.30 am to 5.30 pm (10 am to 4 pm from November through February); entry costs £4.95/2.25. **Speedwell Cavern** (☎ 620512) boasts a long artificially flooded tunnel along which you travel by electric boat to the 'bottomless' pit at the end; before electrification the boatman would propel the boat along the tunnel by 'walking' it with his feet on the tunnel roof. It's open daily from 9.30 am to 5 pm and costs £5/3.

On the other side of the closed section of road by Mam Tor is the impressive **Blue John Cavern** (☎ 620638) where it's thought that Blue John may have been mined in Roman times. One of the cave's chambers has a collection of 19th century mining equipment. It's open daily from 9.30 am to 5.30 pm (dusk in winter); entry costs £5/3.

Experienced potholers can explore other caves, including the **Odin Mine** below Mam Tor, and the **Suicide Cave** and **Old Tor Mine** on Winnats Pass. The remains of prehistoric animals have been found in **Windy Knoll Cave**.

Places to Stay

The large **youth hostel** (☎ 620235, Castle St) across from the church costs £9.75/6.55 for adults/juniors; a few rooms with facilities in the adjoining vicarage cost £11.65/8.

Of the B&Bs, **Cryer House** (☎ 620244), also in Castle St, costs from £19. **Rambler's Rest** (☎ 620125, Mill Bridge) charges from £16. **Bargate Cottage** (☎ 620201, Market Place) is full of character. You'll pay from £21.50, but be prepared for convivial breakfasts.

The slightly pricier **Kelseys Swiss House Hotel** (☎ 621098), on the main road on the Hope side of the village, offers pleasant rooms with bathroom for £29.50/40 a single/double.

CASTLETON & EDALE

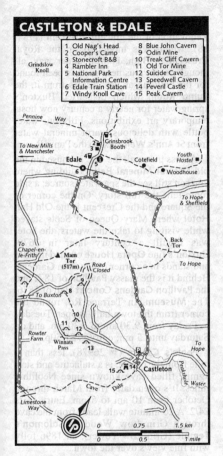

1 Old Nag's Head	8 Blue John Cavern
2 Cooper's Camp	9 Odin Mine
3 Stonecraft B&B	10 Treak Cliff Cavern
4 Rambler Inn	11 Old Tor Mine
5 National Park	12 Suicide Cave
Information Centre	13 Speedwell Cavern
6 Edale Train Station	14 Peveril Castle
7 Windy Knoll Cave	15 Peak Cavern

Places to Eat

The most obvious places to eat are the pubs. The *Castle Hotel* probably does the best meals but the *George* and the *Peak* are also popular. Otherwise there's a *fish and chip shop* round the corner from the hostel, or *Hilary Beth's Tea Room* in Market Place and *Rose Cottage* beside the Blue John Craft Shop for teas and coffees.

If you're after something more formal, the restaurant attached to *Kelseys Swiss House Hotel* does two and three-course

dinners for £10.50/12.95 from 6.30 pm. *Ye Olde Nag's Head Hotel* (☎ 620451) does romantic candlelit suppers for £17.95 and Sunday lunches for £12.95.

Getting There & Away

There's a train station at Hope, 2 miles east of Castleton.

Trent and South Yorkshire PTE buses run to Castleton. Mainline buses run to Sheffield (£2.25).

EDALE
- **pop 350** ☎ 01433

Tiny Edale, the southern terminus of the 250 mile Pennine Way, is easily accessible by train from Sheffield to Manchester. It makes a good starting point for short walks, whether north to Kinder Scout or south to Mam Tor, the ridge overlooking Castleton.

Edale stretches from the main road and train station up to the Old Nag's Head pub. The National Park Information Centre (☎ 670207) is open daily from 9 am to 5.30 pm (5 pm from November through March). The mountain rescue service is based here.

Walks

There are several pleasant short walks from Edale up to the ridge between Mam Tor and Back Tor, overlooking Castleton. Alternatively you can walk north onto the Kinder Plateau; Jacob's Ladder offers the easiest route onto Kinder. If the weather is cooperative, a fine 6 mile walk takes you from the information office, past the youth hostel and up onto the moors along the southern edge of Kinder before dropping back down to Edale.

Places to Stay & Eat

The large *youth hostel* (☎ 670302), at Rowland Cote, Nether Booth, about 2 miles east of the village, costs £9.75/6.55 for adults/juniors.

The small *Fieldhead Camp Site* (☎ 670386) charges £2.85 per person and is right by the information centre. Showers are 50p. To the north of the village, *Cooper's Camp* (☎ 670372) charges £2.25 per person.

MIDLANDS

B&B for £23 a head is available at the *Rambler Inn* (☎ *670268*) right by the train station and at *Stonecroft B&B* (☎ *670262*), past the information centre and church.

The *Old Nag's Head* (official starting point of the Pennine Way) and the *Rambler Inn* serve reasonable pub grub. Cooper's Camp has a small shop for provisions.

HAYFIELD

Hayfield is famous as the starting point of the 1932 'trespass' on Kinder Scout. In good weather an excellent 7 mile walk proceeds east from Hayfield, climbing to the 636m-high (2088 feet) summit of Kinder Scout. Summit is somewhat of a misnomer as there's little difference between the high point and the rest of the Kinder Plateau. From the top, the trail runs north to the Kinder Downfall along the western edge of the Moorland Plateau. It then turns east, still following the plateau edge, before dropping steeply and turning south to Kinder Reservoir near Hayfield.

BUXTON
* **pop 19,500**   ☎ **01298**

Buxton is outside the Peak District National Park boundaries although it makes a fine base for visiting the area. The town has a genteel air to it and is frequently compared to Bath; it even has its own natural spring discovered by the Romans in 78 AD. Buxton's heyday was in the 18th century when there were seven sets of baths about town. By the 1950s all of these had closed and, despite all the New Age shops around town, it seems unlikely they will reopen.

Orientation & Information

Those arriving by train are dropped off near pedestrianised Spring Gardens and the Spring Gardens shopping centre. The TIC (☎ 25106) is beside the newly restored Crescent.

Those arriving by bus are dropped in the Market Place where most of Buxton's eating choices can be found.

The Opera House is the focus for the annual late July to early August Buxton Festival (☎ 70395).

Things to See & Do

Renovation of the graceful **Crescent** (1784-88), which was modelled on the Royal Crescent in Bath, is well under way, although no obvious new use has been found for the building as yet. Across from it, the **Pump Room** which dispensed Buxton's spring water for nearly a century now hosts temporary art exhibitions. Fill your water bottle with delicious warm mineral water from **St Ann's Well**, next to the Pump Room.

Across the road, the TIC is housed in the old **Natural Mineral Baths** building where you can still see the spa water source; a side room tells the full story. On the corner of the Square and the Crescent is the **Old Hall Hotel** where Mary Queen of Scots stayed while visiting to take the waters; the hotel was rebuilt a century later in 1670. Buxton's fine **Opera House** opened in 1903 and stands in a corner of Pavilion Gardens. Behind it is the glassy **Pavilion** of 1871 and the **Pavilion Gardens Concert Hall** of 1876. The **Museum**, in Terrace Rd, round the corner from the town hall, is open Tuesday to Friday from 9.30 am to 5.30 pm, and on Saturday until 5 pm; entry is £1/50p.

Poole's Cavern (☎ 26978), less than a mile from the centre, is a stalactite and stalagmite-filled cave known since Neolithic times. It's open daily from March through October from 10 am to 5 pm. Entry costs £4/2. A 20 minute walk leads from the cave through Grin Low Wood to **Solomon's Temple** (Grin Low Tower), an 1896 folly with fine views over the town.

Places to Stay

The *youth hostel* (☎ *22287, Sherbrook Lodge, Harpur Hill Rd*), south of the centre, costs £7.20/4.95 for adults/juniors. It's usually closed on Sunday.

Cheaper B&Bs for around £15 or £16 per person congregate on Compton and Grange Rds. Places to try on Compton Rd include *Griff Guest House* (☎ *23628*) at No 2, *Compton House* (☎ *26926*) at No 4 and *Templeton Guest House* (☎ *25275*) at No 13. On Grange Rd there's the delightful *Arnemetia*

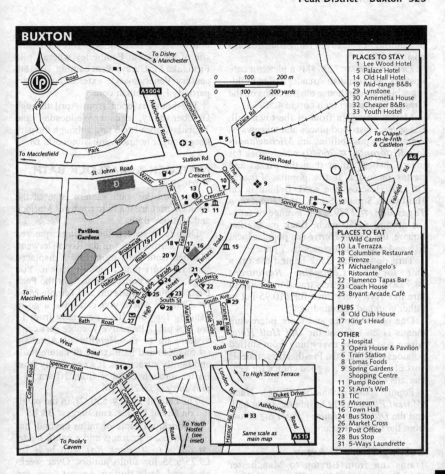

BUXTON

To Disley
& Manchester

To Chapel-
en-le-Frith
& Castleton

To Macclesfield

St Johns Road

The Crescent

Pavilion
Gardens

To Macclesfield

To Poole's
Cavern

To High Street Terrace

To Youth
Hostel
(see
inset)

Same scale as
main map

PLACES TO STAY
1 Lee Wood Hotel
5 Palace Hotel
14 Old Hall Hotel
19 Mid-range B&Bs
29 Lynstone
30 Arnemetia House
32 Cheaper B&Bs
33 Youth Hostel

PLACES TO EAT
7 Wild Carrot
10 La Terrazza
18 Columbine Restaurant
20 Firenze
21 Michaelangelo's
       Ristorante
22 Flamenco Tapas Bar
23 Coach House
25 Bryant Arcade Café

PUBS
4 Old Club House
17 King's Head

OTHER
2 Hospital
3 Opera House & Pavilion
6 Train Station
8 Lomas Foods
9 Spring Gardens
       Shopping Centre
11 Pump Room
12 St Ann's Well
13 TIC
15 Museum
16 Town Hall
24 Bus Stop
26 Market Cross
27 Post Office
28 Bus Stop
31 5-Ways Laundrette

House (☎ *26125*) at No 14 and the non-smoking *Lynstone* (☎ *77043*) at No 3.

Places charging around £20 per person can be found along Broadwalk, a pleasant, traffic-free road overlooking the Pavilion Gardens. There's the *Grosvenor House Hotel* (☎ *72439*) at No 1, the *Hartington Hotel* (☎ *22638*) at No 18 and the nonsmoking *Roseleigh Hotel* (☎ *24904*) at No 19.

The more expensive *Lee Wood Hotel* (☎ *70421*) on the Park has rooms with a bathroom from £40/70 a single/double. The

historic *Old Hall Hotel* (☎ *22841*), that overlooks the Pavilion Gardens and Opera House on the Square, charges £55/80.

Places to Eat

The cheapest cooked meals can be found in the *Bryant Arcade café* (*off Eagle Parade*) where a roast lunch costs £3.95.

Vegetarians should head for *The Wild Carrot.*(☎ *22843, 5 Bridge St*), an excellent health food store with a restaurant upstairs. It opens for lunch every day except Sunday,

MIDLANDS

and for dinner from 6.30 to 11 pm Thursday to Saturday. Typically, a Hungarian goulash costs £4.95.

La Terrazza (☎ *72364*) is a pleasant café upstairs in Cavendish Arcade, a tiled building which used to house the hot baths on the Crescent. A roast lunch costs £4.50.

Market Place, in front of the town hall, has several fast-food places and takeaways. Among the possibilities are *Michaelangelo's Ristorante* (☎ *26640*) which goes for meaty dishes, rather than the pizzas and pastas on offer at the popular *Firenze* (☎ *72203*) across the road. Behind it, on Hardwick Square South, the *Flamenco Tapas Bar* (☎ *27392*) has a range of tapas for around £2.50 each. Back on Market Square, the *Coach House* is a popular local fish and chippie but closes by 7 pm.

Turn down Hall Bank behind the town hall for the *Columbine Restaurant* (☎ *78752*), which offers traditional English fare like Aylesbury duck for £10.95 but in rather cramped surroundings.

One of the longer and more interesting menus is on offer at the *Old Hall Hotel* where you can get everything from stuffed potatoes to full meals. Pre-theatre set meals cost £15.25. There's a good choice for vegetarians too.

Popular pubs include the *King's Head* (*Market Place*), right beside the town hall, and the *Old Club House* (*Water St*) across from the Opera House.

Getting There & Away

Trains run from Buxton to Manchester (£4.60) via New Mills. Change at New Mills to get to Sheffield via Edale.

The TransPeak TP bus service between Nottingham and Manchester stops by Market Place. There are also daily buses to Stoke-on-Trent, Bakewell and Chesterfield, as well as three buses a week to Tideswell and Castleton.

AROUND BUXTON
Lyme Park

For those who saw the popular BBC serialisation of *Pride and Prejudice*, Lyme Park

(☎ 01663-762023, NT), at Disley, 9 miles north-west of Buxton, will forever be the site of the lake at Pemberley where Colin Firth (aka Mr Darcy) went bathing. An 18th century Venetian-style exterior conceals a partially Elizabethan core.

The house is open from April through October daily, except Wednesday and Thursday, from 1 to 5 pm, although the park keeps longer hours. Admission costs £4.

MATLOCK & MATLOCK BATH
☎ 01629

Located on the south-eastern edge of the Peak District are the twin towns of Matlock and Matlock Bath.

Despite its spectacular setting, squeezed into the narrow valley of the River Derwent, Matlock Bath feels more like a displaced seaside resort than a country town. You might want to come here to visit the **Peak District Mining Museum and Temple Mine** (☎ 583834) where you can have a go at panning for gold. It's open daily from 11 am to 4 pm. Alternatively, cable cars carry visitors up to the **Heights of Abraham** (☎ 582365) and its mixture of nature trails and family attractions. It's open daily from Easter through October from 10 am to 5 pm; entry is £6.20/4.10.

The helpful TIC (☎ 55082), in the pavilion on Grand Parade, can suggest B&Bs.

Matlock, a couple of miles beyond, has more shops, restaurants and a *youth hostel* (☎ *582983, 40 Bank Rd*) with beds for £9.75/6.55 for adults/juniors. Over weekends and daily during August, you can travel by steam train through lovely scenery on the restored **Peak Railway** from Matlock Riverside station to Rowsley South. For timetable details phone ☎ 01629-580381. Return fares cost £5/2.50.

Nottinghamshire

There's not much left of Sherwood Forest although Robin Hood, his merry men and the Sheriff of Nottingham have been roped into a variety of amusement parks. Nevertheless, the city of Nottingham is a surprisingly livable Midlands city and there are several other interesting attractions in the county.

NOTTINGHAM
- **pop 275,000 ☎ 0115**

At first glance Nottingham is another of those Midlands disaster areas, a confusing tangle of roads ringing a drab city centre with memories of Robin Hood long forgotten. But as is so often the case, hang around and you'll find it brighter and more interesting than you might have feared.

The Saxon city bore the less than charming name of Snotingham, but modern Nottingham had its moment of glory in the 19th century when the lace industry transformed the city centre. Nottingham was a centre for the Luddite riots of 1811 to 1816. Lace-making declined during the 1890s and was virtually killed off by WWI, although the tourist industry supports some small-scale lace production. The city remains an industrial centre and is home to Raleigh bicycles.

Nottingham's famed Goose Fair dates back to the Middle Ages but these days it's just an outsize funfair which takes place in the Forest Recreation Ground on the first Thursday, Friday and Saturday of October.

The city is also noted for its peculiar Midlands dialect. If someone greets you with a hearty 'eyupmeduck', a suitable response is 'hello'.

Orientation & Information

Like other Midlands cities, Nottingham is chopped in pieces by an inner ring road. The train station is south of the canal on the southern edge of the centre. There are two bus stations: Victoria bus station is hidden away behind the Victoria shopping centre, just north of the city centre, while Broad Marsh bus station is behind Broad Marsh shopping centre to the south.

The TIC (☎ 947 0661) in the Council House is open daily in summer.

Nottingham Castle Museum, the Brewhouse Yard Museum, the Costume Museum and Wollaton Hall are all free during the week but have admission charges at the weekend. Anyone planning to visit the Caves of Nottingham, the Tales of Robin Hood and the Galleries of Justice should consider buying an Explorer Pass (£15.95/9.95) which also covers the other museums at weekends. Passes are available from all the attractions they cover.

Nottingham Castle Museum & Art Gallery

Nottingham Castle was demolished after the Civil War and replaced with a mansion in 1674. This was, in turn, burnt out during the Reform Bill Riots of 1831, but a museum was opened inside the shell in 1875. The museum (☎ 948 3504) describes Nottingham's history and houses some of the alabaster carvings for which Nottingham was noted between 1350 and 1550. Upstairs there's also an art gallery. The castle is open daily from 10 am to 5 pm. At weekends admission costs £1.50/80p. Tours of Mortimer's Hole beneath the castle take place Monday to Friday at 2 and 3 pm for £2/1. There's also a stylish café and an excellent shop.

Caves of Nottingham

Nottingham stands on a plug of Sherwood sandstone which is riddled with man-made caves dating back to medieval times. Rather surprisingly you need to go inside Broad Marsh shopping centre to find the entrance to the most fascinating readily accessible caves (☎ 924 1424). These contain an air-raid shelter, a medieval underground tannery, several pub cellars and a mock-up of a Victorian slum dwelling. They're open Monday to Saturday from 10 am to 5 pm and Sunday from 11 am. Admission costs £2.95/1.95.

The Tales of Robin Hood

The Tales of Robin Hood (☎ 948 3284) at 30-38 Maid Marian Way is a modern tourist attraction which takes you through models of Nottingham Castle and Sherwood Forest in the days when Robin Hood was battling it out with the Sheriff. Afterwards you have time to find out more about the reality

NOTTINGHAM

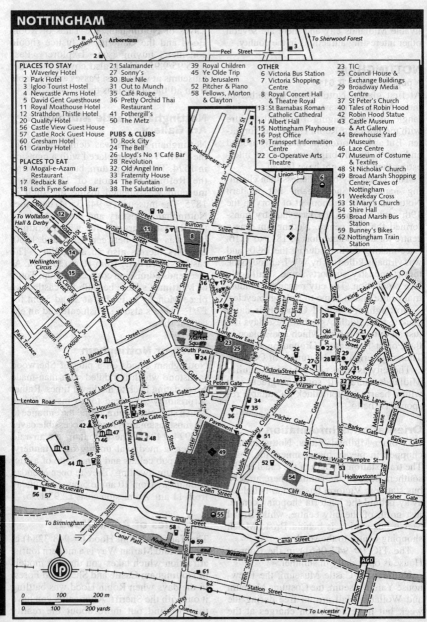

PLACES TO STAY
1   Waverley Hotel
2   Park Hotel
3   Igloo Tourist Hostel
4   Newcastle Arms Hotel
5   David Gent Guesthouse
11 Royal Moathouse Hotel
12 Strathdon Thistle Hotel
20 Quality Hotel
56 Castle View Guest House
57 Castle Rock Guest House
60 Gresham Hotel
61 Granby Hotel

PLACES TO EAT
9   Mogal-e-Azam
    Restaurant
17 Redback Bar
18 Loch Fyne Seafood Bar

21 Salamander
27 Sonny's
30 Blue Nile
31 Out to Munch
35 Café Rouge
36 Pretty Orchid Thai
    Restaurant
41 Fothergill's
50 The Metz

PUBS & CLUBS
10 Rock City
24 The Bell
26 Lloyd's No 1 Café Bar
28 Revolution
32 Old Angel Inn
33 Fraternity House
34 The Fountain
38 The Salutation Inn

39 Royal Children
45 Ye Olde Trip
    to Jerusalem
52 Pitcher & Piano
58 Fellows, Morton
    & Clayton

OTHER
6   Victoria Bus Station
7   Victoria Shopping
    Centre
8   Royal Concert Hall
    & Theatre Royal
13 St Barnabas Roman
    Catholic Cathedral
14 Albert Hall
15 Nottingham Playhouse
16 Post Office
19 Transport Information
    Centre
22 Co-Operative Arts
    Theatre

23 TIC
25 Council House &
    Exchange Buildings
29 Broadway Media
    Centre
37 St Peter's Church
40 Tales of Robin Hood
42 Robin Hood Statue
43 Castle Museum
    & Art Gallery
44 Brewhouse Yard
    Museum
46 Lace Centre
47 Museum of Costume
    & Textiles
48 St Nicholas' Church
49 Broad Marsh Shopping
    Centre; Caves of
    Nottingham
51 Weekday Cross
53 St Mary's Church
54 Shire Hall
55 Broad Marsh Bus
    Station
59 Bunney's Bikes
62 Nottingham Train
    Station

MIDLANDS

behind the legend or to watch clips from the various film versions in the café.

It's open daily from 10 am to 4.30 pm. Admission costs £4.50/3.50. Medieval banquets take place here, too, but you must book and pay the £28.50 fee two weeks in advance.

Wollaton Hall

Built in 1588 by Sir Francis Willoughby, land and coal mine owner, Wollaton Hall (☎ 915 3900) is a fine example of Tudor architecture at its most extravagant. Architect Robert Smythson was also responsible for the equally avant-garde Longleat. Wollaton Hall now houses the **Nottingham Natural History Museum**.

The **Industrial Museum** in the estate buildings has lace-making equipment, Raleigh bicycles, a gigantic 1858 beam engine and oddities like a locally invented 1963 video recorder which never got off the ground. Opening hours for both museums are April to September, Monday to Saturday from 10 am to 4.30 pm, Sunday from 1.30 pm. The Industrial Museum is closed Monday to Wednesday from October through March. Combined entry is £1.50/75p. Wollaton Hall is on the western edge of the city, 2½ miles from the centre; get there on a No 25 bus.

Other Things to See

The **Brewhouse Yard Museum** (☎ 948 3504) is housed in five 17th century cottages on Castle Boulevard virtually below the castle. It re-creates everyday life in 19th century Nottingham with particularly good displays of traditional shops. An underground passageway known as Mortimer's Hole leads from the castle to Brewhouse Yard. Roger Mortimer, who arranged Edward II's murder, is said to have been captured by supporters of Edward III who entered via this passage.

The **Museum of Costume & Textiles** (☎ 948 3504), on Castle Gate, has displays of costumes from 1790 to the mid-20th century arranged in period rooms, as well as tapestries and lace. Across from the castle a

The Legend of Robin Hood

In the Middle Ages most of Nottinghamshire was covered in forest. It was here that Robin Hood and his band of merry men were said to have waged their private war on the wicked Sheriff of Nottingham while Richard I was away crusading.

The Robin Hood story has generated many films, the most recent and successful *Robin Hood Prince of Thieves* with Kevin Costner following in the footsteps of Errol Flynn as Robin and Alan Rickman as the Sheriff. Burnham Beeches in Buckinghamshire stood in for Sherwood Forest, while other scenes were filmed in the church of St Bartholomew-the-Great in London, Peckforton Castle in Preston, Lancashire, and in France.

Nottinghamshire is littered with sites associated with Robin. Nottingham Castle obviously played a key role, as did St Mary's Church. Robin is said to have married Maid Marian in Edinstowe church, while Fountaindale, near Blidworth, is the supposed site of his battle with Friar Tuck.

But did Robin ever really exist? As long ago as 1377 William Langland made fleeting reference to him in his poem *Piers Plowman*, but it was only in the early 16th century that the story began to be fleshed out, most notably in the ballad *A Geste of Robyn Hoode*. In 1795 Joseph Ritson collected all the known accounts of Robin into one volume, since when innumerable authors (including Scott and Tennyson) have turned them into torrid novels and poems.

In spite of all this, researchers have failed to turn up any hard evidence that the outlaw actually existed. He is, for example, said to have been born in Lockesley in Yorkshire or Nottinghamshire but no such place appears on any map. Optimists point to a Loxley in Staffordshire where Hood's father supposedly owned land. But it may be that 'Robin' is no more than a jumbled memory of ancient ideas about forest fairies, or a character made up to give voice to medieval resentments.

small **Lace Centre** (☎ 941 3539) is housed in the medieval Severns building in Castle Rd.

In the impressive Shire Hall building on High Pavement, the **Galleries of Justice** (☎ 952 0558) is being redeveloped to create a new National Museum of Law. The interactive Police Galleries let you visit a pretend crime scene and assess the available evidence, while the Crime & Punishment Galleries look at how offences were handled in Victorian times. It's open Tuesday to Sunday from 10 am to 5 pm; entry is £7.95/4.95.

Places to Stay

The cheapest accommodation is at the *Igloo Tourist Hostel* (☎ 947 5250, 110 Mansfield Rd) a short walk north of Victoria bus station. A bunk bed in a dorm is £8.50; all-you-can-eat breakfast is £2.

The *David Gent Guesthouse* (☎ 947 2414, 16 Clinton Court, North Sherwood St), a modern but anonymous house just a few minutes walk from Victoria bus station, offers great value at from £10 per person. A little farther up is the *Newcastle Arms Hotel* (☎ 947 4616, 68 North Sherwood St) with rooms from £14 per person.

Just south of the castle on Castle Boulevard, the *Castle View Guest House* (☎ 950 0022) at No 85 and the *Castle Rock Guest House* (☎ 948 2116) at No 79 are traditional B&Bs charging around £16 a head.

South of the centre there are some cheap B&Bs near the train station. The *Granby Hotel* (☎ 958 2158, 19 Station St) and the *Gresham Hotel* (☎ 950 1234, 109 Carrington St) both have singles/doubles from around £20/30 per night.

Slightly pricier places north of the centre include the *Park Hotel* (☎ 978 6299, 5-7 Waverley St) right across from the arboretum. Prices start at £25/40. Just off Waverley St, the *Waverley Hotel* (☎ 978 6707, 107 Portland Rd) is similarly priced. It's also worth considering the *Quality Hotel* (☎ 947 5641, George St) that charges from £20 a head for a double.

Over weekends and throughout August, Nottingham's business hotels often offer a special 'Robin Hood Rate' costing from £27.50 per person at hotels like the *Holiday Inn* (☎ 993 5000, Castle Marina Park), to £35 at the *Rutland Square Hotel* (☎ 941 1114, St James St).

Places to Eat

The Hockley area, around Carlton St to the east of the centre, is a good place to start looking for something to eat. *Salamander* (☎ 941 0710, 23 Heathcote St) is an excellent vegetarian restaurant with main courses for around £7. There's more good vegetarian food nearby on Goose Gate where *Out to Munch* is a vegan/vegetarian café above the Hiziki wholefood store. Moroccan stew costs £1.95.

Nearby, classy *Sonny's Restaurant* (☎ 947 3041, 3 Carlton St) has a bright and imaginative menu, with main dishes (very new British) from around £10. In Broad St the *Broadway Media Centre* (☎ 952 6611) has a good, if smoky, café where you can get soup, a baguette and endless coffee for £4.50 from 11 am to 3 pm. The *Blue Nile* (☎ 941 0976, upstairs, 5 Heathcoate St) is an Egyptian restaurant with vegetarian dishes and belly dancing.

Opposite the Castle entrance *Fothergill's* (Castle Rd) has a bar menu as well as a pricier restaurant with main dishes for around £10.

Beside the Theatre Royal, the *Mogal-e-Azam* (☎ 947 2911, 7 Goldsmith St) is an acclaimed Indian restaurant, with biryanis from £5.95.

The *Loch Fyne Seafood Bar* (☎ 950 8481, 17 King St) is a branch of the excellent Scottish oyster and smoked seafood company. Half a dozen oysters cost £4.90. Round the corner, the *Redback Bar* (☎ 953 1531, Queen St) offers good beer and company, plus rooburgers (£2.95) and outback soup (£1.25).

Bridlesmith Gate is a lively cut-through, with a branch of *Café Rouge*. Just off it the *Pretty Orchid Thai Restaurant* (☎ 958 8344) does lunches for £4.50 but dinner will cost more like £15.

Entertainment

Pubs & Clubs *Ye Olde Trip to Jerusalem* is an atmospheric and popular pub below the castle; the upstairs bar is actually cut into the rock. Crusaders are said to have gathered here before setting off to the Holy Land but the existing building is much later than that.

Fellows, Morton & Clayton is an excellent pub near Broad Marsh shopping centre. The *Old Angel Inn* on the corner of Stoney St and Woolpack Lane in the Hockley area is a popular student pub, but *The Fountain (Bridlesmith Gate)* and *Revolution (Broad St)* are two of the hottest places in town. *Gatsby's (Huntingdon St)* is a busy gay bar. At the time of writing the huge redundant church in High Pavement which used to house the Lace Hall had applied for permission to reopen as the *Pitcher & Piano* bar.

New café bars include *Lloyd's No 1 (Pelham St)*, the *Fraternity House (Victoria St)* and *The Metz (Low Pavement)*.

Rock City (☎ 941 2544, Talbot St) is a popular rock venue with a £4 to £12 entry charge.

Theatre, Cinema & Classical Music

The *Broadway* (☎ 952 6611, Broad St) cinema is the city's art-house movie centre. Theatrical venues include the *Co-operative Arts Theatre* (☎ 947 6096, George St) and the *Nottingham Playhouse* (☎ 941 9419, Wellington Circus). The *Royal Concert Hall* and *Theatre Royal* share a booking office (☎ 948 2626) and an imposing building close to the centre.

Getting There & Away

Nottingham is 135 miles from London, around 75 miles from Manchester and Leeds, and 50 miles from Birmingham.

Bus National Express buses operate from the Broad Marsh bus station. A single to London costs £11.75.

For local bus information phone the Buses Hotline on ☎ 924 0000. Sherwood Forester buses (☎ 977 4268) operate to tourist attractions all over Nottinghamshire

in summer. An unlimited travel Ranger Ticket for £3/1.50 gives discounted admission to some attractions. Rainbow Route services by Trent & Barton Buses (☎ 01773-712265) operate to Derby and continue through the Peak District to Manchester (TransPeak). They operate from both bus stations and their one-day Explorer Ticket costs £5.75; one child goes free.

Train Nottingham is not on the main railway routes through the Midlands but regular services to London St Pancras take 1¾ hours.

Getting Around

The Transport Information Centre (☎ 950 3665) in King St, just north of Old Market Square, has information on city bus services. A Day Rider ticket gives you unlimited travel for one day for £2.30.

Bunney's Bikes (☎ 947 2713) at 97 Carrington St near the train station has bicycles from £5 to £8.50 per day.

AROUND NOTTINGHAM
Newstead Abbey

Converted into a home after the dissolution of the monasteries in 1539, Newstead Abbey (☎ 01623-793557) is chiefly notable for being the residence of Lord Byron (1788-1824) but the Byronic connections are sparse.

The façade of the ruined priory church is next to the house, which was already in bad shape when Byron inherited it from his great-uncle. The continuing decline of the family fortune forced him to sell it in 1817. The poet used to hold shooting sessions indoors and a friend commented that a visit was so pleasant it 'made one forget that one was domiciled in the wing of an extensive ruin'.

The house is open April through September, daily from noon to 6 pm; the garden is open year-round. Entry to house and garden is £3.50/1. The house is 12 miles north of Nottingham, off the A60. The Sherwood Forester bus runs right there in summer; otherwise take bus No 63 and walk a mile from the abbey gates.

Southwell Minster

To judge by its magnificent minster/cathedral, medieval Southwell must have had an importance the modern town just doesn't. For those who love Britain's Gothic architecture but loathe the crowds, Southwell Minster (☎ 01636-812649) will come as a great relief. The highlight of the building is the lovely Decorated chapterhouse which is filled with naturalistic carvings of leaves, pigs, dogs and rabbits. Children will also enjoy looking for wooden mice carved by Yorkshire's famous woodcarver Robert Thompson, for whom they acted as a 'signature'.

You can get to Southwell on the twice-daily bus No S3 from Nottingham.

DH Lawrence Birthplace Museum

The birthplace (☎ 01773-763312) of DH Lawrence (1885-1930), Nottingham's controversial author, is at 8A Victoria St in Eastwood, about 10 miles north-west of the city. It's now a museum, open April to October, daily from 10 am to 5 pm, and the rest of the year to 4 pm; entry is £1.50/75p.

Sherwood Forest

Only tiny fragments of Robin Hood's mighty forest remain but a quarter of a million people visit the 180 hectare Sherwood Forest Country Park near the village of Edinstowe every year. At least the hokey Sherwood Forest Visitor Centre (☎ 01623-824490) keeps some of the crowds out of the real woods where Robin is supposed to have hidden in the Major Oak. It's open daily from 10.30 am to 5 pm (4.30 pm from November through March); entry is free.

Sherwood Forester buses run the 20 miles to the park from Nottingham.

Eastern England

With the exception of the city of Cambridge, most of the eastern counties – Essex, Suffolk, Norfolk, Cambridgeshire and Lincolnshire – have been overlooked by tourists. The part of this region known as East Anglia (Norfolk, Suffolk and east Cambridgeshire) has always been distinct, separated from the rest of England by the fens (reclaimed marshlands) and the Essex forests.

To the east of the fens, Norfolk and Suffolk have gentle, unspectacular scenery that can still be very beautiful. John Constable and Thomas Gainsborough painted in the area known as Dedham Vale, the valley of the River Stour. Villages like East Bergholt (Constable's birthplace), Thaxted and Cavendish are quintessentially English, with beautiful churches and thatched cottages.

The distinctive architectural character of the region was determined by the lack of suitable building stone. Stone was occasionally imported for important buildings, but for humble churches and houses three local materials were used: flint, clay bricks and oak. The most unusual of the three, flint, can be chipped into a usable shape, but a single stone is rarely larger than a fist. Often the flint is used in combination with dressed stone or bricks to form decorative patterns.

More than any other part of England, East Anglia has close links with northern Europe. In the 6th and 7th centuries it was overrun by the Norsemen. From the late Middle Ages, Suffolk and Norfolk grew rich trading wool and cloth with the Flemish; this wealth built scores of churches and helped subsidise the development of Cambridge. The windmills, the long, straight drainage canals and even the architecture (especially in King's Lynn) call the Low Countries to mind.

ORIENTATION & INFORMATION

Norwich, Harwich, King's Lynn, Cambridge and Lincoln are all easily accessible from London by train and bus. Harwich is

HIGHLIGHTS

- Visit medieval Lavenham
- Boating on the Norfolk Broads
- Walk around Cambridge University
- Choral Evensong at King's College Chapel
- Punting on the River Cam
- Fitzwilliam Museum
- Ely and Peterborough Cathedrals

the main port for ferries to Germany, Holland, Denmark and Sweden.

There are youth hostels at Cambridge, Lincoln, Brandon, Blaxhall, King's Lynn, Hunstanton, Sheringham, Norwich, Great Yarmouth, Castle Hedingham, Saffron Walden, Harlow and Epping Forest. The East of England Tourist Board (☎ 01473-822922) can provide further information.

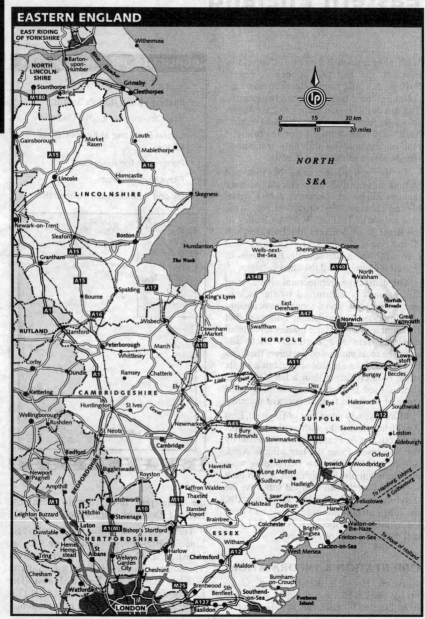

EASTERN ENGLAND

WALKS & CYCLE ROUTES

The Peddars Way and Norfolk Coast Path link to form a 94 mile walking track which crosses the middle of Norfolk to Holme-next-the-Sea and follows the coastline south to Cromer. See the Activities chapter for more information.

This is ideal cycling country. Where there are hills, they're gentle. Bicycles can be hired cheaply in Cambridge and the TICs can suggest several interesting routes. Ask for the *England's Cycling Country* booklet.

OTHER ACTIVITIES
Boating

The Norfolk Broads, a series of inland lakes (ancient, flooded peat diggings) to the east of Norwich, is a popular boating area. Several companies rent out boats of all types – narrow boats, cruisers, yachts and houseboats. See the Norfolk Broads section later in this chapter for information.

GETTING AROUND
Bus

Bus transport around the region is slow and disorganised. For regional timetables and information phone Essex (☎ 0345-000333), Norfolk (☎ 01603-613613), Suffolk (☎ 0645-583358) or Lincolnshire (☎ 01522-553135). For transport information, Cambridgeshire operates an 0891 number (calls are expensive) – ☎ 0891-910910.

Train

From Norwich you can catch trains to the Norfolk coast and Sheringham, but there's an unfortunate gap between Sheringham and King's Lynn (bus or hitch?) which prevents a rail loop back to Cambridge. It may be worth considering an Anglia Plus pass which offers three days travel out of seven for £17, one day for £7.50. For all train information phone ☎ 0345-484950.

Essex

Essex has a serious image problem. Other Brits see the county as nothing more than a number of commuter-belt dormitory towns for the used-car traders of London's East End; in fact, there's even a series of Essex jokes about the people who made their money in the Thatcher boom years. 'Essex Man' drives a hot hatchback with furry dice swinging from the rear-view mirror; 'Essex Girl' preens herself beside him. The jokes don't rate highly on political correctness, and the image is unfair – you're as likely to find stereotypes such as these in any of the other counties surrounding London.

Despite being one of the largest counties in England, Essex has no vital sights. Each year, several million passengers transit the county through Stansted airport and the Harwich ferries. If you are passing through, you should certainly stop in Colchester and the landscape along the border with Suffolk, which inspired the painter Constable, is also worth visiting.

COLCHESTER
- pop 88,000   ☎ 01206

Britain's oldest recorded town, Colchester was the capital of Roman Britain when London was just a minor trading post. It's a surprisingly interesting place with a castle, several museums and the remains of Roman walls.

There was a settlement here for some time before the arrival of the Romans in 43 AD. The Roman town was sacked 17 years later by the infamous Boudicca – also known as Boadicea – of the Iceni tribe. The Iceni had been suppressed by the Romans and Boudicca's husband had been killed. She stormed into town, allegedly in a chariot with swords protruding from its wheel hubs, to mow through the Roman legion and destroy the temple.

The Norman **castle** was built on the foundations of the Roman fort, and boasts the largest castle keep in Europe – bigger than the keep at the Tower of London. The museum contains Roman mosaics and statues. It's open daily (afternoon only on Sunday) and entry is £3.60/2.50.

Holy Trinity Church in Trinity St, is now a museum of social history. Nearby, in

Tymperleys – a magnificent, restored, 15th century building – is the **Clock Museum**. Both museums are open Tuesday to Saturday. It's also interesting to walk around the **Dutch Quarter**, just north of the High St, established in the 16th century by Protestant refugee weavers from Holland.

Orientation & Information

There are two train stations – most services stop at North station, about half a mile north of the town. The bus station is in the centre of town, near the TIC and the castle.

The TIC (☎ 282920) is at 1 Queen St. There are guided walking tours (£2/1) of the town, from June to September, daily at 11 am but times may vary so phone first.

Places to Stay

Colchester Camping (☎ 545551) is on Cymberline Way in Lexden, a 30 minute walk from the city centre. It's £6.90 for a tent and one person.

Scheregate Hotel (☎ 573034, *Osborne St, near St John's St*) offers reasonable B&B in the town centre. Rooms cost from £20/35 for singles/doubles, or £28/40 with a bath. The *Peveril Hotel* (☎ 574001, *51 North Hill*) is also conveniently located on the road to the train station. There are 17 rooms, mostly without bath, from £25/36.

The Old Manse (☎ 545154, *15 Roman Rd*) offers comfortable accommodation for non-smokers. It's in a quiet square beside Castle Park and part of the Roman wall is at the bottom of the garden. Rooms start at £26/38.

The *Rose & Crown Hotel* (☎ 866677, *East St*) is probably the best place to stay. There are 30 rooms – all doubles have a bathroom – from £62.50 to £99. There are cheaper deals for weekend stays.

Places to Eat

The *Rose & Crown Hotel* (see Places to Stay) serves interesting pub grub in the large bar, and there's also an expensive seafood restaurant here. The *Foresters Arms* (*Castle St*) and the *Hole in the Wall* are other good pubs.

There's a branch of *Pizza Express* (☎ 760680) at 1 St Runwald St. *Toto's* (☎ 573235, *57 Museum St*) is a café and takeaway that does steaks, pizzas and pasta. Main dishes are from £5.35. The *Warehouse Brasserie* (☎ 765656, *12 Chapel St North*) is excellent value. There are set lunches for £5.95 (two courses) or £7.95 (three courses) and good vegetarian choices.

Getting There & Away

Colchester is 62 miles from London. There are daily National Express buses from London and frequent rail services between Colchester and London's Liverpool St station.

HARWICH
• **pop 15,000**   ☎ 01255

Although the old harbour is interesting, the only real reason to come here is to catch a ferry to Holland, Scandinavia or Germany. Direct train services to Harwich from London's Liverpool St station take around 70 minutes. See the Getting There & Away chapter at the start of the book.

The TIC (☎ 506139) is at Parkeston Quay. B&Bs near the ferry terminal and train station include *Reids of Harwich* (☎ 506796, *3 West St*) for £16 per person; and *359 Main Rd* (☎ 502635), from £14 per person.

DEDHAM VALE

In the Stour Valley, on the border with Suffolk, Dedham Vale was made famous by the paintings of Constable, who was born here. It's now rapidly being overwhelmed by the number of tour buses that descend on the area. Flatford Mill (not the original) and Willy Lott's House, of *Haywain* fame, are now run by the Field Studies Council, which holds art courses here and at other locations around the country. Phone ☎ 01206-298283 for information.

Bridge Cottage (☎ 01206-298260, NT) also features in some Constable landscapes and now houses a display about the famous painter. It's open daily from May to September from 10 am to 5.30 pm, and for shorter hours (and not every day) the rest of the year. Entry, with guided tour, is £1.80, children free.

Several bus companies operate services from Colchester to East Bergholt, three-quarters of a mile from Bridge Cottage. It's better to come by train (get off at Manningtree), as you get a wonderful 1¾ mile walk along footpaths through Constable country.

THAXTED & SAFFRON WALDEN

These two attractive villages are in the north-western corner of the county. Thaxted dates from Saxon times and prospered in the 15th century through its links with the cutlery industry. The guildhall and some of the half-timbered, colour-washed houses are from this period. There's a small museum and a good view from the early 19th century windmill, open at weekends from 2 to 6 pm.

Saffron Walden is named after the saffron crocus, which was cultivated in the surrounding fields. The church is one of the largest in Essex. The Sun Inn, nearby, is decorated with elaborate plasterwork. On the eastern side of the town is an ancient earthen maze; a path circles for almost a mile, taking you to the centre if you follow the right route. *Saffron Walden Youth Hostel* (☎ 01799-523117, 1 Myddylton Place) is in a 15th century building; beds are £8/5.40 for adults/juniors. The TIC (☎ 01799-510444, 1 Market Place) has accommodation lists for the numerous other places to stay in Saffron Walden and Thaxted.

Stagecoach Cambus (☎ 01223-423554) bus No 22 runs between Cambridge and Saffron Walden. The nearest train station is Audley End, 2½ miles to the west.

AUDLEY END HOUSE

Once one of the largest houses in England, this Jacobean mansion was used as a royal palace by Charles II. Built in the early 17th century, it was described by James I as 'too large for a king'. Set in a fine park landscaped by Capability Brown, the house was originally built for Thomas Howard, Earl of

Suffolk, and was remodelled by Robert Adam after two-thirds of the building had been demolished.

One mile west of Saffron Walden, Audley End House (☎ 01799-522399, EH) is open from April to September, Wednesday to Sunday from 11 am to 6 pm (last entry 5 pm). Entry is £5.75/2.90. Audley End train station is 1¼ miles from the house.

Suffolk

Once one of the richest parts of the country, Suffolk is now something of a backwater – and all the better for it as far as the visitor is concerned. Like most of East Anglia, the county is fairly flat, but the landscape has a serene beauty in parts.

Along the border with Essex is the Stour Valley, made famous by the painters Gainsborough and Constable. Constable enthused about the county's 'gentle declivities, its woods and rivers, its luxuriant meadow flats sprinkled with flocks and herds, its well-cultivated uplands, with numerous scattered villages and churches, farms and picturesque cottages'. The description still holds true for much of the county today.

The region's economic boom as a wool trading centre lasted until the 16th century and has left the county with its magnificently endowed 'wool' churches, many built to support much larger populations than live here now. Some of the villages have changed little since then and Suffolk buildings are famous for their *pargeting* – decorative stucco plasterwork.

IPSWICH

• pop 129,600   ☎ 01473

In Saxon times Ipswich was one of the principal towns in England. Less important now, it's still a major commercial and shopping centre, and Suffolk's county town. Ipswich is a transport hub for the region and, if you're passing through, you should stop to see the Ancient House and Christchurch Mansion.

The TIC (☎ 258070) is in St Stephen's Church, off St Stephen's Lane, near the bus station and the Ancient House. The train station is a 15 minute walk along Princes St and across the roundabout.

Dickens used the *Great White Horse Hotel* (☎ 256558, Tavern St) in *Pickwick Papers*. The 'mouldy, ill-lighted rooms' he mentions are currently undergoing renovations and the hotel will reopen in 1999.

A cheaper option is the *Lochiel Guest House* (☎ 727775, 216 Felixstowe Rd), close to the town centre and with B&B from £15 per person.

There's also very comfortable farmhouse accommodation from around £18 per person at *College Farm* (☎ 652253, Hintlesham), six miles west of Ipswich.

There are some good places to eat by the renovated Wet Dock.

Things to See

The **Ancient House**, now a shop, is one of the finest examples of pargeting in the country, the overhanging upper storey decorated with white stucco. At **Ipswich Museum**, on the High St, there's a replica of the Sutton Hoo ship burial found near Woodbridge, east of Ipswich, in 1939. It was the richest archaeological discovery in the country; the original artefacts are now in the British Museum.

Set in a large park to the north of the town, **Christchurch Mansion** (☎ 253246) is a fine Tudor house built in 1548 and now furnished as a country house. It has a good collection of works by Gainsborough and Constable. It was being restored at the time of writing and should reopen shortly.

Getting There & Away

National Express runs daily coaches to Ipswich. The largest of the several local bus companies is Eastern Counties (☎ 01603-622800).

There are frequent trains from London's Liverpool St station (1¼ hours) and direct connections to Colchester, Bury St Edmunds, Norwich and Lowestoft.

STOUR VALLEY

Running along the border between Suffolk and Essex, the River Stour flows through a soft, pastoral landscape that has inspired numerous painters, of which the most famous are Constable and Gainsborough. For Dedham Vale, the area known as Constable country, see the Essex section.

Long Melford
* **pop 2800**   ☎ 01787

Known for its long High St and timber-framed buildings, Long Melford has a magnificent church with some fine stained-glass windows, two stately homes and the obligatory antique shops.

Melford Hall (☎ 880286, NT) is a turret-ed Tudor mansion in the centre of the village. There's an 18th century drawing room, a Regency library, a Victorian bedroom and a display of paintings by Beatrix Potter, who used to stay here. It's open from May to September; Wednesday, Thursday, Saturday and Sunday from 2 to 5.30 pm; phone for other times; entry is £4/2.

On the edge of the village, down a tree-lined avenue, lies **Kentwell Hall** (☎ 310207), another red-brick Tudor mansion, but one that's privately owned and makes much more of its Tudor origins. Between mid-June and mid-July, over 200 Tudor enthusiasts descend on Kentwell Hall to re-create and live out a certain year in the Tudor calendar. The house is surrounded by a moat, and there's a brick-paved Tudor Rose maze and a rare-breeds farm. It's open daily from April to October from noon to 5 pm; entry is £5.10/3.10, more expensive during the historical re-enactment period.

There are buses to Long Melford from Sudbury and Bury St Edmunds.

Sudbury
* **pop 17,800**   ☎ 01787

Sudbury's prosperity was founded on the cloth industry and it continues to produce silk to this day, although on a much smaller scale than before. The TIC (☎ 881320) is in the town hall, open from April to October, Monday to Saturday.

The painter Gainsborough (1727-88) was born in Sudbury and **Gainsborough's House** (☎ 372958), 46 Gainsborough St, is preserved as a shrine and has the largest collection of his work in the country. It's open from Tuesday to Saturday from 10 am to 5 pm, and on Sunday and bank holiday Mondays from 2 to 5 pm. Entry is £2.80/1.50.

Sudbury has a train station with services to Colchester and London, and there are frequent buses to Cambridge and Norwich.

LAVENHAM
- pop 1700   ☎ 01787

A tourist honey pot, Lavenham can get crowded with bus tours but it's nevertheless worth seeing. It's a beautifully preserved example of a medieval wool town, with over 300 listed buildings. Some are timber-framed, others decorated with pargeting. There are cosy, pink, thatched cottages, crooked houses, antique shops and art galleries, quaint tearooms and ancient inns. When the wool industry moved to the west and north of England in the late 16th century, none of Lavenham's inhabitants could afford to build anything more modern. Today, as long as there are not too many tourists around, you can feel as if you're in a time warp while walking through parts of the village.

The Market Place, off the High St, is dominated by the handsome **Guildhall** (☎ 247646, NT), a superb example of a close-studded, timber-framed building, dating back to the early 16th century. It's now a local history museum with displays on the wool trade and is open daily from Easter to October; entry is £2.80.

Little Hall, which has soft ochre plastering and grey timber, is a private house that can be visited. It's open April to October, on Wednesday, Thursday and at weekends from 2 to 5.30 pm; entry is £1.50/50p.

At the southern end of the village, opposite the car park, is the **Church of St Peter and St Paul**. Its soaring steeple is visible for miles around. The church bears witness to Lavenham's past prosperity at the centre of the local wool trade.

The TIC (☎ 248207), Lady St, has lists of places to stay. One of the most attractive and atmospheric places is *Lavenham Priory (☎ 247404, Water St)*. Once the home of Benedictine monks, then medieval cloth merchants, upmarket B&B is now offered here for £30 to £50 per person.

Since most people come just for the day, there are numerous teashops offering light lunches.

Chambers runs buses from Bury St Edmunds; Ipswich Buses service No 757 runs from Colchester. There are no direct buses from Cambridge; you must go via Sudbury, 7 miles to the south, also the location of the nearest train station.

BURY ST EDMUNDS
- pop 30,500   ☎ 01284

The most attractive large town in Suffolk, Bury is on the Rivers Lark and Linnet amid gently rolling farmland. The town has a distinct Georgian flavour, with street upon street of handsome, 18th century façades which harks back to a period of great prosperity. It's now a busy agricultural centre and cattle, vegetable and fruit markets are held every Wednesday and Saturday. Greene King, the famous Suffolk brewer, is based here.

Centrally placed, Bury is a convenient point from which to explore west Suffolk. The ruined abbey is set in a beautiful garden and is worth seeing. There's also a fascinating clock museum, and recommended guided tours of the brewery.

History
Bury's motto 'Shrine of a King, Cradle of the Law' recalls the two most memorable events in its history. Edmund, a Christian prince from Saxony who was destined to be the last king of East Anglia, was decapitated by the Danes in 856 and his body brought to Bury for reburial in 903. The shrine to the saint became the focal point of the Benedictine monastery. The abbey, now in ruins, became one of the most famous pilgrimage centres in the country; for many

years St Edmund was patron saint of England.

The second memorable episode in Bury's early history took place at the abbey. In 1214, at St Edmund's Altar, the English barons drew up the petition which formed the basis of the Magna Carta.

Orientation & Information

Bury is an easy place to find your way around because it has preserved Abbot Baldwin's 11th century grid layout.

The TIC (☎ 764667), 6 Angel Hill, is open every day from Easter to October and daily except Sunday for the rest of the year. Phone for information and times of the guided walking tours (£2.50/free for children) which start from here.

There are tours around Greene King Brewery (☎ 763222), Crown St, from Monday to Thursday at 2.30 pm. Tickets are £5; tours are popular, so you need to book ahead.

Walking Tour

Outside the TIC on Angel Hill there are many fine Georgian buildings, such as the 18th century Angel Hotel which is covered in thick, Virginia creeper.

The Abbey & Park Although the abbey is very much a ruin, it's a spectacular one set in a beautiful garden. After the dissolution of the monasteries, the townspeople made off with much of the stone – even St Edmund's grave and bones have disappeared.

To reach the abbey, walk right along Angel Hill until you're opposite the second Abbey Gate, which is still as impressive in its austere regality as it was in Norman times. Cross over and walk round the green, which is home to Elizabeth Frink's statue of St Edmund (1976). From here, you can see the remains of part of the west front and Samson Tower, which have houses built into them.

The abbey is open daily until sunset and entry is free. There's a visitors centre, where an excellent 45 minute Walkman tour (£1.50) is available. Alternatively, you can guide yourself around the ruins using the in-formation boards, which help to show how large a community this must have been with its chapels and priory, its chapter house and treasury, abbot's palace and garden. The huge church dominated everything in the vicinity. It was built in the shape of a cross, and contains a crypt and St Edmund's Altar, near which is the plaque commemorating the barons' pledge of 1214.

Walk down to the river, past the old dovecote, before turning back to head for the superb formal gardens. Leave by the Gothic Gate and turn left to reach the cathedral.

St Edmundsbury Cathedral The cathedral dates from the 16th century, but the eastern end was added between 1945 and 1960 and the northern side was not completed until 1990. It was made a cathedral in 1914. The interior is light and lofty with a painted hammerbeam roof. It's open daily from 8.30 am to 8 pm in summer, shorter hours in winter.

St Mary's Church From the cathedral, turn left out of the west door and walk past the Norman Tower to reach St Mary's. Built around 1430, it contains the tomb of Mary Tudor (Henry VIII's sister and one-time queen of France). A curfew bell is still rung, as it was in the Middle Ages.

Manor House Museum On Honey Hill, near St Mary's, is a magnificent museum of horology, art and costume housed in a Georgian building. It's worth being here around noon, when the clocks strike. Manor House (☎ 757072) is open daily except Monday, from 10 am to 5 pm (afternoon only on Sunday); entry is £2.70/1.75.

Art Gallery & Moyse's Hall Retrace your steps on Honey Hill and Crown St, then turn left up Churchgate St, turning right at the end onto Guildhall St. Up the street, on the right, is Market Cross, remodelled in 1774 by Robert Adam and now the Art Gallery. Turn right by the Corn Exchange and continue to the Buttermarket, where Moyse's Hall, dating back to the 12th century, is probably

East Anglia's oldest domestic building. It is now a local museum. Admission is free, and opening times are the same as for the Manor House Museum.

Places to Stay

There's B&B at *Hilltop* (☎ *767066, 22 Bronyon Close, off Flemyng Rd)* for around £15 per person. *Oak Cottage* (☎ *762745, 54 Guildhall St)* has three rooms and charges around £19 per person.

Ounce House (☎ *761779, Northgate St)* is very comfortable, centrally located and non-smoking. Charges range from £34 to £60 per person and rooms have a bathroom, some with garden views.

Charles Dickens stayed at the *Angel Hotel* (☎ *753926)*, in the centre of Bury on Angel Hill. It's an upmarket place with up-market prices, starting at £65/76 for singles/doubles (breakfast extra). Weekend breaks are cheaper at £49 per person B&B or £65 including dinner.

Places to Eat

The *Scandinavia Coffee House* (*30 Abbeygate)* is by the TIC. A smoked-salmon, open Danish sandwich is a good lunch for £4.25; there are also jacket potatoes for £3.85 and a range of cakes. The *Refectory*, at the cathedral, also does teas and light lunches.

Holland & Barrett (☎ *706677, 6 Brentgovel St)* is a vegetarian restaurant and café; most dishes are under £3. It's open from Monday to Saturday until 4.30 pm.

Maison Bleue (☎ *760623, 31 Churchgate St)* is a highly recommended seafood restaurant. Main dishes (brill, sea bass, monkfish etc) range from £8.75 to £14.50, and there's a set menu for £17.95. It's closed on Sunday.

The best known pub in Bury is the *Nutshell*, which is the smallest pub in the country. It's off Abbeygate, on The Traverse.

Getting There & Away

Bury is 75 miles from London, 35 from Norwich and 28 from Cambridge.

There's a daily National Express bus to London, and frequent services to Lavenham

and Colchester. From Cambridge, Stagecoach Cambus (☎ 01223-423554) runs buses to Bury (35 minutes, £4.20 for a day return) every two hours from Monday to Saturday; the last bus back to Cambridge leaves at 5.05 pm.

Bury is on the Ipswich to Ely line, so trains to London (1¾ hours) go via these towns. From Cambridge, it's a little quicker and cheaper to go by bus; there are trains every two hours to Bury (45 minutes, £5.30; £7.50 for a day return).

AROUND BURY ST EDMUNDS
Ickworth House & Park

Three miles south-west of Bury on the A143, Ickworth House is the eccentric creation of the Earl of Bristol. It's an amazing structure, with an immense oval rotunda dating back to 1795. It contains a fine collection of furniture, silver and paintings (Titian, Gainsborough and Velasquez). Outside, there's an unusual Italian garden and a park designed by Capability Brown, with waymarked trails, a deer enclosure and a hide.

Ickworth House (☎ 01284-735270, NT) is open from Easter to October, daily except Monday and Thursday, from 1 to 5 pm. The park is open daily all year from 7 am to 7 pm. Entry is £5.20/2.20 for the house and park, £2/50p for the park alone. To get here by bus, take Eastern Counties buses bound for Haverhill (Nos 141-44), leaving from outside Bury train station.

SUFFOLK COAST

This is a coast of great contrasts that includes traditional seaside resorts like Lowestoft in the north, the busy port of Felixstowe (now freight only – passenger ferries all go from Harwich) in the south, and some of the least visited sections of coastline in Britain in-between. It's a coastline that's being gradually whittled away by the sea – the old section of the village of Dunwich now lies underwater. One of the reasons that it's not well visited is that public transport along the coast is nonexistent in places.

Aldeburgh
- pop 2800   ☎ 01728

The sea is closing in on Aldeburgh, where the beach is now only yards from the village. The place is best known for the Aldeburgh Festival, an annual program of music and the arts that was begun in 1948 by Benjamin Britten and Peter Pears. It takes place each June in venues around Aldeburgh and at Snape Maltings, 3 miles up the river. It's the most important festival in Eastern England. For information and bookings, phone the box office on ☎ 453543.

The TIC (☎ 453637), on the High St, is open from Easter to October. *Blaxhall Youth Hostel* (☎ 688206) is 4½ miles from Aldeburgh, near Snape Maltings; beds are £8/5.40 for adults/juniors. Eastern Counties buses run between Ipswich and Aldeburgh.

Orford
Few visitors get to this little village, 6 miles south of Snape, but there are several worthwhile attractions. The ruins of Orford Castle (EH) date from the 12th century; only the keep has survived.

The other draw is gastronomic. Two smokehouses do good business selling smoked fish, meat and fresh oysters. From Orford Quay, MV *Lady Florence* (☎ 0831-698298) takes diners on 2½-hour brunch cruises (9 to 11.30 am) or four-hour lunch or dinner cruises, year round. The smokehouses supply the food.

Norfolk

Noel Coward once famously remarked that Norfolk was very flat. It is, but he didn't just mean the landscape. Although the nightlife may have become a little more lively in Norwich since then, it's still not Monte Carlo. Once a busy wool-producing and trading area, making use of the ports of King's Lynn and Great Yarmouth, Norfolk is now much quieter and less populated than it was in the Middle Ages. It's a sleepy county, not yet overrun by tourists, with a superb, unspoilt coastline and several nature reserves that attract birdwatchers.

Norwich, the county town, is a very pleasant place with an interesting castle and cathedral; the Norfolk Broads is a network of inland waterways that have long been popular for boating holidays; and King's Lynn is a historic port on the River Ouse, with several very well-preserved buildings. The whole area is easily accessible from Cambridge.

WALKS & CYCLE ROUTES
Several waymarked walking trails cross the county, the best known being the Peddars Way (see the Activities chapter at the start of this book). The Weavers Way is a 57 mile walk from Cromer to Great Yarmouth via Blickling and Stalham. The Angles Way follows the valleys of the Waveney and the Little Ouse for 70 miles. The Around Norfolk Walk is a 220 mile trail linking the Peddars Way, the Norfolk Coast Path, the Weavers Way and the Angles Way. TICs have information leaflets on these walks and on cycle routes.

GETTING AROUND
The public transport county phone line (☎ 01603-613613) has information on bus routes; there are several operators, the largest being Eastern Counties First Bus (☎ 01603-622800).

Norwich, King's Lynn, Cromer and Great Yarmouth are accessible by rail.

NORWICH
- pop 170,000   ☎ 01603

Norfolk's county town (pronounced nor-ridge) was once larger than London. For several centuries, when its prosperity was based on trade with the Low Countries, it was the second-largest town in England.

The East Angles had a fortified centre at Norwich that was burnt down twice by marauding Danes. The Normans built the splendid castle keep, now the best preserved example in the country. Below the castle lies what has been described as the most complete medieval English city. Clustered round the castle and cathedral within the circle of river and city walls are more than 30 parish churches.

Norwich is a surprisingly lively city with a large student population; the University of East Anglia is on the western outskirts.

Orientation & Information

The castle is in the centre of Norwich and the TIC is two blocks west. There are two cathedrals – Roman Catholic to the west and Anglican to the east.

The TIC (☎ 666071) is in the guildhall, Gaol Hill. It's open Monday to Saturday from 9.30 am to 5 pm. Guided walking tours (1½ hours, £2.25/1) take place at various times, including the evening – phone the TIC for details.

Outside the TIC is the market, a patchwork of stall awnings known as tilts. This is one of the biggest and longest-running markets in the country. It was moved here 900 years ago from its original site in Tombland by the now Anglican cathedral.

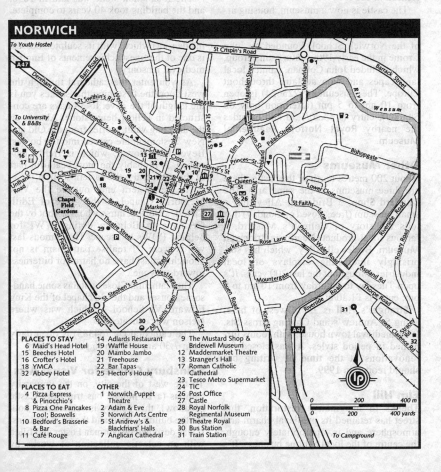

NORWICH

PLACES TO STAY
6 Maid's Head Hotel
15 Beeches Hotel
16 Crofter's Hotel
18 YMCA
32 Abbey Hotel

PLACES TO EAT
4 Pizza Express
  & Pinocchio's
8 Pizza One Pancakes
  Too!; Boswells
10 Bedford's Brasserie
  & Bar
11 Café Rouge

14 Adlards Restaurant
19 Waffle House
20 Mambo Jambo
21 Treehouse
22 Bar Tapas
25 Hector's House

OTHER
1 Norwich Puppet
  Theatre
2 Adam & Eve
3 Norwich Arts Centre
5 St Andrew's &
  Blackfriars' Halls
7 Anglican Cathedral

9 The Mustard Shop &
  Bridewell Museum
12 Maddermarket Theatre
13 Stranger's Hall
17 Roman Catholic
  Cathedral
23 Tesco Metro Supermarket
24 TIC
26 Post Office
27 Castle
28 Royal Norfolk
  Regimental Museum
29 Theatre Royal
30 Bus Station
31 Train Station

Also by the TIC is a convenient Tesco Metro supermarket.

Norwich Castle

Two blocks east of the market square is the massive Norman castle keep. It was built in about 1160 and measures 28m square by 21m high – a solid sentinel on the hill overlooking the medieval and modern cities. It's the best surviving example of Norman military architecture after the Tower of London and has worn pretty well, although it was refaced in 1834.

The castle is now a museum, housing archaeological and natural-history exhibits, as well as providing a gallery for the paintings of the Norwich School. Founded by John Crome in the early 19th century, this group, which included John Cotman, painted local landscapes and won acclaim throughout Europe. The museum (☎ 223624) is open from 10 am to 5 pm (afternoon only on Sunday); entry is £3.20/1.50 and includes the nearby **Royal Norfolk Regimental Museum**.

Other Museums

About 200 metres north of the castle, there are three museums in the same area. **The Mustard Shop**, 3 Bridewell Alley, has a small museum (free, closed on Sunday) that tells the story of Colman's Mustard, a famous local product. Nearby is **Bridewell Museum**, Bridewell Alley, which has surprisingly interesting displays of local industries throughout the last 200 years. It's open Tuesday to Saturday from 10 am to 5 pm; entry is £1.30/60p.

Stranger's Hall is 250m west of here, along St Andrew's and Charing Cross Sts. It's a medieval town house, with rooms furnished in period styles. It was closed for renovations at the time of writing but should reopen in 1999.

Elm Hill

Thanks to imaginative restoration, this street has retained its medieval charm and atmosphere and is, appropriately enough, the centre of the local antique business. It's

one of the most attractive parts of the city. Walk down Wensum St to Tombland, where the market was originally located. 'Tomb' is an old Norse word for 'empty' – hence space for a market.

Norwich Cathedral

The focal point of the city, the Anglican cathedral has retained the appearance and characteristics of a great Anglo-Norman abbey church more than any other English cathedral, apart from Durham.

The foundation stone was laid in 1096, and the building took 40 years to complete. In 1463 it was made fireproof by means of a magnificent stone lierne vault (a kind of inside roof) which, with its sculpted bosses, is one of the finest achievements of English medieval masonry.

As you enter the cathedral through the west door, the first thing that strikes you is the length of the nave. Its 14 bays are constructed in yellow-beige stone. Above, on the amazing vault, stories from the Old and New Testament are carved into the bosses. Beyond the tower, which is richly patterned, is probably the most beautiful part of the cathedral – the eastern section.

At the eastern end, outside the War Memorial Chapel, is the grave of Edith Cavell, a Norfolk nurse who was shot by the Germans in Belgium during WWI for helping POWs to escape. Her famous last words were, 'I realise patriotism is not enough. I must have no hatred or bitterness towards anyone'.

The Cathedral Close contains some handsome houses and the old chapel of the King Edward VI School – which was where Nelson was educated.

The cathedral (☎ 764385) is open daily from 7.30 am to 7 pm (6 pm in winter).

Sainsbury Centre for Visual Arts

To the west of the city, on the university campus (a 20 minute bus trip from Castle Meadow), this gallery is remarkable both for the building itself and the art it contains. It was designed by Norman Foster and filled with an eclectic collection of works by

Picasso, Moore, Bacon and Giacometti, displayed beside art from Africa, the Pacific and the Americas. It's open from Tuesday to Sunday from 11 am to 5 pm; entry is £2/1.

Places to Stay

Camping One mile south of the centre by the A146 on Martineau Lane is *Lakenham Camping* (☎ 620060), which charges £4.50 per person (plus £4 if you're not a C&C member). It's open from Easter through October.

Hostels The *Norwich Youth Hostel* (☎ 627647, 112 Turner Rd) is open every day from April to August; phone for other opening times. The nightly charge is £8.80/5.95 for adults/juniors, and there are some family rooms with two to six beds. It's 2 miles from the train station, on the western edge of the city.

The *YMCA* (☎ 620269, 48 St Giles St) is in a better location. Singles cost £12.50; £8.50 in a dorm. Breakfast is included.

B&Bs & Hotels Most of the B&Bs and cheaper hotels are outside the ring road, along Earlham and Unthank Rds to the west, and around the train station.

The B&Bs along Earlham Rd become more expensive the closer they are to the centre. *Aberdale Lodge* (☎ 502100), at No 211, charges £15 per person with shared bath. *Barton Lodge* (☎ 454874), at No 148, is a 15 minute walk from the centre. There are two singles for £17 with shared bath, and two doubles for £38 with shower.

Edmar Lodge (☎ 615599, 64 Earlham Rd) is a friendly place, with singles from £20 and doubles from £34, some with a bath. Still in Earlham Rd, in the shadow of the Roman Catholic cathedral, *Crofter's Hotel* (☎ 613287), at No 2, has 15 rooms for £44.50/59.50 for singles/doubles, all with bathrooms. Next door, at No 4-6 Earlham Rd, is the comfortable *Beeches Hotel* (☎ 621167). Rooms cost from £54/70 to £60/80; there's a lovely garden.

In the train station area, the *Abbey Hotel* (☎ 612915, 16 Stracey Rd) charges £17/34

with shared bath. There are several other places in this area.

In the centre is the comfortable and historic *Maid's Head Hotel* (☎ 209955), a 700-year-old former coaching inn, on Tombland. Room charges are £79/99 (plus £8.75 for breakfast) during the week, £46 per person including breakfast at weekends (minimum two-night stay).

Places to Eat

The large student population ensures that there's a good range of places to eat in Norwich.

Bar Tapas (☎ 764077, 18 Exchange St) describes itself as 'The rhythm of South America and the taste of Spain' Tapas range from £2.75 to £5.25; a jug of sangria is £11.95. Two streets west, on Lower Goat Lane, is Mexican-Cajun *Mambo Jambo*. A Jambo Dog with chilli, cheese and 'slaw is £5.95.

The *Waffle House* (☎ 612790, 39 St Giles St) specialises in savoury and sweet Belgian waffles. They range in price from £2.05 to £6.25 and there's a wide selection of fillings. On some nights a classical guitarist entertains diners.

The *Treehouse* (☎ 763258, 14 Dove St), above the health food shop, is an excellent vegetarian restaurant serving such delicacies as nut and moonbeam pâté. Main courses come in two sizes – £4.40 and £5.90. It's closed on Sunday.

There's a branch of *Café Rouge* on Exchange St and an excellent *Pizza Express* on St Benedict's St. Almost next door is *Pinocchio's* (☎ 613318), a good Italian place. *Pizza One Pancakes Too!* (☎ 621583, 24 Tombland) is near the cathedral and does as its name says.

Hector's House (☎ 622836, 18 Bedford St) is a café/bar that serves coffee and light lunches. There's no food available in the evening. Almost opposite is *Bedford's Brasserie & Bar*. On the menu are 'sautéed king prawns with chilli jam and a light puff pastry' (£6) – not run-of-the-mill pub grub!

For a splurge, there's *Adlards Restaurant* (☎ 633522, 79 Upper St Giles St) offering classic French cuisine. It's open on Monday for dinner and from Tuesday to Saturday for lunch and dinner; dinner costs £35 for four courses.

Boswells, a wine bar with live jazz or blues most nights, is on Tombland. Serious beer drinkers should head for the *Adam & Eve* on Bishopgate.

Entertainment

ArtEast is a useful Norfolk listings magazine published bimonthly.

The *Theatre Royal* (☎ 630000, Theatre St) features programs by touring drama and ballet companies. Reopening in 1999, *Norwich Arts Centre* (☎ 660352, Reeves Yard, St Benedict's St) features a wide-ranging program of drama, concerts, dance, cabaret and jazz.

On St George's St, *St Andrew's and Blackfriars' Halls*, once home to Dominican Blackfriars, now serve as an impressive civic centre where concerts, antique and craft markets, the Music and Arts Festival and even the annual beer festival are held; there's also a café in the crypt.

The *Norwich Puppet Theatre* (☎ 629921, St James, Whitefriars) is popular, particularly with children. Tickets are around £5/3.75.

Getting There & Away

Cambridge Coach Services (☎ 01223-423900) has four buses a day to Cambridge (two hours, £7; £8 day return), and National Express has a daily bus to Cambridge and London. Eastern Counties (☎ 622800) runs buses to King's Lynn (1½ hours, £4.35), Peterborough and Cromer. There's no bus service to Ely, and for Bury St Edmunds you must change in Diss.

From the train station there are direct services to London, Cambridge, Ely, Cromer and Great Yarmouth.

AROUND NORWICH
Blickling Hall

Anne Boleyn, one of Henry VIII's unfortunate wives, lived in the original Blickling Hall. It's said that on the anniversary of her execution a coach drives up to the house –

drawn by headless horses, driven by headless coachmen and containing the queen with her head on her lap.

The house dates from the early 17th century and is filled with Georgian furniture, pictures and tapestries. There's an impressive Jacobean plaster ceiling in the long gallery. The house is surrounded by parkland offering good walks.

Blickling Hall (☎ 01263-733084, NT) is 15 miles north of Norwich, and is open from Easter to October, Wednesday to Sunday (and also on Tuesday in August), from 1 to 4.30 pm; entry is £6/3. The gardens are open from 10.30 am to 5.30 pm.

Eastern Counties runs buses here from Norwich in summer. Aylsham is the nearest train station, 1¾ miles away.

NORFOLK BROADS

The Norfolk Broads is an area of rivers, lakes, marshland, nature reserves and bird sanctuaries on the Norfolk/Suffolk border. The area, measuring some 117 sq miles, has 'national protected status', which is equivalent to it being a national park.

A broad is a large piece of water formed by the widening of a river. The main river is the Bure, which enters the Broads at Wroxham and is then joined by several other rivers, including the Ant and the Thurne. The Waveney joins the Yare to meet the Bure at Great Yarmouth, where this large network of rivers flows into the sea. What makes this area special is that all these lakes, rivers and their tributaries are navigable. In all, there are 125 miles of lock-free waterways.

There's little variety of scenery, but the ecology of the area means that it's a wonderful place for nature lovers, and for people who like being on or near the water. The habitat includes freshwater lakes, slow-moving rivers, water meadows, fens, bogs and saltwater marshes, and the many kinds of birds, butterflies and water-loving plants that inhabit them.

How Hill, a mere 12m above sea level, is the highest place in the Broads. Since there's nothing to impede the path of sea breezes, this is a good area for wind power.

Many wind pumps (which look like wind-mills) were built to drain the marshland and to return the water to the rivers.

Orientation

The Broads form a triangle with Norwich at the apex, the Norwich-Cromer road as the northern side, the Norwich-Lowestoft road as the southern side and the coastline as the base.

Wroxham, on the A1151 from Norwich, and Potter Heigham, on the A1062 from Wroxham, are the main centres. Along the way, there are plenty of waterside pubs, villages and market towns where you can stock up on provisions, and stretches of river where you can feel you are the only person around.

The Origin of the Broads

For many years the origin of the Norfolk Broads was unclear. The rivers were undoubtedly natural and many thought the lakes were too – it's hard to believe they're not when you see them – but no one could explain how they could have formed.

The mystery was solved when records were discovered in the remains of St Benet's Abbey (on the River Bure). They showed that from the 12th century certain parts of land in Hoveton Parish were used for peat digging. The area had little woodland and the only source of fuel was peat. Since East Anglia was well populated and prosperous, peat digging became a major industry.

Over a period of about 200 years, approximately 1040 hectares were dug up. However, water gradually seeped through causing marshes, and later lakes, to develop. The first broad to be mentioned in records is Ranworth Broad (in 1275). Eventually, the amount of water made it extremely difficult for the diggers and the peat-cutting industry died out. In no other area of Britain has human effort changed the natural landscape so dramatically.

Information

The Broads Authority (☎ 01603-610734), Thomas Harvey House, 18 Colegate, Norwich NR3 1BQ, can supply information about the conservation centres and RSPB bird-watching hides at Berney Marshes, Ranworth, Bure Marshes, Cockshoot Broad, Hickling Broad, Horsey Mere, How Hill, Strumpshaw Fen and Surlingham Church Marsh.

You can also get information about the Broads from the Norwich TIC (☎ 01603-666071). *The Broadcaster* is a visitors' magazine, published annually.

Getting Around

Two companies that operate boating holidays are Blakes (☎ 01603-782911) and Hoseasons (☎ 01502-501010). Costs depend on the boat size, the facilities on the boat, the time of year and the length of the holiday. A boat for two to four people is £399 to £500 for a week – fuel is extra. Short breaks (three to four days) during the off season are much cheaper.

Many boat yards (particularly in the Wroxham and Potter Heigham areas) have a variety of boats for hire by the hour, half-day or full day. Charges still vary according to the season and the size of the boat, but they start from £9 for one hour, £24 for four hours and £40 for one day.

No previous experience is necessary, but remember to stay on the right side of the river, that the rivers are tidal, and to stick to the speed limit – you can get prosecuted for speeding. If you don't feel like piloting your own boat, Broads Tours runs pleasure trips from April to September, with a commentary, for £5.20/3.95 per person. Broads Tours has two bases: The Bridge, Wroxham (☎ 01603-782207), and Herbert Woods, Potter Heigham (☎ 01692-670711).

NORFOLK COAST
Great Yarmouth
• pop 54,800   ☎ 01493

This is one of Britain's most popular seaside resorts, complete with all the tacky trimmings such as amusement arcades and

EASTERN ENGLAND

greasy-spoon cafés, but it's also an important port for the North Sea oil and gas industries.

As well as a wide, sandy beach, other attractions include a number of interesting buildings in the old town. The **Elizabethan House Museum**, South Quay, was a merchant's house and now contains a display of 19th century domestic life. The **Old Merchant's House**, Row 111, South Quay, is a group of typical 17th century town houses. The **Tolhouse Museum**, Tolhouse St, was once the town's courthouse and jail; prison cells can be seen and there's a display covering the town's history. There's also a maritime museum. The TIC (☎ 842195) is on Marine Parade.

There are numerous B&Bs, and *Great Yarmouth Youth Hostel (☎ 843991, 2 Sandown Rd)* is three-quarters of a mile from the train station, near the beach. Charges are £8.80/5.95 for adults/juniors. *Tunstall Camping Barn (☎ 700279, Manor Farm, Tunstall, Halvergate)* is an independent hostel with 20 sleeping platforms in a barn for £3.50 per person. It's about 6 miles from Great Yarmouth, on the Norwich road.

Great Yarmouth is on main bus and rail routes to Norwich. Eastern Counties runs an hourly service between Norwich and Great Yarmouth (40 minutes, £2.65).

Cromer
• pop 4500   ☎ 01263

In the late Victorian and Edwardian eras, Cromer was transformed into the most fashionable resort on the coast. It's now somewhat run-down, but with its elevated seafront, long, sandy beach and scenic coastal walks, it's still worth visiting. Cromer has long been famous for its crabs, and they're still caught and sold here. The TIC (☎ 512497) is by the bus station, and this is one of the few coastal resorts with a train station linked to Norwich.

Two miles south-west of Cromer, **Felbrigg Hall** (☎ 837444, NT) is one of the finest 17th century houses in Norfolk. It contains a collection of 18th century furniture; outside is a walled garden, orangery

and landscaped park. It's open from Easter to October, daily except Thursday and Friday, from 1 to 5 pm; entry is £5.40/2.10.

Cley Marshes

Between Cromer and Wells, Cley Marshes (☎ 0740008) is one of the top birdwatching places in Britain, with over 300 species recorded. There's a visitors centre built on high ground to give good views over the area.

Wells-Next-The-Sea
• pop 2400   ☎ 01328

Set back from the sea, Wells is both a holiday town and a fishing port. It's a pleasant place, with streets of attractive Georgian houses, flint cottages and interesting shops. The TIC (☎ 710885) is in Staithe St and is open daily in summer.

Holkham Hall (☎ 710227) is a most impressive Palladian mansion situated in a 1200 hectare deer park 2 miles from Wells. The grounds were designed by Capability Brown. The house is open daily, except Friday and Saturday, from late May to September; entry is £6/3 and includes the Bygones Museum and the park.

A narrow-gauge steam railway runs 5 miles to **Little Walsingham**, where there's a Catholic shrine that has been an object of pilgrimage for almost 1000 years.

KING'S LYNN
• pop 37,500   ☎ 01553

Situated 3 miles from the sea, on the River Great Ouse, Lynn (as the locals call it) was one of England's chief ports in the Middle Ages. It was also a natural base for fishing fleets and their crews, and home to a number of religious foundations. The old town is a fascinating mixture of these three elements and Lynn is still a port today, though much less busy than it once was.

Orientation & Information

The old town lies along the eastern bank of the river. The train station is on the eastern side of the town. Modern Lynn and the bus station are between them.

The TIC (☎ 763044) should now have moved to the Custom House from the Old Gaol House. There are three market days each week – Tuesday, Friday and Saturday. In July, there's the popular King's Lynn Festival of Music and the Arts.

Walking Tour

This walk takes around 2½ hours. Start in the Saturday Market Place at **St Margaret's** parish church, founded in 1100 with a Benedictine priory. Little remains of the original buildings, but the church is impressive for its size (72m long) and contains two Flemish brasses which are among the best examples in the country. By the west door there are flood-level marks – 1976 was the highest, but the 1953 flood claimed more lives.

Walk south down Nelson St to see a fine collection of domestic and industrial buildings. Their frontages are 17th and 18th century, but their interiors are much older.

On the corner of St Margaret's Lane, and dating back to the 15th century, is a restored building that was once the warehouse or 'steelyard' of the **Hanseatic League** (the Northern European merchants' group).

Continue north-west along Margaret Plain to College Lane and the former Thoresby College, which was founded in 1508 to house priests and is now the youth hostel. Across Queen St is the **town hall**, dating back to 1421. Next to it is the building which houses the town museum and heritage centre. The **Old Gaol House** has been converted into a tourist attraction with self-guided Walkman tours. Lynn's priceless civic treasures, including the 650-year-old King John Cup, can be seen in the basement. It's open daily from Easter to October (Friday to Tuesday for the rest of the year) from 10 am to 5 pm; entry is £2.20/1.60.

Continuing down Queen St you pass **Clifton House**, with its quirky barley-sugar

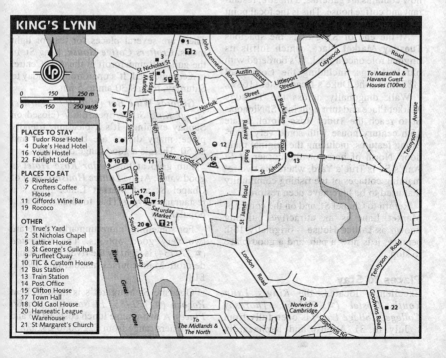

KING'S LYNN

0   150   250 m
0   150   250 yards

PLACES TO STAY
3   Tudor Rose Hotel
4   Duke's Head Hotel
16 Youth Hostel
22 Fairlight Lodge

PLACES TO EAT
6   Riverside
7   Crofters Coffee
    House
11 Giffords Wine Bar
19 Rococo

OTHER
1   True's Yard
2   St Nicholas Chapel
5   Lattice House
8   St George's Guildhall
9   Purfleet Quay
10 TIC & Custom House
12 Bus Station
13 Train Station
14 Post Office
15 Clifton House
17 Town Hall
18 Old Gaol House
20 Hanseatic League
    Warehouse
21 St Margaret's Church

To Marantha & Havana Guest Houses (100m)

To The Midlands & The North

To Norwich & Cambridge

columns and waterfront tower, which was used by merchants scanning the river for returning ships. Walk down the lane to the river past the sturdy, red floodgates. The stately Bank House is on your right. Opposite the square is **Purfleet Quay**, in its heyday the principal harbour. The quaint building with the lantern tower is the **Custom House** (now housing the TIC), which dates back to 1683.

Turn into King St, where the second medieval town begins. It was planned in the latter half of the 12th century and had its own church, guildhall, market and friary. There are many interesting buildings in King St, especially on the left-hand side, where the wealthier merchants built their homes and warehouses on reclaimed land. **St George's Guildhall** is the largest surviving 15th century guildhall in England. It has served as warehouse, theatre, courthouse and armoury (during the Civil War), and now contains art galleries, a theatre, restaurant and coffee house. This is the focal point of the annual King's Lynn   festival.

At the end of King St is the spacious **Tuesday Market Place**, which fulfils its original role once a week. It's bordered with old buildings, including the Corn Hall (1854) and the Duke's Head Hotel (1689).

Walk diagonally across the Tuesday Market Place and turn right into St Nicholas St to reach the **Tudor Rose Hotel**, a late 15th century house with some very interesting features, including the original main door. North of here, on the corner of St Ann's St, is **True's Yard**, where the two remaining cottages of the fishing community that used to be here have been restored.

Return to Chapel St, and on the corner of Market Lane is an attractive building known as **Lattice House** – originally 15th century, it is now a pub, and a good place to stop.

Places to Stay

Excellently located, the *King's Lynn Youth Hostel* (☎ 772461, *Thoresby College, College Lane*) is open fully from 1 July to 31 August and haphazardly

outside that time. A bed costs £8/5.40 for adults/juniors.

Maranatha Guest House (☎ 774596, *115 Gaywood Rd*) has budget accommodation from £12 per person. A double room costs £32 (£34 with a bath). *Havana Guest House* (☎ 772331) is next door at No 117, and has six rooms, four with a bath. It charges from £15 to £20 per person. Both these places are open year-round.

Fairlight Lodge (☎ 762234, *79 Goodwins Rd*) is a comfortable guesthouse with seven rooms, four with a bathroom, which charges £16 to £19 per person.

The *Tudor Rose Hotel* (☎ 762824, *St Nicholas St*) is a 15th century house with B&B from £38.50/50 for a single/double. The town's top hotel is the *Duke's Head Hotel* (☎ 774996), a fine classical building overlooking Tuesday Market. Rooms are £78/90; there are also special weekend deals.

Places to Eat

There are several places for teas or light meals. *Crofters Coffee House*, King St, in the guildhall undercroft at the Arts Centre, is recommended. It's open from Monday to Saturday, from 9.30 am to 5 pm.

Giffords Wine Bar (☎ 769177, *Purfleet St, off King St*) is open daily (closed on Sunday evening). It's a pleasant, friendly place; many dishes are between £4 and £5.50. There's a good range of coffees.

Pub grub at the *Tudor Rose Hotel* is good value. At the *Lattice House*, corner of Chapel St and Market Lane, there's a restaurant serving Thai food as well as a popular pub.

For something more upmarket there are two very good options. The *Riverside* (☎ 773134) is right by the river, near the undercroft. Main courses range from £5.95 to £18.

Opposite St Margaret's is the excellent *Rococo* (☎ 771483, *11 Saturday Market Place*). A two-course lunch costs £9.95 and set dinners range from £22.50 to £32.50.

Getting There & Away
King's Lynn is 43 miles north of Cambridge on the A10.

There are hourly trains from Cambridge (50 minutes, £6.90). Buses are less convenient, with just one National Express service each day, and this must be booked in advance. Eastern Counties (☎ 01603-622800) runs a daily bus service to Norwich (1½ hours, £4.35).

AROUND KING'S LYNN
Castle Rising Castle
The amazingly well-preserved 12th century keep of this castle is set in the middle of a massive earthwork. It was once the home of Queen Isabella, who arranged the murder of her husband Edward II. Open daily from 10 am to 6 pm (4 pm in winter), entry is £2.30/1.20 (☎ 01553-631330, EH). Eastern Counties buses No 410 and 411 run here from King's Lynn, 5 miles to the south.

Sandringham
The Queen's country pile is set in 25 hectares of landscaped gardens and lakes, and it's open to the hoi polloi when the court is not in residence. The house was bought by Queen Victoria in 1862 and the royal family still spends three weeks here from mid-July to early August. The museum contains a collection of vintage cars and other royal trinkets.

Sandringham (☎ 01553-772675) is open from April to September (except when the royal family is here), daily from 11 am to 4.45 pm. Entry is £4.50/2.50, less if you only want to see the grounds and museum. There are buses from King's Lynn, which is 10 miles south-west.

Houghton Hall
Built for Sir Robert Walpole in 1730, Houghton Hall (☎ 01485-528569) is an example of the Palladian style, and is worth seeing for the ornate state rooms alone. It's 12 miles north-east of King's Lynn and is open from April to September on Thursday and Sunday afternoons; entry is £6/3.

Cambridgeshire

Cambridgeshire is best known for its beautiful university town. Cambridge is in the southern part of the county, on the edge of the fens – the flat, fertile region, previously underwater, that covers the rest of the county. Cambridge has the advantage of being smaller and more compact than Oxford and does not have heavy industry. Its position on the River Cam gives it a rural flavour – cattle and horses graze within half a mile of the city centre.

The lack of hills makes this excellent cycling country. A towpath winds all the way from Cambridge to Ely (15 miles), where the superb cathedral, on ground slightly higher than the surrounding plain, is known as the 'ship of the fens'. In the north of the county there's another fine cathedral at Peterborough.

GETTING AROUND
Public transport centres on Cambridge. Rather than phoning the costly council transport helpline (☎ 0891-910910, 50p per minute), get the useful *Cambridgeshire and Peterborough Passenger Transport Map* and contact the bus companies direct.

The main bus companies operating in the area are Stagecoach Cambus (☎ 01223-423554) between Cambridge, Ely and Bury St Edmunds; Cambridge Coach Services (☎ 01223-423900) from Cambridge to Norwich; and Stagecoach United Counties (☎ 01604-620077) from Cambridge to Huntingdon and Peterborough.

Cambridge is only 55 minutes by rail from London. This line continues north through Ely to terminate at King's Lynn in Norfolk. From Ely, a branch line runs east through Thetford and Norwich, and southeast into Suffolk.

CAMBRIDGE
- pop 88,000   ☎ 01223

Cambridge is unquestionably one of the great universities of the world. With over 60 Nobel prizewinners, it is at the top of the research league in British universities; it owns a prestigious publishing firm and a world-renowned examination syndicate; it is the leading centre for astronomy in Britain; its Fitzwilliam Museum contains an outstanding art collection; and its library is used by scholars from around the world.

The university was founded in the 13th century, about a century later than Oxford. There is a fierce rivalry between the two cities and the two universities, and a futile debate over which is best and most beautiful. If you have the time, visit both. Oxford draws many more tourists than Cambridge. Partly because of this, if you only have time for one, and the colleges are open, choose Cambridge. Its trump card is the choir and chapel of King's College, which should not be missed by any visitor to Britain.

Though brimming with history and antiquity, Cambridge is also a bustling, modern market town. Yet it is Cambridge's tranquil, ageless picturesqueness which is hardest to match, and which the visitor will remember best.

History
Neolithic tools and weapons, circa 3000 BC, and ancient burial grounds have been found around Cambridge. There is also an Iron Age fort, Wandlebury, in the Gog Magog hills nearby. In 43 AD, when the Romans needed a road from Colchester to Godmanchester, the River Cam was forded just below Magdalene Bridge and a fort was built on the small hill overlooking it.

The camp became a town, and trading took place by road and river. In the 5th century the Romans withdrew and there followed a series of invasions from Europe – first by the Anglo-Saxons, who didn't do much to develop the town: Ely monks in the 7th century described it as 'desolate'. It was kick-started back into life in the 9th century by the Norse/Danish invaders, who were great traders.

Next, in 1066, came the Normans who replaced the fort with a castle (now a mere mound on Castle Hill) in order to campaign against the bold Saxon leader Hereward the Wake, who lurked in the marshy fens round Ely. The 1086 *Domesday Book* records 400 'burgesses' (full citizens) in Cambridge.

The next two invasions were peaceful ones. The first involved religious orders who radiated out from the great spiritual centre at Ely. The second began in the early 13th century when scholars, many of them from Oxford, arrived to form the nucleus of a university. This gave Cambridge a fresh impetus and signalled a vital new development. The collegiate system, unique to Oxford and Cambridge, came into being gradually with the first college, Peterhouse, founded in 1284 by Hugh de Balsham (later Bishop of Ely). The plan was for tutors and students to live together in a community, much as they would in a monastery.

From the 14th century onwards, a series of colleges was founded by royalty, nobility, leading church figures, statesmen, academics and trade guilds – all for men only. In 1869 and 1871, however, there was a breakthrough for women when Girton and Newnham were founded, though it was only in 1948 that women were actually permitted to graduate. Now, 29 of the 31 colleges are co-residential – two still choosing to maintain their 'women only' status.

Orientation
The colleges and university buildings comprise the centre of the city – like Oxford, Cambridge has no campus. The central area, lying in a wide bend of the River Cam, is easy to get around on foot or by bike. The best known section of the Cam is the Backs, which combines lush river scenery with superb views of six colleges, including King's College Chapel. The other 25 colleges are scattered throughout the city.

The bus station is in the centre on Drummer St, but the train station is a 20 minute walk to the south. Sidney St is the main shopping street, and it changes its name many times.

Information
The TIC (☎ 322640), Wheeler St, is open Monday to Saturday, from 10 am to 6 pm

CAMBRIDGE

PLACES TO STAY
1 Antoni Guest House
2 Lyngamore & Belle
  Vue Guest Houses
3 Arundel House Hotel
4 Aaron House
32 Garden House Hotel
38 University Arms Hotel
43 Lensfield Hotel
45 YMCA
48 Youth Hostel & Six
  Steps Guest House
49 Tenison Towers & Railway
  Lodge Guest Houses
50 Sleeperz

PLACES TO EAT
6 Twenty-two
11 Michel's Brasserie
12 Café Rouge
17 Tatties
18 Clowns
21 Nadia's (King's Parade)
22 Rainbow
23 No 1 King's Parade
  & Eagle Pub
29 Fitzbillies
30 Nadia's (Silver St)
34 Bella Pasta
35 Choices Café
37 Hobb's Pavilion
39 Sticky Fingers Café
40 The Depot
41 Browns
44 Shalimar Restaurant
47 CB1

PUBS
5 Boathouse
9 Rat & Parrot
26 Free Press
33 Granta (& Punt Hire)

OTHER
7 Laundrette
8 Cambridge River Cruises
10 Kettle's Yard
13 Round Church
14 American Express
15 Trinity Punts
16 Great St Mary's Church
19 Senate House
20 King's College Chapel
24 TIC
25 Drummer St Bus Station
27 Post Office
28 St Benet's Church
31 Scudamore's Punt Hire
36 Cambridge Recycles
42 Sub Post Office
46 Mike's Bikes
51 Train Station

(5 pm on Saturday) all year, and also on Sunday (from 11 am to 4 pm) from Easter to September.

It organises walking tours at 1.30 pm every day, all year, with more during summer. Group sizes are limited, so buy your ticket in advance (£6.25 including King's College, £5.75 including St John's College). Private guides are available from the TIC, but arranging the services of an independent guide is cheaper – Pauline Skyrme-Jones (☎ 573441) is recommended.

The university has three eight-week terms: Michaelmas (October to December), Lent (mid-January to mid-March) and Easter (mid-April to mid-June). Exams are held from mid-May to mid-June. There's general mayhem for the 168 hours following exams – the so-called May Week. Most colleges are closed to visitors for the Easter term, and all are closed for exams. Precise details of opening hours vary from college to college and year to year, so contact the TIC for up-to-date information. A few colleges have started charging admission to tourists (£1 to £3). You may, however, find that entry to tourists is now denied entirely at some of the colleges described below. Each year more colleges decide that the tourist bandwagon is just too disruptive.

To collect your email or make cheap international phone calls visit the International Telecom Centre opposite the TIC. There's an American Express office (☎ 351636) at 25 Sidney St, and a laundrette at 12 Victoria Ave, just north of the bridge and near Chesterton Rd.

Walking Tour 1

This three hour walk visits King's College Chapel and the most central colleges, and includes a stretch along the river.

From the TIC, walk one block west to King's Parade, turn right and continue north to **Great St Mary's Church**. This 15th century university church, built in the perpendicular style, has a feeling of space and light inside thanks to its clerestory, wide arch and wood carving. The traditional termly university sermons are preached here. To get your bearings, climb the tower (£1) for a good view of the city. The building across King's Parade, on the right-hand side of the square, is the **Senate House**, designed in 1720 by Gibbs. It's the most beautiful example of pure classical architecture in the city; graduations are held here.

Gonville & Caius Now walk into Trinity St, head north, and turn left into the first gateway to reach this fascinating old college. It was founded twice, first by a priest called Gonville, in 1347, and then again by Dr Caius (pronounced keys), a brilliant physician and scholar, in 1551. Of special interest here are the three gates: Virtue, Humility and Honour. They symbolise the progress of the good student, since the third gate (a fascinating confection with a quirky dome and sundials) leads to the Senate House and thus graduation. Walk through 'Porta Honoris', turn right, then left, to reach King's College Chapel.

King's College Chapel All the college chapels are individually remarkable but King's College Chapel is supreme in its grandeur. It's one of the finest examples of Gothic architecture in England, and comparable with Chartres.

The chapel was conceived as an act of piety by the young Henry VI and dedicated to the Virgin Mary. Its foundation stone was laid by the king in 1446 and building completed around 1516. Henry VI's successors, notably Henry VIII, glorified the interior (and themselves in so doing). Services are led by its choir, originally choristers from Eton College, another of Henry VI's foundations. The choir's Festival of the Nine Lessons and Carols on Christmas Eve is heard all over the world.

Enter through the south porch. Despite the original stained-glass windows, the atmosphere inside is light. Cromwell's soldiers destroyed many church windows in East Anglia but it is believed that, having been a Cambridge student, their leader spared King's.

The stunning interior of 12 bays is about 11m wide, 22m high and 80m long. This vast expanse is the largest in the world canopied by fan vaulting. It's the work of John Wastell, and is a miracle of beauty and skill.

The elaborate carvings, both in wood and stone, include royal coats of arms, intertwined initials, the royal beasts of heraldry, and flowers that were the emblems of Tudor monarchs and related families. Among the Yorkist roses on the western wall is the figure of a woman within a rose. Some claim she is Elizabeth of York, but it's more likely that she's the Virgin Mary.

The ante-chapel and the choir are divided by the superbly carved **wooden screen**, another gift of Henry VIII. The screen bears Henry's initials entwined with those of Anne Boleyn. The work is attributed to Peter the Carver. The one angry human face, almost concealed by the mythical beasts and symbolic flowers, is perhaps his jest for posterity.

Originally constructed between 1686 and 1688, the magnificent organ has been rebuilt and developed over the years, and now its pipes top the screen on which they rest.

The **choir stalls** were made by the same craftsman who worked on the screen, but the canopies are Carolingian. Despite the dark wood, the impression is still of lightness as one approaches the **high altar**, which is framed by Rubens' *Adoration of the Magi* and the magnificent east window.

The excellent **Chapel Exhibition** is in the northern side chapels, to the left of the altar. Here, you can see the stages and methods of building set against the historical panorama from inception to completion. On display are costumes, paintings, illuminated manuscripts and books, plans, tools and scale models, including a full-size model showing how the fan vaulting was constructed.

Entry costs £3/2. The vergers are helpful with information and there are occasional guided tours at the weekend. Tours during the week can be arranged at the TIC. King's College Chapel (☎ 331100) comes alive when the choir sings; even the most pagan heavy-metal fan will find **Choral Evensong** an extraordinary experience. There are services from mid-January to mid-March, mid-April to mid-June, mid-July to late July, early October to early December and on 24 and 25 December. Evensong is at 5.30 pm, Tuesday to Saturday (men's voices only on Wednesday), and at 3.30 pm on Sunday.

Trinity College From King's College Chapel, return to King's Parade and follow it north into Trinity St; the entrance to the college is opposite Heffers bookshop. Henry VIII founded Trinity in 1546, but it was left to Dr Nevile, Master of Trinity (1593-1615) in Elizabeth's reign, to fulfil his wishes.

Walk through the impressive brick gateway, which dates back to 1535, and start reaching for superlatives. The **Great Court** is the largest of its kind in the world. The Gothic ante-chapel is full of huge statues of famous Trinity men, like Tennyson and Newton. The vast hall has a hammerbeam roof and lantern. Beyond the hall are the cloisters of Nevile's Court and the dignified

---

Cambridge – a University Town

Students' lives are centred around their colleges, where they eat, sleep, study and relax – in theory only leaving home for lectures and exams. Colleges are planned, in a monastic manner, as a series of courtyards (known as 'courts', not 'quads' as at Oxford) with study/bedrooms, dining hall, chapel and gardens.

In contrast to the colleges, the university's role is to hold lectures, conduct exams, award degrees and promote research. It owns numerous buildings (lecture halls, laboratories, libraries, museums, administrative centres etc), yet it is not a place but a body of people, encompassing the chancellor all the way down to the undergraduate.

Though town and university have clashed at times – for example, during the Civil War when the university supported the king and the town supported Cromwell – the atmosphere today is largely amicable. Although the university and colleges have continued to infiltrate the town, mainly through building and buying property, this is more integration than domination. The relationship is mutually beneficial, as demonstrated by the town's innovative business and science parks.

Wren Library. The library is open to visitors from noon till 2 pm and is certainly worth visiting, though you may have to queue.

There are some amusing details in Trinity, although much of the college is larger than life (like its founder). On the great gateway, Henry VIII's statue dominates from the top niche, although in one hand he's holding a chair leg instead of the regal sceptre. Students kept removing the sceptre, so the porters thought up this substitute. Newton is reputed to have discovered the Law of Gravity by observing a falling apple; the tree at the entrance is said to be the progeny of this apple. Entry is £1.75.

Along the Backs Walk out of the cloisters and turn right to look at St John's New Court on the western bank. It's a 19th century residence block connected with the rest of **St John's College** by two bridges: Kitchen Bridge and the **Bridge of Sighs** (a replica of the original in Venice). Cross Trinity Bridge and turn left, following the footpath until you come to Garret Hostel Bridge. Pause on top to watch the punts below and look upstream to the bridge at **Clare**. It's ornamented with decorative balls and is the oldest, most interesting bridge on the Backs. Walk on, then turn right into Trinity Hall.

Trinity Hall This is a delightfully small college, wedged among the great and the famous. Despite the name, it has nothing to do with Trinity College. You enter through the newest court, which overlooks the river on one side and has a lovely Fellows' garden on another. Walking into the next court, you pass the quaint 16th century library.

Old Schools As you walk out of the first court, you'll see a tall, historic gate, which receives little attention. It's the entry to Old Schools, the administrative centre of the university. The lower part dates back to 1441, though the upper section was added in the 1860s. You are now back in the heart of the university.

Walking Tour 2

This walk visits Christ's College, Jesus College, the Round Church and Magdalene. This must be a morning tour if you wish to go inside Christ's, which is only open from 9.30 am to noon. The walk should take about two hours and you could continue afterwards to see the Kettle's Yard art gallery. Start outside Christ's, on the corner of St Andrew's and Hobson Sts.

Christ's College Christ's was founded in 1505 by that pious and generous benefactress, Lady Margaret Beaufort, who also founded St John's. It has an impressive entrance gate emblazoned with heraldic carving. The figure of the founder stands in a niche, hovering over all like a guiding spirit. Note the stout oak door leading into First Court, which has an unusual circular lawn, magnolias and wisteria creepers. The court is a mixture of original buildings and 18th century facings and windows. The hall was rebuilt in neogothic style last century, and the chapel's early sections include an oriel window which enabled the founder to join in services from her 1st floor room.

The Second Court has an interesting Fellows' building, dating back to 1643. Its gate leads into a Fellows' garden, which contains a mulberry tree under which Milton reputedly wrote *Lycidas*. Continuing through Iris Court, you're confronted by the stark, grey, modern students' block, which seems totally out of place. Look at the little theatre tucked into the right-hand corner, then walk out past New Christ's into Hobson St; turn right, then left and right into Jesus Lane. You'll pass Westcott, another theological college (not part of the university), then All Saints Church – affectionately dubbed St Op's (St Opposite) by Jesus students.

Jesus College The approach to Jesus via the long 'chimney' is impressive, as is the main gate, which is under a rebus of the founder, Bishop Alcock. A rebus is a heraldic device suggesting the name of its owner: the bishop's consists of several cockerels. The spacious First Court, with its red-brick ranges, is open on the western side – an unusual feature.

The best parts of Jesus are the tiny, intimate cloister court, to your right, and the chapel, which dates back to the St Radegund nunnery. The bishop closed the nunnery, expelled the nuns for misbehaving and founded the new college in its place.

The chapel is inspiring and reflects Jesus' development over the centuries. It has a Norman arched gallery from the nunnery building, a 13th century chancel and beautiful restoration work and Art Nouveau by

Pugin, Morris (ceilings), Burne-Jones (stained glass) and Madox Brown.

The other buildings in Jesus are rather an anticlimax, but the extensive grounds, which include a cricket pitch, are pleasant to walk through.

Round Church Turn right out of Jesus College, go up Jesus Lane, turn right into Park St and left into Round Church St. At the top of this street is the amazing Round Church, or Church of the Holy Sepulchre. It was built in 1130 to commemorate its namesake in Jerusalem and is one of only four in England. It is strikingly unusual, with chunky, round Norman pillars which encircle the small nave. The rest of the church was added later in a different style; the conical roof dates from only the 19th century. No longer a parish church, it's now a brass-rubbing centre. Depending on the size of the brasses, this costs from £3 to £20.

Magdalene College Turn right down Bridge St. It was around Magdalene Bridge that the Romans built the bridge that marked the origins of Cambridge. Boats laden with cargo tied up and unloaded where the block of flats now stands on the river bank. Facing you across the river is Magdalene (pronounced mawdlin), which you enter from Magdalene St.

Originally a Benedictine hostel, the college was refounded in 1542 by Lord Audley. Its river setting gives it a certain appeal, but its greatest asset is the Pepys Library, housing the magnificent collection of books the famous diarist bequeathed to his old college – he was a student here in 1650-53.

Walking Tour 3

Taking in the colleges just to the south of the centre, this walk takes about two to three hours.

Corpus Christi From King's Parade, turn into Bene't St to see the oldest structure in Cambridge – the 11th century Saxon tower of the Franciscan parish church. The rest of the church is newer, but full of interesting features. The church served as chapel to Corpus Christi, next door, until the 16th century. There's an entrance to the college leading into Old Court, which has been retained in its medieval form and still exudes a monastic atmosphere. Christopher Marlowe was a Corpus man, as a plaque, next to a fascinating sundial, bears out. New Court, beyond, is a 19th century creation.

The college library has the finest collection of Anglo-Saxon manuscripts in the world which, with other valuable books, were preserved from destruction at the time of Henry VIII's dissolution of the monasteries.

Queens' College Queens', one of the Backs' colleges, was the first Cambridge college to charge admission – now £1. This was initiated to pay for soundproofing its vulnerable site on this busy street. It takes its name from the two queens who founded it – Margaret and Elizabeth, in 1448 and 1478 respectively – yet it was a conscientious rector of St Botolph's Church who was its real creator.

Its main entrance is off Queens' Lane. The red-brick gate tower and Old Court, which immediately capture your attention, are part of the medieval college. So is Cloister Court, the next court, with its impressive cloister and picturesque, half-timbered President's Lodge (President is the name for the Master). The famous Dutch scholar and reformer Erasmus lodged in the tower early in the 16th century. The Cam is outside Cloister Court, and is crossed by a quaint wooden bridge which brings you into the 20th century Cripps Court.

Peterhouse College Founded in 1284 by Hugh de Balsham, later Bishop of Ely, this is the oldest and smallest of the colleges. It stands to the west of Trumpington St, just beyond Little St Mary's Church (formerly St Peter's, which gave the college its name). A walk through Peterhouse gives you a clear picture of the 'community' structure of a Cambridge college, though, unusually, the Master's house is opposite the college, not within it.

First Court, the oldest, is small, neat and bright, with hanging baskets and window boxes. The 17th century chapel is on the right, built in a mixture of styles which blend well. Inside, the luminous 19th century stained-glass windows contrast with the older eastern window.

The Burrough range, on the right, is 18th century and the hall, on the left, a restored, late 13th century gem. Beyond the hall are sweeping grounds extending to the Fitzwilliam Museum. Bearing right, you enter a court with an octagonal lawn, beyond which are the library, theatre and First Court.

Pembroke College Pembroke has several courts linked by lovely gardens and lawns. As usual, the oldest court is at the entrance. It still retains some medieval corner sections. The chapel, on the extreme right, is an early Wren creation (1666): it is interesting to compare this with his two other Cambridge buildings, the chapel at Emmanuel College and the library at Trinity College.

Crossing Old Court diagonally, walk past the handsome dining hall and into charming Ivy Court. Walk through and round the corner to see a sweeping lawn with an impressive statue of Pitt the Younger (prime minister in the 18th century) outside the ornate library clock tower.

Continue through the garden, past the green where students play croquet after exams in summer, and out, right, into Pembroke St.

Emmanuel College Emmanuel College, on St Andrew's St, was founded in 1584. It's a medium-sized college comprising a community of some 600 people.

If you stand in Front Court, one of the architectural gems of Cambridge faces you – the Wren chapel, cloister and gallery, completed in 1677. To the left is the hall; inside, the refectory-type tables are set at right angles to the high table.

The next court, New Court, is round the corner. It has a quaint herb garden reminis-

cent of the old Dominican priory which preceded the college. There are a few remnants of the priory in the *clunch* (chalk) core of the walls of the Old Library. Turn right to re-enter Front Court and go into the chapel. It has interesting windows, a high ceiling and an Annigoni painting. Near the side door is a plaque to a famous scholar, John Harvard (BA 1632), who was among 30 Emmanuel men who settled in New England. He left money to found the university that bears his name in the Massachusetts town of Cambridge.

Fitzwilliam Museum

Designed by Basevi in 1848, this massive neoclassical edifice, with its vast portico, was a bequest (along with his art treasures) to the university by Viscount Fitzwilliam. It was one of the first public art museums in Britain, and has been called the 'finest small museum in Europe'.

In the lower galleries are ancient Egyptian sarcophagi and Greek and Roman art, as well as Chinese ceramics, English glass and illuminated manuscripts. The upper galleries contain a wide range of paintings, including works by Titian, Rubens, the French Impressionists, Gainsborough, Stubbs and Constable, right up to Cézanne and Picasso. It also has fine antique furniture.

The Fitzwilliam (☎ 332900) is open from Tuesday to Saturday, from 10 am to 5 pm, and on Sunday afternoon, when there are guided tours at 2.30 pm. Admission is free.

Kettle's Yard

Situated on the corner of Northampton and Castle Sts, this gallery was the home of Jim Ede, a former assistant keeper at the Tate Gallery in London. It contains his early 20th century art collection (Gaudier-Brzeska and British). The atmosphere is intimate because the paintings and sculpture are placed amid ceramics, glass and furnishings. There's also an adjoining exhibition gallery.

Kettle's Yard (☎ 352124) was given to the university by the Edes in 1966. Admission is free, and it's open from Tuesday to Sunday, from 2 to 4 pm.

Punting

Taking a punt along the Backs is sublime, but it can also be a wet and hectic experience, especially on a busy weekend. Look before you leap. If you do wimp out, the Backs are also perfect for a walk or a picnic.

Rental prices vary considerably. Cheapest, but not always available, are those at Trinity Punts, behind Trinity College. They charge £6 per hour (plus £25 deposit). Next is the punt hire at the Granta pub, Newnham Rd, for £7 per hour with a £30 deposit. Punts hired by Magdalene Bridge or outside the nearby Rat & Parrot pub cost £8 per hour plus £30 deposit. Down by Silver St, Scudamore's (☎ 359750) charges £10 per hour plus £50 deposit.

Punting the 3 miles up the river to the idyllic village of Grantchester makes a great day out.

Walks & Cycle Routes

The best outing in the area is to Grantchester, 3 miles along the towpath. You can go on foot, by bike or in a punt. For longer walks, the TIC stocks a number of guides, including *Walks in South Cambridgeshire*.

If you're a lazy cyclist, the flat topography makes for ideal biking country, although the scenery can get a little mono-

tonous. *Cycle Routes and the Cambridge Green Belt Area* is a useful guide.

Organised Tours

Guide Friday (☎ 362444) runs hop-on hop-off tour buses round the city, calling at the train station. Tours are daily, year-round; tickets cost £7.50/2 for adults/children, and £6 for students.

Cambridge River Cruises (☎ 300100) run 90-minute cruises from the river near Jesus Green for £6/4. From April to September there's at least one departure daily at 1 pm, with more frequent departures in mid-season.

Places to Stay

Camping *Highfield Farm Camping Park* (☎ 262308, Long Rd, Comberton) is 4 miles south-west of Cambridge. In summer it costs £8 for a two-person tent.

Hostels The *Cambridge Youth Hostel* (☎ 354601, 97 Tenison Rd) has small dormitories and a restaurant near the train station. It's very popular – book ahead. Adult/junior rates are £10.70/7.30. The *Carpenter's Arms* (☎ 351814), on Victoria Rd in the north of the city, has two six-bed dorms and charges £8 per person.

B&Bs & Hotels There are numerous B&Bs to choose from at any time of the year, even more during university holidays from late June to late September. Right outside the train station is *Sleeperz* (☎ 304050), an attractively converted railway warehouse with single/twin rooms for £30/36 with a shower. Rooms with a double bed are larger and cost £45. It's non-smoking and there's wheelchair access to some rooms.

There are several B&Bs on Tenison Rd, including the *Railway Lodge Guest House* (☎ 467688), at No 150, which is good value with rooms from £24/30 for a single/double with bathroom. The *Tenison Towers Guest House* (☎ 566511), at No 148, charges from £20 to £30 per person. The *Six Steps Guest House* (☎ 353968), at No 93, costs from £25 per person. One reader eulogised about

---

How to Punt

1. Standing at the end of the punt, lift the pole out of the water at the side of the punt.

2. Let the pole slide through your hands to touch the bottom of the river.

3. Tilt the pole forward (ie in the direction of travel of the punt) and push down to propel the punt forward.

4. Twist the pole to free the end from the mud at the bottom of the river, and let it float up and trail behind the punt. You can then use it as a rudder to steer with.

5. If you've not yet fallen in, raise the pole out of the water and into the vertical position to begin the cycle again.

the food here: 'the only good bread I tasted in the UK'!

The *YMCA* (☎ *356998, Gonville Place*) charges £21/34 and is good value for weekly stays (£120/207).

The other B&B area is in the north of the city around Chesterton Rd. *Antoni Guest House* (☎ *357444, 4 Huntingdon Rd*) is good, with four singles, four doubles and three triples at £17 to £20 per person. Similarly priced but a bit farther out, *Benson House* (☎ *311594, 24 Huntingdon Rd*) has well-equipped doubles with showers – and a friendly cat.

Closer to the city centre, there's *Lyngamore House* (☎ *312369, 35-37 Chesterton Rd*) with rooms from £15 to £20 per person. The *Belle Vue Guest House* (☎ *351859, 33 Chesterton Rd*) has comfortable doubles for £35. *Arundel House Hotel* (☎ *67701*), at No 53, is a pleasant place to stay. There are 42 single rooms ranging from £39.50 to £67, and 57 doubles from £57 to £89; almost all with bathrooms. *Aaron House* (☎ *314723*), at No 71, is a small place with rooms for £26/42 with bath.

Further east along Chesterton Rd, at No 154, is *Acorn Guest House* (☎ *353888*) with rooms from £20/35 to £25/45, most with bathroom. Vegetarians are catered for. There are several other places nearby, including *Kirkwood House* (☎ *313874*), at No 172, which is similarly priced, and the *Hamilton Hotel* (☎ *365664*), at No 156, which has rooms from £20/40 to £40/59. There's a bar here. At No 245, *Carlton Lodge* (☎ *367792*) is run by widely travelledfriendly, people. Rooms are £19/38.

In the south, near the Fitzwilliam Museum, the *Lensfield Hotel* (☎ *355017, 53 Lensfield Rd*) is well located. It has 32 rooms and charges from £38/65 to £48/68.

The posh *Garden House House (Moat House)* (☎ *259988, Mill Lane*) is by the river, in the centre, and has pastoral views from many rooms. There are 118 luxurious bedrooms with prices to match – £120/150 (not including breakfast), weekend rates of £90 per person per night including dinner and breakfast. The *University Arms Hotel*

(☎ *351241*), on Regent St, overlooking Parker's Piece, is the other top place in town, charging £100/120.

Places to Eat

Cambridge has a good selection of reasonably priced restaurants. Some give student discounts. *Nadia's* is a small chain of bakeries that are excellent value (eg bacon sandwich and coffee for 95p before 10 am). A smoked ham and Emmental cheese baguette is £1.65. There are branches on King's Parade and Silver St.

Choices Café (☎ *360211, Newnham Rd*) will make up picnic hampers for punters, from £3.50 to £4.25 per person.

Across the road from King's College is *Rainbow* (☎ *321551, 9 King's Parade*), a good vegetarian restaurant. Couscous is £5.75. *No 1 King's Parade* (☎ *359506*) is a cellar bar-restaurant opposite King's College. An express two-course lunch costs £6.95. Wild boar and apple sausages cost £8.25.

Clowns (☎ *460453, 54 King St*) is popular with students and serves light meals that are good value. *Hobb's Pavilion* (☎ *67480, Park Terrace*) occupies the old cricket pavilion and specialises in filled pancakes. It's closed on Sunday and Monday.

There's a number of reasonably priced restaurants on Regent St. *The Depot* is stylish yet good value, offering an interesting international menu based around starters. Thai chicken curry is £4.25, potato gnocchi is £4.15. Opposite, at No 26, is Bill Wyman's *Sticky Fingers Café*, walls hung with Stones memorabilia. Also on Regent St is *Shalimar Restaurant* (☎ *355378*), an Indian place offering discounts to students.

CB1 (☎ *576306*) is an Internet café on Mill Rd. It's open from 10 am to 8 pm daily; there are nine terminals and the walls are stacked with second-hand books. Coffee (80p) and cakes are served.

Fitzbillies (☎ *352500, 52 Trumpington St*) is a brilliant bakery/restaurant. The Chelsea buns (80p) are an outrageous experience, and so is the chocolate cake beloved by generations of students, but there are many other temptations in addition to the usual sandwiches and pies – stock up before you go punting. Cakes and buns are also available by mail order.

Tatties (☎ *323399, now at 11 Sussex Gardens*) has long been a budget favourite. It specialises not only in baked potatoes stuffed with a variety of tempting fillings but also in breakfasts, filled baguettes, salads and cakes. The delicious Breakfast Baguette (hot Cambridge sausages) is £2.25.

Browns (☎ *461655, 23 Trumpington St*) is part of the chain that has branches in several university towns. It's not as expensive as it looks. There are also branches of **Bella Pasta** (*Newnham Rd*) and **Café Rouge** (*Magdalene St*).

Michel's Brasserie (☎ *353110, 21 Northampton St*) has set lunches from £6.95 and more expensive à la carte dinners.

Twenty-two (☎ *351880, 22 Chesterton Rd, near the Boathouse pub*) may look like just another house among the hotels and B&Bs on this road, but inside it's a gourmet restaurant. A set dinner costs £22.50.

The city's best cuisine is served overlooking the river on Midsummer Common at **Midsummer House** (☎ *369299*). It's a smart, sophisticated place, said to have one of the most comprehensive wine lists outside Paris. There are set lunch menus at around £25 and set dinners at £39. It's open for lunch from Tuesday to Friday and on Sunday; for dinner, from Tuesday to Saturday. You may need to book several weeks in advance.

Entertainment

The **Corn Exchange** (☎ *357851*), near the TIC, is the city's main centre for arts and entertainment, with shows as diverse as the English National Ballet and Sesame Street Live! The restored **Arts Theatre** (☎ *503333*) is at 6 St Edward's Passage. The King's College Choir is unique to Cambridge – don't miss it.

As you might expect in a city full of students, there are some excellent places for a pint. The **Rat & Parrot** is by the river north of Magdalene Bridge; punts are available from here. The **Granta** (*Newnham Rd*) is another pub with punt hire beside it. The

Boathouse (*14 Chesterton Rd*) can be visited by punt and even has its own mooring place.

The **Free Press** (*Prospect Row*) is a pub and boat club, hence the decorative theme. As well as being a good place to drink, it has some of the best bar food in Cambridge, including good vegetarian choices.

Nobel prizewinning scientists Crick and Watson spent equal time in the laboratory and **The Eagle** (*Bene't St*), so perhaps Greene King, the Suffolk brewers, played a part in the discovery of the structure of DNA. This 16th century pub was also popular with American airmen in WWII; they left their signatures on the ceiling.

Getting There & Away

Cambridge can easily be visited as a day trip from London (although it's worth staying at least a night) or en route north. It's well served by rail, not so well by bus. See the fares tables in the Getting Around chapter.

Bus For bus information, phone ☎ 317740. National Express (☎ 0990-808080) has hourly buses to London, and four buses a day to/from Bristol (two stop at Bath). Unfortunately, connections to the north aren't straightforward. To get to Lincoln or York you'll have to change at Peterborough or Nottingham, respectively. King's Lynn is also only accessible via Peterborough – it's easier to take a train.

Cambridge Coach Services (☎ 423900) runs the Inter-Varsity Link via Stansted airport to Oxford (three hours, six per day, £7/13 for a single/return). It also runs buses to Heathrow (£13) and Gatwick (£17) airports.

Train There are trains every half-hour from London's King's Cross and Liverpool St stations (one hour). Network South-East cards are valid. If you catch the train at King's Cross you travel via Hatfield and Stevenage. There are also regular train connections to Bury St Edmunds, Ely (£2.90) and King's Lynn (£6.70). There are connections at Peterborough with the main northbound trains to Lincoln, York and

Edinburgh. If you want to head west to Oxford or Bath you'll have to return to London first.

Getting Around

Most vehicles are now banned from the centre of Cambridge. It's best to use the well-signposted Park & Ride car parks (£1).

Bus There's a free, gas-powered shuttle service round the town. Cambus (☎ 423554) runs numerous buses around town from Drummer St, including bus No 1 from the train station to the town centre.

Taxi For a taxi, phone Cabco (☎ 312444). Unless you have a lot of luggage, it's not really worth taking one from the train station to the centre. It costs £3.50 and takes about 15 minutes; you can walk it in 20 minutes.

Bicycle It's easy enough to get around Cambridge on foot, but if you're staying out of the centre, or plan to explore the fens, a bicycle can be useful. You don't need a flash mountain bike because there are few hills; most places rent three-speeds. Geoff's Bike Hire (☎ 365629), 65 Devonshire Rd, near the youth hostel, charges £6 per day and £20 per week but gives a 10% discount to YHA members. Cambridge Recycles (☎ 506035), 61 Newnham Rd, charges £5 to £8 per day. Mike's Bikes (☎ 312591), Mill Rd, is cheapest at £5 per day or around £8 per week, for a bike with no gears.

AROUND CAMBRIDGE
Grantchester

Three miles from Cambridge, Grantchester is a delightful village of thatched cottages and flower-filled meadows beside the Granta River (as the Cam is known here). Its quintessential Englishness was recognised by the poet Rupert Brooke, who was a student at King's before WWI, in the immortal lines: 'Stands the church clock still at 10 to three, And is there honey still for tea?' Grantchester's most famous resident is the novelist Jeffrey Archer, who lives in the Old Vicarage.

The Fens

The fens were strange marshlands that stretched from Cambridge, north to The Wash, and beyond into Lincolnshire. They were home to people who led an isolated existence among a maze of waterways; fishing, hunting and farming scraps of arable land. In the 17th century, however, the Duke of Bedford and a group of speculators brought in Dutch engineer Cornelius Vermuyden to drain the fens and the flat, open plains with their rich, black soil were created. The region is the setting for Graham Swift's excellent novel *Waterland*.

As the world's weather pattern changes and the sea level rises, the fens are beginning to disappear underwater again. It's estimated that by the year 2030 up to 400,000 hectares could be lost.

There are teashops, some attractive pubs and the *Orchard Tea-garden*, where cream teas are served under apple trees. The best of the pubs is the *Red Lion*, near the river, which has a very pleasant garden.

Get here via the towpath or hire a punt.

American War Cemetery

Four miles west of Cambridge, at Madingley, is a very moving cemetery with neat rows of white-marble crosses stretching down the sloping site to commemorate the Americans killed in WWII while based in Britain.

Duxford Aircraft Museum

Right by the motorway, 9 miles south of Cambridge, this airfield played a significant role in WWII, especially during the Battle of Britain.

Today, it is home to Europe's biggest collection of historic aircraft, ranging from WWI biplanes to jets, including Concorde. Air shows are frequently held here and battlefield scenes are displayed in the land warfare hall. In 1998 the museum was awarded the Stirling Prize, Britain's most coveted architecture award.

Buses leave regularly for Duxford from Drummer St in Cambridge. Entry is £7/3.50.

Wimpole Hall

Until recently the home of Rudyard Kipling's daughter, Wimpole Hall is now a NT property. It is a large, gracious, 18th century mansion set in 140 hectares of beautiful parkland. Wimpole Home Farm, next to it, was established in 1794 as a model farm; today, it preserves and shows rare breeds.

Wimpole Hall (☎ 01223-207257, NT) is 8 miles south of Cambridge on the A603. Entry is £5.50, or £7.50 including the Home Farm; children half-price. There's no charge to just walk in the park. It's open from Easter to October, daily except Monday and Friday, from 10.30 am to 5 pm.

Whippet service No 175 passes this way from Cambridge. Alternatively, you could try walking the Wimpole Way, a 13 mile waymarked trail from Cambridge. A leaflet is available from the TIC.

ELY
- **pop 9000** ☎ **01353**

Ely (pronounced eelee) is an unspoilt market town with neat Georgian houses, a river port and one of the country's great cathedrals. It stands in the centre of the fens – swamps that extended for miles because the sea level was once higher than the land. Ely used to be an island and derived its name from the eels that frequented the surrounding waters.

Ely is an easy day trip from Cambridge. The TIC (☎ 662062) is in Oliver Cromwell's House. In summer, it's open daily from 10 am to 5.30 pm.

A joint ticket is available for £7 (£5 for students) for the main sights – Ely Cathedral, the stained glass museum, Ely Museum and Oliver Cromwell's House.

Ely Cathedral

The cathedral's origins stem from a remarkable queen of Northumbria called Etheldreda. She had been married twice, but was determined to pursue her vocation to become a nun. She founded an abbey in 673 and, for her good works, was canonised after her death. The abbey soon became a pilgrimage centre.

It was a Norman bishop, Simeon, who began the task of building the cathedral. It was completed in 1189 and remains a splendid example of the Norman Romanesque style. In 1322 – after the collapse of the central tower – the octagon and lantern, for which the cathedral is famous, were built. They have fan vaulting and intricate detail.

Other features of special interest include the Lady Chapel, the largest of its kind in England, which was added in the 14th century. The niches were rifled by iconoclasts, but the delicate tracery and carving remain intact. There's an amazing view from just inside the west door, right down the nave, through the choir stalls and on to the glorious east window – no clutter, just a sublime sense of space, light and spirituality.

Ely was the first cathedral in the country to make an admission charge (now £3.50) and, with funds gathered since 1986, it has managed to restore the octagon and lantern tower. There are free guided tours of the cathedral and also an octagon and roof tour. There's also a stained glass museum (£2.50) in the south triforium. The cathedral (☎ 667735) is open daily from 7 am to 7 pm (5 pm in winter). Sunday services are at 10.30 am and 3.45 pm.

Other Attractions

The area round the cathedral is historically and architecturally interesting. There's the Bishop's Palace, now a nursing home, and King's School, which supplies the cathedral with choristers.

Oliver Cromwell's House (☎ 662062) stands to the west, across St Mary's Green. Cromwell lived with his family in this attractive, half-timbered, 14th century house from 1636-46, when he was the tithe collector of Ely. The TIC, occupying the front room in the house, offers an audiovisual

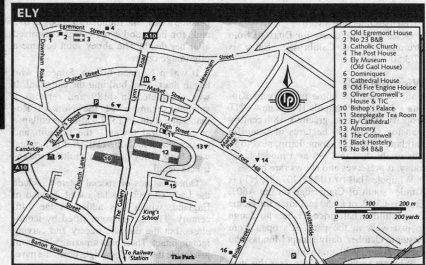

ELY

1 Old Egremont House
2 No 23 B&B
3 Catholic Church
4 The Post House
5 Ely Museum
   (Old Gaol House)
6 Dominiques
7 Cathedral House
8 Old Fire Engine House
9 Oliver Cromwell's
   House & TIC
10 Bishop's Palace
11 Steeplegate Tea Room
12 Ely Cathedral
13 Almonry
14 The Cromwell
15 Black Hostelry
16 No 84 B&B

presentation and an interesting tour of the rooms (£2.50).

The history of the town is told in **Ely Museum**, in the Old Gaol House. Entry is £1.80/1.25; it's closed on Monday.

It's worth walking down to the river by following the signs. There is an interesting **antiques centre** near the river. The **Old Maltings**, which stages exhibitions and has a café, is nearby. The **River Great Ouse** is a busy thoroughfare – swans and ducks compete with boats for river space. The towpath winds up and downstream: for a quiet walk, turn left; turn right for the pub and tea garden. If you continue along this path you'll see the fens stretching to the horizon.

Places to Stay

There are few budget options in Ely. There are several B&Bs on Egremont St. At No 31, **Old Egremont House** (☎ 663118) offers comfortable B&B for £28/44 for singles/doubles in an attractive house with a large garden. At **No 23** (☎ 664557), B&B costs £23/36. **The Post House** (☎ 667184), at 12A, is unmissable with the Union flag

raised outside. The charge is £25/36. On Broad St, **No 84** (☎ 666862) has just one double room for £16/28.

Cathedral House (☎ 662124, 17 St Mary's St) offers very comfortable B&B for £35/50. The **Black Hostelry** (☎ 662612), right by the cathedral on Firmary Lane, is a medieval house where you can stay in very comfortable surroundings. There are two doubles (no singles) at £49.

Places to Eat

Steeplegate Tea Room is right beside the cathedral. Light lunches and baked potatoes from £2.20 are available. Nearby is an attractive garden restaurant, the **Almonry** (☎ 666360), to the left of the Lady Chapel. There's a wide range of teas and coffees here.

Dominiques (☎ 665011, St Mary's St) serves cream teas, as well as lunches and set dinners (£18.25). It's closed on Monday and Tuesday. Totally non-smoking, it has good vegetarian choices.

You can get cheap, filling meals at **The Cromwell** (Fore Hill) where main courses are around £5.

Eels are a local delicacy served in several of the restaurants. A good place to try them is at Ely's best restaurant, the *Old Fire Engine House* (☎ 662582, *St Mary's St*). It seems more like the comfortable house of a friend than a restaurant, but the food is excellent. Main dishes are all about £12. It's open daily except Sunday.

Getting There & Away

Ely is on the A10, 15 miles from Cambridge. Following the Fen Rivers Way (map from TICs), it's a 17 mile walk.

There are frequent trains from Cambridge (15 minutes, £2.90) and buses from Cambridge's Drummer St bus station; they stop on Market St.

PETERBOROUGH
• **pop 113,500 ☎ 01733**

Peterborough may be called the capital city of shopping but it's the wonderful cathedral that is the only point of interest in this city. It's an easy day trip from Cambridge.

The cathedral precinct is an extension of the busy Cowgate, Bridge St and Queensgate. The TIC (☎ 452336), 45 Bridge St, is nearby and the bus and train stations are within walking distance.

Peterborough Cathedral

In Anglo-Saxon times, when the region was part of the kingdom of Mercia, King Peada, a recent convert to Christianity, founded a monastic church here in 655. This was sacked and gutted by the Danes in 870. In 1118, the Benedictine abbot John de Sais founded the present cathedral as the monastic church of the Benedictine abbey. It was finally consecrated in 1237.

As you enter the precinct from Cathedral Square you get a breathtaking view of the early 13th century western front, one of the most impressive of any cathedral in Britain.

On entering you're struck by the height of the nave and the lightness, which derives not only from the mellow Barnack stone (quarried close by and transported via the River Nene), but also from the clerestory windows. The nave, with its three storeys,

is an impressive example of Norman architecture. Its unique timber ceiling is one of the earliest of its kind in England (possibly in Europe) and its original painted decoration has been preserved.

The Gothic tower replaced the original Norman one, but had to be taken down and carefully reconstructed after it began to crack in the late 19th century.

In the north choir aisle is the tombstone of Henry VIII's first wife, the tragic Catherine of Aragon, buried here in 1536. Her divorce, engineered by the king, led to the Reformation in England. Directly opposite, in the south aisle, two standards mark what was the grave of Mary Queen of Scots. On the accession of her son, James, to the throne her body was moved to Westminster Abbey.

The eastern end of the cathedral, known as the New Building, was added in the 15th century. It has superb fan vaulting, probably the work of master mason John Wastell, who worked on King's College Chapel.

The cathedral (☎ 343342) is open from 9 am to 5.15 pm; admission is free (donations are encouraged).

Getting There & Away

Peterborough is 37 miles north of Cambridge. Stagecoach United Counties (☎ 01604-620077) and National Express run buses from Cambridge; some services require a change in Huntingdon. There are hourly trains from Cambridge (55 minutes, £8.60).

Lincolnshire

Sneering southerners who've never visited tend to think of Lincolnshire as flat and boring. The fact that it has few hills of any significance means that it's certainly easy cycling and walking country but it has other attractions that make a visit worthwhile. The unspoiled nature of some of the Lincolnshire towns – cobbled streets, solid stone-built houses with red-tiled roofs – attracts film companies as well as tourists. One of the finest Gothic buildings in Europe and the country, Lincoln Cathedral, has a wealth of beautiful parish churches, built on the proceeds of the flourishing wool trade.

The Lincolnshire Wolds, to the north and east of Lincoln, are comprised of low rolling hills and small market towns. In the south-east of the county are the Lincolnshire Fens, fertile agricultural land reclaimed from the sea.

GETTING AROUND
Regional transport is poor but the main routes are well enough served by train or bus.

The Viking Way is a 140 mile waymarked trail that runs from the Humber Bridge, through the Lincolnshire Wolds, to Oakham in Leicestershire.

Renting a bike in Lincoln, or bringing one with you, is an excellent idea. TICs stock sets of *Lincolnshire Cycle Trails*.

LINCOLN
• pop 81,500   ☎ 01522

Since it's not on a direct tourist route, many people bypass Lincoln, missing an interesting city with a compact medieval centre of narrow, winding streets and a magnificent 900-year-old cathedral (the third-largest in Britain). The suburbs, however, are unattractive and depressed but, perhaps because Lincoln escapes the hordes of visitors that places like York attract, the people are particularly friendly. A new university opened here recently and there's now a large student population.

History
For the last 2000 years, most of Britain's invaders have recognised the potential of this site and made their mark. Lincoln's hill was of immense strategic importance, giving views for miles across the surrounding plain. Communications were found to be excellent – below it is the River Witham, navigable to the sea.

The Romans established a garrison and a town they called Lindum. In 96 AD it was given the status of a colonia, or chartered town – Lindum Colonia, hence Lincoln. Gracious public buildings were constructed and

it became a popular place for old soldiers past their prime to spend their twilight years.

The Normans began work on the castle in 1068 and the cathedral in 1072. In the 12th century the wool trade developed and wealthy merchants established themselves. The city was famous for the cloth known as Lincoln green, said to have been worn by Robin Hood. Many of the wealthiest merchants were Jews, but following the murder of a nine-year-old boy in 1255 for which one of their number was accused, they were mercilessly persecuted and many were driven out.

During the Civil War the city passed from Royalist to Parliamentarian and back again, but it began to prosper as an agricultural centre in the 18th century. In the following century, after the arrival of the railway, Lincoln's engineering industry was established. Heavy machinery produced here included the world's first tank, which saw action in WWI.

Orientation & Information
The cathedral sits on top of the hill in the centre of the old part of the city, with the castle and most of the other things to see conveniently nearby. A 15 minute walk down from the cathedral lies the new town, and the bus and train stations. These two parts of Lincoln are connected by the appropriately named Steep Hill.

The TIC (☎ 529828) is in the old black-and-white building at 9 Castle Hill. It's open Monday to Thursday daily from 9 am to 5.30 pm, and until 5 pm on Friday and at weekends.

Guided walking tours (£2/1) from the TIC take place daily in summer at 11 am and 2 pm, and at weekends in June, September and October. There are also Guide Friday bus tours (☎ 01789-294466).

There's a Co-op supermarket on Silver St, and a laundrette on Rasen Lane.

Cathedral
This superb cathedral is the county's greatest attraction. Its three great towers dominate the city and can be seen from

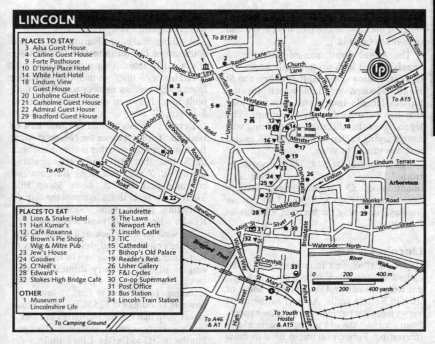

LINCOLN

PLACES TO STAY
3 Ailsa Guest House
4 Carline Guest House
9 Forte Posthouse
10 D'Isney Place Hotel
14 White Hart Hotel
18 Lindum View Guest House
20 Linholme Guest House
21 Carholme Guest House
22 Admiral Guest House
29 Bradford Guest House

PLACES TO EAT
8 Lion & Snake Hotel
11 Hari Kumar's
12 Café Roxanna
16 Brown's Pie Shop; Wig & Mitre Pub
23 Jew's House
24 Goodies
25 O'Neill's
28 Edward's
32 Stokes High Bridge Café

OTHER
1 Museum of Lincolnshire Life
2 Laundrette
5 The Lawn
6 Newport Arch
7 Lincoln Castle
13 TIC
15 Cathedral
17 Bishop's Old Palace
19 Reader's Rest
26 Usher Gallery
27 F&J Cycles
30 Co-op Supermarket
31 Post Office
33 Bus Station
34 Lincoln Train Station

miles around. The central tower stands 81m high, which makes it the second-highest in the country after Salisbury Cathedral. While this is impressive enough, imagine it twice as high, which it was until toppled by a storm in 1547.

Lincoln Cathedral was built on the orders of William the Conqueror and construction began in 1072. It took only 20 years to complete the original building, which was 99m long with two western towers, but in 1185 an earthquake caused severe damage. Only the west front of the old cathedral survived. Rebuilding began under Bishop Hugh of Avalon (St Hugh) and most of the current building dates from the late 12th to late 13th centuries, in the Early English style.

The entrance is below the famous mid-12th century frieze on the **west front**. Unfortunately, the frieze is currently hidden behind the scaffolding of a long-term

restoration project. Emerging into the **nave**, most people are surprised to find a substantial part of the cathedral empty, but this is actually how it would have looked back in 1250 when it was completed. Medieval cathedrals and churches, like mosques and Hindu temples today, did not have pews. This open area is now used for concerts and plays; services take place in St Hugh's choir. The stained glass in the nave is mostly Victorian, but the **Belgian marble font** dates back to the 11th century.

There are interesting stained-glass windows at each end of the transepts. The **Dean's Eye** contains glass that has been here since the 13th century; the glass in the **Bishop's Eye** dates from the 14th century. High above in the central tower, Great Tom is a 270kg bell that still sounds the hours.

St Hugh's Choir was the first section of the church to be rebuilt. The vaulting above is arranged at odd angles, but the canopied stalls of the choir are beautifully carved and over 600 years old.

The **Angel Choir**, named after the 28 angels carved high up the walls under the highest windows, was built as a shrine to St Hugh. Modern pilgrims search for the famous **Lincoln Imp**, a stonemason's joke that has become the city's emblem. The legend goes that this malevolent being was caught trying to chat up one of the 28 angels and was turned to stone.

The cathedral (☎ 544544) is open daily from 7.15 am to 6 pm (5 pm on Sunday); donation of £3 recommended. There's evensong daily at 5.15 pm (3.45 pm on Sunday), and sung Eucharist at 9.30 am on Sunday.

Lincoln Castle

Begun in 1068, just four years before the cathedral, the castle was built over the original Roman town and incorporates some of the old Roman walls. As well as the usual views from the battlements that one expects from a castle, the old prison is particularly interesting. Public executions used to draw crowds of up to 20,000 people, taking place in front of Cobb Hall, a horseshoe-shaped tower in the north-east corner that served as the city's prison for centuries. The red-brick building on the east side replaced it and was used until 1878.

In the same building as the chapel, Lincoln's copy of the Magna Carta is on display.

Lincoln Castle (☎ 511068) is open daily until 5.30 pm in summer, and until 4 pm in winter; £2/1.50.

Walking Tour

After looking round the cathedral and the castle, leave by the castle's west exit. Across the road is **The Lawn**, a former lunatic asylum that now houses a concert hall and several exhibition areas. The **Sir Joseph Banks Conservatory**, in this complex, is a tropical glasshouse containing descendants of some of the plants brought back by this Lincoln explorer who accompanied Captain Cook to Australia.

A short walk up Burton Rd is the **Museum of Lincolnshire Life** (☎ 528448). It's a fairly interesting museum of local social history – displays include everything from an Edwardian nursery to a WWI tank built here. It's open daily from 10 am to 5.30 pm; £2/ 60p.

Return to Westgate and continue east to Bailgate. Turn left to see the **Newport Arch**. Built by the Romans, this is the oldest arch in Britain that still has traffic passing through it. Walk back along Bailgate and continue past the TIC down **Steep Hill**. There are several shops to tempt the tourist, including second-hand bookshops (the Reader's Rest is good) and teashops.

As well as the black-and-white Tudor buildings on Steep Hill, **Jew's House** is of particular interest, being one of the best examples of 12th century domestic architecture in Britain. It's now an upmarket restaurant (see Places to Eat). A few doors down is **Goodies** (☎ 525307), a traditional sweet shop that has 300 varieties in stock – bull's eyes, pear drops, sherbet lemons and humbugs. (Goodies is Lincs dialect for sweets/candy).

Located one block east of Jew's House is **Usher Gallery**, the city's art gallery. It's open daily (afternoon only on Sunday); £2/50p.

Places to Stay

Camping *Hartsholme Country Park* (☎ 686264, *Skellingthorpe Rd*) is about 2 miles south-west of the train station. They charge £4.20 for a tent and two people.

Hostel *Lincoln Youth Hostel* (☎ 522076, *77 South Park Ave*) provides good budget accommodation at £8.80/5.95 for adults/ juniors. It's open daily from February through October, and on Friday and Saturday in November and December.

B&Bs & Hotels On Yarborough Rd there's *Ailsa Guest House* (☎ 534961), at No 161, with B&B at £15/28 for a single/double.

More upmarket is *Carline* (☎ *530422, 1 Carline Rd*). Most of the rooms have a bath and the cost is from £30/40. It's vehemently non-smoking.

There's a good group of B&Bs on West Parade, west of the modern centre of Lincoln. *Linholme Guest House* (☎ *522930*), at No 116, is small with two twins and a double at £18 per person. It's a pleasant place to stay and most rooms have a bathroom.

Parallel to and just south of West Parade is Carholme Rd, with numerous B&Bs. *Carholme Guest House* (☎ *531059*), at No 175, charges £14 or £15 per person. *Admiral Guest House* (☎ *544467*), just off Carholme Rd on Nelson St, charges £17.50 per person.

Lindum View Guest House (☎ *5488943 Upper Lindum St*) is conveniently located east of the cathedral and has rooms, most with a bathroom, at £25/40. South, at 67 Monks Rd, *Bradford Guest House* (☎ *523947*) is good value at £16/30. Some rooms have showers.

The *D'Isney Place Hotel* (☎ *538881, Eastgate*) is small and comfortable, with rooms for £57/72 including breakfast in bed. There's a *Forte Posthouse* (☎ *520341*) right by the cathedral on Eastgate, with rooms for £75 (£59 at weekends).

Lincoln's top hotel is the *White Hart* (☎ *526222*), on Bailgate and also by the cathedral. It's a luxurious place with prices to match – doubles for £90.

Places to Eat

As one might expect in a city of this size, there's a reasonable range of places to eat, some of them particularly good value. There's a good *bakery* on the corner of Westgate and Bailgate.

The *Lion & Snake Hotel* (☎ *523770*) was founded in 1640, which makes it Lincoln's oldest pub. Situated on the Bailgate, it's probably better known for its real ale and good-value, home-made bar food.

Hari Kumar's (☎ *537000, 80 Bailgate*) is a stylish restaurant serving Indian and English food. Saffron breast of chicken is £6.50. Across the road is *Café Roxanna*

(☎ *546464*) where you can choose between a set meal at £6.95 or an international 'game fayre platter' of wild boar, alligator, pheasant, pigeon, kangaroo and ostrich for a mere £69.50 (24 hours notice required).

Brown's Pie Shop (☎ *527330, 33 Steep Hill*) is close to the cathedral and popular with tourists. It's nonetheless worth eating here since pies are a Lincolnshire speciality. Rabbit pie with Dorset scrumpy costs £8.50 but there are cheaper options. The *Wig & Mitre* (☎ *535190, 29 Steep Hill*) is near Brown's Pie Shop. It's a pub with a restaurant, open daily.

A branch of *O'Neill's* dominates the north end of the High St, but a cooler place to hang out is *Edward's*, one block south on High St. At this stylish bar-brasserie you can get everything from a coffee or a beer to a full meal.

Stokes High Bridge Café (☎ *513825, 207 High St*) is popular with tourists since it's in a 16th century timbered building right on the bridge over the River Witham. You can get lunches and teas. It's open Monday to Saturday from 9 am to 5 pm.

Lincoln's top restaurant is the *Jew's House* (☎ *524851, Steep Hill*), occupying a 12th century building that's an attraction in its own right. A three-course set dinner costs £25; set lunches are £12.95.

Getting There & Away

See the fares tables in the Getting Around chapter. Lincoln is 132 miles from London, 85 from Cambridge and 75 from York.

Bus National Express (☎ 0990-808080) operates a daily direct service between Lincoln and London (five hours), via Stamford. There are also direct services to Birmingham and Glasgow. For Cambridge you must change at Peterborough.

The main local bus company is Lincolnshire Roadcar (☎ 532424). It runs hourly buses between Lincoln and Grantham (1¼ hours, £2.35), Monday to Saturday. Only National Express serves Stamford – and you need to book in advance. From Lincoln to

Boston there are buses only on Wednesday and Saturday, run by Appleby's (☎ 533422).

Train There's no direct rail service between Lincoln and London; you must change at Newark or Peterborough on the main London to Edinburgh line. You don't, however, usually have to wait long for a connection. London to Newark takes 1¼ hours, Newark to Lincoln takes half an hour, and there are frequent departures. For York or Edinburgh, a further change is usually necessary at Doncaster. For Cambridge change at Peterborough.

Getting Around
Bus The city bus service is efficient. From the bus and train stations, bus No 51 runs past the youth hostel and Nos 7 and 8 link the cathedral area with the lower town. Fares are around 50p.

Bicycle You can rent everything from a three-speed to a mountain bike from F&J Cycles (☎ 545311), 41 Hungate, but 21 speeds are hardly an essential requirement for cycling in this flat county. Rent a three-speed from £6 per day up to £15 per week.

GRANTHAM
• pop 31,000   ☎ 01476
This pleasant, red-brick town has an interesting parish church, St Wulfram's, with a 85m-high spire, the sixth-highest in England. It dates from the late 13th century. Sir Isaac Newton lived in Grantham, and there's a monument to him in front of the Guildhall. The town's museum, St Peter's Hill, has sections devoted both to him and to Margaret Thatcher who was born in Grantham. Her father's famous corner shop was at 2 North Parade.

Three miles north-east of Grantham on the A607 is Belton House (☎ 566116, NT), one of the finest examples of Restoration country house architecture. Built in 1688 for Sir John Brownlow, the house is known for its ornate plasterwork ceilings and wood carvings attributed to Grinling Gibbons. Set in a 400 hectare park, it's open April to

October, Wednesday to Sunday from 1 to 5.30 pm; £5/2.50. Bus Nos 601 and 609 pass this way.

The TIC (☎ 566444) is by the Guildhall on Avenue Rd. It's open Monday to Saturday from 9.30 am to 5 pm.

Places to Stay & Eat
Grantham was formerly a main stop on the stagecoach route north from London and many pubs and inns still offer cheap accommodation. Try the *Nag's Head* (☎ 563157, Wharf Rd) or the *Black Dog* (☎ 66041, Watergate). Both do B&B from around £16 per person.

The *Beehive* (☎ 404554, Castlegate) is best known for its pub sign – a real beehive full of live bees! The bees have been here since 1830, which makes them one of the oldest populations of bees in the world. Good, cheap lunches are available, and the bees stay away from the customers.

Getting There & Away
Grantham is 25 miles south of Lincoln. Lincolnshire Roadcar runs buses every hour between these two towns, Monday to Saturday. Travelling by train you'll need to change at Newark.

STAMFORD
• pop 16,000   ☎ 01780
This beautiful town of stone buildings and cobbled streets was made a conservation area in 1967 and is one of the finest stone towns in the country. The TIC (☎ 755611) is in the arts centre on St Mary's St.

It's best just to simply wander round the town's winding streets of medieval and Georgian houses, but Stamford Museum (☎ 766317), Broad St, is certainly worth visiting (free). As well as displays charting the history of the town, there's a model of local heavyweight Daniel Lambert, who tipped the scales at 333kg before his death in 1809. It's open daily (afternoon only on Sunday).

Places to Stay & Eat
There's B&B from around £18 per person at *St Peter's Rectory* (☎ 753999, 8 St

Peter's Hill) and at *Stukely House* (☎ *757939, 9 Barn Hill)* for around £15 to £20 per person.

There are a number of historic pubs that also offer accommodation. The *Bull & Swan* (☎ *763558, High St)* does good meals and has rooms with a bathroom for £35/45 for singles/doubles. Across the street, the *George* (☎ *755171)* is the top place to stay. It's a wonderful old coaching inn, parts of the building dating back a thousand years. There's excellent upmarket pub fare, a cobbled courtyard and luxurious rooms for £78/119.

Getting There & Away

Stamford is 46 miles from Lincoln and 21 miles south of Grantham.

National Express serves Stamford from London (2½ hours) and Lincoln (1¾ hours). Lincolnshire Roadcar (☎ 01522-532424) operates buses between Stamford and Grantham (1½ hours, £2.25), Monday to Saturday.

Stamford is on the main rail line between London, York and Edinburgh; services are frequent.

AROUND STAMFORD
Burghley House

Just one mile outside Stamford, this immensely grand Tudor mansion is the home of the Cecil family. It was built between 1565 and 1587 by William Cecil, Queen Elizabeth's adviser.

It's an impressive place with 18 magnificent state rooms. The Heaven Room was painted by Antonio Verrio in the 17th century and features floor-to-ceiling gods and goddesses disporting among the columns. There are over 300 paintings, including works by Gainsborough and Brueghel; state bedchambers, including the four-poster Queen Victoria slept in; and cavernous Tudor kitchens.

The house (☎ 01780-52451) is open from April to early October, daily from 11 am to 4.30 pm. Entry is £5.85 for an adult and there's no additional charge for one accompanying child. It's a pleasant 15 minute

walk through the park from Stamford train station. The Burghley Horse Trials, which take place here over three days in early September, are of international significance.

BOSTON
• pop 34,000   ☎ 01205

A major port in the Middle Ages, Boston lies near the mouth of the River Witham, on the bay known as The Wash. It was from Boston that the Pilgrim Fathers made their first break for the freedom of the New World in 1607. They were imprisoned in the **Guildhall**, where the cells that held them are now a tourist attraction.

Visible for miles around, the 88m-high tower of **St Botolph's Church** is known as the Boston Stump. You can climb the 365 steps for a wonderful view of the fens, and it's open Monday to Saturday from 9 am to 4.30 pm, and also on Sunday between services.

The TIC (☎ 356656) is under the Assembly Rooms on Market Place.

Places to Stay & Eat

A five minute walk from the marketplace, *Park Lea* (☎ *35630985, 85 Norfolk St)* has singles/doubles from £18/30, or £20/32 with a bath. The *White Hart* (☎ *364877, Bridge Foot)* does good pub food and also has some rooms with bathroom at £42.50/55.

Getting There & Away

From Lincoln it's easier to get to Boston by train than by bus, but even that involves a change at Sleaford.

SKEGNESS
• pop 16,000   ☎ 01754

'Skeggy' is a classic English seaside resort, the Blackpool of the east coast. There are rows of jolly B&Bs, bingo every evening and donkeys on the beach. Danny La Rue and Bobby Davro appear at the Embassy Centre and the whole place twinkles with 25,000 light bulbs every night from July to October during the Skegness Illuminations. It's the kind of place the English middle and upper classes wouldn't be seen dead in.

EASTERN ENGLAND

The TIC (☎ 01754-764821), in the Embassy Centre on Grand Parade, has all the information on B&Bs. They can be cheap, from £12 per person. There are direct rail and bus connections to Boston and Lincoln.

North-Western England

North Western England is a mixture of densely populated urban centres and wild remote countryside, with the jam-packed, overdeveloped conurbation that takes in Manchester and Liverpool sandwiched between the relatively sparsely populated, rural county of Cumbria to the north and pretty, prosperous Cheshire to the south.

First-time visitors may not want to linger in the cities, even though both Manchester and Liverpool have pockets of great vitality and interesting old buildings and museums. The walled city of Chester is often used as a staging post for getting from the southern Midlands to the Lake District and Scotland, or to North Wales.

The Lake District, on the other hand, is high on many people's lists of priorities, especially if they're enthusiastic outdoor types. Be warned, though, that locals are just as keen to get out and about, and the lakes can be hideously congested over peak holiday periods.

If you want to experience the tacky taste that is a British seaside resort, big, brash Blackpool fits the bill perfectly. Afterwards you can stop off in Lancaster, a manageably small town with an outsize castle and not too much tourist traffic.

Cheshire

You can scan the stars with the gigantic radio telescope at Jodrell Bank, investigate the canals at the wonderful waterways museum at Ellesmere Port, or return your Roller to its birthplace at Crewe, but when it comes right down to it Cheshire is all about Chester.

CHESTER
• pop 80,000 ☎ 01244

Despite steady streams of tourists Chester remains a beautiful town, ringed by an almost continuous red sandstone wall that dates back to the Roman times. However,

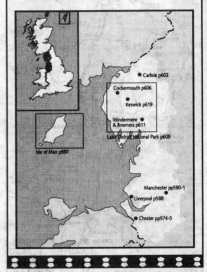

HIGHLIGHTS

- Sampling Manchester's nightlife
- Seeing the industrial past brought back to life at Quarry Bank Mill
- Taking Liverpool's ferry across the Mersey
- Walking Chester's city walls
- Visiting Grasmere out of season
- Hiking in the more remote parts of the Lake District

Carlisle p603
Cockermouth p606
Keswick p619
Windermere & Bowness p611
Lake District National Park p609
Isle of Man p597
Manchester pp580-1
Liverpool p588
Chester pp574-5

appearances can be deceptive – many of the 'medieval'-looking buildings in the centre are actually Victorian.

History
Roman Chester was the fortress city of Deva, a bulwark against the fierce Welsh tribes. It wasn't completely abandoned when the Romans withdrew in the 5th

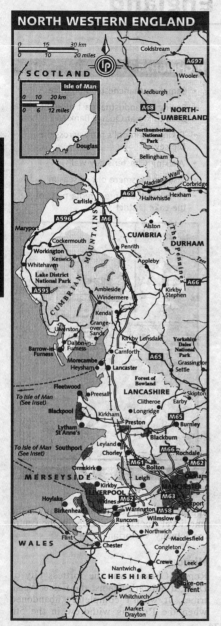

NORTH WESTERN ENGLAND

century, but the Welsh border is only a stone's throw west of Chester and the Welsh remained a threat long after the Romans had gone. It was only in the 14th century that the danger subsided and the regulations which banned the Welsh from the town after dark and stipulated that they couldn't bear arms, hold meetings or enter pubs were withdrawn.

Medieval Chester became the largest port in the north-west but in the Civil War the city took the Royalist side and was besieged for 18 months (1645-46) by Cromwell's forces. It wasn't until the next century that the walls were repaired and took on a new role as a tourist attraction. The first guidebook to Chester was published in 1781!

Orientation

Nestling in a bow formed by the River Dee, the walled centre is now surrounded by suburbs. Most places of interest are inside the walls where the Roman street pattern is relatively intact. From the High Cross (the stone pillar which marks the town centre), four roads fan out to the four principal gates. A nasty ring road, which cuts through the city walls, also encircles the centre.

Information

The TIC (☎ 402111) is in the town hall opposite the cathedral. From May to October it's open Monday to Saturday from 9 am to 7.30 pm, and Sunday from 10 am to 4 pm. Otherwise it's open Monday to Saturday, from 9 am to 5.30 pm. Chester visitors centre (☎ 351609) in Vicars Lane keeps slightly shorter hours. There's also a small TIC at the train station (☎ 322220).

City walks depart daily from Chester visitors centre at 10.30 am and from the town hall at 10.45 am. They cost £3/2.30. From May to October Ghosthunter Trails take place on Thursday, Friday and Saturday at 7.30 pm.

Disabled visitors should head for Dial House (☎ 345655) in Hamilton Place which offers advice and a café. It's open Monday to Friday from 10 am to 4 pm (closed Wednesday afternoon).

A Tour of the City Walls

Chester's walls were originally built around 70 AD to protect the Roman fort of Deva. Between 90 and 120 AD they were rebuilt in stone by the Roman 20th Legion. Over the following centuries they were often altered but their present position was established around 1200. After the Civil War the walls were rebuilt as a fashionable promenade.

Nowadays the 2 mile circuit of the walls makes an excellent introduction to Chester and should take 1½ to two hours. This suggested circuit proceeds clockwise from **Eastgate** at the prominent **Eastgate Clock**, built for Queen Victoria's Diamond Jubilee in 1897.

The **Thimbleby Tower**, also known as the Wolf Tower, was destroyed during the Civil War and never rebuilt. From here you can look down on the foundations of the southeast angle tower of the old Roman fort. Just beyond is **Newgate**, added in 1938 but in medieval style. From here the original Roman fortress walls ran westward, roughly following the course of the modern ring road to **St Martin's Gate**. From Newgate the remains of part of the **Roman Amphitheatre** can be seen.

Outside the walls, the **Roman Gardens** contain a collection of Roman stonework brought here from excavations around Chester. Descend the **wishing steps** at the corner of the wall. They were added in 1785 and local legend claims that your wish will come true if you can run up and down the steps while holding your breath.

Continue past the **Riverside Recorder Hotel** to the **Bridgegate** beside the **Old Dee Bridge**. This oft rebuilt bridge dates from 1387, although parts of it are centuries newer. Just inside the gate is the 1664 **Bear & Billet** pub, once a tollgate into the city.

Beyond Bridgegate the walls disappear for a short stretch. Inside the walls, **Agricola's Tower** is virtually all that remains of the medieval castle. Turn the corner beside the castle ruins.

Cross Grosvenor Rd to where the wall runs alongside the **Roodee**, Chester's ancient horse racing track built on grassland left when the river changed course. The Roodee hosts the country's oldest horse race which, uniquely, is run counter-clockwise. The city wall stands atop a stretch of **Roman Harbour Wall**. Cross **Watergate** and look left to the **Watergate Inn,** where the river once passed.

Continue to the north-west corner, where a short peninsula of wall leads out to the **Water Tower**. **Bonewaldesthorne's Tower**, actually on the corner, once guarded the river at this point but when it shifted course in the 14th century the extension to Water Tower had to be built. In subsequent centuries the river has moved even farther west leaving both towers high and dry.

A little farther on, below the walls, you can see the **Northgate Locks**, a short but steep series of locks built in 1779 by Thomas Telford, the pioneering canal engineer. Continue past **Morgan's Mount** where a Captain Morgan defended the city during the Civil War. Across the canal is the **Blue Coat Hospital (School)**, now closed.

From **Northgate** the walls tower above the **Shropshire Union Canal** which runs in what was once a moat-like ditch constructed by the Romans outside the walls. From **King Charles' Tower** at the corner, Charles I looked out to see his defeated army straggling back from battle in 1645.

Cross the 1275 **Kaleyards Gate** through which monks would go to work in their vegetable gardens outside the walls; it's still ceremonially locked every night at 9 pm. Traces of the original Roman wall are still visible from outside the walls just south of Kaleyards Gate. Continue past **Chester Cathedral** and the **Bell Tower** and you'll be back at the Eastgate Clock.

Chester Cathedral

A Saxon church dedicated to St Werburgh was built here in the 10th century but in 1092 it became a Benedictine abbey and a Norman church replaced the earlier construction. The abbey was closed in 1540 with Henry VIII's dissolution of the monasteries and a year later the building became a cathedral. The 12th century cloister and its

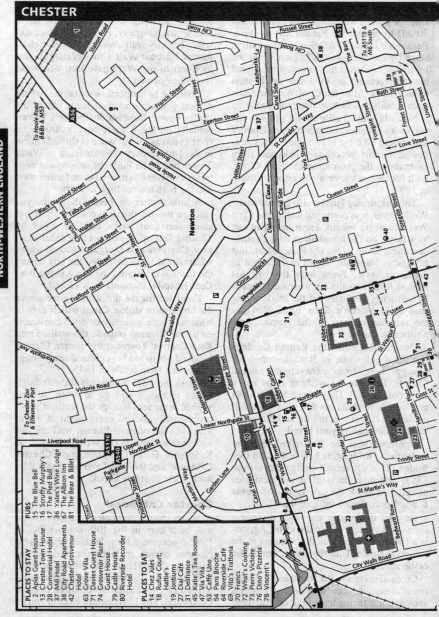

CHESTER

PLACES TO STAY
2 Aplas Guest House
13 Chester Town House
28 Commercial Hotel
37 Mill Hotel
38 City Road Apartments
42 Chester Grosvenor Hotel
63 Grove Villa
71 Davies Guest House
74 Grosvenor Place Guest House
79 Castle House
80 Riverside Recorder Hotel

PUBS
15 The Blue Bell
16 Scruffy Murphy's
17 The Pied Bull
36 Yates's Wine Lodge
67 The Albion Inn
81 The Bear & Billet

PLACES TO EAT
14 Chez Jules
18 Rufus Court;
   Hattie's
19 Jontiums
27 Dial Café
31 Délifrance
45 Katie's Tea Rooms
47 Via Vita
53 Caffè Uno
54 Paris Brioche
64 Riverside Café
69 Vito's Trattoria
70 Francs
72 What's Cooking
73 Pierre Victoire
76 Dino's Pizzeria
78 Vincent's

CHESTER

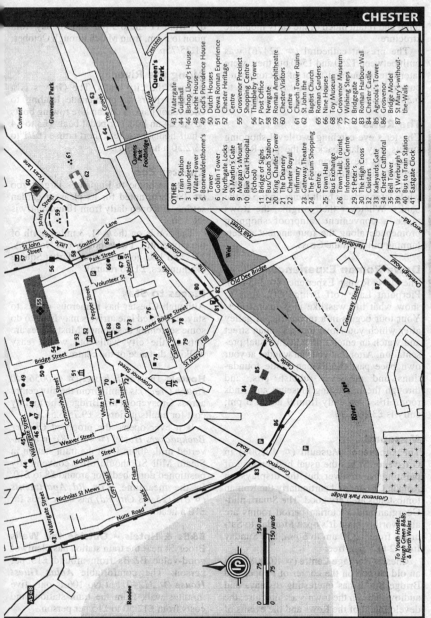

OTHER
1 Train Station
3 Laundrette
4 Water Tower
5 Bonewaldesthorne's Tower
6 Goblin Tower
7 Northgate Locks
8 St Martin's Gate
9 Morgan's Mount
10 Blue Coat Hospital (School)
11 Bridge of Sighs
12 Bus/Coach Station
20 King Charles' Tower
21 The Deanery
22 Chester Royal Infirmary
23 Gateway Theatre
24 The Forum Shopping Centre
25 Town Hall
26 Town Hall; Tourist Information Centre
29 St Peter's
30 The High Cross
32 Cloisters
33 Kaleyards Gate
34 Chester Cathedral
35 Bell Tower
39 St Werburgh's
40 Bus to Train Station
41 Eastgate Clock

43 Watergate
44 Guildhall
46 Bishop Lloyd's House
48 Leche House
49 God's Providence House
50 Dutch Houses
51 Dewa Roman Experience
52 Chester Heritage Centre
55 Grosvenor Precinct Shopping Centre
56 Thimbleby Tower
57 Post Office
58 Newgate
59 Roman Amphitheatre
60 Chester Visitors Centre
61 Church Tower Ruins
62 St John the Baptist Church
65 Roman Gardens
68 Toy Museum
75 Grosvenor Museum
77 Wishing Steps
82 Bridgegate
83 Roman Harbour Wall
84 Chester Castle
85 Agricola's Tower
86 Grosvenor Bridge Model
87 St Mary's-without-the-Walls

surrounding buildings are essentially unaltered and retain much of the early monastic structure.

The present cathedral (☎ 32476) was built between 1250 and 1540 but there were later alterations and a lot of Victorian reconstruction. It's open daily from 7 am to 6.30 pm. Visitors are asked to donate £2.

The Rows

Chester's eye-catching two-level shopping streets may date back to the post-Roman period. As the Roman walls slowly crumbled into rubble, medieval traders may have built their shops against the rubble banks, while later arrivals built theirs on top of the banks. Whatever their origins, the Rows make a convenient rainproof shopping promenade along the four ancient streets fanning out from the Cross.

Dewa Roman Experience

The Dewa Roman Experience (☎ 343407), Pierpoint Lane (off Bridge St), aims to show what life was like in Roman times. Your tour begins in a reconstructed galley after which you move into a Roman street and watch an entertaining audiovisual presentation. After that you can wander at your own pace past the Roman castle foundations and medieval rubbish pits, and through the interesting museum and finds room. It's open daily from 9 am to 5 pm; entry is £3.80/1.90.

Museums

The **Grosvenor Museum** (☎ 402008) in Grosvenor St has the usual hodgepodge of paintings and silver but the displays on Roman Chester and particularly the Roman tombstones are very good. The Stuart, mid-Georgian and Victorian period rooms are also worth seeing. It's open Monday to Saturday from 10.30 am to 5 pm, and Sunday from 2 to 5 pm; free.

Chester Heritage Centre (☎ 402008) is in an old church on the corner of Pepper and Bridge Sts. It has interesting displays and audiovisuals on the town's architecture, the development of the Rows and the events of

the Civil War. It's open Monday to Saturday from 11 am to 5 pm, and Sunday from noon to 5 pm, from March through October; £1.25/75p.

Along the River

Beyond the city walls, The Groves is a popular riverside promenade leading to Grosvenor Park. You can hire rowing boats (£3 to £4 an hour) or pedal boats (£3 to £4 a half-hour), or take a short cruise (£2/1 to £3/2.50 a half-hour).

Chester Zoo

Chester is home to England's largest zoo (☎ 380280), noted for its pleasant garden setting. It's open daily from 10 am; entry is £8/5.50.

The zoo is on the A41, 3 miles north of the city centre. Twice-hourly bus Nos 40A, 11C and 12C go there from Market Square (15 minutes, £1.70 return).

Places to Stay

Although Chester has numerous places to stay, unbooked late arrivals may have to do some searching in summer. Most places are outside the city walls but within easy walking distance of the centre.

Hostels The *youth hostel* (☎ 680056, 40 Hough Green) is a mile from the city centre across Grosvenor Park Bridge. The nightly cost for adults/juniors is £9.75/6.55.

If it ever opens, the proposed *Chester Backpackers Hostel* (☎ 400118), in a converted mill, 400m from the train station in Steam Mill St, should offer conveniently positioned dorm beds for around £8 to £10. In the meantime, *City Rd Apartments* (☎ 813125, 18 City Rd) has basic beds for £10 a head.

B&Bs & Hotels – Outside the Walls

Brook St near the train station has plenty of good-value B&Bs from around £15 per person. The comfortable *Aplas Guest House* (☎ 312401) at No 106 is only five minutes walk from the train station, and costs from £12.50 to £15 per person.

orn Exchange, Leeds

Vhitby harbour

Cathedral, Liverpool

Yorkshire sheep

ictoria Shopping Arcade, Leeds

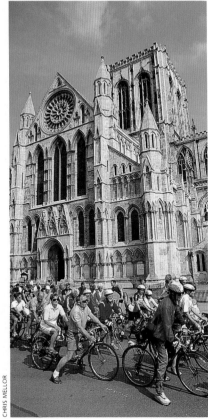
The York Rally outside York Minister, York

Warehouses on the River Ouse, York

Building in the VIctoria quarter, Leeds

River Wharfe at Boston Spa, Yorkshire

Hoole Rd, the road to or from the M53/M56 and beyond the railway lines, is lined with low to medium-price B&Bs within walking distance of the centre. Charging around £15 a head are the *Bawn Park Hotel* (☎ 324971) at No 10, *Glen-Garth Guest House* (☎ 310260) at No 59, the *Ba Ba Guest House* (☎ 315047) at No 65 and *Pear Tree* (☎ 323260) at No 69. The attractive, small *Glann Hotel* (☎ 344800, 2 Stone Place) is off the Hoole Rd and charges from £22 per person.

Grove Villa (☎ 349713, 18 The Groves), right on the River Dee, has rooms with bathroom from £16 to £18 per person. The larger *Mill Hotel* (☎ 350035, Milton St), right beside the canal, boasts a health club and canal cruises as well as singles/doubles from £45/50.

B&Bs & Hotels – Inside the Walls
Grosvenor Place Guest House (☎ 324455) is centrally situated at 24 Grosvenor Place and has rooms at £20/25 or £30/40 with bathroom. Nearby is *Castle House* (☎ 350354) at 23 Castle St. The building dates to the 16th century and comfortable rooms (some with bathroom) cost from £22 per person.

Davies Guest House (☎ 340452, 22 Cuppin St) is a basic but centrally located B&B with rooms from £15. The *Commercial Hotel* (☎ 320749), hidden away in St Peter's Church Yard, offers rooms from £20 per person.

The small *Riverside Recorder Hotel* (☎ 326580, 22 City Walls) is just off Lower Bridge St, near Bridgegate. It has a car park and costs from £28 per person for rooms with a bathroom. The *Chester Town House* (☎ 350021), at No 23 in quiet, pleasantly old-world King St, dates from 1680. Rooms with a bathroom cost £35/48. At *Hotel Romano* (☎ 320841), in lower Bridge St above Dino's pizzeria, rooms cost £40/60.

If you're pushing the boat out, the *Chester Grosvenor Hotel* (☎ 324024) has an unmatchable location in Eastgate. Ask about weekend break deals which bring the prices down to about £80 a head.

Places to Eat
Chester has the usual selection of international fast-food outlets, plus a few centrally located fish and chip places, particularly in Lower Bridge St. *Paris Brioche* and *Delifrance* both turn out good sandwiches and baguettes to eat in or take away.

The cathedral *refectory* serves soup and a sandwich for £3.45 but the best place for a light lunch is *Katie's Tea Rooms* (☎ 400322), spread over three floors of an historic building in Watergate St; something like a salmon rosti costs £5.75. Cheaper is *Hattie's*, a teashop in Rufus Court, near the Northgate. The *Riverside Café* has a pleasant setting by the Queens Park Footbridge. The *Dial Café* (☎ 345655, Hamilton Place) offers disabled access in a town that isn't easy for wheelchair users.

The deservedly popular *Francs* (☎ 317952, 14 Cuppin St) turns out traditional French food every day. Nearby at 14-16 Grosvenor St on the corner of Cuppin St, *What's Cooking* (☎ 346512) offers burgers and other American-style food. *Vito's Trattoria* (☎ 317330, 25 Lower Bridge St) is a standard pizza and pasta specialist. A little farther down at No 51, *Dino's Pizzeria* (☎ 325091) has similar fare while *Vincent's* (☎ 310854) at No 58-60 has Caribbean cuisine – blue marlin for £11.75.

In Rufus Court, the *Abbey Green Restaurant* (☎ 313251) and *Garden House* (☎ 320004) both serve English food; the Garden House has some vegetarian choices. At 2 Abbey Green, *Jontiens* (☎ 313522) serves Thai meals.

Caffé Uno (☎ 400851) is at 29 Bridge St and there's also branch of *Chez Jules* (☎ 400014) at 71 Northgate St.

Pubs serving good, basic food at reasonable prices include *Scruffy Murphy's* and *The Pied Bull* in Northgate St. Also in Northgate St is *The Blue Bell* (☎ 317758) where a two-course meal in the restaurant costs £13.50. The fine Edwardian *Albion Inn* serves reliable English food without chips or fry-ups.

Entertainment

Pubs Pubs with live music include *Yates's Wine Lodge* on Frodsham St which attracts a noisy, young crowd at night, *Scruffy Murphy's* (☎ 321750) in Northgate St, and *Telford's Warehouse* (☎ 390090) at Tower Wharf.

Theatre & Music *Alexander's Jazz Theatre* (☎ 340005, *Rufus Court*) is a combination of wine bar, coffee bar and tapas bar. Entry is sometimes free before 10 pm. Otherwise it costs £2 to £7.50 depending on who's performing.

The *Gateway Theatre* (☎ 340392) is at Hamilton Place beside the Forum Shopping Centre.

Getting There & Away

Chester is 188 miles from London, 85 from Birmingham, 40 from Manchester and 18 from Liverpool. It has excellent transport connections, especially with North Wales.

Bus Just north of the city walls inside the ring road is the National Express (☎ 0990-808080) bus station. It has numerous services: one a day to Glasgow (six hours, £20), three a day to Manchester (1¼ hours, £3.85) and Bristol (four hours, £16); two a day to Llandudno (1¾ hours, £4.80); four a day to Liverpool (one hour, £3.05); and five a day to Birmingham (2½ hours, £7.50) and London (5½ hours, £11.50).

For information on local bus services, ring Cheshire Bus Line (☎ 602666). Local buses leave from Market Square behind the town hall. On Sunday and bank holidays a Sunday Adventurer ticket gives you unlimited travel in Cheshire for £3/2.

Train The train station is a 15 minute walk from the city centre via City Rd or Brook St. City-Rail Link buses are free to people with rail tickets. Otherwise they cost 40p.

There are numerous trains to Shrewsbury (one hour, £4.80); Manchester (one hour, £7.20) and Liverpool (£2.90); Holyhead (2¼ hours, £13.50) via the North Wales

coast, for Ireland; and London Euston (three hours, £38.50).

Getting Around

Much of the city centre is closed to traffic from 10.30 am to 4.30 pm so a car is likely to be a handicap. Anyway, the walled city is easy to walk around and most places of interest are close to the wall walk.

City buses depart from the town hall bus exchange. Call Chester City Transport (☎ 347452) for details. Guide Friday (☎ 347457) offers open-top bus tours of the city; an all-day ticket costs £5.50/1.50; £7/2.50 if you want a half-hour river cruise included.

Davies Cycles (☎ 319204), 6-12 Cuppin St, has mountain bikes for hire at £10 per day.

AROUND CHESTER
Ellesmere Port

The superb Boat Museum (☎ 0151-355 5017) 8 miles north of Chester on the Shropshire Union Canal has a large collection of canal boats as well as indoor exhibits. It's open April to October, daily from 10 am to 5 pm; Saturday to Wednesday from 11 am to 4 pm in winter. Admission costs £4.70/3.

Bus Nos X3, 11C and 12C go there from Chester (40 minutes) or it's a 10 minute walk from Ellesmere Port train station.

Manchester

• pop 460,000   ☎ 0161

Probably best known for its football team, the modern city that produced Oasis, Take That and Simply Red is also a monument to England's industrial history. In the 19th century, Friedrich Engels (co-author of the *Communist Manifesto*) used Manchester to illustrate the evils of capitalism. Someone making a similar study today might uncover disconcerting echoes behind the sometimes glitzy façade.

The 1990s have seen a gradual transformation of parts of the city centre, a process given added impetus by the IRA bomb blast of 1996 that devastated much of the area round the Arndale Shopping Centre. For the time being empty warehouses and factories rub shoulders with stunning Victorian Gothic buildings, rusting train tracks and motorway overpasses with flashy bars and nightclubs – but things are improving as warehouses are given new life as upmarket apartment blocks.

You're unlikely to fall in love with Manchester at first sight, especially if one of your first encounters is with the mess that is Piccadilly Gardens. The longer you stay, the greater the likelihood that you'll find yourself succumbing to the city's hidden charms.

History

Manchester has been important since Roman times. In the 14th century, Flemish weavers (who worked primarily in wool and linen) settled the area. When cotton from the American colonies became available in the 18th century the city, with its weaving tradition, accessible supplies of coal and water and canal links to surrounding towns, became the hub of the new industry and, in effect, of the Industrial Revolution.

As the city grew, demands increased for reform of the parliamentary system and for free trade; the artificial protection of corn prices by the Corn Law tariffs was particularly unpopular. In 1819, 60,000 people assembled in St Peter's Field, a site now occupied by the Free Trade Hall. The authorities ordered mounted troops to arrest the speakers. In the ensuing melee 11 people were killed and 400 injured. The affair came to be known as Peterloo – the poor man's Waterloo – and it provided a rallying point in the battle for reform. Two years after Peterloo, the *Manchester Guardian* was founded to foster parliamentary reform and free trade; today's *Guardian* newspaper is a direct descendent.

The late 19th century brought economic depression as textile exports suffered from growing competition from the USA and Europe. Rather than re-equip themselves with modern machines the mill owners exploited the captive markets of the Empire, a process that continued into the 20th century and led to the industry's final decline.

In an attempt to reduce the loss of its industry to Liverpool and its reliance on cotton, the Ship Canal to the River Mersey was built in 1894. Manchester briefly flourished as Britain's third-largest port until the post-WWII decline.

The city was badly damaged by WWII bombing and then battered by the post-war decline in manufacturing industries. It remains one of Britain's most important commercial and financial centres, with a thriving cultural life. In 1996 central Manchester was badly damaged by an IRA bomb, and work to put right the damage is still going on.

Orientation

Central Manchester is easy to get round on foot or by the excellent Metrolink tramway. The heart of the city, if only because all the buses converge on it, is the depressing, gardenless Piccadilly Gardens. Canal St and Manchester's famous Gay Village (see the boxed text 'Gay & Lesbian Manchester') lie a few streets to the south-west of the Gardens, the Castlefield Urban Heritage Park a little farther to the east. The University of Manchester lies south of the city centre (on Oxford St/Rd). Continue south along Wilmslow Rd and you'll reach the cheap Indian restaurants of Rusholme. East of the university is Moss Side, a ghetto with high unemployment and a thriving drug trade controlled by violent gangs – don't go near it. Farther east again, near the Bridgewater Canal, is Old Trafford, home to Manchester United, England's most famous football team, and to Lancashire County Cricket Club's oval.

Information

The TIC (☎ 234 3157), in the town hall extension off St Peter Square, is open daily. Castlefield has its own visitors centre (☎ 834 4026) at 101 Liverpool Rd, also open daily. There are also two information desks at the airport (☎ 489 6412) and a 24 hour Phone Guide service (☎ 0891-715533) with accommodation details etc. Calls cost 50p a minute.

The TIC sells tickets for guided walks on themes like 'Canals Under the City Streets' and 'King Cotton'. These operate most weekends and almost daily from June to September. They cost £2.50/1.

City Centre

Dominating Albert Square is the enormous Victorian Gothic **town hall**, designed by Albert Waterhouse (of London Natural History Museum fame) in 1876 and with a 85m-high tower. The interior is rich in sculpture and baroque decoration; ask the TIC about occasional tours.

The distinctive circular building on St Peter's Square houses the **Central Library** and the **Library Theatre**. On Peter St, the **Free Trade Hall** is the third to be built on the site of the Peterloo massacre.

Farther west on Deansgate, the gorgeous **John Rylands Library** (☎ 834 5343), built in memory of the wealthy cotton manufacturer, is another good example of Victorian Gothic. It has a fine collection of early printed books (including a Gutenberg Bible, several Caxtons and manuscripts dating back to 2000 BC). It's open Monday to Friday from 10 am to 5.30 pm, and Saturday from 10 am to 1 pm; free. Tours every Wednesday at noon cost £1.

The **Pumphouse People's History Museum** (☎ 839 6061), Bridge St, focuses on social history and the Labour movement. It's open daily except Monday, from 11 am to 4.30 pm; entry is £1 (free on Friday).

The area around King St and St Ann's Square is Manchester's **West End**. It's the most attractive part of the city centre and the pedestrianised streets are lined with classy shops.

On the east side of St Ann's Square is the imposing **Royal Exchange**, originally at the hub of the city's commerce. Trading boards still show the exact price of raw cotton around the world on the day the building closed. It's now home to a café bar and a theatre in the round which has recently

MANCHESTER

PLACES TO STAY
11 Britannia Sachas Hotel
33 Britannia Hotel
36 Malmaison
38 Hotel International; Monroe's Hotel
48 Commercial Hotel
49 Castlefield Hotel
51 Youth Hostel
59 Palace Hotel

PLACES TO EAT
12 Pierre Victoire
13 Grinch's
14 Frankie & Benny's Italian Restaurant
15 Seattle Coffee Company
18 Caffé Uno
19 Armenian Taverna
23 Tampopo
27 Chiang Rai
28 Beer Trading Co
30 Little Yang Sing & Pearl City
31 Giulio's Terrazza
32 Kailash
35 Mash & Air
40 Manto
60 Balearica

PUBS
42 Pitcher & Piano
53 Bar Ça
54 Dukes 92
61 Lass O'Gowrie

OTHER
1 Victoria Station
2 Chetham's Hospital
3 Cathedral
4 Salford Station
5 Pumphouse People's History Museum
6 Barton Arcade
7 Royal Exchange
8 Arndale Shopping Centre
9 Craft Centre
10 Affleck's Palace
16 John Rylands Library
17 Post Office
20 Bus Station
21 Portico Library
22 Town Hall
24 Free Trade Hall
25 Central Library; Library Theatre
26 TIC
29 City Art Gallery
34 Coach Station
37 Piccadilly Station
39 University of Manchester Institute of Science & Technology (UMIST)
41 Bridgewater Hall
43 G-Mex Exhibition Centre
44 Upper Campfield Market
45 Air & Space Gallery

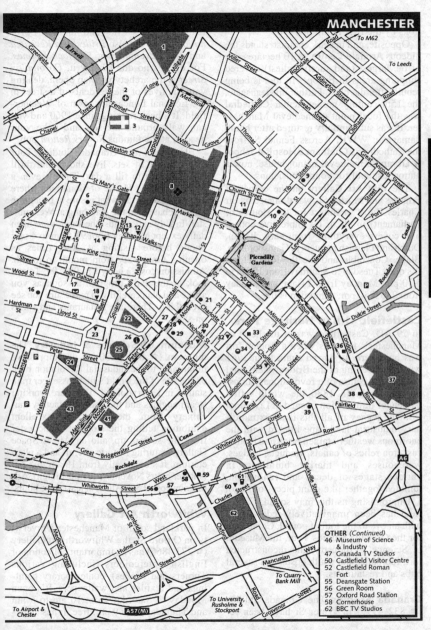

MANCHESTER

To M62

To Leeds

R Irwell

Millgate

Miller Street

Rochdale Road

Addington Street

Swan Street

Oldham Street

Great Ancoats Street

Port Street

Rochdale Canal

Victoria Street

Fennel Street

Long Millgate

Corporation Street

Withy Grove

Shudehill

Thomas Street

Tib Street

Chapel Street

Cateaton St

St Mary's Gate

St Ann St

St Mary's Parsonage

Deansgate

St Ann's Square

King Street

John Dalton St

Hardman St

Lloyd St

Peter Street

Watson Street

Deansgate

Market St

Church Street

Dale Street

Oldham Street

Lever Street

Newton Street

Piccadilly Gardens

York Street

Charlotte St

Mosley Street

Nicholas St

Princess Street

Portland Street

George Street

St James Street

Minshull Street

Chorlton Street

Sackville Street

Major Street

Bloom Street

Canal Street

Whitworth Street

Princess Street

Granby Row

Sackville Street

Fairfield St

London Road

Piccadilly

Aytoun Street

Ducie Street

Dulcie Street

Great Bridgewater Street

Rochdale Canal

Lower Mosley Street

Oxford Street

Whitworth Street West

Charles Street

Cambridge Street

Chester Street

Hulme St

Oxford Road

Mancunian Way

Grosvenor Street

Medlock Street

To Airport & Chester

To University, Rusholme & Stockport

To Quarry Bank Mill

A6

A57(M)

St Peter's Square

Albert Square

Chapel Walks

St Mary's Gate

Metrolink

OTHER (Continued)

46 Museum of Science & Industry
47 Granada TV Studios
50 Castlefield Visitor Centre
52 Castlefield Roman Fort
55 Deansgate Station
56 Green Room
57 Oxford Road Station
58 Cornerhouse
62 BBC TV Studios

reopened after being rocked to its foundations by the IRA bomb of 1996.

Opposite, and in stark contrast, stands the hideous **Arndale Centre**, at 10 hectares one of the largest (and surely ugliest) covered shopping areas in Europe. It, too, is being rebuilt after the blast. Farther up Deansgate, the 15th century perpendicular **Cathedral** was the focal point of medieval Manchester. It was substantially restored after bomb damage in WWII. Across Fennel St from the Cathedral is **Chetham's Hospital School & Library**, a medieval manor house, now a national school for young musicians.

The **City Art Gallery** on the corner of Princess and Mosley Sts was designed by Sir Charles Barry (architect for the Houses of Parliament) in 1824. Its impressive collection covers everything from early Italian, Dutch and Flemish painters to Gainsborough, Blake, Constable and the Pre-Raphaelites. It's open Tuesday to Saturday from 10 am to 5.30 pm; Monday from 11 am; and Sunday from 2 to 5.30 pm; admission is free.

Castlefield Urban Heritage Park

In 79 AD, Castlefield was at the heart of Manchester's fortunes when a Roman fort was built here. It starred again from 1761 when the opening of the Bridgewater Canal put it at the centre of a revolutionary transport network. In 1830 the world's first passenger train station opened in Liverpool Rd. The legacy of all this is an extraordinary industrial landscape littered with the enormous weather-stained brick and rusting cast-iron relics of canals, viaducts, bridges, warehouses and market buildings, in various stages of decay and renovation, tumbled together like giant pieces of Lego.

Unpromising as this may sound, Castlefield has been imaginatively redeveloped with an eye to the tourist pound. Come here for the Granada Studios Tour, the Museum of Science & Industry, the reconstructed fort, footpaths, the youth hostel and several pubs and restaurants.

Granada Studios The Granada Studios (☎ 832 4999) in Water St have been re-
sponsible for many of Britain's best-loved television series – first and foremost *Coronation Street* but also *Brideshead Revisited* and *The Adventures of Sherlock Holmes*. For those who don't know it, *Coronation Street* is the archetypal soap opera, dealing with the lives of the residents of a street in the fictional Lancashire town of Weatherfield. It's been running since 1960 and you can walk around the sets and poke your head in at the famous *Rovers Return* pub.

Elsewhere, the Granada Studios Tour offers a mix of sets, live shows and thrill rides, enough to fill a day. There's even a mock-up of the House of Commons where you can take part in what is sure to be a more polite debate than the real thing at Westminster. In July and August the studios are open daily except Monday from 9.45 am to 4 pm; phone before visiting at other times as opening times vary from month to month. Admission costs a hefty £14.99/9.99. Take a look at the daily program as soon as you arrive and plan carefully to make sure you see everything. There are restaurants and shops on-site.

Museum of Science & Industry The museum (☎ 832 1830) is an impressive monument to the Industrial Revolution built on the site of the world's first passenger train station in Liverpool Rd. There are working steam engines and locomotives, factory machinery from the mills, an excellent exhibition telling the story of Manchester from the sewers up, and an Air & Space Gallery featuring historic aircraft and a planetarium. It's open daily from 10 am to 5 pm (shorter hours November to mid-March). Admission costs £5/3. Allow at least three hours.

Whitworth Art Gallery

In parkland south of Manchester University on Oxford St, the Whitworth Art Gallery (☎ 273 4865) has an important collection of English watercolours (including various Turners and Blakes), contemporary paintings and textiles and wallpapers. It's open Monday to Saturday from 10 am to 5 pm and Thursday until 9 pm; free. It has an excellent gallery bistro with an outdoor terrace for sunny days.

Old Trafford

Manchester United Many regard Manchester United's Old Trafford stadium as holy ground – almost every week supporters demonstrate this literally by asking to have their ashes scattered on the pitch (and they are – behind the goals, where it doesn't matter if it damages the grass).

There are tours (☎ 877 4002) every hour from 10 am to 2 pm (daily except Monday and pre-match and match days). There's also a museum, open daily except Monday from 9.30 am to 4 pm. Admission to the museum and the tour is £7.50/5; and to the museum only is £4.50/3.50. Seats for matches cost around £15. A metro ticket to Old Trafford costs £1.20.

Lancashire County Cricket Club The

Lancashire Club (☎ 872 0261), Warwick Rd, hosts county matches throughout the summer, and international test matches. Admission to county games is £7 to £10.

Places to Stay

There's a reasonable range of places to stay, but most cheap options are some way from the centre. The big central hotels cater to businesspeople during the week and often offer excellent weekend rates. The TIC charges £2 to make bookings; you're better off ringing round yourself.

Note that beds fill up quickly whenever Manchester United is playing at home.

Hostels The stunning new *Youth Hostel* (☎ 839 9960, *Potato Wharf*), across the road from the Museum of Science & Industry in the Castlefield area, has comfortable four-bed dorms for £13/9 for adults/juniors. From late June to late September, the University of Manchester lets student rooms to visitors from around £10 per person. Contact *St Anselm Hall* (☎ 224 7327) or *Woolaton Hall* (☎ 224 7244).

Two miles south of the centre, Stretford has two private hostels. At 17 Greatstone

Rd, tiny *Peppers* (☎ 848 9770) has beds from £8, while at 10 Hornby Rd, the *International Backpackers' Hostel & Guest House* (☎ 872 3499) has beds from £10.

Hotels & B&Bs – Central The *Commercial Hotel* (☎ 834 3504, *125 Liverpool Rd, Castlefield*) is a traditional pub close to the museum with singles/doubles for £20/34. Rather pricier is the modern *Castlefield Hotel* (☎ 832 7073) in Liverpool Rd, with singles/doubles for £49/55 at weekends, including use of its sports facilities.

Opposite Piccadilly train station, *Hotel International* (☎ 236 7484, *34 London Rd*) has rooms with bath for £42/55, and £30/42 without bath. Right next door, *Monroe's* (☎ 236 0564) is popular with a gay clientele.

The *Britannia Hotel* (☎ 228 2288, *Portland St*) is a cotton warehouse that has been converted into a luxury four-star hotel. Rooms are from £31 to £45 for a single, £51 to £65 for a double. The *Britannia Sachas Hotel* (☎ 228 1234, *Tib St*) does singles/doubles from £40/45 at weekends.

On Oxford St near the station is the *Palace Hotel* (☎ 288 1111), converted from a vast 19th century insurance company building and with rooms, some more interesting than others, from £99 per single at weekends.

Across the road from Manchester's Piccadilly station is the luxurious *Malmaison* (☎ 278 1000), with rooms for a flat-rate £99 (£75 at weekends) and a French brasserie.

Hotels & B&Bs – Suburbs Didsbury is an attractive southern suburb, with good local pubs and frequent buses into the city. Wilmslow and Palatine Rds have many hotels in converted Victorian houses.

The pleasant *Baron Hotel* (☎ 434 0941, *116 Palatine Rd, West Didsbury*) is about half a mile from the M63 among a batch of similar standard hotels. Rooms with private bathroom cost from £17/22.

On Wilmslow Rd the comfortable *Elm Grange Hotel* (☎ 445 3336), at No 561, has rooms from £17/36. At No 188, *Fernbank*

Guest House (☎ 01625-523729) is 12 miles from the centre but only 10 minutes from the airport and is comfortable and similarly priced.

The *Crescent Gate Hotel (☎ 224 0672, Park Crescent)* is within walking distance of Rusholme's Indian restaurants and well served by buses into the city centre. Most of the comfortable rooms (£36/50) have bathrooms.

Chorlton also has plenty of B&Bs which are reasonably convenient for Old Trafford to the south-west of the city centre.

Places to Eat

The most distinctive restaurant zones are Chinatown in the city centre and Rusholme in the south. Chinatown is bounded by Charlotte, Portland, Oxford and Mosley Sts, and has lots of restaurants, many but not all of them Chinese, and most not particularly cheap. The most acclaimed is the *Little Yang Sing (☎ 228 7722, 17 George St)*, specialising in Cantonese cuisine. During the day there is a set menu for £8.95, but expect to pay twice that in the evening. Readers also rate *Pearl City (☎ 228 7683, 23 George St)* where dim sum Sunday lunch costs £8.30.

Rusholme, on Wilmslow Rd, the extension of Oxford St/Rd, has numerous cheap, excellent Indian/Pakistani places. Try *Sanam Sweet House & Restaurant (☎ 224 8824, 145 Wilmslow Rd)* which does Karachi chicken for £5.50 as well as an array of mouth-watering sweets. More centrally, *Kailash (☎ 236 1085, 34 Charlotte St)* serves Nepalese and Indian dishes – whole four-course lunches for £5.80.

Café bars have taken off in a big way in Manchester. The first, *Dry 201 (☎ 236 5920, 28 Oldham St)* and *Manto (☎ 236 2667, 46 Canal St)* are still among the best (those worried that Canal St is past its prime, point to a new branch of *Slug & Lettuce* at No 4). The *Beer Trading Co (☎ 228 1818, 55 Mosley St)* does spaghetti bolognese for £4.95, while the *Grinch Wine Bar (☎ 907 3210, Chapel Walk)* serves salmon fishcakes for £5.95 in arty surroundings. The branch of *Pitcher &*

Piano beside the Bridgewater Hall has inviting waterside views.

Albert Square is gradually filling up with places to eat. Alongside branches of *Dôme* and *Caffé Uno*, look out for *Tampopo*, a minimalist noodle bar where mee goreng costs £5.25. More unusual is the basement *Armenian Taverna (☎ 934 9025, 3-5 Princess St)* which will do you an Armenian pizza for £5.50 or a Tbilisi kebab for £7.95; closed on Monday.

In St Ann St *Frankie & Benny's Italian restaurant (☎ 835 2479)* does two-course New York Italian lunches for £5.25. *Guilio's Terrazza (☎ 236 4033, 14 Nicholson St)* dishes up vegetarian lasagne for £5.90. *Chiang Rai (☎ 237 9511, 16 Princess St)* is a deservedly popular Thai restaurant where a couple of courses with drinks will come to about £18.

In a class of its own is Oliver Peyton's four-storey *Mash & Air (☎ 661 6161, 40 Chorlton St)*. This super-trendy place has a café bar with its own brewery on the ground floor and a much posher restaurant upstairs.

Vegetarians could try *On the Eighth Day (☎ 273 4878, 111 Oxford Rd)* next to the Metropolitan University. In nearby Charles St, *Balearica (☎ 273 3722, 42 Charles St)* serves pasta from £6.95 in colourful surroundings.

Entertainment

In keeping with its old Madchester reputation, Manchester comes into its own at night, offering all sorts of high-quality entertainment. *City Life*, an invaluable, fortnightly what's on magazine, has the details.

Pubs & Clubs The *Lass O'Gowrie* pub, *(Charles St)* off Oxford St, is a popular student hang-out, with an excellent small brewery on the premises and good-value bar meals.

The famous scene that spawned Simply Red, The Smiths, Joy Division, New Order, the Stone Roses, The Charlatans and the Happy Mondays continues, although it's more subdued than at its peak. One of the best live music venues is *Band on the*

Wall (☎ *832 6625, Swan St*) which hosts everything from jazz to blues, folk and pop. *Manchester Board Walk* (☎ *228 3555, Little Peter St*) and the *Venue* (☎ *236 0026, 17 Whitworth St*) are also good venues.

There are several popular places to drink in Castlefield, including *Bar Ça* (owned by Mick Hucknall of Simply Red) in Catalan Square with outdoor seating for sunny days, and *Dukes 92*, a popular canalside pub.

Gay nightlife is centred on Canal St but *Paradise Factory* (☎ *273 5422, 112 Princess St*) is a cutting edge club, with gay nights at the weekend.

Theatre, Cinema & Exhibitions The *Green Room* (☎ *236 1677, 54 Whitworth St West*) is the premiere fringe venue and also has a good café bar. There's nearly always something interesting on at the *Royal Exchange* (☎ *833 9833, St Ann's Square or Upper Campfield Market*) or the *Library Theatre* (☎ *236 7110*).

The *Cornerhouse* (☎ *228 2463, 70 Oxford St*) houses a decent cinema, a gallery and a café.

Opposite the Bridgewater Hall, the *G-Mex Centre* (☎ *834 2700*), cleverly converted from the derelict Central train station, hosts exhibitions, concerts and indoor sporting events.

Classical Music Manchester is home to two world-famous symphony orchestras, the cash-strapped Hallé and the BBC Philharmonic. The enormous and impressive Bridgewater Hall (☎ *907 9000*), home to the Hallé, was completed in 1996 at a cost of £42 million.

Shopping

In Oldham St to the north of Piccadilly Gardens, **Affleck's Palace** is a restored warehouse full of stalls, shops and cafés selling clubbing gear from young designers, second-hand clothes, crystals, leather gear, records – you name it. A thriving, buzzy place with a great atmosphere, it's open Monday to Saturday from 10 am to 5.30 pm. Don't miss it.

Gay & Lesbian Manchester

Manchester is the gay capital of the north. The TIC stocks the useful *Gay & Lesbian Village Guide* that lists numerous gay bars, clubs, galleries and groups, including the Lesbian & Gay Centre (☎ 274 3814) on Sydney St. The Lesbian & Gay Switchboard (☎ 274 3999) operates from 4 to 10 pm, daily.

The centre of Manchester's vibrant gay nightlife scene is Canal St. There are said to be over 30 bars and clubs in the so-called 'Gay Village'. The ground-breaker was the Manto Bar (☎ 236 2667, 46 Canal St), which has been copied around the world. Across the canal is Metz (☎ 237 9852), another café bar, and currently more fashionable than Manto. There are several more traditional pubs nearby, including the New Union. On Friday there's a women-only night at the upstairs bar at the Rembrandt Hotel (☎ 236 1311, 33 Sackville St).

The club scene changes so quickly it's difficult to make recommendations but the Paradise Factory (see Pubs & Clubs) is usually popular. Cruz 101 (☎ 237 1554), nearby at 101 Princess St, is the largest gay nightclub in the city.

Britain's biggest gay and lesbian arts festival, It's Queer Up North (IQUP), takes place every two years – next in spring 2000.

One block north in Oak St is Manchester's impressive Craft Centre (☎ 832 4274), housed in the old fish and poultry market building and open Monday to Saturday from 10 am to 5.30 pm.

Getting There & Away

See the fares tables in the Getting Around chapter. Manchester is about 200 miles (three hours) from London, 3½ hours from Glasgow, two hours from York and 35 miles (half an hour) from Liverpool by road.

Air Manchester airport (☎ 489 3000) is the largest outside London, serving 35 countries. It's worth considering if you're heading to/from the north or the Lake District. A train to the airport costs £2.15, a coach £2. The excellent TIC at the airport can recommend nearby B&Bs, some of which will pick you up and drop you off.

Bus National Express (☎ 0990-808080) offers numerous coach links with the rest of the country from Chorlton St coach station in the city centre. Nineteen services a day link Manchester to Liverpool (one hour, £3.50) and Leeds (80 minutes, £4). A coach to London costs £11.50.

Train Piccadilly is the main station for trains to and from the rest of the country, although Victoria station serves Halifax and Bradford. The two stations are linked by Metrolink. A single ticket to Liverpool Lime St costs £6.

Getting Around

For inquiries about local transport, including night buses, phone ☎ 228 7811 (daily from 8 am to 8 pm).

Bus Most local buses start from Piccadilly Gardens where the downside of bus deregulation is obvious in the crush of multicoloured vehicles, all touting different fares to move you about the city. The central Travelshop has timetables but no fares, forcing you to consult each bus driver individually.

Metrolink The Metrolink trams operate on a mixture of disused rail tracks and tracks laid along the city-centre streets. There are frequent links between Victoria and Piccadilly train stations and G-Mex (for Castlefield). Buy tickets from the machines on the platforms. For information phone ☎ 205 2000.

Train Castlefield is served by Deansgate station with rail links to Piccadilly, Oxford Rd and Salford Crescent stations.

AROUND MANCHESTER
Quarry Bank Mill

In Wilmslow, 10 miles south of Manchester, you can visit an 18th century cotton mill in beautiful Styal Country Park. Not only can you see the old waterwheel that used to power the mill and some of the old machinery, but costumed guides in the **Apprentice House** will give you a depressing insight into the life of some of the mill's younger workers, a life of shared beds, and brimstone and treacle cures. The Mill (☎ 01625-527468, NT) is open from April through September from 11 am to 6 pm, closing on Monday and at 5 pm for the rest of the year. The Apprentice House is open Tuesday to Friday from 2 to 4.30 pm. Admission costs £5.50/3.50. To get there take a train (except Sunday) to Styal station and walk for half a mile.

Wigan Pier Heritage Centre

Home to one of Britain's latest big bands The Verve, Wigan is otherwise a dreary Midlands town, famous mainly because George Orwell used it as the basis for his book, *The Road to Wigan Pier*. But forget any thought of fortune-telling booths and kiss-me-quick hats – this pier was never more exciting than a contraption used for tipping coal into barges on the Leeds and Liverpool Canal.

Nevertheless, the site has been used to create a fine heritage centre which attempts to bring to life what it was like to work in a mine in the late 1800s. You can also see inside an old textile mill whose machinery can still be set working for visitors.

The Heritage Centre (☎ 01942-323666) is open Monday to Thursday from 10 am to 5 pm and from 11 am at weekends. Admission costs £5.10/4.10. To get there, take bus No 33 from Manchester city centre, or a train to Wigan station from Manchester or Liverpool.

Tatton Park

Three and a half miles north of Knutsford, Tatton Park (☎ 01565-654822, NT) is a huge estate set around 19th century Wyatt House and a series of gardens, and with a medieval great hall and 1930s-style working farm. From April through October, Wyatt House is open daily except Monday from noon to 4 pm, although the park is open daily from 10 am to 6 pm. Only the house and gardens are free to NT members. Tickets to all the Tatton attractions cost £8.50/5.50.

On Sunday Bus No X2 links Tatton Park with Chester (one hour). Attractive, upmarket Knutsford has a good choice of places to stay and eat.

Merseyside

Liverpool is far and away the most important city in the area known as Merseyside because, of course, the River Mersey flows through it.

LIVERPOOL
• pop 510,000   ☎ 0151

Of all the North Midlands cities, Liverpool has perhaps the strongest sense of its own identity which is closely tied up, as you'll discover on even the shortest visit, with the totems of the Beatles, the Liverpool and Everton football teams, and the Grand National, run at Aintree since 1839.

The city has a dramatic site, rising on a series of steps above the broad River Mersey estuary with its shifting light, its fogs, its gulls and its mournful emptiness. You're bound to be struck by the contrast between the grandeur and the decay, between the decrepit streets and boarded-up windows and the massive cathedrals and imperious buildings.

Liverpool's economic collapse has been even more dramatic than Manchester's which gives the whole city a sharp edge you'd do well not to explore. When people party, they seem to do so with a touch of desperation, certainly with plenty of abandonment. At weekends the city centre vibrates to music from countless pubs and clubs.

It's well worth setting aside time to explore Liverpool properly. The Albert Dock, the Western Approaches Museum, the twin cathedrals and the city streets themselves offer vivid testimony to the city's rugged history and the perverse exhilaration of its present-day decline.

History
Like Bristol, 18th century Liverpool prospered on the back of the infamous triangular trading of slaves for raw materials. From 1700 ships carried cotton goods and hardware from Liverpool to West Africa, where they were exchanged for slaves. The slaves were, in turn, carried to the West Indies and Virginia where they were exchanged for sugar, rum, tobacco and raw cotton, a story retold in an excellent new gallery in the Maritime Museum (see Albert Dock later in this chapter).

As a great port, the city attracted thousands of immigrants from Ireland and Scotland and its Celtic influences are still apparent; but between 1830 and 1930 nine million emigrants – mainly English, Scots and Irish, but also Swedes, Norwegians and Russian Jews – sailed from Liverpool for the New World.

WWII led to a resurgence in Liverpool's importance. Over one million GIs disembarked here before D-day and the port was, once again, hugely important as the western gateway for transatlantic supplies. The city also accommodated the Combined Headquarters of the Western Approaches, which coordinated the transatlantic convoys and the battle against German U-boats.

Liverpool has a long history of left-wing radicalism. The outrageous excesses of 19th century capitalism led to bitter and violent confrontations with increasingly well-organised labour organisations. More recently, unemployment and housing problems have dragged the city down. In the early 80s racial tensions led to rioting in Toxteth, a run-down suburb just south of the city centre.

As elsewhere, the previous Conservative government saw tourism as a way out of Liverpool's problems and money was poured into the redevelopment of the Albert Dock, with an offshoot of the Tate Gallery, several museums and a range of shops and restaurants. But Liverpool remains a depressed city where a great deal more needs to be done to galvanise the local economy.

NORTH-WESTERN ENGLAND

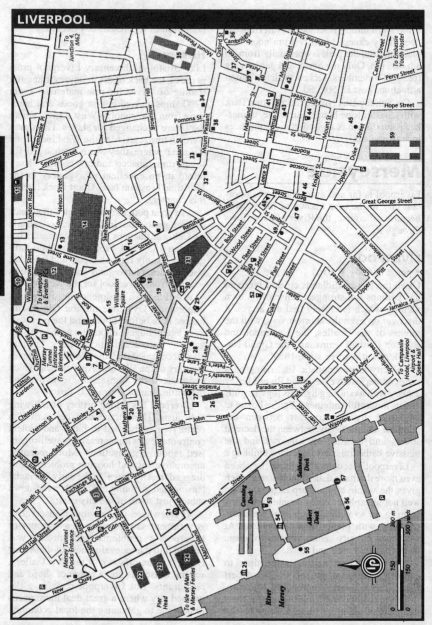

LIVERPOOL

LIVERPOOL

PLACES TO STAY		41	Philharmonic Dining Room	19	Clayton Square Shopping
1	Atlantic Tower Thistle	44	Ye Cracke		Centre
17	Britannia Adelphi Hotel	50	Zanzibar	20	Cavern Club
26	Liverpool Moat House	51	Baa Bar	21	James Street Train Station
32	YMCA	52	Cream	22	Royal Liver Building
33	Aachen Hotel & Belvedere	53	Pumphouse Inn	23	Cunard Building
34	The Feathers Hotel			24	Port of Liverpool Building
36	University of Liverpool,		OTHER	25	Museum of Liverpool Life
	Mulberry Court	2	Western Approaches Museum	27	Bus Station & Parking
38	YWCA	3	Town Hall	28	Bluecoat Arts Centre
58	Youth Hostel	4	Moorfields Train Station	30	Post Office
		7	Post Office	31	Central Train Station
PLACES TO EAT		8	Conservation Centre	35	Metropolitan Cathedral
5	Casa Bella	9	Queen Square Bus Stops	42	Philharmonic Hall
6	Casa Italia	10	Liverpool Museum;	43	Unity Theatre
37	Everyman Theatre & Bistro		Walker Art Gallery	45	Institute for Performing Arts
39	El Macho	11	National Express Coach	47	Blue Angel
40	Becker's Brook		Station	49	Heebiejeebies
46	Far East	12	St George's Hall	54	Merseyside Maritime
48	Café Tabac	13	The Empire		Museum
		14	Lime Street Train	55	Tate Gallery Liverpool
PUBS			Station	56	The Beatles Story
16	American Bar	15	Liverpool Playhouse	57	TIC (Albert Dock)
29	Revolution	18	TIC	59	Anglican Cathedral

Orientation

Liverpool stretches north-south along the River Mersey estuary for more than 13 miles. The main visitor attraction is the Albert Dock on the waterfront west of the city centre. The centre, including the two cathedrals to the east, is quite compact and easy to explore on foot.

Lime St, the main train station, is just to the east of the city centre. The National Express coach station is a few blocks north on the corner of Norton and Islington Sts. The bus station is in the centre on Paradise St.

Information

The main TIC (☎ 709 3631), in the Clayton Square Shopping Centre, is open Monday to Saturday, while the branch in the Albert Dock (☎ 708 8854) is open daily. Both can book accommodation.

Look for the excellent *Liverpool Heritage Walk*, an illustrated guide to the city's landmarks, identified by numbered metal markers set in the footpath.

Both TICs sell tickets for city bus tours. The hop-on hop-off bus tour has 11 stops and costs £5/3. There's also a highly recommended 2¼-hour Beatles tour (see the boxed text 'Doing the Beatles to Death').

If you're planning on visiting several museums make sure to spend £3/1.50 on an NMGM Eight Pass, covering admission to six city centre attractions – Liverpool Museum, Walker Art Gallery, Merseyside Maritime Museum, HM Customs & Excise National Museum, Museum of Liverpool Life and the Conservation Centre – as well as to the Lady Lever Art Gallery in Port Sunlight and to Sudley House (☎ 724 3245) in Aigburth. It's valid for 12 months and is on sale at all the museums.

It pays to be a bit careful in Liverpool. Ideally, avoid walking along side streets or along Duke St, the main drag linking the Anglican cathedral with Hanover St, after dark.

City Centre

At the end of Castle St, the **town hall** was designed by John Wood the Elder of Bath

NORTH-WESTERN ENGLAND

and completed in 1754. Both the dome and the impressive portico and balcony, where the Beatles were received by the Lord Mayor in 1964, were added later.

The confusing **Clayton Square** is a modern shopping centre where you'll find the main TIC. **Bold St**, south of Central station, was once a ropewalk used in the manufacture of ropes for visiting ships.

Once considered one of the world's most luxurious hotels, the **Britannia Adelphi Hotel** in Lime St was completed in 1912 to serve wealthy passengers staying overnight before or after the Atlantic crossing. Farther north along the road is the superb Edwardian pub **Vines**, with its luxurious interior (built in 1907) and the **American Bar**, favoured by the US forces during WWII. In the 19th century, Lime St was famous for prostitution and was immortalised in the song *Maggie May*.

A group of Liverpool's most impressive buildings are clustered together opposite Lime St station, although traffic funnelling into the city and the entrance of the Queensway Mersey Tunnel makes it difficult to appreciate them. Built as a concert hall in 1854, **St George's Hall** is considered one of the world's greatest neoclassical buildings; its exterior is Greek, its interior Roman. Tours take place from mid-July through August daily except Sunday for £1.50.

Liverpool Museum & Walker Art Gallery

Liverpool Museum (☎ 478 4399) is a traditional museum covering everything from archaeology to natural history but also houses a planetarium and hosts interesting temporary exhibitions. As well as its renowned collection of Pre-Raphaelite art, the Walker Art Gallery (☎ 478 4199) has an important collection of Italian and Flemish paintings and some interesting Impressionists and post-Impressionists, including a Degas, Cézanne and Matisse. There's a pleasant café on the ground floor.

The museum and gallery, side by side in William Brown St, are open Monday to Saturday from 10 am to 5 pm, Sunday from noon to 5 pm. Admission to each costs £3/1.50.

Western Approaches Museum

The Combined Headquarters of the Western Approaches (☎ 227 2008), the secret command centre for the Battle of the Atlantic, was buried under yards of concrete beneath an undistinguished building behind the town hall in Rumford Square. At the end of the war the bunker was abandoned with virtually everything left intact. It's open daily, except Friday and Sunday, from 10.30 am to 4.30 pm. Tickets cost £4.75/3.45.

Conservation Centre

Liverpool's latest attraction (☎ 478 4999) is a state-of-the-art exhibition telling the story behind the conservation of the items on display in local museums and art galleries. Hand-held wands allow you to tune into different stories as you walk around and you'll probably be surprised to discover how much fun it all is. Did you know, for example, that a stuffed toucan's bill must be repainted after death? The Conservation Centre is open from 10 am to 5 pm daily in the old Midland Railway Goods Depot in Old Haymarket. Admission costs £3/1.50.

The Cathedrals

As you walk along Hope St you can see Liverpool's twin cathedrals looming on either side of you, the Roman Catholic version to the north, the Anglican to the south.

Metropolitan Cathedral According to Sir Edwin Lutyens' original plans, Liverpool's Roman Catholic cathedral would have been larger than St Peter's in Rome. Unfortunately, the war and Liverpool's decline forced the priests to lower their sights. The present church-in-the-round ('Paddy's Wigwam') was completed in 1967 and incorporates Lutyens' crypt. The soaring exterior is strikingly successful and the interior space impressive, although opinions on the modern decorations vary. With luck, work on repairing the leaky roof will be finished by the time you read this.

The cathedral (☎ 709 9222) is open from 8 am to 6 pm daily.

Anglican Cathedral Work on the red sandstone, neogothic Anglican Cathedral started in 1902 and was finally completed in 1978, by which time it was only exceeded in size by St Peter's and the Milan and Seville cathedrals. The cathedral was the life work of Sir Giles Gilbert Scott (1880-1960) who worked on it until his death. Scott was also responsible for the design of the old red telephone booth which explains why one of these is tucked away upstairs.

Even those who don't usually care for neogothic are likely to be awed by this great, austere sea of space. The best views of Liverpool are from the top of the 101m tower. The cathedral (☎ 709 6271) is open daily from 9 am to 6 pm and a donation of £2 is requested. The tower is open daily from 11 am to 4 pm (£2/1), as is the exhibition of ecclesiastical embroidery (£2/1). The excellent refectory is open from 11 am to 4 pm.

Beside the porch steps, look out for a **memorial** to the 95 Liverpool football fans who died in the crush at Hillsborough Stadium in 1989. The imitation Greek temple nearby is the **Oratory**, designed in 1929 and open to visitors from Easter to September.

Albert Dock

Built between 1841 and 1848, the Albert Dock was one of the earliest enclosed docks in the world. Now 2¾ hectares of water are ringed by a colonnade of enormous cast-iron columns and impressive five-storey warehouses.

In the 1980s the warehouses were restored and now house several outstanding museums, numerous shops and restaurants, offices, studios for Granada TV, a branch of the TIC and several tacky tourist attractions. The site could easily absorb four hours and that's without exploring the impressive buildings north along the waterfront.

Merseyside Maritime Museum This museum (☎ 478 4499) has a large range of imaginatively developed exhibits. Major displays focus on Emigrants to a New World, the WWII Battle of the Atlantic, and Builders of Great Ships. The latest addition is the absorbing Transatlantic Slave Gallery which describes the shameful trade and its repercussions in the form of modern racism. Anything to Declare? is a the gallery devoted to the history of HM Customs & Excise, sounds pretty dry but gives you the chance to find out whether you could catch a smuggler.

The museum is open daily from 10 am to 5 pm. Admission is £3/1.50.

Museum of Liverpool Life This museum (☎ 478 4080) looks at four main themes: Mersey Culture, especially entertainers; Making a Living, showing regional trades; Demanding a Voice, about the growth of unionism and democracy; and A Healthy Place to Live? a look at Liverpool's record on public health. It's open daily from 10 am to 5 pm and entry costs £3/1.50.

Tate Gallery Liverpool It's particularly appropriate that Liverpool should have been chosen as home to this extension of the London Tate Gallery since Henry Tate, benefactor of the original gallery, co-founded the famous Tate & Lyle sugar business here. The newly-refurbished Albert Dock gallery (☎ 709 0507) hosts high-quality changing exhibitions. It's open Tuesday to Sunday from 10 am to 6 pm; free.

The Beatles Story Despite its promising name this attraction fails to capitalise on its subject's potential – fanatics won't discover anything they don't already know, and aside from some old TV clips there's little to kindle excitement for later generations. It's open daily from 10 am to 6 pm, but is questionable value at £5.95/4.25.

North of Albert Dock The area to the north of Albert Dock is known as **Pier Head**, after a stone pier built in the 1760s. This is still the departure point for ferries across the River Mersey (see Getting Around later in

Doing the Beatles to Death

A Victorian warehouse in Mathew St was once home to a music venue called the Cavern Club. Between March 1961 and August 1963, the Beatles played here a staggering 275 times. Other bands like Gerry and the Pacemakers who helped define 'beat' music and the 'Mersey sound' were also regulars. Cilla Black was in charge of the cloakroom.

Turn down Mathew St today and you're hardly able to move for businesses cashing in on the Beatles phenomenon. There's an Abbey Rd Oyster Bar, an Abbey Rd Shop, a Lucy in the Sky With Diamonds café and a Lennon Bar … and that's before you stumble on Cavern Court and the Cavern Walks shopping mall.

The irony is, of course, that the original Cavern Club where the Fab Four started their career was closed in 1973 and the site ruthlessly redeveloped in 1980. A statue of Lennon in his Hamburg period may slouch against the wall of the memorabilia-crammed Cavern Pub (☎ 236 1957) but the present day Cavern Club (☎ 236 9091) at 10 Mathew St only opened in 1984. You may well find it hosting a disco or closed for a private party.

Serious Beatles fans might prefer to head off in search of other Liverpool sites associated with the mopheads. Both TICs sell tickets to the Magical Mystery Tour (☎ 709 3285), a 2¼ hour bus trip taking in Penny Lane, Strawberry Fields and many other landmarks. It departs daily from opposite the Pump House pub in Albert Dock at 2.20 pm and from the main TIC at 2.30 pm. In July and August there are also Saturday tours at 11.50 am. Tickets cost £8.95.

Cheaper, more personal tours can be arranged via the Embassie Youth Hostel.

If you'd rather do it yourself, the TICs also stock the *Discover Lennon's Liverpool* guide and map, and Robin Jones' *Beatles Liverpool*.

this section), and was, for millions of migrants, their final contact with European soil.

Today it's dominated by a trio of self-important buildings dating from the days when Liverpool's star was still in the ascendant. The southernmost, with the dome mimicking St Paul's Cathedral, is the **Port of Liverpool Building**, completed in 1907.

Next to it the **Cunard Building**, in the style of an Italian palazzo, was once HQ to the Cunard Steamship Line. Finally, the **Royal Liver Building** (pronounced liever) was opened in 1911 as the head office of the Royal Liver Friendly Society. It's crowned by the famous 5.5m copper Liver Birds which symbolise Liverpool. Liverpool's original seal depicted an eagle, but over time artists' representations came to look more like a seagull or cormorant!

Football Club Tours

Fans of Everton Football Club will want to head out to Goodison Park to tour the club grounds and find out more about its history. Tours take place Monday, Wednesday, Friday and Sunday at 11 am and 2 pm except on match days, but you must book in advance (☎ 330 2266). They cost £4/3 per person.

Fans of Liverpool FC should head for Anfield Rd where a similar experience is available (☎ 260 6677). To visit the museum and take a tour costs £8/5.

Places to Stay

Note that beds can be hard to find when Liverpool or Everton football clubs are playing at home. You'll also be lucky to find anything if you haven't booked ahead for the third week of August when the Beatles annual convention comes to town.

Hostels The excellent and welcoming *Embassie Youth Hostel* (☎ 707 1089, 1 Falkner Square) is to the west of the Anglican Cathedral but still within walking distance of the centre. Dormitory beds here cost £9.50, including tea and coffee, and facilities include a laundry and TV lounge.

By the time you read this a new *YHA hostel* (☎ 0171-248 5647) should have opened in Chalenor St, across the road from Albert Dock. Beds will cost £15.75/11.75 for adults/juniors, including breakfast.

The YWCA (☎ 709 7791, 1 Rodney St) is off Mount Pleasant and now takes men as well as women and is greatly preferable to the YMCA (☎ 709 9516, 56 Mount Pleasant). Beds cost from £12.

The *University of Liverpool* (☎ 794 3298) has self-catering rooms at Mulberry Court, Oxford St, near the Metropolitan Cathedral, for £15.50 a head; plus B&B (☎ 794 6440) in Greenbank Lane over Easter and from mid-June to mid-September from £14.10.

B&Bs & Hotels There's a handy group of hotels on Mount Pleasant, between the city centre and the Metropolitan Cathedral. The *Feathers Hotel* (☎ 709 9655, 117 Mount Pleasant) is a good mid-range hotel. The 84 rooms boast a variety of facilities. Singles/ doubles (some very small) start at £25/40.

The award-winning *Aachen Hotel* (☎ 709 3477, 89 Mount Pleasant) has well-equipped rooms, most with showers, for £24/38. The smaller and more basic *Belvedere* (☎ 709 2356, 83 Mount Pleasant) is cheaper, with beds from £17.50.

Close to Albert Dock the modern *Campanile Hotel* (☎ 709 8104, Chaloner St) offers flat-rate rooms for £29.95 at weekends, rising to £38 from Sunday to Thursday.

The five-star *Atlantic Tower Thistle* (☎ 227 4444, Chapel) is virtually beside the Royal Liver Building and is a modern multistorey hotel with good views over the River Mersey. Rooms are from £99/111, but there are good-value weekend breaks.

When it was completed in 1912, the 391-room *Britannia Adelphi Hotel* (☎ 709 7200, Ranelagh Place) was considered one of the world's most luxurious hotels. These days there's more competition but it's still worth forking out for bed without breakfast at £49.50/67 in a wonderfully central location.

Places to Eat

The area around Slater St and Bold St is worth trying with a reasonable choice of places to eat. At the eastern end of Bold St *Café Tabac* (☎ 709 3735) is a relaxed café that attracts a young crowd; roasts cost around £4.25.

The *Everyman Bistro* (☎ 708 9545, 5 Hope St), underneath the Everyman Theatre and is highly recommended as a place to tuck into cheap, good food (pizza slices for less than £2 and delicious desserts). Also on Hope St, *El Macho* (☎ 708 6644), at No 23, has a cheerful atmosphere and enormous servings of spicy Mexican food. Most main dishes are around £7.95 but there are three-course set lunches and student specials for £5.95. *Becker's Brook* (☎ 707 0005), a few doors south, does classy new British cookery; a three-course meal costs £17.50.

The *refectory* at the Anglican Cathedral serves great value hot lunches for around £4. There are also excellent cafés in the Walker Art Gallery and the Conservation Centre.

Liverpool's Chinatown has declined since its glory days, but there are still several Chinese restaurants around Berry St. One of the most popular is *Far East* (☎ 709 3141, 27 Berry St), above a Chinese supermarket. Set menus start at £14.50, but you could eat for less – there are plenty of dishes for around £7. Dim sum is popular on Sunday.

At 40 Stanley St, in the centre of town, popular *Casa Italia* (☎ 227 5774) does pizzas from £5. It's open Monday to Saturday. Nearby *Casa Bella* (☎ 258 1800, 25 Victoria St) does pasta from £5.95.

The Albert Dock is also a good place to look for something to eat. *Kaffee und Kuchen* does snacks as well as bratwurst for £4.75.

Entertainment

To find out what's on where, look out for the free monthly entertainment guide *In Touch*.

Pubs & Clubs Liverpool has a thriving, and changeable, nightlife. Wander around Mathew St and south-east to Bold, Seel and Slater Sts and you'll stumble upon an amazing array of clubs and pubs catering to every imaginable taste.

Best known of the clubs is *Cream* (☎ 709 1693), off Parr St, which rings the changes between jazz, samba and techno. The *Blue Angel* (☎ 428 1213, 108 Seel St) is popular with students, as is the downstairs bar at *Casablanca* in Hope St. *Hardy's* (☎ 708 7958, Hardman St) hosts a variety of different club nights.

Zanzibar (☎ 707 0633, 43 Seel St) hosts jazz and funk as does nearby *Heebiejeebes* (☎ 709 2666). Other clubs worth checking

out include *Medication* in Wolstenholme Square, *Mardi Gras* in Bold St and *Krazy House* in Wood St. For indie rock try the *Picket* (☎ 708 5318, 24 Hardman St). The *Irish Centre* (☎ 709 4120) often has live bands. The *Baa Bar* (43 Fleet St) pulls the punters with some beers at £1 a bottle. *Revolution* in Wood St is also popular.

On the corner of Hope and Hardman Sts, the *Philharmonic Dining Room*, built in 1900, is one of Britain's most extraordinary pubs. The interior is resplendent with etched glass, stained glass, wrought iron, mosaics and ceramic tiling – and if you think that's good, just wait until you see inside the men's toilets.

Ye Cracke, on Rice St, has long been favoured by students from the nearby College of Art. John Lennon and Cynthia Powell were regular customers. *Garands* in Eberle St and *The Escape* in Paradise St are popular gay hang-outs.

Theatre & Classical Music The *Everyman Theatre* (☎ 709 4776, Hope St) is one of Britain's most famous repertory theatres and has featured the works of local playwright Alan Bleasdale, among others. The *Liverpool Playhouse* (☎ 709 8363, Williamson Square) or *The Empire* (☎ 709 1555, Lime St) could be staging anything from straight plays to musicals. The *Bluecoat Arts Centre* (☎ 709 5279, School Lane) and the *Unity Theatre* (☎ 709 4988) host innovative, small-scale companies.

The Royal Liverpool Philharmonic Orchestra plays in the *Philharmonic Hall* (☎ 709 3789, Hope St).

Getting There & Away

See the fares tables in the Getting Around chapter. Liverpool is 210 miles from London, 100 miles from Birmingham, 75 miles from Leeds and 35 miles from Manchester.

Air Liverpool airport (☎ 486 8877), 8 miles to the south of the city centre, has flights to Belfast, Dublin and the Isle of Man. A National Express coach to the airport costs £3 (35 minutes).

Bus National Express services (☎ 0990-808080) link Liverpool to most major towns. To get to the town centre from the coach station, turn right up Seymour St and then right again along London Rd. To get to Chester catch bus No X8 from Queen Square in the city centre.

Rail Numerous services run to Lime St station. A train to Wigan costs £3.20, to Chester £2.90 and to Manchester £6.

Boat The Isle of Man Steam Packet Company (☎ 0990-523523) operates a service between Douglas and Liverpool (Pier Head) every weekend throughout the year and more frequently during summer. The journey time is 4¼ hours by ferry or 2½ hours by catamaran. Foot passenger fares start at £23 single. Bicycles are transported free, but a car will cost from £68 each way unless you're eligible for a discounted return fare.

Getting Around
Local public transport is coordinated by Merseytravel (☎ 236 7676), which has a branch in the TIC at Clayton Square. Various zonal tickets are also sold at post offices; an all-zone all-day ticket for bus, train and ferry (except cruises) costs £4.30.

Bus Most local buses leave from Queen Square to the east of St George's Hall. Smart Bus Nos 1 and 5 link Albert Dock with the city centre and the university every 20 minutes.

Taxi Mersey Cabs (☎ 298 222) operates tourist taxi services and has some cabs adapted for disabled visitors.

Ferry The famous ferry across the River Mersey (90p/65p), started 800 years ago by Benedictine monks but immortalised by Gerry & the Pacemakers, still offers one of the best views of Liverpool. Boats for Woodside and Seacombe depart from Pier Head Ferry Terminal, next to the Liver Building to the north of Albert Dock. Special one-hour commentary cruises run

year-round departing hourly from 10 am to 3 pm on weekdays and until 6 pm on weekends (£3.30/1.65). Phone ☎ 630 1030 for more information.

AROUND LIVERPOOL
Port Sunlight
South-east of Liverpool across the River Mersey on the Wirral peninsula, Port Sunlight is a picturesque 19th century village created by the philanthropic Lever family to house workers in its soap factory. The main reason to come here is the wonderful **Lady Lever Art Gallery** (☎ 478 4136) where you can see some of the greatest works of the Pre-Raphaelite Brotherhood, as well as some fine Wedgwood pottery. It's open Monday to Saturday from 10 am to 5 pm and on Sunday from noon. Admission costs £3/1.50.

Also in the village is the **Heritage Centre** (☎ 644 6466), 95 Greendale Rd, which tells the story of the creation of Port Sunlight. It's open Easter to October from 10 am to 4 pm, closing at weekends in winter.

To get to Port Sunlight take a train from Lime St station.

Speke Hall & 20 Forthlin Rd
Six miles south of Liverpool is Speke Hall (☎ 427 7231, NT), a marvellous black and white half-timbered hall, with several priest's holes where Roman Catholic priests could hide in the years of the 16th century when they were forbidden to hold masses. The hall is open April through October daily except Monday from 1 to 5.20 pm, and over winter weekends. Admission costs £4.

Bus No 80 from Queen Square will drop you within a mile of Speke Hall. Visitors to Speke Hall can also go by minibus to 20 Forthlin Rd, Liverpool, once home to Beatle Paul McCartney. It's been restored to its 1950's appearance although there's little directly linked to the great Macca. Tours leave Speke Hall at noon, 12.45, 1.30, 2.15, 3 and 3.45 pm, Wednesday to Saturday, from Easter through October. A combined ticket with Speke Hall costs £4.50/2.50. You *must* prebook by phoning

☎ 0115-486 4006, and note that this is the *only* way to visit this small terraced house.

Isle of Man

- **pop 70,000   ☎ 01624**

Measuring just 33 miles by 12 miles, the Isle of Man is a quirky world of its own. The number one industry is tax avoidance – wealthy Brits can shelter their loot here without having to move to Monte Carlo or the Cayman Islands. And the Isle of Man is a motorcyclist's Mecca; each year's May-June TT (Tourist Trophy) races add 45,000 to the island's small population. Home to the world's oldest continuous parliament, the Isle of Man enjoys special status in Britain, and its annual parliamentary ceremony honours the 1000-year history of the Tynwald (a Scandinavian word meaning 'meeting field'). Douglas, the capital, is a run-down relic of Victorian tourism with fading B&Bs but the countryside can be very beautiful. The Isle of Man also boasts some unique fauna including the tailless Manx cat and the four-horned loghtan sheep.

ORIENTATION & INFORMATION

Situated in the Irish Sea, equidistant from Liverpool, Dublin and Belfast, the Isle of Man is about 30 miles long by 10 miles wide. Ferries arrive at Douglas, the port and main town on the south-east coast. Flights come in to Ronaldsway airport, 10 miles south of Douglas. Most of the island's historic sites are operated by Manx National Heritage, which offers free entrance to NT or EH members. Unless otherwise indicated, Manx Heritage (MH) sites open Easter to September, daily from 10 am to 5 pm. The phone number for all inquiries is ☎ 648000.

The Millennium Way traverses the island north-east to south-west, following the route of a medieval highway.

DOUGLAS

- **pop 20,000   ☎ 01624**

Looking across the Irish Sea towards Black-pool, Douglas is not particularly endearing.

Half the once fine Victorian seafront terraces look ready for demolition, renovation or a good coat of paint. More modern buildings look to have been designed by some of Britain's least inspired architects on their off days.

The Manx Museum (MH) gives an introduction to everything from the island's prehistoric past to the latest TT race winners. It's open Monday to Saturday from 10 am to 5 pm; free.

The TIC (☎ 686766), in the Sea Terminal Building, is open daily and makes free accommodation bookings.

Places to Stay

The TIC's camping grounds information sheet lists sites all around the island. Everything is booked out for TT week, often for years ahead.

There's B&B from £13 per person at *Matlock House* (☎ 676714, 16 Castle Mona Ave) and at several other budget-oriented places nearby.

The seafront promenade is shoulder-to-shoulder with B&Bs where you should find something for under £20 a head. In Loch Promenade, two reasonable places are the *Seabank Hotel* (☎ 674815) at No 21 and, more expensive, the *Modwena Hotel* (☎ 675728) at No 39-40.

The *Sefton Hotel* (☎ 626011, Harris Promenade) is more upmarket, with comfortable rooms at £45/60 for singles/doubles.

Places to Eat

Even the big fast food outlets skip round Douglas, leaving a choice of fish and chip shops, dismal-looking Chinese takeaways and a handful of restaurants.

Scott's Bistro (☎ 623764, John St) is pleasant and moderately priced, while *Blazer's* (☎ 673222), on the corner of North Quay and Bank Hill is a wine bar with pub-style food. It's underneath the pricey *Waterfront* restaurant.

L'Expérience (☎ 623103), at the bottom of Summerhill, is a smart French restaurant that serves *queenies* (local scallops).

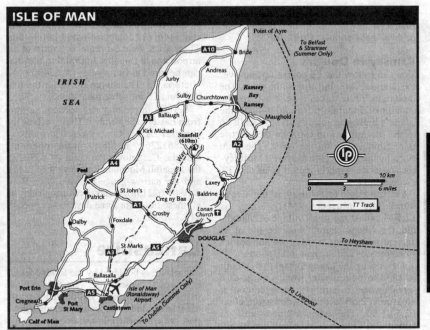

ISLE OF MAN

AROUND THE ISLE OF MAN

Petrol-heads are likely to start their island circuit with motorcycling's Mountain Circuit. At 50 mph some of the long sweeping bends are a delight, at 150 mph they must be terrifying. Fortunately for the unconverted, the island has other attractions, including the 90 mile *Raad ny Foillan*, or Road of the Gull, a coastal walking path which makes a complete circuit of the island.

Castletown & Cregneash

At Castletown, **Castle Rushen** (MH) dates from the 13th century; it's open daily and entry is £3.50/2. There's also a small **Nautical Museum** (MH) here. You can also visit a school dating back to 1570 in **St Mary's church** (MH).

On the southern tip of the island, the **Cregneash Village Folk Museum** (MH) recalls traditional Manx rural life. Admis-

sion is £2.50/1.50. The **Calf of Man**, the small island just off Cregneash, is a bird sanctuary. Calf Island Cruises (☎ 832339) visit regularly during the summer for £6/3 from Port Erin.

Between Castletown and Cregneash, the Iron-Age hillfort at **Chapel Hill** encloses a Viking ship burial site.

Peel

Dating from the 11th century, **Peel Castle** (MH), with its long curtain wall, is stunningly positioned atop St Patrick's Island, joined to Peel by a causeway. The brand-new **House of Manannan** (MH) museum uses interactive displays to explain Manx history and its seafaring traditions. Admission costs £5/2.50.

Just before Peel is the **Tynwald Hill** at St John's where the annual parliamentary ceremony takes place on 5 July.

Peel has several B&Bs. *Kilgallon's Bistro* (☎ 844366) is the best place to eat, or there's the popular *Creek Inn*.

Ramsey to Douglas

You can follow the TT course up and over the mountain or wind around the coast. The mountain route takes you close to the summit of **Snaefell** (621m, 2036 feet), the island's highest point. It's an easy walk up to the summit or you can take the electric tram from Laxey on the coast. The tram stops by the road where **Murray's Motorcycle Museum** displays motorcycles and TT memorabilia.

On the edge of Ramsey is the **Grove Rural Life Museum** (MH); entry is £2.50/1.50. At the small village of **Maughold**, the village church is on the site of an ancient monastery; a small shelter houses stone crosses and ancient inscriptions.

Describing the **Laxey Wheel** (MH), built in 1854 to pump water from a mine, as a 'great' wheel is hardly an exaggeration; it measures 22m across. Admission costs £2.50/1.50. The wheel-headed cross at **Lonan Old Church** is the island's most impressive early Christian cross.

GETTING THERE & AWAY
Air
Manx Airlines (☎ 0345-256256) has frequent connections with Liverpool and Manchester. Jersey European (☎ 0345-676676) connects most frequently with Belfast and Blackpool. There are other smaller operators. Typically, you're looking at around £70 return for a weekend Manchester connection.

Boat
The Isle of Man Steam Packet (☎ 661661) operates regular car ferries and high-speed SeaCat catamarans to Douglas from Dublin, Belfast, Heysham, Fleetwood, Liverpool and Ardrossan. Foot passenger fares start at £23 single but you'll have to pay from £68 to take a car across. The crossing from Liverpool takes 2½ hours by SeaCat or four hours by ferry.

GETTING AROUND
A taxi from the airport into Douglas will cost about £12 compared with £1.50 by bus. There are several car rental operators at the airport and in Douglas. In Douglas, bicycles can be hired at Eurocycles (☎ 624909), 8a Victoria Rd. The charge is £10 for the first day, and £5 for subsequent days.

Several interesting rail services operate from Easter to September. These include the Douglas-Laxey-Ramsey electric tramway (☎ 861226); a steam train operating Douglas-Castletown-Port Erin (☎ 673623); the Snaefell Mountain Railway (☎ 861225); and the narrow-gauge Groudle Glen Railway (☎ 622138). A ticket covering rides on all these trains for three days in seven costs £13.70/6.85.

Lancashire

Lancashire is bordered by the River Mersey in the south, the sea in the west, the Pennines in the east and the Lake District in the north. Manchester and Liverpool, the region's great port, are administered separately.

Business and commerce have gravitated towards southern Lancashire, once famous for its coal and cotton industries, but the depressed industrial towns of Preston (a major transport interchange), Blackburn, Accrington and Burnley offer little to linger for.

Of the traditional seaside resorts serving Manchester and Liverpool, Blackpool lives splendidly, if tackily, on, but Morecambe is in sad decline, worth transiting only to see the Art Deco Midland Hotel crumbling away on the seafront.

LANCASTER
☎ 01524
The historic city of Lancaster is certainly worth a visit. Standing on the banks of the River Lune, it dates back to Roman times but has a wealth of fine Georgian architecture.

The TIC (☎ 32878), at 28 Castle Hill, stocks a comprehensive free guide to Lancaster and Morecambe.

Lancaster Castle & Priory

Lancaster's imposing castle (☎ 64998), part of which is still a prison, was originally built in the 11th century, although what you see now is much newer. Regular tours take in the courtroom and Hadrian's Tower with its display of instruments of torture and the dungeons. One famous trial that took place here was of the so-called Pendle Witches in 1612. It's open daily from Easter to October, from 10.30 am to 4 pm. Admission costs £3.50/2, less at times when court sittings curtail the tours.

Immediately beside the castle is the equally fine **priory church** (☎ 65338), founded in 1094 but extensively remodelled later in the Middle Ages. It's usually open during office hours.

Other Things to See

The **Maritime Museum** (☎ 64637), in the 18th century Custom House on St George's Quay, recalls the days when Lancaster was a flourishing port at the centre of the slave trade. It's open daily from 11 am to 5 pm (12.30 to 4 pm from November to Easter). Admission costs £2/1.

The **City Museum** (☎ 64637), Market Square, has a mixed bag of local historical and archaeological exhibits. It's open Monday to Saturday from 10 am to 5 pm; free.

The **Judges' Lodgings** (☎ 32808), off China St, is a 17th century townhouse containing a Museum of Childhood and some fine furnishings. The **Cottage Museum** (☎ 64637), 15 Castle Hill, has been furnished to show life in an artisan's house in the early 19th century.

Places to Stay & Eat

Lancaster lacks a youth hostel but over Easter and in summer 400 beds are available for B&B at £18.92 a head at the *University College of St Martin* (☎ 384460) accommodation block in Bowerham Rd.

The small *Station House* (☎ 381060, 25 Meeting House Lane)* has singles/doubles for £18/30. *Edenbreck House* (☎ 32464, Sunnyside Lane)* has comfortable rooms with attractive decor for £30/35.

Folly Café, in Castle Park, serves dishes like Lancashire hot pot for £2.95 in a building that doubles as a small art gallery. From Easter to October, teas and lunches are available in the *Priory Refectory*.

Getting There & Away

Lancaster is on the main west-coast railway line and on the Cumbrian Coast Line. A train from Kendal to Lancaster costs £4.70 (30 minutes). There are also National Express links with most local towns.

BLACKPOOL
* **pop 147,000   ☎ 01253**

If you want to see just one of England's brasher resorts, you should probably make it Blackpool, biggest and brashest of them all and still visited by around eight million people a year even though it's well past its heyday.

Blackpool is famous for its Tower, its three piers, its Pleasure Beach and its **Illuminations**, a successful ploy to extend the brief summer holiday season. From early September to early November, 5 miles of the Promenade are illuminated with thousands of electric and neon lights.

Orientation & Information

Blackpool is surprisingly spread out but can still be managed easily without a car because trams run the entire 7 mile length of the seafront Promenade.

'Amusement' centres with slot machines and bingo games stretch all the way along the Golden Mile from the South Pier to the Central and North piers. South Pier, the least impressive, is alongside Blackpool Pleasure Beach and The Sandcastle, an enormous indoor pool complex. The town centre and Blackpool Tower lie between the Central and North piers.

The TIC (☎ 21623) at 1 Clifton St will make free local accommodation bookings. There's a second branch in the Pleasure Beach (☎ 403223).

Blackpool Tower

Europe's second metal tower when built in 1894, the tower (☎ 622242) is Blackpool's best known symbol. It's over 150m high and houses a vast entertainment complex, as well as a laser show and indoor circus.

The highlight is the magnificent, rococo **ballroom**, with extraordinary sculptured and gilded plasterwork, murals and chandeliers. Couples still glide across the floor to the melodramatic tones of a huge Wurlitzer organ from 2 to 11 pm every day. *Saturday Night Fever* might never have happened.

The Tower is open daily from 10 am to 11 pm. Admission costs £5.95/4.95.

Blackpool Pleasure Beach & The Sandcastle

The UK's most visited outdoor attraction, Blackpool Pleasure Beach (☎ 341033) is a 16 hectare funfair packed with rides, the most interesting of them the historic wooden roller coasters – particularly the brilliant Grand National – and a steel roller coaster, the Pepsi Max Big One.

Admission to the park is free. Rides are divided into categories and you can buy tickets for individual categories or for a mixture of them all. It's open daily from 10 am, April through October and at weekends in March.

The pool at **The Sandcastle** (☎ 343602) across the road is open daily from May through October from 10 am to 6 pm (8.30 pm on summer Wednesdays).

Sea Life Centre

Close to Tower World in New Bonny St, is the state-of-the-art aquarium (☎ 622445), open daily from 10 am to 5 pm; £5.95/4.75.

Places to Stay

Blackpool's hundreds of B&Bs and small hotels compete with each other on price so, except at the height of summer, you should have no trouble finding somewhere to stay for less than £15 a head. Good places to start looking are Albert Rd and Hornby Rd, a couple of blocks back from the sea but close to the Tower and the pubs and discos. B&Bs in Albert Rd charging around £18 a head include *Boltonia Hotel* (☎ 620248) at No 124 and *Buxton Manor Hotel*

(☎ 623667) at No 41. *Rosedale Guest House* (☎ 624301, 87 Hornby Rd) charges from £12 a head. In nearby Bright St, pleasant *Hotel Bambi* (☎ 343756) charges £18/33 a single/double.

Quiet Gynn Ave, about half a mile north of North Pier is lined with B&Bs charging around £18 per person. Possibilities include the *Bramleigh Hotel* (☎ 351568) at No 13, the *Haldene Private Hotel* (☎ 353763) at No 4, or *The Austen* (☎ 351784) at No 6.

Places to Eat

Forget gourmet meals – the Blackpool experience is all about stuffing your face with burgers, hot dogs, doughnuts, and fish and chips. Most people eat at their hotels where roast and three vegetables often cost just £3 a head.

There are a few restaurants around Talbot Square (near the TIC) on Queen St, Talbot Rd and Clifton St. The most interesting possibility is the Afro-Caribbean *Lagoonda* (☎ 293837, 37 Queen St) where starters average £3, main meals £9. *Giannini* (☎ 28926, 2 Queen St) does pizza and pasta for around £4.50.

Getting There & Away

Blackpool is approximately 50 miles from both Liverpool and Manchester and 250 miles from London.

Bus One interesting possibility is Primrose Coaches (☎ 0191-232 5567) daily service to/from Newcastle via Kirkby Stephen, Raby Castle, Barnard Castle and Durham (X69).

National Express has services to most major towns in Britain. The central coach station is on Talbot Rd, near the town centre.

Train To get to Blackpool you often have to change in Preston (1½ hours). The journey from London takes about four hours.

Getting Around

To get into the swing of things, hop on and off the vintage trams that run up and down the Promenade. The buses are marginally cheaper but nothing like as much fun.

Cumbria

Much of Cumbria is a scenic feast, with the Lake District National Park at its heart. The mountains, valleys and lakes are beautiful, although ever since they were popularised by the early 19th century Romantics they've been the centre of a major tourism industry. Nonetheless, if you avoid summer weekends and the main roads and do some walking, it's still possible, like Wordsworth, to wander 'lonely as a cloud'.

The M6 and west-coast railway cut the county into an eastern third, which runs into the Yorkshire Dales and Pennine Hills, and a western two-thirds that includes the Lake District National Park and England's highest mountains. Not surprisingly, the western two-thirds draws the largest crowds, although bits of the east, particularly the Eden Valley, are also very beautiful.

WALKS

Cumbria offers some of the best walks in Britain. See the Activities chapter for information on the Cumbria Way, and the Lake District National Park later in this chapter. For more details, see Lonely Planet's *Walking in Britain*.

CYCLE ROUTES

This is also a good area for cycling. Keen cyclists should consider the waymarked 259 mile circular Cumbria Cycle Way. It can be done in five days, but a full week is better. For more details look for *The Cumbria Cycle Way* by Roy Walker and Ron Jarvis. Carlisle TIC also stocks plenty of information.

Another possibility is the 140 mile Sea To Sea (C2C) route from Whitehaven or Workington to Newcastle or Sunderland. Most people will need five days to complete this cross-country route. The *National Cycleway Network Guide* gives all the details.

If you're planning to cycle along Hadrian's Wall, TICs sell the *Hadrian's Wall Country Cycle Map*.

GETTING AROUND

Cumbria Journey Planner (☎ 01228-606000) provides information on all local bus, boat and train services. It's open Monday to Friday from 9 am to 5 pm, and Saturday from 9 am to noon.

Bus

The main operator is Stagecoach (☎ 01946-63222). Its Explorer tickets give unlimited travel on all services, including the No 685 to Newcastle upon Tyne. They cost £5.20/3.85 for one day or £12.99/8.99 for four days but check carefully that you're doing enough travelling to save on the deal.

Train

Three of Britain's most scenic train journeys cross Cumbria. The Cumbrian Coast Line runs right round the west coast from Carlisle to Ulverston and Lancaster (see the Cumbrian Coast Line later in this chapter). A branch line runs from Oxenholme to Windermere. Finally, the Leeds-Settle-Carlisle (LSC) line, which starts in South Yorkshire, enters Cumbria south of Kirkby Stephen on its way to Carlisle.

Tours

The Mountain Goat offers half-day (around £14) and full day escorted tours (around £23) of Cumbria and the Lake District in minivans. If you don't have your own transport this offers a good way of getting to some of the more remote areas, especially out of season. Mountain Goat is at Victoria St, Windermere (☎ 015394-45161) and Central Car Park Rd, Keswick (☎ 017687-73962), but has lots of other pick-up points.

CARLISLE

• pop 72,000 ☎ 01228

Modern Carlisle may be a sleepy small town but for 1600 years it defended the north of England, or the south of Scotland,

The Border Reivers

People who fret about the modern-day crime wave should thank their lucky stars they didn't live in the Border Lands during the 400 years when the rapacious Reivers were king.

The Reivers were brigands whose backgrounds differed but who had in common a complete disregard for the governments of England and Scotland. For the Reivers, sheep rustling and burning the homes of their enemies were a way of life. As a result, northern Cumbria and Northumberland, the southern Scottish Borders and Dumfries & Galloway are littered with minor castles and tower-houses, as people struggled to protect themselves.

It wasn't until James VI of Scotland succeeded Elizabeth I of England and united the two countries that order was finally reasserted. The Reivers are credited with giving the words 'blackmail' and 'bereaved' to the English language. And if your surname is Armstrong, Carruthers, Dixon, Elliot, Henderson, Johnstone, Maxwell, Nixon, Scott, Taylor, Wilson or Young, genealogists would have us believe you could be descended from a Reiver.

depending on who was winning. Although its character was spoilt to some extent by 19th century industrialisation, it's an interesting town and its strategic location can be exploited by visitors to Northumberland, Hadrian's Wall, Dumfries and Galloway, the beautiful Scottish Borders, as well as the Lake District. It's also a hub for five excellent rail journeys.

History

Carlisle's history has been dominated by warfare and it seems miraculous that it could be peaceful today. The Romans under Agricola built a military station here, probably on the site of a Celtic camp or *caer* (preserved in the modern name of Carlisle).

Later, Hadrian's Wall was built a little to the north, and Carlisle became the Roman administrative centre for the north-west. But even the mighty Roman Empire was hard-pressed to maintain control and the Picts sacked the town in 181 and 367.

Carlisle survived into Saxon times, but was under constant pressure from the Scots and was sacked by Danish Vikings in 875. The Normans seized it from the Scots in 1092 and William Rufus began construction of the castle and town walls, but the Scots gained control again between 1136 and 1157. Forty years later the city withstood a siege by the Scottish King William. Sixty years later it managed to repulse William Wallace during the Scottish War of Independence.

The Scottish Borders, or the Debateable Lands as they were known, were virtually ungovernable from the late 13th century to the middle of the 16th century. The great families with their complex blood feuds fought and robbed the English, the Scots and each other. The city's walls and the great gates that slammed shut every night served a very real purpose.

During the Civil War, Carlisle was Royalist, and was eventually taken by the Scottish army after a nine month siege in 1644-45. In 1745 it also surrendered to Bonnie Prince Charlie, who proclaimed his father king at the market cross.

After the Restoration, peace came at last to Carlisle. So, eventually, did industry, cotton mills and railways.

Orientation & Information

The train station is south of the city centre, a 10 minute walk from Town Hall Square and the TIC. The bus station is on Lowther St, one block east of the square.

The TIC (☎ 512444) in Town Hall Square stocks an enormous quantity of literature. Monday to Saturday from May to September, there are 1½-hour guided town walks (☎ 625600) at 2 pm. They cost £2/75p. Sunday walks take place at 2 pm and cost £5.50/2.75. In July and August

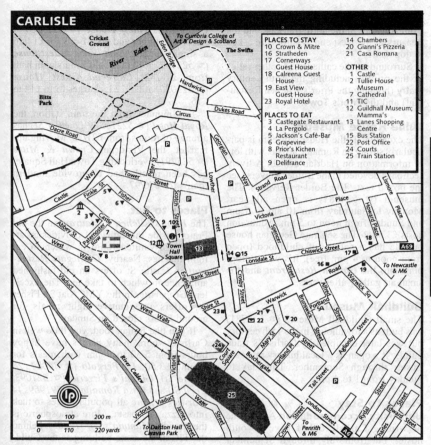

CARLISLE

PLACES TO STAY
10 Crown & Mitre
16 Stratheden
17 Cornerways
   Guest House
18 Calreena Guest
   House
19 East View
   Guest House
23 Royal Hotel

PLACES TO EAT
3 Castlegate Restaurant
4 La Pergolo
5 Jackson's Café-Bar
6 Grapevine
8 Prior's Kichen
   Restaurant
9 Delifrance

14 Chambers
20 Gianni's Pizzeria
21 Casa Romana

OTHER
1 Castle
2 Tullie House
   Museum
7 Cathedral
11 TIC
12 Guildhall Museum;
   Mamma's
13 Lanes Shopping
   Centre
15 Bus Station
22 Post Office
24 Courts
25 Train Station

NORTH-WESTERN ENGLAND

there are 6 pm Tuesday evening tours to Hadrian's Wall for £7.50/4.50.

Carlisle Castle

Probably built on the site of British and Roman fortresses, brooding Carlisle Castle (☎ 591922, EH) is well worth exploring. The fine Norman keep was built in 1092 by William Rufus, and Mary Queen of Scots was briefly imprisoned here in 1568. There's a maze of passages and chambers and great views from the ramparts. Admission costs £2.90/1.50.

Carlisle Cathedral

The small, red sandstone cathedral was originally constructed as a priory church in 1123 but became a cathedral in 1133. During the 1644-45 siege, two-thirds of the nave was torn down to provide stone for repairing the city wall and castle. Serious restoration didn't begin until 1853, but a surprising amount survives, including the east window and part of the original Norman nave.

Features to look out for include the 15th century misericords, including one with a mermaid; the lovely Brougham Triptych from Antwerp in the north transept; and the treasury at the west end. Visitors are asked to donate £2.

Surrounding the cathedral are other relics of the priory, including the 16th century **Fratry** (housing the Prior's Kitchen Restaurant) and the **Prior's Tower**.

Tullie House Museum

The excellent Tullie House Museum is particularly strong on Roman Carlisle, with lots of information on Hadrian's Wall. A lively section is devoted to the Border Reivers (see the boxed text 'The Border Reivers'). The museum (☎ 534781) is open all year, Monday to Saturday from 10 am to 5 pm and Sunday from noon to 5 pm. Admission costs £3.50/2. The separate Georgian house outside has a gallery of childhood (open from noon to 4 pm; free). It's worth dropping into the *Garden Restaurant* and the small art gallery afterwards.

Guildhall Museum

The small Guildhall Museum (☎ 532781) was built as a townhouse in the 15th century but was later occupied by Carlisle's trade guilds. It's open as a local history museum Easter through September, Thursday to Sunday from 1 to 4 pm.

Places to Stay

University Accommodation At the time of writing Carlisle didn't have a youth hostel, but from July through September B&B is available for £15.95 at the *Cumbria College of Art & Design* (☎ 599058, *Brampton Rd*).

Camping The *Dalston Hall Caravan Park* (☎ 710165), just off the B5299 to the south of the city, has van and tent sites from £6.

B&Bs & Hotels With plenty of comfortable B&Bs within walking distance of the centre, you shouldn't have to pay more than £15.

There are several good choices on Warwick Rd. The small and friendly *Stratheden* (☎ 520192) at No 93, has pleasingly decorated rooms from £15 a head. *Cornerways Guest House* (☎ 521733) at No 107, is larger and does B&B for £14/26 a single/double. *East View Guesthouse* (☎ 522112) at No 110, has rooms with bath from £18/32. *Calreena Guest House* (☎ 525020) at No 123, charges from £14 to £16.

Two minutes from the train station, the *Royal Hotel* (☎ 522103, *9 Lowther St*) has a range of rooms from £21/35. Moving up-market, the Victorian *Crown & Mitre* (☎ 525491) overlooking Town Hall Square, has been refurbished to provide modern rooms for £76/97.

Places to Eat

The *Prior's Kitchen Restaurant* in the old Fratry beside the cathedral provides an atmospheric vaulted room in which to eat light lunches. Nearby, *Castlegate Restaurant* in Castle St offers an old-fashioned ambience in which to take tea. The excellent *Grapevine*, in the YMCA at 22 Fisher St, offers imaginative light meals for around £1.50; closed on Sunday.

If you like Italian food, you'll do well in Carlisle where many places have happy hours from 5.30 to 7 pm with meals for around £3.50. *La Pergolo* (☎ 34084, *28 Castle St*), *Gianni's Pizzeria* (☎ 521093, *Cecil St*) and *Casa Romana* (☎ 591969, *44 Warwick St*), are all popular places to tuck into pizza and pasta. More atmospheric is the friendly *Mamma's* (☎ 512305), behind the TIC in the same building as the Guildhall Museum.

A newcomer to the eating scene, *Chambers* (☎ 818353) at the junction of Lonsdale and Lowther streets offers dishes such as paella for £7.25. At the time of writing Carlisle's solitary café bar was *Jackson's* (☎ 596868, *6-8 Fisher St*), which stays open until 2 am and sometimes has live music.

There's a branch of *Delifrance,* offering great sandwiches, behind the TIC.

Getting There & Away

See the fares tables in the Getting Around chapter. Carlisle is 295 miles from London,

98 miles from Edinburgh, 95 miles from Glasgow, 115 miles from York and Manchester and 58 miles from Newcastle upon Tyne.

Bus Numerous National Express connections can be booked at the TIC. There are four buses to/from London (5½ hours, £16) and many to Glasgow (two hours, £11.75). One service a day comes from Cambridge (eight hours, £33) and Bristol (six hours, £36).

For information on Stagecoach bus services phone ☎ 01946-63222. Its X5 Lakeslink service connects Carlisle with Penrith, Keswick, Cockermouth and Whitehaven.

A Rail Link coach service runs from the train station to Hawick, Selkirk and Galashiels in the Scottish Borders.

The Hadrian's Wall Bus No 682/685 connects Carlisle with Haltwhistle, Hexham and Newcastle.

Train Fifteen trains a day link Carlisle with London Euston station (four hours, from £12.50).

Carlisle is the terminus for five famous scenic railways; phone ☎ 0345-484950 for information on day Ranger tickets offering unlimited travel and timetable details.

Leeds-Settle-Carlisle Line cuts south-east across the Yorkshire Dales through beautiful, unspoilt countryside (two hours 40 minutes, £16.40).

Lakes Line branches off the main north-south Preston and Carlisle line at Oxenholme, just outside Kendal, for Windermere; there are plenty of trains daily (20 minutes, £2.65).

Tyne Valley Line follows Hadrian's Wall to/from Newcastle upon Tyne and is useful for visitors to the wall. See the Newcastle upon Tyne and Hadrian's Wall sections (1½ hours, £7.80).

Cumbrian Coast Line (see that section later in this chapter) follows the coast in a great arc around to Lancaster, with views over the Irish Sea, and back to the Lake District (one hour, £16).

Glasgow-Carlisle Line is the main route north to Glasgow and gives you a taste of the spectacular Scottish landscape. Most trains make few stops (1½ hours, £20.50).

COCKERMOUTH
- **pop 7000** ☎ 01900

Lying outside the Lake District National Park, Cockermouth is an attractive small town, well placed for exploring the less populous north-west (especially beautiful Crummock Water and Buttermere). In fact, being outside the park has saved it from the worst excesses of Lakes tourism. It may have been discovered but so far it hasn't been spoilt.

Information
The TIC (☎ 822634) is in the town hall. Fellside Sports (☎ 823071) on Main St stocks outdoor gear.

Wordsworth House
This Georgian country house (☎ 824805, NT), built in 1745, was the birthplace and childhood home of William Wordsworth and his sister Dorothy. It's furnished in 18th century style and contains some Wordsworth memorabilia. It's open April through October, weekdays from 11 am to 5 pm and on summer Saturdays; £2.80/1.40.

Jenning's Brewery
If you appreciate decent beer, you'll very quickly find yourself enjoying Mr Jenning's traditionally brewed products, particularly the Dark Mild and Bitter. From April through October, the brewery alongside the River Cocker (☎ 823214) offers one hour tours (£3/1.50) at 11 am and 2 pm from Monday to Friday, with 12.30 pm tours in July and August, and at 11 am on Saturday from April to mid-September. Children under 12 are not admitted.

Places to Stay
Hostel *Cockermouth Youth Hostel* (☎ *822561, Double Mills*) is in a 17th century water mill on the south edge of town. From Main St follow Station St, then Station Rd. Keep left after the war memorial, then left into Fern Bank Rd. Take the track at the end of Fern Bank. The hostel is open Easter to July and September to October, daily except Tuesday and Wednesday;

NORTH-WESTERN ENGLAND

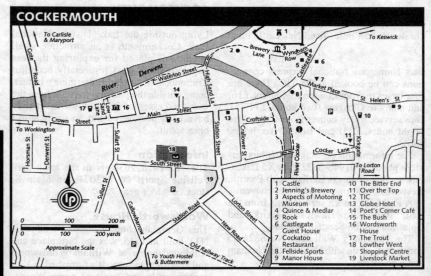

COCKERMOUTH

To Carlisle & Maryport
To Keswick
To Workington
To Lorton Road
To Youth Hostel & Buttermere

1 Castle
2 Jenning's Brewery
3 Aspects of Motoring Museum
4 Quince & Medlar
5 Rook
6 Castlegate Guest House
7 Cockatoo Restaurant
8 Fellside Sports
9 Manor House
10 The Bitter End
11 Over the Top
12 TIC
13 Globe Hotel
14 Poet's Corner Café
15 The Bush
16 Wordsworth House
17 The Trout
18 Lowther Went Shopping Centre
19 Livestock Market

Approximate Scale
0   100   200 m
0   100   200 yards

daily in July and August. Beds cost £7.20/4.95 for adults/juniors.

Camping The nearest camp site is *Violet Bank Holiday Home Park* (☎ 822169, *Simonscales Lane*), off Lorton Rd. Tent pitches cost from £4.90.

B&Bs *Castlegate Guest House* (☎ 826749, *6 Castlegate*) is a beautiful Georgian town house with B&B from £16 to £23 per person. It's opposite the Quince & Medlar restaurant. Readers have also recommended the similarly priced *Rook* (☎ 828496) across the road.

Manor House (☎ 822416, St Helen's St) is another pleasant, central B&B with two family rooms and one single from £16 per person. *Rose Cottage* (☎ 822189), in Lorton Rd (a continuation of Victoria Rd), has beds from £17.50 to £25.

In Main St, *The Globe Hotel* (☎ 822126) has singles/doubles for £25/40. Robert Louis Stephenson stayed here when he visited Cockermouth in 1871.

Places to Eat

Of the various teashops, perhaps the nicest is the *Poet's Corner Café* down an alley off Main St. The tiny but very popular *Over the Top* (☎ 827016) café in Kirkgate is open Tuesday to Saturday from 10 am to 4 pm and Wednesday to Saturday from 7 pm.

The *Quince & Medlar* (☎ 823579) is one of the country's best vegetarian restaurants and booking is advisable. The menu features main dishes like celery and stilton strudel for £8.25, with starters for around £3. The *Cockatoo Restaurant* (☎ 826205) round the corner in Market Place also does vegetarian and vegan food.

The *Trout* in Main St, next to William Wordsworth's birthplace, and the *Bush*, also on Main St, both offer good-value traditional bar meals for under £5. *The Bitter End* in Kirkgate is Cumbria's smallest brewery. Sample Skinners Old Strong or Cockersnoot alongside decent pub grub.

Getting There & Away

Stagecoach Bus No 600 has two or three services a day, Monday to Saturday, to/from

Carlisle (one hour, £2.75). The more frequent X5 service between Whitehaven, Keswick and Penrith also stops at Cockermouth; there are three buses on Sunday between Cockermouth and Keswick.

KENDAL
☎ 01539

On the eastern outskirts of the Lake District National Park, Kendal is a lively town that has had a market since the 12th century. While it's not particularly beautiful, it does have several interesting museums, including the Museum of Lakeland Life, which more than justifies a visit.

The TIC (☎ 725758) is in the town hall in Highgate. As well as the museums and art gallery, you can clamber up to the ruins of Kendal Castle, just to the west of the river, where Henry VIII's last wife Katherine Parr may have lived.

Museums & Galleries

To the south of town, on the banks of the River Kent, you'll find the Museum of Lakeland Life and the Abbot Hall Art Gallery (☎ 722464).

The museum is a delight, with reconstructed period shops and rooms, a model of a local mine and lots of information on lost local industries like bobbin-making. One room is devoted to local author Arthur Ransome who wrote the Swallows & Amazons books, and another to John Cunliffe, more recent creator of Postman Pat who delivers the mail in Greendale (aka Longsleddale).

The Abbot Hall Art Gallery also makes much of local man, artist George Romney (1734-1802), many of whose portraits and drawings are on display. The temporary exhibitions on the 1st floor can be particularly worthwhile.

The **Kendal Museum** (☎ 721374) in Station Rd has collections of natural history and archaeology.

All three museums are open daily from mid-February until Christmas from 10.30 am to 5 pm. Admission to each is £2.80/1.20, although once you've visited one you can see the others for £1.

The Climbers' Friend

Kendal will be best known to many climbers as home of the mint cake, the high nutrition snack that sustained Sir Edmund Hillary and Sirdar Tensing on their successful attempt on the summit of Everest in 1953.

These days there's barely a local sweet-shop, let alone any other kind of shop, that would see its shelves as properly equipped if they weren't piled high with the bars, whether brown, white or even chocolate-coated.

Places to Stay & Eat

Kendal Youth Hostel (☎ 724066, 118 Highgate) is open daily from late March through August, closing on Sunday and Monday at other times. Beds cost £8.80/5.95 for adults/juniors.

Right next door is the **Brewery**, one of those wonderful arts complexes that manages to be all things to all people, with a theatre and cinema (☎ 725133) and an excellent bar-bistro. For £12 you can have a two-course dinner with a cinema ticket thrown in. At other times, soup comes at £1.75 and something like cod and courgette crumble at £3.95.

Other possibilities for light meals include **Castle Dairy** (☎ 721170, Stramongate), **Jackie's Attic Coffee House** in Highgate and the **coffee shop** attached to the Abbot Hall Art Gallery.

Getting There & Away

Kendal is on the branch train line from Windermere to Oxenholme, with connections north to Manchester and south to Lancaster and Barrow-in-Furness. Stagecoach also runs a reasonably frequent service from Windermere to Barrow via Kendal.

Lake District National Park

I wandered lonely as a cloud
That floats on high o'er dales and hills
When all at once I saw a crowd …

William Wordsworth

The Lake District is one of England's most beautiful corners, a magical mix of dainty green dales, stark, rocky mountains and the eponymous lakes. It manages to look beautiful even on the murkiest days – which is just as well since few visitors to the Lakes escape without a soaking! The Cumbrian Mountains are not particularly high – none reach 1000 metres (3280 feet) – but they're much more dramatic than their height would suggest.

Unfortunately, an estimated 14 million people pour into the Lakes every year. The crowds can be so dense and the traffic jams so long that it's debateable whether it's worth visiting on any weekend between May and October, or any time at all from mid-July to the end of August. Stick with weekdays in May and June, or in September to October to make the most of the scenery without having to queue. Fortunately, the National Trust (NT) owns a quarter of the total area. This is partly thanks to Beatrix Potter who sold the NT half of her large estate at cost and bequeathed the rest.

ORIENTATION

The two main bases for the Lakes are Keswick in the north (particularly for walkers) and Windermere and Bowness in the south (two contiguous tourist traps). Coniston is a less hectic alternative. All these towns have youth hostels, plus numerous B&Bs and places to eat.

Ullswater, Grasmere, Windermere, Coniston Water and Derwent Water are often considered to be the most beautiful lakes, but they also teem with boats. Wast Water, Crummock Water and Buttermere are equally spectacular but much less crowded.

In general, the mob stays on the A-roads, and the crowds are much thinner west of a line drawn from Keswick to Coniston.

INFORMATION

The TICs stock a frightening number of guidebooks and brochures about the Lakes. The Windermere and Keswick TICs are good places to start exploring the Lake District; both have lots of information and free local booking services. The national park runs nine TICs in the area, plus a visitors centre (☎ 015394-46601) at Brockhole, on the A591 between Windermere and Ambleside. Altogether there are about 30 dotted around.

If you're staying several days, consider buying a copy of *National Park Walks in the Countryside*, which has 40 walks of all grades, even for kids. *A Walk Round the Lakes* by Hunter Davies will fill in some of the background details. The classic walking guides are the seven hand-written, hand-drawn volumes of Alfred Wainwright's *Pictorial Guide to the Lakeland Fells*, still useful despite their age and cost.

The numerous walking/climbing shops, particularly in Ambleside and Keswick, are other good sources of local information.

WALKS & CYCLE ROUTES

Walking or cycling are the best ways of getting around, but bear in mind that conditions can be treacherous, and the going can be very, very steep. Off-road mountain biking is popular, but there are also some good touring routes. See Getting Around in the Windermere & Bowness section later in this chapter for mountain-bike hire details.

Several outdoor shops and centres hire boots, tents and hiking equipment. Phone the Weatherline on ☎ 017687-75757 before setting out on ambitious excursions. TICs stock free leaflets with basic information on safety in the fells and on the water.

See the Activities chapter for details on the Cumbria Way. The Cumbria section has information on the Cumbrian and Sea To Sea Cycle Ways.

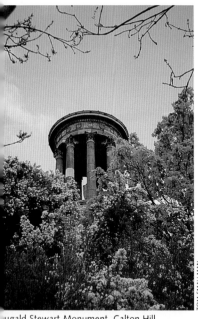

ugald Stewart Monument, Calton Hill

Scottish drummer

Overlooking Edinburgh from Calton Hill

GLENN BEANLAND

Pub entrance on High Street, Edinburgh

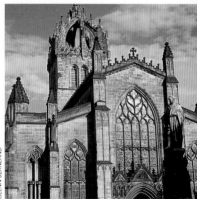

GLENN BEANLAND

St Giles Cathedral, Edinburgh

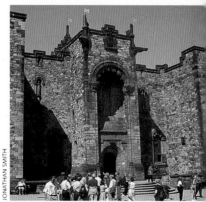

JONATHAN SMITH

Scottish National War Museum, Edinburgh Castle

JONATHAN SMITH

View across North Bridge to Princes Street, Edinburgh

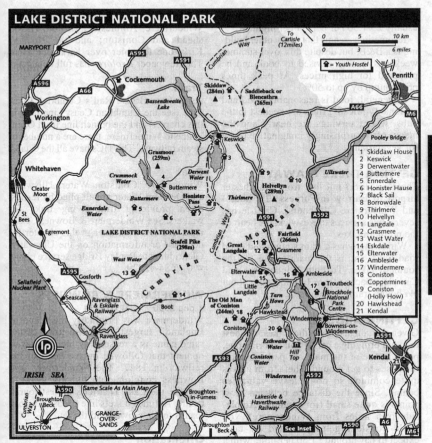

LAKE DISTRICT NATIONAL PARK

To Carlisle (12miles)

Cumbrian Way

MARYPORT

A595

A591

Cockermouth

A596

A66

Workington

Bassenthwaite Lake

Skiddaw (284m) 1

Saddleback or Blencathra (265m)

Keswick

A66

Penrith

M6

Pooley Bridge

Whitehaven

Grasmoor (259m)

Crummock Water

Derwent Water

Keswick

3

Cleator Moor

Buttermere 4

Buttermere

Honister Pass

Helvellyn (289m) 9

10

Ullswater

St Bees

Ennerdale Water

Buttermere 5

6 7 8

Thirlmere

Helvellyn

A591

A592

Egremont

LAKE DISTRICT NATIONAL PARK

Scafell Pike (298m)

Cumbrian Way

Great Langdale

11

12

Fairfield (266m)

Grasmere

Sellafield Nuclear Plant

Gosforth

A595

Wast Water

13

Cumbrian

Mountains

Elterwater

16

Ambleside

17

Troutbeck

Brockhole National Park Centre

Seascale

Ravenglass & Eskdale Railway

Boot

14

Little Langdale

Tarn Hows

Hawkshead

The Old Man of Coniston (244m)

18

15

Coniston

20

Windermere

Bowness-on-Windermere

A591

Ravenglass

Esthwaite Water

Hill Top

Kendal

21

A593

Coniston Water

Windermere

A592

A6

M6

IRISH SEA

A590

Same Scale As Main Map

Cumbrian Way

Broughton Beck

ULVERSTON

GRANGE-OVER-SANDS

Broughton-in-Furness

Broughton Beck

Lakeside & Haverthwaite Railway

See Inset

A590

= Youth Hostel

0   5   10 km
0   3   6 miles

1	Skiddaw House
2	Keswick
3	Derwentwater
4	Buttermere
5	Ennerdale
6	Honister Hause
7	Black Sail
8	Borrowdale
9	Thirlmere
10	Helvellyn
11	Langdale
12	Grasmere
13	Wast Water
14	Eskdale
15	Elterwater
16	Ambleside
17	Windermere
18	Coniston Coppermines
19	Coniston (Holly How)
20	Hawkshead
21	Kendal

NORTH-WESTERN ENGLAND

PLACES TO STAY & EAT

There are over 30 youth hostels in the Lakes, many of them within walking distance of each other. They're very popular so book well ahead in summer.

The Lake District National Park Authority administers 12 camping barns (traditional barns kitted out with basic facilities such as wooden sleeping platform, tap, toilet, table, benches) all in picturesque locations. You can stay in them for £3 a night but need to bring all the usual camping gear

apart from a tent. Contact Keswick Information Centre (☎ 017687-72803), 31 Lake Rd, Keswick CA12 5DQ, for full details.

The NT also operates three excellent camping grounds for tents and vans (not caravans): at the head of Great Langdale, 8 miles from Ambleside on the B5343 (☎ 015394-37668); at the head of Wasdale, on the western shore of Wast Water (☎ 019467-26620); and at Low Wray (☎ 015394-32810) 3 miles south of Ambleside on the western shore of Windermere, access from the B5286. The charge is usually £3/1.50 per person per night.

It sometimes seems that every other building is a B&B, but despite this, over summer weekends, you're advised to book and be prepared for high prices. At peak times prices jump by up to 50%.

In general, food is reasonably good and reasonably priced. Prices are keenest in the pubs, where servings are hearty and the menus often surprisingly imaginative (even for vegetarians).

GETTING THERE & AWAY

There's a direct rail link from Manchester airport to Barrow-in-Furness (2½ hours) and Windermere (2¼ hours). Carlisle has several bus services to Keswick, the heart of the northern lakes.

Windermere has a train station and good road links, and is the main centre for the southern lakes. To both Windermere and Carlisle, coaches from London take about 6½ hours, trains 3½ hours.

GETTING AROUND

Given the congestion in the Lakes, it's best to avoid bringing a car. If you do bring one, put it in one of the main car parks and use the buses to get around. Theft from cars is quite common so don't leave valuables behind. Since the distance between most points is quite small (for example, Ambleside is 5 miles from Windermere), you could consider getting around by taxi; expect to pay around £1.50 per mile, with a minimum charge of £2.

Bus

The innovative Coast to Coast Packhorse (☎ 017683-71680) offers a daily minibus service from St Bees on the west coast to Robin Hood's Bay on the east from Easter to October. See Kirkby Stephen in the North-Eastern England chapter.

Stagecoach (☎ 01946-63222) has some excellent local bus services, including the No 555 Lakeslink between the main towns and Carlisle; the No 505/506 Coniston Rambler minibuses on the Beatrix Potter

Trail – links hourly between Bowness, Windermere, Ambleside, Hilltop, Hawkshead and Coniston; and the No 517 Kirkstone Rambler over Kirkstone Pass. The free paper *Explorer* has full details.

Train

Aside from British Rail's Cumbrian Coast Line (see the Cumbrian Coast Line later in this chapter) and the branch line from Oxenholme to Windermere, there are a number of steam railways. The TICs have all the details.

Boat

Windermere, Coniston Water, Ullswater and Derwent Water are all plied by ferries, often providing time-saving links for walkers. See Windermere & Bowness, Coniston and Keswick later in this chapter for details. For information on the Ullswater, Glenridding to Pooley Bridge service phone ☎ 017684-82229.

WINDERMERE & BOWNESS
- pop 8300   ☎ 015394

Windermere was originally the name of England's largest lake. The town of the same name is a reasonably modern development that followed on the heels of the railway in 1847. The Windermere and Bowness conglomerate quickly grew to become the Lake District's largest tourist centre. At times it feels like a seaside resort, thanks to the crowds and the tat.

Orientation

It's 1½ miles downhill along Main Rd, Lake Rd, Crag Brow and The Promenade from Windermere station to Bowness Pier; a taxi will run you there for around £2.50. All the way along you'll see B&Bs and hotels. Buses and coaches all leave from outside the train station. Most of the places to eat are concentrated in Bowness, which is the livelier place to be in the evening.

Information

Windermere TIC (☎ 46499) in Victoria St is excellent and visitors can even send and receive faxes at reasonable cost. It's open

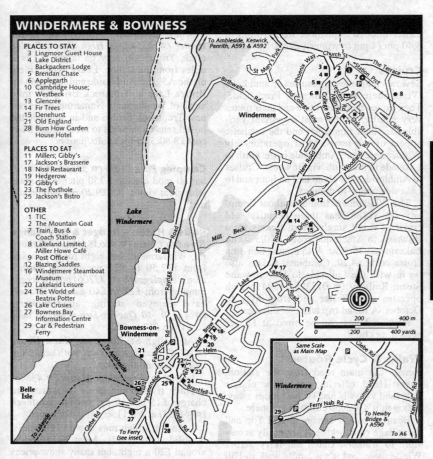

WINDERMERE & BOWNESS

PLACES TO STAY
3 Lingmoor Guest House
4 Lake District Backpackers Lodge
5 Brendan Chase
6 Applegarth
10 Cambridge House; Westbeck
13 Glencree
14 Fir Trees
15 Denehurst
21 Old England
28 Burn How Garden House Hotel

PLACES TO EAT
11 Millers; Gibby's
17 Jackson's Brasserie
18 Nissi Restaurant
19 Hedgerow
22 Gibby's
23 The Porthole
25 Jackson's Bistro

OTHER
1 TIC
2 The Mountain Goat
7 Train, Bus & Coach Station
8 Lakeland Limited; Miller Howe Café
9 Post Office
12 Blazing Saddles
16 Windermere Steamboat Museum
20 Lakeland Leisure
24 The World of Beatrix Potter
26 Lake Crusies
27 Bowness Bay Information Centre
29 Car & Pedestrian Ferry

daily from 9 am to 6 pm (5 pm in winter). The Brockhole National Park Visitor Centre (☎ 46601), 3 miles north of Windermere on the A591, is open daily from April through October from 10 am to 5 pm.

The small Bowness Bay Information Centre, in Glebe Rd south of the Promenade, is only open Friday to Sunday from 10 am to 4 pm.

Lakeland Leisure (☎ 44786), Lake Rd, runs paragliding courses and guided cycling tours.

Things to See

The **Windermere Steamboat Museum** (☎ 45565), Rayrigg Rd, to the north of Bowness on the lakeside, houses a collection of steam and motor boats, including the world's oldest mechanically powered boat. It also offers trips on a small steam launch, the SL *Osprey*. It's open daily from 10 am to 5 pm, Easter to October.

The **World of Beatrix Potter** (☎ 88444), in the Old Laundry in Bowness, cashes in on Pottermania but should keep the kids amused on a wet day. It's open daily from Easter through September from 10 am to 6.40 pm (4 pm in winter); £2.99/1.99.

Cruises

Several companies run cruises around Lake Windermere from Bowness Promenade. Their prices are competitive and their routes very similar, so the most important variables are their timetables and the aesthetic appeal of the boats. Most operators ply Windermere from Ambleside in the north to Lakeside in the south, via Bowness. Cruises to Ambleside take about half an hour and to Lakeside about 40 minutes.

The Windermere Iron Steamboat Company (☎ 31188) has three beautiful old cruisers. Adult single/return tickets from Bowness to Ambleside cost £3.50/5.30; to Lakeside £3.70/5.50. A 45 minute non-stop cruise costs £4.20. Combined tickets also tie in with the Lakeside to Haverthwaite Steam Railway (☎ 015395-31594) which operates over Easter and from May to October. A round trip takes 40 minutes.

Rowing boats can be hired at £2 per person, per hour.

Walks & Cycle Routes

Across the main road from the station, Orrest Head, offering one of the classic Lakeland views is just 1½ half miles away, although it's a steep climb to get there.

Beatrix Potter's cottage at Hill Top and the village of Hawkshead are easily accessible to walkers. Catch the ferry across Windermere, and it's a 2 mile walk to Hill Top. Follow the road around to the western side of Esthwaite Water (turn left at Near Sawrey) for another 2 miles and you reach *Hawkshead Youth Hostel* (☎ 015394-36293). From the hostel it's a mile to Hawkshead and then another 5 miles to Coniston (see Coniston later in this chapter).

Places to Stay

Hostels Within spitting distance of the train station, is the *Lake District Backpackers Lodge* (☎ 46374, High St) that offers beds in small dormitories for £9.50.

Guests have access to a kitchen, lounge and washing machine. *Windermere Youth Hostel* (☎ 43543, at High Cross, Bridge Lane, Troutbeck) may be larger but is 2 miles from the station. Leave Windermere on the A591 to Ambleside and turn right up Bridge Lane at Troutbeck Bridge, a mile north of Windermere. Numerous buses run past Troutbeck Bridge and in summer the hostel sends a minibus to meet trains. Beds cost £8.80/5.95 for adults/juniors.

Camping *Park Cliffe* (☎ 31344, Birks Rd) has all mod cons and 250 pitches on grass with great views. It's £9.20 per two person tent.

B&Bs & Hotels – Budget & Mid-Range *Brendan Chase* (☎ 45638, 1 and 3 College Rd, Windermere) has eight rooms ranging from £12.50 to £25 per person; farther along, *Applegarth* (☎ 43206) has 18 rooms ranging from £22 to £40 a head. Readers have enjoyed staying at *Denehurst* (☎ 44710, 40 Queens Drive) where beds cost from £17 to £22.

At 7 High St, *Lingmoor Guest House* (☎ 44947) has seven rooms, with beds from £12 to £20; non-smoking.

In Oak St, *Cambridge House* (☎ 43846) at No 9, rises to vegetarian breakfasts and charges £15 to £19 per person. *Westbeck* (☎ 44763) at No 11, is similarly priced.

Lake Rd, which runs down to Bowness, is solid with hotels. Most have rooms around £20 a night, but many show prices and vacancies at the front. Cheaper places sometimes lurk down side streets.

Heading down to Bowness, *Fir Trees* (☎ 42272) is a lovely Victorian hotel with eight rooms with private bathroom at £21 to £27 a head. Across the road, *Glencree* (☎ 45822) overlooks woodland and has beds from £20 to £22.50.

B&Bs & Hotels – Top End In the heart of Bowness overlooking the lake, the elegant *Old England* (☎ 42444) is a Georgian country mansion with an open-air heated pool. Singles/doubles usually cost £55/99 but inquire about short-break deals.

Holbeck Ghyll Country House Hotel (☎ *32375, Holbeck Lane*) is in a 19th century hunting lodge overlooking the lake. Prices range from £55 to £85 per person.

Two minutes from the lake, with a mixture of motel-style chalets and rooms and a restaurant in a large Victorian house, **Burn How Garden House Hotel** (☎ *46226, Back Belsfield Rd*) has rooms for £53/76.

Places to Eat

At first sight neither Bowness nor Windermere offers much in the way of gourmet cuisine, although the restaurants at the **Burn How** and **Holbeck Ghyll** hotels offer top-class, expensive cuisine.

Few of the teashops are particularly inspiring, but you could drop into the **Old England** for a cuppa with a lake view. Alternatively try the **Hedgerow Teashop**, above a bookshop on Crag Brow. It does light lunches for around £3.50 but closes at 5.30 pm. In Windermere surprisingly nice cakes can be had in the **Miller Howe Café** in the unlikely surrounds of the Lakeland Limited factory shop behind the station.

Millers in Windermere (☎ *43877, Main Rd*) offers a standard, cheapish tourist menu. During the day **Gibby's**, a few doors down, does lunches.

In the evening, Bowness is more promising. A good place to start looking is pedestrianised Ash St which has Italian and Indian restaurants. Here you'll also find the **Porthole**, a wine buff's paradise with relatively pricey Italian and modern British dishes from £6.50 to £11. Immediately across the street is another branch of **Gibby's** (☎ *43060*), open in the evening and serving a set three-course menu for £6.25.

Just up the road on Crag Brow, the **Nissi Restaurant** (☎ *45055*) is a Greek place selling lobster soup for £3.25, kebabs for £7.50 and vegetarian dishes for £6.95.

Probably the brightest additions to the Bowness eating scene are the two branches of **Jackson's**: **The Brasserie** (☎ *88488, Beresford Rd*) and **The Bistro** (☎ *46264, St Martin's Place*). Snacks cost around £3.60 and a three-course dinner is £10.95.

Getting There & Away

See the fares tables in the Getting Around chapter. Windermere is 265 miles from London, 55 miles from Blackpool, 45 miles from Carlisle and 5 miles from Ambleside.

Bus There are two National Express buses a day from Manchester via Preston (three hours) and on to Keswick. There's also a service from London via Birmingham (seven hours) and on to Keswick.

Stagecoach (☎ *01946-63222*) has several useful services, including the No 555 Lakeslink, which links Lancaster with Keswick, via Kendal, Windermere (train station, Troutbeck Bridge and Brockhole), Ambleside and Grasmere. The No 518 runs between Windermere and Barrow-in-Furness, passing through Newby Bridge, Haverthwaite and Ulverston. No 505/506, links Kendal to Coniston via the Steamboat Museum, Brockhole and Ambleside. The No 599 service runs between Grasmere, Ambleside, Brockhole, Bowness, Windermere train station and Kendal. A Round Robin Ticket allows five breaks of journey between Bowness and Grasmere for £4.20.

Once a week a private bus runs between the Lake District and Bath Backpackers hostels for £15. Phone ☎ *46374* for details.

Train Windermere is at the end of a spur line from Oxenholme which connects with the main line from London Euston to Glasgow. There are 10 trains a day from London Euston station (four hours, £46).

Boat See Cruises earlier in this section. The Windermere ferry plies across the lake from Bowness to Far Sawrey every 20 minutes from around 7 am to 10 pm. A single ticket costs 30p.

Getting Around

Blazing Saddles (☎ *447100*), 61 Quarry Rigg on Lake Rd, Windermere, hires out mountain bikes for £14 a day, reducing to £10 for rentals of three days or more.

AMBLESIDE
☎ 015394

Ambleside is a major centre for climbers and walkers and makes a good base for the southern lakes. But although it has an attractive position half a mile north of the lake, its narrow streets can barely cope with the numbers of walkers in fluorescent outdoor gear who regularly descend on it. Inevitably it's choked with B&Bs, teashops and outdoor equipment shops. Walks head off in every direction. If you need advice on where to go, the TIC (☎ 32582) in Church St is open Easter to October, daily from 9 am to 5 pm, and on Friday and Saturday in winter.

Compston Rd is particularly full of equipment shops, with branches of Rohan (☎ 32946), Hawkshead (☎ 35255) and the YHA Adventure Shop. The vast Climber's Shop (☎ 32297) also hires out camping gear, boots and waterproofs.

The one specific attraction is **The Armitt** (☎ 31212), Rydal Rd, a lavish, if rather specialist exhibition about Lakeland's less famous literary characters. It's open daily from 10 am to 5 pm. Entry costs £2.80/1.80.

Places to Stay & Eat
One mile south of the village, *Ambleside Youth Hostel* (☎ 32304, Windermere Rd – the A591), is open all year; beds cost £10.70/7.30 for adults/juniors. *Low Wray* (☎ 32810), a NT camping site, is 3 miles south of Ambleside on the western shore of Windermere (access from the B5286). The charge is £3 per person per night plus £2 for a car.

B&Bs worth considering include *3 Cambridge Villas* (☎ 32307, Church St), a classic B&B with singles/doubles from £14.50 to £20 per person. In Compston Rd, the *Compston House Hotel* (☎ 32305) has views and comfortable rooms with bathroom from £17.50 to £28.50 per person. *Mill Cottage* (☎ 34830), above a centrally positioned teashop in Rydal Rd, has beds for £19 to £22.

Pippins on Lake Rd is a long-lived café doing breakfasts and snacks. Classier is *Zeffirelli's Wholefood Pizzeria* (☎ 33845, Compston Rd), where you can tuck into pizza before adjourning to the cinema attached; the £14.95 'double feature' menu covers a three-course dinner and cinema ticket. Another stylish addition to the eating scene is *The Glass House* (☎ 32137), attached to the glass-blowing studio in Rydal Rd. It's open for teas, lunches and evening meals; a two-course set lunch costs £5.

GRASMERE & WORDSWORTH COUNTRY
☎ 015394

Grasmere is a picture-postcard village and a lovely place to stay out of season. In summer, its good looks together with its associations with the poet Wordsworth ensure it's overrun with tourists. Most of the buildings date from the 19th and 20th centuries, but the village is actually ancient. St Oswald's Church, with its complicated raftered roof, dates from the 13th century. Wordsworth is buried in the churchyard with his wife Mary and sister Dorothy.

Dove Cottage & Wordsworth Museum
Dove Cottage, just off the A591 on the outskirts of Grasmere, is the main Wordsworth shrine, where he wrote his greatest poems. Once a public house, it has flagstone floors, panelled walls and fine lake views but is far too small for the crush of people who want to see it – do yourself a favour and visit out of season. The half-hour guided tours are particularly worthwhile.

The Wordsworth Museum houses manuscripts and paintings along with personal possessions. The complex (☎ 35544) is open daily, except mid-January to mid-February, from 9.30 am to 5 pm for £4.40/2.20. There have been suggestions that some of the Wordsworth memorabilia will be moved to a larger site. It may be wise to phone and check before visiting.

Rydal Mount

Following his marriage, Wordsworth lived at Rydal Mount from 1812 to 1850. Even then, as many as 100 fans a day would visit in the hope of catching a glimpse of the only Poet Laureate who never wrote a line of official verse. Rydal Mount is a 16th century farmhouse with 18th century additions set in 1¾ hectares of gardens originally landscaped by Wordsworth. It contains some of his furniture as well as manuscripts and possessions.

The house (☎ 33002) is still owned by one of Wordsworth's descendants. It's open March to October daily from 9.30 am to 5 pm, closing at 4 pm in winter and for two weeks in late January. Admission costs £3.50/1, although you can visit the grounds for £1.50.

In spring it's worth diverting through the churchyard below the Mount to see **Dora's Field**, planted with daffodils in memory of Wordsworth's daughter.

Places to Stay & Eat

Grasmere has two youth hostels, one close to the village, the other a mile away in an old farmhouse. *Butterlip How Youth Hostel* (☎ 35316) is just north of the village; follow the road to Easedale for 150 yards, then turn right. It's open daily most of the year except some Mondays. *Thorney How Youth Hostel* (☎ 35591), farther out on Easedale Rd, is open April to August (and other times). Both charge £8.25/5.55 for adults/juniors.

The Wordsworth Trust owns *How Foot Lodge* (☎ 35366), near Dove Cottage, where singles/doubles cost from £35/50, less if you stay more than two nights.

The *Dove Cottage Tea Rooms & Restaurant* (☎ 35268) is an impressive modern vegetarian enterprise offering dishes like vegetable pie for £4.45, as well as a range of cakes and sandwiches. It opens Thursday to Saturday night all year and other days in high season.

In the village itself, *Baldry's Tea Room* is a wholefood place serving hot lunches for around £4.90.

As you leave the churchyard follow your nose to find *Sarah Nelson's Gingerbread Shop* (☎ 35428) which has been trading on the same spot for more than 130 years.

Getting There & Away

Stagecoach Bus No 555 runs from Ambleside to Grasmere, stopping at Rydal church and outside Dove Cottage. A 2½ mile walk links Grasmere and the two Wordsworth shrines.

Elterwater

Elterwater is superbly located at the end of a small lake, tucked in under the Langdales. It's on the Cumbria Way with good walks around and about. There's a wonderful view from Loughrigg Terrace at the southern end of Grasmere, looking north over the lake and the village. Follow the road to High Close Youth Hostel and continue to the east, taking a footpath to the right off the road. It's approximately 3 miles return to Elterwater which has a shop, a good pub and a handful of B&Bs.

There's a nice slate hostel in town, over the bridge. *Elterwater Youth Hostel* (☎ 37245) is open most of the year but closing nights vary; beds cost £8/5.40 for adults/juniors. On the hills to the east, a mile from the village, *Langdale High Close Youth Hostel* (☎ 37313) is a rambling Victorian mansion in extensive gardens with great views. It's open daily from April through October; phone for other times. Beds cost £8.80/5.95.

Barnhowe (☎ 37346), 90m from the village centre, has two doubles and a single from £16 per person. The *Britannia Inn* (☎ 37210) has a pleasant patio overlooking the 'main' street and good-value food; various pies and sausages are around £5. It also has rooms from £19 to £31 per person.

Elterwater is 3½ miles from Ambleside and 5 miles from Coniston.

Hill Top

Beatrix Potter wrote many of her famous children's stories in the 17th century farmhouse at Near Sawrey (☎ 36269, NT), 2 miles south of Hawkshead, which is packed with visitors in summer. It's open from April through October, Saturday to Wednesday, from 11 am to 5 pm; £3.80/1.70. See Walks & Cycle Routes in Windermere & Bowness earlier in this chapter for details of how to get there.

CONISTON

* pop 1800   ☎ 015394

Coniston has the manicured look of a classic Lake District tourist town, but magnificent craggy hills glower over it and there are refreshingly few tourist shops.

Information

The TIC (☎ 41533) is open April to October from 10 am to 5 pm. Summitreks (☎ 41487), 14 Yewdale Rd, next to the TIC, has walking and climbing gear, and is also the base for Coniston Mountain Bikes, which rents bikes for £13 a day.

Boat Trips

Now owned by the NT, the unique and beautiful steam yacht *Gondola*, with its luxurious saloons, was launched on Coniston Water in 1859. The *Illustrated London News* described it as 'a perfect combination of the Venetian gondola and the English steam yacht'.

The *Gondola* (☎ 41288) sails daily from Easter through October and services Brantwood and Park-a-Moor on the eastern side of Coniston. A round trip is £4.50/2.70, although you can also take shorter hops.

The motorised *Coniston Launch* (☎ 36216) also links Coniston with Brantwood House for £3.80 return (£6.80 including entry to Brantwood House).

Brantwood

Brantwood, the house created by the art critic John Ruskin, has a beautiful site overlooking Coniston Water with the Old Man of Coniston behind.

It's open daily from mid-March to mid-November from 11 am to 5.30 pm; Wednesday to Sunday from 11 am to 4 pm in winter. The best way to get there is by the *Gondola* or *Coniston Launch*. Entry is

£3.50 (children free) and there's a good teashop.

Places to Stay

Hostels *Holly How Youth Hostel* (☎ 41323) is a few minutes walk from the town centre, just off Ambleside Rd (the A593). It's open over Easter, from late June to late September and weekends at other times; beds cost £8/5.40 for adults/juniors.

Coppermines Youth Hostel (☎ 41261) has a spectacular mountain setting but is only just over a mile from Coniston; take the minor road between the Black Bull and the Co-op. From June through August it's open daily except Sunday; phone for other times. Beds cost £7.20/4.95.

Camping *Coniston Hall Camp Site* (☎ 41223) has plenty of tent sites (£5.75 per night) beside the lake. Turn left opposite the Catholic church and keep left down to the lake.

B&Bs & Hotels On Yewdale Rd, the *Beech Tree* (☎ 41717), formerly the Old Vicarage, offers vegetarian cooking and six rooms, some with bathroom, from £17 to £25 per person. Also on Yewdale, there's *Oaklands* (☎ 41245), a small, non-smoking place with rates from £16 to £18; and *Orchard Cottage* (☎ 41373), with rooms with private bathroom from £16 to £21.

In Tiberthwaite Ave, east of town, *Lakeland House* (☎ 41303) has seven rooms with beds from £16 to £25 per person; and *Shepherds Villa* (☎ 41337) has rooms with private bathroom from £16 to £22 per person.

The highly regarded *Coniston Lodge Hotel* (☎ 41201) has six rooms with private bathroom from £27.50 to £37 per person.

Places to Eat

The *Sun Hotel* (☎ 41248) is worth the effort of finding it; walk out of town towards Ulverston, cross the bridge and turn right up the hill. Specials include things like vegetable peanut roast for £5.25

and home-made pies from £4.95. It also has rooms with views from £25 per person.

Getting There & Away
Stagecoach's No 505/506 Coniston Rambler service runs from Bowness Pier to Brockhole, Ambleside and Coniston. In summer there are half a dozen services a day and three on Sunday; and in winter only two services on Saturday and none on Sunday.

CUMBRIAN COAST LINE
The Cumbrian Coast railway line, serving the industrial towns and ports of the Cumbrian coast, loops 120 miles around the Cumbrian coast from Carlisle to Lancaster (both cities are on the main line between London Euston and Glasgow). For most of the way it skirts the coast and although parts are beautiful – especially between Ravenglass and Barrow-in-Furness – it also passes some depressing industrial towns in terminal decline.

Although most of it lies outside the park boundary, the line provides useful access points for the western lakes. It's also a potential return link for walkers on the Cumbria Way who've left their vehicles at Carlisle, and walkers on the Coast to Coast Walk who've left their cars at St Bees.

There are five services a day from Monday to Saturday, but none on Sunday. Phone ☎ 0345-484950 for full details.

At Ravenglass you can swap to the private narrow-gauge **Ravenglass to Eskdale** railway, originally built to carry iron ore. The beautiful 7 mile journey costs £6.30/3.30 return. Phone ☎ 01229-717171 for timetable details.

Note that Carnforth station was the one immortalised in the Trevor Howard/Celia Johnson classic film *Brief Encounter* although these days it looks more like an air-raid shelter.

ULVERSTON
☎ 01229
Time seems to have passed Ulverston by – if you're looking for an antidote to the tourist tat of the Lake District towns, this could fit the bill nicely. It's also the starting point for the Cumbria Way.

The TIC (☎ 587120), in Coronation Hall, County Square, can help with making bookings for accommodation along the Cumbria Way.

Things to See
Comedian Stan Laurel was born at 3 Argyle St and fans of Laurel & Hardy will want to make the pilgrimage to 4C Upper Brook St. The **Laurel & Hardy Museum** (☎ 582292) is floor to ceiling with memorabilia. Admission costs £2/1 which lets you sit in on some of the old movies too. It's open daily from 10 am to 4.30 pm except in January.

The small **Heritage Centre** (☎ 580820) in Lower Brook St tells the story of the days before rail and road when getting to Ulverston from Lancaster involved a treacherous journey across the Leven or Kent Sands. It's open Monday to Saturday from 9.30 am to 4.30 pm (closed winter Wednesdays); entry is £2/1.

Coming into town by train you'll see a tower on top of Hoad Hill. This commemorates Sir John Barrow (1764-1848), a local explorer.

Cartmel Priory
Between Grange-over-Sands and Ulverston, Cartmel village grew up around a magnificent 12th century priory. The church was not demolished during the Dissolution and survives as one of the finest in the north-west. It's open daily from 9 am to 5.30 pm (3.30 pm in winter), with guided tours at 11 am and 2 pm on summer Wednesdays.

Places to Stay & Eat
Right in the centre, *Church Walk House* (☎ *582211, Church Walk)* is opposite Stables furniture shop and has rooms with bath from £17.50 per person. *Rock House* (☎ *586879, 1 Alexander Rd)* has three large family rooms and a single for £17 a head. The *Trinity House Hotel* (☎ *587639, Prince's St)* has six rooms for £25/45 a single/double.

NORTH-WESTERN ENGLAND

The *Rose & Crown* in the town centre is a classic pub with excellent food, enormous servings and reasonable prices. The *Farmers Arms*, overlooking the Market Place, has a few outdoor tables for sunny days.

Getting There & Away

You can get to Ulverston on the Cumbrian Coast Line from Lancaster (30 minutes). Alternatively Stagecoach has services linking it to Barrow-in-Furness and to Ambleside, via Windermere (except Sunday). Monday to Friday you can also get to Cartmel from Ulverston by bus (30 minutes).

KESWICK

• pop 5000   ☎ 017687

As the northern centre for the Lakes, Keswick has been on the tourist map for over 100 years and is very busy indeed. An important walking base on the Cumbria Way, it lies between the great rounded peak of Skiddaw and Derwent Water, although the town is cut off from the lake store by a busy main road. Controversy rages over whether Derwent Water, Ullswater or Crummock Water is the most beautiful lake, but Derwent Water is certainly the most accessible for those without private transport. An old market town, Keswick became the centre of a mining industry in the 16th century. These days you can't move for tearooms, B&Bs and outdoor equipment shops.

Information

The busy but helpful TIC (☎ 72645), Moot Hall, Market Square, is open daily all year from 10 am to 4 pm; for most of summer it's open 9.30 am to 5.30 pm, and at peak times to 7 pm.

George Fisher (☎ 72178), 2 Borrowdale Rd, is an enormous outdoor equipment shop with gear for hire. Various outdoor activities and courses, like canoeing, abseiling and cycling, are organised by the Climbing Wall & Activity Centre (☎ 72000), behind the Pencil Museum.

Cruises

Derwent Water has an excellent lake transport service. From March to November (and less frequently from December to February) a regular service calls at seven landing stages around the lake: Ashness Gate, Lodore Falls, High Brandlehow, Low Brandlehow, Hawse End, Nichol End and back to Keswick.

The Keswick on Derwentwater Launch Company (☎ 72263) boats leave every half-hour, one going clockwise, the next going anticlockwise; the round trip takes 50 minutes (£4.75/2); each stage is about 10 minutes (65p/40p). Tickets can be bought at the TIC. The company also hires out rowing boats for £3 an hour.

The launches give access to some excellent walks and provide an exhaustion-saving option for those walking the Cumbria Way (the long walk from Elterwater or Dungeon Ghyll). The walk around the western side of the lake isn't particularly interesting, but Borrowdale is beautiful.

Castlerigg Stone Circle

This beautiful egg-shaped stone circle is set on a hilltop between Skiddaw and Helvellyn, and offers brilliant views. It's a Neolithic and Bronze Age sacred meeting place, with none of the tacky tourist infrastructure asso-

The standing stones at Castlerigg

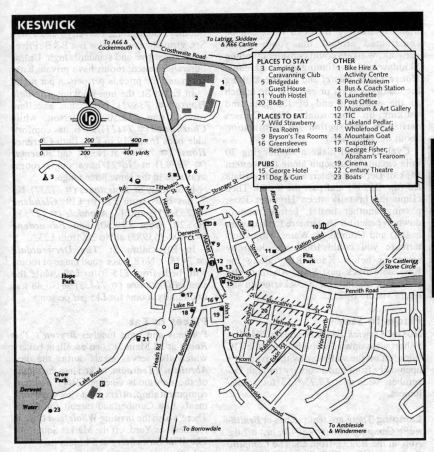

KESWICK

To A66 &
Cockermouth

To Latrigg, Skiddaw
& A66 Carlisle

Crosthwaite Road

PLACES TO STAY	OTHER
3 Camping &	1 Bike Hire &
Caravanning Club	Activity Centre
5 Bridgedale	2 Pencil Museum
Guest House	4 Bus & Coach Station
11 Youth Hostel	6 Laundrette
20 B&Bs	8 Post Office
	10 Museum & Art Gallery
PLACES TO EAT	12 TIC
7 Wild Strawberry	13 Lakeland Pedlar;
Tea Room	Wholefood Café
9 Bryson's Tea Rooms	14 Mountain Goat
16 Greensleeves	17 Teapottery
Restaurant	18 George Fisher;
	Abraham's Tearoom
PUBS	19 Cinema
15 George Hotel	22 Century Theatre
21 Dog & Gun	23 Boats

ciated with other circles. It's 1½ miles east of Keswick and entry is over a fence.

Pencil Museum

In the 16th century graphite was discovered in Borrowdale, leading to the creation of a pencil-making industry which is still going strong even though the components are now imported from as far afield as Sri Lanka and California. The museum attached to the Derwent Watercolour pencil factory tells the whole story with the help of a video. You get to see the world's largest pencil too. The museum and pencil shop (☎ 73626) are open daily from 9.30 am to 4 pm; £2/1.

Other Things to See

The local **Museum & Art Gallery** in Station Rd is open daily from Easter through October from 10 am to 4 pm for £1/50p.

People interested in seeing how novelty teapots are made should drop into **The Teapottery** (☎ 73983) behind the central car park.

Walks & Cycle Routes

Many interesting walks or rides can be constructed around the youth hostel network. Walkers could consider climbing Skiddaw and continuing on to **Skiddaw House Youth Hostel** and Caldbeck along the Cumbria Way, or catching the launch to the southern end of the lake and walking up Borrowdale. (See Cruises earlier in this section for information about the launches.)

Cyclists could make a challenging 30 mile circuit. Head south along the western bank of Derwent Water, along Borrowdale Rd (the B5289) and past the hostel. Then climb the brutally steep Honister Pass, passing another hostel, before running down to beautiful Buttermere (and another hostel) and Crummock Water. From Buttermere you could finish the loop by returning below Knott Rigg along the Keskadale Beck past Stair. Alternatively, you could continue on to Cockermouth and return via the B5292.

Places to Stay

Hostel *Keswick Youth Hostel* (☎ 72484) is a short walk down Station Rd from the TIC (turn left on the walkway by the river). It's open daily from mid-February through December; beds cost £9.75/6.55 for adults/ juniors.

Camping There are tent pitches at *Braithwaite Camping Site* (☎ 78343), just off the A66 on the B5292, from £5. The *Camping & Caravanning Club Site* (☎ 72392), on the lake shore a few minutes walk from town, has van sites and tent pitches from £3 per person.

B&Bs & Hotels One of the best value B&Bs in the Lake District, the *Bridgedale Guest House* (☎ 73914, 101 Main St) has a range of rooms, some with private showers, for just £15 per person. Without breakfast this drops to £12, which is only slightly more than the youth hostel. You can leave your bags here for £1 if you're just passing through on the bus.

To the east of the town centre along Southey, Blencathra, Helvellyn and Eskin Sts, virtually every house is a B&B. Prices are competitive and standards high. Unless otherwise stated, rooms have private bathroom and the price is per person per night.

In Eskin St, the non-smoking *Allerdale House* (☎ 73891), No 1, has excellent rooms from £23.50 per person, while *Charnwood* (☎ 74111), No 6, has comfortable beds from £19 to £25. Both *Clarence House* (☎ 73186) at No 14 and *Braemar* (☎ 73743) at No 21 have single rooms available in the same price range.

In Southey St, *Bluestones* (☎ 74237), No 7, has beds from £14 to £19; *Glendene* (☎ 73548) from £14; *Avondale* (☎ 72735), No 20, from £18.50; and *Edwardene* (☎ 0800-163983) at No 26, from £23.

In Blencathra St, *The Derwentdale* (☎ 74187), No 8, has a good range of rooms with beds from £15.50 to £19, while the small *Blencathra* (☎ 71435) at No 48 has two family rooms for £15 per person.

Places to Eat

For teas and light lunches *Bryson's Tea Room* at 38 Main St is an excellent bakery which also serves meals during the day. *Abraham's Tearoom*, tucked into the rafters of the enormous George Fisher outdoor-equipment shop, offers great views and light meals like Cumberland rarebit for £3.75. There's also the inviting *Wholefood Café* in Hendersons Yard, off the Market Square, or *The Wild Strawberry* at 54 Main St.

In the evening, pubs are probably your best bet. The *Dog & Gun* in Lake Rd is good value, or there's the *George Hotel* at 3 St John's St.

Greensleeves Restaurant (☎ 72932, St John's St) is a large 'tourist' restaurant, but it has a good-value menu with pasta from around £6 and dishes like chicken korma for £7.50.

Getting There & Away

Keswick is 285 miles from London, 31 miles from Carlisle and 15 miles from Penrith.

Bus See Windermere & Bowness earlier in this chapter for information on National Express and Stagecoach buses and connections to Keswick.

In summer, Keswick is also accessible from Penrith train station (three services Monday to Saturday, one on Sunday) with Wright Brothers' (☎ 01434-381200) No 888 service. This service continues across country to Langwathby, on the LSC line, to Hexham and Corbridge, on Hadrian's Wall, and finally to Newcastle upon Tyne.

Stagecoach's Lakeslink (No 555) runs from Carlisle to Lancaster via Keswick, Ambleside, Windermere and Kendal. There are frequent services between Keswick and Kendal. Three a day go on to Carlisle from Monday to Saturday.

Getting Around
Keswick Mountain Bikes (☎ 75202), behind the pencil museum, has bikes for hire from £13. You can also rent them from Lakeland Pedlar (☎ 75752) in Hendersons Yard off the Market Square.

AROUND KESWICK
Places to Stay
There's an excellent network of youth hostels around Keswick, most linked by mountain paths.

Derwentwater Youth Hostel (☎ 77246) is on the eastern side of the lake, 2 miles from Keswick, 5 miles from Thirlmere and 11 miles from Grasmere. Price: £9.75/6.55 for adults/juniors

Longthwaite Youth Hostel (☎ 77257) is at the head of beautiful Borrowdale, 2 miles from Honister, 5 miles from Derwentwater and 7 miles from Buttermere. Price: £9.75/6.55

Thirlmere Youth Hostel (☎ 73224) is at the head of Thirlmere on the A591 to Ambleside, 5 miles from Keswick, 6 miles from Longthwaite, 7 miles from Grasmere and 9 miles from Skiddaw House. Price: £5.85/4

Honister Hause Youth Hostel (☎ 77267) is at the summit of Honister Pass, 3 miles from Black Sail, 2 miles from Longthwaite and 4 miles from Buttermere. Price: £6.50/4.45

Buttermere Youth Hostel (☎ 70245) overlooks Buttermere and is 4 miles from Honister, 7 miles from Longthwaite and 9 miles from Keswick. Price: £8.80/5.95

Black Sail (☎ 0411-108450) is in a remote location at the head of Ennerdale, 3 miles from Honister and Buttermere, and can only be reached on foot. Price: £6.50/4.45

Gillerthwaite Youth Hostel (☎ 01946-861237) is in a quiet wooded valley 3 miles from Buttermere, 4 miles from Black Sail and 7 miles from Honister. Price: £6.50/4.45

Skiddaw House Youth Hostel, Bassenthwaite, Keswick CA12 4QZ (book by post) is in a remote location behind Skiddaw, 6 miles from Keswick and 8 miles from Carrock Fell, and can only be reached on foot. Price: £5.85/4.

North-Eastern England

North-Eastern England is quite different from the rest of the country, although it's misleading to think of it as a single entity. The major sections are Yorkshire to the south; Durham and Northumberland in the north, with the latter area bordering Scotland.

As a rule, the countryside here is harder and more rugged than in the south, and it's as if history reflects this, because every inch has been fought over. The central conflict was the long struggle between north and south, with the battle lines shifting over the centuries.

In the years before the Roman invasion, the area from the Humber River to the Firth of Forth was ruled by a confederation of Celtic tribes known as the Brigantes. The Romans were the first to attempt to delineate a border with Hadrian's Wall, but the struggle didn't end until the 18th century.

In the 9th century the Danes made York their capital and ruled the Danelaw – all of England north and east of a line between Chester and London. Later, their Norman cousin William the Conqueror found the north rebellious and difficult, and he responded with brutal thoroughness. After 500 knights were massacred at Durham, he burnt York and Durham and devastated the surrounding countryside. Seventeen years later, when the royal commissioners arrived to record the tax capacity of Yorkshire (for the *Domesday Book*), they recorded the simple, but frighteningly eloquent, 'waste' beside many parish names. It took the north generations to recover.

Later, the Normans left a legacy of spectacular fortresses and the marvellous Durham Cathedral. The region prospered on the medieval wool trade, which sponsored the great cathedral at York and enormous monastic communities, the remains of which can be seen at Rievaulx and Fountains.

The countryside is a grand backdrop to this human drama, containing three of England's best national parks and some spectacular

HIGHLIGHTS

- The North York Moors
- A trip on the North Yorkshire Moors Railway
- The Yorkshire Dales
- York Minster
- Castle Howard
- The view of Sutton Bank
- Durham Cathedral

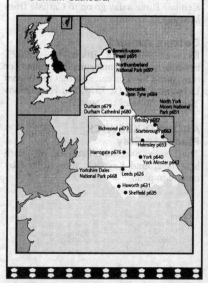

coastline. The Yorkshire Dales is the best known and arguably the most beautiful of the parks, but the North York Moors has a great variety of landscapes, and includes a superb coastline. Both parks can be very crowded in summer, and while it's easier to escape the masses in the North York Moors park, visitors seeking seclusion should opt instead for the Northumberland park.

The Danish heritage survives today, especially in the language, but also, some would argue, in the independent spirit of the people. Place names ending in *thorp*, *kirk* and *by* all have a Danish origin.

ORIENTATION & INFORMATION

The Pennine Hills are the dominant geological feature that form a north-south spine dividing the region from Cumbria and Lancashire in the west and providing the source of major rivers like the Tees and the Tyne.

The major transport routes basically run east of this spine: from York northward to Newcastle upon Tyne and Edinburgh. Newcastle upon Tyne is an important ferry port for Scandinavia.

There are YHA hostels at York and Newcastle upon Tyne and, even more importantly, dozens scattered about the national parks. Make sure you book in summer.

WALKING

There are many great hikes in this region. The most famous is the Pennine Way, which stretches 250 miles from Edale in the Peak District to end at Kirk Yetholm near Kelso in Scotland. Unfortunately, its popularity means that long sections turn into unpleasant bogs, so it is worth considering quieter alternatives. For example, it's possible to walk sections of Hadrian's Wall, or to tackle sections of the difficult 190 mile Coast to Coast Walk which crosses eastward from the Lake District, through the Yorkshire Dales and North York Moors. Alfred Wainwright describes the walk in his inimitable fashion in *A Coast to Coast Walk*.

The Yorkshire Dales and the North York Moors also have numerous walks. See the Activities chapter for information on the beautiful Cleveland Way. In the Dales, consider the relatively easy, but still interesting, Dales Way, which runs 81 miles from Ilkley to Windermere, linking two national parks.

CYCLING

Cycling is a great way to see this part of England; the only disadvantages are the weather, the hills and the fact that, on the weekends, even some of the minor B-roads can be very crowded. On the whole, however, all you need is a good map and some imagination, and you'll have a great time.

One route worth considering is the Dales Way (see Yorkshire Dales National Park later) which mostly follows the rivers, but there are still some steep climbs; it's 130 miles long. There's also an 88 mile Sea to Sea cycle route from Whitehaven on the west coast to Sunderland or Newcastle on the east coast. A good map and accommodation guide is available from Sustrans (☎ 0117-926 8893), 35 King St, Bristol BS1 4DZ.

GETTING THERE & AROUND
Bus

Bus transport around the region can be difficult, particularly around the national parks. For timetables and information covering County Durham, phone ☎ 0191-383 3337; for Northumberland, phone ☎ 01670-533 3128; for North Yorkshire phone ☎ 01609-780780; for the Leeds/Bradford area phone ☎ 0113-245 7676; for the Middlesbrough area phone ☎ 01642-262262 and for the Newcastle area, phone ☎ 0191-232 5325. Numbers for individual operators are given in the various sections that follow. For onward travel into the Scottish Borders, phone Lowland (☎ 01289-307461).

There are several one-day Explorer tickets; always ask if one might be appropriate. The Explorer North East is particularly interesting. It covers a vast area north of York to the Scottish Borders and west to Hawes (in the Yorkshire Dales) and Carlisle. The major operator in the scheme is Northumbria (☎ 0191-212 3000), which can help plan an itinerary. Unlimited travel for one day is £4.95, and there are also numerous admission discounts for holders of Explorer passes. Tickets are available on the buses.

Train

The main-line routes run north to Edinburgh via York, Durham, Newcastle upon Tyne and Berwick-upon-Tweed; and west to

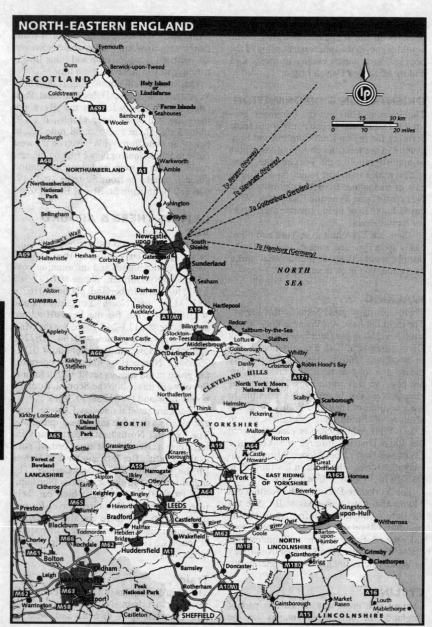

NORTH-EASTERN ENGLAND

Carlisle roughly following Hadrian's Wall. Travelling to/from the south, it may be necessary to make connections at Leeds. Phone ☎ 0345-484950 for all train inquiries.

There are numerous Rover tickets, for single-day travel and longer periods, so ask if one might be appropriate. For example, the North Country Flexi Rover allows unlimited travel throughout the north (but not including Northumberland) for any four days out of eight for £55.

Boat

Norway's Color Line (☎ 0191-296 1313) operates two ferries a week from Newcastle upon Tyne to Stavanger, Haugesund and Bergen in Norway. During summer, Scandinavian Seaways (☎ 0990-333000) operates ferries from Newcastle upon Tyne to Gothenburg, Sweden. See the introductory Getting There & Away chapter.

Leeds & Bradford

For hundreds of years the prosperity of West Yorkshire depended on wool and cloth manufacturing. The industry flourished through the Middle Ages, but was given an added boost by the advent of improved machinery during the Industrial Revolution. A cottage industry that traditionally employed women spinning downstairs while their men wove away upstairs quickly gave way to factories.

By the beginning of the 20th century West Yorkshire, and particularly Leeds and Bradford, dominated the wool industry. Although the industry has almost completely disappeared since WWII, large parts of the landscape are still dominated by reminders of it. Long rows of weavers' cottages (with second-storey windows to provide light for the loom) and workers' houses built along the ridges overlook multistorey mills with towering chimneys in the valleys below. These industrial towns and valleys are separated by the wild stretches of moors so vividly described by the Brontë sisters who lived at nearby Haworth.

The Leeds/Bradford conurbation is one of the biggest in the country, virtually running into the industrial towns of Halifax, Huddersfield and Wakefield.

GETTING AROUND

The Metro public transport network, based in Leeds, organises an effective integrated bus and rail service. The area is particularly well served by rail, with most towns in this section accessible by frequent trains. For extensive travel, buy one of the good-value Metro Dayrover tickets (£1.40).

The Metro Travel Centre at Leeds Central bus station (☎ 0113-245 7676) answers phone inquiries on all public transport during office hours, Monday to Saturday. It also publishes useful maps and timetables, most available in the TICs.

The main bus operators are Yorkshire Coastliner (☎ 01653-692556), Harrogate & District (☎ 01423-566061), and Keighley & District (☎ 01535-603284).

LEEDS

- pop 455,000   ☎ 0113

Of all Britain's big cities, Leeds is certainly one of the most inviting. Not for nothing has it been dubbed the 'Knightsbridge of the North'; indeed, there are so many shops and shopping centres you could be forgiven for assuming every single resident of Leeds is in the business of selling fancy frocks and household goods to other Leeds residents.

Many of the fine Victorian buildings in the city centre have already been given a facelift, and others are being smartened up as you read this. A large student population ensures a thriving nightlife, with the routine line-up of glitzy café bars and restaurants, especially around the Corn Exchange.

Until recently Leeds lacked many blockbuster attractions. Now to the Tetley's tour on Brewery Wharf can be added the Royal Armouries, a multi-million development on the banks of the Leeds-Liverpool Canal. Leeds also makes a good base for excursions to Haworth, Hebden Bridge and Bradford. Unfortunately there's hardly any central accommodation suitable for those on a tight budget.

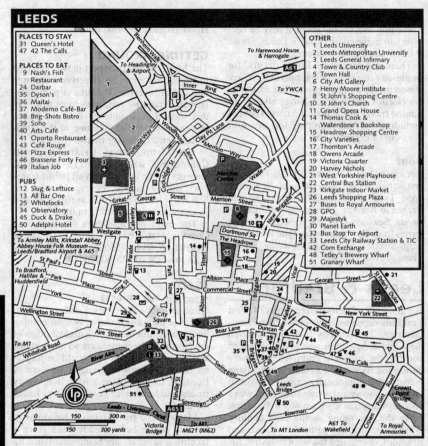

LEEDS

PLACES TO STAY
31 Queen's Hotel
47 42 The Calls

PLACES TO EAT
9 Nash's Fish
     Restaurant
24 Darbar
35 Dyson's
36 Maitai
37 Moderno Café-Bar
38 Brig-Shots Bistro
39 Soho
40 Arts Café
41 Oporto Restaurant
43 Café Rouge
44 Pizza Express
46 Brasserie Forty Four
49 Italian Job

PUBS
12 Slug & Lettuce
13 All Bar One
25 Whitelocks
34 Observatory
45 Duck & Drake
50 Adelphi Hotel

OTHER
1 Leeds University
2 Leeds Metropolitan University
3 Leeds General Infirmary
4 Town & Country Club
5 Town Hall
6 City Art Gallery
7 Henry Moore Institute
8 St John's Shopping Centre
9 St John's Church
11 Grand Opera House
14 Thomas Cook &
     Waterstone's Bookshop
15 Headrow Shopping Centre
16 City Varieties
17 Thornton's Arcade
18 Owens Arcade
19 Victoria Quarter
20 Harvey Nichols
21 West Yorkshire Playhouse
22 Central Bus Station
23 Kirkgate Indoor Market
26 Leeds Shopping Plaza
27 Buses to Royal Armouries
28 GPO
29 Majestyk
30 Planet Earth
32 Bus Stop for Airport
33 Leeds City Railway Station & TIC
42 Corn Exchange
48 Tetley's Brewery Wharf
51 Granary Wharf

Orientation & Information

The city is strung out along the north bank of the River Aire and the Leeds-Liverpool Canal. The train and bus stations are centrally located, but most affordable hotels are a bus ride away. The centre is a nightmare for motorists – there's a ring road with a series of complicated interchanges, the city streets are invariably one-way and some are pedestrianised or closed to private vehicles. Even finding your way to the station can prove tricky.

The Headingley Cricket Ground (for Test cricket fans) is to the north of the city in a pleasant suburb of the same name, along with a large population of students.

The Gateway to Yorkshire TIC (☎ 242 5242) next to the train station is open Monday to Saturday from 9.30 am to 6 pm, and Sunday from 10 am to 4 pm.

Royal Armouries

Leeds' pride and joy is the spectacular new building created to house the Royal Armouries (☎ 0990-106666), in Armouries Drive, on the banks of the Leeds-Liverpool Canal. This grey and white edifice looks remarkably like a fortress, and finding the way in if you've walked along the canal to get there can seem as tricky as trying to penetrate the defences of a medieval castle. Once inside, however, you'll find four floors of exhibits centred on the themes of war, tournaments, self-defence, hunting and the Orient. Outside you can see displays of jousting and falconry from Easter to October. The Menagerie Court shows off the animals who take part in the displays, while the Craft Court allows you to see gun-makers, armourers and leather-workers in action.

The Armouries are open daily from 10.30 am to 5 pm. Admission costs £7.95/4.95 in school holidays; £4.95/4.25 at other times. If you don't want to walk (about 15 minutes from the TIC) you can get there by bus No 63B from outside Lloyd's Bank in Park Row.

Tetley's Brewery Wharf

Tetley's (☎ 243 1888) is a flashy development off Bowman Lane which features a brewery tour (over-14s only), brewery horses, restaurants and various displays that show pub culture through the ages, with actors milling around in costume. It's open from 11 am to 4 pm daily and for £3.95 you can tour the brewery and examine the exhibits on the ground floor. Without the tour, you'll pay £3/1.50.

Other Things to See & Do

Star attraction of the **City Art Gallery** (☎ 247 8248) in Westgate is the Henry Moore Collection, to the right inside the front entrance. One of the century's greatest sculptors, Henry Moore (1898-1986) was a graduate of Leeds School of Art. It's open, free, daily from 10 am to 5 pm, opening at 1 pm on Sunday and closing at 8 pm on Wednesday. The adjoining **Henry Moore Institute** stages periodic exhibitions of 20th century sculpture. Beneath the gallery there's a separate **Craft & Design**

Gallery. Next door the **City Museum** is housed in the same building as the library.

Tucked away off northern Briggate is the redundant **St John's church**, a one-off masterpiece of 17th century design full of elaborate box pews and with a wonderful screen resplendent with huge carvings of the arms of James I and of Charles I as Prince of Wales.

Granary Wharf, behind the train station, is reached via the Dark Arches. It's a cobbled area under vaulted arches at the meeting point of the canal and the river, with art and craft shops, free entertainment and markets selling local, hand-made goods on Friday, Saturday and Sunday.

Headingley

For many people, Leeds means Headingley and Headingley means cricket. The first cricket match was played here in 1890, and it's still a venue for Test matches and home ground to Yorkshire County Cricket Club.

To get to the cricket ground, take bus No 73, 74 or 75 from opposite the town hall or catch a train to Burley Park station, a short walk from the ground. For match bookings (from £17 for a Test match) phone ☎ 278 7394.

Places to Stay

Camping The most convenient camping ground is the *Roundhay Caravan Site* (☎ 265 2354), 4 miles out in Elmete Lane, Roundhay. From March to November it has pitches for tents for £4 per person.

Hostels There are no youth hostels in Leeds; the nearest are in Haworth and York. The alternative is one of two YWCAs which accept both sexes aged 16 to 30. The most central *YWCA* (☎ 245 7840, 22 Lovell Park Hill)* charges £9.45 a head.

B&Bs & Hotels There's a group of B&Bs behind Leeds University on Woodsley Rd but you pay for the (relative) convenience. The *Avalon Guest House* (☎ 243 2545), at No 132, has reasonable décor and is well run and comfortable. Most rooms have private bathroom and singles/doubles are from £20/32. The **Moorlea Hotel** (☎ *243 2653*), at No 146, charges from £23/30 but breakfast is run more for the convenience of the staff than the guests. The **Glengarth Hotel** (☎ *245 7940*), at No 162, charges from £20/34, the **Manxdene Hotel** (☎ *243 2586*), at No 154, from £23/34.

There's another batch of B&Bs on Cardigan Rd, Headingley; once again, rates are around £23/34. Possibilities include the **Ashfield Hotel** (☎ *275 8847*), at No 44; the **Highfield Hotel** (☎ *275 2193*), at No 79; the **Manor Hotel** (☎ *275 7991*), at No 34; and the curiously named **Trafford House & Budapest Hotel** (☎ *275 2034*), at No 16.

The most glamorous hotel in town is *42 The Calls* (☎ *244 0099, 42 The Calls*), a converted Victorian grain mill overlooking the river. Rooms start at £65 regardless of whether you're alone.

Places to Eat

The cheapest snacks can probably be picked up in **Kirkgate Market** but if you're after tea and a bite in more cheerful surroundings, the arcades in the Victoria Quarter harbour several inviting places, including the **Ruskin's Tea Rooms** and **Café Arcade**. Harvey Nichols has an **espresso bar** on the ground floor facing into the arcade. Here, too, you'll find the popular **Indie Joze Coffee Shop** which stays open until 11 pm for drinks and sandwiches.

The streets between the Corn Exchange and the 42 The Calls Hotel contain all sorts of glitzy bars and restaurants. Facing the Corn Exchange in the surviving gatehouse of the White Cloth Hall, a branch of the reliable **Pizza Express** chain produces good-value pizza and pasta. Next door is a branch of **Café Rouge**.

In Call Lane you'll find the extremely popular **Oporto Restaurant** (☎ *243 4008*) where something like chickpea casserole costs £7.95; cheaper bites are available in the adjoining bar. Across the road, **Soho** (☎ *242 9009*) does mushrooms on baked ciabatta for £4.25, while the **Arts Café** (☎ *243 8243*) does fish cakes for £4.75; lunch is considerably cheaper than dinner here.

Briggate is also worth exploring. Unflashy **Maitai** (☎ *243 1989*), at the bottom of Briggate, serves Thai dishes for around £6 each. The **Moderno Café-Bar** has music from 8 to 11 pm to go with its sandwiches and pizzas. Greenery-filled **Brig-Shots Bistro** (☎ *242 5629*) has a pre-theatre menu for £10.50 until 7 pm. Most interesting is **Dyson's** (☎ *234 6444*), which is set round an old clock shop; you can't miss the protruding clock with the Old Father Time figure jutting from the façade. A set meal in these luxurious surroundings costs £18.95.

Nash's Fish Restaurant (☎ *245 7194*), off Briggate, does all-inclusive lunches for £5. Despite the modest doorway, **Darbar** (☎ *246 0381, 16 Kirkgate*) is a very large, very grand restaurant serving Indian and Tandoori specialities. The food is excellent and most curries are from £6.50. The fairly basic **Italian Job** (☎ *242 0185, 9 Bridge End*) offers a good range of Italian food, plus burgers; good-looking lunch buffets cost £5.

Brasserie Forty Four (☎ *234 3232*), attached to the 42 The Calls hotel, is regarded as one of the best restaurants in Leeds. Order by 7.15 pm and be out by 8.15 pm and you can sample a two-course meal for £9.75. The **restaurant** on the top floor of Harvey Nichols is inevitably swish and classy.

Entertainment

The monthly *Leeds Guide* has the lowdown on what's on where. Boar Lane and Call Lane are at the heart of the action, with lots of overdressed young people wandering from pub to pub to bar.

Pubs & Clubs In the centre of the fray, the **Observatory**, 40 Boar Lane, is a trendy bar in a grand building. The ornate Edwardian **Adelphi Hotel**, Leeds Bridge, boasts wood panelling, tiles and engraved glass and attracts a varied clientele.

On Kirkgate, the **Duck & Drake** has an enormous range of real ales, and free bands. Perhaps the most famous Leeds pub is **Whitelocks**, Turk's Head Yard, off Briggate, another classic Edwardian pub with outside tables and traditional pub food like Yorkshire pudding for £1.50.

Clubs worth trying include *Club Uropa* (☎ 242 2224) in Briggate, *Majestyk* and *Planet Earth* overlooking the City Square. For indie rock bands check out the *Town & Country Club* (☎ 280 0100, Cookridge St).

Theatre & Cinema Chaplin and Houdini both performed at the *City Varieties* (☎ 243 0808, Swan St), one of Britain's last old-fashioned music halls. The *West Yorkshire Playhouse* at Quarry Mount (☎ 244 2111) has a good reputation, as does the *Grand Opera House* (☎ 222 6222) in Briggate, where tickets for a wide variety of performances (not just opera) cost from £8.

Shopping

A highlight of any visit to Leeds is a stroll round the magnificent **Victoria Quarter** arcades which are roofed with a stained-glass canopy, paved with mosaics and decorated with marble. The shops are suitably upmarket and intimidating, all the more so since **Harvey Nichols** opened its first store outside London here in 1997.

Just as much fun in a more down-to-earth way is the **Kirkgate Market**, once home of Marks, who later joined Spencer. Here, arcades of wrought iron and ceramic tiles surround stalls piled high with fresh produce and cheap baked goods – ideal for stocking up for a picnic. The market is open from Monday to Saturday, closing at 1 pm on Wednesday. The adjoining open-air markets function on Tuesday, Friday and Saturday.

The wonderful circular **Corn Exchange** (☎ 234 0363), built in 1865, is the place to come if you're into one-off clothes shops and specialities like stencilling. It's open seven days a week.

Getting There & Away

The Metro Travel Centre at the Central bus station (☎ 245 7676), answers inquiries on all public transport.

Air Leeds-Bradford airport (☎ 250 9696), 8 miles north of the city via the A65, offers both domestic and international flights (including to Amsterdam, Paris and Dublin). Bus No 37 operates hourly between the airport and Leeds City Square, next to the train station (£1.50). A taxi will cost around £15.

Bus The Central bus station is a 10 minute walk east of the train station, off St Peter's St National Express has services to most British cities, including nine coaches daily to/from London (3¾ hours).

Yorkshire Coastliner (☎ 244 8976) has a useful service linking Leeds, York, Castle Howard, Goathland and Whitby (Nos 840 and 842). Other services link Leeds, York and Scarborough. A day ticket costs £8.

Train Leeds City station is large and busy, with hourly services to London King's Cross that take as little as two hours. Its also the starting point for the famous Leeds-Settle-Carlisle Line.

Getting Around

You can get a bus to most parts of the city, and to the suburbs, from the Central bus station. Ask about Metro DayRovers which covers trains as well as buses and can be used to get to Bradford, Haworth and Hebden Bridge as well as round the city.

HAREWOOD HOUSE

Harewood is one of Britain's most beautiful stately homes, but it's also extremely popular at peak periods. The building is great, the interiors are over the top and the surrounding park is glorious, but some may find the perfection and commercialisation rather 'cold'.

Harewood has been home to the Lascelles family since it was built between 1759 and 1772. No expense was spared – Capability Brown was responsible for the grounds, Thomas Chippendale for the furniture, and Italy was raided to create an appropriate art collection (including works by Tintoretto, Titian, Bellini and many others).

In addition to the house, there's the Stables Gallery, the Bird Garden and a children's adventure playground. The stables

NORTH-EASTERN ENGLAND

house a pleasant café. Enjoyable walks take you round Harewood Lake and to 15th century **Harewood Church** which is no longer in use (the village it originally served was moved when the house was constructed!) but contains some fascinating tombs and monuments.

The house (☎ 288 6331) is open from April to October, daily from 11 am to 4.30 pm for £6.75/4.50. It's 7 miles north of Leeds on the A61 to Harrogate. Bus No 36 or X35 will get you there from Leeds.

BRADFORD
● pop 296,000   ☎ 01274

The centre of Bradford is 9 miles west of Leeds, but the two cities are virtually continuous. Until WWII Bradford was uncontested capital of the world wool trade. After that the industry collapsed, leaving the city struggling to find a new role. From their rather unpromising material, the Bradford city authorities have worked hard to create a tourism industry. Since the 1960s over 60,000 Indians and Pakistanis have also settled here and helped reinvigorate the city.

The TIC (☎ 753678) is in the newly restored **National Museum of Photography, Film & Television**, right in the town centre with plenty of parking. This is a great place where, as well as learning about the history of photography, you can try out lots of video and graphics technology, and play at being a TV newsreader or cameraperson.

The museum houses one of Britain's few IMAX cinema screens – a massive 20m wide and 16m high – with up to six screenings a day; booking (☎ 727488) is advisable. The museum is open, free, Tuesday to Sunday from 10.30 am to 6 pm.

Other worthwhile sights include the **Colour Museum** (☎ 390955), 82 Grattan Rd, the home of the Society of Dyers and Colourists, which is more interesting than you might expect; the **Industrial Museum** (☎ 631756), Moorside Rd; and the wonderful **Undercliffe Cemetery**, between Undercliffe Lane and Otley Rd, with Britain's best collection of Victorian funerary art.

Well worth a visit is the **Saltaire** suburb, laid out in 1852 to provide decent housing for workers at nearby Salt's Mill, now home to the **David Hockney Gallery** and some interesting shops. At nearby **Bingley** you can also see a series of five 18th century canal locks which raise the Leeds-Liverpool Canal 18m. Bus No 662 goes to Saltaire and Bingley.

In a town that markets 'curry tours', the *Kashmir* (☎ *726513, 27 Morley St*) is a long-standing favourite restaurant, with excellent curries for around £4. The *Mumtaz Paan House* (☎ *571861, 386 Great Horton Rd*) is another classic Indian café. If you're not into subcontinental cuisine, a reader recommended the *Java Café* beside the Alhambra Theatre.

There are frequent trains to Bradford from Leeds (£1.80 day return) and York (£7 day return), as well as regular buses from Leeds.

HAWORTH
● pop 5000   ☎ 01535

As the village that was home to the Brontë family, Haworth rivals Stratford-upon-Avon as England's most important literary shrine. The surrounding countryside seems haunted both by the sisters and their literary creations. Even without this, the old part of the village would still draw tourists; the cobblestoned Main St running steeply down to Bridgehouse Beck (stream) from the parish church provides a quintessential Yorkshire view.

Patrick Brontë and his family moved to the Parsonage in 1820. His wife Maria died of cancer at 38; Maria and Elizabeth died as children; Branwell, Emily and Anne died between the ages of 29 and 31; and Charlotte died at 38. Only Patrick survived to old age, dying in the Parsonage at the age of 84. The Parsonage Museum gives a fascinating insight into their lives.

Orientation & Information

Haworth's development parallels that of the textile industry. The old village, with its cottage-based weavers and spinners, grew up along the ridge above the valley. Then in the 19th century the outworkers were replaced by factories.

The TIC (☎ 642329), 2-4 West Lane, is open daily and has an excellent supply of information on the Brontë family and pleasant walks in the area. The **Brontë Weaving Shed** on North St sells all sorts of expensive woollens.

Brontë Parsonage

Set in a pretty garden, the Parsonage is a Georgian house overlooking the cemetery. The core of the house is furnished and decorated as it would have been when the Brontës lived there. Some of the furnishings are original and there are many personal possessions on display. The museum section houses lots of material, including the fascinating miniature books the children wrote.

The Parsonage (☎ 642323) is open daily from April to September from 10 am to 5 pm (closing at 8 pm on Wednesday in August and at 4.30 pm in winter) for £3.80/2.80.

Keighley & Worth Valley Railway

The K&WV Railway (☎ 645214 for information on timetables) is a favourite movie location with film crews, as much for the six restored stations as for the classic steam engines.

Especially on summer weekends when Haworth can be jam-packed, it's worth parking at Keighley and catching the train and connecting bus to the village. The Brontë Parsonage is a 10 minute walk from the station.

Trains operate virtually hourly on weekends throughout the year. Over school holiday periods there's a daily service too. An all day Rover is £6.50/3.25, a full-line return £5.20/2.60.

Walks

The TIC has information on lots of interesting walks that take in sights associated with the Brontë family. Some of them can be worked in around the K&WV Railway, the Brontë Way (which links Haworth with Bradford and Colne), and the two routes to

NORTH-EASTERN ENGLAND

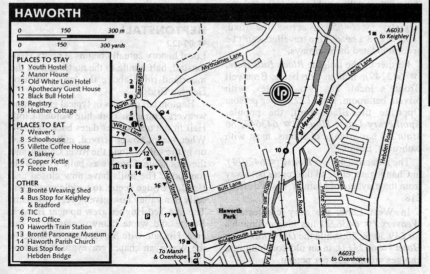

HAWORTH

0 ———— 150 ———— 300 m
0 ———— 150 ———— 300 yards

PLACES TO STAY
1 Youth Hostel
2 Manor House
5 Old White Lion Hotel
11 Apothecary Guest House
12 Black Bull Hotel
18 Registry
19 Heather Cottage

PLACES TO EAT
7 Weaver's
8 Schoolhouse
15 Villette Coffee House & Bakery
16 Copper Kettle
17 Fleece Inn

OTHER
3 Brontë Weaving Shed
4 Bus Stop for Keighley & Bradford
6 TIC
9 Post Office
10 Haworth Train Station
13 Brontë Parsonage Museum
14 Haworth Parish Church
20 Bus Stop for Hebden Bridge

A6033 to Keighley
Mytholmes Lane
Leeds Lane
Changegate
North St
West Lane
Rawdon Road
Main Street
Butt Lane
Belle Isle Road
Bridgehouse Beck
Mill Hey
Victoria Road
Station Road
Prince Street
Hebden Road
Haworth Park
Bridgehouse Lane
Ivy Bank Lane
To Marsh & Oxenhope
A6033 to Oxenhope

Hebden Bridge (see that section). Haworth is just east of the Pennine Way.

Brontë Way by Marje Wilson describes 11 circular walks that cover the entire route of the Way. Particularly interesting is the fairly strenuous 9 mile walk from the Parsonage to Colne/Laneshawbridge via Top Withens (Wuthering Heights), Ponden Hall (Thrushcross Grange) and Wycoller Hall (Ferndean Manor). From Laneshawbridge you can catch a bus to Keighley and complete the loop by catching the K&WV Railway back to Haworth.

Places to Stay

Hostel The *Haworth Youth Hostel* (☎ 642234, Longlands Drive, Lees Lane) closes on Sunday in November and December. Beds cost £8.80/5.95.

B&Bs & Hotels Although there are lots of places to stay, it's still worth booking ahead in summer.

Main St, the most atmospheric part of town, has lots of accommodation but might feel a bit oppressive at the height of the season. At *Heather Cottage* (☎ 644511) those happy with a light breakfast need pay only £12.50 instead of the full £16. *The Registry* (☎ 646503), across the road, charges £18 a head; lone travellers can't be accommodated on Saturdays.

Further up the hill, the *Black Bull Hotel* (☎ 642249), famous for being Branwell Brontë's local, has two doubles, with private bathroom, from £22.50 per person. Opposite the Black Bull, the popular *Apothecary Guest House* (☎ 643642, 86 Main St) has a range of rooms, most with bathroom, from £19.

The attractive *Manor House* (☎ 642911), in Changegate, close to the centre but away from the mayhem of Main St, has beds from £18.

In West Lane, the very comfortable *Weavers* (☎ 643822) has singles/doubles for £49.50/59.50, while the *Old White Lion Hotel* (☎ 642313), in an old coaching inn, charges around £35 per person.

Places to Eat

Main St and West Lane are lined with tea-rooms and restaurants. The *Villette Coffee House & Bakery* is particularly good value with all-day breakfasts for £2.60, and wonderful Yorkshire curd tarts (very sweet, rich and filling) for 75p. The *Copper Kettle* has meals for under £3.

In the *Schoolhouse* where Charlotte Brontë once taught (opposite the church), you can tuck into a ploughman's lunch for £3.50 in rather austere surroundings.

The *Fleece Inn* does good-value lunches, the *Black Bull* decent dinners.

At *Weavers* restaurant starters cost £4.95 while main courses like Yorkshire lamb steak cost £10.95. It's closed Monday.

Getting There & Away

On the Leeds-Settle-Carlisle Line, Keighley is the main jumping-off point for Haworth; it's linked to Haworth by the K&WV Railway and by Keighley & District buses Nos 663, 664, and 665 (☎ 603284). In summer, bus No 500 offers a service four times a day between Todmorden, Hebden Bridge, Haworth and Keighley (Wednesday and Sunday in winter).

HEBDEN BRIDGE & HEPTONSTALL
☎ 01422

Local history actually begins at pretty Heptonstall, half a mile to the north-east on the moorland ridge above the 'new' town of Hebden Bridge.

Heptonstall consists of typical grey-stone weavers' cottages. Yorkshire's oldest Cloth Hall in the main street dates back to 1554. When steam power arrived, mills were set up in the valley along the River Calder, and the Rochdale Canal was built to provide transport. The mills have now closed and Hebden Bridge seems to huddle apologetically in a valley now given over to tourism. The late Ted Hughes grew up near Hebden Bridge and wrote many poems about the area. His late wife Sylvia Plath is buried in the Wesleyan chapel graveyard at Heptonstall.

Orientation & Information

It's easy to get around Hebden Bridge on foot but the steep half mile walk up to Heptonstall is a killer. Better to hang on for a bus unless you're feeling energetic.

The TIC (☎ 843831), 1 Bridge Gate, is open daily and stocks information about walking to Hardcastle Crags, a nearby 400-acre area of woodland.

Calder Valley Cruising (☎ 845557), The Marina on New Rd, offers horse-drawn cruises along the Rochdale Canal.

Walkley Clogs

Walkley Clogs (☎ 842061), a mile west of Hebden Bridge on the Burnley Rd (the A646 to Halifax), is Britain's last working clog factory. Clogs used to be the only shoes the working classes could afford, and clog-making once employed thousands of people. Here you can witness the process first-hand amid a clutter of competing attractions. A passport to get you into all of them costs £4/2.

Heptonstall Old Grammar School

The Old Grammar School (☎ 843738), facing Heptonstall church and its romantic graveyard, has displays of local history in a 17th century school, complete with the old school furniture. It's open at weekends from Easter to October from 1 to 5 pm for £1/50p.

Places to Stay

Camping *Pennine Camp Site* (☎ 842287), at High Greenwood House, Heptonstall, has 50 pitches for tents or vans at £5. The *Jack Bridge Camp Site* (☎ 842795) at Colden, is only really suitable for hiking tents (£2 per person).

Hostel In an ancient manor house in a typical Yorkshire village, *Mankinholes Youth Hostel* (☎ 01706-812340) is near Todmorden, 4 miles south-west of Hebden Bridge, south of the A646 to/from Rochdale, and half a mile from the Pennine Way. From mid-March through October it's usually open daily except Sunday and possibly Monday. Beds cost £7.20/4.95. Trains from Leeds to Manchester stop at Todmorden, 2 miles from the hostel.

B&Bs & Hotels *Redacre Mill* (☎ 885563, Redacre, Mytholmroyd) has two twins and three doubles with private bathroom, in a canalside mill surrounded by gardens, for £37.

The *Robin Hood Inn* (☎ 842593), 2 steep miles out at Pecket Well on the Keighley Rd, has four beautifully decorated rooms with nice views (from £19 per person). The pub also serves good meals. Bus No 500 passes by.

Friendly *Royd Well* (☎ 845304, 35 Royd Terrace) is a three minute walk from town; rooms with shared bathroom cost from £14 per person. *1 Primrose Terrace* (☎ 844747) is similar.

Places to Eat

In Hebden Bridge, *Hebdens* (☎ 843745, Hanginroyd Lane) is a bistro with pizzas for around £5. *Il Mulino* (☎ 844181, Bridge Mill) does standard Italian dishes – spaghetti from £3 – but is closed Monday.

The pubs are probably your best bet – with a car, it's worth driving out to the *Robin Hood Inn* on the Keighley Road. In Heptonstall, the *White Lion* and *Cross in Hand* both do food, or there's a fish and chip shop.

Getting There & Away

Hebden Bridge is within the Leeds Metro area. The rail service runs from Leeds and Bradford to Halifax, Hebden Bridge and Todmorden (for the youth hostel), then continues to Manchester Victoria. Some services run right through from York to Liverpool. There's also a regular rail service linking Halifax, Hebden Bridge and Blackpool.

The buses are slower and less frequent than the trains, but in summer, Keighley & District's bus No 500 offers a handy four times a day service between Todmorden, Hebden Bridge (Hope St), Haworth and Keighley.

NORTH-EASTERN ENGLAND

Sheffield & Around

Until 1997 Sheffield hardly featured on tourist itineraries. Then came the smash-hit film *The Full Monty*, the tale of a group of unemployed steelworkers who turned to stripping for a living, and suddenly the spotlight was turned on this depressed South Yorkshire town. Even now Sheffield's tourist attractions are fairly low-key and, although there are pockets of glamorous redevelopment, much of the city still makes you wish you were somewhere else. But with the Peak District brushing up against its western outskirts, it makes a good base for a day or so. Chesterfield, with its twisted spire, is just a train hop away (see The Midlands chapter).

SHEFFIELD

• pop 475,000   ☎ 0114

Five hundred years ago Sheffield was already renowned for its cutlery production and the words 'Sheffield steel' still have a familiar ring to them. Nowadays the industry employs far fewer people than in the past, but they turn out more knives and forks than ever before.

Victorian Sheffield is synonymous with the worst industrial exploitation. Many buildings were damaged in WWII and postwar rebuilding added little to be admired. Despite this, England's fourth largest city is a lively place. It has an exuberant student population, and the recent redevelopment of the Devonshire Quarter is a hopeful sign for the future.

Orientation & Information

If you arrive by bus you'll find yourself at the vast Sheffield Interchange in Pond St, unattractively ringed with roads and highrises. The train station is clearly signed, three minutes south of the bus stands. There are left-luggage lockers at the Interchange, should you be passing through.

The main TIC (☎ 273 4671) is in Peace Gardens in Union St behind the Town Hall. At the time of writing, the area immediately in front of the Town Hall was being extensively redesigned to create a new Winter Garden and Millennium Gallery. Work will still be in progress when you read this.

Sheffield's main street changes its name from Glossop Rd to West St to Church St to High St as it proceeds from west to east. Immediately south of West St is the area known as the Devonshire Quarter (Devonshire St, Division St and Barker's Pool) where most of the trendy new shops and bars have opened.

Museums & Art Galleries

Given its history, it's not surprising that many of Sheffield's attractions focus on the industrial past.

One mile north of the centre, the **Kelham Island Museum** (☎ 272 2106) covers not just cutlery but the city's wider industrial heritage. It's open Monday to Thursday from 10 am to 4 pm and on Sunday from 11 am to 4.45 pm. Entry is £2.80/1.50.

One mile west of the centre in pleasant Weston Park, the **City Museum & Mappin Art Gallery** (☎ 276 8588) has exhibits on local archaeology and the history of the cutlery industry, as well as a varied collection of art works. It's open, free, Wednesday to Saturday from 10 am to 5 pm.

The **Ruskin Gallery** (☎ 273 5299), at 101 Norfolk St, houses a collection established by the Victorian critic and Gothic-revivalist John Ruskin in 1875 in an attempt to meld art and industry. There's also an exhibition of crafts. It's open, free, Tuesday to Saturday from 10 am to 5 pm.

The nearby **Graves Art Gallery** (☎ 273 5158) displays contemporary British art atop the City Library on Surrey St. It keeps the same hours as the Ruskin Gallery and is also free.

At the time of writing, the fate of the **Abbeydale Industrial Hamlet** (☎ 236 7731), 4 miles south-west on the A621, was uncertain. Ask at the TIC in case it's reopened.

Other Things to See & Do

In 1914 the 15th century church of Saints Peter and Paul on West St was upgraded to **cathedral** status. Note, at the west end, the

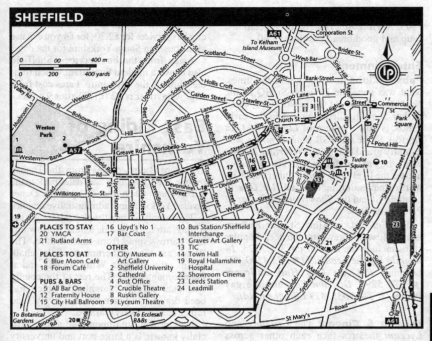

SHEFFIELD

PLACES TO STAY	16 Lloyd's No 1	10 Bus Station/Sheffield
20 YMCA	17 Bar Coast	Interchange
21 Rutland Arms		11 Graves Art Gallery
	OTHER	13 TIC
PLACES TO EAT	1 City Museum &	14 Town Hall
6 Blue Moon Café	Art Gallery	19 Royal Hallamshire
18 Forum Café	2 Sheffield University	Hospital
	3 Cathedral	22 Showroom Cinema
PUBS & BARS	4 Post Office	23 Leeds Station
5 All Bar One	7 Crucible Theatre	24 Leadmill
12 Fraternity House	8 Ruskin Gallery	
15 City Hall Ballroom	9 Lyceum Theatre	

memorial to the crew of the HMS *Sheffield* lost during the Falklands conflict.

In Clarkehouse Rd the **Botanical Gardens** cover 18 acres of ground and contain three recently-restored glasshouses by the Victorian designer Paxton.

Destination Sheffield organises **Full Monty Tours** of sites associated with the film but only if at least six people are interested. Contact the TIC for bookings.

Places to Stay & Eat

Sheffield is sadly lacking in cheap places to stay, especially in the city centre. A notable exception is the *Rutland Arms* (☎ *272 9003, 86 Brown St),* with rooms for £23.50/37 single/double. The big, slightly spartan *YMCA* (☎ *268 4807, 20 Victoria Rd)* caters for both sexes with B&B at £15/24, but it's a fair walk west of the centre. Over Easter and during the summer holidays rooms are

available at the University of Sheffield's *Halifax Hall of Residence* (☎ *222 8811),* 2 miles west of the centre in Endcliffe Vale Rd, for £21.85/33 a single/double.

B&Bs are also concentrated on the west side of town, in Nether Edge and along Ecclesall Rd where *Gulliver B&B* (☎ *262 0729),* at No 167, has singles/doubles for £15/29 while *Abbey House* (☎ *266 7426),* at No 484, charges £17 a head. In Nether Edge, *Lindum House* (☎ *255 2356, 91 Montgomery Rd)* charges from £18 a head for rooms which could do with a bit of maintenance.

When it comes to eating you'd do well to head straight for the Devonshire Quarter. The *Forum Café* (☎ *276 6544)* in the designer-clothes-filled Forum Shopping Centre at the junction of Division St and Eldon St, is hugely popular. A mushroom enchilada will cost you £4.75.

The excellent *Blue Moon Café* (☎ 276 3443, Norfolk Row) caters for vegetarians; soup and good bread cost just £1.80.

Entertainment

Pubs & Clubs In a sad sign of the times, what was once the Division St HQ of the National Union of Mineworkers, when Arthur Scargill ruled the roost in the early 1980s, is now a branch of *Lloyds No 1*. In Norfolk St the old TSB Bank is now a particularly grand branch of *Fraternity House*, while the old fire station in Division St now houses the lively *Bar Coast*. Other café bars worth frequenting include *All Bar One* in Leopold St and the *Showroom Café-Bar* in Paternoster Row.

The *Fat Cat*, in Alma St near Kelham Island Museum, brews its own beer. Popular clubs include the *Capital* (☎ 276 3523, 14 Matilda St), the *Leadmill* (☎ 275 4500, 6-7 Leadmill Rd), the *City Hall Ballroom* (☎ 273 5295, Division Rd), and the gay *Planet* (☎ 244 9033, 429 Effingham Rd).

Theatre & Cinema The *Crucible* and *Lyceum* theatres face each other across Tudor Square and share the same box office (☎ 276 9922). The *Showroom Cinema* (☎ 275 7727), Paternoster Row, shows the most interesting films.

Getting There & Away

Sheffield is 160 miles from London, just off the M1. There are frequent trains from London St Pancras via Leicester and Nottingham or Derby. National Express (☎ 0990-808080) services link Sheffield with London and other major centres in the north. A shuttle bus service links Sheffield with Leeds (1¼ hours, £3).

Sheffield is a jumping-off point for the Peak District. The railway line which cuts through the northern Peak District via Edale runs between Sheffield in the east and New Mills and Manchester in the west. The X23 bus service links Sheffield with Bakewell in the centre of the Peak District and Buxton on its western periphery.

Getting Around

Mainline offers an all day rover ticket for its city bus services for £2.30; for £4 you can use all its buses in South Yorkshire for the day.

Aside from the bus services, Sheffield also boasts a modern Supertram which trundles through the city centre. Fares cost from 60p. A dayrider is £2 (£1.50 after 9 am).

East Riding of Yorkshire

The word Riding comes from the Danish *treding*, meaning 'third' and dates back to the 9th century when the conquering Danes divided Yorkshire into administrative regions.

The county is mostly flat, although the rolling, attractive Wolds extend northwards in a narrow spine from Lincolnshire. The Wolds are the northernmost of the chalk downs originating in Wiltshire and end at Flamborough Head. The rest of the county was once largely marshland, which has been drained and is now intensively (and rather unattractively) farmed.

Hull, or Kingston-upon-Hull as it is officially known, is a large port and university town, with ferries to Zeebrugge (Belgium) and Rotterdam (Netherlands). Ten miles north, on the edge of the Wolds, is the small, unspoilt market town of Beverley, with two superb churches.

GETTING AROUND

The county council has a 24 hour travel line (☎ 01482-884900), or you can contact them on ☎ 01482-884358. The principal bus operators are East Yorkshire (☎ 01482-327146), York Pullman (☎ 01904-608854) and Yorkshire Coastliner (☎ 01653-692556). National Express also runs services to Hull.

Hull is easily reached by rail, and from Hull a line runs north to Beverley, Bridlington, Filey and Scarborough.

HULL (KINGSTON-UPON-HULL)
• pop 332,145 ☎ 01482

Fortunately, only pedants call Hull by its unwieldy official name. Historically, this north-eastern town was a major port, and so it remains today. Hull was hard hit during WWII and initial impressions are not encouraging. But persevere and you'll find more than enough to while away a few hours in the Old Town abutting the modern Marina.

Information & Orientation

Paragon train station is west of Queen Victoria Square, in the centre of town.

The TIC (☎ 223559) in Carr Lane is surrounded by the imposing buildings of Register Square. An excellent town trail from the TIC winds through the Old Town.

All the city's museums and galleries are open Monday to Saturday from 10 am to 5 pm and on Sunday from 1.30 to 4.30 pm. Some are free, others charge £1 admission.

Things To See & Do

Facing Register Square are **Ferens Art Gallery** and **Hull Maritime Museum**, both in impressive Victorian buildings. But the most important museum is waterside **Wilberforce House,** birthplace in 1759 of the anti-slavery crusader William Wilberforce. Wilberforce House was built in 1639 and the museum, which covers the history of slavery and the campaign against it, overflows into several attractive Georgian houses. Next door is the **Streetlife** transport museum with a very pleasant garden.

At the heart of the Old Town, two buildings typify Hull's importance at early stages of its history. **Holy Trinity Church** is a magnificent medieval building with a striking central tower, while **Hull City Council** and the **Law Courts** are housed in a staggeringly over-the-top colonnaded building. Lovely, pedestrianised **Parliament St** suggests what much of 18th century Hull must have looked like.

Stretches of the Hull waterside are faintly reminiscent of the Netherlands, and pubs like the *Baltic Wharf* and *Minerva* with outside tables add to the continental feel. Don't miss the soaring **River Hull Tidal Surge Barrier**, intended to protect the city from flooding.

Finally, the **Princes Quay Shopping Centre**, an imposing glass building set in a

moat and facing the modern marina, exemplifies a Hull which looks to have put the worst years behind it.

Getting There & Away

Hull is on a branch line off the King's Cross to Edinburgh line and has good rail links north and south, and west to York and the Northern Midlands. North Sea Ferries (☎ 377177) has daily services to Zeebrugge and Rotterdam.

BEVERLEY

• pop 20,000   ☎ 01482

At the centre of a rich agricultural region, Beverley is a gem of an 18th century market town, once the capital of the East Riding and hardly marred by modern development. It's dominated by beautiful Beverley Minster, formerly a monastic church and still the equal of many cathedrals in magnificence.

Information

Beverley TIC (☎ 867430), The Guildhall, Register Sq, is well stocked with information and has an accommodation service.

General markets are still held on Wednesday and Saturday. A 400-year-old cattle and pig market is held to the north of the town centre every Tuesday and Wednesday (Wednesday is the big day; selling starts at 10.30 am and finishes by 1 pm).

Beverley Minster

The first church on the site was built in the 7th century; the present building dates from 1220 but construction continued for two centuries spanning the Early English, Decorated and perpendicular periods. The end product is best known for its magnificent perpendicular west front (1420), with its twin towers and wonderful sculpture.

Inside, extraordinary medieval faces and demons peer down from every possible vantage point, while stone angels play a variety of silent instruments. Note particularly a 10th century Frith Stool, or sanctuary chair; the canopy of the Percy Tomb (to the north of the altar); and the 68 medieval misericords (support ledges for choristers).

The minster is open Monday to Saturday from 9 am to 5 pm (later in summer) and Sunday from 2.30 to 5 pm. Donations of £1 are requested. There are sometimes guided tours at 2 pm (£1).

St Mary's Church

Stately St Mary's church would attract all the attention if it were anywhere else but Beverley. Here it inevitably plays second fiddle to the minster. Still, if you like medieval churches, this is a particularly fine example, built in stages between 1120 and 1530. In the ambulatory look out for a carving thought to have inspired Lewis Carroll's White Rabbit.

Places to Stay

Hostel *Friary Youth Hostel* (☎ *881751*), in a beautifully restored 14th century Dominican friary in Friar's Lane, is open daily except Sunday from April through October. Beds are £7.20/4.95.

B&Bs & Hotels Most of the cheaper B&Bs are a short walk south of the minster. *Eastgate Guest House* (☎ *868464, 7 Eastgate*) has singles/doubles from £19.50/32. *York House* (☎ *868617, 4 Ellerker Rd*) offers a single and a twin at £14 per person.

For a splurge, the *Beverley Arms Hotel* (☎ *869241, North Bar Within*) has singles/doubles from £55/75. The *Kings Head Hotel* (☎ *868103, Saturday Market Place*), in a refurbished Georgian building in the town centre, has rooms for £39.50/49.50, but ask about weekend rates.

Places to Eat

There are several teashops on Highgate between the minster and Wednesday Market; *The Tea Cosy* has hot lunch dishes for £4.55. Beside St Mary's church in North Bar Within, *Copperfield's Bistro 22* (☎ *887624*) offers daily specials for £12. Stylish *Wednesdays* (☎ *869727, Wednesday Market*) does starters that double as light meals for around £4; main courses start at £7.75.

Getting There & Away

Beverley is on the railway line from Hull to Scarborough. The train station lies east of the town centre, the bus station north on Sow Hill.

Bus Reasonably regular buses link York (train station) and Hull via Beverley. These services also connect with Leeds and are operated by East Yorkshire Motor Services, Yorkshire Coastliner and York Pullman.

Train There are frequent weekday trains between Hull and York (1¼ hours) and between Hull and Beverley (15 minutes, £2.80 day return). Trains continue from Beverley to Filey and Scarborough every couple of hours except on Sunday.

North Yorkshire

North Yorkshire is one of the largest counties, containing some of the finest monuments, most beautiful countryside and most spectacular coastline in the country. It includes two national parks (the Yorkshire Dales and North York Moors), the medieval city of York, the great monastic ruins of Rievaulx and Fountains abbeys, the classical beauty of Castle Howard, and the grim castles of Richmond and Bolton.

Most of North Yorkshire was untouched by the Industrial Revolution and, to a large extent, the accompanying agricultural revolution. The winter climate is harsh and much of the countryside lends itself to sheep grazing, an activity that has continued largely unchanged from medieval times. Great fortunes – private and monastic – were founded on wool.

In the west the Pennines, including the peaks of Ingleborough and Pen-y-ghent, dominate the beautiful dales, whose flanks are defined by snaking stone walls and overlooked by wild, heather-clad plateaus. In the east, stone villages shelter at the foot of bleak and beautiful moors. These stretch to the high cliffs of the east coast, with its fishing villages and the holiday resort of Scarborough.

GETTING AROUND

North Yorkshire has a transport inquiry line (☎ 01609-780780). Explorer tickets are available on Stagecoach Cumberland (☎ 01946-63222), Harrogate & District (☎ 01423-566061) and Keighley & District (☎ 01535-603284). Ask about day ticket deals. Yorkshire Coastliner (☎ 01653-692556), which has some interesting services around the North York Moors, York, Whitby and Scarborough, has a day Freedom ticket for £8. North East Buses/Tees & District (☎ 01325-355415) has services around Whitby.

YORK

• **pop 123,000   ☎ 01904**

For nearly 2000 years York has been the capital of the north. Its city walls, built during the 13th century, are among the most impressive surviving medieval fortifications in Europe. They encompass a thriving, fascinating centre with medieval streets, grand Georgian town houses, riverside pubs and modern shops. The crowning glory is the Minster, England's largest Gothic cathedral, but there's a bewildering array of things to see and do.

York attracts millions of visitors, and the July and August crowds can get you down; try and visit out of season if you can.

History

The Brigantes probably had a settlement at the meeting point of the rivers Foss and Ouse before the Romans arrived to set up a walled garrison called Eboracum in 71 AD.

Eboracum was strategically important, hence the visits of several emperors: Hadrian used it as a base in 121; Septimius Severus used it to hold Imperial Court in 211; and in 306 Constantius Chlorus died here. He was succeeded by his son Constantine, the first Christian emperor and founder of Constantinople (Istanbul), who was probably proclaimed emperor on the site of the cathedral.

The Anglo-Saxons founded the cathedral city of Eoforwic on the Roman ruins. Eoforwic was the capital of the independent kingdom of Northumbria which, like that of the Brigantes, stretched from the Humber to the Firth of Forth.

In 625 Christianity was brought by Paulinus, a Roman priest who had joined Augustine's Canterbury mission. He succeeded in converting the Saxon king of Northumbria, King Edwin, and his nobles. The first wooden church was built in 627 and became a centre of learning that attracted students from around Europe.

The Danish Vikings captured and burnt the city in 867, but then made it their capital, Jorvik, for nearly 100 years. Under their rule it became an important trading port. Not until 954 did the kings of Wessex succeed in reuniting the Danelaw with the south, but their control remained tenuous. King Harold was forced to tackle a Norwegian invasion-cum-uprising at Stamford Bridge, east of York, immediately before the Battle of Hastings.

William the Conqueror was also faced with rebellion. After the north's second uprising in 1070, he burnt York and Durham and laid waste the countryside … the 'harrying of the North'. Afterwards, the Normans rebuilt the walls and erected two castles and a new cathedral. York once again became an important port, and the centre of the profitable new trade in wool.

In the 15th century the city declined, losing influence and power to London. During the Civil War, York twice came under siege from the Parliamentary army. The first siege was lifted after two months by the arrival of an army under the command of King Charles' nephew Prince Rupert. In the war's bloodiest battle, Prince Rupert chased the retreating Parliamentarians to Marston Moor, where they turned on him and cut his army to pieces, killing 4000 men. The siege was resumed, and the city finally fell in July 1642. Fortunately, the commander of the Parliamentarian forces, Sir Thomas Fairfax, a local man, prevented the troops pillaging the Minster.

The coming of the railway in 1839 once again placed York at the hub of the north-east.

NORTH-EASTERN ENGLAND

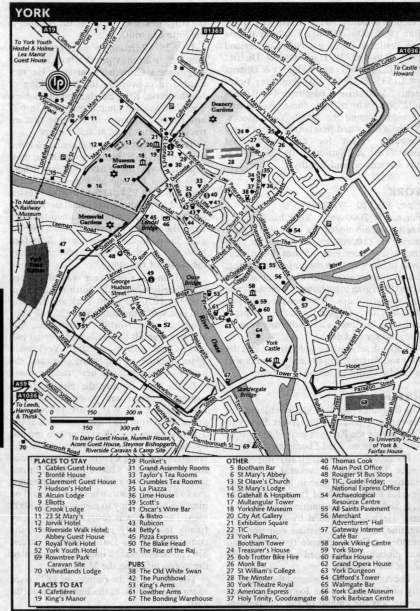

YORK

PLACES TO STAY
1 Gables Guest House
2 Brontë House
3 Claremont Guest House
7 Hudson's Hotel
8 Alcuin Lodge
9 Elliotts
10 Crook Lodge
11 23 St Mary's
12 Jorvik Hotel
15 Riverside Walk Hotel;
   Abbey Guest House
47 Royal York Hotel
52 York Youth Hotel
69 Rowntree Park
   Caravan Site
70 Wheatlands Lodge

PLACES TO EAT
4 Cafetières
19 King's Manor

29 Plunket's
31 Grand Assembly Rooms
33 Taylor's Tea Rooms
34 Crumbles Tea Rooms
35 La Piazza
36 Lime House
39 Scott's
41 Oscar's Wine Bar
   & Bistro
43 Rubicon
44 Betty's
45 Pizza Express
50 The Blake Head
51 The Rise of the Raj

PUBS
38 The Old White Swan
42 The Punchbowl
53 King's Arms
61 Lowther Arms
67 The Bonding Warehouse

OTHER
5 Bootham Bar
6 St Mary's Abbey
13 St Olave's Church
14 St Mary's Lodge
16 Gatehall & Hospitium
17 Multangular Tower
18 Yorkshire Museum
20 City Art Gallery
21 Exhibition Square
22 TIC
23 York Pullman,
   Bootham Tower
24 Treasurer's House
25 Bob Trotter Bike Hire
26 Monk Bar
27 St William's College
28 The Minster
30 York Theatre Royal
32 American Express
37 Holy Trinity, Goodramgate

40 Thomas Cook
46 Main Post Office
48 Rougier St Bus Stops
49 TIC, Guide Friday;
   National Express Office
54 Archaeological
   Resource Centre
55 All Saints Pavement
56 Merchant
   Adventurers' Hall
57 Gateway Internet
   Café Bar
58 Jorvik Viking Centre
59 York Story
60 Fairfax House
62 Grand Opera House
63 York Dungeon
64 Clifford's Tower
65 Walmgate Bar
68 York Castle Museum

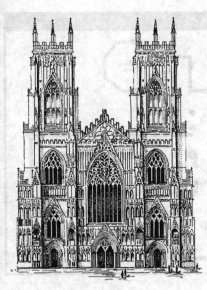

York Minster

Orientation

Although the centre is relatively small, York's streets are a confusing medieval tangle. Remember that in York, *gate* means street, and *bar* means gate.

The city is circled by a ring road. There are five major landmarks in the centre: the wall that encloses the city centre; the Minster at the northern corner; Clifford's Tower, a 13th century castle and mound at the southern end; the River Ouse that cuts the centre in two; and the enormous train station just outside the western corner.

The main bus dropping off point is on Rougier St (off Station Rd, inside the city walls on the western side of Lendal Bridge), but some local and regional buses leave from outside the train station.

Information

The main TIC (☎ 621756), is in De Grey Rooms, Exhibition Square, north of the river near Bootham Bar. It opens daily from 9 am to 6 pm most of the year, but in July and August it opens Monday to Saturday from 9 am to 7 pm, Sunday from 9 am to 6 pm. There's also a small TIC at the train station, and another at 20 George Hudson St near where the long-distance buses stop.

The TICs sell the *York For Less* booklet, giving various discounts on attractions, tours and meals. It also sells the *Disabled Person's Guide to York*.

At the Gateway Internet Cafe-Bar (☎ 646446), 9 Barleycorn Yard, Walmgate, you can explore the Web and exchange emails over a coffee or glass of Black Sheep ale.

York Minster

York Minster (☎ 624426), or the Cathedral & Metropolitan Church of St Peter, is Europe's largest medieval cathedral and one of the world's most inspiring buildings. The word 'minster' suggests that one of the previous buildings was once connected with a monastery. The minster is the seat of the Archbishop of York, who holds the title of Primate of England, and is second only in importance to the Archbishop of Canterbury, the Primate of *All* England!

The cathedral, a time capsule incorporating the remains of seven buildings, is most famous for its extensive medieval stained glass, particularly in the enormous Great East Window (1405-08).

The first church on the site was a wooden chapel built for Paulinus's baptism of King Edwin on Easter Day 627; its site is marked in the crypt. This church, however, was built near the site of a Roman basilica, a vast assembly hall at the heart of Roman military headquarters; parts can be seen in the foundations. A stone church was started, but fell into disrepair after Edwin's death. St Wilfred built the next church, but this was destroyed as part of William's brutal response to a northern rebellion. The first Norman church was built in stages 1060 to 1080; you can see surviving fragments in the foundations and crypt.

The present building, built mainly 1220 to 1480, incorporates several architectural styles. The north transept was built in Early

NORTH-EASTERN ENGLAND

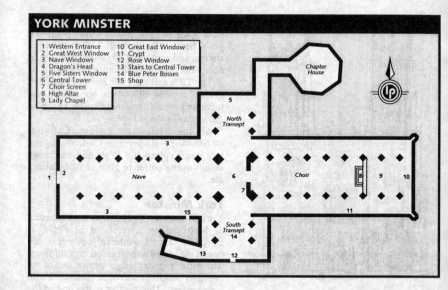

YORK MINSTER

1 Western Entrance
2 Great West Window
3 Nave Windows
4 Dragon's Head
5 Five Sisters Window
6 Central Tower
7 Choir Screen
8 High Altar
9 Lady Chapel
10 Great East Window
11 Crypt
12 Rose Window
13 Stairs to Central Tower
14 Blue Peter Bosses
15 Shop

Chapter House

North Transept

Nave

Choir

South Transept

English style between 1241 and 1260; the nave, choir and octagonal Chapter House were built in Decorated style between 1260 and 1405; and the central, or lantern, tower was the last addition, built in perpendicular style 1460 to 1480.

You enter from the western end. The nave is unusually tall and wide; although the aisles (to the side) are roofed in stone, the central roof is wood painted to look like stone. On both sides of the nave are the shields of nobles who met Edward II at a parliament in York. Also note the **dragon's head** projecting from the gallery – it's a crane believed to have been used to lift a font cover. There are several fine **windows** dating from the early 14th century, but the most dominating is the **Great West Window** from 1338, with beautiful stone tracery.

The transepts are the oldest part of the building above ground, and the **Five Sisters Window**, with five lancets over 15m high, is the cathedral's oldest complete window; most of it is from around 1260. In 1984 the south transept was destroyed in a fire. Six of

the **bosses** in the new roof were designed by children who won a competition sponsored by the popular TV program, *Blue Peter*.

The **Chapter House** is a magnificent example of the Decorated style. Superb stonework decorated with tiny individual stone heads surrounds a wonderful space uninterrupted by a central column.

The heart of the church is dominated by the awesome **central tower**. The 15th century **choir screen** depicts the 15 kings from William I to Henry VI.

The **Lady Chapel** behind the **high altar** is dominated by the **Great East Window**, the largest intact stained-glass medieval window in the world. Created between 1405 and 1408, it illustrates the beginning and end of the world as described in Genesis and the Book of Revelation.

Entered from the south choir aisle, the **crypt** contains fragments from the Norman cathedral. The font shows King Edwin's baptism and marks the site of Paulinus' original wooden chapel.

In the south transept, the **Rose Window** commemorates the union of the royal houses of Lancaster and York through the marriage of Henry VII and Elizabeth of York, which ended the Wars of the Roses and began the Tudor dynasty.

The entry to the stairs up to the tower and down to the Foundations & Treasury is also in the south transept. The queues for the tower are long, but the reward for a steep, claustrophobic climb (275 steps) to the top is an excellent view over York and the surrounding countryside.

The **Foundations & Treasury** shouldn't be missed. In 1967 the foundations were excavated when the central tower threatened to collapse; while engineers worked frantically to save the building, archaeologists uncovered Roman and Norman ruins which now illustrate the site's ancient history – one of the most extraordinary finds is a Roman culvert, still carrying water to the River Ouse. The Treasury houses artefacts from the 11th century, including relics from the graves of medieval archbishops.

To see everything could easily absorb the best part of a day. The cathedral itself is free, but a £2 donation is requested. To visit the Chapter House costs 70/30p; to see the Foundations & Treasury £1.80/70p; to see the crypt 60/30p; and to climb the tower £2/1.

The cathedral opens daily in summer from 7 am to 8.30 pm, in winter from 7 am to 5 pm. The Foundations & Treasury, Chapter House and central tower open at these times Monday to Saturday, from 1 pm Sunday.

Around the Cathedral

Owned by the cathedral since the 15th century, **St William's College** (☎ 637134), College St, is an attractive half-timbered Tudor building housing an excellent restaurant (see Places to Eat).

The **Treasurer's House** (☎ 624247, NT), Minster Yard, was home to the minster's medieval treasurers. Substantially rebuilt in the 17th and 18th centuries, it now houses a fine collection of 18th century furniture. It's open daily from late March to early November from 10.30 am to 5 pm; £3.50/1.75.

City Walls

You can get onto the walls, built in the 13th century, via steps by **Bootham Bar** (on the site of a Roman gate) and follow them clockwise to Monk Bar, a walk offering particularly beautiful views of the Minster.

Monk Bar is the best preserved medieval gate, with a small **Richard III Museum** (☎ 634191) upstairs. The museum sets out the case of the murdered 'Princes in the Tower' and invites visitors to decide whether their uncle, Richard III, killed them. It's open daily from March to October from 9 am to 5 pm (from 9.30 am to 4 pm November to February); admission is £1/50p.

Walmgate Bar is England's only city gate with an intact barbican (built during the reign of Edward III). A barbican is an extended gateway designed to make life difficult for uninvited guests.

Museum Gardens

The Museum Gardens (open daily to dusk) make a peaceful city-centre oasis. Assorted picturesque ruins and buildings include the **Museum Gardens Lodge** (Victorian Gothic Revival, 1874) and a 19th century working **Observatory**. The **Multangular Tower** was the western tower of the Roman garrison's defensive wall. The small Roman stones at the bottom have been built up with 13th century additions.

The **Yorkshire Museum** (☎ 629745), in a classical building completed in 1829, has some interesting Roman, Anglo-Saxon, Viking and medieval exhibits and is worth visiting if there's a good temporary exhibition. It's open April to October, daily from 10 am to 5 pm, November to March, Monday to Saturday from 10 am to 5 pm, Sunday from 1 to 5 pm; £3.60/2.30.

The **Gatehall** was the main entry to **St Mary's Abbey**, a Benedictine monastery founded in 1080 with a later Early English-style church. The ruined 15th century gateway provided access from the abbey to the river. The adjacent **Hospitium** dates from the 14th century, although the timber-framed upper storey is a much-restored survivor from the 15th century; it was used as the abbey guesthouse. **St Mary's Lodge** was built around 1470 to provide VIP accommodation.

St Olave's Church dates from the 15th century, but there has been a church dedicated to the patron saint of Norway on this site since at least 1050.

Merchant Adventurers' Hall

Built in the mid-14th century, the Merchant Adventurers' Hall (☎ 654818), Fossgate (access also from Piccadilly), testifies to the power of the medieval guilds. They controlled all foreign trade into and out of York – a handy little monopoly. The Guild Hall with its massive oak timbers is outstanding.

The hall opens April to mid-November, daily from 8.30 am to 5 pm; mid-November to March, Monday to Saturday from 8.30 am to 3 pm; £1.90/60p.

Jorvik Viking Centre

From 1976 to 1981 excavations in Coppergate uncovered Jorvik, the 9th century

---

Medieval Guilds

In medieval and Tudor times, craftsmen and tradesmen formed themselves into guilds, which were basically a form of trade union or professional association. Crafts and trades were restricted to the members of an appropriate guild except at markets (which were usually weekly) or fairs (which were usually annual).

The guilds checked the quality of the work done, investigated complaints and regulated prices. Competition was only allowed in terms of quality and service. Admission was restricted to those who had served a seven-year apprenticeship and paid a fee. An apprentice was completely bound to his master and received little more than food and board. He couldn't do anything without explicit permission – this included having any relations with the opposite sex.

Viking settlement that preceded modern York. Jorvik Viking Centre (☎ 643211), Coppergate Centre, is one of York's most popular attractions and you may have to queue for up to 30 minutes. You travel in a 'time car' to a smells-and-all recreation of what the Viking town probably looked like, complete with fibreglass figures speaking a language derived from modern Icelandic. At the end of the ride there's a chance to inspect finds from the site.

It's open April to October, daily from 9 am to 5.30 pm; November to March daily from 9 am to 3.30 pm ; £4.99/3.99.

The Jorvik people also run the **Archaeological Resource Centre** (ARC; ☎ 653000), St Saviourgate, which allows hands-on exploration of archaeology for £3.60/2.40.

Clifford's Tower

After laying waste to the north as punishment for its rebellion, William the Conqueror built two mottes (mounds) crowned with wooden towers. The original one on this site was destroyed by fire during anti-Jewish riots in 1190; 150 Jews sheltering in the castle took their own lives. There's not much to see in the building (☎ 646940, EH) but the views over the city are excellent. It opens April to October daily from 10 am to 6 pm (from 9.30 am to 7 pm in July and August); daily from 10 am to 4 pm November to March; £1.70/90p.

York Castle Museum

One of Britain's best museums, York Castle Museum (☎ 653611) contains displays of everyday life complete with Victorian and Edwardian streets, and fascinating reconstructions of domestic interiors. An extraordinary collection of everyday objects from the past 400 years includes old TVs, radios, washing machines, vacuum cleaners and gadgets guaranteed to bring childhood memories flooding back.

The museum is open Monday to Saturday from 9.30 am to 5.30 pm, Sunday from 10 am to 5.30 pm; £4.75/3.30. Allow at least two hours for a visit.

National Railway Museum

This museum (☎ 621261), Leeman Rd, is one of the world's biggest railway museums. The history of railways is traced via an impressive collection of carriages (including Queen Victoria's saloon) and locomotives (including the record-breaking *Mallard*). Allow two hours to do it justice. It's open daily from 10 am to 6 pm; £4.95/3.15.

Medieval Churches

Of York's 41 pre-16th century churches, 20 still survive, often with their stained-glass intact. Finest is **All Saints, North St** which John Betjeman dubbed 'the best reconstruction of a medieval interior', with wonderful glass and all sorts of bits and bobs. It's easily spotted by the octagon rising above its tower.

Just as atmospheric, if more homely, is **Holy Trinity, Goodramgate**, tucked away in a churchyard popular with lunching shopworkers off Goodramgate. Inside, box pews surround an 18th century two-tier pulpit and there's never a straight line in view. It opens Tuesday to Saturday from 9.30 am to 5 pm.

On a busy corner, **All Saints, Pavement**, High Ousegate, has a fine lantern tower and 14th century stained glass.

Other Things to See

In Castlegate, **Fairfax House** (☎ 655543) is a beautiful Georgian house with a renowned collection of 18th century furniture and clocks. It's open March to December, Monday to Thursday and Saturday from 11 am to 5 pm, Sunday from 1.30 to 5 pm; £3.75/1.50.

The **York Story** (☎ 628632), in St Mary's Church in the Coppergate Centre, relates York's history through models and audio-visuals. It's open daily from 10 am to 5 pm (from 1 to 5 pm on Sunday) and costs £1.90/1.30 (50p discount with combined Castle Museum ticket).

York Dungeon (☎ 632599), 12 Clifford St is what you'd expect – a series of gruesome historical reconstructions, intended to scare those who find the Chamber of Horrors tame. It's open daily from 10 am to

5.30 pm (from 4.30 pm October to March) and costs £4.95/3.25.

Opposite the TIC, York's **City Art Gallery** (☎ 551861), Exhibition Square, has a range of paintings, including works by Lely, Reynolds and Lowry. It's open Monday to Saturday from 10 am to 5 pm, Sunday from 2.30 to 5 pm; free.

In the heart of York, the quaintly cobbled **Shambles** hints at what a medieval street might have looked like. It takes its curious name from the Saxon word *shamel*, meaning slaughterhouse. These days the former butchers' shops mainly sell tacky tourist souvenirs.

Organised Tours

Bus For a good overall introduction, York Pullman (☎ 622992), Bootham Tower, Exhibition Square, runs guided double-decker bus tours which circle the city calling at the main sites; you can get on and off where you please (buses run every 20 minutes) and tickets are valid all day. The main starting point is Exhibition Square opposite the TIC and its office is in Bootham Tower. Tickets are £6/2. Guide Friday (☎ 640896), in the TIC on George Hudson St, operates similar tours for £7.50/2.50.

Yorktour (☎ 645151), 8 Tower St, has a range of good-value day tours into the surrounding countryside. These include Castle Howard for £6, North York Moors Railway & Moorland for £18.50, and Yorkshire Dales & Herriot Country for £17.50. Prices don't include admission charges. Children under 16 travel free. Tickets are also available from the TIC.

Boat Yorkboat River Trips operated by the White Rose Line (☎ 623752), Lendal Bridge, has cruises along the River Ouse. Forty-minute round trips depart from King's Staith (behind the fire station) and Lendal Bridge (next to the Guildhall, under Lendal Bridge). February to November trips run every 30 minutes from 11 am; the rest of the year there are three trips a day; £3.50/1.50. March to October, there's even a ghost cruise daily at 7 pm; £5.50/2.75.

Walking Yorkwalk (☎ 622303) offers a series of two-hour themed walks on Roman York, medieval York, the snickelways (alleys) of York, and saints and sinners of York. Each walk costs £4/1 and walkers get a £1 discount off Guide Friday tours. Walks depart from Museum Gardens Gate. The Association of Voluntary Guides has free daily walking tours of the city from Exhibition Square in front of the City Art Gallery at 10.15 am and 2.15 pm.

York has many companies offering ghost walks. The following are the bare bones: the Original Ghost Walk of York (☎ 01759-373090) leaves the Kings Arms at 8 pm daily; the Ghost Trail of York (☎ 633276) leaves the front entrance of the Minster at 7.30 pm daily; the Ghost Hunt of York (☎ 608700) leaves the Shambles at 7.30 pm daily; and the Haunted Walk of York (☎ 621003) leaves from the front of the City Art Gallery daily at 8 pm. All cost £3/2.

Places to Stay

Despite the existence of hundreds of hotels and B&Bs, it can be difficult to find a bed in midsummer or when the races are on. Prices also jump significantly, say from an average of £18 per person to £25 per person, in the high season. The TIC can help with accommodation and in mid-summer it may be worth paying its £3 fee to avoid wasting time.

Camping There are a dozen camping grounds and caravan parks around York but most are at least 4 miles from the centre. The closest is *Rowntree Park Caravan Site* (☎ 658997), over Skeldergate Bridge; it charges £6 a night for a van plus £4 an adult. There's little grass on the sites so although tents are allowed, you'd need something soft to sleep on. *Riverside Caravan & Camp Site* (☎ 704442) is 3 miles south in Ferry Lane, Bishopthorpe.

Hostels *York Youth Hostel* (☎ 653147, Water End, Clifton) opens all year. Once the home of the Rowntree family, this is a large, modern hostel, with four beds in most rooms. It's popular, so book ahead especially in summer. The nightly rate of £14.40/10.95 includes breakfast. It's about a mile north-west of the TIC: turn left into Bootham, which becomes Clifton (the A19), then left into Water End. Alternatively, there's a riverside footpath from the train station.

York Youth Hotel (☎ 625904, 11 Bishophill Senior) in the city centre which is equally popular, particularly with school and student parties. There's a range of rooms, from 20-bed dorms (£9) to twin bunk rooms (£12 per person). Sleeping sheet hire is an additional £1.

The University of York offers accommodation in its halls of residence in holiday times. *Fairfax House* (☎ 432095, 99 Heslington Rd) is a 20 minute walk south-east of the city, has single rooms with washbasins for £20 per person.

B&Bs & Hotels There are lots of B&Bs and hotels in the streets north and south of Bootham (the A19 to Thirsk) to the north-west of the city. There are also quite a few to the south-west in the streets between Bishopthorpe Rd (over Skeldergate Bridge) and the A1036 to Leeds.

B&Bs & Hotels – north-west Leaving Bootham Bar along Bootham, the first main intersection is Gillygate to the right. Turn right and then second left for Claremont Terrace and several reasonably priced guesthouses. *Claremont Guest House* (☎ 625158), at No 18, has double rooms with bath from £28 to £45.

Continue along Bootham and the first street you come to on your left is Marygate, which follows the Museum Gardens down to the river. *Jorvik Hotel* (☎ 653511), at No 50, has a walled garden and 23 comfortable rooms with bath. Doubles cost from £40 to £60 and there's one single from £28. Continue down to the river, where there are a couple of places right on the bank. *Abbey Guest House* (☎ 627782, 14 Earlsborough Terrace) is a standard B&B with rooms from £18 per person. The comfortable *Riverside Walk Hotel* (☎ 620769, 9 Earls-

borough Terrace) has rooms with bath from £24 a head.

Back on Bootham, *Hudson's Hotel* (☎ 621267), at No 60, has 30 rooms with all mod cons in a well-designed, modern annexe and a restaurant and bar in a Georgian town house. Doubles with bath cost from £105.

The next street on the left, St Mary's, has two very pleasant mid-range places: *Crook Lodge* (☎ 655614), at No 26, with doubles only from £44 per room; and *23 St Mary's* (☎ 6226378) with fully equipped singles/doubles from £30/48.

Running along the railway line, Bootham Terrace (south of Bootham) and Grosvenor Terrace (north of Bootham) are virtually lined with B&Bs. Most are standard, but the position is central. Pleasant *Brontë House* (☎ 621066, 22 Grosvenor Terrace) has singles/doubles from £15/32 or £20/50 with private bath.

Inviting places on Sycamore Place, off Bootham Terrace, include *Alcuin Lodge* (☎ 632222), at No 15, which has some rooms with private bath (£45), others with shared facilities (£30), but only doubles and *Elliotts* (☎ 623333), with good rooms and private facilities for £30/48.

There's a whole row of cheapish places together at the bottom of Bootham Crescent. Most have private bathroom and charge from £17 per person, including *The Gables Guest House* (☎ 624381) at No 50.

Several large detached Victorian mansions in St Peter's Grove offer something quiet but reasonably grand. *Holme Lea Manor Guest House* (☎ 623529, 18 St Peter's Grove, Bootham)* is particularly nice and has four doubles from £40.

B&Bs & Hotels – south-west There are more places clustered around Scarcroft Rd, Southlands Rd and Bishopthorpe Rd, the continuation of Bishopgate, which takes off from the southern corner of the wall after Skeldergate Bridge.

On Bishopthorpe Rd itself, *Nunmill House* (☎ 634047), at No 85, is a good place with rooms from £22 per person. Just in from the corner of Bishopthorpe and South-lands Rds, *Acorn Guest House* (☎ 620081, 1 Southlands Rd)* is a decent two-star guesthouse with TV in all rooms and doubles for £28. Next door, *Staymor* (☎ 626935) has beds from £12 per person, while *Bishopgarth* (☎ 635220) charges £13.

Wheatlands Lodge (☎ 654318, 75 Scarcroft Rd)* takes up a whole row of attractive listed Victorian villas. Most rooms are sunny and rates start at £22.50 per person in a double with bath. Vegetarian food is served in the Victorian *Dairy Guest House* (☎ 639367, 3 Scarcroft Rd)*. Singles/doubles start at £28/36. Beside the train station, *Royal York Hotel* (☎ 653681) is a huge Victorian edifice with wonderful grounds and views. Rooms cost £120.50/146 for a single/double with breakfast.

Places to Eat

Restaurants There are several decent restaurants along Goodramgate from Monk Bar. *La Piazza* (☎ 642641) does standard pizzas (£5.30) and pasta (£5.50) in a fine half-timbered Tudor hall. Further along, *Lime House* (☎ 632734) is busy, especially on weekends; mains like sirloin steak are £9 to £11. Up the hill, along Micklegate near the Blake Head Book Shop, *The Rise of the Raj* (☎ 622975) offers a standard range of Indian dishes like chicken tikka masala for £6.55.

Toward the town centre, *St William's College Restaurant* in the college, off College St, is a great spot to relax after exploring the cathedral. It's open from 10 am to 5 pm and does soups for £2.50 and various dishes including vegetarian ones from £5.95. In good weather, the city has few more pleasant spots than its beautiful courtyard.

Atmospheric *Oscar's Wine Bar & Bistro* (☎ 652002, Little Stonegate), has an outdoor area and a wide range of interesting dishes (including vegetarian). Most main meals (for example, smoked-haddock pasta, or chicken tikka masala) are £5 to £8. Across the road *The Rubicon* (☎ 676076, Little Stonegate) is a BYO (bring your own bottle of wine) vegetarian restaurant offering two-course lunches for £5 and three-course meals for £7.

Near Bootham Bar, *Plunket's (☎ 637722, 9 High Petergate)* has mainly Mexican dishes. Chicken burrito is £7.95 or you could have a three-course meal for £14.95.

Petergate has another place that habitually sends queues curling down the street. At *Scott's*, the pork butchers, you can buy pork pies to make the taste buds weep from £1.85. On Gillygate, *Cafetiéres* is a cosy restaurant that does lasagne with garlic bread for £3.95, or more traditional food like chip butties for £1.50.

Beside the City Art Gallery, Exhibition Square, the mainly Tudor *King's Manor* has a student refectory with filling food like gammon and pineapple for under £4. It's open from 10 am to 4 pm, closed weekends.

Pizza Express (☎ 672904, 17 Museum St) serves the usual range of good pizzas in the elegant surroundings of what was once a York gentlemen's club overlooking the Ouse.

Pubs Most pubs serve food. The *King's Arms*, King's Staith, does meals at lunch time and has tables overlooking the river on the south-eastern side of the Ouse Bridge (the middle of the three main bridges). Nearby, the *Lowther Arms*, on the corner of King's Staith and Cumberland St, has bar meals like roast beef and Yorkshire pudding for £3.95 and a restaurant where you pay about £2 more per dish.

Cafés All your sightseeing is likely to make you thirsty. *Betty's* is an very popular, extremely elegant bakery and tearoom in St Helen's Square; depending on your mood you can choose to relax in the spacious, airy upstairs or the wood-panelled no-smoking downstairs. A pot of tea for one is £1.80, sandwiches are £3.40 to £4.20 and hot dishes are around £6.50. Betty's opens from 9 am to 9 pm; a pianist plays from 6 pm. The same menu is also on offer upstairs in *Taylor's*, 46 Stonegate, where queues are as likely as at Betty's. A traditional Yorkshire

high tea here costs £8.50 and would set you up for a week.

You can take tea in even more genteel surroundings in the *Grand Assembly Rooms (☎ 632754)* round the corner in Blake St. The Assembly Rooms are in a basilica-like building lined with paired Corinthian columns and hung with chandeliers. A stilton and pickle sandwich costs £2.95 and beef baguettes £4.45. On Goodramgate in front of Holy Trinity Church, *Crumbles Tea Rooms* is in a 14th century building called Our Lady's Row. It has snacks and pastas for £3.95 and giant Yorkshire puddings with your choice of filling for £2.50. Watch your head as you go in.

The most acclaimed vegetarian café is at the back of the *The Blake Head Bookshop (☎ 623767, 104 Micklegate)*. Soup and a roll costs £2.50, a main-course salad £4.50, a set three-course lunch £7.50. It's open daily from 10 am to 5 pm.

Entertainment

It's worth seeing what's on at *York Theatre Royal (☎ 623568)*, near the TIC; it often has excellent productions. Despite its name, the *Grand Opera House (☎ 671818, Clifford St)* puts on a wide range of productions; ask at the TIC for details. For big-name concerts head for *York Barbican Centre (☎ 656688)*, in an interesting, partly pyramidal modern building in Barbican Rd.

There are several pubs on the south-eastern side of the Ouse Bridge, and some outdoor tables by the river if you want somewhere central to start exploring York's nightlife. Places worth checking out include *The Punchbowl*, in Stonegate, which sometimes has live folk music. There's jazz at *Oscar's Wine Bar* and the *Old White Swan*, Goodramgate, also has bands.

The *Bonding Warehouse* is a pub on Skeldergate beside the bridge and has live music and river views.

Getting There & Away

Bus By road it's about 200 miles to London and Edinburgh, 25 miles to Leeds and Helmsley and 90 miles to Nottingham. See the fares tables in the Getting Around chapter.

National Express (☎ 0990-808080) buses leave from Rougier St, but its office is nearby in the TIC on George Hudson St. There are at least three services a day to London (4½ hours), two a day to Birmingham (4½ hours) and one to Edinburgh (six hours).

For information on local buses (to Castle Howard, Helmsley, Scarborough, Whitby etc), contact York Rider Buses (☎ 624161) at the Rougier St bus terminal (open Monday to Friday from 8 am to 5 pm, Saturday from 9 am to 4.30 pm).

Yorkshire Coastliner (☎ 01653-692556) has buses to Leeds, Malton and Scarborough. A one day Freedom ticket costs £8/5.25.

The best deal if you're heading north or east is the Explorer North East ticket (£4.95), which is valid on most bus services and gives unlimited travel for one day. United Auto (☎ 01325-465252) has a bus north to Ripon where you can link into the network.

Stagecoach Cumberland's (☎ 01946-63222) X9 service runs between York and Keswick via Harrogate (Yorkshire Dales), Skipton, Kendal and Ambleside (Lake District) on Monday, Wednesday, Friday and Saturday. On Saturday the service extends to Grasmere and Keswick.

Train As the ex-headquarters of the York & North Midland Railway, York is well served by rail. There are numerous trains from London's King's Cross (two hours, £54) which continue to Edinburgh (a further 2¾ hours, £44).

North-south trains also connect with Peterborough (1½ hours, £29) for Cambridge and East Anglia (three hours, £36.50). There are good connections with south-west England, via Bristol (4½ hours, £47.50), Cheltenham, Birmingham and Sheffield. There's also a service to Oxford (4½ hours, £42.10), via Birmingham.

Local trains to Scarborough take 45 minutes (£8.40). For Whitby it's necessary to change at Middlesbrough. Trains to/from the west and north-west go via Leeds.

Car The TIC has a full list of car rental possibilities. One good-value option is Practical Car & Van Rental (☎ 01904-624848), 10 Fetter Lane.

Getting Around

Public transport to some of the nearby surrounding attractions can be difficult, so it's worth considering a tour. See Organised Tours earlier.

York gets as congested as most British cities in summer and car parking in the centre can be expensive (up to £7 for a day). There's a Saturday Park & Ride scheme; for details ring ☎ 431388.

Taxi Try Station Taxis (☎ 623332), which has a kiosk outside the train station, ABC Blue Circle (☎ 638787) or Ace Taxis (☎ 638888).

Bicycle You can hire bikes for £9.50 a day from Bob Trotter (☎ 622868) on Lord Mayor's Walk outside Monk Bar.

CASTLE HOWARD

There are few buildings in the world that are so perfect that their visual impact is almost a physical blow – Castle Howard, of *Brideshead Revisited* fame, is one. It has a picturesque setting in the rolling Howardian Hills and is surrounded by superb terraces and landscaped grounds dotted with monumental follies.

Not surprisingly, Castle Howard is a major tourist attraction, and it draws enormous crowds. Outside weekends, however, it's surprisingly easy to find the space to appreciate this extraordinary marriage of art, architecture, landscaping and natural beauty. Wandering about the grounds, views open up over the hills, the Temple of the Four Winds and the Mausoleum, but the great Baroque house with its magnificent central cupola is an irresistible visual magnet.

In 1699 the Earl of Carlisle made an audacious choice when he picked a successful playwright and army captain, Sir John Vanbrugh, as architect. Vanbrugh in turn chose Nicholas Hawksmoor, who had worked for

Christopher Wren, as his clerk of works. This successful collaboration was subsequently repeated at Blenheim Palace.

The house is full of treasures, and the grounds include a superb walled rose garden.

Castle Howard (☎ 01653-648333) is 15 miles north-east of York off the A64 (4 miles). It's open mid-March to October, daily from 10 am (grounds) or 11 am (house) to 4.30 pm. Entry to the house and garden is £7/4, to the garden only £4.50/2.50. All in all, it could absorb the best part of a day; take a picnic.

Getting There & Away

The castle can be reached by several tours and occasional buses from York. Check with the TIC for up-to-date schedules; tours cost £6.50. Yorkshire Coastliner (☎ 01653-692556) has a useful service that links Leeds, York, Castle Howard, Pickering, Goathland and Whitby (Nos 840 and 842). A day return ticket from York costs £3.70.

North York Moors National Park

Only Exmoor and the Lake District rival the North York Moors National Park for natural beauty, but the North York Moors are less crowded than the Lake District and more expansive than Exmoor. The coast is superb, with high cliffs backing onto beautiful countryside. From the ridge-top roads and open moors there are wonderful views, and the dales shelter abbeys, castles and small stone villages.

One of the principal glories of the moors is the vast expanse of heather. July to early September it flowers in an explosion of purple. Outside the flowering season, its browns-tending-to-purple on the hills, in vivid contrast to the green of the dales, give the park its characteristic appearance.

ORIENTATION

The park covers 553 sq miles. The western boundary is a steep escarpment formed by the Hambleton and Cleveland hills; the moors run east-west to the coast between Scarborough and Staithes. Rainwater escapes from the moors down deep, parallel dales – to the Rye and Derwent rivers in the south and the Esk in the north.

After the open space of the moors, the dales form a gentler, greener landscape, sometimes wooded, often with a beautiful stone village or two.

The coastline is as impressive as any in Britain, and considerably less spoilt than most; Scarborough and Whitby are both popular resorts, but Whitby retains more of its charm. Helmsley (near Rievaulx, pronounced reevoh) is the centre for the western part of the park.

INFORMATION

There are visitors centres at Helmsley (☎ 01439-770173) and Danby (☎ 01287-660654). The TICs in Whitby, Pickering and Scarborough are open most of the year. A very useful tabloid visitors' guide is widely available in surrounding towns.

Heather & Grouse

The North York Moors have the largest expanse of heather moorland in England. You can see three species. Ling is the most widespread, has a pinkish-purple flower, and is most spectacular in late summer; bell heather is deep purple; and cross-leaved heather (or bog heather) prefers wet ground, unlike the first two, and tends to flower earlier. Wet, boggy areas also feature cotton grass, sphagnum moss and insect-eating sundew plants.

The moors have traditionally been managed to provide an ideal habitat for the red grouse – a famous game bird. The shooting season lasts from the 'Glorious Twelfth' of August to 10 December. The heather is periodically burned, giving managed moorland a patchwork effect – the grouse nests in mature growth, but feeds on the tender shoots of new growth.

NORTH-EASTERN ENGLAND

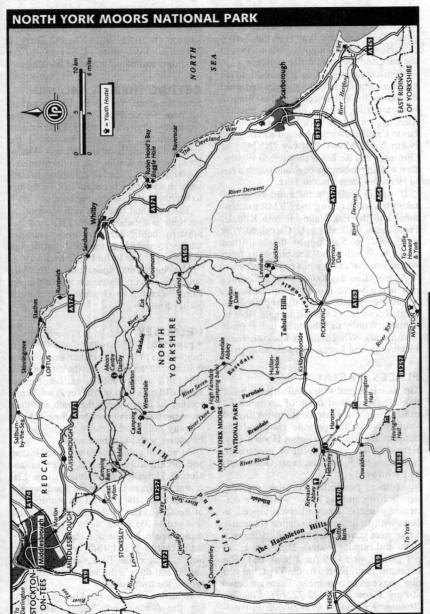

ACTIVITIES

There are a huge number of walks in the park. The Cleveland Way (see the Activities chapter) covers a good cross-section of the park and the spectacular coastline.

With a little imagination, it's possible to put together some interesting itineraries that make the most of the varied scenery and the limited, but interesting, railway lines. One possible itinerary starting at York involves taking a bus to Castle Howard, a bus to Pickering, the North York Moors Railway (NYMR) to Grosmont and the Esk Valley line to Whitby, then walking to Scarborough and taking a bus to Helmsley, then a bus to York.

If you're feeling a bit more energetic, take a bus to Pickering, the NYMR to Grosmont and the Esk Valley line to Kildale. From there, walk along the Cleveland Way north-east to Saltburn-by-the-Sea, then south to Whitby and Scarborough, from where you can catch a bus to Helmsley.

An easy five-day loop, covering 52 miles and using youth hostel accommodation, would be: Scarborough to Boggle Hole (near Robin Hood's Bay); Boggle Hole to Whitby; Whitby to Wheeldale Lodge (near Goathland); Wheeldale to Lockton (near Pickering); and Lockton to Scarborough.

PLACES TO STAY

The park is ringed with small villages, all of which have a good range of accommodation. There's a reasonable sprinkling of youth hostels that provide good walking bases at Boggle Hole, Robin Hood's Bay, Helmsley, Lockton (north of Pickering), Scarborough, Wheeldale (near Goathland) and Whitby.

Another possibility is the growing network of camping barns, which are particularly useful for walkers equipped to cope with basic accommodation (basically a roof over your head, bunk beds perhaps, a toilet and running water). They cost £3.25 per person, or £4.75 for a bunk bed. The barns are administered by the YHA, but you don't have to be a member. There are barns at *Park Farm* (☎ *01642-722135, Kildale*); *Broadgate Farm* (☎ *01287-660259, West-*

erdale); and *Oakhouse* (☎ *01751-433053, High Farndale*). The YHA Northern Region (☎ 01629-825850), PO Box 11, Matlock, Derbyshire DE4 2XA, can provide a leaflet and organise bookings.

GETTING THERE & AROUND

From the south, York is the usual jumping-off point for the North York Moors. From there, buses run to Helmsley, Pickering and Scarborough. There's a reasonable bus service between Scarborough and Whitby. From the north, Darlington, on the main east-coast railway line, and Middlesbrough, at the western end of the beautiful Esk Valley line to Whitby, are good starting points.

The excellent free brochure *Moors Connections* is available from TICs and is a must for public-transport users. Transport on the A-roads is quite good, but beyond them you'll have to find your own way.

The North York Moors Railway (NYMR) cuts across an interesting section of the park from Pickering to Grosmont on the Esk Valley line.

HELMSLEY

• pop 1500   ☎ 01439

Helmsley is a classic Yorkshire market town, built around the expansive Market Place that still hosts a busy Friday market. Narrow Etton Gill runs west of Market Place, before joining the River Rye in the south, and there are some fascinating cottages along its banks – many built traditionally in grey-yellow limestone with red pantile roofs.

Almost all elements of the moors' history and architecture come together in and around Helmsley: the ruins of a 12th century Norman castle stand south-west of Market Place; the superb 12th century ruins of the Cistercians' Rievaulx Abbey shelter in Ryedale 3½ miles west; a 16th century manor house, Nunnington Hall, is 4½ miles south-east; a grand 18th century country house, Duncombe Park, lies beyond the castle; and there's the vernacular architecture of the town itself.

Helmsley makes an ideal base for exploring the North York Moors. There are numerous short walks in the surrounding countryside that take in the aforementioned sights, and, for the more ambitious, Helmsley is the starting point for the Cleveland Way.

Orientation & Information

Everything radiates out from the central Market Place – the parish church is to the north-west, and the castle and Duncombe Park are to the south-west.

The TIC (☎ 770173) opens April to October, daily from 9.30 am to 6 pm, November to March, weekends from 10 am to 6 pm. It has a particularly good range of information on the North York Moors National Park, the Cleveland Way and local cycling routes.

Helmsley Castle

The castle (☎ 770442, EH) is most famous for its extensive surrounding earthworks – huge earthen banks and ditches – but parts of the curtain wall, the keep and a 16th century residential wing survive. Begun in the early 12th century, various additions were made

through to the Civil War when, after a three-month siege in 1644, it surrendered.

A retired London banker bought the castle in 1689 and later built neighbouring Duncombe Park. Once the castle was no longer used as a residence it fell into disrepair, but it still makes a picturesque sight; admission is £2.20/1.10.

Duncombe Park

Duncombe Park dates from 1713 and was built for retired London banker, Thomas Duncombe, by William Wakefield, a friend of Vanbrugh. The building is neoclassical and is beautifully located in 600 acres of landscaped parkland. There are enormous lawns and terraces with views across the moors and surrounding countryside (see Rievaulx Terrace & Temples); the park has a number of walks.

The entrance to the house (☎ 770213) is signposted from the A170 to/from Thirsk. It's open May to September, Sunday to Friday from 11 am to 6 pm; Sunday to Thursday in April and October; tickets for

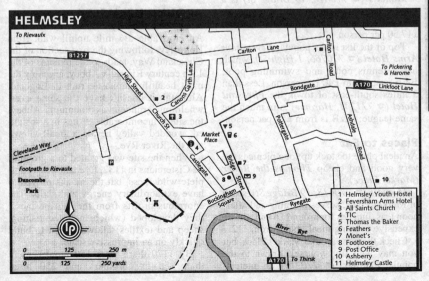

HELMSLEY

1 Helmsley Youth Hostel
2 Feversham Arms Hotel
3 All Saints Church
4 TIC
5 Thomas the Baker
6 Feathers
7 Monet's
8 Footloose
9 Post Office
10 Ashberry
11 Helmsley Castle

the house and grounds are £5.50/2.50; entry to the grounds only is £3.50/1.50.

Places to Stay

Camping Two miles south-east of town, *Foxholme Caravan Park* (☎ 770416, *Harome*) has 60 individual pitches amongst trees from £6.50 per day.

Hostel *Helmsley Youth Hostel* (☎ 770433, *Carlton Lane*) is a purpose-built hostel a quarter of a mile east of Market Place. To get there, take Bondgate from the north-eastern corner of the place and turn left at Carlton Rd. Opening times vary, so phone ahead. The nightly rate is £8 for adults and £5.40 for juniors.

B&Bs & Hotels There are several places on Ashdale Rd; leave Market Place at the north-eastern corner along Bondgate, and Ashdale Rd is the second street on the right. *Ashberry* (☎ 770488), at No 41, is a traditional B&B with shared facilities from £16 per person. Also on Ashdale Rd, the modern *Argyle House* (☎ 770172) has several rooms from £15.

Monet's (☎ 770618, *19 Bridge St*) is a good-value restaurant with three rooms offering B&B accommodation above; from £17.50 per person.

Top of the list is the popular *Feversham Arms Hotel* (☎ 770766, *1 High St*), which has a tennis court and swimming pool; B&B costs from £40 per person. Less than 3 miles south-east of town, the *Pheasant Hotel* (☎ 771241, *Harome*) is in much the same league; B&B is from £53 per person.

Places to Eat

An ideal place to stock up for a picnic is the very good and cheap *Thomas the Baker* (*Market Place*).

Monet's (☎ 770618, *19 Bridge St*), south of Market Place, serves morning and afternoon teas, lunches for around £6 and a more expensive evening meal, mains from £12.

Check the pubs around Market Place, but you may well find yourself drawn to the popular *Feathers* (☎ 770275), an interesting old inn with excellent bar food (most mains from £6.50 to £7.50). The *Feversham Arms* also has excellent bar meals.

Getting There & Away

Helmsley is 25 miles from York, 16 miles from Malton and 14 miles from Pickering and Thirsk.

Bus Stephenson's (☎ 01347-838990) bus No 57 runs twice daily between York and Helmsley (1¼ hours). There are three slow buses a day between Malton train station (on the York-Scarborough line) and Helmsley (No 94, one hour), in this case operated by Yorkshire Coastliner (☎ 01653-692556).

Scarborough & District (☎ 01723-369331) has six buses a day Monday to Saturday, three on Sunday, between Helmsley and Scarborough via Pickering (bus No 128, 1¾ hours).

Getting Around

Ring A&R (☎ 771040) or Bob's (☎ 771081) for a taxi. Footloose (☎ 770886), Borogate, hires mountain/hybrid bicycles for £10/7.50 per day. Booking is advisable.

AROUND HELMSLEY
Rievaulx Abbey

An enjoyable 3½ mile uphill walk from Helmsley, following the first section of the Cleveland Way, leads to the remains of the 13th century Rievaulx Abbey, arguably the most beautiful monastic ruin in England. Although it doesn't have the same overwhelming grandeur as Fountains Abbey, the site is incomparable. It lies in a secluded, wooded valley beside a small village and the River Rye.

When the site was granted to a group of 12 Cistercians in 1132, Ryedale was a complete wilderness, but the monks proved to have extraordinary energy and skills. The enormous profits from the 'agribusiness' they developed (which included fishing, sheep and textiles) allowed them to build quickly on an impressive scale.

By 1170 there were 150 monks, more than 250 lay brothers and 250 hired workmen. By the end of the century most of the building was completed (the nave is Norman, the transepts are transitional and the choir is Early English). By the dissolution in 1539, however, there were only about 20 monks. Many of the surrounding buildings, including much of pretty Rievaulx village, were constructed from stone pillaged from the ruins.

Rievaulx Abbey (☎ 798228, EH), on the B1257 to Stokesley, opens daily April to October from 10 am to 6 pm; daily July and August from 9.30 am to 7 pm; daily in winter from 10 am to 4 pm; £2.90/1.50.

Rievaulx Terrace & Temples

In the 1750s Duncombe Park was landscaped to create a romantic series of views overlooking Rievaulx Abbey, Ryedale and the Hambleton Hills. Rievaulx Terrace & Temples (☎ 798340, NT) consists of a half-mile-long grass-covered terrace with carefully planned openings into the surrounding woods. There's no access to the abbey from the terrace. The terrace opens April to October, daily from 10.30 am to 6 pm (or dusk if earlier); last admissions are at 5 pm; £2.80/1.40.

Nunnington Hall

Nunnington Hall (☎ 748283, NT) is an attractive manor house on the banks of the River Rye, about 4½ miles south-east of Helmsley. It includes sections from the 16th century, but most of the building dates from the 17th. There's a tearoom and an attractive garden. It's open May to September, Wednesday to Sunday from 1.30 to 6 pm and Sunday from noon to 6 pm, to 5.30 pm in April and October; £4/2.

THIRSK & AROUND

Thirsk is a small market town outside the western edge of the national park, below the Hambleton Hills in the Vale of Mowbray. It's the fictional 'Darrowby' of James Herriot's stories of life as a Yorkshire vet, but part of its charm lies in the fact that it remains a normal, untouristy place. Hope-

fully, this won't change too much when the new **James Herriot Centre** opens.

The helpful, volunteer-run TIC (☎ 01845-522755), 14 Kirkgate, opens March to October, Monday to Saturday 9.30 am to 5 pm, Sunday from 2 to 4 pm.

On the A170 between Thirsk and Helmsley, **Sutton Bank** is the western escarpment of the Hambleton Hills, with magnificent views across the Vale of Mowbray to the Pennines and Yorkshire Dales. From the car park on the top there are walks to Lake Gormire and the Kilburn White Horse and along the Cleveland Way. The National Park Visitors Centre (☎ 01845-597426) opens Easter to October, daily from 10 am to 5 pm; November to March, weekends only from 11 am to 4 pm.

Thirsk TIC's accommodation guide quotes James Herriot on Sutton Bank:

I must have stopped at this very spot thousands of times because there is no better place for a short stroll along the green path which winds around the hill's edge with the wind swirling and that incredible panorama beneath. I know I keep saying these things about Yorkshire but this is the finest view in England.

In Thirsk, the *Three Tuns Hotel* (☎ 01845-523124, Market Place) has bar and restaurant meals from £4.95, including vegetarian options; it also has rooms with bathroom from £30. The *Golden Fleece* (☎ 01845-523108), nearby, is a bit swisher with a good variety of bar meals £5.75 to £6.50; it also has rooms.

Between Thirsk and Helmsley, Stephenson's (☎ 01347-838990) bus No 57 runs once daily, Monday, Friday and Saturday (50 minutes). Thirsk is on the main east-coast rail line between London's King's Cross and Edinburgh, and on the trans-Pennine route between York and Newcastle.

DANBY

Danby (sometimes referred to as Danby-in-Cleveland) is at the head of Eskdale, and the surrounding countryside is particularly beautiful. Fourteenth century Danby Castle can be seen from the road; Danby Beacon, 2 miles north-east, has great views; and Duck Bridge, downstream from the village, is a 14th century packhorse bridge.

The Moors Centre (☎ 01287-660654), the main headquarters for the national park, is in Danby, half a mile from the village proper. There are displays, information, an accommodation-booking service and tea-rooms in an 18th century manor house. The centre opens April to October, daily from 10 am to 5 pm; November to March, week-ends only from 11 am to 4 pm. There are five short circular walks from the centre.

Places to Stay & Eat

Some local farms have good-value B&B, costing around £15; these include *Crag Farm (☎ 01287-660279)* and *Danby Castle Farm (☎ 01287-660164)*.

Danby Watermill (☎ 01287-660330), near the train station, is the last working mill on the River Esk; it's an interesting place with a coffee shop and some bed-rooms (including a single) from £15 per person. The *Duke of Wellington* pub *(☎ 01287-660351)* has good bar meals, and rooms for around £24 per person.

Getting There & Away

There are only four trains a day on the Esk Valley line from Monday to Saturday; though once threatened with closure it's now used principally by tourists and schools.

STAITHES

Tucked beneath high cliffs and running back along the steep banks of a small river, the old fishing village of Staithes is one of the most picturesque on the English coast. The idyll is somewhat spoiled, though, by the large potash mine in the hills behind.

In some ways, the village seems un-touched by the 20th century, focusing still on its centuries-old battle with the sea. James Cook served as an apprentice grocer in a shop that has since been reclaimed by the sea; the shop and the street have been recre-ated in the **Staithes Heritage Centre**. Legend

says that fishermen's tales of the high seas and bad treatment by his master led him to steal a shilling from the till and run away to Whitby. There's accommodation in the two pubs and in a couple of guesthouses.

WHITBY
• pop 15,000   ☎ 01947

Somehow Whitby transcends the amuse-ment arcades, coaches and fish and chip shops – the imposing ruins of an abbey loom over red-brick houses that spill down a headland to a beautiful estuary harbour. This small town has had a disproportionate impact on world history, both as the site for the Synod of Whitby, which determined the nature of the medieval English church, and as the starting point for the maritime career of one of the world's greatest explorers – Captain James Cook.

Whitby is one of the most interesting and attractive towns on the British coast and among the highlights of a trip to the north. It's the perfect base from which to explore the cliffs, coves, fishing villages and beaches to the east and west, which are amongst the most spectacular on this island.

Salmon come up the River Esk in the spawning season and are followed by seals which feed on them.

The town itself combines the colour of a working harbour on the estuary of the Esk, a muddle of medieval streets with a range of restaurants and pubs, the silhouette of the abbey which seems to float over the town, and the paraphernalia of a seaside resort. It attracts a diverse group of people – not just retirees and young families.

The past is powerfully evoked, particu-larly when mists roll up the Esk valley, but also when it's at its sunniest and loveliest.

History

The Romans had a signal station on the high cliffs east of town. Over 200 years after their departure Celtic Christianity was firmly es-tablished in the kingdom of Northumbria by St Aidan. In 635 he founded the great Lin-disfarne monastery (see Holy Island later). In 657 St Hilda, a Northumbrian princess,

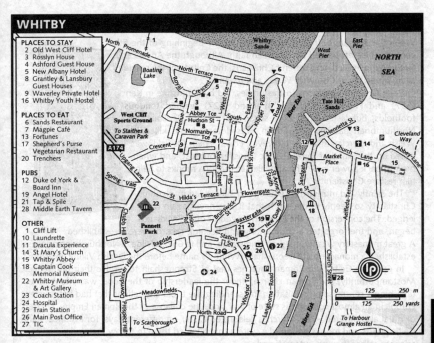

WHITBY

PLACES TO STAY
2 Old West Cliff Hotel
3 Rosslyn House
4 Ashford Guest House
5 New Albany Hotel
8 Grantley & Lansbury Guest Houses
9 Waverley Private Hotel
16 Whitby Youth Hostel

PLACES TO EAT
6 Sands Restaurant
7 Magpie Café
13 Fortunes
17 Shepherd's Purse Vegetarian Restaurant
20 Trenchers

PUBS
12 Duke of York & Board Inn
19 Angel Hotel
21 Tap & Spile
28 Middle Earth Tavern

OTHER
1 Cliff Lift
10 Laundrette
11 Dracula Experience
14 St Mary's Church
15 Whitby Abbey
18 Captain Cook Memorial Museum
22 Whitby Museum & Art Gallery
23 Coach Station
24 Hospital
25 Train Station
26 Main Post Office
27 TIC

established a monastery at Streoneshalh (as Whitby was known before the Danish Viking invasions). In 664 the Celtic and Roman churches met at the abbey to resolve their differences. Eventually, the grand bishops, monks and nuns of the Whitby Synod (or council) on their windy headland decided the future of the English church in favour of Rome and its organisation based at Canterbury.

The Danish destroyed the abbey in 867, but they recognised Whitby's potential as a port. The abbey was refounded by Benedictines in 1078 and flourished until the Dissolution in 1539 – the Benedictine ruins survive today.

From the Middle Ages, the importance of Whitby as a maritime centre increased; Whitby-built and Whitby-crewed ships were to serve generations of Whitby traders, whalers, fishermen and explorers.

In 1746, the 18-year-old James Cook arrived in the town as an apprentice to a local shipowner. For nine years Cook worked on Whitby cats – unique Whitby-built colliers that carried coal south from the Durham coalfields to London. These sturdy flat-bottomed vessels were specially designed to allow them to be beached for loading and off-loading.

In 1755 Cook joined the navy, and in 1768 he began the first of three voyages of discovery. On all three voyages the ships he chose to use, including the *Endeavour*, were Whitby cats.

Orientation & Information

Old Whitby grew up along the steep sides of the Esk estuary. Until the 18th century, the eastern bank was the most important, but in the 19th century a new town, catering to the new seaside tourist industry with

Christianity & the Synod of Whitby

When the Romans withdrew from Britain at the beginning of the 5th century, they left behind the Christian faith. Although the Angles and Saxons who arrived next weren't Christians, the Celts kept the religion alive, especially in Cornwall, Wales and Ireland.

Pope Gregory's missions to the Angles, led by Augustine in Kent (597) and Paulinus in Northumberland (627), gained tenuous footholds, but lasted only six years in the case of Paulinus. His Northumbrian patron, King Edwin, was defeated and killed by Welsh and Mercian invaders. However, Edwin's heir, Oswald, was exiled on the island of Iona, a Celtic Christian outpost, and when he won back power in 635 he appealed to the Iona monks to help him restore Christianity.

The saintly Aidan met this request and succeeded in planting Christianity so deeply in the north that it was never again challenged. The conversion of the Mercian kingdoms of the Midlands began, and the forgotten arts of writing and keeping records were re-established.

A great monastery was founded on Lindisfarne, and in 657 St Hilda, a Northumbrian princess, established a monastery at Streoneshalh (Whitby's name before the Danish Viking invasions).

In 664, the Celtic and Roman churches met at Streoneshalh to resolve their differences. Most importantly, the Roman church, under the leadership of the pope, was intent on establishing a centralised organisation transcending the tribal distinctions that had left much of Europe in an almost continuous state of war since the collapse of the Roman Empire. Matters of ritual also differed – the churches celebrated Easter on different days, for instance – and Celtic priests and monks preferred a system that allowed them to follow their individual consciences rather than an autocratic rule.

Eventually, the synod decided in favour of the Roman church's rites and organisation, although the decision wasn't entirely one-sided. The Roman Archbishop of Canterbury, Theodore, allowed a number of Celtic practices to continue, including divorce and remarriage in certain cases, and the private confession of sins rather than confession in front of a congregation.

terraced crescents, grew up on the western side, and this is also where most 20th century development has occurred.

To confuse matters, one street sometimes has two names; for example, the southern side of one street is Hudson St, while the northern side is Abbey Terrace.

The TIC (☎ 602674), Langborne Rd, opposite the train station, opens May to September daily from 9.30 am to 6 pm, October to April daily from 10 am to 4.30 pm. Inexplicably, it closes on busy public holiday weekends, like Easter. It has infor-

mation on self-catering possibilities in the North York Moors National Park and along the coast.

There's a small laundrette at the top of Skinner St. The cliff lift operates May to September.

Whitby Abbey & St Mary's Church

Nothing survives of the Saxon abbey founded by St Hilda; it lay a little to the north of the existing ruins. A Benedictine abbey was re-established on the site in 1078, and the remains visible today are of the Benedictine church built in the 13th and 14th centuries (mainly in the Early English style).

In many ways, the nearby St Mary's Church is more interesting than the abbey ruins. It's a lovely medieval church with a low Norman tower and an atmospheric, extraordinary interior full of skewwhiff Georgian galleries and box pews. The nautical term 'crow's nest' may have come from the name given to the high pulpit from which the priest, dressed in black, gave his sermon.

The abbey (☎ 603568, EH) opens daily April to October from 10 am to 6 pm (to 4 pm the rest of the year); £1.70/90. The church opens daily; admission is free. Those with vehicles pay £1.50 for parking.

Captain Cook Memorial Museum

The museum is in the harbourside house below the abbey once owned by John Walker, the Quaker captain to whom Cook was apprenticed. Cook sometimes lodged in the attic. It's well worth a visit for the house itself and for the interesting displays on Cook's life and voyages.

The museum opens daily April to November from 9.45 am to 5 pm. In March it is only open at weekends from 11 am to 3 pm. Admission is £2.30/1.60.

Whitby Museum

Whitby Museum (☎ 602908), Pannett Park, was founded in 1823 and is a traditional place full of dusty glass cabinets that are themselves full of fascinating stuff. It has a good collection of fossils including ones of a crocodile and a dinosaur, both found locally. It's surrounded by a beautiful, steep garden with views (partly marred by an ugly block of modern flats) that give you another perspective on the town.

The museum opens May to September, weekdays from 9.30 am to 5.30 pm, Sunday from 2 to 5 pm; October to April, Tuesday from 10 am to 1 pm, Wednesday to Saturday from 10 am to 4 pm, Sunday from 2 to 4 pm; £1.50/1. There's also a small art gallery open the same hours; free.

Walks

Consider attempting the 5½ mile cliff-top walk south to Robin Hood's Bay; the last Tees & District bus returns to Whitby around 4 pm. There are also some beautiful small fishing villages, like Staithes, to the north.

Other Things to See & Do

The connection is fairly tenuous, but, apparently, the **Dracula Experience** (☎ 601923), Pier Rd, is the most popular tourist attraction in Whitby.

Several companies along the eastern bank of the estuary, across from the Angel Hotel, offer boat and fishing trips.

April to September, interesting evening ghost walks depart from the Arts Centre, Market Place on Church St, in the evening at 8 pm (£2/1.50).

Places to Stay

There are plenty of places to stay, but beware the Easter weekend, Whitby Festival (mid-June) and Whitby Regatta (August), when the place can be booked out.

Camping *Sandfield House Farm Caravan Park* (☎ 602660), on Sandsend Rd (the A174), has five tent sites and 50 touring pitches from £6.50 per night.

Hostels Beside the abbey, *Whitby Youth Hostel* (☎ 602878), East Cliff at the top of 199 steps (used by Dracula in the novel), has great views over the town. It's open daily late May to early September, but closes during the day until 5 pm. For opening times

Dracula

Bram Stoker wrote the story of *Dracula* while staying in a B&B in Whitby. In the story, Dracula himself was a brief visitor when, in the shape of a black dog, he leapt off the wreck of the Russian ship, *Demeter of Varna*, and up the steps toward Whitby Abbey.

the rest of the year ring ahead; £7.20 /£4.95 for adults/juniors.

The alternative is the well designed and well positioned **Harbour Grange Hostel** (☎ 600817, Spital Bridge) on the eastern side, opposite the marina (£7, £1 for linen). It's open all year and during the day.

B&Bs & Hotels A number of places in the centre of the medieval town, on the eastern side of the river offer B&B. There is accommodation above the **Shepherd's Purse Vegetarian Restaurant** (☎ 820228, 95 Church St) with pleasant rooms, including a vegetarian breakfast, from £16 per person.

Most accommodation, however, is on the western side, the part of town that developed in Victorian times. A walk along Royal Crescent, Crescent Ave, Hudson St/Abbey Terrace and East Terrace will turn up many decent possibilities.

The **New Albany Hotel** (☎ 603711, 3 Royal Crescent) has rooms with sea views for £23 per person. **Ashford Guest House** (☎ 602138), at No 8, is an unspoilt place, with sea views and a range of rooms, from £18 per person.

Waverley Private Hotel (☎ 604389, 17 Crescent Ave) has doubles from £18.50 per person. In a nice old Victorian building, the **Old West Cliff Hotel** (☎ 603292, 42 Crescent Ave) has six rooms with bathroom for £27/46 a single/double.

Possibilities on Hudson St/Abbey Terrace include **Lansbury Guest House** (☎ 604821, 29 Hudson St), with basic singles and doubles from £19 per person; **Grantley House** (☎ 600895), at No 26, £19 per person; and **Rosslyn House** (☎ 604086, 11 Abbey Terrace), with rooms from £17/30.

The **Old Hall Hotel** (☎ 602801, Ruswarp) is in a Jacobean house built in 1603, and overlooks the Esk Valley. There's quite a range of rooms, some with bathroom, from £20 to £30 per person.

Places to Eat

There are plenty of reasonable eating places in Whitby, with a predictable emphasis on seafood.

It's claimed that the **Magpie Cafe** (☎ 602058, 14 Pier Rd) does the best fish and chips in the world, but unfortunately most of the world knows, so there are often long queues. Staff will fry, grill or poach the fish of your choice (from £6 to £10); there are also some vegetarian meals. It's open from 11.30 am to 9 pm. **Trenchers** (☎ 603212), near the train station is also highly regarded for its fish – it can get busy.

There are numerous other fish and chips places in town, costing around £2 less – just take your pick.

Overlooking the sea, **Sands Restaurant**, on the cutting that links the western cliffs and the old town, is a spic-and-span, efficient operation with vegetarian meals for £5.95 and cod, chips, peas and tea for £5.25.

On the eastern side of the river, the **Shepherd's Purse Vegetarian Restaurant** (☎ 820228, 95 Church St) is at the back of the wholefood shop opposite Market Place. It has starters like stilton and onion soup for £2.50 and mains like stuffed avocado for £5.95. Takeaways are available and it also has an outside courtyard – and pleasant rooms (see Places to Stay).

At the end of Church St and overlooking the harbour, there are two pubs that offer good-value bar meals. The **Duke of York** is more atmospheric than the **Board Inn**. At one time or other when you're in Whitby you will be duty bound to try some crab, either in a salad or sandwich; salads are £5.95 at the Duke of York. You can get cod & chips for £4.95.

Although you can't eat there, one of the most famous contributors to English cuisine is **Fortunes** (Henrietta St), a small family company that has produced and sold kippers since 1872. Kippers are fish (traditionally herring) that have been salted and smoked. The 'Two Fat Ladies' bought some here for one of their TV cooking shows.

Entertainment

There are several quite lively pubs; if the inclination for music and Tetleys (beer) strikes, go for a wander. The **Angel Hotel**, New Quay, has live music, as does the **Tap**

& *Spile*, opposite the train station. For a quieter pint away from the crowds try *Middle Earth Tavern* on Church St.

Things to Buy

Jet (black fossilised wood) is found around Whitby; in Victorian times over 200 workshops produced jet jewellery; only a few still do so today. Some shops around town sell it.

Getting There & Away

Whitby is 20 miles from Scarborough, 230 miles from London and 45 miles from York.

Bus Tees & District (☎ 602146) has a number of services in the Whitby area. There are regular buses, Nos 93 and 93A (via Robin Hood's Bay), to/from Scarborough (one hour, £2.50). Yorkshire Coastliner (☎ 01653-692556) has an interesting service (bus Nos 840 and 842) between Whitby and Leeds via Goathland, Pickering (the latter two on the NYMR) and York.

Train Although it's not, in some ways, particularly efficient, you can get to Whitby by train, and the Esk Valley line from Middlesbrough is one of the most attractive in the country – more interesting scenically than the much-promoted NYMR (see that section).

En route, it's possible to connect with the northern terminal of the NYMR at Grosmont (to visit Danby) and Kildale (a possible starting or finishing point for the Cleveland Way). There are only four trains daily, Monday to Saturday.

Alternatively, you can catch a train to Scarborough from York, then a bus from Scarborough.

Getting Around

Taxi The main taxi rank is beside the TIC, opposite the train and bus station, Harrison Taxis (☎ 600606) is one of the main operators. The minimum fare is £1.50 and you can get to most places around Whitby for under £3.

COOK COUNTRY

Explorer and navigator Captain James Cook was born and raised in the north of this area, and there are a number of museums and monuments commemorating his life. The Cook Country Walk, a 40 mile hike, links the most important sites of Cook's early years. The first half basically follows the northern flanks of the Cleveland Hills east from Marton (near Middlesbrough), then the superb coast south from Staithes to Whitby. It's designed to be broken into three easy days.

The **Captain Cook Birthplace Museum** (☎ 01642-311211), Stewart Park, Marton, Middlesbrough, is an excellent museum open April to October, Tuesday to Sunday from 10 am to 5.30 pm, November to March, Tuesday to Sunday from 9 am to 4 pm; £2/1.

There are railway links to Saltburn-by-the-Sea and Whitby, on the Cleveland Way, and to Marton (Esk Valley line) for the start of the Cook Country Walk. There are also regular connections to Darlington for the main north-south line.

ROBIN HOOD'S BAY
☎ 01947

Bay or Baytown, as the locals call it, probably has a lot more to do with smugglers than with the Sherwood Forest hero, but it's a picturesque haven. A steep road drops from the coastal plateau down to the sea. There's compulsory parking at the top – don't even think about cheating and driving down, because there's hardly even room to turn at the bottom.

The village is a honeycomb of cobbled alleys and impossibly small houses that seem to hide in secret passages. There are a few gift shops and a trail of pubs (start from the bottom and work your way up), but really this is a place to just sit and watch the world go by, preferably out of season.

Unless you book, or are prepared to walk a mile (along the beach at low tide, or the cliff at high) to the popular *Boggle Hole Youth Hostel* (☎ 880352, *Mill Beck, Fylingthorpe*) don't plan on staying. *The Dolphin*, accessed from King St, has huge bar meals from £5.25, while *The Laurel*, halfway down Main St, serves excellent real ales.

There's an hourly Tees & District (☎ 602146) service between Whitby and Scarborough which stops at the Bay. In summer the Coast to Coast Packhorse (☎ 017683-71680) service runs from St Bees Head on the west coast to the Bay, delivering backpacks and/or bodies along the route of Alfred Wainwright's Coast to Coast Walk (see Kirkby Stephen).

SCARBOROUGH

- pop 39,000   ☎ 01723

Scarborough is a large, often kitsch, seaside resort. Unlike Blackpool (and many other places of that ilk), however, it has a long history and, most importantly, a spectacular site. These, combined with the traditional trappings of an English seaside holiday resort, make it an appealing, enjoyable place.

Although some parts are a bit run-down and you don't get a good impression as you arrive, it has, for the most part, survived the 20th century and the impact of cheap package holidays to the Mediterranean. It remains a classic resort, with two beautiful bays separated by a castle-crowned headland, but has added sufficient mod cons and amusements to remain attractive to young families and the elderly from all round the north. Unfortunately, there seem to be few visitors between the ages of 18 and 25.

History

The headland that separates the North and South bays has been an impressive defensive position and has been occupied since Celtic times. A fishing village was, according to tradition, established by Vikings in the 9th century around what is now known as the Old Harbour. The Normans built their castle from around 1130, and it survived until 1648, when it was slighted by the Parliamentarians. It was also bombarded by a German battleship in 1914.

The medieval fishing and market town grew up around the Old Harbour. Mineral springs were discovered in 1620 and it was transformed into a fashionable spa town. It became one of the first places in Britain where sea bathing was popular, and from the mid-18th century it has been a successful seaside resort. It therefore has a legacy of fine Georgian, Victorian and Edwardian architecture.

Orientation & Information

Modern suburbs sprawl west of the town centre, which is above the old town and the South Bay. The town is on a plateau above the beaches; three cliff lifts, steep streets and footpaths provide the link. The Victorian development to the south is separated from the town centre by a steep valley, which has been landscaped and is crossed by high bridges.

The railway is conveniently central with the coach station behind it.

The busy TIC (☎ 373333), Valley Bridge Rd, opens May to September daily from 9.30 am to 6 pm, and October to April daily from 10 am to 4.30 pm.

Things to See & Do

Well it's a beach resort, innit? So there are all the things the British do at beaches, plus some bonuses.

Scarborough Castle (☎ 372451, EH), approached via a 13th century barbican, survives, as do the curtain walls dating from around 1130 and the shell of a keep built around 1160. There are excellent views; £2.20/1.10. Below the castle is **St Mary's Church** from 1180, rebuilt in the 15th and 17th centuries, with some interesting 14th century chapels. Anne Brontë is buried in the churchyard. The old town lies between the church and castle and the Old Harbour.

Places to Stay

Camping *Scalby Manor Caravan Park* (☎ 366212, Burniston Rd) is 3 miles north of town, past the youth hostel. It's a large park with plenty of touring pitches for vans and tents; up to £8.50 for a site.

Hostel The *White House Youth Hostel* (☎ 361176, Burniston Rd) (the A166 to

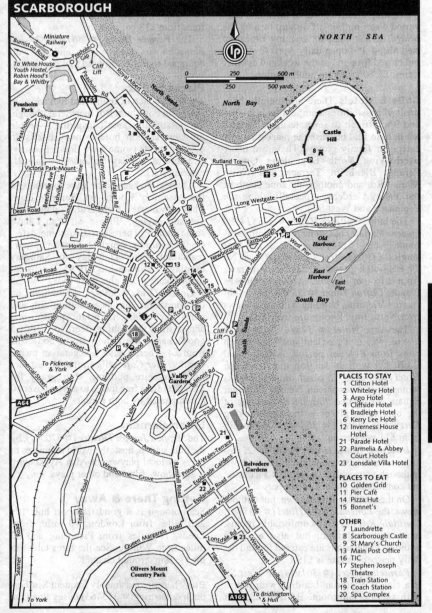

SCARBOROUGH

NORTH SEA

North Bay

Castle Hill

North Sands

Peasholm Park

To White House Youth Hostel, Robin Hood's Bay & Whitby

Victoria Park·Mount

Dean Road

Prospect Road

To Pickering & York

To York

Sandside

Old Harbour

East Harbour

South Bay

East Pier

West Pier

South Sands

Valley Gardens

Belvedere Gardens

Olivers Mount Country Park

To Bridlington & Hull

PLACES TO STAY
1 Clifton Hotel
2 Whiteley Hotel
3 Argo Hotel
4 Cliffside Hotel
5 Bradleigh Hotel
6 Kerry Lee Hotel
12 Inverness House Hotel
21 Parade Hotel
22 Parmelia & Abbey Court Hotels
23 Lonsdale Villa Hotel

PLACES TO EAT
10 Golden Grid
11 Pier Café
14 Pizza Hut
15 Bonnet's

OTHER
7 Laundrette
8 Scarborough Castle
9 St Mary's Church
13 Main Post Office
16 TIC
17 Stephen Joseph Theatre
18 Train Station
19 Coach Station
20 Spa Complex

Whitby; catch a No 3 or 10 minibus from the centre), 2 miles north of town in a converted water mill, is off a sharp turn by the bridge. It has complex opening times, so ring ahead. It's open daily April to August but closed for parts of the weekend at other times; £7.20/£4.95 for adults/juniors.

B&Bs & Hotels There are literally hundreds of possibilities, competition is intense and it's difficult to separate them. Singles are hard to find because the market largely caters for family groups. There are many overlooking North Bay along Queens Parade, Blenheim Terrace and North Marine Rd, and another big zone south of the Valley Gardens, especially along the Esplanade and West St.

The large **Whiteley Hotel** (☎ *373514, 99 Queens Parade)* has some rooms with bathroom from £16.50 per person. It has four singles. *Cliffside Hotel* (☎ *361087)*, at No 79, is a well kept traditional place with rates from £16 per person. Also on Queens Parade, *Clifton Hotel* (☎ *375691)* is a substantial Victorian building with great views over North Bay. Rooms are from £35.

The *Argo Hotel* (☎ *375745, 134 North Marine Rd)* is a pleasant small hotel with rates from £14 per person. A traditional B&B, but with no singles, the *Bradleigh Hotel* (☎ *364596, 35 North Marine Rd)* has rooms for £14 per person. Nearby Trafalgar Square is crowded with B&Bs and one of the best value places is the non-smoking *Kerry Lee Hotel* (☎ *363845)*, at No 60; from £11 per person.

Inverness House Hotel (☎ *369770, 22 Aberdeen Walk)* has a great position in the town (although you sacrifice a view). It's a classic but comfortable place; £14 per person.

On the southern side of town, but without views, the *Lonsdale Villa Hotel* (☎ *363383, Lonsdale Rd)* has nine comfortable rooms, most with bathroom, but also a single without. Vegetarians are catered for and the daily per person rate is £19.

Parmelia Hotel (☎ *361914, 17 West St)* is a classic Victorian building with rooms with private bathroom. B&B is £21 per person. Next door, the *Abbey Court* (☎ *360659)*, at No 19, is good value with rates from £18 per person.

The *Parade Hotel* (☎ *361285, 29 Esplanade)* has great views and 17 well equipped rooms for around £24 per person.

Places to Eat

There's a bunch of traditional fish and chip places on Foreshore Rd. In general, though, the possibilities aren't inspiring – people must eat at their hotels, many B&Bs do evening meals (some have liquor licences) and lots of holiday-makers stay in self-catering flats.

Charles Dickens once gave readings in the Assembly Rooms on Huntriss Row. They now house a *Pizza Hut*. You may find yourself saying, 'Please Sir, can I have some more?' There are also some cafés. One is *Bonnet's*, which also has an upstairs restaurant open Thursday to Saturday evenings where steak is £10.95. It sells delicious hand-made chocolate too.

Golden Grid (☎ *360922, 4 Sandside)*, on the foreshore, has been selling fish and chips since 1883. It's bright, popular and across from the fishing fleet, so there's a good chance the fish is fresh; cod costs from £4. There's also a vegetarian menu. Nearby, *Pier Cafe* sells simple honest fare like Yorkshire pudding with gravy for £1.50. It offers free meals to anyone over 80 accompanied by both parents!

Entertainment

The *Stephen Joseph Theatre* (☎ *370541)*, by the train station, hosts the world premieres of plays by local playwright Alan Ayckbourn. It also shows films and other plays.

Getting There & Away

Scarborough is a good transport hub. It's 230 miles from London, 70 miles from Leeds, 16 miles from Pickering and 22 miles from Whitby. See the fares tables in the Getting Around chapter.

Bus There are reasonably frequent Scarborough & District (☎ *375463)* buses along the

A170 to Pickering and Helmsley (No 128, 1½ hours). They leave from Westborough.

Tees & District (☎ 01947-602146) has regular buses to/from Whitby (Nos 93 and 93A; one hour, £2.50) via Robin Hood's Bay. Yorkshire Coastliner (☎ 01653-692556) has a frequent service between Leeds and Scarborough (No 843) via York.

Train Scarborough is connected by rail with Leeds (£13.80) via Harrogate, Knaresborough and York, and Kingston-upon-Hull via Filey and Beverley. The journey from Leeds shows a good cross section of Yorkshire, with potential stopovers in attractive Knaresborough and majestic York worth considering.

Getting Around
Bus Local buses leave from the western end of Westborough pedestrian mall and outside the train station.

Taxi There's a taxi rank outside the train station; or contact Station Taxis (☎ 361009/ 366366), a 24 hour service; £3 should get you most places.

PICKERING
- **pop 5315**   ☎ 01751

Once you get away from the traffic along the A170, Pickering is a surprisingly attractive little town. As the main starting point for trips on the NYMR, it also draws an enormous number of tourists.

The helpful and award-winning TIC (☎ 473791), Eastgate car park, opens April to October daily from 9.30 am to 6 pm, and November to March from 10 am to 4.30 pm. It has loads of information on the NYMR, walks and mountain biking on the moors.

Pickering Castle (☎ 474989, EH) was founded by William the Conqueror, but the remaining ruins date from a later period. Some of the curtain walls with towers, and part of the keep on a 40-foot-high motte, survive. It's a beautiful site, with good views over the town; £2.20/1.10.

The nearest youth hostel is the *Old School Youth Hostel* (☎ 460376, Lockton),

about 4 miles north on the A169 between Pickering and Whitby. It's about 2 miles from the NYMR station at Levisham, and is passed by Yorkshire Coastliner's bus No 840 between Leeds/York and Whitby. The hostel makes a good walking base. April to June and in September it opens Monday to Saturday, July and August daily; £5.85/£4 for adults/juniors.

The *Black Swan* (☎ *472286, 18 Birdgate*) is a popular pub so don't expect to sleep before closing time. B&B starts at £26/47 a single/double; allow a couple more pounds if you want a bathroom.

The cheapest option for food is the excellent *Thomas of Pickering* bakery, Market Place – stock up for picnics, train rides and walks. The *Rose* pub, on Bridge St near the NYMR station, has a pleasant beer garden beside the river and cheap food; seafood platter is £4.95.

For excellent fish and chips (£2.30), try the *Little Scarboro Restaurant*, Hungate, west of the roundabout on the A170.

As well as the Yorkshire Coastliner's service mentioned above, Scarborough & District (☎ 369331) bus No 128 runs reasonably frequently along the A170 between Helmsley and Scarborough (2½ hours).

NORTH YORKSHIRE MOORS RAILWAY
Aside from appealing to railway enthusiasts with some magnificent restored engines and carriages, the NYMR cuts across an interesting section of the moors and opens up some excellent day walks. And it can still fulfil its original function of providing a link to Whitby.

History
The line from Pickering to Whitby was the third passenger line opened in Yorkshire, coming 10 years after the Stockton-Darlington Railway. For the first 10 years of its life, carriages on the Pickering-Whitby line were pulled by horses, except at Beck Hole, where the 1:15 incline was conquered by a balancing system of water-filled tanks, and on downhill stretches

where the horses were put in a carriage and the train freewheeled! The first steam locomotive was used in 1847.

In the 1950s the increasing domination of private cars led to the first closures, and after 1965 only the Esk Valley line remained in operation. Thousands of locals opposed the 'rationalisation' however, and in 1967 a volunteer preservation society was formed to restore and operate the Grosmont-Pickering line. Today the NYMR carries 300,000 passengers a year.

Orientation & Information

The NYMR runs north-south and links Grosmont (on British Rail's Esk Valley line between Whitby and Middlesbrough) with Pickering. It's 18 miles long and the full journey takes an hour and costs £8.60.

The main station is at Pickering (☎ 01751-472508). At all stations there's information about waymarked walks, designed as family strolls lasting between one and four hours. The railway, Pickering and the surrounding countryside can easily absorb a day. Look for the *Walks from the Train* booklet.

May to September several special dining trains operate. Each Saturday one leaves Grosmont station at 7.20 pm; dinner is served and it returns at 9.45 pm (don't forget the long summer evenings). The train and meal price is £32.

The timetable is too complicated to repeat here, but there's a recorded timetable (☎ 01751-473535). Roughly speaking, there are up to eight trains a day between Easter and early November.

The Journey

Most passengers begin and end their journey at Pickering.

From Pickering the line follows Pickering Beck. The first stop is **Levisham station**, 1½ miles west of beautiful **Levisham** village, which in turn faces **Lockton** across a steep valley. Lockton, off the A169 between Whitby and Pickering, has *The Old School Youth Hostel* (see the Pickering section).

Goathland is a picturesque village 152m above sea level amongst the heather-clad moors. Most passengers get off here to view the village because it's used in the TV series *Heartbeat*. There are several good walks from the station.

You can camp at *Abbott's House Farm* (☎ 01947-896270) for £5, and at *Brow House Farm* (☎ 01947-896274) for £4. *Wheeldale Lodge Youth Hostel* (☎ 01947-896350) is 3 miles south-west of Goathland station. It's open Friday to Tuesday in September and from April to June; Thursday to Tuesday in July and August; £5.80/£4 for adults/juniors.

Mallyan Spout Hotel (☎ 01947-896486) has good bar food, and B&B from £65 per person.

The sleepy, little village of **Grosmont** (pronounced growmont) has accommodation at *Hazelwood Tea Rooms* (☎ 01947-895292), one pub, the *Station Tavern*, and that's about it.

Getting There & Away

It's possible to connect with the Esk Valley line at Grosmont, but considerable waits might be involved. The Esk Valley line doesn't operate on Sunday; Whitby and Middlesbrough-bound trains stop at Grosmont.

Tees & District (☎ 01947-602146) has two buses Monday to Friday from Whitby to Goathland. Yorkshire Coastliner (☎ 01653-692556) has an interesting service (bus Nos 840 and 842) between Whitby and Leeds via Goathland, Pickering and York.

Yorkshire Dales National Park

Austere stone villages with simple, functional architecture; streams and rivers cutting through the hills; wide, empty moors and endless stone walls snaking over the slopes – this is the region made famous by James Herriot and the TV series *All Creatures Great and Small*.

The landscape is completely different from that of the Lake District – the overwhelming impression is of space and openness. The high tops of the limestone hills are exposed moorland, and the sheltered dales between them range from Swaledale, which is narrow and sinuous, and Wensleydale and Wharfedale, which are broad and open, to Littondale and Ribblesdale, which are more rugged.

The Yorkshire Dales are very beautiful, but in summer, like the Lake District, they are extremely crowded. Avoid weekends and the peak summer period, or try to get off the beaten track. The famous Pennine Way runs to the area and can be unbelievably busy while other local footpaths are deserted.

ORIENTATION

The Yorkshire Dales can be broken into northern and southern halves: in the north, the two main dales run parallel and east-west. Swaledale, the northernmost, is particularly beautiful. If you have private transport, the B6270 from Kirkby Stephen to Richmond is highly recommended. Parallel and to the south is broad Wensleydale.

In the south, north-south Ribblesdale is the route taken by the Leeds-Settle-Carlisle (LSC) railway line, which provides access to a series of attractive towns. Wharfedale is parallel and to the east.

Skipton is the most important transport hub for the region, although apart from its castle it isn't very interesting. Richmond, handy for the north, is a beautiful town. For visitors without transport, the best bet will be those places accessible on the LSC line; Kirkby Stephen, Dent and Settle all have nearby YHA hostels.

INFORMATION

The main National Park Visitors Centre (☎ 01756-752774), in Grassington, 6 miles north of Skipton, is open daily from May to October, but only on weekends from November to April. It publishes the useful *Visitor* newspaper.

WALKS

There's a huge range of walks from easy strolls to extremely challenging hikes; the TICs are good places to get information on day walks.

The Pennine Way crosses the park; it's a demanding and deservedly popular walk to the rugged western half. Another possibility is the Dales Way which begins in Ilkley, follows the rivers Wharfe and Dee to the heart of the Dales, and finishes at Bowness-on-Windermere in the Lake District. If you started at Grassington, it would be an easy five day, 60 mile walk.

CYCLE ROUTES

Outside busy summer weekends, the Dales provide ideal cycling country. Most roads follow the rivers along the bottom of the dales, so, although there are still some steep climbs, there's also plenty on the flat.

The CTC (see the Activities chapter) and the National Park Visitors Centre at Grassington have information about the 131 mile Yorkshire Dales Cycle Way that loops through some of the lesser known dales, following small B-roads.

The first 24 mile stage is from Skipton to Malham: start by heading east to Bolton Abbey, then north to Appletreewick, then north-west to Grassington and Malham.

The second 22 mile stage starts by heading north to Malham Tarn, then continues west to Settle, Clapham and Ingleton.

The third 23 mile stage heads north to Dent along Kingsdale, then east along Dentdale and on to Hawes.

The fourth 20 mile stage runs east along Wensleydale to Askrigg, where it turns north over the moors to Swaledale, then east to Grinton.

The fifth 22 mile stage turns south to Bolton Castle, east to Wensley, then south-west down Coverdale to Kettlewell.

The final 20 mile stage back to Skipton follows Wharfedale south to Grassington, then retraces the route through Appletreewick and Bolton Abbey.

GETTING THERE & AROUND

For public-transport users from the south, the Dales are best accessed from Leeds using the LSC line to Skipton, which also gives

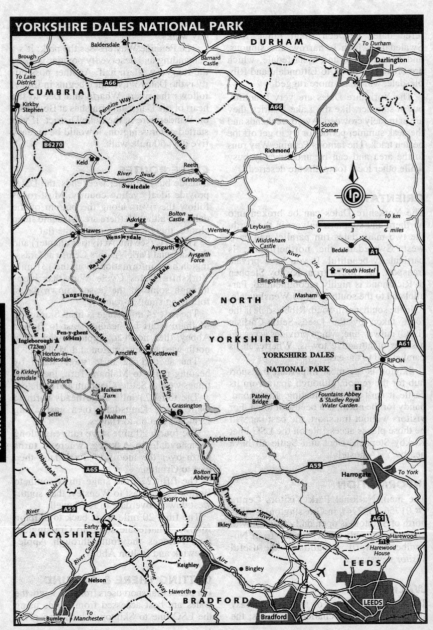

YORKSHIRE DALES NATIONAL PARK

good access to the west. This line also makes Carlisle a jumping-off point in the north-west. Life is more difficult in the north-east and east, although buses run from Darlington to Richmond and Barnard Castle, and Harrogate and Ripon are also accessible.

As a rule, however, public transport is grim. Bus users need a copy of the *Dales Connections* timetable, available from TICs. Cycling is an excellent way to get around.

LEEDS-SETTLE-CARLISLE LINE

The Leeds-Settle-Carlisle (LSC) line was one of the greatest engineering achievements of the Victorian era, and it takes passengers across some of the best countryside in England. It services a number of attractive market towns (several with nearby youth hostels) and gives excellent access to the western dales.

Orientation & Information

The LSC line runs between Leeds and Carlisle, from Leeds along the Aire Valley, then to Ribblesdale, Dentdale and the western edge of the Dales. There are good walks from some of the small stations along the way and free guided walks each Saturday and some Sundays and Wednesdays.

There are trains roughly every two hours Monday to Saturday all year, and three on Sunday April to October. The entire journey takes three hours one way and costs £18 for a day return.

The Journey

The first section of the journey is along the Aire Valley from **Leeds**.

Keighley (see the separate section) is the starting point for the Keighley & Worth Valley steam railway to Haworth (of Brontë fame).

Skipton is considered the gateway to the southern dales. After Skipton the railway crosses the moors to Ribblesdale and the attractive market town of **Settle** (near which is a youth hostel).

Next is the spectacular Ribblehead Viaduct and Blea Moor Tunnel, linking Ribblesdale to Dentdale. *Dentdale Youth*

Hostel (☎ 015396-25251), an old shooting lodge beside the River Dee, is 2 miles south of Dent station. The attractive and popular village of Dent is 4 miles west. The hostel opens Friday to Wednesday, April to August, and Friday to Tuesday in September and October; £8/5.40 for adults/juniors.

After Garsdale, the train reaches its highest point (356m) at Ais Gill. Before **Kirkby Stephen** (which has a youth hostel) are the ruins of Pendragon Castle, built in the 12th century and reputed to be the home of King Arthur's father.

Appleby is home to the famous Gipsy Horse Fair, held the second Wednesday of June. After Appleby and to the east is Cross Fell, at 893m (2930 feet), the highest point on the Pennines. **Langwathby** is just northwest of Penrith, a jumping-off point for the Lakes, connected by bus to Keswick and Newcastle (see Getting There & Away). Armathwaite Viaduct is above the village and castle of **Combe Eden**, after which you reach **Carlisle** (which has a youth hostel).

Getting There & Away

For information about connecting services, see the Leeds and Carlisle sections. Another interesting possibility is the summer-only trans-Pennine bus service between Newcastle upon Tyne and Keswick, which connects with the LSC line at Langwathby train station. The service is operated by Wright Brothers (☎ 01434-381200). There are three services Monday to Saturday and one on Sunday going across country from Newcastle upon Tyne to Keswick, via Langwathby, on the LSC line, and Hexham and Corbridge, on Hadrian's Wall.

SKIPTON

• pop 13,000   ☎ 01756

Skipton is a popular gateway to the Dales and a market town, so it can get very busy on summer weekends. The TIC (☎ 01756-792809), 9 Sheep St, opens Monday to Saturday from 9.45 am to 5 pm, and Sunday in summer from 2 to 5 pm.

Skipton Castle is considered to be one of the best preserved medieval castles in

Britain. It's open daily from 10 am to 6 pm (from noon Sunday); £3.80/1.90.

Pennine Boat Trips (☎ 790829), Coach St by the bridge, runs hour-long trips along the canal daily Easter to October at 11.30 am, 1.30, 3 and 4.30 pm; £3.40/1.70.

Most accommodation is on Keighley Rd. *Craven House* (☎ 794657), at No 56, has rooms with shared bathroom for £17.50 per person. At *Highfield Hotel* (☎ 793182), No 58, all rooms have a bathroom and go for £18.50 per person. A little larger is the *Unicorn Hotel* (☎ 01756-794146) which has singles/doubles with bathroom for £24.50/32.

Beside the canal, *Bizzie Lizzies* (☎ 793189, 36 Swadford St) is a modern, large restaurant and takeaway locally celebrated for the quality of its fish and chips (£4.50). South of town on Keighley Rd *Eastwood's Fish Restaurant & Takeaway* is similar, with an extensive menu of fish dishes as well as traditional fish and chips.

There are National Express (☎ 0990-808080) buses direct to/from London. Keighley & District (☎ 01535-603284) has regular buses to Keighley (Nos 78 and 79) and Grassington (Nos 71 and 72). Pennine Motors (☎ 01535-749215) runs a service (No 580) to Settle, while Harrogate & District (☎ 01423-566061) goes to Harrogate and York (No X50).

During summer, Stagecoach Cumberland's (☎ 01946-63222) bus No X9 service runs between York and Ambleside (Lake District) via Kirkby Lonsdale, Settle, Skipton and Harrogate (Yorkshire Dales) on Monday, Wednesday, Friday and Saturday.

The train station is about half a mile out of town on Swadford Rd (A59). Skipton is on the famous LSC line, and is only three stops north of Keighley (for the Keighley & Worth Valley Railway (☎ 01535-645214) to Haworth).

GRASSINGTON
☎ 01756

Grassington is an attractive village that makes an excellent base for exploring the Dales, especially Upper Wharfedale.

There's a useful National Park Visitors Centre (☎ 752774), open April to October daily from 10 am to 5 pm, south of the village, with a large car park. It has an accommodation booking service and lots of information on walks and cycle routes.

Linton Youth Hostel (☎ 752400, Linton) is three-quarters of a mile south of Grassington, in the adjoining hamlet of Linton. It's open Monday to Saturday April to September (daily July and August); telephone for its complicated opening schedule the rest of the year; £8.80/5.95 for adults/juniors.

The attractive *Burtree Cottage* (☎ 01756-752442, Hebden Rd) is a short walk from the village centre; it has only two rooms for £16 per person. *Raines Close* (☎ 01756-752678, 13 Station Rd) has comfortable doubles and twins from £19 to £25 per person.

From Skipton train station, Keighley & District (☎ 01535-603284) bus Nos 71 and 72 depart several times a day Monday to Saturday. There's a Sunday service April to September.

SETTLE & AROUND
☎ 01726

Settle is a pleasant market town in Ribblesdale, on the edge of the geological fault that delineates the limestone to the north and the gritstone to the south.

The TIC (☎ 825192) in The Shambles opens daily April to September from 10 am to 5 pm, closing at 2 pm the rest of the year.

The Three Peaks

The countryside to the north is dominated by the well known Three Peaks, which are part of a challenging 26 mile circuit involving 5000 feet (1500m) of ascent. Beginning at Horton-in-Ribblesdale, you follow the Pennine Way to **Pen-y-ghent** (693m, 2273 feet), with a distinctive sphinx-like shape.

Next is **Whernside** (736m, 2414 feet), actually the northernmost peak, then finally, **Ingleborough** (723m, 2373 feet), which has a distinctive flat top of gritstone and was the site for a Celtic settlement – hut circles and parts of a defensive wall can still be seen.

Stagecoach Cumberland's bus No X9 service stops at Ingleton for the Peaks, with a bus Wednesday, Friday and Saturday during summer only.

Places to Stay & Eat

Knight Stainforth Hall (☎ *822200, Stackhouse Lane)*, opposite the high school, is about 3 miles from town and has tent sites from £7.75. *Stainforth Youth Hostel* (☎ *823577, Stainforth)* is 2 miles north of Settle on the B6479 to Horton-in-Ribblesdale. It's open daily April to September, Friday and Saturday the rest of the year; £8 /£5.40 for adults/juniors.

The *Royal Oak* (☎ *822561, Market Place)* is a good pub with bar meals starting around £5, including plenty of vegetarian dishes and salads; it also has B&B from £28.50 per person.

Penmar Court (☎ *823258, Duke St)*, east of Market Place, has six rooms from £16 per person.

Getting There & Away

For Stagecoach Cumberland's bus No X9 service see Skipton. Settle is on the LSC line.

KIRKBY LONSDALE
* pop 1800   ☎ 015242

Kirkby Lonsdale is a beautiful, unspoilt market town with an excellent position midway between the Lakes and the Dales. In common with quite a few of the Lake District towns, it's rather artfully unspoilt, a bit cutesy and a bit unreal.

Orientation & Information

Kirkby Lonsdale is actually a part of Cumbria. It's outside the park borders, but for visitors it's essentially a Dales town, both in appearance and as a useful touring centre.

The excellent TIC (☎ 71437), 24 Main St, opens Easter to October daily from 9 am to 1 pm and from 2 to 5 pm, and November to March Thursday to Sunday the same hours.

Places to Stay & Eat

The *Copper Kettle Restaurant* (☎ *71714, Market St)* has a large traditional English menu (with plenty of roasts), with dishes from £4 to £9. There are also four comfortable rooms from £16 per person. The *Sun Hotel* (☎ *71965, Market St)* is a very old inn, dating to the 17th century, with interesting meals in its *Mad Carews* restaurant. Its steak and kidney in red wine pudding costs £6.95.

The *Snooty Fox Tavern* (☎ *71308, Main St)* is well known for good food, with an imaginative menu ranging from £6 to £14; it also has rooms for £30/45 a single/double.

Getting There & Away

Kirkby Lonsdale is 17 miles from Settle and 15 miles from Windermere; the nearest railway connection is at Oxenholme (12 miles).

For Stagecoach Cumberland's bus No X9 service, see Skipton.

KIRKBY STEPHEN
* pop 1600   ☎ 017683

Kirkby Stephen is a classic market town with stone Georgian-style houses flanking an attractive High St. There's nothing very remarkable about the place, but in some ways that adds to its appeal – it isn't inundated with visitors.

Orientation & Information

Kirkby Stephen is actually part of Cumbria. It's outside the park borders, but for visitors it's a useful touring centre for the Dales and the surrounding Eden Valley.

The excellent TIC (☎ 71199), Market Square, opens Easter to October, Monday to Saturday from 9.30 am to 5.30 pm, Sunday from 10 am to 4 pm; the rest of the year Monday to Saturday from 10 am to noon (and from 2 to 4 pm Monday).

Walks & Cycle Routes

Kirkby Stephen is the central point on Alfred Wainwright's 190 mile **Coast to Coast Walk** which runs from St Bees Head on the west coast to Robin Hood's Bay on the east. Following the walk east, it's 13 miles from Kirkby Stephen to Keld, which also has a youth hostel. Following the walk west, the next stops are Orton, Shap, Patterdale and Grasmere.

Places to Stay
Hostel *Kirkby Stephen Youth Hostel* (☎ *71793, Fletcher Hill, Market St)* is in a converted chapel in the centre of town, south of Market Square. It's open Thursday to Monday from April to June; daily July and August; and Wednesday to Sunday during September and October; £8/£5.40 for adults/juniors.

B&Bs The *Old Court House* (☎ *71061, High St)* has excellent accommodation, and yes, it's in the Old Court House. There are rooms from £15 per person. At the *Jolly Farmers House* (☎ *71063, 63 High St)*, all rooms have a bathroom and cost £18 per person.

Places to Eat
There are several excellent bakeries and good-value tearooms. The *Pennine Hotel (Market St)* is a straightforward pub with straightforward bar meals like Cumberland sausage and chips from £4.60. The *Old Forge Bistro* (☎ *71832, 39 North Rd)* serves excellent lunchtime vegetarian dishes like savoury aubergine and apple moussaka for around £3.50. In the evening, tzatziki with pitta is £6.

Getting There & Away
Kirkby Lonsdale is 25 miles away, Hawes is 16 miles away and Carlisle is 50 miles away.

Bus Primrose Coaches (☎ 0191-232 5567) has a daily No X69 service between Newcastle upon Tyne and Blackpool via Durham, Barnard Castle, Raby Castle and Kirkby Stephen.

Coast to Coast Packhorse Kirkby Stephen is home to the innovative Coast to Coast Packhorse (☎ *71680)*, a daily minibus that runs from St Bees Head to Robin Hood's Bay from Easter to October.

It has several services including to some of the villages and towns along the route of Alfred Wainwright's Coast to Coast Walk. These towns include Penrith, Keswick, Cockermouth, Whitehaven, St Bees and back through Ennerdale, Rosthwaite, Keswick, Grasmere, Patterdale and Shap to Kirkby Stephen. Another route is Kirkby Stephen through Keld, Richmond, Blakey and Grosmont to Robin Hood's Bay.

The minibus takes bodies or backpacks or both. Backpacks (and bodies where appropriate) are delivered to a pick-up point at the next stop on the walk. Packs cost £3 per stop if booked, £3.50 unbooked; it's £51 (booked) from St Bees to Robin Hood's Bay.

Getting Around
Bicycle The well-organised Mortlake Mountain Bikes (☎ 71666, or ☎ 71993 after hours), 32 Market St near the TIC, hire bikes, organise tours and can suggest routes. Mountain bikes cost £15 per day.

RICHMOND
• **pop 8000**   ☎ **01748**

Richmond is one of the most beautiful towns in England – and surprisingly few people know. A ruined castle perches high on a rocky outcrop overlooking a rushing stream, and looms over the steeply sloping Market Square surrounded by Georgian buildings. Cobbled streets, closely lined with stone cottages, radiate from the square and run down to the river, providing exhilarating glimpses of the surrounding hills and moors.

Orientation & Information
Richmond is actually outside and to the east of the national park, but makes an excellent touring base for the park and it's definitely in the Yorkshire Dales.

The TIC (☎ 850252), Friary Gardens, Victoria Rd, opens April to October daily from 9.30 am to 5.30 pm, and November to March, Monday to Saturday from 9.30 am to 4.30 pm. It has good brochures showing walks around the town and surrounding countryside (including to Easby Abbey, which is recommended).

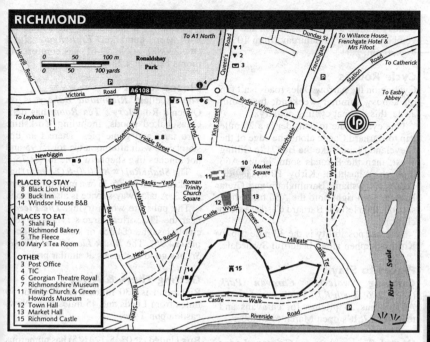

RICHMOND

0   50   100 m
0   50   100 yards

To A1 North

Ronaldshay Park

To Willance House,
Frenchgate Hotel &
Mrs Fifoot

Dundas St

To Catherick

To Easby Abbey

Victoria Road A6108

To Leyburn

Ryder's Wynd

Newbiggin

Finkle Street

Market Square

Roman
Trinity
Church
Square

Thornhills Banks—Yard

Castle Wynd

Tower St

Millgate

Castle Ter

River Swale

New Road

Castle — Walk

Riverside Road

PLACES TO STAY
8   Black Lion Hotel
9   Buck Inn
14 Windsor House B&B

PLACES TO EAT
1   Shahi Raj
2   Richmond Bakery
5   The Fleece
10 Mary's Tea Room

OTHER
3   Post Office
4   TIC
6   Georgian Theatre Royal
7   Richmondshire Museum
11 Trinity Church & Green
    Howards Museum
12 Town Hall
13 Market Hall
15 Richmond Castle

Finkle St, off Market Square, has some interesting shops including Alt-Berg, for outdoor gear.

Richmond Castle

Begun in 1071, Richmond Castle (☎ 822493, EH) has surviving 11th century curtain walls, a gatehouse, a chapel and what is believed to be the oldest surviving Norman great hall (Scollard's Hall). The impressive keep (1171), beside the gatehouse, is in remarkably good condition. It has been refloored and reroofed to give an idea of what it was like in medieval times.

It's a dramatic ruin so it's not surprising that legends (however unlikely) cling to it like moss: some say an underground tunnel links it to Easby Abbey, and that King Arthur and his knights are in a magical sleep here and will wake when the country needs them.

It's open April to October daily from 10 am to 6 pm, November to March daily from 10 am to 4 pm; £2.30/1.10.

Museums

There are three small but interesting museums in Richmond. The **Georgian Theatre Royal** (☎ 823710), Victoria Rd, was built in 1788 and is the oldest theatre in the UK surviving in its original form. It's open for guided tours April to October, Monday to Saturday from 10.30 am to 3.45 pm, Sunday from 11 am to 1.15 pm; £1.50/1. **Richmondshire Museum** (☎ 825611), Ryder's Wynd, is an interesting local museum open Good Friday to late October daily from 11 am to 5 pm; £1.50/1. The **Green Howards Museum** (☎ 822133), Trinity Church Square, shows the history of the Green Howards, a famous Yorkshire regiment; open April to October, Monday to Saturday from 9.30 am to 4.30 pm, Sunday from 2 to 4.30 pm, March and November, Monday to Saturday, from 10 am to 4.30 pm; £2/1.

Cycle Routes

Cycling on the narrow Dales roads isn't fun on a busy summer weekend; that point aside, this is great cycling country.

One cycle route to consider is a 20 mile trip to Barnard Castle along the edge of the Cleveland Plain. Take the B6271 to Gilling West, then the B-roads south of the A66 through Whashton, Kirby Hill, Gayles, Dalton, Newsham, Barningham and Greta Bridge. Turn right onto the A66 for a short section, then left for Barnard Castle (a steep climb).

Another possibility is the 33 mile trip to Kirkby Stephen along beautiful Swaledale.

Places to Stay

Camping *Swaleview Caravan Park* (☎ 823106, Reeth Rd), 3 miles west on the A6108, has 25 pitches for caravans and tents for £7. It's open March to October.

Hostel The nearest is *Grinton Lodge Youth Hostel* (☎ 01748-884206, Grinton), 10 miles west, and south of the B2670 between Richmond and Reeth. Built as a shooting lodge, the hostel is high on the moors. It's open January to March except Sunday and Monday, April to August daily, and September to October except Sunday and Monday; £8/5.40 for adults/juniors.

B&Bs & Hotels *Windsor House B&B* (☎ 823285, 9 Castle Hill) has a great position near the square; the charge is a reasonable £15 per person, £18 with bathroom.

The *Buck Inn* (☎ 822259, 27 Newbiggin) is a nice old pub with rooms from £22 per person, while the large *Black Lion Hotel* (☎ 823121, 12 Finkle St) has decent rooms from £21 per person. There's a batch of pleasant places in 17th and 18th century town houses on cobbled Frenchgate. Near the top of the street, *Willance House* (☎ 824467), at No 24, has doubles with

bathroom and a twin for £20. *Mrs Fifoot* (☎ 823227), at No 58, has one double for £40. More upmarket, *Frenchgate Hotel* (☎ 822087), at No 59-61, has comfortable rooms between £26.50 and £37.

Places to Eat

The excellent *Richmond Bakery* is on Queen's Rd. *Mary's Tea Room* has delicious baked goods, including Yorkshire curd tarts and game pies. There's an upstairs café with afternoon tea for £3.95 and hot lunches like shepherd's pie for £3.75.

The *Shahi Raj* (☎ 826070, 8 Queen St) has chicken baltis for £5.35 or a mushroom curry for £3. A takeaway service is also available.

The pubs are worth trying. *The Fleece*, near the TIC, offers large servings of vegetable lasagne (£4.55) or steak and kidney pie (£4.95). The *Black Lion Hotel* (Finkle St) has good bar meals at similar prices.

Getting There & Away

Richmond is 230 miles from London, 50 miles from Leeds and 45 miles from Newcastle upon Tyne.

Bus United (☎ 0345-124125) has numerous regular services (bus Nos 27, X27, 28, 35 and 35A) to Darlington, which has a train station. Stagecoach (☎ 01325-384573) also has an express bus (No X90) to Darlington and Newcastle upon Tyne.

Train The nearest station is 12 miles northeast in Darlington, which is on the main east-coast line from London's King's Cross to Edinburgh.

FOUNTAINS ABBEY & STUDLEY ROYAL WATER GARDEN

Sheltered in a secluded valley, with a number of monumental buildings surrounded by extensive parkland and gardens, this complex in the narrow valley of the River Skell is a World Heritage Site.

It includes the magnificent ruins of Fountains Abbey, a 12th century Cistercian abbey; Fountains Hall (1610), a five storey Jacobean mansion; St Mary's Church, a sumptuous Victorian church built in the 1870s; and a number of 18th century follies. These are all set within a beautiful, 18th century, 800 acre, landscaped park built around a series of artificial lakes and designed to feature the abbey ruins.

History

Fountains Abbey began as a small breakaway group of 13 monks from the Benedictine abbey of St Mary's in York. In 1132 the Archbishop of York granted them land in what was virtual wilderness. Lacking assistance from any established abbey or order, they turned to the Cistercian order for help.

The Cistercians were often called the White Monks because they wore a habit of undyed wool, reflecting the austerity and simplicity of their order. They were committed to long periods of silence and eight daily services. Clearly, this didn't leave much time for practical matters. So the Cistercians ordained lay brothers who lived within the monastery, but pursued the abbey's ever-growing business interests – wool, lead mining, quarrying, animal breeding and so on.

Sadly, the idealism and purity didn't last long. After economic collapse in the 14th century, the monks rented their lands to tenant farmers and replaced lay brothers with servants. By the beginning of the 16th century the vast abbey had a population of only 30 monks.

After the dissolution the estate was sold into private hands and between 1598 and 1611 Fountains Hall was built with stone from the abbey ruins. The hall passed through several families until it and the ruins were united with the Studley Royal Estate in 1768.

The main house of Studley Royal burnt down in 1946, but the superb landscaping survives virtually unchanged from the 18th century. Studley Royal was owned by John Aislabie, who spent 20 years creating an extensive park. Major engineering works were required to create the lakes and to control the flow of the river.

Orientation & Information

Fountains Abbey lies 4 miles west of Ripon off the B6255. There are two entrances, one leaving the B road 1½ miles from Ripon, for the Canal Gates entrance, and one at 3 miles for the impressive visitor centre (☎ 01765-608888, NT).

The abbey, garden and visitor centre open, April to September, daily from 10 am to 7 pm, and from 10 am to 5 pm during the rest of the year. The deer park opens daily until dusk. Fountains Hall and St Mary's Church open April to September daily from 1 to 5 pm.

Admission to the abbey, hall and garden is £4.20/2; the deer park and St Mary's Church are free.

There are free one-hour guided tours April to October at 2.30 pm, and at 11 am and 3.30 pm May to September. There's no public transport but a limited bus service from Ripon may be operating soon.

HARROGATE
- **pop 65,500**   ☎ **01423**

After the grimy cities of the Midlands and parts of Yorkshire, Harrogate is reminiscent of the more prosperous south. Primarily built in the 19th century as a fashionable spa town, it has managed to remain affluent although its original excuse for existence – the health-giving effect of mineral spring water – is no longer convincing.

The town is famous for its spring/summer floral displays, but the extensive gardens flanked by stately Victorian terraces are beautiful at any time of year. There are numerous high-quality hotels and B&Bs (we're definitely not talking nylon sheets in Harrogate). Even more remarkably, there's a wide range of interesting restaurants – but not many decent pubs.

Orientation & Information

Harrogate is actually outside and south-east of the national park, but makes an excellent touring base. The town is almost surrounded by gardens, in the south by the 200 acre Stray. The bus and train stations are on Station Parade.

HARROGATE

To Ripon & Skipton

Coppice Drive

A61

Springfield Avenue

Duchy Road

Ripon Road

Franklin Mount

Franklin Road

Kirkby

Dragon Avenue

Dragon Parade

Dragon Road

Skipton Road

A59

York Road

Cornwall Road

Swan Road

Crescent Road

Parliament Street

Cheltenham Road

Cheltenham Parade

King's Road

Commercial Street

Bower Road

East Parade

Park View

Walkers Passage

Kingsway

Harcourt Road

Harcourt Drive

Woodside

Chelmsford Road

Station Parade

Oxford Street

Cambridge Street

James Street

Albert Street

Raglan Street

Victoria Avenue

Station Bridge

North Park Rd

South Park Rd

East Park Rd

To Knaresborough & York

Knaresborough Rd

Valley Gardens

Esplanade

Montpellier Hill

Prospect Gardens

St Mary's Walk

Valley Drive

Valley Mount

Cold Bath Road

Victoria Road

Beech Grove

West Park Stray

West Park

Tower St

Robert Street

York Place

Leeds Road

Otley Road

To Leeds

Leeds Road

Stray Rein

Stray

The Stray

0   150   300 m
0   150   300 yards

PLACES TO STAY
1 Alexander Guest House
2 Franklin Hotel
3 Almscliffe B&B
5 Daryl House Hotel
6 Dragon House
7 Old Swan Hotel
17 Cavendish Hotel
19 The Imperial

PLACES TO EAT
9 Fino's Tapas Bar
10 The Blue Piano
11 Graveley's
12 Rajput
18 Betty's

OTHER
4 Conference & Exhibition Centre
8 TIC
13 Bus Station
14 Main Post Office
15 Royal Pump Room Museum
16 Sun Colonnade
20 Train Station

The TIC (☎ 537300), in the Royal Baths Assembly Rooms, Crescent Rd, opens Monday to Saturday from 9 am to 6 pm, Sunday from noon to 3 pm. It has an accommodation booking service and details of free guided walking tours (April to September, daily except Fridays and Saturdays).

Things to See & Do

There are no particularly important sights in Harrogate, but the town is, nonetheless, an attractive place. Strolling in the gardens and taking tea seem to be the principal activities. A wander should start at the **Royal Pump Room Museum** (☎ 503340), Crown Place, built in 1842 over the most famous of the sulphur springs. It gives quite a curious insight into the phenomenon. It's open April to October, Monday to Saturday from 10 am to 5 pm, Sunday from 2 to 5 pm (to 4 pm the rest of the year); £1.75/1.

The **Valley Gardens**, the site for the town's flower show, are attractive. They're flanked by a 180m-long glass-covered walk.

At the top of Montpellier Hill, **Betty's** is a classic Edwardian tearoom that has been in business since 1919 (see Places to Eat).

The Harrogate Flower Show is held in April.

Places to Stay

Camping Two miles north of town, *Bilton Park* (☎ *863121, Village Farm, Bilton*) has sites for tents for £7.50; open April to October.

B&Bs & Hotels One of the best streets for cheaper options is Franklin Rd, which is lined with B&Bs. *Almscliffe* (☎ *507027*), at No 5, is standard but Thelma and Neville are welcoming, with doubles from £18. Nearby, *Franklin Hotel* (☎ *569028*), at No 25, has rooms for £16 per person. *Alexander Guest House* (☎ *503348*), at No 88, is comfortable and has rooms for £24/ 45.

There are two good-value places in Dragon Parade: *Dragon House* (☎ *569888*) at No 6 and *Daryl House Hotel* (☎ *502775*) at No 42. Rooms are without bathroom; from £16 per person.

There are a number of comfortable, medium-priced hotels overlooking the beautiful Valley Gardens; most have private bathroom. Amongst others, the *Cavendish Hotel* (☎ *509637, 3 Valley Drive*) is from £32/50; *Ashbrooke House* (☎ *564478*), at No 140, is from £23/45.

At the top, *The Imperial* (☎ *565071, Prospect Place*) is a very grand hotel in the centre of town; rooms cost from £82/97. The *Old Swan Hotel* (☎ *500055, Swan Rd*) is an ivy-clad 18th century coaching house. This is where Agatha Christie chose to hide from the world when she went missing in 1926; rooms cost £108/138.50.

Places to Eat

There's a wide range of possible eating places. *Betty's* (☎ *502746, 1 Parliament St*) is a classic Yorkshire tearoom, open from 9 am (for breakfast) to 9 pm. It has a large variety of teas, coffees and teacakes and reasonably priced soups, sandwiches and main meals (under £7). A pianist plays from 6 pm.

Walk up Cheltenham Parade for Spanish food at *Fino's Tapas Bar* (☎ *565806*) or for mixed and matched food from around the world – Cajun, Chinese, Japanese, Mediterranean – at *The Blue Piano* (☎ *530448*). Both charge under £5 for main dishes.

Indian food is available a few doors up at *Rajput* (☎ *562113*) for £4.50 to £5.50. Across the road, *Graveley's* (☎ *507093*) serves a good-value, tasty fish and chips meal with tea and bread for £4.95.

Getting There & Away

Harrogate is roughly between Leeds (15 miles) and York (22 miles), 75 miles from Newcastle upon Tyne and 210 miles from London.

Bus Harrogate & District (☎ 566061), 20A Station Parade, is the most important local operator. There are frequent buses to Knaresborough (Nos 1, 2, 55 and others; 20 minutes), Leeds (Nos 36, 36A, 36C; 40 minutes) and Ripon. The No X50 runs daily between Skipton via Harrogate and York.

For Stagecoach Cumberland's No X9 service, see Skipton.

Train Harrogate is on the Harrogate line from Leeds (30 minutes, £3.30); this runs on to York (£3.30) hourly.

Durham & Around

The Durham area includes some of the most beautiful parts of the northern Pennines, one of the greatest Christian buildings in the world, and an ancient mining heritage that has left a legacy of uninspiring half-towns.

Although its history isn't as turbulent as that of neighbouring Northumberland (which actually formed Durham's defensive buffer), Durham has known its fair share of bloodshed. In the Middle Ages it was still sufficiently wild to warrant the Prince Bishops of Durham having virtually limitless power. They combined lay and religious responsibilities as the rulers of a palatinate (a kingdom within a kingdom). The Prince Bishop (aka the Count Palatine) had the right to have his own army, nobility, coinage and courts. His great cathedral and castle was once described by Sir Walter Scott as, 'Half church of God, half castle 'gainst the Scot.'

The Prince Bishops did bring peace to Durham, and this allowed the county to develop long before Northumberland, a fact reflected in the higher population density and the neat hedges and stone-walled fields. The western half of the county is dominated by the heather-covered hills of the northern Pennines, while the eastern half was, from the 18th century, the centre for a major coal mining industry which has now largely disappeared.

GETTING AROUND

The Durham County Council transport inquiry line (☎ 0191-383 3337) is open weekdays from 8.30 am to 5 pm, to 4.30 pm Friday. The Explorer North East ticket (see the North-Eastern England Getting Around section) is valid on many services in the county.

DURHAM
* pop 83,000   ☎ 0191

Durham is the most dramatic cathedral city in Britain, with a massive Norman cathedral dominating a wooded promontory high above a bend in the River Wear. Other cathedrals are more refined but none have more impact – it's an extraordinary structure built to survive, with utter confidence in the enduring qualities of faith and stone.

The story of Durham begins with the monks of Holy Island (Lindisfarne) fleeing from Viking raiders with their most precious treasures, St Cuthbert's body and the illuminated Lindisfarne Gospels. The Lindisfarne monastery had thrived for 240 years, but in 875 the monks began a search for a safer site. Finally, in 995 they found a perfect, easily defended position above the River Wear. The current cathedral is the third church to be built on the site; its foundation stone was laid on 12 August 1093.

The Prince Bishops reached the peak of their power in the 14th century, and although they survived with great pomp and ceremo-ny into the 19th century, their real influence ebbed away. In 1836 the last privileges were returned to the Crown and the last Count Palatine gave the castle to the newly founded Durham University (1832), the third-oldest university in England. Durham is still the centre for local government.

Orientation

Durham is surprisingly small. The centre of town is limited by the space available on the teardrop-shaped peninsula, and although the city, especially the university, has now overflowed to some extent, everything is within easy walking distance.

The Market Place (and TIC), castle and cathedral are all on the peninsula surrounded by the River Wear. The train station is above and north-west of the cathedral on the other side of the river. The bus station is also on the western side. Using the cathedral as your landmark, you can't really go wrong.

Information

The TIC (☎ 384 3720), Market Place, a short walk north of the castle and cathedral, opens Monday to Saturday from 10 am to 5 pm. There's also a Thomas Cook office on Market Place.

Durham Cathedral

Built as the shrine for St Cuthbert, Durham Cathedral dates almost entirely from the 12th century and is the most complete and spectacular example of Norman architecture. The Romanesque style as developed by the Normans had a monumental simplicity, characterised by great scale, round arches, enormous columns and zigzag chevron ornament – all shown at their best in Durham. The cathedral's vast interior is like a cave that is only partly artificial, its exterior like time-worn cliffs.

A number of walks give good views of the exterior; perhaps the two most famous are from Framwelgate Bridge and Prebend's Bridge, although the approach across Palace Green is also impressive.

History The choir, transepts and nave of the cathedral were built between 1093 and 1133

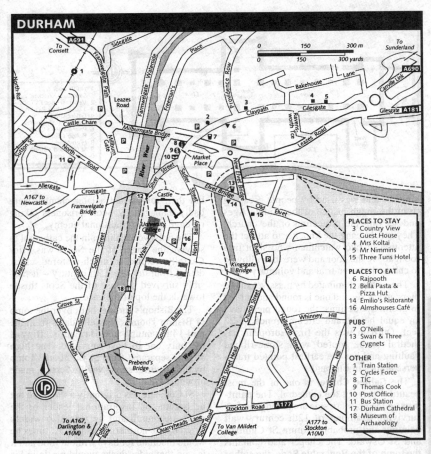

DURHAM

PLACES TO STAY
3 Country View
  Guest House
4 Mrs Koltai
5 Mr Nimmins
15 Three Tuns Hotel

PLACES TO EAT
6 Rajpooth
12 Bella Pasta &
   Pizza Hut
14 Emilio's Ristorante
16 Almshouses Café

PUBS
7 O'Neills
13 Swan & Three
   Cygnets

OTHER
1 Train Station
2 Cycles Force
8 TIC
9 Thomas Cook
10 Post Office
11 Bus Station
17 Durham Cathedral
18 Museum of
   Archaeology

and still survive in uncompromised Romanesque form. There have been four major additions, all successful: the beautiful Galilee Chapel, with its slim pillars of Purbeck marble at the western end, built between 1170 and 1175; the western towers, built from 1217 to 1226; the Chapel of Nine Altars, with the pointed arches and carved capitals of the Early English style, built between 1242 and 1280; and the central tower, which was rebuilt between 1465 and 1490.

Information The cathedral (☎ 386 4266) opens May to August daily from 7.15 am to 8 pm, September to April from 7.15 am to 6 pm; a donation is requested. There are tours (£2) late May to early September, Tuesdays and Thursdays at 10.30 am. Evensong is at 5.15 pm weekdays (not Monday) and at 3.30 pm Sunday.

Inside the Cathedral The main entry is through the **north door**. Note the great bronze knocker. This was a sanctuary

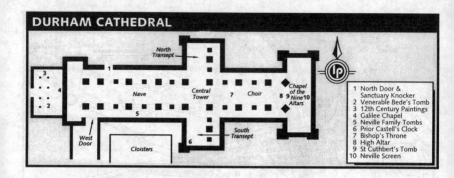

DURHAM CATHEDRAL

1 North Door & Sanctuary Knocker
2 Venerable Bede's Tomb
3 12th Century Paintings
4 Galilee Chapel
5 Neville Family Tombs
6 Prior Castell's Clock
7 Bishop's Throne
8 High Altar
9 St Cuthbert's Tomb
10 Neville Screen

knocker and was used by people escaping from the rough justice of the Middle Ages and seeking the protection of the church. They would bang the knocker to attract the attention of two watchmen who slept in a room above the door and were then allowed to choose between trial and voluntary exile.

The nave is dominated by massive carved piers; every second one is round and carved in geometric designs; the round piers have an equal height and circumference of 22 feet. Durham was the first European cathedral to be roofed with stone-ribbed vaulting and has the earliest pointed transverse arches in England.

The **Galilee Chapel** is one of the most beautiful parts of the cathedral. The **paintings** on the northern side are among the few surviving examples of 12th century wall painting and probably feature St Cuthbert and St Oswald. The chapel also contains the **tomb of the Venerable Bede**, the author of the *Ecclesiastical History of the English People*. Bede was an 8th century Northumbrian monk, a great historian and polymath whose work held a pre-eminent role in Latin literature for four centuries and is still the prime source of information on the development of early Christian society and institutions in Britain. Amongst other things, he began the practice of dating years from the birth of Jesus.

The Lords of Raby, the great Neville family, were the first lay people to be buried in the cathedral (in the late 14th century),

but their **tombs** and a later chantry were badly damaged by Scots prisoners taking revenge on their traditional enemy.

The only wooden item in the cathedral to survive the anger of the Scots was **Prior Castell's Clock**, a much-restored clock dating from the late 15th century – it possibly survived because of the Scots thistle towards the top of the case.

The **Bishop's throne**, built over the tomb of Bishop Thomas Hatfield, dates from the mid-14th century, and Hatfield's effigy is the only one to have survived. The **high altar** is separated from **St Cuthbert's tomb** by the beautiful stone **Neville Screen**, made around 1375.

St Cuthbert was originally a shepherd but he became an inspirational leader of the northern church and he was also widely loved by the northern peasants. At times he would meditate for days without food and it is said that eider ducks would nestle in his clothing. He died in 687 and when the Viking raids made Lindisfarne untenable, the monks carried his miraculously preserved body with them. His reputation attracted many pilgrims to Durham.

The Chapel of the Nine Altars actually did once have nine altars – in order to facilitate giving Mass to all the monks!

Cloisters The monastic buildings are centred on the cloisters. They were heavily rebuilt in 1828. The west door to the cloisters is particularly famous for its 12th century ironwork. On the western side is a monastic dormitory, now a library, and an undercroft which now houses the Treasury and restaurant.

Treasury Museum The Treasury Museum is definitely worth visiting as it includes relics of St Cuthbert from the 7th century and a collection of illuminated manuscripts and cathedral 'paraphernalia'. At the time of research it was closed for refurbishment but should be open again by the time you read this.

Durham Castle

The castle was begun in 1072 and served as the home for Durham's Prince Bishops. It has been substantially rebuilt over the years, but still preserves the fundamental layout of a Norman motte-and-bailey castle. It is now a residential college for the university, and it is possible to stay here during summer holidays (see Places to Stay). Late March to September there are guided tours Monday to Saturday from 10 am to 12.30 pm and from 2 to 4 pm, Sunday from 2 to 4 pm, and the rest of the year from 2 to 4 pm on Monday, Wednesday, Saturday and Sunday; £3/2.

Museum of Archaeology

In an old fulling mill on the banks of the Wear between Framwelgate and Prebend's bridges, the Museum of Archaeology (☎ 374 3623) has a collection illustrating the history of the city. It's open April to October daily from 11 am to 4 pm; November to March, Monday, Thursday and Friday from 12.30 pm to 3 pm, Saturday and Sunday from 11.30 am to 3.30 pm; £1/50p.

Walks

There are superb views back to the cathedral and castle from the outer bank of the river; walk around the bend between Elvet and Framwelgate bridges, or hire a boat at Elvet Bridge.

Cruises

The Prince Bishop River Cruiser (☎ 386 9525), Elvet Bridge, offers one-hour cruises along the river. Trips run June to September at 12.30, 2 and 3 pm; £3/1.50.

Rowing boats can be hired for £2.50 per person per hour from Browns Boathouse (☎ 386 3779) below Elvet Bridge.

Places to Stay

The TIC makes local bookings free, which is useful since convenient B&Bs aren't numerous; the situation is particularly grim during graduation week in late June.

Camping *Grange Camping & Caravan Site (☎ 384 4778, Meadow Lane)* is 2 miles from the city centre. A car, two people and a tent costs from £9.70.

B&Bs & Hotels Several colleges rent their rooms during the university holidays (particularly July to September). The most exciting possibility is *University College (☎ 374 3863)*, in the old Durham Castle grounds, which has B&B singles/doubles for £20 per person. *Van Mildert College (☎ 374 3900)* has rooms for £18.

There are a few unpretentious B&Bs starting around £15 per person on Claypath and Gilesgate. Leave the market square from its northern end and cross over the A690 onto Claypath, where you'll find *Country View Guest House (☎ 386 1436)* with rooms for £21/35. Claypath becomes Gilesgate, where *Mrs Koltai (☎ 386 2026)*, at No 10, has three rooms at £15 per person; and *Mr Nimmins (☎ 384 6485)*, at No 14, has two family rooms at the same rate. *Mrs Elliot (☎ 384 1671)*, at No 169, has doubles for £35.

In the town centre, the *Three Tuns Hotel (☎ 386 4326, New Elvet)* is a historic hotel with luxury facilities and singles/doubles from £95/115.

Places to Eat

Most of the eating possibilities are within a short walk of the market square. *Emilio's Ristorante (☎ 384 0096)*, just over the old Elvet Bridge, is good value with pizzas and pastas from £4.95. On the other side of the peninsula, *Pizza Hut* and *Bella Pasta*, on the eastern side of Framwelgate Bridge, have good views over the river; most pizzas are from £5 and pastas £6.

The **Almshouses Café (Palace Green)** serves some simple but very good food. It's open from 9 am to 5 pm and June to September it closes at 8 pm. Choices include salmon, cod and haddock pie with salad (£3.20) and celery soup with roll (£2.45).

Rajpooth (☎ 3861496, 80 Claypath) has a good reputation for Indian food; £4.50 for four-course lunch and £5 to £7 for curries.

Entertainment

It's worth checking what's going on; a half an hour walk will give you an idea and the TIC has a list of pub entertainment. There are a couple of pubs on Gilesgate, including the pleasant **Travellers Rest**. **O'Neills**, on Claypath, is an Irish pub with live music (not always Irish). There are a couple of rowdy possibilities on the western side of Framwelgate including the **Coach & Eight**. The **Swan & Three Cygnets**, Old Elvet Bridge, is a bright riverside pub with tables overlooking the river and good bar food.

Getting There & Away

See the fares tables in the Getting Around chapter. Durham is 260 miles from London, 75 miles from Leeds and 15 miles from Newcastle upon Tyne.

Bus There are five National Express (☎ 0990-808080) buses a day to London (4½ hours), three to Edinburgh (five hours), and numerous buses to/from Birmingham (5¾ hours) and Newcastle upon Tyne (50 minutes). There's one bus a day (No 370) between Durham and Edinburgh via Jedburgh and Melrose in the Scottish Borders.

Primrose Coaches (☎ 232 5567) has a daily service between Newcastle upon Tyne and Blackpool via Durham, Barnard Castle, Raby Castle and Kirkby Stephen (No X69). It leaves Durham from the Sutton St bus stop.

Train There are numerous trains to York (one hour, £17.50), many of which continue to London (three hours, £70.15) via Peterborough (for Cambridge). Frequent trains from London continue through to Edinburgh (three hours).

Getting Around

Taxi Pratt's Taxis (☎ 386 0700) charge a minimum of about £1.80.

Bicycle Contact Cycle Force (☎ 384 0319) at 29 Claypath.

BEAMISH OPEN AIR MUSEUM

Beamish (☎ 01207-231811) was founded on the ruins of Durham's coal industry; overheard from a grizzled ex-miner sitting in the sun at the entrance waiting for his grandchildren to return, 'Spent half my life down a pit. No way am I going to pay seven quid to go down one again!'

Visitors can go underground, and explore mine heads, a working farm, cottages, a school, a pub and shops.

Beamish opens April to October daily from 10 am to 5 pm (until 6 pm from late July to early September and 4 pm in winter). Allow a minimum of two hours to do the place justice. Ticket prices range from £3/2 in winter to £8/5 in summer.

Beamish is about 8 miles north-west of Durham; it's signposted from the A1 (take the A691 west). Bus Nos 709, 720, 775 and 778 run to the museum. Late July to early September, a special Sunday bus service runs between Durham train station and Beamish (No X79, half an hour).

BARNARD CASTLE
• pop 6070   ☎ 01833

Barnard Castle isn't as self-contained and picturesque as Richmond, but it's still an attractive market town, and it makes a good base for exploring Teesdale and the northern Pennines. The TIC (☎ 630272/690909), Flats Rd, opens daily year round.

The ruins of Barnard Castle (☎ 638212, EH), on the banks of the Tees, cover almost six acres and testify to its importance; it was founded by Guy de Bailleul and rebuilt by his nephew around 1150; £2/1.50.

Housed in a wholly unexpected 19th century French château 1½ miles west of town, **Bowes Museum** (☎ 690606) contains a magnificent collection of artworks, including paintings by El Greco and Goya. A prime exhibit is the 18th century mechanical silver swan in the hall; ask when you can see it in operation. At present the museum opens daily from 10 am to 5.30 pm (Sunday from 2 to 5.30 pm), but may close (at least temporarily) through lack of funding. Admission is £3/2.

Accommodation can be hard to find in summer, so the TIC's accommodation-booking service can be particularly useful. *Mrs Wilkinson (☎ 631383, 2 Wesley Terrace)* has a single and double from £15 per person. The *Old Well* pub *(☎ 690130, 21 The Bank)* is downhill from the Market Cross, which also has interesting food, has doubles with bathroom for £50.

Primrose Coaches (☎ 0191-232 5567) has a daily service between Newcastle upon Tyne and Blackpool via Durham, Barnard Castle, Raby Castle and Kirkby Stephen (Nos X79/71). United (☎ 0191-384 3323) has four services Monday to Saturday to/from Durham (via Bishop Auckland and Raby Castle). Go OK (☎ 0845 606 0260) has regular buses to Bishop Auckland.

AROUND BARNARD CASTLE

A mile south of Barnard Castle, the ruins of Egglestone Abbey are on a lovely bend of the Tees. The countryside around Barnard Castle is beautiful, especially **Teesdale** to the north-west. In particular, **High Force** waterfall, where the River Tees jumps 15m, is considered one of the best in Britain. There are a number of popular walks, including several sections of the Pennine Way.

Raby Castle

Raby Castle (☎ 660202) is a romantic-looking 14th century castle, a stronghold of the Neville family until the Rising of the North. Most of the interior has been substantially altered, but the exterior remains true to the original design, built around a courtyard and surrounded by a moat. The castle and its beautiful grounds open May and June, Wednesday and Sunday from 1 to

---

The Rising of the North

Barnard Castle played its most important role in 1569 during the reign of Elizabeth I. The Percys (Earls of Northumberland) and the Nevilles (Earls of Westmoreland) plotted at nearby Raby Castle to release Mary Queen of Scots from Bolton Castle in Wensleydale, where she was imprisoned, place her on the throne and restore Roman Catholicism.

Sir George Bowes remained loyal to Elizabeth, however, and he and other loyalists held Barnard Castle. On 2 December, 5000 rebels besieged Barnard. On 8 December, the walls were breached and Bowes retreated to the Inner Ward. On 12 December, Bowes was finally forced to surrender, but the delay had allowed the Earl of Sussex to assemble his forces at York and the rebels were defeated.

---

5 pm, and July to September, Sunday to Friday from 1 to 5 pm; £4/1.50. It's 6 miles north-east of Barnard Castle off the A688 (see Barnard Castle for bus transport).

NEWCASTLE UPON TYNE
• **pop 210,000 ☎ 0191**

Newcastle is the largest city in the northeast. It grew famous as a coal-exporting port, and in the 19th century became an important steel, shipbuilding and engineering centre – all industries that went into serious decline after WWII. It had a dour struggle to survive, but retains some 19th century grandeur, and the famous six bridges across the Tyne are an arresting sight.

There are no major tourist attractions, although both St Nicholas' Cathedral and Castle Garth are worth visiting.

Orientation

Although Newcastle is dauntingly large, the city centre is easy to get around on foot, and the Metro (convenient for the hostel and B&Bs) is cheap, efficient and pleasant to use.

NORTH-EASTERN ENGLAND

NORTH-EASTERN ENGLAND

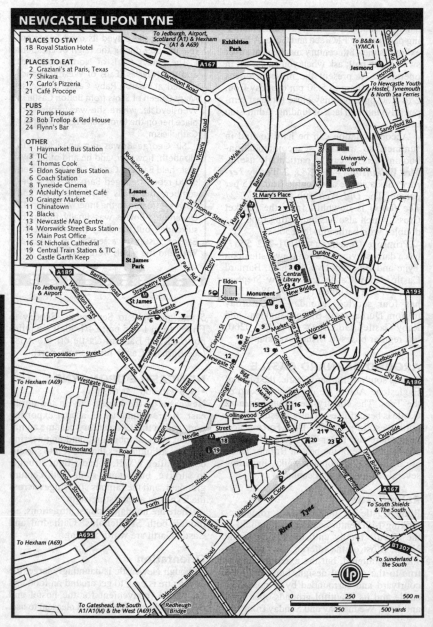

NEWCASTLE UPON TYNE

PLACES TO STAY
18 Royal Station Hotel

PLACES TO EAT
2 Graziani's at Paris, Texas
7 Shikara
17 Carlo's Pizzeria
21 Café Procope

PUBS
22 Pump House
23 Bob Trollop & Red House
24 Flynn's Bar

OTHER
1 Haymarket Bus Station
3 TIC
4 Thomas Cook
5 Eldon Square Bus Station
6 Coach Station
8 Tyneside Cinema
9 McNulty's Internet Café
10 Grainger Market
11 Chinatown
12 Blacks
13 Newcastle Map Centre
14 Worswick Street Bus Station
15 Main Post Office
16 St Nicholas Cathedral
19 Central Train Station & TIC
20 Castle Garth Keep

The Central train station is just to the south of the city centre. The coach station is on Gallowgate. Local buses leave from Eldon Square, buses for the north leave from Haymarket, and buses for Beamish leave from Worswick St.

Information

The convenient train station TIC (☎ 230 0030) opens October to May, Monday to Saturday from 10 am to 5 pm; and June to September, Monday to Friday to 8 pm, Saturday from 9 am to 5 pm, Sunday from 10 am to 4 pm. There is also a main office (☎ 261 0610) in the Central Library and a desk at the airport. They all have a free map, guide and accommodation list and a free booking service.

Thomas Cook (☎ 261 2163) has an office on the corner of Northumberland St and New Bridge. Blacks (☎ 261 8613), the outdoor equipment chain, has a shop at 81-83 Grainger St and The Newcastle Map Centre (☎ 261 5622), 55 Grey St, has a good supply of maps and guides.

You can eat and surf the Net at McNulty's Internet Café (☎ 232 0922), 26-30 Market St, which offers special packages for tourists.

Castle Garth Keep

Castle Garth is the 'new' castle from which the city gets its name. The original was built in wood, but the current construction dates from 1168. It is a fine example of a square keep, with good views and some interesting displays on the history of the city. Open daily (except Mondays) from 9.30 am to 5.30 pm from April to September; to 4.30 pm the rest of the year; £1.50/50p.

Tyne Bridges & Sightseeing Cruises

The most famous view in Newcastle is of the six bridges over the Tyne, and the most famous of the bridges is the **Tyne Bridge**, built in 1925-28, about the same time as, and reminiscent of, Sydney Harbour Bridge in Australia. Perhaps the most interesting is the **Swing Bridge**, which pivots in the middle. The **High Level Bridge**, designed by Robert Stephenson, was the world's first road and railway bridge and was opened in 1849.

Sightseeing cruises run from Quayside pier May to early September Sundays at 2 pm. They last three hours and cost £7/5.

Markets

When it opened in the 1830s **Grainger Market**, in a magnificent building on Grainger St, was Europe's largest undercover shopping centre, a position now claimed by the MetroCentre. It mainly sells fruit and vegetables, but there are other interesting stalls, including the Marks & Spencer Original Penny Bazaar. **Quayside Market**, a popular flea market, is held beneath the Tyne Bridge on Sunday from 9 am to 2.30 pm. **Bigg Market** is held in the street of the same name on Tuesday, Thursday and Saturday.

Jarrow

The eastern suburb of Jarrow is embedded in labour history for the 'Jarrow Crusade' in 1936, when 200 men set out to walk all the way to London to protest against the appalling conditions brought about by unemployment.

Today's visitors to this grim district might think little has changed. However, Jarrow is also famous as the home of the Venerable Bede (author of the *History of the English People*), and parts of St Paul's Church date back to the seventh century. Together with a museum and Jarrow Hall, it forms part of **Bede's World** (☎ 489 2106), a park with many reconstructed medieval buildings. It's open April to October, Tuesday to Saturday from 10 am to 5.30 pm, Sunday from noon to 5.30 pm, and November to March Tuesday to Saturday from 11 am to 4.30 pm, Sunday from 2.30 to 5.30 pm. Admission is £3/1.50. Jarrow and Bede's World are accessible via the Metro.

Places to Stay

Camping The nearest sites in South Shields are *Sandhaven* (☎ 454 5594, *Bents Park Rd*), where sites are £6.20 and *Lizard*

Lane (☎ *454 4982, Marsden*), where sites are £5.70 for a two person tent.

Hostel The *Newcastle Youth Hostel* (☎ *281 2570, 107 Jesmond Rd*), north of the city centre, opens February to November (and other times); £8.80/5.95 for adults/ juniors. Call in advance, as it can be busy.

North East YMCA (☎ *281 1233, Jesmond House, Clayton Rd*) accepts male and female guests at £16.50 per person. Turn left on Osborne Rd from Jesmond station and take the second street on the right.

B&Bs & Hotels A lot of places have cheaper rates at weekends. There are quite a number of B&Bs along Osborne Rd. To get there, catch the Metro to Jesmond station, or catch bus Nos 33/33B from Central train station, Grainger St or the corner of New Bridge and Pilgrim St.

Beside Central station, the impressive *Royal Station Hotel* (☎ *232 0781, Neville St*) has rooms from £60/72, as well as cheaper weekend deals.

Osborne Rd has the greatest concentration of B&Bs. At the top end, the *Cairn Hotel* (☎ *281 1358*), at No 97, is a large four-star hotel with rooms from £57/72, dropping by £20 on weekends.

Mere mortals hunting on Osborne Rd should consider the *Gresham Hotel* (☎ *281 4341*), at No 92, a medium-sized, comfortable hotel from £24/34, although at that price in Newcastle you still share a bathroom. The *Minerva Hotel* (☎ *281 0190*), at No 105, is a small place with decent prices; £21.50/35.

Fern Ave is the fifth street on the right if you head down Osborne Rd from Jesmond station. *Gowan Hotel* (☎ *281 3129*), at No 88, is an attractive terraced house with a number of rooms at £22.50/35. The *Adelphi Hotel* (☎ *281 3109*), at No 63, is similar. *Westland Hotel* (☎ *281 0412, 27 Osborne Ave, off Osborne Rd*) has 15 rooms from £22.50/42 a single/double.

Places to Eat

Newcastle has a most un-English attitude to food. Geordies believe in going out to eat

and they believe the food should be cheap. As a result, Newcastle has a remarkable number of good restaurants. Many places have 'happy hours' early in the evening when you can often get cheap specials.

Restaurants are widely scattered. There are some at the northern end of town (handy for the university and the youth hostel), and Chinatown is on Stowell St to the west of Eldon Square. Perhaps the most interesting zone to explore, however, is south of the city centre. Walk south down Grey St (lined with beautiful Georgian and Victorian offices), which becomes Dean St and takes you down to the River Tyne and Quayside.

On Grey St itself, *Carlo's Pizzeria* (☎ *233 2300*) is reasonable value, with pizzas and pastas at around £5. *Café Procope* (☎ *232 3848, 35 The Side*) has an imaginative modern menu, with plenty of vegetarian dishes, with prices £8 to £10.

There are a number of interesting pubs at the bottom of the hill. *Flynns Bar* (*63 Quayside*) has a beer garden and cheap food and drink, but check out the *Pump House*, *Bob Trollop* and *Red House* which have pub meals for about £3.

At the other end of town, *Graziani's at Paris, Texas* (☎ *261 5084, St Mary's Place*) is a lively rock café with pizzas and pastas under £5 and even better specials before 7 pm and at lunch time.

One of the most acclaimed restaurants is *Shikara* (☎ *233 0005, 52 St Andrew's St*), serving excellent Indian food; it's cheap for lunch, most mains in the evening costing £6 to £10. There are more Indian restaurants in Dean St.

Entertainment

Newcastle caters to most tastes, with high culture and low. On weekends young people come from other parts of the country to enjoy Newcastle's nightlife. There are a number of guides to what's on: *Paint it Red* and *the crack* (free), and the *Evening Chronicle* on Wednesday.

The Royal Shakespeare Company is a regular visitor to the superb *Theatre Royal* (☎ *232 0997, 100 Grey St*) but there are also fringe companies like the *Live Theatre* (☎ *232 1232, 27 Broad Chare, Quayside*). *Tyneside Cinema* (☎ *232 8289, 10 Pilgrim St*) is worth checking out.

Geordies take going out, drinking beer and dancing seriously (though not necessarily in that order). The Bigg Market area is notorious for the crowds of young people it attracts – especially on Friday nights when groups of scantily-clad young women and increasingly drunken young men circulate the street ogling each other. Be prepared for queues, thick-necked bouncers and infuriating dress codes – runners or sneakers will be out, and some places insist on a collar and tie.

The pubs and clubs around Quayside are more relaxed. The *Cooperage* (☎ *232 8286, 32 The Close, Quayside*) is a popular with a wide-ranging clientele; £3.50 admission. In Waterloo St, *Rockshots II* (☎ *232 9648*) is free and *Powerhouse Nightclub* (☎ *261 4507*) is a gay and lesbian venue.

Things to Buy
Shopaholics might be tempted by the Metro-Centre at Gateshead, an enormous shopping centre – the largest in Europe – with 350 shops, 50 places to eat (mostly fast food) and fairground rides. Eldon Square shopping centre in Newcastle itself is another enormous modern shrine to consumerism. Needless to say, the markets like old Grainger Market are *much* more interesting.

Getting There & Away
Newcastle is 275 miles from London (about five hours by car), 105 miles from Edinburgh (about 2½ hours), 57 miles from Carlisle, 35 miles from Alnwick and 15 miles from Durham. It's a major transport hub, so travellers have many options, including air and sea links.

Air Newcastle international airport (☎ 286 0966) is 7 miles north of the city, linked by the Metro and 20 minutes by car off the A696. There are direct scheduled services to Aberdeen, London, Cardiff, Dublin, Belfast, Oslo, Amsterdam, Paris and Brussels. The standard one way fare to London is £126.

Bus There are numerous National Express connections with virtually every major city in the country. There are buses every two hours to London (5¼ hours, £15) and Edinburgh (3¼ hours, £7.50), and a number of buses each day from York (2¼ hours, £12).

For local buses around the north-east, don't forget the excellent-value Explorer North East ticket, valid on most services. Northumbria Buses (☎ 212 3000) has details on services to Berwick-upon-Tweed (No 501) and along Hadrian's Wall (No 685); see the appropriate sections.

April to September, Keswick can be reached with Wright Brothers' (☎ 01670-533128) daily No 888 service.

Train Newcastle is on the main London-Edinburgh line so there are numerous trains; Edinburgh (1¾ hours), London's King's Cross (four hours), York (1¼ hours). Berwick-upon-Tweed and Alnmouth (for Alnwick) are north on this line.

There's also the interesting, scenic Tyne Valley Line west to Carlisle. See the Hadrian's Wall section.

Boat See the Getting There & Away chapters for details of ferry links to Stavanger and Bergen in Norway, Gothenburg (Sweden) and Hamburg (Germany).

Getting Around
There's a large bus network but the best means of getting around is the excellent, cheap, underground railway known as the Metro, with fares from 50p. A DaySaver ticket is £2.80 or you can get a day Network Travel Ticket, covering all modes of transport, for £3.60. For advice and information ring the travel line (☎ 232 5325).

Driving in and around Newcastle isn't fun thanks to the web of roads and motorways, the bridges and the one-way streets in the centre – avoid peak hours.

To/From the Airport The airport is linked to town by the excellent Metro system. There are frequent services daily, and the cost is £1.60.

NORTH-EASTERN ENGLAND

To/From the Ferry Terminal Bus No 327 links the ferry (at Tyne Commission Quay), the central train station and Jesmond Rd (for the youth hostel and B&Bs). It leaves the train station 2½ and 1¼ hours before each sailing; £2.75/1.50.

There's a taxi rank at the terminal; £10.

Taxi Taxis can be hard to come by on weekend nights; try Noda Taxis (☎ 222 1888 or ☎ 232 7777), which has a kiosk outside the entrance to Central station.

Northumberland

Taking its name from the Anglo-Saxon kingdom of Northumbria (north of the River Humber), Northumberland is one of the wildest, least spoilt of England's counties. There are probably more castles and battle-field sites here than anywhere else in England, testifying to the long, bloody struggle with the Scots.

The Romans were the first to attempt to draw a line separating north from south: Hadrian's Wall, stretching 73 miles from Newcastle upon Tyne to Bowness-on-Solway near Carlisle, was the northern frontier of the empire for almost 300 years. It was abandoned around 410, but enough remains to bring the past dramatically alive.

After the arrival of the Normans, large numbers of castles and fortified houses, or *peles*, were built. Many changed hands several times as the Scottish border was pushed back and forth for the next 700 years. Most have now lapsed into peaceful ruin, but others, like Bamburgh and Alnwick, were converted into great houses, which can be visited today.

Northumberland National Park lies north of Hadrian's Wall, incorporating the open, sparsely populated Cheviot Hills. The walks cross some of the loneliest parts of England and can be challenging. The most interesting part of Hadrian's Wall is also in-cluded (along the southern boundary) – see the Hadrian's Wall section.

GETTING AROUND

The excellent *Northumberland Public Trans-port Guide* is available from local TICs or from the Section Manager Public Transport (☎ 01670-533128), Northumberland County Council, County Hall, Morpeth NE61 2EF. Transport options tend to be sparse, with the exception of the link between Carlisle and Newcastle and along the east coast to Berwick-upon-Tweed. The principal operator is Northumbria Buses (☎ 0191-212 3000) and there are many other smaller operators.

WARKWORTH
☎ 01665

Warkworth is a picturesque small village beneath the formidable remains of a 14th century castle and set in a loop of the River Cocquet. Of interest are the impressive ruins of **Warkworth Castle** (☎ 711423, EH); £2.20/1.10.

The village has a number of B&Bs, in-cluding *Bide a While* (☎ *711753, 4 Beal Croft)*, with rooms for £17.50 per person and *Roxbro House* (☎ *711416, 5 Castle Terrace)*, for £18/35 a single/double.

Warkworth is served by Northumbria Buses (☎ 0191-212 3000) bus No X18 linking Newcastle upon Tyne, Warkworth, Alnmouth and Alnwick. There's a train station on the main east-coast line, about 1½ miles west of town.

ALNWICK
• pop 7000   ☎ 01665

Alnwick (pronounced annick) is a charming market town that has grown up in the shadow of magnificent Alnwick Castle. The attrac-tive old town still has a medieval feel with narrow, cobbled streets and a market square.

The castle is on the northern side of town and overlooks the River Aln. The TIC (☎ 510665), at The Shambles, the tradition-al location for butchers' stalls, adjacent to the market, opens Monday to Saturday from 9 am to 5 pm, Sunday from 10 am to 4 pm.

Alnwick Castle

Outwardly the castle hasn't changed much since the 14th century, but the interior has been substantially altered, most recently in the 19th century. If you enjoy castles, don't miss this one.

The six rooms open to the public – state rooms, dining room, guard chamber and library – have an incredible display of Italian paintings, including 11 Canalettos and Titian's *Ecce Homo*. There are also some fascinating curiosities, including Oliver Cromwell's camp pillow and night cap, and a hairnet used by Mary Queen of Scots which is actually made from her hair!

The castle (☎ 510777) opens Easter to September, Saturday to Thursday from 11 am to 5 pm; £5.95/3.50. For a great view back to the castle, looking up the River Aln, take the B1340 towards the coast.

Places to Stay & Eat

Aln House (☎ 602265, South Rd, the A1 Newcastle road), near the roundabout, is an Edwardian house with rooms for £18 per person. Bondgate Without, just outside the town's medieval gateway, has several accommodation options. The small *Lindisfarne Guest House (☎ 603430),* at No 6, has rooms for £20 with a vegetarian breakfast option.

The pubs present the best options for a meal; wander around town before making a choice. *Market Tavern (Fenkle St),* near the market square, is friendly and the food is good and generous; poached salmon is £5.50. Nearby, *King's Place (2 Market Place)* is a clean but twee coffee house and restaurant with a wide range of meals from £3 to £6.

Getting There & Away

Alnwick has reasonable transport links since it's on the A1 between Newcastle upon Tyne and Edinburgh. Northumbria Buses (☎ 0191-212 3000) has a number of services linking Newcastle upon Tyne and Berwick-upon-Tweed. Bus No X18 has services to the attractive towns of Warkworth and Alnmouth (also stopping at the train station there, which is the nearest to Alnwick).

FARNE ISLANDS

Owned and managed by the NT, the Farne Islands lie 3 to 4 miles offshore from Sea-

houses. Despite being basically bare rock, they provide a home for 18 species of nesting sea birds, including puffins, kittiwakes, Arctic terns, eider ducks, cormorants and gulls. There are also colonies of grey seals. There are few places in the world where you can get so close to nesting sea birds. It's an extraordinary experience.

St Cuthbert, of Lindisfarne fame, died on the islands in 687, and there's a tiny chapel to him on Inner Farne, where it's possible to land. The best time to go is in the breeding season (roughly May to July), when you can see chicks being fed by their parents.

Crossings can be rough – and may not be possible at all in bad weather. Tours take between two and three hours; inexplicably, they use open boats with no proper cabin, so make sure you've got warm, waterproof clothing if there's a chance of rain.

There are various tours and tour operators. There's really nothing to separate the operators, but it's definitely worth landing on one of the islands – preferably Inner Farne. April to August, tours start at 10 am. A three hour tour around the islands and a landing on Inner Farne costs £7/5; there's an additional £3.90/1.90 fee payable to the NT (if you're not a member).

Tickets are available from booths beside the pier in Seahouses, a couple of miles along the coast from Bamburgh. Operators include W McKay (☎ 01665-721144), Billy Shiel (☎ 01665-720308) and Hanvey & Sons (☎ 01665-720388).

BAMBURGH
☎ 01668

Bamburgh is an unspoilt hamlet just inland from miles of magnificent sandy beaches, and dominated by the romantic profile of an enormous castle.

Bamburgh Castle

This fortress, impressive-looking by day but even more so by night, sits on a basalt crag rising from the sea and dominates the coast for miles. The site has been occupied since prehistoric times, but the current castle is largely a 19th century construction and isn't particularly interesting inside. The castle (☎ 214515) opens April to October daily from 11 am to 5 pm; £3/1.50, plus 70p to park your car.

Places to Stay

Bradford Caims Caravan Park (☎ 214366) has grass pitches and all mod cons, including showers and laundrette. The price of a pitch varies according to the season from £7 to £8. *Burton Hall* (☎ 214213) is open year round and offers B&B for £18 per person.

Getting There & Away

Northumbria's bus No 501 runs from Alnwick to Berwick-upon-Tweed via Seahouses and Bamburgh; Monday to Saturday there are three services a day. Bus No 401 from Alnwick stops in Bamburgh.

HOLY ISLAND (LINDISFARNE)

The most exciting part of Holy Island (or Lindisfarne as it was once known) is the drive from the mainland over a causeway that crosses 3 miles of fascinating muddy flats. Even in the off season, the windswept 2 mile square island is full of tourists but seems to have few facilities for them.

St Aidan founded a monastery here in 635, and it became a major centre of Christianity and learning. The exquisitely illustrated *Lindisfarne Gospels*, which originated here, can be seen in the British Library. Saint Cuthbert lived on Lindisfarne for a while, but even he didn't like it and went to the Farne Islands after a couple of years.

Lindisfarne Priory (☎ 01289-389200, EH) consists of the remains of the priory's church and the later 13th century St Mary the Virgin Church. The museum next to these shows the remains of the first monastery and how monks used to live. It's open April to October daily from 10 am to 6 pm, closing at 4 pm during the winter; £2.70/1.40.

Lindisfarne Castle (☎ 01289-389244, NT) was built in 1550, and restored and converted by Sir Edward Lutyens in 1903. Note that it is half a mile from the village, and

there's no toilet. It's open April to October, Saturday to Thursday from 1 to 5.30 pm; £4.

It's possible to stay on the island, but try to book. Probably the best bet (of a small selection) is the *Crown & Anchor* pub (☎ 01289-389215), which has reasonable pub meals and B&B from £20 per person. There aren't many other places to eat.

Lindisfarne can be reached by bus No 477 from Berwick-upon-Tweed and is 14 miles from Berwick-upon-Tweed train station. The sea covers the causeway and cuts the island off from the mainland for about five hours each day. Tide times are printed in local papers.

BERWICK-UPON-TWEED
• pop 13,000   ☎ 01289

The stone-built town of Berwick, the northernmost town in England, has a dramatic site flanking the estuary of the River Tweed. The river, often graced with flotillas of swans, is crossed by a low stone bridge (built in 1634), the soaring arches of the railway bridge (1850) and a concrete span for road traffic (1928).

From the 12th to the 15th centuries, Berwick changed hands between the Scots and the English 13 times. This merry-go-round ceased prior to the construction of massive Elizabethan ramparts that still enclose the town centre – although, reflecting geographical realities, the football team still plays in the Scottish League!

Berwick is a great place to explore on foot. There are several small museums, but there's nothing, apart from the walls, that must be seen.

Orientation & Information

The fortified town of Berwick proper is on the northern side of the Tweed; the three bridges link with the suburbs of Tweedmouth, Spittal and Eastcliffe. The town centre is compact and easy to walk around, but some B&Bs are quite far-flung.

The TIC (☎ 330733), Castlegate car park, opens Monday to Saturday from 10 am to 5 pm.

The Walls

Berwick has had two sets of walls: little remains of the first which were built during the reign of Edward II; the ones guarding the town today were begun in 1558 and are still intact. They represented the most advanced military technology of the day and were designed both to house the increasingly effective artillery (in arrow-head shaped bastions) and to withstand it (the walls are low and massively thick).

It's possible to walk virtually the entire length of the walls, and this is a must for visitors. There are some wonderful views and the entire circuit takes about 1½ hours. The TIC has a brochure describing the main sights. Easter to October there are recommended guided tours, Monday to Saturday at 11.15 am, Sunday 2.30 pm (£2.50/free).

Places to Stay

The cheapest B&Bs tend to be south of the river in Tweedmouth, Spittal and Eastcliffe; fortunately there are frequent buses. The B1 runs from the main bus station on Marygate (High St) across the bridge to Tweedmouth, before turning off and heading to Spittal.

Mrs Mary Law (☎ 304454, 4 The Crescent, Spittal) is the last house to the south, but it's a great B&B with views out to sea and a warm welcome; from £15 per person.

There's a group of places on North Rd: *Dervaig* (☎ 307378), at No 1, has two double rooms with bathroom from £20 per person; the friendly, non-smoking *Four North Road* (☎ 306146), at No 4, has clean rooms from £17 per person and large breakfasts.

It's preferable to stay in the centre of town, but it can be hard to find a room. *Alletsa Guest House* (☎ 308199, 66 Ravensdowne) has nine rooms; from £18. Similarly priced is *Wallace House* (☎ 306539, 1 Wallace Green).

The four-star *Berwick Walls Hotel* (☎ 330770, 34 Ravensdowne) provides well-equipped rooms from £20 per person.

Places to Eat

At the time of research *Humble Pie* (☎ 303223), in a lane running off Marygate,

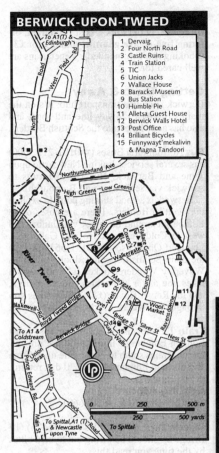

BERWICK-UPON-TWEED

1 Dervaig
2 Four North Road
3 Castle Ruins
4 Train Station
5 TIC
6 Union Jacks
7 Wallace House
8 Barracks Museum
9 Bus Station
10 Humble Pie
11 Alletsa Guest House
12 Berwick Walls Hotel
13 Post Office
14 Brilliant Bicycles
15 Funnywayt'mekalivin
   & Magna Tandoori

was closed for refurbishment but the menu features cheap, simple vegetarian meals.

Union Jacks (☎ 306673, Wallace Green) has a large variety of meals, some with a military name, for around £5.50; the dish called Officers Messroom is chicken in breadcrumbs.

Magna Tandoori (☎ 302736, 39 Bridge St) has good-quality tandoori dishes: most mains are £5.50 to £7, so with a side dish and a beer you should be able to eat for around £10.

Funnywayt'mekalivin (☎ *308827, 41 Bridge St)* is Berwick's best restaurant, offering five-course gourmet dinners for £31 (booking is recommended). Vegetarians are well cared for.

Getting There & Away

Berwick is quite a transport hub; it's on the main east-coast railway line and road, and also has good links into the Scottish Borders.

Bus Northumbria Buses (☎ 0191-212 3000) has several services linking Newcastle upon Tyne and Berwick. Bus No 501 runs to Alnwick via Seahouses and Bamburgh.

Berwick is a good starting point to explore the Scottish Borders. There are buses on to Edinburgh around the coast via Dunbar and west to Coldstream, Kelso and Galashiels. Lowland Omnibuses (☎ 0131-663 1945) is the main Scottish operator; look out for its Waverley Wanderer ticket (£11.50), which takes you as far as Peebles and Edinburgh, and the Reiver Rover (£8), which takes you through the Borders, nearly as far as Carlisle.

Train Berwick is on the main east-coast London-Edinburgh line, and there are numerous trains south to Newcastle upon Tyne and north to Edinburgh (£11.30 day return).

Getting Around

Taxi Try Blue Star (☎ 305660).

Bicycle Brilliant Bicycles (☎ 331476), 17 Bridge St, should be hiring out hybrid bikes by the time you read this.

Hadrian's Wall

Hadrian's Wall was the most monumental attempt in the island's history to divide the north from the south. It cuts 73 miles across the narrow neck of the country, from Solway Firth in the west, virtually to the mouth of the Tyne in the east, through beautiful, varied countryside. It is a World Heritage Site, and although mainly foundations survive, the ruins and their beautiful locations are extraordinarily evocative.

The wall was the greatest single engineering project undertaken by the Roman Empire – it involved moving two million cubic yards of soil and took over six years (from 122) to build.

The section from Newcastle upon Tyne to the River Irthing was built of stone, turf blocks were used on the section to Solway – roughly 10 feet thick and 15 feet high. A 10-foot-deep, 30-foot-wide ditch and mound were excavated immediately in front (except where there were natural defences). Every Roman mile (1620 yards) there was a gateway guarded by a small fort (milecastle) and between each milecastle were two observation turrets. Milecastles are numbered right across the country, starting with Milecastle 0 at Wallsend and ending with Milecastle 80 at Bowness-on-Solway. The intermediate turrets are tagged A and B, so Milecastle 37 (quite a good one) will be followed by Turret 37A, Turret 37B and then Milecastle 38. A second ditch (the vallum) and a military road were built between 200 and 500 feet to the south.

A series of forts were developed as bases some distance south (and may actually predate the wall), and 16 actually lay astride it. The prime remaining forts on the wall are Cilurnum (Chesters), Vercovicium (Housestead) and Banna (Birdoswald). The best forts behind the wall are Corstopitum, at Corbridge, and Vindolanda, at Chesterholm.

Today it's possible to visit a number of picturesque surviving sections of the wall, milecastles, forts and turrets, and some excellent museums. Several attractive small towns make good touring bases.

HISTORY

By building the wall, Emperor Hadrian intended simultaneously to establish control over a clearly delineated frontier and reduce the demand on manpower. He came to Britain in 122 to see it started, and the actual building was undertaken by Roman legions. The wall was primarily a means of controlling the movement of people across the frontier – it could easily have been breached by a determined attack at any single point – and of preventing low-level border raiding.

No one knows when the troops finally abandoned their posts; it's most likely that around 400 AD Britain was simply set adrift as the Roman Empire fragmented. When pay stopped arriving the soldiers remaining on the wall would simply have left for greener pastures.

ORIENTATION

Hadrian's Wall crosses beautiful, varied country. Starting in the lowlands of the Solway coast, it crosses the lush hills east of Carlisle to the ridge of basalt rock known as Whin Sill (which is bleak and windy, still) overlooking Northumberland National Park, and ends in the urban sprawl of Newcastle upon Tyne. The most spectacular section is between Brampton and Corbridge.

Carlisle, in the west, and Newcastle upon Tyne, in the east, are good starting points, but Brampton, Haltwhistle, Hexham and Corbridge all make good bases.

The B6318 basically follows the course of the wall from the outskirts of Newcastle upon Tyne to Birdoswald; from Birdoswald to Carlisle it pays to have a detailed map. The main A69 road and the railway line follow 3 or 4 miles to the south.

INFORMATION

Carlisle and Newcastle upon Tyne TICs are good places to start gathering information, but there are also TICs in Hexham and Haltwhistle open all year, and in Corbridge and Brampton open seasonally. The Northumberland National Park Visitor Centre (☎ 01434-344396) off the B6318 at Once Brewed, opens daily mid-March to October from 9.30 am to 5 pm.

See the Activities chapter for information on walking Hadrian's Wall.

PLACES TO STAY & EAT

See the Newcastle upon Tyne and Carlisle sections. Brampton and Corbridge are the most attractive small towns close to the wall, but Haltwhistle is also convenient, and

bustling Hexham is another good possibility. All have plentiful B&Bs. There are also three usefully placed youth hostels (book in summer): Greenhead, Once Brewed and Acomb.

GETTING THERE & AROUND
Bus

West of Hexham the wall runs parallel to the A69, between Carlisle and Newcastle upon Tyne. Bus No 685, operated jointly by Northumbria (☎ 0191-212 3000) and Stagecoach Cumberland (☎ 01946-63222), runs between those cities on the A69 hourly. It passes relatively near the youth hostels and 2 to 3 miles south of the main sites.

Late May to September the special hail-and-ride Hadrian's Wall Bus (No 682) runs between Hexham and Haltwhistle train stations, connecting with trains. It follows the B6318, which runs close to the wall, calling at the main sites, and the Northumberland National Park Visitor Centre and youth hostel at Once Brewed. This puts the youth hostels at Acomb and Greenhead within easy reach. For further information contact Hexham TIC (☎ 01434-605225).

Explorer tickets on all theses services cost £4.95/3.75.

The easy option is to take a tour from Carlisle, where the TIC (☎ 01228-512444) organises coach tours.

Train

The railway line between Newcastle upon Tyne and Carlisle has stations at Corbridge, Hexham, Haydon Bridge, Bardon Mill, Haltwhistle and Brampton. This service runs daily, but not all trains stop at all stations.

Taxi

Henshaw Garage (☎ 01434-344272) operates a Hadrian's Wall taxi service from Bardon Mill to most sites in the area – Bardon Mill to Housesteads is £7 each way. Sproul's (☎ 01434-321064) in Haltwhistle has a similar service.

CORBRIDGE

* pop 3500   ☎ 01434

Corbridge vies with Brampton as the most attractive town near the wall. It's on the banks of a beautiful stretch of the River Tyne, 17 miles west of Newcastle upon Tyne, and has attractive stone houses (some very old) lining tree-shaded cobbled streets. It has an ancient history beginning with the Romans. An Anglo-Saxon monastery followed and the town thrived despite being burnt three times in border clashes.

St Andrew's Church, mostly rebuilt in the 13th century but with some Anglo-Saxon features, also has a fascinating 14th century pele tower (a fortified vicarage) in its grounds. The TIC (☎ 632815), Hill St, opens April to September, Monday to Saturday from 10 am to 1 pm and from 2 to 6 pm, Sunday from 1 to 5 pm.

Corbridge Roman Site & Museum

Corbridge (or Corstopitum to the Romans) was a garrison town. There were a succession of forts and supply depots, and a surrounding civil settlement. It lies south of the wall on what was the main road from York to Scotland.

The site (☎ 632349, EH) is half a mile west of Corbridge off Trinity Terrace (just over a mile from Corbridge train station). Open April to October daily from 10 am to 6 pm, November to March daily from 10 am to 4 pm; £2.70/1.40.

Places to Stay & Eat

There are several attractive hotels, most with rooms and bar meals. The 17th century *Angel Inn* (☎ 632119), on the main street, has comfortable rooms with bathroom for £42 per person. *Holmlea* (☎ 01434-632486, *Station Rd*) near the station, is a terraced house with a comfortable double and family room from £18 per person. *Town Barns* (☎ 633345), off Trinity Terrace, offers a single, a double and a family room for £20 per person.

The pubs are probably your best bet for food. The *Angel Inn* serves good, quite adventurous food and offers three-course meals for £12. The *Golden Lion (Hill St)* is cheaper with filling meals for under £4. You could also try *Corbridge Tandoori*, on the central square, where mains are £5.40 to £7.50.

Getting There & Away

Bus No 685 between Newcastle upon Tyne and Carlisle comes through Corbridge, as does bus No 602 from Newcastle upon Tyne's Eldon Square to Hexham. The town is also on the Newcastle-Carlisle railway line.

HEXHAM

* pop 11,300   ☎ 01434

Hexham is quite an interesting town, but is rather marred by being a busy shopping centre. The TIC (☎ 605225), Hallgate, opens mid-May to September, Monday to Saturday from 9 am to 6 pm, Sunday from 10 am to 5 pm, and the rest of the year Monday to Saturday from 9 am to 5 pm.

Hexham Abbey, surrounded by a park, is considered a fine example of Early English architecture. The crypt survives from St Wilfrid's Church, which was built in 674, and inscribed stones from Corstopitum can be seen in its walls.

Hexham's size means it's the best place near the wall for accommodation and places to eat. *West Close House* (☎ 603307, *Hextol Terrace*), off Allendale Rd (the B6305), has a range of comfortable rooms from £18 per person. The *Beaumont Hotel* (☎ 602331, *Beaumont St*) overlooks the abbey and has high-quality accommodation from £45 per person.

There are several bakeries on Fore St and, if you turn left into the quaintly named Priestpopple near the bus station, you'll find some decent restaurants. Possibilities include *Restaurant Fortini*, with pizza and pasta from £4.40, and next door, the *Coach & Horses*, a pleasant pub with a beer garden and bar meals from £4.25. Across the road, *Diwan-E-Am Tandoori* has mains for £4.60 to £8.

Bus No 685 between Newcastle upon Tyne and Carlisle comes through Hexham, and the town is also on the Newcastle-Carlisle railway line.

HEXHAM TO HALTWHISTLE
Chesters Roman Fort & Museum

Chesters (☎ 01434-681379, EH) is even more extensive and well preserved than Housesteads, but although the surroundings are attractive, they're not as dramatic as the latter's. The remains are of a Roman cavalry fort and include part of a bridge across the River North Tyne (very complex and beautifully constructed), an extraordinary bathhouse and a well-preserved under-floor heating system. The museum has an extensive collection of Roman sculpture and stone inscriptions. Open April to October daily from 10 am to 6 pm, November to March daily from 10 am to 4 pm; £2.70/1.40.

Chesters is half a mile west of Chollerford on the B6318 and 5½ miles from Hexham.

Brunton Water Mill (☎ *01434-681002, Chollerford*) is just a stone's throw from Chollerford bridge and B&B costs from £20 per person. At the much pricier but pleasant *George Hotel* (☎ *01434-681611*), beside the bridge, B&B costs from £80/110. The Chesters fort site has an excellent small café, *Lucullus Larder*, and the George Hotel has a restaurant.

Housesteads Roman Fort & Museum

Perched high on a ridge overlooking the moors of Northumberland National Park, Housesteads (☎ 01434-344396, EH) is one of the best known, best preserved and most dramatic of the sites on the wall. The fort covers five acres and the remains of many buildings, including granaries, barracks, latrines and a hospital, can be seen. This is the starting point for some excellent walks and the one to Steel Rigg is considered the most spectacular section of the entire wall.

Housesteads is 2½ miles north of Bardon Mill on the B6318, and about 3 miles from Once Brewed. It's popular, so try to visit outside summer weekends. It opens April to September daily from 10 am to 6 pm,

October to March daily from 10 am to 4 pm; £2.50/1.90.

Vindolanda Roman Fort & Museum

Vindolanda (☎ 01434-344277), 1½ miles north of Bardon Mill between the A69 and B6318 and a mile from Once Brewed, is an extensively excavated fort (excavations are still continuing) with accompanying civil buildings. There are reconstructions of the stone wall with a turret, a length of turf wall and a timber milecastle gate. The museum has some extraordinary relics, including a leather shoe and a fragment of a letter on a wooden writing tablet that talks of socks and underclothes being sent to a soldier on the wall. Nothing has changed: in this climate you can never have too many.

It's managed by the Vindolanda Trust and opens daily at 10 am but closes at different times during the year: March and October at 5 pm, April and September at 5.30 pm, May and June at 6 pm, July and August at 6.30 pm and November to February at 4 pm. Entry is £3.50/2.50 or £5.25/3.65 with a joint ticket for the Roman Army Museum (see Haltwhistle to Brampton later).

Hostels

Once Brewed Youth Hostel (☎ *01434-344360, Military Rd, Bardon Mill*) is a modern, well equipped hostel central for both Housesteads Fort (3 miles) and Vindolanda (1 mile). Northumbria bus No 685 (which you can catch at Hexham or Haltwhistle train stations) will drop you at Henshaw, 2 miles south, or you could leave the train at Bardon Mill 2½ miles southeast. It's open daily April to October, weekdays only in November, February and March; £9.75 for adults.

Acomb Youth Hostel (☎ *01434-602864, Main St*) is on the edge of Acomb village about 2½ miles north of Hexham and 2 miles south of the wall. Hexham can be reached by bus or train. It's open mid-March to mid-July, September and October, Tuesday to Sunday, and daily from mid-July to August; £5.85/4.

Set in 18 acres of countryside, *Hadrian's Wall Backpackers* (☎ *01434-688688, North Rd, Haydon Bridge*) is just north of the A69, and is accessible by bus or train. Dorm beds cost £8, or £12.50 with breakfast. It's open daily April to October.

HALTWHISTLE
* pop 3750   ☎ 01434

Haltwhistle, just north of the A69, is a small market town that straggles some distance along Main St. It's a pleasant enough place, but doesn't have quite the charm of either Brampton or Corbridge.

The TIC (☎ 322002), at the train station, opens in April from Monday to Saturday from 10 am to 5 pm, Sunday from 1 to 5 pm; mid-May to October, Monday to Saturday from 10 am to 6 pm, Sunday from 1 to 6 pm; November to March, Monday to Friday from 10 am to 3.30 pm.

Ashcroft (☎ *320213, Lanty's Lonnen*) is an attractive B&B with rooms from £16 to £25 per person. *Hall Meadows* (☎ *321021, Main St*) in the centre of town, charges £15 to £16. *Manor House Hotel* (☎ *322588, Main St*) is central, very friendly and has good pub food; B&B starts at £12.50 per person and goes up to £20 per person.

Bus No 685 between Newcastle upon Tyne and Carlisle comes through Haltwhistle, as does Hadrian's Wall bus Nos 682 and 890. The town is also on the Newcastle-Carlisle railway line. Local taxi services include Turnbull's (☎ 320105) and Sproul's (☎ 321064).

HALTWHISTLE TO BRAMPTON
Roman Army Museum
One mile north-west of Greenhead near Walltown, the museum (☎ 016977-47485) has models and reconstructions featuring the Roman army and the troops that garrisoned the wall. Children will enjoy it. It's open the same hours as Vindolanda Fort & Museum. Entry is £2.80/1.90, or £5.25/3.65 if you have a joint ticket with Vindolanda.

Birdoswald Roman Fort
Birdoswald (☎ 016977-47602, EH) is one of the most interesting of the ruins along the wall, with a well-preserved fort on an escarpment overlooking the beautiful Irthing Gorge. The Willowford bridge abutment, across the river, is worth seeing. There's also a good stretch of wall and a new exhibition centre is being built. It's on a minor road off the B6318 about 3 miles west of Greenhead. It's open daily Easter to October from 10 am to 5.30 pm; £1.95/1.

Places to Stay
Greenhead and nearby Gilsland have pubs and B&Bs. *Greenhead Youth Hostel* (☎ *016977-47401*) is in a converted Methodist chapel 3 miles west of Haltwhistle train station. It's also served by Northumbria's bus No 685 (see the Hadrian's Wall introductory Getting There & Around section for this and other transport possibilities). It's open April to June Monday to Saturday, July and August daily, September to mid-December Thursday to Tuesday (also other times); £7.20/4.95.

BRAMPTON
☎ 016977

Brampton is a charming market town built in the red Cumbrian sandstone and surrounded by beautiful countryside. The town is particularly interesting on market day (Wednesday). It would make a great base for exploring Hadrian's Wall, and it's on the Cumbrian Cycle Way.

The TIC (☎ 3433) opens Easter to October, Monday to Friday from 10 am to 5 pm, Saturday from 9.30 am to 5 pm.

The *White Lion Hotel* (☎ *2338, High Cross St*) is one of several pubs serving good bar meals from around £5; gammon steak here is £5.95. It also has comfortable rooms with bathroom from £17 to £27.50 per person. *The Nook* (☎ *41879*) is a Tudor-style B&B with a couple of rooms for £16.50 per person.

Bus No 685 between Newcastle upon Tyne and Carlisle comes through Brampton, and the town is also on the Newcastle-Carlisle railway line. Mountain bikes are available from Bentley's Border Bikes (☎ 2458), Capon Hill, for £15 per day.

Northumberland National Park

Northumberland National Park covers 398 sq miles of some of the emptiest country in the British Isles. The landscape is characterised by windswept grassy hills cut by streams, and is almost empty of human habitation.

After the Romans left, the region remained a contested zone between Scotland and England, and home to warring clans and families. Few buildings constructed prior to the 18th century survive, partly because few were built. The cattle-farming families lived in simple structures of turf that could be built quickly and cheaply, and be equally quickly abandoned. Peace came in the 18th century, but coincided with new farming practices, so the tenant farmers were dispossessed, leaving large estates. Unlike the rest of England, this area has no scattering of villages, few stone walls and few small farms. Scenically, it has a bleak grandeur, with wide horizons and vast skies.

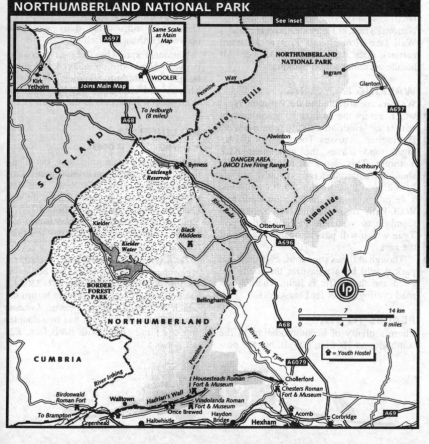

NORTHUMBERLAND NATIONAL PARK

See Inset

Same Scale as Main Map

A697

WOOLER

Joins Main Map

Kirk Yetholm

To Jedburgh (8 miles)

A68

NORTHUMBERLAND NATIONAL PARK

Ingram

Glanton

Pennine Way

Cheviot Hills

Alwinton

A697

SCOTLAND

Byrness

DANGER AREA (MOD Live Firing Range)

Rothbury

Catcleugh Reservoir

River Rede

Simonside Hills

Kielder

Black Middens

Otterburn

A696

Kielder Water

BORDER FOREST PARK

Bellingham

LP

0   7   14 km
0   4   8 miles

NORTHUMBERLAND

Pennine Way

River North Tyne

A68

A6079

⌂ = Youth Hostel

CUMBRIA

River Irthing

Birdoswald Roman Fort

Walltown

Hadrian's Wall

Housesteads Roman Fort & Museum

Vindolanda Roman Fort & Museum

Chollerford

Chesters Roman Fort & Museum

To Brampton

Greenhead

Haltwhistle

Once Brewed

Haydon Bridge

Hexham

Acomb

Corbridge

A69

ORIENTATION & INFORMATION

The park runs from Hadrian's Wall in the south, takes in the Simonside Hills in the east and runs into the Cheviot Hills along the Scottish border. There are few roads.

For more information, contact the Information Officer (☎ 01434-605555), Eastburn, South Park, Hexham, Northumberland NE46 1BS.

There are several visitor centres: Ingram (☎ 01655-78248) for the Cheviots, open April to September; Rothbury (☎ 01669-20887) for the central area, open mid-March to October; and Once Brewed (☎ 01434-344396) for the Hadrian's Wall area, open mid-March to October. There's also a centre (☎ 01434-344525), in partnership with the National Trust, at Housesteads on Hadrian's Wall (see Housesteads Fort & Museum earlier), open daily April to October. All handle accommodation bookings.

WALKING & CYCLING

Walkers are attracted to the **Pennine Way**, which enters the park at its south-eastern corner on Hadrian's Wall, continues to Bellingham, crosses The Cheviot (814m high), and leaves the park near Kirk Yetholm. This is a demanding walk and should be undertaken only if you're properly equipped to deal with tough conditions.

In preparation is the 81 mile **Hadrian's Wall Path** from Bowness-on-Solway in Cumbria to Wallsend in Newcastle upon Tyne which will pass through the south of the park.

Though at times strenuous, cycling in the park would be a pleasure; the roads are good and the traffic is light. There's off-road cycling in Border Forest Park.

PLACES TO STAY

There's plenty of accommodation in the south around Hadrian's Wall, but the pos-sibilities further north are extremely limited. There are a few B&Bs in Bellingham and Otterburn, and hostels in Bellingham and Byrness (on the Pennine Way). *Byrness Youth Hostel (☎ 01830-520425)* opens April to mid-July and September, Wednesday to Monday, mid-July to August daily; £6.50/4.45.

GETTING THERE & AROUND

Public-transport options are limited, aside from buses on the A69. Bus No 808 operates four times a day Monday to Friday (once a day, weekends) between Otterburn and Newcastle upon Tyne. Postbus No 815, operated by the Royal Mail (☎ 01325-38112, Darlington) runs twice daily weekdays between Hexham and Bellingham.

National Express has three services a day between Newcastle upon Tyne and Edinburgh via Otterburn, Byrness, Jedburgh, Melrose and Galashiels. See the Hadrian's Wall section for access to the south.

BELLINGHAM

- **pop 900**   ☎ 01434

Bellingham is a plain little town, but is surrounded by beautiful countryside, particularly south towards Hadrian's Wall. The TIC (☎ 220616), Main St, opens Easter through October, Monday to Saturday from 10 am to 1 pm and from 2 to 6 pm, Sunday from 1 to 5 pm; November to March, Monday to Friday from 2 to 5 pm.

Bellingham Youth Hostel (☎ 220313, Woodburn Rd) is fairly spartan but cosy; £6.50/4.45. *Westfield House (☎ 220340)* has three rooms, all with private bathroom, which cost from £19 per person. *Lyndale Guest House (☎ 220361)* has two doubles and one family room with B&B from £20 per person.

SCOTLAND

Facts about Scotland

No visitor to Britain should miss the chance to visit Scotland. Despite its official union with England and Wales in 1707, it maintains an independent national identity that extends much further than the occasional display of kilts and bagpipes.

It is also very beautiful. The wild Highlands, in particular, are extraordinary.

There's a combination of exhilarating open space and a rain-washed quality to the light that illuminates a wonderful range of colours – subtle purples, browns and blues, interspersed with vivid greens and gold.

The weather is sometimes harsh, but 'bad' weather, with scudding clouds and water spilling from storm-wrapped mountains and

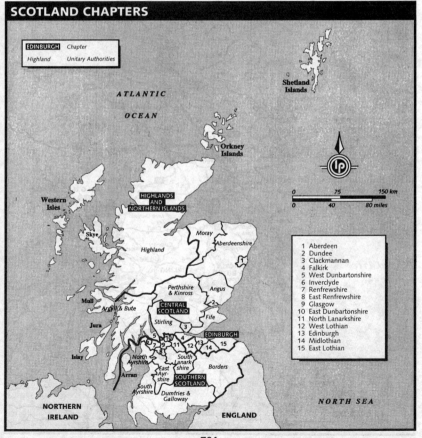

SCOTLAND CHAPTERS

EDINBURGH Chapter
Highland Unitary Authorities

ATLANTIC
OCEAN

Shetland Islands

Orkney Islands

Western Isles

HIGHLANDS AND NORTHERN ISLANDS

Skye

Highland

Moray
Aberdeenshire

Perthshire & Kinross
Angus

Mull
Argyll & Bute
CENTRAL SCOTLAND
Fife

Jura
Stirling

EDINBURGH

Islay
North Ayrshire
South Lanarkshire
Borders
East Ayrshire
SOUTHERN SCOTLAND
Arran
South Ayrshire
Dumfries & Galloway

NORTHERN IRELAND
ENGLAND
NORTH SEA

1 Aberdeen
2 Dundee
3 Clackmannan
4 Falkirk
5 West Dunbartonshire
6 Inverclyde
7 Renfrewshire
8 East Renfrewshire
9 Glasgow
10 East Dunbartonshire
11 North Lanarkshire
12 West Lothian
13 Edinburgh
14 Midlothian
15 East Lothian

0   75   150 km
0   40   80 miles

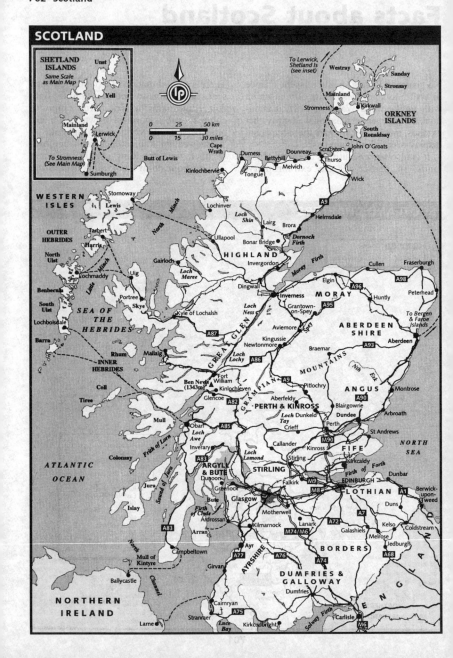

hills, can be spectacular. It's not an easy country, and even Scottish engineers and 20th century technology have failed to tame it completely. When the winds howl, a human being can still feel extremely vulnerable. At times, it's hard to imagine how human settlement has survived here for so many thousands of years.

But then the clouds break, and shafts of sunlight play across the landscape, highlighting snow-capped mountains and heather-covered hills, vast lochs and fast-running streams. And then come the balmy, sunny days, when the countryside is as seductive as anywhere on earth.

It's hardly a secret, but for a country with an interesting history and some of the world's most dramatic scenery, Scotland is curiously underrated and unknown.

Scottish culture survives particularly strongly in the countryside and on the islands, but the urban centres are also unique: Edinburgh is one of the world's most beautiful cities; Glasgow is a vibrant cultural centre, vigorously reinventing itself after the collapse of its traditional industries; St Andrews is a beautiful coastal university town and prosperous Aberdeen surveys the North Sea (and its oilfields) with proprietorial interest.

HISTORY
First Immigrants
Scotland's earliest inhabitants were hunter-gatherers who began arriving about 6000 years ago from England, Ireland and northern Europe. Over the next few thousand years these colonisers came in waves to different parts of the country. There are indications of Baltic cultures in east Scotland and Irish cultures on the islands of the west. Mesolithic flints from northern France have been found at many sites.

Prehistoric Civilisations
The Neolithic era, beginning in the 4th millennium BC, brought a new way of life, with agriculture, stockbreeding and trading. Unprecedentedly large populations were the result and more complex patterns of social organisation evolved to control them. With organised groups of workers, more ambitious construction projects were possible.

Scotland is rich in Neolithic sites; in fact, some of the most impressive in Europe are in Orkney, Shetland and the Western Isles. The chiefs who led these growing populations built elaborate tombs like the great passage grave at Maes Howe, Orkney, constructed from carefully dressed boulders. Stone circles date from the late Neolithic and Bronze Age; the Ring of Brodgar and the Standing Stones of Stenness, both in Orkney, are magnificent examples. At Callanish, on Lewis, there's a stone circle similar to that at Avebury in England.

Neolithic people usually built wooden houses, and it's only in treeless regions where they were forced to use stone that their architecture has survived. The northern islands contain rare examples of Neolithic domestic architecture; there's an entire village at Skara Brae in Orkney dating from around 3100 BC.

Between the late Neolithic and the early Bronze Age the Beaker People reached the British Isles from mainland Europe. They were so named because of the shape of their earthenware drinking vessels that were customarily buried with their dead. They also introduced bronze for knives, daggers, arrowheads and articles of gold and copper. Many of Scotland's standing stones and stone circles can be accredited to the Beaker People. Some sources claim that they were the original Celts.

The Iron Age reached Scotland around 500 BC, with the arrival of Celtic settlers from Europe. In the Highlands, which escaped Roman influence, it lasted well into the Christian era.

Roman Attempts at Colonisation
The Romans didn't have much success in the north of Britain. In 80 AD, the Roman governor Julius Agricola marched north and spent four years trying to subdue the wild tribes the Romans called the Picts (from the Latin pictus, meaning painted). The Picts were the most numerous of many Celtic

peoples occupying this area at the time and probably reached Scotland via Orkney.

In the far north, Orkney was a centre of maritime power and posed a threat to the Romans as well as the other northern tribes. For defence against raiding parties, *brochs* (fortified stone towers) were constructed. Broch architecture was perfected in Orkney in the 1st century BC, and there are over 500 examples, concentrated in Shetland, Orkney, the Western Isles and the north of Scotland. The best preserved, at Mousa in Shetland, dates from around 50 BC.

By the 2nd century, Emperor Hadrian decided that this inhospitable land of mists, bogs, midges and warring tribes had little to offer the Roman Empire so the Roman presence in southern Scotland was pulled back. Hadrian built the wall (122-28) that took his name as a defence against the pressures from the northern tribes.

Feuding Celtic Tribes in Alba

When the Romans left Britain in the 4th century, there were two indigenous Celtic tribes in northern Britain, then known as Alba: the Picts, and the Britons from the south.

The historian, Bede, attributes Christianity's arrival in Scotland to St Ninian who established a centre in Whithorn in 397. It's likely, however, that some of the Romanised Britons in southern Scotland adopted Christianity after the religion was given state recognition in 313. St Columba founded a second important early Christian centre on the tiny island of Iona, off Mull, in 563.

In the 6th century a third Celtic tribe, the Gaels later known as the Scots, reached Scotland from northern Ireland (Scotia). In the 7th century Anglo-Saxons from northeast England colonised south-east Scotland.

In the 790s, raiding Norsemen in longboats sacked the religious settlement at Iona, causing the monks to flee inland with St Columba's bones to found a cathedral in the Pictish Kingdom at Dunkeld. The Norsemen continued to control the entire western seaboard until Somerled of the Isles broke their power at the Battle of Largs in 1263.

Kenneth MacAlpin & the Makings of a Kingdom

In 843 Kenneth MacAlpin, king of the Scots of Dalriada, took advantage of the Pictish custom of matrilineal succession to make himself king of Alba. Thereafter the Scots gained cultural and political ascendancy and the Pictish culture disappeared.

The only material evidence of the Picts comprises their unique symbol stones set up to record Pictish lineages and alliances. These boulders, engraved with mysterious symbols of an otherwise unknown people, are found in many parts of eastern Scotland.

Canmore Dynasty

Shakespeare's Malcolm was Malcolm III, a Canmore, who killed Macbeth at Lumphanan in 1057. With his English queen, Margaret, he founded a dynasty of able Scottish rulers. They introduced Anglo-Norman systems of government and religious foundations, and David I (1124-53) increased his influence by adopting the Norman feudal system, granting land to great Norman families in return for their acting as what amounted to a government police force. By 1212 Walter of Coventry remarked that the Scottish court was 'French in race and manner of life, in speech and in culture'.

Clans & Feudalism

The old society was based on ties of kinship between everyone in the tribe, or clan, and its head. Unlike a feudal lord, a chief might still command the loyalty of his clan whether he was a landowner or not.

Although the initial reception was bloody, the feudal system was eventually grafted onto the old system in the Lowlands and Highland fringes. It created families and clans who were enormously powerful in terms of land ownership and loyal fighting men.

Highlands & Lowlands

However, inaccessible in their glens, the Highland clans remained a law unto themselves for another 600 years. A cultural and linguistic divide grew up between Gaelic-speaking Highlanders, and the Lowland

JONATHAN SMITH

Piper on parade at Glamis Castle

TOM SMALLMAN

St Michaels, on the road to Linlithgow Palace

BRYN THOMAS

Discovery, Scott's polar research ship, Dundee

NEIL WILSON

Roofless nave of Jedburgh Abbey

Crail Harbour, Fife

River Tummel, Killiecrankie

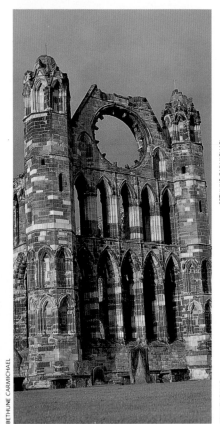

Elgin Cathedral

Mull Mile Marker

Tanistry: Finding a King

Unlike the matrilineal Picts, the Scots preferred tanistry – selection of a suitable male heir from anyone in the family who could claim a king as great-grandfather. The chosen successor was known as the tanist. As Shakespeare demonstrated to great effect in *Macbeth*, this had dire consequences for Scottish history, with many successions decided by the murder of one's predecessor. While the play isn't historically or geographically accurate, it certainly manages to evoke the dark deeds, bloodshed and warring factions of the period.

Scots who spoke Lallans, a language made up of English, Norse and Gaelic constituents.

In the Lowlands, small commercial centres like Berwick, Roxburgh, Stirling, Edinburgh and Forfar grew up through the trading activities of Angles, Scandinavians and Flemings. These centres later became independent, self-governing burghs, trading wool from the monasteries of the Borders for Flemish cloth or wine from Burgundy. Most of the population, however, eked out a subsistence from the land. Until the 20th century, the rural Scots' diet consisted largely of oatmeal, barley, milk, cheese, herrings, rabbits, grouse and kail (cabbage).

Wars of Independence

Two centuries of the Canmore dynasty effectively ended in 1286 when Alexander III fell to his death into the Firth of Forth at Kinghorn, Fife. There followed a dispute over the succession and by 1291 there were no less than 13 'tanists' or contestants for the throne. Edward I of England took advantage of the Scottish monarchy's weakness. He began the attempted conquest of Scotland that earned him the title Hammer of the Scots, and there followed a long struggle for independence from English domination.

In 1291 Edward travelled the country forcing the clan leaders to sign a declaration of allegiance to him. In a final blow to Scottish pride he removed the Stone of Destiny, the coronation stone on which the kings of Scotland had been invested for centuries, and sent it from Scone to London. Resistance broke out throughout the country, some incidents more serious than others. In 1296 he laid siege to and captured Berwick.

In 1297, William Wallace's forces defeated the English at the Battle of Stirling Bridge. After further skirmishes he was captured and subjected to barbaric execution – hung, drawn, emasculated, burnt and quartered – at Smithfield in London in 1305. He's still remembered as the epitome of patriotism and a great hero of the resistance movement.

Robert the Bruce emerged as a contender for the throne. He murdered his rival John Comyn (also known as Red Comyn) in February 1306 and crowned himself king of Scotland in March. However, he was defeated in battle first at Methven in June and then at Dalry in August. According to myth, while Bruce was on the run he was inspired to renew his own efforts by a spider's persistence in spinning its web. He went on to defeat the English at the Battle of Bannockburn in 1314, a turning point in Scotland's fight for independence from England.

After his death, the country was ravaged by endless civil disputes and plague epidemics. The Wars of Independence strengthened links with France and Europe; the Auld Alliance first agreed with France in 1295 was constantly renewed up to 1492.

The Stewarts & the Barons

Bruce's son became David II of Scotland, but was soon caught up in battles with Scots disaffected by his father and aided by England's Edward III. He suffered exile and imprisonment, but was released after agreeing to pay a huge ransom. He appointed Edward's son as his heir, but when David II died in 1371 the Scots quickly crowned

Robert Stewart (Robert the Bruce's grandson), the first of the Stewart dynasty.

The early Stewart kings were ruthless in their attempts to break the power of the magnates. These were not peaceful years. Time and again the king met with an untimely death and clans like the Douglases and the Donalds (Lords of the Isles after the Norsemen were driven from the Hebrides in 1266) grew to wield almost regal power.

James IV & the Renaissance

James IV married the daughter of Henry VII of England, the first of the Tudor monarchs, thereby linking the two families. This didn't, however, prevent the French from persuading James to go to war with his in-laws. He was killed at the battle of Flodden Hill in 1513, along with 10,000 of his subjects.

Renaissance ideas flourished in Scotland during James's reign. Scottish poetry thrived. The intellectual climate was fertile ground for the ideas of the Reformation, a critique of the medieval Catholic church, and the rise of Protestantism.

Much graceful Scottish architecture dates from this time, and examples of the Renaissance style can be seen in alterations made to the palaces at Holyrood, Stirling, Linlithgow and Falkland. The building of collegiate churches and universities brought opportunity for education at home, along French lines. St Andrews University was founded in 1410, Glasgow in 1451 and Aberdeen in 1495.

Mary Queen of Scots & the Reformation

In 1542, James V died – broken-hearted, it's said, after his defeat by the English at Solway Moss. His baby daughter, Mary, became Queen of Scots.

At first the country was ruled by regents, who rejected Henry VIII's plan that Mary should marry his son and sent her to France. Henry was furious and his armies ravaged the Borders and sacked Edinburgh in a failed attempt to force agreement – the Rough Wooing, as it was called. Mary eventually married the French dauphin and became queen of France as well as Scotland.

While Mary, a devout Catholic, was in France, the Reformation of the Scottish church was under way. The wealthy Catholic church was riddled with corruption and the preachings of John Knox, pupil of the Swiss reformer, Calvin, found sympathetic ears. In 1560 the Scottish Parliament created a Protestant church that was independent of Rome and the monarchy. The Latin mass was abolished and the pope's authority denied.

Following her husband's death, Mary returned to Scotland. Still only 18 and a stunning beauty, she was a headstrong Catholic and her conduct did nothing to endear her to the Protestants. She married Henry Darnley and gave birth to a son. However, domestic bliss was short-lived and, in a scarcely believable train of events, Darnley was involved in the murder of Mary's Italian secretary Rizzio (rumoured to be her lover). Then Darnley himself was murdered, presumably by Mary and her lover and future husband, the Earl of Bothwell.

Forced to abdicate in favour of her son, James VI, Mary was imprisoned in the castle in the middle of Loch Leven, but escaped to England and her cousin, the Protestant Elizabeth I. Since Mary had claims to the English throne, and Elizabeth had no heir, she was seen as a security risk and Elizabeth kept her locked in the Tower of London. It took her 19 years to agree to sign the warrant for Mary's execution. When Elizabeth died in 1603, James VI of Scotland united the crowns by also becoming James I of England.

Religious Wars of the 17th Century

Religious differences led to civil war in Scotland and England. The fortunes of the Stuarts (spelt the French way following Mary's Gallic association) were thereafter bound with the church's struggle to establish independence from Rome. To complicate matters, religious reform in Scotland was divided between Presbyterians, who shunned all ritual and hierarchy, and less-extreme Protestants who were more like the Anglicans south of the border. The question of episcopacy (rule of the bishops) was particularly divisive.

Earning himself the nickname of the Wisest Fool in Christendom, James VI pursued a moderate policy despite the reformers' fervour. But he also insisted that his authority came directly from God (the Divine Right of Kings) and was therefore incontestable, and encouraged the paranoia which led to witch hunts, with many innocent people, set up as scapegoats, suffering appalling deaths by torture and burning.

In 1625 James was succeeded by his son, Charles I, a devout Anglican who attempted to impose a High Anglican form of worship on the church in Scotland.

In 1637 the Dean of St Giles Cathedral in Edinburgh was reading from the English prayer book (a symbol of episcopacy) when he was floored by a stool thrown by Jenny Geddes, an Edinburgh greengrocer. The common people wanted a common religion and riots ensued which ended with the creation of a document known as the National Covenant. The Covenanters sought freedom from Rome and from royal interference in church government, the abolition of bishops and a simpler ritual.

The dispute developed into civil war between moderate royalists and radical Covenanters. The Marquis of Montrose is still remembered as a dashing hero who, though originally a Covenanter, eventually held out for the king. He was betrayed to the English Republicans while hiding at Ardvreck Castle in Loch Assynt and executed as a traitor in 1650.

In the meantime, civil war raged in England. Charles I was defeated by Oliver Cromwell and beheaded in 1649. His exiled son, Charles, was offered the crown in Scotland as long as he signed the Covenant. He was crowned in 1650 but soon forced into exile by Cromwell.

After Charles II's restoration in 1660, episcopacy was reinstated. Many of the clergy rejected the bishops' authority and

started holding outdoor services, or Conventicles. His successor, James II, a Catholic, appeared to set out determinedly to lose his kingdom. Among other poor decisions, he made worshipping as a Covenanter a capital offence.

The prospect of another Catholic king was too much for the English Protestants, so they invited·William of Orange, a Dutchman who was James' nephew and married to his oldest Protestant daughter, to take power. In 1689 he landed with a small army; James broke down and fled to France. In the same year, episcopacy was abolished.

Union with England in 1707

The wars left the country and economy ruined. During the 1690s, famine killed up to a third of the population in some areas.

Anti-English feeling ran high. The Jacobite, Graham of Claverhouse (Bonnie Dundee), raised a band of Highlanders and routed the English troops at Killiecrankie (1689), near Pitlochry. The situation was exacerbated by the Darien Disaster, the failure of an investment venture in Panama set up by the Bank of England to boost the economy, which resulted in widespread bankruptcy in Scotland.

In 1692, people were horrified by the treacherous massacre, on English government orders, of MacDonalds by Campbells in Glencoe, for failing to swear allegiance to William. The massacre became Jacobite (Stuart) propaganda that still resonates today.

In this atmosphere, the lure of trade concessions to boost the economy and the preservation of the Scottish church and legal system offered by the Act of Union of 1707 (along with financial inducements) persuaded the Scottish Parliament to agree to the Act of Union in 1707. This act united the two countries under a single parliament but the union was unpopular with most ordinary Scots.

The Jacobites (1715-45)

The Jacobite rebellions, most notably of 1715 and 1745, were attempts to replace the Hanoverian monarchy (chosen by parliament to succeed the house of Orange) with Catholic Stuarts. Despite Scottish disenchantment with the Act of Union, however, there was never much support for the Jacobite cause outside the Highlands, owing to the fear of inviting Catholicism back into Scotland.

James Edward Stuart, the Old Pretender, was the son of the exiled James VII. With support from the Highland clans he made several attempts to regain the throne but fled to France after the unsuccessful 1715 rebellion. In an effort to impose control on the Highlanders, General Wade and the English military (the Redcoats) were sent to construct roads into the previously inaccessible glens.

In 1745, James's son, Charles Edward Stuart (Bonnie Prince Charlie, the Young Pretender) landed in Scotland to claim the crown. He was at first successful, getting as far south into England as Derby, but back in Scotland after retreating north, the prince and his Highland supporters suffered catastrophic defeat at Culloden (1746). Dressed as a woman, he escaped via the Western Isles assisted by Flora MacDonald.

After 'the '45' (as it became known), the government banned private armies, wearing the kilt and playing the pipes. Many Jacobites were transported or executed, or died in prison; others forfeited their lands.

Beginnings of the Industrial Revolution

From about 1750, Lowland factories began to draw workers out of the glens. The tobacco trade with America boomed before the War of Independence (1776-83) and then gave way to the textile industry. People came to work in the cotton and linen mills in Glasgow and Lanarkshire. Established in 1759, the Carron ironworks became the largest ironworks in Britain. The jute trade developed in Dundee and shipyards opened on the Clyde in the early 19th century.

Scottish Enlightenment

In the flowering of intellectual life known as the Scottish Enlightenment of the 18th

century, the philosophers David Hume and Adam Smith emerged as influential thinkers nourished on generations of theological debate.

After the bloodshed and fervent religious debate of the Reformation, people applied themselves with the same energy and piety to the making of money and the enjoyment of leisure. There was a revival of interest in vernacular literature, reflected in Robert Fergusson's satires and Alexander MacDonald's Gaelic poetry. The poetry of Robert Burns, a man of the people, achieved lasting popularity. Sir Walter Scott, the prolific poet and novelist, was an ardent patriot.

Highland Clearances & the 19th Century

With the banning of private armies, the relationship of chief to clansman in the late 18th and early 19th centuries became one of economic, not military, consideration. The kelp industry (the production of soda ash from seaweed) was developed and Highland populations continued to grow.

By the mid-19th century, overpopulation, the collapse of the kelp industry and the potato famine of the 1840s led to the Highland Clearances. People were forced off the land and shipped or tricked into emigrating to North America, Australia and New Zealand. Those who remained were moved to smallholdings, known as *crofts*. Rents were extortionate and life for the crofters was extremely precarious. Common grazing ground was confiscated for sheep or deer runs. In 1886, however, the Crofters Commission was set up to ensure security of tenure and to fix fair rent for smallholders.

In the 19th century, it became fashionable for wealthy southerners to holiday in the Highlands to shoot deer and grouse. Queen Victoria built Balmoral Castle in 1848 and spent a great deal of time there after Prince Albert died, disguising herself as a simple Scotswoman and promenading in the company of her Scots servant, John Brown. Their relationship was depicted in the 1997 film *Mrs Brown*.

Elsewhere, the new urban society saw a growing bourgeoisie take precedence in politics over the still powerful landed aristocracy. Political life was more closely integrated with England. Two Scotsmen had a significant impact on British politics. The popular Liberal, William Gladstone, was prime minister four times and Keir Hardie was the first leader of the British Labour Party.

There was much constitutional and parliamentary reform throughout the Victorian era. Legislation to improve the education system was connected with reform and dissension in the church. Desire for betterment might send a farmer's child, barefoot and with a sack of oatmeal on their back, to the university. The education system remains distinct from England's.

In the great industrial cities, conditions among the working classes were hard. In the notorious Glasgow Gorbals, where typhoid epidemics were rife, people lived in overcrowded tenements on barely subsistence wages. Despite prosperity from the thriving shipyards, coal mines, steel works and textile mills, Glasgow and Clydeside still harboured many unemployed, unskilled immigrants from Ireland and the Highlands.

The Economy in the 20th Century

Industry continued to thrive through WWI, with Clydeside a munitions centre. The postwar slump wasn't felt in Scotland until the 1920s, but the Great Depression of the 1930s hit so hard that heavy industry never recovered. In fact, the seeds of Scotland's 20th century economic failure could be said to lie in the success of the preceding industrial era.

The discovery of oil and gas in the North Sea in the 1970s brought prosperity to Aberdeen and the surrounding area, and to the Shetland Islands. However, most of the oil revenue was siphoned off to England. This, along with takeovers of Scottish companies by English ones (which then closed the Scottish operations, stripped them of their assets

and transferred the jobs to England), fuelled increasing nationalist sentiment in Scotland.

Light engineering and high-tech electronics companies replaced the defunct coal mines and steel works of the Central Lowlands, but many are foreign owned. The fishing industry, profitable until Britain joined the European Union (EU), is in decline, crippled by fishing quotas imposed from Brussels and by over-fishing.

Depopulation of the rural areas continues although grant schemes subsidise new business initiatives away from agriculture and fishing.

Self-Rule

In 1967 the Scottish National Party (SNP) won its first seat, and support for it grew during this period. Both the Labour Party and the Conservatives had toyed with offering Scotland devolution, or a degree of self-government.

In 1979 Scots voted in a referendum to establish a directly elected Scottish Assembly, but failed to get the necessary majority. From 1979 to 1997, Scotland was ruled by a Conservative government for which the majority of Scots hadn't voted. Nationalist feelings, always present, grew stronger.

Following the landslide victory of the British Labour Party in May 1997, another referendum was held over the creation of a Scottish Parliament. This time voters were overwhelmingly in favour. The new parliament will be in Edinburgh and, following elections in 1999, will convene in the year 2000. Although devolution is occurring *within* the UK, the prospect of a totally independent Scotland doesn't seem as unlikely as it once did.

GEOGRAPHY & GEOLOGY

Scotland covers 30,414 sq miles, about half England's size. It can be divided into three areas: Southern Uplands, Central Lowlands, and northern Highlands and Islands.

South of Edinburgh and Glasgow are the Southern Uplands, with fertile coastal plains and ranges of hills bordering England. The Central Lowlands comprise a triangular slice from Edinburgh and Dundee in the east to Glasgow in the west, and contain the industrial belt and most of the population.

The Highland Boundary Fault, a geographical division, runs north-east from Helensburgh (west of Glasgow) to Stonehaven (south of Aberdeen) on the east coast. North of it are the Highlands and Islands, roughly two-thirds of the country and an area that includes mountain ranges of sandstone, granite and metamorphic rock. Mountains over 900m (3000 feet) – there are almost 300 of them in Scotland – are known as Munros, after the man who first listed them. Some rise directly from the steep sea fjords, or lochs, of the west coast. Ben Nevis, in the western Grampians, is Britain's highest mountain, at 1343m (4406 feet).

The main Highlands watershed is near the west coast, giving long river valleys running east, many containing freshwater lochs and some arable areas. The Great Glen, a fault line running from Fort William to Inverness, contains a chain of freshwater lochs (including Loch Ness) connected by the Caledonian Canal.

Of Scotland's 790 islands, 130 are inhabited. The Western Isles comprise the Inner Hebrides and the Outer Hebrides. To the north are two other island groups, Orkney and Shetland, the northernmost reaches of the British Isles.

Edinburgh is the capital and financial centre, Glasgow the industrial centre and Aberdeen and Dundee the two largest regional centres.

CLIMATE

'Varied' is a vague but accurate way to describe Scotland's cool temperate climate. The weather changes quickly – a rainy day is often followed by a sunny one. There are also wide variations over small distances; while one glen broods under a cloud, the next may be basking in sunshine. May and June are generally the driest months, but expect rain at any time.

Considering how far north the country lies (Edinburgh is on the same line of latitude as Moscow), you might expect a colder

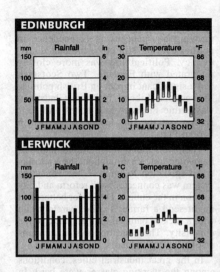

climate, but the winds from the Atlantic are warmed by the Gulf Stream. The east and west coasts have relatively mild climates. The east coast tends to be cool and dry – rainfall averages around 650mm, and winter temperatures rarely drop below 0°C, although winds off the North Sea can rattle your teeth. The west coast is milder and wetter, with over 1500mm of rain and average summer highs of 19°C.

In the Highlands, rainfall can be as much as 3000mm; the average summer high is 18°C.

ECOLOGY & ENVIRONMENT

Though much of Scotland's wild, open countryside looks natural, it isn't. It's almost entirely 'spoilt', as much of the original forest (ie 99%) has gone.

In many areas you'll notice thick evergreen plantations. In recent decades governments encouraged landowners to plant these fast-growing trees, despite serious ecological drawbacks. As well as destroying wildlife habitat, conifers increase acidity in soil and may have a detrimental effect on weather patterns. In the far north, bog land has been destroyed.

This also causes increased water run-off and, hence, flooding downstream.

Tourism can have damaging effects on the landscape. The Cairngorm Chairlift Company wants to replace its ageing chairlift with an all-weather, year-round funicular railway. Scottish Natural Heritage (SNH) initially opposed it, but now backs this controversial scheme. Visitors won't be permitted to leave the top station of the funicular! However, the project breaches certain European Union (EU) regulations and the controversy continues.

Waste from Sellafield, the nuclear power station in northern England, has an adverse effect on fish off the west coast of Scotland. In Caithness, the Dounreay nuclear reprocessing plant, has had seepage problems, and in 1998 had to shut down temporarily because of power failure.

Red Grouse

FLORA & FAUNA

Although much of the country was once covered by the Caledonian forest – a mix of Scots pine, oak, silver birch, willow, alder and rowan, with heather underfoot – deforestation has reduced this mighty forest to a few small pockets of indigenous trees.

Almost three-quarters of the country is uncultivated bog, rock and heather. In mountainous areas like the Cairngorms, alpine plants thrive; in the far north there are lichens and mosses found nowhere else in Britain. Acidic peat covers almost 2,000,000 acres, most notably in the Flow Country of Caithness and Sutherland, a conservation area.

Although the thistle is commonly associated with Scotland, the national flower is the harebell or bluebell. Yellow flag, wild thyme and yarrow abound in the summer. Purple coloured heather is probably the most noticeable of Scottish flowering plants.

Red deer are found in large numbers, but the reindeer, beaver, auroch (wild ox) and wolf are extinct. Once nearly extinct, wild boars have been reintroduced in the southwest. There are still some wildcats but, like wild goats, they're rarely seen.

Sheep graze the grass-covered hills, and much of the Lowlands is given over to agriculture. Hairy Highland cattle are well adapted to survive the cold. Take care in approaching these diminutive bovines – they have foul tempers.

Foxes and red squirrels are found throughout the country, with pine martens in the forests. Otters are rare, though less so than in England; and minks, escaped from fur farms, are multiplying fast.

Large numbers of grouse graze the heather on the moors, and gamekeepers burn vast areas to encourage the new shoots that attract this small game bird. In heavily forested areas you may be lucky enough to see a capercaillie, a black, turkey-like bird, the largest member of the grouse family. Birds of prey like the eagle, osprey, peregrine falcon and hen harrier are protected. Millions of greylag geese winter on the Lowland stubble fields.

Since 80% of Britain's coastline is in Scotland, it's not surprising to find millions of sea birds here. Whale-watching trips follow more substantial photographic prey, and seals are frequently seen. The major rivers attract anglers from around the world to fish for the famed Scottish salmon.

Endangered Species

Scotland is home to many animals and birds that are rare elsewhere in the UK but they

The Monarch of the Glen

The red deer, the Monarch of the Glen, is causing a serious ecological problem in Scotland. Unlike many species, it isn't hurtling
towards extinction but multiplying way out of control. There are
over 300,000 and huge areas of vegetation are being damaged.

Fencing off woodland isn't the answer as it reduces the territory of
the deer and leads to even heavier grazing of these
areas. In some parts of Scotland, no new trees have
been able to grow since deer populations started to
increase about 300 years ago.

The balance of nature was upset when the
natural predator of the red deer, the wolf, was
eradicated in the 17th century. In recent years,
too few deer have been culled by farmers and
estate managers, and, with milder winters,
fewer deer have died from lack of food. If
nothing is done to reduce deer numbers, the
last few areas of indigenous forest in the country may be destroyed.

too are constantly threatened by the changing environment. The habitat of the once
common corncrake, for example, has
almost been completely destroyed by
modern farming methods. Farmers now
receive a subsidy for mowing in corncrake-
friendly fashion. Other threats don't even
have an economic justification; the osprey
nest at Boat of Garten has to be watched to
prevent egg collectors taking the eggs.

Conservation Areas

Scotland doesn't have national parks, but
does have large areas under protection designated variously as national scenic areas,
forest parks, areas of outstanding natural
beauty and sites of special scientific interest. The National Trust for Scotland is
responsible for areas of natural importance
as well as historic monuments etc.

GOVERNMENT & POLITICS

For the time being Scotland is still ruled
from London. The Secretary of State for
Scotland, a member of the British Cabinet,
is responsible for Scotland's administration

in the five departments – education and
health; development; planning; agriculture
and fisheries; and the judicial system. Some
laws in the British Houses of Parliament are
passed exclusively for Scotland.

There are 72 Scottish members in the
Westminster House of Commons and Scottish peers have a seat in the House of Lords.
There are 32 administrative regions, roughly
corresponding to the old counties (eg
Argyll, Perthshire etc) which existed prior to
the 1974 reforms.

The main political parties are the same as
for the rest of Britain with the addition of
the Scottish Nationalist Party. As a result of
the 1997 British general election there were
no remaining Conservative MPs in Scotland. The Conservative Party was the only
party opposed to devolution, although the
long-term goal of the Scottish Nationalists
is complete independence.

Elections for the new Scottish Parliament
(under a system of partial proportional representation) will be held in 1999 and the
parliament will convene in 2000. It'll have
129 members, will sit for four-year terms
and be responsible for levying income

Radical Politics

The radical Scottish tradition that produced John Knox and other church reformers also generated some later influential political thinkers.

The trade unions produced James Keir Hardie, who helped form the Scottish Labour Party (1888), the Independent Labour Party for Great Britain (1893) and the Labour Representative Committee (1900) forerunner of the British Labour Party. Scottish statesman Ramsey MacDonald became Britain's first Labour prime minister in 1924.

The economic distress of the 1930s pushed Scottish political opinion further to the left and several major players in the Communist Party of Great Britain were Scots.

The formation in 1934 of the Scottish National Party (SNP) was initiated by several distinguished men of letters – Hugh MacDiarmid, Eric Linklater, Sir Compton Mackenzie, Neil Gunn and Lewis Grassic Gibbon. This party achieved political success only relatively recently, most Scots being traditional Labour supporters. After elections to the new Scottish Parliament it may be the majority party. It sees the new parliament as only a stepping stone to complete independence, for which it has a target date of 2007 – the 300th anniversary of the Act of Union.

taxes, education, health and other domestic affairs. Westminster will still control areas like defence, foreign affairs and social security.

ECONOMY

Not all is well with Scotland's economy. Many coal mines and steel works have closed. Oil and gas are still extracted from North Sea platforms, but the oil-boom days in Shetland, Invergordon and Aberdeen are over.

The old heavy industries are being replaced by less labour-intensive high-tech engineering projects (Scotland has its Silicon Glen), electronics, finance and service industries. Unemployment is generally higher than the UK average and is much higher in some regions. Tourism is a growth industry, and Edinburgh is an important international finance centre.

Some traditional industries survive and thrive. Woollens, tweeds and tartans from Harris and the Borders are world renowned, as are the whisky distilleries.

In the Highlands some sheep and cattle farming continues, although the grouse moors, deer forests and salmon rivers are a better bet economically. The fertile lowland plains produce barley, oats, wheat, potatoes, turnips, cattle and sheep. EU policy, however, requires farmers to put around 15% of arable land out of production. Scotland catches over two-thirds of UK fish and shellfish even with EU fishing quotas.

POPULATION & PEOPLE

Scotland has just over five million people, around 9% of the UK's total population. Glasgow is the largest city with 689,000 people, followed by Edinburgh with 409,000, Aberdeen with 217,000, and Dundee with 177,000. The Highland region is Britain's most sparsely populated administrative area, with an average of 20 people per sq mile.

Early history describes a belligerent people of mixed origin. Invading Romans, raiding Vikings, avaricious English kings and clan warfare never gave them a chance to settle down. Centuries-old disagreements between clans are remembered, and even today a Colquhoun won't sit with a MacGregor because of the massacre of Colquhouns by Rob Roy and a band of MacGregors 300 years ago. Religious differences also play a part (see Religion later in this chapter).

Influences from different parts of Europe have created a country of people who are far from homogeneous. The 'hurdy-gurdy' accent of Shetlanders and Orcadians betrays their Scandinavian roots. Gaelic is still spoken in parts of the Highlands and

Scots Abroad

'The Scotsman is never at home but when he's abroad', goes the saying. That's why someone like Sean Connery can claim to be a Scottish nationalist while living in the Bahamas.

Scots have emigrated to all corners of the globe for hundreds of years. There are now 25 million people of Scottish extraction living outside the country, compared to five million within it.

Evicted Highlanders were sent to Canada, Free Church supporters went to Dunedin in New Zealand, others joined the Hudson's Bay Company and the East India Company. Large numbers of Scots were among those who colonised the countries of the British Empire, well prepared by the hardship of existence in Scotland for the pioneering life. The missionary zeal of the Presbyterians was great in Africa; Dr Livingstone, explorer of the source of the Nile, is one example of many. Some, like Andrew Carnegie in the USA, had a disproportionate influence on their adopted country.

Scotland also provided the empire with large numbers of soldiers. The bravery of the Highland regiments is legendary; and the red hackle (plume of red feathers) and dark tartan of the Black Watch, Scotland's top regiment, were seen in many battles fought by the British during the last three centuries.

Islands, and Highland society is very different to the anglicised Lowlands. In the 20th century, immigrants, including Irish, Italians, Jews, Poles and Asians, have settled mostly in the larger towns.

EDUCATION

Scotland's education system was one of the best in the world, the Scottish love of learning and pride in education being a by-product of the church reformation. Education was controlled by the church for a long time and the great universities were set up to provide a source of educated churchmen. By the 17th century there was a school in every parish and standards continued to rise until the Industrial Revolution, when the use of child labour increased. Basic education became compulsory in 1872.

The 1962 Education Act introduced a uniform system preserving the broader-based Scottish system from erosion by anglicisation. Schools today are run by the Scottish Education Department and follow a curriculum and examination system different from England's. There are many independent, fee-paying schools run along English lines.

Many young people leave school without qualifications, but educational standards aren't really falling as some have claimed. It's just that the educational results of other countries are improving.

ARTS

Between them, Edinburgh and Glasgow dominate the arts in Scotland. Both have an energetic cultural scene, partly reflected by their respective festivals, which showcase an extraordinary range of performers and artists. Historically, however, although the Scots have had a disproportionate impact on science, technology, medicine and philosophy, they are, except perhaps for literature, under-represented in the worlds of art and music.

The arts never seem to have caught the Scottish popular imagination – or at least not in a form recognised by modern culture vultures. Perhaps the need for creative expression took different, less elitist paths – in the *ceilidh* (see Society & Conduct later in this chapter), in folk music and dance, oral poetry and folk stories.

Literature

Scotland's literary heritage is so rich that most parts of the country have a piece of writing that captures its spirit.

Sir Walter Scott's prodigious output did much to romanticise Scotland and its historical figures. *Rob Roy* portrays the cattle rustler/blackmailer rather rosily; the descriptions of the Trossachs, in which the MacGregor family operated, are more accurate.

Several Robert Louis Stevenson novels have Scottish settings; *Kidnapped*, set on the island of Mull, Edinburgh and Rannoch Moor, captures the country most vividly.

Sir Compton Mackenzie's *Whisky Galore* is required reading for long Hebridean ferry rides; it's the witty tale of what happens when a cargo of whisky runs aground on one of the islands during WWII, something that really happened. Derek Cooper's more serious *Hebridean Connection* is also recommended.

If you're visiting Orkney, you should try to read at least one of George Mackay Brown's novels. *Greenvoe* is a wonderfully poetic description of an Orkney community. His short story collection *A Calendar of Love* is delightful.

Muriel Spark's shrewd portrait of 1930s Edinburgh, *The Prime of Miss Jean Brodie*, was made into an excellent film. In sharp contrast, Irvine Welsh's *Trainspotting* takes the reader on a tour of the modern city's underworld of drugs, drink and despair.

The grim realities of contemporary Glasgow are vividly conjured up in James Kelman's short story collection, *Not not while the giro*. Kelman won the 1994 Booker Prize with *How late it was, how late*, but the language it was written in provoked controversy. Alasdair Gray's acclaimed *Lanark* is also set in a run-down city based on modern Glasgow. Duncan McLean's *Bucket of Tongues* is an equally disturbing short story collection set in assorted depressed urban locations.

Journalist Isla Dewar's novels are spirited accounts of small town life in modern Scotland. Titles include *Women Talking Dirty* and *Giving up on Ordinary*.

In *A Scot's Quair*, Lewis Grassic Gibbon evocatively recaptures early 20th century village life in Aberdeenshire. His *Sunset Song* is a literary classic.

Nigel Tranter is a prolific historical novelist whose books are set in Scotland. His most recent novel *High Kings and Vikings* is set in the 10th century and tells the story of one Cormac Mac Farqhar, Thane of Glamis.

Collections of ballads and poems by the popular national bard Robert Burns are widely available. Another 18th century poet, Alexander MacDonald, wrote in Gaelic. Sorley MacLean and Norman McCaig were also exceptional poets. Scotland's finest modern poet is Hugh MacDiarmid. Perhaps the worst is William MacGonagall, who is celebrated for the sheer awfulness of his rhymes. His *Poetic Gems* offers a taster.

Visual Arts

There are few internationally known figures in the visual arts, although the National Gallery in Edinburgh and the galleries in Glasgow, Aberdeen, Perth and Dundee have important Scottish collections. Since the 19th century, Glasgow has dominated the Scottish scene, partly thanks to the Glasgow School of Art, which has produced several outstanding artists, including Charles Rennie Mackintosh.

Architecture

Scottish architecture can be divided into six periods: Celtic (to the 11th century), Anglo-Norman (to the 16th century), post-Reformation or Renaissance (to the 17th century), Georgian (18th century), Victorian Baronial (19th century) and 20th century (which so far evades simple characterisation).

Interesting buildings can be seen throughout Scotland, but Edinburgh has a particularly remarkable heritage of superb architecture from the 12th century to the present day.

Celtic Few Celtic buildings survive, although the Islands have some of the best surviving examples in Europe. The best known are the stone villages of Skara Brae (from 3100 BC) in Orkney, Jarlshof (from 1500 BC) in Shetland, and the characteristic *brochs* (stone towers), probably built by chieftains, that can be seen in some places, including Carloway in Lewis and Mousa in Shetland.

The crofters' blackhouses of the High-lands and Islands were probably little changed from Celtic times through to the 19th century, but only a few remain. Origin-ally they were circular, but at some point they came to be long, low rectangular build-ings. They had thick dry-stone walls, and thatched roofs, sometimes augmented with skins and canvas, tied down with ropes and nets. There were no chimneys; smoke from a central peat fire simply leaked through the thatch. The kitchen and communal area was in the centre; the family slept to one side, the animals to the other.

Anglo-Norman The Normans were great builders, and their Romanesque style – with its characteristic round arches – can still be seen in David I's church (1128) at Dun-fermline and the 12th century church at Leuchars.

Military architecture was also influenced by the Normans in castles like Caerlave-rock (1290) and, later, at Stirling (1496). Most feudal lords, however, built more modest tower, or peel houses, like Threave and Smailholm (14th century). These had a single small entrance, massively thick stone walls and a single room at each of about five levels.

As the Gothic style developed in England and Europe, it was brought to Scotland and adapted by religious orders. The character-istic pointed arches and stone vaulting can be seen in Glasgow Cathedral (13th century) and the ruins of great border abbeys like Jedburgh (12th century).

Post-Reformation After the Reformation most churches were modified to suit the new religion, which frowned on ceremony and ornament. In some areas, tower houses and castles became less relevant because of the increasing effectiveness of artillery. The gentry therefore had the luxury of expand-ing their houses and at the same time making them more decorative. Features like turrets, conical roofs, garrets and gables became popular in buildings like Castle Fraser (1636) and Thirlestane Castle.

Georgian The greatest exponent of the austere, symmetrical Georgian style in Scotland was the Adam family, in particu-lar Robert Adam. Among other buildings, he designed Hopetoun, Mellerstain and Culzean Castle in the mid-18th century.

Victorian Baronial As the Scottish iden-tity was reaffirmed by writers like Burns and Scott, architects turned to the towers and turrets of the past for inspiration. Fan-ciful buildings like Balmoral, Scone Palace and Abbotsford were created, and the fashion is also exhibited in many civic buildings.

20th Century Scotland's most famous 20th century architect and designer is Charles Rennie Mackintosh of Glasgow, one of the most influential exponents of Art Nouveau. His best known work is Glasgow School of Art, which still looks modern 90 years after it was built.

In general, the quality of modern build-ing has been poor, although there are notable exceptions like the impressive gallery housing the Burrell Collection in Glasgow. The larger towns and cities have been badly affected by the onslaught of the motor car and the unsympathetic impact of large-scale office blocks and shoddy council housing. Traditional houses suf-fered badly from dampness. They've been demolished in large numbers, but many remain.

SCIENCES

Scottish scientists include John Napier, the inventor of logarithms; Lord Kelvin, who described the second law of thermodynam-ics; and James Clerk Maxwell, who described the laws of electromagnetism.

The technologists include James Watt, who revolutionised steam power; John Dunlop, who invented the pneumatic tyre; John McAdam, who invented the road surface that bears his name (though spelt dif-ferently); Charles Mackintosh, who invented waterproof material; Alexander Graham Bell, who invented the telephone; John

Logie Baird, who invented television; and Sir Robert Watson Watt, who invented radar.

Doctors include John and William Hunter, who pioneered anatomy; Sir Joseph Lister, who pioneered the use of antiseptics; and Alexander Fleming, who discovered penicillin.

The philosophers and thinkers include David Hume and Adam Smith.

Many reasons have been given for this extraordinary roll-call, but one of the most obvious is the long tradition of high-quality education that can be traced back as far as the earliest monastic institutions.

SOCIETY & CONDUCT

Outside Scotland, Scots are often portrayed as being a tight-fisted bunch, but nothing could be further from the truth – they're extremely generous. They appear reserved, but are passionate in their beliefs whether it's politics, religion or football. They generally treat visitors courteously, and the class distinctions that so bedevil England are less prevalent. The influence of religion is declining. But in the Highlands and Islands it still affects daily life, and sectarian tension between Protestant and Catholic occasionally erupts in violence.

The Scots take their drinking seriously, spending an average 9% of their weekly income on booze and cigarettes, the highest consumption in Britain.

Traditional Culture

Bagpipes One of the oldest musical instruments still used is the bagpipe.

Scottish Inventions & Discoveries

The inventiveness of the Scots is remarkable, given Scotland's size. Some academics say that the Scots have produced more geniuses than any other people. Perhaps it was the weather that caused thinking Scots to remain indoors pondering life, the universe and all that is within it. The long list of things they either discovered or invented includes:

anaesthetics	penicillin
breech-loading rifles	pneumatic tyre
bicycles	postage stamp (adhesive)
carbon dioxide	radar
colour photography	refrigeration
decimal fraction point	shrapnel
electric light	speedometers
fire alarms	steam engines
gas masks	steel ships
grand pianos	tarmacadam roads (McAdam)
golf	telephones
insulin	telescopes
lawn mowers	television
logarithms	thermos flasks
mackintosh	ultrasound
marmalade	water softeners
morphine	

Among Scottish Nobel Prizewinners are Sir William Ramsay, John Macleod, Charles Wilson, Sir Alexander Fleming, John Orr, Alexander Robertus Todd and Sir James Black.

Although no piece of film footage on Scotland is complete without the drone of the pipes, their origin probably lies outside the country. The Romans used bagpipes in their armies, and modern versions can be heard as far away from the Highland glens as India and Russia.

The Highland bagpipe is the type most commonly played in Scotland. It comprises a leather bag inflated by a blowpipe and held under the arm; the piper controls the flow of air through the pipes by squeezing the bag. Three pipes, appropriately known as the drones, play all the time without being touched by the piper. The fourth, the chanter, is the one on which tunes are played.

Ceilidh The Gaelic word *ceilidh* (pronounced kaylee) means 'visit' – a ceilidh was originally a social gathering in the house after the day's work was over. A local bard (poet) presided over the telling of folk stories and legends; there was also music and song. Today, a ceilidh means an evening of entertainment including music, song and dance.

Clans A clan is a group of people who claim descent from a common ancestor. In the Highlands and Islands, where the Scottish clan system evolved between the 11th and 16th centuries, many unrelated families joined clans to be under the clan chief's protection. So, although they may share the same name, not all clan members are related by blood.

Clan members united in raiding the more prosperous Lowlands or neighbouring glens to steal other clans' cattle. After the Jacobite rebellions the suppression of Highland culture brought the forced breakdown of the clan system, but the spirit of clan loyalty remains strong, especially among the 25 million Scots living abroad. Each clan still has its own chief, like the Queen merely a figurehead, and its own tartan (see Tartans later in this chapter).

Crofting In the Highlands and Islands, a few acres of land supporting some sheep or cows, or a small market garden, is known as a croft.

Crofting has always been a precarious way of life. In the 19th century crofters were regularly forced off the land by landlords demanding extortionately high rents. In the 20th century, unrealistic demands upon the land by agricultural economists almost killed off the crofting tradition.

Now, however, there's increased interest in crofting, and some communities support more people than they have done since the mid-19th century.

Highland Games Highland Games take place throughout the summer, and not just in the Highlands. Assorted sporting events with piping and dancing competitions attract locals and tourists alike.

The original games were organised by clan chiefs and kings who recruited the strongest competitors for their armies and as bodyguards. Even now the Queen never fails to attend the Braemar Gathering, the best known and most crowded of all Highland Games, in September.

Some events are peculiarly Scottish, particularly those that involve the Heavies in bouts of strength testing. The apparatus used can be primitive – tossing the caber involves heaving a tree trunk into the air. Other popular events in which the Heavies take part are throwing the hammer and putting the stone. (See Spectator Sports in the Regional Facts for the Visitor chapter.)

Tartans The oldest surviving piece of tartan, a patterned woollen material now made into everything from kilts to key-fobs, dates back to the Roman period. Today, tartan is popular the world over, and beyond – astronaut Al Bean took his MacBean tartan to the moon and back. The *plaid* is the traditional dress, with a long length of tartan wrapped around the body and over the shoulder. Particular *setts* (patterns) didn't come to be associated with certain clans until the 17th century, although today every clan, indeed every football team, has a distinctive tartan.

The wearing of Highland dress was banned after the Jacobite rebellions but revived under royal patronage in the following century. For their visit in 1822, George IV and his English courtiers donned kilts. Sir Walter Scott, novelist, poet and dedicated patriot, did much to rekindle interest in Scottish ways. By then, however, many of the old setts had been forgotten – some tartans and the modern kilt are actually Victorian creations.

Dos & Don'ts

Though using the term British is fine, the Scots don't like being called English (see the boxed text 'What's in a Name?' in the Regional Facts for the Visitor chapter) especially in the Highlands and Islands where Scottish nationalism is strongest.

The mixture of religion and football creates intense rivalry especially between Protestant Glasgow Rangers and Catholic Glasgow Celtic. If someone approaches you, in a bar for example, and asks which team you support it may be wise to tell them you don't follow football. Whenever subjects like religion or Scottish nationalism come up, as a visitor it's probably a good time for you to practise your listening skills.

RELIGION

Religion has probably played a more influential part in Scotland's history than in other parts of Britain. This remains true today. While barely 2% of people in England and Wales regularly attend church services, the figure for Scotland is 10%.

Christianity reached Scotland in the 4th century although in some places vestiges of older worship survived. As recently as the 18th century, Hebridean fishing communities conducted superstitious rites to ensure a good catch. With the Reformation the Scottish Church rejected the pope's authority. Later a schism developed among Scottish Protestants – the Presbyterians favouring a simplified church hierarchy without bishops, unlike the Episcopalians.

Two-thirds of Scots belong to the Presbyterian Church (or Kirk) of Scotland.

There are two Presbyterian minorities: the Free Church of Scotland (known as the Wee Frees) and the United Free Presbyterians, found mainly in the Highlands and Islands. Their strict adherence to the scriptures means that ferries aren't always allowed to operate on Sunday. The Episcopal (Anglican) Church of Scotland, once widespread north of the Tay, now has only about 35,000 members, many of them from the landed gentry.

There are about 800,000 Catholics, mainly around Glasgow, many descended from 19th century Irish immigrants. Some islands, like Barra, and areas of Aberdeenshire and Lochaber, were converted to Roman Catholicism as a result of secret missionary activity after the Reformation. Sectarian tensions can be felt in Glasgow, especially when the Protestant Rangers and Catholic Celtic football teams play.

LANGUAGE

Ancient Picts spoke a language that may have been of non Indo-European origin. It survives mainly in place names prefixed by 'Pit' (eg Pitlochry). With the coming of Gaelic-speaking Celts (Gaels, later called Scots) from northern Ireland from the 4th to 6th centuries, Gaelic became the language spoken in most of Scotland. This predominance lasted until the 9th or 11th centuries when Anglo-Saxons arrived in the Lowlands. Gaelic then went into a long period of decline, and it was only in the 1970s that it began to make a comeback.

Lallans or Lowland Scots evolved from Anglo-Saxon and has Dutch, French, Gaelic, German and Scandinavian influences. It's the language of Robert Burns and Sir Walter Scott and it too is undergoing a revival. And then there's English. Aye, but the Scots accent can make English almost impenetrable to the *Sassenach* (an English person or a Lowland Scot) and other foreigners, and there are numerous Gaelic and Lallan words that linger in everyday English speech. Ye ken?

See the Scottish Gaelic section in the language guide at the back of this book.

Facts for the Visitor

PLANNING
When to Go

Whenever you visit Scotland, you're likely to see both sun and rain. The best time to visit is from May to September. April and October are also acceptable weather risks, though many things close in October. In summer, daylight hours are long; the mid-summer sun sets around 11 pm in the Shetland Islands and even in Edinburgh, the evenings are seemingly endless.

Edinburgh becomes impossibly crowded during the festival in August. Book well ahead if you plan to visit then; alternatively, stay in Glasgow (or elsewhere) and travel into Edinburgh.

In winter the weather's cold and daylight hours are short. Though travel in the Highlands can be difficult, roads are rarely closed and Scotland's five ski resorts are popular then. Although many facilities close for the season, there's always one Tourist Information Centre (TIC) open for an area (though several within that area may close) and more B&Bs and hotels are staying open year round. Travel in the islands can be a problem then because high winds easily disrupt ferries. Edinburgh and Glasgow are still worth visiting in winter. See also Climate in the Facts about Scotland chapter.

What Kind of Trip

Many visitors to Scotland restrict themselves to Edinburgh but the rest of the country is too beautiful to overlook.

It's easy to get to the main centres by bus or train, and if you're driving, the country's A-road dual-carriageway system offers plenty to see and can be travelled at the national speed limit of 70mph. However, getting around the more remote parts is time-consuming because of the twisty, single-track roads; give yourself time to do them justice, especially if you want to take in some of the islands too.

For a short stay, your best bet might be to take one of the hop-on, hop-off bus transport-only tours operated by Go Blue Banana or Haggis Backpackers (see the Getting Around chapter). The same companies offer more formal three and six day tours of the main highlights. These are specifically designed for backpackers, aged roughly 18 to 30.

Maps

If you're driving north from England you'll probably have a road atlas showing Scotland in adequate detail for touring. Alternatively, TICs have free maps at a scale of at least one inch to 10 miles.

You'll need an Ordnance Survey map for greater detail. Its Landranger maps at 1:50,000 or about 1¼ inches to one mile are adequate for walkers, but if you want more detail it also publishes Pathfinder/Tourist maps at 2½ inches to one mile. TICs usually stock a selection.

For general touring the clear *Leisure Map – Touring Scotland* shows most tourist attractions. Munro-baggers should look out for the Bartholomew map of the Munros.

What to Bring

Bring some form of waterproof clothing or an umbrella. If you're going walking, it's worth treating your boots with a waterproofing agent as some trails cross boggy ground. In summer you'll need insect repellent to ward off the midges (see Dangers & Annoyances later in this chapter and also in the Regional Facts for the Visitor chapter).

TOURIST OFFICES

Outside Britain, contact the British Tourist Authority (BTA).

Local Tourist Offices

The Scottish Tourist Board (STB) (☎ 0131-332 2433, fax 0131-315 4545) has its headquarters at 23 Ravelston Terrace (PO Box 705), Edinburgh EH4 3EU. In London, contact the STB (☎ 0171-930 8661), 19 Cockspur St, London SW1 5BL, off Trafalgar Square, for routes, detailed information and reservations.

Most towns have TICs that open weekdays from 9 am to 5 pm, often opening at weekends in summer. In small places, particularly in the Highlands, TICs only open from Easter to September.

VISAS & DOCUMENTS

No visas are required if you arrive from England or Northern Ireland. If you arrive from the Republic of Ireland or any other country, normal British customs and immigration regulations apply (see the Regional Facts for the Visitor chapter).

CONSULATES & HIGH COMMISSIONS

Edinburgh's consulates and high commissions include:

Belgium
(☎ 01968-679969)
21b The Square, EH26 8LH
Denmark
(☎ 0131-556 4263)
4 Royal Terrace, EH7 5AB
Canada
(☎ 0131-245 6013)
30 Lothian Rd, EH1 2DH
France
(☎ 0131-225 7954)
11 Randolph Crescent, EH3 7TT
Germany
(☎ 0131-337 2323)
16 Eglinton Crescent, EH12 5DG
Italy
(☎ 0131-226 3631)
32 Melville St, EH3 7HA
Japan
(☎ 0131-225 4777)
2 Melville Crescent, EH3 7HW
Netherlands
(☎ 0131-220 3226)
53 George St, EH2 2HT
Spain
(☎ 0131-220 1843)
63 North Castle St, EH2 3LJ
Sweden
(☎ 0131-554 6631)
6 Johns Place, Leith, EH6 7EP
Switzerland
(☎ 0131-226 5660)
66 Hanover St, EH2 1HH
USA
(☎ 0131-556 8315)
3 Regent Terrace, EH7 5BW

MONEY
Costs

Backpacker accommodation is more readily available in Scotland than England, so you'll be able to keep costs down. Edinburgh is more expensive than most other mainland towns, but prices rise steeply in remote parts of the Highlands and on the Islands where supplies depend on ferries. Petrol can cost 10p to 15p a litre more on the Islands than in the central Lowlands. Throughout this book admission costs are given as adult/child.

Currency

The pound sterling is valid on both sides of the border, but the Clydesdale Bank, Royal Bank of Scotland and Bank of Scotland issue their own banknotes, including pound notes. You won't have any trouble changing Scottish notes in shops etc immediately south of the Scotland-England border, but elsewhere it may be difficult.

Cards

You can use MasterCard Worldwide card in ATMs belonging to the Royal Bank of Scotland and Clydesdale Bank; with a Visa card you can use the Bank of Scotland, Royal Bank of Scotland, Clydesdale Bank and TSB; American Express card-holders can use the Bank of Scotland.

If you have a UK bank account in England, then you can use a National Westminster or Midland cash card at Clydesdale, and a Lloyds or Barclays cash card at Royal Bank of Scotland or Bank of Scotland.

INTERNET RESOURCES

You can access the Scottish Tourist Board's Web site at www.holiday.scotland.net. Edinburgh Fringe Festival-goers can check out www.edfringe.com; information on all

Edinburgh festivals can be found at www
.go-edinburgh-.co.uk.

BOOKS
Lonely Planet
Lonely Planet's *Walking in Britain* has two
chapters on Scottish trails. Also check out
the *Scotland* and *Edinburgh* guides.

Guidebooks
There are numerous local guidebooks, the
most useful mentioned in the text. See also
Books in the Regional Facts for the Visitor
chapter.

Travel
One of the greatest Scottish travelogues is
*The Journal of a Tour to the Hebrides with
Samuel Johnson*, by James Boswell. This
famous lexicographer and his Scottish biographer visited Skye, Coll and Mull in
1773, and met Flora MacDonald (who had
helped Bonnie Prince Charlie escape after
the battle of Culloden).

Native Stranger (1995), by Alistair Scott,
recounts the efforts of a Scot who knew
'more about the Sandinistas' to learn about
the realities of modern Scotland by travelling throughout the country.

In *Danziger's Britain* (1997), Nick
Danziger describes the grim reality of life
for many marginalised people in the Highlands and Glasgow.

History
Michael Lynch's *Scotland – A New History*
provides a good historical background up to
the early 1990s. Tom Steel's *Scotland's
Story* is readable and well illustrated but
stops in the early 1980s. *A Short History of
Scotland*, by Richard Killeen, is a concise
up-to-date introduction.

To flesh out some of the great figures of
Scottish history, there are many well-
written biographies, including Antonia
Fraser's *Mary Queen of Scots* and Fitzroy
Maclean's *Bonnie Prince Charlie*. John
Prebble has written passionate accounts of
the Highland Clearances, the massacre in
Glen Coe or the battle of Culloden.

General
Gavin Maxwell wrote several books about
his life among otters and other wildlife in the
Highlands; *Ring of Bright Water* is probably
best known. The naturalist, Mike Tomkies,
wrote an evocative series of books, including
A Last Wild Place, about his experiences
while living in a remote West Highland

Scotland on Film

Scotland has been the setting for many
films. Earlier ones include *The Prime of
Miss Jean Brodie* (1969) and *Kidnapped*
(1972). Time was when the film most
closely associated with Scotland was probably *Local Hero* (1983), Bill Forsyth's
gentle story of an oil magnate turned con-
servationist for love of the scenery. His
other great success was *Gregory's Girl*
(1980), about an awkward teenage
schoolboy's romantic exploits. A sequel is
now in production.

When *Braveheart*, the Mel Gibson spin
on the William Wallace saga, won an
Oscar in 1996 the Scottish Tourist Board
cheered, anticipating a boom in tourists
lured by the glorious scenery in the background. What the STB wasn't shouting
about, however, was that though it was
partly filmed around Fort William, most of
Braveheart was shot in Ireland which had
been wooing Hollywood film-makers with
tax breaks.

The same year saw the release of *Loch
Ness*, a romantic comedy focussing on the
monster myth, following fast on the
success of *Trainspotting*, the grim film rendition of Irvine Welsh's novel set in
Edinburgh. All this, when memories of *Rob
Roy*, the 1995 rendition of the outlaws'
tale, starring Liam Neeson and Jessica
Lange with wonky Scottish accents, were
only just fading.

Billy Connolly's accent was real enough
when he played John Brown, Queen Victoria's Scottish servant in *Mrs Brown*
(1997).

cottage in the 1980s. *The Silver Darlings*, Neil Gunn's story of the north-east's great fishing communities in the days before European Union quotas, is worth seeking out.

NEWSPAPERS & MAGAZINES

The Scots have published newspapers since the mid-17th century. Scotland's home-grown dailies include the *Scotsman*, a Liberal Democrat paper; the *Herald*, formerly the *Glasgow Herald*; and the tabloid *Daily Record*. The *Sunday Post* is the country's best-selling Sunday paper. Most papers sold elsewhere in Britain are available in Scotland, some designed specifically for Scottish readership.

The monthly *Scots Magazine*, with articles on all aspects of Scottish life, has been in circulation since the 18th century.

RADIO & TV

Radio and TV stations are linked to the national network, although there are considerable regional variations. Scottish Television (STV) carries Gaelic-speaking programs.

USEFUL ORGANISATIONS
Scottish Youth Hostel Association (SYHA)

The SYHA (see also Accommodation later in this chapter) markets an Explore Scotland ticket and Scottish Wayfarer ticket, that represent a worthwhile saving, especially if you're not a student; see the Getting Around chapter for details. The SYHA head office (☎ 01786-891400) is at 7 Glebe Crescent, Stirling, FK8 2JA.

Historic Scotland

Historic Scotland (HS) (☎ 0131-668 8800), Longmore House, Salisbury Place, Edinburgh EH9 1SH, manages more than 330 historic sites, including top attractions like Edinburgh and Stirling castles. A year's membership costs £22/16 for an adult/child, giving free entry to HS sites and half-price entry to English Heritage properties in England, and Cadw properties in Wales. It also offers short-term 'Explorer' membership – seven/14 days for £12.50/17.

There are standard HS opening times. From April to September properties open daily from 9.30 am to 6.30 pm. From October to March they close two hours earlier. Last entry is 30 minutes before closing time.

In this book, the initials HS indicate a Historic Scotland property – and, unless indicated otherwise, standard opening times apply.

National Trust for Scotland

The National Trust for Scotland (NTS) (☎ 0131-226 5922), 5 Charlotte Square, Edinburgh EH2 4DU, is separate from the National Trust (England, Wales and Northern Ireland), although there are reciprocal membership agreements. The NTS cares for over 100 properties and 185,000 acres of countryside.

A year's membership of the NTS costing £25 (£10 if you're aged under 26) offers free access to all NTS and NT properties. Short-term membership (touring ticket) costs £16/24 for one/two weeks. YHA members and student-card-holders get half-price entry to NTS properties.

In this book, the letters NTS indicate a National Trust for Scotland property.

DANGERS & ANNOYANCES

Edinburgh and Glasgow have all the usual big-city problems, so normal caution is advised.

Highland hikers should be properly equipped and cautious: the weather can become vicious at any time of the year. After rain peaty soil can become boggy; always wear stout shoes and carry a change of clothing.

Midges

The most infuriatingly painful problem facing visitors to the west coast and Highlands is midges. These tiny blood-sucking flies are related to mosquitoes. From late May to mid-September (especially from mid-June to mid-August) they can be prolific. It's at least partly thanks to them that much of Scotland remains a wilderness. They're at their worst in the evening or in cloudy or shady conditions.

There are several possible defences. Cover up, particularly in the evening; wear light-coloured clothing (midges are attracted to dark colours); and, most importantly, buy a reliable insect repellent containing DEET or DMP.

Church Regulations

In the Highlands and Islands the Free Church of Scotland (the Wee Frees) and the United Free Presbyterians, adhere so strictly to the scriptures that in some areas on Sundays the public toilets are padlocked and ferries aren't always allowed to operate.

RAF Jets

The sudden appearance and sound of RAF jets is both frightening and annoying. It's something you never get used to.

Racial Discrimination

Few visitors will be aware of anti-English feelings but they exist, fanned by organisations that try to dissuade the English (and other nationalities) from buying property in the Highlands.

BUSINESS HOURS

Minimum banking hours are weekdays from 9.30 am to 3.30 pm; a few places close from 12.30 to 1.30 pm, but the tendency is to longer hours. Post offices and shops open weekdays from 9 am to 5.30 pm; post offices close at 1 pm on Saturday. Shops in small towns sometimes have an early-closing day midweek, while in cities there's often late night shopping Thursday till 7 or 8 pm.

In the Highlands and Islands many pubs have the infuriating habit of closing for two hours mid-afternoon (usually from 2 to 4 pm).

PUBLIC HOLIDAYS

Although bank holidays are general public holidays in England, in Scotland they only apply to banks and some other commercial offices. Bank holidays occur at the start of January, the first weekend in March, the first and last weekend in May, the first weekend in August and Christmas Day and Boxing Day.

New Year's Day and Good Friday are general holidays, and Scottish towns normally have a spring and autumn holiday. Dates vary not only from year to year but also from town to town.

ACCOMMODATION
Camping

You can camp free on public land (unless it's specifically protected). Commercial camping grounds are geared to caravans and vary widely in quality. A tent site costs around £6.50. If you plan to use a tent regularly, invest in *Scotland: Camping & Caravan Parks*, available from most TICs. Camping and caravan parks are graded by the STB, reflecting the level and quality of facilities.

Bothies, Camping Barns & Bunkhouses

Bothies are simple shelters, often in remote places. They're not locked, there's no charge, and you can't book. Take your own cooking equipment, sleeping bag and mat. Users should stay one night only, and leave it as they find it.

A camping barn – usually a converted farm building – is where walkers can stay for around £3 per night. Bunkhouses are a grade or two up from camping barns, have stoves for heating and cooking and may supply utensils. They may have mattresses, but you'll still need a sleeping bag. Most charge from £6.50.

Hostels
Scottish Youth Hostel Association (SYHA)

The SYHA (π 01786-891400, fax 01786-891333), 7 Glebe Crescent, Stirling FK8 2JA, is separate from the YHA. Its hostels are generally cheaper and often better than those in England. The SYHA produces a handbook (£1.50) giving details on around 80 hostels, including transport links. In big cities, costs are £11.50/9.95 for adults/juniors; the rest range from £4.65/3.85 to £8.60/7.10.

Independent & Student Hostels

There's a growing number of independent hostels/bunkhouses, with prices averaging around £9.50. The *Independent Hostel Guide – Backpackers Accommodation*, available from some TICs, lists over 90 hostels in Scotland. Alternatively, you can send a stamped, addressed envelope to Pete Thomas, Croft Bunkhouses & Bothies, 7 Portnalong, Isle of Skye IV47 8SL.

In university towns, cheap accommodation is usually available in student hostels during college holidays. Local TICs have details.

B&Bs, Guesthouses & Hotels

B&Bs and guesthouses tend to be cheaper than their English counterparts; budget travellers are unlikely to have to pay more than £18 per person.

At the other end of the scale, however, there are some wonderfully luxurious places, including country-house hotels in superb settings, and castles complete with crenellated battlements, grand staircases and the obligatory rows of stags' heads. For these you can pay from around £60 to well over £100 per person.

TICs have local booking services (usually £1) and a Book-A-Bed-Ahead (BABA) scheme (£3). A refundable deposit is also required for most bookings. The service is worth using in July and August, but isn't necessary otherwise, unless you plan to arrive in a town after business hours when the local TIC is closed. If you arrive late, it may still be worth going to the TIC, since some leave a list in the window showing which B&Bs had rooms free when they closed.

Short-Term Rental

There's plenty of self-catering accommodation but, in summer at least, the minimum stay is usually one week. Details are in the accommodation guides available from TICs. Alternatively, buy a copy of the STB's *Scotland: Self-Catering Accommodation*.

FOOD

Scotland's chefs have an enviable range of fresh meat, seafood and vegetables at their disposal. The country has gone a long way to shake off its once dismal culinary reputation. Most restaurants are reasonably good while some are internationally renowned.

The Scots' high rate of heart disease partly results from their high consumption of alcohol and cigarettes, but also from many poorer Scots eating a less healthy diet – high on fried foods, refined sugar and white bread – than previous generations. However, restaurants don't usually serve greasy, fatty foods.

The quality of cooking at hotel restaurants and B&Bs that provide evening meals is variable. In small villages the alternatives are usually bleak, although village bakeries have a good range of pies, cakes and snacks. In towns there are Indian and Chinese alternatives, as well as fast food chains and the classier Pierre Victoire and Littlejohn's.

Lunch is served from 12.30 to 2 pm, dinner from 7 to around 9 pm. An alternative to dinner is high tea (from about 4.30 to 6.30 pm), when a main dish is served with tea and cakes.

Some of the best places to eat are members of the Taste of Scotland scheme. The STB's annual *Taste of Scotland Guide* is worth buying to track down these restaurants and hotels.

Many restaurants have at least one vegetarian dish on the menu.

Scottish Breakfast

You'll rarely be offered porridge in a B&B. Generally, a glass of fruit juice accompanies a bowl of cereal or muesli, followed by a cooked breakfast which may include: bacon, sausage, black pudding (a type of sausage made from dried blood), grilled tomato, grilled mushrooms, fried bread or tattie (potato) scones (if you're lucky), and an egg or two. More upmarket hotels may offer porridge followed by kippers (smoked herrings). As well as toast, there may be oatcakes (oatmeal biscuits) to spread your marmalade upon. In the Aberdeen area there may also be butteries – delicious butter-rich bread rolls.

Snacks

As well as ordinary scones (similar to American biscuits), Scottish bakeries usually offer milk scones, tattie scones and girdle scones. Bannocks are a cross between scones and pancakes. Savoury pies include the *bridie* (a pie filled with meat, potatoes and sometimes other vegetables) and the Scotch pie (minced meat in a plain round pastry casing – best eaten hot).

Dundee cake, a rich fruit cake topped with almonds, is highly recommended. Black bun is another type of fruit cake, eaten over Hogmanay (New Year's Eve).

Soups

Scotch broth, made with barley, lentils and mutton stock, is highly nutritious and very good. Cock-a-leekie is a substantial soup made from a cock, or chicken, and leeks.

You may not be drawn to *powsowdie* (sheep's-head broth) but it's very tasty. More popular is *cullen skink*, a fish soup containing smoked haddock.

Meat & Game

Steak eaters will enjoy a thick fillet of world-famous Aberdeen Angus beef, while beef from Highland cattle is much sought after. Venison, from the red deer, is leaner and appears on many menus. Both may be served with a wine-based or creamy whisky sauce.

Game birds like pheasant and grouse, traditionally roasted and served with game chips and fried breadcrumbs, are also available. They're definitely worth trying, but watch your teeth on the shot, which is not always removed before cooking. Then there's haggis, Scotland's much-maligned national dish …

Fish & Seafood

Scottish salmon is well known but there's a big difference between farmed salmon and

---

Haggis – Scotland's National Dish

A popular rhyme, penned by an English poet, goes:

For the land of Burns
The only snag is
The haggis

Scotland's national dish is frequently ridiculed by foreigners because of its ingredients which don't sound too mouth watering. However, once you get over any delicate sensibilities towards tucking in to chopped lungs, heart and liver mixed with oatmeal and boiled in a sheep's stomach, with the accompanying glass of whisky it can taste surprisingly good.

Haggis should be served with tatties and neeps (mashed potatoes and turnips, with a generous dollop of butter and a good sprinkling of black pepper).

Although it's eaten year round, haggis is central to the celebrations of 25 January in honour of Scotland's national poet, Robert Burns. Scots worldwide unite on Burns Night to revel in their Scottishness. A piper announces the arrival of the haggis and Burns' poem *Address to a Haggis* (otherwise known as the Selkirk Grace) is recited to this 'Great chieftan o' the puddin-race'. The bulging stomach is then lanced with a *dirk* (dagger) to reveal the steaming offal within.

Vegetarians (and quite a few carnivores, no doubt) will be relieved to know that veggie haggis is available in some restaurants in Scotland.

---

the leaner, more expensive, wild version. Both are available either smoked (served with brown bread and butter) or poached. Smoked brown trout is cheaper, and also good.

As an alternative to kippers (smoked herrings) you may be offered Arbroath smokies (lightly smoked fresh haddock), traditionally eaten cold. Herrings in oatmeal are good if you don't mind the bones. *Krappin heit* is cod's head stuffed with fish livers and oatmeal. Mackerel paté and smoked or peppered mackerel (both served cold) are also popular.

Prawns, crab, lobster, oysters, mussels and scallops are available in coastal towns and around lochs, although much is exported.

Cheeses

The Scottish cheese industry is growing. Cheddar is its main output but there are a speciality cheese-makers whose products are worth sampling. Many are based on the islands.

Brodick Blue is a ewes' milk blue cheese made on Arran. Lanark Blue is rather like Roquefort. There are several varieties of cream cheese (Caboc, St Finan, Howgate) that are usually rolled in oatmeal.

Scottish oatcakes make the perfect accompaniment for cheese.

Puddings

Traditional Scottish puddings are irresistibly creamy, calorie-enriched concoctions. *Cranachan* is made with toasted oatmeal, raspberries, or some other fresh fruit, and whisky, all mixed into thick cream. *Atholl brose* is similar but without the fruit – rather like English syllabub. Clootie dumpling is delicious, a rich steamed pudding filled with currants and raisins.

DRINKS
Nonalcoholic Drinks

On quantity drunk, tea probably qualifies as Scotland's national drink, but coffee is widely available and catching up. Definitely an acquired taste is the virulent orange-coloured fizzy drink, Irn-Bru; it's 100% sugar plus some pretty weird flavouring.

Alcoholic Drinks

Whisky First distilled in Scotland in the 15th century, whisky (spelt without an 'e' if it's Scottish) is Scotland's best-known product and biggest export; over 2000 brands are now produced.

There are two kinds of whisky: single malt, made from malted barley, and blended whisky, distilled from unmalted grain (maize) and blended with selected malts. Single malts are rarer (there are only about 100 brands) and more expensive than blended whiskies. Although distilleries exist all over the country, there are concentrations around Speyside and on the isle of Islay.

As well as blends and single malts, there are also several whisky-based liqueurs like Drambuie. If you must mix your whisky with anything other than water try a whisky-mac (whisky with ginger wine). After a long walk in the rain there's nothing better to warm you up.

When out drinking, Scots may order a dram (measure) of whisky as a chaser to a pint of beer. Only tourists say 'Scotch' – what else would you be served in Scotland?

Beer Most popular is what the Scots call 'heavy', a dark beer similar to English bitter. Most Scottish brews are graded in shillings so you can tell their strength, the usual range being 60 to 80 shillings (written 80/-). The greater the number of shillings, the stronger the beer.

The market is dominated by the big brewers: Youngers, McEwans, Scottish & Newcastle and Tennent's. Look out for beer from local breweries, some of it very strong – the aptly-named Skullsplitter from Orkney is a good example. Caledonian 80/-, Maclays 80/- and Bellhaven 80/- are others worth trying.

Long before hops arrived in Scotland, beer was brewed from heather. Reintroduced, heather ale is surprisingly good and available in some pubs.

ENTERTAINMENT

In Scotland the pub is the place to go and you'll get a warm reception at most. Ask at your hostel, B&B or hotel for local recommendations. Larger cities like Edinburgh, Glasgow, Aberdeen and Dundee have theatres, concert halls and cinemas, and Glasgow and Edinburgh have lively club

The Malt Whisky Trail

Roughly 45 Scottish whisky distilleries open to the public and you should certainly try to visit one while you're in Scotland.

In some, showing tourists around has become a slick marketing operation, complete with promotional videos, free drams, gift shops that rival the distillery in size and an entry charge of around £3. Eight Speyside distillers – Glenfiddich, Cardhu, Glenfarclas, Glen Grant, The Glenlivet, Strathisla, Tamdhu and Tamnavulin – promote themselves in the Malt Whisky Trail, a pleasant drive around Speyside, although visiting all eight might be overkill. You can also create your own malt whisky trail – on the island of Islay, six distilleries can be visited.

The process of making malt whisky begins with malting. Barley is soaked in water and allowed to germinate so that enzymes are produced to convert the starch in the barley to fermentable sugar. The barley is then dried in a malt kiln over the peat fire that gives malt whisky its distinctive taste. Since most distilleries now buy in their malted barley, tourists rarely see this part of the process.

The malt is milled, mixed with hot water and left in a large tank, the mash tun. The starch is converted into sugar and this liquid, or 'wort', is drawn off into another large tank, the washback, for fermentation.

This weak alcoholic solution, or wash, is distilled twice in large copper-pot stills. The process is controlled by the stillman, who collects only the middle portion of the second distillation to mature in oak barrels. The spirit remains in the barrels for at least three years, often much longer. During bottling, water is added to reduce its strength.

Some recommended distillery tours include: Glenfiddich, The Glenlivet and Strathisla on Speyside; any of the Islay distilleries; and Highland Park on Orkney, one of the few distilleries where you still see the barley malting process.

scenes. In Glasgow or Edinburgh, look out for *The List*, a fortnightly listings magazine.

Many tourist centres stage a ceilidh or Highland show featuring Scottish song and dance, most nights during the summer. Some local restaurants also combine a floor show with dinner.

If you fancy an eightsome reel, ceilidhs with dancing that you can join in usually take place Friday or Saturday. Ask at the local TIC for details. It's not as difficult as it looks and there's often a 'caller' to lead everyone through their paces.

SHOPPING

Making things to sell to tourists is big business in Scotland, and almost every visitor attraction seems to have been redesigned to funnel you through the gift shop. Amongst the tourist kitsch are some good-value, high-quality goods.

If you're interested in visiting mills, factories and craft shops, pick up a copy of the STB publication *See Scotland at Work*.

Tartan, Tweed & Other Textiles

Scottish textiles, particularly tartans, are popular and tartan travelling rugs or scarves are often worth buying. There are said to be over 2000 designs, some officially recognised as clan tartans. Many shops have a list and can tell you if your family belongs to a clan, but these days if you can pay for the cloth you can wear the tartan. There are some universal tartans, like the Flower of Scotland, that aren't connected with a clan. For about £350 to £400, you can have a kilt made in your clan tartan, but this shouldn't be worn without a *sporran* (purse), which can cost from £40 for a plain version up to £1000 for an ornate silver-dress sporran. Full kilts are traditionally worn only by men, while women wear kilted or tartan skirts.

There are mill shops in many parts of Scotland, but the best-known textile manufacturing areas are the Borders and Central regions, particularly around Stirling and Perth. Scotland is also renowned for a rough woollen cloth known as tweed – Harris tweed is world famous. There are various places on this Hebridean island where you can watch your cloth being woven.

Sheepskin rugs and jackets are also popular.

Knitwear

Scottish knitwear can be great value and is sold throughout Scotland. Shetland is most closely associated with high-quality wool, and at knitwear factory shops you can buy genuine Shetland sweaters for as little as £11. The most sought-after sweaters bear the intricate Fair Isle pattern – the genuine article from this remote island costs at least £25.

Jewellery & Glassware

Silver brooches set with cairngorms (yellow or wine-coloured gems from the mountains of the same name) are popular. Jewellery decorated with Celtic designs featuring mythical creatures and intricate patterns is particularly attractive, although some pieces are actually made in Cornwall. Glassware, particularly Edinburgh crystal and Caithness glass, is another good souvenir.

Food & Drink

Sweet, butter-rich Scottish shortbread makes a good gift. The biggest manufacturer, Walkers, bakes such prodigious quantities of the stuff that the Speyside town of Aberlour smells of nothing else. Dark, fruity Dundee cake lasts well and is available in a tin, but heavy to take home by air. Heather honey can give you a reminder of Scotland when your visit is over.

If you haven't far to go, smoked salmon or any other smoked product (venison, mussels etc) are worth buying, but some countries don't allow you to import meat and fish.

As for souvenir bottles of whisky, you're better off buying it duty-free at the airport than in High Street shops, unless it's a rare brand. If you go on a distillery tour, you may be given £1 or so discount to buy a bottle there. Miniature bottles make good presents.

Getting There & Away

AIR

There are direct air services from London and other European cities to Edinburgh, Glasgow, Dundee, Aberdeen, Inverness or Kirkwall, and from North America to Glasgow. The standard one-way fare from New York to Glasgow is around US$590 (£385).

Travelling from Europe it's often better flying to London then taking a train or bus north. The standard return flights from London to Glasgow or Edinburgh cost around £265. No frills one-way tickets can, however, be as low as £29. See the Getting Around chapter at the start of the book.

Within the UK, British Airways (☎ 0345-222111) has flights from London's Heathrow, Gatwick and Stansted, and from Birmingham, Manchester and Belfast; KLM UK (☎ 0990-074074) flies from Stansted; and British Airways Express/Loganair (☎ 0345-222111) from Manchester. Easyjet (☎ 0990-292929) flies from London's Luton airport. British Midland (☎ 0345-554554) flies from Heathrow.

Flying time from London to Edinburgh is about one hour, but adding the time taken to get between the airports and the city centres, and boarding time, the four-hour centre-to-centre rail trip takes only about an hour more in actual travelling time.

LAND

Bus

Long-distance buses (coaches) are usually the cheapest method of getting to Scotland. The main operator is Scottish Citylink (☎ 0990-505050), part of the Britain-wide National Express group, with numerous regular services from London and other departure points in England and Wales (see the Edinburgh chapter, and Glasgow in the Southern Scotland chapter).

Fares on the main routes are competitive, with new operators undercutting National Express. From London, advance-purchase tickets cost from £14/26 single/return.

The budget bus company Slow Coach, that operates between youth hostels in England, ventures into Scotland as far as Edinburgh. See this book's introductory Getting Around chapter.

Train

InterCity services can take you from London's King's Cross to Edinburgh in as little as four hours, or to Glasgow in five hours (see those sections). Call ☎ 0345-484950 for fare and timetable information.

The cheapest adult return ticket between London and Edinburgh or Glasgow is the SuperApex, which costs only £35. Numerous restrictions apply to these tickets, which must be purchased 14 days in advance and are difficult to get hold of in summer. Apex tickets (£49 return) must be bought seven days in advance and are more readily available. See also the Getting Around chapter at the beginning of this book.

Car & Motorcycle

The main roads are busy and quick. Edinburgh is 373 miles from London, and Glasgow is 392 miles from London. Allow eight hours for the trip. It makes more sense to break the journey en route, perhaps in York or Chester, or in the Lake District.

Hitching

It's easy enough, though not necessarily wise, to hitch to Scotland along the A68 (to Edinburgh) or the A74 (to Glasgow). The coastal routes are slow. See also Hitching in the Getting Around chapter at the start of this book.

SEA

For more details on the following ferry services see the Getting There & Away chapter at the start of this book.

Northern Ireland

Scotland has ferry links to Larne, near Belfast, from Cairnryan (P&O, ☎ 0990-980666) and from Stranraer (Stena Line, ☎ 0990-707070), both are south-west of Glasgow. A high-speed catamaran also operates between Stranraer and Belfast. There's a ferry from Campbeltown (Argyll & Antrim Steam Packet Company, ☎ 0345-523523) in Argyll to Ballycastle in County Antrim.

Scandinavia

From late May to early September, P&O (☎ 01224-572615) operates one ferry a week between Bergen (Norway), Lerwick (Shetland Islands) and Aberdeen. From Bergen the ferry leaves at 3 pm Tuesday, arriving in Lerwick at 1.30 am on Wednesday.

Once a week from late May to early September, Smyril Line runs between Lerwick, Bergen, Tórshavn (Faroes) and Seydisfjördur (Iceland) calling at Lerwick once weekly. P&O is the agent for Smyril Line. See the Getting There & Away chapter at the start of this book for more details.

To make a fascinating northern sea route, you could link these two ferry services.

Getting Around

PASSES

If you're not a student, it's worth considering the Freedom of Scotland Travelpass – see the passes table in this chapter for details. For more information contact ScotRail (☎ 0345-484950), which administers the scheme. Tickets are available from the Scottish Travel Centre, at London's Victoria and King's Cross train stations, and from the main stations in Glasgow and Edinburgh.

The Scottish Youth Hostels Association (SYHA; ☎ 01786-891400) markets an Explore Scotland ticket. It includes a Citylink bus pass and seven nights' SYHA accommodation, a bus timetable, a Scotpass discount card, free SYHA membership and a handbook and a Historic Scotland pass for £155/250 for five/eight days travel. The Scottish Wayfarer ticket gives a similar package but includes travel by rail and on Caledonian MacBrayne's west-coast and Strathclyde PT ferries. It costs £160/270/299 for four/eight/12 days travel.

AIR

It might be worth flying to Barra to experience landing on a beach. Otherwise, flying is a pricey way to get round relatively short distances. It's worth checking whether any passes are available.

Several carriers, including British Airways Express/Loganair (☎ 0345-222111), British Airways (☎ 0345-222111) and Air UK (☎ 0345-666777), connect the main towns, the Western Isles, Orkney and Shetland.

BUS

Scotland's internal bus network has one major player, Scottish Citylink (☎ 0990-505050), part of the Britain-wide National Express group, and numerous smaller regional companies that come and go with astonishing rapidity.

From June to September, Haggis Backpackers (☎ 0131-557 9393), 11 Blackfriars St, Edinburgh, runs a daily service on a circuit between hostels in Edinburgh, Perth, Pitlochry, Aviemore, Inverness, Loch Ness, Isle of Skye, Fort William, Glencoe, Oban, Inverary, Loch Lomond and Glasgow (although there's no obligation to stay in the hostels). You can hop on and off the minibus wherever and whenever you like, booking up to 24 hours in advance. There's no fixed time for completing the circuit, but you can only cover each section of the route once. At other times of the year there are still five or six departures a week. Go Blue Banana (☎ 0131-556 2000), 16 High St, Edinburgh, also runs a jump-on, jump-off service on the same circuit. See the Scottish Transport Passes table for more information.

Both companies also offer excellent-value three-day Highlands tours for £75, leaving from Edinburgh.

The National Express Tourist Trail Pass (see the Getting Around chapter at the start of this book) can be used on Scottish Citylink services. Citylink also honours European under-26 cards, including the Young Scot card (£7), which provides discounts all over Scotland and Europe.

If they don't have one of these cards, full-time students and people aged under 26 have to buy the so-called Smart Card, the equivalent to the National Express Discount Coach Card (see the Getting Around chapter at the start of the book). On presentation of proof of age, or student status (an NUS or ISIC card), a passport photo and an £8 fee, you get the Smart Card to add to your collection. It entitles you to a 30% discount, so chances are you'll be ahead after buying your first ticket.

Royal Mail postbuses can be useful for walkers. For information and timetables contact Communications (☎ 0131-228 7407), Royal Mail Scotland, 102 West Port, Edinburgh EH3 9HS.

Most buses don't carry bicycles.

TRAIN

Scotland has some stunning train routes but they're limited and expensive, so you'll probably have to use other modes of transport too. The West Highland line through Fort William to Mallaig, and the routes from Stirling to Inverness, Inverness to Thurso, and Inverness to Kyle of Lochalsh are some of the best in the world. You can make ScotRail bookings by credit card on ☎ 0345-550033.

The BritRail pass, which includes travel in Scotland, must be bought outside Britain. ScotRail's Freedom of Scotland Travelpass

Scottish Transport Passes		
Pass Name	Cost (Prices for adults/ discount card holders)	Bus/train/ferry services offered
Freedom of Scotland Travelpass	£64 for 4 days out of 8 consecutive days £93 for 8 days out of 15 consecutive days £122 for 12 days out of 15 days consecutive days	Unlimited travel on trains, CalMac ferries and Strathclyde ferries. 33% discount on postbuses and most important regional bus lines. 33% discount on P&O Orkney to Scrabster ferry, 20% discount on P&O Aberdeen to Shetland, Aberdeen to Orkney. £1.50 off Guide Friday city tours of Edinburgh, Glasgow and Dundee.
National Express Tourist Trail Pass	As for Britain – see Getting Around chapter	All National Express and Scottish Citylink buses.
National Express Discount Coach Card (full time students; under 26; over 50)	£8	30% off adult fares on all Scottish Citylink buses.
Explore Scotland (SYHA)	£155 for 5 days £250 for 8 days	Includes Citylink bus pass, with 7 nights SYHA accommodation and a Historic Scotland pass, plus other benefits.
Scottish Wayfarer (SYHA)	£160 for 4 days £270 for 8 days £299 for 12 days	Similar to Explore Scotland, but also includes rail travel and CalMac west coast and Strathclyde PT ferries.
Young Person's or Senior's Railcard	£18 per annum	33% off rail throughout Britain.
Go Blue Banana Haggis Backpackers	Both £85	Jump on, jump off circuit route.
Flexipass	As for Britain	

(see the Scottish Transport Passes table) and Regional Rover tickets can be bought in Britain, including from most train stations in Scotland.

The Highland Rover ticket covers the West Highlands and Inverness-Kyle line (£42 for four out of eight consecutive days). The Festival Cities Rover covers the central area (£26 for three out of seven consecutive days).

Reservations for bicycles (£3.50) are compulsory on many services.

Sometimes the cheap day-return fare is cheaper than the full one-way fare.

CAR & MOTORCYCLE

Scotland's roads are generally good and not as busy as those in England, so driving is more enjoyable. The fast A9, that runs up the centre, is the busiest road. In the Highlands and Islands the main hazards are suicidal sheep … and the distracting beauty of the landscape!

In some areas, roads are only single track, with passing places indicated by a pole. It's illegal to park in these places. In the same areas petrol stations are few and far between and sometimes closed on Sunday. Petrol prices also tend to rise as you get further from main population centres.

HITCHING

Hitching is reasonably easy in Scotland, with the average wait 30 to 40 minutes. Although the north-west is more difficult because there's less traffic, waits of over two hours are unusual (except on Sunday as the Sabbath is still widely observed in areas

of the north and west). Public transport doesn't stop on the A9 (except in villages); otherwise, buses will usually stop and rescue you if they're not full. See also Hitching in the Getting Around chapter at the start of this book.

BOAT

Caledonian MacBrayne (CalMac; ☎ 0990-650000) is the most important ferry operator on the west coast, with services from Ullapool to the Outer Hebrides, and from Mallaig to Skye and on to the Outer Hebrides. Its main west-coast port, however, is Oban, with ferries to the islands of Barra, South Uist, Coll, Tiree, Lismore, Mull and Colonsay.

As an example, a single passenger fare from Oban to Lochboisdale, South Uist (Hebrides), is £17.30. However, it pays to plan your complete trip in advance since CalMac's Island Hopscotch tickets are usually the best deal, with ferry combinations over 15 set routes. CalMac also has Rover tickets, offering unlimited travel for eight and 15 days (£39/56).

P&O (☎ 01224-572615) has ferries from Aberdeen and Scrabster to Orkney, and from Aberdeen to Shetland. From June to August, the cheapest one-way tickets to Stromness (Orkney) cost £14 from Scrabster, £37 from Aberdeen. Between Aberdeen and Shetland, the standard fare is £55. There's a 10% student discount.

Taking a car on the ferries is expensive. You can save some money by hiring once you get onto the islands.

Edinburgh

- **pop 409,000** ☎ **0131**

Edinburgh has an incomparable location, studded with volcanic hills, on the southern edge of the Firth of Forth. Its superb architecture ranges from extraordinary 16th century tenements to monumental Georgian and Victorian masterpieces – all dominated by a castle on a precipitous crag in the city's heart. Sixteen thousand buildings are listed as architecturally or historically important, in a city which is a World Heritage Site.

The geology and architecture combine to create an extraordinary symphony in stone. The Old Town, with its crowded tenements, stands in contrast to the orderly grid of the New Town with its disciplined Georgian buildings. There are vistas from every street – sudden views of the Firth of Forth, the castle, the Pentland Hills, Calton Hill with its memorials, and rugged Arthur's Seat.

All the great dramas of Scottish history have played at least one act in Edinburgh, the royal capital since the 11th century. Even after the union of 1707 it remained the centre for government administration (now the Scottish Office), the separate Scottish legal system and the Presbyterian Church of Scotland.

In some ways, however, it's the least Scottish of Scotland's cities, partly because of the impact of tourism, partly because of its closeness to England and partly because of its multicultural, sophisticated population.

Edinburgh has a reputation for being civilised and reserved, especially in comparison with intense, gregarious Glasgow. Nevertheless, there's a vibrant pub scene, and the dynamism of the world's greatest arts festival every August.

The flip side to the gloss is the grim reality of life in the bleak council housing estates surrounding the city, the thriving drug scene, prostitution and a distressing AIDS problem.

HISTORY

Castle Rock, a volcanic crag with three vertical sides, dominates the city centre. This natural defensive position was probably

735

EDINBURGH

what first attracted settlers; the earliest signs of habitation date back to 850 BC.

Northumbrian Angles captured Lothian in the 6th century, rebuilding a fortress, known as Dun Eadain, on Castle Rock. This served as the Scots' southern outpost until 1018 when Malcolm II established a frontier at the River Tweed. Nonetheless, the English sacked the city seven times.

Edinburgh began to grow in the 11th century when markets developed at the foot of the fortress and from 1124 when David I held court at the castle and founded the abbey at Holyrood.

The first effective town wall was constructed around 1450 and circled the Old Town and the area around Grassmarket. This restricted, defensible zone became a medieval Manhattan, forcing its densely packed inhabitants to build tenements that soared to 12 storeys.

A golden era that saw the foundation of the College of Surgeons and the introduction of printing ended with the death of James IV at the Battle of Flodden in 1513. England's Henry VIII attempted to force a marriage between Mary (James V's daughter) and his son, but the Scots sent the infant Mary to France to marry the dauphin. The city was sacked by the English, and the Scots turned to the French for support.

The Scots were increasingly sympathetic to the ideas of the Reformation and when John Knox returned from exile in 1555 he found fertile ground for his Calvinist message.

When James VI of Scotland succeeded to the English crown in 1603, he moved the court to London, and for the most part, the Stuarts ignored Edinburgh. When Charles I tried to introduce episcopacy (the rule of the bishops) in 1633 he provoked the National Covenant (see Greyfriars Kirk & Kirkyard) and more religious turmoil which finally ended in triumph for Presbyterianism.

The Act of Union in 1707 further reduced Edinburgh's importance, but cultural and intellectual life flourished. In the second half of the 18th century a new city was created across the ravine to the north. The population was expanding, defence was no longer vital and the thinkers of the Scottish Enlightenment planned to distance themselves from Edinburgh's Jacobite past.

The population exploded in the 19th century – Edinburgh quadrupled in size to 400,000, close to today's figure – and the Old Town's tenements were taken over by refugees from the Irish famines. A new ring of crescents and circuses was built south of the New Town, and grey Victorian terraces sprung up.

In the 20th century the slum dwellers were moved into new housing estates which now foster massive social problems. But a new era is beginning for Edinburgh with the decision to locate the new Scottish Parliament in the city; it's due to begin sitting in the year 2000.

ORIENTATION

The most important landmark is Arthur's Seat, the 251m-high rocky peak south-west of the city centre. The Old and New Towns are separated by Princes St Gardens, with the castle dominating both of them.

The main shopping street, Princes St, runs along the northern side of the gardens. Buildings are restricted to its north side, which has the usual High St shops. At the east end, Calton Hill is crowned by several monuments. The Royal Mile (Lawnmarket,

---

The Flodden Wall

In 1513 the English defeated the Scots at the Battle of Flodden, and King James IV and 10,000 of his followers were killed. The citizens of Edinburgh were thrown into such despair by this episode that they decided to separate their city from the outside world altogether. To that end they built the Flodden Wall across High St between what are now the World's End and Royal Archer pubs. Part of the wall can still be seen in the basement of the World's End.

Inverness Castle

GLENN BEANLAND

Puffin

BRYN THOMAS

The Black Cullin, Isle of Skye

GARETH McCORMACK

Slioch, Wester Ross

GRAEME CORNWALLIS

Duncansby Stacks near John o'Groats

NEIL WILSON

Italian Chapel, Orkney Islands

BRYN THOMAS

The Mamores from Ben Nevis

GARETH McCORMACK

High St and Canongate) is the parallel equivalent in the Old Town.

The TIC is beside Waverley train station, above the Waverley Market Shopping Centre on Princes St. The bus station in the New Town is trickier to find; it's off the north-east corner of St Andrew Square, north of Princes St.

The foldout map produced by the Scottish Tourist Board, and available from the TIC, is good enough to get you to most places.

INFORMATION
Tourist Offices

The busy main TIC (☎ 557 1700), Waverley Market, Princes St, opens November to March, Monday to Saturday from 9 am to 6 pm, plus, in April and October, Sunday from 1 to 6 pm; May, June and September, daily from 9 am to 7 pm (Sunday from 11 am); July and August, daily from 9 am to 8 pm. There's also a branch (☎ 333 2167; credit card bookings possible) at Edinburgh airport.

It has information about all of Scotland, and sells the *Essential Guide to Edinburgh*. Its accommodation service charges a steep £3 and only books one night ahead (hopeless during busy periods when forward planning is essential). Instead, get the free accommodation brochure and ring yourself.

For £5, three branches of Thomas Cook also make hotel reservations: the Edinburgh airport office (☎ 333 5119); the office (☎ 557 0905) in Waverley Steps near the TIC; and the office (☎ 557 0034) on Platform One of Waverley train station.

At the Backpackers Centre (☎ 557 9535), 6 Blackfriars St beside Haggis Backpackers, you can get information about hostels and tours, and book tickets for National Express, Stena Line, P&O and other services.

Consulates & High Commissions

See the Scotland Facts for the Visitor chapter.

Money

The TIC *bureau de change* opens the same hours as the TIC and charges 2.5% commission with a minimum of £2.50. American Express (☎ 225 7881), 139 Princes St, opens Monday to Friday from 9 am to 5.30 pm, Saturday to 4 pm. Thomas Cook (☎ 465 7700), 26-28 Frederick St, opens Monday to Saturday from 9 am to 5.30 pm.

Post

The main post office is inconveniently tucked away inside the sprawling St James' Shopping Centre, off Leith St. It's open Monday from 9 am to 5.30 pm, Tuesday to Friday from 8.30 am to 5.30 pm, and Saturday from 8.30 am to 6 pm. Items addressed to poste restante are sent here and can be picked up from any counter.

Email & Internet Access

Web 13 Internet Café (☎ 229 8883), 13 Bread St, offers online access for £5 per hour. It opens weekdays from 9 am to 10 pm, Saturday to 6 pm, Sunday from noon to 6 pm. Cyberia (☎ 220 4403), 88 Hanover St, charges £2.50 per half-hour.

Bookshops

The Stationery Office Bookshop (☎ 228 4181), 71 Lothian Rd, has an excellent selection of books and maps on Scotland. Waterstone's and James Thin each have several shops around town including on Princes St.

Left Luggage

Left-luggage facilities are available at Waverley train station (from £2.50 all day) and at St Andrew Square bus station (£1 to £2 all day).

Camping & Outdoor Gear

Tiso's (☎ 225 9486), 121 Rose St, is a well stocked outdoor equipment shop; it has a discount warehouse (☎ 554 0804) at 13 Wellington Place off Commercial St, Leith.

Emergency

The free emergency numbers are ☎ 999 or ☎ 112.

ROYAL MILE

Following a ridge that runs from Edinburgh Castle to Holyrood Palace, the Royal Mile is

EDINBURGH

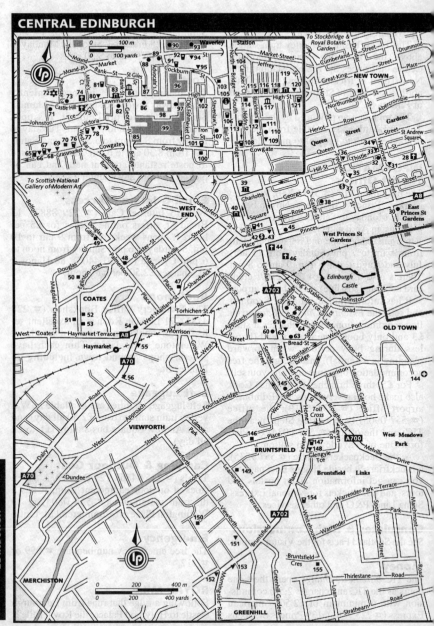

CENTRAL EDINBURGH

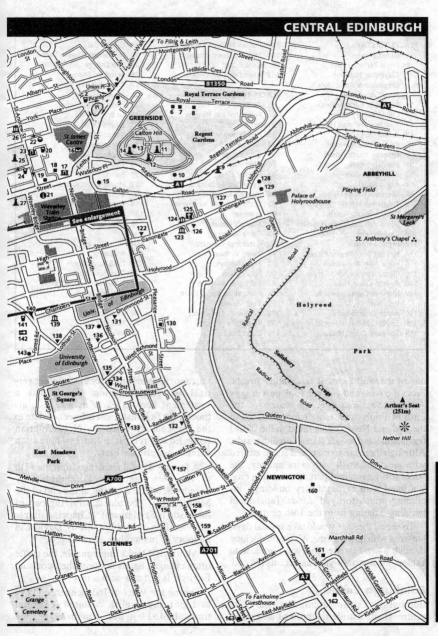

CENTRAL EDINBURGH

CENTRAL EDINBURGH

PLACES TO STAY
1 Sibbet House
6 Royal Terrace Hotel
7 Claymore, Halcyon,
   Greenside & Adria Hotels
8 Ailsa Craig Hotel
18 Princes St Backpackers
19 Old Waverley Hotel
47 Kinnaird Christian Hostel
48 Palmerston Lodge
49 Belford Youth Hostel
50 Eglinton Youth Hostel
51 Boisdale Hotel
52 Beresford Hotel
53 Argus Hotel
59 Sheraton Grand Hotel
70 Thistle Inn Hotel
100 Central Youth Hostel
103 Edinburgh Backpackers Hostel
104 Carlton Highland Hotel
112 High St Hostel
114 Holiday Inn Crowne Plaza
116 Royal Mile Backpackers
130 Pleasance Youth Hostel
146 Averon Guest House
149 Menzies Guest House &
   Villa Nina
150 Aaron Guset House
155 Bruntsfield Youth Hostel
159 Salisbury Guest House

160 Pollock Halls of Residence
161 Millfield Guest House
162 Casa Buzzo
163 Avondale Guest House

PLACES TO EAT
3 Giuliano's
4 Ferri's Italiano Pizzeria
31 Bar Napoli
33 Henderson's
34 Gringo Bill's
35 Café Rouge
36 Chez Jules
43 Bewley's
55 Verandah Restaurant
56 Howie's Restaurant
62 Dario's Pizzeria Restaurant
64 Jasmine
66 Mama's Pizzas
68 Pierre Victoire
69 Ristorante Gennaro
78 Pierre Victoire
79 Beppe Vittorio
80 Polo Fusion
87 Patisserie Florentin
94 Doric Wine Bar & Bistro
95 Viva Mexico
102 Elephant's Sufficiency
109 Black Bo's
115 Dubh Prais

118 Gustos Café
120 Netherbow Theate Café
122 The Grange
126 Brambles Tearoom
127 Clarinda's Tea Room
131 Khushi's
132 Howie's Restaurant
133 La Bonne Vie
135 Susie's Diner
136 Kebab Mahal
138 Negociant's
140 Elephant House
148 Efes
151 Parrots
152 Howie's Restaurant
153 Montpelier's
156 Chinese Home Cooking
157 Kalpna
158 Metropole

PUBS
2 Mathers
20 Café Royal Bar
24 Tiles Bar-Bistro
41 Whigham's Wine Cellars
65 Beehive Inn
67 White Hart Inn
76 Last Drop
77 Bow Bar
81 Jolly Judge

one of the world's most fascinating streets. From the west end you can look past craggy Arthur's Seat and over the waters of the Firth of Forth, with tantalising glimpses of the Old and New Towns through the *closes* (entrances) and *wynds* (lanes) on either side. Although there are tourists and shops stuffed with tacky Scottish souvenirs aplenty, the street still feels a real part of a thriving city. It's lined with extraordinary buildings, including multistoreyed *lands* (apartment buildings) dating from the 15th century.

To see all the sites would take several days, but even with limited time, it's worth ducking through a *pend* (arched gateway) or close to explore the narrow wynds and courts beyond.

Edinburgh Castle

Edinburgh Castle dominates the city centre. It sits astride the core of an extinct volcano, its three sides scoured almost vertical by glacial action. There was a settlement here as early as 850 BC, although the first historical references date to the 6th century when the Northumbrian King Edwin rebuilt a fortress here as a defence against the Picts.

A favoured royal residence from the 11th to the 16th centuries, Edinburgh only became Scotland's capital at the end of the Middle Ages. The oldest surviving part of the castle is St Margaret's Chapel, a simple stone edifice, probably built by David I in memory of his mother around 1130.

Although it looks impregnable, the castle often changed hands between the Scots and English. It last saw action in 1745.

During the Wars of Independence (1174 to 1356), the English captured it several times. In 1313 it was demolished by the

CENTRAL EDINBURGH

91	Malt Shovel Inn	
92	Hebrides Bar	
101	Green Tree	
106	Ceilidh House	
108	Bannerman's	
113	The Vaults	
121	World's End	
134	Pear Tree	
141	Greyfriars Bobby's Bar	
147	Bennet's Bar	
154	Ye Olde Golf Tavern	

OTHER

5	Playhouse Theatre
9	Burns Monument
10	Royal High School
11	National Monument
12	Nelson Monument
13	City Observatory
14	Monument to Dugald Stewart
15	Venue Night Club
16	St James Shopping Centre & Main Post Office
17	Register House
21	TIC & Waverley Market
22	St Andrew Bus Station
23	Dundas House
25	Melville Monument
26	Scottish National Portrait Gallery & Museum of Antiquities

27	Sir Walter Scott Monument
28	St Andrew's & St George's Church
29	National Gallery
30	Royal Scottish Accademy
32	Cyberia
37	Thomas Cook
38	Tiso's
39	Georgian House
40	West Register House
42	American Express
44	St John's Church
45	Waterstone's Bookshop & Starbucks Café
46	St Cuthbert's Church & Watchtower
54	Melville's Car Hire
57	Usher Hall
58	Royal Lyceum Theatre
60	Filmhouse
61	Stationery Office Bookshop
63	Web 13 Internet Café
71	Scotch Whisky Heritage Centre
72	Ramsay Garden
73	Camera Obscura
74	Church of Scotland General Assembly Hall (Temporary Scottish Parliament)
75	Tolbooth Kirk
82	Brodie's Close

83	Gladstone's Land
84	Lady Stair's House
85	National Library
86	Heart of Midlothian
88	Edinburgh Festival Box Office
89	Traveline
90	LRT Travel Shop
93	Tattoo Office
96	Edinburgh City Chambers
97	Mercat Cross
98	St Giles Cathedral
99	Parliament House
105	Tron Kirk
107	City Café
110	Edinburgh Cycle Hire
111	Backpackers Centre
117	Museum of Childhood
119	John Knox's House
123	Huntly House Museum
124	The People's Story
125	Canongate Kirk
128	Queen Mary's Bath House
129	Abbey Lairds
137	Edinburgh Festival Theatre
139	Royal Museum of Scotland
142	Greyfriars Kirk
143	Campus Travel
144	Royal Infirmary
145	Central Cycle Hire

Scots as part of Robert the Bruce's scorched earth policies and wasn't rebuilt until 1371 (by David II). Little of this work survives, however, because the castle was strengthened and renovated in the 16th, 17th and 18th centuries.

From the 16th century the royal family built more comfortable domestic accommodation at places like Holyrood and the castle developed as a seat of government and military power. However, in 1566 Mary Queen of Scots underlined its continuing symbolic importance when she chose to give birth to her son in the castle. In 1573 much of it was destroyed when loyalists attempted to hold it for Mary; the oldest substantial work, including the Half Moon Battery and Portcullis Gate, survives from the subsequent rebuilding. The castle was then taken in turn by the Covenanters

(in 1640), Cromwell (in 1650) and King William and Queen Mary (the last true siege, in 1689). In 1715 and 1745 the Stuarts tried unsuccessfully to recapture it. In the gaps between sieges more defences were added, and by the mid-18th century the castle looked much as it does today.

Partly thanks to Sir Walter Scott, in the 19th century the castle began to recover its importance as a Scottish symbol. Efforts were made to improve its appearance and to restore important buildings, including St Margaret's Chapel, then in use as a powder magazine. In the 1920s the massive Scottish National War Memorial was added to the complex.

The castle crawls with tourists and, although the views are great, you may decide it's more impressive from the outside looking in.

EDINBURGH

Visitors enter from the Esplanade, a parade ground where the Military Tattoo takes place each August. The changing of the guard also takes place here on the hour. Inside the castle, the most important sights are the **Stone of Destiny**, **St Margaret's Chapel**, the **Mons Meg** (a 500-year-old siege cannon), the **Palace** (including the Scottish crown jewels and the room where Mary gave birth to James) and the **Scottish National War Memorial**.

The castle (☎ 225 9846) opens daily from 9.30 am to 6 pm, April to September, and to 5 pm in winter. The admission price of £6/1.50 includes provision of an audio tape commentary.

Scotch Whisky Heritage Centre

If you'd like to know how whisky is manufactured the Scotch Whisky Heritage Centre (☎ 220 0441), Castle Hill, offers a tour with audiovisual presentations followed by a ride in a car past a tableau explaining the history of the 'water of life'. If you're pushed for time you can take the ride only (15 minutes) for £3.80/2. Either do the full tour or put the money toward the purchase of one (or more) of the hundreds of different brands of

---

The Stone of Destiny

Alleged to have accompanied the Scots in all their mythical journeys, the original Stone of Destiny (the Fatal Stone) was a carved block of sandstone on which the Scottish monarchs placed their feet during the coronation.

Stolen by Edward I in 1296, this venerable talisman was incorporated into the Coronation Chair, used by all English (and later British) monarchs, in London's Westminster Abbey. Apart from being taken to Gloucester during the air raids in WWII, the Stone lay undisturbed for centuries.

On Christmas Eve 1950, however, a plucky band of Scottish students drove down from Glasgow, jemmied the door of Westminster Abbey and made off with the Stone. English officialdom was outraged. The border roads had roadblocks on them for the first time in 400 years, but while Scots living in London jeered the English police as they searched the Serpentine Lake and the River Thames, the Stone was being smuggled back to Scotland.

King George VI was 'sorely troubled about the loss', but the students issued a petition affirming their loyalty to him, stating that they would give back the Stone as long as it could remain on Scottish soil. The authorities refused to negotiate and, three months after it was stolen, the Stone turned up on the altar of the ruined Abbey of Arbroath. It was here, in 1320, that the Arbroath Declaration had been signed, reaffirming the right of Scots to self-rule and independence from England. Before the public were aware that the Stone had even been found, it was back in London. No charges were brought and Ian Hamilton, the student who led this jolly caper, published his story in *The Taking of the Stone of Destiny*.

Many Scots, however, hold that the original Stone is safely hidden somewhere in Scotland, and that Edward I was fobbed off with a shoddy imitation. This is possibly true, for descriptions of the original state that it was decorated with carvings, not that it was a plain block of sandstone. Given that Scottish nationalism is running high, this powerful symbol of Scotland would surely have been brought out by now if it hadn't been quite so safely hidden.

Imitation or not, the Scottish Secretary and Conservative MP Michael Forsyth arranged for the return of the sandstone block to Edinburgh Castle, with much pomp and circumstance, in 1996. If it was an attempt to boost his flagging political standing, it failed dismally; Forsyth lost his seat in the House of Commons in the May 1997 general election.

whisky sold in the shop. The centre opens daily from 10 am to 5.30 pm; the full experience costs £4.95/2.50.

Camera Obscura

On the corner of Ramsay Lane, Camera Obscura (☎ 226 3709) offers great views over the city. The 'camera' is a curious device (originally dating from the 1850s, although improved in 1945) a bit like a periscope, using lenses and mirrors to throw a 'live' image onto a large interior bowl. The accompanying 'guided tour' is entertaining, and the whole exercise has a quirky charm. It's open Monday to Friday from 9.30 am to 6 pm, weekends from 10 am; £3.85/1.95.

Highland Tolbooth Kirk

With the tallest spire (73m) on one of Edinburgh's highest points, the Highland Tolbooth Kirk is an important feature of the skyline. It was built in the 1840s by James Graham and Augustus Pugin (architect of the London Houses of Parliament). It's being refurbished and will be the new home of the Edinburgh Festival office.

Beside the kirk are the **Assembly Rooms** of the Church of Scotland; they'll be the temporary home of the Scottish Parliament until the new building is constructed.

Ramsay Garden

Constructed around the mid-18th century home of the poet Alan Ramsay, the attractive apartments overlook The Esplanade and the small garden from which they get their name. They were designed in the 1890s by an early town planner called Patrick Geddes in an attempt to revitalise the Old Town. They're now very expensive, very wonderful private apartments.

Gladstone's Land

Gladstone's Land (☎ 226 5856, NTS), 477 Lawnmarket, gives a fascinating glimpse of the past. The house was built in the mid-16th century and extended around 1617 by wealthy merchant Thomas Gledstanes. Its comfortable interior contains fine painted walls and beams and some splendid furniture. It's open April to October, Monday to Saturday from 10 am to 5 pm, Sunday from 2 to 5 pm; £2.80/1.90.

The Writers' Museum

The Writers' Museum (☎ 529 4901) is housed in **Lady Stair's House**, built in 1622, and contains manuscripts and memorabilia belonging to Robert Burns, Sir Walter Scott and Robert Louis Stevenson. The static displays will only interest enthusiasts of these writers but it's open Monday to Saturday from 10 am to 5 pm and, during the Edinburgh Festival, Sunday from 2 to 5 pm; free.

Brodie's Close

Brodie's Close is named after the father of the notorious William Brodie, a deacon and respected citizen by day, a burglar by night. Brodie was the inspiration for Robert Louis Stevenson's *The Strange Case of Dr Jekyll and Mr Hyde* and, some would say, a dramatic reflection of Edinburgh's schizophrenic undercurrents. He met his end on the gallows in 1788.

Parliament Square

Lawnmarket ends at the crossroads of Bank St and George IV Bridge; at the south-east corner, brass strips set in the road mark the site of the scaffold where public hangings took place until 1864. From here the Mile continues as High St.

Parliament Square, largely filled by St Giles Cathedral, the High Kirk of Edinburgh, is on the south side. This was the heart of Edinburgh until the 18th century, and a cobblestoned **Heart of Midlothian** is set in the ground. Passers-by traditionally spit on it for luck. This was the site of the entrance to the Tolbooth, originally built to collect tolls, but subsequently a meeting place for parliament, the town council and the General Assembly of the Reformed Kirk, then law courts and, finally, a prison and place of execution.

The 19th century **Mercat Cross** takes the place of the original 1365 cross and marks the spot where merchants and traders met to transact business and Royal Proclamations were read.

The square's southern side is flanked by **Parliament House** which was the meeting place of the Scottish Parliament from 1639; its neoclassical façade was added in the early 19th century. After the Act of Union in 1707 the building became the centre for the Scottish legal system – the Court of Session and High Court – which retained its independence. The most interesting feature is **Parliament Hall**, where the parliament actually met, which is now used by lawyers and their clients as a meeting place.

St Giles' Cathedral

There has been a church on this site since the 9th century. A Norman-style church was built in 1126, but this was burnt by the English in 1385; the only substantial remains are the central piers that support the tower. The present church was then built in stages, with the crown spire completed in 1495.

Inside, near the entrance is a life-size statue of John Knox, minister from 1559 to 1572; from here he preached his uncompromising Calvinist message and launched the Scottish Reformation. The new austerity this ushered in led to changes in the building's interior – decorations, stained glass, altars and the relics of St Giles were thrown into the Nor Loch.

The High Kirk of Edinburgh was at the heart of Edinburgh's struggle against episcopacy. A tablet marks the spot where, in 1637, Jenny Geddes threw a stool at the dean who was using the English prayer book (a symbol of episcopacy). According to popular belief this led to the signing of the National Covenant at Greyfriars the following year; a copy is displayed on the wall.

One of the most interesting corners of the kirk is the **Thistle Chapel** built 1909-11 for the Knights of the Most Ancient and Most Noble Order of the Thistle. The carved Gothic-style stalls have canopies topped with the helms and arms of the 16 knights.

Entry to the kirk is free, but a £1 donation is requested.

Edinburgh City Chambers

The City Chambers were originally built by John Adam (brother of Robert) in 1761 to replace the Mercat Cross and serve as a Royal Exchange, but the merchants continued to prefer the street. The building has been used by the town council since 1811.

Tron Kirk

At the south-western corner of the intersection with South Bridge, Tron Kirk owes its name to a salt *tron* or public weighbridge that stood on the site. It was built in 1637 on top of Marlin's Wynd which has been excavated to reveal a cobbled street with cellars and shops on either side. The church acts as a visitors centre for the Old Town. It's open early April to mid-June, Thursday to Monday from 10 am to 5 pm; and mid-June to early September, daily from 10 am to 7 pm.

John Knox's House

Perhaps the most extraordinary building on the Royal Mile, John Knox's House (☎ 556 9579) dates from 1490. The outside staircase, overhanging upper floors and crow-stepped gables are typical of a 15th century town house. John Knox is thought to have occupied the 2nd floor from 1561 to 1572. The labyrinthine interior has an interesting display on his life including a recording of his interview with Mary Queen of Scots, whose mother was a target of his diatribe *First Blast of the Trumpet Against the Monstrous Regiment of Women*. It's open Monday to Saturday from 10 am to 4.30 pm; £1.95/75p.

Museum of Childhood

This museum (☎ 529 4142), 42 High St, attempts to cover the serious issues related to childhood – health, education, upbringing and so on – but more enjoyable is the enormous collection of toys, dolls, games and books which fascinates children and, for adults, brings childhood memories back. The museum opens Monday to Saturday from 10 am to 5 pm, and, during the Edinburgh Festival only, Sunday from 2 to 5 pm; free.

Netherbow Port

High St ends at the intersection with St Mary's and Jeffrey Sts. The city's eastern gate, Netherbow Port, no longer exists, although it's marked by brass strips set in the road. The next stretch of the Mile, Canongate, takes its name from the canons (priests) of Holyrood Abbey. From the 16th century, it was home to aristocrats attracted to Holyrood Palace. Originally governed by the canons, it remained an independent burgh until 1856.

The People's Story

Canongate Tolbooth, with its picturesque turrets and projecting clock, is an interesting example of 16th century architecture. Built in 1591, it served successively as a collection point for tolls (taxes), a council house, a courtroom and a jail. It now houses a fascinating museum (☎ 331 5545) telling the story of the life, work and pastimes of ordinary Edinburgh folk from the 18th century to the present day. It opens Monday to Saturday from 10 am to 5 pm, and, during the Edinburgh Festival only, Sunday from 2 to 5 pm; free.

Huntly House Museum

Huntly House, built in 1570, is a good example of the luxurious accommodation that aristocrats built for themselves along Canongate; the projecting upper floors of plastered timber are typical of the time. It now contains a local history museum (☎ 529 4143) with some interesting displays, including a copy of the National Covenant of 1638. It opens Monday to Saturday from 10 am to 5 pm, and, during the Edinburgh Festival only, Sunday from 2 to 5 pm; free.

Canongate Kirk

Attractive Canongate Kirk was built in 1688. In 1745 Prince Charles Stuart (the Young Pretender) used it to hold prisoners taken at the Battle of Prestonpans. Several famous people are buried in the churchyard, including the economist Adam Smith, author of *The Wealth of Nations*, who lived nearby in Panmure Close.

Abbey Lairds

On the north side of Abbey Strand, flanking the entrance to Holyrood Palace, the Abbey Lairds provided sanctuary for aristocratic debtors from 1128 to 1880. They could avoid prison as long as they remained within the palace and Holyrood Park, although they were allowed out on Sunday.

Queen Mary's Bath House

Further to the north is this small, 16th century turreted lodge where, according to legend, Queen Mary used to bathe in white wine and goat's milk – as frequently as twice a year! It's more likely to have been a summer house or dovecot.

Palace of Holyroodhouse & Holyrood Abbey

The Palace of Holyroodhouse developed from a guesthouse attached to medieval Holyrood Abbey. It was a royal residence at various times from the 16th century, and is still the Queen's official residence in Scotland, so access is very restricted. You can only view a few apartments, walk around part of the grounds and visit the abbey ruins.

The abbey, founded by David I in 1128, was probably named after a fragment of the Cross (*rood* is an old word for cross) said to have belonged to his mother St Margaret. As it lay outside the city walls it was particularly vulnerable to English attacks, but the church was always rebuilt and survived as Canongate parish church until it collapsed in 1768. Most of the surviving ruins date from the 12th and 13th centuries, although a doorway in the far south-eastern corner survives from the original Norman church.

James IV extended the abbey guesthouse in 1501 to create more comfortable living quarters than in bleak, windy Edinburgh Castle; the oldest surviving section of the building, the north-west tower, was built in 1529 as a royal apartment. Mary Queen of Scots spent 16 eventful years living in the tower. During this time she married Darnley (in the abbey) and Bothwell (in what is now the Picture Gallery), and this is

EDINBURGH

where she debated with John Knox and witnessed the murder of her secretary Rizzio.

Although Holyrood was never again a permanent royal residence after Mary's son James VI departed for London, it was further extended during Charles II's reign.

Although you're carefully shepherded through a limited part of the palace, there's a certain fascination to following in Mary's footsteps and seeing the room where Rizzio was cut down.

Opening hours are normally April to October, daily from 9.30 am to 5.15 pm; November to March, daily from 9.30 am to 3.45 pm. Entry is £5.30/2.60. However, the complex sometimes closes for state functions or when the Queen is in residence, usually in mid-May, and mid-June to around 7 July; phone ☎ 556 7371 to check.

Close to Holyrood, construction is under way for the new purpose-built **Scottish Parliament** and the **Dynamic Earth** exhibition on the geology of the planet.

Holyrood Park & Arthur's Seat

Edinburgh is blessed in having a real wilderness on its doorstep. Holyrood Park covers 260 hectares of varied landscape, including mountains, moorland, lochs and fields. The highest point is the 251m-high extinct volcano, Arthur's Seat.

You can circumnavigate the park by car or bike and it has several excellent walks. Opposite the palace's southern gate, a footpath named Radical Rd runs along the base of the Salisbury Crags, but is partly blocked because of danger from falling rocks. An easy half-hour walk leads from Dunsapie Loch to the summit of Arthur's Seat, with magnificent views. Duddingston Loch, the one natural lake, is a bird sanctuary.

SOUTH OF THE ROYAL MILE

The area south of the Royal Mile includes some of the oldest, most crowded and atmospheric parts of the Old Town at the foot of Castle Rock and the Mile. Around the university and the beautiful Meadow Park it opens up to run into sturdy Victorian suburbs like Bruntsfield, Marchmont and Grange.

One of the city's main traffic arteries (carrying traffic to/from the A68 and A7), with many shops, restaurants and guesthouses, runs down the eastern side – beginning as North Bridge and becoming successively South Bridge, Nicolson St, Clerk St, Newington Rd, Minto St, Mayfield Gardens and Craigmillar Park.

Grassmarket

Grassmarket is one of Edinburgh's nightlife centres, with numerous restaurants and pubs, including the White Hart Inn (patronised by Robert Burns). An open area hedged by tall tenements and dominated by the looming castle, it can be approached from George IV Bridge, via Victoria St, an unusual two-tiered street clinging to the ridge below the Royal Mile, with some excellent shops.

The site of a market from at least 1477 to the start of the 20th century, Grassmarket was always a focal point for the Old Town. This was the main place for executions and over 100 hanged Covenanters are commemorated with a cross at the east end. The notorious murderers Burke and Hare operated from a now vanished close off the west end. In around 1827 they enticed at least 18 victims here, suffocated them and sold the bodies to Edinburgh's medical schools.

Leading off the south-east corner, Candlemaker Row climbs back up to George IV Bridge and Greyfriars Kirk.

Greyfriars Kirk & Kirkyard

At the bottom of a stone canyon made up of tenements, churches, volcanic cliffs and the castle, Greyfriars Kirkyard is one of Edinburgh's most evocative spots – a peaceful oasis dotted with memorials and surrounded by Edinburgh's dramatic skyline.

The kirk was built on the site of a Franciscan friary and opened for worship on Christmas Day in 1620. The National Covenant was signed here in 1638, rejecting Charles I's attempts to reintroduce episcopacy and a new English prayer book, and affirming the independence of the Scottish church. Many of those who signed were later executed in Grassmarket and, in

1679, 1200 Covenanters were held prisoner in terrible conditions in an enclosure in the yard.

Tour groups, however, come to pay homage to a tiny statue of **Greyfriars Bobby** (in front of the nearby pub). Bobby was a Skye terrier who maintained a vigil over the grave of his master from 1858 to 1872, a story immortalised as a novel by Eleanor Atkinson in 1912 and later turned into a film. Inside the kirk you can buy *Greyfriars Bobby – The Real Story at Last*, Forbes Macgregor's debunking of some of the myths.

Cowgate

Cowgate, which runs off the eastern end of Grassmarket parallel to the Royal Mile, is less a canyon than a bleak tunnel, thanks to the bridges that were built above it. Once a fashionable place to live, it now has a couple of Fringe Festival venues and one or two good pubs.

University of Edinburgh

The University of Edinburgh is one of Britain's oldest, biggest and best universities. Founded in 1583, it has around 17,000 undergraduates. The students make a major contribution to the lively atmosphere of Grassmarket, Cowgate, and the nearby restaurants and pubs. The university sprawls for some distance, but the centre is the Old College, at the junction of South Bridge and Chambers St, a Robert Adam masterpiece designed in 1789.

Royal Museum of Scotland

The Royal Museum of Scotland (☎ 225 7534), Chambers St, houses a comprehensive collection covering geology and fossils, Egyptology, Chinese, Islamic and European decorative art, and even technology, with one section featuring the world's oldest steam locomotive.

The new **Museum of Scotland** beside it opened in 1998, and houses the collection from the old Museum of Antiquities. It shows the history of Scotland in chronological order starting with the country's earliest history in the basement, to the most recent on the top floor.

They're open Monday to Saturday from 10 am to 5 pm (to 8 pm Tuesday), Sunday from noon to 5 pm; £3/free.

CALTON HILL

Calton Hill, at the east end of Princes St, is another distinctive component of Edinburgh's skyline, 100m high and scattered with grandiose memorials mostly dating from the first half of the 19th century. Here you get one of the best views of Edinburgh, taking in the entire panorama – the castle, Holyrood, Arthur's Seat, the Firth of Forth, the New Town and Princes St.

Approaching from Waterloo Place, you pass the imposing **Royal High School**, Regent Rd, dating from 1829 and modelled on the Temple of Theseus in Athens. Former pupils include Robert Adam, Alexander Graham Bell and Sir Walter Scott. Now called St Andrew's House, it's home to the Scottish Office. Further up, on the other side of Regent Rd, is the **Burns Monument** (1830), a small round temple commemorating the Scottish bard.

The largest structure on Calton Hill is the **National Monument**, an over-ambitious attempt to replicate the Parthenon, in honour of Scotland's dead in the Napoleonic Wars. Construction began in 1822, but funds ran dry when only 12 columns were complete.

The **City Observatory** (1818) houses the **Edinburgh Experience** (☎ 556 4365), a 20 minute, 3-D portrayal of Edinburgh's history. It's open April to October, daily from 10 am to 5 pm; £2/1.20.

Looking a bit like an upturned telescope, the **Nelson Monument** was built after Nelson's death at Trafalgar. It's open (for great views) April to September, Monday from 1 to 6 pm, Tuesday to Saturday from 10 am to 6 pm; October to March, Monday to Saturday from 10 am to 3 pm; £2.

There are also two historic observatories, and the small, circular **Monument to Dugald Stewart** (1753-1828), an obscure professor of philosophy.

NEW TOWN

New Town, dating from the 18th century, lies north of the Old Town, separated from it by Princes St Gardens and occupying a ridge that runs below, but parallel to, the Royal Mile. It's in complete contrast to the tangle of streets and buildings that evolved in the Old Town, and typifies the values of the Scottish Enlightenment.

Despite being confined behind city walls, the Old Town was still periodically sacked by the English or torn by civil wars and disputes. The overcrowding and non-existent sanitation gave it its nickname, Auld Reekie. So when the Act of Union in 1707 brought the prospect of long-term stability, aristocrats were keen to find healthier, more spacious surroundings. Cowgate was bridged to open up the south, Nor Loch at the northern foot of Castle Rock was drained and the North Bridge was constructed.

In 1767, 23-year-old James Craig won a competition to design a New Town. His plan was brilliant in its simplicity. George St followed the line of the ridge between Charlotte and St Andrew Squares. Building was restricted to one side of Princes St and Queen St only, so the town opened onto the Firth of Forth to the north, and to the castle and Old Town to the south.

The New Town continued to sprout squares, circuses, parks and terraces, and some of its finest neoclassical architecture was designed by Robert Adam. Today, the New Town is the world's most complete and unspoilt example of Georgian town planning and architecture.

Princes St

Princes St was originally envisaged as the back of the New Town, as it was literally and figuratively turning away from its Jacobite past. However, the transport links and stunning outlook soon led to its development as Edinburgh's principal thoroughfare.

The main train station at the east end is now overshadowed by the uninspiring **Waverley Market shopping centre**, with the entrance to the main TIC via the street level piazza.

The street's north side is lined with standard High St shops, and few 18th century buildings survive. One exception is the beautiful **Register House** (1788), designed by Robert Adam to hold Scotland's official records, opposite North Bridge. About halfway along, the massive Gothic spire of the **Sir Walter Scott Monument**, built by public subscription after his death in 1832, testifies to a popularity largely inspired by his role in rebuilding pride in Scottish identity. At the time of writing it was closed for refurbishment, but when it reopens you'll be able to climb the 287 steps to the top.

Princes St Gardens are cut by **The Mound**, a mound of earth dumped during the construction of the New Town which provides a road link between the Old and New Towns. The Royal Scottish Academy and the National Gallery of Scotland are also here (see later in this section).

St John's Church, at the western end of Princes St, stands above some interesting shops and the Cornerstone Coffee House. **St Cuthbert's Church**, round the corner, has a watchtower in the graveyard – a reminder of the Burke and Hare days when graves had to be guarded against robbers.

Royal Scottish Academy

Built in Grecian style in 1826, the academy (☎ 225 6671) hosts temporary exhibitions throughout the year. It's open Monday to Saturday from 10 am to 5 pm, Sunday from 2 to 5 pm; free (although there are charges for some exhibitions).

National Gallery of Scotland

The National Gallery (☎ 556 8921) is an imposing classical building dating from the 1850s. It houses an important collection of European art from the 15th century Renaissance to 19th century post-Impressionism. There are paintings by Tintoretto, Titian, Holbein, Rubens, El Greco, Poussin, Rembrandt, Constable, Gainsborough, Turner, Monet, Pissaro, Gauguin and Cézanne but perhaps the most interesting section shows specifically Scottish art in the basement. Look out, too, for Antonio Canova's statue of the Three Graces (room X), owned jointly with London's Victoria and Albert Museum. More than £7 million was raised to purchase this single sculpture. It opens Monday to Saturday from 10 am to 5 pm, Sunday from 2 to 5 pm; free.

George St & St Andrew Square

George St was originally envisaged as the main thoroughfare of the residential New Town. It's now home to highly successful Scottish financial institutions which control billions of pounds. **St Andrew's & St George's Church**, built in 1784, boasts a wonderful oval plaster ceiling.

Dominated by the **Melville Monument**, St Andrew Square isn't particularly architecturally distinguished, but the Royal Bank of Scotland is in the impressive **Dundas House** which has a spectacular dome, visible from inside, and frieze.

Charlotte Square & the Georgian House

At the western end of George St, Charlotte Square was designed in 1791 by Robert Adam and is regarded as the jewel of the New Town. The Church of St George is now **West Register House**, an annexe to Register House in Princes St and home to Scottish records and occasional exhibitions.

On the north side is one of Robert Adam's masterpieces. Number 7, the **Georgian House** (☎ 225 2160, NTS), has been beautifully restored and refurnished to show how Edinburgh's elite lived at the end of the 18th century. A 35 minute video brings it to life rather well. It's open April to October, Monday to Saturday from 10 am to 5 pm, Sunday from 2 to 5 pm; £4.20/2.80.

Scottish National Portrait Gallery

The gallery (☎ 556 8921) is in a large Italian-Gothic building dating from 1882 (at the junction of St Andrew and Queen Sts). The hall is decorated with a frieze showing the main protagonists in Scottish history and the balcony with frescos of important moments in Scottish history painted by William Hole in 1897.

The gallery records Scottish history through portraits and sculptures of its most important players. The subjects are probably the main source of interest, but some portraits are also fine paintings. It's open Monday to Saturday from 10 am to 5 pm, Sunday from 2 to 5 pm; free. *Queen Street Café* in the gallery serves delicious home-baked cooking from 10 am to 4.30 pm.

WEST END

The last part to be built, the West End is an extension of the New Town. Huge **St Mary's Episcopal Cathedral**, Palmerston Place, built in the 1870s, was Sir Gilbert Scott's last major work.

Alongside the Water of Leith, **Dean Village** is an odd corner of Edinburgh – once a milling community, it has been taken over by yuppies. A pleasant walk begins on the left bank of the Water of Leith at Belford Bridge. The footpath takes you up onto the Dean Path, then onto Dean Bridge, from where you can look down on the village. You continue on the right bank of the Leith, through Stockbridge, and can then detour to the Royal Botanical Garden.

Scottish National Gallery of Modern Art

Beyond the West End and Dean Village, the Scottish National Gallery of Modern Art (☎ 556 8921), Belford Rd, repays the effort of getting there (take bus No 13 from George St). It's housed in an impressive classical building and surrounded by a sculpture park. The collection concentrates on 20th century art, with work by Matisse, Picasso, Miro, Kirchner, Magritte, Mondrian and Giacometti. It's small enough not to overwhelm and opens Monday to Saturday from 10 am to 5 pm, Sunday from 2 to 5 pm; free.

NORTH OF THE NEW TOWN

The New Town's Georgian architecture extends north to Stockbridge and the Water of Leith, a rewarding area to explore since it's well off the tourist trail. **Stockbridge** is a trendy area with its own distinct identity, some interesting shops and a good choice of pubs and restaurants.

North of Stockbridge is the lovely **Royal Botanic Garden** (☎ 552 7171) on Inverleith Row. It's worth visiting for the different perspective you get on the Edinburgh skyline from the *Terrace Café*. The garden opens November to January, daily from 10 am to 4 pm; February and October to 5 pm; March and September to 6 pm; April to August to 7 pm; free. Bus Nos 8, 19, 23, 27 and 37 get you there.

BUS TOURS

Open-topped buses leave from Waverley Bridge outside the main train station and offer hop-on, hop-off tours of the main sights. Guide Friday charges £7.50 and LRT's Edinburgh Classic Tour £5.50. They're a good way of getting your bearings – although with a bus map and a Day Saver bus ticket (£2.20) you could do the same thing, without a commentary.

SPECIAL EVENTS

The **Edinburgh International Festival** is one of the world's largest, most important arts festivals, with the best performers playing to capacity audiences.

The **Fringe Festival** grew in tandem to showcase would-be stars. It claims to be the largest such event in the world, with over 500 amateur and professional groups presenting every possible kind of avant-garde performance. To make sure that every B&B for 40 miles around is full, the **Military Tattoo** is held at the same time.

It's a great time to be in Edinburgh. The city is at its best and the Fringe isn't at all elitist. In most cases the performers and front of house people are friendly and relaxed, they're grateful to have an audience, so there's no need to feel intimidated. Just be prepared to take the bad with the good ...

The International and Fringe festivals run from mid-August to early September. The last week is a good time to go, because the Tattoo finishes at the end of August, reducing the number of visitors. If you want to

attend the International Festival, it's best to book ahead; the program is published in April and is available from the Edinburgh Festival Office (☎ 226 4001), 21 Market St, EH1 1BW. Prices are generally reasonable, and any unsold tickets are sold half-price on the day of performance (from 1 to 5 pm) from the venue one hour before each performance or from the Festival Box Office in Market St. (The box office is scheduled to move to the Highland Tolbooth Kirk on the Royal Mile; check with the TIC.)

The Fringe is less formal, and many performances have empty seats left at the last moment. It's still worth booking for well-known names, or if the production has good reviews. Programs are available, from June, from the Festival Fringe Society (☎ 226 5257), 180 High St, EH1 1QS.

To book for the Military Tattoo, an extravaganza of regimental posturing, contact the Tattoo Office (☎ 225 1188; fax 225 8627), 33-34 Market St, EH1 1QS.

Hogmanay, the Scottish celebration of the New Year, is another major fixture in Edinburgh's festival calendar. Plans are under way to celebrate the year 2000 with the street party to end all parties. For details call ☎ 557 1700.

For all these festivals, booking accommodation months ahead is strongly advised.

PLACES TO STAY

Edinburgh has masses of accommodation, but the city can still fill up quickly over the New Year, at Easter and between mid-May and mid-September, particularly while the festivals are in full swing. Book in advance if possible, or use an accommodation booking service (see Information earlier).

Camping

Mortonhall Caravan Park (☎ 664 1533, off Frogston Rd East, Mortonhall) is 15 minutes south-east of the centre. It's open March to October, sites are £6.75/£10.50.

Hostels & Colleges

There's a growing number of independent backpackers' hostels. The long-established, well equipped *High St Hostel* (☎ *557 3984, 8 Blackfriars St)* is popular, although some have found it noisy. Beds cost £9.50 per night in a 10 bed dorm, plus £1.50 for breakfast. It's opposite the Haggis Backpackers tour-booking office.

Nearby is *Royal Mile Backpackers* (☎ *557 6120, 105 High St)* beside Gustos Café; it charges £9.90 for beds in dorms of up to 10 beds. *Edinburgh Backpackers Hostel* (☎ *220 1717, 65 Cockburn St)* is close to all the action; dorm beds cost from £10 and doubles are £35.

Princes St Backpackers (☎ *556 6894, 5 West Register St)* is also well positioned, behind Princes St and close to the bus station. Entry is next to the Guildford Arms pub and you have to negotiate 77 exhausting steps to reach reception. Dorm beds cost £9.50, doubles £24. A full breakfast costs £2, and Sunday night dinner is free!

Belford Youth Hostel (☎ *225 6209, 6 Douglas Gardens)* is in a converted church and although some people have complained of noise, it's well run and cheerful with good facilities. Dorm beds cost £8.50, and there are a couple of doubles for £27.50.

Quiet *Palmerston Lodge* (☎ *220 5141, 25 Palmerston Place)* on the corner of Chester St, is in a listed building that was once a boarding school. The rates, which include a continental breakfast, start at £10 for a dorm bed; singles/doubles with bathroom are £30/40.

There are four good SYHA hostels. *Eglinton Youth Hostel* (☎ *337 1120, 18 Eglinton Crescent)* is about a mile west of the city near Haymarket train station; beds cost £12.50/9.95 for adults/juniors. Walk down Princes St and continue on Shandwick Place which becomes West Maitland St; veer right at the Haymarket along Haymarket Terrace, then turn right into Coates Gardens which runs into Eglinton Crescent.

Bruntsfield Youth Hostel (☎ *447 2994, 7 Bruntsfield Crescent)* is trickier to get to; it has an attractive location overlooking Bruntsfield Links about 2½ miles from Waverley train station. Catch bus No 11 or 16 from the garden side of Princes St and

alight at Forbes Rd just after the gardens on the left. It's closed in January and rates are £8.60/7.10.

The other two are summer only (late June to early September): *Central Youth Hostel* (☎ *337 1120, Robertson's Close and College Wynd, Cowgate)* and *Pleasance Youth Hostel* (☎ *337 1120, New Arthur Place)*. Book in advance.

Women and married couples are welcome at the *Kinnaird Christian Hostel* (☎ *225 3608, 13-14 Coates Crescent)* where beds in a Georgian house cost from £14.

During university holidays *Pollock Halls of Residence* (☎ *667 0662, 18 Holyrood Park Rd)* has modern (often noisy) single rooms from £23.90 per person including breakfast.

B&Bs & Guesthouses

On a tight budget the best bet is a private house; get the TIC's free accommodation guide and phone around. Outside festival time you should get something for around £16, although it'll probably be a bus ride away in the suburbs. Places in the centre aren't always good value if you have a car, since parking in the New Town is severely restricted.

Guesthouses are generally two or three pounds more expensive than private rooms, and to get a private bathroom you'll have to pay around £25. The main concentrations are around Pilrig St, Pilrig; Minto St (a southern continuation of North Bridge), Newington; and Gilmore Place and Leamington Terrace, Bruntsfield.

There are a couple of places in Eyre Place, north of the New Town near Stockbridge and the Water of Leith, a mile from the centre. *Ardenlee Guest House* (☎ *556 2838)*, No 9, has beds from £22 to £26 per person (£2 more for a private bath). *Blairhaven Guest House* (☎ *556 3025)*, No 5, does B&B from £18.

Pilrig St, left off Leith Walk (veer left at the east end of Princes St), has lots of guesthouses, all within easy reach of the centre. *Balmoral Guest House* (☎ *554 1857)*, No 32, is a terraced Georgian house with beds from

£17 to £20 per person. Similar is the *Barrosa* (☎ 554 3700), No 21, with rooms from £19.50/23.50 per person without/with bath. At No 94, the attractive, detached, two-crown *Balquhidder Guest House* (☎ 554 3377) has rooms with bath from £18 to £30 a head.

There are lots of guesthouses on and around Minto St/Mayfield Gardens in Newington, south of the city centre, with plenty of buses to the centre. The best places are in the streets on either side of the main road.

Salisbury Guest House (☎ 667 1264, 45 *Salisbury Rd*) is east of Newington, 10 minutes from the centre by bus, and is quiet and comfortable. Rooms with a bath cost from £23 to £30 per person. The welcoming *Avondale Guest House* (☎ 667 6779, 10 South *Gray St)*, west of Minto St, is a comfortable, traditional B&B with singles/doubles from £19/32. *Fairholme Guest House* (☎ 667 8645, 13 Moston Terrace)*, east of Mayfield Gardens, is a pleasant Victorian villa with free parking. The range of rooms includes a single from £15.

In Bruntsfield, busy *Averon Guest House* (☎ 229 9932, 44 Gilmore Place)* is within walking distance of Princes St, and has beds from £20. Using the same bus stop as for Bruntsfield Youth Hostel, you can get to *Menzies Guest House* (☎ 229 4629), down Leamington Terrace at No 33. It's reasonably well run and has rooms from £20 to £28 per person, though you only have one choice of cereal. Similar is *Villa Nina* (☎ 229 2644) at No 39.

There are several quiet guesthouses in Hartington Gardens, off Viewforth, itself off Bruntsfield Place. *Aaron Guest House* (☎ 229 6459)*, at the end of the street, is handy for drivers since it has a private car park. Beds go for £20 to £35 per person in comfortable *en suite* rooms.

Casa Buzzo (☎ 667 8998, 8 Kilmaurs Rd)*, east of Dalkeith Rd, is quite a way out. It has two doubles for £16 per person. *Millfield Guest House* (☎ 667 4428, 12 Marchhall Rd)*, also east of Dalkeith Rd past Pollock Halls of Residence, is a pleasant, two-storey, Victorian house with rooms from £18/33.

Hotels

The international hotels in the centre are extremely expensive, although there can be good deals outside summer, especially at weekends.

There's a handy batch of mid-range places on Coates Gardens, off Haymarket Terrace near Haymarket train station. Comfortable *Boisdale Hotel* (☎ 337 1134), No 9, has rooms with bath from £25 to £45 per person. Other possibilities include *Argus Hotel* (☎ 337 6159), No 14, and *Beresford Hotel* (☎ 337 0850) at No 32.

Rothesay Hotel (☎ 225 4125, 8 Rothesay *Place)* is in a quiet, central street in the West End and has pleasantly spacious rooms, mostly with bathroom, from £30 to £80 per person.

Royal Terrace has a great position on the north side of Calton Hill. *Ailsa Craig Hotel* (☎ 556 1022)*, No 24, is a refurbished Georgian building. Rooms, often with bath, cost from £30/55. The *Claymore Hotel* (☎ 556 2693)*, No 7, *Halcyon Hotel* (☎ 556 1032)*, No 8, *Greenside Hotel* (☎ 557 0022)*, No 9, and *Adria Hotel* (☎ 556 7875)*, No 11, are similar. Also in Royal Terrace is the thoroughly swish *Royal Terrace Hotel* (☎ 557 3222)* with rooms from £120/160.

Thistle Inn Hotel (☎ 220 2299, 94 *Grassmarket)* is in the heart of the Old Town in one of the city's nightlife centres. Rooms with bath and TV cost from £33/56. The entrance is next to Biddy Mulligan's pub, and every floor is accessible by lift. (Don't confuse it with the more expensive King James Thistle Hotel beside the shopping centre, Leith St.)

Old Waverley Hotel (☎ 556 4648, 43 *Princes St)* has a prime site opposite Waverley station, and many rooms have castle views. Rooms with bath cost from £90/144.

Holiday Inn Crowne Plaza (☎ 557 9797, *80 High St)* is a purpose-built hotel whose exterior mimics the Royal Mile's 16th century architecture. The interior is, nonetheless, as modern as you could hope for. Rates are from £125/144.

The *Sheraton Grand Hotel* (☎ 229 9131, *1 Festival Square)* is opposite the Royal

Lyceum Theatre, off Lothian Rd, west of the castle. You pay for, and get, luxury. Rooms cost from £155/195.

More personal than these chain hotels is **Sibbet House** (☎ *556 1078, 26 Northumberland St)* where prices of £80 to £90 per person might include an impromptu bagpipe recital by your host.

PLACES TO EAT

There are good-value restaurants scattered all round the city. For cheap eats, the best areas are Union Place, near the Playhouse Theatre; around Grassmarket, south of the castle; near the university around Nicolson St, the extension of North/South Bridge, and in Bruntsfield. Most restaurants offer cheap set menus at lunchtime. Many close on Sunday evening, so ring ahead to make sure.

Royal Mile

Despite being a tourist Mecca, the Royal Mile has lots of good-value, enjoyable eating oases.

Restaurants The excellent, small **Polo Fusion** (☎ *622 7722, 503 Lawnmarket)* is reasonably priced by Edinburgh standards, and specialises in Asian dishes. Noodle dishes are good value at £5.50 to £6.50; Thai barbecued duck costs £10.50.

Viva Mexico (☎ *226 5145, Cockburn St)* is a cheerful, atmospheric restaurant. Some tables have views across to the New Town, and the food is good quality. Nachos cost from £2.50, burritos from £8.95.

Doric Wine Bar & Bistro (☎ *225 1084, 15 Market St)* has a good-value bar menu (meals from £2.50 to £3.50) from noon to 6.30 pm. The small upstairs bistro offers classic Scottish dishes like haggis, neeps and tatties for £8.95.

Pleasant **Black Bo's** (☎ *557 6136, 57 Blackfriars St)* offers an imaginative vegetarian menu. Main courses like mushrooms and olives baked in filo pastry with red wine and green pepper sauce cost around £8.95.

You can sample traditional Scottish cooking at **The Grange** (☎ *558 9992, 267 Canongate)* where you can enjoy mains like venison in a prune and wine glaze for £15.35. **Dubh Prais** (☎ *557 5732, 123 High St)* is considered one of the best places to try Scottish cuisine and is popular with locals and tourists. The menu features dishes like asparagus and Parmesan risotto for £4.90 and pan-seared salmon for £13.

Cafés *Patisserie Florentin (St Giles St)* attracts a rather self-consciously Bohemian crowd, but has excellent light meals and pastries; filled baguettes are £3 and good coffee £1. It stays open till the early hours during the festival.

Lower Aisle Restaurant, beneath St Giles' Cathedral in Parliament Square, is peaceful outside peak lunchtimes. Soup and a roll costs £1.50.

Elephant's Sufficiency (☎ *220 0666, 170 High St)* is a bustling lunch spot. Try the Orkney burger for £3.75 or the elephant burger for £4.95.

The enormously popular **Elephant House** (☎ *220 5355, 21 George IV Bridge)* is a café with newspapers, delicious pastries, some of the best coffee in Edinburgh … and elephants in all shapes and sizes.

Gustos Café (☎ *558 3083, 105 High St)* does delicious gourmet sandwiches from £1.95 and filled focaccia from £2.80. The **Netherbow Theatre Café**, beside John Knox's House, serves cheap breakfasts in an outdoor courtyard until noon, then lunches (big portions), salads and quiche for £3.15.

Clarinda's Tea Room *(69 Canongate)* lurks at the rather inhospitable Holyrood end of the Mile. There are a variety of teas from 50p and delicious cakes from 93p. **Brambles Tearoom**, opposite the People's Story, does soup and a roll for £1.50.

Grassmarket

The lively pubs and restaurants on the north side of Grassmarket cater to a young crowd – it's a good starting point for a night out.

Ristorante Gennaro (☎ *226 3706)*, No 64, has standard Italian fare, with minestrone at £2.20 and pizzas from £4.70 to £7.

Popular, informal *Mamma's Pizzas* (☎ 225 6464), No 28, does excellent pizzas with imaginative toppings (from £3.95).

Pierre Victoire (☎ 226 2442, 38 Grassmarket) is part of the chain that serves good-value French food. There's also a branch at *10 Victoria St*, which curves up to George IV Bridge from the north-east corner of Grassmarket. Also part of Pierre's empire, *Beppe Vittorio* (☎ 226 7267, 7 Victoria St) follows the same formula – authentic, good-value food – although in this case it's Italian. Minestrone is £1.50, and you can mix and match sauces and pastas from £5.

Princes St & Around

Midway along Princes St are two pleasant cafés. On the 2nd floor of the huge Waterstone's bookshop, near the corner of South Charlotte St, is a branch of *Starbucks*. It has a bow window overlooking Princes St and serves good coffee. Nearby, *Bewley's Café* (☎ 220 1969, 4 South Charlotte St) is a branch of the Irish chain of traditional cafés. Sandwiches are £1.95 to £2.50, pastries £1.20; it also serves lunch and breakfast.

New Town

The New Town is neither particularly well endowed with eating places nor a particularly interesting part of town at night, but there are a few reasonable options, especially in Hanover St.

Henderson's (☎ 225 2131), downstairs at No 94, is an Edinburgh institution which has been churning out vegetarian food for more than 30 years. Hot dishes start at £3.50 but it's worth checking if there's a lunch or dinner special. At No 110, *Gringo Bill's* (☎ 220 1205), with its bright yellow entrance, does a meal and a drink at lunchtime for £5. *Bar Napoli* (☎ 225 2600), No 75, is a cheerful Italian restaurant, open until 3 am, with pasta and pizza for £4 to £6.

Chez Jules (☎ 225 7893, 61 Frederick St) is a spin-off from Pierre Victoire, offering similar simple, cheap, but good-quality French food. Soup is £1 and a three-course lunch is £5.90. In the same French vein

there's a branch of the popular *Café Rouge* chain nearby.

Leith Walk

Several places on Leith Walk pitch for Playhouse Theatre-goers, including some Italian options. Pick of the bunch is friendly, informal *Giuliano's* (☎ 556 6590, 18 Union Place) opposite the theatre. It's open to 2 am, serving pastas and pizzas for under £6. *Ferri's Italiano Pizzeria* (☎ 556 5592, 1 Antigua St) does pasta or pizza at similar prices and has a good vegetarian selection.

There's a branch of *Pierre Victoire* (☎ 557 8451, 8 Union St) with a relaxed style and main courses for around £8.

Dalry Rd (West End)

A few places on Dalry Rd are convenient for those staying in or near the West End.

The branch of *Howie's Restaurant* (☎ 313 3334), at No 63, is so popular that advance booking is wise. A two course lunch is a bargain at £6.95; the set evening menu is £15.95. House specialities include banoffi pie.

At the north end of Dalry Rd, the *Verandah Restaurant* (☎ 337 5828), No 17, is an excellent tandoori restaurant with tasty food and a three course lunch for £5.95.

Stockbridge

Village-like Stockbridge is popular with the young and affluent and has some enjoyable pubs and restaurants. *Caffe Italia*, at the junction of Dean St and Raeburn Place, has some outside tables and is often packed with shoppers; pastas cost £4 to £6. *Patisserie Florentin* (☎ 220 0225, 5 North West Circus Place) has excellent baguettes, pastries and coffee like its sister shop on St Giles St, off the Royal Mile.

Lothian Rd

A few places around the southern end of Lothian Rd cater for the Royal Lyceum Theatre's clientele. Big, jolly *Dario's Pizzeria Ristorante* (☎ 229 9625), No 85, opens until 5 am daily. Set lunches cost £4 and, in the evening, pasta and pizzas start from around £5.

Opposite the entrance to the theatre, *Jasmine* (☎ 229 5757, 32 Grindlay St) has excellent Chinese cooking, especially seafood. You'll be able to eat well for under £15. A weekday three course lunch costs £6.

Bruntsfield

There's a batch of moderately priced restaurants on Home and Leven Sts (which lead to Bruntsfield Place), but some of the more interesting places are further south around the junction of Bruntsfield Place, Montpelier Park and Murchison Place.

Efes (☎ 229 7833, 42 Leven St) has various kebabs and pizzas. They're cheaper to take away but if you eat in, a doner kebab costs £6.50 and starters like hummus are around £2.80.

Parrots (☎ 229 3252, 3 Viewforth), off Bruntsfield Place, is a popular non-smoking restaurant selling excellent-value evening meals in pleasant parrot-themed surroundings. The extensive menu offers everything from baltis for £5.95, to mushroom and nut fettuccine for £3.75. It's even possible to eat alone here without feeling like a leper. It's closed Sunday and Monday. Further south, *Montpelier's* (☎ 229 3115, 159 Bruntsfield Place) serves cappuccinos and cakes all day, and excellent Scottish breakfasts. The interesting dinner menu has things like swordfish in mango sauce for £8.95.

There's a branch of *Howie's Restaurant* (☎ 221 1777, 208 Bruntsfield Place) in an old bank (see the Dalry Rd section for details).

University

There are lots of places near the university. Many student favourites are between Nicolson St and Bristo Place at the end of George IV Bridge.

Kebab Mahal (☎ 667 5214, 7 Nicolson Square) is a legendary source of cheap sustenance with excellent kebabs from £2.25, and curries from £3.25. You sit at a counter bathed in fluorescent light.

Vegetarians should look for *Susie's Diner* (☎ 667 8729, 51 West Nicolson St) which has good, inexpensive food – mains costs £3.45 to £4.75 – and a belly dancer for entertainment in the evenings.

Negociant's (☎ 225 6313, 45 Lothian St) is a hip café and music venue with good-value food – main courses from £5.95 for Cajun salmon to £6.50 for beef chilli. The basement bar opens until 3 am.

Spartan, atmospheric *Khushi's* (☎ 556 8996, 16 Drummond St) is the original Edinburgh curry house and not much has changed since it opened in 1947. Lamb bhuna at £4.60 is said to be the local favourite, and you can bring your own beer.

Kalpna (☎ 667 9890, 2 St Patrick's Square) is a highly acclaimed, reasonably priced Gujarati (Indian) vegetarian restaurant. On Wednesday nights it lays on a gourmet buffet (£8.95) of 20 dishes from one region of India – the region varies each week.

Newington & Around

If you're staying in Minto St or Mayfield Gardens, you need to head toward the centre to find several good choices on either side of the main road.

The Metropole, on the corner of East Newington Place, is a large café with a wide choice of coffees and teas from 85p and good pies and pastries. It's a good place to relax with a newspaper or book.

Chinese Home Cooking (☎ 668 4946, 34 West Preston St) is a real bargain BYO restaurant with spartan décor but filling, tasty food. Starters cost £1.20 to £3.60, mains £4 to £9, but its three-course lunch is a bargain at £4.

There's also another branch of *Howie's Restaurant* (☎ 668 2917, 75 St Leonards St) near the corner of Montague St.

La Bonne Vie (☎ 622 9111, 113 Beccleuch St) is a highly regarded restaurant specialising in vegetarian and seafood dishes. Vegetarian strudel is £5.75.

ENTERTAINMENT

For full coverage of films, theatre, cabaret, music and clubs, buy *The List* (£1.90), Edinburgh's and Glasgow's fortnightly events guide.

EDINBURGH

Theatre & Cinema

Probably because of the frantic festival activity, Edinburgh has more than its fair share of theatres. The *Edinburgh Festival Theatre* (☎ *529 6000, 13-29 Nicolson St*) stages everything from ballet to the Chippendales. The *Royal Lyceum Theatre* (☎ *229 9697*), opposite Festival Square, hosts concerts, children's shows and ballet. Nearby *Usher Hall* (☎ *228 1155*) puts on classical and popular concerts.

Across the road, *Filmhouse* (☎ *228 2688, 88 Lothian Rd*) shows films that are less-mainstream.

Pubs

Edinburgh has over 700 pubs and bars which are as varied as the population … everything from Victorian palaces to rough and ready drinking holes.

Royal Mile & Around The pubs on the Royal Mile aren't very inspiring, although there are some classics along the side streets. The *Jolly Judge* (*7A James Court*) retains its distinctive 17th century character, has live music and there's a cheering fire in cold weather. The *Malt Shovel Inn* (*13 Cockburn St*) has a good range of beers and whiskies, jazz on Tuesday nights and tables outside in fine weather.

One of Edinburgh's most entertaining pubs is *The Ceilidh House* below the Tron Tavern, Hunter Square. It's the atmospheric home to the Edinburgh Folk Club. Most nights, there are informal, but high-quality, jam sessions. The *Hebrides Bar* (*17 Market St*) provides a mix of Scottish and Irish folk music on Friday and Saturday night, while on Sunday afternoon anyone is invited to come along and play.

Grassmarket & Around The blue-painted *Bow Bar* (*80 West Bow*) is a popular pub serving real ales. Despite its picturesque name, *The Last Drop* (*74 Grassmarket*) actually commemorates the executions that used to take place nearby. The *Beehive Inn* at No 18 is another popular watering hole.

There's a couple of cheerful, friendly places on Cowgate, that runs off the southeast corner of Grassmarket. The *Green Tree*, No 182, is a student hang-out and has a beer garden. *Bannerman's*, No 212, attracts students, locals and backpackers, and there's often live music or disco.

Further south, *Greyfriars Bobby's Bar* (*Candlemaker Row*) and the *Pear Tree* (*West Nicolson St*) are popular student hang-outs with reasonable food. The Pear Tree's large outdoor courtyard is pleasant in warm weather.

New Town Rose St may have lots of pubs, but they're not all worth frequenting. Two exceptions are the *Abbotsford*, No 3, which has Victorian décor, and the *Rose St Brewery*, No 55, which has a good range of beers, most brewed on the premises.

It's worth sticking your nose through the door of *Café Royal Bar* (*17 West Register St*) to see its amazing stained-glass windows, Victorian interior and ceramic portraits of famous people. Nearby in Andrew St, *Tiles Bar-Bistro* is similarly lavish and serves good food.

Mathers, in trendy Broughton St near Leith Walk, is good for a quiet drink, and has inexpensive real ales and a huge selection of malts.

At the west end, in Hope St between Princes St and Charlotte Square, *Whigham's Wine Cellars* is an old (and pricey) wine bar in atmospheric cellars.

Bruntsfield *Bennet's Bar* (*8 Leven St*), beside the King's Theatre, is a Victorian pub whose chief feature is the large curved mirrors with the tiled surrounds. *Ye Olde Golf Tavern* (*30 Wright's Houses*), parallel to Bruntsfield Place and overlooking Bruntsfield Links, is decorated with golfing memorabilia; there's a good selection of whiskies.

Clubs

There are some interesting music/club venues in old vaults under the George IV and South bridges. *The Vaults* (☎ *558*

9052, 15 Niddry St, under South Bridge) has a café as well as a variety of reliable club nights offering reggae, rap, R&B etc.

It's a bit hard to categorise the *City Café* (☎ 220 0125, 19 Blair St). It's a seriously cool bar, but there are also meals, snacks and all-day breakfasts (£4.75). Downstairs, there's a dance floor, *City 2*, with different music depending on the night.

The *Venue Night Club* (☎ 557 3073, 17 Calton Rd) has live music and is well worth checking out. Its fortnightly *Disco Inferno* is one of the favourite sessions with disco music on three floors.

Scottish Evenings
Several places offer an evening of eating, singing and dancing. The *Carlton Highland Hotel* (☎ 472 3000, North Bridge) has a *Hail Caledonia* night for £35.50 which includes five courses, entertainment and a nip of whisky. The action kicks off at 7.30 pm and ends around 10.20 pm, depending on how much the audience gets into the swing of things.

GETTING THERE & AWAY
Edinburgh is 378 miles from London, 46 from Glasgow, 105 from Newcastle upon Tyne, and 194 from York. See the introductory Scotland and Britain Getting Around chapters.

Air
Edinburgh airport (☎ 333 1000), 6½ miles west of the city, has domestic services and a limited number of international services. Air UK, British Airways and British Midland all have regular services.

Bus
Buses from London are competitive and you may be able to get cheap promotional tickets. See Glasgow in the Southern Scotland chapter; prices are the same and the journey takes about seven hours.

There are numerous links with cities in England, including Newcastle (2¾ hours, £8 one way) and York (5½ hours, £20.25 one way).

Buses and coaches leave from the St Andrew Square bus station where Scottish Citylink has an inquiry and ticket counter. Scottish Citylink (☎ 0990-505050) has buses to virtually every major town in Scotland. Most west-coast towns are reached via Glasgow. There are numerous buses to Glasgow, with peak/off-peak returns for £5/7, and to St Andrew, Aberdeen and Inverness.

Train
The main train station is Waverley in the heart of the city, although most trains also stop at Haymarket station, which is convenient for the West End.

There are up to 20 trains a day from London's King's Cross; apart from Apex fares which must be booked in advance, they're expensive, but they're also quicker and more comfortable than buses.

ScotRail has two northern lines from Edinburgh: one that cuts across the Grampians to Inverness (3½ hours) and on to Thurso, and another that follows the coast around to Aberdeen (three hours) and on to Inverness. All services are non-smoking. There are numerous trains to Glasgow (50 minutes, £7.10 one way). For rail inquiries, phone ☎ 0345-484950.

GETTING AROUND
To/From the Airport
Frequent LRT buses run from Waverley Bridge near the train station to the airport, taking 35 minutes and costing £3.20/5 one way/return. A taxi costs around £14 one way.

Bus
Bus services are frequent and cheap, but two main companies, Lothian Regional Transport (LRT) and Scottish Motor Traction (SMT), compete with each other and their tickets aren't interchangeable. You can buy tickets when you board buses, but on LRT buses you must have exact change. For short trips, fares are 50p to 65p. A Day Saver ticket (£2.20), available from bus drivers when you board, covers a whole day's travel. After midnight there are special night buses. The free *Edinburgh*

EDINBURGH

Travelmap shows the most important services and is available from the TIC, or during weekdays contact Traveline (☎ 225 3858 or 0800 232323), 2 Cockburn St.

Train

Trains heading west and north link Waverley station with Haymarket, but it's cheaper to catch a bus down Princes St. Eastward to North Berwick the first stop is Musselburgh.

Taxi

There are numerous central taxi ranks; costs are reasonable and £6 gets you almost anywhere. Local companies include Capital Taxis (☎ 228 2555), Central Radio Taxis (☎ 229 2468), City (☎ 228 1211) and Radiocabs (☎ 225 9000).

Car Rental

In addition to the big national operators, the TIC has details of reputable local car rental companies. Practical Car & Van Rental (☎ 346 4545), 23 Roseburn St, has weekly rates of £70 (plus insurance) for its smallest cars with unlimited mileage. Melville's (☎ 337 5333), 9 Clifton Terrace, has small Fiat Seicentos with unlimited mileage from £115 per week including insurance.

Bicycle

Although there are plenty of steep hills to negotiate, Edinburgh is ideal for cycling – nothing is more than half an hour away and the traffic is fairly tolerable.

Edinburgh Cycle Hire (☎ 556 5560), 29 Blackfriars St, hires out city bikes for £5 a day, mountain and hybrid bikes for £10 to £15 a day, or £50 a week. It hires out tents and touring equipment like panniers, and arranges cycling tours of the city for £10 for three hours. It also sells used bikes and buys them back, the price depending on the state they come back in.

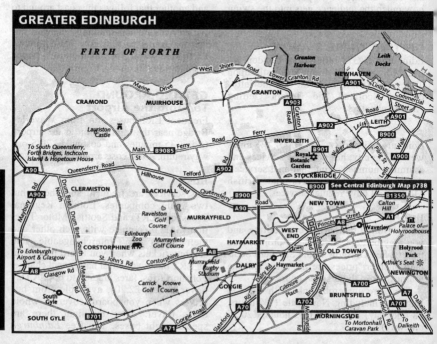

GREATER EDINBURGH

Central Cycle Hire (☎ 228 6333), Lochrin Place off Home St, near Tollcross, operates from the Bike Trax shop and has touring/mountain bikes for £10/15 per day.

Around Edinburgh

CRAIGMILLAR CASTLE

Edinburgh's suburbs are beginning to surround the castle, and the approach road, Craigmillar Castle Rd, is strewn with litter. Nevertheless, massive Craigmillar Castle (☎ 244 3101, HS), about 2½ miles south of the city centre off the A68 to Dalkeith, is still impressive.

Dating from the 15th century, the tower house rises above two sets of walls that enclose a 0.6-hectare area. Mary Queen of Scots took refuge here after the murder of Rizzio; here too plans to murder her husband Darnley were laid. Look for the

prison cell complete with built-in sanitation, something some British prisons only finally managed in 1996. It's open April to September, daily from 9.30 am to 6.30 pm; October to March, Monday to Saturday from 9.30 am to 4.30 pm, Sunday from 2 to 4.30 pm; £1.80/75p. Bus Nos 14, 21, C3 and C33 pass by.

LEITH

Leith is and was Edinburgh's main port, although it remained an independent burgh until the 1920s. It's still among Britain's busiest ports, but in the 1960s and 70s it fell into a sad state, abandoned to council housing, a prey to drug dealers, and blighted by AIDS.

Since the 1980s a revival has been taking place and the area is now noted for its eateries with a number of interesting restaurants and pubs.

Parts are still rough – as are sections of Leith Walk, the main approach – but it's a distinctive corner of Edinburgh. The most interesting parts are bounded by North/Great Junction, Commercial and Constitution Sts, but the prettiest area is around The Shore, where the Water of Leith path south-west to Balerno starts.

Malmaison Hotel (☎ 468 5000, 1 Tower Place), in a 19th century sailor's home, is a wonderfully stylish hotel, with rooms from £95. It has both a café bar and a brasserie where mains, including plenty of vegetarian options, cost £8.50 to £16.50.

Other places to eat along The Shore include *The Shore* (☎ 553 5080) with three-course lunches for £7.95 and live traditional music Wednesday and Saturday at 9 pm, and *Fishers Bistro* (☎ 554 5666) in a 17th century signal tower, where mains (£12 to £16) include marinated swordfish.

You can eat on the cruise ship *Edinburgh*, moored in the dock, on weekends; a full breakfast including haggis is £5.75. Bar meals and real ales are available in two historic pubs, the *Malt & Hops,* the oldest in Leith, and *King's Wark*. Take bus No 87, 88 or 88A from St Andrew Square.

FIRTH OF FORTH

RESTALRIG

Salamander Street

Seafield

Portobello

PORTOBELLO

To Musselburgh, Prestonpans & North Berwick

Musselburgh Rd

DUDDINGSTON

Duddingston Golf Course

Dunsapie Loch

Duddingston Loch

Prestonfield Golf Course

CRAIGMILLAR   To Craigmillar Castle

EDINBURGH

BRITANNIA

You'll find the former royal yacht *Britannia* (☎ 555 5566 for ticket reservation) moored in Leith harbour, just off Ocean Drive (the ship will be relocated at the new Ocean Terminal, also in Leith, in 2001). Allow at least 1½ hours to look around, and note that the use of cameras on board is prohibited.

Britannia is open daily, except Christmas Day, from 10.30 am to 6 pm (last admission at 4.30 pm). Entry to the visitors centre and the ship costs £7.50/5.75/3.75 for adults/seniors/children and there's an £18 family ticket for two adults and two children. Tickets should be reserved in advance by telephone or purchased from the Tattoo Office, 32 Market St.

NEWHAVEN

Immediately west of Leith is Newhaven, once a small, distinctive fishing community, now part of the Edinburgh conurbation. The old fish-market building houses the Newhaven Heritage Museum (☎ 556 7371) which is worth a visit. A 15 minute video reveals the astonishingly tribal lifestyle that survived here until the 1950s when overfishing ended the traditional source of income. The museum opens daily from noon to 5 pm; free.

Most people come here, however, to taste the delights of the enormously popular *Harry Ramsden's* (☎ 551 5566), purveyor of fish and chips, next to the centre. Take bus No 7 or 11 from Princes St.

EDINBURGH ZOO

Parents of young children will be relieved to know there's a zoo (☎ 334 9171) to provide relief from all the museums. It's open Monday to Saturday from 9 am to 6 pm (to 5 pm October and March, to 4.30 pm November to February), and Sunday from 9.30 am. Admission costs £6/3.20. It's 3 miles west of the centre on the A8 road to Glasgow. Bus Nos 2, 26, 31, 69, 85 and 86 pass by.

LAURISTON CASTLE

Three miles north-west of the centre, Lauriston Castle (☎ 336 2060), Cramond Rd South, started life in the 16th century but was 'modernised' in 19th century baronial style.

There are 40-minute guided tours April to October, Saturday to Thursday from 11 am to 5 pm; November to March, weekends only, from 2 to 4 pm; £4/3. Bus Nos 40 and 41 from Hanover St pass by.

SOUTH QUEENSFERRY & THE FORTH BRIDGES

South Queensferry lies on the south bank of the Firth of Forth, at its narrowest point. From early times it was a ferry port, but no more – it's now overshadowed by two bridges.

The magnificent Forth Rail Bridge is one of the finest Victorian engineering achievements. Completed in 1890 after seven years work and the deaths of 58 men, it's over a mile long and the 50,000 tons of girders take three years to paint. The Forth Road Bridge, completed in 1964, is a graceful suspension bridge.

In the pretty High St there are several places to eat and the small South Queensferry Museum (☎ 331 5545) contains some interesting background info on the bridges. The prize exhibit is a model of the Furry Man; on the first Friday of August, some hapless male still has to spend nine hours roaming the streets covered from head to toe in burrs and clutching two floral staves in memory of a medieval tradition. It's open Thursday to Saturday from 10 am to 1 pm and 2.15 to 5 pm, Sunday from noon to 5 pm; free.

The *Maid of the Forth* (☎ 331 4857) leaves from Hawes Pier and cruises under the bridges to Inchcolm Island (see Inchcolm Island & Abbey) and Deep Sea World (☎ 01383-411411), the huge aquarium in North Queensferry. There are daily sailings mid-July to early September (weekends only April to June and October). In summer, evening cruises with jazz or folk music cost £9.50 a head.

You can reach South Queensferry by the frequent trains to Dalmeny station (15 minutes). There are also numerous buses from St Andrew Square, including Nos 43, 47, X47 and 47A.

INCHCOLM ISLAND & ABBEY

Inchcolm Island has one of Scotland's best preserved medieval abbeys which was founded for Augustinian priors in 1123. In well tended grounds stand remains of a 13th century church and a remarkably well preserved octagonal chapter house with stone roof.

It's half an hour to Inchcolm, and you're allowed 1½ hours ashore. Admission to the abbey is £2.30/1, included in the £7.50/3.60 ferry cost (HS members should show their cards for a reduction); non-landing tickets cost £5.20/2.60 and allow you to see the island's grey seals, puffins and other seabirds.

HOPETOUN HOUSE

Two miles west of South Queensferry, Hopetoun House (☎ 331 2451), one of Scotland's finest stately homes, has a superb location in lovely grounds beside the Firth of Forth. There are two parts, the older built to Sir William Bruce's plans between 1699 and 1702 and dominated by a splendid stairwell, the newer designed between 1720 and 1750 by three members of the Adam family, William and sons Robert and John. The rooms have splendid furnishings and staff are on hand to make sure you don't miss details like the revolving oyster stand for two people to share.

The Hope family supplied a Viceroy of India and a Governor-General of Australia so the upstairs museum displays interesting reminders of the colonial life of the ruling class. Even further up there's a viewing point on the roof, ideal for photos.

The house is open April to September, daily from 10 am to 5.30 pm; £4.70/2.60 (for the grounds only it's £2.60/1.60).

You can reach Hopetoun House from South Queensferry, or from Edinburgh – turn off the A90 onto the A904 just before the Forth Bridge Toll and follow the signs.

Southern Scotland

Southern Scotland is a large and beautiful region, although in many ways it's something of a 'no man's land'. Historically, it was the buffer between the rambunctious, imperialist English and the equally unruly Scots.

Although today's inhabitants are proudly and indisputably Scottish they are, in fact, unique – like but unlike the Scots further to the north, like but unlike the northern English to the south. This duality perhaps isn't incompatible with the fact that this region was home to the two men – Burns and Sir Walter Scott – who, in the late 18th and early 19th centuries, did most to re-invent and popularise Scottishness.

The Romans attempted to draw a clean line across the map with Hadrian's Wall, leaving the Celtic Picts to their own devices. The great Anglo-Saxon kingdoms of Bernicia and Northumbria, however, dominated the east and the south-west and succeeded in driving many Celts farther north. Another wave of Anglo-Saxons arrived from northern England after 1066, bringing with them a language that evolved into Lowlands Scots – like but unlike English, as Burns so vividly illustrated.

The Norman invasion of England led to war with the Scots, although in times of peace, especially in the south, the aristocracy intermarried, leading to complicated land holdings on both sides of the border. The wars of Scottish independence fought at the end of the 13th century to the late 14th century, took a terrible toll on southern Scotland. Although the Scots succeeded in consolidating their independence, and great monastic estates were established, the south was still periodically trampled by opposing armies.

Worse still, large parts of today's Scottish Borders and Dumfries & Galloway regions were allowed to go to hell – neither the English nor the Scottish had any real interest in bringing stability to their enemy's border. There were periods of relative calm

HIGHLIGHTS

- Tweed Valley
- Jedburgh
- Melrose and the Eildon Hills
- Dryburgh Abbey
- Traquair House
- The Burrell Collection
- Mackintosh architecture in Glasgow
- The Tenement House, Glasgow
- Culzean Castle
- The beautiful scenery of Dumfries & Galloway

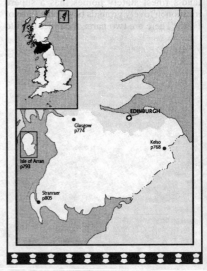

when great monasteries were constructed, but the Debateable Lands, as they were known, were virtually ungoverned and ungovernable from the late 13th to the mid-17th century. The great families with their complex blood feuds fought and robbed the English, the Scots and each other. This continuous state of guerrilla warfare, it's been argued by some, had an indelible effect on the region and its people.

Following the union in 1707, peace allowed a new surge of development. The Scottish Borders, partly thanks to the abbeys, had traditionally been an important wool growing and processing region, and during the 19th century the knitting and weaving industries that survive today were created.

The countryside varies from gentle open fields in the east, to beautiful hilly countryside flanking the River Tweed, to the high Glenken and Galloway hills in the west. The region certainly isn't undiscovered by tourists, but it's easy to escape the crowds, particularly in the south-west. Away from the main roads there's little traffic, which makes for good cycling.

ORIENTATION

Southern Scotland can effectively be divided into four quarters. The southern uplands divide the region into northern and southern halves. In the north-west, the region is divided into North and South Lanarkshire, and North, South and East Ayrshire, plus smaller unitary authorities around Glasgow. The Lothians are in the north-east (linked with Edinburgh). The Scottish Borders, in the south-east, also look to Edinburgh, and there are good bus links with that city. With the exception of the main routes to Stranraer (for Northern Ireland ferries), Dumfries & Galloway in the south-west is quite isolated.

Ayrshire was the birthplace of Scotland's national poet, Burns, though it's the least spectacular part of the region. In Dumfries & Galloway the coast and mountains approach the grandeur of the north. The Scottish Borders have beautiful countryside, particularly around the River Tweed, and pleasant towns built around monastic ruins. The Lothians, most of which are easily accessible on day trips from Edinburgh, have some wild, bleak hills and a beautiful coastline to the east.

INFORMATION

Every small town has an excellent TIC with free accommodation booking services (Book-A-Bed-Ahead, £3) and an excellent range of brochures. Southwaite TIC (☎ 01697-473445/6), on the M6 south of Carlisle, has a lot of information on southern Scotland; it's open April to September, daily from 10 am to 6 pm; October to March, Monday to Friday from 10 am to 5 pm, and Saturday from 10 am to 2 pm. There's another useful TIC, the Gretna Gateway to Scotland (☎ 01461-338500), on the A74.

The TICs have information on car touring routes, including the Burns Trail, starting from near Ayr where Burns was born to Dumfries where he died; the Solway Coast Heritage Trail, from Gretna Green around the beautiful coast to Ayr; and the Scottish Borders Woollen Trail, taking in the mills and mill shops.

SYHA hostels are scarce and, in general, not very accessible unless you have a car. The exceptions are at Melrose, Minnigaff (near Newton Stewart) and Ayr. There are also SYHA hostels at Kendoon, Wanlockhead, Broadmeadows, Kirk Yetholm (near Kelso), Abbey St Bathan's and Coldingham Bay.

WALKS

In the valley of the Tweed especially, there are numerous circular walks around the small towns; the TICs have information.

The most famous is the **Southern Upland Way**, Britain's first official coast-to-coast footpath. It runs 212 miles from Portpatrick on the south-west coast (near Stranraer) to Cockburnspath on the east coast.

The route includes some long, extremely demanding stretches, so walkers tackling the entire length must be both fit and experienced. Parts of the route are sparsely populated, with shelter and transport virtually nonexistent. Proper equipment is essential; in summer you can expect to experience everything from snow to a heat wave. Although the entire route is waymarked, walkers must be able to navigate

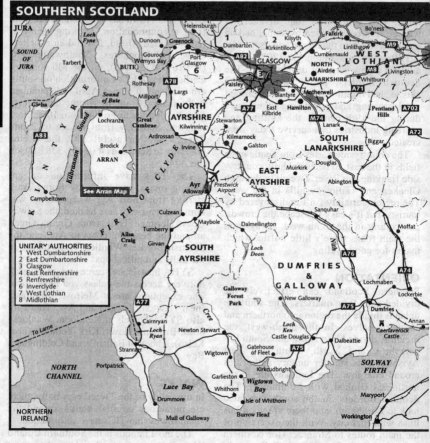

SOUTHERN SCOTLAND

UNITARY AUTHORITIES
1 West Dumbartonshire
2 East Dumbartonshire
3 Glasgow
4 East Renfrewshire
5 Renfrewshire
6 Inverclyde
7 West Lothian
8 Midlothian

with map and compass when visibility is bad. Walkers are advised to walk from west to east. The walk could take anything between 10 and 20 days, although 14 is a fair guess. The way incorporates cliff-top paths, old Roman roads, hill ridges and droving trails. It passes over high hilltops and wide moors, through valleys, forests, farms and villages.

The excellent official guide to the walk, *Southern Upland Way*, is published by the government Stationery Office and comes complete with two 1:50,000 Ordinance Survey route maps. It's available from bookshops, TICs and Stationery Office bookshops in London and Edinburgh.

Accommodation is difficult to find in some parts and many walkers use tents. Book accommodation in advance, especially in the busy summer months. Local TICs can help, and supply a free accommodation leaflet.

Shorter, less demanding sections of the walk can be undertaken. Two suggestions

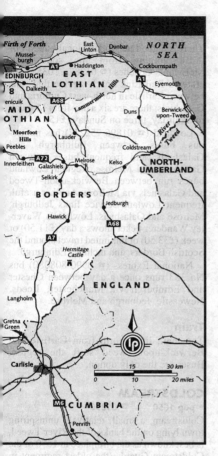

countryside, makes this ideal cycling country. Remember the prevailing winds are from the south-west. Local TICs have information on possible routes.

The **Tweed Cycle Way** is a waymarked route running 62 miles along the beautiful Tweed Valley following minor roads from Biggar to Peebles (13 miles); to Melrose (16 miles); to Coldstream (19 miles); and to Berwick-upon-Tweed (14 miles). Jedburgh TIC (☎ 01835-863435), Murray's Green, Jedburgh TD8 6BE, has information.

Another interesting route is outlined in the guide *Scottish Border Cycle Way*, although this isn't a waymarked route. It runs 210 miles coast to coast from Portpatrick to Berwick-upon-Tweed. Contact Jedburgh TIC for information. Another route is in the guide *Four Abbeys Cycle Route*, a 55 mile circular tour taking in Melrose, Dryburgh, Kelso and Jedburgh.

A decent map will reveal numerous other possibilities. The Tweed Valley is hard to ignore, but the Galloway Hills (north of Newton Stewart) and coastal routes to Whithorn (south of Newton Stewart) are also excellent.

GETTING AROUND
Bus
Bus transport is excellent around Glasgow and Ayrshire, in the Borders and Lothians, reasonable on the main north-south routes and the A75 to Stranraer, but limited elsewhere in Dumfries & Galloway. The relevant inquiry lines and the telephone numbers for the major operators are given in the following sections. Various explorer tickets are available. These can be bought from bus drivers or bus stations, and are nearly always your best-value option if you're travelling reasonably extensively.

Train
Train services are limited. There are stations at Berwick-upon-Tweed (in Northumberland on the English side of the border, but the natural jumping-off point for the Tweed Valley) on the main east-coast line; at Dumfries on the main west-coast line; and at

are Portpatrick to New Luce (23 miles) and Yair Bridge to Melrose (7½ miles).

Another long-distance walk is the 100 mile **St Cuthbert's Way**, inspired by the travels of St Cuthbert, which runs from Melrose in the Scottish Borders, east to Lindisfarne in Northumberland.

CYCLE ROUTES
With the exception of the main north-south A-roads and the A75 to Stranraer, traffic is sparse, which, along with the beauty of the

Stranraer, which is linked to Glasgow. For rail inquiries call (☎ 0345-484950).

Scottish Borders

There's a tendency to think that the real Scotland doesn't start until you're north of Perth, but the castles, forests and glens of the Scottish Borders have a romance and beauty of their own. The region survived centuries of war and plunder and was romantically portrayed by Burns and Scott.

Although areas, especially to the west, are wild and empty, the fertile valley of the River Tweed has been a wealthy region for over 1000 years. The population was largely concentrated in a small number of *burghs* (towns, from burh, meaning a defensive ring of forts), which also supported large and wealthy monastic communities. These provided an irresistible magnet during the border wars and were destroyed and rebuilt numerous times.

The monasteries met their final fiery end in the mid-16th century, burnt by the English yet again, but this time English fire combined with the Scottish Reformation and they were never rebuilt. The towns thrived once peace arrived and the traditional weavers provided the foundation for a major textile industry, which still survives.

If you pause here on your way north, you'll find the lovely valley of the Tweed, rolling hills, castles, ruined abbeys and sheltered towns. This is excellent cycling and walking country. Two walking possibilities are St Cuthbert's Way and the challenging coast-to-coast Southern Upland Way. For cyclists there's the Tweed Cycleway among others (see the Walks and Cycle Routes sections at the start of this chapter).

The Scottish Borders region lies between the Cheviot Hills along the English border, and the Pentland, Moorfoot and Lammermuir Hills, which form the border with the Lothian region and overlook the Firth of Forth. The most interesting country surrounds the River Tweed and its tributaries.

GETTING AROUND
Bus
There's a good network of local buses. For those coming from the south-west, McEwan's Coaches (☎ 01387-710357) operates a Rail Link coach service that runs between Carlisle in north-west Cumbria and Galashiels; there are six a day from Monday to Saturday, three on Sunday (£15).

Lowland (☎ 01896-752237) has numerous buses between Edinburgh and Galashiels, and frequent buses between Galashiels and Melrose. Regular Lowland buses run between Berwick-upon-Tweed and Galashiels via Melrose. Another useful, frequent Lowland service links Jedburgh, Melrose and Galashiels. Lowland's Waverley Wanderer ticket allows a day (£11.50) or week (£33.50) of unlimited travel around the Scottish Borders, and includes Edinburgh.

National Express (☎ 0990-808080) bus No 383 runs once a day between Chester and Edinburgh via Manchester, Leeds, Newcastle, Jedburgh and Melrose.

Train
The main lines north from Carlisle and Berwick-upon-Tweed skirt the region. Buses are the only option.

COLDSTREAM
• pop 1650   ☎ 01890

Coldstream, a small, relatively uninspiring town lying on the banks of the River Tweed, is best known as the birthplace in 1650 of the Coldstream Guards (the oldest regiment in continuous existence). The TIC (☎ 882607), Town Hall, opens daily April to September and from Monday to Saturday in October.

The history of the regiment is covered in the **Coldstream Museum** (☎ 882630), off High St in Market Square, open Easter to October; £1/50p.

Coldstream Caravan & Camping Site (☎ 883376) has a beautiful grassy site beside the river; it's £8 for a cyclist and tent.

The Georgian *Crown Hotel* (☎ 882558, *Market Square*) near the museum, is a family-run hotel with good-value bar meals.

Coldstream Guards

The Coldstream Guards, formed in 1650 for duty in Scotland as part of Oliver Cromwell's New Model Army, took their name from the town where it was stationed in 1659. The regiment played a significant part in the Restoration of the monarchy in 1660, and remains the oldest regiment in continuous existence in the British army. The regiment's emblem is the Star of the Order of the Garter and its regimental motto is *nulli secundus* (second to none).

Single/double rooms cost £18/34 (£26/46 with bathroom).

There's a regular bus service between Kelso and Berwick-upon-Tweed via Coldstream – about six a day from Monday to Saturday. The main operator is Swan (☎ 01289-306436).

KELSO

• **pop 6045**   ☎ **01573**

Kelso is a prosperous market town with a broad cobbled square, flanked by Georgian buildings, at the hub of narrow cobbled streets. There's an interesting mix of architecture and the town has a lovely position at the junction of the Tweed and Teviot rivers. It's busy during the day, but dies completely in the evening. It's a real town, however, not a tourist trap.

The TIC (☎ 223464), Town House, The Square, opens daily from April to October. Accommodation can be difficult to find during local festivals and markets held during late June to mid-September; ring ahead to be sure.

Kelso Abbey

Kelso Abbey was built by Tironensians, an order founded at Tiron in Picardy, and brought to the Scottish Borders around 1113 by David I. Once one of the richest abbeys in southern Scotland, English raids in the 16th century reduced it to ruins.

Today there's little to see, although the abbey precincts are attractive and the nearby octagonal **Kelso Old Parish Church** (1773) is intriguing. The abbey opens April to September, Monday to Saturday from 9.30 am to 6 pm, Sunday from 2 to 6 pm; October to March it closes at 4 pm; free.

Floors Castle

Floors Castle (☎ 223333), Scotland's largest inhabited house, overlooks the River Tweed about a mile west of Kelso. Built by William Adam in the 1720s, the original Georgian simplicity was 'improved' during the 1840s with the addition of rather ridiculous battlements and turrets. Floors makes no bones about being in the tourist business, and although the Roxburgh family is still in residence, there's no sense that this is a real home – visitors are restricted to 10 rooms and a busy restaurant.

Floors Castle opens Easter to late October daily from 10 am to 4.30 pm; £4.50/2.50. Follow Cobby Riverside Walk to reach the entrance to the castle grounds.

Walks

The **Pennine Way**, which starts its long journey at Edale in the Lake District, ends at Kirk Yetholm Youth Hostel, about 6 miles south-east of Kelso on the B6352. Less ambitious walkers should leave The Square by Roxburgh St, and take the signposted alley to **Cobby Riverside Walk**, a pleasant ramble along the river (past some expensive fishing spots) to Floors Castle (although you have to rejoin Roxburgh St to gain entry).

Places to Stay

Kirk Yetholm Youth Hostel (☎ *420631*), is in a Georgian mansion 6 miles south-east of Kelso; dorm beds for adults/juniors cost £6.10/4.95. From Monday to Saturday, bus No 81 runs up to six times daily to/from Kelso.

In Kelso, *Wester House* (☎ *225479, 155 Roxburgh St*) has singles/doubles for £12/30, or doubles with bath for £36. The attractively decorated, central *Old Priory & Coach House* (☎ *223030, 12 Abbey Row*)

SOUTHERN SCOTLAND

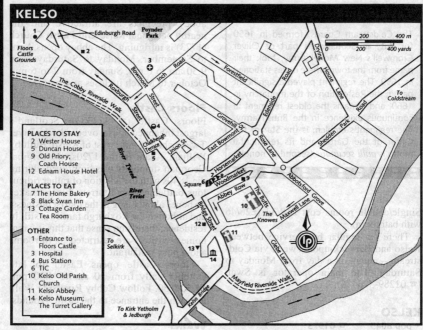

KELSO

Scale: 0 – 200 – 400 m / 0 – 200 – 400 yards

PLACES TO STAY
2 Wester House
5 Duncan House
9 Old Priory;
   Coach House
12 Ednam House Hotel

PLACES TO EAT
7 The Home Bakery
8 Black Swan Inn
13 Cottage Garden
   Tea Room

OTHER
1 Entrance to
   Floors Castle
3 Hospital
4 Bus Station
6 TIC
10 Kelso Old Parish
   Church
11 Kelso Abbey
14 Kelso Museum;
   The Turret Gallery

---

has eight rooms all with bathrooms from £18.50 per person.

Duncan House (☎ 225682, *Chalkheugh Terrace*) is an old house near the town centre, but with a view over the Tweed and Teviot rivers. There's a double, a twin and a family room, and private bathrooms, with rates from £15.50 per person.

The top place to stay is the comfortable *Ednam House Hotel* (☎ 224168, *Bridge St*), a Georgian house with fine gardens overlooking the river. It has a range of rooms, including singles, all with bathrooms. B&B is from £52/73.

Places to Eat

The *Home Bakery* (*Horsemarket*) sells delicious quiches, pies and the like. The *Cottage Garden Tea Room* (*7 Abbey Court*), tucked away in a quiet corner near the museum, has some outdoor seating. It serves tea, coffee and light lunches; a ploughman's lunch is £3.50.

The *Black Swan Inn* (☎ 224563, *Horsemarket*) has decent, generous bar meals from around £5; it doesn't look too prepossessing outside, but it's comfortable inside. It also has B&B from £19 per person.

Bar lunches at the *Ednam House Hotel* are reasonably priced from £4.50 to £5.50; dinners aren't too bad either with a main dish and coffee or tea for £11.50.

Getting There & Away

Kelso is 340 miles from London, 44 from Edinburgh, 18 from Galashiels, 11 from Jedburgh, and nine from Coldstream.

Bus Lowland's bus No 20 is a good service linking Kelso, Jedburgh and Hawick; there are six buses Monday to Friday, three Sunday. It has of buses to/from Galashiels via Melrose; one goes via Smailholm village and Mellerstain House (see Around Kelso).

See the Coldstream section for details on the service to Berwick-upon-Tweed.

AROUND KELSO
Bus No 65 between Melrose and Kelso stops in Smailholm village and passes within a mile or so of Mellerstain House.

Smailholm Tower
Smailholm Tower (☎ 01573-460365, HS) is one of the most evocative sights in the Borders. Perched on a rocky knoll above a small lake with a panoramic view from the top, the narrow stone tower brings the bloody uncertainties of the Borders alive.

The nearby farm, Sandyknowe, was owned by Scott's grandfather. Scott's imagination was fired by the ballads and stories he heard at Sandyknowe as a child, and by the ruined tower of his ancestors a stone's throw away. You pass through the farmyard to get to the tower.

The tower is 6 miles west of Kelso, a mile south of Smailholm village on the B6937. It's open standard hours; £1.80/75p.

Mellerstain House
Mellerstain House (☎ 01573-410225), considered to be Scotland's finest Robert Adam designed mansion, is particularly famous for its ornate interiors. Completed in 1778, it has a classically elegant style. It's open May to September, Sunday to Friday from 12.30 to 4.30 pm; £4/2.

MELROSE
- **pop 2275**   ☎ 01896
Melrose, the most charming of the Border towns, lies at the feet of the three heather-covered Eildon Hills. It's a spic-and-span little town, with a classic market square, some attractive parks and rugby ovals (home to the famous Melrose Sevens competition), and one of the great abbey ruins. Unfortunately, urban sprawl from Galashiels is lapping at its western edges.

There are many attractive walks in the surrounding Eildon Hills, and St Cuthbert's Way and the coast-to-coast Southern Upland Way pass through.

Information
The TIC (☎ 822555), Abbey House, opens April and May, Monday to Saturday from 10 am to 5 pm, Sunday from 10 am to 1 pm; June and September, Monday to Saturday from 10 am to 5.30 pm, Sunday from 10 am to 2 pm (one hour less in October and extended hours in July and August).

Melrose Abbey
Founded by David I in 1136 for Cistercian monks from Rievaulx in Yorkshire, the abbey was repeatedly destroyed by the English in the 14th century. It was rebuilt by Robert the Bruce whose heart is buried here. The ruins date from the 14th and 15th centuries and were repaired by Scott in the 19th. They're pure Gothic and are famous for their decorative stonework. The adjoining museum isn't particularly interesting.

The abbey (☎ 822562, HS) opens April to September daily from 9.30 am to 6.30 pm; October to March, Monday to Saturday from 9.30 am to 4.30 pm, Sunday from 2 to 4.30 pm; £2.80/1.

Next to the abbey are the sheltered **Priorwood Gardens** (☎ 822493, NTS), featuring plants used for dried flower arrangements (£1 donation requested).

Places to Stay
Hostel *Melrose Youth Hostel* (☎ 822521) is in a large Georgian mansion on the edge of town. From the market square, follow the signposting for the A68. It's open Easter to September; dorm beds cost £7.75/6.50 (adults/juniors).

B&Bs & Hotels Melrose B&Bs and hotels aren't cheap by Scottish standards, but are of a high standard – this wouldn't be a bad place to treat yourself. There aren't that many, so consider booking.

Friendly *Birch House* (☎ 822391, *High St*) is a large, open place with a double and a twin for £16 per person; breakfasts are substantial and include a choice of fresh fruit.

Near the abbey, *Braidwood* (☎ *822488, Buccleuch St*) is an excellent B&B with high-standard facilities and a warm welcome. There's a single, double and twin, and rates are from £18 per person.

Burts Hotel (☎ *822285, Market Square*) dates from the late 18th century and offers upmarket B&B from £41 per person. Opposite, *Bon Accord Hotel* (☎ *822645, Market Square*) is a small comfortable hotel where singles/doubles cost £42/68 with bathroom.

Places to Eat

There's excellent pub food in town. The *Kings Arms* has substantial mains for £5 to £9; poached salmon steak is £8.95. In Market Square *Burts Hotel* has good food (mains cost £4 to £8), as does the *Bon Accord Hotel* (☎ *822645*) opposite, where soup of the day is £1.70 and pork fillet £7.50. All provide vegetarian meals.

The acclaimed *Melrose Station Restaurant* (☎ *822546, Palma Place*) opens for lunch from Wednesday to Sunday, and evening meals from Wednesday to Saturday. Book for evening meals. Lunches, which include haggis in whisky and mushroom sauce for £3.25, are cheaper.

Getting There & Away

Melrose is 340 miles from London, 38 from Edinburgh, and 12 from Kelso and Jedburgh.

Bus Lowland has numerous, regular bus links to Galashiels, an important transport hub in the Scottish Borders, Kelso and Jedburgh. Bus No 62 runs regularly to Peebles, while bus No 65 to Kelso travels via Smailholm and close to Mellerstain House (see Around Kelso).

AROUND MELROSE
Dryburgh Abbey

The most beautiful, most complete Border abbey is Dryburgh, partly because the neighbouring town of Dryburgh no longer exists (another victim of the wars), and partly because it has a lovely site in a sheltered valley by the River Tweed. The abbey belonged to the Premonstratensians, a religious order founded in France, and dates from about 1150.

The pink-hued stone ruins were chosen as the burial place for Scott and later for Earl Haig, the WWI allied commander. There are some beautiful picnic spots.

The abbey (☎ 01835-822381, HS) is 5 miles south-east of Melrose on the B6404, which passes famous **Scott's View** overlooking the valley. It's open April to September, Monday to Saturday from 9.30 am to 6.30 pm, Sunday from 2 to 6.30 pm; from October to March it closes two hours earlier; £2.30/1. Bus No 67 passes nearby.

Abbotsford

The home of Scott isn't an architectural masterpiece – the best one can say is that it's disjointed – but it's in a beautiful setting, and is quite fascinating. There's an extraordinary collection of the great man's possessions making it well worth visiting. It opens late March to October, Monday to Saturday from 10 am to 5 pm, Sunday from 2 to 5 pm (Sunday from 10 am June to September); £3.50/1.80.

The house (☎ 01896-752043) is about 3 miles west of Melrose between the River Tweed and B6360. Frequent buses run between Galashiels and Melrose; alight at the Tweedbank traffic island and walk 15 minutes.

Thirlestane Castle

Thirlestane (☎ 01578-722430) is one of the most fascinating of Scotland's castles. The massive original keep was built in the 13th century, but was refashioned and extended in the 16th century with fairytale turrets and towers – achieved without compromising the scale and integrity of the building. It's still very much a family home and as a visitor you feel almost as if you're prying.

It's open during Easter, May, June and September on Sunday, Monday, Wednesday and Thursday; July and August, daily except Saturday. The castle opens from 2 to 5 pm (from noon July and August); the grounds open from noon to 5 pm; £4.

The castle is 10 miles north of Melrose, near Lauder, off the A68. Bus Nos 29 and 30 go to Lauder.

GALASHIELS
* pop 13,765   ☎ 01896

Galashiels is a busy, unprepossessing mill town strung along the A6091, 3 miles east of Melrose. It's something of a transport hub and there's quite a bit of accommodation available, but there's little reason to stay. The town virtually closes down by 6 pm.

The TIC (☎ 755551), 3 St John St, opens April to September, Monday to Saturday from 10 am to 5 pm, Sunday from 1 to 3 pm (extended hours in July and August); and in October from Monday to Saturday.

Lowland (☎ 752237) is the main operator with frequent buses to/from Edinburgh, Melrose, Hawick, Kelso and Peebles.

SELKIRK
* pop 5950   ☎ 01750

Selkirk is an unusual little town that climbs a steep ridge above Ettrick Water, a tributary of the River Tweed. Mills came to the area in the early 1800s, but it's now a quiet place (much quieter than Galashiels or the textile centre of Hawick).

The TIC (☎ 720054), Halliwell's House, opens April to October, Monday to Saturday from 10 am to 5 pm, Sunday from 2 to 4 pm (extended hours in July and August). The adjoining local **Halliwell's House Museum** is interesting.

County Hotel (☎ 721233, 3-5 High St, Market Square) has accommodation from £23 per person and good bar meals; beef and Guinness pie is £4.50.

Lowland's bus No 95 runs between Hawick, Selkirk, Galashiels and Edinburgh.

JEDBURGH
* pop 4090   ☎ 01835

Jedburgh, the most visited of the Scottish Borders towns has some interesting sites

that it has capitalised on with efficiency. It's an attractive town, and many old buildings and *wynds* (narrow alleys) have been intelligently restored.

The large, efficient TIC (☎ 863435), Murray's Green, opens daily March to October; and from Monday to Saturday, November to February. Early-closing day is Thursday.

Jedburgh Abbey
Jedburgh Abbey dominates the town. Founded in 1138 by David I as a priory for Augustininan canons, it was the site for a royal wedding and a coronation, but suffered the usual cycle of sacking and rebuilding. The red sandstone ruins are roofless, but comparatively complete.

The abbey (☎ 863925, HS) opens daily April to September from 9.30 am to 6.30 pm; October to March, Monday to Saturday from 9.30 am to 4.30 pm, Sunday from 2 to 4.30 pm; £2.80/1.

Mary Queen of Scots House
Mary stayed here in 1566 after her famous ride to Hermitage Castle to visit the injured Earl of Bothwell, her future husband. It's a beautiful 16th century tower house and worth a visit – the sparse displays are interesting and evoke the sad saga of Mary's life. The house (☎ 863331) opens March and November, Monday to Saturday from 10.30 am to 3.30 pm, Sunday from 1 to 4 pm; April to October, Monday to Saturday from 10 am to 4.30 pm, Sunday from noon; £2/1.

Places to Stay
Camping *Elliot Park Camping & Caravanning Club Park* (☎ 863393, Edinburgh Rd), about a mile north of the centre, has sites for £6.90.

B&Bs & Hotels *Castlegate Restaurant* (☎ 862552, 1 Abbey Close) on the corner of High St near the abbey has large clean rooms from a reasonable £15 per person.

Kenmore Bank (☎ 862369, Oxnam Rd) overlooks the abbey and is good value. Twins, doubles and family rooms all have

SOUTHERN SCOTLAND

bathrooms and cost from £18 per person. The very comfortable *Glenfriar's Hotel (☎ 862000, Friarsgate)* has two singles, two twins and two doubles, all with bathrooms, for £35/64.

Places to Eat

Castlegate Restaurant has a traditional menu, with dishes like steak and kidney pie. It's a good place for either a full meal (BYOB) or just a cup of tea. The *Pheasant Lounge Bar (☎ 862708, 61 High St)* has a good range of bar meals from around £5 to £7, with interesting offerings like breast of pheasant with lemon and apple sauce.

Getting There & Away

Jedburgh is 330 miles from London, 45 from Edinburgh, 17 from Galashiels and Selkirk, and 11 from Kelso.

Bus Jedburgh has good bus connections around the Borders. Lowland (☎ 01896-752237) in Galashiels is the main operator. There are many connections to Hawick, Galashiels and Kelso. Bus No 23 runs to/from Berwick-upon-Tweed via Kelso and Coldstream. Bus Nos 29 and 30 run six times daily between Edinburgh and Jedburgh in each direction.

PEEBLES
* pop 7080   ☎ 01721

Peebles is a prosperous little town set among rolling wooded hills on the banks of the River Tweed. The TIC (☎ 720138), High St, opens April to October, Monday to Saturday from 10 am to 5 pm, Sunday from 10 am to 2 pm (extended hours in July and August); November to March, Monday to Saturday from 9.30 am to 12.30 pm and 1.30 to 4.30 pm.

There's a broad, attractive High St, the interesting local **Tweeddale Museum**, and although it's not particularly notable, Peebles is a pleasant place to stay.

Places to Stay & Eat

Rowanbrae (☎ 720630, Northgate) has only two rooms but it's very pleasant. B&B costs £16 per person.

Green Tree Hotel (☎ 720582, 41 Eastgate) is a well-organised, tidy hotel. There's a range of rooms, including singles, most with bathrooms. The nightly rate is £23 to £28 per person. *The County Hotel (☎ 720595, 35 High St)* is a downbeat but good pub, often with live music in the evening. It has some B&B (£19 per person), decent bar meals from around £5 and a more expensive restaurant.

Two miles from Peebles on the A703, *Cringletie House (☎ 730233)* is a comfortable country house hotel with an excellent restaurant. Rooms start at £55 per person. There are set lunches for £16, set dinners for £28.

Getting There & Away

Bus The bus stop is beside the post office. Lowland bus No 95 runs hourly to Edinburgh, Galashiels and Melrose.

Bicycle Scottish Border Trails (☎ 720336), Glentress, organises bicycle tours – both on and off road. It also hires mountain bikes from £16 per day and tourers from £10. Pre-booking is recommended; bikes are delivered to you free in the Peebles area.

AROUND PEEBLES
Neidpath Castle

Neidpath Castle is a tower house perched on a bluff above the River Tweed, a mile west of Peebles on the A72. It's a lovely spot, although there's not much to see inside. The castle (☎ 01721-720333) opens Easter to September, Monday to Saturday from 9.30 am to 6.30 pm, Sunday from 2 to 6.30 pm; £2.50/1.

Traquair House

Traquair (pronounced trakweer) is one of Britain's great houses; there are many that are more aesthetically pleasing, but this one has a powerful, atmospheric beauty – and exploring it is like time-travelling.

Parts of the building are believed to have been constructed long before the first official record of its existence in 1107. The massive tower house was gradually expanded over the next 500 years, but has remained virtually unchanged since 1642.

Since the 15th century, the house has belonged to various branches of the Stuart family whose unwavering Catholicism and loyalty to the Stuart cause is largely why development ceased when it did. The family's estate, wealth and influence was gradually whittled away after the Reformation, and there was neither the opportunity, nor, one suspects, the will, to make any changes.

One of the most fascinating rooms is the concealed priest's room where priests secretly lived and gave mass – up to 1829 when the Catholic Emancipation Act was finally passed. Other beautiful timeworn rooms hold fascinating relics, including the cradle used by Mary Queen of Scots for her son, James VI of Scotland (who was also James I of England), and many letters written by the Stuart pretenders to their supporters.

In addition, there's a maze, an art gallery, a small brewery producing Bear Ale and an active craft community.

Traquair (☎ 01896-830323) is 1½ miles south of Innerleithen, about 6 miles southeast of Peebles. It's open June to August, daily from 10.30 am to 5.30 pm; April, May and September, daily from 12.30 to 5.30 pm; and in October, Friday to Sunday from 12.30 to 5.30 pm. Entry is £4.50/2.25.

HERMITAGE CASTLE

Hermitage Castle is a massive collection of stone with a heavy cubist beauty, and sits isolated beside a rushing stream surrounded by bleak, empty moorland. Dating from the 13th century, but substantially rebuilt in the 15th, it embodies the brutal history of the Scottish Borders; the stones themselves almost speak of the past. It was Scott's favourite castle.

It's probably best known as the home of the Earl of Bothwell, and the spot where Mary Queen of Scots rode in 1566 to see him after he had been wounded in a border raid. It's also where, in 1338, Sir William Douglas imprisoned his enemy Sir Alexander Ramsay and deliberately starved him to death. Ramsay survived for 17 days by

eating grain that trickled into his pit (which can still be seen) from the granary above.

The castle (☎ 013873-76222, HS) is 5½ miles north-east of Newcastleton off the A7. It's open April to September, daily from 9.30 am to 6.30 pm; October to March, Monday to Wednesday and Saturday from 9.30 am to 4.30 pm, Thursday from 9.30 am to 1 pm, and Sunday from 2 to 4.30 pm; £1.50/75p.

Glasgow

• pop 689,000   ☎ 0141

Although Glasgow lacks the instantly inspiring beauty of Edinburgh, it's one of Britain's largest, liveliest, most interesting cities, with a legacy of appealing Victorian architecture and several distinguished suburbs of terraced squares and crescents. 'Glasgow – The Friendly City' say the billboards, and it's true.

In the early 1970s, the name Glasgow became synonymous with unemployment, economic depression and urban violence. It was known for bloody confrontations that occurred between rival supporters of Protestant Rangers and Catholic Celtic football teams, and as the home of the Glasgow Kiss (a head butt). Over the following years, however, the city reinvented itself, rediscovering its rich cultural roots and proclaiming a new pride through a well-orchestrated publicity campaign. By 1990, it was elected European City of Culture and in 1999 served as the UK's City of Architecture & Design. Glasgow has become the third most popular destination in Britain for foreign tourists, after London and Edinburgh.

Although influenced by thousands of Irish immigrants, Glasgow is the most Scottish of cities, with a unique blend of friendliness, urban chaos, black humour and energy. In the 80s and 90s, the city saw an incredible outburst of musical talent and produced such groups as Simple Minds, Tears for Fears, Deacon Blue, Aztec Camera, Wet Wet Wet and Texas, as well as comedians like Billy Connolly and Stanley Baxter.

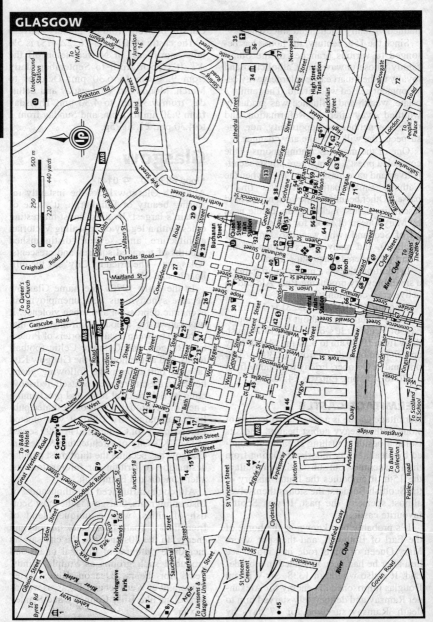

GLASGOW

PLACES TO STAY		62	Café Gandolfi	OTHER	
4	Glasgow Backpackers Hostel	67	Change at Jamaica	1	Hunterian Museum
5	Glasgow Youth Hostel	69	The Granary	11	Tenement House
6	Woodlands House			20	Centre for Contemporary Arts
7	Alamo Guest House	PUBS		21	Glasgow School of Art
8	Smiths Hotel	3	Uisge Beatha	25	Glasgow Film Theatre
12	McLay's Guest House	9	Halt Bar	27	Theatre Royal
13	Baird Hall	23	Brunswick Cellars	28	Glasgow Royal Concert Hall
14	Berkeley Globetrotters	30	Austin's	29	Buchanan Bus Station
17	Charing Cross Tower Hotel	32	Sadie Frost's Café, Bar &	34	Provand's Lordship Museum
18	Willow Hotel; Hampton		Restaurant	35	Glasgow Cathedral
	Court Hotel	41	The Horse Shoe	36	St Mungo's Museum
19	Victorian House	43	King Tut's Wah Wah	38	City Chambers
33	University of Strathclyde		Hut	39	Bank of Scotland Buildings
37	Cathedral House Hotel	47	The Waterloo Bar	40	Post Office
46	Glasgow Marriott	48	Bar 10	42	American Express Office
		50	The Bank	45	SECC
PLACES TO EAT		52	The Jenny	49	Princes Square
2	Shalimar	55	Bennet's Nightclub	51	Gallery of Modern Art
10	Insomnia Café	57	Polo Lounge, Café Del	53	TIC
15	Mitchell's Bistro & Bon		Monica's; Café Latte	54	Hutchesons' Hall
	Accord Pub	58	The Court Bar	56	Trades House
16	Ristoro Ciao Italia; Loon Fung	61	Babbity Bowster	59	Sheriff Court House
22	Bradford's Bakery	63	Blackfriars	60	City Halls
24	Willow Tearoom	66	MacSorleys	64	Tobacco Exchange
26	Delifrance	68	Glasgow Gay & Lesbian	65	St Enoch Travel Centre
31	Balbir's		Centre; QC's Bistro	71	Tron Theatre
44	The Buttery Restaurant	70	Scotia Bar	72	The Barrows Market

The city also boasts excellent art galleries and museums, most of them charging no entry fee, including the famous Burrell Collection as well as numerous good value restaurants, countless pubs and bars and a lively arts scene.

History

Glasgow grew around the cathedral founded by St Kertigan, later to become St Mungo, in the 6th century. In 1451, it became the site of the University of Glasgow, the second university in Scotland. Unfortunately, with the exception of the cathedral, virtually nothing of the medieval city remains. It was swept away by the energetic people of a new age – the age of capitalism, the Industrial Revolution, and the British empire.

In the 18th century, much of the tobacco trade between Europe and the USA was routed through Glasgow and provided a great source of wealth. Other New World imports included rum and sugar. Even after the tobacco trade declined in the 19th century, the city continued to prosper as a centre of textile manufacturing, shipbuilding and the coal and steel industries.

The new industries created a huge demand for labour and peasants poured in from Ireland and the Highlands to crowd the city's tenements. In the mid-18th century the population was 17,500 and by the end of the century it had risen to 100,000. After 20 years that figure had doubled and by 1860 it was home to 400,000 people. The outward appearance of prosperity, however, was tempered by the dire working conditions in the factories, particularly for women and children. In the second half of the 19th century the city experienced four major cholera outbreaks and the average life expectancy was a mere 30 years.

While the workers suffered, the textile barons and shipping magnates prospered, and Glasgow could justifiably call itself the second city of the empire. Grand Victorian public buildings were constructed and some of the wealthier citizens spent their fortunes on amassing the large collections of art that now form the basis of the city's superb galleries.

In the first half of the 20th century Glasgow was the centre of Britain's munitions industry, supplying arms and ships for the two world wars. After those boom years, however, the port and heavy industries began to decline and by the early 1970s, the city looked doomed. Glasgow has always been proud of its predominantly working class nature, but unlike middle-class Edinburgh with its varied service industries, it had few alternatives when recession hit and unemployment spiralled.

Certainly there's now renewed confidence in the city but behind all the optimism, the standard of living remains low for the UK and life continues to be tough for those affected by relatively high unemployment, inadequate housing and generally poor diet.

Orientation

Glasgow's tourist sights are spread over a wide area. The city centre is built on a grid system on the north side of the River Clyde. The two train stations (Central and Queen St), Buchanan St bus station and the TIC are all within a couple of blocks of George Square, the main city square. Running along a ridge in the northern part of the city, Sauchiehall St (first syllable pronounced soch as in loch) has a pedestrian mall with numerous High St shops at its eastern end, and pubs and restaurants at the western end. Merchant City is the commercial district, east of George Square.

The Glasgow University and the SYHA hostel are near Kelvingrove Park, northwest of the city centre in an area known as the West End. Pollok Country Park and the Burrell Collection are in South Side, southwest of the centre.

Motorways bore through the suburbs and the M8 sweeps round the western and northern edges of the centre. The airport lies 10 miles west of the centre.

Information

Tourist Offices The main TIC (☎ 204 4400), 11 George Square, has a £2 accommodation booking service and a *bureau de change*. It's open Monday to Saturday from 9 am to 6 pm; 9 am to 7 pm in June and September; and 9 am to 8 pm in July and August. It's also open Sunday, Easter to September from 10 am to 6 pm. There's another branch at Glasgow airport.

Travel information is also available from the St Enoch Square Travel Centre (☎ 226 4826), St Enoch Square. It's open Monday to Saturday from 9.30 am to 5 pm.

Money American Express (☎ 221 4366), 115 Hope St, opens during commercial hours from Monday to Friday and until noon on Saturday.

Emergency

Like the rest of Britain, the free emergency numbers are ☎ 999 or ☎ 112.

George Square & The Merchant City

The TIC is on George Square, a good starting point for exploring the city. The square is surrounded by imposing Victorian architecture, including the post office, the Bank of Scotland and the City Chambers. There are statues of Burns, James Watt, Lord Clyde and, atop a 24m-high doric column, Scott.

The grand City Chambers (☎ 221 9600), the seat of local government, was built in the 1880s at the high point of the city's wealth. The interior is even more extravagant than the exterior, and the chambers are sometimes used as a movie location to represent the Kremlin or the Vatican. There are free tours lasting 45 minutes from the main entrance, Monday to Friday at 10.30 am and 2.30 pm.

A Walk Through Merchant City An interesting hour-long walk can be taken from

George Square to Glasgow Cathedral through The Merchant City, a planned 18th century civic development. The Tobacco Lords were the entrepreneurs who opened up European trade with the Americas, importing tobacco, rum and sugar in the 18th century and their profits went to build these warehouses, offices and gracious homes. The redevelopment trend has turned the warehouses into apartments for Glaswegian yuppies and stylish shopping malls such as the Italian Centre have sprung up to serve their retail needs.

Once you've seen the City Chambers, cross George Square and walk one block south down Queen St to the **Gallery of Modern Art**. Built in 1827, this four-storey colonnaded building was originally the Royal Exchange, where business transactions were negotiated.

The gallery faces Ingram St, which you follow east for two blocks. To the right, down Garth St, is **Trades House**, designed by Robert Adam in 1791 to house the trades guild. This is the only surviving building in Glasgow by this famous Scottish architect. A farther two blocks east along Ingram St brings you to **Hutchesons' Hall**. Built in 1805 to a design by David Hamilton, this elegant building is maintained by the National Trust for Scotland. It's open Monday to Saturday from 10 am to 5 pm.

Retrace your steps one block and continue south down Glassford St past **The Warehouse**, a distinctive Art-Nouveau building that houses designer clothes shops. Turn right into Wilson St and first left along Virginia St, lined with the old warehouses of the Tobacco Lords. The **Tobacco Exchange** became the Sugar Exchange in 1820 and many of the old warehouses are now being converted into flats.

Back on Wilson St, the bulky **Sheriff Court House** fills a whole block. It was originally built as Glasgow's town hall. Continue east past **Ingram Square**, another warehouse development, to the **City Halls**, now used for concerts. The city's markets were once held here. Turn right from Albion St into Blackfriars St. Emerging onto High St, turn left and follow the street up to Glasgow Cathedral.

Glasgow Cathedral & Precincts

The oldest part of the city is centred on Glasgow Cathedral, east of the modern centre. The area was given a face-lift with the opening of St Mungo's Museum of Religious Life and Art. The money for the restoration of the cathedral was sensibly spent on updating the heating system rather than giving the blackened exterior a high-pressure hose-down. Nearby, Provand's Lordship, the city's oldest house, completes a trio of interesting sights.

The crumbling tombs of the city's rich and famous crowd the renovated necropolis behind the cathedral.

It takes about 15 to 20 minutes to walk from George Square but numerous buses pass by. Bus Nos 11, 12, 38 and 51 follow Cathedral St; bus No 2 runs from Argyle St via High St.

Glasgow Cathedral   Glasgow Cathedral (☎ 552 6891), is a shining example of pre-Reformation Gothic architecture and the only mainland Scottish cathedral to survive the Reformation. Most of the current building dates from the 15th century – only the western towers were destroyed in the turmoil.

This has been hallowed ground for over 1500 years. The site was blessed for Christian burial in 397 by St Ninian. In the following century St Mungo accompanied the body of a holy man from Stirlingshire to be buried here. He stayed to found a monastic community and built a simple church. The first building was consecrated in 1136, in the presence of King David I, but it burned in 1197 and was rebuilt as the lower church.

Entry is through a side door into the **nave**, hung with regimental colours. The wooden roof above has been restored many times since its original construction but some of the timber dates from the 14th century. Much of the cathedral's stained glass is modern and to your left, you'll see Francis Spear's 1958 work *The Creation*, which fills the west window.

The cathedral is divided by a late 15th century stone choir screen, decorated with seven pairs of figures representing the Seven Deadly Sins. Beyond is the choir. Also by Francis Spear, the four stained-glass panels of the east window depicting the apostles are particularly effective. At the north-east corner is the entrance to the 15th century **upper chapter house**, where Glasgow University was founded. It's now used as a sacristy.

The lower church is the most interesting part of the cathedral and is reached by a stairway. Its forest of pillars creates a powerful atmosphere around St Mungo's tomb, the focus of a famous medieval pilgrimage that was believed to be as meritorious as a visit to Rome. Edward I paid three visits to the shrine in 1301.

The cathedral opens to visitors Monday to Saturday from 9.30 am to 6 pm, and Sunday from 2 to 5 pm. In winter it closes at 4 pm daily. Sunday services are held at 11 am and 6.30 pm.

St Mungo's Museum of Religious Life & Art

The award-winning St Mungo Museum (☎ 553 2557), near the cathedral, was opened in 1993. From its inception, it has been a highly controversial project – it's understandably challenging to select works of art outlining all the world's main religions – but the result is well worth a look and is small enough not to be overwhelming.

The building may look like a restored antiquity, in fact it's a £6.5 million reconstruction of the bishop's palace that once stood here, and is only a few years old. A 10 minute video provides an overall view before you delve into the exhibits. There are three galleries representing religion as art, religious life and, on the top floor, religion in Scotland. In the main gallery, Dalí's *Christ of St John of the Cross* hangs beside statues of the Buddha and Hindu deities. Outside, you'll find Britain's only Zen Buddhist garden.

There's a good restaurant downstairs serving both vegetarian and meat dishes. Soup and a roll cost £1.25 and main dishes are £3.50.

The museum opens daily from 10 am to 5 pm (from 11 am on Sunday); entry is free.

Provand's Lordship Across the road from St Mungo Museum, Provand's Lordship (☎ 552 8819) is the oldest house in Glasgow. Built in 1471 as a manse for the chaplain of St Nicholas Hospital, it's said to have been visited by Mary Queen of Scots, James II and James IV. It's now a museum of various period displays connected with the house. These are as diverse as a 16th century room of one of the chaplains who lived here, and a 20th century sweet shop. Once the current conservation work is finished, Provand's Lordship will open daily until 5 pm; entry is free.

Burrell Collection

Glasgow's top attraction, the Burrell Collection (☎ 649 7151), was amassed by wealthy industrialist Sir William Burrell before it was donated to the city. It's now housed in a prize-winning museum in Pollok Country Park, 3 miles south of the city centre. This idiosyncratic collection includes everything from Chinese porcelain and medieval furniture to paintings by Renoir and Cézanne. It isn't so big as to be overwhelming, and the stamp of the collector creates an intriguing coherence.

The building was the result of a design competition in 1971. If it hadn't been run during a postal strike, necessitating an extension of the closing deadline, Barry Gasson's winning entry wouldn't have been completed. The result is a building that from the outside seems somewhat of a hybrid, but the truly spectacular interior provides a fitting setting for an exquisite collection of tapestries, oriental porcelain, paintings and European stained glass. Floor-to-ceiling windows admit a flood of natural light, and the trees and landscape outside only enhance the effect created by the exhibits.

Carpeted floors mean silence to contemplate the beautifully displayed treasures. Carved-stone Romanesque doorways are incorporated into the structure so one actually walks through them. Some galleries are reconstructions of rooms from Hutton Castle, the Burrell residence. Even the public seating is of superb design and production quality.

The light and airy café on the lower ground floor includes the same floor-to-ceiling windows, hung with heraldic glass medallions.

The Burrell Collection opens Monday to Saturday from 10 am to 5 pm, and from 11 am to 5 pm on Sunday. Admission is free, but parking costs a hefty £1.50. There are occasional guided tours. Numerous buses pass the gates (including bus Nos 45, 48A and 57 from the centre), and there's a twice-hourly bus service between the gallery and the gates (a pleasant 10 minute walk). Alternatively, catch a train to Pollokshaws West from Central station (four per hour; the second station on the light blue line south, trains destined for East Kilbride or Kilmarnock).

Pollok House

Also in Pollok Country Park, and a 10 minute walk from the Burrell Collection, Pollok House contains a fine collection of Spanish paintings, including works by El Greco and Goya. The house is Georgian and parts have been redecorated with historically correct but bizarre-looking colour schemes. There's a tearoom in the old kitchens. The house was closed at the time of research but it's likely to be taken over and re-opened by the National Trust for Scotland (NTS). Opening times will probably be daily from 10 am to 5 pm (shorter hours in winter) and there'll be a moderate admission charge. Contact the NTS (☎ 616 2266) for the latest information.

Mackintosh Buildings

There are some superb Art-Nouveau buildings designed by the Scottish architect and designer, Charles Rennie Mackintosh (CRM). There are day tours of several of these buildings from May to October (once or twice a month), and at weekends, for £30 per day. Contact the CRM Society (☎ 946 6600) for details.

Glasgow School of Art Widely recognised as Mackintosh's greatest building, the Glasgow School of Art (☎ 353 4526), 167 Renfrew St, still houses the educational institution. It's hard not to be impressed by the thoroughness of the design – the architect's pencil seems to have shaped every- thing inside and outside the building. The interior design is strikingly austere, with simple colour combinations (often just black and cream) and those uncomfortable-looking high-backed chairs for which he is famous. The library, designed as an addition in 1907, is a masterpiece of rectangular pillars, horizontal beams and Mackintosh's characteristic linear style.

There are guided tours Monday to Friday at 11 am and 2 pm, and on Saturday at 10.30 am (£3.50/2). Parts of the school may be closed to visitors if they're in use.

Willow Tearoom The Willow Tearoom (☎ 332 0521), 217 Sauchiehall St, is more Mockintosh than Mackintosh – a reconstruction of the tearoom Mackintosh designed and furnished in 1904 for restaurateur Kate Cranston. The restaurant closed in 1926 and the premises were occupied by a series of retail businesses. Reconstruction took two years and the Willow opened as a tearoom again in 1980. Sauchiehall means 'lane of willows', hence the choice of a stylised willow motif.

Queues for light meals and tea (see Places to Eat) often extend into the gift shop and jeweller's downstairs.

Queen's Cross Church Now the headquarters of the CRM Society, Queen's Cross Church (☎ 946 6600), 870 Garscube Rd, is the only one of Mackintosh's church designs to be built. The simplicity of the design is particularly inspiring. There's an information centre, a small display and a gift shop.

It's open to visitors Monday to Friday from 10 am to 5 pm, Saturday from 10 am to 2 pm, and Sunday 2 to 5 pm. For adults, a donation is suggested; it's free for students.

Charles Rennie Mackintosh

The quirky, linear and geometric designs of this famous Scottish architect and designer have had almost as much influence on the city as have Gaudi's on Barcelona. Many of the buildings Mackintosh designed in Glasgow are now open to the public, and you'll see his tall, thin, Art-Nouveau typeface repeatedly reproduced.

Born in 1868, he studied at the Glasgow School of Art. In 1896, when he was aged only 27, his design won a competition for the School of Art's new building. The first part was opened in 1899 and is considered to be the earliest example of Art Nouveau in Britain, and Mackintosh's supreme architectural achievement. This building demonstrates his skill in combining function and style.

Mackintosh applied himself to every facet of design, from whole façades to the smallest window fastener. As a furniture designer and decorative artist, he designed the interiors for Kate Cranston's chain of Glasgow tearooms between 1896 and 1911. The Willow Tearoom, 217 Sauchiehall St, has now been fully restored and reopened as a tearoom.

Although Mackintosh's genius was quickly recognised on the Continent (he contributed to a number of exhibitions in France, Germany and Austria), he did not receive the same encouragement in Scotland. His architectural career here lasted only until 1914 when he moved to England to concentrate on furniture design. He died in 1928, but it's only in the last thirty years that Mackintosh's genius has been widely recognised. If you want to know more about the man and his work, contact the Charles Rennie Mackintosh Society (☎ 0141-946 6600, fax 0141-945 2321), Queen's Cross, 870 Garscube Rd, Glasgow, G20 7EL.

Other Mackintoshiana The principal rooms from Mackintosh's house have been reconstructed as the **Mackintosh House** at the Hunterian Art Gallery.

At the Art Gallery and Museum in Kelvingrove Park there's a display of Mackintosh paintings, furniture and decorative art.

Scotland Street School (☎ 429 1202), 225 Scotland St, is an impressive Mackintosh building dominated by two glass-stair towers. It's now a museum of education, which may sound dull but is actually fascinating. It's open Monday to Saturday from 10 am to 5 pm, and on Sunday from 2 pm to 5 pm; admission is free.

Although designed in 1901 as an entry to a competition run by a German magazine, the **House for an Art Lover,** (☎ 353 4770), Bellahoustonn Park, Drumbreck Rd, wasn't completed until 1996. It has permanent Mackintosh displays and a café. It's open Saturday and Sunday from 10 am to 5 pm; for weekday access details call (☎ 353 4449). Admission is £3.50/2.50.

Twenty-three miles north-west of Glasgow at Helensburgh is **Hill House** (☎ 01436-673900), Mackintosh's domestic masterpiece, now in the hands of the National Trust for Scotland.

The Tenement House

For an extraordinary time capsule experience, you can visit the small apartment in the Tenement House (☎ 333 0183), 145

Buccleuch St. It gives a vivid insight into middle-class city life at the turn of the 20th century with box-beds, an original kitchen range and all the fixtures and fittings of the family who lived here for more than 50 years. It's an interesting place but very National Trust – surely the Toward family wouldn't have kept it quite so squeaky clean and orderly as the National Trust for Scotland manages to now.

Despite the additional exhibition area in the ground-floor flat, it can get crowded. The flat opens March to October, daily from 2 to 5 pm; entry is £3/2.

West End

In the West End you'll find Glasgow University, several museums and galleries, lots of restaurants and the extensive Kelvingrove Park. The area swarms with students during term time, but is quieter during holidays.

Hunterian Museum & Art Gallery Part of the university, and now housed in two separate buildings on either side of University Ave, the Hunterian was opened in 1807 as Scotland's first public museum. It houses the collection of William Hunter (1718-83), famous physician, medical teacher and one time student of the university.

The Hunterian Museum (☎ 330 4221), in the university building, comprises a disparate collection of artefacts including a notable coin collection, fossils and minerals, dinosaur eggs, Romano-British stone slabs and carvings, a display detailing the archaeological history of Scotland, and some of Captain Cook's curios from his voyages to the South Seas.

The Hunterian Art Gallery (☎ 330 5431) is nearby at 82 Hillhead St. Behind a pair of imposing cast-aluminium doors created by Edinburgh-born Paolozzi is the art collection. The Scottish colourists – Peploe, JD Fergusson, Cadell – are well represented, including McTaggart's Impressionistic Scottish landscapes, and a gem by Thomas Millie Dow. There's a special collection of James McNeill Whistler's limpid prints, drawings and paintings. Some of his own

furniture and household goods are also here, and it's interesting to compare them to the contents of the **Mackintosh House**, the final section in the gallery.

Set up as a reconstruction of the architect Mackintosh's Glasgow home, which had to be demolished, the style of the Mackintosh House is quite startling even today. You ascend from the gallery's gloomy ground floor into the cool, white austere drawing room. There's something otherworldly about the very mannered style of the beaten silver panels, the long-backed chairs, and the surface decorations echoing Celtic manuscript illuminations. The Northampton guest bedroom is impossibly elegant and dazzling in blue and white stripes.

The Hunterian opens Monday to Saturday from 9.30 am to 5 pm; Mackintosh House closes from 12.30 to 1.30 pm; entry is free. There's a coffee bar by the museum's entrance and the student refectory is next to the art gallery. Bus Nos 44 and 59 pass this way from the city centre (Hope St).

Art Gallery & Museum, Kelvingrove Opened in 1902, this grand Victorian cathedral of culture (☎ 357 3929) shouldn't be missed, particularly for its excellent collection of Scottish and European art.

The impressive central hall is dominated at one end by organ pipes; recitals are an integral part of the museum program. An authentic museum smell emanates from the natural history of Scotland section, popular with school tours. Downstairs there's a rather dowdy presentation of some interesting artefacts, including archaeological finds of prehistoric Scotland, European arms and armour, and silver.

The art gallery upstairs houses the city's art collection of 19th and 20th century works. Scottish painters of luminous landscapes and still lifes are comprehensively represented – Melville, McTaggart, Cadell, Crawhall; and, among the moderns, Paolozzi, Bruce McLean, Hockney and Jasper Johns. Other paintings include Rembrandt's wonderful *Man in Armour* and works by Botticelli, Monet, Van Gogh and Picasso.

Grandly set back from the road in Kelvingrove Park, west of Kelvin Way, the art gallery and museum open daily from 10 am to 5 pm, and from 11 am to 5 pm on Sunday; entry is free. Any bus for Dumbarton Rd passes this way, such as bus Nos 6, 6A, 57, 64 and 64A; Kelvin Hall is the nearest underground station. There's an inexpensive café.

Museum of Transport Across Argyle St from the Art Gallery and Museum is the surprisingly interesting and comprehensive Museum of Transport (☎ 357 3929). Exhibits include a reproduction of a 1938 Glasgow street scene, a display of cars made in Scotland, plus assorted railway locos, trams, bikes and model ships. One of the model ships is the unique circular ship, the *Livadia*. It's open daily from 10 am to 5 pm, and from 11 am to 5 pm on Sunday; entry is free.

Other Things to See

On Glasgow Green, the city's oldest park, **The People's Palace** (☎ 554 0223) was built in the late 19th century as a cultural centre for Glasgow's East End. It's now a splendid museum of social history, telling the story of the city from 1175 to the present. The adjoining Winter Gardens are also worth seeing. It's open daily from 10 am to 5 pm, and from 11 am to 5 pm on Sunday, with free admission.

The Barrows (pronounced barras), Glasgow's flea market on Gallowgate, shouldn't be missed. There are almost 1000 stalls and people come here just for a wander as much as for shopping, which gives the place a holiday air. It takes place only on Saturday and Sunday. The Barrows is known for copycat designer gear – don't expect the real thing! Watch your wallet in this area.

Walks & Cycle Routes

There are numerous green spaces within the city. **Pollok Country Park** surrounds the Burrell Collection with many woodland trails. Nearer the centre of the city, the Kelvin Walkway follows the River Kelvin through Kelvingrove Park, the Botanic Gardens and on to Dawsholm Park.

There are several long-distance pedestrian/cycle routes that originate in Glasgow and follow off-road routes for most of the distance. The TIC has a range of maps and leaflets detailing these routes, most of which start from Bell's Bridge (by the SECC). For the latest information on the expanding National Cycle Network, contact Sustrans (☎ 0117 929 0888).

The **Glasgow-Loch Lomond Route** traverses residential and industrial areas following a disused train line to Clydebank, the Forth and Clyde canal *towpath* (path beside a canal or river) to Bowling, then a disused train line to Dumbarton. It reaches Loch Lomond via the towpath by the River Leven. There's an extension to this route all the way to Inverness, from Balloch via Aberfoyle, Loch Vennacher, Callander and Strathclyde to link with the Glen Ogle Trail, Killin, Pitlochry and Aviemore (the entire route should be open by 2000).

The **Glasgow-Greenock Route** runs via Paisley, the first section mainly on roads. From Johnstone to Greenock the route follows a disused train line; the final section to Gourock is yet to open. Sculpture from the Sustrans public arts project brightens parts of the way.

The **Glasgow-Irvine/Ardrossan and West Kilbride Cycle Way** runs via Paisley, then off-road as far as Glengarnock. From there to Kilwinning it follows minor roads, then the route is partly off-road. Ferries to the Isle of Arran, popular with cyclists, leave from Ardrossan.

The long-distance footpath, the **West Highland Way**, begins in Milngavie, 8 miles north of Glasgow, and runs for 95 miles to Fort William (see the Activities chapter).

Organised Tours

In summer, Discovering Glasgow (☎ 204 0444) runs tourist buses every 20 minutes along the main sightseeing routes. You get on and off as you wish; fares are £6.50/5 for a day ticket. Guide Friday (☎ 556 2244) is similar with a slightly longer route.

Special Events

Like Edinburgh, Glasgow has developed several festivals of its own, starting each January with a two-week **Celtic Music Festival** (☎ 332 6633). **Maydaze,** in early May, is an arts and dance festival; for details call Performing Arts (☎ 287 5429). The **West End Festival** (☎ 341 0844) of music and the arts runs for two weeks in June and is Glasgow's biggest festival. The excellent **International Jazz Festival** (☎ 400 5000) is held in July.

Other festivals include the **Scottish Proms** (☎ 332 6633, classical music) in mid-June and the **World Pipe Band Championships** (☎ 221 5414) in mid-August with over 100 pipe bands competing.

Places to Stay

Finding somewhere decent in July and August can be difficult – for a B&B get into town reasonably early and use the TIC's booking service. Unfortunately, Glasgow's B&Bs are expensive by Scottish standards – you may have to pay up to £20. At weekends many expensive business hotels slash prices by up to 50%, making them great value for tourists.

Camping *Craigendmuir Caravan Park* *(☎ 779 4159, Campsie View, Stepps)* is the nearest, but it's still a 15 minute walk from Stepps station. It takes vans and tents for £6.50 (two people).

Hostels & Colleges *Glasgow Youth Hostel (☎ 332 3004, 7 Park Terrace)* has mainly four-bed rooms, many with *en suite* facilities, as well as four doubles; book in summer. It's open all day and the nightly charge for adults/juniors is £12.50/10.95, including continental breakfast. From Central station take bus No 44 or 59 and ask for the first stop on Woodlands Rd.

Berkeley Globetrotters (☎ 221 7880, 63 Berkeley St) has beds from £7.50 (£6.50 if

you have your own bedding) in dorms, £9.50 in twin rooms. Phone ahead for bookings. Berkeley St is a western continuation of Bath St (one block south of Sauchiehall St). The hostel's just past Mitchell Library.

Near the SYHA hostel, *Glasgow Backpackers Hostel (☎ 332 5412, Kelvin Lodge, 8 Park Circus)* is one of the university's halls of residence, so it's only open from July to September. Beds are from £8.90. This is an Independent Backpackers Hostel and is very popular. Nearby, at 4, 5 and 12A Woodlands Terrace, *Woodlands Houses (☎ 332 2386)* provides backpacker accommodation for around £10. It also only opens in summer.

The *University of Glasgow (☎ 330 5385)* has a range of B&B accommodation at £21 per head and self-catering at £12.50 from mid-March to mid-April, and from July to September.

The *University of Strathclyde (☎ 553 4148)* also opens its halls of residence to tourists mid-June to mid-September. In the *Campus Village (☎ 552 0626, 24 hours)* opposite Glasgow Cathedral, backpacker accommodation costs £9.50 (sleeping bag required). If you don't mind staying farther out of town, the university's cheapest B&B accommodation is at *Jordanhill Campus (76 Southbrae Drive).* Comfortable rooms are £19.50/29, and bus No 44 from Central station goes to the college gates. The university's impressive *Art-Deco Baird Hall (460 Sauchiehall St),* offers some B&B accommodation in a great location year round. It has singles for £23.50 and doubles for £39.

The *YMCA Glasgow Aparthotel (☎ 558 6166, David Naismith Court, 33 Petershill Drive, Springburn)* is a characterless tower block north of the M8. With continental breakfast the nightly charge is £17/28 or £107.10/176.40 per week.

B&Bs & Hotels – City Centre *McLay's Guest House (☎ 332 4796)* is labyrinthine, but brilliantly located at 264 Renfrew St behind Sauchiehall St. Considering the location, you can't quibble at £21 for a single room without bathroom, or £25 with. There are doubles for £38, or £44 with bath.

If you can't get in there try *The Victorian House* (☎ *332 0129, 212 Renfrew St)* – down from the School of Art. It's a large guesthouse; prices are £23/38 with shared bathroom, £29/48 with bathroom. There are several other similarly priced places along this street, including the *Willow Hotel* (☎ *332 2332)* at No 228. *Hampton Court Hotel* (☎ *332 6623)* at No 230, is slightly cheaper. Singles without bath are £17, with bath they're £25; doubles are £40 with bath.

Babbity Bowster (☎ *552 5055, 16 Blackfriars St)* is a very lively pub/restaurant (see Entertainment) with six bedrooms. Singles/doubles with bathrooms cost £45/65. It's a great place to stay but forget it if you like to turn in early with a nice cup of cocoa.

Charing Cross Tower Hotel (☎ *221 1000, 10 Elmbank Gardens)*, in the newly renovated tower above Charing Cross train station, offers room-only rates of £44.50/59.50 with bath. At weekends, prices drop to £34.50/50. A full Scottish buffet breakfast costs £6.95.

Glasgow Marriott (☎ *226 5577, 500 Argyle St)* is a comfortable city centre hotel. Rooms cost £89 to £145 per person during the week, and start at £59 at the weekend.

B&Bs & Hotels – East There's a batch of reasonable-value B&Bs east of the Necropolis. *Brown's Guest House* (☎ *554 6797, 2 Onslow Drive)* has rooms from £15/26. *Craigpark Guest House* (☎ *554 4160, 33 Circus Drive)* charges from £16/28. *Seton Guest House* (☎ *556 7654, 6 Seton Terrace)* has rooms from £16.50/29.

One of the best places is the small *Cathedral House Hotel* (☎ *552 3519, 28 Cathedral Square)*. Housed in a Victorian baronial-style building complete with turrets, it's very close to the cathedral and easily accessible from the M8. There's a pleasant café bar, and Glasgow's only Icelandic restaurant where diners cook at the table on hot rocks. The well-appointed rooms cost from £49/69, all with bath.

B&Bs & Hotels – West End Many places in this area are on or around Great Western Rd. There are several B&Bs on Hillhead St (south of Great Western Rd and near Byres Rd), including *Chez Nous Guest House* (☎ *334 2977)*, at No 33, with rooms from £18.50/37 to £25/50 and *Iona Guest House* (☎ *334 2346)*, at No 39, which is smaller with similar prices.

Kelvin View Guest House (☎ *339 8257, 411 North Woodside Rd)* is north of Great Western Rd and the M8. Rooms are from £17/32; some with bathrooms. There are several other similarly priced B&Bs on this road.

The highly recommended *Kirklee Hotel* (☎ *334 5555, 11 Kensington Gate)* is more upmarket and you'll probably be treated as carefully as the plants in the window boxes. Rooms with shower/bath cost £45/59. Off Great Western Rd, a little nearer the city centre at 14 Belhaven Terrace, is the comfortable *Terrace House Hotel* (☎ *337 3377)*. There are 13 rooms, all with bathrooms. It charges £47/60 during the week, £39/50 at weekends. In the same area, *The Town House* (☎ *357 0862, 4 Hughenden Terrace)* is similar to these last two, very well run and an excellent choice. Rooms are from £58/68.

There are other places just south of Kelvingrove Park. *Alamo Guest House* (☎ *339 2395, 46 Gray St)* with rooms from £18/32 is good value. *Smith's Hotel* (☎ *339 6363, 963 Sauchiehall St)* charges £19/34 for its budget rooms.

Probably the best hotel in Glasgow is *One Devonshire Gardens* (☎ *339 2001)*, address the same, off Great Western Rd. Sumptuously decorated and occupying three classical terrace houses, the atmosphere is that of a luxurious country house. There are 27 well appointed rooms at £140/165. At the weekend, doubles are £125 per person. As one might expect, there's also an excellent restaurant.

B&Bs & Hotels – South of the Clyde On and around Pollokshaws Rd, on the way to Pollok Country Park and the Burrell

Collection, there are several places to stay in this quiet suburb. *Regent Guest House* (☎ *422 1199, 44 Regent Park Square*) has B&B accommodation from £20 per person. Some rooms have baths. *Reidholm Guest House* (☎ *423 1855*) farther down the terrace at No 36 is about the same price.

On the other side of Pollokshaws Rd, south of Queen's Park, *Boswell Hotel* (☎ *632 9812, 27 Mansionhouse Rd, off Langside Ave*) can be an entertaining place to stay. The Boswell is better known as a watering hole, with three bars and live jazz or R&B on occasion. Singles/doubles are £42.50/60 during the week, £30/50 at weekends; all with bath/showers.

North of Pollok Country Park, in the Bellahouston area between the M8 and M77, there's a couple of small B&Bs. *Mr Bristow's* (☎ *427 0129, 56 Dumbreck Rd*) costs from £25/34 and opens year-round. *Mrs Ross's* (☎ *427 0194, 3 Beech Ave*) has rooms from £25/40 with shower.

Places to Eat

Glasgow not only has an excellent range of places to eat but many are also very moderately priced. The West End probably has the greatest range of restaurants, everything from Glasgow's most famous place to eat, the upmarket Ubiquitous Chip, to cheap cafés where chips really are served with everything. In the city centre, however, and along Sauchiehall there's also no shortage of eateries. If you're on a budget, have your main meal at lunch time – the set lunches offered by many restaurants are usually very good value at £3 to £5.

West End The main restaurant/pub area in the West End is about three-quarters of a mile west of the youth hostel, around Byres Rd. The nearest underground station is Hillhead.

Off Byres Rd, on the east side, Ashton Lane is packed with places to eat. Cheapest is the *Grosvenor Café* (☎ *339 1848*), at No 35, where you can get soup, filled rolls and hot meals all day. Try the pizza with fried egg for £1.10. This is a popular student hang-out.

Some of Glasgow's top restaurants are also on Ashton Lane. *The Ubiquitous Chip* (☎ *334 5007*), No 12, has earned a solid reputation for its excellent Scottish cuisine, fresh seafood and game, and for the length of its wine list. A three-course dinner with coffee costs £24. This is an excellent place for a night out. There's a cheaper restaurant here, *Upstairs at the Chip*, where two courses at lunch time cost less than £10. *Mitchells* (☎ *339 2220*), No 35, is an informal bistro with excellent Scottish dishes. Main courses range from £8 to £12.

Back on Byres Rd, *The University Café* (☎ *339 5217*), No 87, is a university institution. It's cheap with all meals under £4; there's fish and chips and salad (£3.70), excellent pizza and superb home-made ice cream.

On the west side of Byres Rd directly across from Ashton Lane is Ruthven Lane, with some interesting places to eat among the whacky shops. At *Back Alley* (☎ *334 7165, 8 Ruthven Lane*) students get a 10% discount. Mexican and Indian mains are normally £7 to £9 and there are vegetarian options. At No 11 is the *Puppet Theatre* (☎ *339 8444*) a classy, expensive place featuring Scottish cuisine. Dinner is £27.95 for three courses; lunch £12.95 for two. Down the lane at No 61 is *Di Maggio's* (☎ *334 8560*), good for pizzas and pasta from £5 to £7 (with vegetarian options).

In the Kelvingrove Park area you'll find a scattering of restaurants on and around Gibson St and Great Western Rd. *Shalimar* (☎ *339 6453, 25 Gibson St*) is a large Indian restaurant that offers a five-course buffet dinner for £8.95 or £9.95 at weekends.

The vegetarian *Bay Tree Café* (☎ *334 5898, 403 Great Western Rd*) is excellent value. Filling main dishes cost less than £4, salads are generous, and there's a good range of hot drinks. The café is famous for its all-day Sunday brunch, served from 11 am to 8 pm, including vegetarian burger, tattie scone, mushrooms, beans and tomato for £3.50. Open Tuesday to Sunday, it closes at 9 pm (8 pm on Sunday). It also serves takeaway.

Insomnia Café (☎ 332 5500, 38 Woodland Rd) has never closed since it first opened in October 1995. There are sandwiches from £1.15, a wide range of meals (mains are £4 to £6.25), herbal teas and coffees in Scotland's first 24-hour café.

Near the Kelvingrove Art Gallery and Museum, Dutch-run *Janssens (☎ 334 9682, 1355 Argyle St)* serves good lunches, everything from interesting sandwiches to full meals. Mains are £6 to £11, but pizzas start at £4.

City Centre There are some good choices elsewhere on Sauchiehall St. *Ristoro Ciao Italia (☎ 332 4565)*, No 441, is an efficient Italian restaurant where you should be able to eat and drink for around £10. One block east, *Loon Fung (☎ 332 1240)*, No 417, is one of the best Chinese places in town. There are set dinners from £17; a three-course lunch is £6.30.

There's a pleasant café with sandwiches (£4.95), salads and main courses (£5 to £6.25) at the *Centre for Contemporary Arts (☎ 332 7521, 346 Sauchiehall St)*.

The main branch of Glasgow's best known bakery chain, *Bradford's*, is at No 245. There's a good tearoom upstairs where light meals are available (£4 to £5).

The *Willow Tearoom (☎ 332 0521, 217 Sauchiehall St)* above a jewellery shop, was designed as a tearoom by Mackintosh in 1903. Last orders are at 4.15 pm, and for lunch and tea the queues can be long. Avoid them by arriving when it opens at 9 am (noon on Sunday) and splash out on a superior breakfast of smoked salmon, scrambled eggs and toast for £5.10.

Continuing east along Sauchiehall, there's a branch of the patisserie chain, *Delifrance (☎ 353 2700)*, at No 119. The filled baguettes (from £1.85) are good.

Glasgow's first balti restaurant, the *Balti Bar (51 West Regent St)* has amalgamated with the *Bombay Bistro (☎ 331 1980)* upstairs. It's still good value with a daily

three-course pre-theatre menu costing only £6.75.

At Princes Square, the stylish shopping centre on Buchanan St, one floor is given over to restaurants and food stalls ranging from Caribbean to Chinese. There are more upmarket options here, too. Nearby, there's *The Jenny (☎ 204 4988, 18 Royal Exchange Square)*. This tearoom and bistro has a pavement café in summer, and is highly recommended. Try the savoury buns (£4.45 to £5.85) or two-in-one pies (£5.25).

Near St Enoch Centre is the pleasant, inexpensive *Granary (☎ 226 3770, 82 Howard St)*. It's mainly vegetarian but has a few non-veg choices. Mains are £3 to £4.

In the Merchant City, near the City Halls, is *Café Gandolfi (☎ 552 6813, 64 Albion St)*. Once part of the old cheese market, it's now an excellent bistro and upmarket coffee shop – very much the place to be seen. Mains cost £4 to £12.

One of the best restaurants is *The Buttery (☎ 221 8188, 652 Argyle St)* just west of the M8. The menu is Scottish, a three-course dinner costs around £30, and it's closed on Sunday. Downstairs is the cheaper bistro, the *Belfry (☎ 221 0630)*; reservations are advised. A two-course, pre-theatre dinner (6.30 to 7.30 pm) costs £9.95.

Mitchell's (☎ 204 4312, 157 North St) near the Mitchell Library, is an excellent bistro. Lunch mains are £5 to £11.

Entertainment

Some of Scotland's best nightlife is found in the pubs and clubs of Glasgow. Most pubs also do food, although many stop serving at around 8 pm. For the latest information, get a copy of *The List* (£1.90), Glasgow's and Edinburgh's invaluable fortnightly guide to films, theatre, cabaret, music – the works. Also look out for the freebie magazine, *city live*, a monthly listing of Glasgow's live music scene.

If it's a wee bit of Scottish dancing you're after rather than a night in the pubs or clubs, go to the *Riverside (☎ 248 3144, Fox St)*, off Clyde St, on Friday or Saturday evening for the *ceilidh* (pronounced kaylee, informal evening entertainment and dance). Doors open at 8 pm and the band starts at 9 pm. It's good clean fun for £5.

Owing to an unusual law in force in Glasgow you may not be allowed entry to a club after 1 am. Check the clubs recommended in this section for the current regulations.

Pubs – West End The *Halt Bar (160 Woodlands Rd)*, is a popular university pub that hasn't been tarted up. There's free live music most nights, a great atmosphere, and it's open until midnight on Friday and Saturday, 11 pm other nights.

Farther along Woodlands Rd there's *Uisge Beatha (☎ 564 1598)*, No 246, which keeps the same hours. The name's Gaelic for whisky (literally, water of life). It's friendly, with eclectic décor and four bar areas.

Bar Oz (☎ 334 0884, 499 Great Western Rd) is an Australian theme pub offering a good range of bottled beers, lagers and wines from down under.

There are numerous pubs on or around Byres Rd. *Curlers (☎ 334 1284)*, No 256, is popular with students who come for the bargain three-course set lunch (£3.25) and stay for the live jazz (midweek). There's also *Cul de Sac (☎ 334 4749)*, the place to be seen in Ashton Lane, at No 44; meals are inexpensive – £3.45 to £5. The *Ubiquitous Chip*, No 12, also has a bar.

Pubs – City Centre By the Union St exit of Central station is the basement *Underworld (☎ 221 5020)*. It's a quirky, stylish, but not too pretentious place, with a restaurant area serving Tex-Mex food.

Bar 10 (☎ 221 8353, 10 Mitchell Lane off Buchanan St) is a stylish, popular café bar. It was designed by Ben Kelly who was responsible for Manchester's famous Dry Bar and Hacienda.

The subterranean *Brunswick Cellars (☎ 572 0016, 239 Sauchiehall St)* is a popular bar that also does excellent value lunches (mains £4 to £5). Between 3 and 8 pm drinks cost £1 to £1.20 per pint.

Scotia Bar (☎ 552 8681, 112 Stockwell St) Glasgow's oldest pub, opened in 1792. It serves real ales and bar lunches. There's live folk music on Wednesday evenings and live blues on Sunday afternoons.

Babbity Bowster (☎ 552 5055, 16 Blackfriars St) is a popular Merchant City pub with a good range of real ales, excellent pub grub from £4 to £6 and live folk music on Sunday. There's also a hotel here, and a restaurant noted for its Scottish cuisine.

The Horse Shoe (☎ 221 3051, 17 Drury Lane) may have one of the longest bars in Europe, but its more important attraction is what's served over it – real ale and good food that's also good value. The pub's been here for over 100 years and is largely unchanged.

By Mitchell's on North St, is the traditional *Bon Accord (☎ 248 4427)* with 14 real ales and 18 malt whiskies. There's also great pub grub – doorsteps (large toasted sandwiches) cost £2.25.

Lots of city centre pubs do live music, including *The Bank (☎ 248 4455, 35 Queen St)*; *Blackfriars (☎ 552 5924, 36 Bell St)*; *The Drum & Monkey (☎ 221 6636, 93 St Vincent St)*; and *MacSorley's (☎ 572 0199, 42 Jamaica St)*.

Clubs Glasgow's club scene rivals London and Manchester, but it changes so quickly it's difficult to make recommendations. The following places, however, seem to remain popular. Check *The List* and ask around for the latest places.

Glaswegians hit the clubs after the pubs have closed, so many clubs offer discounted entry and cheaper drinks if you go before 10 or 11 pm. Most also usually give discounts for students. Don't arrive in running shoes or you'll be turned away from most places.

Off Jamaica St and under Central station, *Arches (☎ 221 9736)* is the place to go at weekends – there's Slam Un-cut on Friday (£6, students £5, 11 pm to 3.30 am) and various other sessions (Love Boutique, Colours, Cool Lemon, £10 to £15) on Saturday.

King Tut's Wah Wah Hut (☎ 221 5279, 272 St Vincent St) has live music most nights from local, national and, occasionally, international bands. Tickets cost £3.50 to £10.50; buy tickets for bigger events in advance. The downstairs bar opens daily.

The Tunnel (☎ 204 1000, 84 Mitchell St) is a stylish club in the West End. The gents' loos are famous for their designer waterworks. This is one Glasgow attraction women might have to miss!

Victoria's (☎ 332 1444, 98 Sauchiehall St) is a large glitzy nightclub with two discos (music from the 60s to the 90s), a second floor piano bar with a resident cabaret, and a cabaret room featuring Scotland's foremost artistes. The club opens Wednesday to Sunday; admission costs £7.95 to £11.95, depending on the day.

Glasgow has a lively gay scene of pubs, cafés and clubs. The *Waterloo Bar (306 Argyle St)* is Scotland's oldest gay bar. Other pubs include *Austins (183 Hope St)*, the *Court Bar (69 Hutcheson St)* and *Sadie Frost's* (☎ 332 8005, 8 West George St). The *Polo Lounge* (☎ 553 1221, 84 Wilson St) is a bar popular with women and the funky *Del Monica's Bar (68 Virginia St)* serves food from noon to 10 pm. *Café Latte (63 Virginia St)* opens daily from 9 to 1 am. *QC's Bistro Bar* (☎ 204 5418), at the Glasgow Gay & Lesbian Centre (☎ 221 7203), is also an option. Some of the straight clubs do crossover gay nights, while *Bennet's* (☎ 552 5761, 80 Glassford St) is a gay club popular with men in their 20s.

And then? On Friday and Saturday head for *Change at Jamaica* (☎ 429 4422, 11 Clyde Place) where infamous breakfasts are served from 10 pm to 5 am. This café is south of the river, under the train bridge.

Concerts, Theatre & Cinema For tickets phone the Ticket Centre (☎ 227 5511).

The *Theatre Royal* (☎ 332 9000), Hope St, is the home of Scottish Opera, and the Scottish Ballet often performs here. The Royal Scottish National Orchestra plays at the modern *Glasgow Royal Concert Hall* (☎ 227 5511, 2 Sauchiehall St).

Rock and pop bands on the international circuit usually play at the *Scottish Exhibition & Conference Centre* (SECC, ☎ 248 3000), a modern aircraft hangar of a place by the river. Some bands choose the *Barrowland Ballroom* (☎ 552 4601, 244 Gallowgate), a vast dance hall in the East End that's far funkier.

Citizens' Theatre (☎ 429 0022, Gorbals St) is one of the top theatres in Scotland and it's well worth trying to catch a performance here. The *Tron Theatre* (☎ 552 4267, 63 Trongate) stages contemporary Scottish and international performances.

The *Centre for Contemporary Arts* (☎ 332 7521, 350 Sauchiehall St) is an interesting centre for the visual and performing arts. A couple of blocks east, the *Glasgow Film Theatre* (☎ 332 8128, 12 Rose St, off Sauchiehall St) screens new releases, classics and popular re-runs.

Getting There & Away

See the fares tables in the Getting Around chapter. Glasgow is 405 miles from London, 97 from Carlisle, 42 from Edinburgh and 166 from Inverness.

Air Glasgow international airport (☎ 887 1111), 10 miles west of the city, handles domestic traffic and international flights.

Bus Long-distance buses arrive and depart from Buchanan St bus station. Buses from London are competitive. Silver Choice (☎ 333 1400) is currently the best deal at £13/25 for a single/return. Departures are daily at 11 pm from Victoria coach station, London and Buchanan St bus station in Glasgow; the run takes eight hours. The service is popular so you'll need to book.

National Express (☎ 0990-808080) also leaves from both Victoria and Buchanan St and has four or five daily services for £18/28. The best option is to catch the 8 am bus from London, so that you arrive in good time to organise accommodation. There's one daily direct bus from Heathrow airport.

There are numerous links with other English cities. National Express services include: three or four daily buses from Birmingham (5½ hours); one from Cambridge (nine hours); numerous from Carlisle (two hours); two from Newcastle (four hours); and one from York (6½ hours).

National Express/Scottish Citylink (☎ 0990-505050) has buses to most major towns in Scotland. There are numerous buses to Edinburgh every 15 minutes during the day (1¼ hours, singles/returns £4.50/5 off-peak). Around 18 buses run per day to Stirling (45 minutes), 12 to Inverness (from 3½ hours), three or four to Oban (three hours), 18 to Aberdeen (3¼ to four hours), four or five to Fort William (three hours) and three to Portree on Skye (6¼ to seven hours). There's a twice-daily service from mid-May to mid-October to Stranraer, connecting with the ferry to Larne in Northern Ireland (six hours).

Fife Scottish (☎ 01592-261461) runs buses to Anstruthers (three hours, six per day, £5.50), St Andrews (2¼ hours, hourly, £5) and Dundee (2½ hours, hourly, £5) via Glenrothes.

Walkers should check out Midland Bluebird (☎ 01324-613777), which runs hourly buses to Milngavie (30 minutes, £1.45), the starting point of the West Highland Way.

Train As a general rule, Central station serves southern Scotland, England and Wales, and Queen St serves the north and east. There are buses every 10 minutes between the two (40p or free with a through train ticket). There are up to seven direct trains daily from London's Euston station; they're not cheap, but they're much quicker (five to six hours) and more comfortable than the bus. There are also up to seven direct services from London King's Cross.

ScotRail has the West Highland Line north to Oban and Fort William (see those sections) and direct links to Dundee, Aberdeen and Inverness. There are numerous trains to Edinburgh (50 minutes, £7.10 single). For rail inquiries call (☎ 0345-484950).

Car There are numerous car rental companies; the big names have offices at the airport. Melvilles Motors (☎ 632 5757), 192 Battlefield Rd, charge £26.40 per day for a Micra, Punto or Corsa.

Cabervans (☎ 01475-638775), Caberfeidh, Cloch Rd, Gourock, has motor homes for rent from around £300 per week. They can collect you from Glasgow, Prestwick or Edinburgh airports or Gourock train station.

Getting Around

Get a copy of the *Visitors Transport Guide Map* (free) from the TIC.

The Roundabout Glasgow ticket (£3.40/ 1.70) covers all underground and public transport in the city for a day; the Roundabout Glasgow Plus ticket (£5.80/ 2.90) also includes the Discovering Glasgow hop-on hop-off tourist buses that run along the main sightseeing routes.

To/From the Airport There are buses every 30 minutes (15 minutes in summer) from the airport to Buchanan St bus station (25 minutes, £2.20). A taxi costs about £13.

Bus Bus services are frequent. You can buy tickets when you board buses, but on most you must have exact change. Routes are shown on the *Visitors Transport Guide Map*. For short trips in the city, fares are 65p. After midnight there are limited night buses from George Square.

Train There's an extensive suburban network; tickets should be bought before travel if the station is staffed, or from the conductor if it isn't.

There's also an underground line that serves 15 stations in the centre, west and south of the city (65p). An Underground Heritage Trail Pass (£2) gives unlimited travel on the system for a day.

Taxi There's no shortage. If you order a taxi from Glasgow Wide Taxis (☎ 332 6666) by phone you can pay by credit card.

Bicycle West End Cycles (☎ 357 1344), 16 Chancellor St, at the southern end of Byres Rd, rents mountain bikes for £12/50 per day/week. Two IDs are required and a £50 deposit.

Around Glasgow

Glasgow is surrounded by a grim hinterland of post-industrial communities. Industrial archaeologists could have a field day here and some might see a perverse beauty in the endless suburbs of grey council house architecture. It's here, possibly, that the Glasgow area's gritty black sense of humour is engendered.

PAISLEY
• pop 78,000   ☎ 0141

This town gave its name to the well-known fabric design of swirling stylised teardrops or pine cones called the Paisley Pattern. The famous design was, in fact, copied from shawls brought back from India. Now really a suburb west of Glasgow, Paisley grew up around **Paisley Abbey**, heavily 'restored' by the Victorians, which was founded here in 1163. By the 19th century the town was a major producer of printed cotton and woollen cloth. At one time, Paisley was the largest producer of cotton thread in the world; the Coats family of thread makers have enjoyed a long association with the town.

The history of the Paisley Pattern is outlined in an interesting exhibition at the **Museum & Art Galleries** (☎ 889 3151), on High St, with a large display of Paisley shawls. It's open Monday to Saturday from 10 am to 5 pm; free.

The helpful TIC (☎ 889 0711) is in the Lagoon Leisure Centre, Christie St, but may move to Gilmour St. There's no need to stay here overnight but, should you wish to, the TIC has the usual accommodation lists. Trains leave Glasgow's Central station up to eight times an hour for Paisley's Gilmour St station; there are also frequent buses.

FIRTH OF CLYDE

The ghosts of once great shipyards still line the banks of the Clyde west of Glasgow. Ten miles downstream, the impressive Erskine Bridge links the north and south banks. The only place of any interest along the coast west of here is Greenock, although in the otherwise unprepossessing town of **Port Glasgow** you could stop to see the replica of the *Comet*, Greenock Rd, Europe's first commercial steamship.

GREENOCK
• pop 57,325   ☎ 01475

James Watt, who perfected the steam engine, was born in this large town, 27 miles from Glasgow. In the **Mclean Museum & Art Gallery** (☎ 723741), 15 Kelly St, displays chart the history of steam power and Clyde shipping. The museum opens Monday to Saturday from 10 am to 5 pm; free. The **Custom House Museum** (☎ 726331) on the quay traces the history of the Customs & Excise service. Burns and Adam Smith were former employees. Worth a visit, it's open Monday to Friday from 10 am to 4 pm; free.

There are three trains an hour from Glasgow Central and hourly buses. The Glasgow to Greenock pedestrian/cycle route follows an old train track for 10 miles (see the Glasgow section).

GOUROCK
• pop 11,000   ☎ 01475

From the run-down seaside resort of Gourock, 3 miles west of Greenock, Cal-Mac ferries (☎ 650100) leave frequently every day for Dunoon (20 minutes, £2.45) on Argyll's Cowal peninsula. Clyde Marine (☎ 721281) runs a passenger-only service to Kilcreggan (12 minutes, 13 per day, £1.55) and Helensburgh (40 minutes, four per day, £1.55), Monday to Saturday.

Lanarkshire

South and east of Glasgow are the large satellite towns of East Kilbride, Hamilton, Motherwell and Coatbridge. Farther upstream, the Clyde passes through central Lanarkshire, once an important coal mining district and still important for its fruit farms.

Plums from the area around Crossford and strawberries from Kirkfieldbank are particularly tasty.

BLANTYRE
• pop 18,531   ☎ 01698

This town's most famous son was David Livingstone, the epitome of the Victorian missionary-explorer, who opened up central Africa to Europe. Born in the one-roomed tenement that now forms part of the David Livingstone Centre, he worked by day in the local cotton mill from the age of 10, educated himself at night, and qualified with a medical degree in 1840 before setting off for Africa.

The **David Livingstone Centre** (☎ 823140), 165 Station Rd, tells the story of his life from a youngster in Blantyre to his later days as missionary and explorer, his battle against slave traders, and his famous meeting with Stanley. It's by the River Clyde and opens daily from 10 am to 5 pm (Sunday from 12.30 pm); £2.95/1.95. There's an African theme café serving reasonably priced snacks and meals.

It's a 20 to 30 minute walk down the river to **Bothwell Castle** (☎ 816894; HS), Uddingston. It was much fought over during the Wars of Independence and is regarded as the finest 13th century castle in Scotland. Built of red sandstone, the substantial ruins include a massive circular keep standing above the river. It's open standard hours from April to September. The rest of the year it's closed on Thursday afternoon and Friday; entry is £1.80/1.30.

It's best to come by train (20 minutes from Glasgow Central, £2.40 off-peak return) as the David Livingstone Centre is a short walk from Blantyre station. Buses stop on Main St, a 15 minute walk away.

LANARK & NEW LANARK
• pop 9000   ☎ 01555

Below the market town of Lanark, in an attractive gorge by the River Clyde, are the excellent restored mill-buildings and warehouses of New Lanark. This was once the largest cotton spinning complex in Britain

but it was better known for the pioneering social experiments of Robert Owen, who managed the mill from 1800. An enlightened capitalist, he provided his workers with housing, a co-operative store (that was the inspiration for the modern co-operative movement), a school with adult education classes, and a social centre he called The New Institute for the Formation of Character.

Orientation & Information
The TIC (☎ 661661), Horsemarket, Ladyacre Rd, Lanark, near the bus and train stations is open all year. The 20 minute walk down to New Lanark is worth it for the views, but there's a daily bus service from the train station (hourly, but two-hourly on Monday to Saturday afternoons). Returning to Lanark, the last bus leaves New Lanark at 5.03 pm.

Things to See
There's a **Visitor Centre** (☎ 661345) in New Lanark, and £3.75/2.50 gets you entry to Robert Owen's home, a restored millworkers' house, the Annie McLeod Experience (a high-tech, audiovisual ride where the spirit of a 10-year-old mill girl recalls life here in 1820) and the 1920s-style village store. It's open daily from 11 am to 5 pm. There are craft shops in the restored buildings and good-value woollens on sale.

Probably the best way to get the feel of this impressive place is to wander round the outside of the buildings, then walk up to the **Falls of Clyde** through the nature reserve. Visit the **Falls of Clyde Wildlife Centre** (☎ 665262) by the river in New Lanark first. It's open Easter to October, weekdays from 11 am to 5 pm, weekends from 1 to 5 pm, the rest of the year weekends only (closed January). Admission to the centre is £1/50p but the reserve is free. Walk for a couple of miles to the power station, then half a mile to the beautiful **Cora Linn** (waterfalls), and beyond them, **Bonnington Linn**.

Places to Stay & Eat
New Lanark Youth Hostel (☎ 666710, *Wee Row*) is very pleasantly located near the river. Nightly charges are £9.75/8.50 for

adults/juniors with continental breakfast; open year-round. The recently opened *New Lanark Mill Hotel* (☎ 667200) has singles/doubles from £40/60, all with bath.

If you want to stay in Lanark, the TIC has a free accommodation list for the area. There are numerous B&Bs, including *Mrs Buchanan's* (☎ 661002, *5 Hardacres*) who charges from £16 per person, and *Mrs Allen's* (☎ 662540, *9 Cleghorn Rd*) with rooms from £20/34 a single/double.

In the New Lanark Visitor Centre there's the *Mill Pantry* for snacks and light meals; try the *hotel bar* and *restaurant* for something more substantial.

In Lanark, the *Crown Tavern* (☎ 662465, *17 Hope St*) does good bar meals. Self-caterers can stock up at the large Somerfield supermarket conveniently situated by the TIC.

Getting There & Away

Lanark is 25 miles south-east of Glasgow. Hourly trains run daily between Glasgow Central and Lanark (£3.70).

Ayrshire

The rolling hills and farmland of Ayrshire are best known as the birthplace and home of poet Burns. These rich pastures were once also famous for the Ayrshire breed of dairy cattle, now largely replaced by Frisians. Parts of the coast comprise attractive sandy beaches and low cliffs overlooking the mountainous island of Arran.

There are famous golf courses at Troon and Turnberry. It was at Prestwick Golf Club that the major golf tournament, the British Open Championship, was initiated in 1860.

NORTH AYRSHIRE
Isle of Great Cumbrae
• pop 1200   ☎ 01475

Included here because it's reached from North Ayrshire, the island is administered as part of Argyll & Bute. There's actually nothing very great about it – it's only 4 miles long – but it's bigger than the privately owned Little Cumbrae island just south.

A frequent 15 minute CalMac ferry ride links the town of Largs with Great Cumbrae. Buses meet the ferries for the 3½ mile journey to Millport, which has two sandy beaches. The town boasts Europe's smallest cathedral, **The Cathedral of the Isles** (☎ 530353), open daily, and the interesting **Robertson Museum & Aquarium** (☎ 530581), where admission costs £1.50/1. There's a seasonal TIC (☎ 530753), 28 Stuart St (on the waterfront), and several bike hire places including Mapes (☎ 530444), 3 Guildford St (£2.40 for two hours).

Ardrossan
• pop 11,000   ☎ 01294

The main reason for coming here is to catch a CalMac ferry to Arran. Trains leave Glasgow Central (one hour, £4.10) five times a day to connect with ferries (see Arran section). If you need a B&B, try *Edenmore Guest House* (☎ 462306, *47 Parkhouse Rd*) off the main A78 road. Singles/doubles cost from £16.50/30.

ISLE OF ARRAN
• pop 4800   ☎ 01770

'Scotland in miniature' they call it, and parts of this island certainly are reminiscent of other areas of the country. There are challenging walks in the mountainous northern part of the island, often compared to the Highlands. The landscape in the south is gentler, similar to the rest of southern Scotland.

Since Arran is easily accessible from Glasgow and the south of the country, being only an hour's ferry ride from Ardrossan, it's very popular. Despite its popularity the 20 mile long island seems to be big enough to absorb everyone. The bucket and spade brigade fills the southern resorts, cyclists take to the island's circular road and hikers tackle the hills, the highest being Goat Fell (860m/2820 feet). With seven golf courses, Arran is also popular with golfers.

Orientation & Information

The ferry from Ardrossan docks at Brodick, the island's main town. To the south, Lamlash is actually the capital, and, like nearby Whiting Bay, a popular seaside resort. From the village of Lochranza in the north there's a ferry link to Claonaig on the Kintyre peninsula.

Near Brodick pier, the TIC (☎ 302140) opens June to September daily from 9 am to 7.30 pm (10 am to 5 pm on Sunday); and shorter hours at other times of the year.

The week-long Arran Folk Festival takes place in early June. Phone (☎ 302341) for information.

Arran is known for its local cheeses, and Arran mustard is also worth buying. Watch out for the woollens, though. Real Aran (one 'r') sweaters come from the Irish island of Aran, not this one.

Things to See

The town of **Brodick** isn't particularly interesting, but it's in a pleasant location. Taking the road 1½ miles north you come to the small **Heritage Museum** (☎ 302636), open April to October, daily from 11 am to 4 pm (June to August from 10 am to 5 pm); £2/1.25.

Brodick Castle (☎ 302202) and park is 2½ miles north of town. The ancient seat of the dukes of Hamilton is now in the hands of the NTS. It's an interesting stately home, with rather more of a lived-in feel than some NTS properties. The kitchens and scullery, complete with displays of peculiar kitchen devices, are well worth a look. The grounds, now a country park with various trails among the rhododendrons, have an attractive walled garden. The house opens April to October from 11.30 to 4.30 pm; entry to the castle and park is £4.80/3.20. The park opens year-round, daily from 9.30 am to sunset (£2.40/1.60 for the park only).

As you go round Brodick Bay, look out for seals, which are often seen on the rocks around Merkland Point. Two types live in these waters, the Atlantic grey and the common seal. They're actually quite easy to tell apart – the common seal has a face like

a dog; the Atlantic grey seal has a Roman nose.

The road follows the coast to the small village of **Corrie**, and one of the tracks to Goat Fell starts here. After **Sannox**, where there's a sandy beach, the road cuts inland.

Lochranza is a village in a small bay at the north of the island. In summer there's a ferry link to the Kintyre peninsula from here. There's also a youth hostel, camping ground and several B&Bs. On a promontory stand the ruins of the 13th century **Lochranza Castle**, said to be the inspiration for the castle in *The Black Island*, Hergés Tintin adventure. Also in Lochranza is Scotland's newest distillery, Isle of Arran Distillers (☎ 830264), opened in 1995. Tours run daily from 10 am to 5 pm (£3.50). Two miles beyond Lochranza, the white-washed cottages of **Catacol** are known as the Twelve Apostles.

On the west side of the island, reached by the String Rd across the centre (or the coast road), are the **Machrie Moor standing stones**. It's an eerie place, and these are the most impressive of the six stone circles on the island. There's another group at nearby **Auchagallon**.

Blackwaterfoot is the largest village on the west coast with a shop/post office and two hotels. From here, you can walk down to the **King's Cave** via Drumadoon Farm – Arran is one of several islands that lays claim to a cave where Robert the Bruce, on the run after his defeat at the Battle of Glentrool, was inspired by a spider's persistence in spinning its web. Myth has it that this small act spurred him on to future success including the defeat of the English at Bannockburn. This walk could be combined with a visit to the Machrie standing stones.

The landscape in the southern part of the island is much gentler; the road drops into little wooded valleys, and it's particularly lovely around **Lagg**. At **Kildonan** there are pleasant sandy beaches, a camp site, two hotels and the ruin of an ivy-clad castle.

North of Whiting Bay is **Holy Island**, owned by the Samyé Ling Tibetan Centre (Dumfriesshire) and used as a retreat, though it does allow day visits. One ferry runs from Whiting Bay (☎ 700382, May to September, 15 minutes, three daily, £6), the other goes from Lamlash (☎ 0860-235086, 30 minutes, five daily, £6). No dogs, alcohol or fires are allowed on the island. There's a good walk to the top of the hill (314m/1030 feet), a two to three hour round trip. **Lamlash** is a sailing centre.

Walks & Cycle Routes

The walk up **Goat Fell** takes five to six hours for the round trip and, if the weather is good, there are superb views from the 874m (2866 feet) summit. It can, however, be very cold and windy up here so come well prepared. There are paths from Brodick Castle and Corrie. Another good walk on a marked path goes up to **Coire Fhionn Lochan** from Mid Thundergay; it takes about 1½ hours to reach the loch.

More moderate walks include the trail through **Glen Sannox** from the village of Sannox up the *burn* (creek), a two hour return trip. From Whiting Bay Youth Hostel there are easy one-hour walks through the forest to the **Giant's Graves** and **Glenashdale Falls** and back.

The 50 mile circuit on the coastal road is popular with cyclists and has few serious hills – more in the south than the north. Traffic isn't too bad, except at the height of the season.

Places to Stay

Camping Camping without the permission of the land owner isn't allowed, but there are several camping grounds (open April to October). When choosing a site note that midges (similar to mosquitos) can be a major nuisance in sheltered spots.

Two miles from Brodick, you can camp at *Glen Rosa Farm* (☎ 302380) from £4 for a tent and two people. In Kildonan, *Breadalbane Lodge* (☎ 820210) charges campers £3.50 each; it's very pleasantly located and the breeze here keeps the midges away. *Lochranza Golf* (☎ 830273, Lochranza) costs from £8 for a tent and two people.

Hostels *Lochranza Youth Hostel* (☎ 830631), in the north of the island, is an excellent place to stay. It's a self-catering hostel open all year except January. The nightly charge for adults/juniors is £7.75/6.50. In the south there's *Whiting Bay Youth Hostel* (☎ 700339), £6.10/4.95, open from March to October.

B&Bs & Hotels – Brodick It's best to get out of Brodick to some of the smaller villages, although there are numerous places to stay in this town.

The *Douglas Hotel* (☎ 302155), near the pier, charges from £20 to £30 per person and is convenient if you're catching an early ferry. Some rooms have baths. Along Shore Rd, guesthouses include *Tigh-na-Mara* (☎ 302538), which charges from £18 per person; and *Belvedere* (☎ 302397, Alma Rd) where rooms are from £16. Half a mile from the centre of Brodick **Rosaburn Lodge** (☎ 302383) is a comfortable B&B with three rooms for £24 to £28, all with baths.

B&Bs & Hotels – Glen Coy The island's best hotel, the **Kilmichael Country House Hotel** (☎ 302219, Glen Coy) is also its oldest building. It's a small, elegant hotel, 2 miles outside Brodick with six rooms from £60 to £65 for a single, £78 to £124 for a double. There's also an excellent restaurant here.

B&Bs & Hotels – Corrie & Sannox **Corrie Hotel** (☎ 810273) has rooms from £21/42 with shared bathroom, £26/52 with bathroom. The seafront **Blackrock Guest House** (☎ 810282) opens from March to October and offers B&B from £19 per person in rooms with shared baths. **Sannox House** (☎ 810230, Sannox) is a fine place with *en suite* singles from £17.50 and doubles from £46; dinner costs an extra £10.

B&Bs & Hotels – Lochranza This is a great place to stay. **Benvaren** (☎ 830647), overlooking the bay and near the ferry slipway, has rooms for £18 to £20 per person. **Castlekirk** (☎ 830202), a converted church, has two rooms for £18 per person and an in-house darkroom for photographers (phone for information on art courses run here). **Kincardine Lodge Guest House** (☎ 830267) charges £18 to £20 per person and some rooms have baths. The best place to stay is **Apple Lodge** (☎ 830229), with three double rooms for £50 to £60. You'll be well looked after in very comfortable surroundings.

B&Bs & Hotels – Kilmory Kilmory House (☎ 870342) is a converted 17th century flax mill with three rooms from £15 per person.

B&Bs & Hotels – Kildonan Kildonan is a very peaceful spot. The friendly **Breadalbane Hotel** (☎ 820284) has holiday flats with bedrooms, bathroom and kitchen, sleeping four to six people. It charges from

£80 to £200 per week depending on the season – outside the high season it may let a flat for less than a week. **Drimla Lodge** (☎ 820296) has rooms with shower from £22 to £30 per person.

Places to Eat

The award-winning **Creelers Seafood Restaurant** (☎ 302810) is 1½ miles north of Brodick by the Arran Aromatics shopping centre. It's a bistro-style place with some outdoor seating, open Tuesday to Sunday. The imaginative menu includes main dishes from £6 to £16. There's also a shop here selling seafood and smoked foods. You can stock up on local cheeses from the cheese shop opposite.

Back in Brodick, **Stalkers Eating House** (☎ 302579) along the waterfront does good-value meals. Home-made steak pie is £5.50, jacket potatoes are from £1.50, and there are solid British puddings like fruit crumble and sherry trifle. **Duncan's Bar** at the Kingsley Hotel on Shore Rd does good pub grub. **Ormidale Hotel** (☎ 302293, Glen Cloy) is similar with mains for £5 to £10, and occasional live music.

Two miles from Lochranza, the bar at **Catacol Bay Hotel** (☎ 830231) does excellent bar food, with mains from £4.50 to £7. The restaurant here does a Sunday afternoon buffet for £8.50. In summer there are often ceilidhs and live music.

In Kildonan, the **Breadalbane Hotel** (☎ 820284) does great home-made bar food; main courses cost from £3.25 to £10. **Carraig Mhor** (☎ 600453, Shore Rd), Lamlash, is recommended for its seafood.

Getting There & Away

CalMac (☎ 302140) runs a daily car ferry between Ardrossan and Brodick (55 minutes, four to six daily, £3.95); summer services between Claonaig and Lochranza (30 minutes, 10 daily, £3.35); and summer services on Monday, Wednesday and Friday between Brodick and the Isle of Bute (1½ hours, one each-way, £4.35).

If you're going to visit several islands it's worth planning your route in advance.

CalMac has a wide range of tickets including Island Hopscotch fares that work out cheaper than buying several single tickets.

Getting Around

The island's efficient bus services are operated by Western Buses (☎ 302000) and Royal Mail (☎ 01463-256200). There are about four to six buses a day from Brodick Pier to Lochranza (40 minutes, £1.55). A Daycard costs £3. For a taxi phone ☎ 302274 in Brodick or ☎ 600725 in Lamlash.

In Brodick there are several places to rent bikes, including Mini Golf Cycle Hire (☎ 302272) on Shore Rd with bikes from £9 per day. You can also rent three-speeds from Sandy Kerr (☎ 830676) near Lochranza Youth Hostel (£4.50/15 for adults/juniors, per day/week).

SOUTH AYRSHIRE

Ayr

- **pop 49,500   ☎ 01292**

Ayr's long sandy beach has made it a popular family seaside resort since Victorian times. It's also known for its racecourse, the top course in Scotland, with more racing days than any other in Britain. Ayr is the largest town on this coast and makes a convenient base for a tour of Burns territory.

Information

The TIC (☎ 288688), opposite the train station on Burns Statue Square, opens September to June, Monday to Saturday from 9.15 am to 5 pm, Sunday from 11 am to 5 pm (possibly closed at weekends, November to March). In July and August, the TIC opens Monday to Saturday from 9.15 am to 6 pm, Sunday from 10 am to 5 pm.

Things to See

Sights in Ayr are mainly Burns related. The bard was baptised in the **Auld Kirk** (old church) off High St. Several of his poems are set in Ayr. In his *Twa Brigs*, Ayr's old and new bridges argue with one another. The **Auld Brig** was built in 1491 and spans the river just down from the church. In Burns' poem *Tam o'Shanter*, Tam spends a boozy evening in the pub at 230 High St that now bears his name.

Cycle Routes

With few steep hills, the area is well suited to cyclists. See the Glasgow section for the cycle way from that city. The TIC has a useful leaflet.

From Ayr, you could cycle to Alloway and spend a couple of hours seeing the Burns sights before continuing via Maybole to Culzean. You could either camp here after seeing Culzean Castle, or cycle back along the coast road to Ayr, a round trip of about 22 miles.

In Ayr, AMG Cycles (☎ 287580), 55 Dalblair Rd, rents bikes for £10 per day (24 hours).

Places to Stay

There's a smart caravan park in town but it doesn't take campers. *Crofthead Caravan Park* (☎ 263516), 2 miles east of Ayr near the A70, charges from £5.50 for a small tent and two people.

Ayr Youth Hostel (☎ 262322, 5 Craigweil Rd) is in a magnificent turreted mansion by the beach and is less than a mile south of the train and bus stations. It's open from March to October; the nightly charge is £7.75/6.50 for adults/juniors.

There are numerous B&Bs and hotels. *Eglinton Guest House* (☎ 264623, 23 Eglinton Terrace) is a short walk west of the bus station and has rooms for £16/30 a single/double.

A five to 10 minute walk from the station brings you to a crescent of upmarket B&Bs and small hotels. On Park Circus, *Belmont Guest House* (☎ 265588) at No 15 has *en suite* rooms for £19/36. *Lochinver Hotel* (☎ 265086) at No 32 is a homely sort of place and charges from £15.50 per person. *Richmond Hotel* (☎ 265153) at No 38 is a small, friendly and efficient place with rooms from £25/36.

Park Circus continues into Bellevue Crescent and there are also several places to stay along here.

Robert Burns

Best remembered for penning the words of *Auld Lang Syne*, Robert Burns is Scotland's most famous poet, and a popular hero whose birthday (25 January) is celebrated as Burns Night by Scots around the world.

He was born in 1759 in Alloway. Although his mother was illiterate and his parents poor farmers, they sent him to the local school where he soon showed an aptitude for literature and a fondness for the folk song. He began to write his own songs and satires, some of which he distributed privately. When the problems of his arduous farming life were compounded by the threat of prosecution from the father of Jean Armour, with whom he'd had an affair, he decided to emigrate to Jamaica. He gave up his share of the family farm and published his poems to raise money for the journey.

The poems were so well reviewed in Edinburgh that Burns decided to remain in Scotland and devote himself to writing. He went to Edinburgh in 1787 to publish a second edition, but the financial rewards were not enough to live on and he had to take a job as a customs officer in Dumfriesshire. He contributed many songs to collections published by Johnson and Thomson in Edinburgh, and a third edition of his poems was published in 1793. Burns died in Dumfries in 1796, aged 37, after a heart attack.

While some dispute Burns' claim to true literary genius, he was certainly an accomplished poet and songwriter, and has been compared to Chaucer for his verse tale *Tam o'Shanter*. Burns wrote in Lallans, the Scottish Lowland dialect of English that is not very accessible to the foreigner. Perhaps this is part of his appeal. He was also very much a man of the people, satirising the upper classes and the church for their hypocrisy.

Many of the local landmarks mentioned in *Tam o'Shanter* can still be visited. Farmer Tam, riding home after a hard night's drinking in a pub in Ayr, sees witches dancing in Alloway churchyard. He calls out to the one pretty witch but is pursued by them all and has to reach the other side of the River Doon to be safe. He just manages to cross the Brig o'Doon, but his mare loses her tail to the witches.

The Burns connection in southern Scotland is milked for all it's worth and TICs have a *Burns Heritage Trail* leaflet leading you to every place that can claim some link with the bard.

Places to Eat

The Hunny Pot (☎ 263239, 37 Beresford Terrace), a short walk from the TIC, is a pleasant place serving good teas and light meals (£4 to £5) from 9 am to 10 pm. There's a branch of that reliable Edinburgh chain *Pierre Victoire* (☎ 282087) at 4 River Terrace. The set three-course lunch in this French restaurant costs £5.90.

The best place in town is *Fouters Bistro Restaurant* (☎ 261391, 2A Academy St) opposite the town hall. It specialises in Ayrshire produce and local seafood. Main dishes are £9.50 to £14, and there's a cheaper bistro menu. It's closed on Sunday and Monday.

Getting There & Away

There are at least two trains an hour from Glasgow Central to Ayr (50 minutes, £4.80) and some trains continue south to Stranraer (1½ hours from Ayr, £13.70). The main bus operator in the area is Western Buses (☎ 613500) – its hourly X77 service from Glasgow to Girvan/Stranraer via Ayr costs £3 (Glasgow to Ayr).

Alloway

Three miles south of Ayr, Alloway is where Burns was born in 1759. Even if you're not a fan it's still worth a visit, since the Burns related exhibitions give a good impression of life in Ayrshire in the late 18th century. All the sights are within easy walking distance of each other and come under the umbrella title **Burns National Heritage Park**.

Burns Cottage & Museum (☎ 01292-441215) stands by the main road from Ayr. Born in the little box bed in this cramped thatched cottage, the poet spent the first seven years of his life here. There's a good museum of Burnsiana by the cottage exhibiting everything from his writing compendium to a piece of wood from his coffin. Light meals are available in the tearoom. The museum opens April to October, daily from 9 am to 6 pm; November to March, Monday to Saturday from 10 am to 4 pm, Sunday from noon to 4 pm. Entry is £2.50/1.25; the ticket also permits entry to the Burns Monument & Gardens.

From here you can visit the ruins of **Alloway Auld Kirk**, the setting for part of *Tam o'Shanter*. Burns' father, William Burnes (his son dropped the 'e' from his name) is buried in the kirkyard.

The nearby **Tam o'Shanter Experience** (☎ 01292-443700) has audiovisual displays (£2.50/1.25) and a bookshop/gift shop. It opens April to October, daily from 9 am to 6 pm (9 am to 5 pm the rest of the year). The restaurant does excellent home-made soup. The **Burns Monument & Gardens** (opening hours as for the Burns Cottage) are nearby. The monument was built in 1823 and affords a view of the 13th century **Brig o'Doon**. There are also statues of Burns' drinking cronies in the gardens.

Brig O'Doon House (☎ 01292-442466) has a brasserie doing three-course dinners for around £15. Conveniently located, as its name suggests, rooms are £80/100. *Northpark House Hotel* (☎ 01292-442336) is off the road to Ayr. It's a small, luxurious hotel with a fine restaurant; rooms cost from £60/80.

Western Buses (☎ 613500) run hourly from Monday to Saturday between Alloway and Ayr, until 5.50 pm (No 57, £1.50 return). Otherwise, rent a bike and cycle here.

Culzean Castle & Country Park

Well worth seeing, Culzean (pronounced cullane), 12 miles south of Ayr, is one of the most impressive of Scotland's great stately homes. Perched dramatically on the edge of the cliffs, this 18th century mansion was designed by Robert Adam to replace the castle built here in the 16th century.

The original castle belonged to the Kennedy clan, who, after a feud in the 16th century, divided into the Kennedys of Culzean and Cassillis, and the Kennedys of Bargany. Because of the American connection (Eisenhower was a frequent visitor) most people wrongly assume that the Culzean Kennedys are closely related to JFK. Culzean Castle was given to the National Trust for Scotland in 1945.

Robert Adam was the most influential architect of his time, renowned for his meticulous attention to detail and the elegant classical embellishments with which he decorated his ceilings and fireplaces. The beautiful oval staircase here is regarded as one of his finest achievements.

On the first floor, the opulence of the circular saloon contrasts splendidly with the views of the wild sea below. The other rooms on this floor are also interesting and Lord Cassillis' bedroom is said to be haunted by a lady in green, mourning for a lost baby. Even the bathrooms are palatial, the dressing room beside the state bedroom being equipped with a state-of-the-art shower that directs jets of water from almost every angle.

Set in a 563-acre park combining woodland, coast and gardens, there's much more to see than just the castle. An interesting exhibition in the Gas House explains how gas was produced for the castle. There's also a visitors centre, ice house, swan pond and aviary.

Culzean Castle (☎ 01655-760269) is the NTS's most visited property and can get quite crowded on summer weekends. It's open April to October from 10.30 am to 5.30 pm. The park opens year-round from 9.30 am to sunset. Entry is £6.50/4.40 (£17 for a family ticket), or £3.50/2.40 if you want to visit the park only.

It's possible to stay in the castle from April to October, but gracious living doesn't come cheap. A night for two in the Eisenhower suite costs £300 and the cheapest rooms are £100/150 a single/double. If you're not in that league there's a *Camping & Caravanning Club* (☎ 01655-760627) in the park. It costs £4 per person plus £4 for nonmembers per night.

Maybole is the nearest train station, but since it's 4 miles away it's best to come by bus from Ayr (11 per day, Monday to Saturday, 30 minutes, £1.95). The bus passes the park gates but it's still a 20 minute walk through the grounds to the castle.

Turnberry

To play the world-famous golf course here you must usually stay at the luxurious *Turnberry Hotel* (☎ 01655-331000). Singles cost £158 to £250, while doubles are £184 to £340. If you can afford that, dinner in the award-winning restaurant is a snip at £45.

Ailsa Craig

From much of South Ayrshire, you can see curiously shaped Ailsa Craig, looking like a giant bread roll floating out to sea. Granite rock quarried from here is used for *curling* (game played on ice) stones. It's now a bird sanctuary and taking a cruise from Girvan on the MV *Glorious* (☎ 01465-713219) is normally about as close as you'll get to the gannets that crowd this 340m-high (1114 feet) rocky outcrop.

Dumfries & Galloway

The tourist board bills this region as Scotland's surprising south-west, and it is surprising if you expect beautiful mountain and coastal scenery to be confined to the Highlands. Only the local architecture disappoints; otherwise, with mountains (which reach over 2000 feet/600m), lochs and an interesting coastline, it's reminiscent in some ways of the Lake District. There are even stone walls running up hill and down dale. This is, however, one of the forgotten corners of Britain, and beyond the main transport routes to Stranraer, traffic and people are sparse.

Dumfries & Galloway covers the southern half of Scotland's southern elbow. Warmed by the Gulf Stream, this is the mildest corner of Scotland, a phenomenon that has allowed the development of some famous gardens. There are notable historic and prehistoric attractions linked by the Solway Coast Heritage Trail (information from TICs). Caerlaverock Castle, Threave Castle and Whithorn Cathedral & Priory are just three of many. Kirkcudbright is a beautiful town, and would make a good base.

This is excellent cycling and walking country, and it's crossed by the coast-to-coast Southern Upland Way (see Walks and Cycle Routes at the beginning of this chapter).

Dumfries & Galloway lies south of the Southern Uplands. Stranraer is the ferry port to Larne in Northern Ireland; it's the shortest link from Britain to Ireland. There are youth hostels at Newton Stewart, Kendoon and Wanlockhead and a backpacker hostel at Castle Douglas.

GETTING THERE & AROUND

The regional council has a travel information line (☎ 0345-090510), Monday to Friday from 9 am to 5 pm.

Bus

National Express (☎ 0990-808080) has coaches from London, Birmingham (via Manchester and Carlisle), and Glasgow/Edinburgh to Stranraer. These service the main towns and villages along the A75 (including Dumfries, Kirkcudbright and Newton Stewart). Stagecoach Western (☎ 01387-253496) and MacEwan's (☎ 01387-710357) provide a variety of local bus services. Sometimes different bus companies have services along the same route but charge different prices, so ring the travel information line for more info.

The Day Discoverer (£5) is a useful day ticket valid on most buses in the region and on Stagecoach Cumberland in Cumbria.

Train

Two lines from Carlisle to Glasgow cross the region, via Dumfries and Moffat respectively. The line from Glasgow to Stranraer runs via Ayr. Call ☎ 0345-484950.

DUMFRIES

• pop 31,000   ☎ 01387

Dumfries is a large town with a strategic position that placed it smack in the path of vengeful English armies. As a result, although it has existed since Roman times, the oldest standing building dates from the 17th century.

It has escaped modern mass tourism, although it was the home of Burns from 1791 to his death in 1796, and there are several important Burns-related museums. The centre is rather run-down and uninspiring, but there are some pleasant 19th century suburbs built in the area's characteristic red sandstone.

Orientation & Information

The main bus station is by the new bridge; the train station is a 10 minute walk north-east. The TIC (☎ 253862), 64 Whitesands opposite the car park by the river, opens daily June to September from 9.30 am to 6 pm; from 9.30 am to 5 pm the rest of the year. You can book National Express/Citylink buses here. Early-closing day is Thursday.

Burnsiana

On Burns St, **Burns House** (☎ 255297) is a place of pilgrimage for Burns enthusiasts. It's here the poet spent the last years of his life and there are some interesting relics, and original letters and manuscripts. It's open April to September, Monday to Saturday from 10 am to 5 pm, Sunday from 2 to 5 pm; October to March, Tuesday to Saturday from 10 am to 1 pm and from 2 to 5 pm; free.

The **Robert Burns Centre** (☎ 264808), Mill Rd, is an award-winning museum on the banks of the River Nith in an old mill.

It tells the story of Burns and Dumfries in the 1790s. There's also a café/gallery. It's open April to September, Monday to Saturday from 10 am to 8 pm, Sunday from 2 to 5 pm; October to March, Tuesday to Saturday from 10 am to 1 pm and 2 to 5 pm; free (£1.20/60p for the audiovisual presentation).

Burns' **mausoleum** is in the graveyard at St Michael's Kirk. Back in the centre at the top of High St is a **statue** of the bard.

Places to Stay

There are some good-value B&Bs in a quiet, pleasant suburb near the train station. **Cairndoon** (☎ 256991, 14 Newall Terrace) has spacious, comfortable rooms with TVs and a delightfully warm welcome for £19 per person. On Lovers Walk, you could try the **Fulwood Hotel** (☎ 252262), No 30, with singles/doubles for £18/32, or **Torbay Lodge Guest House** (☎ 253922) with rooms from £16 per person.

You'll find several accommodation options on Lauriknowe including **Edenbank Hotel** (☎ 252759), No 17, a short walk from the centre of town. It's a small, family-run, renovated hotel with a range of rooms including two singles, all with bathrooms, for £45/58.

Places to Eat

Olivers on the High St mall has a range of good-value baked goods, sandwiches and baked potatoes. **Doonhamer Restaurant** (17 Church Crescent) serves snacks and hot meals from fish and chips to pizza (£3.25) including vegetarian dishes.

The set lunch menu at **Pierre** (☎ 265888, 113 Queensbury Rd) is excellent value at £4.95. It also does good-quality seafood; fresh halibut is £7.90.

The Italian **Bruno's** (☎ 255757, 3 Balmoral Rd) is one of the best places to eat. Lasagne della casa is £4.95. Next door is the highly recommended **Balmoral Fish & Chicken Bar**, run by the same family.

The **Globe Inn** (56 High St), a traditional pub said to be Burns' favourite watering hole, has bar meals and a restaurant.

Getting There & Away
Dumfries is 330 miles from London, 75 from Edinburgh, Glasgow and Stranraer and 35 from Carlisle.

Bus National Express bus No 920 runs thrice daily between London and Belfast, via Birmingham, Manchester, Carlisle, Dumfries, the towns along the A75, and Stranraer. Local buses run regularly to Kirkcudbright and towns along the A75 to Stranraer (three hours, £3.50). Stagecoach Western has two buses daily (No 100) to/from Edinburgh.

Train Dumfries is on a line that leaves the main west-coast line at Gretna, and from Dumfries runs north-west along Nithsdale to join the Glasgow-Stranraer line at Kilmarnock. You can join the service at Carlisle or Glasgow; Monday to Saturday there are frequent trains between Carlisle and Dumfries (35 minutes, £6.40), and six between Dumfries and Glasgow (1½ hours, £16.40); there's a reduced service on Sunday.

Getting Around
Taxi Try Hastings Taxi (☎ 252664).

Bicycle Grierson & Graham (☎ 259483), 10 Academy St, and Nithsdale Cycle Centre (☎ 254870), 46 Brooms Rd, hire bikes with rates from £6 per three hours.

AROUND DUMFRIES
Caerlaverock Castle
The ruins of Caerlaverock Castle (☎ 01387-770244, HS), on a beautiful stretch of the Solway coast, are among the loveliest in Britain. Surrounded by a moat, lawns and stands of trees, the unusual pink-hued triangular stone castle looks impregnable – in fact it fell several times. The present castle dates from the late 13th century. Inside, there's an extraordinary Scottish Renaissance façade to apartments that were built in 1634.

It's open April to September, daily from 9.30 am to 6.30 pm; October to March, Monday to Saturday from 9.30 am to 4.30 pm, Sunday from 2 to 4.30 pm; £2.30/1. Monday to Saturday, the castle can be reached from Dumfries by Stagecoach Western's bus No 371.

You can combine a visit to the castle with one to **Caerlaverock Wildlife & Wetlands Centre** (open daily from 10 am to 5 pm; £4.25/2.50) a mile away, which protects 1350 acres of salt marsh and mud flat, the habitat for barnacle goose and other birds. There are hides and observatories.

NEW GALLOWAY & AROUND
* pop 290 ☎ 01644
New Galloway is a quaint little town, surrounded by beautiful countryside. There's nothing much to bring you here, except to get away from it all. Tourist information is available from The Smithy teashop on High St.

South-west is **Galloway Forest Park**, with great whale-backed heather-covered mountains (although, sadly, the lower slopes have been clear-felled by the Forestry Commission). The countryside to the south-east and north is particularly beautiful and unusual. You feel as if you're on a high plateau, surrounded by tumbling short-pitched hills. There's a sense of space unusual in Britain.

On High St, the refurbished *Kenmure Arms* (☎ 420240) has rooms from £16.50 per person, while opposite, the *Leamington Hotel* (☎ 420327), has rooms with bathrooms from £15 to £24 per person.

MacEwan's bus No 521 runs twice a week (Wednesday and Saturday) to Dumfries.

CASTLE DOUGLAS & AROUND
* pop 3500 ☎ 01556
Castle Douglas is an open, attractive little town that was laid out in the 18th century by Sir William Douglas, who had made a fortune in the Americas. Beside the town is the small but beautiful Carlingwark Loch. At the Loch's western end is **Threave Garden** (NTS), which is spectacular in spring. It's open daily all year; £4.

The TIC (☎ 502611), in a small park on King St, opens daily April to June and September to October from 10 am to 4.30 pm, July and August from 10 am to 6 pm.

Threave Castle

Three miles west of Castle Douglas, off the A75, Threave Castle (HS) is an impressively grim tower on a small island in the middle of the lovely River Dee. It's only a shell, but it's a romantic ruin nonetheless. Built in the late 14th century it became a principal stronghold for the Douglases.

It's a 10 minute walk from the car park, and visitors are ferried across to the island in a small boat. The castle opens April to September, daily from 9.30 am to 6.30 pm, £1.80/75p, including the ferry.

Places to Stay

Lochside Caravan & Camping Site (☎ 502949), an attractive spot alongside Carlingwark Loch, has sites for vans and tents from £7.10. On the shore of Loch Ken, north of Parton village, *Galloway Sailing Centre* (☎ 420625) offers backpacker accommodation year-round; dorms are £7.50.

Craigvar House (☎ 503515, 60 St Andrew St) is a comfortable B&B, with rooms from £20 per person. *Douglas Arms Hotel* (☎ 502231, King St) has good food and a range of comfortable rooms, most with bathrooms, from £35/65 a single/double.

Getting There & Around

MacEwan's bus No 501 between Dumfries and Kirkcudbright calls in frequently (only twice on Sunday). Ace Cycles (☎ 504542), 11 Church St, hires touring and mountain bikes for £10 per 24 hours.

KIRKCUDBRIGHT

- pop 3500 ☎ 01557

Kirkcudbright (pronounced kirkoobree), with its dignified streets of 17th and 18th century merchants' houses and its interesting harbour, is the ideal base to explore the beautiful southern coast. The lovely surrounding countryside has distinctive hummocky hills covered in gorse – it's almost as if they've been heaped up to make a golf course.

Orientation & Information

The town is on the River Dee and everything is within easy walking distance. The TIC (☎ 330494), Harbour Square, opens Easter to October, daily from 10 am to 5 pm. There are some useful brochures outlining walks and car tours in the surrounding district. Early-closing day is Thursday.

Things to See

The modest sights have charm and provide an excuse for exploring the town. **McLellan's Castle**, near the harbour and TIC, is a large ruin, built in 1577. Nearby, the 17th century Broughton House contains **Hornel Art Gallery**, a reminder of the town's 19th century artist's colony, featuring paintings by Australian-born EA Hornel and a beautiful Japanese garden. **Tolbooth Arts Centre** caters to today's local artists, and the **Stewartry Museum** is a particularly interesting local museum; entry to each is £1.50/free.

Places to Stay & Eat

Silvercraigs Caravan & Camping Site (☎ 330123) overlooks the town and has great views. It has sites from £6.60.

Parkview (☎ 330056, 22 Millburn St) is a small blue-painted B&B charging £17 per person. *Gladstone House* (☎ 331734, 48 High St) offers upmarket B&B to non-smokers from £30/50 a single/double in an attractively-decorated Georgian house.

The large, well-run *Royal Hotel* (☎ 331213, St Cuthbert St) offers rooms with bathrooms for £22.50/38. It has good-value bar meals, including an all-you-can-eat buffet for £4.95 noon to 2.30 pm. The *Selkirk Arms Hotel* (☎ 330402, High St) has well-equipped rooms, all with bathrooms, for £48/75. It also has good bar meals, plus a more expensive dining room.

The best place to eat is the *Auld Alliance* (☎ 330569, 5 Castle St) open daily for dinner only. A reference to the political alliance between Scotland and France, here it means a combination of local fresh Scots produce (such as small scallops known as queenies) and French cooking and wine. Main dishes range from £5.90 to £14; booking is advised.

Getting There & Away

Kirkcudbright is 25 miles from Dumfries, 50 from Stranraer. There are regular MacEwan's bus services to Dumfries (£2.50) and Stranraer (£4.90).

GATEHOUSE OF FLEET

- **pop 900** ☎ **01557**

Gatehouse of Fleet is an attractive little town, on the banks of the Water of Fleet and surrounded by partly wooded hills – completely off the beaten track. The TIC (☎ 814212), High St, opens daily Easter to October from 10 am to 4.30 pm. A mile south-west on the A75, **Cardoness Castle** (☎ 814427) is a classic 15th century tower house with good views (£1.80/75p). The *Bank O' Fleet Hotel* (☎ 814302, 47 High St) has B&B rooms with bathroom from £23.50 per person and good bar meals; savoury mince and tatties are £4.25. MacEwan's bus Nos 500 and X75 run regularly to Dumfries and Stranraer.

NEWTON STEWART

- **pop 3200** ☎ **01672**

Surrounded by beautiful countryside, and set on the banks of the River Cree, Newton Stewart is a centre for hikers and anglers. The TIC (☎ 402431), Dashwood Square, opens April and October, daily from 10 am to 4.30 pm; from 10 am to 5 pm in May, June and September; and from 10 am to 6 pm in July and August.

Many walkers head for Glen Trool in the Galloway Hills in **Galloway Forest Park** – 300 sq miles of lochs, mountains and forest. If you're interested in renting fishing gear, contact Creebridge House Hotel (see Places to Stay & Eat).

Places to Stay & Eat

Creebridge Caravan Park (☎ 402324), about 300 yards from the bridge, charges £2.30 for a tent plus £2 per person. In the adjoining town, *Minnigaff Youth Hostel* (☎ 402211) opens from April to September; dorm beds cost £6.10/4.95 for adults/juniors.

On the banks of the River Cree is the friendly *Flowerbank Guest House* (☎ 402629, Millcroft Rd, Minnigaff) five

minutes from town. B&B starts from £16.50 per person (£20 with bathroom).

Creebridge House Hotel (☎ 402121) is a magnificent 18th century mansion built for the Earl of Galloway. There's a good restaurant and huntin', shootin' and fishin'. The rooms, all with bathrooms, are tastefully decorated; prices range from £42/72 to £48/84 for singles/doubles.

Getting There & Away

Newton Stewart is served by buses running between Stranraer and Dumfries, including bus No 920 (National Express) and bus Nos 500 and X75 (various operators, at least two a day). It's also a starting point for buses south to Wigtown and Whithorn.

Getting Around

Bike hire is available from Belgrano (☎ 403307), 6 Church Lane, for £10 for 24 hours up to £25 for a week.

WIGTOWN

- **pop 1000** ☎ **01988**

Overlooking Wigtown Bay and the Galloway Hills, Wigtown has expansive views and is surrounded by attractive rolling countryside. Economically run-down, the town's revival has begun with the decision to make it Scotland's first 'Booktown'. Over the next few years new bookshops will be set up, offering the widest selection of books in Scotland.

Craigmount Guest House (☎ 402291), on the edge of town, has a range of rooms overlooking the bay, including a single and a couple with private bathrooms. B&B is from £17 per person. *County Hotel*, on South Main St, has bar meals; high tea is £5.50.

WHITHORN

- **pop 1000** ☎ **01988**

Whithorn has a broad, attractive High St virtually closed at both ends – designed to enclose a medieval market. Economic hard times have hit the town and there are virtually no facilities – just a couple of shops and pubs. It's worth visiting, however, because it has a fascinating history.

In 397, while the Romans were still in Britain, St Ninian established the first Christian mission beyond Hadrian's Wall (predating St Columba on Iona by 166 years) in Whithorn. The modest ruins of Whithorn Cathedral Priory, once the focus of an important medieval pilgrimage, are now the centre point for the **Whithorn Dig** (☎ 500508). The substantial remains of the old monastic settlement are being excavated and there are exhibitions and an audiovisual display. There's also a museum with some important finds and early Christian sculpture. It's open April to October, daily from 10.30 am to 5 pm; £2.70/1.50.

Stagecoach Western's bus No 415 runs regularly to/from Newton Stewart.

ISLE OF WHITHORN

The Isle of Whithorn – once an island but now part of a peninsula – is a curious, raggedy place with an attractive harbour. **St Ninian's Chapel**, probably built for pilgrims who landed nearby, is on the windswept, rocky headland.

The 300-year-old *Dunbar House* (☎ 01988-500336, Tonderghie Rd) overlooking the harbour has B&B in large rooms for £18 per person. On the quayside, the *Steam Packet Inn Hotel* (☎ 01988-500334) has popular, excellent-value bar meals – everything from soup of the day to fresh lobster; most mains cost around £5. There's also B&B in rooms with bathrooms from £22.50 per person.

Stagecoach Western's bus No 415 runs regularly to/from Newton Stewart.

PORTPATRICK
* **pop 600   ☎ 01776**

Portpatrick is a charming port on a rugged stretch of coast. Until the mid-19th century it was the main port for Northern Ireland, so it's quite substantial. It's now a lifeboat station, a quiet resort, and the starting point for the **Southern Upland Way**.

It's possible to follow the Southern Upland Way virtually to Stranraer (9 miles). It's a cliff top walk, followed by sections of farmland and heather moor.

Start at the Way's information shelter at the north end of the harbour. The walk is waymarked until a half-mile south of Stranraer, where you get the first good views of the town. The way continues south-eastwards. From Stranraer, walk westward along High St, turn left into Glebe St and follow the Portpatrick road. A waymarker points to the right shortly after reaching the top of the hill.

There are **fishing** trips from Portpatrick on the *Cornubia* for £8 for half a day; call Mr Tyerman (☎ 810468).

Places to Stay

There are lots of places to stay on North Crescent, which curves around the harbour. *Knowe Guest House & Tea Room* (☎ 810441), No 1, is a charming place overlooking the harbour; B&B with private bathroom is £17 per person. *Ard Choille Guest House* (☎ 810313, 1 Blair Terrace) has doubles, including one with a private bathroom. Rates start at £15 per person.

Formerly the customs house, *Harbour House Hotel* (☎ 810456, 53 Main St) is a popular pub with a range of rooms, some with bathrooms, from £24 per person.

Getting There & Away

Stagecoach Western bus No 367 runs regularly Monday to Saturday to Stranraer.

STRANRAER & CAIRNRYAN
* **pop 10,000   ☎ 01776**

Although a little run-down, Stranraer is rather more pleasant than the average ferry port. There's no pressing reason to stay, unless you're catching a ferry. Make for the south coast (maybe nearby Portpatrick) or Glasgow.

Orientation & Information

In Stranraer, the bus and train stations, accommodation and TIC are close to the Stena Sealink and SeaCat terminals. The TIC (☎ 702595), 28 Harbour St, opens April to June, September and October, Monday to Saturday from 9.30 am to 5 pm, Sunday from 10 am to 4 pm; July and

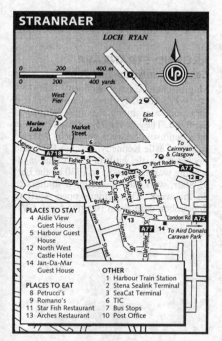

STRANRAER

LOCH RYAN

PLACES TO STAY
4   Aislie View
    Guest House
5   Harbour Guest
    House
12 North West
    Castle Hotel
14 Jan-Da-Mar
    Guest House

PLACES TO EAT
8   Petrucci's
9   Romano's
11 Star Fish Restaurant
13 Arches Restaurant

OTHER
1   Harbour Train Station
2   Stena Sealink Terminal
3   SeaCat Terminal
6   TIC
7   Bus Stops
10 Post Office

August daily from 9.15 am to 6 pm; November to March, Monday to Saturday from 10 am to 4 pm. Early-closing day is Wednesday.

Places to Stay

Aird Donald Caravan Park (☎ 702025 London Rd) is the nearest camping ground that takes vans and tents. Sites start from £7.

Harbour Guest House (☎ 704626, Market St) on the harbour front near the town centre, has rooms for £17 per person. There's a string of standard places along Agnew Crescent facing the harbour, including the low-key *Aislie View Guest House (☎ 705792)*, No 8, which has good views of Loch Ryan and B&B from £15 per person.

Jan-Da-Mar Guest House (☎ 706194, 1 Ivy Place, London Rd) is conveniently located, and has a range of rooms (some with bathrooms). Singles/doubles are from

£18/32. The most luxurious hotel in Stranraer is *North West Castle Hotel (☎ 704413)*, formerly the home of Arctic explorer Sir John Ross. It's expensive but good, with singles/doubles from £52/74.

If you fancy a night in a lighthouse, *Corsewall Lighthouse Hotel (☎ 853220)* is an unusual place to stay, 10 miles north of Stranraer at Corsewall Point. Rooms are from £45/70, all with bathroom; one room is specially equipped for disabled travellers.

Places to Eat

There are reasonable pizzas and other fast food at two places in George/Charlotte St. *Petrucci's*, opposite St John's Tower, has pizzas from £2.25, and *Romano's* does a fish and chips special for £4.25. Another option is *Star Fish Restaurant, (14 Charlotte St)* with Scotch pie for £2.50; open until midnight.

The *Arches Restaurant (Hanover St)* is a bright, popular café with main dishes from £4.95. The best restaurant is at *North West Castle Hotel (☎ 704413)*, where a set four-course dinner costs £21, including a vegetarian choice.

Getting There & Away

Stranraer is 390 miles from London, 120 from Edinburgh, 80 from Glasgow and 75 from Dumfries.

Sea See the introductory Getting There & Away chapter for details on services to Northern Ireland. There are three alternatives: P&O (☎ 0990-980777) ferries from Cairnryan to Larne; Stena Line (☎ 0990-707070) ferries from Stranraer to Larne and Belfast; and fast SeaCat (☎ 0990-523523) catamarans from Stranraer to Belfast.

The Cairnryan to Larne service is used mainly by motorists and hauliers. Cairnryan is 5 miles north of Stranraer on the northern side of Loch Ryan. Bus No 303 runs there from Stranraer four times daily from Monday to Saturday. For a taxi (around £4) phone Central Taxis (☎ 704999).

Stena Line ferries for Larne connect directly with rail and bus services. The train station is on the ferry pier. The SeaCat terminal is south of the ferry pier.

Bus National Express runs thrice daily between London and Belfast, via Birmingham, Manchester, Carlisle, Dumfries, the towns along the A75 and Stranraer. Stagecoach Western runs hourly buses to Glasgow (three hours, £7). There are also regular local buses to Kirkcudbright and the towns along the A75, like Newton Stewart (£1.95) and Dumfries.

Train There are up to four trains daily between Stranraer and Belfast (Donegall Quay) via Larne (nine hours); and regular services to Glasgow (2½ hours, £19.50).

AROUND STRANRAER
Castle Kennedy Gardens

Magnificent Castle Kennedy Gardens (☎ 01776-702024), several miles east of Stranraer, are among the most famous in Scotland. They cover 75 acres and are set on a peninsula between two lochs and two castles (Castle Kennedy, burnt in 1716, and Lochinch Castle, built in 1864). The landscaping was undertaken in 1730 by the Earl of Stair, who used unoccupied soldiers to do the work. The gardens open April to September, daily from 10 am to 5 pm; £2/1.

Central Scotland

The Highland line, the massive geological fault that divides the Highlands from the Lowlands, runs across the central section of Scotland, making this possibly the most scenically varied region in Britain. To the south are undulating hills and agricultural plains; to the north, the wild, bare Highland peaks.

The town of Stirling, 26 miles north of Glasgow, has witnessed most of the great battles in the Scottish struggle against English domination. The spectacular castle, dramatically perched on a rock as is Edinburgh's castle, was of paramount strategic importance for centuries, controlling the main routes in the area.

Less than 20 miles north of Glasgow are the famous 'bonnie, bonnie banks' of Loch Lomond, straddling the Highland line. Tourists have been visiting this area and the Trossachs (the lochs and hills east of Loch Lomond) for over 150 years – Queen Victoria among them. She had set her heart on adding a Highland residence to her list of royal properties and eventually purchased the Balmoral estate in Aberdeenshire.

In the south-east, Fife was for centuries an independent kingdom. The attractive seaside town of St Andrews, its capital, was once the ecclesiastical centre of the country, but is now better known for its university and as the home of golf.

Perth is on the direct route from Edinburgh and Glasgow to Inverness. Now just a busy town, it was once the capital of Scotland. Dunkeld and Pitlochry, to the north, are appealing (though touristy) villages, and useful as walking bases. Frequent buses and trains service this route.

Following the coast to Aberdeen from Perth or St Andrews, you quickly reach Dundee, one of Scotland's largest cities. Despite its excellent location, it hasn't recovered from modern development and the loss of its jute and shipbuilding industries. It's worth pausing in Dundee to visit Cap-

HIGHLIGHTS

- Stirling Castle
- St Andrews
- Walking the West Highland Way
- Scone Palace, Perth
- Blair Castle
- Discovery Point, Dundee
- Glamis Castle
- The Whisky Trail
- Kilmartin Glen
- The Isles of Islay & Jura
- The Isles of Mull, Iona & Staffa

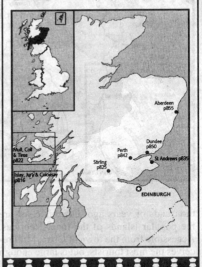

Aberdeen p855

Dundee p850

Perth p842

St Andrews p835

Stirling p825

EDINBURGH

Mull, Coll & Tiree p822

Islay, Jura & Colonsay p816

tain Scott's Antarctic ship, *Discovery*, moored near the Tay Bridge.

To the west is Argyll & Bute and the western coastline, which is indented by long inlets and sea lochs forged by glaciers

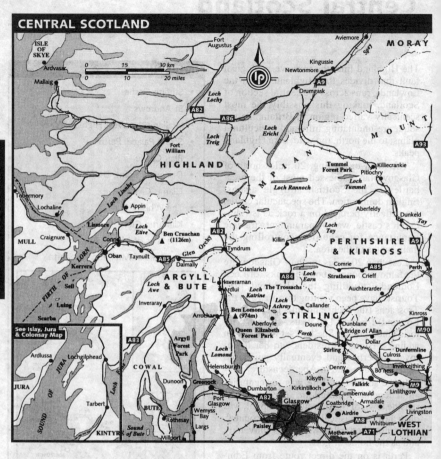

CENTRAL SCOTLAND

thousands of years ago. Off this coast are the popular islands of the Inner Hebrides. Accessible from the town of Oban, Mull receives the most tourists, but is large enough to absorb them. There are some wonderful mountain walks up Mull's challenging 900m peaks. Off the furthest tip of Mull is the Isle of Iona, where St Columba, having sailed from Ireland, came to build his Christian foundation. To the west of Mull lie Coll and Tiree – long, low islands, seen from the ferry on a summer's day as a blue haze

tinged with the silver of their sandy beaches. South-west of Oban are the isles of Colonsay, Islay and Jura. The latter's breast-shaped mountains are known as the Paps of Jura, and are visible from far away on a clear day. Islay is more agricultural and is famous for its whisky distilleries.

The eastern Highlands is a great elbow of land that juts into the North Sea between Perth and the Firth of Tay in the south, and Inverness and Moray Firth in the north. There are excellent hill walks in the

fattened on the proceeds of a long history of sea trade and, currently, the North Sea oil industry, for which it's the onshore base.

Few people visit the small fishing villages of the north coast, but some are very pretty. Further west along this coast, experiments with alternative lifestyles continue at the Findhorn Foundation, an international spiritual community that welcomes outsiders. Further spiritual guidance is provided in neighbouring Speyside, where whisky distilleries welcome visitors with tours and free drams.

ORIENTATION & INFORMATION

This central section of the country comprises the administrative regions of Fife, Stirling, Perthshire & Kinross, Angus, Aberdeenshire, Moray, and Argyll & Bute.

The main mountain range is the Grampians, rising to over 1060m; the Cairngorms (1220m) border the Highland region. Off the western coast, the islands of the Inner Hebrides – Islay, Jura, Colonsay, Mull, Iona, Coll and Tiree – are accessible from Oban.

There are TICs in all the main tourist centres, many open daily in summer. Smaller TICs close from October to Easter. Most TICs charge for booking local accommodation, usually around £1 or £2; most ask only for a 10% advance.

WALKS & CYCLE ROUTES

The West Highland Way, possibly the finest long-distance walk in Britain, cuts across the centre of this region from Milngavie (near Glasgow) to Fort William. (See the Activities chapter at the start of the book.)

There's some superb hill walking in the Highland areas of central Scotland; Braemar is one of a number of good bases – there's a challenging walk from here through the Cairngorms to Aviemore. The isles of Mull and Jura have wild, mountainous areas and are excellent for walking holidays. When completed, the Fife Coastal Path will run for 78 miles between the Forth Bridges and the Tay Bridge.

Away from the busy A9, the side roads are refreshingly free of traffic and excellent

Grampians, and the Cairngorm plateaus are as bleak and demanding as any Scottish mountains. The coastline, especially from Stonehaven to Buckie, is particularly attractive. The valley of the Dee – the Royal Dee thanks to the Queen's residence at Balmoral – has sublime scenery. Braemar is surrounded by good walking country, and every September hosts Scotland's most important Highland Games, the Braemar Gathering.

The largest city in the north-east is prosperous Aberdeen, a lively, attractive place

for cycling. There's an official cycle trail –
the Glasgow, Loch Lomond & Killin Cycle
Way – which follows forest trails, small
roads and disused rail routes.

GETTING AROUND

Although the larger towns are easy to reach
by bus and train, travel into the Grampians
and other interesting walking areas is often
difficult without your own transport. The
division between the eastern and western
Highlands reflects the transport realities –
there are few coast-to-coast links across
central Scotland. You can hire cars in the
larger towns.

Bus

Scottish Citylink (☎ 0990-505050) links the
main towns in the area; Perth is a major hub
for its services. Away from the population
centres there are few buses and, as already
mentioned, travelling east to west is difficult. Bus transport around the north-eastern
coast, however, is reasonable.

Midland Bluebird (☎ 01324-613777) and
Bluebird Buses (☎ 01224-212266) operate
local services. There are some day passes,
such as Midland Bluebird's Heart of Scotland Explorer ticket (£7.30), which also
gives you half-price travel with bus companies in neighbouring regions.

For information on local buses phone
Argyll & Bute (☎ 0141-2264826); Dundee
(☎ 01382-433125); Aberdeenshire and
Moray (☎ 01224-664581); Stirling (☎ 01324-
613777); and Fife (☎ 01592-414141,
extension 3103).

Train

The rail system in central Scotland has three
lines running north to south, connected by
a fourth running north-east from Glasgow
through Stirling, Perth, Dundee and Aberdeen. It's a reasonably efficient service, but
has a major flaw – east-west travel across
central Scotland is impossible. You must
return to Glasgow.

The West Highland line, possibly the
most spectacular train journey in Britain,
runs north from Glasgow to Fort William

and Mallaig. A branch line from Crianlarich
connects Oban to the system, and overnight
trains run between London and Oban for
ferries to the Hebridean islands.

Another scenic train journey runs from
Perth to Inverness and includes a beautiful
climb through the Cairngorms from Dunkeld
to Aviemore.

ScotRail's regional Rover tickets cover
parts of the system. The Highland Rover
ticket allows travel on the West Highland
line (from Glasgow) and the North Highland lines (from Aberdeen or Aviemore) for
four days out of eight and cost £42. The
Festival Cities Rover (£26), valid for three
days out of seven, allows travel between
Edinburgh, Glasgow, Falkirk and Stirling.

For rail information phone ☎ 0345-
484950.

Boat

From Aberdeen, P&O (☎ 01224-572615)
has departures Monday, Wednesday,
Thursday and Friday leaving in the evening
for Lerwick (Shetland). In summer, there
are departures at noon on Tuesday and Saturday to Lerwick via Stromness (Orkney).
See Aberdeen for more information.

Ferries to the Hebridean islands off the
west coast are mostly run by Caledonian
MacBrayne, or 'CalMac' (☎ 01475-
650100). Most routes depart from Oban, but
there are some services from Kennacraig on
the Kintyre peninsula. If you plan to island
hop, you'll save money by planning your
trip in advance and buying one of CalMac's
Island Hopscotch tickets covering set routes.
There are also Island Rover Passes covering
the whole system – £39 for eight days, £56
for 15 days. Taking a car can be expensive.
Contact CalMac at the Ferry Terminal,
Gourock PA19 1QP, for a free timetable and
fare structure – also available from TICs.

Argyll & Bute

The northern section of Strathclyde was
renamed Argyll & Bute in 1996 and it
stretches from the tip of the Kintyre peninsula (Paul McCartney's 'Mull of Kintyre')

almost to Glen Coe, and east to Loch Lomond. It includes the Isle of Bute, parts of the Western Highlands, and the islands of the Inner Hebrides – Islay, Jura, Colonsay, Mull, Coll and Tiree.

This area is centred on the ancient kingdom of Dalriada, named by the Irish settlers (known as the Scots) who claimed it around the 5th century. From their headquarters at Dunadd, in the Moine Mhor (great bog) near Kilmartin, they gained ascendancy over the Picts and established the Kingdom of Alba, which eventually became Scotland.

Just 20 miles from Glasgow, Loch Lomond is a very popular destination. Its western bank, where most of the tourist activity takes place, lies in Argyll & Bute; the eastern bank is in Stirling.

The Firth of Clyde, to the south, is a complex system of long, deep fjords, or sea lochs, such as Loch Long and Loch Fyne. This pattern of glacial valleys, drowned by the incoming sea, continues up the western coast of Scotland, creating hundreds of miles of indented coastline. The area records some of the highest rainfall in Britain.

Most people heading for the islands pass through the pleasant town of Oban, the only place of any size in the area. Ferries leave for the popular Isle of Mull (nothing to do with the Mull of Kintyre). It's a great place to hike, with peaks over 900m. There are two interesting castles, Torosay and Duart, near the eastern port of Craignure, and a narrow-gauge railway. The pretty fishing port of Tobermory is in the north of the island.

A five minute ferry trip to the west of Mull is the tiny Isle of Iona, where St Columba arrived from Ireland in the 6th century. Boat trips leave for the uninhabited Isle of Staffa, where the incredible fluted pillars of Fingal's Cave inspired Felix Mendelssohn to compose the *Hebrides Overture*.

Ferries continue from Tobermory to the islands of Coll and Tiree. South from Oban they link Colonsay and Islay. The latter is the most southerly island in the Hebrides and is famous for its whisky distilleries, which produce wonderfully peaty single malts. Beside Islay is the wild Isle of Jura,

where George Orwell wrote *1984*. There are ferry links from Islay to the Kintyre peninsula and the mainland.

For accommodation guides and information contact Argyll, the Isles, Loch Lomond, Stirling & Trossachs Tourist Board (☎ 01786-470945, fax 01786-471301).

GETTING AROUND

The main bus companies in the area are Scottish Citylink and Oban & District Buses (☎ 01631-562856).

There's only one railway line: the scenic branch line off the West Highland line from Crianlarich to Oban.

Most ferries to the islands are run by CalMac. Its Island Hopscotch tickets, based on 23 route combinations, are much better value than single tickets, but require advance planning. For example, the Wemyss Bay to Rothesay (Isle of Bute) and Colintraive to Rhubodach ticket costs £3.45 (£15.80 for a car), a saving of 9% on regular fares. Bicycles are carried free with a Hopscotch ticket.

The Argyll Tourist Route is a driving route marked with brown signposts. It runs from Tarbet on Loch Lomond through Inveraray, Lochgilphead, Oban, Connel and Balachulish to Fort William.

ISLE OF BUTE

The resort of Rothesay is Bute's only town, built around the substantial ruins of **Rothesay Castle**. Mock Gothic **Mount Stuart House** (☎ 503877), the Marquess of Bute's house, is well worth seeing. It's open May to mid-October, from 11 am to 4.30 pm; £6/2.50.

The TIC (☎ 01700-502151), 15 Victoria St, has lists of B&Bs and hotels, but there's no youth hostel on the island. The main beach is in the south by Kilchattan Bay. In late July there's a popular folk festival on Bute.

Frequent CalMac ferries ply between Wemyss Bay and Rothesay (30 minutes, £2.95) on Bute. Another ferry crosses between Rhubodach in the north of the island and Colintraive (five minutes). On Monday, Wednesday and Friday there's a ferry link with the Isle of Arran (two hours).

CENTRAL SCOTLAND

LOCH LOMOND

After Loch Ness, this is perhaps the most famous of Scotland's lochs. Measuring 27½ sq miles, Loch Lomond is the largest single inland waterway in Britain. Its proximity to Glasgow means that parts of the loch get quite crowded in summer. The main tourist focus has always been on the western coast, along the A82, and the southern end, around Balloch, which can be a nightmare of jet skis and motorboats. The eastern coast north of Rowardennan, which the West Highland Way follows, receives few visitors.

The loch, formed by the action of glaciers, lay at the junction of the three ancient Scottish kingdoms of Strathclyde, Dalriada and Pictland. Some of the 37 islands in the loch made perfect retreats for early Christians. The missionary St Mirrin spent some time on Inchmurrin, the largest island, which is named after him.

The loch crosses the Highland line and its character changes quite distinctly as you move from north to south, with the most dramatic scenery in the north. The highest mountain in the area is Ben Lomond (974m) on the eastern coast.

Orientation & Information

Loch Lomond is 22 miles long and up to 5 miles wide. The A82, a major route north, follows the western coast through Tarbet and on to Crianlarich. The main thoroughfare on the eastern coast is just a walking trail, the West Highland Way, but it's reached by road from Drymen and Aberfoyle.

There are TICs at Balloch (☎ 01389-753533), Balloch Rd, open April to October; Drymen (☎ 01360-660068), in the library on the square, open May to September; and Tarbet (☎ 01301-702260), at the A82/83 junction, open April to October.

Walks & Cycle Routes

The big walk is the West Highland Way, but it's easy to access parts of the trail for shorter walks. (See the Activities chapter at the start of the book.)

From Rowardennan you can tackle Ben Lomond (974m), a popular five to six hour round trip. The route begins from the car park by the Rowardennan Hotel, and you can return via Ptarmigan (731m) for good views of the loch.

The main cycle route in the area is the Glasgow to Killin Cycle Way, which reaches the loch at Balloch and Inversnaid. Most of the route is set back to the east of the loch, through the Queen Elizabeth Forest Park. Along the western coast, the A82 is very busy in summer, but there are sections of the old road beside it that are quieter.

Boat Trips

The main centre for boat trips is Balloch, where Sweeney's Cruises (☎ 01389-752376) and Mullen's Cruises (☎ 01389-751481) offer a wide range of trips from £4.50/2 an hour, for an adult/child. There's a 2½ hour cruise (£6.50/3) to the village of Luss, allowing 30 minutes ashore. If this twee village looks like a film set, that's because it is. The village is popular with Scottish visitors hoping to catch a glimpse of the stars of the soap *Take the High Road*.

Cruise Loch Lomond (☎ 01301-702356) operates from Tarbet, and MacFarlane & Son (☎ 01360-870214) from Balmaha.

Places to Stay

Camping For campers, *Tullichewan Caravan Park* (☎ *01389-759475, Balloch*) costs £8 per tent and two people; the popular and well located *Forestry Commission Cashel Campsite* (☎ *01360-870234*), on the eastern shore, costs £7.90; and the *Ardlui Caravan Park* (☎ *01301-704243*) costs £8 to pitch a tent – you can also rent boats here.

Near the station in Ardlui, there's a *backpacker's camp site* (☎ *01301-704244*) which charges £4 per tent.

Hostels A very impressive hostel is *Loch Lomond Youth Hostel* (☎ *01389-850226*), in an imposing building set in beautiful grounds 2 miles north of Balloch, near Arden. It's open all year and the nightly charge is £8.60/7.10 for adults/juniors. You need to book in advance in summer. And yes, it's haunted.

Rowardennan Youth Hostel (☎ 01360-870259) is across the loch, halfway up the eastern coast, by the water. It's also an activity centre, and opens late January to the end of October. Beds are £7.75/6.50. It's the perfect base for climbing Ben Lomond.

B&Bs & Hotels There are numerous B&Bs, centred on Balloch, Luss, Inverbeg and Tarbet.

There is one pub you shouldn't miss. The *Drover's Inn (☎ 01301-704234)*, in Inverarnan at the northern end of the loch, has smoke-blackened walls, bare wooden floors, a grand hall filled with moth-eaten stuffed animals, and wee drams served by barmen in kilts. It's a great place for serious drinking; and you can stay here for £17 per person B&B. However, it's up for sale, so it could be quite different when you get there.

Getting There & Away
There are several Scottish Citylink buses a day (Nos 915/16/35) from Glasgow to Balloch (40 minutes, £3); other services continue up the west coast to Luss (55 minutes), Tarbet (65 minutes), Ardlui (1¼ hours) and, north of the loch, Crianlarich.

There are two railway lines. From Glasgow, one serves Balloch (35 minutes, £2.90); the other is the West Highland Line to Oban and Fort William (three daily), which follows the loch from Tarbet to Ardlui.

Getting Around
Ferry services run between Mid-Ross (a mile north of Arden) and Inchmurrin Island; Balmaha and the nature reserve on Inchcailloch Island; Inverglas and Inversnaid; and Inverbeg and Rowardennan.

INVERARAY
• pop 704   ☎ 01499

On the shores of Loch Fyne, Inveraray is a picturesque, small town with some interesting attractions. It's a planned town, built by the Duke of Argyll when he revamped his nearby castle in the 18th century. The TIC (☎ 302063) is on the street beside the loch.

Inveraray Castle
Inveraray Castle (☎ 302203) has been the seat of the chiefs of Clan Campbell, the dukes of Argyll, since the 15th century. The current 18th century building includes whimsical turrets and fake battlements. Inside is the impressive armoury hall, whose walls are patterned with more than 1000 pole arms, dirks, muskets and Lochaber axes. The dining and drawing rooms have ornate ceilings and there's a large collection of porcelain.

Near the castle, the Combined Operations Museum (☎ 500218) relates the town's role in the training of Allied troops for the D-day landings.

The castle opens early April to mid-October, Saturday to Thursday (but open Friday in July and August), from 10 am to 1 pm and from 2 to 5.45 pm (afternoon only on Sunday). Entry is £4.50/2.50; it's well worth visiting.

Inveraray Jail
The Georgian jail and courthouse, in the centre of town, have been converted into an entertaining tourist attraction, where you sit in on a trial, try out a cell, and discover the meaning of 'picking oakum'. Chatty warders and attendants in 19th century costume accost visitors. The jail (☎ 302381) opens daily from 9.30 am to 6 pm (last entry 5 pm); tickets are £4.30/2.10.

Inveraray Maritime Museum
The *Arctic Penguin*, a three-masted schooner built in 1911 and one of the world's last iron sailing ships, is now a 'unique maritime experience'. There are displays on the maritime history of the Clyde, piracy and the Highland Clearances, archive videos, and activities for children. Open daily from 10 am to 6 pm (5 pm in winter), entry is £3/1.50

Places to Stay & Eat
Inveraray Youth Hostel (☎ 302454) is a modern building on Dalmally Rd. Open mid-March to September, the nightly charge is £6.10/4.95 for adults/juniors.

There are several B&Bs. *Mrs Campbell's* (☎ *302258, Main St South*) opens April to October and charges £15 per person. The *Old Rectory* (☎ *302280*) has nine rooms from £14/28 for singles/doubles, and opens year-round.

The *Argyll Hotel* (☎ *302466*) looks out over the loch and offers pub meals from £4.50; B&B costs from £32.50 per person.

The best place to eat in the area is *Loch Fyne Oyster Bar* (☎ *600236*), 6 miles north of Inveraray. Half a dozen oysters are £4.90 and there's a good range of smoked fish and fresh seafood. Cheaper fish is sold in the attached shop.

Getting There & Away
There are six Citylink buses a day (three on Sunday) from Glasgow (1¾ hours, £5.80). There are also buses to Oban (1¼ hours).

KILMARTIN GLEN
This magical glen is the centre of one of the most concentrated areas of prehistoric sites in Scotland. The Irish invaders founded Dalriada and formed the kingdom of Alba here, which eventually united a large part of the country, so this part of mid-Argyll is seen as the cradle of modern Scotland.

The nearest TIC (☎ 01546-602344) is at Lochgilphead, 8 miles south of Kilmartin.

The oldest monuments date from 5000 years ago and comprise a linear cemetery of burial cairns, running south of Kilmartin village for 1½ miles. There are also two stone circles at Temple Wood which is three-quarters of a mile south-west of Kilmartin. Three miles north of Lochgilphead, at Kilmichael Glassary, elaborate designs are cut into rock faces; their purpose is unknown.

The hill fort of Dunadd, 4 miles north of Lochgilphead, overlooks the boggy plain that is now the Moine Mhor Nature Reserve. It was the royal residence of the first kings of Dalriada, and was probably where the Stone of Destiny, used in the investiture ceremony, was located. The faint rock carvings – an ogham inscription (ancient script), a wild boar and two foot-prints – were probably used in some kind of inauguration ceremony.

There are some 10th century Celtic crosses in Kilmartin churchyard. Beside the church, Kilmartin House (☎ 01546-510278) is an interesting centre for archaeology and landscape interpretation with artefacts from the sites, reconstructions, interactive displays and guided tours. The project was partly funded by midges – the curator exposed himself in Temple Wood on a warm summer's evening and was sponsored per midge bite! It opens March to December, daily from 10.30 am to 5.30 pm; £3.90/1.20.

Places to Stay & Eat
At *Burndale* (☎ 01546-510235) there's B&B in an old manse – £16 to £20 per person. *Kilmartin Hotel* (☎ 01546-510250) charges £18 per person (£25 with bath) and has a restaurant and bar; there's folk music here some weekends. *Cairn Restaurant* (☎ 01546-510254), nearby, does good lunches and dinners.

At Ardfern, adjacent to Craobh Haven and in an idyllic, peaceful location overlooking the Isles of Shuna and Luing, is *Lunga* (☎ 01852-500237), a grand 17th century mansion. The hospitable laird offers B&B from £15.50 to £19.50 per person. There are also self-catering apartments on this 1200 hectare estate. Lunga is about 10 miles north of Kilmartin.

Getting There & Away
For the 8 miles from Lochgilphead to Kilmartin there's only one daily bus in summer (not Sunday), leaving at 9.10 am (15 minutes, £1.50). From Oban to Kilmartin (1¼ hours, £3.30), the bus leaves at 1.45 pm.

KINTYRE
Forty miles long and 8 miles wide, the Kintyre peninsula is almost an island, with only a narrow strand to connect it to the wooded hills of Knapdale at Tarbert. Magnus Barefoot the Viking, who was allowed to claim any island he circumnavigated, made his men drag their longship across this strand to validate his claim.

Tarbert is the gateway to Kintyre. It's a busy fishing village that also attracts the yachting crowd. The TIC (☎ 01880-820429) is by the harbour. Above Tarbert is a small, crumbling castle built by Robert the Bruce.

Apart from Scots, who pack the B&Bs and camping grounds of Machrihanish, few other tourists venture down here and public transport is very limited. There are CalMac ferry terminals at Kennacraig (☎ 01880-730253) for Islay, and at Claonaig (no ☎) for Arran.

From Tayinloan, there are hourly ferries (20 minutes, £4.30 return) to the Isle of Gigha (pronounced ghee-a), a flat island 6 miles long by about a mile wide. It's known for the subtropical gardens of Achamore House (☎ 01583-505254), open daily from 9 am to dusk; entry is £2/1. Gigha cheese is sold in many parts of Argyll and is recommended, though not cheap. There are island walks and bikes can be rented from Gigha Stores. Several places do B&B: the *Post Office (☎ 01583-505251)* charges around £18 per person. The *Gigha Hotel (☎ 01583-505254)* has rooms for £34 to £40 per person, and a good restaurant and bar.

Campbeltown was left to decay slowly, but the new ferry to Northern Ireland is bringing in the tourists. There's a TIC (☎ 01586-552056) by the quay. A narrow, winding road leads to the Mull of Kintyre, popularised by the song – and the mist does indeed roll in. A lighthouse marks the spot closest to Ireland, 12 miles across the water. Campbeltown is linked by daily Scottish Citylink buses to Glasgow. From May to early October the Argyll & Antrim Steam Packet Company (☎ 0345-523523) runs a twice-daily ferry to Ballycastle in Northern Ireland (three hours).

ISLE OF ISLAY
- pop 4000   ☎ 01496

The most southerly of the islands of the Inner Hebrides, Islay (pronounced eye-lah) is best known for its single malt whiskies, which have a highly distinctive, smoky flavour. There are six distilleries, some of which welcome visitors with guided tours.

Since it's further from the coast than Arran or Mull, Islay receives fewer visitors than they do, but it's definitely worth the trip.

Orientation & Information
Port Askaig is the ferry terminal opposite Jura. Port Ellen is a larger place, with three distilleries nearby. Bowmore is the island's capital. It's 10 miles from both Port Askaig and Port Ellen, on the island's western coast. Around the top of Loch Indaal is the attractive village of Port Charlotte.

The TIC (☎ 810254), The Square, Bowmore, opens March to October.

Things to See
The island has a long history, which is related at the Museum of Islay Life (☎ 850358) in Port Charlotte. It was an early focus for Christianity. The exceptional 8th century Kildaton Cross, at Kildaton Chapel, 5 miles north-east of Port Ellen, is the only remaining Celtic High Cross in Scotland. Islay was also a seat of secular power for the Hebrides, and the meeting place of the Lords of the Isles during the 14th century. At Finlaggan (☎ 840644) are the ruins of the castle from which the powerful MacDonald Lords of the Isles administered their considerable island territories. At Bowmore, the Round Church was built in 1767 in this curious shape to ensure that the devil had no corners to hide in.

With over 250 recorded bird species, Islay also attracts birdwatchers. It's an important wintering ground for white-fronted and barnacle geese. There are also miles of sandy beaches and good walks.

Places to Stay & Eat
Port Charlotte has several B&Bs and a hostel, the *Islay Youth Hostel (☎ 850385)* which opens March to October and has beds for £5.40/4.40 for adults/juniors. *Mrs Halsall's (☎ 850431, Nerabus)* has rooms with bath from £17.50 per person.

In Port Ellen, the pleasant *Trout Fly Guest House (☎ 302204)* has rooms from £16.50 per person; evening meals are £10.50 (residents only). You can eat at the

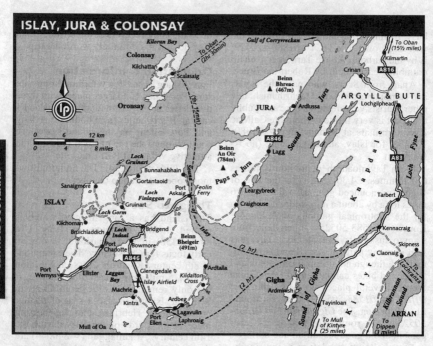

ISLAY, JURA & COLONSAY

White Hart Hotel (☎ *302311*), with main courses and vegetarian dishes from £5 to £12. The hotel has live music weekly in summer. The *Davaar Café* does good take-aways; fish and chips are £2.80. The *Harbour Inn* (☎ *810330*) in Bowmore, has a good seafood restaurant; B&B is £35/55 a single/double. *Tiree* (☎ *810633, Jamieson St*) offers B&B from £16.

Getting There & Away

CalMac (☎ 302209) has a ferry from Kennacraig to Port Ellen (2¼ hours, £6.45) and another to Port Askaig (two hours, £6.45). They operate daily except Wednesday, when there's only a ferry to Port Askaig, and Sunday, when there's only a ferry to Port Ellen. On Wednesday in summer there's a ferry between Colonsay and Port Askaig.

Getting Around

A limited bus service operates between Port Ellen, Bowmore and Askaig. Bowmore post office (☎ 810366, 810653) hires out mountain bikes for £10/50 per day/week.

ISLE OF JURA

- **pop 195**   ☎ **01496**

Jura is a magnificently wild and lonely island and one can understand why Orwell chose it as a retreat. He spent several months at Barnhill, a house in the north. It's a wonderful place to walk – in fact, there's really nothing else to do here, apart from visiting the Craighouse distillery in the island's only village. The mountain scenery is superb and the distinctive shapes of the Paps of Jura are visible from miles around.

North of the island, between Scarba and Jura, is the epicentre of a great tide race known as the Corryvreckan whirlpool.

Caused by the tide running out more slowly on the landward side of the islands, it can be heard roaring on a still day. Although stags have been known to swim it, and quite small boats to slip through, it has claimed many victims who didn't calculate the tides properly. It's most impressive an hour after low tide.

Walks

The Paps of Jura provide a tough hill walk that requires good navigational skills and takes eight hours, although the record for the Paps of Jura fell race is just three hours! Look out for adders – the island is infested with them, but they are shy snakes that will move away as you approach.

A good place to start is by the bridge over the River Corran, north of Lergybreck. The first pap you reach is Beinn a'Chaolais (734m), the second is Beinn an Oir (784m) and the third is Beinn Shiantaidh (755m). Most people also climb Corra Bheinn (569m), before joining the path that crosses the island to descend to the road.

Places to Stay & Eat

In Craighouse, there's B&B from £17 to £19 per person at *Gwen Boardman's* (☎ 820379, 7 Woodside). The *Jura Hotel* (☎ 820243) is a great place to stay and the place to drink on Jura. It charges from £30 per person; try to get the rooms at the front for the views. There's pub grub, and full set meals are £16.95.

Getting There & Away

You reach Jura via Islay. Western Ferries (☎ 840681) shuttles between Port Askaig and Feolin roughly hourly, Monday to Saturday, less often on Sunday (five minutes, 80p). The ferry also takes cars.

ISLE OF COLONSAY
• pop 106   ☎ 01951

North of Islay is the remote isle of Colonsay. It's an unspoilt island of varied landscapes which has a good sunshine record and receives only half the rainfall of the Argyll mainland. As well as cliffs and a rocky coast-

line, there are several beaches of white sand, the most spectacular being Kiloran Bay.

The island is of particular interest to ornithologists, with more than 150 species of birds recorded, including golden eagles. Botanists will appreciate the subtropical gardens of Colonsay House, known for their rhododendrons. Grey seals are often seen around the coast and wild goats inhabit some of the neighbouring islets.

At low tide you can walk across the strand to Oronsay, a small island to the south, where the ruins of the priory date from the 14th century.

Places to Stay & Eat

There are few places to stay (none of them cheap), and camping is not allowed. For B&B, there's *Seaview* (☎ 200315), on the rugged western coast, charging £22 per person. The *Isle of Colonsay Hotel* (☎ 200316), open March to October, is the only hotel. Most people stay there on a B&B and dinner basis; rates are around £60 per person, including bicycle hire.

Getting There & Away

CalMac has ferries Monday, Wednesday and Friday to Colonsay from Oban (2¼ hours, £9.30), and Wednesday from Islay's Port Askaig (1¼ hours, £3.15) and from Kennacraig on the Kintyre peninsula (3½ hours, £9.30).

OBAN & AROUND
• pop 8517   ☎ 01631

Oban can be inundated by visitors but, as the most important ferry port on the west coast, it manages to hold its own. By Highlands standards, it's quite a large town, but you can easily get around on foot. There isn't a great deal to see or do, but it's on a beautiful bay, the harbour is interesting and there are some good coastal and hill walks in the vicinity.

Orientation

The bus, train and ferry terminals are all grouped together by the side of the harbour, on the southern edge of the bay. Argyll Square is one block east of the train station, and George St leads north past the North Pier. From the pier, Corran Esplanade runs round the northern edge of the bay.

From Inveraray, the A85 brings you into the northern end of town.

Information

Oban TIC (☎ 563122) is on Argyll Square, next to the site of the Tolerable Inn, where Johnson and Boswell stayed on 22 October 1773 on their travels through the Western Isles. The TIC opens July and August, Monday to Saturday from 9 am to 9 pm, and Sunday until 7 pm; May, June and September until 5.30 pm (5 pm on Sunday); Mondays to Saturdays the rest of the year.

Things to See

Crowning the hill above the town is **McCaig's Tower**, built at the end of the 19th century. It was intended to be an art gallery, but was not completed and now looks like an ugly version of Rome's Colosseum. There are, however, good views over the bay from beside this peculiar structure. It's always open and there's no entry charge. There's an even better view from **Pulpit Hill**, south of the town.

Since 1794, **Oban Distillery** (☎ 572004) has been producing Oban single malt whisky in the centre of the town. There are tours (£3) Monday to Friday, year-round, and also on Saturday from Easter to October. Even if you don't want the tour or the whisky, it's worth visiting the distillery for the small exhibition in the foyer.

At Kilninver, 8 miles south of Oban, **World in Miniature** is a bit twee with its miniature houses and tableaux but shows considerable skill. It's open Easter to October, daily from 10 am to 5 pm; £1.80/1.30.

Walks & Cycle Routes

It's a pleasant 20 minute walk north from the youth hostel along the coast to **Dunollie Castle**, built by the MacDougalls of Lorne in the 15th century. It's open all the time and very much a ruin. You could continue along this road to the beach at Ganavan Sands, 2½ miles from Oban.

A TIC leaflet lists local bike rides. They include a 7 mile Gallanach circular tour, a 16 mile route to Seil Island, and routes to Connel, Glenlonan and Kilmore.

Organised Tours

On Sunday, Oban & District (☎ 562856), the local bus company, operates a range of half-day tours to Loch Etive, Inveraray, Glencoe, Kilmartin and the Sea Life Centre (10 miles to the north).

Day trips from Oban to Mull and Iona now use the CalMac ferry to Mull. Bowman & MacDougall's Tours (☎ 563221), 3 Stafford St, has a Mull and Iona tour for £16/10; a Mull, Iona, Staffa and Ulva tour for £26/16; and a coach tour to Tobermory for £10.

Places to Stay

Camping & Hostels The nearest camp site is *Gallanachmore Farm Caravan & Camping Park* (☎ 562425), 2½ miles south of Oban on the road to Gallanach. It's by the sea and costs around £6.

The popular *Oban Backpackers Lodge* (☎ 562107, Breadalbane St) charges £8.90 (including sheets). From the train station and ferry terminal walk north to the end of George St, past the cinema, and veer right into Breadalbane St. It's a friendly place with a communal kitchen. Breakfast costs £1.40.

Oban Youth Hostel (☎ 562025) is on the Esplanade, north of town, across the bay from the terminals. Beds are £8.60/7.10 for adults/juniors, and it's open February to December.

B&Bs & Hotels The cheapest B&B is *Jeremy Inglis'* (☎ 565065, 21 Airds Crescent), across the square from the TIC. Jeremy Inglis (alias Mr McTavish's Kitchens) charges around £7 per person – including continental breakfast – so gets booked up quickly. There are some double and family rooms.

Near the ferry terminal is *Maridon House* (☎ 562670, Dunuaran Rd), a large blue house with 10 rooms. B&B ranges from £13 to £19 per person. Book in advance in summer.

The main area for guesthouses and B&Bs is at the northern end of George St, along Dunollie Terrace and Breadalbane St. *Sand Villa Guest House (☎ 562803, Breadalbane St)* is an efficient place with 15 rooms, charging from £12.50 to £20 per person.

North of the town, Corran Esplanade is lined with more expensive guesthouses and small hotels, all facing seaward and most offering rooms with bathrooms. *Glenrigh Private Hotel (☎ 562991)* offers B&B from £23 per person. *Kilchrenan House (☎ 562663)*, near the youth hostel, is an excellent place, charging from £23 to £32 per person. At the far end of the Esplanade is *Barriemore Hotel (☎ 566356)*, another recommended place, with B&B from £25 to £30 per person. It does an excellent dinner.

There are a number of B&Bs below McCaig's Tower. *Mrs Frost's (☎ 566630, Laurgiemhor, Laurel Rd)* is the white building that looks like a castle, nearest to the tower. There are superb views and great breakfasts, but only one single and a double. B&B is around £15 per person. *Crathie Guest House (☎ 562619, Duncraggan Rd)* has seven rooms priced from £14/28 for a single/double. There are good views from *Invercloy Guest House (☎ 562058, Ardconnel Terrace)*. It offers B&B from £12/24 to £22/44.

In the centre, the *Palace Hotel (☎ 562294, George St)* has B&B from £16 to £25 per person, and most rooms have a bathroom.

Just north of the North Pier, on the Esplanade, the *Regent Hotel (☎ 562341)* is Oban's attempt at Art Deco. B&B in a room with bath costs £25 to £50 per person.

The top hotel is the *Manor House (☎ 562087, Gallanach Rd)*, south round the bay. Built in 1780, this house was originally part of the estate of the Duke of Argyll. It's worth eating in the hotel's restaurant if you're staying here. B&B and dinner ranges from £47 to £92 per person. Also highly recommended is *Heatherfield House* (see Places to Eat), which has been described as a restaurant with rooms.

Places to Eat

There's no shortage of places to eat in Oban. Most are along the bay between the train station and the North Pier, and along George St.

You can't miss the highly publicised, central *McTavish's Kitchens (☎ 563064, George St)*. There's a self-service café, and a Scottish show in the restaurant each night (see Entertainment).

Opposite the Oban Distillery, the *China Restaurant (☎ 563575)* does takeaways and table service, with most dishes under £6.

Studio Restaurant (☎ 562030, Craigard Rd, off George St) continues to deserve its good reputation. Local cuisine includes pâté and oatcakes, roast Angus beef and Scottish cheeses. A three course dinner costs £10.75 between 5 pm and 6.30 pm, £11.95 until 10 pm.

North of the North Pier, along Corran Esplanade, is *Coasters Pub*, a popular place with cheap food such as fish and chips, and curries for under £6.

The *Waterfront Restaurant (☎ 563110)*, by the train quay, is an excellent place for seafood. Most courses are from £10.25 to £16.50 (eg Scallops Tobermory with prawns in cream sauce, £12.75), but there's also a cheaper bar menu.

The best place to eat is *Heatherfield House (☎ 562681, Albert Rd)*. There's a set dinner in the non-smoking dining room for £16.50; the owners bake their own bread, cure their own hams and all seafood is locally caught. There are a few rooms here, from £43.50 to £50 per person including dinner, B&B.

Entertainment

The nightly Scottish show at *McTavish's Kitchens* (see Places to Eat) packs 'em in. It starts at 8.30 pm and there's dancing, a live band and a piper. It costs £1.50/75p for adults/children if you also eat here, £3/1.50 if you don't; there are also set meals from £7.95 including the show.

The *Gathering Restaurant & O'Donnells Bar (☎ 564849, Breadalbane St)* has live entertainment most nights. It's open from noon to 1 am; the restaurant specialises in steaks (prices up to £15), but the bar is cheaper.

The best pub is the *Oban Inn,* overlooking the harbour by the North Pier. It's a lively place which dates from the 18th century. It has a good range of single malt whiskies and the bar food includes breaded scampi (£4.95).

Getting There & Away

See the fares table in the Getting Around chapter. Oban is 504 miles from London, 123 from Edinburgh, 115 from Inverness, 93 from Glasgow and 50 from Fort William.

Bus Scottish Citylink runs two to four buses a day to Oban from Glasgow (three hours, £10). Oban to Inveraray is a 1¼ hour journey (£5). Another service follows the coast via Appin to Fort William (1¾ hours; £6) to Inverness.

Train Oban is at the end of a scenic branch line that leaves the West Highland line at Crianlarich. Up to three trains a day leave Glasgow for Oban (three hours, £17). There's a *Window Gazer's Guide* available on the train.

To get to other parts of Scotland from Oban, the train is not much use. To reach Fort William requires a trip via Crianlarich round three sides of a rectangle – take the bus.

Boat Numerous CalMac (☎ 562285) boats link Oban with the Inner and Outer Hebrides. There are services to Mull (up to seven a day), Colonsay (three times a week), Coll and Tiree (daily except Thursday and Sunday), Barra and South Uist (five services a week). See the island entries for details.

There are also up to four services Monday to Saturday to the nearby island of Lismore (five minutes, £2.15).

Getting Around

Oban & District (☎ 562856), the local bus company, has services up to McCaig's Tower and to the beach at Ganavan Sands.

Oban Cycles (☎ 566996), Craigard Rd, rents out mountain bikes for £2/10 per hour/day.

ISLE OF MULL
• pop 2678

It's easy to see why Mull is so popular with tourists. As well as having superb mountain scenery, two castles, a narrow-gauge railway and being on the route to the holy isle of Iona, it's also a charmingly endearing place. Where else would you find a police station that uses gerbils to shred documents (really), or a stately home where notices encourage you to sit on the chairs? And there can be few places left where the locals don't lock their doors. Despite the numbers of visitors, the island seems large enough to absorb them all; and many stick to the well worn route from Craignure to Iona, returning to Oban in the evening.

Orientation & Information

Two-thirds of Mull's population is centred on Tobermory, in the north. Craignure, on the eastern coast where most people arrive, is very small.

There are TICs at Craignure (☎ 01680-812377), opposite the quay, and at Tobermory (☎ 01688-302182), Main St. In summer, they're both open daily until at least 6 pm.

Things to See

There's little at **Craignure** apart from the ferry quay and the TIC. The Mull & West Highland Railway (☎ 01680-812494) is a toy train that takes passengers 1½ miles south to **Torosay Castle** (10 minutes, £3.40/1.40 single). Torosay Castle (☎ 01680-812421) is a Victorian house in the Scottish Baronial style. 'Take your time but not our spoons', advises the sign, and you're left to wander at will. Set in a beautiful garden, the house opens Easter to mid-October, daily from 10.30 am to 5 pm; entry is £4.50/2.

A 40 minute walk beyond Torosay is **Duart Castle** (☎ 01680-812309), a formidable fortress dominating the Sound of Mull.

The seat of the Maclean clan, this is one of the oldest inhabited castles in Scotland. The keep was built in 1360 and the castle was lost to the Campbells in 1745. In 1911, Sir Fitzroy Maclean bought and restored the castle. It has damp dungeons, vast halls, and bathrooms with ancient fittings. Lady Mac will take your £3.50 at the door (£1.75 for children) and in the excellent tearoom you can try to get her Aussie employees to reveal what goes into Lady Maclean's Chocolate Specials. The castle opens daily May to September, from 10.30 am to 6 pm.

In the north of the island is the beautiful little fishing port of **Tobermory**, Mull's capital. The brightly painted houses, reflected in the water, make this one of the most picturesque villages in Scotland. There are few things to see other than a small **Mull Museum** and the **Tobermory Distillery**, open only on weekdays, Easter to October. You can't pass the doors of the chocolate factory without going in. Somewhere out in the bay is the wreck of a ship that was part of the Armada, sunk here in 1588. No one is sure if the ship was the *Florida*, the *San Juan* or the *Santa Maria*, but rumours of a cargo of gold have kept treasure hunters looking ever since.

Eight miles west of Tobermory, at Dervaig, is **Mull Little Theatre** (☎ 01688-400245). With only 43 seats, it's Britain's smallest. There are regular shows in summer and the place has a good reputation.

One mile north of Dervaig, at Torrbreac, Sea Life Surveys (☎ 01688-400223) operates the UK's only **whale research centre**. It has cetacean displays and skeletons and is open April to October, daily except Saturday, from 10 am to 4 pm (closed from 1 to 2 pm).

Walks

The highest peak on the island, Ben More (966m), has spectacular views across to the surrounding islands when the weather is clear. If it's overcast or misty, wait until the next day because Mull's weather is notoriously changeable. A trail leads up the mountain from Loch na Keal, by the bridge on the A486 over the Abhainn na h-Uamha – the river 8 miles south of Salen. Allow five to six hours for the round trip.

Places to Stay & Eat

Tobermory has the best choice of places to stay. *Tobermory Youth Hostel* (☎ 01688-302481, *Main St*) opens mid-March to October. Beds are £6.10/4.95 for adults/juniors.

On Old Dervaig Rd, *The Cedars* (☎ 01688-302096) offers B&B for £16/30 a single/double. *Tom-A-Mhuillin* (☎ 01688-302164, *Salen Rd*) charges £14.50 to £18 per person. *Failte Guest House* (☎ 01688-302495, *Main St*) is in a central location and has rooms from £22 to £30, all with bath.

Mishnish Hotel (☎ 01688-302009, *Main St*) is the place to drink and the food's good value. Main dishes range from £4.50 to £12.50. There's often live music and sometimes a disco.

One of the top hotels on Mull is the *Western Isles Hotel* (☎ 01688-302012), with superb views over the bay. It costs from £38 to £87.50 per person, and there's a good restaurant. Run by Sea Life Surveys, *Mucmara Lodge* (☎ 01688-400223, *Torrbreac, Dervaig*) has rooms from £18/36. Also in the Dervaig area, beside the theatre, is the upmarket *Druimard Country Hotel & Restaurant* (☎ 01688-400345), which charges from £57.50 per person. A three course set meal is £22.50.

In the Craignure area, *Fois-An-Iolaire* (☎ 01680-812423) is only 350m from the ferry; B&B costs around £21/24 per person.

Getting There & Away

There are up to seven CalMac (☎ 01631-566688) ferries a day from Oban to Craignure; the trip takes 40 minutes and costs £3.25/22.70 for a passenger/small car. Smaller boats from Oban's North Pier ferry passengers out to Duart Castle; this is the cheapest way to reach Mull.

There's another ferry link between Fishnish and the mainland at Lochaline (20 minutes, £1.95), and boats run at least hourly every day. There are also Steading Holidays

MULL, COLL & TIREE

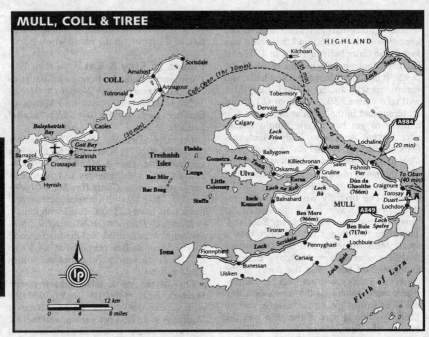

(☎ 01972-510262) ferries from Tobermory to Kilchoan (35 minutes, £4), Monday to Friday. The Oban-Coll-Tiree ferry doesn't currently call at Tobermory, but that may change.

Getting Around

There's a basic bus service run by Essbee Coaches (☎ 01631-566999) connecting the ferry points and main villages. The Craignure to Tobermory service (one hour, £2.65) goes up to five times a day all week (only once on Sunday). The Craignure to Fionnphort service (1¼ hours, £3.10) is equally frequent.

Cycling is a good way to get around and you can rent bikes from a number of places. In Salen, try On Yer Bike (☎ 01680-300501); it also has an outlet in the craft shop near the ferry terminal in Craignure. In

Tobermory, contact Mrs MacLean at Tom-A-Mhuillin (☎ 01688-302164), Salen Rd.

AROUND MULL
Isle of Iona

• pop 130   ☎ 01681

A five minute ferry ride (£3 return) from Fionnphort on the south-western tip of Mull brings you to Iona. St Columba landed here from Ireland in 563, before setting out to convert Scotland. A monastery was established, and it was here that the Book of Kells – the prize attraction of Dublin's Trinity College – is believed to have been transcribed. It was taken to Kells in Ireland when Viking raids drove the monks from Iona.

The monks returned and the monastery prospered until its destruction in the Reformation. The ruins were given to the Church of Scotland in 1899, and by 1910 the **Iona Abbey** (☎ 700404) was reconstructed by priests who established the Iona Community. It's still a flourishing spiritual community holding regular courses and retreats.

Iona is indeed a very special place, but the stampeding hordes that pile off the tour buses make it difficult to appreciate. The best advice is to spend the night here. After the crowds have gone, you can walk to the top of the hill, go to an evening service or look around the ancient graveyard where 48 of Scotland's early kings, including Macbeth, are buried. The grave of former Labour leader John Smith is also here, and is a focus for tour groups.

For B&B try *Bishop's House* (☎ 700306), opposite the ferry landing, or *Cruachan* (☎ 700523), half a mile from the ferry. Both are around £16 per person. The *Argyll Hotel* (☎ 700334) is the island's best and charges from £36/88 for a comfortable single/double.

Isle of Staffa

This uninhabited island is a truly magnificent sight, and you'll understand why it inspired Mendelssohn. It's the eastern end of the geological phenomenon in Northern Ireland known as the Giant's Causeway – huge, many-sided basalt pillars form the sides and line the walls of the cathedral-like **Fingal's Cave**. You can land on the island and walk into the cave. Staffa is also visited by a sizeable puffin colony. The TIC books tickets for the boat trips (2¼ hours, £10), most of which leave from Fionnphort.

ISLE OF COLL
• pop 172   ☎ 01879

There's a good walking trail round this little island, which has a good sunshine record but can be very windy. On the western coast the wind has formed sand dunes 30m high. There's the RSPB **Totronald Reserve** and two castles, both known as **Breacachadh Castle** and both built by the Macleans.

Near the castles, and 4½ miles from where the ferry docks at Arinagour, *Garden House* (☎ 230374, *Castle Gardens*) offers B&B from £17 per person, plus £12 for the evening meal. *Isle of Coll Hotel* (☎ 230334, *Arinagour*) has singles/doubles for £40/60

and a good restaurant serving lobster (£15) and scallops, the local specialities. A set dinner is £25.

CalMac ferries (☎ 230347) run Monday to Wednesday and Friday and Saturday to Tiree (one hour, £2.60) and Oban (from 2½ hours, £10.50). Sailings to Tobermory may resume in future.

You can hire mountain bikes from Tammie Hedderwick (☎ 230382), Coll Ceramics, Arinagour, for £7.50 per day.

ISLE OF TIREE
• pop 768   ☎ 01879

A low-lying island with some beautiful, sandy beaches, Tiree has one of the best sunshine records in Britain, particularly during early summer. It can also get fairly breezy, which makes it an excellent location for windsurfing – there are competitions each October. Call the windsurfing school (☎ 220399).

If you want to camp, make sure you get the landowner's permission first. *Mrs Cameron's* (☎ 220503, *The Shieling, Crossapol*), 3 miles from Scarinish, does B&B for £16 per person. *Scarinish Hotel* (☎ 220308), on the harbour, has rooms with bathroom for £25/46 a single/double.

Tiree airport (☎ 220309) has links to Glasgow. CalMac ferries are as for Coll.

Stirling & Around

Stirling includes countryside on both sides of the Highland line: agricultural and industrial Lowlands to the south and the bare peaks of the Highlands to the north. Stirling was formerly known as Central region, a name appropriate not only for its location, but also for the pivotal role it has played in Scotland's history.

The administrative capital, also known as Stirling, has a superb castle at the head of the Firth of Forth and the main route into the Highlands – and is the most strategically important spot in the country.

Loch Lomond lies on the western edge of the region (see Argyll & Bute). The

Trossachs, Rob Roy country, is another busy tourist destination. The mountainous north of the region gets far fewer visitors; public transport here is patchy in some parts, nonexistent in others.

For accommodation guides and information, contact Argyll, the Isles, Loch Lomond, Stirling & Trossachs Tourist Board (☎ 01786-470945, fax 01786-471301).

GETTING AROUND

For local transport information in the Stirling administrative region, phone ☎ 01786-442707. Midland Bluebird (☎ 01324-613777) is the main operator. Its Heart of Scotland Explorer ticket (£7.30) gives you one day's travel on all its services in the Stirling region, West Lothian and Kincardine, and half-price travel in Fife, Lothian and Strathclyde.

The Trossachs Trundler (☎ 01877-330969) is a useful summer bus service circling Aberfoyle, Callander and the pier on Loch Katrine. Some Day Rover tickets (eg from Glasgow) are valid on this bus; connecting fares from Stirling (with Midland Bluebird) are available.

Stirling town is the rail hub but the lines skirt round the region, so you'll be relying on buses if you don't have your own transport.

The West Highland Way cuts along the western region from Glasgow to Fort William (see the Activities chapter at the start of the book). There are numerous other walks in the area. Bartholomew's *Walk Loch Lomond & the Trossachs* is a useful guide available from TICs.

The Glasgow to Killin Cycle Way crosses the region from the centre of Glasgow via Balloch on the southern tip of Loch Lomond, Aberfoyle and Callander in the Trossachs, Loch Earn, Killin and Loch Tay. There are detours through Queen Elizabeth Forest Park and round Loch Katrine. It's a good route for walkers as well as cyclists because it follows forest trails, old train routes and canal towpaths. A brochure showing the route is available from TICs.

STIRLING

- **pop 37,000   ☎ 01786**

Stirling is such a strategic site that there's been a fortress here since prehistoric times. It was said that whoever held Stirling controlled the country, and Stirling has witnessed many of the struggles of the Scots against the English. The castle is perched high on a rock and dominates the town. It's one of the most interesting castles in the country, better even than Edinburgh Castle.

Two miles north of Stirling, and visible for miles around, the Wallace Monument commemorates William Wallace. Mel Gibson's movie *Braveheart* revived interest in this hero of the wars of independence against England. You can climb this Victorian tower for a panoramic view of seven battle ground's – one of them at Stirling Bridge, where Wallace beat the English in 1297.

A more famous battlefield is 2 miles south of Stirling at Bannockburn where, in 1314, Robert the Bruce and his small army of determined Scots (outnumbered four to one) put Edward II's English force to flight and reclaimed Stirling Castle. This victory turned the tide of fortune sufficiently to favour the Scots for the following 400 years, in the long struggle against the threat of English domination.

Although you can fit the main sights of Stirling into a day trip from Edinburgh or Glasgow, it's a very pleasant place to stay. There's an excellent youth hostel near the castle, and the town lays on enjoyable medieval markets and numerous other activities in the summer.

Orientation

The largely pedestrianised old town slopes up from the train station and nearby bus station to the castle, which sits 75m above the plain atop the plug of an extinct volcano. Stirling University's modern campus is to the north, by Bridge of Allan.

Information

The TIC (☎ 475019), 41 Dumbarton Rd, opens daily, July and August, from 9 am to 7.30 pm (to 6.30 pm Sunday), and shorter

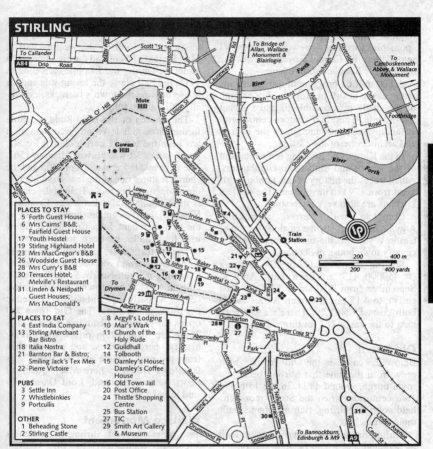

STIRLING

PLACES TO STAY
5 Forth Guest House
6 Mrs Cairns' B&B;
  Fairfield Guest House
17 Youth Hostel
19 Stirling Highland Hotel
23 Mrs MacGregor's B&B
26 Woodside Guest House
28 Mrs Curry's B&B
30 Terraces Hotel;
  Melville's Restaurant
31 Linden & Neidpath
  Guest Houses;
  Mrs MacDonald's

PLACES TO EAT
4 East India Company
13 Stirling Merchant
  Bar Bistro
18 Italia Nostra
21 Barnton Bar & Bistro;
  Smiling Jack's Tex Mex
22 Pierre Victoire

PUBS
3 Settle Inn
7 Whistlebinkies
9 Portcullis

OTHER
1 Beheading Stone
2 Stirling Castle

8 Argyll's Lodging
10 Mar's Wark
11 Church of the
  Holy Rude
12 Guildhall
14 Tolbooth
15 Darnley's House;
  Darnley's Coffee
  House
16 Old Town Jail
20 Post Office
24 Thistle Shopping
  Centre
25 Bus Station
27 TIC
29 Smith Art Gallery
  & Museum

hours, Monday to Saturday, the rest of the year. As well as guided walks of the town, the TIC has details of the popular ghost walks (£5/3) that take place Tuesday to Saturday.

The town puts on an entertaining program of events in summer, including ceilidhs at the guildhall on Monday and Saturday evening, pipe bands on Tuesday and Saturday, and medieval markets. There are also 'living history' plays performed in and around the castle.

Stirling Castle

The location, architecture and historical significance of Stirling Castle combine to make it one of the grandest of all Scottish castles. It commands superb views across the surrounding plains.

There has been a fortress of some kind here for several thousand years, but the current building dates from the late 14th to the 16th centuries, when it was a residence of the Stuart monarchs. The Great Hall and Gatehouse were built by James IV. The spectacular palace was constructed in the reign of James V; French masons were responsible for the stonework. James VI remodelled the Chapel Royal and was the last king of Scotland to live here.

A £20 million program of improvements at the castle is still in progress, but enough of the castle is accessible to make a visit worthwhile. There's a visitors centre with an audiovisual introduction to the history and architecture of the castle.

In the King's Old Building is the **museum** of the Argyll and Sutherland Highlanders, which charts the history of this famous regiment from 1794 to the present. The castle's kitchens are also very interesting.

Complete with turrets, spectacular **Argyll's Lodging** – by the castle at the top of Castle Wynd – is the most impressive 17th century town house in Scotland.

Stirling Castle and Argyll's Lodging (☎ 450000, HS) are open daily, April to September from 9.30 am to 5.15 pm (last entry); to 4.15 pm in winter. Admission to both costs £4.50/1.20. There's a car park next to the castle (£2 for three hours).

Old Town

Below the castle is the Old Town, which grew from the time that Stirling became a royal burgh, around 1124. In the 15th and 16th centuries, when the Stuart monarchs held court in Stirling, rich merchants built their houses here.

Stirling has the best surviving **town wall** in Scotland and it can be followed on the **Back Walk**. It was built around 1547 when Henry VIII of England began what became known as the 'Rough Wooing' – attacking the town to force Mary Queen of Scots to marry his son in order to unite the kingdoms.

The walk follows the line of the wall from Dumbarton Rd (near the TIC) to the castle, continuing round Castle Rock and back to the Old Town. There are great views from the path, and you could make a short detour to Gowan Hill to see the **Beheading Stone**, now encased in iron bars to keep ritual axe murderers away. **Mar's Wark**, on Castle Wynd at the head of the Old Town, is the ornate façade of what was once a Renaissance-style town house commissioned in 1569 by the wealthy Earl of Mar, Regent of Scotland during James VI's minority. During the Jacobite Rebellion in 1715, the Earl chose the losing side and his house became the town's barracks, eventually falling into ruin.

The **Church of the Holy Rude** is a little further down Castle Wynd, in St John St. It has been the town's parish church for 500 years. James VI was crowned here in 1567. The nave and tower date from 1456 and the church features one of the few surviving medieval open-timber roofs. Behind the church is the **Guildhall** (also known as Cowane's Hospital), built as an almshouse in 1637 by the rich merchant John Cowane. It's now used for ceilidhs, banquets and concerts.

The **Mercat Cross**, in Broad St, is topped with a unicorn and was once surrounded by a bustling market. Nearby is the **Tolbooth**, built in 1705 as the town's administrative centre. A courthouse and jail were added in the following century. The **Old Town Jail** opens daily from 9.30 am to 6 pm; £2.75/2. There are displays on prison life, 'living history' performances, and a good view from the roof. At the end of Broad St is **Darnley's House**, where Mary Queen of Scots' second husband, Lord Darnley, is said to have stayed.

Wallace Monument

Two miles north of Stirling is Scotland's Victorian monument to Sir William Wallace, who was hung, drawn and quartered by the English in 1305. The view from the top is as breathtaking as the climb up to it, and the monument contains interesting displays including a parade of other Scottish heroes and Wallace's mighty two-handed sword. Clearly the man was no weakling.

The Wallace Monument (☎ 472140) opens March to May (and October), daily from 10 am to 5 pm; June and September, from 10 am to 6 pm; July and August, from 9.30 am to 6.30 pm; November and December, from 10 am to 4 pm; and from 10 am to 4 pm at weekends in January and

February. In summer, an open-top tour bus links the monument with Stirling Castle, but you could also walk (see Walks & Cycle Routes).

Bannockburn

On 24 June 1314 the greatest victory in Scotland's struggle to remain independent took place at the Battle of Bannockburn. At the Bannockburn Heritage Centre (☎ 812664, NTS), the story is told with audiovisual displays. Outside is the Borestone site, said to be Robert the Bruce's command post before the battle. There's also his grim-looking statue, dressed in full battle gear and mounted on a charger.

The site, 2 miles south of Stirling, never closes but the heritage centre opens daily, April to October, from 10 am to 5.30 pm; the last audiovisual show is at 5 pm. In March, November and December, it's open daily from 11 am to 3 pm. Entry is £2.30/1.50.

Cambuskenneth Abbey

The only substantial remnant of this Augustinian abbey, founded in 1147, is the belfry. In medieval times, Cambuskenneth became one of the richest abbeys in the country, and its high status is supported by the fact that Robert the Bruce held his parliament here in 1326, and James III and his queen are both buried here. The abbey is a mile from both Stirling Castle and the Wallace Monument. It's open at all times; entry is free.

Walks & Cycle Routes

The best way to reach the Wallace Monument is on foot (45 minutes) or by bike; it takes about to walk there. Cross the railway line on Seaforth Place, continue straight ahead into Forth Crescent and Abbey Rd. There's a footbridge over the River Forth to Cambuskenneth, where you should visit the ruins of the abbey. The Wallace Monument is a mile north of here; follow Adysneuk Rd and turn left at the junction with Alloa Rd.

Organised Tours

From May to early September an open-top bus tour runs daily between the castle and

the Wallace Monument; there are two buses every hour. A day ticket costs £5.50/2.

Places to Stay

Camping *Witches Craig Caravan Park* (☎ 474947) is on the edge of the Ochil Hills in Blairlogie, 3 miles east of Stirling by the A91. Tent pitches cost from £4.

Hostels The façade of a 19th century church conceals *Stirling Youth Hostel* (☎ 473442), which is in a perfect location in the old part of town in St John St. Open year-round, it's a superb modern hostel with 126 beds in small dorms; the £11.50/9.95 charge for adults/juniors includes continental breakfast. The hostel has a less attractive annexe in Union St, open summer only.

Stirling Holiday Campus (☎ 467140), on the edge of Bridge of Allan, 3 miles north of town, lets student rooms in the summer for £18. There are only single rooms – 1030 of them – and there's also a pub, golf course and cinema on the landscaped campus.

B&Bs & Hotels There's a clutch of B&Bs on Linden Ave (just off Burghmuir Rd), which is fairly close to the bus station and less than half a mile from the train station. *Linden Guest House* (☎ 448850), at No 22, charges £15 to £22 per person. *Neidpath Guest House* (☎ 474840), at No 24, offers B&B for £15. *Mrs MacDonald's* (☎ 473418), at No 28, charges £15 to £17 per person.

Across the road from the TIC is *Woodside Guest House* (☎ 475470, 4 Back Walk), where B&B costs from £20/38 for singles/doubles with bathroom. Equally close to the TIC, at 1 Albert Place, *Mrs Curry's* (☎ 451002) has three rooms and charges around £18. Convenient *Mrs MacGregor's* (☎ 471082, 27 King St), does B&B from £18/30. Dinner is £7 extra.

A short walk north of the train station is the excellent *Forth Guest House* (☎ 471020, 23 Forth Place), just off Seaforth Rd. It's a small Georgian terrace house with a tiny rose-filled front garden and three comfortable rooms, all with bath. B&B costs from

£19.50 per person and evening meals are available for £13.

Central *Mrs Cairns'* (☎ *479228, 12 Princes St*) is an easy walk from the train station. B&B costs from £17 per person, with bath. *Fairfield Guest House* (☎ *472685, 14 Princes St*) has six rooms, five with bathroom, from £20/40.

Friendly *Terraces Hotel* (☎ *472268, 4 Melville Terrace*) is popular with businesspeople during the week, and rooms cost £55/72. It's an efficient hotel with good food and real ales.

The smartest hotel in town is the *Stirling Highland Hotel* (☎ *475444, Spittal St*), a sympathetic refurbishment of the old high school. B&B costs £95/123 in summer, but there are special offers available. B&B packages for over 60s cost from £51 per person.

Places to Eat

There are good views from the restaurant at *Stirling Castle* but it's rather overpriced. Down the hill from the castle, at the end of Broad St in Darnely's House, is *Darnley Coffee House* (☎ *474468*), a convenient pit stop as you walk around the Old Town.

Barnton Bar & Bistro (*3½ Barnton St*), opposite the main post office, is a popular student hang-out serving excellent all-day breakfasts. Open daily and until 1 am at weekends, it's a great place to eat or drink. *Smiling Jack's Tex Mex* (☎ *462809, 17 Barnton St*) does chicken nachos for £4.30.

Italia Nostra (☎ *473208, 25 Baker St*) is a busy Italian place that also does takeaways. There's also a branch of *Pierre Victoire* (☎ *448171, 41 Friars St*). Its £5.90 three course set lunch is reasonable value but the wooden chairs are a bit hard.

The *East India Company* (☎ *471330, 7 Viewfield Place*) is a good Indian restaurant and takeaway. There's a cheaper Balti bar upstairs.

Close to the castle, *Stirling Merchant Bar Bistro* (☎ *473929, 39 Broad St*) was formerly the town's bathhouse. It now serves contemporary Scottish cuisine and specialist ales and wines. It's open daily to midnight (11 pm in winter). *Herman's* (☎ *450632, 32 St John's St*) is around the corner at the Tolbooth. It's an excellent Scottish-Austrian restaurant with a two course set lunch for £7.95.

Popular *Melville's* (☎ *472268*), at the Terraces Hotel, has good-value bar meals from £3.75. A steak with brandy and cream sauce is £12.50.

Entertainment

Pubs *Portcullis* (☎ *472290, Castle Wynd*), below the castle, serves pub meals all day and has a good range of malt whiskies.

There are two pubs further down St Mary's Wynd: *Whistlebinkies* and the very popular *Settle Inn* – the oldest pub in Stirling. *Barnton Bar & Bistro* (see Places to Eat) is another popular place for a drink.

Getting There & Away

Stirling is 26 miles north of Glasgow, 35 from Edinburgh and 420 from London.

Bus Scottish Citylink has a number of services, usually hourly, from Glasgow (45 minutes, £3). Some buses continue to Aberdeen via Perth and Dundee. Stirling to Aberdeen takes 3½ hours and costs £11.90; you'll probably need to change at Perth. Local services are operated by Midland Bluebird (☎ *446474*).

Train ScotRail runs services to Edinburgh (50 minutes, £4.70) twice an hour most of the day, Monday to Saturday, hourly on Sunday. Not all services are direct. There are hourly trains from Glasgow (40 minutes, £3.70) and frequent services to Perth (35 minutes, £7.10), Dundee (one hour, £10.90) and Aberdeen (2¼ hours, £29).

Car For car hire contact Arnold Clark (☎ *478686*), Kerse Rd. Cheapest is a Nissan Micra at £16 per day.

Getting Around

It's easy to walk around the central part of the town. From the train station to the castle is about three-quarters of a mile. Check with the TIC to see if the shuttle bus has been reinstated if you want to save your feet on this uphill walk.

Woodside Taxis (☎ 450005) can organise sightseeing trips for up to eight people at around £18 per hour.

AROUND STIRLING
Dunblane

Dunblane, 5 miles north of Stirling, will for many years to come be associated with the horrific massacre that took place in the primary school in 1996. There's a seasonal TIC (☎ 01786-824428) on Stirling Rd.

The main interest is **Dunblane Cathedral**. Beloved of Ruskin, it's a simple, elegant, sandstone building – a superb example of the Gothic style. The lower parts of the walls date from Norman times; the rest is mainly 13th to 15th century. The roof of the nave collapsed in the 16th century, but the cathedral was saved from ruin by a major restoration project in the 1890s. It's open daily from 9.30 am to 6.30 pm (closing at 4.30 pm October to March, and closed Thursday afternoon and Friday in winter).

The small **cathedral museum**, on the square, relates the history of both cathedral and town. It opens May to October, Monday to Saturday, from 10 am to 12.30 pm and from 2 to 4.30 pm; free. You can walk to **Bridge of Allan** from Dunblane along the Darn Rd, an ancient path used by the monks. Alternatively, there are frequent buses from Stirling.

Doune

Seven miles north-west of Stirling, Doune is now a quiet rural town. It was once the capital of the ancient kingdom of Menteith, and was later famous as a centre for the manufacture of sporrans and pistols.

Doune Castle (☎ 01786-841742) is one of the best preserved 14th century castles in Scotland, having remained largely unchanged since it was built for the Duke of Albany. It was a favourite royal hunting lodge, but was also of great strategic importance because it controlled the route between the Lowlands and Highlands.

Mary Queen of Scots stayed here, as did Bonnie Prince Charlie – the first as a guest, the second as a prisoner. There are great views from the castle walls and the lofty gatehouse is very impressive, rising nearly 30m. The castle is open standard HS hours (but in winter it's closed Thursday afternoon and all day Friday); entry is £2.30/1.

A mile west from the castle is **Doune Motor Museum** (☎ 01786-841203), the Earl of Moray's collection of 50 vehicles, including the second-oldest Rolls Royce in the world and Scotland's only production model racing car, the JP Special. From April to September it's open daily from 10 am to 5 pm; entry is £3.50/2.50.

There are buses every hour or so to Doune from Stirling (£2.40); less frequently on Sunday.

Dollar

About 11 miles east of Stirling, in the foothills of the Ochil Hills that run east into Perthshire, is the small town of Dollar. **Castle Campbell** (☎ 01259-742408) is a 20 minute walk into the hills above the town. It's a spooky old stronghold of the dukes of Argyll and stands between two ravines; you can clearly see why it was known as Castle Gloom. There's been a fortress of some kind on this site from the 11th century, but the present structure dates from the 15th century. Opening hours and charges are as for Doune Castle.

There are buses to Dollar from Stirling and Alloa. From Kinross, the R5 service runs three times each Wednesday and Friday only.

THE TROSSACHS

The narrow glen between Loch Katrine and Loch Achray is named the Trossachs, but it's now used to describe a wider scenic area around the southern border of the Highlands.

As the tourist literature repeatedly informs you, this is Rob Roy country. Rob Roy Macgregor (1671-1734) was the wild leader of the wildest of Scotland's clans, Clan Gregor. Although he claimed direct descent from a 10th century king of the Scots and rights to the lands the clan occupied, these Macgregor lands stood between powerful neighbours. Rob Roy became notorious for his daring raids into the Lowlands to carry off cattle and sheep, but these escapades led to the outlawing of the clan – hence their sobriquet 'Children of the Mist'. He also achieved a reputation as a champion of the poor. He lies buried in the churchyard at Balquhidder, by Loch Voil.

Walter Scott's historical novel *Rob Roy* brought tourists to the region in the 19th century. Loch Katrine was the inspiration for Scott's *Lady of the Lake* and, since the beginning of the 20th century, the SS *Sir Walter Scott* has been taking visitors across Loch Katrine. The main centres in the area are Aberfoyle and Callander. During the summer months, a vintage bus, the Trossachs Trundler, links these two places with Loch Katrine.

Aberfoyle
* pop 545   ☎ 01877

Known as the southern gateway to the Trossachs, Aberfoyle is on the eastern edge of the Queen Elizabeth Forest Park, which stretches across the hills beside Loch Lomond. The TIC (☎ 382352), Main St, opens April to October.

Three miles east is one of Scotland's two lakes, Lake Menteith. The substantial ruins of the priory where Mary Queen of Scots was kept safe as a child, during Henry VIII's 'Rough Wooing', are on Inchmahome Island. A ferry takes visitors from the village to the priory. It's open April to September, Monday to Saturday from 9.30 am to 6.30 pm, Sunday from 2 to 6.30 pm; entry is £2.80/2.10 including the ferry.

About half a mile north of Aberfoyle, on the A821, is the **Queen Elizabeth Forest Park Visitors Centre** (☎ 382258), which has information about the numerous walks and cycle routes in and around the park.

Walks & Cycle Routes Waymarked trails start from the visitors centre on the hills above the town.

There's an excellent 20 mile circular cycle route that links with the ferry (☎ 376316) across Loch Katrine. From Aberfoyle, join the Glasgow-Killin Cycle Way on the forest trail, or take the A821 over Duke's Pass. Following the southern shore of Loch Achray, you reach the pier on Loch Katrine. The ferry should drop you at Stronachlachar, on the western shore (note that afternoon sailings don't stop here). From Stronachlachar, follow the B829 via Loch Ard to Aberfoyle.

Places to Stay & Eat *Cobleland Campsite* (☎ 382392) is off the A81, 2 miles south of Aberfoyle; tent pitches are £4.20. In Aberfoyle, *Mrs Oldham's* (☎ 382845, *Mayfield, Main St*) offers B&B from just £15 to £17 per person, with bath.

In the middle of the village, the *Forth Inn* (☎ 382372, *Main St*) does B&B; £27/46 in singles/doubles with bath. Bar meals are available all day.

Getting There & Away Midland Bluebird has up to five buses a day from Stirling. The Trossachs Trundler has a day ticket that includes Callander and Stirling for £8.10.

Callander
* pop 2300   ☎ 01877

Fourteen miles north of Stirling, Callander is a large tourist town that bills itself as the eastern gateway to the Trossachs. It has been pulling in the tourists for over 150 years, and tartan shops now line the long main drag.

The **Rob Roy & Trossachs Visitor Centre** (☎ 330342) is also the TIC. A Rob Roy audiovisual is shown daily May to September, from 9.30 am to around 9 pm (7 pm on Monday, Wednesday and Friday), and from 10 am to 5 pm the rest of the year; entry is £2.50/1.75.

Places to Stay & Eat There are numerous places to stay. *Trossachs Backpackers* (☎ 331200) is about a mile along Invertrossachs Rd, which runs on the south side of the river draining Loch Vennachar; beds are £10 to £12, including sheets and breakfast.

Ben A'an Guest House (☎ *330317, 158 Main St)* has five rooms and charges £16 per person. North of town, *Arden House* (☎ *330235, Bracklinn Rd)* has B&B from £20 per person. It's an excellent place and was used as the setting for the TV series *Doctor Finlay's Casebook*. Evening meals are available. Upmarket *Roman Camp Hotel* (☎ *330003)*, beautifully located by the river, dates from 1625 and has a good restaurant. Rooms cost £45 to £85 per person.

Getting There & Away Midland Bluebird operates buses from Stirling (45 minutes, £2.90). The Trossachs Trundler calls here and reaches the pier on Loch Katrine 35 minutes later.

Loch Katrine & Loch Achray

This rugged area, 6 miles north of Aberfoyle and 10 miles west of Callander, is the heart of the Trossachs. From April to September, SS *Sir Walter Scott* (☎ 01877-376316) sails Loch Katrine from Trossachs Pier at the eastern tip of the loch; tickets are £4.95/3.25.

NORTH CENTRAL REGION
Crianlarich & Tyndrum

These villages are little more than service junctions on the main A82 road, although they're both in good hiking country and on the West Highland Way.

At Crianlarich there's a train station and nearby *Crianlarich Youth Hostel* (☎ *01838-300260, Station Rd)*, where beds cost £7.75/6.50 for adults/juniors; it opens February to December. Tyndrum has a TIC (☎ 01838- 400246) in the car park of the Invervey Hotel.

Killin

In the north-eastern corner of the region, just west of Loch Tay, Killin is a pleasant village to use as a base for exploring the hills and glens of the surrounding area. There's a TIC (☎ 01567-820254) in the Breadalbane Folklore Centre, Main St. Killin is a popular destination for tour buses

that bring people to see the pretty **Falls of Dochart** in the centre of the village.

Walks & Cycle Routes Killin is at the northern end of the cycle way from Glasgow (see Getting Around at the start of Stirling & Around).

Five miles north-west of Killin, **Ben Lawers** (1214m) rises above Loch Tay. There's a visitors centre and trails lead to the summit (see West Perthshire under Perthshire & Kinross).

Places to Stay & Eat *Killin Youth Hostel* (☎ *01567-820546)*, open March to October, charges £6.10/4.95 for adults/juniors.

There are numerous B&Bs and hotels. At the *Falls of Dochart Cottage* (☎ *01567-820363)*, in the middle of the village, there's B&B for £15 per person; dinner is £8. *Clachaig Hotel* (☎ *01567-820270)* overlooks the falls; most rooms have bathrooms and cost around £21 per person.

Getting There & Away Getting to Killin by bus is tricky. Midland Bluebird operates a service on school days only from Stirling (1¾ hours, £4.45) via Callander. There's no bus from Pitlochry to Killin, but there's a daily (except Sunday) postbus service between Aberfeldy and Killin (three hours to Killin, 1¾ hours to Aberfeldy).

Fife

This region between the Firths of Forth and Tay refers to itself as the Kingdom of Fife – it was home to Scottish kings for 500 years.

Despite its integration with the rest of Scotland, it has managed to maintain an individual Lowland identity, quite separate from the rest of the country. As they still say outside the region, 'It takes a long spoon to sup with a Fifer'.

To the west, the Lomond Hills rise to over 500m; the eastern section is much flatter. Apart from a few notable exceptions inland, the main attractions in Fife are around the coast. For visitors, the focus of the region is undoubtedly St Andrews – an

CENTRAL SCOTLAND

ancient university town and ecclesiastical centre that is also world famous as the home of golf. To the south, along the indented coastline of East Neuk, are picturesque fishing villages. This coast is pleasant walking country, and at Anstruther there's the interesting Scottish Fisheries Museum.

GETTING AROUND

If you're driving from the Forth Road Bridge to St Andrews, a slower but much more scenic route than the M90/A91 is along the signposted Fife Tourist Route, via the coast.

Fife Council (☎ 01592-414141, ext 3103) has information about buses and produces a useful map guide, *Getting Around Fife*, available from TICs. Fife Scottish (☎ 01334-474238) is the main bus operator.

Trains are less useful in Fife than in some regions as the rails no longer run as far as St Andrews; the nearest station is at Leuchars, 5 miles from the town.

WEST FIFE
Culross
• pop 460   ☎ 01383
Around the 17th century, Culross (pronounced cooross) was a busy little community trading in salt and coal. Now it's the best preserved example of a Scottish burgh and the NTS owns 20 of the buildings, including the palace. It's a picturesque village with small, red-tiled, whitewashed buildings lining the cobbled streets.

Culross has a long history. As the birthplace of St Mungo, the patron saint of Glasgow, Culross was an important religious centre from the 6th century. The burgh developed as a trading centre under the businesslike laird George Bruce (a descendant of Robert the Bruce), whose mining techniques involved digging long tunnels under the sea to reach coal. A vigorous sea trade developed between Culross and the Forth ports and Holland. From the proceeds Bruce built the palace, completed in 1611. When a storm flooded the tunnels and mining became impossible the town switched to making linen and shoes.

The NTS Visitors Centre (☎ 880359), in the lower part of the Town House, has an exhibition on the history of Culross. You can visit **Culross Palace**, more a large house than a palace, which features decorative, painted woodwork and an interior largely unchanged since the early 17th century. The **Town House** and the **Study**, also early 17th century, are open to the public, but the other NTS properties can only be viewed from the outside. Ruined **Culross Abbey**, founded by the Cistercians, is on the hill; the choir of the abbey church is now the parish church.

Culross is 12 miles west of the Forth Road Bridge, off the A985. It's open May to September from 11 am to 5 pm (the Town House and Study open from 1.30 to 5 pm, and October weekends 11 am to 5 pm); £4.20/2.80. Fife Scottish (☎ 621249) bus Nos 14/14A runs hourly, every day, between Glasgow, Stirling, Culross and Dunfermline.

Dunfermline
• pop 52,000   ☎ 01383
Six Scottish kings, including Robert the Bruce, are buried at Dunfermline Abbey. Once the country's capital, Dunfermline is now a large regional centre surrounded by suburbs that aren't particularly attractive, but the abbey's worth a visit. The TIC (☎ 720999), 13 Maygate, opens year-round.

In the 12th century David I built **Dunfermline Abbey** on the hill here as a Benedictine monastery. It grew into a major religious centre, eclipsing the island of Iona (off Mull) as the favourite royal burial ground. Most of the abbey, having fallen into ruins, has been absorbed into the parish church, but the wonderful Norman nave, with its ornate columns, remains. Robert the Bruce is buried near the pulpit.

Next to the abbey are the ruins of **Dunfermline Palace**, rebuilt from the abbey guesthouse in the 16th century for James VI. It was the birthplace of Charles I, the last Scottish king born on Scottish soil. Both buildings (☎ 739026, HS) are open daily (closed Thursday afternoon and Friday in

Colourful Fishguard

Swansea Castle against the modern Swansea

Cliffs in the Pembrokeshire Coast National Park

Dylan Thomas statue, Swansea

The Cliff Railway in Aberystwyth

Abergavenny Castle

Llanthony Priory, Brecon Beacons

winter), standard HS hours; £1.80/1.30.

Dunfermline's most famous former inhabitant was Andrew Carnegie, who was born in a weaver's cottage, now a museum, in 1836. He emigrated to America in 1848 and by the late 19th century had accumulated enormous wealth, US$350 million of which he gave away. Dunfermline benefited by his purchase of Pittencrieff Park, beside the palace. **Andrew Carnegie Museum** (☎ 724302), Moodie St, opens daily April to October, from 11 am to 5 pm (afternoon only on Sunday), June to August from 10 am, and from 2 to 4 pm in winter; £1.50/free.

Dunfermline is a major transport hub, with frequent buses to Glasgow, Edinburgh, Stirling and Dundee. It's a half hour train ride from Edinburgh, and there's one direct train an hour. The train and bus stations are within walking distance of the abbey.

SOUTH COAST
Aberdour
• **pop 1800**   ☎ **01383**

It's worth pausing in this popular seaside town to see **Aberdour Castle** (☎ 860519, HS). It was built by the Douglas family in 1342 and the original tower was extended in the 16th and 17th centuries. By the 18th century, it was partly in ruins and abandoned by its owners. The east wing is still in use, however. An impressive feature of the castle is its attractive walled garden. There's a fine circular dovecote (called a doocot in Scotland), shaped like a beehive, dating from the 16th century. **St Fillan's Chapel**, in the grounds, dates from the 12th century. The castle opens standard HS hours (but closes on Thursday afternoon and on Friday in winter); £1.80/75p.

Bus No 57 runs every two hours to Edinburgh, daily; there are two No 7 buses an hour to Dunfermline.

Kirkcaldy
• **pop 49,570**   ☎ **01592**

Another town worth stopping in, Kirkcaldy (pronounced kirkoddy) sprawls along the edge of the sea for several miles. It has an attractive promenade and an interesting

museum and art gallery. In the second half of the 19th century it was the world's largest manufacturer of linoleum.

The TIC (☎ 267775), 19 Whytecauseway, opens year-round.

Kirkcaldy Museum & Art Gallery (☎ 412860) is a short walk from the train and bus stations. As well as covering the town's history, there's an impressive collection of Scottish and English paintings from the 18th and 19th centuries and an exhibition on the political economist Adam Smith, who was born here. It's open daily from 10.30 am to 5 pm (afternoon only on Sunday); free.

After looking around the museum, you could walk along the Esplanade to ruined **Ravenscraig Castle**, in the park by the sea. Two miles north of Kirkcaldy, in Dysart, is the **MacDouall Stuart Museum** (☎ 260732), the birthplace of the engineer and explorer who in 1862 became the first person to cross Australia from the south coast to the north. It's open June to August, from 2 to 5 pm; entry is free. Bus Nos K7 and K8 from Kirkcaldy centre pass this way twice every hour.

If you want to stay, *Invertiel House* (☎ 264849, 21 Pratt St), just south of the centre by Beveridge Park, is a comfortable place with B&B from £17 per person.

A major transport hub, Kirkcaldy is on the main Edinburgh/Glasgow to Dundee/Aberdeen rail line. There are two trains an hour to Edinburgh (30 minutes, £4.50). There are numerous buses from Hill St bus station (☎ 642394), two blocks inland from the Esplanade.

CENTRAL FIFE
Falkland
• **pop 1120**   ☎ **01337**

Below the soft ridges of the Lomond Hills in the centre of Fife is Falkland, an attractive village surrounded by rich farmland and with many buildings of architectural or historical importance. A very pleasant place to stay, it's known for its superb 15th century **Falkland Palace** (☎ 857397), a country residence of the Stuart monarchs. Mary Queen of Scots is said to have spent the happiest days of her life 'playing the country girl in the woods and parks' at Falkland.

French and Scottish craftspeople were employed to create this masterpiece of Scottish Gothic architecture, built between 1501 and 1541 to replace a castle dating from the 12th century. The chapel, which has a beautiful painted ceiling, and the king's bedchamber have both been restored; you can also look around the keeper's apartments in the gatehouse.

The wild boar that the royals hunted, and the Fife forest that was their hunting ground, have now disappeared. One feature of this royal leisure centre still exists: the oldest royal tennis court in Britain, built in 1539 for James V, is in the grounds and still in use. Although the palace still belongs to the Queen, it's administered by the NTS.

Falkland Palace opens April to October, Monday to Saturday, from 11 am to 5.30 pm, Sunday from 1.30 to 5.30 pm; £4.30/3.20.

Places to Stay & Eat *Falkland Youth Hostel* (☎ 857710, *Back Wynd*) opens mid-March to early October; beds are £4.65/3.85 for adults/juniors. Opposite the palace, there's *Ladieburn Cottage* (☎ 857016, *High St*) offering B&B with two *en suite* rooms costing from £20/36 a single/double. Evening meals are £7.

Getting There & Away Falkland is 11 miles north of Kirkcaldy. There are three buses a day Monday to Saturday to Kinross (see Perthshire & Kinross), and buses roughly every two hours from Perth and Cupar. The nearest train station is 5 miles away at Markinch, on the Edinburgh-Dundee line.

Cupar & Around
• pop 7610   ☎ 01334

Cupar is a pleasant market town and the capital of the region. The main reason to visit is to see the **Hill of Tarvit Mansion House** (☎ 653127, NTS), 2½ miles south of town. It was rebuilt for Frederick Sharp in the late 1800s by Scottish architect Robert Lorimer. Sharp was a wealthy Dundee jute manufac-

turer who bought the house as a showcase for his valuable collection of furniture, Dutch paintings, Flemish tapestries and Chinese porcelain. A 15 minute walk takes you to the top of the Hill of Tarvit, which has an excellent panoramic view. The house opens daily, May to September and October weekends, from 1.30 to 5.30 pm; £3.70/2.50.

Cupar is a busy transport centre with direct bus services to St Andrews, Dundee and Edinburgh. It's also on the Edinburgh-Dundee rail line.

ST ANDREWS
• pop 13,900   ☎ 01334

St Andrews is a beautiful, unusual seaside town – a concoction of medieval ruins, obsessive golfers, windy coastal scenery, tourist glitz and a contradictory university where wealthy English undergraduates rub shoulders with Scottish theology students.

Although St Andrews was once the ecclesiastical capital of Scotland, both its cathedral and castle are now in ruins. For most people the town is the home of golf. It's the headquarters of the game's governing body, the Royal & Ancient Golf Club, and the location of the world's most famous golf course, the Old Course.

History
St Andrews is said to have been founded by the Greek monk St Regulus in the 4th century. He brought important relics from Greece, including some of the bones of St Andrew, who became Scotland's patron saint.

The town soon grew into a major pilgrimage centre for the shrine of the saint. The Church of St Regulus was built in 1130 (only the tower remains); the adjacent cathedral was built in 1160. St Andrews developed into an ecclesiastical centre and, around 1200, the castle (part fortress, part residence) was constructed for the bishop.

The university was founded in 1410, the first in Scotland. James I received part of his education here, as did James III. By the mid-16th century there were three colleges: St Salvator's, St Leonard's and St Mary's.

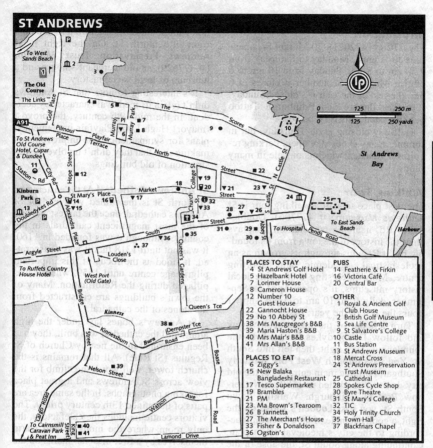

ST ANDREWS

To West Sands Beach

The Old Course

The Links

A91

To St Andrews Old Course Hotel, Cupar & Dundee

Kinburn Park

To Ruffets Country House Hotel

To Cairnsmill Caravan Park & Peat Inn

St Andrews Bay

To East Sands Beach

Harbour

To Hospital

Golf Place

Pilmour Place

Playfair Terrace

Hope Street

City Road

Station Rd

Doubledykes Rd

Alexandra Place

Bridge Street

Kinnessburn Road

Nelson Street

Watson Ave

King Street

Lamond Drive

Murray Pl

Murray Park

North Street

St Mary's Place

Market Street

South Street

Argyle Street

Louden's Close

West Port (Old Gate)

Queen's Gardens

Queen's Tce

College St

Church St

N Castle St

S Castle St

Abbey St

Abbey Road

The Scores

St Mary's Place

Kinness

Kinnessburn

Burn

Boase Road

Dempster Tce

To St Andrews Old Course Hotel, Cupar & Dundee

PLACES TO STAY	
4	St Andrews Golf Hotel
5	Hazelbank Hotel
7	Lorimer House
8	Cameron House
12	Number 10 Guest House
22	Gannoch House
29	No 10 Abbey St
38	Mrs Macgregor's B&B
39	Maria Haston's B&B
40	Mrs Mair's B&B
41	Mrs Allan's B&B

PLACES TO EAT	
6	Ziggy's
15	New Balaka Bangladeshi Restaurant
17	Tesco Supermarket
19	Brambles
21	PM
23	Ma Brown's Tearoom
26	B Jannetta
27	The Merchant's House
33	Fisher & Donaldson
36	Ogston's

PUBS	
14	Featherie & Firkin
16	Victoria Café
20	Central Bar

OTHER	
1	Royal & Ancient Golf Club House
2	British Golf Museum
3	Sea Life Centre
9	St Salvatore's College
10	Castle
11	Bus Station
13	St Andrews Museum
18	Mercat Cross
24	St Andrews Preservation Trust Museum
25	Cathedral
28	Spokes Cycle Shop
30	Byre Theatre
31	St Mary's College
32	TIC
34	Holy Trinity Church
35	Town Hall
37	Blackfriars Chapel

CENTRAL SCOTLAND

Although golf was being played here by the 15th century, the Old Course dates from the following century. The Royal & Ancient Golf Club was founded in 1754 and the imposing clubhouse was built a hundred years later. The British Open Championship, which was first held in 1860 in Prestwick, on the west coast near Glasgow, has taken place regularly at St Andrews since 1873.

Orientation

St Andrews preserves its medieval plan of parallel streets with small closes leading off them. The most important parts of the old town, lying to the east of the bus station, are easily explored on foot. The main streets for shops are Market and South Sts, running east-west. Like Cambridge and Oxford, St Andrews has no campus – the university buildings are integrated into the central part of the town. There's a small harbour near the cathedral and two sandy beaches: East Sands extends south from the harbour and the wider West Sands is north of the town.

Information

The TIC (☎ 472021), 70 Market St, opens June to August, Monday to Saturday from 9.30 am to 8 pm, Sunday from 10 am to 6 pm; in May and September it closes at 6 pm; the rest of the year it's closed Sunday. It makes theatre and Edinburgh Tattoo bookings and sells NTS passes.

Half-day closing is on Thursday, but in summer many shops stay open. Parking requires a voucher, which is on sale in many shops.

Walking Tour

The best place to start a walking tour is **St Andrews Museum** (☎ 477706), Doubledykes Rd, near the bus station. Displays chart the history of the town from its founding by St Regulus through its growth as an ecclesiastical, academic and sporting centre. More interesting than some local history museums, it's open April to September, daily from 10 am to 5 pm, shorter hours the rest of the year; free.

Turn left out of the museum driveway and follow Doubledykes Rd back to the roundabout. Turn right, then left into South St. You pass through **West Port**, formerly Southgait Port, the main entrance to the old city. It was remodelled in 1589 on Netherbow Port in Edinburgh. Walking down South St, you pass **Louden's Close** on the right, a good example of the closes built according to the city's medieval street plan. Continuing along South St, the apse of the 16th century **Blackfriars Chapel** stands in front of Madras College.

Opposite the Victorian town hall is **Holy Trinity**, the town's parish church, built in 1410. On the same side of the street as the town hall is **St Mary's College**, founded in 1537; beside it is the university library. The oak tree in the courtyard is over 250 years old.

Cross over to cobbled Market St – parallel (one street north) to South St – via Church St. Street markets are held around **Mercat Cross**, although the cross is now a fountain. The TIC is nearby, at No 70. At the TIC, follow Market St down to the junction with South Castle St, turn left, and then right into North St. On the right is **St Andrews Preservation Trust Museum** (☎ 477629), an old merchant's house and a museum of local social history.

It's interesting to note that St Andrews didn't retain its medieval character by accident. In the mid-19th century, the provost (mayor) Hugh Lyon Playfair implemented plans for sympathetic civic improvements making sure that they didn't involve the destruction of old buildings.

St Andrews Cathedral At the eastern end of North St is the ruined west end of St Andrews cathedral, once the largest and one of the most magnificent cathedrals in the country. Although it was founded in 1160, it was not until 1318 that it was consecrated. It stood as the focus of this important pilgrimage centre until 1559, when it was pillaged during the Reformation. Many of the town's buildings are constructed from the stones of the cathedral.

St Andrew's bones lay under the high altar; until the cathedral was built, they had been enshrined in the nearby Church of St Regulus (St Rule). All that remains is the **church tower**, well worth the climb for the view across St Andrews and a great place for taking photographs. In the same area are parts of the ruined 13th century **priory**. The visitors centre includes the calefactory, the only room where the monks could warm themselves by a fire; masons' marks on the red sandstone blocks, identifying who shaped each block, can still be seen clearly. There's also a collection of Celtic crosses and gravestones found on the site.

The cathedral site is open standard HS hours; tickets are £3.50/1.25 including entry to the castle. If you only want to visit the cathedral, it's £1.80/75p.

St Andrews Castle Round from the cathedral, above the sea, St Andrews castle was founded around 1200 as the fortified home of the bishop. In the 1450s the young king James II often stayed here. A visitors centre gives a good audiovisual introduction and has a small collection of Pictish stones.

In 1654 part of the castle was pulled down to provide building materials for the harbour wall. Enough survives to give you an idea of what each of the chambers was used for. After the execution of Protestant reformers in 1545, other reformers retaliated by murdering Cardinal Beaton and taking over the castle. The cardinal's body was hung from a window in the Fore Tower before being tossed into the bottle-shaped dungeon. The reformers then spent almost a year besieged in the castle; one of the most interesting things to see is the complex of **siege tunnels**, said to be the best surviving example of siege engineering in Europe. You can walk along the damp, mossy tunnels, lit by electric lights.

The castle opens standard HS hours and entry is either £2.30/1, or as part of the combined cathedral ticket (£3.50/1.25).

The Scores From the castle, follow The Scores west past St Salvator's College. At the western end is the **Sea Life Centre** (☎ 474786), which has the usual displays of marine life; entry is £4.25/3.25 and it's open daily from 10 am to 6 pm (from 9 am to 7 pm in July and August).

Nearby is the **British Golf Museum** (☎ 478880), open daily April to October, from 9.30 am to 5.30 pm, and with reduced hours in winter when it's closed Tuesday and Wednesday; entry is £3.75/1.50. It's an interesting, modern museum with audiovisual displays and touch screens, as well as golf memorabilia.

Opposite the museum is the **clubhouse** of the Royal & Ancient. Outside the club is the **Old Course**, and beside it stretch the sands of the beach made famous by the film *Chariots of Fire*.

Walks & Cycle Routes

The TIC has a list of local walks and sells OS maps. You could walk from St Andrews to Crail along the coast, but it's about 15 miles and you'd have to take care not to get caught by the tide. There are some excellent

Playing the Old Course

Golf has been played at St Andrews since the 15th century, and by 1457 was apparently so popular that James II had to place a ban on it because it was interfering with his troops' archery practice. Everyone knows that St Andrews is the home of golf, but few people realise that anyone can play on the Old Course, the world's most famous golf course. Although it lies beside the exclusive, all-male Royal & Ancient Golf Club, the Old Course is a public course and is not owned by the club.

However, getting a tee-off time is something of a lottery. Unless you book months in advance, the only chance you have of playing here is by entering a ballot before 2 pm on the day before you wish to play. Be warned that applications by ballot are normally heavily oversubscribed, and green fees are a mere £72. There's no play allowed on Sunday. You must present a handicap certificate or letter of introduction from your club to the St Andrews Links Trust (☎ 01334-466666). If you want to make a booking yourself, write a year in advance (for summer and autumn reservations) to The Secretary, St Andrews Links Trust, Pilmour Cottage, St Andrews, Fife, KY16 9SF.

If your number doesn't come up, there are five other public courses in the area, none with quite the cachet of the Old Course, but all of them significantly cheaper. Fees are as follows: New £31, Jubilee £29, Eden £21, Strathtyrum £16 and Balgove £7.

shorter walks along the southern part of the East Neuk coast (see East Neuk later in this chapter).

Since there are few steep hills in eastern Fife, cycling is pleasant and there are some good rides along the quiet side roads. Kellie Castle and Hill of Tarvit mansion are within easy cycling distance. We don't advise cycling the narrow, busy coast road from St Andrews to Crail due to dangerous bends and no verges in places.

Organised Tours

Guided walks of the town are run in summer (the University Tour, ☎ 462245) or all year (the Witches Tour, ☎ 655057).

Places to Stay

Camping & University Accommodation

From April to October you can camp at *Cairnsmill Caravan Park* (☎ 473604), a mile from St Andrews on the A915, for £6.50 for a tent and two people.

There's no youth hostel, but there's a bunkhouse 9 miles away near Anstruther (see Anstruther later in this chapter). Between June and September, however, you can stay for £10, room only, at the university's *Gannochy House* (☎ 464870, *North St*), next to Younger Hall. It has 40 single rooms, but there's no kitchen. You must check in between 2 and 6 pm.

B&Bs The cheapest B&Bs are south of the centre. *Maria Haston's* (☎ 473227, 8 *Nelson St)* is one of the closest and excellent value at £12 to £13 per person. Closer to the centre, *Mrs Macgregor's* (☎ 474282, *8 Dempster Terrace)* has just one room with three single beds for £16 per person.

Further south, on King St, there's *Mrs Allan's* (☎ 476326), at No 2, from £15; and *Mrs Mair's* (☎ 472709), at No 10, which charges £18/32 for a single/double. Both open year-round.

No 10 Abbey St (☎ 474094) is a bigger place with one single and two twin rooms. It's near the Byre Theatre, and charges £14 to £22.50 per person.

Almost every house on Murray Park and Murray Place is a B&B. The area couldn't be more convenient but prices are on the high side – most places charge around £22 per person. Rooms tend to have bathrooms. During summer you need to book in advance, but at other times it's probably best to knock on a few doors and pick what you like. *Lorimer House* (☎ 476599, 19 Murray Park)

opens year-round and charges from £18 to £26 per person. *Cameron House* (☎ 472306, 11 Murray Park)* offers B&B from £19 to £26 per person in comfortable rooms.

Number Ten Guest House (☎ 474601, *10 Hope St)* is a good place to stay. There are 10 rooms, all with bathroom for £25 per person.

Hotels Facing the bay, more expensive hotels line The Scores. At No 28, *Hazelbank Hotel* (☎ 472466) has rooms from £25 to £85 per person. *St Andrews Golf Hotel* (☎ 472611, 40 The Scores) is an excellent upmarket hotel 200m from the Old Course. Prices start from £78/130 for a single/double. There are also cheaper two-night breaks. The hotel has a bar and excellent restaurant.

Under 2 miles west of the town centre, *Rufflets Country House Hotel* (☎ 472594, *Strathkinness Low Rd)* is a top class hotel with a recommended restaurant. B&B and dinner ranges from £75 to £90.

If money's no object, stay at *St Andrews Old Course Hotel* (☎ 474371), the imposing building by the golf course at the western end of town. Rooms at this luxurious establishment range from £195/244 to £360. There are resident golf pros and a team of therapists and beauticians providing massage for both body and ego. If you're planning to drop in out of the sky, note that you need prior permission to use the helipad.

Places to Eat

If you're on a tight budget, *PM*, on the corner of Market and Union Sts, does breakfast, burgers and fish and chips from £1.85. For more upmarket snacks, head for *Fisher & Donaldson*, which sells Selkirk bannocks (rich fruit bread), cream cakes and a wonderful range of pastries.

Ma Brown's Tearoom (24 North St) is the place for coffee, cream tea or a light lunch. One of the busiest places at lunchtime is *Brambles (5 College St)*, which has excellent salads and vegetarian dishes. It's not open in the evening. *The Merchant's House* (☎ 472595, 49 South St) is in a venerable building. It serves delicious home-made soup (£1.50) and opens from 10 am to 5.30 pm.

The *New Balaka Bangladeshi Restaurant* (☎ 474825, 3 Alexandra Place) is recommended for curries. A three course meal costs around £15.

Ziggy's (☎ 473686, 6 Murray Place) is popular with students and has burgers from £3.95 and a range of Mexican dishes and seafood. *Ogston's* (☎ 473473, 116 South St) is a trendy café, bar and bistro.

Apart from the pricey restaurant at *St Andrews Old Course Hotel* (see Places to Stay), you need a car to reach the top restaurants in the area. The recommended *Peat Inn* (☎ 840206), south-west of St Andrews on the B940 (turn right off the A915), opens Tuesday to Saturday for lunch and dinner. Four-course set lunches are £18.50; set dinners, including excellent fresh seafood, cost £28 per person, excluding wine.

Finally, don't leave town without sampling one of the 52 varieties of ice cream from *B Jannetta* (31 South St). Don't confuse this main branch with the smaller shop at the other end of South St. This is a St Andrews institution. Most popular flavour? Vanilla. Weirdest? Irn Bru!

Entertainment

In July and August the Royal Scottish Country Dance Society holds dances and will show novices the steps. Contact the TIC for information. There are also other country dances in summer.

The *Byre Theatre* (☎ 476288, Abbey St) is being completely rebuilt and should reopen by 2000. In the meantime the company is performing in local halls – contact the TIC.

St Andrews has a good supply of pubs, reflecting its varied population. The *Central Bar (Market St)* is all polished brass and polished accents, full of rich students from south of the border. The *Featherie & Firkin (5 Alexandra Place)* has live music on Thursday and Friday. The *Victoria Café (St Mary's Place)* is popular with all types of students.

Getting There & Away

St Andrews is 55 miles north of Edinburgh and 16 miles south of Dundee.

Bus Fife Scottish (☎ 474238) has a half-hourly bus service from St Andrew Square, Edinburgh, to St Andrews (two hours, £5; £3.40 for students) and on to Dundee (30 minutes, £2).

Train The nearest station to St Andrews is Leuchars (one hour from Edinburgh, £6.80), 5 miles away on the Edinburgh-Dundee-Aberdeen-Inverness line. There are three direct trains to London each day. Bus Nos X59 and X60 leave every half-hour to St Andrews.

Car Ian Cowe Coachworks (☎ 472543), 76 Argyle St, rents Fiats from £27 per day.

Getting Around

Try Golf City Taxis (☎ 477788), 23 Argyle St. A taxi between the train station at Leuchars and the town centre costs around £7.

You can rent bikes at Spokes (☎ 477835), 77 South St; mountain bikes and hybrids cost from £8.50 per day.

AROUND ST ANDREWS
Kellie Castle

Kellie Castle (☎ 01333-720217) is a magnificent example of Lowland Scottish domestic architecture and is well worth a visit. It's set in a beautiful garden and many rooms contain superb plasterwork. The original part of the building dates from 1360; it was enlarged to its present dimensions around 1606. Robert Lorimer worked on the castle in the late 1800s, when it was not in good shape. It was bought by the NTS in 1970.

Kellie Castle is 3 miles north-west of Pittenweem on the B9171. It's open daily at Easter and May to September, from 1.30 to 5.30 pm, and October weekends from 1.30 to 5.30 pm. Entry is £3.70/2.50.

Fife Scottish (☎ 01333-426038) runs bus Nos 61A and 61B from St Andrews to

Arncroach, past the castle gates, four times daily Monday to Saturday (one hour).

Scotland's Secret Bunker

Three miles north of Anstruther is a fascinating attraction – what would have been one of Britain's underground command centres and a home for Scots leaders if nuclear war had broken out. Hidden 30m underground and surrounded by reinforced concrete are the operation rooms, communication centre and dormitories. An audiovisual display explains how it would have been used.

The bunker and museum (☎ 01333-310301), at Troy Wood by the B9131, is 5 miles south of St Andrews. It's open Easter to October, from 10 am to 5 pm daily; £5.95/3.25.

Fife Scottish (☎ 01333-426038) run nine buses daily (except Sunday) between St Andrews and Arncroach, Earlsferry or Leven, via Troy Wood and Anstruther.

EAST NEUK

The section of the south Fife coast that stretches from Leven east to the point at Fife Ness is known as East Neuk. There are several picturesque fishing villages and some good coastal walks in the area.

Crail

- pop 1290   ☎ 01333

One of the prettiest of the East Neuk villages, Crail, 10 miles from St Andrews, has a much-photographed harbour surrounded by white cottages with red-tiled roofs. There are far fewer fishing boats in the harbour now than there once were, but you can still buy fresh lobster and shellfish.

The TIC (☎ 450869), 62 Marketgait, opens Easter to September. The village's history and involvement with the fishing industry are outlined in the Crail Museum (☎ 450310), in the same building as the TIC.

Anstruther

- pop 3270   ☎ 01333

A large former fishing village 9 miles south of St Andrews, Anstruther is worth visiting for the Scottish Fisheries Museum (☎ 310628), by the harbour. Displays include a cottage belonging to a fishing family and the history of the herring and whaling industries that were once the mainstay of the local economy. It's open April to October, daily from 10 am to 5.30 pm (from 11 am to 5 pm Sunday), shorter hours the rest of the year. Entry is £3.50/2.50.

From the harbour there are sea angling trips or visits to the Isle of May, a nature reserve. You can make reservations for both at the kiosk (☎ 310103) near the museum. A three hour fishing trip costs £10. A five hour excursion to the Isle of May is £12/5; the crossing takes just under an hour. From April to July, the cliffs are packed with breeding kittiwakes, razorbills, guillemots, shags and puffins. Inland are the remains of St Adrian's Chapel, a 12th century monastery.

The helpful TIC (☎ 311073), by the Scottish Fisheries Museum, opens April to September, daily from 10 am to 5 pm (from noon to 5 pm on Sunday).

Places to Stay & Eat The *Bunkhouse* (☎ 310768, West Pitkierie) is 1½ miles out of Anstruther on the B9131. Beds cost £6.50, and it's best to book ahead in summer.

Just uphill from the museum, *Mrs Smith* (☎ 310042, 2 Union Place) charges £15 to £17 for B&B. The *Spindrift* (☎ 310573, Pittenweem Rd) is a very comfortable guesthouse a short walk from the village centre. All rooms have bathrooms and cost from £26.50 per person.

As well as basic cafés, Anstruther boasts one of Scotland's top places to eat. *The Cellar Restaurant* (☎ 310378, 24 East Green), behind the museum, is famous for its seafood – crabs, lobster, scallops, langoustine, monkfish, turbot etc. Advance bookings are essential. Lunch mains start at £6.50 and there's a set dinner for £28.50.

Getting There & Away The hourly Fife Scottish (☎ 426038) bus No 95 runs daily from Dundee to Leven via St Andrews, Crail, Anstruther (harbour), St Monans and Elie.

Pittenweem
- **pop 1640   ☎ 01333**

This is now the main fishing port on the East Neuk coast, and there are lively fish sales in the early morning at the harbour. The village name means 'place of the cave', referring to the cave in Cove Wynd which was used as a chapel by the 7th century missionary St Fillan. He was a saint who possessed miraculous powers – when he wrote his sermons in the dark cave his arm would illuminate his work by emitting a luminous glow.

Perthshire & Kinross

This area includes most of the former region of Tayside – the area covered by the River Tay and its tributaries. It contains as many variations in terrain as Scotland itself in miniature, from the bleak expanse of Rannoch Moor in the west, to the rich farmland of the Carse of Gowrie between Perth and Dundee.

From 838, Scotland's monarchs were crowned at Scone. Robert the Bruce signed a declaration of independence from England at Arbroath Abbey in 1320. Mary Queen of Scots was imprisoned in Lochleven Castle, and at Killiecrankie the Jacobites repelled the government forces.

The county town of Perth, built on the banks of the Tay, has a medieval church and many fine Georgian buildings. West of Perth there's attractive Strath Earn, with small towns and villages including the wealthy former resort of Crieff. Blairgowrie lies north of Perth, in an area known for fruit growing.

The Highland line cuts across this region – in the north and north-west are the rounded, heathery Grampians. North of Blairgowrie, the twisty road to Braemar follows Glen Shee and crosses the Cairnwell Pass, Britain's highest main road pass.

Flowing out of Loch Tay, in West Perthshire, the River Tay runs eastwards through hills and woods towards Dunkeld, where there's a cathedral on the riverbank. Queen Victoria, when looking for a place to buy, was quite taken by the Pitlochry area,

particularly the view over Loch Tummel. North of Pitlochry, at Blair Atholl, is Blair Castle, ancestral seat of the dukes of Atholl.

GETTING AROUND
The A9, Scotland's busiest road, cuts across the centre of this region through Perth and Pitlochry. It's the fast route into the Highlands and to Inverness – watch out for speed traps.

Perth is a major transport hub; phone Perth & Kinross Council's Public Transport Traveline on ☎ 0845-3011130. The main bus operators in the area include: Scottish Citylink (☎ 0990-505050), Stagecoach (☎ 01738-629339), Fife Scottish (☎ 01334-474238) and Strathtay Scottish (☎ 01382-484950).

Trains run alongside the A9, destined for Inverness. The other main line connects Perth with Stirling (in the south) and Dundee (in the east).

KINROSS & LOCH LEVEN
- **pop 4032   ☎ 01577**

Kinross lies in the extreme south of Perth & Kinross region, on the western shore of Loch Leven. It's the largest loch in the lowlands, known for its extensive bird life.

The helpful Kinross Services TIC (☎ 863680), by Junction 6 of the M90, opens all year (closed Sunday in winter).

Loch Leven Castle (☎ 01786-450000, HS), on an island in the loch, served as a fortress and prison from the late 14th century. Its most famous captive was Mary Queen of Scots, who spent almost a year incarcerated there from 1567. Her infamous charms bewitched Willie Douglas, who managed to get hold of the cell keys to release her then row her across to the shore. The castle is now roofless but basically intact. It's open standard HS hours, April to September; entry is £2.80/2.10, including the ferry trip from Kinross.

Gallowhill Farm Caravan Park (☎ 862364), open April to October, is 2 miles from Kinross, near the A91. Camping charges start at £4. There's basic B&B at the *Roxburghe Guest House* (☎ 862498, 126

High St) from £15 to £20 per person. Four miles from the M90 (Junction 6), near Milnathort, there's comfortable *Warroch Lodge* (☎ 863779). B&B costs £18 per person and evening meals are available for £9.

Scottish Citylink has an hourly service between Perth and Kinross (30 minutes, £2.50).

PERTH

- **pop 42,086   ☎ 01738**

In *The Fair Maid of Perth*, Sir Walter Scott extolled the virtues of this county town. 'Perth, so eminent for the beauty of its situation, is a place of great antiquity', he wrote, and this is still true.

Perth's rise in importance derives from Scone (pronounced scoon), 2 miles north of the town. In 838, Kenneth MacAlpine became the first king of a united Scotland and brought the Stone of Destiny, on which all kings were ceremonially invested, to Scone. An important abbey grew up on the site. From this time on all Scottish kings were invested here, even after Edward I of England carted the sacred talisman off to London's Westminster Abbey. In 1996 the stone was returned to Scotland, but it went to Edinburgh Castle rather than Scone.

Built on the banks of the River Tay, Perth grew into a major trading centre, known for weaving, dyeing and glove-making. It was originally called St John's Toun, hence the name of the local football team, St Johnstone. From the 12th century Perth was Scotland's capital, and in 1437 James I was murdered here. There were four important monasteries in the area and the town was a target for the Reformation movement in Scotland.

Perth is now a busy market town and centre of service industries. It's the focal

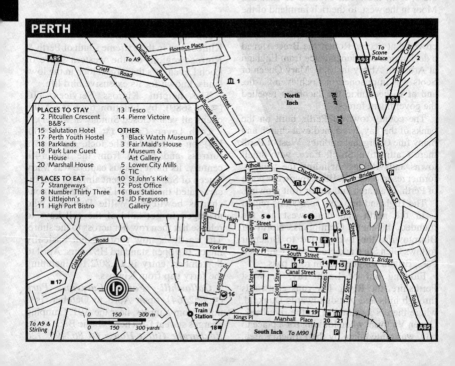

PERTH

PLACES TO STAY
2 Pitcullen Crescent B&B's
15 Salutation Hotel
17 Perth Youth Hostel
18 Parklands
19 Park Lane Guest House
20 Marshall House

PLACES TO EAT
7 Strangeways
8 Number Thirty Three
9 Littlejohn's
11 High Port Bistro

13 Tesco
14 Pierre Victoire

OTHER
1 Black Watch Museum
3 Fair Maid's House
4 Museum & Art Gallery
5 Lower City Mills
6 TIC
10 St John's Kirk
12 Post Office
16 Bus Station
21 JD Fergusson Gallery

point for this agricultural region and there are world famous cattle auctions of the valuable Aberdeen Angus breed. The bull sales in February draw international buyers.

The top attraction in the area is Scone Palace, but the town itself has a number of interesting things to see, including an excellent art gallery, housing the work of local artist JD Fergusson.

Orientation & Information

Most of the town lies on the western bank of the Tay; Scone Palace and some of the B&Bs are on the eastern bank. There are two large parks: North Inch, the scene of the infamous battle of the clans in 1396, and South Inch. The bus and train stations are next to each other, near the north-western corner of South Inch.

The TIC (☎ 638353), 45 High St, opens daily, April to October, and Monday to Saturday the rest of the year. Buy tickets here for the hop-on, hop-off bus service (£5/2) that takes in Scone Palace.

Scone Palace

Two miles north of Perth, Scone Palace (☎ 552300), the home of the Earl and Countess of Mansfield, shouldn't be missed. It was built in 1580 in the grounds of a former abbey; the abbey was destroyed in 1559 by a crowd inflamed by John Knox's sermon in St John's Kirk. With the destruction of the abbey buildings, the land passed to the Gowrie family, then to the Murrays.

In 1803 the palace was enlarged, and it now houses a superb collection of French furniture, including Marie Antoinette's writing table. Displays of 16th century needlework include bed hangings worked by Mary Queen of Scots. In the library is a valuable collection of 18th and 19th century porcelain. The palace is surrounded by parkland, including rare pine trees.

Scone Palace opens April to October, daily from 9.30 am to 5.15 pm. Entry is £5.20/3 for the house and grounds, half-price for the grounds only. The hop-on, hop-off bus (contact the TIC for tickets) goes this way, as does bus No 58.

Other Things to See

From the TIC, walk one block south to **St John's Kirk**. Founded in 1126, and surrounded by cobbled streets, this is still the centrepiece of the town. In 1559, John Knox preached a powerful sermon here that helped begin the Reformation and the resulting destruction of monasteries, including the one at Scone. The kirk was restored in the 1920s.

Four blocks south is the Round House, the old waterworks building on the edge of South Inch that now houses the **JD Fergusson Gallery** (☎ 441944). This Perthshire artist, one of the Scottish Colourists, was noticeably influenced by French styles after spending much of his life in France in the early part of the 20th century. The gallery is well worth seeing; it's open Monday to Saturday, from 10 am to 5 pm; free.

Two blocks north of the TIC is the **Museum & Art Gallery** (☎ 632488), which charts local history. There are displays of Perth art glass, an impressive silver collection and natural history displays. It's open the same hours as the Fergusson Gallery.

Nearby, on Curfew Row, is the **Fair Maid's House**, the house chosen by Sir Walter Scott as home for Catherine Glover, the novel's romantic heroine. The novel was set in the 14th century, but this house dates from the 16th, when it was a meeting hall for the town's glove manufacturers.

South-west of the Fair Maid's House, **Lower City Mills** (☎ 627958) is a restored Victorian mill. In the town's north, Balhousie Castle houses the **Black Watch Museum** (☎ 621281), charting the military campaigns since 1740 of Scotland's foremost regiment.

Places to Stay

The excellent *Perth Youth Hostel* (☎ 623658, 107 Glasgow Rd) opens late February to the end of October. Beds cost £7.75/6.50 for adults/juniors.

The main B&B areas are along Glasgow Rd, Dunkeld Rd, Dundee Rd and Pitcullen Crescent. *Iona Guest House* (☎ 627261, 2 Pitcullen Crescent) charges from £17/34 for singles/doubles; all with private showers.

Similar *Achnacarry Guest House* (☎ 621421), at No 3, charges £19.50 to £26 per person. Somewhat cheaper is *The Darroch Guest House* (☎ 636893), also on Pitcullen Crescent, which costs from £15/30 and has some en suite rooms. At No 17, *Pitcullen Guest House* (☎ 626506) charges from £20 per person.

Closer to the centre, there are several places along Marshall Place, overlooking South Inch. *Marshall House* (☎ 442886), at No 6, has three rooms with private showers and charges £15 per person. The very comfortable *Park Lane Guest House* (☎ 637218), at No 17, offers B&B for around £23 per person.

The *Salutation Hotel* (☎ 630066, 34 South St) was reputedly used as a headquarters by Bonnie Prince Charlie during the 1745 rebellion. Rooms cost up to £95, but if business is slack at weekends it sometimes offers B&B for as little as £30 per person.

Small but luxurious *Parklands (☎ 622451, St Leonards Bank)* is one of the top hotels and all rooms have baths, one with a spa. B&B starts at £37.50/70.

Places to Eat

There's a good coffee shop and restaurant at *Scone Palace*.

Littlejohn's (☎ 639888, 24 St John's St) provides the same standard menu it offers at other branches. Starters range from £1.65 to £6.45, mains £4.25 to £12.75. Vegetarian choices include lasagne (£4.45) and vegetable fajitas (£7.95). There's also a branch of *Pierre Victoire* (☎ 444222, 38 South St), with the usual three course lunch for £5.90. Over the road, *High Port Bistro* (☎ 444049), at No 47, serves three-course lunches for £5.50.

Strangeways (☎ 628866, 24 George St) is a bistro that's open daily. It's a good place to have a drink in the evening, but it stops serving food at 5 pm.

Number Thirty-three (☎ 633771, 33 George St) has a good oyster bar and restaurant specialising in seafood. Popular menu items include Mary's seafood soup and sticky toffee pudding with butterscotch sauce, both £2.95. A three course meal costs around £21.

Getting There & Away

Scottish Citylink operates regular buses from Perth to Glasgow (1½ hours, £6.80), Edinburgh (one to 1½ hours, £4.50), Dundee (35 minutes, £3), Aberdeen (2½ hours, £9) and Inverness (2½ hours, £9).

There's an hourly train service from Glasgow's Queen St (one hour, £11.40), two-hourly on Sunday, and numerous trains from Edinburgh. See also the fares tables in the Getting Around chapter.

STRATHEARN

West of Perth, the wide *strath* (valley) of the River Earn was once a great forest where medieval kings hunted. The Earn, named after a Celtic goddess, runs from St Fillans (named after the mystic who lived on an island in Loch Earn), through Comrie and Crieff and eventually into the Tay near Bridge of Earn. The whole area is known as Strathearn, an attractive region of undulating farmland, hills and lochs. The Highlands begin in the western section of Strathearn and the so-called Highland line runs through Comrie and Crieff, and through Kirriemuir and Edzell to Stonehaven.

Crieff

- pop 6359   ☎ 01764

Attractively located on the edge of the Highlands, Crieff has been a popular resort town since Victorian times. Until 1770 it was the scene of a large cattle fair; some vendors would come from as far away as Skye – swimming the cattle across to the mainland. There's a TIC (☎ 652578) in the High St, open all year.

The main attraction now is the **Glenturret Distillery** (☎ 656565), about a mile from the centre of town. Its visitors centre opens daily from 9.30 am to 6 pm (afternoon only on Sunday); the last tour is at 4.30 pm. It's all fairly touristy but a free dram is included in the price of £3.50.

Braincroft Bunkhouse (☎ 670140) has basic accommodation in small rooms for £8 per person. Braincroft is 5 miles from Crieff, 2 miles from Comrie, on the A85.

Auchterarder

- pop 2932   ☎ 01764

In the south of Strathearn, this small town stands in the centre of a rich agricultural area. Overlooking Auchterarder are the Ochil Hills, which run north-east into the Sidlaws. The TIC (☎ 663450), 90 High St, opens all year and houses an interesting heritage centre.

The town is probably best known for the internationally famous hotel on its outskirts. Splendid *Gleneagles Hotel* (☎ 662231) has three golf courses (including a championship course), a swimming pool, jacuzzi, sauna, gym, and tennis and squash courts. Room charges, including full use of the leisure facilities, range from £140/260 a single/double to £1250 for the Royal Lochnagar Suite (complete with antiques, silk-lined walls and hand-woven carpets). The hotel even has its own train station, 50 minutes (£8.80) from Glasgow, and there's complimentary transport between the station and hotel. However, if you can afford to stay here you can afford the limousine from the airport (£130).

PERTH TO AVIEMORE

There are several major sights strung out along the A9, the main route north to Aviemore in the Highlands. Frequent buses and trains run along this route; most stop at the places described in this section.

Dunkeld & Birnam

- pop 1050   ☎ 01350

Fifteen miles north of Perth, Dunkeld is an attractive town on the Highland line. There are some excellent walks in the surrounding wooded area. Dunkeld TIC (☎ 727688) is at The Cross.

Dunkeld Cathedral must be among the most beautifully sited cathedrals in the country. Half of it is still in use as a church, the rest is in ruins. The oldest part of the original church is the choir, completed in 1350. The 15th century tower is also still standing. The cathedral was damaged during the Reformation and burnt in the battle of Dunkeld in 1689.

On High and Cathedral Sts is a collection of 20 **artisans' houses** restored by the NTS. Across the bridge is Birnam, made famous by *Macbeth,* but there's not much left of Birnam Wood.

Good local walks include the Hermitage Woodland Walk from the car park, a mile west of Dunkeld. The well marked trail follows the River Braan to the Black Linn Falls, where the Duke of Atholl built a folly, **Ossian's Hall**, in 1758.

Scottish Citylink buses between Glasgow/Edinburgh and Inverness stop at the train station (by Birnam) four or five times daily.

Pitlochry

- pop 2439   ☎ 01796

Despite the tourist shops, Pitlochry is a pleasant town and makes a useful base for exploring the area. There are good transport connections if you don't have your own wheels.

The TIC (☎ 472215), 22 Atholl Rd, opens daily (except Sunday in winter). From late May to mid-September, it opens from 9 am to 8 pm.

If you haven't yet been on a tour of a whisky distillery, Pitlochry has two. **Bell's Blair Athol Distillery** (☎ 472234) is at the southern end of town; £3. **The Edradour** (☎ 472095) is Scotland's smallest distillery, 2½ miles east of Pitlochry; free.

When the power station was built on the River Tummel, a **fish ladder** was constructed to allow the salmon to swim up to their spawning grounds. It's at the north-eastern end of town, and you can walk up from the Pitlochry Festival Theatre to watch the fish, April to October, daily from 10 am to 5.30 pm. May and June are the best months.

Walks & Cycle Routes The TIC sells the useful publication *Pitlochry Walks*, which lists four short and four long local walks.

The Edradour walk (2 miles) goes past the distillery and the Black Spout waterfall. An 8½ mile hike goes round Loch Faskally, past the theatre and fish ladder, and up to the Pass of Killiecrankie. A 7 mile hike

CENTRAL SCOTLAND

takes you to Blair Castle; you could catch the bus back, but check times with the TIC before you go. There's a steep, 3 mile round trip to 400m-high Craigower, a viewpoint above Pitlochry. For a more spectacular view, tackle Ben Vrackie (841m), a steep, 6 mile walk from Moulin (on the A924).

Places to Stay & Eat Pitlochry is packed with places to stay, but anything central tends to be pricey. *Pitlochry Youth Hostel* (☎ 472308, Knockard Rd) overlooks the town centre and has great views. It's open year-round and beds cost £7.75/6.50 for adults/juniors.

The cheapest B&Bs are in Moulin, just over a mile to the north on the A924. At *Craig Dubh Cottage* (☎ 472058, Manse Rd), B&B costs around £14 per person; there's one double with bath for £30. Also on Manse Rd is *Lavalette* (☎ 472364), which is similarly priced.

There are plenty of places to stay along Atholl Rd, which runs through the town centre. *Craig Urrard Hotel* (☎ 472346), at No 10, charges from £20 to £28 per person. At No 8, the luxurious *Acarsaid Hotel* (☎ 472389) has 19 rooms, all with bath, from £25 to £40 per person.

One of the top places is the *Pitlochry Hydro Hotel* (☎ 472666, Knockard Rd), which has singles/doubles for £55/100.

The café at the *Festival Theatre* is recommended. The *Old Smithy* (☎ 472356, 154 Atholl Rd) is also quite good; braised pheasant flambéed in brandy is £9.95, and there are vegetarian choices.

Getting There & Away Scottish Citylink runs buses approximately hourly between Inverness and Glasgow/Edinburgh. Journey times and prices to destinations from Pitlochry are: Inverness (two hours, £7), Aviemore (1¼ hours, £5.50), Perth (40 minutes, £4.50), Edinburgh (2¾ hours, £6.30) and Glasgow (2¼ hours, £6.80).

Pitlochry is on the main rail line from Perth to Inverness. There are five trains a day from Perth (30 minutes, £7.10), fewer on Sunday.

Pass of Killiecrankie

The first skirmish of the Jacobite Rebellion took place in 1689 in this beautiful, rugged gorge 3½ miles north of Pitlochry. Highland soldiers led by Bonnie Dundee routed government troops led by General Mackay. As they fled, one of the soldiers is said to have jumped across the gap now known as Soldier's Leap to evade capture. An NTS visitors centre has a display on the battle.

Blair Castle & Blair Atholl

One of the most popular tourist attractions in Scotland, Blair Castle (☎ 01796-481207) is the seat of the Duke of Atholl. Outside this impressive, white castle, set beneath forested slopes above the River Garry, a piper pipes in the crowds each day. In 1996, the 10th duke died, leaving the castle and its 28,000 hectares to a charitable trust and only the title to his heir, a distant cousin in South Africa. Since the new duke has refused to acknowledge his title and has no plans to move to Scotland, it's unlikely that he will take his cousin's place at the annual May parade of the Atholl Highlanders, the only private army in the country.

The original tower was built in 1269, but the castle has undergone significant remodelling since then. In 1746, it was besieged by the Jacobites, the last castle in Britain to be subjected to siege.

Thirty-two rooms are open to the public and they are packed with paintings, arms and armour, china, lace, and embroidery, presenting a wonderful picture of upper-class Highland life from the 1500s to the present. One of the most impressive rooms is the ballroom, which has a wooden roof and walls covered in antlers.

Blair Castle is 7 miles north of Pitlochry, and a mile from Blair Atholl village. It's open daily, April to October, from 10 am to 6 pm (last entry 5 pm); tickets cost £5.50/4.50.

Other attractions in Blair Atholl village include a working **water mill** (☎ 01796-481321) by the river.

You can hire bikes from Atholl Mountain Bikes (☎ 01796-481646). It has a leaflet listing cycle routes in the area, including a

16 mile ride along an estate road up Glen Tilt, a 12 mile ride around Bruar Falls and Old Struan, or a 6 mile ride to Killiecrankie Pass and back.

The *Atholl Arms* (☎ *01796-481205)* is a pub near the station; B&B is £32.50 per person.

Elizabeth Yule Buses (☎ 01796-472290) runs a service two to four times daily between Pitlochry and Blair (20 minutes, £1.10). There's a train station in the village, but not all trains stop here.

For a continuation of this route, see Aviemore in the Highlands & Northern Islands chapter.

WEST PERTHSHIRE

The lochs and hills of this remote area can be reached by public transport, but buses are usually once-a-day postal services.

From the A9, south of Pitlochry, the A827 heads west to Crianlarich and the western coast. At **Aberfeldy** there's a TIC (☎ 01887-820276), The Square, open all year. **Castle Menzies** (☎ 01887-820982), 1½ miles west of town, is the seat of the Chief of the Clan Menzies; it's open daily. West of Aberfeldy, the pretty village of **Fortingall** is famous as the birthplace of Pontius Pilate.

The bulk of Ben Lawers (1214m) rises above Loch Tay. It's in the care of the NTS, which has a visitors centre on the slopes of the mountain. A trail leads to the summit from the centre, but a more interesting, seven hour route is up Lawers Burn from Machuim Farm, just north of Lawers villages. You can walk around the ridges via Meall Garbh to the summit, but you should take a good map (OS sheet 51).

At the western end of Loch Tay is the village of Killin (see Stirling & Around earlier in this chapter).

Dundee & Angus

Formerly part of the region of Tayside, Dundee and Angus are now two separate unitary authorities.

Dundee was once a whaling port and the centre of the thriving jute industry. It's now a victim of 20th century decline and chronic unemployment, but has several interesting attractions for visitors, including Captain Scott's ship *Discovery*.

The main draw in Angus is Glamis Castle of *Macbeth* fame. Angus is an attractive county of peaceful glens running down to the sea. The area was part of the Pictish kingdom in the 7th and 8th centuries, and there are interesting Pictish symbol stones at Aberlemno.

GETTING AROUND

Angus Council publishes an annual *Public Transport Map & Guide*, available from TICs. For information on buses within the Dundee & Broughty Ferry area phone ☎ 01382-433125. For services outside this area contact Strathtay Scottish (☎ 01382-228054).

DUNDEE

- **pop 177,540** ☎ **01382**

Poor Dundee. This grey city is an unfortunate example of the worst of 1960s and 70s town planning – ugly blocks of flats and office buildings joined by unsightly concrete walkways. Once, there were more millionaires per head in Dundee than anywhere else in Britain. Today it's Dole City, with the highest rate of unemployment in Scotland, second in the UK only to Liverpool.

In 1993 the city decided to stake all its tourist fortunes on one main attraction – Captain Scott's polar research ship *Discovery*, but the city's main asset is its people. Despite the feeling of desolation here, the vigour that remains in the city is in the hearts of Dundonians, who are among the friendliest, most welcoming and most entertaining people you'll meet anywhere in the country.

It's worth staying here awhile. Dundee's hotels and restaurants are good value, there are some great drinking places and 4 miles east of the city is the seaside suburb of Broughty Ferry.

Pictish Symbol Stones

The Romans permanently occupied only the southern half of Britain up to 410. Caledonia, the section north of Edinburgh and Glasgow, was mostly left alone, especially after the mysterious disappearance of the Ninth Legion. Caledonia was the homeland of the Picts, about whom little is known. In the 9th century they were culturally absorbed by the Scots, leaving a few archaeological remains and a scattering of Pictish place names beginning with Pit-. However, there are hundreds of mysterious standing stones decorated with intricate symbols, mainly in the north-east. The capital of the ancient Southern Pictish kingdom is said to have been at Forteviot in Strathearn, and Pictish symbol stones are to be found throughout this area and all the way up the eastern coast of Scotland into Sutherland and Caithness.

It's believed that the stones were set up to record Pictish lineages and alliances, but no-one is yet quite sure exactly how the system worked. The stones fall into three groups. Class I, the earliest, are rough blocks of stone, carved with any combination from a basic set of 28 symbols. Class II are decorated with a Celtic cross as well as with symbols. Class III, dating from the end of the Pictish era (790-840), have only figures and a cross.

With your own transport, it's possible to follow a number of symbol-stone trails in the area. Starting at Dundee (visit the McManus Galleries first), drive north-east to Arbroath. On the outskirts of Arbroath is St Vigeans Museum which contains several interesting stones. Continue north along the A92 to Montrose, where there are more stones in the local museum. Along the A935, in Brechin Cathedral, is a good example of a Class III stone. From Brechin, take the B9134 to Aberlemno, where there are excellent examples of all three classes. Along the A94, at Meigle, there's a museum with one of the best collections of stones in the country.

For more information, it's worth getting a copy of *The Pictish Trail* by Anthony Jackson (Orkney Press), which lists 11 driving tours, or his more detailed *Symbol Stones of Scotland*, both available in TICs.

History

Dundee first began to grow in importance as a result of trade links with Flanders and the Baltic ports. It was awarded the first of its royal charters by King William in the late 12th century.

In its chequered history, Dundee was captured by Edward I, besieged by Henry VIII and destroyed by Cromwellian forces in the 17th century. It became the second most important trading city in Scotland (after Edinburgh).

In the 19th century, Dundee was a major player in the shipbuilding and railway engineering industries. Linen and wool gave way to jute and, since whale oil was used in the production of jute, whaling developed alongside. At one time there were as many as 43,000 people employed in the textile industry, but as the jute workers became redundant, light engineering, electronics and food processing provided employment.

Dundee is often called the city of the three 'Js' – jute, jam and journalism. No jute is produced here any more, and when the famous Keiller jam factory was taken over in 1988 production was transferred to England. There is still journalism, and DC Thomson, best known for its comics (such as the *Beano*), is the city's largest employer.

Orientation

Most people approach the city from the Tay Road Bridge or along the A85 from Perth; both routes take you right into the centre. The train station and Captain Scott's ship *Discovery* are near the bridge; the bus station is a short walk to the north, just off Seagate. Four miles east of Dundee is Broughty Ferry, Dundee's seaside resort. It's connected by regular buses and is a pleasant place to stay.

Information

The very helpful TIC (☎ 434664), 4 City Square, opens from May to September, Monday to Saturday from 9 am to 6 pm, and Sunday from 10 am to 4 pm; from October to April, it's open Monday to Saturday only, from 9 am to 5 pm. As well as the usual bed booking facility (£1 for local bookings), it sells Scottish Citylink and National Express tickets. Pick up a copy of *What's On*.

Discovery Point

Make an effort to see the much-publicised visitor attraction, centred on Captain Scott's famous polar expedition vessel, the research ship *Discovery* (☎ 201245). The ship was constructed here in 1900 with a hull more than half a metre thick to survive the Antarctic pack ice. Scott sailed for the Antarctic in 1901 and, in a not uneventful voyage, spent two winters trapped in the ice.

After viewing the interesting exhibitions and audiovisual displays in the main building, go on board the ship to see the cabins used by Scott and his crew. The complex is on the bank of the Firth of Tay, near the Tay Road Bridge. It's open daily from 10 am to 5 pm (to 4 pm November to March); entry is £4.50/3.45.

HM Frigate Unicorn

Unlike the *Discovery*, Dundee's other floating tourist sight retains the atmosphere of an old ship. Built as a warship in 1824, the *Unicorn* (☎ 200900) is the oldest British-built warship still afloat – perhaps because it never saw action. By the mid-19th century, sailing ships were outclassed by steam and the *Unicorn* served as storage for gunpowder, then later as a training vessel. When it was proposed to break up the historic ship for scrap in the 1960s a preservation society was formed.

Wandering around the four decks gives you an excellent impression of what it must have been like for the crew to live in such cramped conditions. The *Unicorn* is berthed in Victoria Dock, just east of the Tay Bridge. It's open daily from 10 am to 5 pm (November to February, weekdays only, from 10 am to 4 pm); tickets are £3/2 including a guided tour.

Other Sights

The **McManus Galleries** (☎ 432020), Albert Square, is a solid Victorian Gothic building designed by Gilbert Scott, containing the city's art collection and museum. The interesting exhibits are well displayed and include the history of the city from the Iron Age. There's an impressive display of Scottish Victorian paintings, furniture and silver. Look out for the display on William McGonagall, Scotland's worst poet, whose lines about the Tay Rail Bridge disaster are memorably awful. The galleries open Tuesday to Saturday from 10 am to 5 pm (from 11 am Monday); entry is free.

Over the road is the **Howff Burial Ground**, a historic graveyard given to the people of Dundee by Mary Queen of Scots. The carved gravestones feature the signs and symbols of the old craft guilds and date back to the 16th century.

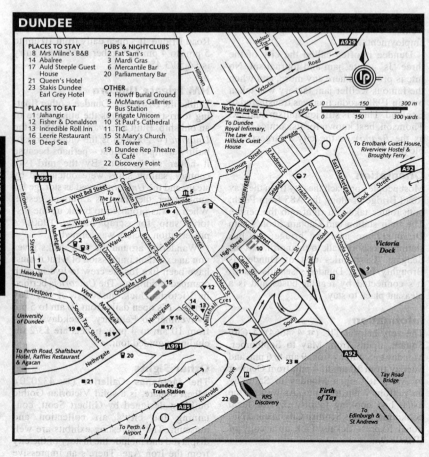

DUNDEE

PLACES TO STAY	
8	Mrs Milne's B&B
14	Abalree
17	Auld Steeple Guest House
21	Queen's Hotel
23	Stakis Dundee Earl Grey Hotel

PLACES TO EAT	
1	Jahangir
12	Fisher & Donaldson
13	Incredible Roll Inn
16	Leerie Restaurant
18	Deep Sea

PUBS & NIGHTCLUBS	
2	Fat Sam's
3	Mardi Gras
6	Mercantile Bar
20	Parliamentary Bar

OTHER	
4	Howff Burial Ground
5	McManus Galleries
7	Bus Station
9	Frigate Unicorn
10	St Paul's Cathedral
11	TIC
15	St Mary's Church & Tower
19	Dundee Rep Theatre & Café
22	Discovery Point

CENTRAL SCOTLAND

It's worth the hike up to **The Law** – at 174m, the highest point in the city. It's the remains of an ancient volcanic plug and there are great views over the city and across to Fife.

You also get a good view of the two bridges over the Tay. The 1½ mile road bridge was opened in 1966. The railway bridge, at just over 2 miles long, is the longest in Europe. It was built in 1887, replacing a section destroyed by a storm in 1879. Moments after the collapse a train at-

tempted to cross and plunged into the firth, killing 75 people.

Broughty Ferry

This pleasant suburb is 4 miles east of Dundee. There's a long, sandy beach (though not exactly spotless) and a number of good places to eat and drink.

Claypotts Castle (☎ 01786-450000), built in the late 16th century, was once in the country but has now been absorbed into suburbia. Looking like a house perched on top of a castle, it's actually one of the most complete Z-plan tower houses. Phone for details of opening hours.

Broughty Castle Museum (☎ 776121) is a reconstructed 16th century tower guarding the entrance to the Firth of Tay. It has an interesting display on the local whaling industry. Admission is free, but it closes Friday.

Walking Tours

Guided walks (☎ 532754) are available with a minimum charge of £10 per hour per group (minimum four people) – a heritage and industrial walk, a maritime walk, and other possibilities can be catered for.

Places to Stay

Hostels & Colleges *Riverview* (☎ 450565, 127 Broughty Ferry Rd) is a 10 minute walk east of the bus station. It's open all year; reservations are recommended since there are only 17 beds. You'll pay £10 per person (£12 with breakfast).

During university holidays you can stay in the halls of residence at *Dundee University* (☎ 647171, West Park), 1½ miles from the centre. Single/twin rooms cost from £20/30.

B&Bs & Guesthouses *Abalree* (☎ 223867, 20 Union St) is a basic guesthouse but you couldn't be more central, and overnight B&B costs around £17/28. Around the corner, and much more upmarket, is *Auld Steeple Guest House* (☎ 200302, 94 Nethergate). It charges £22/36 with bath, £18/34 without.

In the north of the city, a 10 minute walk from the bus station, is *Mrs Milne's* (☎ 225354, 8 Nelson Terrace), which has B&B for around £14. *Hillside Guest House* (☎ 223443, 43 Constitution St, off Constitution Rd) charges £20 to £30 per person.

In the east, *Errolbank Guest House* (☎ 462118, 9 Dalgleish Rd) charges £17.50 to £25 per person.

There's a good range of places to stay in Broughty Ferry. *Auchenean* (☎ 774782, 177 Hamilton St) charges £17/34. Dinner is available from £6.50. It's a pleasant place five minutes walk from the beach. *Hollies*

Orchard (☎ 776403, 12 Castle Roy Rd) does *en suite* B&B for £25 per person.

Hotels On the western side of Dundee, just off the Perth Rd and about 1½ miles from the city centre, is the *Shaftesbury Hotel* (☎ 669216, 1 Hyndford St). It's a former jute baron's mansion, and an excellent place to stay; it's popular with businesspeople. B&B costs from £44.50/58, but there are bargain midweek and weekend rates available. There's a good restaurant and the set dinner is £14.90.

The two main business hotels in the city centre are the *Queen's Hotel* (☎ 322515, 160 Nethergate), a grand Victorian hotel with B&B from £40/58; and the waterfront *Stakis Dundee Earl Grey Hotel* (☎ 229271), by the Tay Bridge, which charges from £45 to £125.50 per person. The lowest rates apply at the weekend.

Places to Eat

There's a surprising number of interesting places to eat in Dundee and prices are competitive. For a snack, the *Incredible Roll Inn*, Whitehall Crescent, is a good sandwich shop with a wonderful range of hot and cold filled rolls from 80p.

Het Theatre Café (☎ 200813) is at the Dundee Rep Theatre on Tay Square. It's a European-style coffee bar, open daily except Sunday, and a great place for coffee, a drink or a meal.

The *Deep Sea* (81 Nethergate) is the oldest fish and chip shop in Dundee, but it doesn't stay open late. Nearby, the *Leerie Restaurant* (Nethergate) is cheap, with mains from £4. More upmarket, *Fisher & Donaldson* is an excellent bakery/patisserie with a café attached.

It's worth going to *Jahangir* (☎ 202022, 1 Session St) for the décor alone. This extraordinary Indian restaurant looks like a nightclub from the outside; inside, it's pure Moghul Hollywood, with an over-the-top tent and fountain. The food's good and it also does takeaways. Chicken curries start at £4.10. It's open until 1 am at the weekends, midnight during the week.

There are lots of interesting places along Perth Rd, although some are a fair walk from the centre. However, the best restaurant in Dundee, *Raffles Restaurant* (☎ 201139, 18 Perth Rd), isn't far and main courses are good value at £8 to £11.75. The most interesting restaurant is the *Agacan* (☎ 644227, 113 Perth Rd), part Turkish restaurant, part art gallery, and a great place to spend the evening.

In Broughty Ferry, *Visocchi's (Gray St)* is an Italian ice-cream shop and café that's an institution. *Gulistan Balti & Tandoori Restaurant* (☎ 738844, Queen St) is in an old church hall; in the early evening (from 5 to 7 pm, not Saturday) it has a set menu for £7.95.

Entertainment

The *Dundee Rep Theatre* (☎ 223530, Tay Square) hosts touring companies and also stages its own performances. Some of the Dundee Jazz & Blues Festival (June) is held here.

The *Parliamentary Bar* (☎ 202658, 134 Nethergate) is a large, stylish pub popular with students. There's live jazz Saturday afternoon. The *Mercantile Bar* (☎ 225500, 100 Commercial St) is a lively city centre pub.

In Broughty Ferry, the beer is good at the *Fisherman's Tavern (12 Fort St)*. Another good place to drink is the *Ship Inn (121 Fisher St)*, which also serves pub grub.

Dundee has several nightclubs. *Fat Sam's* (☎ 228181, South Ward Rd) is popular with students. Nearby, there's *Mardi Gras* (☎ 205551).

Getting There & Away

See the fares tables in the Getting Around chapter. Dundee is 472 miles from London, 83 from Glasgow, 62 from Edinburgh, 67 from Aberdeen and 21 from Perth. If you're driving over the Tay Road Bridge from Fife, it's toll-free in that direction only.

Air The airport (☎ 643242), Riverside Drive, is close to the centre, with flights to Aberdeen, Manchester and Denmark.

Bus National Express (☎ 0990-808080) operates four services a day (two direct) to Dundee from London, including one night service.

Scottish Citylink has hourly buses from Edinburgh (two hours, £6.50) and Glasgow (2¼ hours, £7.80). On some services, you may have to change in Perth. There are also hourly services to Perth (20 minutes, £3) and Aberdeen (1¾ hours, £6.50). To get to the western coast is a major pain – you must go via Glasgow to reach Fort William or Oban.

Train From Edinburgh (1¼ hours, £14) and Glasgow (1½ hours, £18.50), trains run at least once an hour, Monday to Saturday; hourly on Sunday to Edinburgh, every two hours on Sunday to Glasgow. For Aberdeen (1¼ hours, £16.40), trains run via Arbroath and Stonehaven. There are two trains an hour, fewer on Sunday.

Car Rental companies include Arnold Clark (☎ 225382), Trades Lane, and Mitchell's Self Drive (☎ 223484), 90 Marketgait.

Getting Around

Most city centre buses pass along the High St, stopping by St Mary's Church. It's possible to catch a train to Broughty Ferry, but buses (15 minutes, 80p) are much more frequent. Phone Tele Taxis (☎ 889333) if you need a cab.

GLAMIS CASTLE

Looking every bit a Scottish castle, with turrets and battlements, Glamis Castle (pronounced glarms) was the legendary setting for Shakespeare's *Macbeth*. The Grampians and an extensive park provide a spectacular backdrop for this family home of the Earls of Strathmore and Kinghorne. Glamis (☎ 01307-840242) has been a royal residence since 1372; the Queen Mother (née Elizabeth Bowes-Lyon) spent her childhood here and Princess Margaret (the Queen's sister) was born here.

The five-storey, L-shaped castle was given to the Lyon family in 1372, but was significantly altered in the 17th century. The most impressive room is the drawing room, with its arched plasterwork ceiling. There's a display of armour and weaponry in the crypt (haunted) and frescoes in the chapel (also haunted). Duncan's Hall is where King Duncan was murdered in *Macbeth*. You can also look round the royal apartments, including the Queen Mother's bedroom.

Glamis Castle is 12 miles north of Dundee. It's open daily April to October, from 10.30 am to 5.30 pm (last entry 4.45 pm). You're escorted on an hour-long tour which leaves every 15 minutes. Tickets are £5.20/2.70. There are up to five buses a day from Dundee (35 minutes, £2.10), operated by Strathtay Buses (☎ 01382-228054).

ARBROATH
* **pop 23,528** ☎ **01241**

Source of the famous Arbroath smokie (smoked haddock), this fishing port was established in the 12th century. Nowadays, the town is impoverished and unemployment is high, but it's no less interesting for all that. There's an all-year TIC (☎ 872609) in Market Place.

The settlement grew up around **Arbroath Abbey** (☎ 878756), founded in 1178 by King William the Lion, who is buried here. It was at the abbey that Robert the Bruce signed Scotland's famous declaration of independence from England in 1320. Closed following the Dissolution, the fortified abbey fell into ruin but enough survives to make this an impressive sight. There's a tall gable in the south transept, with a circular window that once held a shipping beacon. Parts of the nave and sacristy are intact. The abbey is open standard HS times; entry is £1.80/1.30.

For sea fishing trips, contact the skipper of the *Girl Katherine* (☎ 874510).

There are places to stay and eat around the harbour, including *Harbour House Guest House* (☎ 878047), charging £15 to £18 per person.

Scottish Citylink has frequent buses from Edinburgh and Dundee, but it's best to go by train because it's a scenic trip along the coast from Dundee (20 minutes, £3, two trains an hour).

Aberdeenshire & Moray

Known from 1974 to 1996 as the Grampian region, the area is (not surprisingly) bound to the west and south by the Grampians. The largest place is prosperous Aberdeen, a tidy city of impressive granite architecture, still benefiting from the North Sea oil industry.

Aberdeenshire incorporates the valley of the grand River Dee, Royal Deeside – royal because Queen Victoria liked it so much that she bought Balmoral. The royal family still spends part of every summer here, appearing at the Braemar Gathering, the best known of the Highland Games.

Around the coast are the fertile plains, immortalised by Lewis Grassic Gibbon in his trilogy the *Scots Quair,* which was based on the life of a farming community early in the 20th century. The east coasters, and particularly the Aberdonians, have always had a reputation for being hard-working and thrifty. Certainly anyone living near, or making a living from, the North Sea would have to be tough.

There is a vigorous culture in the north-east quite separate from the rest of Scotland. Much of it is expressed in lively anecdotal or poetic form (in dialect). The *both y* ballads and bands which provided home entertainment among the workers on the big farms still get high billing on local radio and TV.

Along the northern coast of Banff and Moray are small fishing ports which have neat, little streets looking out to sea, with nothing between them and Scandinavia to the north. This sandy coastline gets a lot of sun and not much rainfall and the unspoilt, small towns have a brisk, no-nonsense feel.

There are many castles in the characteristic Scottish baronial style in this area. In the north-west, and across the border in the Highlands, the biggest industry is the distilling of whisky – many distilleries offer tours followed by drams.

GETTING AROUND

For information on buses around Aberdeen phone ☎ 01224-664581. Bluebird Buses (☎ 01224-212266) is the main bus company in the area. Its Day Rover ticket (£8.50) covers all its services.

The only rail line runs from the south to Aberdeen and continues through Inverurie, Huntly and Elgin to Inverness.

There are some superb walks in the mountains in the south-western part of this region. TICs sell the useful *Hillwalking in Grampian Highlands*.

ABERDEEN

- **pop 217,260** ☎ **01224**

Aberdeen is an extraordinary symphony in grey. Almost everything is built of grey granite, including the roads, which are paved with crushed granite. In the sunlight, especially after a shower of rain, the stone turns silver and shines like a fairytale, but with low, grey clouds and rain scudding in off the North Sea it can be a bit depressing.

Aberdeen was a prosperous North Sea trading and fishing port centuries before oil was considered a valuable commodity. After the townspeople supported Robert the Bruce against the English at the Battle of Bannockburn in 1314, the king rewarded the town with land for which he had previously received rent. The money was diverted into the Common Good Fund, to be spent on town amenities, as it still is today. It finances the regimented floral ranks that have won the city numerous awards, and helps keep the place spotless. As a result, the inhabitants have been inculcated with an almost overbearing civic pride.

The name Aberdeen is a combination of two Pictish-Gaelic words, 'aber' and 'devana', meaning the meeting of two waters. The area was known to the Romans and was raided by the Vikings when it was an increasingly important port, with trade conducted in wool, fish, hides and fur. By the 18th century, paper and rope-making, whaling and textile manufacture were the main industries; in the following century it was a major herring port.

Since the 1970s, Aberdeen has become the main onshore service port for one of the largest oilfields in the world. Unemployment rates, once among the highest in the country, dropped dramatically, but have since fluctuated with the rise and fall of the price of oil.

Aberdeen is certainly worth a visit. It's a very lively city – there are more bars than would seem even remotely viable. Start with almost 200,000 Scots, then add multinational oil workers and a large student population – the result: a thriving nightlife.

Orientation

Aberdeen is built on a ridge that runs east-west to the north of the train and bus stations and the ferry quay. The bus and train stations are next to each other, off Guild St. Old Aberdeen and the university are to the north of this area. To the east lies a couple of miles of clean, sandy beach; at the southern end is Footdee (pronounced fittee), a fishing community at the mouth of the River Dee.

Information

The TIC (☎ 632727), St Nicholas House, Broad St, opens daily May to September, from 9 am to 5 pm (extended hours July and August). October to May it's closed Sunday. As well as the usual bed-booking facility, there's a *bureau de change*.

The Harbour

The harbour has always been a busy place. From dawn until about 8 am the fish market operates as it has for centuries.

Maritime Museum Situated in Provost Ross's House, the oldest building in the city, the Maritime Museum (☎ 585788) explains Aberdeen's relationship (almost exclusively commercial) with the sea. There are some interesting displays about shipbuilding and the whaling and fishing industries. Speedy Aberdeen clippers were a 19th century shipyard speciality which were attractive to British tea merchants in China for the transportation of emigrants to Australia and, on return, the importation of

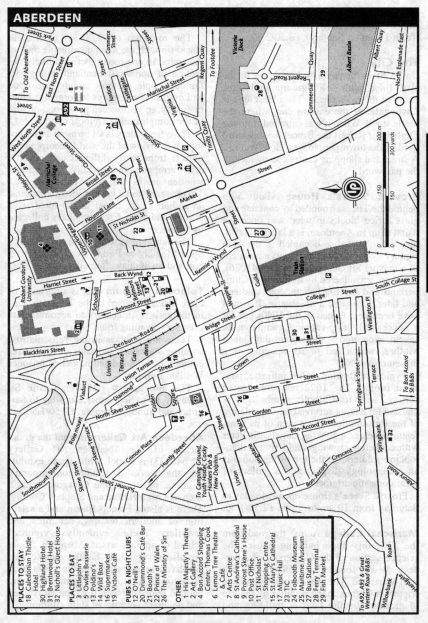

ABERDEEN

CENTRAL SCOTLAND

PLACES TO STAY
18 Caledonian Thistle Hotel
30 Highland Hotel
31 Brentwood Hotel
32 Nicholl's Guest House

PLACES TO EAT
3 Littlejohn's
5 Owlies Brasserie
13 Poldino's
14 Wild Boar
16 Supermarket
19 Victoria Café

PUBS & NIGHTCLUBS
12 O'Neill's
20 Drummond's Café Bar
21 Booth's
22 Prince of Wales
26 The Ministry of Sin

OTHER
1 His Majesty's Theatre
2 Art Gallery
4 Bon Accord Shopping Centre; Thomas Cook
6 Lemon Tree Theatre & Café
7 Arts Centre
8 St Andrew's Cathedral
9 Provost Skene's House
10 Post Office
11 St Nicholas' Shopping Centre
15 St Mary's Cathedral
17 Music Hall
23 TIC
24 Tolbooth Museum
25 Maritime Museum
27 Bus Station
28 Ferry Terminal
29 Fish Market

tea, wool and exotic goods (opium, for instance). It opens daily, from 10 am to 5 pm (from 11 am on Sunday); £3.50/2.50.

The City

Union St is the main thoroughfare in the city, lined with solid granite buildings, many of them Victorian. The oldest area is **Castlegate**, at the eastern end, where the castle stood. When it was captured from the English for Robert the Bruce, the password used by the townspeople was 'Bon Accord'. A street and shopping centre commemorate the password.

Provost Skene's House About 50m behind the TIC, surrounded by concrete and glass office blocks in what was once the worst slum in Aberdeen, is a late medieval, turreted town house occupied in the 17th century by the Provost (the Scots equivalent of a mayor) Sir George Skene (☎ 641086). It was commandeered by the Duke of Cumberland and his English redcoat soldiers, and later it became a dosshouse. It would have been demolished in the 1940s but for a successful, long-running campaign to save it, supported by the present-day Queen Mother, which led to its opening as a museum in 1953.

Typical of its kind, it has intimate, panelled rooms. The 1622 tempera-painted ceiling, with its Catholic symbolism, is unusual for having survived the depredation of the Reformation. It's a gem of its time, featuring earnest looking angels, St Peter with cockerels crowing, and Cromwellian-looking soldiers. At the top of the house is an archaeology display and a gallery of local domestic artefacts.

Provost Skene's House opens Monday to Saturday from 10 am to 5 pm; £2.50/1.50.

Marischal College Across the road from the TIC, this huge building houses the science section of the University of Aberdeen. It was founded in 1593 by the 5th Earl Marischal. The present building is late Victorian Gothic, made peculiar by the use of granite. It's the kind of building you

either love or hate, but cannot avoid being impressed by.

The **museum** (☎ 273131) is straight ahead through the main quadrangle and up the stairs. In one room, there's a lively depiction of north-east Scotland through its famous people, customs, architecture, trade and myths. The displays are organised thematically, so visitors can get a good picture of the complex and rich local culture.

The other gallery is set up as an anthropological overview of the world, incorporating objects from vastly different cultures. It's also arranged thematically (Polynesian wooden masks alongside gasmasks etc). There are the usual bizarre Victorian curios, an Indian kayak found in the local river estuary and some Eskimo objects collected by whalers.

The museum is well worth visiting. It's open Monday to Friday from 10 am to 5 pm, and on Sunday afternoon; entry is free.

Tolbooth Museum This is a museum of civic history, housed in the Tolbooth built in the early 17th century to accommodate prisoners awaiting trial.

There are displays in the cells, narrow winding staircases and tales of escape recounted by an animated model of prisoner William Baird.

The museum (☎ 621167), Castle St, opens April to September, Tuesday to Saturday and Sunday morning; £2.50/1.50.

Aberdeen Art Gallery Behind the grand façade of the Aberdeen Art Gallery (☎ 646333) is a cool, white space exhibiting the work of young contemporary painters, mostly of the Glasgow School, such as Gwen Hardie and Stephen Conroy. There is also a Francis Bacon and a selection of modern textiles, ceramics and jewellery. There's evidently a vigorous school of applied arts in Aberdeen. There are also several Joan Eardley landscapes; she lived in a cottage on the cliffs near Stonehaven in the 1950s and 60s and painted tempestuous oils of the North Sea and poignant portraits of slum children.

Among the Pre-Raphaelites upstairs is a collection of 92 small portraits of artists, many of them self-portraits of now forgotten painters. The collection was begun around 1880 by George Macdonald on the instigation of John Millais.

Downstairs, a large, empty, white, circular room, with fish-scaled balustrades evoking the briny origins of Aberdeen's wealth, commemorates the 165 people who lost their lives in the Piper Alpha oil rig disaster in 1988.

The gallery, on Schoolhill, opens Monday to Saturday from 10 am to 5 pm, Sunday from 2 to 5 pm.

Old Aberdeen

Old Aberdeen is a suburb 1½ miles north of the city centre. The name is somewhat misleading, since the area around the harbour is actually older; it's called Alton in Gaelic, meaning village by the pool, and this was anglicised to Old Town. The university buildings and St Machar's Cathedral are at the centre of this peaceful area.

It was here that Bishop Elphinstone established King's College, Aberdeen's first university, in 1495. Earl Marischal founded the college in the city centre in 1593 but it wasn't until the 19th century that the two colleges were united as the University of Aberdeen. The 16th century **King's College Chapel** (☎ 272137) is easily recognisable by its crowned spire. The interior of the chapel is largely unchanged – the stained-glass windows and choir stalls are impressive. It's closed weekends. **King's College Visitors Centre** (☎ 273702) houses a multimedia display on the university's history. It's open Monday to Saturday from 10 am to 5 pm, and on Sunday afternoon, year-round; free.

The 15th century **St Machar's Cathedral** (☎ 485988), with its massive twin towers, is one of the few examples in the country of a fortified cathedral. According to legend, St Machar was ordered to establish a church where the river takes the shape of a bishop's crook, which it does just here. The cathedral is best known for its impressive heraldic ceiling, dating from 1520, which has 48 shields of kings, nobles, archbishops and bishops. It's open daily from 9 am to 5 pm; services on Sunday are at 11 am and 6 pm.

Places to Stay

Camping The nearest camping ground is *Hazelhead Caravan Park & Campsite* (☎ 321268), 4 miles west of the centre and near the A944, with pitches for £4.30 in a woodland setting. Phone for directions.

Hostels *Aberdeen Youth Hostel* (☎ 646988, 8 Queen's Rd) is a mile west of the train station. It's open all year; beds cost £8.60/7.10 for adults/juniors in small dormitories (£1 surcharge in July and August). Walk west along Union St and take the right fork along Albyn Place until you reach a roundabout; Queen's Rd continues on the western side.

During the university holidays some colleges let rooms to visitors. The list of colleges offering accommodation changes from year to year – check with the TIC. *Robert Gordon's University* (☎ 262140, *Woolmanhill Residence*) has *en suite* singles for £15 per person (with cooking facilities). The *Scottish Agricultural College* (☎ 711195, *Craibstone Estate, Bucksburn*), north-west of Aberdeen, has rooms from £18 to £24 per person.

B&Bs & Hotels There are clusters of B&Bs on Bon Accord St and Springbank Terrace (both close to the centre), and Great Western Rd (the A93, a 25 minute walk). They are more expensive than is usually the case in Scotland and, with all the oil industry workers here, single rooms are at a premium. Prices tend to be lower at the weekend.

The more expensive guesthouses are at the city end of Bon Accord St. At No 154, *Applewood Guest House* (☎ 580617) charges from £18 to £24 per person for B&B. *Crynoch Guest House* (☎ 582743, *164 Bon Accord St*) has singles/doubles for £19/34. The two guesthouses next door are both similarly priced: *Denmore Guest*

House (☎ *587751)* at No 166, and *Dunrovin Guest House* (☎ *586081)* at No 168.

Nearby, at 63 Springbank Terrace, *Nicholl's Guest House* (☎ *572867)* is a recommended, friendly place with rooms at around £20/31 (£28/43 with bath). There are plenty of other alternatives in the area.

There are numerous places along Great Western Rd. At No 189, *Penny Meadow Private Hotel* (☎ *588037)* is a small, friendly place. Rooms with bath are from £30/40. The *Corner House Hotel* (☎ *313063)*, at No 385, is a solid, turreted building with off-street parking and evening meals if required. It charges from £35/46 for *en suite* rooms.

For non-smokers only, *Strathisla Guest House* (☎ *321026, 408 Great Western Rd)* is a comfortable place. All rooms have a bath, and charges are around £25/40. *Klibreck Guest House* (☎ *316115)*, at No 410, charges from £20/30. *Aurora Guest House* (☎ *311602, 429 Great Western Rd)* is another small, family-run B&B. There are five rooms, ranging from £19/30 to £20/34, all with shared bathroom.

Back in the centre of Aberdeen, the friendly *Brentwood Hotel* (☎ *595440, 101 Crown St)* is comfortable, but often full during the week. Rooms cost from £69/77; about 50% less at weekends. The hotel has a good bar and restaurant.

The *Atholl Hotel* (☎ *323505, Kings Gate)*, an elegant granite building on the western edge of the town, has an excellent reputation. Luxurious rooms range from £46/54 at weekends to £78/88 during the week.

A fine place to stay in the centre of town is the *Caledonian Thistle Hotel* (☎ *640233, Union Terrace)*, with 80 rooms. Its published tariff starts from £115/135 but cheaper rates are available.

Places to Eat

Aberdeen has an excellent range of places to eat, from branches of the big-name fast-food chains to expensive gourmet restaurants.

The *Ashvale Fish Restaurant* (☎ *596981, 46 Great Western Rd)* is a fish and chip shop that's well known outside the city, having won several awards. Ask for mushy peas with your haddock and chips (from £3.10 to take away) – they don't taste as bad as they sound. The *New Dolphin (3 Chapel St, just off Union St)* isn't a Chinese take-away, but it's an excellent fish and chip shop with a sit-in section. Haddock and chips is £3.20 and it's open to 3 am Thursday to Sunday.

The café at the *Lemon Tree* (☎ *642230)*, the theatre at 5 West North St, does excellent coffee, meals and cakes. It's open Wednesday to Sunday from noon to 3 pm.

The *Victoria Café* (☎ *621381, 140 Union St)* does snacks and sandwiches from £2. Just around the corner, the *Wild Boar* (☎ *625357, 19 Belmont St)* is a popular, stylish bistro. Cake fanatics will have a great time here. Main courses range from £4.25 to £9.95, with vegetarian choices; couscous is £5.45.

Poldino's (☎ *647777, 7 Little Belmont St)* is an upmarket Italian restaurant. Pizza and pasta cost £6.60 to £7.30. It's open Monday to Saturday for lunch and dinner.

Owlies Brasserie (☎ *649267, Littlejohn St)* is highly recommended, good value and, consequently, very popular. It produces tasty food with unusual flavours – try the couscous Marocain (£7.20). It also has a good range of vegetarian and vegan food.

There's a branch of the chain *Littlejohn's* (☎ *635666, 46 School Hill)*, with all the usual diversions, including the toy train. Retraining in hospitality would be better than gimmicks. There are burgers from £4, and other main dishes (eg char-grilled chicken) from around £8.

For a splurge, there are a number of choices. *Silver Darling Restaurant* (☎ *576229)*, at the southern end of the Beach Esplanade on Pocra Quay, North Pier, Footdee, is renowned for its seafood and superb location overlooking the port entrance. A three course dinner costs at least £20. The excellent *Faradays Restaurant* (☎ *869666, 2 Kirk Brae, Cults)* is 4 miles from the centre. The cuisine is a combination of traditional Scottish and French, with lots of fresh, local ingredients. It's open Tuesday to Saturday.

Entertainment

A listings guide, *What's on in Aberdeen*, is available from the TIC. There's also the bimonthly *Aberdeen Arts & Recreation Listings*. You can book tickets for most plays and concerts on the Aberdeen Box Office line (☎ 641122).

Theatre & Music The city's main theatre is *His Majesty's* (☎ 637788, *Rosemount Viaduct*), which hosts everything from ballet and opera to musicals and pantomimes. The *Music Hall* (☎ 632080, *Union St*) is the main venue for classical music concerts. The *Arts Centre* (☎ 635208, *King St*) stages exhibitions at its gallery and drama in its theatre.

The *Lemon Tree* (☎ 642230, *5 West North St*) usually has an interesting program of dance, music or drama. It hosts festivals, has an excellent café, and often has rock, jazz and folk bands playing.

Pubs & Nightclubs Aberdeen is a great city for a pub crawl – it's more of a question of knowing where to stop than where to start. Note that many pubs don't serve food in the evening.

The *Prince of Wales* (☎ 640597, *7 St Nicholas Lane*) is possibly the best known Aberdeen pub. Down an alley off Union St, it boasts the longest counter in the city, a great range of real ales and good-value pub grub at lunchtime. It can also get very crowded. Nearby, on Back Wynd, *Booth's* is a better place for a pub lunch. It has a good range of traditional pies.

Cocky Hunters (☎ 626720, *504 Union St*) is a great place with regular live music. *Drummond's Café Bar* (☎ 624642, *Belmont St*) serves meals during the day, but it's more of a student pub in the evening.

There are numerous nightclubs but most won't let you in if you're wearing runners and some will turn you away if you're wearing jeans. *The Ministry of Sin* (☎ 211661, *Dee St*) is in a deconsecrated

church. It attracts 20 to 35-year-olds and is a fairly good club. One of the wildest clubs is upstairs at *O'Neill's* pub (☎ 621456, *9 Back Wynd*), open daily until 2 am.

Getting There & Away

See the fares tables in the Getting Around chapter. Aberdeen is 507 miles from London, 129 from Edinburgh and 105 from Inverness.

Air Aberdeen airport is 6 miles north-west of the city centre. The oil industry ensures that there are flights to numerous cities in the UK, including Orkney and Shetland, and international flights to the Netherlands and Norway.

For airport information, phone ☎ 722331. Bus Nos 27 and 27A run from the city centre to the airport, taking about 35 minutes.

Bus National Express (☎ 0990-808080) has daily buses from London, but it's a tedious 12 hour trip (from £24.50 one way). Scottish Citylink runs direct services to Dundee (two hours, £6.50), Perth (2½ hours, £9), Edinburgh (four hours, £13), Stirling (3½ hours, £12.80) and Glasgow (4¼ hours, £13.30).

Bluebird Buses is the major local operator.

Train There are numerous trains from London's King's Cross station, taking an acceptable seven hours, although they're considerably more expensive than buses. Other destinations served from Aberdeen by rail include Edinburgh (2¾ hours, £32), Glasgow (2¾ hours, £35.10), Perth (1¾ hours, £19.50), Stirling (2¼ hours, £29), Dundee (1¼ hours, £16.40) and Inverness (2¼ hours, £18.50).

Car Try Arnold Clark (☎ 249159), Girdleness Rd, or Morrison Brothers (☎ 826300), Broadfield Rd, Bridge of Don.

Boat The passenger terminal is a short walk east of the train and bus stations. P&O (☎ 572615) has daily evening departures from Monday to Friday leaving for Lerwick

(Shetland). The trip takes approximately 14 hours or 20 hours (some sailings go via Orkney). A reclining seat costs £49/55 in the low/high season, one way.

From June to August, there are departures Tuesday and Saturday to Stromness (Orkney); 10 hours, £37/40.

Getting Around

Bus The *Aberdeen Passport* is available from the TIC and gives basic details of city bus services; for full details, you'll need the *Travel Guide to Aberdeen*. For local bus information phone the Grampian Busline (☎ 650000). The most useful services are bus Nos 18, 19 and 24 from Union St to Great Western Rd, No 27 from the bus station to the youth hostel, and Nos 20 and 26 for Old Aberdeen. If you're using the buses frequently, get a prepaid farecard (like a phonecard).

Taxi For a taxi, phone Mair's (☎ 724040). A trip to the airport costs £10 to £11.

Bicycle Bikes can be rented from Alpine Bikes (☎ 211455), 64 Holburn St. It's open daily and charges £8/12 per half/full day during the week, £24 for the weekend (Friday evening to Monday morning).

DEESIDE & DONSIDE

The region around the Rivers Dee and Don, eastwards from Braemar to the coast, is castle country and includes the Queen's residence at Balmoral. There are more fanciful examples of Scottish baronial architecture here than anywhere else in Scotland. The TICs have information on a Castle Trail, but you really need private transport to follow it.

The River Dee, flowing through the southern part of this area, has its source in the Cairngorm mountains, to the west. The River Don follows a shorter, but almost parallel, course. The best walking country is around Braemar and Ballater, in upper Deeside.

Ballater

- **pop 1260**   ☎ 01339

This small town supplies nearby Balmoral Castle with provisions, hence the shops

sporting 'By Royal Appointment' crests. The TIC (☎ 755306), Station Square, opens Easter to October.

The place has been famous for its spring water since the 19th century. There are no great sights, but there are some pleasant walks in the surrounding hills. The woodland walk up Craigendarroch (400m) takes just over an hour, but it's quite steep. Morven (872m) is a more serious prospect, taking around six hours, but has good views from the top.

B&Bs include *Mrs Cowie's* (☎ 755699, *Celicall, 3 Braemar Rd*), for around £17/30 a single/double. The *Alexandra Hotel* (☎ 755376, 12 Bridge Square) is a friendly and comfortable hotel offering B&B from £24 to £30 per person.

Bluebird Buses (☎ 755422) run almost every hour from Aberdeen (1¾ hours, £5.50); every two hours on Sunday. The service continues to Braemar.

Balmoral Castle

Eight miles west of Ballater, Balmoral Castle (☎ 01339-742334) was built for Queen Victoria in 1855 as a private residence for the royal family. The grounds and an exhibition of paintings and other royal trinkets in the ballroom are open; the rest of the castle is closed to the prying eyes of the public. On the edge of the estate is Crathie Church, which the royals use when they're here.

Balmoral opens 28 April to 3 August, daily from 10 am to 5 pm (closed on Sunday in April and May), and attracts large numbers of visitors. Admission costs £3/2.50. It's by the A93 and can be reached on the Aberdeen-Braemar bus (see Braemar).

Braemar

- **pop 410**   ☎ 01339

Braemar is an attractive village surrounded by mountains; it makes an excellent walking base. There's a helpful TIC (☎ 741600), The Mews, Mar Rd, open all year. It has lots of useful information on walks in the area.

North of the village, turreted **Braemar Castle** (☎ 741219) dates from 1628, and was a garrison post after the 1745 Jacobite

Rebellion. It's open Easter to October, Saturday to Thursday, from 10 am to 6 pm; entry is £2/1.50.

Walks An easy walk from Braemar is up Creag Choinnich (538m), a hill to the east above the A93. There are route markers and the walk takes about 1½ hours. For a longer walk (three hours) and superb views of the Cairngorms, climb Morrone (859m), the mountain south of Braemar.

Special Events On the first Saturday in September, Braemar is invaded by 20,000 people, including the royal family, for the Braemar Gathering (Highland Games); bookings are essential.

Places to Stay & Eat *Braemar Youth Hostel* (☎ 741659), south of the centre, opens year round and charges £7.75/6.50 for adults/juniors. *Braemar Bunkhouse* (☎ 741242, 15 Mar Rd) has dorm accommodation from £7.

Craiglea (☎ 741641, Hillside Dr) has rooms for around £18 per person, while *Wilderbank* (☎ 741651, Kindrochit Drive) charges a little less. *Callater Lodge Hotel* (☎ 741275, 9 Glenshee Rd) is a small hotel set in its own grounds; most rooms have baths and cost around £27 per person – evening meals are available. The top place to stay is *Braemar Lodge* (☎ 741627, Glenshee Rd), a restored Victorian shooting lodge on the outskirts of the town. B&B costs from £25 to £36 per person.

The pubs are the best places for food and entertainment: *Fife Arms Hotel* has a daily carvery and bar meals, and *Invercauld Arms Hotel* is a reasonable place for a pint.

Getting There & Away It's a beautiful drive between Perth and Braemar but public transport is limited. From Aberdeen to Braemar (2¼ hours, £5.50), there are several buses a day operated by Bluebird Buses (☎ 01224-212266) which travel along the beautiful valley of the River Dee.

Inverey

Five miles west of Braemar is the little settlement of Inverey. Numerous mountain walks start from here, including the adventurous Lairig Ghru walk – 21 miles over the pass to Aviemore. The Cairngorm peaks of Cairn Gorm and Ben Macdui (see Aviemore in the Highlands & Northern Islands chapter) are actually just this side of the regional border.

Inverey Youth Hostel (no ☎) opens mid-May to early October; beds cost £4.65/3.85 for adults/juniors. There's an afternoon postbus (not Sunday) from Braemar to the hostel, Linn of Dee and Linn of Quoich.

Glenshee

Glenshee is Scotland's largest skiing area, on the border of Perthshire and Aberdeenshire. The A93 ploughs through the middle of the resort. Blairgowrie is the main accommodation centre for Glenshee, although there's a small settlement 5 miles south of the ski runs at Spittal of Glenshee. There's a TIC (☎ 01250-872960) at Blairgowrie, 26 Wellmeadow, which opens all year.

Places to Stay & Eat Apart from the accommodation centres of Braemar and Blairgowrie, places to stay are strung out along the A93 around Glenshee. At the Blairgowrie end you could try the *Blackwater Inn* (☎ 01250-882234, Blackwater), where B&B costs around £18 per person. *Compass Christian Centre* (☎ 01250-885209, Glenshee Lodge) charges around £13.50 per person for B&B, and only £5 more for dinner.

The *Spittal of Glenshee Hotel* (☎ 01250-885215) offers B&B in rooms with bath from £17.50 to £27 per person. Grand *Dalmunzie House Hotel* (☎ 01250-885224, Glenshee) boasts the highest nine hole golf course in Britain, and is set in a 2400-hectare estate 1½ miles off the main road. B&B costs from £50/78 a single/double.

Getting There & Away Strathtay Scottish (☎ 01382-228054) operates a service from Perth to Blairgowrie (50 minutes, £2.05), hourly Monday to Saturday, six times a day on Sunday. The only service from Blair-gowrie to the Glenshee area is the postbus (☎ 01250-872766) to Spittal of Glenshee (no Sunday service).

INLAND ABERDEENSHIRE & MORAY

The direct, inland rail and road route from Aberdeen to Inverness cuts across rolling agricultural country that, thanks to a mild climate, produces everything from grain to flower bulbs. The grain is turned into that magical liquid known as malt whisky. You may be tempted by the **Malt Whisky Trail**, a 70 mile signposted tour which gives you an inside look and complimentary tastings at a number of famous distilleries (including Cardhu, Glenfiddich and The Glenlivet). TICs stock a leaflet covering the tour. See also Food & Drink in the Scotland Facts for the Visitor chapter.

This is also castle country, and there's a *Castle Trail* leaflet to guide you around. **Castle Fraser** (☎ 01330-833463, NTS), 3 miles south of Kemnay, looks rather like a French chateau and dates from the 16th century. **Haddo House** (☎ 01651-851440, NTS), 19 miles north of Aberdeen, was designed by William Adam in 1732. It's best described as a classic English stately home transplanted to Scotland. **Fyvie Castle** (☎ 01651-891266), 8 miles south of Turriff, is a magnificent example of Scottish baronial architecture. There are numerous other castles in various states of preservation.

Huntly
• pop 4150   ☎ 01466

This small town, with an impressive ruined castle, is in a strategically important position on a low-lying plain, along the main route from Aberdeen into the Strathspey and Moray regions. The TIC (☎ 792255), The Square, opens daily April to October.

On the northern edge of town, **Huntly Castle** (☎ 793191, HS), the former stronghold of the Gordons, is on the banks of the River Deveron. Over the main door is a superb carving that includes the royal arms and the figures of Christ and St Michael.

The castle opens standard HS hours; entry is £2.30/1.75.

The Aberdeen to Inverness Bluebird bus (No 10) passes through Huntly hourly, and the town is on the rail line that follows the same route.

Dufftown
• pop 1700   ☎ 01340

Founded only in 1817 by James Duff, 4th Earl of Fife, Dufftown is 14 miles west of Huntly. It's a good place to start the Malt Whisky Trail – there are seven working distilleries in Dufftown alone! The TIC (☎ 820501), in the clock tower in the square, opens Easter to October.

North of town is **Glenfiddich Distillery Visitors Centre** (☎ 820373). Visitors are guided through the process of distilling, and can also see whisky being bottled – the only Highland distillery where this is done on the premises. It's open all year, Monday to Saturday, from 9.30 am to 4.30 pm; also, Easter to October, Sunday from noon to 4.30 pm. There's no entry charge – your free dram really is free.

Bluebird Buses link Dufftown to Elgin, among other places.

GRAMPIAN COAST

The Grampians meet the sea at Stonehaven, home to spectacular Dunnottar Castle. Continuing around the coast from Aberdeen, there are long stretches of sand and, on the north coast, some magical fishing villages – like Pennan, where the film *Local Hero* was shot.

Stonehaven
• pop 9310   ☎ 01569

Originally a small fishing village, 'Stanehyve' became the county town of Kincardineshire in 1600 and is now a seaside resort. If you want to stay, the TIC (☎ 762806), 66 Allardice St, has a list of B&Bs. Stonehaven is on the main bus and rail routes between Dundee and Aberdeen.

The most pleasant way to reach **Dunnottar Castle** (☎ 762173), 1½ miles south, is on foot; the TIC has a walking leaflet. The castle ruins are spread out across a flat rock rising 45m above the sea – as dramatic a film set as any director could wish for. It was last used for Zeffirelli's *Hamlet*, starring Mel Gibson. The original fortress was built in the 9th century; the keep is the most substantial remnant, but the Drawing Room is more interesting. The castle must have supported quite a large community, judging from the extent of the ruins.

The castle opens Easter through September, Monday to Saturday from 9 am to 6 pm, and Sunday from 2 to 5 pm; November to March, Monday to Friday from 9 am to sundown and Sunday from 2 pm to sundown. Entry is £3/1 and last admission is half an hour before closing.

Aberdeen to Fraserburgh

There are attractive beaches at Cruden Bay and Newburgh along this section of the coast, but little to hold the visitor. The remains of a once-great fishing industry are now based in Peterhead.

At Fraserburgh, **Scotland's Lighthouse Museum** (☎ 01346-511022) is a recommended attraction with guided tours to the top of Kinnaird Head lighthouse. It's open Monday to Saturday from 10 am to 6 pm (Sunday from 12.30 pm), closing at 4 pm from November to March; £2.50/2.

Banff & Macduff

* **pop 8170 (combined)**   ☎ 01261

A popular seaside resort, the twin towns of Banff and Macduff are separated by Banff Bridge. Interesting Banff could be an attractive little town, but there's vandalism and neglect here. Nearby Macduff is a busy fishing port. The TIC (☎ 812419), High St, Banff, opens daily April to October and has a free Walkman tour to encourage you to look around the town.

Duff House (☎ 818181), in Banff upstream from the bridge, is an impressive Georgian Baroque mansion designed by William Adam, and completed in 1749. It's been a hotel, hospital and POW camp and is now an art gallery housing a collection of paintings from the National Gallery of Scot-

land. It's open daily from 10 am to 5 pm (closed Monday to Wednesday from October to March); £3/2.

Bluebird Buses runs an infrequent service to Fraserburgh and there are hourly buses to Aberdeen and Elgin.

Elgin

* **pop 20,000**   ☎ 01343

At the heart of Moray, Elgin has been the provincial capital since the 13th century. The TIC (☎ 542666), 17 High St, opens all year.

In medieval times, Elgin was of greater importance than it is now. The great **Elgin Cathedral** (☎ 547171), known as the 'lantern of the north', was consecrated in 1224. In 1390 it was burnt down by the infamous Wolf of Badenach, the illegitimate son of Robert II, following his excommunication by the bishop. It was rebuilt, but ruined once more in the Reformation. It opens April to September, Monday to Saturday from 9.30 am to 6.30 pm, Sunday from 2 to 6.30 pm; for the rest of the year, closing Sunday at 4.30 pm and closed Thursday afternoon and Friday; £1.80/1.30.

Places to Stay A few minutes walk from the centre of the town, *Mrs McMillan's* (☎ *541515, 14 South College St)* has rooms from £16 to £25 per person, with bath. *Southbank Guest House* (☎ *547132, 36 Academy St)* has 11 rooms and charges from £16 to £25 per person. Just west of the centre, *Rosemount* (☎ *542907, 3 Mayne Rd)* offers comfortable B&B in two *en suite* rooms for £20 to £28 per person.

Getting There & Away Bluebird Buses runs services along the coast to Banff and Macduff, south to Dufftown, west to Inverness, and south-east to Aberdeen. A local bus runs to Lossiemouth, passing near Spynie Palace. Trains run five to 10 times daily from Elgin to Aberdeen and Inverness.

Findhorn & Forres

Old and new hippies should check out the Findhorn Foundation (☎ 01309-673655),

Forres IV36 0RD. The Foundation is an international spiritual community founded in 1962. There are about 150 members and many more sympathetic souls who have moved into the vicinity. With no formal creed, the community is dedicated to creating 'a deeper sense of the sacred in everyday life, and to dealing with work, relationships and our environment in new and more fulfilling ways'. In many ways it's very impressive, although it can become a bit outlandish. A recent course was entitled 'Towards Inner Peace and Planetary Wholeness' (has this anything to do with Lonely Planet?).

There are daily tours at 2 pm in summer. The community isn't particularly attractive itself – it started life in the Findhorn Bay Caravan Park and still occupies one end of the site. Far more attractive are the nearby fishing village of Findhorn (1 mile north) and the town of Forres (2½ miles). It's possible to stay in *Findhorn Bay Caravan Park* (☎ 01309-690203), which has camping from £5. There are also week-long residential programs from £250 to £395, including food and accommodation. Findhorn is 4 miles north of Forres, which is on the main bus and rail route between Inverness and Elgin and has lots of places to eat.

Plas Newydd, Llangollen

Penrhyn Castle

The smallest house in Britain, Conwy

Ruins of Brittania copper mine, Mt Snowdon

Route
73
to and from
Oxford Street

73 Islington Kings Cross
Euston Oxford Street
Hyde Park Corner

STOKE NEWINGTON

Route
73
to and from
Oxford Street

73

NML 632E

CHRIS MELLOR

A London bus

Highlands & Northern Islands

Forget the castles, forget the towns and forget the villages. The Highlands and northern islands are all about mountains, sea, heather, moors, lakes – and wide, empty, exhilarating space. This is one of Europe's last great wildernesses and it's more beautiful than you can imagine.

The Highlands is an imprecise term for the upland area which covers the far west and northern half of mainland Scotland. This chapter covers the administrative region known as Highland, the Isle of Skye and the islands of the northern Inner Hebrides, the Outer Hebrides (Western Isles), Orkney and Shetland.

The east coast is dramatic, but it's the north and west, where the mountains and sea collide, that exhaust superlatives. Some of the most beautiful areas can only be reached by many miles of single-track road, by boat or on foot. Make the effort and you'll be rewarded!

ORIENTATION & INFORMATION

The Great Glen, with a series of deep, narrow lochs (including mysterious Loch Ness) cuts across the country south-west to north-east, from Fort William to Inverness, neatly dividing the southern Highlands from the north. East of Loch Ness are the Monadhliath and Cairngorm Mountains' Arctic plateaus, with Aviemore as the main tourist resort. Ben Nevis dominates the town of Fort William in the west.

Most population centres in the rugged, wild Highlands are dotted around the coast, but several island groups are linked to the Highlands. The Orkney Islands are off the north-eastern corner, and farther north are the remote Shetland Islands. West are the Outer Hebrides, while closer, between the Hebrides and the mainland, the beautiful Isle of Skye is a stone's throw from the mainland coast – to which it's connected by a bridge. For the Isle of Mull and other

HIGHLIGHTS

- Callanish Standing Stones (Lewis)
- Plockton
- Cromarty's gabled cottages
- Glen Shiel
- The train from Fort William to Mallaig
- Ullapool
- The boat ride to Cape Wrath
- Glen Coe
- Eilean Donan Castle (outside only)
- Walking around the Quiraing and the Old Man of Storr on Skye
- The prehistoric sites of Orkney
- Coastal walks in Orkney – Hoy and Yesneby
- Birdwatching in the Shetlands
- Sitting among the puffins in North Unst, the northernmost point in Britain

HIGHLANDS & NTH ISLANDS

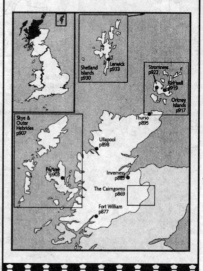

HIGHLANDS & NORTHERN ISLANDS

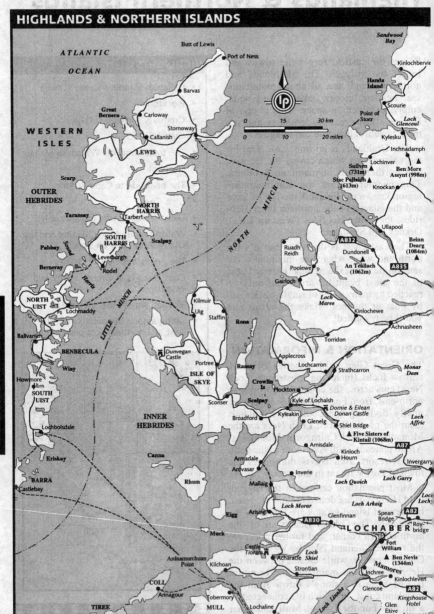

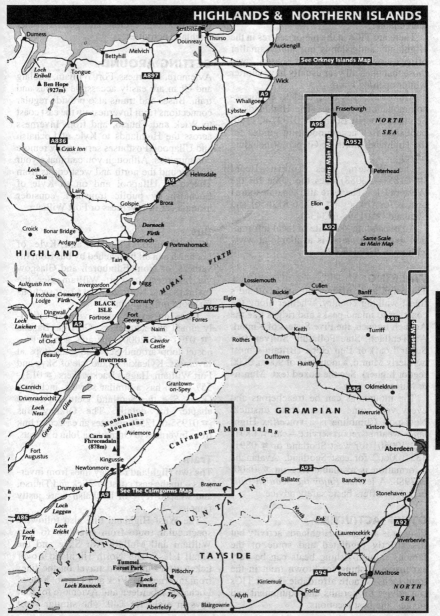

HIGHLANDS & NORTHERN ISLANDS

Dumess
Scrabster
Dounreay
Thurso
Auckengill

Bettyhill
Melvich

Loch Eriboll
Tongue

▲ Ben Hope (927m)

A897

Wick

See Orkney Islands Map

Whaligoe
Lybster

A9

A836

Crask Inn

Dunbeath

Loch Shin

NORTH SEA

Fraserburgh

A98

A952

Peterhead

Lairg

Golspie
Brora

Helmsdale

A9

Ellon

A92

Same Scale as Main Map

Croick
Bonar Bridge
Ardgay

Dornoch Firth
Dornoch
Portmahomack

Tain

HIGHLAND

Aultguish Inn
Inchbae Lodge
Cromarty Firth
Invergordon
Nigg
Cromarty

MORAY FIRTH

Lossiemouth
Buckie
Cullen
Banff

Elgin

A96

Dingwall
BLACK ISLE
Fortrose
Fort George

Forres

Keith

Turriff

A98

See Inset Map

Loch Luichart
Muir of Ord
A9

Nairn

Rothes

Dufftown

Huntly

A96

Oldmeldrum

Beauly

Inverness

Cawdor Castle

Cannich
Drumnadrochit

Grantown-on-Spey

GRAMPIAN

Inverurie
Kintore

Loch Ness

Great Glen

Monadhliath Mountains

Aberdeen

Fort Augustus

Carn an Fhreiceadain (878m)

Aviemore

Cairngorm Mountains

Ballater

A93

Banchory

Kingussie
Newtonmore

See The Cairngorms Map

Braemar

Stonehaven

A92

Drumgask

A9

M O U N T A I N S

North Esk

Laurencekirk

Inverbervie

A86

Loch Laggan

Loch Ericht

TAYSIDE

A94

Brechin

Montrose

Loch Treig

Tummel Forest Park
Pitlochry

Loch Tummel

Kirriemuir

Forfar

NORTH SEA

G R A M P I A N

Loch Rannoch

Tay

Alyth

Blairgowrie

Aberfeldy

HIGHLANDS & NTH ISLANDS

islands to the south, see the Central Scotland chapter.

There are TICs in the major centres in the Highlands and islands but many smaller offices close during the low season; even those that open all year usually have shorter winter opening hours.

Almost all TICs charge £1 to £2 for accommodation bookings. The Highlands of Scotland Tourist Board (☎ 01997-421160) publishes free accommodation guides for the Highlands north of Glencoe (including Skye).

The Western Isles Tourist Board (☎ 01851-703088) does the same for the Western Isles. There are also separate tourist boards for Orkney (☎ 01856-872856) and Shetland (☎ 01595-693434).

An expanding Web site of local information, including maps, is available at www .cali.co.uk/HIGHEXP/.

WALKING

The Highlands offer some of Scotland's finest walking country, whether along the coast, or to inland peaks and ridges like the Aonach Eagach, the Five Sisters of Kintail, An Teallach, Stac Pollaidh, Suilven (the Sugar Loaf) or Ben Hope (Britain's most northerly Munro, a mountain of 900m, 3000 feet or higher). See the boxed text 'Munros & Munro Bagging'.

The mountains can be treacherous and every year some walkers come unstuck. Nevisport Climbline is a voice/fax Highlands weather-report service – call ☎ 0891-333-100601 for west Scotland or ☎ 0891-333-100602 for east Scotland. Avalanche information is available free on ☎ 0800-987988. A leaflet, *Enjoy the Scottish Hills in Safety*, offers basic safety advice.

OTHER ACTIVITIES

Fishing is a popular Highlands activity but it's strictly regulated and some of the famous salmon fishing beats can be very expensive. Fishing for brown trout in the trout lochs is more affordable. Local TICs can advise on permits and equipment and suggest the best locations.

Thurso has some of Europe's best surf. Pony trekking, cycling and golf are other Highland activities.

GETTING AROUND

Aviemore, Inverness, Fort William, Mallaig and Oban are easily accessible by bus and train. Buses and trains also provide regular connections from Inverness up the east coast to Wick and Thurso, and from Inverness across the Highlands to Kyle of Lochalsh and Ullapool. Postbuses serve many remote communities. Although you can make your way around the north and west coasts from Thurso to Ullapool and on to Kyle of Lochalsh by public transport, consider hiring a car in Inverness or Fort William.

Bus

Wick, Thurso, Ullapool and Kyle of Lochalsh can all be reached by bus from Inverness, or from Edinburgh and Glasgow via Inverness or Fort William. See the Inverness and North & West Coast sections for more information.

There are several bus services specifically aimed at backpackers. Go Blue Banana (☎ 0131-556 2000) operates a hostel-to-hostel loop around Scotland with stops at Inverness, Kyleakin on the Isle of Skye and Fort William. Haggis Backpackers (☎ 0131-557 9393) has a similar service, including Oban. See the Scotland Getting Around chapter for details. The Orkney Bus (☎ 01955-611353) operates an east coast link from Inverness to Orkney via John o'Groats.

Train

The two Highland railway lines from Inverness – up the east coast to Wick and Thurso, and west to Kyle of Lochalsh – are justly famous.

The West Highland line also follows a spectacular route from Glasgow to Fort William and Mallaig (for Skye and the Small Isles). The North Highland Rover ticket offers unlimited travel on the lines from Inverness to Wick and Thurso, Kyle of Lochalsh, Aberdeen and Aviemore for four days in eight for £40. The similar West

Highland Rover ticket (£40) covers Glasgow, Oban, Fort William and Mallaig.

For rail information phone ☎ 0345-484950.

The Cairngorms

The magnificent Cairngorms, Britain's highest range and most popular skiing area, soar above forests of regenerating native Caledonian pine in the upper reaches of Strathspey (Speyside). Far more attractive than the regimented Forestry Commission conifer plantations, these native woodlands are home to rare animals like pine martens and wildcats. Red squirrels, ospreys and capercaillie survive here, as does Britain's only herd of reindeer.

The Cairngorm summits provide Britain's only Arctic tundra vegetation, inhabited by birds like snow buntings, ptarmigans and dotterels. What's more, even non-hikers can reach the high peaks, as the Cairngorm chair lift operates year-round.

Aviemore, popular with skiers, hikers and cyclists, is the main resort town. The top hiking routes include the 24 mile Lairig Ghru walk through the peaks and right down to Braemar in the Grampians. If you prefer to avoid the crowds, the lovely but less dramatic Monadhliath (pronounced mona-lee-a) Range, west of the River Spey, sees fewer tourists.

The 100 mile Spey, one of Scotland's top salmon rivers, attracts anglers from all over the world. Pure mountain water from its tributaries provides a basic ingredient for whisky production, and some distilleries can be visited. North of Grantown-on-Spey, the Spey joins the River Avon (pronounced ahn) and continues out of the Cairngorms into Morayshire. For information, including

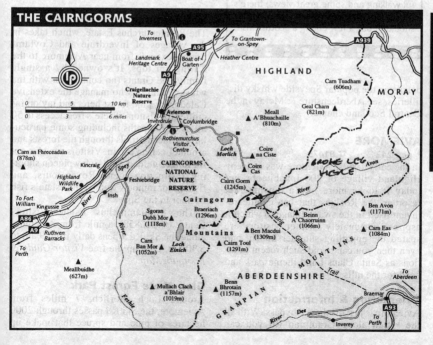

THE CAIRNGORMS

HIGHLANDS & NTH ISLANDS

Munros & Munro Bagging

In 1891 Sir Hugh T Munro published his list of 283 mountains higher than 3000 feet (314m). The list has been argued about ever since – when is a summit a subsidiary 'top' of a mountain as opposed to being a mountain in its own right. The current list of 'Munros' stands at 284. The practice of Munro bagging, climbing the 314m-plus peaks, must have started soon after the list was first published because by 1901 Reverend AE Robertson had climbed the lot. These days, Munro bagging has become a national passion: speculate on a Munro record and it's probably been attempted, from 'first person to climb the lot with a mountain bike' to 'first woman to climb the lot in a single circuit'. The fastest circuit, occurring in 1988 and involving all Munro peaks, took 66 days. Madness it may be, but Munros offer some wonderful walking and some great views; there's no reason why any reasonably fit visitor shouldn't bag a few during a Scottish visit.

❂ ❂ ❂ ❂ ❂ ❂ ❂ ❂ ❂ ❂ ❂ ❂

details on the popular Speyside whisky distilleries, see Aberdeenshire & Moray in the Central Scotland chapter.

AVIEMORE
- pop 2421   ☎ 01479

In the early 1960s, Aviemore was a sleepy Highland village of 200 inhabitants, but today it looks more like a downmarket resort in the Rockies that can't quite reinvent itself in the swank image to which it aspires. Fortunately, winter visitors are spared the appalling summer kitsch, and even then you can avoid such recent additions as Santa Claus Land theme park and head for the hills.

Orientation & Information
Aviemore is just off the A9 bypass. With all the kitsch along Grampian Rd you can hardly get lost. The train station, banks and eateries are on this road. The Cairngorm skiing/hiking area is 8 miles east of Aviemore at the end of the Ski Rd which runs through two large forest estates: Rothiemurchus and Glen More.

The busy TIC (☎ 810363), 500m south of the centre on Grampian Rd, is open year-round, with extended hours in July and August (Monday to Saturday until 7 pm and Sunday until 6 pm). The local accommodation guide is free, but you'll pay £1.50 for bookings through the TIC. There's a *bureau de change* at the TIC. It sells a good range of books and maps, including the yellow Ordnance Survey (OS) Outdoor Leisure Map *Aviemore & the Cairngorms* which covers the whole area, while Ernest Cross' *Walks in the Cairngorms* describes the main hikes.

Of the outdoor-equipment shops along Grampian Rd, try Ellis Brigham (☎ 810175), at No 9, which organises equipment hire and ski lessons.

Rothiemurchus Estate
The Rothiemurchus Estate, which takes in the villages of Inverdruie and Coylumbridge, extends from near Aviemore to the Cairngorm tops. It's owned by a single family, the Grants (no connection with the whisky family), who manage the extensive Caledonian pine forest here, and lay on facilities for visitors. There's free access to 50 miles of footpaths including some particularly attractive trails through the forests and around Loch an Eilein. Visitors can also opt for ranger-guided walks, clay pigeon shooting instruction, Land Rover tours, and fishing for rainbow trout at the estate's fish farm or in the Spey.

The Rothiemurchus Estate Visitors Centre (☎ 810858), a mile from Aviemore along the Ski Rd, opens daily from 9 am to 5.30 pm. Pick up the free *Visitor Guide & Footpath Map*.

Glen More Forest Park
Around Loch Morlich, 7 miles from Aviemore, the Ski Rd passes through 2000 hectares of pine and spruce that make up

Glen More Forest Park. Attractions include a pleasant sandy beach and a popular **water sports centre** (☎ 861221) offering canoeing, windsurfing, sailing and fishing. At the **Cairngorm Reindeer Centre** (☎ 861228), the warden will take you to see and feed the reindeer. Walks leave daily at 11 am (and 2.30 pm in summer); the cost is £4/3.

The visitors centre (☎ 861220) near the loch has the *Glen More Forest Guide Map* detailing local walks.

Activities

Walks To get straight to the best views, take the chair lift (☎ 861261) to the Cairngorm plateau. It starts from the car park at the end of the Ski Rd and ascends in two sections to the 1097m (3600 feet) level, where you'll find Britain's highest café. It operates daily from 9.15 am to 5.15 pm and costs £5/3 return. Plans to replace the lift with a funicular railway have still not been finalised, and the controversy rumbles on.

From the top station, it's a relatively short climb to the summit of Cairngorm (1225m, 4084 feet). You can continue south to climb Ben Macdui (Britain's highest peak at 1309m, 4296 feet), but this can take six to eight hours, including the chair lift ride up.

The **Lairig Ghru walk**, which can take up to eight hours, is a demanding 24 mile route from Aviemore over the Lairig Ghru Pass to Braemar. If you're not doing the full route, it's still worth taking the six hour return hike up to the pass.

Hikers will need a lunch, plenty of liquids, a map, a compass and a windproof jacket. The weather can change almost instantly and snow, even in midsummer, isn't unknown.

Skiing Aviemore isn't Aspen or Val d'Isère but with 28 runs it's Britain's biggest ski area, and when the snow is optimum and the sun's shining, you can close your eyes and imagine you're in the Alps. The season runs from January until the snow melts which can be at the end of April.

The ski area is about 9 miles from Aviemore centre and lifts start from the main Coire Cas car park, and are connected to the more distant Coire na Ciste car park by free shuttle bus. A Cairngorm Day Ticket costs £17/14.50 for adult/concession and under 18s pay £8.50. The TIC distributes the free *Cairngorm Piste Map & Ride Guide* leaflet with advice for safe skiing and snowboarding.

During the ski season the TIC displays relevant avalanche warnings. Call the Ski Hotline (☎ 0891-654655) or tune into Ski FM on 96.6 for reports on snow conditions.

As well as downhill skiing, there are also several cross-country routes.

For more information on skiing see the Activities chapter.

Fishing Fishing is a major sport, both on the Spey and in most of the lochs. Ask the TIC for information on beats and permits. At local shops, fishing permits for salmon cost £20 to £30 per day, while trout permits cost £12. Alvie Estate (☎ 01540-651255) hires rods for £5 per day.

Places to Stay

Camping The nearest camping ground is *Rothiemurchus Camping & Caravan Park* (☎ 812800, Coylumbridge), 1½ miles along the Ski Rd. It charges from £6 per tent. *Glenmore Camping & Caravan Park* (☎ 861271), 5 miles farther along the road near Loch Morlich, charges £7.50 per site.

Hostels The *Aviemore Youth Hostel* (☎ 810345, 25 Grampian Rd) offers upmarket hostelling in a refurbished building from late December to mid-November. It's near the TIC and the start of the Ski Rd; beds cost £8.60/7.10 for adults/juniors (with a £1 surcharge in July and August).

In Glen More Forest Park, 7 miles from Aviemore, the popular *Loch Morlich Youth Hostel* (☎ 861238) has a great location but prebooking is essential. It's open year-round and charges £7.75/6.50. North of Loch Morlich and a mile from the Ski Rd, *Badaguish Outdoor Centre* (☎ 861285) has dormitory accommodation from £5 to £8 and camping from £2.

B&Bs & Hotels – Centre Just off Grampian Rd on Craig na Gower Ave, 350m north of the train station, there's an enclave of B&Bs. Most offer single/double rooms with private baths for around £17/34. Try *Mrs Sheffield's* (☎ 810698), in Dunroamin Cottage. *Karn House* (☎ 810849) charges from £16 per person. *Kila* (☎ 810573, Grampian Rd in the centre) is open year-round and charges from £18/32 for *en suite* rooms.

On Dalfaber Rd are two larger guest-houses. *Kinapol Guest House* (☎ 810513) charges from £16/30; *Ardlogie Guest House* (☎ 810747) has rooms with bath for £17 to £20 per person.

Pleasant *Balavoulin Hotel* (☎ 810672, Grampian Rd) has eight well-equipped double rooms with bath for £18 to £22.50 per person.

In the centre is the recommended *Cairngorm Hotel* (☎ 810233, Grampian Rd), otherwise known as the Cairn, which charges £23 per person for B&B.

One mile from Aviemore, on the Lynwilg road, is an excellent small country-house hotel, *Lynwilg House* (☎ 811685). B&B is £27 to £35 per person, or £45 to £57 for B&B and a dinner to write home about.

B&Bs & Hotels – Ski Rd The excellent *Corrour House Hotel* (☎ 810220, 1½ miles from Aviemore), with splendid views of the Lairig Ghru Pass, opens December to October and charges £24 to £35 per person for rooms with bath.

In Inverdruie, the small *Avondruie Guest House* (☎ 810267) charges from £19 per person for rooms with bathroom. Just beyond Inverdruie on Dell Mhor are several B&Bs.

Mrs Mackenzie (☎ 810235) at No 1, *Mrs Bruce* (☎ 810230) at No 2 and *Mrs Harris* (☎ 810405) at No 5 all offer single/double B&B for around £15/28.

Perhaps the finest of the resort hotels is *Stakis Coylumbridge* (☎ 811811), which enjoys an excellent location just outside Aviemore. Rates start at £55/70.

Places to Eat

There's no shortage of places to eat, but few are particularly inviting. If you prefer to self-cater, Aviemore has an enormous *Tesco supermarket*. For smoked trout, venison, paté and other delicacies visit the *Rothiemurchus Fish Farm* shop (☎ 810703), a short way along the Ski Rd.

Asha Indian Restaurant (☎ 811118, 43 Grampian Rd) near the TIC does vegetarian dishes from £7, and takeaways. *Smiffy's Fish & Chip Restaurant*, nearer the station, does takeaways and a reasonable fry-up, with cod and chips at £2.25. The nearby *Sheffield's Café Bar* (☎ 811670) opens daily from 9 am to 10 pm; bar meals start at £4.50.

Farther north along Grampian Rd, opposite the police station, a branch of *Littlejohn's* (☎ 811633) serves steaks, pizzas, burgers, ribs, potato skins, vegetable fajitas etc in slightly offbeat surroundings. Main dishes are from £4.25. Over the road at No 9, the *Ski-ing Doo* (☎ 810392) serves a range of steaks, including 285g sirloins (£11.29). The *Winking Owl* (☎ 810646, Grampian Rd) has a reasonable choice of pub food and great outdoor seating.

The highly recommended *Old Bridge Inn* (☎ 811137, Dalfaber Rd) near the youth hostel does an excellent salmon and dill tart (£5.95).

There's a small *café* along the Ski Rd in Glen More Forest Park. The *snack bar and restaurant* at the ski resort day lodge in Coire Cas serves snacks, meals and drinks until 4.30 or 5 pm in the winter and until 11 pm in July and August.

Entertainment

From Easter to the end of October every Tuesday at 7 pm, the *Old Bridge Inn* (☎ 811137) hosts a Highland Evening. For £17.50 you get a four course Scottish meal (including soup, haggis, salmon and the delicious Scottish pudding, cranachan), a piper, Highland dancers and live music. Advance booking is advisable.

Aviemore Mountain Resort (☎ 810624) is a large leisure complex, signposted from the centre, with ice rink, dry ski slope, cinema, bars, restaurants and a swimming pool. However, it's a bit of an eyesore and may soon be demolished.

Getting There & Away

Aviemore is 33 miles from Inverness, 62 miles from Fort William, 127 miles from Edinburgh and 505 miles from London.

Bus Buses stop on Grampian Rd; you can make bookings at the TIC.

Scottish Citylink connects Aviemore with Inverness to the north (45 minutes, £4); and to the south to Kincraig (10 minutes), Kingussie (20 minutes), Newtonmore (30 minutes), Dalwhinnie (45 minutes), Pitlochry (1¼ hours), Perth (two hours), Glasgow (3½ hours) and Edinburgh (3½ hours). For Aberdeen, you change to a Midland Bluebird bus at Inverness.

There's one direct daytime service to London's Victoria coach station (11 hours, £39), an overnight service and an early morning service requiring a change in Glasgow. There are also overnight services to Heathrow and Gatwick airports.

Train There are direct train services to London (7½ hours, normally from £61 but bargain singles are £24), Glasgow/Edinburgh (three hours, £20) and Inverness (40 minutes, £8.80).

Strathspey Steam Railway (☎ 810725) operates between Aviemore, Boat of Garten and Nethy Bridge and work has begun on an extension to Grantown. The station is over the tracks from the main train station.

Car MacDonald's Self Drive (☎ 811444), 13 Muirton, rents cars from £30 a day and will deliver/collect from your hotel.

Getting Around

Cairngorm Chairlift Company (☎ 861261) buses link Aviemore and Cairngorm, three to six times daily from late October to April (£2.20/1.10).

Several places in central Aviemore hire out mountain bikes. You can also hire bikes in Rothiemurchus Estate and in Glen More

Forest Park. Most places charge £9 to £14 per day. Aviemore Mountain Bikes (☎ 811007), 45A Grampian Rd, organises guided bike tours.

AROUND AVIEMORE
Kincraig

Kincraig, 6 miles south-west of Aviemore, is another good Cairngorm base. Run by the Royal Zoological Society of Scotland, **Highland Wildlife Park** (☎ 01540-651270), about a mile south of the village, features breeding stocks of local wildlife. There's a drive-through safari park, then several woodland walks offering most people their best opportunity to come face-to-face with an elusive wildcat or furiously displaying male capercaillie. Admission costs £5 for a car with two people and £10 for a car with four. It's open April to October daily from 10 am to 6 pm (7 pm June to August), the rest of the year from 10 am to 4 pm.

At Kincraig, the River Spey widens into **Loch Insh**, home of the Loch Insh Watersports Centre (☎ 01540-651272) which offers canoeing, windsurfing, sailing, bike hire and fishing. There's also B&B accommodation from £16 a head in comfortable rooms with baths. Food here is good, especially after 6.30 pm when the lochside café transforms into a restaurant.

Glen Feshie extends east into the Cairngorms. About 5 miles from Kincraig, *Glen Feshie Hostel* (☎ 01540-651323) is a friendly, independent 14 bed hostel that's very popular with hikers. The nightly charge of £8 includes bed linen and a steaming bowl of porridge to start the day.

Carrbridge

- **pop 543**　　☎ 01479

At Carrbridge, 7 miles north-east of Aviemore, the **Landmark Highland Heritage Centre** (☎ 841614), set in a forest of Scots pines, offers a few novel and worthwhile concepts, such as the raised Treetop Trail which allows you to view red squirrels, crossbills and crested tits. Most of it, however, seems rather tacky. It's open daily year-round, with extended hours in summer. Admission costs £5.95/4.20.

You'll find the ultimate in humpback bridges in the village centre. Built in 1717, it now looks decidedly unsafe, but remains impressive.

In September, the village hosts a Celtic music festival (☎ 841242) and a series of ceilidhs.

Boat of Garten

Eight miles north-east of Aviemore, Boat of Garten is known as the Osprey Village, since these rare birds of prey nest at the Royal Society for the Protection of Birds (RSPB) **Loch Garten Osprey Centre** (☎ 01479-831694) in Abernethy Forest. RSPB volunteers guard the site throughout the nesting season to deter egg collectors. The hide is open to visitors from late April to August, daily from 10 am to 6 pm. Admission for nonmembers is £2.

The best way to get here is on the Strathspey Steam Railway (☎ 01479-810725) which runs at least five times daily from Aviemore – a ticket in 3rd class costs £4.60 return.

Dulnain Bridge & Skye of Curr Bridge

At the Heather Centre (☎ 01479-851359) in Skye of Curr, 2 miles south-west of Dulnain Bridge, you'll learn about the innumerable uses of heather over the centuries. After strolling around the garden centre, you can sample one of 21 recipes for Scottish dumpling (rich fruit cake steamed in a *cloot* or linen cloth) in the adjacent *Clootie Dumpling Restaurant*; the Heather Centre Special comes with cream, ice cream, heather cream liqueur, chopped nuts and blackberry preserve for £3.20.

GRANTOWN-ON-SPEY
* pop 2000   ☎ 01479

This Georgian town on the Spey, which attracts throngs of coach tourists in summer, lies amid an angler's paradise. Most hotels can either kit you up for a day of fishing or put you in touch with someone who can.

The TIC (☎ 872773), 54 High St, opens daily from April to October.

Places to Stay & Eat

Grantown's accommodation reflects its clientele, with plenty of comfortable up-market hotels notable for their food, although there are some budget options.

The *Grantown-on-Spey Caravan Park* (☎ 872474), half a mile from the centre, charges £5 to £10 per vehicle. *Speyside Backpackers* (☎ 872529, 16 The Square), also known as the Stop-Over, has dorm beds for £8.50 per person, but you need your own sleeping bag.

Crann Tara Guest House (☎ 872197, High St) has singles and doubles from £16 per person with shared bath. *Bank House* (☎ 873256, 1 The Square), in the Bank of Scotland, does B&B from £16 to £18 per person.

Highly commended *Ardconnel House* (☎ 872104, Woodlands Terrace) is in a Victorian villa known for its French/Scottish cuisine and elegant atmosphere. Dinner and B&B costs from £42 to £49 per person, and all rooms have private baths. Similarly deluxe *Ravenscourt House Hotel* (☎ 872286, Seafield Ave), near the main square, has *en suite* accommodation for £35 to £45 per person.

Getting There & Away

Highland Country Buses (☎ 01463-233371) runs six to eight buses daily, Monday to Saturday, between Grantown and Aviemore (35 minutes, £3.25). To or from Inverness, you can take the Highland Bus & Coach (☎ 01463-233371) service two or three times daily except Sunday (1¼ hours, £3.40). Also, work is in progress to extend the Strathspey Steam Railway to Grantown-on-Spey.

KINGUSSIE
* pop 1461   ☎ 01540

The tranquil Speyside town of Kingussie (pronounced king-yewsie) is best known as the home of one of Scotland's finest folk museums. The TIC (☎ 661297), just off

High St in King St, opens daily from late May to September.

Highland Folk Museum

Kingussie's Highland Folk Museum (☎ 661307), Duke St, comprises a collection of historical buildings and relics revealing all facets of Highland culture and lifestyles. The 18th century Pitmain Lodge holds displays of ceilidh musical instruments, costumes and washing utensils. The village-like grounds also include a traditional thatch-roofed Isle of Lewis blackhouse, a water mill, a 19th century corrugated iron shed for smoking salmon, and assorted farm implements. In summer, you can watch spinning, woodcarving and peat-fire baking demonstrations. It's open March to September, Monday to Saturday from 10 am to 6 pm, Sunday from 2 to 6 pm; entry is £3/2.

Ruthven Barracks

Built in 1719 on the site of an earlier 13th century castle, Ruthven Barracks (pronounced rivven) was one of four fortresses constructed after the first Jacobite rebellion of 1715 as part of a Hanoverian scheme to take control of the Highlands. Given the long-range views, the location makes perfect sense. The barracks were last occupied by Jacobite troops awaiting the return of Bonnie Prince Charlie after the Battle of Culloden. Learning of his defeat and subsequent flight, they destroyed the barracks before taking to the glens. There's free admission to the ruins, which are floodlit at night.

Walks

The Monadhliath Range, north-west of Kingussie, attracts fewer hikers than the nearby Cairngorms, and makes an ideal destination for walkers seeking peace and solitude. However, during the deer-stalking season (August to October), you'll need to check with the TIC before setting out.

The recommended six hour circular walk to the 878m (2881 feet) summit of Carn an Fhreceadain above Kingussie begins north of the village. It continues to Pitmain Lodge and along the River Allt Mór before climb-ing to the cairn on the summit. You can then follow the ridge east to the twin summits of Beinn Bhreac before returning to Kingussie via a more easterly track.

Places to Stay & Eat

You can camp at the **Caravan Park** (☎ 661600) by the golf course, which costs from £6 per tent. **Lairds Bothy Hostel** (☎ 661334, 68 High St) lies behind the Tipsy Laird pub. There are four family rooms and several eight-bed dorms which cost £8 per person.

Mrs Jarratt's (☎ 661430, St Helens, Ardbroilach Rd) has double rooms from £20 per person. On the western outskirts friendly **Homewood Lodge** (☎ 661507, Newtonmore Rd) does B&B for £18 to £20 per person. You'll have views just outside the front door.

The **Osprey Hotel** (☎ 661510, on the corner of Ruthven Rd) charges £24 per person for B&B in a comfortable Victorian house with good home cooking.

If you're feeling flush, **The Cross** (☎ 661166, Tweed Mill Brae, Ardbroilach Rd) is one of the Highlands' top hotel-restaurants (closed Tuesday). Dinner and B&B costs from £85 per person.

Rather cheaper are pub meals at the **Tipsy Laird** in High St. The most promising of the High St cafés is **La Cafetière**, which does soup and home-made seed bread or herb scone and butter for £1.50, and toasties from £2.10.

Getting There & Away

Kingussie is 120 miles from Edinburgh, 75 miles from Perth and 40 miles from Inverness. It's on the main Edinburgh/Glasgow to Inverness route, so all trains and most Scottish Citylink buses stop here.

KINGUSSIE TO FORT WILLIAM

Just north of Kingussie there's a choice of routes south. The A9 continues to Perth, leaving the Highland region via the bleak Pass of Drumochter. You could detour to visit **Dalwhinnie Distillery** (☎ 01528-522208) which claims to be Scotland's highest distillery. It's open Monday to Friday from 9.30 am to 4.30 pm (Saturday in summer); tours cost £3.

The A86 to Fort William leaves the A9 at Kingussie, continuing through Newtonmore to run along Loch Laggan and **Loch Moy**, a particularly fine stretch of water, with views of Ben Nevis.

The railway joins the road at Tulloch station and follows Glen Spean to the Great Glen, through **Roybridge** and **Spean Bridge**. In Roybridge, the independent *Roybridge Inn Hostel* (☎ 01397-712236), also known as Grey Corrie Lodge, charges £9 per night. Two miles away at Auchluachrach is the recommended hostel, *Aìte Cruinnichidh* (☎ 01397-712315), with beds for £7.

Six miles north of Fort William the **Nevis Range** ski area (☎ 01397-705825) skirts the slopes of Aonach Mór (1221m, 366 feet). Except for from November to Christmas, the gondola cable car to the top station (655m, 2150 feet) operates year-round (£6.25/5.60 return). The *Snowgoose Restaurant* does hearty inexpensive meals. There are walking routes from the Snowgoose and through nearby **Leanachan Forest**. At the base station you can rent bikes for £8.50/12.50 for a half/full day.

The Great Glen

The Great Glen is a natural fault line running across Scotland from Fort William to Inverness as a series of lochs – Linnhe, Lochy, Oich and Ness – linked by the Caledonian Canal. It has always been a communication (and invasion) route and General George Wade built a military road along the south side of Loch Ness from 1724. The modern A82 road along the north side was completed in 1933.

The 80 mile Great Glen Cycle Route from Fort William to Inverness via Fort Augustus follows canal towpaths and gravel tracks through forests to avoid busy roads where possible. The *Cycling in the Forest* leaflet, available from TICs or the Forestry Commission, gives details.

GETTING AROUND
Bus
Scottish Citylink (☎ 0990-505050) has several daily services along the loch between Fort William and Inverness (two hours, £6.30). Inverness Traction (☎ 01463-239292) has day tours from Inverness to Loch Ness costing £9.75/7.75.

FORT WILLIAM
* **pop 10,774**   ☎ 01397

Fort William, which lies beside Loch Linnhe amid some of Britain's most magnificent mountain landscapes, has one of the finest settings in the country. Although insensitive civic planning compromised its appeal for many years, the conversion of the High St to a mall and the determination of its people have turned it into a rather pleasant little town. As a major tourist centre, it's easily accessed by rail and bus lines, and makes a great base for exploring the mountains and glens of Lochaber.

Magical Glen Nevis begins near the north end of the town and extends west below the slopes of Ben Nevis. 'The Ben' – Britain's highest mountain at 1342m (4406 feet) – and neighbouring mountains are a magnet for hikers and climbers. The glen is popular with movie-makers – part of Mel Gibson's Oscar-winning *Braveheart* was filmed here.

Orientation & Information
The town meanders along the edge of Loch Linnhe for several miles. The centre, with its small selection of shops, takeaways and pubs, is easy to get around on foot unless you're booked into a far-flung B&B.

The busy TIC (☎ 703781), in Cameron Square, has a good range of books and maps. For local walks, its leaflet series of *Great Walks* incorporating a map and basic information are handy, but you'll need an OS map for more adventurous hikes, such as Ben Nevis. More information is available from the Glen Nevis Visitors Centre, Ionad Nibheis, 1½ miles up the glen from town; entry £1.

As you might expect, Fort William has well-stocked outdoor-equipment shops.

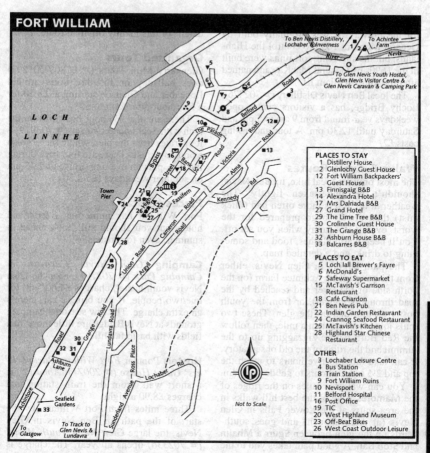

FORT WILLIAM

LOCH LINNHE

To Ben Nevis Distillery, Lochaber & Inverness

To Achintee Farm

River Nevis

To Glen Nevis Youth Hostel, Glen Nevis Visitor Centre & Glen Nevis Caravan & Camping Park

The Parade

Town Pier

Ashburn Lane

Seafield Gardens

To Glasgow

To Track to Glen Nevis & Lundavra

Not to Scale

PLACES TO STAY
1 Distillery House
2 Glenlochy Guest House
12 Fort William Backpackers' Guest House
13 Finnisgaig B&B
14 Alexandra Hotel
17 Mrs Dalriada B&B
29 The Lime Tree B&B
30 Crolinnhe Guest House
31 The Grange B&B
32 Ashburn House B&B
33 Balcarres B&B

PLACES TO EAT
5 Loch Iall Brewer's Fayre
6 McDonald's
7 Safeway Supermarket
15 McTavish's Garrison Restaurant
18 Café Chardon
21 Ben Nevis Pub
22 Indian Garden Restaurant
24 Crannog Seafood Restaurant
25 McTavish's Kitchen
28 Highland Star Chinese Restaurant

OTHER
3 Lochaber Leisure Centre
4 Bus Station
8 Train Station
9 Fort William Ruins
10 Nevisport
11 Belford Hospital
16 Post Office
19 TIC
20 West Highland Museum
23 Off-Beat Bikes
26 West Coast Outdoor Leisure

HIGHLANDS & NTH ISLANDS

Nevisport (☎ 704921), near the train station, has a marvellous range of books and maps for mountaineers. West Coast Outdoor Leisure (☎ 705777) is at the other end of High St.

West Highland Museum

Beside the TIC, this museum (☎ 702169) is packed with Highland memorabilia. Of particular interest is the secret portrait of Bonnie Prince Charlie. After the Jacobite rebellions, all things Highland were banned,

including pictures of the exiled leader. This picture looks like nothing more than a smear of paint until placed next to a curved mirror, when it reflects a likeness of the prince. The museum opens all year, Monday to Saturday, until at least 4 pm (5 pm from May to September) and in July and August on Sunday afternoon; entry is £2/1.50.

Other Things to See

There's little left of the original **Fort William** from which the town takes its name, as it was pulled down in the 19th century to make way for the railway. It was originally built by General Monk in 1635 to control the Highlands, but the surviving fort ruins were built in the 1690s by General MacKay and named after the king, William III.

The local **Ben Nevis Distillery** (☎ 702476), Lochy Bridge, has a visitors centre open weekdays year-round from 9 am to 5 pm and Saturday until 12.30 pm. A tour and tasting costs £2.

Walks & Cycle Routes

The most obvious local hike, up **Ben Nevis**, shouldn't be undertaken lightly. The weather at the top is more often bad (thick mist) than good, so go prepared for the worst, even if it's sunny when you set off. You'll need warm clothes, food and something to drink, and a detailed map.

The path begins in Glen Nevis, either from the car park by Achintee Farm (on the north side of the river and reached by the road through Claggan), or from the youth hostel on the road up the glen. These two trails join after less than a mile, then follow the Red Burn before zigzagging up to the summit and the ruins of the old observatory. It can take three to five hours to reach the top and 2½ to four hours to get down again.

You can walk for miles on the ridges of the **Mamores**. One of the best hill walks in the area starts at the Lower Falls in Glen Nevis (at Achriabhach) and goes southwards up the glen between **Sgurr a'Mhaim** and **Stob Ban**. A good path takes you to the tiny loch below the **Devil's Ridge**, zigzags up the steep slope north-east of the loch and turns left along the spectacular ridge for Sgurr a'Mhaim (1099m, 3605 feet). The round trip takes about six hours.

There are pleasant (far less strenuous) walks along Glen Nevis through the gorge at the east end to beautiful **Steall Meadows**. You could also walk part of the **West Highland Way** from Fort William to Kinlochleven via Glen Nevis (14 miles) or even to Glencoe (21 miles to the junction with the A82).

The 80 mile **Great Glen Cycle Route** links Fort William and Inverness. The

Forestry Commission's free leaflet gives details of this mainly off-road route.

Organised Tours

Glengarry Mini Tours (☎ 01809-501297) does half-day or full-day tours around Lochaber and Glencoe starting at £8.50 for a four hour afternoon tour.

There are also 1½ hour boat trips on the loch with Seal Island Cruises (☎ 703919) – it operates from the pier, where there's also a booking kiosk. There are four trips during the day, plus an evening cruise at 7.45 pm on summer weekdays (£5/2.50).

Places to Stay

Fort William has numerous B&Bs and hotels but you should still book ahead in summer, even for hostels.

Camping *Glen Nevis Caravan & Camping Park* (☎ 702191), near the Glen Nevis youth hostel, charges £4.60/5.60 for one/two people. If you bring a car, there's an extra charge. The few seasonal camping grounds at Nevis Bridge are little more than fields with basic facilities.

Hostels Popular *Fort William Backpackers' Guest House* (☎ 700711, Alma Rd) is a short walk from the train station and charges £8.90 a night.

Three miles from Fort William, by the start of the path up Ben Nevis in Glen Nevis, the large *Glen Nevis Youth Hostel* (☎ 702336) opens all year. The charge is £8.60/7.10 for adults/juniors. Across the river, *Ben Nevis Bunkhouse* (☎ 702240, Achintee Farm) is a good alternative (£8).

In Corpach, 4 miles along the Mallaig road north of Fort William, there's *Smiddy Bunkhouse* (☎ 772467, Station Rd), an independent hostel charging from £8.50. The attached activity centre organises mountaineering, kayaking and sailing trips.

B&Bs & Hotels Several B&Bs in and around Fassifern Rd are closest to the train and bus stations. Try *Finnisgaig* (☎ 702453, Alma Rd), which charges from £14 for a double, or *Mrs Dalriada* (☎ 702533, 2 Caberfeidh, Fassifern Rd), where B&B costs £15 to £21 for a double. Achintore Rd, which runs south along the loch, is packed with B&Bs and hotels, but some seem large and characterless.

More interesting is the B&B-cum-art gallery at the *Lime Tree* (☎ 701806), which has beds for around £14. The comfortable *Ashburn House* (☎ 706000) has rooms with bath for £25 to £35 per person.

Several B&Bs just off Achintore Rd offer pleasant loch views, including *Balcarres* (☎ 702377), which charges from £16 to £25.

On Grange Rd, parallel to Achintore Rd, there are two very comfortable guesthouses whose owners' attention to detail has earned them the top tourist-board rating. The excellent three room *Grange* (☎ 705516) and the *Crolinnhe* (☎ 702709) next door charge from £33 to £35 per person (double).

The *Alexandra Hotel* (☎ 702241, The Parade) is a large, traditional hotel with comfortable doubles with bath from £34.50. The *Grand Hotel* (☎ 702928, High St) is the other large, central hotel, with rooms from £25 per person.

Distillery House (☎ 702980, the old Glenlochy Distillery) opposite the road into Glen Nevis is thoroughly recommended. Rooms with baths cost £25/44, to £35/64 for *en suite* singles/doubles.

The wonderfully grand five-star *Inverlochy Castle* (☎ 702177), in 200-hectare grounds 3 miles north of Fort William, is an opulent Victorian creation completed in 1865. It has everything you'd expect to find in a castle – crenellated battlements, stags' heads, log fires and a wide staircase. Luxurious rooms cost from £180/250. Reservations are requisite.

Glen Nevis offers several more places to stay, including *Achintee Farm* (☎ 702240), which has B&B accommodation as well as the bunkhouse. Rooms cost from £16 to £22 per head.

Places to Eat

With the honourable exception of the Crannog Seafood Restaurant, Fort William is

pretty much a culinary desert. For those on a tight budget, the *Safeway Coffee Shop* near the bus and train stations is good value – filled jacket potatoes cost from £2. It's open until 8 or 9 pm weekdays, 6 pm at weekends. Across the road, *Loch Iall Brewer's Fayre* (☎ 703707) does a range of main courses from £4.35.

Nevisport Bar & Restaurant (☎ 704921), in the outdoor-equipment shop, does cheap meals but closes at 7.30 pm Monday to Saturday; Sunday it closes even earlier. Bar meals, including vegetarian options, start at £4.

Most other places to eat line the High St. *Café Chardon*, upstairs in P Maclennan's store, has soup for £1.85, filled ciabatta sandwiches for £2.50 and focaccia for £3.05.

McTavish's Kitchen (☎ 702406, High St) has the same menu and floor show (see Entertainment) as the Oban branch. There's a self-service café downstairs. On High St, *McTavish's Garrison Restaurant* (same phone number) offers food only.

Indian Garden Restaurant (☎ 705011, 88 High St) is popular and not too expensive. It does takeaways for around £5, and stays open late. You can also get takeaways from the town's only Chinese restaurant, the *Highland Star* (☎ 703905, 155 High St), which has a good reputation.

The best restaurant in town is *Crannog Seafood Restaurant* (☎ 705589), on the pier, giving diners an uninterrupted view over the loch. A two course set lunch is £7.50, and main courses cost from £10 to £15.

Entertainment

McTavish's Kitchen (☎ 702406) takes the pile 'em high, sell 'em cheap approach to Scottish cuisine and culture, but the music's good and it can be fun as long as you get into the spirit of things. Shows are staged nightly at 8.30 pm, with dancing, a live band and a piper. It costs £1.50/1 with a meal, £3/1.50 without, and set meals start at £8, including the show. A disco operates on

Friday and Saturday from 10.30 pm (cover charge £3).

On the opposite side of High St, the Jacobite Bar in the **Ben Nevis** pub is a popular music venue and a good place for a drink or inexpensive meal. The **Nevisport Bar**, in the Nevisport complex, beckons walkers and climbers.

Getting There & Away

Fort William is 597 miles from London, 146 miles from Edinburgh, 104 miles from Glasgow and 66 miles from Inverness. If you've got a spare week the best way to get here is on foot, along the 95 mile West Highland Way from just north of Glasgow (see the Activities chapter).

Bus Scottish Citylink (☎ 0990-505050) has four or five direct daily buses to Glasgow (three hours, £10) via Glencoe, with connections to London. There are three direct daily Citylink buses between Fort William and Kyle of Lochalsh (two hours, £9). It also has two or three buses daily between Fort William and Oban (1¾ hours, £6). There are also several daily services along Loch Ness to Inverness (two hours, £6.30) and two or three daily except Sunday to and from Mallaig (1½ hours, £4.50), via Glenfinnan. Another useful Monday to Saturday service runs to Glencoe (30 minutes, £1.40).

Highland Country Buses (☎ 702373) runs six daily services to Kinlochleven (45 minutes, £2.10) via Glencoe.

Train The spectacular West Highland line runs from Glasgow via Fort William to Mallaig. There's a particularly wonderful wild section across bleak Rannoch Moor. There's no direct rail connection between Oban and Fort William; use the Scottish Citylink bus services to avoid backtracking to Crianlarich.

There are two or three trains daily from Glasgow to Fort William (3½ hours, £22.70), and one to four trains between Fort William and Mallaig (1½ hours, £7.20). The Highland Rover ticket (£42) allows un-

limited travel on four days in eight consecutive days.

An overnight train connects Fort William and London Euston (from £79 including the sleeper) but you'll miss the views.

Car The TIC has a leaflet listing car hire places. Try MacRae & Dick (☎ 702500), on the road to the Isles Filling Station, Lochy Bridge.

Getting Around

Bus Highland Country Buses runs from the bus station up Glen Nevis to the youth hostel (10 minutes, £1.10), leaving roughly hourly from 8 am to 11 pm, Monday to Saturday from June to September. Buses to Corpach (15 minutes) are more frequent.

Bicycle Off-Beat Bikes (☎ 704008), 117 High St and also at the Nevis Range base station, has mountain bikes for £8.50/12.50 for a half/full day. It also runs guided bike tours of the area for around £40, excluding bike hire.

FORT WILLIAM TO GLEN COE

South of Fort William, the A82 follows Loch Linnhe as far as **Inchree**. Accommodation includes *Inchree Bunkhouse* (☎ 01855-821287), with beds from £7 and a pub/restaurant on the site. It's easy to get here by bus as this is the main route between Fort William and Glasgow or Oban. For something more stylish, there's the *Lodge on the Loch* (☎ 01855-821237) in nearby Onich, with luxurious singles/doubles from £44/88 and a good restaurant.

At North Ballachulish you can either cross the bridge and continue along the A82 into Glencoe village or take the side road that runs up Loch Leven to Kinlochleven and back to Glencoe along the southern shore.

GLEN COE

Scotland's most famous glen was written into the history books in 1692 when Mac-Donalds were murdered by Campbells in what became known as the Massacre of Glencoe. (See the boxed text 'The Glen Coe

The Glen Coe Massacre

The brutal murders that took place here in 1692 were particularly shameful, perpetrated as they were by one Highland clan on another (with whom they were lodging as guests).

In an attempt to quash remaining Jacobite loyalties among the Highland clans, William III had ordered that all chiefs take an oath of loyalty to him by the end of the year (1691). Maclain, the elderly chief of the MacDonalds of Glen Coe, was late in setting out to fulfil the king's demand, and going first to Fort William rather than Inverary made him later still.

The Secretary of State for Scotland, Sir John Dalrymple, declared the MacDonalds should be punished as an example to other Highland clans, some of whom had not bothered to even take the oath. A company of 120 soldiers, mainly of the Campbell clan, was sent to the glen. Since their leader was related by marriage to Maclain, the troops were billeted in MacDonald homes. It was a long-standing tradition for clans to provide hospitality to passing travellers.

After they'd been guests for 12 days, the order came for the soldiers to put to death all MacDonalds under the age of 70. Some Campbells alerted the MacDonalds to their intended fate, while others turned on their hosts at 5 am on 13 February, shooting Maclain and 37 other men, women and children. Some died before they knew what was happening, while others fled into the snow, only to die of exposure.

The ruthless brutality of the incident caused a public uproar and after an inquiry several years later, Dalrymple lost his job. There's a monument to Maclain in Glencoe village and members of the MacDonald clan still gather here on 13 February each year.

Massacre'.) However, it's also one of the country's most beautiful glens, with steeply sloping sides and narrow-sided valleys that provided the cattle-rustling Highlanders with the perfect place to hide their stock. The glen is dominated by three massive, brooding spurs, known as the Three Sisters of Glencoe.

There are wonderful walks in this highly atmospheric glen, much of which is owned by the National Trust for Scotland (NTS), and some excellent accommodation.

Glencoe Village
- pop 360   ☎ 01855

Standing by Loch Leven, at the entrance to the glen, the village is 16 miles from Fort William on the main Glasgow road. There's an NTS visitors centre (☎ 811307) 1½ miles from the village along the road into the glen. It's open daily April to October from 10 am to 5 pm, and from 9.30 am to 5.30 pm mid-May to August. It's worth paying the 50/30p entry fee to see the 14 minute video on the Glencoe Massacre. The small thatched **Glencoe Folk Museum** aside, there's little to see in the village.

Places to Stay & Eat You can camp at *Invercoe Caravans* (☎ 811210) where sites cost from £8 to £12 per night, or you can rent a caravan by the week.

Glencoe Youth Hostel (☎ 811219), a 1½ mile walk from the village on the north side of the river, is popular, particularly with climbers, so you'll need to book ahead. Open all year, the nightly charge is £7.75/6.50 for adults/juniors.

Nearby, *Leacantuim Farm Bunkhouse* (☎ 811256) has bunkhouse accommodation for £7.50, or £6 in the Alpine Barn. It also runs *Red Squirrel Campsite*, charging campers £3.50 each.

Two and a half miles from the village is *Clachaig Inn* (☎ 811252) offering B&B in rooms with private bath from £18 to £32 a head. There's a pub, good food and live music several times a week.

On the village outskirts, *Glencoe Guest House* (☎ *811244, Strathlachan*) charges £15 to £18 per person.

Getting There & Away Highland Country Buses (☎ 01397-702373) runs buses from Fort William to Glencoe (30 minutes). Scottish Citylink buses run to Glasgow (2½ hours, £8.80).

Glencoe Ski Centre

About 1½ miles from Kingshouse Hotel, on the other side of the A82, is the car park and base station for this ski centre, where commercial skiing in Scotland first started in 1956. At the base station there's a **Museum of Scottish Skiing & Climbing** (☎ 01855-851226); among the relics is the ice axe Chris Bonington used to climb Everest.

The chair lift (☎ 01855-851226) operates all week in summer (late June to August) from 9.30 am to 5 pm; it costs £3.75/2.50 return. The chair lift is the easiest way to get to the 640m-high (2099 feet) viewpoint and several good walks.

Kingshouse Hotel

Scotland's oldest established inn, this isolated hotel (☎ 01855-851259) has been a landmark for so long that it now appears on maps, marked simply as 'Hotel'. It's on the West Highland Way at the east end of the glen, and hikers stop here to tuck into a plate of haggis, tatties and *neeps* (turnips) and a refreshing drink in the bar. It's a good place to stay, with rooms from £23.50/53 plus £7 for breakfast.

Walks

This is serious walking country and you'll need maps, warm clothes, and food and water. The NTS visitors centre stocks lots of useful information.

A great six hour hike leads through the Lost Valley to the top of **Bidean nam Bian** (1141m, 3742 feet). Cross the footbridge below Allt-na-Reigh and follow the gorge up into the Lost Valley, continuing up to the

rim, then along it to the right, to the summit. You need to be very careful crossing to Stob Coire nan Lochan as there are steep scree slopes. Descend the west side of this ridge and round into Coire nan Lochan, where a path heads back to the road.

For something less strenuous, hike this route as far as the **Lost Valley**, a hidden mountain sanctuary. Allow three hours for the return trip.

Aonach Eagach, the glen's northern wall, is said to be the best ridge walk on the Scottish mainland, but it's difficult in places and you need a good head for heights. Some parts could almost be graded a rock climb. It's best done from east to west, and there's a path up the hillside north of Allt-na-Reigh and down from Sgor nam Fiannaidh towards Loch Achtriochtan. The more direct gully that leads to Clachaig Inn isn't a safe way down. It takes six to eight hours.

FORT WILLIAM TO FORT AUGUSTUS

It's 33 miles along the A82 from Fort William to Fort Augustus, but it's worth taking the slightly longer B8004 route at first to see **Neptune's Staircase**, a flight of eight locks which raises the water in the Caledonian Canal by 19.5m. Scottish engineer Thomas Telford's canal was built from 1803 to 1822 to connect the east and west coasts of Scotland, from Inverness to Fort William. The lochs make up 38 miles of the canal's total 60 miles and there are 29 locks.

This side trip rejoins the A82 at the **Commando Memorial** to the WWII military force that trained here. The road then runs along the south-eastern shore of **Loch Lochy** before crossing the canal by the Laggan Locks to run along the northern shore of narrow **Loch Oich**. At the head of Loch Oich, the **Well of the Heads** details the summary justice handed out to seven 16th century murderers by their victims' aggrieved family.

FORT AUGUSTUS

• pop 600   ☎ 01320

Fort Augustus, at the junction of four of General Wade's military roads, was the headquarters for his road-building operations from 1724.

The TIC (☎ 366367) in the car park opens from Easter to October and charges £2 for local bookings.

Fort Augustus Abbey

Between 1729 and 1742, as part of his plan to pacify the Highlands, General Wade built a fort where the River Tarff joined Loch Ness. Although it was captured and later damaged by the retreating Jacobites, it remained occupied until 1854. In 1876, Benedictine monks took over the building and founded Fort Augustus Abbey. The adjoining Catholic boys' school was closed in 1994. The abbey shut late in 1998.

Other Things to See

At Fort Augustus, boats using the **Caledonian Canal** are raised and lowered 13m by **five locks**. When the swing bridge is opened, however, it can cause long delays on the busy A82. The promontory between the canal and the River Oich affords a fine view over Loch Ness. Tiny **Cherry Island**, on the Inverness side of Fort Augustus, was originally a *crannog* or artificial island settlement.

Cruises on Loch Ness on the *Catriona* (☎ 366233) operate April to October. The 50 minute trip costs £4.

Places to Stay & Eat

The *Abbey* (☎ 366233) offers B&B from £16 per person; the attached *Abbot's Table* restaurant does everything from soup and a roll to main courses and is highly recommended. There's also a good choice of B&Bs for £13 to £19 per person, including *Appin* (☎ 366541, Inverness Rd) and *Greystone's* (☎ 366736, Station Rd).

The *Coffee House* (☎ 366361) opposite the car park offers café-style food by day but becomes a restaurant in the evening. Near the canal the *Jac-O-Bite* tearoom deserves a visit for its name alone; jacket potatoes cost £2 to £3. The *Bothy Bite* (☎ 366710) is an alternative lunch spot with canal views.

Loch Ness Monster

Although there's a tale of St Columba meeting Nessie (the Loch Ness Monster) in the 6th century, the craze has only really developed since 1933, when the A82 road was completed along the loch. The classic monster photograph of a dinosaur-like creature's long neck emerging from the water was taken in 1934, and from then on the monster hunt was on. In recent years there have been sonar hunts, underwater cameras and computer studies, but unfortunately no monster has turned up. The loch is very deep and very murky, so the Nessie tourist business has to pedal very hard to make a go of it. Keep your camera handy – you could be the one to prove the monster does exist.

Getting There & Away

Scottish Citylink runs five or six buses daily between Inverness and Fort William, stopping at Fort Augustus en route. To get to either town takes an hour and costs £5.80.

LOCH NESS

Dark, deep and narrow Loch Ness stretches 23 miles from Fort Augustus at its southern end nearly as far as Inverness. Its bitterly cold waters have been extensively explored for Nessie, the elusive Loch Ness monster, and although some visitors get lucky, most see only a cardboard cut-out form. Along the north-western shore runs the congested A82, while the more tranquil and extremely picturesque B862 follows the south-eastern shore. A complete circuit of the loch is about 70 miles, and you'll have the best views travelling anticlockwise.

DRUMNADROCHIT
- **pop 600**   ☎ 01456

Exploitation of poor Nessie reaches fever pitch at Drumnadrochit where two 'Monster' exhibitions vie for the tourist dollar. The villages of Milton, Lewiston and

HIGHLANDS & NTH ISLANDS

Strone are adjacent with Drumnadrochit while Urquhart Castle is immediately south.

Monster Exhibitions

The prominent **Official Loch Ness Monster Exhibition Centre** (☎ 450218) is the better of the two Nessie theme exhibitions, featuring a 40 minute audiovisual presentation plus exhibits of equipment used in the various underwater monster hunts. In summer, it's open daily from 9.30 am to 6.30 pm, with shorter winter hours. Admission costs £4.50/3.50. Children over seven are charged £2.50; students must have ID. The nearby **Original Loch Ness Monster Centre** (☎ 450342) shows a marginal 30 minute Loch Ness video for £3.50/2.75. The video portion comes with multilingual headsets. It's open June to September daily from 8.30 am to 9.30 pm, with shorter hours during the rest of the year.

Urquhart Castle

Urquhart Castle (☎ 450551, HS), one of Scotland's best known castles, was taken and lost by Edward I, held by Robert the Bruce against Edward III and fought over by everyone who passed this way. Not only was the castle repeatedly sacked, damaged and rebuilt over the centuries but the unfortunate inhabitants of the Great Glen were also regularly pillaged and robbed in the process.

Destruction and reconstruction followed so regularly that it's hard to trace the full story of the castle's development. By the 1600s it had become redundant, superseded by more palatial residences and more powerful fortresses at Fort William and Inverness. It was finally blown up in 1692 to prevent Jacobites using it and its remains perch dramatically on the edge of the loch, approached by a steep path from the roadside car park.

The castle was entered by a drawbridge that led into the gatehouse. The summit of the upper bailey (outmost wall) at the southern end was probably used as a hillfort over 1000 years ago but by the 15th century the nether bailey at the northern end had become the focus of fortifications. The five

storey tower house at the extreme northern end is the most impressive remaining fragment and offers wonderful loch views.

From April to September hours are daily from 9.30 am to 6.30 pm, and from October to March it closes at 4.30 pm; entry is £3.50/2.80.

Places to Stay & Eat

Loch Ness Backpackers (☎ 450807, East Lewiston) lies within walking distance of Drumnadrochit and Urquhart Castle. Dorm beds cost from £8.50. *Loch Ness Youth Hostel* (☎ 01320-51274), 13 miles down the loch at Glenmoriston, costs £6.10/4.95. There are numerous B&Bs in Drumnadrochit but single rooms are in short supply. If you're driving, try the welcoming *Drumbuie Farm* (☎ 450634), on the right as you enter Drumnadrochit from Inverness. It has comfortable rooms for £16 to £20 per person.

Glen Café (☎ 450282), and the more expensive *Fiddler's Café Bar* (☎ 450678) with traditional Scottish fare, are both near the village green. The restaurant at the *Drumnadrochit Hotel* (☎ 450218) is noted for its fine cuisine and service. Well-appointed rooms start at £24.50 per person.

Getting There & Around

Scottish Citylink (☎ 0990-505050) has five or six daily services along the loch between Fort William and Inverness, via Drumnadrochit.

Fiddler's Café Bar hires good-quality mountain bikes for £12/45 per day/week, all-inclusive.

INVERNESS
• pop 41,800   ☎ 01463

Inverness has a great location on the Moray Firth at the northern end of the Great Glen. The town was probably founded by David I in the 12th century and is now the capital and transportation hub of the Highlands. In summer it overflows with visitors intent upon monster-hunting at nearby Loch Ness. However, it's worth spending some time strolling and birdwatching along the picturesque River Ness or cruising on the

Moray Firth in search of its 100 or so bottlenose dolphins.

Orientation & Information

The River Ness, which links Loch Ness and the Moray Firth, flows through the heart of town. The bus and train stations and hostels are east of the river, within 10 minutes walk of each other. The TIC (☎ 234353) is beside the museum on Castle Wynd just off Bridge St, and you'll find a smaller tourist office at North Kessock on the A9 north.

Inverness Museum & Art Gallery

The Inverness Museum & Art Gallery (☎ 237114) contains wildlife dioramas, geological displays, period rooms with historic weapons, Pictish stones and a missable art gallery. It's entered through Castle Wynd off Bridge St and opens Monday to Saturday from 9 am to 5 pm. Entry is free.

Inverness Castle

In the 11th century a timber castle probably stood to the east of the present castle site. In

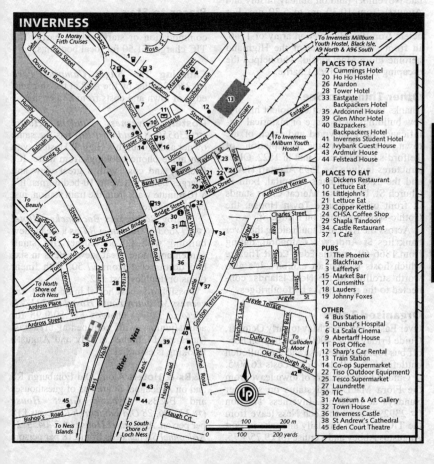

INVERNESS

PLACES TO STAY
7 Cummings Hotel
20 Ho Ho Hostel
26 Mardon
28 Tower Hotel
33 Eastgate
   Backpackers Hotel
35 Ardconnel House
39 Glen Mhor Hotel
40 Bazpackers
   Backpackers Hotel
41 Inverness Student Hotel
42 Ivybank Guest House
43 Ardmuir House
44 Felstead House

PLACES TO EAT
8 Dickens Restaurant
10 Lettuce Eat
11 Littlejohn's
21 Lettuce Eat
23 Copper Kettle
24 CHSA Coffee Shop
29 Shapla Tandoori
34 Castle Restaurant
37 1 Café

PUBS
1 The Phoenix
2 Blackfriars
3 Laffertys
15 Market Bar
17 Gunsmiths
18 Lauders
19 Johnny Foxes

OTHER
4 Bus Station
5 Dunbar's Hospital
6 La Scala Cinema
9 Abertarff House
11 Post Office
12 Sharp's Car Rental
13 Train Station
14 Co-op Supermarket
22 Tiso (Outdoor Equipment)
25 Tesco Supermarket
27 Laundrette
30 TIC
31 Museum & Art Gallery
32 Town House
36 Inverness Castle
38 St Andrew's Cathedral
45 Eden Court Theatre

HIGHLANDS & NTH ISLANDS

the 12th century it was replaced with a stone castle, which was then rebuilt in the 15th century. It was repaired in 1718 and expanded in 1725, only to be taken by the Jacobites in 1746 and blown up. The present rose-coloured structure was constructed between 1837 and 1847.

Today it serves as the local Sheriff's Court and most of the youths hanging around outside are waiting for their cases to be heard. The Drum Tower now houses the **Castle Garrison Encounter** (☎ 243363), which opens Monday to Saturday, Easter to late November (and on Sunday in July and August) from 10.30 am to 5.30 pm. For £3/2.70 you meet actors representing characters from the Hanoverian army of 1746. In front stands a statue of the Highland heroine Flora MacDonald, who helped the escaping Bonnie Prince Charlie.

Other Things to See

Thanks to Inverness' often violent history, few buildings of real age or historical significance have survived and much of the town dates from the completion of Telford's Caledonian Canal in 1822. Older structures include the 1593 **Abertaff House** and the 1668 **Dunbar's Hospital**, both in Church St. Inverness' **Mercat Cross** stands in front of the ornate **Town House**, the Gothic-style town hall on Bridge St.

Across the river and south along the river bank lies **St Andrew's Cathedral**, dating from 1866-69, and the **Eden Court Theatre** which hosts regular art exhibits. It's also worth strolling to the **Ness Islands**, connected to the river banks by footbridges.

Organised Tours

Over Easter and from May to early October, Guide Friday (☎ 224000) runs hop-on hop-off bus tours of Inverness and the Culloden battlefield. An all-day ticket costs £6.50/5.

Guided walking tours of town leave from the Flora MacDonald statue on summer Sundays at 10.30 am. Inverness Traction (☎ 239292) tours to Loch Ness leave from the TIC at 10.15 am daily and take in Fort Augustus Abbey and a cruise for £9.75/7.75.

From Tomnahurich Bridge, the *Jacobite Queen* (☎ 233999) cruises Loch Ness for £9/7 to £12/9. A one-way trip to Urquhart Castle, including entry, costs £9.50/8.

Moray Firth Cruises (☎ 717900) offers 1½ hour wildlife cruises to see dolphins, seals and bird life. Sightings aren't guaranteed but it's still enjoyable, especially on fine days. Follow the signs to Shore St Quay from the far end of Chapel St. Trips cost £10/8 and leave between 10.30 am and 4.30 pm (6 pm in July and August). Buses leave from the TIC 15 minutes before sailings.

Places to Stay

In the peak season, either prebook your accommodation or start looking early. The TIC charges £1.50 for local bookings.

Camping The *Bught Camping Park* (☎ 236920) lies by the A82 at the southern edge of town and costs from £3 per site.

Hostels *Inverness Student Hostel* (☎ 236556, 8 Culduthel Rd) has the same owner as Edinburgh's High St Hostel – you can make phone bookings from there. It's friendly and cosy with a great view and charges £8.50 in five to 10-bed dorms. It's a 10 minute walk from the train station, just past the castle.

Nearby *Bazpackers Backpackers Hotel* (☎ 717663, 4 Culduthel Rd) is a clean, new building with a wood-burner fire, small garden and more great views. Beds in six-bed dorms cost from £7.50, with linen; twins or doubles cost £12.

Possibly the best hostel in Scotland, *Inverness Millburn Youth Hostel* (☎ 231771, Victoria Drive) charges £11.50/9.95 for adults/juniors with continental breakfast (rates are £1 higher in July and August). Booking is essential.

B&Bs & Hotels Along Old Edinburgh Rd and on Ardconnel St are lots of guesthouses and B&Bs. *Ivybank Guest House* (☎ 232796, 28 Old Edinburgh Rd) costs £18 per person. *Ardconnel House* (☎ 240455, 21 Ardconnel St) has beds from £18 per person.

Just off Old Edinburgh Rd, *Leinster Lodge Guest House* (☎ 233311, 27 Southside Rd) has rooms for under £20 per person.

On Kenneth St, west of the river, and adjoining Fairfield Rd, you'll find several B&Bs, including *Mardon* (☎ 231005, 37 Kenneth St) which charges £14/20 per person without/with bath.

On Church St in the centre, the four-star *Cummings Hotel* (☎ 232531) has rooms, most with bath, from £30 to £45 per person.

For a few pounds more it's possible to have a river view in Ardross Terrace/Ness Walk, along the west side of the river, or Ness Bank, along the east side.

Ardmuir House (☎ 231151, 16 Ness Bank) has singles/doubles from £32.50/53, all with private bath. *Felstead House* (☎ 231634), at No 18, has rooms with and without bath from £20 per person. The larger *Glen Mhor Hotel* (☎ 234308), at No 10, has *en suite* rooms from £29 to £72 per person.

Across the river, the *Tower Hotel* (☎ 232765, 4 Ardross Terrace) has rooms from £30/50. West of the river, and just off the A82, the *Moyness House Hotel* (☎ 233836, 6 Bruce Gardens) offers B&B with bath for £26 to £34 per person and exceptional meals for £18.

Places to Eat

The museum has a small *coffee shop*, open Monday to Saturday from 10 am to 4 pm. Pub-style food and snacks including soup and a roll for £1.50 are found in the *Copper Kettle* (☎ 233307, 50 Baron Taylor's St), above the Eagle Bar. For takeaway sandwiches from 75p, try *Lettuce Eat* (☎ 715064, 7 Lombard), with another store in Church St.

Littlejohn's (☎ 713005, 28-30 Church St) is bright and noisy, with amusing décor and a highly descriptive pasta-Mexican-burger menu. Pizzas start at £4.25, burritos at £7.25. Upmarket *Dickens Restaurant* (☎ 713111, 77-79 Church St) has a good reputation and specialises in seafood, international cuisine and vegetarian dishes from £6.

The *Castle Restaurant* (☎ 230925, 41 Castle St), near the youth hostel, is a traditional café which prides itself on plentiful portions and low prices; main dishes cost from £3 to £8. The more upmarket *1 Café* (☎ 226200) nearby attempts to be a bit classier. Braised rump steak with onions costs around £9. The recommended *Shapla Tandoori Restaurant & Takeaway* (☎ 241919, 2 Castle Rd) does Indian specialities, including chicken tikka masala for £6.95.

Entertainment

Blackfriars and *The Phoenix* are popular pubs on Academy St near *Laffertys*, one of the new-style themed Irish pubs. The small *Market Bar* upstairs in the *Old Market Inn* (Market Hall, just off Church St) has live folk music nightly. *Gunsmiths* (Union St) also has live bands from Tuesday to Saturday.

From June to September, Scottish Showtime at the *Cummings Hotel* (☎ 232531, Church St) costs £12/11. *Eden Court Theatre* (☎ 221718, Ness Walk) has regular theatre performances. *Riverside Screen*, at the same location, is Inverness' art-house cinema. *La Scala* (Strother's Lane) shows mainstream films.

Getting There & Away

See the fares table in the Getting Around chapter. Inverness is 155 miles from Edinburgh, 110 miles from Aberdeen and 135 miles from Dundee.

Air Inverness airport (☎ 232471), Dalcross, offers flights to Glasgow, Edinburgh, Stornoway and other centres.

Bus For Inverness bus station phone ☎ 233371. Scottish Citylink (☎ 0990-505050) has connections with major centres in England, including London (13 hours, £24.50) via Perth and Glasgow. There are numerous buses to/from Glasgow (3½ hours, £11.50), Edinburgh via Perth (four hours, £12.30) and Aberdeen (three hours, £9.50).

In summer there are several buses daily to Ullapool (1½ hours, £7), connecting with

HIGHLANDS & NTH ISLANDS

the CalMac ferry to Stornoway on Lewis (not Sunday).

There are three or four daily Citylink services via Wick to Thurso and Scrabster (from three hours, £9) for ferries to Orkney. The Citylink bus leaving Inverness at 1.30 pm connects at Wick with a Highland Country Buses service to John o'Groats. There are connecting ferries and buses from John o'Groats to Burwick and Kirkwall in the Orkney Islands. It also runs regular daily services along Loch Ness to Fort William (two hours, £6.30).

Citylink/Skye-Ways (☎ 01599-534328) operates three buses a day (two on Sunday) from Inverness to Kyle of Lochalsh and Portree, on Skye. The journey takes three hours and costs £10.50.

It's possible to head to the north-west through Lairg. Inverness Traction (☎ 239292) has a Monday to Saturday service to Lairg (Sunday also in summer). In summer, daily buses run through to Durness. There's also a Monday to Saturday postbus service (☎ 256228), travelling Lairg-Tongue-Durness.

Train London to Inverness costs £61 most weekdays and takes from eight hours. There are direct trains from Aberdeen (£18.50), Edinburgh and Glasgow (£28.90).

The line from Inverness to Kyle of Lochalsh offers one of the greatest scenic journeys in Britain. There are three trains a day (none on Sunday); it takes 2½ hours (£14.30). Some trains to Thurso (3¾ hours, £12.20) connect with the ferry to Orkney.

Car The TIC has a handy *Car Hire* leaflet. The big boys charge from around £33 per day or you could try Sharp's Car Rental (☎ 236694), 1st floor, Highland Rail House, Station Square, for cheaper cars and vans.

Getting Around

To/From the Airport The twice-daily airport bus connects with Stornoway and London flights, takes 20 minutes and costs £2.45. A taxi costs around £10.

Bus Inverness Traction and Highland Country Buses operate buses to places around Inverness including Nairn, Forres, the Culloden battlefield, Beauly, Dingwall and Lairg. An Inverness Traction Day Rover Highland ticket costs £6.50/3.25, while a Highland Bus Day Rover ticket costs £6/3. The Highland Buses return fare to Culloden is £1.30; to Cawdor it's £3.85.

Bicycle There are great cycling opportunities out of Inverness and several rental outlets, including Ho Ho Hostel (☎ 221225), 23A High St, Wilder Ness (ask at Bazpackers Backpackers Hostel) for £7.50/10 for a half/full day and Bught Camping Park.

AROUND INVERNESS
Beauly
• **pop 1800**   ☎ **01463**

In 1584, Mary Queen of Scots is said to have given this village its name when she exclaimed, in French, 'quelle beau lieu!' (What a beautiful place!). Founded in 1230, the red-sandstone **Beauly Priory** is now an impressive ruin; entry is £1/75p (get the key from the Priory Hotel).

Inverness Traction (☎ 239292) operates hourly services daily from Dingwall and Inverness (only four run on Sunday).

Black Isle & Cromarty

Actually a peninsula rather than an island, Black Isle can be reached from Inverness by a short cut across the **Kessock Bridge**. You'll find the vaulted crypt of a 13th century chapterhouse and sacristy, and ruinous 14th century south aisle and chapel, at **Fortrose Cathedral**. In Rosemarkie the **Groam House Museum** (☎ 01381-620961) has a superb collection of Pictish stones incised with designs like those on Celtic Irish stones. It's open Easter and from May to September, Monday to Saturday from 10 am to 5 pm, Sunday from 2 to 4.30 pm (2 to 4 pm at weekends in winter); entry is £1.50/50p.

The Cromarty Firth is famous for the huge offshore oil rigs which are built at Nigg before being towed out to the North Sea. Dolphin Ecosse (☎ 01381-600323) runs boat trips along the firth to see bottlenose dolphins and other wildlife.

At the peninsula's north-eastern end, the pretty village of Cromarty has many fascinating 18th century stone houses. In Church St, **Cromarty Courthouse** (☎ 01381-600418) has a thoroughly interesting local history museum, open April to October, daily from 10 am to 5 pm (shorter hours in winter). The £3/2 admission fee includes the loan of headsets for a recorded tour of Cromarty's other historic buildings. Next to the courthouse is **Hugh Miller's Cottage** (☎ 01381-600245, NTS). This well-known author's thatched-roof home opens May to September, daily from 11 am to 1 pm and 2 to 5 pm (afternoon only on Sunday); entry is £2/1.30.

Several places offer B&B from £15 a head including *Mrs Robertson (☎ 01381-600488, 7 Church St)*. You'll find the pleasant *Binnies Teashop* in High St, the inviting *Thistles Restaurant (☎ 01381-600471, Church St)* and *The Cromarty Arms*, a good pub with bar meals and live music, also in Church St.

The Cromarty to Nigg ferry is currently not operating. Highland Bus & Coach (☎ 01463-233371) runs buses Monday to Saturday from Inverness to Fortrose and Rosemarkie. Some continue to Cromarty (55 minutes, £4.40).

Cawdor

Cawdor Castle (☎ 01667-404615), the 14th century home of the Thanes of Cawdor, was reputedly the castle of Shakespeare's Macbeth and the scene of Duncan's murder. The central tower dates from the 14th century but the wings are 17th century additions. It's open May to October, daily from 10 am to 5 pm; entry is £5.20/4.20.

Cawdor Tavern (☎ 01667-404777) in the nearby village is worth a stop. Deciding what to drink can be difficult as it stocks over 100 varieties of whisky. There's also reasonable pub grub, with most specials under £7.

Culloden

Culloden is about 6 miles east of Inverness. The Battle of Culloden in 1746, the last fought on British soil, saw the defeat of Bonnie Prince Charlie and the slaughter of over 1200 Highlanders in a 68 minute rout. The Duke of Cumberland won the label Butcher Cumberland for his brutal treatment of the defeated Scottish forces. The battle sounded the death knell of the old clan system, and the horrors of the Clearances soon followed (see the boxed text 'Crofting & the Clearances' later in this chapter). The sombre 49 hectare moor where the conflict took place has scarcely changed to this day. The site, with its many markers and memorials, is always open.

The visitors centre (☎ 01463-790607, NTS) offers a 15 minute audiovisual presentation on the battle. It's open in summer, daily from 9 am to 6 pm with shorter hours in winter; closed completely in January. Admission is £3/2.

Clava Cairns

Clearly signposted 1½ miles east of Culloden, the Clava Cairns are a picturesque group of cairns and stone circles dating from the late Neolithic period (around 4000 to 2000 BC). There's a superb railway viaduct nearby.

Fort George

Covering much of the headland is a virtually unaltered 18th century artillery fortification, one of the best examples of its kind in Europe. It was completed in 1769 as a base for George II's army. The mile-plus walk around the ramparts offers fine views out to sea and back to the Great Glen. Given its size, you'll need several hours to look around. The visitors centre (☎ 01667-462777, HS) opens year-round. Admission costs £3/2.30.

Brodie Castle

The castle (☎ 01309-641371, NTS) is 8 miles east of the small town of Nairnset, set in 70 hectares of parkland. Although the Brodies have lived here since 1160, the present structure dates from the 16th century. You can look around several rooms, some with extravagant ceilings, and there's

HIGHLANDS & NTH ISLANDS

a large collection of paintings and furniture. Don't miss the huge Victorian kitchen.

The castle opens April to September from 11 am to 5.30 pm (1.30 to 5.30 pm Sunday); admission is £4.20/2.80. There are also woodland walks and an observation hide by the pond. Bluebird Bus No 10 runs every half-hour, taking 45 minutes to reach Brodie from Inverness via Culloden.

East Coast

The east coast starts to get interesting once you leave behind Invergordon's industrial development. Beyond this, great heather-covered hills heave themselves out of the wild North Sea, with pleasant little towns moored precariously at their edge.

DINGWALL TO BONAR BRIDGE

Located at the head of Cromarty Firth, **Dingwall** (population 5000) is the legendary birthplace of Macbeth. Local military hero Sir Hector MacDonald features in the **Dingwall Museum** (☎ 01349-865366), High St (open May to September only) and in a monument overlooking the town.

Sir Hector Munro, another military hero, commemorated his most notable victory, the capture of the Indian town of Negapatam in 1781, by erecting the Fyrish Monument, a replica of the town's gateway, high above nearby **Evanton**. Turn towards Boath off the B9176; from the car park it's a 45 minute walk along the Jubilee Path.

Invergordon is the main centre for repairing North Sea oil rigs in the Cromarty Firth.

Tain was a centre for the management of the Clearances and has a curious 16th century tollbooth in the town centre. St Duthac was born in Tain, died in Armagh (Ireland) in 1065 and is commemorated by the 11th to 12th century ruins of St Duthac's Chapel, as well as by St Duthus Church, now part of the **Tain Through Time** heritage centre (☎ 01862-894089), open daily April to October from 10 am to 6 pm, noon to 4 pm in November, December and March; entry is £3.50/2.

The A9 crosses Dornoch Firth. Alternatively, from Ardgay at the head of Dornoch Firth, a road leads 10 miles up Strathcarron to **Croick**, scene of notorious evictions during the 1845 Clearances. Refugee crofters from Glencalvie scratched their sad messages on the east windows of Croick Church.

Another detour from Ardgay along the Kyle of Sutherland leads to **Carbisdale Castle** (dating from 1914), which now houses Scotland's largest *Youth Hostel* (☎ *01549-421232*). It's open from March to October and charges £11.50/9.95 for adults/juniors. The sweeping **Bonar Bridge** then crosses the head of the firth to rejoin the A9 just before Dornoch.

DORNOCH
- **pop 1000**   ☎ **01862**

On the coast, 2 miles off the A9, Dornoch is a pleasant seaside town clustered around **Dornoch Cathedral**. The original building was destroyed in 1570 during a clan feud. Despite some patching up, it wasn't completely rebuilt until 1835 to 1837.

The TIC (☎ 810400), open year-round, is in the main square.

Dornoch has several camping grounds and plenty of B&Bs. If you want to stay in grand *Dornoch Castle* (☎ *810216)*, the 16th century former Bishop's Palace, expect to pay from £34 per person. *Sutherland House* (☎ *811023*) just off the square has cheap pub-style food (burgers from £4.50), or you can dine in style at Dornoch Castle for £22.

South of Dornoch, seals are often visible on the sand bars of **Dornoch Firth**. North of Dornoch the A9 crosses the head of **Loch Fleet** on the Mound, an embankment built by Telford from 1815 to 1816.

DUNROBIN CASTLE

One mile north of Golspie, Dunrobin Castle (☎ 01408-633177), the largest house in the Highlands (187 rooms), dates back to around 1275. Additions were made in the mid-1600s and late 1700s, but most of what you see today was built in French style between 1845 and 1850. One of the homes of the Earls and Dukes of Sutherland, it's

Crofting & the Clearances

Many Highland settlements are described as crofting communities. The word croft comes from the Gaelic *croitean*, meaning a small enclosed field. Highland land was generally owned by clan chiefs until the early 19th century, and their tenants farmed land on the 'run-rig' system. The land was divided into strips which were shared among the tenants. The strips were periodically shuffled around so no tenant was stuck with bad land or always enjoyed the good land. Unfortunately, it also meant they might end up with several widely scattered strips and with no incentive to improve them because they knew they would soon lose them. Accordingly, the system was changed and the land rented out to the tenants as small 'crofts', averaging about 1.2 hectares. Each tenant then built their own house on their croft and the former tight cluster of homes became scattered. Crofters could also graze their animals on the common grazings, land which was jointly held by all the local crofters.

Crofting remained a precarious lifestyle. The small patch of land barely provided a living and each year the tenancy could be terminated and the crofter lose not only the croft but the house they had built on it. During the Highland Clearances, that was what happened – many clan chiefs decided sheep farming was more profitable than collecting rent from poverty-stricken crofters. The guidebook to Dunrobin Castle, seat of the Sutherland family, blithely notes that they 'proceeded to make large-scale improvements to Sutherland's communications, land and townships which involved the clearance of some 5000 people from their ancestral dwellings'. Crofting tenancies still exist but complex regulations now protect the crofters.

richly furnished and offers an insight into their opulent lifestyle.

Judging by the numerous hunting trophies and animal skins, much family energy went into hunting. The house also displays innumerable gifts from farm tenants (probably grateful that they hadn't been evicted as part of the Sutherlands' Clearance). Behind the house formal gardens slope down to the sea, and a museum – once a summerhouse – offers an eclectic mix of archaeological finds, natural history exhibits and more big-game trophies.

The house opens April to October, Monday to Saturday from 10.30 am to 4.30 pm, Sunday from noon, and June to September daily from 10.30 am to 5.30 pm; entry is £5/3.50.

BRORA & HELMSDALE

Between Dunrobin and Brora, the **Carn Liath Broch** is a well-preserved Iron Age fort.

Brora, at the mouth of a river famed for its salmon, has a fine beach and plenty of B&Bs.

Helmsdale, with its pretty harbour and salmon river, is busy in summer. The TIC (☎ 01431-821640) is by the A9 on the south side of the village. The **Timespan Heritage Centre** (☎ 01431-821327) has details of the 1869 Strath of Kildonan gold rush and a model of Dame Barbara Cartland. It's open Easter to mid-October, Monday to Saturday from 9.30 am to 5 pm, Sunday from 2 to 5 pm (6 pm in July and August); entry is £3/2.40.

There are several B&Bs, or a bed at the *Helmsdale Youth Hostel* (☎ 01431-821577) costs £4.65/3.85 for adults/juniors. It's open mid-May to September, but book well ahead for July or August.

Cartland, queen of pulp romance novelists, has been holidaying in Helmsdale for over 60 years. You're unlikely to spot her, but Nancy Sinclair, proprietor of *La Mirage* fish and chip shop in Dunrobin St, is a dead

HIGHLANDS & NTH ISLANDS

ringer for Cartland – they share the same hairdresser.

HELMSDALE TO LATHERON

North of Helmsdale, the road climbs to a fine viewpoint at the **Ord of Caithness**. About 7 miles north of Helmsdale, a 15 minute walk from the A9 takes you to **Badbea**, where the ruins of crofts are perched on the cliff top. **Berriedale** has a llama farm and in early summer puffin colonies inhabit the shoreline. Just north of Dunbeath, **Laidhay Croft Museum** (π 01593-731244) re-creates crofting life from the mid-1800s to WWII. It's open April to October, daily from 10 am to 6 pm; entry is £1/50p.

At **Clan Gunn Centre** (π 015932-731370) in Latheron you learn that it was really a Scot, not Christopher Columbus, who discovered America. It's open June to September, Monday to Saturday from 11 am to 5 pm; and in July and August, Sunday from 2 to 5 pm; £1.20/75p.

CELTIC SITES

There are several Celtic sites between Dunbeath and Wick. Turn north on the A895 at Latheron, and at Achavanich, wedged between Loch Rangag and Loch Stemster, double back on the road to Lybster to the 40 or so **Achavanich Standing Stones**.

Just beyond Lybster, a turn-off leads to the **Grey Cairns of Camster**, 5 miles north of the A9. Dating from between 4000 and 2500 BC, the burial chambers are hidden in long, low mounds rising from an evocatively desolate stretch of moor. The Long Cairn is 61 by 21m. You can enter the main chamber but you must crawl into the well-preserved Round Cairn. Afterwards, continue 7 miles north on this remote road to approach Wick on the A882.

The **Hill o'Many Stanes** just beyond the Camster turn-off is a curious, fan-shaped arrangement of 22 rows of small stones probably dating from around 2000 BC. Nearer to Wick at Ulbster (Whaligoe), the **Cairn o'Get** is a quarter-mile off the A9, and then a 2 mile walk. Steps lead down to

small, picturesque **Whaligoe** harbour, directly opposite the Cairn o'Get.

WICK

- **pop 8000**   π **01955**

Wick, with its boarded-up buildings, hasn't always been so dismal. A century ago, it was the world's largest herring fishing port, its harbour crammed with fishing boats and larger ships to carry barrels of salted herring abroad, and thousands of seasonal workers streaming into town to pack the catch. After WWI the herring began to disappear and by WWII the town had died.

Wick's massive harbour was the work of Telford, who designed Pulteneytown, the model town commissioned by the engagingly named British Society for Extending the Fisheries & Improving the Sea Coasts of the Kingdom. A failed attempt to add a breakwater was the work of Thomas Stevenson, father of author Robert Louis Stevenson.

Information

The TIC (π 602596) is in Whitechapel Rd, off High St on the road leading to the Safeway supermarket car park.

Wick Heritage Centre

The town's award-winning local museum (π 605393) in Bank Row deserves all the praise heaped upon it. It tracks the rise and fall of the herring industry and displays everything from fishing equipment to complete herring fishing boats.

The Johnston photographic collection is the museum's star exhibit. From 1863 to 1977, three generations of Johnstons photographed everything that happened around Wick, and the 70,000 photographs are an amazing portrait of the town's life. The museum even displays the Johnstons' photo studio; prints of superb early photos are for sale. It's open May to September, Monday to Saturday from 10 am to 5 pm; entry is £2/50p.

Other Things to See

A path leads a mile south of town to the 12th century ruins of **Old Wick Castle**, with the spectacular rock formations of the **Brough** and the **Brig**, or **Gote o'Trams**, just to the south. In good weather, it's a fine coastal walk to the castle.

Just past Wick airport, on the north side of town, you can watch the glass-blowing operations in **Caithness Glass Visitors Centre** (☎ 602286), Monday to Friday from 9 am to 4.30 pm. The shop here stays open until 5 pm daily (opening at 11 am Sunday, from Easter to December).

Places to Stay

Close to the centre, *Riverside Caravan Club Site* (*☎ 605420, Riverside Drive*) charges £3.55 to £7.50 per tent.

For a central B&B, try *Wellington Guest House* (*☎ 603287, 41 High St*) behind the TIC. It has singles/doubles with bathroom for £25/40. Close to the waterfront, *Harbour Guest House* (*☎ 603276, 6 Rose St*) has rooms from £18/32. By the A9 at the southern edge of town on South Rd, *The Clachan* (*☎ 605384*) charges from £22/36 and is recommended.

Places to Eat

There's a *Harbour Chip Shop* on Harbour Quay, but most places are along High St and its continuation, The Shore. On High St, the *Home Bakery & Café* does snacks (from 40p) and baked potatoes from £1. *Cabrelli's Café* (*134 High St*) does good pasta dishes from £3 and other mains from £2.50. *Carter's Bar* (*☎ 603700, 2 The Shore*) does pub-style food, and the *Waterfront* (*☎ 602550*) is a cavernous disco/nightclub but its restaurant is best avoided.

Getting There & Away

Wick is 280 miles from Edinburgh and 125 miles from Inverness.

GillAir and British Airways Express fly to Wick from Aberdeen, Edinburgh, Orkney and Shetland. There are regular bus and train services from Inverness to Wick and on to Thurso (see the Inverness section earlier in this chapter for details). Highland Country Buses (☎ 01847-893123) runs the connecting service to John o'Groats for the passenger ferry to Burwick, Orkney.

Getting Around

Richard's Garage (☎ 604123) on Francis St rents cars and bicycles.

JOHN O'GROATS

Disappointingly the coast at the country's north-east tip isn't particularly dramatic, and modern John o'Groats is little more than a ramshackle tourist trap. Its name comes from Jan de Groot, one of three brothers commissioned by James IV to operate a ferry service to Orkney in 1496 for just four pence.

Two miles east of John o'Groats is **Duncansby Head**, home to many seabirds at the start of summer. A path leads to **Duncansby Stacks**, a spectacular natural rock formation soaring over 60m (197 feet) above the sea. There is a series of narrow inlets and deep coves on this wonderful stretch of coast.

The TIC (☎ 01955-611373) opens April to October. There are also shops and a crafts complex.

Places to Stay & Eat

Three miles west of John o'Groats at Canisbay, the *John o'Groats Youth Hostel* (*☎ 01955-611424*) opens from late March to October and costs £6.10/4.95 for adults/juniors. There are several B&Bs in John o'Groats and nearby Canisbay and a couple of camping grounds. The big *John o'Groats House Hotel* (*☎ 01955-611203*) has a reasonable restaurant, and the adjacent *Groats Inn* serves pizzas.

Getting There & Away

Highland Country Buses (☎ 01847-893123) runs up to seven daily buses to John o'Groats from Wick or Thurso from Monday to Saturday, and on Sunday from mid-May (£2.10). Harrold Coaches (☎ 01955-631295) runs from Thurso to John o'Groats several times daily from Monday to Saturday (£2.30).

From May to September, MV *Pentland Venture* (☎ 01955-611353) shuttles across

HIGHLANDS & NTH ISLANDS

to Orkney. The single fare to Burwick is £15/7.50 and day tours around Orkney cost £30/15.

See the Inverness section for details on transport straight to the islands from Inverness. See the Orkney Islands section later in this chapter for ferry details.

DUNNET HEAD

Contrary to popular belief, John o'Groats isn't the mainland's most northerly point, an honour which goes to Dunnet Head, a few miles west. The head is marked by a lighthouse that dates from 1832. The tricky Pentland Firth, the strait between Orkney and the mainland, stretches from Duncansby Head to Dunnet Head. *Dunnet Head Tearoom* (☎ *01847-851774*) offers inexpensive food including meals for vegetarians, and B&B from £13 a head.

Just past Dunnet Head and a magnificent stretch of sandy beach, there's a turning to the tiny harbour at **Castlehill** where a heritage trail explains the evolution of the local flagstone industry.

North & West Coast

From just beyond Thurso, the coast round to Ullapool is mind-blowing. Everything is massive – vast, empty spaces, enormous lochs and snow-capped mountains. Ullapool is the most northerly town of any significance and there's more brilliant coast round to Gairloch, along the incomparable Loch Maree and down to Kyle of Lochalsh (a short hop from Skye).

From there you're back in the land of the tour bus; civilisation (and main roads) and this can be quite a shock after all the empty space.

Local tourist offices have excellent information leaflets about the coast route. Look for *Scotland's North Coast* (John o'-Groats to Durness), *West Sutherland Coastal Route* (Durness to Elphin, just before Ullapool) and *Wester Ross Coastal Route* (Elphin to Kyle of Lochalsh).

Banks and petrol stations are few and far between in this corner of Scotland, so check your funds and fuel before setting out.

GETTING AROUND

Public transport in the north-west is very patchy. Getting to Thurso or Kyle of Lochalsh by bus or train is easy, but it can be difficult to follow the coast between these places.

In July and August, Highland Country Buses (☎ 01847-893123) runs a once-daily bus from Thurso to Durness. At other times of the year, Highland Country Buses and Rapson's (☎ 01408-621245) have Monday to Saturday services from Thurso to Bettyhill. There's also a postbus (☎ 01463-256228) from Tongue to Durness once daily from Monday to Saturday.

The alternative is to come up from Inverness via Lairg. There are trains daily to Lairg, and Inverness Traction (☎ 01463-239292) buses from Monday to Saturday. In summer, the buses continue to Durness. May to early October, the Heatherhopper bus runs once daily from Monday to Saturday between Lairg and Ullapool, connecting with the Inverness-Ullapool-Durness service at Ledmore Junction.

Monday to Saturday postbus services operate the Lairg-Tongue-Durness and Lairg-Kinlochbervie-Durness routes and from Lairg to Lochinver. There are also services around the coast from Elphin to Scourie, Drumbeg to Lochinver, Shieldaig to Kishorn via Applecross, and Shieldaig to Torridon and Strathcarron, but always with gaps between towns.

There are regular bus services between Inverness and Ullapool.

Renting a car or hitching are perhaps better options.

THURSO & SCRABSTER
• pop 9000   ☎ 01847

The most northerly town on the mainland, Thurso is a fairly large, fairly bleak place looking across Pentland Firth to Hoy in Orkney. Medieval Thurso was Scotland's major port for trade with Scandinavia.

Today, ferries cross from Scrabster, 2½ miles west of Thurso, to Orkney. The ferry aside, Scrabster is little more than a collection of BP oil storage containers.

Information

The TIC (☎ 892371), Riverside Rd, opens from April to October, daily in summer.

Things to See & Do

There's a **Heritage Museum** (☎ 892459) in Thurso Town Hall (open June to September). The ruins of **Old St Peter's Kirk** date mainly from the 17th century, but the original church on the site was founded around 1220. The small round building over the **Meadow Well** marks the site of a former well.

Thurso is an unlikely surfing centre but the nearby coast has arguably the best and most regular surf in Britain. There's an excellent right-hand reef break on the east side of town, directly in front of Lord Caithness' castle, and another shallow reef break 5 miles west at Brimms Ness.

North of Scrabster harbour, there's a fine cliff walk along Holborn Head. Take care in windy weather.

Places to Stay

Ormlie Lodge (☎ 896888, *Ormlie Rd*) opens all year and charges £6/8 for dorm beds without/with sheets. In July and August *Thurso Youth Club* (☎ 892964, *Old Mill, Millbank*) has basic dorm accommodation for £8 including linen; phone ahead to check though. *Thurso Camping Site* (☎ 607771), by the coast on the edge of Thurso towards Scrabster, charges from £7.25 per tent.

Thurso has many moderately priced B&Bs; the TIC charges £1.50 for local bookings. *Pathecia* (☎ 894751, *3 Janet St*) costs £17 per person, with another £1 to use the spa bath. Also central is the large *Pentland Hotel* (☎ 893202, *Princes St*), with singles/doubles from £30/54. The *Royal Hotel* (☎ 893191, *Traill St*) has singles from £30 to £50, and doubles from £50 to £90.

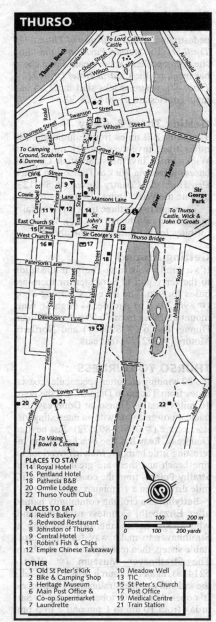

THURSO

PLACES TO STAY
14 Royal Hotel
16 Pentland Hotel
18 Pathecia B&B
20 Ormlie Lodge
22 Thurso Youth Club

PLACES TO EAT
4 Reid's Bakery
5 Redwood Restaurant
8 Johnston of Thurso
9 Central Hotel
11 Robin's Fish & Chips
12 Empire Chinese Takeaway

OTHER
1 Old St Peter's Kirk
2 Bike & Camping Shop
3 Heritage Museum
6 Main Post Office &
　 Co-op Supermarket
7 Laundrette
10 Meadow Well
13 TIC
15 St Peter's Church
17 Post Office
19 Medical Centre
21 Train Station

Places to Eat

Basic cafés include *Reid's Bakery* in the pedestrian mall and *Johnston of Thurso (10 Traill St)*. The *Stewart Pavilion* at the camp site does excellent-value meals. For a cheap bar meal, try the *Central Hotel (☎ 893129, Traill St)*, where snacks start at £1.45 and main courses are £3.90 to £5.50.

Getting There & Away

Thurso is 290 miles from Edinburgh, 130 miles from Inverness and 21 miles from Wick. From Inverness, Scottish Citylink buses operate via Wick to Thurso (3½ hours, £9). Highland Country Buses (☎ 893123) operate the Wick-Thurso-Dounreay route.

There are two or three train services daily in summer (3½ hours, £12.20), but space for bicycles is limited so book ahead.

Getting Around

It's a 2 mile walk from Thurso train station to the ferry port at Scrabster, or there are buses for 90p. The Bike & Camping Shop (☎ 896124), The Arcade, 34 High St, rents mountain bikes from £6.50 a day. William Dunnet & Co (☎ 893101) and Northern Motors (☎ 892777) rent cars.

THURSO TO DURNESS

It's 80 winding and often spectacular coastal miles from Thurso to Durness. On the coast 10 miles west of Thurso, at **Dounreay**, is a nuclear power station with an interesting visitors centre (☎ 01847-802572). Just beyond Dounreay, **Reay** has fine beaches and an interesting little harbour. **Melvich** overlooks a fine beach and there are great views from **Strathy Point** – from the coast road, it's a 2 mile drive, then a 15 minute walk.

Bettyhill is a crofting community named after Elizabeth, Countess of Sutherland, who kicked her tenants off their land at Strathnaver to make way for more profitable sheep, then resettled the tenants here. The **Strathnaver Museum** (☎ 01641-521418), in an old church in Bettyhill, tells the sad story of the Strathnaver Clearances. It's open April to October, Monday to Saturday from 10 am to 1 pm and 2 to 5 pm;

entry is £1.90/1.20. There's a Pictish cross in the graveyard behind the museum. From Bettyhill the B871 turns south for Helmsdale, through **Strathnaver**.

The wonderful beach at **Coldbackie** is overlooked by the Watch Hill viewpoint. Only 2 miles farther on is **Tongue**, overlooked by the 14th century ruins of Castle Varrich. Down by the causeway, *Tongue Youth Hostel (☎ 01847-611301)* has a spectacular location looking up and down the Kyle of Tongue (a kyle is a narrow strait) for a nightly cost of £6.10/4.95 for adults/juniors.

From Tongue it's 30 miles to Durness – you can take the causeway across the **Kyle of Tongue** or the beautiful old road which climbs up to the head of the kyle. A detour to **Melness** and **Port Vasgo** may be rewarded with the sight of seals on the beach. Continuing west, the road crosses a desolate moor past **Moine House** to the northern end of **Loch Hope**. A 10 mile detour south along the loch leads to **Dun Dornaigil**, a preserved *broch* (defensive tower) in the shadow of **Ben Hope** (927m, 3041 feet). If you'd like to bag this Munro it's a three to four hour round trip along the route from the car park, which is 2 miles before the broch. Beyond Loch Hope, **Heilam** has stunning views out over **Loch Eriboll**, Britain's deepest sea inlet.

DURNESS

- pop 300   ☎ 01971

Durness is one of the best located Scottish villages. The TIC (☎ 511259) opens April to October, and has slide shows at the Village Hall and guided walks in summer.

Things to See

There's a path down to **Smoo Cave**, a mile east of the village centre. The vast cave entrance stands at the end of an inlet, or *geo*, and a river cascades right through its roof and then flows out to sea. You can take a boat trip (£2.50/1.25) into the cave, although after heavy rain the waterfall can make it impossible to get past.

Durness has several beautiful beaches, starting at Rispond to the east, and the sea offers some superb scuba-diving sites complete with wrecks, caves, seals and whales.

A disused radar station at **Balnakeil**, less than a mile beyond Durness, has been turned into a scruffy craft village. A walk along the beach to the north leads to **Faraid Head**, where you can see puffin colonies in early summer.

Places to Stay & Eat

Durness Youth Hostel (☎ 511244) is at Smoo, on the east side of the village. It's open from mid-March to early October and costs £4.65/3.85 but is pretty basic. *Sango Sands Caravan Park (☎ 511222)* has camping grounds and the *Oasis Café* is one of the few places to eat in Durness. The pub food is unexceptional (£3.60 to £10.25). *Smoo Cave Hotel (☎ 511227)* does B&B from £15.50 per person and pub grub, including a vegetarian selection. Durness also has several private B&Bs, like *Morven* (☎ 511252) or *Puffin Cottage (☎ 511208)* from £16 per person.

DURNESS TO ULLAPOOL

It's 69 miles from Durness to Ullapool, with plenty of side trips and diversions to make along the way.

Cape Wrath

The cape is crowned by a lighthouse (dating from 1827) and stands close to the seabird colonies on Clo Mor Cliffs, the highest sea cliffs on the mainland. Getting to Cape Wrath involves a ferry ride (☎ 01971-511376) across the Kyle of Durness (£2.25 return) and a connecting minibus (☎ 01971-511287) for the 11 miles to the cape (40 minutes one way, £6 return). Services operate May to September daily, and up to eight times a day in July and August.

South of Cape Wrath, **Sandwood Bay** boasts one of Britain's most isolated beaches. It's about 2 miles north of the end of a track from Blairmore (approach from Kinlochbervie), or you could walk south from the cape (allow eight hours) and on to Blairmore.

Handa Island & Scourie

Boats go out to Handa Island's important seabird sanctuary from Tarbet. You may see skuas and puffins, as well as seals. You can see the **Old Man of Stoer** across Eddrachillis Bay. Scourie is a pretty crofting community with a well-known herd of Highland cattle.

Kylesku & Loch Glencoul

Cruises on Loch Glencoul pass seal colonies and the 213m drop of **Eas a'Chual Aulin**, Britain's highest waterfall. In summer, the MV *Statesman* (☎ 01571-844446) runs two-hour trips at 11 am and 2 pm from Kylesku Old Ferry Pier for £9/3. While you wait, you can have a pint and a snack or meal in *Kylesku Hotel (☎ 01971-502231)* overlooking the pier.

It's a fine three hour, 6 mile (round trip) walk to the top of the falls, starting from beside Loch na Gainmhich at the top of the climb out of Kylesku towards Ullapool. The OS Landranger No 15 map shows the route.

The Old Man of Stoer

It's a roughly 30 mile detour off the main A894 to the Point of Stoer and the Rhu Stoer Lighthouse (1870) and back to the main road again. Along the coast road you need to be prepared for single-car-width roads, blind bends and summits ... and sheep. The rewards are spectacular views, pretty villages and excellent beaches along the way. From the lighthouse, it's a good one hour cliff walk to the Old Man of Stoer, a spectacular sea stack (a tower of rock rising from the sea). There are more good beaches between Stoer and Lochinver.

Lochinver & Around
- pop 560   ☎ 01571

This popular little fishing port has a TIC (☎ 844330), open from April to October. The **Hills of Assynt** near Lochinver are popular with walkers and include peaks like Suilven (731m, 2399 feet), Quinag (808m, 2651 feet), Ben More Assynt (998m, 3273 feet) and Canisp (846m, 2779 feet). The *Assynt Field Centre (☎ 822218)* on the

Lochinver-Lairg Rd in Inchnadamph has 50 beds from £8.50. It's ideal for walkers and climbers.

The detour to the Old Man of Stoer and Lochinver returns to the main road at **Skiag Bridge**, by Loch Assynt.

Lochinver has a camping ground and *Achmelvich Youth Hostel (☎ 01571-844480)*, 4 miles away at Achmelvich that costs £4.65/3.85 for adults/juniors. There are numerous B&Bs and the sprawling waterfront *Culag Hotel (☎ 844270)*, with beds from £25. The *Lochinver Larder & Riverside Bistro (☎ 844356)* has interesting local food, especially fish, to eat in or take away.

Knockan & Inverpolly Nature Reserve

There's an SNH information centre (☎ 01854-666234) and geological and nature trails at Knockan, beside Inverpolly Nature Reserve, which has numerous glacial lochs and the three peaks of Cul Mor (849m, 2786 feet), Stac Polly (613m, 2010 feet) and Cul Beag (769m, 2523 feet). There are good views of Isle Martin from just before Ardmair and then of the Summer Isles, Loch Broom and Ullapool.

Reached by a circuitous route around Loch Lurgainn, Achiltibuie's **Hydroponicum** (☎ 01854-622202) grows tropical fruit and flowers. From April to September tours operate on the hour from 10 am to 5 pm and cost £4/3.25. Boat trips (☎ 01854-622200) also operate to the Summer Isles from Achiltibuie.

ULLAPOOL
• **pop 1000**   ☎ **01854**

Ullapool is a pretty fishing village from where ferries sail to Stornoway on the Isle of Lewis. Small though it is, Ullapool is the biggest settlement in Wester Ross. Although it's a long way around the coast in either direction, Ullapool is only 59 miles from Inverness via the A835 along beautiful Loch Broom.

The TIC (☎ 612987), 6 Argyle St, opens April to November (daily May to September). The only bank is the Royal Bank of Scotland in Ladysmith St. The Ullapool Bookshop opposite the Seaforth Inn on

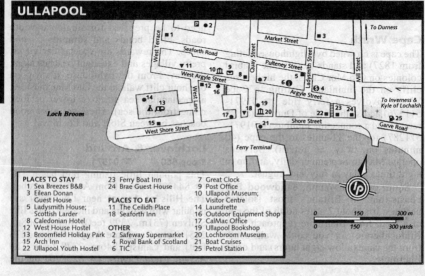

ULLAPOOL

PLACES TO STAY	23 Ferry Boat Inn	7 Great Clock
1 Sea Breezes B&B	24 Brae Guest House	9 Post Office
3 Eilean Donan		10 Ullapool Museum;
Guest House	PLACES TO EAT	Visitor Centre
5 Ladysmith House;	11 The Ceilidh Place	14 Laundrette
Scottish Larder	18 Seaforth Inn	16 Outdoor Equipment Shop
8 Caledonian Hotel		17 CalMac Office
12 West House Hostel	OTHER	19 Ullapool Bookshop
13 Broomfield Holiday Park	2 Safeway Supermarket	20 Lochbroom Museum
15 Arch Inn	4 Royal Bank of Scotland	21 Boat Cruises
22 Ullapool Youth Hostel	6 TIC	25 Petrol Station

Quay St is excellent and has lots of books on Scottish topics.

Ullapool Museum & Visitor Centre, in a church in West Argyle St, opens April to October, Monday to Saturday from 9.30 am to 5.30 pm, noon to 4 pm in winter; entry is £2/1.50.

Places to Stay

Broomfield Holiday Park (☎ 612664) has camping from £5 (hiker and tent) up to £10 (car and tent). The harbourside *Ullapool Youth Hostel* (☎ 612254) opens all year except most of January. Dorm beds cost £7.75/6.50; booking is advisable at Easter and in summer. *West House Hostel* (☎ 613126, West Argyle St) charges from £8.50 per bunk.

There are lots of B&Bs and guesthouses along Seaforth Rd and Pulteney St, and on Argyle St near the Quay St junction. *Arch Inn* (☎ 612454, 11 West Shore St) has rooms from £18 to £27 per person. Also right on the waterfront in Shore St, *Brae Guest House* (☎ 612421) has rooms with and without bath from £19 per person.

The friendly *Eilean Donan Guest House* (☎ 612524, 14 Market St) has rooms from £15 per person. Nearby, *Ladysmith House* (☎ 612185, 24 Pulteney St) charges from £14 per person. At *Sea Breezes* (☎ 612520, 2 West Terrace) singles/doubles cost from £16/30.

The *Ferry Boat Inn* (☎ 612103, Shore St) has pleasant hotel rooms with views up the loch for £31/58. The big *Caledonian Hotel* (☎ 612306, Quay St) offers rooms with private bath from £30 to £47 a single, and £50 to £84 a double.

Places to Eat

Upstairs at the junction of Quay and Shore Sts, *Seaforth Inn* (☎ 612122) does good fish and chips. *Arch Inn* (☎ 612454) and *Ferry Boat Inn* (☎ 612366), both in Shore St, do pub food at lunch time and early evening. The *Scottish Larder* (☎ 612185, 24 Pulteney St) does all sorts of pies from £4.95. For excellent but pricier restaurant meals *Morefield Hotel* (☎ 612161) does full menus, with fish main courses from £6.50.

The *Ceilidh Place* (☎ 612103) has a daytime café (from 10 am) with soup and snacks from £1.95 and a much pricier evening restaurant (it's a bit of a tourist trap). It's also Ullapool's main entertainment centre, with live music most nights in summer.

Getting There & Around

Ullapool is 215 miles from Edinburgh and 60 miles from Inverness. See the Inverness section for information on bus and train links with the ferry to Stornoway on Lewis.

Bikes can be rented from the West House Hostel for £10/6.50 per day/half-day.

ULLAPOOL TO KYLE OF LOCHALSH

Although it's less than 50 miles as the crow flies from Ullapool to Kyle of Lochalsh, it's more like 150 miles along the circuitous coastal road, with fine views of beaches and bays backed by mountains all along the way.

Falls of Measach

The A832 doubles back to the coast from the A835, 12 miles from Ullapool. Just before the junction, the Falls of Measach ('ugly' in Gaelic) spill 45m into the spectacularly deep and narrow Corrieshalloch Gorge.

Inverewe Gardens

At Poolewe on Loch Ewe, the subtropical Inverewe Gardens (☎ 01445-718229, NTS) are a testament to the warming influence of the Gulf Stream. The gardens were founded by Osgood Mackenzie in 1862 – a barren, windswept peninsula was gradually transformed into a luxuriant, colourful, 26 hectare garden. They're open daily year-round from 9.30 am to sunset; entry is £4.80/3.20. There's a pleasant restaurant for soup and sandwich lunches.

Gairloch

Gairloch is a group of villages around the inner end of a loch of the same name. The

TIC (☎ 01445-712130) is at the car park in Auchtercairn; it's normally open all year. The **Heritage Museum** (☎ 01445-712287) tells of life in the west Highlands, complete with a typical crofting cottage. It's open Easter to October, Monday to Saturday from 10 am to 5 pm; entry is £1.50/50p.

For accommodation, there's the remote *Carn Dearg Youth Hostel* (☎ 01445-712219), 3 miles west of Gairloch on the road to Melvaig, which costs £6.10/4.95 for adults/juniors. At the end of the road, 13 miles from Gairloch, you can stay at the *Ruadh Reidh Lighthouse* hostel (☎ 01445-771263) for £7.50. In Gairloch there's plenty of B&B accommodation and bigger hotels like the *Myrtle Bank Hotel* (☎ 01445-712004), which has rooms with bathroom from £36 to £42 per person.

Loch Maree & Victoria Falls

The A832 runs alongside craggy Loch Maree, sprinkled with islands and with a series of peaks along the north shore culminating in 980m-high (3217 feet) Ben Slioch. The Victoria Falls (commemorating Queen Victoria's 1877 visit) tumble down to the loch between Slattadale and Talladale. Look for the 'Hydro Power' signs to find them.

Kinlochewe to Torridon

Small Kinlochewe is a good base for outdoor activities. From here the road follows Glen Torridon, overlooked by the multiple peaks of Beinn Eighe (1010m, 3309 feet) and Liathach (1055m, 3456 feet). The road reaches the sea at Torridon, where an NTS countryside centre offers information on walks in this rugged area. *Torridon Youth Hostel* (☎ 01445-791284) charges £7.50/6.50 for adults/juniors.

Applecross & Loch Carron

A long side trip abandons the A896 to follow the coast road via the remote seaside village of Applecross. Turning inland from Applecross, the road climbs to the Bealach-na Bo Pass (626m), then drops steeply to rejoin the A896. This winding, precipitous road can be closed in winter.

The A896 continues through the village of Lochcarron, then skirts Loch Carron itself.

PLOCKTON
• pop 400   ☎ 01599

From Stromeferry, there are two routes to Kyle of Lochalsh, from where ferries used to cross to Skye. The coastal route detours via idyllic Plockton, once a clearing centre for those displaced in the Clearances. This is a delightful place to stay, its main street lined with palms and whitewashed houses, each with a seagull perched on its chimney-stack gazing out at the sea. The steady throughput of visitors is augmented by viewers of the popular TV series *Hamish Macbeth* coming in search of scenes from the stories.

From May to September, Leisure Marine (☎ 544306) runs seal-watching cruises for £3.50/2. Sea Trek Marine (☎ 544356) operates similar tours.

Places to Stay & Eat

Plockton Station Bunkhouse (☎ 544235), open all year, charges £10 including sheets. There are several pleasant places to stay in Harbour St; try *An Caladh* (☎ 544356) at No 25 with beds from £16 a head. Right by the sea *The Sheiling* (☎ 544282) charges about the same. *Craig Highland Farm* (☎ 544205), 2 miles east of Plockton, is a delightful conservation centre with beds from £15 a head. There are lots of animals around and if you don't want to stay you can still visit for £1.50/1.

Plockton Hotel (☎ 544274, Harbour St) isn't the village's prettiest building but its pub food is popular; fish dishes start at about £6. Good, home-made food is available at *Off The Rails* (☎ 544423, Plockton Station). During the day you can get things like baked potatoes for £2.30; in the evening, meals like haggis, neeps and tatties cost around £5 to £7. The best food is at the *Haven Hotel* (☎ 544223) where four-course meals cost £24.

KYLE OF LOCHALSH
- pop 800   ☎ 01599

Until the Skye Bridge opened in 1995, Kyle of Lochalsh was the main jumping-off point for trips to Skye. Now, however, its many B&B owners have to watch most of their trade whizzing past without stopping.

The TIC (☎ 534276) is beside the main seafront car park and opens April through October and stocks useful information on Skye.

The *Seagreen Restaurant & Bookshop* (☎ *534388, Plockton Rd*), less than a mile from Kyle, has wonderful wholefood. Alternatively you could try the pricier *Seafood Restaurant* (☎ *534813*) in Kyle station.

Kyle can be reached by bus and train from Inverness (see Getting There & Away under Inverness), and by direct Scottish Citylink buses from Glasgow (five hours, £14.80), which continue across to Kyleakin and on to Portree (one hour, £5.80) and Uig (1½ hours, £6.80), for ferries to Tarbert on Harris and Lochmaddy on North Uist.

The 82 mile train ride between Inverness and Kyle of Lochalsh (2½ hours, £14.30) is one of Scotland's most scenic. From May to September you can enjoy the view from the observation saloon, or the view and a meal from the dining car.

KYLE TO THE GREAT GLEN
It's 55 miles via the A87 from Kyle to Invergarry, which is between Fort William and Fort Augustus on Loch Oich.

Eilean Donan Castle
Photogenically sited at the entrance to Loch Duich, Eilean Donan Castle (☎ 01599-85202) is Scotland's best-looking castle, and you get an excellent new exhibition and history display panels inside for your £3/2. It was ruined in a Jacobite uprising in 1719 and not rebuilt until 1932. It's open late March through October, daily from 10 am to 5.30 pm.

Citylink buses from Fort William and Inverness to Portree stop opposite the castle.

Glen Shiel & Glenelg
From Eilean Donan Castle, the A87 follows Loch Duich into the spectacular Glen Shiel valley, with 1000m (3000 feet) peaks soaring up on both sides of the road. Turn off towards Glenelg to see two fine ruined Iron Age **brochs**, Dun Telve and Dun Troddon. From Glenelg round to **Arnisdale** the scenery becomes even more spectacular.

ROAD TO THE ISLES
The scenic, 46 mile Road to the Isles (the A830) runs from Fort William via Glenfinnan to Arisaig and Mallaig. Just outside Fort William, at Banavie, is **Neptune's Staircase**; see the Fort William to Fort Augustus section earlier.

At **Glenfinnan**, a visitors centre (☎ 01397-722250, NTS) recounts the story of Prince Charles Edward Stuart, or Bonnie Prince Charlie, whose 1745 uprising started here and ended near here 14 months later when he fled to France. A lookout tower offers fine views over Loch Shiel. The centre opens April to October, daily from 10 am to 1 pm and 2 to 5 pm; entry is £1.50/1.

From **Arisaig**, the MV *Shearwater* (☎ 01687-450224) runs day trips to the islands of Rhum, Eigg and Muck. From Arisaig, the road winds around attractive bays, and the beaches known as the **Silver Sands of Morar**. Morar village is at the entrance to **Loch Morar**, Britain's deepest body of fresh water. It's thought to contain its own monster, named Morag.

MALLAIG
- pop 900   ☎ 01687

The lively fishing village of Mallaig makes a nice stopover between Fort William and Skye or the Small Isles. The TIC (☎ 462170) opens April to October.

Mallaig Marine World (☎ 462292) is an aquarium of mainly local species. From June to September it's open daily from 9 am to 9 pm (5.30 pm the rest of the year); entry is £2.75/2. **Mallaig Heritage Centre** opens Tuesday to Saturday from 1 to 4 pm; entry is £1.80/1.20. Minch Charters (☎ 462304), Harbour Slipways, runs **whale and**

dolphin-watching cruises several times weekly from May to September (seven hours, £40).

There are several pleasant B&Bs, and **Sheena's Backpacker's Lodge** (☎ *462764, Harbour View*) has dorm beds from £6 to £8.50, doubles for £11 per person.

From July to September, Scottish Citylink operates two or three buses daily (except Sunday) between Fort William and Mallaig (1½ hours, £4.50). The beautiful West Highland railway line between Fort William and Mallaig (£7.20) operates four times a day, Monday to Saturday, and once on Sunday, with connections to Glasgow. In July, one train each day is steam-operated.

Ferries run from Mallaig to Skye and the Small Isles year-round.

The Interior

It's easy to think of northern Scotland as a coast and to forget the interior highlands, even though their presence is always so visible. Access into this bleak but inspiring high country is provided by only a few roads, some single-track.

From June to September, just south of Lairg, at the southern end of Loch Shin, you can watch salmon leaping the **Falls of Shin** on their way upstream. From Lairg, single-track roads run north to Tongue, Laxford Bridge (between Durness and Kylesku) and Ledmore (between Kylesku and Ullapool). The A836 from Lairg to Tongue passes Ben Klibreck (721m, 2366 feet) and Ben Loyal (765m, 2509 feet). Ben Hope lies just to the west, at the head of Loch Hope.

From Monday to Saturday, Inverness Traction buses (☎ 01463-239292) run from Inverness to Lairg via Tain. Postbus services (☎ 01463-256228) connect Lairg to the coast; see the North & West Coast section.

Isle of Skye

• pop 8200

Skye is a rugged, convoluted island, 50 miles from end to end. It's ringed by beau-

Over the Bridge to Skye

'Speed bonny boat like a bird on the wing ... over the sea to Skye.' The words of the Skye Boat Song immortalised the flight of Bonnie Prince Charlie after the Battle of Culloden (disguised as Flora MacDonald's maid), and in doing so romanticised the idea of the boat trip to Skye.

The Caledonian MacBrayne ferry was hardly a rowing boat but did at least stick with the spirit of the song. Then in 1995 the new Skye Bridge from Kyle of Lochalsh to Kyleakin opened, a big concrete arch apparently depriving Skye of its island identity – but you can still take ferries from Glenelg (in summer) and Mallaig.

The very idea of a bridge was bad enough, but when the tolls were announced (£4.30 rising to £5.20 in the peak season), there was outrage. Some people objected to the principle of having to pay for what was theoretically just another part of the Scottish road network; while others pointed out that Skye was an area of high unemployment whose residents could ill afford the toll. The toll had been matched to the previous, artificially high ferry fare for cars.

The toll soon turned into a mini version of the 1990s poll tax rebellion. SKAT (Skye and Kyle Against the Toll) encouraged people to refuse to pay, even if it meant going to court. Dingwall's Sheriff Court is still working its way through the cases.

tiful coastline and dominated by the Cuillin, immensely popular for the sport of Munro bagging (see the boxed text 'Munros & Munro Bagging' in this chapter). Tourism is a mainstay of the island economy, so until you get off the main roads, don't expect to escape the hordes. Come prepared for changeable weather; when it's nice it's very, very nice, but often it isn't!

Portree and Broadford are the main population centres. Getting around the island midweek is fairly straightforward, with postbuses supplementing normal bus services. But here as much as in the Highlands, transport dwindles to nothing at weekends, particularly in winter and even more dramatically (so it seems) when it rains.

Gaelic is still spoken by half of Skye's residents.

There are two ways to travel over the sea to Skye. In summer CalMac (☎ 01678-462403) operates from Mallaig to Armadale (30 minutes, cars from £14.45, passengers £2.50). There's also a six car Glenelg to Kylerhea (☎ 01599-511302) service from April to October (not always on Sunday), taking 10 minutes and costing £5.50 for car, driver and four passengers, 60p for foot passengers.

PORTREE (PORT RIGH)
☎ 01478

Port Righ is Gaelic for King's Harbour, named after a 1540 call paid by James V to pacify local clan chieftains. Portree is Skye's biggest settlement with most of the facilities like banks, petrol stations and a post office with foreign exchange facilities. The harbour itself is particularly pretty.

The TIC (☎ 612137), just south of Bridge Rd, is open all year.

On the southern edge of Portree, the **Aros Experience** (☎ 613649) offers a lively introduction to Skye life. It's open daily from 9 am to 6 pm (11 pm in summer). Admission is £3.50/2.50.

Places to Stay
Portree Harbour Backpackers (☎ 613332) is a basic backpacker's hostel on waterfront Douglas Row with beds for £7.50. Alternatively, there's *Portree Independent Hostel* (☎ 613737), in the old post office near Somerled Square (£8.50), and *Portree Backpackers Hostel* (☎ 613641), on the Dunvegan Rd (from £7.50).

Portree hotels include the *Tongadale* (☎ 612115, Wentworth St), with rooms from £20 to £30 per person. On Somerled Square, the friendly *Isles Hotel* (☎ 612129) costs from £24 to £35 per person, while *Portree Hotel* (☎ 612511) is slightly pricier.

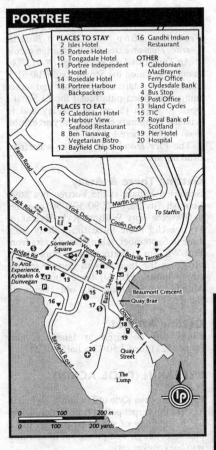

PORTREE

PLACES TO STAY
2 Isles Hotel
5 Portree Hotel
10 Tongadale Hotel
11 Portree Independent Hostel
14 Rosedale Hotel
18 Portree Harbour Backpackers

PLACES TO EAT
6 Caledonian Hotel
7 Harbour View Seafood Restaurant
8 Ben Tianavaig Vegetarian Bistro
12 Bayfield Chip Shop
16 Gandhi Indian Restaurant

OTHER
1 Caledonian MacBrayne Ferry Office
3 Clydesdale Bank
4 Bus Stop
9 Post Office
13 Island Cycles
15 TIC
17 Royal Bank of Scotland
19 Pier Hotel
20 Hospital

Rosedale Hotel (☎ 613131), on the waterfront, costs from £35 to £45 per person.

Places to Eat
The *Caledonian Hotel* is popular with locals and does bar meals for £2.50 to £7. *Bayfield Chip Shop* does good takeaway fish and chips for £2.75. The *Harbour View Seafood Restaurant* (☎ 612069, *Bosville Terrace*) is reasonable. There's pub food from £5.50 at the *Portree* and *Tongadale* hotels. You can even sample curry at the

HIGHLANDS & NTH ISLANDS

Gandhi Indian Restaurant (☎ 612681, Bayfield Rd). The excellent *Ben Tianavaig Vegetarian Bistro (☎ 612152, 5 Bosville Terrace)* has an extensive vegetarian menu.

An Tuireann Art Centre Café (☎ 613306) is out of town on the Struan road (B885). It caters for vegetarians and vegans and serves things like filled pitta bread for £3.50. It's open to 8 pm (5 pm on Sunday and in winter). Temporary contemporary art exhibitions are held here.

The *Pier Hotel* is a popular waterfront drinking spot.

Getting There & Away

Somerled Square is the Portree bus stop. Scottish Citylink (☎ 0990-505050) operates a Glasgow-Fort William-Kyle-Kyleakin-Portree-Uig route three times daily from June to September, taking three hours from Fort William to Portree and costing £12. It also runs the Inverness to Portree service (three hours, £10.50) three times a day Monday to Saturday, but only twice on Sunday.

Getting Around

Bikes can be hired at Island Cycles (☎ 613121) for £7.50/12 a half/full day.

KYLEAKIN (CAOL ACAIN)
☎ 01599

Even more than Kyle of Lochalsh, Kyleakin has had the carpet pulled from under its feet by the opening of the Skye Bridge. It's a pleasant enough wee place, but it's turning into backpacker city.

Castle Moil Seal Cruises (☎ 544235) charges £5.50/2.50 for a 1¼ hour cruise to see a seal colony on Eilean Mhal.

Kyleakin Youth Hostel (☎ 534585) charges £8.60/7.10 (£1 more in July and August) and is just doors from the friendly *Skye Backpackers (☎ 534510)*, where beds cost from £7 to £8.90. *Pier Coffee House* does snacks and meals for 90p to £5.25.

KYLERHEA (CAOL REITHE)

Kylerhea is about 4 miles south-east of Kyleakin and there's a car ferry from there to Glenelg on the mainland. Before crossing to Glenelg, you can follow a 1½ hour nature trail offering the chance to see otters from a shoreline hide (☎ 01320-366581); entry is free. Even if the otters elude you, you should still see basking seals and assorted birds.

The ferry (☎ 01599-511302) operates April to mid-May, Monday to Saturday from 9 am to 6 pm; mid-May to August, daily from 9 am to 8 pm (Sunday from 10 am to 6 pm); and September and October, daily from 9 am to 6 pm (Sunday first ferry at 10 am). A car and four passengers costs £5.50, a foot passenger 60p.

ARMADALE (ARMADAL)
☎ 01471

It's still possible to arrive on Skye by boat from Mallaig. If you do that you'll wind up in remote Armadale. If you visit the **Clan Donald Centre** (☎ 844305), in ruined Armadale Castle, a guided tour will tell you all you ever wanted to know about the MacDonald clan. It's open Easter to November, daily from 9.30 am to 5.30 pm; entry is £3.50/2.50. There's a pleasant restaurant serving homemade soup and snacks for under £2.

It's just 350m from the Armadale ferry terminal to the SYHA *Youth Hostel (☎ 844260)*, which opens Easter to September and costs £6.10/4.95 for adults/juniors. Four miles along the road is *Hairy Coo Backpacker Hotel (☎ 833231)*, a big, basic place with dorm beds for £8.50.

You can hire a bike from the Ferry Filling Station (☎ 844249) for £6/30 per day/week.

BROADFORD (AN T-ATH LEATHANN)
☎ 01471

Broadford's TIC (☎ 822361) is by the large Esso petrol station. There's nothing much to detain you in Broadford except the **Serpentarium** (☎ 822209) where you can see and touch all sorts of snakes, most of them illegally imported, impounded by customs and given refuge here. It's open Easter to October (£2.25/1.25).

The *Youth Hostel (☎ 822442)* opens February to December and charges £7.75/6.50

for adults/juniors. *Fossil Bothy (☎ 822644)* hostel, at nearby Lower Breakish, charges £7 a head.

You can hire a bike from Fairwinds Cycle Hire (☎ 822270) for £7 a day or rent a car from Skye Car Rental (☎ 822225).

THE CUILLINS & MINGINISH PENINSULA
☎ 01478

The rocky Cuillin Hills, west of Broadford, provide spectacular walking and climbing country. The complete traverse of the Black Cuillin ridge requires two days and involves real climbing; make sure you're properly equipped. Sgurr Alasdair, at 993m (3257 feet), is the highest point.

At Carbost, the **Talisker Distillery** (☎ 640314) opens Monday to Saturday from July to September (£3).

The camping ground (☎ 650333) at **Sligachan (Sligeachan)** is a popular jumping-off point for Cuillin climbers. There are two hostels in **Portnalong (Port nan Long)**: *Croft Bunkhouse (☎ 640254)*, 3 miles from Talisker Distillery, charges £6.50 (less for campers); *Skyewalker Independent Hostel (☎ 640250)*, at the Old School in Fiskavaig Rd, costs £7.

NORTH-WEST SKYE
☎ 01470

On the west side of the Waternish Peninsula, magnificent **Dunvegan Castle** (☎ 521206) dates back to the 13th century, although it was restored in Romantic style in the mid-19th century. Inside, you can visit the dining room, lounge, a decidedly alarming dungeon and, next door, an excellent drawing room. The castle opens daily from 10 am to 5.30 pm (11 am to 4 pm in winter); entry is £5/4.50.

Of several possible places to stay in Dunvegan, *Roskhill Guest House (☎ 521317)* has beds from £24.50, and the *Tables Hotel (☎ 521404)*, a mile from the castle, has beds from £25.

From Monday to Friday, you can get to Dunvegan by a Skyeways Travel (☎ 01599-534328) bus from Portree, leaving at 10 am

and returning from the castle at 12.52 pm (you get two hours at the castle).

TROTTERNISH PENINSULA
☎ 01470

North of Portree, Skye's coastal scenery is at its finest in the Trotternish Peninsula. Look out in particular for the rocky spike of the **Old Man of Storr**, the spectacular **Kilt Rock** and the ruins of **Duntulm Castle**. Near Staffin (Stamhain) the spectacular **Quiraing** also offers dramatic hill walking.

At the north end of the peninsula at Kilmuir (Cille Mhoire), the **Skye Museum of Island Life** (☎ 252213) re-creates crofting life in a series of cottages overlooking marvellous scenery. It's open April to October, Monday to Saturday from 9.30 am to 5.30 pm; entry is £1.50/1.

The biggest settlement is tiny **Staffin** where you can stop for lunch or a drink at *The Oystercatcher (☎ 562384)*, except on Sunday.

Three miles north of Staffin in even tinier **Flodigarry (Flodaigearraidh)** you can stay at the historic *Flodigarry Country House Hotel (☎ 552203)*, with singles from £49 to £55, doubles from £98 to £170. The home of **Flora MacDonald** is now part of the hotel and her grave at Kilmuir indicates that she is a real victim of tourism. The 1955 memorial records that of the original memorial 'every fragment has been removed by tourists'.

The *Dun Flodigarry Hostel (☎ 552212)* is much cheaper at £7.50 a head.

UIG (UIGE)
☎ 01470

Uig has a TIC (☎ 542404) in the bus terminal.

The *youth hostel (☎ 542211)* opens late March to October and costs £6.10/4.95 for adults/juniors. There's a cluster of bungalow B&Bs with beds for around £15. The *Old Ferry Inn (☎ 542242)* is pricier at £25 a head, the *Uig Hotel (☎ 542205)* pricier still at £35 a single but both have fine positions overlooking the bay.

From Uig pier, CalMac has services daily to Lochmaddy on North Uist (1¾ hours,

Flora MacDonald

The Isle of Skye was home to Flora Mac-Donald, who became famous for helping Bonnie Prince Charlie escape his defeat at the Battle of Culloden.

Flora was born in 1722 at Milton in South Uist and a memorial cairn marks the site of one of her early childhood homes. After her mother's abduction by Hugh MacDonald of Skye, Flora was reared by her brother and educated in the home of the Clanranald chiefs.

In 1746, she helped Bonnie Prince Charlie escape from Benbecula to Skye disguised as her Irish servant. With a price on the Prince's head, their little boat was fired on, but they managed to land safely and Flora escorted the Prince to Portree where he gave her a gold locket containing his portrait before setting sail for Raasay.

Waylaid on the way home, the boatmen admitted everything. Flora was arrested and imprisoned in the Tower of London. She never saw or heard from the Prince again.

In 1747, she returned home, marrying Allan MacDonald of Skye and going on to have nine children. Dr Samuel Johnson stayed with her in 1773 during his journey round the Western Isles, but later poverty forced her family to emigrate to North Carolina. There her husband was captured by rebels. Flora returned to Kingsburgh on Skye where she died in 1790 and was buried in Kilmuir churchyard, wrapped in the sheet in which Bonnie Prince Charlie and Dr Johnson had slept.

cars from £37, passengers £7.85) and Monday to Saturday to Tarbert on Harris (same times and prices).

ISLE OF RAASAY
- **pop 163**   ☎ **01478**

This long, narrow, quiet island is reached by CalMac ferry from Sconser, between Portree and Broadford. From April to October the ferry operates up to 10 times a day, Monday to Saturday only. Cars cost £8.45, passengers £2. There's no petrol on Raasay. Forest Enterprise publishes a free leaflet with suggested walks and forest trails.

To camp at **Raasay Outdoor Centre** (☎ 660266) costs £4. There are bikes available for hire. **Raasay Youth Hostel** (☎ 660240) opens late March to October and costs £4.65/3.85 for adults/juniors.

Outer Hebrides

Synonymous with remoteness, the Outer Hebrides (Western Isles) are a string of islands running in a 130 mile arc from north to south, shielding the north-western coast of Scotland. Bleak, isolated, treeless and exposed to gales that sweep in from the Atlantic, the Outer Hebrides are almost irresistibly romantic. They form one of Europe's most isolated frontiers and have a fascinating history, signposted by Neolithic standing stones, Viking place-names, empty crofts and folk memories of the Clearances.

Immediate reality can be disappointing, however. The towns are straggly, unattractive and dominated by stern, austere churches. Although the ruins of traditional blackhouses (named after the soot left on the walls by the burning peat fire in the centre) can still be seen, they've been supplanted by unattractive (though no doubt more comfortable) concrete-block bungalows. Rugged and apparently inhospitable though the islands are, they support a surprisingly large and widely distributed population and in summer CalMac ferries disgorge a daily cargo of tourists.

The landscapes can be mournful, but they're also spectacular, with wide horizons of sky and water, dazzling white beaches, azure bays, wide peat moors, and countless lochs, mountains and stony hills. These are islands that reward an extended stay, especially if you travel on foot or by bike; a rushed tour will be less satisfying, and

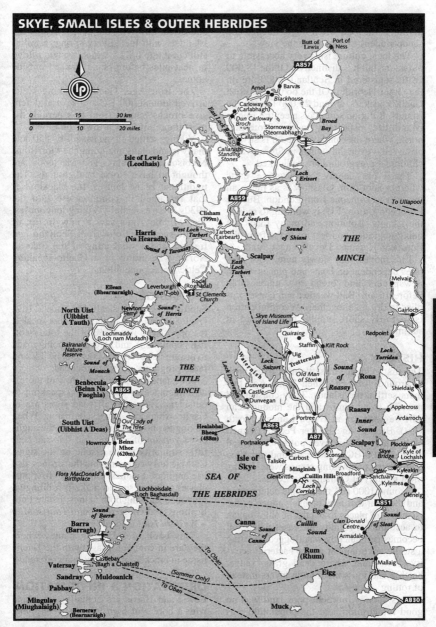

SKYE, SMALL ISLES & OUTER HEBRIDES

Butt of Lewis
Port of Ness
A857
Arnol
Barvas
Blackhouse
Carloway
(Carlabhagh)
Dun Carloway
Broch
Stornoway
(Steornabhagh)
Broad Bay
Callanish
Uig
Callanish
Standing
Stones
Isle of Lewis
(Leodhais)
East Loch Loch
Loch
Erisort
To Ullapool
A859
Clisham
(799m)
Loch
of Seaforth
Harris
(Na Hearadh)
West Loch
Tarbert
Tarbert
(Tairbeart)
Sound
of Shiant
THE
MINCH
Sound of Taransay
Scalpay
Melvaig
East
Loch
Tarbert
Ellean
(Bhearnaraigh)
Leverburgh
(An T-ob)
Rodel
(Roghadal)
St Clements
Church
Gairloch
Newton
Ferry
Sound
of Harris
Skye Museum
of Island Life
Redpoint
North Uist
(Uibhist
A Tauth)
Lochmaddy
(Loch nam Madadh)
Quiraing
Staffin
Kilt Rock
Loch
Torridon
Balranald
Nature
Reserve
Sound of
Monach
THE
LITTLE
MINCH
Waternish
Loch
Snizort
Trotternish
Old Man
of Storr
Sound
of
Raasay
Rona
Shieldaig
Benbecula
(Beinn Na
Faoghla)
A865
Loch Dunvegan
Dunvegan
Castle
Dunvegan
Portree
Raasay
Inner
Sound
Applecross
Ardarroch
South Uist
(Uibhist A Deas)
Our Lady of
The Isles
Healabhal
Bheag
(488m)
A863
Portnalong
A87
Scalpay
Plockton
Skye
Bridge
Kyle of
Lochalsh
Howmore
Beinn
Mhor
(620m)
Talisker
Carbost
Sconser
Broadford
Otter
Sanctuary
Kyleakin
Flora MacDonald's
Birthplace
SEA OF
Isle of
Skye
Minginish
Cuillin Hills
Glenbrittle
Loch
Corruisk
Kylerhea
Glenelg
Lochboisdale
(Loch Baghasdail)
THE HEBRIDES
Elgol
A851
Sound
of Sleat
Sound of Barra
Canna
Cuillin
Sound
Clan Donald
Centre
Barra
(Barragh)
Sound
of
Canna
Armadale
Mallaig
Castlebay
(Bagh a Chaisteil)
To Oban
Vatersay
Sandray
Muldoanich
(Summer Only)
Rum
(Rhum)
Eigg
Pabbay
To Oban
Mingulay
(Miughalaigh)
Berneray
(Bearnaraigh)
Muck
A830

0   15   30 km
0   10   20 miles

when driving you have to pay too much attention to the road (often single-tracked and sheep-ridden) to appreciate the views.

The local culture isn't very accessible to outsiders, but it is distinctive. Of the 18,000 crofts registered in Scotland, 6000 are on the Outer Hebrides. Of the 66,000 Scottish Gaelic speakers, around 25,000 live on the islands. Religion still plays a central role in island life, especially in the Protestant north, where the Sunday Sabbath is strictly observed – even the swings in Stornoway's children's playground are padlocked.

These are deeply conservative parts where a Scot from Glasgow is as much an incomer as someone from London. But the European Union (EU) is working to reduce the islands' isolation and many roads are being upgraded courtesy of loans from the European Regional Development Fund.

Life moves very slowly here, with supplies dependent on boats and planes. Often newspapers and bread are unavailable before 10 am. Bad weather can cause supplies to dry up altogether. Accommodation is in fairly short supply; book ahead in summer.

HISTORY

The first evidence of settlement dates back to around 4000 BC when Stone Age farmers settled the islands. They constructed massive stone tombs and the mounds can still be seen (as at Barpa Langas, North Uist). Bronze Age Beaker People (named after their distinctive pottery) arrived around 1800 BC, and it's around this time that groups of standing stones were set up, most notably at Callanish on Lewis.

Around 1000 BC, the climate deteriorated and the peat that now blankets much of the islands – in places to depths of 6m – began to accumulate. Acidity increases when soil becomes permanently waterlogged, creating a sterile environment where bacterial activity slows, and where dead grass, sedge, heather and moss build up in layers instead of rotting.

This spongy, nutrient-poor land was no good for farming, and the population was forced onto the coastal fringe. When cut and dried, however, the peat provided the islanders with fuel. Every spring, families still cut it into bricks, which are wind-dried in neat piles before being stacked outside homes.

The Iron Age, Gaelic-speaking Celts arrived around 500 BC and several defensive brochs remain from this period, the most impressive at Carloway on Lewis.

Vikings settled on the islands by 850, and many island clans, including the Morrisons, Nicolsons, MacAulays and Macleods, are thought to have Norse backgrounds. The traditional island houses, the blackhouses that remained in common use into the 1930s, were essentially Viking longhouses. The Middle Ages saw a new influx of Gaelic-speaking Celts from Scotland and Ireland, and a weakening of the links to Norway, resulting in a Gaelic-speaking Celtic/Norse population.

LANGUAGE

Scottish Gaelic is basically the same as Irish Gaelic. About 75% of the islanders speak it (as opposed to just 1.5% of the total Scottish population), and efforts are being made to ensure its survival. Many Gaelic TV and radio programs are now produced.

All islanders speak English, and there's no reluctance to use it when speaking to outsiders. However, all road signs are in Gaelic which can cause confusion. When talking to outsiders, islanders use the anglicised version of a name, but this can bear little similarity to the Gaelic on the signs. CalMac ferry company and the airlines also use anglicised names. One of the first purchases a visitor should make is a bilingual road map showing both names; Estate Publications' red-covered *Official Tourist Map – Western Isles* is ideal.

This book uses English names where they are in common usage with the Gaelic name in brackets at the first main reference.

ORIENTATION & INFORMATION

Lewis and Harris are actually one island with a border of high hills between them.

The Wee Frees & Other Island Creeds

Religion plays a complex and important role in island life and priests and ministers enjoy powerful positions in the community. The split between the Protestants to the north of Benbecula and the Catholics to the south creates, or perhaps reflects, a different communal atmosphere.

Hebridean Protestants have developed a distinctive fundamentalist approach, with Sunday being devoted to religious services, prayer and Bible reading. On Lewis and Harris, virtually everything closes down. In general, social life is restricted to private homes and, as public drinking is frowned upon, pubs are mostly uninspiring.

The Protestants are further divided into three main sects, with convoluted, emotionally charged histories. The Church of Scotland, the main Scottish church, is state-recognised or 'established'. The Free Presbyterian Church of Scotland and the Free Church of Scotland (or Wee Frees) are far more conservative and intolerant, permitting no ornaments, organ music or choirs. Their ministers deliver uncompromising sermons (usually in Gaelic) from central pulpits, and *precentors* lead the congregation in unaccompanied, but atmospheric, psalm singing. Visitors are welcome to attend services, but due respect is essential.

The most recent split occurred in 1988 when Lord Mackay, Lord Chancellor and a prominent Free Presbyterian, committed the awful crime of attending a friend's Catholic requiem mass. The church elders threatened him with expulsion, and he and his supporters responded by establishing the breakaway Associated Presbyterian Church!

The Catholic Church south of Benbecula survived the Reformation. The priests were expelled early in the 17th century but, despite several missionary attempts, Protestantism failed to take hold. The Sunday Sabbath on South Uist and Barra is more easy-going, and the attitude towards the demon drink more relaxed.

The northern half of Lewis is low and flat with miles of peat moors; southern Lewis and Harris are rugged, with some impressive stony mountains and glorious beaches. Stornoway, on Lewis, is the largest town in the Outer Hebrides, with a reasonable range of facilities.

North Uist, Benbecula and South Uist are joined by bridge and causeway. These are low, flat, green islands half-drowned by sinuous lochs and open to the sea and sky. Benbecula has a large army and air force base.

There are TICs in every ferry port, open April to mid-October for ferry arrivals up to midnight.

The main Western Isles Tourist Board (☎ 01851-703088), 26 Cromwell St, Stornoway, Lewis PA87 2DD, produces a brochure showing all accommodation possibilities, from hotels to B&Bs and self-catering cottages. *The Outer Hebrides Handbook & Guide*, written by local experts, gives lots of data on the islands' history, culture, flora and fauna.

ACCOMMODATION & FOOD

Camping grounds with facilities are scarce, but free camping is usually allowed, provided you get permission from the nearest house and remove all rubbish. Some landowners may ask a small fee.

There are a few basic hostels in old crofts scattered around the islands, but most are difficult to get to without transport or a readiness to hike. Most are run by the SYHA or Gatliff Hebridean Hostels Trust, 71 Cromwell St, Stornoway, Lewis PA87 2DG, in association with the SYHA. Charges are the same as for SYHA grade 3 hostels. The Gatliff Trust hostels have bunk beds, blankets, cooking equipment, cold

HIGHLANDS & NTH ISLANDS

running water and open fires. Bring a sleeping bag and eating utensils. Local crofters look after them, but no advance bookings are accepted and they prefer people not to arrive or depart on a Sunday.

In recent years, several independent hostels have opened. These tend to be clean, modern and, consequently, more expensive than the Gatliff Trust or SYHA hostels.

B&Bs provide an otherwise rare opportunity to meet the islanders, who are famous both for their hospitality and the size of their breakfasts. Few offer private bathrooms, but they're usually comfortable and clean and offer hearty dinners as well. Most B&B hosts, especially on Lewis and Harris, appreciate guests booking ahead if they're going to stay on Sunday night.

A few B&Bs are handy for the ferry ports, but most are scattered around the countryside. The ports themselves are generally uninspiring, but always have at least one pub where meals are available. If you stay in the countryside – which is recommended – check whether there's a convenient pub, make arrangements to eat at your B&B, or take your own provisions to a hostel.

Self-catering cottages must be booked in advance.

Options for eating out centre on the pubs, which are few and far between and not particularly cheap. The picture for vegetarians is improving; most hotels manage at least one suitable dish.

GETTING THERE & AWAY
Air
British Airways Express (☎ 0345-222111) flies to the islands, and there are airports at Stornoway, on Lewis, and on Benbecula and Barra. The main airport, 4 miles east of Stornoway, is served by regular BA flights from Glasgow and Inverness (Monday to Saturday). British Airways Express also has flights to Benbecula and Barra from Glasgow Monday to Saturday, with additional Sunday flights in peak summer months. British Airways Express also links Barra and Benbecula with Stornoway. At Barra the planes land on the beach, so the timetable depends on the tides.

Bus
Regular bus services to Ullapool, Uig and Oban connect with the ferries. The main operator to Ullapool and Oban is Scottish Citylink (☎ 0990-505050).

Train
Spectacular train services run as far as Oban, Mallaig and Kyle of Lochalsh from Glasgow and Edinburgh. To get to Ullapool, take the train to Inverness, then a bus to Ullapool.

Boat
CalMac runs comfortable car and passenger ferries from Ullapool to Stornoway on Lewis (2½ hours, two or three times a day Monday to Saturday); from Uig, on Skye, to Tarbert on Harris and Lochmaddy on North Uist (around 1¾ hours, once or twice a day six or seven days a week); and from Mallaig and Oban to Lochboisdale on South Uist and Castlebay on Barra (3¼ to seven hours, almost daily).

The timetables are complicated and, especially during summer, car space can fill up fast. Advance booking is essential, although foot and bicycle passengers should have no problems.

There are eight different Island Hopscotch fares for set routes in the Outer Hebrides, offering worthwhile savings. Island Rover Passes give unlimited travel on all CalMac routes for eight or 15 days; convenient certainly, but make sure you use enough services to recoup the cost. For reservations and service details, contact Caledonian MacBrayne (☎ 01475-650000 for reservations, ☎ 01475-650100 for inquiries), The Ferry Terminal, Gourock PA19 1QP.

A one-way ticket from Stornoway to Ullapool is £12 for each passenger or driver, plus £54 for a car. From Otternish to Leverburgh it's £4.30/20; from Lochboisdale to Castlebay £4.90/27.50; and from Lochboisdale or Castlebay to Oban £17.30/61. For a passenger this totals £38.50, for a car

£162.70 – as against £35 and £147 for the equivalent Hopscotch ticket. Allow at least a week to tackle this full north-south route. Bikes are carried free with a Hopscotch ticket (otherwise £7).

GETTING AROUND
Bus
Bus transport is extremely limited, although a bare-bones service allows crofters to get to the shops in the morning and return in the afternoon. TICs have up-to-date timetables and you can contact Stornoway bus station (☎ 01851-704327) for information about Lewis and Harris services. Visitors without their own transport should anticipate a fair amount of hitching and walking.

Car
Most roads are single-track and the main hazard is posed by sheep wandering onto the roads. Petrol stations are far apart, expensive and usually closed on Sunday.

Cars can be hired from around £20 per day from Arnol Motors (☎ 01851-710548), Arnol, Lewis; Mackinnon Self Drive (☎ 01851-702984), 18 Inaclete Rd, Stornoway; Harris Car Services (☎ 01859-502280), Scott Rd, Tarbert; Maclennan's Self Drive (☎ 01870-602191), Balivanich, Benbecula; Ask Car Hire (☎ 01870-602818), Liniclate, Benbecula; and Laing Motors (☎ 01878-700267), Lochboisdale, South Uist.

Bicycle
Cycling north to south is quite popular, but allow at least a week for the trip. The main problems are difficult weather, strong winds (you hear stories of people cycling downhill and freewheeling uphill) and sheep that believe they have right of way.

Bikes can be hired from Alex Dan's Cycle Centre (☎ 01851-704025), 67 Kenneth St, Stornoway, Lewis; Barra Cycle Hire (☎ 018714-284), 29 St Brendan's Rd, Castlebay, Barra; and DM Mackenzie (☎ 01859-502271), Pier Rd, Tarbert, Harris. Booking is advisable.

Hitching
Hitching is feasible, although traffic is light and virtually stops on Sunday, especially on Harris and Lewis. The islanders are generally hospitable, and hitching is definitely safer than around big cities. See Hitching in the Getting Around chapter at the start of this book.

LEWIS (LEODHAIS)
☎ 01851

The northern half of Lewis (combined population with Harris 21,737) is low, flat and dominated by the vast Black Moor, a peat moor dotted with numerous small lochs. The coastal fringes have some arable land and are surprisingly densely populated, if not particularly attractive.

The old blackhouses may have gone, but most holdings are crofts that follow a traditional pattern dating back to medieval times. Most are narrow strips, designed to give everyone an equal share of good and bad land. Usually they run back from the foreshore (with its valuable seaweed), across the machair (the grassy sand dunes that were the best arable land) and back to the peaty grazing land.

Nowadays few crofts are economically viable, so most islanders supplement what they make from the land with other jobs. Many travel away to work on oil rigs or ships, and others work in the fishing industry (including a growing number in fish farming), service industries, or the traditional tweed weaving industry.

South of Stornoway and Barvas, the island is mountainous and beautiful, reminiscent of parts of the mainland's north-west coast. Three of the Outer Hebrides' most important sights – Arnol Blackhouse, Dun Carloway Broch and Callanish Standing Stones – are also here.

Stornoway (Steornabhagh)
• pop 8100
The island's only sizeable town, Stornoway lies on a beautiful natural harbour, but it's not one of the most pleasant places in Scotland. There's a bit of a drugs problem,

perhaps because there's so little else to do. For tourists there are reasonable facilities and the small **Museum nan Eilean** (☎ 703773), in Francis St, but most people will want to escape as quickly as possible.

Stornoway is the Outer Hebrides' administrative and commercial centre, and the base for the Western Isles Council (Comhairle nan Eilan), a hospital and the islands' Gaelic TV and radio stations. There's an airport and a ferry link with Ullapool (see Getting There & Away earlier in the Outer Hebrides section).

Orientation & Information The ferry docks in the town centre, which is compact and easy to get around on foot. The bus station is on the foreshore to the east of the ferry terminal. For ferry information, phone CalMac (☎ 702361).

Some of the residential areas (and B&Bs) are a fair hike without a car, and many people commute in from communities around the island to work and shop, so there's more traffic than you might expect.

The main Western Isles Tourist Board (☎ 703088) is a short walk from the ferry pier. In theory you could use this office to book B&Bs around the islands, but in practice it's best to take the free accommodation list and make the calls yourself.

Places to Stay & Eat *Laxdale Holiday Park* (☎ 703234, 6 Laxdale Lane) is 1½ miles north of town off the A857. Charges start at £6.50 per person.

Stornoway Backpackers Hostel (☎ 703628, 47 Keith St) is a five minute walk from the ferry and bus station – walk east along pedestrianised Point St, which becomes Francis St, pass the post office, then turn left into Keith St. Dorm beds are £8 including breakfast, and there's a self-catering kitchen.

B&Bs are widely scattered. *Hollsetr* (☎ 702796, 29 Urquart Gardens) is a long walk from the centre, but it's immaculate and welcoming, with a single, twin and family room from £16 per person. There are a few pleasant places on Matheson Rd,

within walking distance of the ferry: *Ravenswood* (☎ 702673), at No 12, has a double and twin with bath from £18 a head, while *Fernlea* (☎ 702125), at No 19, charges similarly.

Park Guest House (☎ 702485), with beds from £21 to £29, and *Tower Guest House* (☎ 703150), with beds from £18, are two comfortable guesthouses in Victorian homes in James St. To find them follow the waterfront east, then veer left at the signpost for the A866.

The old-fashioned *County Hotel* (☎ 703250, Francis St), east from the pedestrian mall, is a reasonable hotel; singles/doubles are £40/60.

During the day *Merchants Coffee House*, opposite the TIC, does snacky meals in pleasant surroundings. After 6 pm you'll only get food at the pub-hotels and a few takeaway places. You can get a curry at the *Stornoway Balti and Kebab House* (☎ 706116, 24 South Beach St) from around £6; it does takeaways and opens on Sunday. The *Royal Hotel* (☎ 702109, Cromwell St) has prices starting at £4.50, and a more expensive restaurant with a seafood slant. The *Crown Hotel* (☎ 703181, Castle St) also does bar meals.

Butt of Lewis (Rubha Robhanais)

Lewis's northern tip is windswept and rugged, with a lighthouse and large colonies of nesting fulmars. To get there, drive across the bleak expanse of Black Moor to **Barvas (Barabhas)**, then follow the densely populated west coast to the north-east. **St Moluag's Church** is an austere, barn-like structure believed to date from the 12th century, but still used by the Episcopal Church. **Port of Ness (Port Nis)** is an attractive harbour with a popular sandy beach.

Arnol Blackhouse Museum

The most interesting and beautiful part of Lewis is south of Barvas and Stornoway. Situated just west of Barvas off the A858, Arnol Blackhouse Museum (☎ 710395, HS) is the only authentically maintained, traditional blackhouse – a combined byre, barn and home – left on the islands. Built in 1885, it was inhabited until 1964 and now offers a wonderful insight into the old crofting way of life. It's open April to September, Monday to Saturday from 9.30 am to 6.30 pm, and October to March, Monday to Thursday (and Saturday) from 9.30 am to 4.30 pm; entry is £1.80/1.30.

At nearby **Bragar** a pair of whalebones form an arch by the road with the rusting harpoon that killed the whale dangling from the centre.

Carloway (Carlabagh)

Carloway looks across a beautiful loch to the southern mountains and has a post office and small store. At nearby **Garenin (Gearrannan)** some fascinating, ruined blackhouses are quietly mouldering alongside new concrete cottages. Also here is the *Gearrannan Crofters' Hostel*, itself a restored blockhouse (£4.65/3.85 for adults/juniors). To get to the hostel from the war memorial by the church, cross the bridge and turn left. Don't take the road that passes under the bridge. Pass the shop, but don't turn left; continue straight on at the next junction. The hostel is half a mile farther on at the end of the road. The warden, Mrs Pat Macgregor, lives at 3 Uraghag, one of the modern houses (with a large black and white cartwheel at its side) by the last road junction en route to the hostel.

Carloway Broch (Dun Charlabhaigh) is a well-preserved, 2000-year-old dry-stone defensive tower, in a beautiful position with panoramic views. The new **Dun Carloway Interpretative Centre** will be open by the time you read this.

Callanish (Calanais)

The construction of the **Callanish Standing Stones** began around 4000 years ago, so they predate the Pyramids by 1000 years. Fifty-four large stones are arranged in the shape of a Celtic cross on a promontory overlooking Loch Roag. This is one of the most complete stone circles in Britain. Its great age, the mystery of its purpose, its impressive scale and its undeniable beauty

have the dizzy effect of dislocating you from the present day.

The new **Calanais Visitor Centre** (☎ 621422) is a *tour de force* of discreet design and provides a rare place to eat in the area. It's open (free) daily, April to September from 10 am to 7 pm (4 pm the rest of the year). There's an exhibition about the stones for £1.50/1.

There are a couple of pleasant B&Bs nearby; try *Mrs Morrison (☎ 621392)* in the house right by the stones (from £18), or the attractive *Eschol Guest House (☎ 621357)*, half a mile back towards Carloway (from £25). *Tigh Mealros (☎ 621333)* does light lunches in summer from £2 and evening main courses from £7.50, including wild local scallops.

Mealista (Mealasta)

The road to Mealista (the B8011 south-west of Callanish, signposted to Uig) takes you through the most remote parts of Lewis. Follow the road right round towards Breanais for some truly spectacular white-sand beaches, although the surf can make swimming treacherous. The famous 12th century walrus-ivory Lewis chess pieces were discovered in the sand dunes here in 1831; of the 78 pieces, 67 wound up in the British Museum in London.

HARRIS (NA HEARADH)
☎ 01859

Harris has the islands' most dramatic scenery, combining mountains, magnificent beaches, expanses of machair (grass and wildflower-covered dunes) and weird rocky hills and coastline.

North Harris is actually the mountainous southern tip of Lewis, beyond the peat moors south of Stornoway – the Clisham is the highest point at 799m (2600 feet). South Harris, across the land bridge at Tarbert, is also mountainous but has a fascinating variety of landscapes and great beaches.

Harris is famous for Harris Tweed, high-quality woollen cloth still hand-woven in islanders' homes. The industry employs 400 millworkers and 750 independent

HIGHLANDS & NTH ISLANDS

weavers. Tarbert TIC can tell you about weavers and visitable workshops.

Tarbert (Tairbeart)
• pop 500

Tarbert is a village port midway between North and South Harris with ferry connections to Uig on Skye. Not in itself particularly inspiring, it has a spectacular location, overshadowed by mountains on the narrow land bridge between two lochs. Tarbert has basic facilities: a petrol station, Bank of Scotland and two general stores. The Harris Tweed Shop stocks a wide range of books on the islands.

The TIC (☎ 502011) is signposted up the hill and to the right from the ferry. For ferry information, phone CalMac (☎ 502444). While you wait, *Firstfruits* tearoom, open April to September, does a few hot dishes as well as sandwiches and cakes. It's opposite the TIC.

A good B&B is the cosy *Tigh na Mara* (☎ 502270), a five minute walk from the ferry, with views of the east loch and beds from £15 to £16 per person. Closer to the ferry terminal, *Waterstein House* (☎ 502358), a bland building with three rooms, charges £14 per person.

Harris Hotel (☎ 502154) has a range of rooms, some with bath, from around £28 a head. It also has a good range of whiskies and serves good-value pub meals (including something for vegetarians) from around £5.

North Harris

North Harris is the most mountainous part of the Outer Hebrides. Only a few roads run through the region, but there are many opportunities for climbing and walking.

The small village of **Rhenigidale (Reinigeadal)** is accessible by road. *Reinigeadal Crofters' Hostel* can also be reached on foot (three hours and 6 miles from Tarbert). It's an excellent walk, but take all necessary supplies. From Tarbert, take the road to Kyles Scalpay for 2 miles. Just beyond Laxdale Lochs, at a bend in the road, a signposted track, marked on OS maps, veers off to the left across the hills. The hostel

is a white building standing above the road on the east side of the glen; the warden lives in the house closest to the shore. Beds cost £4.65/3.85 for adults/juniors.

South Harris

Beautiful South Harris is ringed by a tortuous 45 mile road. The beaches on the west coast, backed by rolling machair and mountains, with views across to North Harris and to offshore islands, are stunning.

The town of **Leverburgh (An T-ob)** is named after Lord Leverhulme (the founder of the conglomerate Unilever), who bought Lewis and Harris in 1918 and 1919. He had grand plans for the islands, particularly Obbe, as Leverburgh was then known, which was to be a major fishing port. It's now a sprawling, ordinary place but with a shop and several pleasant B&Bs; try *Caberfeidh House* (☎ 520276), which charges £15 per person or *Garryknowe* (☎ 520246), which has doubles for £16, or £18 with bathroom.

A passenger ferry goes from Leverburgh to Berneray and North Uist. From April to October, it runs Monday to Saturday three or four times a day; in winter, once daily (one hour, £4.30, £20 for a car). Tarbert TIC has information, or phone CalMac (☎ 01475-650100).

Three miles east at attractive **Rodel (Roghadal)** stands **St Clement's Church**, mainly built between the 1520s and 1550s, only to be abandoned in 1560 after the Reformation. Inside there's the fascinating tomb of Alexander MacLeod, the man responsible for the initial construction. Crude carvings show scenes of hunting, a castle, a galleon and various saints including St Clement clutching a skull.

The east, or Bays, coast is traversed by the Golden Road, derisively nicknamed by national newspapers that didn't think so much money should be spent on building it. This is a weird, rocky moonscape, still dotted with numerous crofts. It's difficult to imagine how anyone could have survived in such an inhospitable environment, but they did, and do. The SYHA operates *Stockinish*

Youth Hostel (☎ *530373*) in the small village of Caolas Stocinis. It's 7 miles from Tarbert, costs £4.65/3.85 for adults/juniors, and you should bring all your supplies.

NORTH UIST (UIBHIST A TUATH)
• pop 1404   ☎ 01876

North Uist is half-drowned by lochs, but has some magnificent beaches on the west side. There are also some great views north to the mountains of Harris. The landscape is a bit less wild than Harris but it has a sleepy, subtle appeal. For birdwatchers this is an earthly paradise, with huge populations of migrant waders – oystercatchers, lapwings, curlews and redshanks at every turn.

Lochmaddy (Loch nam Madadh)

There isn't much to keep you in tiny Lochmaddy, but it has the ferry terminal for sailings to Uig on Skye, and there are a couple of stores, a Bank of Scotland, a petrol station, a post office and a pub. There's also the interesting **Taigh Chearsabhagh** museum and arts centre (☎ 500293), open March to December, Monday to Saturday from 10 am to 5 pm (8 pm from June to September). The next door café does soups and sandwiches.

The TIC (☎ 500321) opens April to mid-October, Monday to Saturday from 9 am to 5 pm, and for late ferry arrivals. For ferry information, phone CalMac (☎ 500337).

Lochmaddy Youth Hostel (☎ *500368*), half a mile from the docks (signposted), opens mid-May to September and costs £6.10/4.95 for adults/juniors. An independent hostel at *Uist Outdoor Centre* (☎ *500480*) has beds in four-bed rooms for £6.

The *Old Court House* (☎ *500358*) is a comfortable B&B with two singles, a twin and a double, costing from £18 per person; the similarly priced *Old Bank House* (☎ *500275*) is also good. Extremely comfortable and well presented is *Stag Lodge* (☎ *500364*) in a pleasing whitewashed building; beds start at £18 and are well worth it. There's also a small restaurant here.

Lochmaddy Hotel (☎ *500331*) is a traditional hotel with a range of rooms (some with bath) from around £30 per person. Its restaurant serves excellent fish and seafood, or you can get bar meals (most under £5.50) until 8.30 pm. It's also a good place to stay if you're into fishing (and North Uist is famous for fishing); you can buy permits here.

Car ferries for Leverburgh, on South Harris, leave from Otternish, near the Berneray causeway – see earlier under South Harris.

Balranald Nature Reserve

Eighteen miles west of Lochmaddy off the A865 is an RSPB nature reserve (☎ 510730) where you can watch migrant waders and listen for rare corncrakes. From April to September, a basic visitors centre provides refuge if it's raining.

Bharpa Langass & Pobull Fhinn

The chambered Neolithic burial tomb of Bharpa Langass stands on a hillside 6 miles south-west of Lochmaddy, just off the A867. It's believed to date back 5000 years. Take care as the path can be boggy.

Pobull Fhinn (Finn's People) is a stone circle of similar age accessible from a path beside Langass Lodge Hotel. There are lovely views over the loch, where seals can sometimes be seen.

BENBECULA (BEINN NA FAOGHLA)
• pop 1803   ☎ 01870

Blink and you'll miss Benbecula, a low-lying island that's almost as much water as land, connected by bridge and causeway to North and South Uist. Although the number of British soldiers based here is declining, they still hang on at a missile firing range.

The troops and their families are quartered around hideous **Balivanich (Baile a'Mhanaich)** where the big Naafi/Spar Store opens usual hours and on Sunday (until 1 pm). You can get good food in the *Stepping Stone Restaurant* (☎ *603377*), with lunch time main courses under £4. There's one flight a day, Monday to Saturday, to Glasgow.

HIGHLANDS & NTH ISLANDS

SOUTH UIST (UIBHIST A DEAS)

- **pop 2106**   ☎ **01878**

South Uist is the second largest island in the Outer Hebrides. Once again, it lacks the drama of Harris, but although it's unassuming, there's an expansiveness that has its own magic. The west coast is low, with machair backing an almost continuous sandy beach. The east coast is quite hilly, with **Beinn Mhor** reaching 620m (2030 feet), and cut by four large sea lochs. This island rewards those who explore beyond the main north-south road.

As you drive from Benbecula, watch for the granite statue of **Our Lady of the Isles** standing on the slopes of the Rueval hill.

Lochboisdale (Loch Baghasdail)

Lochboisdale has ferry links to Oban and Mallaig on the mainland and Castlebay on Barra.

The TIC (☎ 700286) opens April to mid-October, Monday to Saturday from 9 am to 5 pm, and for late ferry arrivals. For ferry information phone CalMac (☎ 700288). There's a branch of the Royal Bank of Scotland and petrol supplies.

Of the B&Bs, friendly *Lochside Cottage* (☎ 700472) has beds from £13, while *Riverside* (☎ 700250) starts at £14. *Bay View* (☎ 700329) is nearer the pier and charges from £14 to £20 per person. *Lochboisdale Hotel* (☎ 700332), above the ferry terminal, has a variety of rooms, all with bath, for £36 to £42 a head. The pub has good food; bar meals and snacks range from £2 to £5.50.

Howmore (Tobha Mor)

An attractive west coast village, Howmore has the *Tobha Mor Crofters' Hostel* (£4.65/3.85 for adults/juniors). To get to it, take the turn-off from the A865 to Tobha Mor – the hostel is the white building with a porch by the church at the road's end. The warden lives at Ben More House, at the junction with the main road.

The South

The southern tip of the island looks across to the islands of Eriskay and Barra. From Ludag, there's a car ferry (☎ 720261) to Eriskay and a passenger ferry (☎ 720238) to Eoligarry on Barra's northern tip.

BARRA (BARRAIGH)

- **pop 1244**   ☎ **01871**

Barra is a tiny island, just 12 miles around and ideal for exploring on foot. With beautiful beaches, machair, hills, Neolithic remains and a strong sense of community, it could be said to encapsulate the Outer Hebridean experience.

The TIC (☎ 810336) in **Castlebay (Bagh a Chaisteil)**, the largest village, is open April to mid-October. In the village, **Kisimul Castle** (☎ 810336) was built by the MacNeil clan in the 12th century. It was sold in the 19th century and restored in the 20th century by US architect Robert MacNeil, who became clan chief. A standard flies above the castle when his son and heir is in residence.

With only about 20 B&Bs scattered around the island and some ferries arriving late in the evening, it's best to book ahead. In Castlebay, try *Suidheachan* (☎ 890243), the former home of *Whisky Galore* author Sir Compton Mackenzie, with rates from £16, or *Faire Mhaoldonaich* (☎ 810441), where rooms with bath cost from £16. *Craigard Hotel* (☎ 810200) has a range of rooms, some with bath, from £29 to £32 per person.

For ferry information, phone CalMac (☎ 8103060).

Orkney Islands

Just 6 miles off the north coast of the Scottish mainland, this magical group of islands is known for its dramatic coastal scenery, ranging from 300m cliffs to white, sandy beaches, for its abundant marine bird life, and for a plethora of prehistoric sites, including an entire 4500-year-old village at Skara Brae.

Sixteen of the 70 islands are inhabited. Kirkwall is the main town and Stromness is a major port – both are on the largest island, which is known as Mainland. The land is virtually treeless, but lush, cultivated and

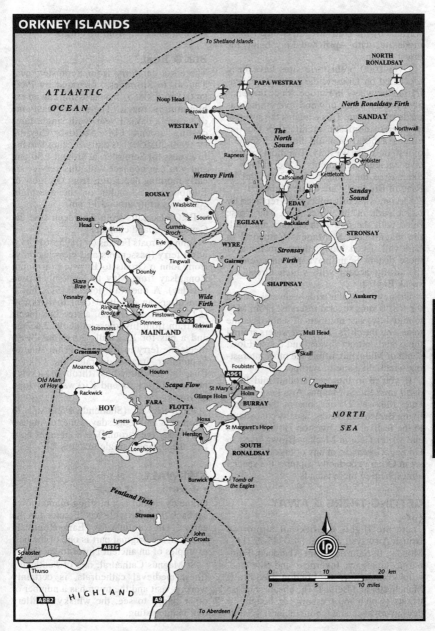

level rather than rugged. The climate, warmed by the Gulf Stream, is surprisingly moderate, with April and May being the driest months.

Over 1000 prehistoric sites have been identified on Orkney, the greatest concentration anywhere in Europe. Since there has always been a lack of wood, everything was made from stone. This explains the survival of ancient domestic architecture that includes a 5000-year-old house, Europe's oldest, on Papa Westray. The most impressive ancient monuments – the village of Skara Brae, the tomb of Maes Howe and the Ring of Brodgar – are all on Mainland.

Orkney's Pictish rulers were replaced by Norse earls in the 9th century. The Norse ruled until the mid-13th century and built the magnificent St Magnus Cathedral in Kirkwall. Even today, there are hints of those distant Scandinavian connections in the lilting accent with which Orcadians speak English.

Orkney is popular with birdwatchers and the RSPB runs several reserves. From May to mid-July, vast numbers of seabirds come to nest on the cliffs. The clear waters around the islands attract divers, and Scapa Flow, south of Mainland, offers the most interesting wreck dive site in Europe.

If you're in the area around mid-June, don't miss the St Magnus Arts Festival. Sir Peter Maxwell Davies, one of the greatest living British composers, usually contributes to the festival – he lives on Hoy. The poet and writer George Mackay Brown lived in Orkney. *Greenvoe*, or any of his other books set in Orkney, perfectly captures the special atmosphere of these islands.

GETTING THERE & AWAY
Air
There are flights to Kirkwall airport on British Airways/Loganair (☎ 0345-222111) Monday to Saturday from Aberdeen, Edinburgh, Glasgow, Inverness and Shetland, with connections to London Heathrow, Manchester and Belfast. The cheapest return tickets (which must usually be bought 14 days in advance and require at least a Satur-

day night stay in Orkney) cost £214 from London and £113 from Inverness.

Bus & Boat
There's a car ferry from Scrabster, near Thurso, to Stromness, operated by P&O (☎ 01856-850655). The crossing can be exhilaratingly rough. There's at least one departure a day all year, with single fares costing around £14. Scottish Citylink (☎ 0990-505050) has daily coaches leaving Inverness for Scrabster, at around 1.30 pm, and you can connect with this service on early morning departures from Glasgow or Edinburgh, or London on the overnight coach departing around 11 pm.

P&O also sails from Aberdeen (see the Central Scotland chapter).

John o'Groats Ferries (☎ 01955-611353) has a ferry (passengers and bicycles only) from John o'Groats to Burwick on South Ronaldsay from May to September (two per day). A one-way ticket is £15, but it also offers an excellent deal to Kirkwall (£25 return). In Thurso, a free bus meets the train from Inverness at about 2.45 pm and a bus for Kirkwall (20 miles away) meets the ferry in Burwick. From June to September, it also operates the Orkney Bus, a bus/ferry/bus through service between Inverness and Kirkwall via John o'Groats.

From Lerwick (Shetland), P&O sails to Stromness on Wednesday (June to August) and Friday (year-round). It's an eight hour trip; the cheapest single ticket is £37.

KIRKWALL
* pop 6100   ☎ 01856
Orkney's capital is a bustling market town set back from the wide bay. Founded in the early 11th century by Earl Rognvald Brusson, the original part is one of the best examples of an ancient Norse town.

St Magnus Cathedral, one of Scotland's finest medieval cathedrals, is certainly worth a visit and the town has a number of other things to see; the whisky distillery tour is interesting.

Orientation & Information

Kirkwall is fairly compact and it's easy enough to get around on foot. The cathedral and most of the shops are set back from the harbour on Broad St, which changes its name several times along its length. Ferries leave from the harbour for the northern Orkney islands.

The helpful TIC (☎ 872856), 6 Broad St by the cathedral, opens April to September, daily from 8.30 am to 8 pm; and October to March, Monday to Saturday from 9.30 am

to 5 pm. It has a good range of publications on Orkney, and you can also change money. A recommended walking guide is *Walks in Orkney* by Mary Welsh.

St Magnus Cathedral

Founded in 1137 and constructed from local red sandstone and yellow Eday stone, St Magnus Cathedral (☎ 874894) was built by masons who had worked on Durham Cathedral. The interior is particularly impressive and, although much smaller than

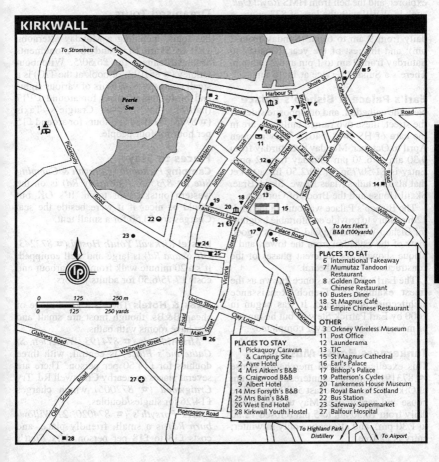

KIRKWALL

PLACES TO EAT
6   International Takeaway
7   Mumutaz Tandoori Restaurant
8   Golden Dragon Chinese Restaurant
10 Busters Diner
18 St Magnus Café
24 Empire Chinese Restaurant

OTHER
3   Orkney Wireless Museum
11 Post Office
12 Launderama
13 TIC
15 St Magnus Cathedral
16 Earl's Palace
17 Bishop's Palace
19 Patterson's Cycles
20 Tankerness House Museum
21 Royal Bank of Scotland
22 Bus Station
23 Safeway Supermarket
27 Balfour Hospital

PLACES TO STAY
1   Pickaquoy Caravan & Camping Site
2   Ayre Hotel
4   Mrs Aitken's B&B
5   Craigwood B&B
9   Albert Hotel
14 Mrs Forsyth's B&B
25 Mrs Bain's B&B
26 West End Hotel
28 Kirkwall Youth Hostel

HIGHLANDS & NTH ISLANDS

the great cathedral at Durham, the same powerful atmosphere of a very ancient faith pervades the place.

Earl Rognvald Kolsson commissioned the cathedral in the name of his martyred uncle, Magnus Erlendsson, who was killed by Earl Hakon Paulsson on Egilsay in 1115. The building is the result of 300 years of construction and alteration, and includes Romanesque, transitional and Gothic styles.

The bones of Magnus are interred in one of the pillars in the cathedral. Other memorials include a statue of John Rae, the Arctic explorer, and the bell from HMS *Royal Oak*, sunk in WWII with the loss of 833 crew.

The cathedral opens April to September, daily from 9 am to 6 pm (Sunday from 2 pm); and the rest of the year, Monday to Saturday from 9 am to 1 pm and 2 to 5 pm. There's a Sunday service at 11.15 am.

Earl's Palace & Bishop's Palace

Near the cathedral, and on opposite sides of the street, these two ruined buildings are in the care of HS (☎ 875461). They're open April to October, Monday to Saturday from 9.30 am to 6.30 pm (Sunday from 2 pm). Entry is £1.50/75p, or £9/2.50 for a ticket that also includes Maes Howe, Skara Brae, Skaill House and the Broch of Gurness.

The Bishop's Palace was built in the mid-12th century to provide comfortable lodgings for Bishop William the Old. There's a good view of the cathedral from the tower, and a plaque showing the different phases of the construction of the cathedral.

The Earl's Palace was once known as the finest example of French Renaissance architecture in Scotland. It was begun in 1600 by Earl Patrick Stewart but he ran out of money and it was never completed.

Tankerness House Museum

This excellent, restored merchant's house (☎ 873191) contains an interesting museum of Orkney life over the last 5000 years. The house and garden open May to September, daily from 10.30 am to 5 pm (closed 12.30 to 1.30 pm), and afternoons only in winter; entry is £2/free.

Highland Park Distillery

Not only is Highland Park a fine single-malt, but the tour of the world's most northern whisky distillery (☎ 874619) is also one of the best. You'll see the whole whisky-making process – this is one of the few distilleries that still does its own barley malting.

There are tours of the distillery April to October, Monday to Friday, every half-hour from 10 am to 4 pm, and weekends in July and August. In winter there are weekday tours at 2 pm (and by appointment). Your free dram's not free, though – tickets cost £3.

Organised Tours

Go Orkney (☎ 874260) has a selection of bus tours, including a Monday afternoon visit to Skara Brae and the monuments around Stenness for £6.50/5. Wildabout Orkney (☎ 851011, or book at the TIC) is a small company with tours of various sights and birdwatching areas for around £9/17 (half/full day). Also, Craigie's Taxis (☎ 872817) offers taxi tours for around £15 per hour for four people.

Places to Stay

Camping *Pickaquoy Caravan & Camping Site (☎ 873535, Pickaquoy Rd)* is on the western outskirts of town. It's OK but would be nicer if it were beside the sea. Charges are £3.50 for a small tent.

Hostel *Kirkwall Youth Hostel (☎ 872243, Old Scapa Rd)* is large and well equipped. It's a 20 minute walk from the harbour and costs £7.75/6.50 for adults/juniors.

B&Bs & Hotels There's a good range of cheap B&Bs, though most are small and few have rooms with baths.

Mrs Aitken's (☎ 874193, Whiteclett, St Catherine's Place) is central, with three doubles for £14.50 per person. There are several places on nearby Cromwell Rd. Try *Craigwood (☎ 872006)* which charges £14/26 for singles/doubles.

Mrs Forsyth's (☎ 874020, 21 Willowburn Rd) is a small, friendly place, and costs £13 to £18 per person. *Mrs Flett's*

(☎ 872747, Briar Lea, 10 Dundas Crescent) is a comfortable B&B with two singles and two doubles for £15 to £17 per person.

Mrs Bain's (☎ 872862, 6 Frasers Close) is down a quiet lane near the bus station. There are three rooms, one with bath, costing £13 to £15 per person.

The *West End Hotel* (☎ 872368, Main St) dates from 1824 and has rooms for £34/54, all with baths. It does good bar meals. The *Albert Hotel* (☎ 876000, Mounthoolie Lane) is central and has a couple of lively bars. Rooms cost from £35/45 to £55/75.

The harbourfront *Ayre Hotel* (☎ 873001) is the top place to stay. It's a very comfortable town house hotel, built 200 years ago. B&B costs £54/80; the most pleasant rooms are those with a sea view.

Places to Eat

St Magnus Café (☎ 873354), in the Kirkwall & St Ola Community Centre across the road from the cathedral, has good, cheap food – quiches, bacon rolls etc. It's open Monday to Saturday from 9.30 am to 4 pm and 7 to 10 pm, and also on Sunday afternoons in July and August.

There are several places to eat around Bridge St, near the harbour. *Mumutaz Tandoori Restaurant* (☎ 873537, 7 Bridge St) has a wide range of main dishes from £6 to £12, and it does takeaways. Opposite, *International Takeaway* dishes up fairly good fish and chips for £2.70.

For Chinese food there are a couple of restaurants that also do takeaways: the *Golden Dragon* (☎ 872933, 25A Bridge St) and the *Empire Chinese Restaurant* (☎ 872300, 51 Junction Rd).

Busters Diner (☎ 876717, 1 Mounthoolie Place) is an American/Italian/Mexican place serving pizzas, burgers and hotdogs (from £3.90). It's open daily until at least 10 pm, and also does takeaways.

The restaurant at the *Ayre Hotel* is recommended but expensive. At the *Albert Hotel*, three-course set meals cost £18. For a really special occasion, go to the *Creel Restaurant* in St Margaret's Hope (see South Ronaldsay later).

Entertainment

The bar at the *Albert Hotel* is probably the liveliest place to drink, and you can also get meals. On Thursday, Friday and Saturday there's a disco – Matchmakers. The *West End Hotel* has a pleasant bar.

Getting There & Away

The airport (☎ 872494) is 2½ miles from the town centre. See Getting There & Away at the start of the Orkney Islands section for flight information. For flights and ferries to the northern islands, see the individual island sections.

From the bus station, JD Peace (☎ 872866) runs buses to Stromness (35 minutes, £2). There are eight buses a day on weekdays, six on Saturday. For Orphir and Houton (25 minutes, £1.20), it also has at least three buses a day, Monday to Saturday. Causeway Coaches (☎ 831444) runs buses to St Margaret's Hope (£2), South Ronaldsay. Rosie Coaches (☎ 751227) operates the service to Tingwall and Evie. Note that no buses run on Sunday in Orkney.

Getting Around

There are several car rental places. Charges are from around £28 per day, or £150 per week. Try Scarth Hire (☎ 872125), Great Western Rd, or John G Shearer & Sons (☎ 872950).

Patterson's (☎ 873097), Tankerness Lane, rents mountain bikes for £7/42 a day/week.

WEST & NORTH MAINLAND
Stromness

• pop 2400   ☎ 01856

P&O ferries dock at this attractive little greystone village. As a place to stay, many visitors prefer Stromness to Kirkwall – it's smaller, it has more of the feeling of a working fishing village, and it's convenient for the island of Hoy. There are some excellent places to stay, and the winding main street has a most civilised selection of shops that includes no less than three bookshops and even a place that does tarot readings.

Although Stromness was officially founded in 1620, it had been used as a port

HIGHLANDS & NTH ISLANDS

by the Vikings in the 12th century, as well as by earlier visitors. Its importance as a trading port grew in the 18th century and in the 19th century it was a busy centre for the herring industry. Until the beginning of the 20th century, ships from the Hudson's Bay Company would stop to take on fresh water from Login's Well.

The TIC (☎ 850716) is in the ferry terminal and opens daily all year, staying open later when ferries dock.

Places to Stay *Ness Point Caravan & Camping Site* (☎ 873535) overlooks the bay at the south end of town, although it can be a little breezy. It costs £3.50 for a small tent.

Stromness Youth Hostel (☎ 850589, Hellihole Rd) is a 10 minute walk from the ferry terminal; £6.10/4.95 for adults/juniors. *Brown's Hostel* (☎ 850661, 45 Victoria St) is open year-round and is a popular independent place. It has 14 beds (£7.50 each) and there's no curfew.

For B&B try *Mrs Hourston's* (☎ 850642, 15 John St) from £15 per person. Out towards the camping ground, there's *Mrs Worthington's* (☎ 850215, 2 South End) with singles/doubles from £19/34. *Stenigar* (☎ 850438, Ness Rd), a little farther south, is a pleasant old house with views of Hoy. B&B here costs from £25/30.

With good harbour views, the *Braes Hotel* (☎ 850495, Hellihole Rd) has rooms, some with bath, from £17/34. Near the harbour, the *Ferry Inn* (☎ 850280) has rooms, most with baths, from £18/34.

Places to Eat *The Café* (☎ 850368, 22 Victoria St) does toasties (from £1.40), pizzas, burgers and baked potatoes – to eat in or take away. There's a fish and chip shop near the Royal Hotel.

There's a good bar at the *Ferry Inn* and a restaurant serving seafood with mains from around £6. For a pint try Orkney Dark Island or Red McGregor, two of the local brews. The bar at the *Stromness Hotel* does meals from £5. The most popular place to drink is the *Royal Hotel*, mainly because it stays open late. The top place to eat is the

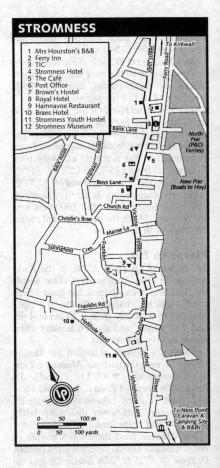

STROMNESS

1 Mrs Hourston's B&B
2 Ferry Inn
3 TIC
4 Stromness Hotel
5 The Café
6 Post Office
7 Brown's Hostel
8 Royal Hotel
9 Hamnavoe Restaurant
10 Braes Hotel
11 Stromness Youth Hostel
12 Stromness Museum

Hamnavoe Restaurant (☎ 850606, 35 Graham Place). Main dishes at this excellent seafood restaurant are around £9.50. It's closed Monday.

Getting There & Away For information on ferries to Scrabster, Lerwick and Aberdeen, see Getting There & Away at the start of the Orkney section. For boats to Hoy, see that section later.

JD Peace (☎ 872866) runs buses to Kirkwall (35 minutes, £2), Monday to Saturday.

Shalder Coaches (☎ 850809) has a bus to Birsay (90p) on Monday only.

Stenness

This village is little more than a petrol station (with a shop that sells outrageous hats). A mile east, however, are some of the most interesting prehistoric monuments on Orkney. Since the road between Stromness and Kirkwall passes through, you can travel by bus, Monday to Saturday.

Maes Howe Constructed about 5000 years ago, Maes Howe is the finest chambered tomb in Western Europe. A long stone passage leads into a chamber in the centre of an earth-covered mound which is over 6.7m high and 35m across. The passage is aligned with sunset in midwinter.

No remains were found when the tomb was excavated in the 19th century. It's not known how many people were originally buried here or whether they were buried with any of their worldly goods. In the 12th century, however, Vikings returning from the Crusades broke into the tomb, searching for treasure. They found none, but left a wonderfully earthy collection of graffiti, carved in runes on the walls. Some of it's pretty basic – 'Thorni bedded Helgi Carved', but 'Many a woman has walked stooping in here' is a little more subtle – you have to stoop to get through the passage.

Maes Howe opens April to September, Monday to Saturday from 9.30 am to 6.30 pm (Sunday from 2 pm), and for shorter hours in winter; entry is £2.30/1. There's also a combined ticket for £9/2.50 that includes Skara Brae, Skaill House, the Broch of Gurness, the Brough of Birsay and the Bishop's and Earl's Palaces. Get your ticket in Tormiston Mill, on the other side of the road from Maes Howe, where there's a café, gift shop and small exhibition.

Standing Stones of Stenness Near Maes Howe stand only four of the original 12 mighty boulders that once formed a ring. They were erected around 2500 BC; one is over 5m high. There's no entrance charge.

Ring of Brodgar About a mile along the road from Stenness towards Skara Brae is a wide circle of standing stones, some over 5m tall. Thirty-six of the original 60 stones are still standing among the heather. It's an impressive sight and a powerful place. These old stones, raised skyward 4500 years ago, still attract the forces of nature – on 5 June 1980, one was struck by lightning.

There's no entrance charge and the monument is always open.

Skara Brae

Idyllically situated by a sandy bay 8 miles north of Stromness, Skara Brae (☎ 01856-841815) is northern Europe's best preserved prehistoric village. Even the stone furniture – beds, boxes and dressers – has survived the 5000 years since a community first occupied it. It was hidden under the sand until 1850, when a severe storm blew the sand and grass away, exposing the houses underneath.

Skara Brae is in the care of HS; opening times are as for Maes Howe; entry costs £4/1.20. It's worth buying the guidebook, which gives a guided tour involving eight viewpoints.

You need your own transport, except on Monday when there's a bus to Birsay. Alternatively, it's possible to walk along the coast from Stromness via Yesnaby and the Broch of Borwick.

Yesnaby Sea Stacks

Six miles north of Stromness are some spectacular coastal walks. Less than half a mile south of the Yesnaby car park is Yesnaby Castle, a sea stack similar to the Old Man of Hoy. Watch out during the nesting season in early summer, as seabirds will dive-bomb you to scare you away from their nests.

Birsay

The small village of Birsay is 6 miles north of Skara Brae. The ruins of the **Earl's Palace** (always open; free) are in the centre of Birsay. The palace was built in the 16th century on an even grander scale than the palace in Kirkwall.

When the tide is low, you can walk out to the **Brough of Birsay**, three-quarters of a mile from the Earl's Palace. It's a Norse settlement built around the 12th century St Peter's Church, of which the foundations remain.

Birsay Hostel (☎ 01856-873535, ext 2404) was formerly the village school but now provides accommodation for groups only (minimum 12) at £6.10 a head. It's open all year. There's B&B accommodation at *Primrose Cottage (☎ 01856-721384)*, overlooking Marwick Bay, for £14/28 a single/double or £36 for a double with bathroom.

Evie

About 1½ miles down a track from the tiny village of Evie, and past a sandy beach, is the **Broch of Gurness**. Although not nearly as impressive as Mousa Broch in Shetland, this is the best preserved example of a fortified stone tower in Orkney. Built around 100 BC, it's surrounded by the remains of a large village. Standard HS hours apply; entry is £2.30/1.75.

The *Eviedale Centre (☎ 01856-751270)*, in the village, has a small *bothy* (hut) with four beds (£5 each), and a camping ground. The centre offers a range of outdoor activities, including canoeing and windsurfing. *Woodwick Stores* has a restaurant and serves high teas.

EAST MAINLAND, BURRAY & SOUTH RONALDSAY

After a German U-boat sneaked into Scapa Flow and sank the battleship HMS *Royal Oak* in 1939, Sir Winston Churchill ordered better protection for the naval base. Using concrete blocks and old ships, the channels between some of the islands around Scapa Flow were blocked. The **Churchill Barriers**, as they're known, now link the islands of Lamb Holm, Glimps Holm, Burray and South Ronaldsay to Mainland. There are good sandy beaches by Barriers No 3 and 4.

East Mainland is mainly agricultural. There are large colonies of nesting seabirds at Mull Head and Gultak, and the shores of Deer Sound attract wildfowl.

On the island of Lamb Holm, the **Italian Chapel** (☎ 01856-781268) is all that remains of a POW camp that housed the Italian prisoners who worked on the Churchill Barriers. They built the chapel in their spare time, using two Nissen huts, scrap metal and their considerable artistic and decorative skills. One of the artists returned in 1960 to restore the paintwork. It's definitely worth seeing.

On Burray, the road passes the **Orkney Fossil & Vintage Centre** (☎ 01856-731255), a quirky collection of local furniture and clothes, and 360-million-year-old fish fossils. Entry is £2/1 and the tea shop is excellent.

The main village on South Ronaldsay is St Margaret's Hope, named after Margaret, the Maid of Norway, who was to have married Edward II of England but died here in 1290. The **Orkney Wireless Museum** (☎ 01856-874272), Junction Rd, is a fascinating jumble of communications equipment. Entry is £2/1.

Highly recommended is a visit to the **Tomb of the Eagles** (☎ 01856-831339), Liddle Farm, Isbister. The 5000-year-old burial chamber was discovered by local farmers, the Simisons, who now run this privately owned visitors' attraction. It's as interesting for their entertaining guided tour as for the tomb itself. After handling some of the skulls and eagles' claws found in the tomb, you walk across the fields, put on kneepads and crawl down the entrance passage. It's well worth the £2 ticket.

The summer-only ferry from John o'-Groats docks in Burwick, on the south coast of South Ronaldsay. See Getting There & Away at the start of the Orkney Islands section for details.

Places to Stay & Eat

Mrs Watt's (☎ 01856-731217, Ankersted) is an excellent B&B on Burray, with rooms with bath for £16/30 for singles/doubles. Diving trips – experienced divers only – can be organised here.

St Margaret's Hope, South Ronaldsay, is a good place to stay. *Bellevue Guest House (☎ 01856-831294)* charges £15/30 for a room without bath, £18/36 with one. The *Creel Restaurant (☎ 01856-83311, Front Rd)* is ar-

Scapa Flow Wrecks

The wrecks that litter these clear waters make Scapa Flow the best diving location in Europe. Enclosed by Mainland, Hoy and South Ronaldsay, this is one of the world's largest natural harbours and has been used by vessels as diverse as King Hakon's Viking ships in the 13th century and the NATO fleet of today.

It was from Scapa Flow that the British Home Fleet sailed to meet the German High Seas Fleet at the Battle of Jutland on 31 May 1916. After the war, 74 German ships were interned in Scapa. Conditions for the German sailors were poor and there were several mutinies as the negotiations for the fate of the ships dragged on. When the terms of the armistice were agreed on 6 May 1919 with the announcement of a severely reduced German navy, Admiral von Reuter, who was in charge of the German fleet in Scapa Flow, decided to take matters into his own hands. On 21 June, a secret signal was passed from ship to ship and the British watched incredulously as every German ship began to sink.

Most of the ships were salvaged, but seven vessels remain to attract divers. There are three battleships – the *König*, the *Kronprinz Wilhelm* and the *Markgraf* – which are all over 25,000 tonnes. The first two were subjected to blasting for scrap metal, but the *Markgraf* is undamaged and considered one of the best dives in the area. Four light cruisers (4400 to 5600 tonnes) – the *Karlsruhe*, *Dresden*, *Brummer* and *Köln* – are particularly interesting as they lie on their sides and are very accessible to divers. The *Karlsruhe*, though severely damaged, is only 9m below the surface. Its twisted superstructure has now become a huge metal reef encrusted with diverse sea life.

As well as the German wrecks, numerous other ships litter the Scapa Flow sea bed. HMS *Royal Oak*, which was sunk by a German U-boat in October 1939, with the loss of 833 crew, is now an official war grave.

If you're interested in diving in Scapa Flow, contact the following: Dolphin Scuba Services (☎ 01856-731269), Garisle, Burray; the Diving Cellar (☎ 01856-850055), 4 Victoria St, Stromness; or Scapa Scuba (☎ 01856-851218), 13 Ness Rd, Stromness. Scapa Scuba runs half-day courses for beginners.

guably the best place to eat in town and has B&B accommodation for £40/60. Main dishes are £15.50; there's a three course dinner for £26. The Orcadian fish stew is excellent. It's open daily, April to September. *Wheems Bothy* (☎ *01856-831537, Wheems, Eastside*) is a pleasant hostel offering basic bed and organic breakfast for £5.50. You can camp if the hostel is full.

Getting There & Away

Between Kirkwall and St Margaret's Hope, Causeway Coaches (☎ 01856-831444) runs four buses a day on weekdays, two on Saturday (£2). Shalder Coaches (☎ 850809) runs the Kirkwall-Burwick service that connects with the ferries.

HOY

The highest hills in Orkney are on Hoy (the name means High Island), the second largest island in the group. There's spectacular cliff scenery, including some of the highest vertical cliffs in Britain. St John's Head rises 346m (1136 feet) on the west coast. The island is probably best known for the **Old Man of Hoy**, a 137m-high rock stack that can be seen from the Scrabster-Stromness ferry.

The best scenery is in the northern part of the island, maintained as a nature reserve by the RSPB since 1983. There are some excellent walks, the most popular being to the edge of the cliffs opposite the Old Man of Hoy. Allow about seven hours for the return trip from Moaness Pier. There's basic hostel accommodation in Rackwick, a two hour walk from the pier through beautiful **Rackwick Glen**. You pass the 5000-year-old **Dwarfie Stone**, the only example of a rock-cut tomb in Britain, and **Berriedale Wood**, the country's most northerly native forest.

Lyness, on the eastern side of Hoy, was an important naval base during both world wars, when the British Grand Fleet was based in Scapa Flow. With the dilapidated remains of buildings and an uninspiring outlook towards the Elf Oil Terminal on Flotta Island, this isn't a pretty place, but the **Scapa Flow Visitors Centre** (☎ 01856-791300) is well worth a visit. It's a fascinating naval museum and photographic display in an old pumphouse. It's open year-round, weekdays from 9 am to 4 pm, and mid-May to September on weekends also, from 10.30 am to 4 pm; entry is £2/1.

Places to Stay & Eat

Hoy Outdoor Centre (☎ 01856-873535, ext 2404) is just over a mile from Moaness Pier. Beds cost £6 to £6.50 per person. BYO sleeping bag and supplies. Near the post office and the pier, *Hoy Inn* (☎ 01856-791313) is a bar with a restaurant serving good seafood; the garlic clams are excellent. The RSPB has a small information centre here.

In Rackwick Glen, the *Rackwick Youth Hostel* (☎ 01856-873535, ext 2404) has eight beds in two dorms; bring your own sleeping bag. The nightly charge is £6.10/4.95 for adults/juniors and the warden comes by to collect it each evening.

There are several B&Bs on the island, with accommodation at around £16 per person. At Lyness, *Mrs Budge's* (☎ 01856-791234) has two rooms with bath. The *Anchor Bar* (☎ 01856-791356), at Lyness, does bar meals and there's a *café* at the Scapa Flow Visitors Centre.

Getting There & Away

Orkney Ferries (☎ 01856-850624) runs a passenger ferry between Stromness and Moaness Pier (30 minutes, £2.30), at 7.45 and 10 am and 4.30 pm weekdays, and 9.30 am and 6 pm on weekends, with a reduced schedule from mid-September to mid-May. In the other direction, the service departs five minutes after its arrival on Hoy. All boats can call at Graemsay Island.

Orkney Ferries (☎ 01856-811397) also sails to Hoy (Lyness and Longhope) and the island of Flotta from Houton on Mainland, up to seven times a day Monday to Saturday, for £2.30 each way (£6.90 for a car). The more limited Sunday service runs from May to September. Flotta and Houton are 20 minutes and 45 minutes from Lyness respectively.

NORTHERN ISLANDS

The group of windswept islands that lies north of Mainland provides a refuge for migrating birds and a nesting ground for seabirds; there are several RSPB reserves. Some of the islands are also rich in archaeological sites. However, the beautiful scenery, with wonderful white-sand beaches and lime-green to azure seas, has to be the main attraction.

The TICs in Kirkwall and Stromness have a useful brochure, *The Islands of Orkney*, with maps and details of these islands. Note that the pronunciation of the 'ay' ending of each island name is 'ee' (ie Shapinsay is pronounced shapinsee).

Orkney Ferries (☎ 01856-872044) operates an efficient ferry service. From Kirkwall you can day-trip to many of the islands (except North Ronaldsay; see that section later) most days of the week, but it's really worth staying for at least a few nights.

Shapinsay

Just 20 minutes by ferry from Kirkwall, Shapinsay is a highly cultivated, low-lying island. **Balfour Castle**, completed in 1848 in the Scottish Baronial style, is the most impressive sight and there are tours on Wednesday and Sunday afternoon, May to September. These must be arranged in advance at the TIC in Kirkwall.

There's B&B for £16/32 a single/double at *Mrs Wallace's* (☎ *01856-711256, Girnigoe)*. With home-made bread and jam, the breakfasts at this farmhouse are excellent, they also do four-course dinners. At *Balfour Castle* (☎ *01856-711282)*, dinner and B&B costs £88 per person. A private boat is available.

There are about six sailings every day (except Sunday from mid-September to mid-May) between Kirkwall and Shapinsay (20 minutes).

Rousay

This hilly island, with a population of around 200 people, is known as 'the Egypt of the North' for its numerous archaeological sites. It also has the important **Trumland RSPB Reserve** and three lochs for trout fishing.

West of the pier are four prehistoric **burial cairns** – the two storey Taversoe Tuick, the stalled cairns of Yarso and Blackhammer, and Midhowe Cairn. Containing the remains of 25 people and dating from the 3rd millennium BC, the 'Great Ship of Death', as Midhowe Cairn is called, is the longest chambered cairn in Orkney. Nearby, **Midhowe Broch** is the best example of a broch in Orkney.

The TICs on Mainland have a useful leaflet, *Westness Walk*, describing the mile walk from Midhowe Cairn to Westness Farm. Bikes can be rented for £5.50 per day from ABC (☎ 01856-821293), near the pier, and the island's one road makes a pleasant circuit of about 13 miles.

Places to Stay & Eat *Rousay Farm Hostel* (☎ *01856-821252, Trumland Farm)* is half a mile from the ferry. There's excellent dormitory accommodation for £6 (bring a sleeping bag) and tent sites for £2.50. You can get bar meals at the *Pier Restaurant* (☎ *01856-821359)* by the pier.

Taversoe Hotel (☎ *01856-821325)*, about 2 miles south-west of the pier, does B&B at around £25 per person. There are superb views from its restaurant and a good selection of malt whiskies in the bar. It's closed Monday.

Getting There & Away A small car ferry connects Tingwall (Mainland) with Rousay (30 minutes, £2.30 for a passenger, £6.90 for a car) and the other nearby islands of Egilsay and Wyre about six times every day. For bookings phone ☎ 01856-751360.

Egilsay & Wyre

These two small islands lie 1½ miles east of Rousay. On Egilsay, a cenotaph marks the spot where Earl Magnus was murdered in 1116. After his martyrdom, pilgrims flocked to the island and St Magnus Church, now roofless, was built.

Wyre is even smaller than Egilsay. In the mid-12th century it was the domain of the Viking baron Kolbein Hruga ('Cubbie Roo'). The ruins of his castle and St Mary's Chapel can be visited free.

These two islands are reached on the Rousay-Tingwall ferry (see Rousay above), but you must ask if you wish to land.

Stronsay

In the 18th century, the major industry on this island was the collection and burning of seaweed to make kelp, which was exported for use in the production of glass, iodine and soap. In the 19th century, it was replaced by herring-curing, and Whitehall harbour became one of Scotland's major herring ports.

A peaceful and attractive island, Stronsay now attracts seals, migratory birds and tourists. There are good coastal walks and, in the east, the **Vat o'Kirbister** is the best example of a *gloup* (natural arch) in Orkney.

Places to Stay & Eat *Stronsay Hotel* (☎ *01857-616213)* in Whitehall has rooms for £12 per person. In the bar you can get reasonable pub grub from around £4. At *Stronsay Bird Reserve* (☎ *01857-616363)*, on Mill Bay, there's B&B for £14; you can also camp.

Getting There & Away BA Express (☎ 01856-872494) has two flights a day, Monday to Friday, from Kirkwall (£29/58 a single/return).

A ferry service links Kirkwall with Stronsay (1½ hours, two per day, £4.60), and Stronsay with Eday (35 minutes, one per day, £2.30). There's a reduced service on Sunday.

Eday

Eday supplied some of the stone for St Magnus Cathedral in Kirkwall, and peat to most other northern islands. It has a hilly centre and cultivated fields around the coast. Occupied for at least the last 5000 years, Eday has numerous chambered cairns, and also one of Orkney's most impressively located standing stones, the **Stone of Setter**.

It's worth getting hold of the *Eday Heritage Walk* leaflet, which details an interesting four hour ramble from the Community Enterprises shop up to the Cliffs of Red Head in the north of the island.

Places to Stay The basic *Eday Youth Hostel* (☎ 01857-622283), run by Eday Community Enterprises, is 4 miles north of the ferry. There are 24 beds for £4.65 per night; BYO sleeping bag. *Mrs Cockram's* (☎ 01857-622271), in a comfortable farmhouse at Skaill, near the church, charges around £29 per person for dinner and B&B.

Getting There & Away There are flights from Kirkwall (£29 one way) to London airport – that's London, Eday – on Wednesday only. The ferry service from Kirkwall sails via Stronsay (1¼ to two hours, £4.60). There's a link between Sanday and Eday on Monday, Friday and Sunday.

Sanday

This island is aptly named, for the best beaches in Orkney are here – dazzling white sand of the sort you'd expect in the Caribbean. The island is 12 miles long and almost entirely flat, apart from the cliffs at Spurness.

There are several archaeological sites, the most impressive being the **Quoyness**

chambered tomb, similar to Maes Howe, and dating from the 3rd millennium BC.

The island is known for its knitwear, which is sold in Lady village at the Wool Hall.

Places to Stay With permission, you can camp on the island, but there's no hostel. There's comfortable accommodation at the *Belsair Hotel* (☎ 01857-600206), which has six rooms, three with baths, from £19 per person.

Getting There & Away Flights from Kirkwall (£29 one way) operate to Sanday and Westray twice daily Monday to Friday, once on Saturday. There's at least one ferry a day between Kirkwall and Sanday (1½ hours, £4.60) from mid-September to mid-May.

Getting Around Cars can be hired from Kettletoft Garage (☎ 01857-600321). For bicycle hire, try Bernie Flett (☎ 01857-600418).

Westray

This is the largest of the northern islands, with a population of around 700. It's quite a varied island, with prehistoric sites, some sandy beaches, impressive cliff scenery and the ruins of **Noltland Castle** (a fortified Z-plan house). It's also famous for the RSPB reserve at Noup Head Cliffs, which attracts vast numbers of breeding seabirds.

Pierowall is the main village and one of the best natural harbours in Orkney, once an important Viking base. Ferries from Kirkwall dock at Rapness, about 7 miles south of Pierowall.

Places to Stay & Eat With permission, you can camp almost anywhere. Several places offer B&B from around £15/30 for singles/doubles. Try *Mrs Groat's* (☎ 01857-677374, at Sand o'Gill) where there are a couple of bikes for rent; she also has a six berth caravan from £50 to £80 per week. The *Pierowall Hotel* (☎ 01857-677208) is a popular pub with accommodation from £16/30.

The most comfortable place to stay is *Cleaton House Hotel* (☎ *01857-677508*), a refurbished Victorian manse 3 miles south of Pierowall. B&B costs £29 to £32 per person. It serves good bar and restaurant meals.

Getting There & Away For information on flights, see under Sanday. A ferry service links Kirkwall with Rapness and Pierowall on Westray, and Papa Westray. There's at least one service a day (1½ hours, £4.60) in each direction.

Papa Westray
This tiny island (4 miles long and a mile wide) attracts superlatives – Europe's oldest domestic building is the **Knap of Howar** (built about 5500 years ago), the world's shortest scheduled flight is the two minute hop over from Westray, and the largest colony of Arctic terns in Europe is at North Hill. The island was also the cradle of Christianity in Orkney – **St Bonieface's Church** was founded in the 8th century.

Places to Stay & Eat The excellent *Papa Westray Hostel* (☎ *01857-644267*), just over a mile from the ferry, opens all year. There are 16 beds and the nightly charge is £7.75. The community co-op, which runs the hostel, also has four comfortable rooms with bathrooms on a B&B basis for £26/46 for singles/doubles. It also runs a small shop and restaurant.

Getting There & Away Flying to Papa Westray or North Ronaldsay from Kirkwall is an amazing deal compared to other flights in Orkney – about twice the distance for half the price. To either island it's £14/28 for a single/return, with flights twice daily Monday to Saturday.

There's a ferry from Pierowall on Westray to Papa Westray, two to six times a day in summer (25 minutes, £4.60). On Tuesday and Friday, there's a through service from Kirkwall (1¾ hours, £4.60). This service isn't operated by Orkney

Ferries from the end of October to May. During this period a private ferry company runs from Pierowall to Papa Westray by arrangement. Contact Thomas Rendall (☎ 01857-677216).

North Ronaldsay
Pity the poor sheep on this remote, windswept island – they're kept off the rich farmland by a wall and forced to feed only on seaweed, which is said to give their meat a unique flavour.

North Ronaldsay (population 50) is only 3 miles long and almost completely flat. The island is an important stopover point for migratory birds. The *Bird Observatory* (☎ *01857-633200*) offers solar-powered accommodation and ornithological activities at £24 to £27 per person including dinner. *Mrs Muir* (☎ *01857-633244; Garso Guest House*), about 3 miles from the pier, charges £25 per head for dinner and B&B.

See Papa Westray for details of flights. There's also a weekly sailing from Kirkwall, not always on the same day of the week. Phone ☎ 01856-872044 for details.

Shetland Islands

Sixty miles north of Orkney, the Shetland Islands remained under Norse rule until 1469, when they were given to Scotland as part of a Danish princess's dowry. Even today these remote, windswept, treeless islands are almost as much a part of Scandinavia as of Britain – the nearest mainland town is Bergen, Norway.

Much bleaker than Orkney, Shetland is famous for its varied bird life and teeming seabird colonies, for a 4000-year-old archaeological heritage that includes the ancient settlement of Jarlshof, and for its rugged, indented coastline that offers superb cliff-top walks.

Almost everything of interest is on the coast rather than inland, so you're much more aware of the presence of the sea than on Orkney's Mainland. In fact, in Shetland it's impossible to get farther than 3 miles from the sea. There are some impressively

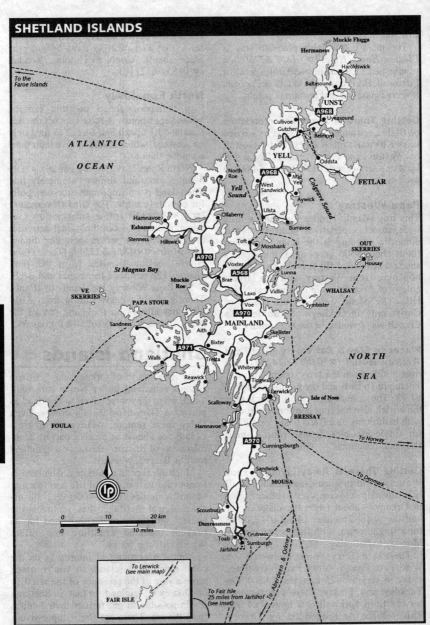

SHETLAND ISLANDS

Muckle Flugga
Hermaness
Haroldswick
Baltasound
UNST
A968
Cullivoe   Uyeasound
Gutcher   Belmont
YELL
Oddsta
FETLAR
North
Roe
A968   Mid
West   Yell
Sandwick
Aywick
Ollaberry   Ulsta
Yell Sound   Burravoe

To the
Faroe Islands

ATLANTIC

OCEAN

Colgrave Sound

Hamnavoe
Eshaness
Stenness   Hillswick
A970
St Magnus Bay   Voxter
Muckle   A968
Roe   Brae
VE   Laxo
SKERRIES   PAPA STOUR   Voe
A970
Sandness   MAINLAND
Aith   Skellister
Bixter
A971
Walls   Tresta
Reawick   Whiteness
Tingwall
Scalloway   Lerwick
Hamnavoe   BRESSAY
A970
FOULA   Cunningsburgh

Toft   Mossbank
Lunna
Vidlin
WHALSAY
Symbister

OUT
SKERRIES
Housay

NORTH

SEA

Isle of Noss

To Norway

To Denmark

Sandwick
MOUSA
Scousburgh
Dunrossness
Toab   Grutness
Jarlshof   Sumburgh

0   10   20 km
0   5   10 miles

To Lerwick
(see main map)

FAIR ISLE

To Fair Isle
25 miles from Jarlshof
(see inset)

To Aberdeen & Orkney Is

Birdwatching in the Shetlands

Lying on the north-south and east-west migration routes, this island group is internationally famous for its bird life, and is one of Britain's top birdwatching locations. As well as the islands being a stopover for migrating Arctic species, there are large seabird breeding colonies. Of the 24 seabird species that nest in the British Isles, 21 are found here. June is the height of the breeding season. The bird population vastly outnumbers the human population of 24,000 – there are said to be around 30,000 gannets, 140,000 guillemots, 250,000 puffins and 300,000 fulmars.

The Royal Society for the Protection of Birds maintains reserves on south Mainland at Loch of Spiggie, which attracts wildfowl in autumn and winter; Lumbister on Yell, a 1600 hectare moorland reserve; and on the remote island of Fetlar, which supports the richest heathland bird community, known particularly for its snowy owls.

There are national nature reserves at Hermaness, where you can't fail to be entertained by the clownish antics of the almost tame puffins – known here as the tammy norrie – and on the Isle of Noss, which can be reached from Lerwick. Fair Isle, owned by the National Trust for Scotland, supports large seabird populations and you can stay at the bird observatory.

Lerwick TIC has lots of ornithological leaflets. Take care when birdwatching, as the cliff-edge sites can be dangerous. Also watch out for skuas (bonxies) that will dive-bomb you if you go near their nests. Since they aim for the highest part of your body, it's wise to walk with a stick, pointing it above your head if they approach. And don't get too close to nesting fulmars or you'll be the target for their smelly, oily spittle!

located places to stay, and budget accommodation includes six camping *böds* (barns).

Of the 100 islands, 15 are inhabited. Mainland is by far the largest; Lerwick is the capital. Shetland is the base for the North Sea oilfields, and pipelines feed Europe's biggest oil refinery at Sullom Voe, in north Mainland. Oil has brought a certain amount of prosperity to these islands; there are well-equipped leisure centres in many villages.

GETTING THERE & AWAY

Unlike Orkney, Shetland is relatively expensive to get to from mainland Britain.

Air

The oil industry ensures that air connections are good. The main airport is at Sumburgh, 25 miles south of Lerwick. There are at least four flights daily between Sumburgh and Aberdeen (50 minutes), on British Airways (☎ 0345-222111) and Busi-

ness Air (☎ 0500-340146). The standard fare is around £130 return. You can also fly direct from Inverness, Glasgow, Edinburgh, Belfast and London.

British Airways operates low-flying ATPs daily between Orkney and Shetland (35 minutes, £85 return).

Boat

P&O (☎ 01224-572615) runs car ferries from Lerwick to Aberdeen and Stromness (Orkney); see those sections for details. For details of the ferry link between Lerwick and Bergen (Norway) see the Getting There & Away chapters to Scotland and at the start of this book.

GETTING AROUND
Bus

There are several bus operators. For information on all services call ☎ 01595-694100.

Car

Shetland's wide roads seem like motorways after Orkney's tiny, winding lanes. It's cheaper to rent a car in Lerwick than at the airport. Try Star Rent A Car (☎ 01595-692075), 22 Commercial Rd, opposite the Lerwick bus station, or John Leask & Son (☎ 01595-693162), The Esplanade.

Bicycle

If it's fine, cycling on the islands' excellent roads can be an exhilarating way to experience the stark beauty of Shetland. It can, however, be very windy (wind speeds of up to 194mph have been recorded!) and there are few places to shelter. Eric Brown at Grantfield Garage (☎ 01595-692709), North Rd, Lerwick, hires bikes for £6/35 per day/week.

LERWICK
* pop 7500   ☎ 01595

A pleasant town of grey-stone buildings built around a natural harbour, Lerwick is the only place of any size in Shetland.

Although the Shetland Islands have been occupied for several thousand years, Lerwick was established only in the 17th century. Dutch herring fleets began to shelter in the harbour, in preference to Scalloway, which was then the capital. A small community grew up to trade with them and by the late 19th century this was the largest herring town in northern Europe. Today, it's the main port of entry into the Shetlands and transit point to the North Sea oil rigs.

Orientation & Information

The main ferry terminal is a 20 minute walk north of the old harbour, which forms the focus of the town and is now used by visiting yachts and pleasure cruisers. Commercial St, one block back from the waterfront, is the main shopping street, dominated by the Victorian bulk of the Grand Hotel.

The TIC (☎ 693434), on Market Cross, opens April to September, Monday to Friday from 8 am to 6 pm, Saturday to 4 pm (plus Sunday from 10 am to 1 pm, June to August). From October to March it opens

weekdays from 9 am to 5 pm. There's a *bureau de change* here. The TIC has a good range of books and maps, as well as brochures on everything from Shetland pony stud farms to lists of safe anchorages for yachts. *Inter-Island Transport Timetable* (70p) is an invaluable publication listing all local air, sea and bus services. *Walks on Shetland* by Mary Welsh is a good walking guide. There's a seasonal TIC at the main ferry terminal.

Eight countries have consulates in Shetland. The consulates for Denmark, Iceland, Netherlands and Sweden can be contacted on ☎ 692533; those for Finland, France, Germany and Norway on ☎ 692556.

Lerwick Laundry (☎ 698043) is on Market St but it's not do-it-yourself.

Things to See

Above the town, there are good views from the battlements of **Fort Charlotte**, built in 1653 by troops from the Cromwellian fleet. There's not much to see in the fort itself, which housed the town prison in the 19th century and now provides the headquarters for the Territorial Army. It's open daily from 9 am to 10 pm; entry is free.

It's worth visiting the **Shetland Museum** (☎ 695057), above the library on Lower Hillhead, for an introduction to the island's history. There are replicas of the St Ninian's Isle treasure, and displays detailing the fishing, whaling and knitting industries. It opens Monday, Wednesday and Friday from 10 am to 7 pm, and until 5 pm Tuesday, Thursday and Saturday; entry is free.

The **Up Helly Aa Exhibition**, off St Sunniva St, explains the Viking fire festival that takes place on the last Tuesday in January, when locals dress up as Vikings and set fire to a ship built here. Opening hours are limited: mid-May to mid-September, Tuesday from 2 to 4 pm and 7 to 9 pm, Friday from 7 to 9 pm, Saturday 2 to 4 pm; entry is £2.

The fortified site of **Clickimin Broch**, about a mile west of the town centre, was occupied from the 7th century BC to the 6th century AD. It's always open and entry is free.

LERWICK

PLACES TO STAY
11 Fort Charlotte Guesthouse
12 Grand Hotel
14 Lerwick Youth Hostel;
    Isleburgh House Café
15 Clickimin Leisure Centre;
    Caravan & Camp Site
16 Mrs Gifford's B&B
19 Queen's Hotel
24 Carradale &
    Solheim Guesthouses
25 Kveldsro House Hotel
26 The Old Manse

PLACES TO EAT
2 Raba Indian Restaurant
5 Happy Haddock
9 Havly Centre
10 Fort Café
17 Golden Coach
22 Monty's Deli & Bistro
23 Caffe Latte

OTHER
1 Grantfield Garage
  Bike Hire
3 Viking Bus Station
4 Lerwick Laundry
6 Up Helly Aa Exhibition
7 Police Station
8 Fort Charlotte
13 Shetland Museum
18 Post Office
20 TIC
21 The Lounge
27 Hospital
28 Clickimin Broch

HIGHLANDS & NTH ISLANDS

The **Böd of Gremista**, about a mile north of the ferry terminal, was the birthplace of Arthur Anderson, one of the founders of P&O. It's been restored as an 18th century fishing booth and there's also a small exhibition about Anderson. It's open June to mid-September, Wednesday to Sunday from 10 am to 1 pm and 2 to 5 pm; £1.50/1.

Special Events

It's worth being here for the Folk Festival in April/May, or the Fiddle and Accordion Festival in October. See also Up Helly Aa in the Things to See section.

Places to Stay

Camping *Clickimin Caravan & Camp Site* (☎ 741000) is behind Clickimin Leisure Centre by the loch on the western edge of town. It charges £5.60 for a small tent and includes use of the shower in the centre.

Hostel *Lerwick Youth Hostel* (☎ 692114, *King Harald St)*, in the centre of town, is clean and well maintained though the kitchen is small. It opens mid-April to October and the nightly charge is £7.75/6.50 for adults/juniors.

B&Bs & Hotels Most of Lerwick's B&Bs and guesthouses are small, cosy places with only two or three rooms.

Although *Mrs Gifford's* (☎ 693554) address is 12 Burgh Rd, the house is actually in a small lane off Burgh Rd. B&B is from £17 per person. The excellent *Solheim Guest House* (☎ 695275, 34 King Harald St) offers a good range of options for breakfast including yoghurt and fruit. Large, clean rooms with shared bathroom cost £18/32 a single/double. Next door at No 36, *Carradale Guest House* (☎ 692251) is similar with rooms for £19/36; it also offers evening meals on request.

Dating from 1685, the charming *Old Manse* (☎ 696301, 9 Commercial St) is recommended. B&B in singles is £18, or £20 per person in a double with bathroom. Squeezed between Commercial St and the fort, *Fort Charlotte Guesthouse* (☎ 695956, 1 Charlotte St) has four rooms, all with bathroom, for £25/40.

Queen's Hotel (☎ 692826, Commercial St) is right by the harbour and, if you can get a room with a view over the water, a very pleasant place to stay. Rooms are £59/90.

At the top end is *Kveldsro House Hotel* (☎ 692195), just off Greenfield Place, overlooking the harbour; the small, narrow streets can make it difficult to find. Pronounced kelro, it's a very comfortable, small hotel with 17 rooms for £88.50/105.50. If it isn't busy at the weekend you may be able to negotiate a special deal.

Places to Eat

Although there's good fresh fish, Shetland is no place for gastronomes. Restit is the best known local dish – lumps of mutton cured with salt and made into a soupy, salty stew traditionally eaten in the long winter months. It tastes quite as awful as it sounds and consequently rarely appears on menus.

Fish and chips can be good – as they should be in the heart of a fishing community. There are several takeaways. Try *Fort Café* (☎ 693125, 2 Commercial St), north of the centre, which has a cheap restaurant as well as a takeaway, or the *Happy Haddock*, farther round on Commercial Rd.

Islesburgh House Café (☎ 692114), in the same building as the youth hostel on King Harald St, serves good-value, wholesome food. Soup and bread is £1.15, lasagne £3.60. It opens Monday to Thursday from 11 am to 9 pm, Friday and Saturday from 11 am to 5 pm.

Recommended is the *Havly Centre* (9 Charlotte St), a Norwegian Christian centre with an excellent café, and they don't quiz you on your religious beliefs. It serves mainly snacks (baked potatoes are £2.50) and its gooey cakes are heavenly; it closes Sunday and Monday.

Caffe Latte (Mounthooly St) is a small café at the side of the Westside Pine building. It serves open sandwiches for £3 and a wide range of delicious coffees and teas. Just down from here is *Monty's Deli & Bistro* (☎ 696555), which serves good cheap snacks and meals during the day – smoked salmon is £3.20; in the evening mains are £7.20 to £13.50. It's closed Sunday.

Raba Indian Restaurant, near the bus station, is the best curry house in Shetland. The large *Golden Coach* (☎ 693848, Hillhead) is the only Chinese restaurant; lunch time mains are around £5.

There's a good restaurant at the *Queen's Hotel*, with four-course dinners for £15.75, but secluded *Kveldsro House Hotel* is the place to go for a really special occasion. It serves a four course dinner plus coffee/tea for £23.50.

Entertainment

The best place to drink is at *The Lounge*, Mounthooly St near the TIC. There's live music some evenings and Saturday lunch times. The town's only nightclub is *Posers*, at the Grand Hotel. The Shetland Fiddlers play at a number of locations and it's worth attending their sessions – inquire at the TIC.

Shopping

Best buys are the woollen jerseys, cardigans and sweaters for which Shetland is world famous. There are numerous shops selling woollens, but for bargains you must go to the factories. One is Judane (☎ 693724), on the industrial estate north past the power station. It sells plain sweaters for £11, patterned ones for £15. Most sought-after are real Fair Isle sweaters, which cost from £25.50. To qualify as such, they must not only have the distinctive OXOXO pattern, but must also have been made on Fair Isle.

Getting There & Away

See the Getting There & Away section to Shetland and the Getting There & Away chapters for Scotland and Britain.

Ferries dock at Holmsgarth terminal, a 20 minute walk from the town centre. From the main airport at Sumburgh, Leask's (☎ 693162) runs regular buses to meet flights (£1.90 one way).

AROUND LERWICK

Two islands lie across the water from Lerwick: **Bressay** (pronounced bressah), and beyond it the National Nature Reserve (NNR) of **Noss**, which is well worth visiting to see the seabirds nesting on its 180m-high cliffs.

From the dock below Fort Charlotte in Lerwick, there are hourly ferries (☎ 01426-980317) daily to Bressay (five minutes, £1.10). It's then a 2½ mile walk across the island; some people bring rented bikes from Lerwick. An inflatable dinghy shuttles across the water between Bressay and Noss (£2.50/1 return) daily, except Monday and Thursday, from 10 am to 5 pm. Check with the TIC before leaving Lerwick as the Noss dinghy doesn't operate in bad weather, or after August. There's B&B accommodation on Bressay at the *Maryfield Hotel* (☎ 01515-820207), near the ferry terminal, but you can't stay on Noss. There are also afternoon cruises from Lerwick around Noss; check with the TIC.

Six miles west of Lerwick, **Scalloway** (pronounced scallowah), the former capital of Shetland, is a busy fishing village with the ruins of **Scalloway Castle**, built in 1600, rising above the warehouses of the port. The small **Scalloway Museum** nearby is interesting for its displays on the 'Shetland Bus', the boats which the Norwegian resistance movement operated from Scalloway during WWII. Buses run regularly from Lerwick (20 minutes, 95p), except on Sunday.

SOUTH MAINLAND
Sandwick & Around

Opposite the small but scattered village of Sandwick is the Isle of Mousa, on which stands the impressive double-walled fortified tower **Mousa Broch**. The best preserved broch in Britain, it was built between 100 BC and 100 AD. From April to September there are regular boat trips (15 minutes, £5/2.50 return), allowing 2½ hours on the island. Phone Tom Jamieson (☎ 01950-431367) in advance for reservations. There are five buses a day, Monday to Saturday, between Lerwick and Sandwick (25 minutes, £1.30).

Sumburgh

At the southern tip of Mainland, this village is the location of the international airport and **Jarlshof** (☎ 01950-460112, HS), Shetland's most impressive archaeological attraction. This large prehistoric and Norse settlement was hidden under the sand until exposed by a gale at the turn of the 20th century. You should buy the short guide which interprets the ruins from a number of vantage points. It's an interesting place, but modernity impinges with the airport and hotel so close. It's open April to September, daily from 9.30 am to 6.30 pm; entry is £2.30/1.

Near Jarlshof you can visit **Sumburgh Head** where large colonies of kittiwakes, fulmars, guillemots and razorbills nest.

Sumburgh Hotel (☎ 01950-460201) is a large, upmarket hotel with a bar and restaurant, next to Jarlshof. Single/double rooms cost from £40/58. To get here from Lerwick take the airport bus (50 minutes, £1.90) and get off at the second last stop.

NORTH MAINLAND

The red, basalt lava cliffs of **Eshaness**, in the north-west of Mainland, form some of the most impressive coastal scenery in Shetland; this is good walking country. *Johnny Notions Camping Böd* (£3 per night, book at Lerwick TIC) is at Hamnavoe nearby.

Buses from Lerwick run (evenings only) as far as **Hillswick**, 7 miles from Eshaness, where there's B&B accommodation in the *St Magnus Bay Hotel* (☎ *01806-503372*). *Booth Restaurant & Café* (☎ *01806-503348*) is Shetland's oldest pub, but only opens weekends; it serves vegetarian food and has live music.

There's B&B accommodation at **Brae**, 11 miles along the road back to Lerwick. *Busta House Hotel* (☎ *01806-522506*), just outside Brae, is a luxurious country-house hotel with singles/doubles from £53.50/8. The restaurant, considered to be the best in Shetland, offers four-course dinners of £25.

YELL & UNST

Yell and Unst are connected with Mainland by small car ferries between Toft and Ulsta, and Gutcher and Belmont. Each ferry costs £2.80 for a car and although you don't need to book in advance, from May to September traffic is constant so it's wise to do so. Call ☎ 01957-722259.

Yell is a desolate, heather-covered peat moor, but there are some good coastal and hill walks. *Windhouse Lodge* (£3, book at Lerwick TIC) is a camping böd in the centre of the island below the haunted ruins of **Windhouse**.

Unst is the northernmost part of Britain. Fittingly, its northernmost point is a wonderfully wild and windy nature reserve, **Hermaness**, where you can sit on the cliffs, commune with the puffins and gaze across the sea into the Arctic Circle. Robert Louis Stevenson wrote *Treasure Island* while living on Unst – his uncle built Muckle Flugga lighthouse. There's B&B accommodation at *Mrs Ritch's* (☎ *01957-711323, Gerratoun, Haroldswick*) and at *Mrs*

Firmin's (☎ *01957-755234, Prestegaard, Uyeasound*).

Haroldswick is 55 miles from Lerwick, and if you don't have a car you must spend the night on Unst as buses only run twice a day. From Lerwick, if you catch the 8 am bus to South Yell you can make connections with ferries and other buses to reach Haroldswick before noon. It's then 2 miles to the Hermaness car park. Pause to mail a card from Britain's most northerly post office.

OTHER ISLANDS

Regular ferries connect Yell and Unst with **Fetlar**, where there's an RSPB reserve. West of Shetland is **Foula**, a windy island supporting a community of 40 people, 1500 sheep and 500,000 seabirds amid dramatic cliff scenery. It's reached by twice-weekly ferries (☎ 01595-753232) from Walls and planes (£40 return) from Tingwall (☎ 01595-840246).

Fair Isle is Britain's most remote inhabited island. Known for its patterned knitwear, still produced in the island's cooperative, it's also a birdwatchers' paradise. Twenty-four miles from Sumburgh and only three by 1½ miles in size, it was given to the National Trust for Scotland in 1954. Accommodation must be booked in advance and includes meals. The *Fair Isle Lodge & Bird Observatory* (☎ *01595-760258*) has full-board accommodation, charging £25 in the dorm and £40/70 for singles/doubles. Locals also offer rooms with meals, at around £28/50. Try *Mrs Riddiford* (☎ *01595-760250*) in Schoolton.

From Tingwall (☎ 01595-840246) there are two flights a day there and back (25 minutes, £70 return) on Monday, Wednesday, Friday and Saturday. A day return allows about six hours on the island (seven on Monday). From May to September, a ferry sails from Grutness (near Sumburgh) to Fair Isle (2½ hours, £19.68) on Tuesday, Saturday and alternate Thursdays, and from Lerwick (4½ hours) on alternate Thursdays. Book with JW Stout (☎ 01595-760222).

WALES

WALES

Facts about Wales

'Every day when I wake up I thank the Lord I'm Welsh', run the lyrics of Catatonia's title track on *International Velvet*. There's a remarkably upbeat feeling in Wales today. In 1979 the majority of the people voted against home rule; yet in the 1997 referendum they said yes to a Welsh Assembly to be based in Cardiff from 1999. In the Welsh lyrics of *International Velvet*, however, Catatonia urge Wales to 'wake up ... the weakness is deep'. The country has been subservient to its dominating neighbour for almost a thousand years now.

Wales has had the misfortune to be so close to England that it could not be allowed its independence, and far enough away to be conveniently forgotten. It is almost miraculous that anything Welsh should have survived the English onslaught, but the culture has proved to be remarkably enduring, and the language stubbornly refuses to die.

Wales' appeal lies in its countryside. In general, the towns and cities are not particularly inspiring. The best way to appreciate the great Welsh outdoors is by walking, cycling, canal boating, or using some other form of private transport. Simply catching buses or trains from one regional hub to another is not recommended. Instead, base yourself in a small town or farm B&B, and explore the surrounding countryside for a few days. Hay-on-Wye, Brecon, St David's, Dolgellau, Llanberis and Betws-y-Coed are possibilities that come to mind.

Although parts of the country are still breathtakingly beautiful, Wales can sometimes feel rather like England's unloved backyard – a suitable place for mines, pine plantations and nuclear power stations. Even the most enduring of its symbols – the grim mining towns and powerful castles – represent exploitation and colonialism.

Much of the most attractive countryside is now protected by the Pembrokeshire Coast National Park, the Brecon Beacons National Park and the Snowdonia National Park, but the Gower peninsula and the Llŷn peninsula are also outstanding. Outside the national parks, and particularly in the north, however, miles of coastline have been ruined by shoddy bungalows and ugly caravan parks.

Wales has an unsurpassed legacy of magnificent medieval castles. Edward I built a string of fortresses in the north-west – Caernarfon, Conwy, Beaumaris and Harlech are listed as UNESCO World Heritage List sites and should not be missed.

WALES CHAPTERS

MID WALES Chapter
Powys Counties & Unitary Authorities

1 Swansea	7 Blaenau Gwent
2 Neath & Port Talbot	8 Torfaen
3 Bridgend	9 Newport
4 Rhondda Cynon Taff	10 Cardiff
5 Merthyr Tydfil	11 Vale of Glamorgan
6 Caerphilly	

HISTORY
Prehistory & the Celts
Wales is among the oldest countries in the world. Some of the rocks within its borders

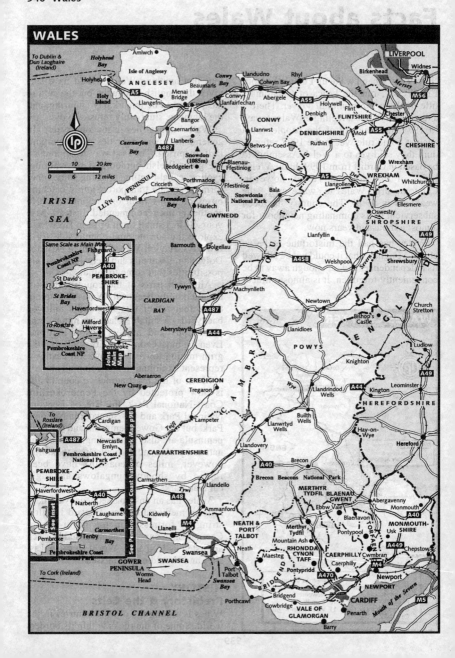

WALES

were formed over 3000 million years ago, and evidence of human habitation stretches back nearly 200,000 years. The stone frames of cromlechs (burial chambers) left by Neolithic people can still be seen in several parts of the country – Pentre Ifan in Pembrokeshire, for example. The Celts arrived from Europe sometime after 600 BC. Little is known about them, although it is to their Celtic forebears that the modern Welsh attribute national characteristics like eloquence, warmth and imagination.

The Romans

From 60 AD, the region – for it was not yet Wales – was occupied by the Romans, who for the next 300 years kept close control over the tribes from the garrison towns at Chester and Caerlon. In his *Historia Britonum* (circa 800), Nennius suggests that the people revered their Roman governors. One of the Romans, Magnus Maximus, is transformed into a near mythical hero called Maxen Wledig, with an elaborate genealogy. This embroidering seems so much part of Welsh history that little of it is verifiable, and fact slides readily into fantasy.

Irish Invaders

Around 400, people from the Brythonic kingdom of Gododdin in Scotland arrived, led by Cunedda. They came ostensibly to drive out the Irish in north-west Wales, but stayed and settled in the area that became Gwynedd. In fact, the two main features of Welsh history in the Dark Ages after the Romans left are the struggle of the native Brythons against these raiding Irish pirates along the coast and, around the same time, the coming of Christianity. At this time, the country was made up of kingdoms, possibly remnants of administrative units set up under the Romans.

The Arrival of Christianity

The western sea routes were important for Wales. They brought the earliest settlers from the south and, later, traders from the Mediterranean. Christian missionaries came, probably from Ireland in the 5th century. Among them was a monk named Dewi, who sought converts in the south – in the Norman period, he became known as David, patron saint of Wales. A French connection is also to be found in the monastic character of the church, and in some of the inscriptions on early Christian stones.

Christianity was grafted on to the old Celtic belief system, with its sacred wells, holy men and hermit saints in the contemplative tradition, remembered in place names with the prefix Llan (enclosed place or church) and Merthyr (burial place of a saint). In 768, however, Christians became subject to the Church of Rome, which then dominated the western world.

King Arthur & the Anglo-Saxons

From the 5th century to the 11th, the people in this region were under almost constant pressure from the Anglo-Saxon invaders of England. By the 8th century, the Brythons had been cut off by these invaders from their compatriots to the north in Cumbria, and it is around this time that they started to call themselves Cymry or fellow countrymen.

The legendary King Arthur is thought to have led the Brythons against the Anglo-Saxons some time during this period. It seems that he was Christian and, as many of the Welsh were, Romanised. Scarcely a contemporary historical record of him survives and yet he has inspired a huge body of poetry and literature, not least by the Welsh in *The Mabinogion*. He is said to be buried on the 'Isle of Avalon' (Glastonbury) in England. The legends of his court at Camelot, with his knights of the Round Table, have sparked many a fruitless search into the annals for more than a tantalising scrap of evidence of his historical existence.

We do know that in the 8th century, Offa, the king of Mercia (one of the most powerful of the Anglo-Saxon kingdoms in southern Britain), constructed a dyke marking the boundary between the Welsh and the Mercians. Offa's Dyke can still be seen today, in fact you can walk its length (see the Activities chapter at the beginning of this book).

The legendary King Arthur

Early Unification of Wales

The 9th and 10th centuries were the time of savage attacks on the coasts by Danish and Norse pirates raiding into the south. It was also the time when the small kingdoms of Wales began unifying, through necessity, to repel the Vikings.

Rhodri Mawr (who died in 878) defeated a Viking force off Anglesey and began the unification process. His grandson Hywel the Good is known as the lawgiver, thought to have been responsible for drawing up a unified set of laws between the kingdoms. Although the earliest written records of these laws date from the 13th century, they probably originate in this much older society.

Ironically, as Wales was becoming a recognisable entity, so did it fall further under the aegis of the English crown. In 927, faced with the destructive onslaught of the Vikings, the Welsh kings recognised Athelstan, the Anglo-Saxon king of England, as their overlord in exchange for an alliance against the Vikings.

The Normans & Edward I

By the time the Normans arrived in England, the Welsh had returned to their warring, independent ways. To secure his new kingdom, William the Conqueror set up powerful, feudal barons along the Welsh borders at Chester, Shrewsbury and Hereford. The Lords Marcher, as they were known, developed virtually unfettered wealth and power and began to advance on the lowlands of South and Mid Wales.

Llywelyn the Great (who died in 1240) attempted to set up a state in Wales along the lines of the new feudal system in England. However, it was his grandson Llywelyn the Last who got himself recognised as the first Prince of Wales, by Henry III of England in 1267. The tide turned with Henry's successor, the great warrior king Edward I, who descended on the country in a bloody campaign. Wales became a dependent principality, owing fealty and allegiance under feudal rules to England. In 1302, the title of Prince of Wales was given to the monarch's eldest son, a tradition that continues today. To maintain his authority, Edward built the great castles of Conwy, Beaumaris, Caernarfon and Harlech. English boroughs, settled by colonists, were established around these, and the country was broken up into counties English-style.

Owain Glyndŵr

In 1400, driven by economic and social frustration, Owain Glyndŵr (Owen Glendower to the English) headed a rebellion. As a descendant of the princes of northern Powys, head of the royal house of Deheubarth in the south-west, he thus had a good claim to the principality of Wales. Although his rebellion was crushed by Henry IV, feelings were roused that rankled for many years after. Punishments were severe. The Welsh were barred from public life, and the lords of the manor suffered heavy fines and loss of rents, and much farming land was devastated. Glyndŵr died an outlaw in 1416.

Acts of Union

By the time the half-Welsh Henry Tudor picked the crown of England off a battlefield in 1485 and became king, the Welsh were only too grateful to enjoy the consequences – preferential treatment at the English court and new career opportunities in English public life.

Likewise, the Acts of Union of 1536-43, under Tudor's son Henry VIII, were welcomed by an aspiring Welsh gentry, bringing as they did English law, parliamentary representation for Wales, plenty of trade opportunities and participation in government. The Welsh language, however, ceased to be recognised in the law courts.

With James I of Great Britain came the Stuart kings. James exchanged the Welsh lion, which Henry VII had incorporated into the royal coat of arms, for the Scottish unicorn. However, the Welsh did remain loyal to the monarchy throughout the Civil War of the 17th century.

Industrial Revolution & Methodism

Puritanism was not a force in Wales until the 1730s brought Methodism and the Great Awakening. They were by-products of the Industrial Revolution, and the character of modern Wales is coloured by the social and economic changes that started at this time. The great centres of Methodism were the Welsh mining valleys and the factory towns of the English Midlands.

By 1811, the Calvinistic Methodists had broken away from the Church of England, and in 1851 nonconformists accounted for 76% of the church-going population. By this time, copper, iron and slate were being extracted and ironworks were in operation in the Merthyr Tydfil and Monmouth areas. The 1860s saw the Rhondda valleys opened up for coal mining, and Wales soon became a major exporter of coal. By 1875, most of the world's tin plate was produced in Wales.

Economic & Political Change

The population increased phenomenally with industrialisation. What had been almost exclusively a fragmented, rural population became concentrated in the south in mining and industrial communities, with a character and toughness of their own – vigorous, close-knit, self-reliant and nonconformist. Strikes and occasional violence broke out, as did protests against low wages and bad working conditions, but it was much later that a trade union movement began to emerge.

Tension grew between the nonconformists and the anglicised 'squirearchy', who were the traditional ruling class. The church became a target for reform; the established church was seen as being unrepresentative and expensive to maintain. Nonconformism began to ally itself politically with liberalism, which favoured nationalism and the disestablishment of the church. It was not until 1920, while David Lloyd George, Welsh Liberal and champion for home rule in Wales, was prime minister of Britain, that the church was disestablished.

From around 1900, support began to grow for the Labour Party in South Wales. Keir Hardie was elected to parliament from Merthyr Tydfil, and through the economic depression of the 1930s and after, this support increased. The severity of the Depression led to 242,000 people leaving the valleys.

Welsh Nationalism

In 1925, Plaid Cymru, the Welsh National Party, was formed by six men in a hotel room during the National Eisteddfod. Political independence through language and cultural differences was the goal of a small minority. The Welsh Language Society, for instance, resorted to civil disobedience to press their point, with the result that in 1942 the Welsh language was made legally acceptable.

The colleges of Aberystwyth, Cardiff and Bangor had been united in 1893 as the University of Wales, and the eisteddfod had become a focus for the preservation of the language and culture. In 1955, Cardiff was made the official capital of Wales. In 1964, a Welsh minister of state was appointed with cabinet rank in the British government, and in 1966 a Welsh Nationalist was elected to parliament. By 1978, a Labour-dominated parliament passed an act to create an elected Welsh assembly with power over some Welsh domestic affairs, but a referendum in 1979 showed the enthusiasm of the 1960s had waned, and the subject was dropped. The country finally got a Welsh-language TV channel when S4C started in 1982.

Wales Today

The 20th century, especially the 1960s, 70s and 80s, saw the coal industry and the associated steel industry collapse. Large-scale unemployment persists as Wales attempts to move to more high-tech and service industries. Coal is king no more – Tower Colliery, Wales' last large coal mine, closed in 1994, although it was reopened a year later as a smaller, private concern.

Tourism is now a major industry, accounting for 10% of all jobs in the principality. Wales is currently experiencing something of a tourist boom with record numbers of visitors.

GEOGRAPHY

Covering an area of 8017 sq miles, Wales is approximately 170 miles long and 60 miles wide. Surrounded by sea on three sides, its border to the east with England still runs roughly along Offa's Dyke, the giant earthwork constructed in the 8th century.

Wales has two major mountain systems: the Black Mountains and Brecon Beacons in the south and the mountains of Snow-donia in the north-west. At 1113m (3650 feet), Snowdon is the highest peak in England and Wales and more rugged than the rounded Brecon Beacons to the south. These glaciated mountain areas are deeply cut by narrow river valleys. Rolling moorlands between 180m and 600m stretch from Denbigh in the north to the Glamorgan valleys in the south, ending on the west coast in spectacular cliffs and the plains of river estuaries. The population is concentrated in the south-east, along the coast between Cardiff and Swansea and in the old mining valleys that run north into the Brecon Beacons.

CLIMATE

Although Welsh weather is as difficult to second-guess as anywhere else in Britain, it's probably fair to say that it suffers from an excess of rainfall; it would be unwise to arrive without rainproof clothing and mud-proof footwear. Westerly and south-westerly winds can also make life pretty miserable, especially when it's raining as well. That said, the closeness of the mountains to the coast means that you can encounter very different climatic conditions within a relatively short geographical distance. It's also slightly warmer – but not so you'd notice – along the south coast.

ECOLOGY & ENVIRONMENT

Anyone returning to South Wales who'd last seen the place in its coal mining days would scarcely recognise the valleys now. The mines have closed, many of the ugly slagheaps have been grassed over and the air is cleaner than it's been for centuries.

It's not been all good news for the environment over the past few years, though. In February 1996 Pembrokeshire hit the world news when the supertanker *Sea Empress* broke up off the Pembrokeshire Coast National Park, releasing 76,000 tonnes of light crude oil into the sea. More than 120 miles of coastline were covered with oil and although this soon dispersed, it will be decades before the ecology completely recovers. The

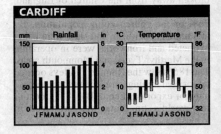

real damage to the environment is always less obvious – a population of rare starfish was wiped out in West Angle Bay, for example. As long as there's an oil refinery at Milford Haven, in the centre of the national park, there will always be a risk of further pollution.

Wales is experiencing largely similar environment problems as the rest of Britain: the overuse of pesticides on fields, the destruction of hedgerows and an ever increasing number of vehicles on the roads. Tourism is taking its toll, too. The increase in numbers of tourists in national parks, particularly in Snowdonia, has led to footpath erosion that is serious in places.

One of the biggest tourist attractions in the country is the eco-friendly Centre for Alternative Technology, just outside Machynlleth in Mid Wales.

FLORA & FAUNA

Like Scotland, much of Wales was once covered by forest, mainly sessile oak, but very little remains and none of it is completely untouched. Most has long since been cleared for agriculture, or chopped down for shipbuilding, charcoal burning or construction – not least for pit props in the mines. Overgrazing also makes it hard for new oak saplings to take root; in Snowdonia the rampant spread of wild rhododendron bushes prevents them even seeding. Imported oaks, like the Turkey oak, actually seem to fare better. Pengelli Forest in Pembrokeshire is as close as you'll get to untouched Welsh woodland nowadays.

Ash trees are also native to Wales and are common everywhere, especially along rivers and in woods and thickets in the Gower peninsula and the Brecon Beacons. In their shade grow primroses, common dog violets and several species of orchid. Hornbeams were once restricted to south-east Wales but are now found elsewhere, too. You'll see plenty of wild cherry trees and field maples, and churchyards often harbour yew trees, as in England. Nor could anyone miss the massed stands of sitka spruce, popular with plantation-owners seeking a

quick-growing source of timber, but far from ideal as habitats for native birds and mammals, the sturdy pine marten aside.

Wales' mountainous terrain has made it a perfect breeding ground for fragile alpine-Arctic plants, including the unique Snowdon lily, which brightens the slopes of Mt Snowdon between the end of May and the middle of June. Easier to spot are saxifrage plants and moss campion growing on the rocks. Amid the coastal sand dunes, you may find evening primroses, sea spurge, sea bindweed and marram grass, while the Gower peninsula is a good place for thrift, samphire and sea lavender. Around Tenby, you might even find the unique Tenby daffodil.

Like Scotland, Wales' lengthy coastline ensures it a sizeable seabird population. Grassholm harbours one of the world's largest gannet colonies, with 30,000 breeding pairs. Wales also has 150,000 pairs of Manx shearwaters, 30% of the world's population. The rock faces of Skomer and Skokholm islands in particular are densely filled with colonies of guillemots, razorbills, storm petrels, kittiwakes and puffins. There are also a few pairs of rare choughs on Ramsey and Bardsey islands, and passing migrants include the occasional great northern diver.

In general, the Welsh inland bird population mirrors that of England, with a few notable exceptions. It does have the only red kites left in Britain (100 breeding pairs), mainly in the Elan Valley of Mid Wales. The mammal population is also similar to England's, although the greater horseshoe bat is now confined to Wales and corners of south-western England, and Skomer boasts a unique species of vole. Red squirrels are vanishing fast throughout Britain, but a few survive around Lake Vyrnwy. Otters, once very rare, are re-establishing themselves along the River Teifi and in the border area of Montgomeryshire. A colony of grey seals is breeding successfully on the west coast of Ramsey Island.

With so many fast-flowing rivers, it's hardly surprising that Wales has a wide variety of fish, including salmon (in the Usk and Wye), brown trout and char. Bala Lake also boasts a unique species, the white gwyniad, said to have been hanging around since the Ice Age. Cockles are still harvested at low tide in the Burry Inlet on the Gower peninsula and made into pies by the locals.

National Parks

The three national parks in Wales could not be more different from each other. The rolling hills of the Brecon Beacons National Park are in the southern part of Mid Wales, the Pembrokeshire Coast National Park is Britain's only coastal park and lies in the extreme south west, and the dramatic mountains of Snowdonia National Park dominate the north.

GOVERNMENT & POLITICS

Wales is a principality and since 1302, when Edward I invested his son as Prince of Wales, the British sovereign's eldest son has been given the title. In 1969, Charles was formally invested as Prince of Wales at Caernarfon Castle. It goes without saying that few Welsh Nationalists are openly supportive of this state of affairs.

In 1997, the people of Wales voted to be governed by a Welsh Assembly based in Cardiff from May 1999, rather than from the House of Commons in London. Until then, Wales continues to return 38 MPs to Westminster, the majority from the Labour Party. The country is as resoundingly Labour in its attitudes as Scotland, no doubt because of its industrial history. Plaid Cymru is the largest opposition party in Wales, with four MPs at Westminster. Wales also returns four MEPs to the European Parliament.

Wales is represented in the British government by a secretary of state for Wales, who has overall responsibility for a wide range of functions including health, social services, education, local government, housing, tourism and the environment.

For the purposes of local government, the country is divided into 22 'unitary authorities' or counties. Most are Labour-controlled but Plaid Cymru holds 120 seats and is the governing party of Gwynedd county.

The likelihood of Wales emerging as a nation independent of the rest of the UK is currently small – certainly smaller than Scotland's, which has independent judicial and education systems.

ECONOMY

Research carried out by the Wales Tourist Board (WTB) suggests that people who have never visited Wales imagine it a grim, grey country scarred by the ugly paraphernalia and detritus of heavy industry, primarily coal mining, steel manufacture and slate quarrying. In some ways nothing could be further from the truth; although the steel industry and slate quarrying linger on around Port Talbot and Blaenau Ffestiniog, coal mining has more or less vanished, turned into little more than an adjunct of the much cleaner heritage-tourism industry. The scale of the change is typified by the Rhondda Valley, where 50 pits once employed 40,000 men. There are now no large working pits left there.

Mass unemployment and the ensuing social disruption in parts of the South Wales valleys have led some commentators to draw not altogether ridiculous comparisons with the developing world. Probably the most successful modern industry – aside from agriculture and forestry – is tourism, but unfortunately that can rarely make up for the loss of well paid manual jobs in the areas worst affected by the 1980s and 90s pit closures. Two-thirds of Welsh jobs are now in the service industries.

In 1976, the Welsh Development Agency (WDA) was set up to help Wales make the awkward transition to new sources of employment. It's been phenomenally successful in attracting foreign investment, particularly from Japanese companies, among them Sony, National Panasonic, Aiwa and Toyota. There has also been a mini-boom in new financial businesses opening or moving to Wales, a fact confirmed by a glimpse at the name-boards going up around Cardiff Bay. Although Wales has only one-twentieth of the UK's population, since 1986 it's succeeded in attracting one-sixth of inward investment.

POPULATION & PEOPLE

Wales has a population of around 2.9 million, about 5% of the population of the UK. The largest centre of population is Cardiff, with 265,000 residents. Swansea and Newport, also in South Wales, are the other main population centres. Mid Wales is the least densely populated part of the country, although it's interesting to note that the population of Powys, the emptiest area, actually grew between 1981 and 1991, as people deserted the cities in favour of the countryside and an alternative lifestyle.

The caricature Welshman of English imagination was a coal miner who went to chapel on Sunday and spent his spare time singing or playing rugby. His wife wore long skirts with a pinafore and shawl, and a tall black top hat. The 1980s and 90s saw the mining part of this picture laid to rest, and the chapel-going, too, has died as much of a death in Wales as in England. The only places you're likely to see women in national costume nowadays are at the eisteddfodau or the Welsh Folk Museum. That said, the Welsh do remain a people apart, if only because of their accents and the fact that their language is still very much alive.

The long struggle of the Welsh to stay separate from England probably accounts for some of the continued sense of 'difference', not to mention the hostility some (but not many) visitors claim to experience in the Welsh-speaking enclaves of the northwest. As a foreign visitor, you're unlikely to experience any hostility, although the Welsh can sometimes be as reserved as the English when it comes to introducing themselves to strangers.

The indigenous Welsh are of Celtic stock who seem to have arrived from the European mainland around 600 BC. During the Industrial Revolution, the population make-up was drastically altered as wealthy investors moved to Wales to take advantage of its mineral wealth, recruiting in their wake a large non-Welsh working force. It was at this time that the Welsh language began a decline that has only recently been halted.

Wales has a small ethnic, minority population, mainly concentrated in Cardiff, Newport and Swansea. But you'll probably be amazed at how many English people live in Wales and, in particular, how many of them make a living out of tourism: running B&Bs, craft centres, cafés and other attractions. In fact, if you're not careful, you could spend more time talking to English incomers than to native Welsh people.

EDUCATION

In most ways, the Welsh education system mirrors the English one. However, the recent revival of interest in the Welsh language makes for some inevitable differences. There are, for example, special Welsh-medium schools where the normal curriculum is taught in Welsh, and English is treated as a second language to be introduced at about age seven. Although there are plenty of Welsh-medium primary and junior schools, many parents chicken out when it comes to secondary education. In any case, there are currently too few Welsh-medium secondary schools to accommodate all the children coming up from the elementary schools. The status of Welsh in the national curriculum, introduced in 1990, seems, like so much else, to fluctuate from year to year.

There are universities at Cardiff, Aberystwyth, Bangor, Lampeter, Swansea and Treforest.

ARTS
Music & Literature

Wales is seen as a country positively bursting at the seams with lusty male voice choirs, mysterious eisteddfodau and pretty female harpists. Everyone has heard of Dylan Thomas, even if they've never read *Under Milk Wood* or seen it performed, and Richard Burton and Anthony Hopkins have stamped Wales firmly into theatrical history.

Welsh bands are currently enjoying considerable success around the world; the best known being Manic Street Preachers and Catatonia.

Painting

The country hasn't been so blessed when it comes to the visual arts, with few Welsh artists other than Augustus and Gwen John achieving real fame. Graham Sutherland did, nevertheless, settle in Wales and do much of his work at Picton Castle. As if to make up for this dearth of indigenous talent, Gwendoline and Margaret Davies ploughed the money they inherited from their father (who created Barry Docks) into amassing a stunning collection of impressionist paintings, including Monets, Manets, Sisleys and Pisarros, which are now on show at the National Museum of Wales in Cardiff.

Architecture

On the architectural front, Wales is best known for the great medieval castles in various states of ruination that ring the coasts and Marches (border areas). Ironically, most of them were built by the English to ward off Welsh nationalists of the medieval kind. The finest of all are the ones Edward I had built in North Wales such as Caernarfon, Harlech, Conwy and Beaumaris but wherever you go in South or North Wales there'll be a ruined castle within reasonable reach. It's also worth making a special trip to see some of the following castles: Rhuddlan, Denbigh, Cricieth, Raglan, Pembroke, Kidwelly, Chepstow and Caerphilly. Most of them are cared for by Cadw, the Welsh Historic Monuments Agency (see Useful Organisations in the Wales Facts for the Visitor chapter).

The ruined castles aside, Wales is not noted for its wonderful architecture. Although the history of Christianity in Wales stretches back to the 5th century, medieval Wales never shared in the prosperity that led to the blossoming of splendid churches and cathedrals in England. Cadw cares for atmospheric ruined abbeys at Tintern, Neath, Strata Florida and Valle Crucis, and the cathedral at St David's is as splendid as many in England. There are also some pleasing towered churches in Pembrokeshire and Gwent, but the real boom in Welsh church building came after the Industrial Revolution as people flooded into the newly industrialising areas.

This population growth coincided with the high point of interest in nonconformist religion. Wales is scattered from end to end with Methodist, Baptist and Congregationalist chapels, and since none of these sects believed in lavish church building, their legacy is a landscape of small, plain chapels. What's more, none of these sects has gone to such lengths as the Anglican Church to conserve its redundant premises, so wherever you go in Wales you'll see chapels boarded up, crumbling or converted for some wholly irreligious new function.

There are also a few fine houses, like Tredegar outside Newport, Williams Hall at Bodelwyddan, which now houses the National Portrait Gallery's Victorian collection, and Plas Newydd, the half-timbered house once occupied by the Ladies of Llangollen (see the Llangollen section). Some of the finest houses are in the care of the National Trust for England and Wales. Cardiff also boasts two more unusual 'castles' – Cardiff Castle and Castell Coch – designed by the Victorian architect William Burges, who specialised in love-it-or-hate-it repro Gothic.

Not surprisingly, Wales has an abundance of industrial architecture, and attitudes to this have changed enormously. The great colliery towers and winding gear once regarded as eyesores are now seen through the rose-tinted glasses of nostalgia, especially once they've been cleaned up and made presentable for their visitors. In South Wales it's well worth visiting Big Pit at Blaenafon or the Rhondda Heritage Centre, and in Mid Wales you can visit old slate-quarrying sites at Blaenau Ffestiniog.

SOCIETY & CONDUCT
Eisteddfodau

The eisteddfod is a thoroughly Welsh institution that tends to leave the non-Welsh mystified. Its precise origins are shrouded in legend, but the word means a gathering of bards, and the traditional eisteddfod was a contest involving poetry and music. The first recorded event seems to have taken place at Cardigan in 1176, but after the Act of Union in 1536, eisteddfodau seem to have become less frequent and less lively, a process accentuated in the 17th and 18th centuries as the dour nonconformist sects got their claws into Wales.

All this changed in the 1860s when the National Eisteddfod Society was established to revive the old traditions. There are now three major annual eisteddfodau: the International Music Eisteddfod in purpose-built premises at Llangollen every July; the Royal National Eisteddfod, which moves between North and South Wales each August; and the newer Urdd (Youth – under 25s only) Eisteddfod, which also alternates between sites in North and South Wales each May.

For details of the International Music Eisteddfod in Llangollen, phone ☎ 01978-860236. The Royal National Eisteddfod

---

Male Voice Choirs

The Welsh male voice choir (*cor meibion*) is something of an institution, and most closely associated with the coal mining communities of the South Wales valleys. Perhaps surprisingly, it was the nonconformist sects, particularly Methodism, which breathed life into these choirs, so their repertoires are stronger on hymns than might be anticipated.

The collapse of the old coal mining communities presents a threat to the survival of the choirs, but so far they're hanging in. The Wales Tourist Board booklet *Welsh Male Voice Choirs* lists rehearsal nights for village choirs that are happy to host visitors. There are choirs in all the main towns, but the largest concentration is in the south. As a sign of the times, some of them now boast female voices, too.

(☎ 01222-763777) will be at Llanbedr Goch (Anglesey) in 1999 and Llanelli in 2000. The Urdd National Eisteddfod (☎ 01970-623744) will take place at Lampeter in 1999 and in Conwy county (probably Llandudno Junction) in 2000. Accommodation is likely to be in short supply around festival dates; book ahead.

If you'd like to see an eisteddfod but can't make any of the big competitions, it's still worth contacting the WTB for its events booklet, which also lists local contests.

Alternative Culture

In the 1980s, parts of Mid Wales in particular became popular refuges for people in search of an alternative lifestyle. At its most extreme, this has meant setting up tepee camps in remote valleys; at its most moderate, it has led to a rash of alternative bookshops and restaurants in small towns like Llanidloes and Machynlleth.

Near Machynlleth, the Centre for Alternative Technology (CAT) has brought together many of the characteristics of this craving for something different: organic farming, wind and water power, and the recycling of virtually everything, in a communal setting.

Dos & Don'ts

Probably the greatest insult you can give the Welsh is to refer to them as English, or tell them how much you like being 'here in England', when you mean 'here in Wales'.

RELIGION

Christianity is believed to have been introduced to Wales in the 5th century, going its own way until the time of the Reformation, when the Welsh Church was reorganised to become part of the regular Anglican Church. In 1588, Bishop Morgan translated the Bible into Welsh.

As the population grew in the 18th century, the new industrial working classes proved fertile recruiting ground for various Protestant nonconformist sects, particularly the Baptists, Methodists and Congregationalists. An 1851 survey discovered that almost 80% of the population was nonconformist, and in

1920 the Anglican Church actually ceased to be the established church of Wales. The nonconformist tradition brought a puritanical strain to Welsh life that might account for the rather dour image of its people. Until recently, it wasn't just shops that stayed shut on Sunday in Wales – pubs did too.

But all that has changed, and now it would be hard to argue that Wales is any more actively religious than England. The most recent survey found 108,400 people identifying themselves as members of the Anglican Church, 60,600 as Roman Catholics and 220,300 as Methodists, Baptists and assorted other nonconformists.

LANGUAGE

The one thing that marks Wales out so distinctly from the rest of Britain is the survival of Welsh as a living language. Despite its weird and seemingly unpronounceable double 1s and consecutive consonants, Welsh is an Indo-European language, from a Celtic offshoot. Its closest linguistic cousins are Cornish and Breton.

During the Roman occupation, people in positions of authority probably spoke Latin, even if everyone else spoke Welsh. Gradually, a bilingual Latin/Welsh-speaking population emerged, and the influence of Latin on Welsh is clear, as is the influence of French (from the Norman period) and English. The language as it is spoken today seems to have been more or less fully developed by the 6th century, making it one of Europe's oldest languages.

Following the Act of Union in 1536, people were forbidden to hold high office unless they spoke English as well as Welsh. Bishop Morgan's translation of the Bible in 1588 is thought to have played an important part in keeping the language alive.

During the 17th and 18th centuries, the nonconformist sects that made such headway in Wales also supported the native language. However, the Industrial Revolution brought a whole new class of industrial landlords and employers, few of whom spoke Welsh. From then on, the number of native Welsh speakers went into steep decline. At the start of the 19th century, 80% of the population probably spoke Welsh, but by 1901 this had sunk to 50%. Now, only about 20% of the population speak Welsh. Welsh speakers are concentrated particularly in the north-western and western parts of the country where up to 75% of the population of a given locality may speak it. In contrast, only 2.4% of people living in Monmouthshire know more than the odd word.

Reasons for the decline in the number of people speaking Welsh are not hard to find: television, better communications, emigration, mixed marriages and tourism are just some of those commonly cited. Perhaps what is more surprising is that so many people have continued to speak the language despite all these threats. Indeed, in the 1980s and 90s there was revived interest in the language, not least among incomers.

Since the 1960s the importance of Welsh has been officially recognised, and in 1967 the Welsh Language Act ensured that Welsh speakers could use their own language in court. Since then an increasing number of publications have been bilingual and it's rare nowadays to see a road sign in just one language. In 1982 Channel 4 set up S4C, which broadcasts daily Welsh television programs and has even made the odd feature film. Radio Cymru also transmits in Welsh, and roughly 400 books a year are published in the language.

In 1988 a Welsh Language Board was set up to advise the secretary of state for Wales on everything to do with the language, while in 1994 a new Welsh Language Act gave equal validity to Welsh as a language for use in public-sector businesses.

If all this sounds almost too good to be true, there are those who would argue that is the case and that the cause of the Welsh language has been espoused by middle class interlopers as a way of ensuring grants and jobs. There are also English visitors who get very hot under the collar when they visit Welsh-speaking areas and find themselves unable to understand what is being said.

See also Welsh in the Language section at the back of this book.

Facts for the Visitor

HIGHLIGHTS

For most visitors, the highlights of Wales are its countryside and castles.

With several national trails and hundreds of miles of beautiful coastline Wales is an excellent place for walking. In fact it's popular for outdoor activities of all types (see Activities later in this chapter).

The best way to appreciate the countryside is to base yourself for several days in a village in one of the national parks and explore the surrounding countryside. Hay-on-Wye and Brecon (Brecon Beacons National Park), St David's (Pembrokeshire Coast National Park), Dolgellau, Llanberis and Betws-y-Coed (Snowdonia National Park) all make good bases.

From Snowdonia, it's easy to visit some of the magnificent medieval castles built by Edward I. Caernarfon, Conwy, Beaumaris and Harlech are listed as UNESCO World Heritage List sites. Conwy is particularly worth visiting and there are several other interesting sights in the little town.

SUGGESTED ITINERARIES

If you have a week to spend in Wales, base yourself in Snowdonia National Park and visit Conwy. Alternatively, base yourself in the Pembrokeshire Coast National Park and visit St David's. The Brecon Beacon's National Park is convenient for shorter stays because it's fairly easily accessible from London and southern England.

PLANNING
When to Go

Spring and autumn are probably the best times to visit Wales if you want to avoid the July and August crowds. The roads are least busy, and accommodation is emptiest in winter, but many of the attractions close in mid-October and don't open again until Easter. Some of the mountain passes can be snowbound in winter.

See also the Climate section in the Facts about Wales chapter.

Maps

The Wales Tourist Board's *Wales Tourist Map* is available at all TICs. If you don't have a car you'll find the *Wales – Bus, Rail and Tourist Map & Guide*, updated annually and available free from TICs, absolutely invaluable.

For walkers, large-scale Ordnance Survey (OS) maps relevant to the area are usually stocked by local TICs.

What to Bring

If you're walking, bring not only a waterproof jacket but also waterproof over-trousers since it may be windy as well as wet. In summer a swimming costume is also useful; the sea can be surprisingly warm.

RESPONSIBLE TOURISM

The tourist pressure in the national parks is considerable. Use public transport where possible and stick to the footpaths.

TOURIST OFFICES

Outside Britain, contact the BTA for information. The Wales Tourist Board (WTB, ☎ 01222-499909) has its headquarters on the 12th floor of Brunel House, 2 Fitzalan Rd, Cardiff CF2 1UY, and also operates a branch in the British Travel Centre (☎ 0171-808 3838), 1 Regent St, Piccadilly Circus, London SW1Y 4XT.

Most major towns in Wales have TICs that are open weekdays from 9 am to 5 pm, with hours sometimes extending to weekends in summer. In small places, TICs only open from Easter to September.

The WTB has a range of very comprehensive free publications on walking, cycling and other activities. It also publishes *Discovering Wales Accessible* (free) for disabled travellers.

VISAS & DOCUMENTS

No visas are required if you arrive from England. If you arrive from any other country, normal British regulations apply (see the Regional Facts for the Visitor chapter at the beginning of this book). There are several diplomatic missions in Cardiff.

MONEY

Wales has the same currency as England and you will find the same banks and ATMs.

In surveys of value-for-money European destinations, Cardiff consistently comes out tops, with prices on average from 5 to 10% less than in England.

Throughout this book admission costs are given as adult/child.

INTERNET RESOURCES

For services covering Britain as a whole, see Facts for the Visitor at the start of the book. The Wales Tourist Board also has a useful Internet site at (www.tourism.wales .gov.uk).

BOOKS
Guidebooks

You'll come across a wide range of detailed guidebooks and books on Welsh life as you travel around Wales. Many are stocked by the larger TICs and by bookshops at visitor attractions like Cardiff Castle and the National Museum of Wales. See also the Books and Maps section in the Regional Facts for the Visitor chapter.

General

If you want to get to grips with Welsh mythology, the book to start with is *The Mabinogion*, a collection of tales that date back to the mystic Celtic past, but which were not actually written down until the 14th century, or translated until the 19th.

Two other oldies you might want to dip into are *The Journey Through Wales* and *The Description of Wales*, medieval travel tales written by the 12th century monk Giraldus Cambrensis (Gerald of Wales) as he journeyed round Wales looking for recruits for the Third Crusade. If you find the ori-

ginals heavy going, Cadw publishes *A Mirror of Medieval Wales*, that picks out the highlights of Gerald's prose. A more recent picture of Wales is in George Borrow's *Wild Wales*. The author walked around the country in 1854 and wrote an account some would regard as condescending.

For an impressionistic and entertaining description of Wales and its history, look for Jan Morris's *The Matter of Wales*, a modern travel writer's account of her home country. John Davies' *A History of Wales* fills in the more prosaic facts and figures.

Probably the best-known Welsh author remains Dylan Thomas, whose play *Under Milk Wood*, about life in a small Welsh seaside town, is required reading for anyone heading for his home in Laugharne. Your appetite once whetted, you could also try his *Collected Stories*, which includes 'Quite Early One Morning,' the story that grew up to become *Under Milk Wood*, and *Portrait of the Artist as a Young Dog*.

Only a little less well known is Richard Llewellyn, whose *How Green Was My Valley* is just the first of a set of four novels describing the life of a boy growing up in a South Wales mining community, which did much to create the mystique of the tough life it portrayed. Another excellent read is Bruce Chatwin's acclaimed novel *On The Black Hill*, which describes the life of twin farmers living and working on the English-Welsh border.

A quirky book to look out for if you're visiting Llangollen is Elizabeth Mavor's *The Ladies of Llangollen*, describing the equally quirky lesbian couple who eloped from Ireland to Wales and settled down in Plas Newydd, and were to receive visits and gifts from many of the 18th century's great and good.

Of the Welsh-language authors, one of the best selling is Kate Roberts. *Feet in Chains: A Novel* and *Living Sleep* are both available in English.

NEWSPAPERS & MAGAZINES

You can buy the standard London published daily and weekly newspapers in Wales, although you may want to sample local papers to find out what's going on or to pick up local gossip. The *Western Mail* is a reasonable Welsh national daily, with *Wales on Sunday* taking over at weekends. In Cardiff, it's worth glancing at the *South Wales Echo*, while in Swansea you might want to pick up the *Swansea Evening Post*, not because it's a lively read (it isn't particularly) but because it's the paper on which Dylan Thomas cut his journalistic teeth.

RADIO & TV

Radio and TV stations are linked into the national network although Wales does have its own alternative to Channel 4, Sianel Pedwar Cymru (S4C), that broadcasts Welsh-language (but not exclusively) programs daily. BBC Radio Wales offers daily news and features on Wales, while BBC Radio Cymru transmits the same in Welsh.

USEFUL ORGANISATIONS
Youth Hostels Association

Membership of the YHA (Hostelling International) for England covers Wales as well.

For more details, see the Accommodation section in the Regional Facts for the Visitor chapter.

Cadw

Cadw (☎ 01222-500200), the Welsh Historic Monuments agency, looks after most of the ruined abbeys and castles in Wales, including the group of castles (Caernarfon, Harlech, Conwy and Beaumaris) in North Wales that has been designated a UNESCO World Heritage List site.

A one year membership for an adult costs £20 and gives free admission to all Cadw sites. A young person (aged from 16 to 20) can join for £14, and a child for £12. Family membership, covering two parents and children aged under 21, is excellent value at £38. Cadw members are also eligible for half-price admission to EH and HS sites (free in the second year of Cadw membership).

Three-day/seven-day Explorer Passes are also available, costing £9/15 per adult, £16/25 for two people, £21/30 for a family. Wheelchair-users, the visually-impaired

---

Sianel Pedwar Cymru's Success

Currently receiving a subsidy of £74 million a year, making it the world's most heavily subsidised public television channel, Sianel Pedwar Cymru (SC4 – Channel 4 Wales) might not sound like a success story. The benefits of this Welsh-language TV service, on the air since the early 1980s, are only now becoming obvious to its critics, who thought the money could be better spent elsewhere.

SC4 came into being not through the benevolence of Whitehall, but after heavy campaigning by Cymdeithas yr Iaith Cymraeg (the Welsh Language Society), which included a hunger strike by Gwynfor Evans, the Welsh nationalist. Since then the channel has played an important part in rejuvenating the language, and it's now estimated that 32% of children in Wales can speak at least some Welsh. Accountants are no doubt pleased to see that the channel's benefits are not only cultural. SC4 has been successful in selling its programs to other TV channels, and film makers from abroad are starting to choose Welsh locations and use production companies based there.

The long-running Welsh soap *Pobol y Cwm* (People of the Valley) has been transmitted with subtitles to the rest of Britain on BBC2. Other acclaimed productions have included the children's cartoon *SuperTed*. SC4's greatest success to date, however, is *Hedd Wynn*, which won an Oscar in 1994 for Best Foreign Language Film.

and their assisting companion, are admitted free to all Cadw monuments.

Most Cadw sites have standard opening times. From April to late October the properties are open daily from 9.30 am to 6.30 pm. In winter they're open Monday to Saturday from 9.30 am to 4 pm, and Sunday from 2 to 4 pm. Last admissions are 30 minutes before closing time. Occasionally, opening times may vary, so before making a long trip to a remote site, it's as well to double check. In this book a Cadw-run property is indicated by the word Cadw, usually following a phone number.

National Trust

The NT covers England and Wales, so taking out membership in England will entitle you to free entry to Welsh properties too. For more details see Useful Organisations in Regional Facts for the Visitor. Bear in mind that in winter, some NT properties stay closed or have reduced opening times.

DANGERS & ANNOYANCES

Levels and types of crime in Wales are similar to those in the rest of Britain and it's wise to take the same precautions when hitching or walking in city centres at night. The Cardiff Bay area used to have an unenviable reputation for drunken violence, but nowadays is probably no worse than any other inner-city area.

Away from the towns, the annoyances you're most likely to experience relate to the weather. The general wetness aside, it's as well to treat the Brecon Beacons and Snowdonia national parks with the respect they deserve. Mists can come down with a startling suddenness, and you shouldn't venture to the heights without checking weather forecasts first. What's more, you should certainly make sure you're sensibly and warmly clad and shod, and that you have food, water and a compass for emergencies. Ideally, make sure someone knows where you're heading if it's off the beaten track or in dubious climatic conditions.

Some English visitors work themselves into a quite unnecessary frenzy over the alleged 'unfriendliness' of Welsh-speaking natives. You might be unlucky and bump into a raving nationalist who wants to take issue with you if you mouth the wrong opinion in the wrong place. This is pretty unlikely, though. For the most part, the Welsh are as friendly and welcoming as most people, especially if you visit out of the high season, when the slower pace of life leaves more time for chatting.

BUSINESS HOURS & PUBLIC HOLIDAYS

Business hours and holidays are the same as in England. In the countryside, shops often close early on Wednesday. Pubs no longer close on Sunday.

ACTIVITIES

See the Activities chapter at the beginning of this book for more detailed information on activities.

Wales has done much to promote itself as the country to come to for activity holidays and there are activity centres everywhere. You can trek, walk, climb, raft, ride, birdwatch, swim and otherwise indulge yourself all year-round. TICs will have details of what's possible in their vicinity.

Wales has numerous popular **walks**; the most challenging are in the rocky Snowdonia National Park (around Llanberis and Betws-y-Coed) and the grassy Brecon Beacons National Park (around Brecon). The most famous of the long distance paths in Wales are the Pembrokeshire Coast Path (189 miles) and Offa's Dyke Path (177 miles). Less well known and slightly less busy are the Cambrian Way (274 miles), that runs across the Cambrian Mountains, and Owain Glyndŵr's Way (120 miles), that cuts through Mid Wales. See Lonely Planet's *Walking in Britain* for more information.

The south-west coast of Wales has a number of good **surfing** spots. From east to west, try Porthcawl, Oxwich Bay, Rhossili, Manorbier, Freshwater West and Whitesands.

Pony trekking centres are spreading like wildfire through the Welsh countryside, as

European Union (EU) subsidies to farmers are cut back and farm owners struggle to find alternative uses for their land. For more information, see the WTB free guide *Discovering Wales on Horseback.*

There are plenty of rivers suitable for **canoeing** and **white-water rafting** in Snowdonia, and Llangollen on the River Dee has carved out quite a niche as a canoeing centre. There's a National Whitewater Centre on the River Tryweryn, near Bala.

ACCOMMODATION
Hostels
The YHA (England and Wales) publishes a single accommodation guide, available from YHA Adventure Shops and from many hostels. It lists more than 40 hostels in Wales, most of them in Snowdonia, the Brecon Beacons and along the coast. Generally speaking, these hostels are likely to offer the cheapest accommodation around, although some of it can be pretty basic. It's essential to book ahead for busy periods: May to September, Easter and the Christmas/New Year period.

To book hostels in advance in the west Wales area and along the Pembrokeshire Coast Path phone the West Wales Booking Bureau (☎ 01437-720345).

As well as the YHA/HI hostels, there are around 30 independent hostels in Wales. Many are mentioned in this book but see the *Independent Hostel Guide* for full details.

Camping
Camping grounds, too, are concentrated in the national parks and along the coast. The TICs have a free *Wales Touring Caravan and Camping* leaflet with sites graded for facilities and quality by the WTB. Expect to pay about £6 a night for a tent, although on some sites prices go much lower, especially out of high season. Most sites are only open from March or April to October, so phone before going out of your way at other times.

B&Bs, Guesthouses & Hotels
Wherever you go in Wales, you'll find reasonably priced, comfortable B&Bs, with prices from around £13. Outside Cardiff, Swansea and Newport, you're unlikely to have to pay more than £16 a head, even in high season. In national park areas, many of the guesthouses are used to walkers and climbers and serve breakfasts big enough to set them up for their day's activities; travel in winter and you'll also find many of them with big, welcoming log fires. Many (but not all) of these places are listed in the WTB publication *Wales Bed and Breakfast*; establishments listed have been inspected and graded by the WTB, although the descriptions are provided by the hotel proprietors. As in England and Scotland, crowns (listed, one, two, three, four, five) are awarded for facilities, services and equipment; grades (approved, commended, highly commended and deluxe) refer to quality.

You can phone any B&B or hotel and book it yourself; alternatively, TICs will be happy to do this for you. Local bookings cost nothing, although a deposit is required. This is a service you might want to make use of if you arrive in July and August without having booked in advance; at other times, it's probably not necessary.

Short-Term Rental
There's plenty of rental accommodation all round Wales, much of it of a high standard, but often you have to be prepared to book for periods of a week at a time. If you're after something out of the ordinary, there are even self-catering cottages at Portmeirion (☎ 01766-770228), Clough Williams-Ellis' Italianate fantasy estate near Porthmadog. TICs will have all the details and stock the WTB's *Wales Self-Catering.*

FOOD
Outside Wales, it could hardly be claimed that Welsh cuisine has a high profile. Pressed, people might remember the lamb, the leeks and the rarebits, but that's about it.

Taste of Wales was set up in 1988 to try and change all that, and TICs should be able to supply you with the *Taste of Wales Gazetteer*, listing 400 restaurants where you can eat good food with a Welsh tang. It also contains a list of delicatessens and markets where you'll be able to buy traditional Welsh produce.

Traditional Welsh dishes include *cawl*, a thick vegetable broth, often flavoured with meat; and laverbread, not a bread at all, but seaweed that is often served mixed up with oatmeal and bacon on toast – a surprisingly tasty combination.

Welsh rarebit is a sophisticated variation of cheese on toast, with the cheese seasoned and flavoured with butter, milk and a little beer. Rarebit is a modern name – originally it was called Welsh rabbit.

Glamorgan sausages are made from cheese, breadcrumbs, herbs and chopped leek, making them good for vegetarians. Bara brith is spicy fruit loaf, made with tea and marmalade as well as the more conventional ingredients, while Welsh cakes are fruity griddle scones.

There's not much Caerphilly cheese being made in Caerphilly these days, but cheese-making generally has undergone a recent revival. If you're keen on cheese, it's worth combing the delis for Caws Ffermdy Cenarth, Llanboidy, Llangloffan, Skirrid, St Illytd or Y Fenni.

The big towns have the usual range of Pizza Huts, Burger Kings and McDonald's, as well as dingy cafés, majoring in greasy egg and chips. In popular tourist areas, choices will be better, with vegetarians increasingly catered for. In smaller places, don't hold your breath for gourmet delights, particularly if you arrive late in the day.

DRINKS

From the visitor's point of view, things are looking up on the alcohol front, in as much as the archaic licensing laws that had pubs closing on Sunday have finally been dropped.

Don't leave Cardiff without downing a pint of Brains, the local brew.

ENTERTAINMENT

As everywhere in Britain, pubs tend to be the focal point of local social life and vary enormously in their décor and atmosphere. In country areas, you'll find cosy watering

Lovespoons

All over Wales, craft shops are turning out wooden spoons with contorted handles in a variety of different designs, at a speed that would have left their original makers – village lads with their eyes on a lady – gawking in astonishment. The carving of these spoons seems to date back to the 17th century, when they were made by men to give to women to mark the start of courtship. Various symbols were carved into the spoons; their meanings are as follows:

Anchor – I want to set up home with you
Ball – child (the number of balls corresponds to the number of children desired)
Bell – wedding
Chain – forever together
Cross – faith
Double Spoon – side by side forever
Flowers – love and affection
Heart – take my heart
Horseshoe – luck
Key – my house is yours
Vine – our love is growing
Wheel – I will work for you forever

If you want to see some carving in progress, the Welsh Folk Museum at St Fagans can usually oblige. Any number of shops will be happy to sell you the finished product.

holes with big fires, inviting menus and the TV tuned in to S4C.

In the high season, so many tourists pass through that the locals keep pretty much to themselves; if you visit at other times of the year, however, you'll find people happy to linger and chat. In Cardiff and other big cities, you'll need to pick and choose carefully; some of the city centre places are decidedly uninviting, especially for women travelling alone.

Whatever time of year you choose there's bound to be a festival or special event taking place nearby; check with the local TIC for details. Particularly important ones to catch are the eisteddfodau (see Culture in the Facts about Wales chapter); the International Eisteddfod is held in Llangollen every July, while the Royal National Eisteddfod occupies a different site every August. At the end of May, it's worth trying to catch the St David's Cathedral Festival, with music recitals taking place in the glorious cathedral. Throughout the summer, the Mid Wales Festival of the Countryside spawns all manner of activities in the country's least visited region (phone ☎ 01686-625384 for more details).

SHOPPING

The recent revival of craft industries in craft centres all over Wales has provided plentiful shopping fodder for visitors with a yen for pottery, knitwear and lovespoons. Indeed, there can be hardly a visitor attraction left that doesn't have its shop selling commemorative T-shirts, pencils, stationery, books and souvenir fudge. Even the industrial sites have got in on the act, hawking repro miner's lamps, coal sculptures and similar artefacts. Prices are often high, and quality variable, but among the furry red dragons there are some classy items to be had.

Getting There & Away

AIR

The international airport (☎ 01446-711111) at Cardiff is mainly used for holiday charter flights, although there are some scheduled flights to Aberdeen, Amsterdam, Belfast, Brussels, the Channel Islands, Dublin, Edinburgh, Glasgow, the Isle of Man, Manchester and Paris.

LAND

Bus

Long-distance buses (coaches) are the cheapest method of getting to Wales. National Express (☎ 0990-808080) has routes from London and Bristol along the south coast through Cardiff to Pembroke (for ferries to Ireland), from Birmingham through Shrewsbury to Aberystwyth, and from Chester and the Midlands along the north coast to Holyhead (for ferries to Ireland).

London to Cardiff is £18.25 (£4 more if you travel on a Friday). As in England, return tickets usually cost only a fraction more than singles. London to Pembroke takes six hours and costs £22.50 (£27 on a Friday).

Train

Great Western InterCity services can take you from London Paddington to Cardiff in as little as 1¾ hours, or to Fishguard (for the Ireland ferry) in four hours. A SuperSaver return ticket from Cardiff to London will cost £34/35 for a single/return. There's also a line between London's Waterloo and Cardiff but journey time is longer at almost three hours. Fast InterCity trains also link south Wales with Birmingham, York and Newcastle.

There are also trains from London's Euston station to north Wales and Holyhead via Birmingham, Chester and Llandudno. There are about five trains a day from Euston to Holyhead; they take 4½ hours and a SuperSaver ticket costs £49.50/50.50 for a single/return.

For rail inquiries phone ☎ 0345-484950.

Car & Motorcycle

Motorways bring you into Wales quickly and easily. The three mile-long Second Severn Crossing, Britain's longest bridge, opened in June 1996 downstream from the old Severn Bridge. The M4 travels west from London, across the bridge (£4 toll, westbound traffic only) and deep into south Wales. London to Cardiff is 155 miles and takes about three hours.

The A55 coastal expressway whisks traffic along the north coast. Access to Mid Wales is trickiest and slowest, with no major roads to get you there quickly.

Hitching

Hitching along the M4 and A55 is relatively easy, although not necessarily wise for women. Heading into Mid Wales with your thumb sticking out, you should probably pack a good book.

See also Hitching in the Getting Around chapter at the start of this book.

SEA

There are ferry links with Ireland from four towns in Wales: Holyhead, in the north-west, to Dublin (Irish Ferries) and Dun Laoghaire, near Dublin (Stena Line); Pembroke, in the south-west, to Rosslare in south-east Ireland (Irish Ferries); Fishguard, in the south-west, to Rosslare (Stena Line); and, from March to early January, from Swansea to Cork (Swansea Cork Ferries).

Getting Around

Distances in Wales are small, but with the exception of links around the coast, public transport users have to fall back on infrequent and complicated bus timetables. There are no internal flights in Wales.

Sniff out a copy of *Wales – Bus, Rail and Tourist Map & Guide*, sometimes available from TICs. This invaluable map lists bus and train routes, journey times and operators.

BUS

The major operators serving Wales are Arriva Cymru (☎ 01492-596969), for the north and west, and First Cymru (☎ 01792-580580) in the south. There are Rover tickets available that can be very good value. For example, Arriva Cymru have Rover tickets for one/three/five days for £4.80/9/14 covering all their services and also including some buses across the border into the Midlands.

Arriva has a particularly useful daily Traws Cambria service, but there's only one bus a day each way. The 701 (west coast) link runs between Cardiff, Swansea, Carmarthen, Aberystwyth, Porthmadog, Caernarfon and Bangor. Cardiff to Aberystwyth (four hours) costs £10.95; Aberystwyth to Porthmadog (two hours) costs £8.

Bus Gwynedd (☎ 01286-679535) is a network of buses operating in the north-west corner of Wales – from Llandudno to Machynlleth, including all of Snowdonia. Those using a Regional Railways North and Mid Wales Rover ticket can travel free on these buses as well. Bus Gwynedd public transport guide-maps are available at TICs.

A more unusual way of getting round, especially in remote Mid Wales, is to make use of the Royal Mail postbuses that link up the villages. Local post offices should be able to help with details.

Hairy Hog (☎ 01222-666900), 98 Neville St, Riverside, Cardiff CF1 8LS, is a backpackers bus service that offers tours of Wales for two/five days for £49/125. See www.hairyhog.co.uk for more information.

Bushwakkers (☎ 0181-573 3330, bushwakkers@msn.com), 15 Chartwell Ct, 145 Church Rd, Hayes, Middx UB3 2LP, is a London-based company offering weekend adventure trips to Wales by minibus. Prices are around £69, accommodation is in tents and activities include walking, mountainbiking, canoeing and horse riding.

TRAIN

Wales has some fantastic train lines – both mainline (☎ 0345-484950) and private, narrow-gauge survivors. Apart from the main lines along the north and south coasts to the Irish ferry ports, there are some interesting lines that converge on Shrewsbury (see Getting There & Away in the Shrewsbury section of the Northern Midlands chapter). The lines along the Cambrian (west) coast and down the Conwy valley are exceptionally attractive.

There are several Rover tickets, including the Freedom of Wales Rover/Flexi Pass – see the passes table in this chapter for details. See also Getting There & Away in the Shrewsbury section of the Northern Midlands chapter.

CAR & MOTORCYCLE

Getting around north and south Wales is made simple by the M4 and A55 respectively. Away from these highways, roads are still good but generally slower, especially in the mountainous areas and Mid Wales. Bear in mind that some of the highest roads may be snowbound in winter. Even when the snow clears, ice can linger to make driving conditions treacherous, especially on windy, narrow mountain roads, which are often single-track affairs with passing places at intervals.

Welsh Transport Passes

Pass Name	Cost (Prices for adult/child)	Bus/train/ferry services offered
Freedom of Wales Rover/ Flexi Pass	£69/45.55* for 8 days out of 15	Unlimited travel on all trains and some buses.
Regional Rover/Flexi Rover for example North and Mid-Wales	£39.90/26.35* for 7 days £25.70/16.95* for 3 days out of 7	All train travel north of Aberystwyth and Shrewsbury plus Blaenau Ffestiniog Railway plus most bus services in the area.
Young Person's or Senior's Railcard	£18 per annum	33% off rail travel throughout Britain.
National Express Tourist Trail Pass	As for Britain and Scotland	Unlimited travel on all National Express and Scottish Citylink bus services.
National Express Explorer Pass	As for Britain and Scotland	Unlimited travel on all National Express and Scottish Citylink bus services.
National Express Discount Coach Card (full-time students; under 26; over 60)	£8	30% off adult fares on all National Express and Scottish Citylink bus services.

* A railcard will get you a third off these prices but it can't be used during the summer.

BICYCLE

Travelling around Wales by bike is increasingly popular, although the hilly terrain is really only suitable for experienced cyclists. Most towns have at least one shop where you can hire a bike for about £10 a day. If you're bringing your own, don't forget that you may need to book space to transport it on a train, and that you're rarely allowed to take bikes on trains during rush hours.

HITCHING

Hitching along the M4 and A55 and down to the ferry ports may be fairly quick and easy, but in the quieter, more remote areas you could be waiting a long time for lifts, especially on Sunday when traffic often fades away completely.

See also Hitching in the Getting Around chapter at the start of this book.

BOAT

You're most likely to use boats to get out to the islands off the Pembrokeshire coast (Skomer, Skokholm, Grassholm and Ramsey), or off the Llŷn peninsula (Bardsey). The *Dale Princess* plies back and forth between Skomer, Skokholm and Grassholm during the summer; details can be obtained from Dale Sailing Co (☎ 01646-

The Great Little Trains of Wales

Wales' narrow-gauge steam railways are survivors from its industrial heyday, when mine and quarry owners needed to move their produce more quickly than horses could manage in terrain that defied normal standard-gauge trains. In the 20th century, as these lines gradually lost their *raison d'être*, train enthusiasts took many of them over and now run steam-hauled services on them, particularly in summer. Most of these lines run through glorious scenery, primarily in North and Mid Wales, so they're worth checking out even if you're not a rail buff.

Schedules vary depending on the time of year. The TICs usually have timetables for the routes nearest to them. Otherwise, contact any of these numbers for details: Bala Lake Railway (☎ 01678-540666), Brecon Mountain Railway (☎ 01685-722988), Ffestiniog Railway (☎ 01766-512340, www.festrail.co.uk), Llanberis Lake Railway (☎ 01286-870549), Vale of Rheidol Railway (☎ 01970-625819), Talyllyn Railway (☎ 01654-710472), Welsh Highland Railway (☎ 01766-513402), and Welshpool & Llanfair Railway (☎ 01938-810441).

Wanderer tickets are available for all eight railways from 1 April to 31 October. A pass giving four days travel in any eight days costs £28/14 for adults/children; for eight days travel in any 15 days it's £38/19. Passes are sold at the main stations of the participatory railways, or write to GLTW, The Railway Station, Llanfair Caereinion, Powys SY21 0SF. Holders of some mainline rail passes may be eligible for discounts. Some of the railways operate Santa Specials over the Christmas period.

601636), Brunel Quay, Neyland, Pembrokeshire, or from the Wildlife Trust West Wales (01437-765462). Voyages of Discovery (☎ 01437-720285) operates boats to Ramsey. Sailings (and accommodation arrangements) for Bardsey are controlled by the Bardsey Island Trust (☎ 01758-730740).

For canal cruises contact Llangollen Wharf (☎ 01978-860702) and Montgomery Canal Cruises (☎ 01938-553271).

South Wales

Stretching from the Wye Valley on the border with England, west to Pembrokeshire, this area includes the capital of Wales, Cardiff, the second-largest town in Wales, Swansea, and the 230-square-mile expanse of the Pembrokeshire Coast National Park.

The south coast from Newport to Swansea is heavily industrialised, but there are still stretches of beautiful coastline such as the Glamorgan Heritage Coast. This protected coastline stretches 14 miles from Aberthaw to Porthcawl.

The valleys running north into the Black Mountains and the Brecon Beacons National Park are still struggling to come to grips with the loss of the coal-mining industry. Even so, the little villages that form a continuous chain along the valleys have their own stark beauty, more attractive now that the old slagheaps are being grassed over and the people are particularly friendly.

The Pembrokeshire Coast National Park is the only largely coastal national park in Britain – it's also the smallest. Despite many scenic attractions in the area, only the places on the milder southern part of the coastline have been developed into tourist resorts – the more exposed northern coast is still virtually unspoilt and offers some of the best walking in Britain.

South-Eastern Wales

This part of the country contains over half the population and most of Wales' factories. Hidden among the urban sprawl, however, are some interesting places. There's the Wye Valley and, between the traditional market town of Monmouth and the dramatically located castle at Chepstow, there are the scenic ruins of Tintern Abbey.

To the west is Cardiff, a surprisingly lively city. The Welsh are proudly defensive of their capital, which has been rapidly transformed from a dull provincial backwater into a prosperous university city with an increasingly lively arts scene.

Swansea was where the poet and writer Dylan Thomas grew up. It's the gateway to

HIGHLIGHTS

- Cardiff Castle
- The Museum of Welsh Life at St Fagans
- Wye Valley and Tintern Abbey
- Chepstow Castle
- The Mumbles Mile – pub crawl in the suburbs of Swansea
- Dylan Thomas Boathouse
- Pembrokeshire Coast National Park
- St David's
- Pwll Deri Youth Hostel
- Fishguard

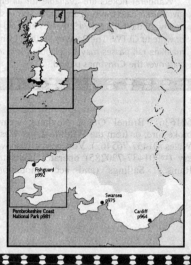

the Gower, a sparsely populated peninsula with long, sandy beaches and attractive cliff scenery.

GETTING AROUND

Bus and train services are good in this part of Wales, although the country's mountainous geography means that direct journeys from South to North Wales are tricky and time-consuming. For information on buses in the Cardiff area, phone ☎ 01222-396521; in the Swansea area, phone ☎ 01792-580580.

Some bus companies sell day passes that are also valid on services run by other companies. First Cymru's Roverbus ticket costs £5 and is valid for a day's travel throughout South Wales on services run by First Cymru, Rhondda, Red & White and Silverline Coaches. It's not valid on the Cardiff-Swansea Shuttle but you can use it on the slow X1 service between Cardiff and Swansea.

For rail information, phone ☎ 0345-484950. Cardiff Valley Lines has a one day unlimited travel ticket for £5.40/2.70 allowing rail travel in the Cardiff area and the Valleys. On this ticket you could visit Cardiff Bay, Caerphilly Castle, the Rhondda Heritage Park and along the Taff and Rhymney rivers.

The Wye Valley Walk is a 107 mile way-marked trail, which runs alongside the river from Chepstow to Rhayader. There are youth hostels along the way at St Briavels, Monmouth and Welsh Bicknor. For more information visit the Chepstow TIC, which also has a permanent exhibition on walks in the Wye Valley.

CARDIFF (CAERDYDD)

• pop 280,000 ☎ 01222

As Glasgow did in the early 1990s, the Welsh capital is busy re-inventing itself as 'the fastest growing capital city in Europe'. Much of the city is currently under redevelopment but this shouldn't put you off visiting. Cardiff has a striking city-centre castle, a world-class museum and art gallery, a newly renovated docks area, and pockets of beautiful architecture.

WARNING

The telephone area code 01222 is changing to 029. Local 6-digit numbers in the 01222 area are being prefixed with 20 to make local 8-digit numbers.

Numbers 01222-XXXXXX will become 029-20XX XXXX. From 22 April 2000 you must use either the new 8-digit number or the old number preceded by the old area code when dialling locally.

The giant freshwater marina in Cardiff Bay is nearing completion. Environmentalists point out that this is at the price of losing the mud flats that have traditionally provided feeding grounds for thousands of wading birds. Another major project has been the impressive 75,000-seater Millennium Stadium built for the Rugby World Cup, to be held in Cardiff in October 1999. Sadly, plans for architect Zaha Hadid's opera house, designed as a dazzling 'crystal necklace' of glass, were scotched by a campaign orchestrated by the local press. A more conservative multi-purpose building will take the place of the one that could have done for Cardiff what the Opera House did for Sydney.

Cardiff is a good base for visiting a few sites in the surrounding area, including the Rhondda Heritage Park, the Museum of Welsh Life at St Fagans, the castles at Caerphilly and Castell Coch and the Big Pit Mining Museum at Blaenavon. Transport links are good, with the M4 linking Cardiff to Swansea and Bristol.

History

The Romans first settled the area to the east of the River Taff, but once they pulled out of Britain the site, it seems, became abandoned until after the Norman conquest. Robert Fitzhamon was responsible for the motte and bailey castle, remains of which still stand in the grounds of the later Cardiff Castle. Throughout the Middle Ages there was a settlement at Cardiff (St John's

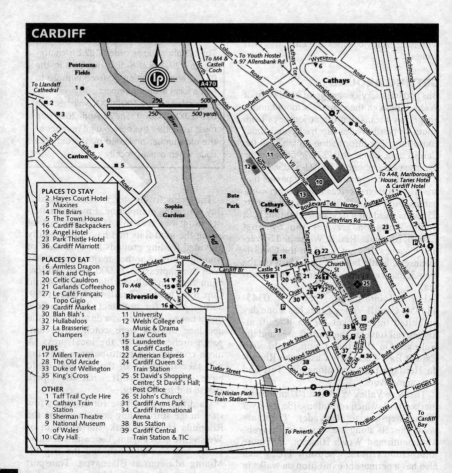

CARDIFF

Pontcanna
Fields

To Llandaff
Cathedral

To M4 &
Castell
Coch

To Youth Hostel
& 97 Allensbank Rd

Wyeverne

Cathays

Senghenydd

Canton

Sophia
Gardens

Bute
Park

Cathays
Park

Boulevard de Nantes

To A48, Marlborough
House, Tanes Hotel
& Cardiff Hotel

Greyfriars Rd

Riverside

Cowbridge   Road

Cardiff Br

Castle St

Queen

Church
St

Westgate

Quay

Tudor Street

To Ninian Park
Train Station

To Penarth

Wood Street

Central Sq

To
Cardiff
Bay

To Penarth

Tresillian   Way

PLACES TO STAY
2 Hayes Court Hotel
3 Maxines
4 The Briars
5 The Town House
16 Cardiff Backpackers
19 Angel Hotel
23 Park Thistle Hotel
36 Cardiff Marriott

PLACES TO EAT
6 Armless Dragon
14 Fish and Chips
20 Celtic Cauldron
21 Garlands Coffeeshop
27 Le Café Français;
Topo Gigio
29 Cardiff Market
30 Blah Blah's
32 Hullabaloos
37 La Brasserie;
Champers

PUBS
17 Millers Tavern
28 The Old Arcade
33 Duke of Wellington
35 King's Cross

OTHER
1 Taff Trail Cycle Hire
7 Cathays Train
Station
8 Sherman Theatre
9 National Museum
of Wales
10 City Hall

11 University
12 Welsh College of
Music & Drama
13 Law Courts
15 Laundrette
18 Cardiff Castle
22 American Express
24 Cardiff Queen St
Train Station
25 St David's Shopping
Centre; St David's Hall;
Post Office
26 St John's Church
31 Cardiff Arms Park
34 Cardiff International
Arena
38 Bus Station
39 Cardiff Central
Train Station & TIC

Church in the city centre is a reminder of this period) but it was very small; even in 1801, the census figures suggest barely 1000 people lived here.

Cardiff really owes its development to the coal mining in the valleys to the north. In 1839, the Marquis of Bute had the first docks built in Cardiff, and the Bute family, who owned much of the land on which coal had been found, were able to insist all exported coal was traded through their ports. Cardiff boomed, and by the end of the 19th century there were probably about 170,000 people living here. However, hard times returned in the 20th century, especially during the slump of the 1930s. The city was also badly damaged by bombs during WWII, which explains some of the nastier modern development in the centre. The South Wales coal industry has now disappeared – the last mines seen off in the years since the catastrophic 1984 strike.

It was only in 1955 that Cardiff was designated the capital of Wales, a status which brought it renewed prosperity as government agencies concerned with Wales relocated their headquarters here. However, the docks could never recover their lost importance and it wasn't until the creation of the Cardiff Bay Development Corporation in 1987 that serious efforts were made to revive the area. With the recent announcement that the new Welsh Assembly will be located by Cardiff Bay, it looks as if the revival is complete.

Orientation

Cardiff originally grew up around Tiger Bay, but the city centre gradually migrated northwards as the port trade dried up. Consequently, Cardiff has two 'centres' as far as tourists are concerned.

Buses and trains arrive just south of the main thoroughfare of St Mary/High St, with the castle forming a useful landmark. Behind the castle stretches Bute Park, the city's main open space, with the River Taff running through it. Opposite the castle lies the main shopping area, where the most interesting places tend to be tucked away inside the network of 19th and early 20th century arcades. The National Museum of Wales is grouped with the Law Courts, the Civic Hall and University College, east of the castle. Cardiff Bay and the docklands museums are a dreary half-hour's walk south. Take a bus.

Cardiff Central train station is off Penarth Rd; the main bus terminal is right in front of it. Some local train services leave from Queen St station to the east. Bute St station is within walking distance of Cardiff Bay.

Information

The TIC (☎ 227281) is inside Cardiff Central station. It's open daily from 9 am to 6.30 pm (from 10 am on Tuesday, and from 10 am to 4 pm on Sunday).

The TIC sells the Cardiff Card (£11/18/24 for 24/48/72 hours), which gives unlimited travel on buses and Valley Lines trains, free entry to Cardiff Castle, the National Gallery, Techniquest, the Big Pit & Rhondda Heritage Park as well as seven

other attractions, and discounts at other attractions and at some restaurants.

The Buzz is a free bimonthly magazine with information about events in all the city venues. Available from the TIC, it's also good on Cardiff's nightspots.

Thomas Cook (☎ 224886) is at 16 Queen St, and there's a branch of Campus Travel (☎ 220744) inside the YHA Adventure Shop at 13 Castle St.

The main post office is in St David's Shopping Centre. There's a laundrette near Cardiff Backpackers.

Parking in the centre of Cardiff is usually subject to restriction. Many places require you to display vouchers, which you need to buy in advance from local shops. A 60p voucher lasts one hour.

Cardiff Castle

It would be hard to miss the castle, which is ringed by a low wall with sculpted bears, lions and wolves crawling all over it. Although excavations on the site indicate it was first occupied by the Romans, the first substantial remains (a motte and bailey castle) date back to Norman times. The present Cardiff Castle is, however, much newer. It was designed for the third Lord Bute by the Victorian architect William Burges (1827-81), who specialised in Victorian Gothic. The outrageous interior is now more Hollywood than medieval, but you'll only get to explore the Banqueting Hall, the Arab Room and the Fairytale Nursery on a guided tour.

The castle (☎ 878100) is open from 9.30 am to 6 pm, March to October, with tours at 20-minute intervals; in winter, the grounds are open from 9.30 am to 4.30 pm, but there are only five daily tours, the first at 10.30 am and the last at 3.15 pm. A visit and tour is £4.80/2.40; to explore only the grounds costs £2.40/1.20.

National Museum of Wales

In Cathays Park, the National Museum forms a pleasing turn-of-the-century grouping of grey-white buildings with the City Hall and the Law Courts. For anyone with children, this place is a must. There's also a wonderful exhibition on the evolution of Wales, complete with mammoths that wave their trunks and waggle their ears.

The natural-history galleries are also excellent; in particular, look out for the rooms housing the skeleton of a young humpback whale washed up near Aberthaw in 1982 and the remains of a giant leatherback turtle found dead on the beach at Harlech in 1988.

On the fourth floor is a magnificent collection of paintings, including Gwendoline and Margaret Davies' bequest of Impressionist paintings, with some Monet *Waterlilies* and works by Sisley, Pisarro, Manet and Degas. There's also a version of Rodin's *The Kiss* and an even nicer model of *The Earth and the Moon*.

The museum (☎ 397951) is open Tuesday to Sunday from 10 am to 5 pm; entry is £4.25/2.50.

St John's Church

Jutting up incongruously from the tacky shopping precinct surrounding it is the graceful 15th century tower of St John's Church. The church is a haven from the bustle outside and one of the few reminders of Cardiff's pre-Victorian past.

Cardiff Bay

The area once called Tiger Bay is now more prosaically named Cardiff Bay. On a sunny day, it's a pleasant place for a stroll, with works of sculpture dotted around the promenade, although there will inevitably be some noise and disruption until all the redevelopment is completed.

The most striking edifice is the Pierhead Building, a huge, red-brick, Victorian masterpiece. A little away from the Bay itself, off James St, is Mount Stuart Square, which has some imposing Victorian architecture. It's a haven of restored grandeur amid the general drabness of Butetown.

Bus No 8 runs from the city centre to Cardiff Bay, or you can get a train to Bute St station and walk.

Welsh Industrial & Maritime Museum

Closed for renovation in 1998, this museum

(☎ 481919) contains exhibits relating to South Wales' industrial and maritime history.

One of the most interesting parts of the museum, containing old house and shop interiors, is still open and housed separately at 126 Bute St. It's open from 10 am to 5 pm, Tuesday to Saturday, and from 2.30 to 5 pm Sunday; tickets cost £1.25/75p.

Techniquest Techniquest (☎ 475475) is the UK's largest hands-on science exhibition, with everything from a machine that blows smoke rings to a wet area with exhibits pertaining to liquid. Just across from the Welsh Industrial and Maritime Museum, there's also a planetarium and science theatre.

It's open from 9.30 am to 4.30 pm, Monday through Friday and from 10.30 am to 5 pm at weekends; entry is £4.75/3.50.

Cardiff Bay Visitors Centre Little more than a way of soft-soaping visitors into buying the Cardiff Bay Development Corporation's view of things, the visitors centre is at least housed in an imaginative building (a long, white tube that acts like a giant telescope overlooking the bay). Entry is free and it's open from 9.30 am to 4.30 pm, Monday to Friday, and from 10.30 am to 5 pm at weekends.

Llandaff Cathedral

If Cardiff seems too busy and brash for comfort, hop on bus No 133 or 65X along Cathedral Rd to Llandaff, a peaceful, pretty northern suburb where Llandaff Cathedral sits in a dip in the landscape.

Dating from 1130, it was largely rebuilt in the 19th century, and extensively restored again after being damaged by a land mine in 1941. The west-end towers epitomise the cathedral's fragmented history; one was built in the 15th century, the other in the 19th. Nowadays, the most striking internal feature is the giant central arch carrying the organ and Jacob Epstein's striking *Majestas*. Fans of the Pre-Raphaelites will be interested in the Burne-Jones reredos in St Dyfrig's chapel and the stained glass by Rossetti and

William Morris' company. Outside, the heads of the British monarchs are carved along the top of the south aisle wall; look out for the uncrowned head of Edward VIII, who abdicated before his coronation.

Organised Tours

During the summer, hop-on hop-off, open-top bus tours, run by Leisurelink (☎ 522202), circle 11 points around the city, from Llandaff in the north to Cardiff Bay in the south. If you stay on the bus for the whole tour, it takes one hour. Tickets cost £6/2.50 (£5 for students) and give you a 10% discount at Cardiff Castle.

Places to Stay

Hostels The cheapest option is *Cardiff Youth Hostel* (☎ 462303, 2 Wedal Rd, Roath Park), where a bed costs £9.75/6.55 for adults/juniors. It's open daily from January through November. The hostel is 2 miles north of the city centre – bus Nos 78, 80 and 82 run this way from Cardiff Central train station.

Cardiff Backpackers (☎ 345577, 98 Neville St, Riverside) is an independent hostel less than a mile from the train and bus stations. The cheapest beds are £12.50 in small dorms, and there are singles (£16), doubles (£29) and triples (£35). A light breakfast is included, and there's also a bar. 'Cleanest backpackers' place I've ever stayed in', said one visitor. It's well-run and popular – book ahead. Hairy Hog (☎ 666900) backpacker tours are based here.

B&Bs & Hotels Cardiff has the usual range of B&Bs from around £16 a head; most of them can be found along Cathedral Rd, to the west, and Newport Rd, to the east. Both these roads are busy with traffic.

Maxines (☎ 220288, 150 Cathedral Rd) does B&B from £18/32 for a single/double. *The Briars* (☎ 340881), at No 126, is similarly priced. On Newport Rd, good bets are *Tanes Hotel* (☎ 493898), at No 148, for £18/32, or the *Cardiff Hotel* (☎ 491964), at No 138, which costs from £18/29 for the most basic rooms. Out of season, many of the hotels along these two roads bring their prices down – look for offers in the windows. A quieter option is the guesthouse at *97 Allensbank Rd* (☎ 621230) in Heath, to the north, where rooms cost £15/28.

Middle-range hotels are also concentrated in Cathedral and Newport Rds. In Cathedral Rd, *The Town House* (☎ 239399), at No 70, is American-run and a comfortable place to stay. All rooms have a bathroom and range from £39.50/49.50 to £59.50/69.50. The *Hayes Court Hotel* (☎ 230420), at Nos 154-64, has rooms for £35/50 with bath. On Newport Rd, the *Marlborough House* (☎ 492385), at No 98, has rooms for £32/45 with shared bath and £45/55 with bathroom.

The *Cardiff Marriott* (☎ 399944, Mill Lane) is centrally located by the café quarter. Rooms are £90 during the week, £57 at weekends for doubles. Breakfast is extra.

The *Angel Hotel* (☎ 232633), opposite the castle in Castle St, has grand public rooms and charges £92/105. At the weekend, however, it does B&B for £36 per person. The *Park Thistle Hotel* (☎ 383471, Park Place), off Queen St shopping centre, is conveniently located and charges £102/115. Weekend breaks are cheaper.

Places to Eat

If you're on a tight budget, head for Cardiff Market in The Hayes, where there are several snack bars. The market is the place to come if you're after cheese, cold meats, laverbread and rolls for a picnic. Convenient for Cardiff Backpackers, there's *Fish and Chips* on Lower Cathedral Rd.

Immediately opposite the castle, in Castle Arcade, is the *Celtic Cauldron*, where you can sample traditional Welsh dishes like laverbread (£4.30), cawl (£3.30) and oatmeal pancakes. It does good vegetarian meals, and you can also get glasses of spicy fruit punch (£1.10). It's open Monday to Saturday from 8.30 am to 9 pm and on Sunday from 11 am to 4 pm.

In Duke St Arcade, *Garlands Coffeeshop* is a pleasant place for coffee, tea and light snacks. Coronation chicken salad is £4.40.

SOUTH WALES

On Church St, just off High St, there are several eating options. Opposite St John's Church is *Le Café Français* (☎ 645188). The baguettes are delicious and fillings include smoked salmon and dill dressing (£2.50) and sliced ham, brie and grapes (£2.35). Takeaways are cheaper. Cardiff's strong Italian community guarantees plenty of pizza and pasta places to choose from. *Topo Gigio (12 Church St)* is not necessarily the cheapest but it's pretty reliable.

On High St, *Blah Blah's* is a subterranean bar serving good-value food. Half a roast chicken and chips is £3.95. Many of the pubs in this area serve cheap lunches for £3 or £4. South of High St, on St Mary St, *Hullabaloos* (☎ 226811) is a BYO restaurant.

More upmarket, although not in a very upmarket area, is the *Armless Dragon* (☎ 382357, 97 Wyeverne Rd). The à la carte menu is pretty pricey – dinner would set you back around £20 – but there are good-value set lunches (£7.90/9.90 for two/three courses and coffee).

At 60-61 St Mary St, there are two informal restaurants run by the same management – *La Brasserie* (☎ 372164) and *Champers* (☎ 373363) – offering a range of Spanish, French and Welsh food, balanced with a good choice of seafood. Main courses range from £5 to £15 (suckling pig), or £25 (lobster).

The best French restaurant in Cardiff is *Le Cassoulet* (☎ 221905, 5 Romilly Crescent), off Llandaff Rd in the west of the city. Start your evening with one of the excellent cocktails. Set lunches are £12.50/15 for two/three courses. In the evening there's an à la carte menu (£13 to £17 per dish). It's open Tuesday to Saturday.

There are numerous places springing up in the Cardiff Bay area. The *Caribbean Restaurant* (☎ 252102, 14 West Bute St, Mount Stuart)* does good-value food. Lamb curry is £4.20; steak, rice and veg costs £7.50. It's a popular place, open daily from noon to 2 pm and from 5 to 11 pm (1 am at weekends). The fish and chip chain *Harry Ramsden's* (☎ 463334) has a branch on Stuart St, and opening in late 1999 is the much-hyped *Sports Café* beside the new St David's Hotel.

Also in Cardiff Bay, the reconstructed Norwegian Church near the visitors centre has been turned into a cosy *teashop*, doing excellent cakes, waffles and sandwiches. Children's author Roald Dahl was christened here.

Entertainment

Pubs The local brew is Brains SA (Special Ale or Skull Attack depending on how many pints you have). There are numerous places to try it. The *Wellington (Mill Lane)* is in the centre of the so-called Café Quarter (otherwise known as Drunk's Alley). The *King's Cross* on the corner Caroline St and Mill Lane, is a busy gay bar.

The Old Arcade (Church St) is a good traditional pub. Just off Lower Cathedral Rd, *Millers Tavern* is convenient if you're staying in the area.

Clubs For the latest on the growing club scene check *The Buzz*. Popular clubs and music venues include *Clwb Ifor Bach* (☎ 232199, 11 Womanby St), *Sam's* (☎ 345189) at the St Mary St end of Mill Lane, and the *Cardiff University Students Union* (☎ 387421, Park Place).

Other Entertainment Cardiff's best-known entertainment is rugby, which takes place on Saturday afternoon at Cardiff Arms Park (☎ 390111).

If you're after something less frenetic in warmer surroundings, *St David's Hall* (☎ 878444, The Hayes) offers a full range of theatrical events. There are also two smaller theatres, the *Sherman Theatre* (☎ 230451, Senghennydd Rd, Cathays), and the *New Theatre* (☎ 878889, Park Place), currently the home of the Welsh National Opera.

Most imaginative cinema programs tend to be at the *Chapter Arts Centre* (☎ 399666, Market Rd, Canton). It's popular with students; get there on bus Nos 12, 14 and 16.

There are regular classical music concerts in St David's Hall, and less frequent ones in Llandaff Cathedral and St John's

Although the Welsh play conventional football (soccer), it's really rugby union that marks Wales out from England. During the 1970s, the Welsh national team was immensely successful, winning six out of 10 Five Nations Championships. Since then however, things haven't gone quite so swimmingly, and in 1991 Wales went down to ignominious defeat (63-6) at the hands of Australia. In 1994, however, Wales did win the Five Nations Championship, in which Wales, England, Scotland, Ireland and France competed against each other. Perhaps (like France's did when it held the World Cup soccer finals in 1998) Wales' fortunes will soar when the 1999 Rugby World Cup is held in Cardiff in October.

If you'd like to see Wales play, its stadium is at Cardiff Arms Park in the centre of Cardiff, where the new Millennium Stadium is nearing completion. Tickets for normal fixtures are easy to obtain at reasonable prices (around £8 to £10 in the stands; phone ☎ 01222-390111 for details), although those for big events sell out months in advance of the match.

The most successful club sides are Cardiff, Swansea, Neath and Llanelli, and you can catch their matches between September and Easter. Most of the former mining valley towns also have their own sides.

Church. The *Cardiff International Arena* (☎ 224488, Mary Ann St) hosts large scale pop concerts of the Barry Manilow type. The stately *Coal Exchange (Mount Stuart Square, Cardiff Bay)* takes the smaller gigs.

Getting There & Away

See the fares tables in the introductory Getting Around chapter. Cardiff is 155 miles from London, 50 from Bristol and 48 from Swansea.

Air Cardiff airport (☎ 01446-711111) is 12 miles south-west of the centre.

Bus National Express (☎ 0990-808080) runs coaches every two hours between London (Victoria) and Cardiff (three hours, from £19 single). There are hourly services linking Cardiff and Bristol (£4). Via Birmingham, there are twice-daily services between Cardiff and Llandudno (seven hours, £37.75) and Cardiff and Rhyl (6¼ hours, £27.20).

The First Cymru Shuttle (☎ 01792-580580) links Cardiff with Swansea almost hourly (one hour, £6 single or return). Twice a day there are also services to Bristol (£9.50 single) and Bath (£12 single). Bicycles are taken free.

The daily Traws Cambria 701 connects Cardiff with Holyhead (nine hours, £20) via Swansea, Aberystwyth, Caernarfon and Bangor. For more information, phone ☎ 01248-351879.

Train Cardiff Central is on the main Inter-City London to Swansea route: London to Cardiff costs £34 one way (two hours, hourly services), and Cardiff to Swansea costs £7.60 (one hour). Regional Railways' Alphaline also offers direct services between Cardiff and London's Waterloo, which are timed to connect with international services through the Channel Tunnel.

Direct train services connect Cardiff and Manchester, Liverpool, Birmingham, Nottingham and the ports at Portsmouth and Southampton. Trains to Chester continue to Holyhead (£49.90) for Dun Laoghaire. There are trains connecting Cardiff and Pembroke Dock via Tenby (£13.60), Milford Haven via Haverfordwest (£13.60), and Fishguard Harbour (for Rosslare, £13.60).

Cardiff Valley Lines' services (from Cardiff Central or Queen St) link Cardiff with Merthyr Tydfil, Aberdare, Pontypridd, Treherbert, Rhymney and Coryton. The free bus map from Cardiff Bus Office includes a map of the valley rail routes.

Car & Motorcycle The M4 loops round Cardiff, linking it to Swansea, Bristol and

London. The new Peripheral Distributor Rd across Cardiff Bay provides direct links to the M4, bypassing the city centre.

Boat In summer, you can get to Penarth, 3 miles from Cardiff, on the *Balmoral* or *Waverley* ships operating from Bristol.

Getting Around

Cardiff's sights are scattered around the city, so walking is really only feasible to get around the centre, parts of which are pedestrianised.

Bus Orange and white Cardiff Bus services provide quick, cheap access to most parts of town. Most want exact fares; the only way you'll get any change is to ask for a change ticket and either use it on another service or wait two days before cashing it in at the city bus office.

Capital Day Out tickets (£3.30, available from the driver) are available all day and can be used to get round the city centre, Penarth, Castell Coch, St Fagans, Llandaff and Cardiff Bay. There are weekly tickets for £9.50 (photo required).

Cardiff Bus Office (☎ 396521) is in St David's House, Wood St, right in front of the bus terminal. Its excellent free map shows not just the city bus routes but also the local train lines as well.

Train There are local train stations at Queen St, Cathays, Llandaff, Ninian Park and Bute Rd (for the bay).

Bicycle Cardiff is at the southern end of the Welsh National Cycle Route, Lôn Las Cymru, which runs the full length of Wales to end in Holyhead, Anglesey. From Cardiff the route follows the Taff Trail (see Brecon Beacons National Park in the Mid Wales chapter).

Taff Trail Cycle Hire (☎ 398362) is by the Cardiff Caravan Park, off Cathedral Rd. Bike rental costs £8 per day. It has some adapted bikes for disabled cyclists.

AROUND CARDIFF
Castell Coch

Rising up among the beech trees on a hill just north-west of the city, Castell Coch looks more like a Loire château than a standard Welsh castle. The summer retreat of the Bute family, it was designed by Burges (like Cardiff Castle) in gaudy Victorian Gothic. Particularly interesting are the sitting room, with designs based on Aesop's Fables; the bedroom, which has a sink that swings up to empty out the water; and the kitchen, which has a fine Welsh dresser.

Castell Coch (☎ 01222-810101, Cadw) is open daily from 9.30 am to 6.30 pm; entry is £2.50/2. Cardiff Bus No 26 will take you to Tongwynlais: it's a 10 minute walk from there.

Caerphilly Castle

Nine miles north of Cardiff, Caerphilly is a fairytale ruined medieval castle complete with moat – although its setting is somewhat marred by the ugly development of Caerphilly itself, right on its doorstep.

The castle was built in stages between 1268 and 1277 by Gilbert de Clare, under constant threat of attack from Prince Llywelyn. It has a long external wall with a gatehouse opening onto a causeway over the moat. This leads to the keep, which stands on a platform. The castle was in a dismal state in the 19th century, when the Bute family offered funds to restore it to its present state.

Caerphilly Castle (☎ 01222-883143, Cadw) is open Easter to October, daily from 9.30 am to 6.30 pm; and from 9.30 am to 4 pm, Monday to Saturday, and from 11 am to 4 pm on Sunday for the rest of the year; entry is £2.40/1.90. Caerphilly train station is a quarter of a mile from the castle and there are frequent trains, or you can get there on Bus Nos 71 and 72.

Museum of Welsh Life at St Fagans

Four miles west of Cardiff along the A4232, St Fagans is a small village with a vast tourist attraction. The 40-hectare museum is a collection of 30 reconstructed buildings brought from all over the country. Among them are a tollhouse, a cockpit, a chapel and assorted houses, cottages, and a row of Victorian shops brought here from the valleys.

Craftspeople still work in many of the buildings, allowing visitors to see how clogs, barrels, cider and wooden artefacts were made. In the grounds, you can also see examples of peculiarly Welsh breeds of livestock and poultry. History is regularly brought to life here, especially on public holidays when the site can get horribly cluttered with families tucking into hot lamb sandwiches.

The museum (☎ 01222-569441) is open daily from 10 am to 6 pm; tickets cost £5.20/3. Cardiff Bus Nos 32, 32A and 56 run to St Fagans.

Penarth

A relatively demure seaside resort, Penarth has a Victorian pier from which you can take summer boat trips across to England – to Clevedon, Minehead, Ilfracombe and many other destinations. Some trips are on the last surviving operational paddle steamer, PS *Waverley*. For details of boat departures, phone ☎ 01446-720656.

In Penarth, you can visit the **Turner House Gallery**, an offshoot of the National Museum of Wales, which displays *objets d'art* and touring exhibitions. You can get to Penarth on Cardiff Bus Nos L1, P2, P10 and P20 or by train.

Barry

- pop 45,000 ☎ 01222
(029-20 from 22 April 2000)

Eight miles west of Cardiff, Barry is an uninspiring dormitory town for commuters to the capital. If you've got children, however, Barry does boast a **Pleasure Beach** – a funfair on the Blackpool model, a **Rollerdome** and a **Quasar Centre**. Trains from Cardiff run directly to the fair (get off at Barry Island station) and Cardiff Bus offers hourly services (No 304) from Central station. In summer, boats link Barry with Bristol across the Bristol Channel.

Rhondda Valley & Heritage Park

If you're interested in the industrial history of the valleys, don't miss the Rhondda Heritage Park, 10 miles north-west of Cardiff, between Pontypridd and Porth. This was the centre of the late coal-mining industry in South Wales; the Heritage Park is built on the site of Lewis Merthyr colliery, which closed in 1983. Here, an exhibition brings the old colliery buildings back to life and tries to explain what life was like for those who worked here and their families. You can descend in a cage to the coalface, with a retired miner as your guide.

The park (☎ 01443-682036) is a half-hour train ride north from Cardiff Central station. The site is open daily from 10 am to 6 pm (except Monday from October to Easter); entry is £5.25/4.

Newport

- pop 116,000 ☎ 01633

Newport is a busy industrial and commercial centre, one of the biggest in Wales. The **town museum**, in the same building as the TIC, has interesting displays on the Roman fortress of Caerleon, and about the history of mining in the area. Also of interest is **Tredagar House**, a restored 17th century mansion set in a park on the western outskirts of the town.

The fact that Newport is a major transport junction means that you may find yourself changing trains or buses here. The train station is about 500m north of the bus station. The TIC (☎ 842962), John Frost Square, is across the road from the southern end of the bus station, in the same building as the museum and art gallery. The Newport Centre (☎ 662662), at Kingsway, hosts big pop concerts. Trains link Cardiff and Newport daily until just before midnight.

Caerleon Roman Fortress

At Caerleon, 4 miles north of Newport, is the most important Roman site in Wales. It was known as Isca in Roman times, after the River Usk that flows past the town.

There's an impressive amphitheatre dating from AD 90, fortress baths, and the

SOUTH WALES

only legionary barracks on display in Europe. There are excellent displays in the Roman Legionary Museum (☎ 01633-423134, Cadw). It's all very well-presented and well worth a visit.

The amphitheatre is always open and free; joint entry to the baths and museum is £3.30/2.

WYE VALLEY

The River Wye flows 154 miles from its source at Plynlimon in Mid Wales to meet the River Severn at Chepstow. From the mossy spring where the water rises, it runs through the mountains to Rhayader, past Glasbury and Builth Wells, on through Hay-on-Wye (see the Brecon Beacons National Park section in the Mid Wales chapter), Hereford and Ross-on-Wye (see the Hereford & Worcester section of the Midlands chapter) and down through Monmouth, past the picturesque ruins of Tintern Abbey, to Chepstow. The Wye Valley Walk (see Getting Around at the start of this section) follows the river from Rhayader to Chepstow, and the section of the river from Monmouth to Chepstow is particularly attractive.

Monmouth

- pop 7500   ☎ 01600

While Monmouth is a town of few distinctions, it's the attractive centre of an agricultural region. It has a beautiful and unique 13th century bridge with a busy cattle market nearby. The town is on the Welsh side of the border with England.

The Normans built a castle on the town's easily defended site. It was the birthplace of Henry V, but was later destroyed and Great Castle House, still standing, was built from its stones. Occupied by both Royalists and Roundheads during the Civil War, Monmouth subsequently became the county town of Monmouthshire, prospering from livestock and country markets, and as the site of the regular Assize Court.

Monmouth's shape is governed by its position at the confluence of the Rivers Monnow, Wye and Trothy. The town is centred on Agincourt Square. From here, Monnow St, the principal thoroughfare, lined with shops, descends to the Monnow Bridge. Above the square, along a number of smaller lanes, are bookshops and pubs. The TIC (☎ 713899) is under the portico of the Shire Hall on Agincourt Square.

Things to See The symbol of the town is the **Monnow Bridge**, unique in Britain as the only complete example of a late 13th century stone-gated bridge. Built as part of the city defences, it was also a toll bridge.

The centre of the town is **Agincourt Square**, an irregularly shaped hub with the arcade of the Shire Hall, built in 1724, on one side. In front of it is the statue of Charles Rolls, Monmouth son and co-founder of the Rolls-Royce car and aero-engine company.

The **Nelson Museum & Local History Centre** (☎ 713519), on Priory St, houses an extraordinary collection of memorabilia relating to the great admiral, even though he had only the most tenuous of connections with the town. The collection includes letters to his mistress, Emma Hamilton. It's open all year, Monday to Saturday from 10 am to 5 pm, and on Sunday from 2 to 5 pm. Entry is £1/75p.

Places to Stay & Eat *Monmouth Youth Hostel* (☎ 715116, Priory St School, Priory St) is in the town centre. It's open from March to October and the nightly charge is £7.20/4.95 for adults/juniors. *Monnow Bridge Caravan & Camping* (☎ 714004) is beside the river and near the bridge. It charges £3 for a tent and one camper.

There are many hotels in the surrounding area, but few in the town itself. *Steeples* (☎ 712600), over the café on Church St, charges £25/45 for singles/doubles – all rooms have a bathroom. The *Riverside Hotel* (☎ 715577, Cinderhill St) is the smartest place in town. It's just over the Monnow Bridge from the centre; rooms with bath are £48/68.

There are a number of places to eat around or near Agincourt Square – the *Punch House* (☎ 713855) is an attractive pub. Alternatively, there's takeaway at *Pick-a-Pizza* (☎ 714998). For a more expensive and sophisticated meal, try the *French Horn Brasserie* (☎ 772733, St Mary St).

Getting There & Away There are regular buses to Chepstow (No R69), Lydney and Coleford.

There's no train station but there are bus links, Monday to Saturday, to the nearest stations at Hereford and Newport, both 16 miles away.

Tintern Abbey

The tall walls and empty, arched windows of this 14th century Cistercian abbey on the edge of the River Wye have been painted by Turner and lauded by Wordsworth. It's one of the most beautiful ruins in the country. As a result, the village of Tintern swarms with visitors in summer. The abbey ruins are indeed an awe-inspiring sight, though best visited towards the end of the day, after the crowds have dispersed.

This Cistercian house was founded in 1131 by Walter de Clare, but the present building dates largely from the 14th century. It lasted until the dissolution and, compared to other religious sites that were laid to waste at this time, a remarkable amount remains.

The abbey (☎ 01291-689251, Cadw) is open from late March to late October, daily from 9.30 am to 6.30 pm, November to March, Monday to Saturday, from 9.30 am to 4 pm, and from 11 am to 4 pm on Sunday. Entry is £2.20/1.70. The Walkman tours (£1/50p) are highly recommended.

The town follows the course of the River Wye with the abbey ruins located on the west bank. The TIC (☎ 01291-689566) is north of the town at the old station, a long walk from the abbey.

Stagecoach Red & White bus No 69 runs every two hours between Chepstow and Monmouth, Monday to Saturday only.

Raglan Castle

Seven miles west of Monmouth on the road to Abergavenny, Raglan Castle is a very impressive and atmospheric ruin. Constructed in the 15th and 16th centuries, it was the last medieval castle to be built in the country. It's particularly interesting to see how castle design had evolved by this time to include flamboyant embellishments (such as the gargoyles and heraldic stonework on the gatehouse).

The castle (☎ 01291-690228) is open standard Cadw times; entry is £2.40/1.90.

CHEPSTOW

• **pop 9000**   ☎ **01291**

Just over the border from England, Chepstow is an attractive, small town near the confluence of the Rivers Wye and Severn. It's noted for its superb castle, but is also well known for its racecourse. Although a day is certainly sufficient to explore the town, Chepstow is a good base from which to explore the area.

Essentially a Norman town, Chepstow (from Old English *chepe* and *stowe*, meaning marketplace) was developed as a base for the Norman conquest of south-east Wales. It later prospered as a port for the timber and wine trades but as river-borne commerce declined, so Chepstow's importance diminished to that of a typical market town.

Orientation & Information

The centre of Chepstow tapers upwards from the river in a wedge shape, with the castle on a bluff to the west and the A48 to the east. The main streets are Bridge St, High St and the pedestrianised St Mary St. The TIC (☎ 623772) is at the bottom of Bridge St, in the castle car park.

Things to See

The main attraction is **Chepstow Castle**, which is fairly well preserved in its dramatic location on a cliff overlooking the River Wye – best seen as a whole from the English side of the river. Construction began in 1067, making it the first stone castle in Wales, perhaps in Britain – a sure sign of its importance. Its massive fortifications were added in the 12th century, followed by mostly domestic construction in the 13th century. Towards the end of the Civil War, it was used as a prison; by 1690, when the garrison was dispersed, it had become all but an irrelevance. The castle (☎ 624065, Cadw) is open daily from 9.30 am to 6.30 pm in summer, and until 4 pm in winter; entry is £3/2.

The well-preserved, 13th century city wall – the **Port Wall**, or Customs Wall – was built more as a means of controlling entry than for defence. It can best be seen from the main car park off Welsh St or the vicinity of the train station. The Town Gate, originally part of the Port Wall, was much restored in the 16th century.

Chepstow Museum (☎ 625981) is near the TIC in an 18th century town house. Mostly devoted to the history of the port, it also has a collection of 18th and 19th century prints and drawings of the Wye Valley. It's open from 10.30 am to 1 pm and from 2 to 5.30 pm, Monday through Saturday, and from 2 to 5.30 pm on Sunday; £1/free.

The handsome Wye River Bridge, made of iron, was built in 1816.

Places to Stay

Cobweb Cottage (☎ 626643, Belle Vue Place, Steep St) is a small place charging £20 per person for B&B. *Langcroft* (☎ 625569, 71 St Kingsmark Ave) is a short walk from the centre and has rooms at £15.

There are several B&Bs and hotels along Bridge St. The *Afon Gwy Hotel* (☎ 620158) has rooms overlooking the river, with bathroom, for £33/45 a single/double. The restaurant is recommended. The *Castle View Hotel* (☎ 620349), also on Bridge St, has rooms for £39.50/56.50 (breakfast is extra).

On Welsh St, the *Coach & Horses* (☎ 622626) is a pub close to the castle and has rooms from £19/34. With bathroom a double is £38.

The top place to stay is the *George* (☎ 625363), next to the city gate. The George dates back to 1610 and its comfortable rooms cost £70/80. There's also a weekend B&B rate of £45 per person.

Places to Eat

St Mary's Tea Rooms (5 St Mary St) does very good snacks and well-priced meals and cakes.

The *Coach & Horses* (☎ 622626, Welsh St) does excellent pub grub, and bar meals are also available from the *Three Tuns Inn* (☎ 623497), by the castle. The *Castle View Hotel* (see Places to Stay) offers substantial meals; rump steak is £11.95.

The restaurant at the *Afon Gwy Hotel* (see Places to Stay) is an excellent place to eat. There's a set menu for £12.95 (three courses).

Getting There & Away

Chepstow has good bus connections. Stagecoach Red & White (☎ 01633-266336) and Badgerline (☎ 0117-955 3231) run hourly buses to Bristol (one hour, £2.45) from Chepstow bus station. The X15 service goes to Monmouth via Tintern on Wednesday only. There are also services to Newport (45 minutes, every half-hour), Gloucester (1¼ hours) and Cardiff.

From the train station, there are direct services to Cardiff (25 minutes, £5.10), Gloucester (30 minutes, £5.20) and Newport.

SWANSEA (ABERTAWE)
• pop 190,000   ☎ 01792

Swansea is the second-largest town in Wales, and the gateway to the superb coastal scenery of the Gower Peninsula. Thomas grew up in Swansea and later called it an 'ugly, lovely town'. It certainly is in a lovely location on the bay, but some of the concrete developments here are distinctly ugly. Among all this, though, are attractions that make it worth pausing in Swansea, including an excellent maritime museum beside the regenerated dockland, an interesting local art galley, a literary centre and, around the bay at Mumbles, a mile of pubs that constitute one of the best pub-crawls in Britain.

The Vikings named this area Sveins Ey (Swein's Island), probably referring to the sandbank in the mouth of the river. The Normans built the castle, but Swansea's heyday didn't come until the Industrial Revolution, when it rapidly developed into a centre for the smelting of copper. Ore was imported first from Cornwall, easily accessible across the Bristol Channel by boat. By the 19th century, this was Copperopolis – the world centre for the nonferrous-metal's refining industry. Ore came from Chile, Cuba and the USA, while Welsh coal was sold in return.

By the 20th century, the heavy-industry base of the town had declined but the oil refinery and numerous factories were still judged a worthy target for the Luftwaffe, which devastated the centre of Swansea in 1941.

Orientation & Information

The train station is about half a mile north of the town centre, while the bus station is central, in West Way. Swansea University

is to the west. About 4 miles farther west around Swansea Bay is the seaside village of Oystermouth, also known as Mumbles. Its many pubs are as popular with today's students as they were with Thomas.

The TIC (☎ 468321) should have returned to its rebuilt premises on Singleton St, near the bus station, by the time you read this. Until then it's just round the corner in the bus station car park. It's open Monday to Saturday from 9.30 am to 5.30 pm. It can be found on the Web at www.swansea.gov.uk. There's also a seasonal TIC (☎ 361302) on the seafront in Mumbles.

There's a laundrette on Bryn-y-Mor Rd, and a large Sainsbury's supermarket by the river.

Swansea Castle

The castle, originally Norman, dates from the 14th century. The ruins look picturesque

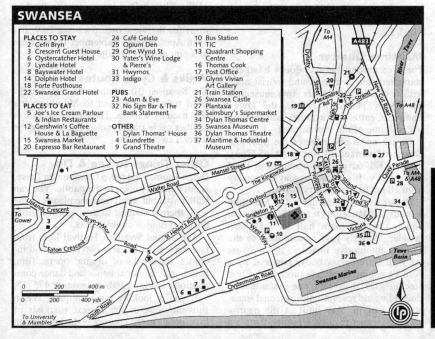

SWANSEA

PLACES TO STAY	24 Café Gelato	10 Bus Station	
2 Cefn Bryn	25 Opium Den	11 TIC	
3 Crescent Guest House	29 One Wynd St	13 Quadrant Shopping	
6 Oystercatcher Hotel	30 Yates's Wine Lodge	Centre	
7 Lyndale Hotel	& Pierre's	16 Thomas Cook	
8 Bayswater Hotel	31 Hwyrnos	17 Post Office	
14 Dolphin Hotel	33 Indigo	19 Glynn Vivian	
18 Forte Posthouse		Art Gallery	
22 Swansea Grand Hotel	**PUBS**	21 Train Station	
	23 Adam & Eve	26 Swansea Castle	
PLACES TO EAT	32 No Sign Bar & The	27 Plantasia	
5 Joe's Ice Cream Parlour	Bank Statement	28 Sainsbury's Supermarket	
& Indian Restaurants		34 Dylan Thomas Centre	
12 Gershwin's Coffee	**OTHER**	35 Swansea Museum	
House & La Baguette	1 Dylan Thomas' House	36 Dylan Thomas Theatre	
15 Swansea Market	4 Laundrette	37 Maritime & Industrial	
20 Expresso Bar Restaurant	9 Grand Theatre	Museum	

reflected in the mirrored glass of the surrounding tower blocks but are not substantial. Most of the castle was destroyed by Cromwell in 1647; what remained was converted into a prison in the 19th century. Swansea Castle is open year-round; entry is free.

Glynn Vivian Art Gallery

This gallery (☎ 655006), located on Alexandra Rd, rightly claims to be 'one of Britain's liveliest provincial galleries'. There are works by Welsh artists, a display of Swansea china, European ceramics and clocks, and temporary exhibitions. The gallery is open Tuesday to Sunday from 10 am to 5 pm; entry is free.

Plantasia

Eight hundred species of plants from around the world, plus attendant insects and reptiles, are housed in the three climatic zones of Plantasia's striking pyramidal greenhouse. Plantasia (☎ 474555), off The Strand, is open daily from 10 am to 5 pm; entry is £1.95/1.25.

Maritime Quarter

The area around the old docks has been converted into a marina and tourist area, with dockside apartments, two museums, the Dylan Thomas Theatre, the Dylan Thomas Centre and a rather odd-looking seated statue of the man himself.

On the north-east edge of the Maritime Quarter, **Swansea Museum** (☎ 653763), Victoria Rd, covers 200 centuries of local archaeology. It's open Tuesday to Sunday from 10 am to 5 pm; entry is free.

Rather more interesting is the **Maritime & Industrial Museum** (☎ 650351), Museum Square. In the main hall is a Gilbern Invader, Wales's first contribution to the world's automotive industry. It's a sports car with a fibreglass body, powered by a Ford V6 engine. Even less successful, Clive Sinclair's C5, the plastic one-seater that he claimed would revolutionise personal transport in Britain, was built at the nearby vacuum-cleaner factory. Upstairs, there's a

collection of boats, including the circular Welsh coracle, and machinery from the Neuth Abbey wool mill. Moored nearby are a lightship and a steam tug. In an annexe is the restored town tram that plied between Swansea and Mumbles on the world's first public passenger train from 1804 to 1960. Opening hours are the same as the Swansea Museum; entry is free.

The **Dylan Thomas Centre** (☎ 463980), the National Literature Centre for Wales, was opened by Jimmy Carter in 1995. Off Somerset Place, it's open Tuesday to Sunday from 10.30 am to 4.30 pm, facilities include a theatre, exhibition galleries, bookshops, restaurant and bar. Should the desire take you, you can even get married here.

Oystermouth Castle

Five miles west of Swansea centre, in Mumbles, Oystermouth Castle was the stronghold of the Norman Lords of Gower, who established a wooden fort here in the 1180s. They built a stone castle in the late 13th century; it's worth walking up to these ruins for the view over Swansea Bay. It's open April through September from 11 am to 5 pm; entry is £1/80p.

Walks & Cycle Routes

The Swansea Bike Path is a 5 mile beach-front trail that runs out to Mumbles; it's also used by walkers. The Riverside Path is another cycle trail, running north along the River Tawe.

Other Things to See & Do

Dylan Thomas' house, 5 Cwmdonkin Drive, is not currently open to the public. You can walk past it but, apart from the plaque on the wall, there's nothing to distinguish it from the other houses on this street.

The annual **Swansea Festival** lasts from late September to early November, and includes six weeks of drama, opera, film, ballet, jazz, classical music and dance competitions. For information, phone ☎ 475715.

If you're looking for a uniquely Welsh souvenir, one of the largest stockists of lovespoons in the country is the **Lovespoon**

Gallery, 492 Mumbles Rd, Oystermouth; examples range from £3 to £300.

Places to Stay

Central Swansea There's no youth hostel in Swansea; the nearest is 13 miles away on the Gower (see Gower Peninsula later in this chapter).

Conveniently situated outside the train station, *Swansea Grand Hotel (☎ 650541)* has good-value doubles at £25, although it's a bit shabby. Singles are £20.

Oystermouth Rd, on the seafront, is lined with B&Bs and guesthouses. At No 322, the *Bayswater Hotel (☎ 655301)* has rooms from £18/28 for a single/double. At No 324, the *Lyndale Hotel (☎ 653882)* offers sea views from most rooms, which cost £18/32, less for longer stays. The *Oystercatcher Hotel (☎ 456574)*, at No 386, has 14 rooms, mostly with bathroom, and charges £17 per person. There's also a bar here, and evening meals are available.

In the rather more upmarket neighbourhood of Uplands, there's another clutch of B&Bs along Uplands Crescent and Eaton Crescent. *Cefn Bryn (☎ 466687, 6 Uplands Crescent)* charges £25/45 for comfortable rooms with bathroom. *Crescent Guest House (☎ 466814, 132 Eaton Crescent)* has six rooms, all with bath, for £27/44.

The *Forte Posthouse (☎ 651074, 39 Kingsway)* is centrally located. Double rooms are £85; there's a gym and pool. If it's quiet at weekends there are sometimes special room deals as low as £40. The *Dolphin Hotel (☎ 650011, Whitewalls)* is also central and popular with businesspeople. It charges £49.50/60 during the week, £39.50/49.50 at weekends.

Mumbles There are several guesthouses along Mumbles Rd, overlooking Swansea Bay. At No 708, the *Coast House (☎ 368702)* is run by a friendly family; B&B costs from £19/36. At No 734, *Beach House Hotel (☎ 367650)* has rooms from £23/40, some with bathroom.

One of the most pleasant places to stay is the *Hillcrest Hotel (☎ 363700, 1 Higher Lane)*. It has a plain exterior but very comfortable bedrooms based on highly imaginative themes. Rooms are £48/60 with bathroom. The Safari room (£80) at the front is best, complete with four-poster bed, an imitation leopard-skin cover and African bush décor. The hotel also has an excellent restaurant.

Places to Eat

Self-caterers should head for the Swansea Market, which has been operating at the same site since 1830. It's interesting to wander round even if you're not buying. In the centre, stalls sell Pen-clawdd cockles (70p) along with that other local delicacy, laverbread (seaweed). You'll find cockles with bacon and laverbread on the menus of many hotels and restaurants, and it's a delicious dish. The market is open Monday to Saturday from 8.30 am to 5.30 pm.

Opposite the train station is the *Expresso Bar Restaurant*, a greasy spoon serving all-day breakfasts, plus tea and toast, for a bargain £1.99. On Castle St, *Café Gelato* is marginally more stylish and does more than coffee and ice cream. A pie and chips is £2.70.

There are several places on Singleton St, close to the TIC. *Gershwin's Coffee House* does breakfasts, lunches, cream teas and good coffee. Nearby, *La Baguette* offers what it says, from £1.60 to £2.45 to take away; cappuccino is 90p.

Wynd St (Wind St) is the up-and-coming café quarter. Almost opposite the castle is *Yates's Wine Lodge*. At No 66 is *Pierre's (☎ 470520)*, a former Pierre Victoire restaurant that continues to offer good-value lunches for £4.90 (two courses). A few doors down is *The Bank Statement*, an impressive new branch of the Wetherspoon pub chain. A pint of beer priced at £1.30 and set meals for two at £5.95 help pull the punters in. Down the alley off Wynd St is *Indigo*, a Mediterranean bar-bistro with set lunches for £6.25, and tapas on the menu.

One Wynd St (☎ 456996) is an upmarket restaurant serving Welsh and continental cuisine. Main dishes are around £7 at lunch;

in the evening there are set dinners (£17 for two courses). It's closed Sunday and Monday. *Hwyrnos* (☎ *641437, Green Dragon Lane)*, off Wynd St, puts on a Welsh night some evenings, with roast lamb in honey, cider and herbs eaten to the accompaniment of live harp music and folk songs.

The *Opium Den* (☎ *456161, 20 Castle St)* is a recommended Cantonese restaurant.

On the western side of town is a line of Indian restaurants popular with students. The *Anarkhali*, the *Moghul Brasserie* and the *Bengal Balti House*, all on St Helen's Rd, battle out the curry wars trying to outdo each other with special offers. The Sunday all-you-can-eat buffets (around £7) are very popular. Nearby, *Joe's Ice Cream Parlour* has been producing excellent, really creamy ice cream since 1922.

The *Hillcrest House Hotel Restaurant* (☎ *363700, 1 Higher Lane, Mumbles)* is an excellent place to eat. There's a set two course dinner for £15.95 or £17.95 for three courses. Also in Mumbles is *L'Amuse* (☎ *366006, 2 Woodville Rd)*, a good French restaurant where the set lunches are from £6.95, set dinners £20.50.

Entertainment

Pubs At weekends, the students head west to the many pubs that line Mumbles Rd in Oystermouth. This is certainly the most lively place to drink. To do the Mumbles Mile you have to have a drink in all 11 pubs, between Newton Rd and Bracelet Bay, in one night. Start with the *White Rose* and work your way via the new *Knab Rock* rock and roll pub to end at *Cinderella's* or *Neptune's*, the nightclubs. There are even T-shirts for those who finish. The Mumbles pub where Thomas used to drink is now called *Dylan's Tavern*, and is fairly touristy.

The *No Sign Bar* (*56 Wynd St)* is a traditional pub with sawdust on the floor. It's a pleasant place for a pint, although its claim to be the 'best pub north of Salzburg' may be stretching things. Next door is *The Bank Statement* (see Places to Eat). On High St, the *Adam & Eve* is another good place to drink.

Other Entertainment *Dylan Thomas Theatre* (☎ *473238, Gloucester Place)* is near his statue on Swansea Marina; his works are often performed here. The *Taliesin Arts Centre* (☎ *296883)* stages a varied program of music, theatre, dance and film at Swansea University, Singleton Park, on the west side of town. *Swansea Grand Theatre* (☎ *475715, Singleton St)* is the town's main theatre, hosting everything from pantomimes to ballet.

Getting There & Away

The Swansea-Cardiff Shuttle (☎ 580580) runs between these two cities (one hour, £6 return) hourly, Monday to Saturday; less often on Sunday.

Swansea is on the main line to London Paddington via Cardiff and Bath. Swansea to Cardiff takes 50 minutes and costs £7.60. There are also direct trains to Fishguard for ferries to Ireland. An interesting cross-country line runs from Swansea, north-east through Llandrindod, Knighton and Craven Arms, to Shrewsbury (four hours).

Daily except Tuesday, there are ferries to Cork (Ireland) in summer, less frequent departures in winter, on Swansea-Cork Ferries (☎ 456116). It charges from £22 to £32 per person. The terminal is on the opposite side of the river to the town centre. In midsummer, there are ferries to Ilfracombe in Devon.

Getting Around

Bus There's an efficient local bus service, with colour-coded routes, run by First Cymru. A Swansea multiride ticket offers all-day bus travel in the Swansea and Mumbles area for £3.10. Bus Nos 2 and 2A run to Oystermouth and Mumbles (£1.30).

Taxi For a taxi try Abba Cabs (☎ 702333). It's about £6.50 to Mumbles from the train station.

GOWER PENINSULA

Extending 15 miles east of Mumbles, the Gower Peninsula was the first part of Britain to be officially designated an Area of Outstanding Beauty, and it well deserves its title. A favourite haunt of Thomas, it has some superb sandy beaches and beautiful cliff scenery – good walking country. In summer, however, it can get very crowded.

Much of the Gower is owned by the NT. On the south coast is **Oxwich Bay**, the first sandy beach of any size you come to. Around Oxwich Point is **Port Eynon**, which has camping grounds and a youth hostel by the beach. The extreme western tip is known as **Worm's Head**, an apt name for this elongated, rocky headland. You can walk out across the causeway onto the Worm only during the two-hour period either side of low tide.

Rhossili is the village above Worm's Head. To the north stretch the 3 miles of the Gower's best and biggest beach, Rhossili Bay. Hang-gliders soar off the cliffs onto the wide expanse of sand. The **Rhossili Visitor Centre** (☎ 01792-390707), at the start of the path to Worm's Head, is run by the NT.

In the 18th century, smugglers landed brandy and tobacco from France on these beaches and secret coves. The seas around this area are treacherous: over 250 boats have been lost off the Gower. On Rhossili Beach, the bows of the *Helvetica*, wrecked in 1880, stick out of the sand.

Walks
Circular Walks in Gower is a useful publication stocked by TICs. For a good five hour ramble, start in the car park on the eastern side of Middleton, walk down to Worm's Head and back up to the visitors centre at Rhossili. Then climb up to the beacon on Rhossili Down, walk down to Hillend and then back to Rhossili and Middleton along the beach. You can phone the visitors centre to check the tide times for crossing to Worm's Head. While you're there you could have lunch or tea at the Worm's Head Hotel.

Places to Stay & Eat
Hotels and guesthouses tend to be more expensive on the Gower Peninsula than in Swansea and Mumbles.

The *Port Eynon Youth Hostel* (☎ 01792-390706) is an old lifeboat house superbly situated right on the beach at Port Eynon, 15

miles from Swansea. It's open from April to October, daily except Sunday but does open on Sunday on bank holiday weekends and in midsummer. The nightly charge is £7.20/4.95 for adults/juniors. There's also the summer-only *Stouthall Youth Hostel* (☎ 01792-391086) at Reynoldston. *Carreglwyd Camping Site* (☎ 01792-390795) is at Port Eynon; £6 for an adult and a tent.

The *Worm's Head Hotel* (☎ 01792-390512) is in a splendid location overlooking Worm's Head and Rhossili Bay. B&B costs £40/60 for a single/double room with bath. Most rooms, and the restaurant, have sea views. There's also a bar.

Getting There & Away
From Swansea bus station, First Cymru bus Nos 18 and 18A run to South Gower, Port Eynon, Rhossili (£2.20) and Horton, daily except Sunday. Bus No 16 runs to North Gower, Llanrhidian and Llangennith.

CARMARTHEN (CAERFYRDDIN)
• pop 14,200   ☎ 01267

It's difficult to believe that this unexciting place, Carmarthenshire's county town, was where Merlin the magician from the Arthurian legends was born. At least it's a little more Welsh than Swansea and Cardiff – you'll hear the language spoken here. There's no real reason to stop, but since it's an important transport hub, you may have to.

Carmarthen lies on the north side of the River Towy. The TIC (☎ 231557) is at 113 Lammas St, in the centre of the town; buses stop along Blue St. The train station is across the bridge, on the southern bank.

Getting There & Away
From Swansea, bus Nos X11 and X30 run hourly to Carmarthen (£3.30), and you can connect with bus No 222 to Laugharne for the Dylan Thomas Boathouse.

Carmarthen is on the main train line from London Paddington, which goes through Cardiff and Swansea. West of Carmarthen, the line divides: one route continues to Pembroke Dock, another to Milford Haven and a third to Fishguard.

LAUGHARNE
- **pop 1000   ☎ 01994**

Pilgrims on the Dylan Thomas trail come to this little town on the west side of the Taff estuary to see the house where he lived, the pub where he perfected the drinking habit that finally killed him and the churchyard where he is buried. Even if you're not particularly a fan, it's an attractive place to visit.

Dylan Thomas Boathouse (☎ 427420) is built into the hillside, a 15 minute walk down a steep lane from the town. He spent the last four years of his life here with his wife Caitlin, and the house is preserved as a shrine. There are photographs, manuscripts and recordings of the poet reading from his own works. Above the house, you can look through the window in the old wooden shed – 'The Shack', he called it – where he wrote *Under Milk Wood*. Beside the house is a tearoom on the terrace, where you can look out across the 'heron priested shore' that inspired some of Thomas' best work. The Dylan Thomas Boathouse is open daily from Easter to October, from 10 am to 5 pm, and in winter from 10.30 am to 3 pm; entry is £2.50/1.50.

Laugharne is a pleasant town of Georgian houses and has the remains of a 12th century castle. The poet's simple grave is in the churchyard of St Martin's Church. *Brown's Hotel* was where Thomas drank, and it's still a serious drinking place – no DT cocktails here for the visitors.

Getting There & Away
Bus No 222 runs hourly from Carmarthen, Monday to Saturday. You can get here from Swansea via Carmarthen for £5 using a Rover bus ticket.

Pembrokeshire Coast National Park

Most of the coastline of the Pembrokeshire Coast National Park consists of rugged cliffs, broken up by stretches of superb sandy beaches – the best in Wales – and rocky coves. Pembrokeshire has some of the oldest rocks in the world, formed over 3000 million years ago.

The park is probably best known for the 189 mile Pembrokeshire Coast Path (see the Activities chapter), which runs from Amroth in the south to Poppit Sands in the north. But as well as excellent walks, there are numerous other outdoor activities – climbing, mountain biking, bird-watching, pony trekking, surfing, sea kayaking and canoeing.

The Preseli Hills are the only upland area in the park. Ancient trade routes run through them, and hill forts, standing stones and burial chambers are all evidence of the prehistoric people who once lived here.

The offshore islands of Skomer, Skokholm and Grassholm were given their names by Viking raiders. They're now inhabited by seabird colonies – puffins, guillemots, razorbills (the emblem of the park) and gannets. Ramsey and Skomer islands are breeding grounds for the grey seal. Caldey Island is owned and farmed by Cistercian monks. All of the islands can be visited.

Anyone who comes to Pembrokeshire should not miss St David's, where the superb cathedral, the most impressive in Wales, is a shrine to the country's patron saint.

The area's warm, sunny climate makes it a place that you can visit all year-round. In July and August, the main tourist areas can be very crowded. May and September are probably the best months for clear days and lack of crowds.

ORIENTATION
The park covers about 230 square miles and includes 180 miles of rocky coastline. Within the park you're never more than 10 miles from the sea. The park can be divided into four separate sections – the coastline east of Fishguard to Cardigan and inland to the Preseli Hills; the coastline west of Fishguard down to Milford Haven; the upper stretches of the Milford Haven waterway; and the coastline round the south of Pembroke peninsula. The industrial coastline

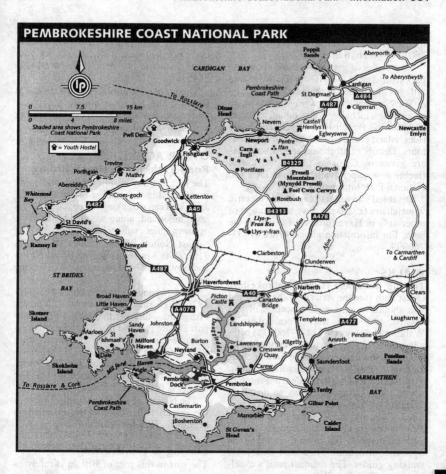

PEMBROKESHIRE COAST NATIONAL PARK

(map) Shaded area shows Pembrokeshire Coast National Park

🏠 = Youth Hostel

around Pembroke and Milford Haven is not part of the park.

The highest point in the park is Foel Cwm Cerwyn in the Preseli Hills, which rises to 536m (1758 feet). The hills are now acknowledged as being the source of the blue stones that form the inner circle of Stonehenge.

The southern part of Pembrokeshire is often known as 'Little England beyond Wales', because of the 50 castles built by the English invaders. The invasion con-

tinues today – resorts such as Tenby are very popular with English holiday-makers. Many of the B&Bs and guesthouses are run not by the Welsh but by incomers.

INFORMATION

The head office for the Pembrokeshire Coast National Park (☎ 01437-764636) is at Winch Lane, Haverfordwest.

There are National Park Information Centres at St David's (☎ 01437-720392), in the TIC and open year-round; Newport

(☎ 01239-820912), also in the TIC; and in the centre of Haverfordwest (☎ 01437-760136), 40 High St.

You can also get information about the park from any of the TICs in the towns and villages mentioned in this section

The National Park organises a wide range of activities, including walks (along the coast and into the Preseli Hills), cycle and horse rides, island cruises, canoe trips and minibus tours. Details of all the organised activities are given in *Coast to Coast*, the useful freebie newspaper available from TICs and National Park Information Centres.

Disabled travellers can hire electric wheelchairs (£2.50 per day) and a range of other aids in Haverfordwest for use in the park. For information phone ☎/fax 01437-760999.

WALKS

The big walk here is the Pembrokeshire Coast Path (see the Activities chapter), and you should at least walk a section of this superb 189 mile trail. Pembrokeshire Walking Holidays (☎ 01437-760075) offer a luggage carrying service for lazy walkers.

Guides that cover the whole route include Dennis Kelsall's *Pembrokeshire Coastal Path*, which follows the route from south to north; the recommended way to do it. CJ Wright's *A Guide to the Pembrokeshire Coast Path*, and the *National Trail Guide – Pembrokeshire Coast Path*, both have more detailed mapping but cover the route in the opposite direction. TICs also sell local walking guides. The national park's excellent *Six Circular Walks* series cover St David's, Strumble Head, Newport, Broad Haven and Saundersfoot. National Park rangers lead guided walks. A half-day walk costs from £2 and a full-day from £3.50. There is even a 14 day guided walk of the complete Coast Path for £100. See the *Coast to Coast* newspaper for details.

CYCLE ROUTES

Although bikes are not allowed on the Pembrokeshire Coast Path, local lanes and bridleways offer excellent cycling. In the north of the country there are more difficult routes for mountain bikes. If you plan to cycle off the roads, it's best to check your route with the National Park (☎ 01437-764636).

There are several places in the area – St David's and Newport among them (see those sections) – where you can hire touring and mountain bikes.

OTHER ACTIVITIES
Pony Trekking & Horse Riding

The fact that this is an ideal area for riding is reflected in the number of stables in the area. You can ride along the beaches, across open moorland, along wooded bridleways, or down quiet country lanes.

East Nolton Riding Stables (☎ 01437-710360) is 3 miles from both Broad Haven and Newgale. To ride here costs £13 for one hour.

Maesgwynne Riding Stables (☎ 01348-872659) charges £8 for one hour. It's near Fishguard – turn off the A40 in Fishguard past Pendre pub and it's 200m down Maesgwynne lane on the left. Pembrokeshire Riding Centre (☎ 01646-682513), Penny-bridge Farm, Hundleton, is 2½ miles south-west of Pembroke on the B4320. The charge is £10 for an hour.

The National Park also organises rides in the Preseli Hills. Contact the information centres or TICs for details.

Surfing & Windsurfing

The surf in this part of Britain is rarely as consistent as in Cornwall, but surfies are still drawn to the beaches at Whitesand, Newgale, Manorbier and Freshwater West.

Windsurfing is popular off many beaches and also on the sheltered waters of Milford Haven. Most of the villages near the coast have a place where you can hire equipment.

Haven Sports (☎ 01437-781354), Marine Rd, Broad Haven, rents windsurfers and runs courses; Newsurf (☎ 01437-721398), at the filling station at Newgale, rents boards and wet suits. They're open every day.

Sea Kayaking & Canoeing

The Pembrokeshire coast is regarded as one of the best sea-kayaking areas in Britain, although you should be aware that rips and currents here can be powerful. For peaceful canoeing, head for the tranquil waters of the Dauggleddau estuary (the Milford Haven waterway).

Boating

Boat trips to see the wildlife on the island nature reserves are very popular and highly recommended. Boats to Ramsey Island, off St David's, depart from St Justinian or Whitesand Bay. Trips to Skomer, Skokholm and Grassholm islands are also possible from St Justinian, or from Martin's Haven. Boats to Caldey Island go from Tenby. As well as trips on small ex-fishing boats, there are also excursions on high-speed water-jet propelled inflatables.

Charges vary according to the length of the trip and the number of islands visited, but you should expect to pay £10 to £20 for a day trip.

Fishing

To fish the rivers you must have a rod licence (£1.50 to £5) from the Environment Agency (☎ 01437-760081) and the permission of the land/fishery owner. Clubs or associations may give day tickets. On small rivers, approach local farmers.

There's good sea fishing – Newgale is one of the best beaches in Wales to fish from. However, you'll need permission first if you want to fish off dock or harbour walls.

OTHER ATTRACTIONS

If you have children, the largest theme park in the area is Oakwood (☎ 01834-891376), just off the A40 between Carmarthen and Haverfordwest, at Canaston Bridge. The wooden roller coaster ride is Europe's largest, topping 80km/h, with 11 crossovers and a maximum drop of 25m.

PLACES TO STAY & EAT

There's no shortage of accommodation and places to eat in this area, particularly in the more developed seaside resorts on the southern coast. At the cheaper end, there are camping grounds (from about £3 per tent) and plenty of youth hostels.

If you're booking two or more of the hostels in Pembrokeshire, you can use the West Wales Booking Service at *St David's Youth Hostel* (☎ *01437-720345*). The service costs £2.50 and bookings must be made two weeks in advance. The other hostels in Pembrokeshire are: *Pentlepoir* (☎ *01834-812333*), near Saundersfoot; *Manorbier* (☎ *01834-871803*); *Lawrenny* (☎ *01646-651270*), 12 miles from Pembroke; *Marloes Sands* (☎ *01646-636667*); *Broad Haven* (☎ *01437-781688*); *Solva (Pen-y-Cwm)* (☎ *01437-720959*); *Trevine (Trefin)* (☎ *01348-831414*); *Pwll Deri* (☎ *01348-891233*), at a wonderful location on cliffs 2¾ miles south of Strumble Head; *Newport* (☎ *01239-820080*), a new hostel and *Poppit Sands* (☎ *01239-612936, St Dogmaels*).

GETTING THERE & AWAY

There's a twice-daily National Express (☎ 0990-808080) bus from London to Haverfordwest (£24).

From London Paddington there's an hourly InterCity service as far as Swansea, where you may need to change to catch less frequent trains to Narberth, Kilgetty, Tenby, Penally, Saundersfoot, Manorbier, Lamphey and Pembroke. Some services from London continue beyond Swansea in summer.

Trains from Swansea also go to Haverfordwest and Fishguard. The service to Haverfordwest runs about seven times a day (less frequently on Sunday). The service to Fishguard goes twice a day. Trains from Swansea to Pembroke go approximately every two hours (1¾ hours, £8).

GETTING AROUND

Bus services around Pembrokeshire are reasonably good. Timetables are available from TICs. For transport information phone ☎ 01437-764551, extension 5227.

The three main local operators are Richards Brothers (☎ 01239-613756), who run services from Haverfordwest to Newgale, St David's, Fishguard and Newport; First Cymru (☎ 01792-580580) and Silcox Motor Coach Co (☎ 01646-683143), who offers services to Pembroke, Tenby and other places south of Haverfordwest.

The West Wales Rover ticket (£4.60/3.40) allows unlimited travel for one day on services in Pembrokeshire, Carmarthenshire and Ceredigion. It can be bought on the bus. Richards Brothers also has its own Day Explorer ticket (£3.20/2.10), only valid on those services.

Trains are less useful for getting round the area. There's no service to St David's in the west or connecting with the northern end of the coast path. You could, however, use the train to get from Tenby to Pembroke, and from Haverfordwest to Milford Haven or Fishguard. For rail inquiries, phone ☎ 0345-484950.

TENBY (DINBYCH Y PYSGOD)
• pop 5500   ☎ 01834

The Welsh name for this genteel seaside town, built around a beautiful bay, is as charming as Tenby itself. It means Little Fort of the Fishes.

The Normans built the castle on the promontory above the two sandy beaches. The town was fortified in the 13th century after several unsuccessful attempts by the Welsh to recapture it. It grew as a port and in the 19th century developed into a holiday resort. Unlike many other seaside resorts in Britain, Tenby has managed to avoid being overtaken by amusement arcades and fish and chip shops. Tenby gets crowded in summer but is nonetheless worth visiting, and the coast path runs right through the town.

Orientation & Information
The town extends east of the castle on the promontory, with the harbour and North Beach on one side and South Beach on the other. The train station is on the western side, at the bottom of Warren St. The bus station is one block south of Warren St on Upper Park Rd.

There's a TIC (☎ 842404) in The Croft, open in July and August, daily from 10 am to 9 pm, and for shorter hours the rest of the year.

To collect your email visit The Cyberpoint (☎ 844700), Nelson's Walk.

Things to See
Tall, elegant Georgian houses, most of them now hotels, rise above the pretty harbour. The most interesting building to look round is the **Tudor Merchant's House** (☎ 842279, NT), Quay Hill, a late 15th century house that shows how a merchant lived in this time. The remains of three frescoes can be seen on the interior walls. The house is open from April to October, daily except Wednesday and Saturday, from 10 am to 5 pm, and on Sunday from 1 to 5 pm; entry is £1.80/90p.

Other things to see in Tenby include the **castle ruins** (good for views over the bay) and the **Museum & Art Gallery** on Castle Hill.

When the tide is down, you can walk across the sand to **St Catherine's Island**. The Victorian fortress here is not open to the public. A popular boat trip from Tenby harbour is across to Caldey Island (see Around Tenby).

Places to Stay
There are no youth hostels in Tenby, but there is one 4 miles east at Pentlepoir (see Saundersfoot), and another about 6 miles west at Skrinkle Haven (Manorbier).

There's a good choice of cheaper B&Bs along Harding and Warren Sts, near the train and bus stations. *Weybourne* (☎ 843641, 14 Warren St) charges from £13 in winter to £16 in summer.

Myrtle House Hotel (☎ 842508) is a comfortable non-smoking hotel on St Mary's St. All rooms have a bath or shower; B&B is around £24 per person.

There's no shortage of places to stay along the Esplanade, above the South Beach, and on Victoria St, Picton Terrace and Sutton St, which lead off it. Prices range from £20 to £30 per person, depending on the size of the room and whether it has a sea view. On the Esplanade you will find the *Clarence House Hotel* (☎ 844371), *Esplanade Hotel* (☎ 843333) and also the *Panorama Hotel* (☎ 844976).

The *Fourcroft Hotel* (☎ 842886, The Croft) is a comfortable place that's been run by the same friendly family for the last 58 years. It's £44 per person in rooms with bathroom and sea view; without the view it's £39, and in winter rates drop to £29 per person. The hotel overlooks the bay and has a pool and private garden above the beach.

The *Atlantic Hotel* (☎ 842881, The Esplanade) is an excellent place, with a heated pool, and a private garden leading onto the beach. B&B costs £55/78 for singles/doubles.

Places to Eat

In summer, Tenby has a glut of teashops and cafés serving overpriced snacks and lunches. *Celtic Fare Tea Rooms* (St Julian's St) is open from 10 am to 6 pm and has cream teas and some traditional Welsh dishes. For excellent ice cream, head for *Adrianne Fecci's Ice Creamery* (Upper Frog St), one block west of High St, which has over 50 varieties of the stuff and also does snacks.

The *Bay Tree* (Tudor Square) is a bistro with main dishes from £7.95 to £10.95 and occasional live music.

Plantagenate Restaurant (☎ 842350, Quay Hill) is by the Tudor Merchant's House and claims to be the oldest house in town. As well as being an interesting building it's an excellent place to eat. Crab sandwiches cost £3.95; main dishes range from £9.95 to £14.95, and there are good vegetarian choices.

Most of the larger hotels have restaurants that are open to nonguests.

Getting There & Away

An hourly bus service, No 358/9, runs between Haverfordwest and Tenby (1½ hours, £2.65), from Monday to Saturday. There's also a direct train service from Swansea (1½ hours, £8).

AROUND TENBY
Caldey Island

A 20 minute boat trip from Tenby, Caldey Island is home to a small community of 20 Cistercian monks, seals and sea birds. The monks make a variety of products for sale, including perfume, dairy products and chocolate – industries that now employ people from the mainland. There are guided tours of the monastery twice a day (men only), and great walks around the island, with good views from the lighthouse. Make sure you visit the old priory and **St Illtyd's Church**, with its oddly shaped steeple. Inside is a fascinating ogham stone, with inscriptions in this ancient Irish script.

There are regular services to the island (£4.95, including landing fee), from Easter to October, Monday to Friday (and Saturday from May to September). Tickets are sold from the kiosk in Castle Square, above the harbour.

Saundersfoot
- pop 2200   ☎ 01834

Situated 3 miles north of Tenby, the attractive village of Saundersfoot was once a fishing port, which was also involved in the export of anthracite. It's now a busy seaside resort with a good beach. There's a TIC (☎ 813672), open seven days a week, near the harbour car park.

Pentlepoir Youth Hostel (☎ 812333) is 1½ miles inland from Saundersfoot, in the old schoolhouse in Pentlepoir village. It's open daily in July and August; phone for other opening days. The nightly charge is £6.50/4.45 for adults/juniors. There are also numerous B&Bs and guesthouses in the area.

Buses run to Saundersfoot from Tenby (15 minutes, £1). The train station is a mile north of the town.

Manorbier

Above this village are the ruins of **Manorbier Castle**, with superb views over the sea. This 12th century fortification was the birthplace of Giraldus Cambrensis, Gerald of Wales, one of the country's greatest scholars and tutor to both Richard the Lion-Heart and King John. 'In all the broad lands of Wales, Manorbier is the best place by far', he wrote. In some of the castle's rooms you'll find waxworks in period costume – a job lot of rejects from Madame Tussaud's in London. Look for the two figures that were originally Prince Philip – in one room he's dressed in chain mail, and he pops up again in another, this time disguised as a 'Welsh Lady' beside a spinning wheel! The castle is open Easter through September, daily from 10.30 am to 5.30 pm; entry is £2/1.

The impressive *Manorbier Youth Hostel* (☎ 01834-871803) is 200m from the sandy beach at Skrinkle Haven, on the east side of the village; you can also camp here. It's open daily from mid-February through October. The nightly charge is £9.75/6.55 for adults/juniors and the hostel is 1½ miles south of Manorbier train station. Bus service No 358/9 runs daily from Manorbier to Tenby (20 minutes) and Pembroke (30 minutes).

Carew Castle & Tidal Mill

Looming romantically over the River Carew, with its wide, empty windows reflected in the still water, Carew Castle is an impressive sight. These rambling ruins began as an early 12th century castle, built by Gerald de Windsor, Henry I's constable of Pembroke. It was eventually converted into an Elizabethan country house. Abandoned in 1690, the castle is still home to a large number of bats, including the protected greater horseshoe bat. In summer a program of events is held, which includes battle re-enactments and open-air theatre performances.

On the causeway nearby is the Elizabethan Tidal Mill. It was used to grind corn until WWI and is one of three working tidal mills in Britain; it was restored using its original machinery. The rising tide fills the millpond and, when the tide falls, a head of water is released through a sluice. This turns the main millwheel, which in turn powers the machinery in the mill.

The castle and mill (☎ 01646-651782) are open Easter to October, daily from 10 am to 5 pm. Entry to the castle only is

£1.70/1.20; a combined ticket that includes the mill costs £2.50/1.60.

There's a fine **Celtic Cross**, dating from the 11th century, not far from the castle entrance. The nearby *Carew Inn* is a cosy pub, serving food (seafood pie £6.50) from noon to 2 pm.

Carew is 4 miles from Pembroke and 5 from Tenby. Bus No 361 runs between Tenby and Pembroke via Carew Cross about three times a day.

PEMBROKE
* pop 15,400　☎ 01646

Founded over 900 years ago, Pembroke's medieval street plan has survived along with its castle, the oldest in west Wales. Although there are other castles in the country that have more atmosphere, this one is certainly worth a visit, but Pembrokeshire's county town need not delay you for much more than half a day.

Just over 2 miles to the west of Pembroke is **Pembroke Dock**, where ferries leave for Rosslare (Ireland). The dock is on the south bank of the Milford Haven waterway, and on either side of this wide, natural harbour is some ugly development, including oil refineries and a power station. Plans to convert this power station to orimulsion (potentially far more polluting than crude oil) are causing considerable controversy.

Pembroke grew into an important trading centre after the castle was built in 1093. In 1154, local traders gained a monopoly in the area when an Act of Incorporation was passed, making it illegal to land goods in the Milford Haven waterway at anywhere other than Pembroke. The castle was home to the early Tudors, and the future King Henry VII was born here. During the Civil War, it was besieged by Cromwell for 48 days before it fell.

The Pembroke Visitors Centre and TIC (☎ 622388) is south of the castle on Commons Rd. It's open Easter through October, daily from 10 am to 5.30 pm; and on Tuesday, Thursday and Saturday in November, February and March. As well as the usual TIC services, there's an interpretive display about the town. It stocks a *Town Trail* walking guide.

At Pembroke Dock, there's a TIC (☎ 622246) in the restored Gun Tower, Front St.

Pembroke Castle

Pembroke's main attraction dominates the western end of town. Although a fort was established here in 1093 by Arnulph de Montgomery, the current buildings mainly date from the 12th and 13th centuries. The fort was in use until 1945, and was the home of the Earls of Pembroke for over 300 years.

The massive walls enclose a large area of grass and an ugly tarmac parade ground. Passages run from tower to tower, and a plaque in one marks the birthplace (in 1456) of Harry Tudor, who defeated Richard III to become Henry VII.

In the centre of the castle grounds stands a 23m-high tower. One hundred steps lead to the top and a glorious view, as long as you don't look in the direction of the Texaco oil refinery or the power station. If it's windy, the tower is closed.

The castle (☎ 681510) is open April to September, daily from 9.30 am to 6 pm; in March and October, daily until 5 pm; and in November, daily until 4 pm. Entry is £3/2.

Museum of the Home

The Museum of the Home (☎ 681200), just across the road from the Castle at 7 Westgate Hill, is worth visiting. It has a great collection of toys and games, including Roman die and the first snakes and ladders board, as well as cooking and eating implements and other objects of past eras, in a domestic setting. There are no labels, you're shown round by the enthusiastic owners. It's open May to September, Monday to Thursday from 11 am to 5 pm; £1.20/90p.

Places to Stay & Eat

Wisteria-clad *Beech House* (☎ 683740, 78 Main St) does B&B for £14 per person in very comfortable surroundings. With rather more character, *Merton Place House* (☎ 684796, 3 East Back, by Main St) is a good place, with B&B from £15/30 for singles/doubles.

High Noon Guest House (☎ 683736, Lower Lamphrey Rd) is comfortable and welcoming. With bathroom, rooms are £19/39.

The *Kings Arms Hotel* (☎ 683611, Main St) does B&B from £32.50/45 and is an excellent example of an old county town hotel. There's a good restaurant and the bar food is about the best in Pembroke. Steak pie and chips is £4.50.

Henry's Gift & Coffee Shop (☎ 622293) is the unmissable pink building near the Kings Arms. It's a good place for lunches and teas and has an excellent range of cakes. It's open Monday to Saturday from 9 am to 5 pm. There are several other cafés near the castle.

The *Watermans Arms*, just over the bridge and by the river, has lovely views of the castle, and the terrace is a good place for a drink. More serious drinking is done in the *Old Cross Saws (Main St)*.

Getting There & Away

Bus service No 359 operates every two hours, Monday to Saturday, from Haverfordwest to Pembroke (50 minutes, £1.95). Service No 358 also goes to Pembroke but takes longer. Both services go to Pembroke Dock and stop near Pembroke centre. First Cymru (☎ 01792-580580) service No 333 runs from Swansea to Pembroke Dock via Carmarthen and Tenby, from Monday to Saturday. The No 361 goes to Saundersfoot and Kilgetty and is operated by Silcox Motors (☎ 683143).

Pembroke is connected to the branch train line that runs through Tenby and terminates at Pembroke Dock.

Irish Ferries (☎ 0990-171717) runs two ferries a day to Rosslare in Ireland from Pembroke Dock.

HAVERFORDWEST (HWLFFORDD)

• pop 13,700   ☎ 01437

Although this market town is not within the borders of the park, it's the commercial centre of the area and a focal point for public transport.

The town was founded beside the Western Cleddau River in about 1110, as a Flemish settlement. Overpopulation in Flanders had forced some of the inhabitants to seek other land, and the Flemings who reached Wales were granted land around this river. A castle was built at the time the town was founded. The port remained important until the arrival of the railway in the mid-19th century.

There's not much to see in Haverfordwest today – the castle ruins are fairly plain. The **Castle Museum & Art Gallery** (☎ 763087) is in the outer ward of the castle.

The TIC (☎ 763110) is near the bus station on Old Bridge St. The National Park Information Centre (☎ 760136) is at 40 High St.

Places to Stay & Eat

Villa House (☎ 762977, St Thomas Green) has B&B from £15 per person. There are several other places in this area.

The excellent *Penrhlwllan* (☎ 769049, Well Lane, Prendergast) is a small B&B a short walk from the bus station. Rooms are £21 per person with bath, £18 without.

The *Castle Hotel* (☎ 769322, Castle Square) charges £37.50/50 for a single/double with bath. There's a good restaurant, and bar meals in the pub downstairs include boozy pie (£4.95). The *Pembroke Yeoman* (5 Goat St) serves ploughman's lunches for around £3. *The Fishguard Arms* (Old Bridge St) is a pleasant place for a drink.

Getting There & Away

Haverfordwest is 249 miles from London and about 7 from Milford Haven. There are buses from here to many parts of Pembrokeshire. Richards Brothers (☎ 01239-613756) No 412 runs from Haverfordwest via Fishguard to Cardigan (1¾ hours, £2.95), hourly Monday to Saturday, and twice on Sunday. Other services link Haverfordwest with St David's and Pembroke.

There are about seven trains a day from Swansea (fewer on Sunday). The journey takes about 1½ hours and costs £8.10.

ST BRIDES BAY (BAE SAIN FFRAID)

St Brides Bay is at the western end of the 'landsker', the invisible boundary between the Welsh and Anglicised parts of Pembrokeshire. The best beaches in Wales line this wide bay, and they're big enough to absorb the crowds of holiday-makers they attract at the height of the summer season. There are numerous camping grounds, and most of the farmers will be happy to let you use one of their fields for a couple of pounds; you must ask permission first.

Skomer, Skokholm & Grassholm Islands

These islands, lying off the coast on the south side of the bay, are nature reserves populated mainly by sea birds. The bird colonies are busiest between April and mid-August. It's possible to visit the islands and bookings can be made through any National Park Information Centre, or through Dale Sailing Company (☎ 01646-601636). Costs are from £12 to £20 per person.

Easiest to reach is Skomer, and from Martin's Haven there are departures daily except Monday, at 10 and 11 am and at noon. Boats return from about 3 pm, allowing several hours on the island. There's no shop or café so you need to bring a picnic.

Skokholm is famous for its Manx shearwaters and, with Skomer, provides shelter for 45% of the world's population of this bird. There are services to the island on Monday only, from early June to mid-August. The largest gannetry in the northern hemisphere is on Grassholm, a small island 10 miles offshore. There are boat trips (£20) on Monday and Friday in summer.

Broad Haven

This is a lively seaside village with several caravan parks and camping grounds. Also here is the modern *Broad Haven Youth Hostel* (☎ 01437-781688), which is open daily from mid-February through October; the nightly charge is £9.75/6.55 for adults/juniors.

Haven Sports (☎ 01437-781354), Marine Rd, rents mountain bikes from £3 per hour, and £16 per day.

Newgale

This tiny village is beside the biggest beach in the area, popular with both swimmers and surfers. At very low tides, the fossil remains of a prehistoric forest can be seen. You can hire surf skis, boards, boogey boards and wet suits from Newsurf Hire Centre (☎ 01437-721398) at Newgale Filling Station. Body boards cost £2 for one hour, £4 for four hours.

Places to Stay & Eat There are several excellent camping grounds. *Newgale Camp Site (☎ 01437-710253)* is across the road from the beach; it charges from £2.50 per person. There's a café and a store nearby.

Penycwm (Solva) Youth Hostel (☎ 01437-720959) is not at Solva but 1½ miles north of Newgale at Whitehouse. It's open from March to October and beds cost £8.80/5.95 for adults/juniors. There's also B&B at this hostel and there are excellent meals available. There's more accommodation at Solva, Simpsons Cross and Nolton.

Getting There & Away Newgale is a stop on Richards Brothers hourly service No 411/412 (only two journeys on Sunday) from Haverfordwest to St David's and Fishguard. The journey from Haverfordwest takes 25 minutes (£1.45) and it's 20 minutes from there to St David's.

ST DAVID'S (TY-DDEWI)
• pop 1450   ☎ 01437

There's something very special about St David's that even the crowds of holiday-makers in summer fail to extinguish. The magic must have worked for Dewi Sant (St David), who chose to found the first monastic community here in the 6th century only a short walk from where he was born. St David is dear to the hearts of the Welsh – he's their patron saint and his relics are kept in a casket in the cathedral.

Although St David's is no bigger than a village, with only one square and a few side roads leading off it, the cathedral's presence earns it the right to be called a city. As you approach the place you're unaware of the cathedral, which is just as its builders intended, for it was hidden in the depression below the square in the vain hope that passing Norse raiders might miss it. It's a magnificent sight, and if you visit only one cathedral in Wales, make it this one.

Information

The National Park Visitors Centre and TIC (☎ 720392) should now have moved farther up High St into its purpose-built exhibition and visitors centre; open daily.

The St David's Arts Festival, held in the first half of August, includes open-air Shakespeare plays in the Bishop's Palace that are well worth seeing. There's a music festival centred on the cathedral in late May.

St David's Cathedral

St David's Cathedral was built in the late 12th century, but there has been a church on this site since the 6th century. Norse pirates ransacked the site at least seven times, and various bishops added to the building between the 12th and 16th centuries. In the Middle Ages, two pilgrimages to the shrine of St David's were said to equal one to Rome – thus the cathedral has seen a constant stream of visitors.

Inside the cathedral, there's an atmosphere of great antiquity. The floor slopes 1m upwards and the pillars keel over drunkenly, the result of an earthquake in 1248. In the Norman nave is a superbly carved oak ceiling, installed in the 16th century. St David's shrine is by the north choir aisle. This cathedral is the only one in the UK in which the reigning monarch has a permanently reserved stall.

Services are held at 7.30 and 8 am during the week, and on some days at 6 pm. On Sunday there are services throughout the morning, and a choral evensong at 6 pm. Some services are held in Welsh. Entry to the cathedral (☎ 720517) is free, although a donation of £2/1 is suggested; there are also photography charges.

Bishop's Palace

Beside the cathedral are the extensive ruins of the Bishop's Palace (☎ 720517, Cadw), largely built by Henry de Gower between 1328 and 1347. Until the 16th century, this was a grand residence. It now provides a spectacular setting for the open-air plays held in the summer. Most of the walls still stand – the ruins are substantial and impressive, and there are two small exhibitions on the site.

Entrance to the palace is £1.70/1.20; it's open Easter to October, daily from 9.30 am to 6.30 pm, and in winter from 9.30 am to 4 pm daily (afternoon only on Sunday).

St Non's Bay

St David is said to have been born three-quarters of a mile south of the cathedral, beside the bay that was later named after his mother. A small spring is said to have emerged on the site just as he emerged into the world. The shrine still attracts pilgrims, and the water is believed to have curative powers. Also here are the 13th century ruins of St Non's Chapel, a modern chapel and a building used as a retreat.

Walks & Cycle Routes

Incorporating sections of the coast path, there are some excellent two to three-hour walks around St David's peninsula.

From St David's, you could walk south-west to the coast at Porthclais, follow the coast path to Caerfai Bay and return to St David's – a walk that will probably take less than two hours.

A wonderful 4½ hour walk takes you from St David's to Porthclais, where you pick up the coast path. Continue right around the western tip of the peninsula (opposite Ramsey Island) to St Justinian, where you follow the road back to St David's.

The quiet lanes that run parallel to the north coast of Pembrokeshire are perfect for cycling. Voyages of Discovery, on the square, can give advice about routes.

Other Things to See & Do

Two sea life centres battle it out for the customers. There was originally just one but the partners fell out and started competing. The bigger of the two is the **Oceanarium** (☎ 720453), 42 New St; entry is £3/1.80.

Thousand Islands Expeditions (☎ 721686), Cross Square, offers several boat tours. The Two Hour Spectacular on a water-jet boat is £20/10. Boats are booked here and depart from Whitesand Bay or St Justinian.

TYF Adventure Days (☎ 721611), 1 High St, does canoeing, sea-kayaking, climbing and surfing trips. Also here is Voyages of Discovery (☎ 721911), which runs the *Viking Voyager*, an inflatable craft fitted with underwater video cameras, enabling you to see the sea life and wrecks on a trip to Ramsey Island (see St David's to Fishguard later in this chapter). Charges are £12/7.

St David's Scuba Diving Centre (☎ 721788), Caerfai Bay Rd, is a PADI and BSAC diving school.

Places to Stay

Hostel *St David's Youth Hostel* (☎ 720345) is 1½ miles north-west of St David's, near Whitesand Bay. It's open daily in July and August, and daily except Thursday between May and September. The charge is £6.50/4.45 for adults/juniors.

Camping Closest to St David's is *Caerfai Farm Camp Site* (☎ 720548), a 20 minute walk away. It's 400m from the beach and charges from £3.

The *Hendre Eynon Caravan & Camping Site* (☎ 720474) is 2 miles north-east of St David's, situated between the Dowrog Common Nature Reserve and the coastal path, and is open from May to September.

You can also camp at *Pencarnan Farm Caravan & Camping Site* (☎ 720324, Porthsele) 2 miles from St David's, and at *Lleithyr Farm* (☎ 720245, near Whitesand Bay).

B&Bs & Hotels *Ty Olaf* (☎ 720885, Mount Gardens) is an excellent place offering very comfortable B&B from £14 (winter) to £16 (summer) per person.*Siop y Dywfrwr (☎ 720333, 43 Nun St)* is a friendly B&B above a shop selling Welsh and Celtic books. Rooms are £16.50 per person, £18.50 with bath.

The *Old Cross Hotel (☎ 720387)* is in Cross Square, which is set back from the old market square. All rooms have a bathroom, and there's a restaurant and bar. B&B costs £44/76 for singles/doubles (£36/66 outside the summer season).

The excellent *Ramsey House (☎ 720321, Lower Moor)*, half a mile from the cathedral, has seven rooms and is open all year. During the high season it does only dinner, bed & breakfast deals at £43 per person. Out of season, B&B costs from £25.

Places to Eat

There are several teashops to choose from. The *Sampler Coffee Shop (Nun St)* offers light lunches and teas. Its Pembrokeshire clotted cream tea includes bara brith, a scone and tea for £3.

Cartref Restaurant (☎ 720422, Cross Square) is built round a 17th century stone cottage. Main dishes range from £2.70 to £12. *Dyfed Café (☎ 720250)*, also in the square, serves lunches and suppers and also has a fish and chip shop if you want takeaway.

For an upmarket meal, *Morgan's Brasserie (☎ 720508, 20 Nun St)* does excellent seafood and has an imaginative Welsh menu. Main dishes, including wild boar and sea trout, cost from £9 to £14.

The *Farmer's Arms (Goat St)* is the place to drink. It has excellent bar meals and there's a pleasant terrace.

For a pricey, high-calorie snack, you can't miss *Chapel Chocolates*, on the way down to the cathedral.

Getting There & Away

Bus service No 411/412 goes hourly from Haverfordwest, Monday to Saturday, and twice daily on Sunday in summer (45 minutes, £1.85), continuing to Fishguard.

Getting Around

Voyages of Discovery (☎ 721911), on the square, rents bikes for £10 per day.

ST DAVID'S TO FISHGUARD

The coast from St David's to Fishguard is far less touristy than the southern part of Pembrokeshire. The coves and beaches, if they're accessible at all, are reached by tiny, winding lanes and footpaths. If you're only going to walk part of the Pembrokeshire Coast Path, this would be an excellent section to tackle.

Two miles north of St David's is **Whitesand Bay**, one of the finest beaches in Wales, and popular with surfers. It can get quite crowded but there's an excellent secluded beach at **Porthmelgan**, a 15 minute walk north.

Lying off St David's Head, **Ramsey Island** is an RSPB reserve with beautiful cliff scenery and varied bird life, which includes a healthy population of choughs. Ramsey Island Pleasure Cruises (☎ 01437-720285) operates cruises around the island from April to September. They depart daily from St Justinian (3 miles from St David's), at around 10 am and return at 3.30 pm; tickets are £10/6. If you're there between late August and mid-November, you may see seal pups. Thousand Islands Expeditions (see the St David's section) does trips that land on the island, but you'll probably see more wildlife from the boat.

Porthgain is an interesting old coastal village, a former brickworks and slate centre. People now come here primarily to eat and drink. In an age of theme-pubs, the *Sloop Inn* is famous for its old-fashioned ordinariness. It's a fantastic place for a pint and there are interesting photos showing what the village was like in its industrial heyday. There are good pub meals – the smoked bacon and melted cheese baguette (£3) is excellent. Across the car park there's the more upmarket *Harbour Lights Restaurant (☎ 01348-831549)*; three courses for £23.

On the route between St David's and Fishguard are two well-located hostels, and numerous farmhouse B&Bs. *Trevine Youth Hostel* (☎ *01348-831414*) is in the old school in the centre of **Trevine**, half a mile from the sea. It's 11 miles along the coast path from Whitesand Bay. Also in the village is the *Old Court House* (☎ *01348-837095*), a vegetarian guesthouse and walking holiday centre. There's B&B for £19.50 per person and delicious veggie dinners for £12.50.

Eight miles further east from Trevine along the path is *Pwll Deri Youth Hostel* (☎ *01348-891233*), in a spectacular location overlooking the bay.

FISHGUARD (ABERGWAUN)
• pop 3200   ☎ 01348

Ferry ports tend to be ugly, depressing places, but Fishguard stands out as an exception to the rule. It's on a beautiful bay, and the old part of town (Lower Fishguard) was the location for the 1971 film version of *Under Milk Wood*, which starred Burton and Elizabeth Taylor.

In February 1797, a band of French mercenaries and convicts landed at Carregwastad Point near Fishguard and conducted a series of undisciplined raids on houses in the Pen Caer area.

During one particular raid, the invaders came upon large stocks of Portuguese wine, which proved their undoing. With the invaders in a state of drunkenness, the local people were soon able to round them up. Appropriately, the surrender was signed in the Royal Oak Inn.

In 1997, the town commemorated the bicentenary of the last invasion of Britain with a 30m tapestry telling the story of the invasion. The tapestry is now on display at St Mary's Town Hall (☎ 874997), open daily from 10 am to 5 pm (2 to 5 pm on Sunday); entry is £1.20/50p.

Orientation & Information
The train station and harbour (for Stena Line ferries to Rosslare, Ireland) are at Goodwick, a 20 minute walk down the hill from Fishguard proper. To the east, the road winds round the picturesque harbour of Lower Fishguard.

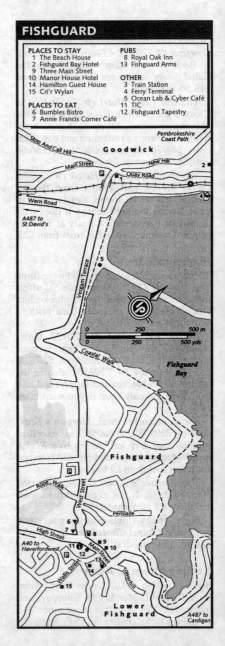

FISHGUARD

PLACES TO STAY
1 The Beach House
2 Fishguard Bay Hotel
9 Three Main Street
10 Manor House Hotel
14 Hamilton Guest House
15 Cn'r Wylan

PLACES TO EAT
6 Bumbles Bistro
7 Annie Francis Corner Café

PUBS
8 Royal Oak Inn
13 Fishguard Arms

OTHER
3 Train Station
4 Ferry Terminal
5 Ocean Lab & Cyber Café
11 TIC
12 Fishguard Tapestry

Open daily, the TIC (☎ 873484) is in the Town Hall on Market Square.

In late July, Fishguard stages a music festival, which includes classical and jazz musicians, some from abroad. For information, phone the festival office (☎ 873612).

You can send and collect your email at Ocean Lab's Cyber Café (☎ 874737), by the Watersports Leisure Centre, between Fishguard and Goodwick.

Places to Stay

Hamilton Guest House & Backpackers Lodge (☎ 874797, 21 Hamilton St) is near the TIC in Fishguard. It's a very friendly place, open 24 hours, with 20 beds in small dormitories for around £9 per person. There's a kitchen for self-caterers, a TV lounge and laundry. The nearest *HI hostel* is at Pwll Deri, 4 miles west of Goodwick.

You can camp at *Fishguard Bay Caravan Park* (☎ 811415), 6 miles to the east, between Fishguard and Newport on the headland at Dinas Cross. It's well situated for the coastal path, and open from March to January; £4 for a tent and one person.

In Goodwick, *The Beach House* (☎ 872085) is just off Quay Rd above the train line – it overlooks the bay and is a five minute walk from the ferry. It's remarkably welcoming given the constant flow of visitors – B&B is around £15 per person.

There are several other B&Bs in this area, and also the large *Fishguard Bay Hotel* (☎ 873571), formerly the Great Western Railways Hotel. Single/double rooms with bath cost £44/65.

The excellent *Gifach Goch Farmhouse* (☎ 873871) is 2 miles north of Fishguard on the road to Cardigan – the Cardigan bus stops at its gate. The farmhouse has six rooms and a lovely garden and offers B&B for £23; it's open from March to November.

Back in Fishguard, there's comfortable B&B at *Cri'r Wylan* (☎ 873398, Penwallis), a short walk from the TIC. The charge is from £16 per person and it's a small place. On Main St, *Manor House Hotel* (☎ 873260) has sea views from the back

rooms. B&B is from around £22 per person, £26 for a room with a view.

Nearby *Three Main Street* (☎ 874275) is recommended. It has only three doubles, all with bath, for £30 per person. There's a superb restaurant here.

Places to Eat

Annie Francis Corner Café, on the square, is cheap and cheerful. Nearby on West St is *Bumbles Bistro*, where you can get cream teas, light lunches, and, in the summer, dinner from 6 to 10 pm.

The famous *Royal Oak Inn* (☎ 872514) is on the square, and full of invasion memorabilia. The *Fishguard Arms (Main St)* is where the serious drinking is done.

There's a good restaurant at *Manor House Hotel* (see Places to Stay). *Three Main Street* (☎ 874275) is one of the best restaurants in South Wales. Set dinners are £21 for two courses, £25 for three. You'll probably need to book.

Getting There & Away

Richards Brothers (☎ 01239-820751) operates an hourly service, Monday to Saturday, from Haverfordwest (45 minutes, £1.90). It also runs buses to St David's and Cardigan.

Fishguard is the northern terminus of a branch of the train line that crosses South Wales. Fishguard to London costs £49.50 (Super Saver single).

Stena Line (☎ 0990-707070) runs a ferry and catamaran several times a day to Rosslare, Ireland.

Getting Around

Bus service No 410 runs on a regular circuit from Fishguard Square to Goodwick Square, Fishguard Harbour and back to Fishguard Square; it operates Monday to Saturday, every half hour.

NEWPORT (TREFDRAETH)

- pop 1200   ☎ 01239

This small town grew up around the castle, and the rocky outcrop **Carn Ingli**, which dominates the town and beach. The castle is Norman but there's evidence of much earlier settlements in the area. Newport makes a very pleasant base for walks along the wild coast or into the Preseli Hills to the south. It's also a pleasant walk up Carn Ingli, from where there are great views over the bay. There are several beaches – **Parrog**, close to the town, and the better **Newport Sands**, across the river and around the bay.

The National Park Visitors Centre (☎ 820912), Bank Cottages, Long St, is open Monday to Saturday. Bikes can be hired for £12 per day from Newport Mountain Bikes (☎ 820008) at Llysmeddyg Guest House, East St.

Places to Stay & Eat

The recently established *Newport Youth Hostel (☎ 820080, Lower St Mary's St)* is open daily except Wednesday and Thursday from April to June and September and October, and daily in July and August. The charge is £8/5.40 for adults/juniors.

Two miles from Newport, on the Cilgwyn road, is *Brithdir Mawr (☎ 820164)*, where bunkhouse beds cost from £4. *Morawelon Caravan & Camping Park (☎ 820565)* is west of Newport at Parrog Beach.

There's B&B from £16 at *2 Springhill (☎ 820626, Parrog Rd)*, 400m from the coastal path, and with good sea views. It's open year-round.

On the outskirts of Newport, and 100m from the coast path, is the excellent *Grove Park Guesthouse (☎ 820122, Pen-y-Bant)*. Charges are around £20 per person for B&B.

There are several places you could try for accommodation and also for a meal in East St. The *Golden Lion Hotel (☎ 820321)* does B&B from £20/35 for singles/doubles and it has a bar, and restaurant. *Cnapan Country House (☎ 820575)* has five rooms for £26 per person, and is open from March to January. It also has a good restaurant (closed on Tuesday).

Llysmeddyg Guest House (☎ 820008, East St) is a comfortable, efficiently run B&B in a most attractive building. The cost is £19 per person and you can rent bikes here.

The *Llwyngwair Arms (☎ 820267, East St)* is the best pub. It also has a restaurant

specialising in Indian food (curries from £5.50) and takeaways.

Ffronlas Café, (Market St), does excellent lunches – home-made pâtés, soups and salads. Bring your own wine from the Spar shop opposite. There are herbal teas, coffees, scones and cakes. It's open Tuesday to Saturday from 10 am to 5 pm.

Getting There & Away

Newport is 7 miles from Fishguard and 12 from Cardigan.

Richards Brothers (☎ 820751) operates an hourly service (No 412) to Haverfordwest (1¼ hours, £2.30) and Cardigan (30 minutes, £1.90). The service to Haverfordwest runs via Fishguard.

AROUND NEWPORT
Nevern

Situated 2 miles east of Newport, this little village, with its overgrown castle and the **Church of St Brynach**, makes an interesting excursion. St Brynach was a 5th century Irish holy man who lived in a hut on Carn Ingli, above Newport.

The church is best known for its carved stones. The Maglocunus Stone is thought to date from the 5th century and has an inscription in ogham (an ancient Celtic script) and Latin. In the idyllic churchyard are two more stones, one with another ogham inscription, and the other one of the most impressive Celtic crosses in Wales, dating from the 10th century. Some of the gravestones are interesting, and one of the yew trees is known as the 'bleeding yew', for the blood-like red sap that oozes from it.

Castell Henllys

Located 2 miles south-east of Nevern, this site was originally occupied 2500 years ago and has now been reborn as the **Castell Henllys Iron Age Settlement**.

Some of the buildings – roundhouses, animal pens, a smithy and a grain store – have been partially reconstructed. The settlement is open March through October, daily from 10 am to 5 pm; tickets are £2.50/1.60.

To get there by bus, take the hourly service (No 412) from Newport towards Cardigan. Get off at the Melina Rd stop and it's a half-mile walk.

Pentre Ifan

Pentre Ifan is a 4500-year-old cromlech in a remote site, with views across to the sea –

to the south stretch the Preseli Hills. Said to be the best-preserved Neolithic burial chamber in Wales; the 5m-high capstone is supported by 2m-high boulders. Situated 2 miles south of Nevern, Pentre Ifan is accessible by taking the bus to the same stop for Castell Henllys and then walking south down the side roads for a mile.

Mid Wales

The majority of visitors to this part of Wales head for the grass-capped mountains of the Brecon Beacons National Park, leaving the quiet valleys of Mid Wales to the Welsh.

This is unspoilt walking country – farming land interspersed with bare, rolling hills and small lakes. The 120 mile Glyndŵr's Way is a walking trail that visits the Welsh hero's associated sites, between Knighton (on Offa's Dyke Path) and Welshpool via Machynlleth.

Aberystwyth, the only place of any size on the west coast, is a remarkably pleasant university town with good transport connections. Steam trains run through the Vale of Rheidol to Devil's Bridge, with spectacular views of the nearby waterfalls. Several of Wales' other Great Little Trains are found in Mid Wales.

Machynlleth is an attractive market town that makes a good base for exploring the region. On the outskirts of the town, the Centre for Alternative Technology experiments with green living in an interesting working community that welcomes visitors.

Brecon Beacons National Park

Formed in 1957, Parc Cenedlaethol Bannau Brycheiniog covers 522 sq miles of high, grassy ridges, including the highest mountains in southern Britain, interspersed with wooded valleys. Most of the park is privately owned and the slopes provide grazing for thousands of sheep. Pen-y-Fan, at 886m (2906 feet) the highest point, and the 3200 hectares surrounding it are in the hands of the NT.

Although they're referred to as mountains, the Brecon Beacons are hardly the Himalaya, and the countryside is less dramatic than Snowdonia to the north. Nevertheless, these bare escarpments are undeniably beautiful, rising in a series of

HIGHLIGHTS

- Pony trekking in the Brecon Beacons
- Brecon Jazz Festival
- Browsing for books in Hay-on-Wye
- Centre for Alternative Technology, Machynlleth
- Vale of Rheidol Steam Railway from Aberystwyth to Devil's Bridge

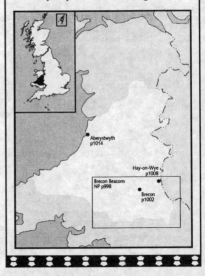

great, green waves above the plains to the north and the former mining valleys to the south. From their crests, hikers are rewarded with spectacular views.

Two long paths pass through the park: Offa's Dyke Path, along the eastern border, and the Taff Trail, south from Brecon. Most people come here to walk, but the region offers numerous other outdoor activities. Lôn Las Cymru, the Welsh National Cycle Route, passes through the park on quiet minor roads and cycling paths, from Cardiff to Brecon (77 miles), and on through Glasbury and Builth Wells.

This is perfect pony trekking country, and you can also rent canoes or narrowboats on the Monmouthshire & Brecon Canal, go fishing, mountaineering or hang-gliding. To the south of the park, cavers are attracted to some of the deepest black holes in Britain.

On the northern edge, the eccentric town of Hay-on-Wye, where almost every other shop sells second-hand books, is well worth a visit. Just south of the park at Blaenavon is the Big Pit Mining Museum, and the guided tours which venture deep into this old coal mine are highly recommended. Just north of Merthyr Tydfil, vintage steam locos still operate on a short section of the Brecon Mountain Railway.

Since the park is only 30 miles from the M4 bridges over the River Severn, it's easily accessible from London and the south of England. In spite of this, if you avoid the popular central Brecon Beacons area in summer, it can be far less crowded than Snowdonia.

ORIENTATION

The park is a mere 15 miles from north to south and 45 miles from west to east, yet it comprises four mountain ranges and a variety of terrain.

In the centre is the Brecon Beacons, the range that gives the park its name; the high ridges here form the focal point for hikers. To the west is Fforest Fawr, an area of hills, valleys and, to the south, waterfalls. Farther west is the isolated Black Mountain. In the east are the confusingly named Black Mountains (plural), running north to south between Hay-on-Wye and Abergavenny.

The town of Brecon is the main urban centre within the park's boundaries and it makes a good base, although the nearest train stations are at Abergavenny and Merthyr Tydfil. The Monmouthshire & Brecon Canal follows the valley of the River Usk from Brecon through Abergavenny, which is a good base for the eastern area of the park. Hay-on-Wye, on the northern edge, also has a wide range of accommodation.

INFORMATION

The National Park Visitors Centre (☎ 01874-623366) is in open countryside near Libanus, 5 miles south-west of Brecon off the A470. It's open daily, except Christmas Day, from 9.15 am, closing at 6 pm in July and August, 4.30 pm in winter and 5 pm at other times. There's also a gift shop and café here.

The National Park Information Centres at Brecon (☎ 01874-623156) and Abergavenny (☎ 01873-853254) may be more convenient. Although they're open only from April to October, they're in the same buildings as the TICs, which are open year-round. The TICs also have information about the park.

There's an information centre at Llandovery (☎ 01550-720693), open from April to September, and at Pen-y-cae (☎ 01639-730395, Craig-y-nos Country Park), open in the summer.

A large range of publications and maps is on sale at these information centres and at TICs in the area. Harveys Superwalker maps cover the park in two 1:25,000 sheets. The park's walking booklets cover the main areas in enough detail for most people spending a few days here. The park even has the *Aircraft Crashes in the National Park* guide. Leaflets describing walks and other activities are listed in the following sections.

Check the weather forecast before setting out on a mountain hike. Take a sweater and waterproof clothing with you, even if it's a sunny day when you start, and be prepared to turn back if the mist comes down. Whatever the weather, it can be very windy on the exposed ridges. Bring something to eat with you, but resist the temptation to share it with the sheep or ponies, especially in unfenced areas, as they may become attracted to cars on the roads and cause accidents.

WALKS & CYCLE ROUTES

There's an almost infinite number of walks in the park, ranging from a strenuous mountain climb to a gentle stroll along the canal towpath.

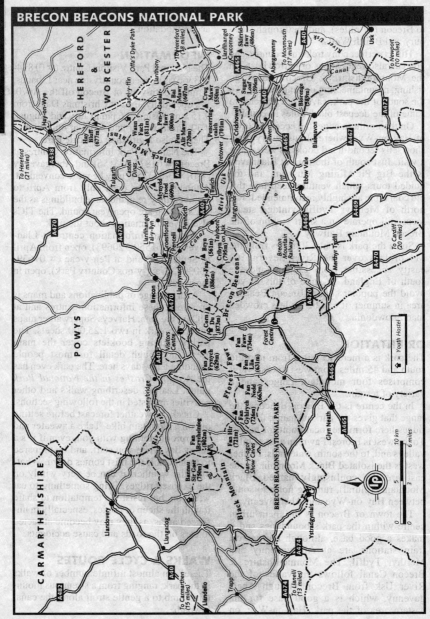

BRECON BEACONS NATIONAL PARK

= Youth Hostel

In summer, traffic on the A-roads can make cycling hazardous, so stick to smaller roads. The Lôn Las Cymru/Taff Trail is the most interesting cycle route between Cardiff and Brecon.

Cycle hire is available in some towns (see Brecon, Abergavenny, Hay-on-Wye, Llanwrtyd Wells, Aberystwyth). Bicycle Beano (☎ 01982-560471) organises cycle camping holidays, with vegetarian wholefood catering. Mountain Bike Guided Treks & Tours (☎ 01874-658242) offers half-day, day and weekend tours, and can arrange accommodation.

Brecon Beacons

The classic walk in the park is to the top of the highest of these ridges, Pen-y-Fan, but this area gets crowded in the summer and at weekends. The many routes up are covered in the leaflet *Walks in the Brecon Beacons Area*.

The shortest trail is from the car park at Pont ar Daf or from the Storey Arms, a mile north (and no longer a pub). They're both on the bus route along the A470 between Brecon and Merthyr Tydfil. From here it's a 2½ hour hike to the top and back. If you're starting from the Llwyn-y-Celyn Youth Hostel, allow three hours for the return trip. Walking from Brecon it will take five to six hours; follow the side road out of town to the trailhead at Cwm Gwdi.

Directly below Pen-y-Fan, in the natural amphitheatre formed 10,000 years ago during the last Ice Age, there are less strenuous walks around the small lake with the tongue-twisting name of Llyn-cwm-Llwch (pronounced hlin-coom-hlooch).

Taff Trail & Lôn Las Cymru

Linking canal towpaths, disused railways and paths, the 77 mile trail between Cardiff and Brecon forms the first section of the Lôn Las Cymru, the Welsh National Cycle Route that runs across the country to Anglesey. From Cardiff the waymarked route follows the River Taff north via Castell Coch, the market town of Pontypridd, Merthyr Tydfil, the Pontsticill Reservoir and Talybont-on-Usk to the canal at Pencelli,

where there's a choice of routes into Brecon. You can either continue along the canal or follow the side road via Llanfrynach.

Usk Valley

The least demanding walks in the park are along the towpath of the Monmouthshire & Brecon Canal, which follows the valley of the River Usk. It's possible to walk the full 33 mile length of the canal between Brecon and Pontypool. Crickhowell, just north of the canal, would make an excellent overnight stop but there are numerous other villages along the route offering accommodation in B&Bs or pubs. Most walkers just hike the 20 mile Abergavenny to Brecon section.

Black Mountains

Some of the best views on the entire 168 mile length of Offa's Dyke Path are from the 17 mile section that runs through the Black Mountains from Pandy to Hay-on-Wye. Pandy is on the A465, on the bus route between Abergavenny and Hereford. The route is along a high, exposed grassy ridge that can be very windy.

It's definitely worth dropping down to visit the ruins of Llanthony Priory, where the remaining buildings now house a pub and a delightfully atmospheric hotel. Farther north up this valley is the Capel-y-ffin Youth Hostel. As a less strenuous alternative to walking along the ridge, you could follow the River Honddu from Llanfihangel, lower down in the valley. TICs stock the two leaflets that cover walks in the north and south parts of this area.

The highest point in the Black Mountains is Waun Fach (811m, 2660 feet). If you've got a car, it's best to drive via Patrishow (an interesting 13th century church in an idyllic location) to the end of the track in the Mynydd Du Forest. Follow the old railway track up to Grwyne Fawr Reservoir, where a path runs up Waun Fach. Alternatively, the peak can be reached by climbing from Llanbedr up to the ridge that runs north via Pen-y-Gadair-fawr.

Around Abergavenny

There are rewarding walks up any of the three hills near Abergavenny, described in detail in *Thirty Walks in the South Black Mountains & the Abergavenny Area*, available from the TIC.

Three miles to the north is the cone-shaped Sugar Loaf (596m, 1955 feet). It's a steep climb to the top. A couple of miles south of the town is Blorenge (559m, 1834 feet), also popular as a launching pad for hang-gliders. Three miles north-east of Abergavenny is Skirrid-fawr (486m, 1594 feet); from the top there are good views of Sugar Loaf, the Usk Valley and the Black Mountains.

Fforest Fawr & Waterfall Walks

There is a great variety of scenery in this area, which was once a Norman hunting ground. In the north there are mountain walks in terrain similar to that of the Brecon Beacons.

The youth hostel at Ystradfellte makes a good base, and along the rivers and streams to the south there are a number of attractive waterfalls in this wooded area. The most attractive is Sgwd-yr-eira (the spout of snow), where you can actually view the falls from behind the water. It's an easy 2 mile walk south of Ystradfellte, on the River Hepste. There are other falls at Ponteddfechan and Coelbren. Look out for the leaflet on *Waterfall Walks* at the TICs.

Black Mountain

It's not surprising to find another Black Mountain in this range – when the weather is bad, any bare piece of high ground in the Brecon Beacons deserves the name. This western section of the park contains the wildest, least visited walking country. The highest point, Fan Brycheiniog (802m, 2630 feet), can be reached from the youth hostel at Llanddeusant or along a path that leads off the side road just north of the Dan-yr-ogof Show Caves.

OTHER ACTIVITIES

The Talybont Venture Centre (☎ 01874-676458) in Talybont-on-Usk, 5 miles south-east of Brecon, offers a range of activities, including abseiling, caving, rock climbing, mountain biking and orienteering.

For **cavers**, there are several limestone cave systems in the south of the park, including some of the longest and deepest in Britain. Pick up a copy of the leaflet *Caving* from TICs and, unless you know what you're doing, contact one of the outdoor activity centres (such as Talybont Venture Centre). If a subterranean sound and light show with stalagmites illuminated in pretty colours is more your idea of going underground, the Dan-yr-ogof Show Caves are in the south-west area of the park.

Gliders are available for hire from the Black Mountains Gliding Club (☎ 01874-711463), near Talgarth, which offers introductory courses. The Welsh Hang Gliding Centre (☎ 01873-832100), Bryn Bach Park, Merthyr Rd, Tredegar, offers one-day courses in hang-gliding for £60.

There are good **fishing** rivers in this area. Just to the north of the park, and flowing through Hay-on-Wye, the River Wye is reputed to be the finest salmon river south of the border with Scotland. In the park, the River Usk is among the best waters in Wales for brown trout and salmon fishing. Many of the reservoirs, including the Usk and the Talybont, are stocked with trout and there's coarse fishing in the canal and Llangorse Lake. You'll need a permit from the owner of the fishing rights as well as a Water/Environment Agency licence.

Pony Trekking & Horse Riding

The open hillsides make this ideal pony trekking country and there are numerous trekking centres. Charges are from £11 to £16 for two hours, £23 for a full day, and many of the centres are on farms which also offer B&B accommodation. Places to try include the Grange Pony Trekking Centre (☎ 01873-890215) at Capel-y-ffin, and Llangorse Riding Centre (☎ 01874-658272) near Brecon.

Llangorse Riding Centre will also cater to serious riders interested in a superior mount, as will Cwmfforest Riding Centre (☎ 01874-711398) at Talgarth. Cwmfforest offers a range of riding holidays, including the six day Trans Wales Trail, with all food and accommodation, for £695.

Canal Cruising

The Monmouthshire & Brecon Canal links Brecon with Pontypool in Gwent. There are only six locks along its 33 mile length, and there's one lock-free section of 22 miles. Built for the iron industry in the early 19th century, it fell into disuse in the 1930s but has now been restored and opened to recreational traffic.

Traditional narrowboats can be hired by the hour, day or week from Cambrian Cruisers (☎ 01874-665315), Ty Newydd, Pencelli, near Brecon. Dragonfly Cruises (☎ 0831-685222), in Brecon, operates 2½ hour cruises on Wednesday, Thursday, Saturday and Sunday at noon and 3 pm, for £5/3. The 1½ hour cruises (£3.25/2.50) run by Water Folk (☎ 01874-665382), Old Storehouse, Llanfrynach, are more traditional, since the boats are horse-drawn.

PLACES TO STAY & EAT

There are five YHA youth hostels in the national park – Ty'n-y-Caeau (2½ miles from Brecon), Llwyn-y-Celyn (by the A470 Merthyr Tydfil to Brecon road), Capel-y-ffin (8 miles south of Hay-on-Wye, and attached to a pony trekking centre), Ystradfellte (in the waterfall and caving district) and isolated Llanddeusant below the Black Mountain.

There are 15 independent bunkhouses in the area. Some are mentioned here, but contact TICs or the Association of Bunkhouse Operators (☎ 07071-780259) for the full list.

With the permission of the farmer or landowner, it's possible to camp almost anywhere in the park, but not on NT land. TICs have lists of camping grounds with full facilities.

There's a good range of B&Bs and hotels in and around the main centres of Brecon, Abergavenny and Hay-on-Wye, as well as in the villages along the Usk Valley. Some hotels offer all-inclusive activity holidays, including fishing or riding.

GETTING THERE & AWAY

It takes three to four hours to drive to the Brecon Beacons from London, via the M4 over the River Severn and along the A4024 from Newport.

Stagecoach Red & White (☎ 01633-266336) buses run between Cardiff, Merthyr Tydfil and Abergavenny; Brecon, Hay-on-Wye and Hereford; and Brecon, Abergavenny, Pontypool and Newport. First Cymru (☎ 01792-580580) runs buses between Swansea and Brecon.

There are rail services to Abergavenny (via Newport) and Merthyr Tydfil (via Cardiff) but not to Brecon. Phone ☎ 0345-484950 for information.

Between smaller villages, public transport is severely limited. Distances are not great, however, and if you're not prepared to walk it's worth considering a taxi.

Explore the Brecon Beacons is a useful free guide available from TICs. It lists bus and train timetables plus walks that can be linked to public transport routes.

BRECON (ABERHONDDU)
* pop 7000   ☎ 01874

The principal centre in the park is the attractive, historic market town of Brecon. It makes an excellent base for exploring the area, and has a good range of accommodation for all budgets, including a youth hostel just outside the town, and plenty of places to eat.

The Celtic hill forts of Pen-y-Crug and Slwch attest to the fact that the area was occupied long before the Romans arrived in 75 AD. The remains of their camp at Y Gaer, 3 miles west of the town, can be visited. It was not until Norman times that Brecon began to grow. The local Welsh chieftain was overthrown by Bernard de Newmarch, the Norman lord who built the castle and church.

This sober, grey-stoned town seems an unlikely venue for a music festival of any kind, but on one weekend in mid-August, multicoloured awnings and flags transform the place for the Brecon Jazz Festival. This has become one of Europe's leading jazz festivals and it attracts thousands for what is essentially one long party. One famous jazz

MID WALES

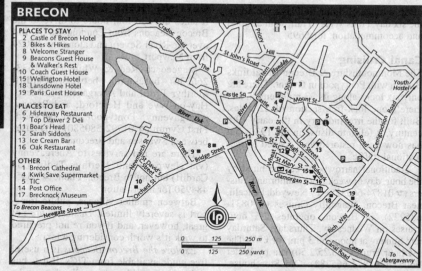

BRECON

PLACES TO STAY
2 Castle of Brecon Hotel
3 Bikes & Hikes
8 Welcome Stranger
9 Beacons Guest House
   & Walker's Rest
10 Coach Guest House
15 Wellington Hotel
18 Lansdowne Hotel
19 Paris Guest House

PLACES TO EAT
6 Hideaway Restaurant
7 Top Drawer 2 Deli
11 Boar's Head
12 Sarah Siddons
13 Ice Cream Bar
16 Oak Restaurant

OTHER
1 Brecon Cathedral
4 Kwik Save Supermarket
5 TIC
14 Post Office
17 Brecknock Museum

musician you may see in town is George Melly, who has a house nearby.

Orientation

Brecon is a compact town with everything within walking distance. There's no train or bus station – most buses leave and arrive at the Bulwark in the centre, close to the TIC. B&Bs are in two groups: around the Watton Rd and across Bridge St in Llan Faes, the western area of Brecon.

Information

The TIC (☎ 622485), open daily from 10 am to 6 pm, is in the Cattle Market car park. The National Park Information Centre (☎ 623156) shares the same office and is open daily from Easter to October – at other times, the TIC can help with information. A good range of books, maps and other information is available.

For information on the Jazz Festival contact the festival office (☎ 625557). Some performances are hosted in the new Theatr Brycheiniog (☎ 611622), by the canal on Canal Rd.

Mountain bikes can be rented from Bikes & Hikes (see Places to Stay). Rates are £9/13 for a half/full day, and there are tandems for £15/20.

Brecon Cathedral

Built in the 11th century above the River Honddu in the north of Brecon, on the site of an earlier church, all that remains of the Norman building is parts of the walls of the nave. The tower, choir and transepts date from the 13th century. In the mid 1860s the church was restored by Sir Gilbert Scott. In the west end of the nave is a stone cresset (an ancient lighting device), the only one that exists in Wales. The 30 cups each held oil to illuminate the church lamps.

There's an exhibition about the cathedral in the heritage centre (☎ 625222), housed in the restored tithe barn in Cathedral Close. A £1 donation is requested from visitors.

Brecknock Museum

This is one of the more interesting museums of the old county of Brecknockshire. Brecon was the county town, but the district is now absorbed into Powys.

The museum has an old dugout canoe found in Llangorse Lake, a re-created Welsh kitchen, a complete Victorian assize court and the town stocks. There's also a collection of that peculiar Welsh utensil (now reborn as a tourist souvenir), the lovespoon. The museum is open Monday to Saturday from 10 am to 5 pm; admission is 50p.

Walks
For information on walks and other activities see Information under Brecon Beacons National Park earlier. The Monmouthshire & Brecon Canal and the Taff Trail both start in Brecon.

Places to Stay
Camping *Brynich Caravan Park* (☎ 623325) is 2½ miles east of Brecon and costs from £4 per person.

During the jazz festival, open areas around the town are turned into temporary camping grounds.

Hostel The *Ty'n-y-Caeau Youth Hostel* (☎ 665270) is in a large country house near the caravan park. Open from April to October, it's closed on Sunday except on bank holiday weekends and the middle of summer; phone for other opening days. The nightly charge is £8/5.40.

There are several bunkhouses in the area, all charging £7.50 to £9. Under a mile from Brecon is *Canal Barn* (☎ 625361, *Ty Camlas, Canal Bank*). Three miles southeast of Brecon, there's *The Held* (☎ 624646, *Cantref*). There's more bunkhouse accommodation, and a riding centre, at *Upper Cantref Farm* (☎ 665223).

B&Bs & Hotels The *Beacons Guest House* (☎ 623339, 16 Bridge St) has a large range of rooms, with singles/doubles from £25/36. The *Walker's Rest* (☎ 625993, 18 Bridge St) charges around £15 per person. Nearby is *Welcome Stranger* (☎ 622188, 7 Bridge St), a friendly B&B charging around £16 per person. There's also a restaurant

here. *Bikes & Hikes* (☎ 610071, 10 The Struet) does B&B for £15 per person.

The *Coach Guest House* (☎ 623803, Orchard St) is a highly commended B&B with doubles for £40, with bathroom. Smokers are not welcome.

Along the Watton, the *Paris Guest House* (☎ 624205), at No 28, has rooms for £15/30. Rooms with bath are from £27.50/47.50 at the *Lansdowne Hotel* (☎ 623321) at No 39, and there are several other hotels and B&Bs in the Watton area.

Just off the Watton, peacefully located on the canal, there's *Ty Gardd* (☎ 623464) where rooms cost £16/32 or £38 for the double with bath.

The *Wellington Hotel* (☎ 625225) is right in the centre of town on the Bulwark. It's a comfortable place with a good range of facilities including a pub, coffee shop and wine bar. B&B is £35/55.

The only part of the Norman castle that you can visit has been incorporated into the *Castle of Brecon Hotel* (☎ 624611), although there's not much left of the old building. Rooms in the main hotel are £49/64, and in the lodge nearby they're £40/54, all with bath or shower.

The *Griffin Inn* (☎ 754241) at Llyswen (about 8 miles from Brecon on the A470) is a good place to stay and an excellent place to eat. B&B costs around £35 per person. Distinctly superior pub grub includes wood pigeon, jugged hare, braised wild duck and partridge with game chips. Most main dishes cost from £9.90 to £12.75.

Places to Eat
For self-catering, there's the *Kwik Save supermarket* opposite Mount St, or the *Top Drawer 2 Deli* (High St), which stocks a wonderful range of breads (the pumpkin seed rolls are recommended) and Welsh cheeses. The *Ice Cream Bar*, in the alley opposite the TIC, is always busy. Everything is home-made and very good.

There are several tearooms that also do reasonably priced meals, but they close early in the evening. *Hideaway Restaurant & Tea Rooms* (High St) is the perfect place for a cream tea and it serves superb chocolate gateau, and light lunches. *Oak Tea Rooms* (☎ 625501), on the Bulwark, is a little more upmarket, and has a pleasant garden patio. Leek and bacon pie is £4.95.

The restaurant at the *Beacons Guest House* (☎ 623339) is open to nonresidents and the food is all home-made and very good. There's a three course dinner for £15.50 to £17.50. The dining room at the upmarket *Castle of Brecon Hotel* is more expensive but recommended.

Entertainment

The town has a good selection of pubs. Locals head for the *Boar's Head*, Ship St, and the *Sarah Siddons*, on the Bulwark. Sarah Siddons, one of the most famous actresses of the 18th century, was born in Brecon. The bar at the *Wellington Hotel* is recommended and there's live jazz here some evenings.

Getting There & Away

Brecon is 167 miles from London, 45 miles from Cardiff, 48 miles from Bristol and 20 miles from Abergavenny. The nearest train stations are at Abergavenny and Merthyr Tydfil (from Cardiff). Taxis charge about £15 to Merthyr Tydfil.

National Express (☎ 0990-808080) has daily links to Brecon from most parts of southern Britain via Cardiff (1½ hours, £2.60). First Cymru operates daily coaches between Brecon and Merthyr Tydfil (35 minutes) and Swansea (85 minutes).

The Stagecoach Red & White (☎ 01633-266336) service No 39/40 runs between Brecon and Hereford via Hay-on-Wye five times a day (twice on Sunday).

BRECON TO ABERGAVENNY
Crickhowell

* pop 2000   ☎ 01873

This little village on the bus route between Brecon and Abergavenny is another good walking base. The TIC (☎ 812105) is on Beaufort St, by the main A40.

There's a camping ground in the village, the *Riverside Caravan Park* (☎ 810397,

New Rd); charges are £3 per tent, plus £2 per person. The most central B&B is *Mrs Morgan's* (☎ 811177, 2 Greenhill Villas, Beaufort St)*, with rooms from £18/32 for a single/double.

The *Bear Hotel* (☎ 810408) is the best place to stay in the town, and rates range from £45 to £85 for a single, £59 to £110 for a double. Some rooms have jacuzzis. There's excellent bar food and a good restaurant.

Tretower Court & Castle

Three miles north-west of Crickhowell, Tretower combines a large, medieval manor house and, across the meadow, the 13th century tower, part of the castle. The house has been considerably restored and was originally the home of the Vaughan family; the best known member of the family was the metaphysical poet, Henry Vaughan.

Tretower Court (☎ 01874-730279, Cadw) is open daily from 10 am to 5.30 pm. Entry is £2.20/1.70 and there's an excellent Walkman tour included in the price.

ABERGAVENNY (Y FENNI)

* pop 10,000   ☎ 01873

Standing by the eastern edge of the park surrounded by hills, this busy market town styles itself as the 'Gateway to Wales'. It's a good base for walking in the Black Mountains, with a wide range of accommodation and, unlike Brecon, a train station.

The town's history goes back 4000 years, when there was a Neolithic settlement here. The Romans established Gobarium Fort nearby and stayed from 57 to 400 AD, but Abergavenny only really began to grow after Hamelin de Ballon built his castle in 1090. Eventually falling into ruin, the keep was heavy-handedly restored by the Victorians and now houses a small **museum** of local history. Entry is £1/free.

Among the former visitors who have enjoyed the town's rural position was Rudolf Hess in 1941. Although he wasn't here on holiday, his wardens did allow him a weekly hike up Pen-y-Fan.

The TIC (☎ 857588) is by the bus stand in Swan Meadow, and open year-round. In the same building is a National Park Visitors Centre (☎ 853254).

Places to Stay

Two miles north of Abergavenny, in the village of Pantygelli, is *Smithy's Bunkhouse* (☎ 853432), down the farm track opposite the Crown Inn. There are two dormitories at this well-equipped bunkhouse; charges are around £7 per person. There's a laundry, common room and kitchen. The nearest HI youth hostel to Abergavenny is at Capel-y-ffin, 15 miles north on the road to Hay-on-Wye.

In the north of the town, the 200-year-old *Aenon House* (☎ 858708, 34 Pen-y-Pound) is a very pleasant place to stay. Rooms are £15 per person. Award-winning *Pentre House* (☎ 853435, Brecon Rd) is another good choice, with singles/doubles for £25/34. Evening meals are £10. 'Best place I stayed in,' wrote one reader.

There are several other B&Bs around the train station. On Holywell Rd, *Belchamps Guest House* (☎ 853204) charges £20/36.

Park Guest House (☎ 853715, 36 Hereford Rd) is a Georgian building with six rooms at £18/32. The *Guest House* (☎ 854823, 2 Oxford St) is nearby, with comfortable rooms for £19.50/34 and evening meals.

The *Great George Hotel* (☎ 854230, Cross St) charges £20 per person, room only, or £25 including breakfast. The top place in town is the *Angel Hotel* (☎ 857121, Cross St). Rooms are £65/80 and there are cheaper two-night deals at weekends.

Places to Eat

On Market St there's *Market St Fish & Chips* (☎ 855791) for takeaways. The *Greyhound Vaults* (☎ 858549) is on the same street. There are filled rolls, pasta, salads and steaks, and it's open daily (closed Monday evening).

Three miles north-east of Abergavenny at Llandewi Skirrid is the *Walnut Tree Inn* (☎ 852797), reputed to be the best restaurant in Wales. The chef is Italian, the cuisine international and the ingredients, as far as possible, Welsh. The menu might include anything from vincigrassi (pasta, béchamel, ceps, truffles) to bubble and squeak. It's closed on Sunday and Monday, and very busy when it's open, so you must book. After a memorable dinner for two, including drinks and service, don't expect any change out of £80.

Getting There & Away

There's no direct National Express service from London; you must change at Hereford. Stagecoach Red & White (☎ 01633-266336) runs services to Brecon or Cardiff.

The train station is just off Monmouth Rd, a 15 minute walk from the bus station and TIC. There are services to Cardiff every hour (£7.10), and direct trains to Manchester. London requires a change at Newport. For information phone ☎ 0345-484950.

Getting Around

For a taxi try P Taxis (☎ 850712). You can rent bikes from McCarthy's Cycle Hire (☎ 850390), 16 Monk St, for £10 per day.

AROUND ABERGAVENNY
Blaenavon

Five miles south-west of Abergavenny, Blaenavon is home to the **Big Pit Mining Museum**, created inside a real mine which ceased production in 1980, 100 years after the first miners began work there.

You can descend the 90m to the pit floor in an old mine lift, to inspect the tunnels and coalfaces. Safety precautions are treated seriously, so you'll be decked out in a hard hat and with a heavy power pack attached to your waist to light your helmet lamp. Some of the men who guide you were once miners who cut coal here. It's not a trip for the claustrophobic. As well as the mine itself, you can see the old pithead baths, the blacksmith's workshop and other colliery buildings.

The Big Pit (☎ 01495-790311) is open daily from 9.30 am to 5 pm, March to November, with one hour underground tours (popular with school parties) from 10 am (last tour 3.30 pm). It's cold at the bottom of the

ABERGAVENNY TO HAY-ON-WYE

Llanfihangel Crucorney

This little village, 5 miles from Abergavenny off the road between Abergavenny and Hereford, attracts lots of tourists. They mainly come to see the *Skirrid Mountain Inn* (☎ 01873-890258), which claims to be the oldest pub in Wales. From the early 12th century until the 17th century this was the courthouse, where almost 200 prisoners were hanged; the rope marks on one of the beams can still be seen.

The most pleasant place to stay in the area is wonderful *Penyclawdd Court* (☎ 01873-890719), a tastefully restored Tudor manor house below Bryn Arw mountain. B&B costs £45/72 for a single/double and you must book ahead. Modern conveniences such as electricity are provided in the bedrooms, but not in the dining room where delicious four course meals are served by candlelight.

Llanthony

The ruins of the Augustinian priory church and the monastic buildings of **Llanthony Priory** (Cadw) are set in a beautiful location in the Ewyas Valley. There's a superb walk from the car park up onto the bare ridge above. Offa's Dyke runs along the ridge.

The *Abbey Hotel* (☎ 01873-890487) is built into some of the surviving abbey buildings. Like Penyclawdd Court in Llanfihangel Crucorney, it's recommended for its atmosphere. There's a public bar in the vaulted crypt that serves basic meals. It's open daily from Easter to October, and on weekends in winter. Rooms are let only as doubles, and they're £46 during the week and £110 for a minimum two night stay (for two people) at weekends.

Capel-y-Ffin

Farther up the valley is Llanthony Monastery, founded in 1870. It was unoccupied by the 1920s when Eric Gill, artist and typographer, started a commune in it. It's now a private residence.

Capel-y-ffin Youth Hostel (☎ 01873-890650) is a mile north of the village, by the road to Hay-on-Wye. Its opening hours are complex – phone for details – but it's usually open daily in July and August and closed in December and January. The nightly charge is £6.50/4.45.

There's a riding school by the hostel – this is excellent pony trekking country. Offa's Dyke Path is 1½ miles from the hostel on the ridge. The walk to Hay is highly recommended.

HAY-ON-WYE

* pop 1600   ☎ 01497

On 1 April 1977 Hay-on-Wye declared independence from Britain – just one publicity stunt this eccentric little bookshop town has used to draw attention to itself.

Most of the publicity has been generated by bookseller Richard Booth, the colourful, self-styled King of Hay, who was largely responsible for Hay's evolution from just another market town on the Welsh-English border to the second-hand bookshop capital of the world.

A day browsing among the shops is definitely recommended. With its small centre made up of narrow sloping lanes, the town itself is also interesting, and the people it attracts certainly are. On the north-eastern corner of the national park, Hay makes an excellent base for the Black Mountains.

History

Most events in the history of Hay have been connected with its location as a Marches town, on the border of Wales and England. In fact, during the Norman period the town was administered as English Hay (the town proper) and Welsh Hay (the countryside to the south and west of the town).

A castle had already stood in the town before the construction of the present one, built in about 1200 by the treacherous William Breos II (one of the Norman barons, or Lords Marcher, granted vast tracts of land on border country to consolidate conquered

The Town of Books

There are now over 30 second-hand book-shops in Hay, containing literally hundreds of thousands of books – 400,000 in Richard Booth's Bookshop alone. British publishers churn out more than 80,000 new titles each year, and this country has a long history of publishing. According to the experts, quantity rather than quality is what you'll find in most places in Hay.

Some of these bookshops specialise in esoteric fields – for example, B & K Books (☎ 820386), Newport St, boasts the world's finest stock of books on apicul-ture. Rose's Books (☎ 820013), 14 Broad St, stocks rare and out-of-print children's books. Lion St Bookshop (☎ 820121), 1 St John's Place, deals in militaria and anar-chism. There's theology and church history at Marches Gallery (☎ 821451), Lion St. Murder and Mayhem (☎ 821613), 5 Lion St, is filled with detective fiction, true crime and horror.

Many bookshops, however, cover everything – the most famous being Richard Booth's (☎ 820322), 44 Lion St, and the Hay Cinema Bookshop (☎ 820071), Castle St. Some shops will carry out searches to locate out-of-print books. Booksearch (Hay-on-Wye, Here-ford HR3 5EA) deals only by post. There are regular book auctions at Y Gelli Auc-tions (☎ 821179), Broad St.

territory). From then until the final acquisi-tion of Wales by the English crown, Hay changed hands many times. It subsequently became a market town, employing a large number of people in the flannel trade during the 18th century.

The first large-scale second-hand book-shop opened in 1961, the vanguard of a new industry.

The castle, complete with the Jacobean mansion built within its Norman walls, was purchased by Booth in 1971 but a fire in 1977 left it in its present dilapidated state.

Orientation & Information

Hay's compact centre contains the castle and most of the bookshops, within a roughly square perimeter. The main central thorough-fare is Castle St, which links Oxford Rd with Lion St.

The TIC (☎ 820144), open every day, is on Oxford Rd, on the edge of town and just by the main car park. It's open from 10 am to 5 pm from Easter to October, and from 11 am to 4 pm at all other times. It closes for lunch from 1 to 2 pm.

Most bookshops stock the useful free town plan that locates and describes all the bookshops in Hay. The annual Festival of Literature takes place in May/June and is a very popular and entertaining affair.

Bikes can be hired from Paddles & Pedals (☎ 820604), Castle St, for £7.50 per half-day, £12.50 for the first full day with subsequent days cheaper. It also hires out Canadian canoes (for two/three people).

Places to Stay

Radnors End Campsite (☎ 820780) is 550m from the bridge over the River Wye, on the road to Clyro. The charge is £3 per person.

Hay has a fair number of B&Bs and hotels, but the nearest youth hostel is at Capel-y-ffin, 8 miles south (see the earlier Abergavenny to Hay-on-Wye section). To stay at *Joe's Lodge* (☎ 01874-711845, Hay Rd, Talgarth), 8 miles south-west of Hay, you need to book in advance. It's an inde-pendent hostel, and B&B costs around £9.50. Also in Talgarth, there's an upmarket B&B at *Upper Trewalkin Farm* (☎ 01874-711349, Pengenffordd), for £20 per person. Evening meals (£12) are excellent.

Back in Hay, *La Fosse* (☎ 820613, Oxford Rd) is a comfortable place charging £37 for a double room (no singles) with bathroom. *Belmont House* (☎ 820718, Belmont Rd) is well located, with rooms for £18/30 (£36 for a double with bathroom). At *Cwm Dulais* (☎ 820640, Heoly-Dwr), also central, there's B&B for £18 per person.

Kilvert's Hotel (☎ 821042) is right in the centre on the Bull Ring, with rooms at around £30 per person.

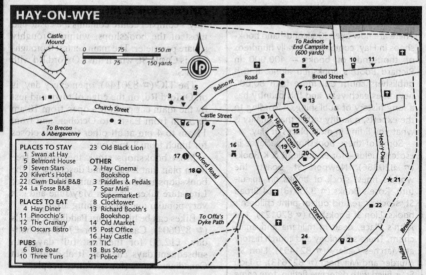

HAY-ON-WYE

PLACES TO STAY	23 Old Black Lion
1 Swan at Hay	
5 Belmont House	**OTHER**
9 Seven Stars	2 Hay Cinema
20 Kilvert's Hotel	Bookshop
22 Cwm Dulais B&B	3 Paddles & Pedals
24 La Fosse B&B	7 Spar Mini
	Supermarket
PLACES TO EAT	8 Clocktower
4 Hay Diner	13 Richard Booth's
11 Pinocchio's	Bookshop
12 The Granary	14 Old Market
19 Oscars Bistro	15 Post Office
	16 Hay Castle
PUBS	17 TIC
6 Blue Boar	18 Bus Stop
10 Three Tuns	21 Police

The **Seven Stars** (☎ *820886, Broad St*) is an excellent place to stay. As well as comfortable rooms for £17.50 to £30 per person, it even has a swimming pool and sauna.

The **Swan at Hay** (☎ *821188, Church St*) is more conventionally luxurious and charges £50 for a single, and between £65 and £90 for a double room.

Two miles from Hay, at Llanigon and near Offa's Dyke Path, is the **Old Post Office** (☎ *820008*), an excellent vegetarian B&B with rooms for £15 per person with shared bathroom, £20 with private bathroom.

Places to Eat

For such a small place, there's a lot of variety. **Hay Diner**, on Castle St, is good for a coffee, a beer or a full meal – and there's a takeaway next door. Hay Diner is open daily from 10 am to 10 pm. A chicken kebab is £4.95; a lentil and walnut burger costs £3. There's some seating in the garden.

For something informal, yet substantial, the **Granary** (☎ *820790, Broad St*) is an excellent and popular choice. A large steak and kidney pie costs £7.50, and there are

good vegetarian dishes – the Tibetan roast is recommended. It also has some interesting puddings, including the classic summer pudding, with raspberries and blackberries. It's open daily from 10 am to 10 pm (during the day only in winter).

Oscars Bistro (☎ *821193, High Town*) is central and offers very reasonably priced dishes (including vegetarian). It also has excellent filled baguettes for £3.

Pinocchio's (☎ *821166, 2 Broad St*) is a good Italian restaurant with excellent pizza.

The tiny **Three Tuns** (*Broad St*) is a wonderful old pub and cider house, popular with locals. The **Blue Boar** (☎ *820884, Castle St*) has a wide selection of bar food, and there's upmarket pub grub at the **Old Black Lion** (*Lion St*). **Kilvert's Hotel** (see Places to Stay) also has good pub food and an à la carte restaurant.

There's a **Spar minisupermarket** on Castle St.

Getting There & Away

The nearest train station is in Hereford. There are six buses a day to Hereford (one hour, £3.10), Monday to Saturday, and three buses on Sunday. Departures are from Oxford Rd and there are additional services from the clock tower on Broad St. For Brecon (40 minutes), there are six buses a day, Monday to Saturday, and two on Sunday.

Offa's Dyke Path passes beside Hay.

Powys

Powys is a large and sparsely populated county, stretching from Brecon Beacons National Park in the south up to Snowdonia in the north. In the local government border reorganisation of 1974, Brecknockshire in the south, the central county of Radnorshire and Montgomeryshire in the north were combined to create the new county of Powys. The northern section is often still referred to as Montgomeryshire.

There are few specific sights in the county – Powis Castle and the Centre for Alternative Technology are probably the main tourist attractions – but there's superb open walking country.

WALKS
The best known walk in the area is **Offa's Dyke Path**, the 168 mile national trail that runs the length of Wales, following the eastern border of Powys. See the Activities chapter at the start of this book for more information.

The 120 mile **Glyndŵr's Way** is through beautiful countryside and has the added interest of following in the footsteps of the Welsh hero Owain Glyndŵr. Contact the Planning Information Service, Powys County Council, County Hall, Llandrindod Wells, Powys LD1 6GG, for a series of leaflets covering the trail. There's also a guidebook: *Owen Glyndŵr's Way* by Richard Sale.

It takes five to nine days to walk from Knighton to Welshpool via Machynlleth, and the walk can be done in either direction. Some sections are along roads, which you could cut out by using public transport.

GETTING AROUND
Public transport in this area is limited. To visit the more remote areas, a certain amount of advance planning is necessary.

Bus
Arriva Cymru (☎ 01970-617951) operates bus services to and from many areas in Mid Wales. It has Rover tickets for £4.80/9/14 which allow unlimited travel for one/three/five days on its services except for the 701. You can also use this pass on Arriva Midland services across the border in England.

Train
Rail services are sparse. The Cambrian Main Line runs through Shrewsbury and Machynlleth to terminate in Aberystwyth; the Heart of Wales Line brushes across the south-east corner from Shrewsbury via Llandrindod Wells and Builth Wells and south to Swansea.

A useful ticket is the North & Mid Wales Rover, valid for seven days (£39.90/26.35) or for any three out of seven days (£25.70/16.95) on main-line services between Aberystwyth and Shrewsbury, Shrewsbury to Crewe and Crewe to Holyhead, and also on most bus services in the area. The Rover also entitles the holder to discounts on some of the private railways. However, it doesn't include services on the Shrewsbury-Llandrindod Wells-Swansea line.

LLANWRTYD WELLS
• pop 500   ☎ 01591
Llanwrtyd Wells was developed as a spa town in the 18th century when the health benefits of the local sulphur spring (still flowing) were discovered. This small attractive town is surrounded by beautiful countryside, with the Cambrian Mountains to the north-west and the Mynydd Eppynt to the south-east. As well as walking, mountain biking and pony trekking, the town hosts a number of less orthodox events and pastimes – see the boxed text 'World Bog Snorkelling Championships' in this chapter.

There's a TIC (☎ 610666) on the square. The **Stonecroft Hostel** (☎ 610332) is a friendly self-catering guesthouse near the centre of town on Dol-y-coed Rd. It's a good place with dormitory accommodation for £9, and rooms from £10.50 per person. There's a kitchen, riverside garden and TV room. Breakfast (£2.50) is available next door at the **Stonecroft Inn**, which is also an excellent place for a pint and good pub grub. The **Neuadd Arms** (☎ 610236), on the square, does B&B for £24 per person (£27 with bathroom). It rents mountain bikes for £12 per day.

LLANDRINDOD WELLS

- pop 4300   ☎ 01597

Roman remains at Castell Collen nearby show that people were here long before Llandrindod was reinvented as a spa town in the 18th and 19th centuries. The town's architecture – towers, balustrades, balconies – and ironwork reflect the tastes and style of the time. You can still take the water outside the Pump Room in Rock Park though no treatments are available. Once a year there's a Victorian Festival where the townspeople dress up in Victorian clothes.

The town is now the administrative centre for Powys. The TIC (☎ 822600) is in the Old Town Hall, Memorial Gardens, Temple St. The **Llanerch** (☎ 822086, Waterloo Rd) is a traditional pub known for its good-value bar food.

KNIGHTON

On the border with England, Knighton lies on Offa's Dyke, at the junction of Offa's Dyke Path and Glyndŵr's Way.

The Offa's Dyke Centre & TIC (☎ 01547-528753), West St, is open daily from Easter to October. For B&B try **Pilleth Court** (☎ 01547-560272, Whitton), where it's £18 to £20 per person.

Knighton is located on the Shrewsbury-Llandrindod Wells-Swansea train line.

WELSHPOOL

- pop 5000   ☎ 01938

This town, situated in the Severn Valley, was originally called Pool, but the name was changed to avoid confusion with Poole in Dorset. Really the only reason to come here is to get to Powis Castle or ride the narrow-gauge railway.

The TIC (☎ 552043) is in the Vicarage Gardens car park. There's a livestock market every Monday which dates back to 1263.

Things to See & Do

The **Welshpool & Llanfair Light Railway** (☎ 810441) was originally built to take local people to market with their sheep and cattle. The line was closed in 1956 but reopened by enthusiasts in 1960. It runs on an 8 mile journey from Raven Square and operates between Easter and early October – but not every day (phone for timetables). The return fare is £7.50/3.75.

World Bog Snorkelling Championships

Llanwrtyd Wells hosts numerous alternative activities. There's the Real Ale Wobble, a cycling event held in conjunction with the beer festival, and the Man vs Horse Marathon, in which runners and horses compete. In 1982, the sponsors very nearly had to hand over the £10,000 prize money to man, as horse won by only four minutes.

The most alternative of all events held here, however, must be the World Bog Snorkelling Championships. Held over the August bank holiday, competitors must swim two lengths of a specially prepared peat bog trench 55m long using a snorkel and fins. They may surface only twice for navigational purposes. Anyone can enter and they come from all over the world to do so. Amazingly, it's the only event of its kind in the world.

One mile south of Welshpool is **Powis Castle** (☎ 554336, NT). The castle is an impressive sight with its red walls and beautiful terraced gardens. The museum contains treasures that Clive of India brought back from India – his family married into the Herberts of Powis. The castle is open Wednesday to Sunday from early April to the end of October. In July and August it's also open on Tuesday. The gardens are open from 11 am to 6 pm, and the castle from noon to 5 pm. Entry to the castle and gardens is £7.50/3.75, and to the gardens only it's £5/2.50.

Five miles south of Welshpool, at Berriew, is the **Andrew Logan Museum of Sculpture** (☎ 01686-640689), open May to October at weekends (Wednesday to Sunday in July and August) from 2 to 6 pm. In November and December it's open Sunday only. Entry is £2/1. Andrew Logan is one of Britain's top modern sculptors and this whacky, slightly camp collection is highly entertaining.

Getting There & Away

Welshpool is on the Shrewsbury to Aberystwyth line. From Shrewsbury to Welshpool takes 30 minutes (£4.20) with departures approximately every two hours Monday to Saturday, less often on Sunday.

MACHYNLLETH

- **pop 2000**   ☎ **01654**

On the western edge of Montgomeryshire, Machynlleth (pronounced mahuncliff) holds an important place in Welsh history as it was here that Glyndŵr set up his parliament. In recent years it's become better known as a centre of green living, mainly due to the influence of the Centre for Alternative Technology on the edge of the town.

Machynlleth is in the Dyfi Valley, and there's good cycling in this area. Mountain bikes can be hired from Greenstiles (☎ 703543), just behind the clock tower in the town centre, for £12 (50% off for visitors to the Centre for Alternative Technology).

The TIC is in the Canolfan Owain Glyndŵr Centre (☎ 702401). It sells a leaflet to walks on Cadair Idris, which is about 7 miles north of Machynlleth.

Things to See & Do

The **Glyndŵr Parliament House** (☎ 702827) is open daily from April to September and has displays showing life in the Middle Ages in Wales, as well as on Glyndŵr's fight for Welsh independence.

Despite the fact that the Celts have played a defining role in the culture of Europe, the first museum devoted solely to them was

---

The Centre for Alternative Technology

If you're anywhere in the area don't miss the Centre for Alternative Technology (CAT, ☎ 01654-702400) three miles north of Machynlleth. Founded in 1975 by a group of environmentalists on a 16 hectare site that was once a slate mine, it's now a self-sufficient working community. It's probably the most interesting eco centre in Europe.

There are more than 50 exhibits: working displays of wind, water and solar power, a low-energy self-built house and an organic garden, as well as an underground display on the world of soil (complete with giant mole) and a transport maze. The displays are interesting and fun yet also educational. There's a water powered cliff railway (closed in winter in case of frost), bookshop and excellent vegetarian restaurant.

The centre is open daily from 10 am to 7 pm (last entry is 5 pm or at dusk if earlier). Entry is £5.70/2.80. Arrive by bike and entry is half-price. There are also discounted tickets available when you buy rail or bus tickets – inquire on buses or at the train station.

CAT runs residential courses throughout the year. Basic accommodation and meals are provided.

opened only in 1996, in Machynlleth. **Celtica** (☎ 702702), Y Plas, Aberystwyth Rd, is an interpretive centre and exhibition, that highlights not only Wales' Celtic roots but includes all the Celtic groups of Europe. The main exhibition is a multimedia entertainment (£4.65/3.50) devised by the people that created the Jorvik Centre in York. There's a Celtic settlement, magic forest and a meeting with a druid. It's actually rather more entertaining than it sounds. The interpretive centre is good and there is also a bookshop and restaurant. Celtica is open daily from 10 am to 6 pm (last entry is at 4.30 pm).

Places to Stay

At Corris, 5 miles north of Machynlleth, the energy efficient **Corris Youth Hostel** (☎ 761686) is in the Old School. It's open daily from March through October. The nightly charge is £8/5.40.

In Machynlleth, five minutes from the clock tower there's B&B for around £15 per person at **Haulfryn** (☎ 702206, Aberystwyth Rd).

Maenllwyd (☎ 702928, Newtown Rd) charges £38 for a double room and is a very pleasant place to stay; vegetarian breakfasts are served if required. **Pendre Guest House** (☎ 702088, Maengwyn St) has four rooms, two with a bath, and charges from £16.50.

Try the **Glyndŵr Hotel** (☎ 703989, Doll St); B&B is from £16 per person. There's an excellent farm B&B available outside the town at **Mathafarn** (☎ 01650-511226, Llanwrin) for £17.50 per person.

Places to Eat

The wonderful **Wholefood Café** (Maengwyn St) serves vegetarian food and uses organic ingredients where possible. Cheesy broccoli filo pie is £3.95. **Bwyty Maengwyn** (☎ 702126, 57 Maengwyn St) uses local produce including Welsh lamb. A vegetable bake (eg leek and potato pie) is £3.59. The Sunday lunch (£6.50) is popular.

At the Celtica exhibition, there's a good **tearoom** with light lunches. Welsh leek soup and a roll is £2.20.

Getting There & Away

Machynlleth is on the Shrewsbury to Aberystwyth line. Services from Shrewsbury (1½ hours, £6.90) operate almost every two hours. Arriva Cymru's (☎ 01970-617951) No 32 bus from Aberystwyth (40 minutes, £3.60) operates every two hours from Monday to Saturday, and once on Sunday.

Ceredigion

Ceredigion (Cardiganshire) is the county that encompasses the southern coastal section of Cardigan Bay, and which extends inland to Powys. For three out of every five people who live here, Welsh is their first language.

The county includes 50 miles of coastline, much of which is protected by heritage coast status. The capital is the university town and classic seaside resort of Aberystwyth, certainly the most happening place in Ceredigion.

GETTING AROUND
Bus

There are a couple of Rover tickets covering services in Ceredigion and neighbouring counties. The West Wales Rover ticket (£4.60) includes most services in Ceredigion, Pembrokeshire and Carmarthenshire. Arriva Cymru (☎ 01970-617951) also operates bus services in North and Mid Wales. It also has a Rover ticket (£4.80/9/14 for one/three/five days).

Train

There are few lines in Ceredigion. The only main-line service is into Aberystwyth via Machynlleth from Shrewsbury (see the Powys section). There's a popular private line, the Vale of Rheidol Railway, which takes tourists from Aberystwyth up to Devil's Bridge.

CARDIGAN (ABERTEIFI)
• pop 4000   ☎ 01239

This was the county town of Cardiganshire. The Welsh name refers to the town's position at the mouth of the Teifi, an important seafaring and trading centre until the harbour silted up.

The first competitive National Eisteddfod was held in the castle here in 1176. A strong local interest in the arts continues and the town has a good alternative theatre and arts centre, Theatr Mwldan (☎ 621200). The TIC (☎ 613230) is in the same building, on Bath House Rd. In summer it's open daily from 10 am to 7 pm.

Places to Stay & Eat

The newly renovated *Poppit Sands Youth Hostel (☎ 612936)* is 4 miles from Cardigan, by the start of the Pembrokeshire Coast Path. It's open from March to October, daily except some Sundays and Mondays; beds are £7.20/4.95.

There are several good places to stay on Gwbert Rd, in the north of the town. *Maes-a-Môr (☎ 614929, Park Place, Gwbert Rd)* is opposite the King George V Park. B&B is £18 per person in a room with a bath, cheaper off-season. No smoking is permitted. A few doors down is *Brynhyfryd Guest House (☎ 612861)*, where B&B costs £17 per person. If you're on the bus from Aberystwyth, it stops at the end of Gwbert Rd.

Two miles from Cardigan Bay is the very comfortable *Penbontbren Farm Hotel (☎ 810248, Glynarthen)*. All rooms have a bath and cost £40/74. Dinner, bed and breakfast costs £49 per person.

For a light meal, the *Theatr Mwldan Café*, in the theatre building, is excellent. A five grain vegie burger costs £2.20 and there's a good range of herbal teas. The *Black Lion Hotel (High St)* pulls a reasonable pint and has good-value lunches on Sunday and bar food during the week. Round the back, *Go Mango Wholefoods (Black Lion Mews)* is a wholefood shop serving snacks to take away.

If the catering students are at Coleg Ceredigion you can taste their experiments at the *Gordon Edwards Restaurant (☎ 612032, Park Place)*. Set lunches are around £6 and dinners cost about £11.

Getting There & Away

Cardigan is not accessible by rail. The easiest way to get there is to go to Aberystwyth and then take the No 550 bus service, which runs every two hours, Monday to Saturday (two hours, £4.80). There's only one service on Sunday. The route is covered by two operators – Richards Brothers (☎ 613756) and Arriva Cymru (☎ 01970-617951).

Alternatively, you could go to Haverfordwest or Carmarthen and take the hourly No 412 service via Fishguard to Cardigan (1½ hours, £2.85), which runs Monday to Saturday.

ABERYSTWYTH
* pop 9000   ☎ 01970

On the central coast of Wales, Aberystwyth combines the attractions of a traditional seaside resort with a lively university town.

Like many other towns in the area, it was founded by Edward I when he started building a castle at the mouth of the River Rheidol in Ceredigion Bay in 1277. It was captured by Glyndŵr in 1404 and destroyed by Oliver Cromwell's forces in 1649. By the beginning of the 19th century, the walls and gates had virtually disappeared. Now a pretty unimpressive ruin by day, it's quite attractive when floodlit at night.

The town developed a fishing industry, and silver and lead-mining industries were also important in the area. With the arrival of the railway in 1864, it became a fashionable resort. In 1872 Aberystwyth was chosen as the site of the first college of the University of Wales, and in 1907 it became home to the National Library of Wales.

The TIC (☎ 612125) is located at the junction of Terrace Rd and Bath St. It's open daily from 9 am to 7 pm during summer, from 10 am to 5 pm in winter.

There's Internet access at the Web Café, on Terrace Rd, near the train station. It's open daily from 10 am to 8 pm (noon to 5 pm on Sunday). At the junction of Northgate St and North Parade is a laundrette, open daily from 8 am to 8 pm.

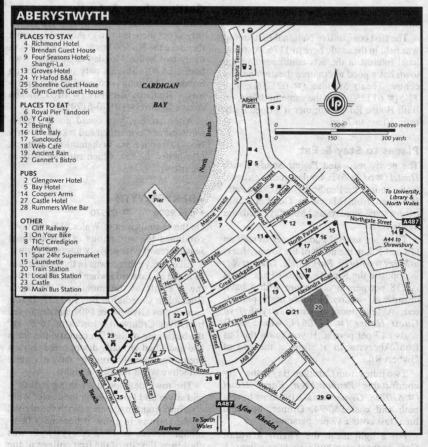

ABERYSTWYTH

PLACES TO STAY
4 Richmond Hotel
7 Brendan Guest House
9 Four Seasons Hotel;
   Shangri-La
13 Groves Hotel
24 Yr Hafod B&B
25 Shoreline Guest House
26 Glyn Garth Guest House

PLACES TO EAT
6 Royal Pier Tandoori
10 Y Graig
12 Beijing
16 Little Italy
17 Sunclouds
18 Web Café
19 Ancient Rain
22 Gannet's Bistro

PUBS
2 Glengower Hotel
5 Bay Hotel
14 Coopers Arms
27 Castle Hotel
28 Rummers Wine Bar

OTHER
1 Cliff Railway
3 On Your Bike
8 TIC; Ceredigion
   Museum
11 Spar 24hr Supermarket
15 Laundrette
20 Train Station
21 Local Bus Station
23 Castle
29 Main Bus Station

CARDIGAN
BAY

North Beach

Albert Place

Victoria Terrace

To University,
Library &
North Wales

Northgate Street

A487

A44 to
Shrewsbury

Marine Terrace

Bath Street

Queen's Road

Portland Road

North Road

Terrace Road

Portland Street

North Parade

Cambrian Street

Pier

King Street

Castle Street

Eastgate

Great Darkgate Street

Laura Place

New Street

Bridge Street

High Street

Queen's Street

Gray's Inn Road

South Road

Castle Terrace

Rheidol Tce

Quay Road

South Marine Terrace

South Beach

Alexandra Road

Elm Tree Avenue

Trinity Road

Mill Street

Park Avenue

Glyndwr Road

Riverside Terrace

A487

Afon Rheidol

To South
Wales

Harbour

Things to See & Do

The **Cliff Railway** (☎ 617642) is the longest electric cliff railway in Britain, running from the Promenade to the top of Constitution Hill. The hill offers good views over the bay and a **Camera Obscura** (free). This is a simple optical instrument like a projecting telescope which almost gives you a peek at the inside of locals' houses. Trains depart daily every few minutes, Easter to October from 10 am to 6 pm; tickets cost £2/1 return.

The **National Library of Wales** (☎ 623800) holds over five million books in a variety of languages and various ancient manuscripts and pictures. It's open Monday to Friday from 9.30 am to 6 pm, and on Saturday until 5 pm.

Ceredigion Museum (☎ 617911) is in the Coliseum, Terrace Rd, by the TIC. It has an entertaining collection of folk material based on the three main occupations of the people of Ceredigion – agriculture, seafaring and lead mining. There are also temporary exhibitions showing works by local artists. Entry is free, and it's open Monday to Saturday from 10 am to 5 pm.

The **Vale of Rheidol Railway** (☎ 625819) runs from Aberystwyth to Devil's Bridge, a journey of 11¾ miles, and is hauled by a narrow-gauge steam train. The railway was constructed to take the lead and timber from the Rheidol Valley, and the engines were built by the Great Western Railway in 1923.

The station is adjacent to Aberystwyth's main-line station and the ticket office opens at 10 am. The service operates daily from Easter to October, but there are no services on Friday in April and May, nor after the second Friday in September, nor on Friday, Saturday and Monday in October. Trains usually go twice a day in each direction (11 am and 2.30 pm from Aberystwyth, 1 and 4.30 pm from Devil's Bridge) but there are four a day on certain days in July and August. The return fare is £10.50/5.

Places to Stay

Borth Youth Hostel (☎ 871498) is 9 miles to the north, near a wide sandy beach. It's open from April to September; the nightly charge is £8.80/5.95.

Yr Hafod (☎ 617579, 1 South Marine Terrace) is an excellent little B&B charging from £17 to £22 per person. *Shoreline Guest House* (☎ 615002, 6 South Marine Terrace) nearby offers B&B from £15 per person. There are 11 rooms, all with satellite TV. It's a good place.

Glyn Garth Guest House (☎ 615050, South Rd) is a comfortable place with B&B from £18 to £24 per person.

The *Four Seasons Hotel* (☎ 612120, 50-54 Portland St) has 17 bedrooms, most with a bath, for £50/75. Nearby, *Shangri-La* (☎ 617659, Portland St) has B&B for £15/28 without bath.

The *Richmond Hotel* (☎ 612201, 44-45 Marine Terrace) has B&B for £45/65. *Brendan Guest House* (☎ 612252), also in Marine Terrace, charges £18/36 (£20/40 with bath). Most rooms have sea views.

The *Groves Hotel & Restaurant* (☎ 617623, 44 North Parade) has rooms at £45/60, all with bathroom. There are also a couple of cheaper singles at £32.

Places to Eat

The student presence ensures that there are plenty of good, cheap places to eat in Aberystwyth.

Y Graig (34 Pier St) is a very popular wholefood restaurant for vegetarians, vegans and meat-eaters. It's also a good place to find out what's going on locally. The other veggie place is *Ancient Rain* (Cambrian St). A melted cheese baguette is £2.20.

There are numerous Chinese restaurants and takeaways. The best is the *Beijing* (Portland Rd). The best of the several Indian restaurants is the *Royal Pier Tandoori*, in a great location at the end of the pier. Lunch is excellent value at £4.95.

Sunclouds (North Parade) has a good range of coffees and does light lunches. A Spanish omelette, salad and half a baguette costs £2. Nearby is *Little Italy* (☎ 625707) with pasta and pizzas from £4.95.

Gannet's Bistro (☎ 617164, 7 St James Square) has evening main dishes from £5 to £10. It does some reasonable traditional food, such as beef Wellington (£9.95).

On Terrace Rd is a *Spar supermarket* open 24 hours.

Entertainment

Rummers Wine Bar (Bridge St) is right by the river, and there are seats outside. It's open from 7 pm to midnight.

The *Castle Hotel* (Castle Terrace) is a good traditional pub, and the *Coopers Arms* (Northgate St) has live jazz some nights. The *Glengower Hotel* (Victoria Terrace) and the *Bay Hotel* (Marine Terrace) both attract students.

Getting There & Away

National Express (☎ 0990-808080) operates one service a day from London (seven hours, £21.50).

Arriva Cymru's bus No 701 connects Bangor with Bristol and passes through Aberystwyth. There are two buses a day between Aberystwyth and Cardiff (3¾ hours,

£10.90) and one a day to/from Bangor (three hours).

Service No 550 runs between Aberystwyth and Cardigan (hourly Monday to Saturday, once on Sunday) and takes two hours. Service No 2 goes between Aberystwyth and Caernarfon (change at Dolgellau) approximately every two hours. It's a three hour trip and can be covered with a Rover ticket (£4.80).

Aberystwyth is at the end of the Cambrian line from Shrewsbury. There are departures every two hours, Monday to Saturday, less frequently on Sunday.

Getting Around

On Your Bike (☎ 626996) offers cycle hire for £10/15 for a mountain bike/tandem for a day. It's based in the Old Police Yard, Queen's Rd.

AROUND ABERYSTWYTH
Devil's Bridge

Devil's Bridge is situated at the head of the Rheidol Valley in the Pumlumon Hills. The fast-flowing rivers Mynach and Rheidol meet in a gorge below the village. The River Mynach drops 90m in a series of spectacular waterfalls.

The Mynach is also notable for the three stone bridges which have been built on top of one another. The first is believed to have been built by the Knights Templars before 1188, the second in 1753 and the last more recently.

The Rheidol Valley Steam Railway goes to Devil's Bridge (see Things to See & Do in the Aberystwyth section).

Places to Stay & Eat The *Ystumtuen Youth Hostel* (☎ 890693, *Glantuen*) is 1½ miles from Devil's Bridge and is open from Easter to October; the nightly charge is £5.85/4.

The excellent *Mount Pleasant Guest House* (☎ 890219) is 200m from the Rheidol Steam Railway. It charges £25/40, with continental breakfast (£2 extra for a cooked breakfast). *Hafod Arms Hotel* (☎ 890232) is also about 200m from the railway and was originally a shooting lodge. B&B costs £28/45, or £32/50 with a bathroom.

North Wales

North Wales is dominated by the beautiful Snowdonia Mountains, which loom over the coastline. Unfortunately, this coast is the holiday playground for much of the English Midlands. 'From the train, north Wales looked like holiday hell – endless ranks of prison camp caravan parks ...' wrote Bill Bryson in *Notes from a Small Island*.

Heading west from Chester, the country is industrialised and uninteresting until you reach Llandudno. Llandudno is virtually contiguous with Conwy – either spot would make a good base. From Llandudno and Conwy you can catch buses or trains into the Snowdonia National Park. The park is also accessible from the coastal market town of Porthmadog on the Ffestiniog Railway. From Porthmadog, you can loop back to Shrewsbury along the Cambrian coast.

The remote Llŷn Peninsula in the west escapes the crowds to a large extent; start from Caernarfon, with its magnificent castle, or Pwllheli. To the north is the island of Anglesey, joined to the mainland by bridges – Holyhead is one of the main ferry ports for Ireland. Near Porthmadog is whimsical Portmeirion, an entire village built in the Italianate style – very attractive but crowded in summer.

This section of Wales includes the counties of Gwynedd, Anglesey, Conwy, Denbighshire, Flintshire and Wrexham.

GETTING AROUND

Gwynedd Public Transport Maps and Timetables is invaluable and includes the Llŷn Peninsula and all of Snowdonia. It's available from TICs, bus stations or the Transport Unit (☎ 01286-679535). For Anglesey, phone ☎ 01248-752458. For the eastern half of North Wales, Flintshire County Council (☎ 01352-704035) produces bus timetables covering all the services within its area.

Rail services in North Wales include the North Wales Coast Line from Chester via

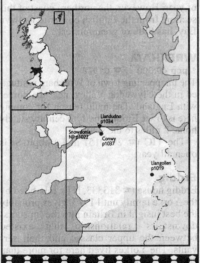

HIGHLIGHTS

- Plas Newydd, Llangollen
- Snowdonia National Park
- Hiking up Mt Snowdon
- Riding the Ffestiniog narrow-gauge railway
- The seaside at Llandudno
- Llŷn Peninsula

Llandudno Junction, Conwy and Bangor, terminating by the ferry terminal at Holyhead. By using trains that cross Snowdonia (Conwy Valley line, Ffestiniog Railway and Cambrian Coast line), you can link with the service that runs halfway along the Llŷn Peninsula to Pwllheli. Phone ☎ 0345-484950 for rail inquiries.

A North & Mid Wales Day Ranger (£16.90) covers most rail and bus services in this area.

See Snowdonia National Park later in this chapter for information on transport in that region.

North-Eastern Wales

Most travellers pass through this area of Wales to reach Snowdonia, but along the valley of the River Dee are a number of places worth stopping at. The International Musical Eisteddfod is held in Llangollen in July, although the town has enough alternative attractions to merit a visit at any time of year. However, the northern coast of this section, from the English border to Colwyn Bay, has little of great interest.

WREXHAM
• pop 40,000   ☎ 01978

The unappealing town of Wrexham is situated in the Clywedog Valley, near the border with England. The main reason for coming here is to see Erddig, the 17th century stately home 2 miles to the south.

The TIC (☎ 292015) in Lambpit St is open all year.

Erddig

Erddig house (☎ 313333, NT), inhabited by the Yorke family until 1973, gives probably the best insight in Britain into the 'upstairs-downstairs' relationship that existed between the upper classes and their servants. The Yorkes lived here for more than 200 years, and were known for the respect with which they treated their servants. Upstairs is a fine collection of furniture and an impressive state bed. Downstairs are photographs of servants through the ages and an interesting collection of household devices, such as the box mangle, which was filled with heavy stones and rolled over the laundry. Outside is an 800-hectare country park, where there are pleasant walks.

Erddig house and grounds are open from early April to late October, daily except Thursday and Friday, from 11 am to 6 pm for the grounds and from 12 to 5 pm for the house. Last admission to the house is at 4 pm. During October, the house is open from noon to 4 pm (last entry 3 pm).

Because Erddig is very popular, timed entry tickets may be issued. Entry to the grounds, family rooms and below stairs is £5.60/2.80, while entry to the grounds and below stairs only costs £3.60/1.80.

Places to Stay

Grove Guest House (☎ *354288, 36 Chester Rd*) charges from £16 per person for B&B. *Abbotsfield Priory Hotel* (☎ *261211, 29 Rhosddu Rd*) offers B&B for £27/40 for a single/double.

Getting There & Away

National Express has one service a day from London (£20). Arriva Cymru operates service No 1 from Chester to Wrexham, from Monday to Saturday every 15 minutes, and hourly on Sunday.

Wrexham is accessible by train from London via Shrewsbury, and also from Liverpool. There are departures every two hours from Shrewsbury (40 minutes, £4.30).

LLANGOLLEN
• pop 2600   ☎ 01978

Llangollen is famous for its International Musical Eisteddfod. The six-day music and dance festival attracts folk groups from around the world.

This attractive town makes an excellent base for outdoor activities, such as walks to ruined Valle Crucis Abbey and the Horseshoe Pass, horse-drawn canal boat trips and canoeing on the River Dee.

Orientation & Information

Covering both banks of the River Dee, Llangollen is small enough to walk around. The TIC (☎ 860828), in the Town Hall, Castle St, is open daily from 10 am to 6 pm during the summer, 9.30 am to 5 pm in winter.

There's a laundrette on Regent St, and a Spar supermarket (open daily from 8 am to 11 pm) on Castle St.

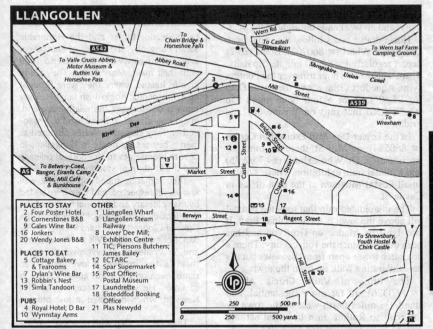

LLANGOLLEN

PLACES TO STAY
2   Four Poster Hotel
6   Cornerstones B&B
9   Gales Wine Bar
16 Jonkers
20 Wendy Jones B&B

PLACES TO EAT
5   Cottage Bakery
    & Tearooms
7   Dylan's Wine Bar
13 Robbin's Nest
19 Simla Tandoori

PUBS
4   Royal Hotel; D Bar
10 Wynnstay Arms

OTHER
1   Llangollen Wharf
3   Llangollen Steam
    Railway
8   Lower Dee Mill;
    Exhibition Centre
11 TIC; Piersons Butchers;
    James Bailey
12 ECTARC
14 Spar Supermarket
15 Post Office;
    Postal Museum
17 Laundrette
18 Eisteddfod Booking
    Office
21 Plas Newydd

International Musical Eisteddfod

The International Musical Eisteddfod was first held in 1947. It now takes place in a purpose-built venue by the river over six days every July. It's a massive affair, with over 12,000 performers – choirs, musicians, folk singers and dancers – and crowds of more than 120,000. Phone ☎ 860236 for details. The booking office is in the centre of town.

Plas Newydd

Plas Newydd (☎ 861314) was the home of the so-called Ladies of Llangollen, Lady Eleanor Butler and Sarah Ponsonby, who lived here from 1780 to 1829. In their own words, the women were 'seized with the oak-carving mania' and they set about transforming their house into a bizarre combination of Gothic and Tudor romantic styles. They added stained-glass windows and carved oak panels, and created formal gardens. The black and white timbering was, however, an alteration made by the next owner.

Sir Roy Strong, former director of the Victoria and Albert Museum in London, called Plas Newydd 'an early monument to architectural salvage'. It's a fascinating place. South-east of the town centre, the house is open Easter to October, daily from 10 am to 5 pm; entry is £2/1.

Other Things to See

ECTARC (☎ 861514), Castle St, is the European Centre for Traditional & Regional Cultures, and stages exhibitions on the cultures of lesser-known European groupings. It's open daily from 10 am to 6 pm (11 am to 5 pm on Sunday). Admission is free.

Llangollen Steam Railway (☎ 860979) runs over a 7 mile line via Berwyn and the Horseshoe Falls to Glyndyfrdwy and

Carrog (£7/ 3.50), from April to October daily, and on weekends throughout the year.

Horse-drawn boats follow the canal from **Llangollen Wharf** (☎ 860702). Boats (£3/2) depart regularly for the 30 minute trip daily. There's also a two hour trip over the Pontcysyllte Aqueduct (38m above the River Dee) for £5.50/4.50, or a four hour round trip (£6.50/5.50) that runs on Wednesday and Friday.

In the **Lower Dee Mill Exhibition Centre** (☎ 860584), on Mill St, there are other attractions – a Dr Who exhibit (£4.75/2.75) and a model train exhibition. There's also a small **Postal Museum** at the post office in Castle St.

The dilapidated ruin that tops the conical hill above the town is **Castell Dinas Bran**. It was built by Madoc ap Gruffydd and has been deserted since the 16th century. There's not much to see apart from the views but it's an exhilarating walk up from the town.

The ruins of **Valle Crucis Abbey** (☎ 860326) are far more substantial, and stand 1½ miles north-west of the town by the road to Ruthin. In a beautiful setting, Valle Crucis is rather like a smaller version of Tintern Abbey (see the South Wales chapter). In the care of Cadw, it's open daily April to September from 10 am to 5 pm; entry is £1.70/1.20. Along the road out here you pass a small **Motor Museum**.

Chirk Castle (☎ 01691-777701) is a magnificent Marcher fortress, 5 miles south-east of Llangollen and with superb views over the surrounding country. It was built in 1310, and adapted for more comfortable living from about the 16th century. It's open from April to October, daily except Monday and Tuesday (October weekends from noon to 5 pm only); entry is £4.60/2.30. There are buses to Chirk from Llangollen.

Activities

The two best walks in the area are along the canal to the Horseshoe Falls or up to Dinas Bran.

Llangollen is well known for canoeing and there are several centres. Jim Jayes (☎ 860763), Mile End Mill, Berwyn Rd,

---

The Ladies of Llangollen

Lady Eleanor Butler and the Honorable Sarah Ponsonby, the Ladies of Llangollen, lived in Plas Newydd from 1780 to 1829 with their maid, Mary Carryl. They fell in love in Ireland where they were brought up in aristocratic Anglo-Irish families. Their families discouraged the relationship and, in a desperate bid to be allowed to live together, they eloped to Wales disguised as men. They set up home in Llangollen, to devote themselves to 'friendship, celibacy and the knitting of stockings'.

Their romantic friendship became well known yet respected, and they were visited by many literary and national figures of the day, including the Duke of Wellington, the Duke of Gloucester, Richard Brinsley Sheridan, Robert Southey, William Wordsworth and Sir Walter Scott. Wordsworth called them 'sisters in love, a love allowed to climb, even on this earth above the reach of time'. He was less accepting of Plas Newydd, which he called 'a low browed cot'.

Their relationship with their maid, Mary Carryl, was also close – most unusual for those days. She managed to buy the freehold of Plas Newydd and left it to them when she died. They erected a large monument to her in the graveyard at the Church of St Collen in Bridge St, where they are also buried. Lady Eleanor died in 1829, Sarah Ponsonby two years later.

---

half a mile from Llangollen, charges from £7 to £13 per person per hour. You can also go white-water rafting, which costs £9 per person. There's bunkhouse accommodation here (see Places to Stay).

Places to Stay

There are plenty of places to stay, but for accommodation in July around the time of the Eisteddfod, you should book long in advance. If you're coming to Llangollen for the canoeing, some of the canoe centres also offer cheap accommodation.

The **Llangollen Youth Hostel & Activity Centre** (☎ 860330) is in Tyndwr Hall, a Victorian manor house 1½ miles east of the centre. It's open daily from mid-February through October, and the nightly charge is £8.80/5.95 for adults/juniors. The **Mill Café & Bunkhouse** (☎ 869043, Mile End Mill, Berwyn Rd), half a mile from Llangollen, charges £6 to £8 per person for dormitory accommodation.

Eirianfa Camp Site (☎ 860919) charges £6 for a tent and two people. It's about a mile from Llangollen, towards Betws-y-Coed. **Wern Isaf Farm** (☎ 860632) is across the river and to the east, half a mile from the school.

Wendy Jones (☎ 860882, 1 Bodwen Villas, Hill St) offers B&B at around £17 per person.

Right in the centre is **Cornerstones** (☎ 861569, 15 Bridge St) with singles/doubles for £20/38. **Gales Wine Bar** (☎ 860089, 18 Bridge St,) has 15 very comfortable rooms at £38/50 with bathroom. It's one of the most pleasant places to stay and is right in the centre of town. There's good-value food in the wine bar.

An interesting place to stay is **Jonkers** (Chapel St), where there's a single room for £18.50, a double for £32 and a triple for £42.

The **Four Poster Hotel** (☎ 861062, Mill St) specialises in four-posters, charging from £24 per person.

Places to Eat

Piersons Butchers, beside the TIC, is good for a snack, and sells hot barbecued chicken. The nearby delicatessen **James Bailey** does good home-made pies. Try a Welsh Oggie (meat, potato and onion pasty). **Cottage Bakery & Tea Rooms** (Castle St) does good cream teas.

Dylan's Wine Bar (☎ 861569, Bridge St) has a wide range of well-priced dishes. Thai green chicken curry is £5.80. **Robbin's Nest** (☎ 861425, Market St) does jacket potatoes and light lunches. A three-course dinner is £10.95.

Gales Wine Bar (☎ 860089, 18 Bridge St) is an excellent place for a meal. There are baked potatoes, salads, seafood and steaks. The home-made ice cream is highly recommended. The **Simla Tandoori** (Hill St) is a good curry house.

The **Wynnstay Arms** on Bridge St is a good place to drink. The **D Bar** at the Royal Hotel is probably the most happening place in Llangollen.

Meals on wheels are available at weekends on the Llangollen Steam Railway (see Other Things to See). A three course lunch is £22.50, dinner costs £30.50.

Getting There & Away

Llangollen is 10 miles from Wrexham and there are frequent buses between these two places. There's a daily National Express bus to London (☎ 0990-808080).

Bryn Melyn (☎ 860701) runs bus services from Llangollen to Ruabon, Wrexham, Oswestry and Horseshoe Falls. Public transport to Snowdonia is very limited. Bus No 94 runs to Dolgellau where you can pick up the No 701 for Aberystwyth.

The train station here only serves the Llangollen Steam Railway; the nearest mainline station is at Ruabon, on the Shrewsbury to Chester main line. Services operate every two hours from Shrewsbury to Ruabon (30 minutes, £4.10). A taxi from Ruabon costs about £6 – contact Llangollen Taxis (☎ 861018).

Snowdonia National Park

Snowdonia is the second-largest national park in Britain, after the Lake District. Although the Snowdonia Mountains cover a fairly compact area, in the north they loom over the coast and are undeniably spectacular.

The area around Mt Snowdon, at 1085m the highest peak in Britain south of the Scottish Highlands, is the busiest part of the park. About half a million people climb, walk or take the train to the summit each

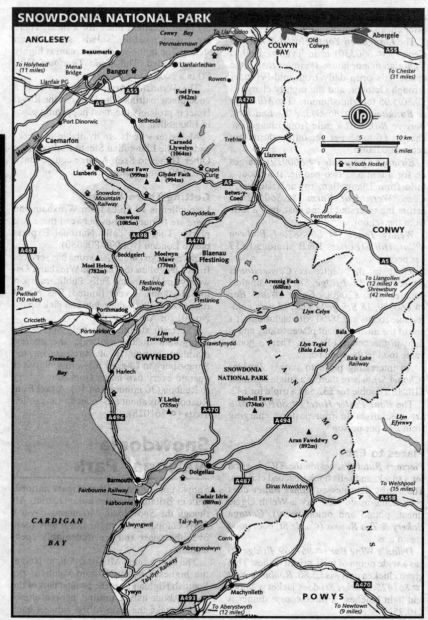

SNOWDONIA NATIONAL PARK

NORTH WALES

= Youth Hostel

year. This was the area where members of the first successful attempt on Mt Everest trained, and it's been the training ground for many of Britain's best-known mountaineers since then.

The Welsh name for Snowdon is Yr Wyddfa, which means 'great tomb' – legend says that a giant who was killed by King Arthur is buried on the summit. The English name is said to have been derived from an old word for snow, which crowns the peaks in winter.

As well as impressive mountains, the park contains a wide variety of other natural features – rivers, lakes, waterfalls, forests, moorlands, glacial valleys and a lovely coastline.

Despite the inhospitable nature of this rugged area, Snowdonia has provided both a home and a store of valuable natural resources for people since it was shaped by the retreating glaciers of the Ice Age. There are Stone Age burial chambers at Dyffryn Ardudwy and Capel Garmon; Bronze Age burial cairns at Bryn Cader Faner near Talsarnau; a hill fort at Pen-y-Gaer; Roman forts at Caerhun, Tomen-y-Mur and Caer Gai; and Welsh and Norman castles. The mountains sheltered Llywelyn ap Gruffydd in the 13th century and Owain Glyndŵr in the 15th, during their struggles to reclaim Wales from the English.

The remains of the huge mining and quarrying operations that were once a major industry can still be seen. There's now more money to be made from tourism, and so the former slate quarries and gold and copper mines are being turned into visitor attractions. Blaenau Ffestiniog now has two slate mines open to the public.

Snowdon and the nearby town of Llanberis form the main target for most visitors, but there's good mountain walking in many other parts of the park. Above Dolgellau in the south, Cadair (Cader) Idris rises to around 900m. There are hikes in the forests and hills around Betws-y-Coed in the east.

While the main reason for coming to the park is to walk, there are numerous other activities – climbing, white-water rafting,

pony trekking and windsurfing. Several of Wales' 'Great Little Railways' are found in Snowdonia, including the famous Ffestiniog Railway.

Rainfall in the area is very high, with over 500mm some years. By way of comparison, the town of Leicester in England manages an annual average of only 63mm. There are several lakes in Snowdonia and some are used for water storage for hydroelectric power. The largest pumped storage scheme in Europe is on the edge of the park near Tanigrisau. Hikers must be prepared to deal with hostile conditions at any time of the year. You should never go walking without rain gear, even if the day starts with a cloudless sky.

ORIENTATION

Although it takes its name from the mountain range in the north, the park extends far south of Mt Snowdon. It covers 840 square miles (2200 sq km), including much of North Wales and parts of Mid Wales.

Most of the land in the park is privately owned and used for hill farming. Herds of wild goats are sometimes seen on the higher ground, and sheep and cattle graze on the more accessible grass of the lower slopes and in the valleys.

INFORMATION

There are National Park Information Centres at Aberdovey (☎ 01654-767321), Betws-y-Coed (☎ 01690-710426), Blaenau Ffestiniog (☎ 01766-830360), Dolgellau (☎ 01341-422888) and Harlech (☎ 01766-780658). All are open from 9.30 am to 6 pm in the high season, and the centre at Betws-y-Coed is also open in winter from 10 am to 4.30 pm. The head office (☎ 01766-770274) is at Penrhyndeudraeth.

All the information centres have accommodation lists, a free bed-booking service and public transport timetables, as well as leaflets about walks and other activities in the area.

There are TICs at Barmouth (☎ 01341-280787), Tywyn (☎ 01654-710070), the Craft Centre in Corris (☎ 01654-761244),

Scaling Snowdon

Despite the fact that 500,000 people tramp up Snowdon every year, it's still a worthwhile hike to the 1085m (3558 feet) high summit. Views are stupendous on a clear day, and even if it's cloudy you often find you're above the clouds – they swirl beneath your feet, occasionally clearing to give brief glimpses of the valley far below. It's probably not a great idea to choose a midsummer weekend for this walk or you may be inclined to agree with Prince Charles who, on seeing the crowds, the litter and the café at the summit, declared it to be the 'highest slum in Europe'.

There's a choice of seven paths to the top. The easiest are the Llanberis Path (5½ hours), which follows the train track from Llanberis, and the Snowdon Ranger Path (five hours), which starts at the Snowdon Ranger Youth Hostel (near Beddgelert).

From Pen-y-Pass there are three routes. The Miners' Track (five hours) is the easiest of them, while the Pyg Track (5½ hours) includes some easy climbing and the Snowdon Horseshoe combines the two with a spectacular ridge walk that can take up to nine hours.

The Watkin Path (seven hours) is a tough walk from the south. The Rhyd Ddu Path (five hours) approaches Snowdon from the west, and is easier.

All these walks start from roads that are served daily by the Snowdon Sherpa bus.

Llanberis (☎ 01286-870765) and Machynlleth (☎ 01654-702401).

Available from TICs, *Snowdonia* is a useful free newspaper, listing guided walks and other activities in the region. It's published annually.

WALKS

The National Park publishes a useful series of leaflets on many of the mountain walks, including one on each of the six routes up Snowdon. They're available from TICs and information centres.

Although there are walks of all grades, you should be aware that even some walks described as easy may follow paths that go near very steep slopes and over loose scree. Take the Pyg Path up Snowdon and you'll find yourself literally climbing parts of it. Inevitably, with so many people on the mountains, accidents happen – usually on the way down. Each year, an average of 70 serious incidents occur and about 10 people end their lives up here. Be properly equipped before setting out, with food, drink, warm clothing and waterproofs.

The National Park organises a wide variety of 5 to 6-mile guided walks at various levels of difficulty. Charges are usually £1.50/50p.

CYCLE ROUTES

The high level of use of bridleways for off-road cycling to the summit of Snowdon has led to erosion and fears for walkers' safety. A ban is now in place and cycling is not allowed between 10 am and 5 pm, June to September.

There are biking routes through the following forests: Coed-y-Brenin, between Dolgellau and Ffestiniog, Gwydyr Forest near Betws-y-Coed, and Beddgelert Forest Park.

OTHER ACTIVITIES
Pony Trekking & Horse Riding

There are many stables offering escorted and unescorted rides. Snowdonia Riding Stables (☎ 01286-650342) is based at Waunfawr, on the western edge of the park near Caernarfon. It offers escorted rides only – one hour costs £10 and a full day £40. The stables are near the bus stop in Waunfawr, and the Snowdon Sherpa bus service between Caernarfon and Llanberis stops here.

Meifod Isaf Riding & Trekking Centre (☎ 01341-247651), on the outskirts of Dyffryn Ardudwy, between Harlech and Barmouth, is open Easter to October and offers rides from £8 for one hour to £15 for an afternoon.

Narrow-Gauge Railway Journeys

One of the features of this area is the number of narrow-gauge railways. The Ffestiniog Railway runs from Porthmadog to Blaenau Ffestiniog, Snowdon Mountain Railway from Llanberis to the summit, and Talyllyn from Tywyn to Abergynolwyn. Shorter lines include the Llanberis Lake Railway, the Fairbourne Railway, the Bala Lake Railway and the Welsh Highland Railway. See the later sections of this chapter for details.

PLACES TO STAY

There are 13 youth hostels in and around the park, among them some of the best in the country.

Around Mt Snowdon, there are hostels at Pen-y-Pass (☎ 01286-870428), near Llanberis on the Pyg and Llyn Llydaw Miners' tracks up to the summit; Llanberis (☎ 01286-870280); Bryn Gwynant (☎ 01766-890251), Nant Gwynant, 4 miles from Beddgelert near the Watkin Path up Snowdon; Snowdon Ranger (☎ 01286-650391), 5 miles from Beddgelert at the starting point for the Ranger Path; and Idwal Cottage (☎ 01248-600225), Nant Ffrancon, near Bethesda.

There are also hostels at Capel Curig (☎ 01690-720225), 5 miles from Betws-y-Coed; Lledr Valley (☎ 01690-750202), on the main road between Betws-y-Coed and Ffestiniog; Rowen (☎ 01492-530627), 5 miles from Conwy; Conwy (☎ 01492-593571), Sychnant; Llanbedr (☎ 01341-241287), Plas Newydd (near Harlech); and Kings (☎ 01341-422392), Penmaenpool, near Dolgellau.

In addition to the hostels, there are bunkhouses and camping grounds. To camp on a non-official site, you need to get the permission of the landowner.

Within the park, Betws-y-Coed has the most B&Bs and guesthouses; others are found in smaller villages and on farms.

GETTING THERE & AWAY
Bus

National Express (☎ 0990-808080) has services from London to Llandudno (seven hours, £17) and Bangor twice daily, and from London to Aberystwyth once daily.

Arriva Cymru (☎ 01492-596969) operates the Traws-Cambria service (No 701) daily from Bristol through Cardiff, Machynlleth, Dolgellau and Caernarfon to Bangor.

Train

There's a regular InterCity service from London's Euston station via Crewe (where you may have to change) to Llandudno Junction and Bangor, with at least one train an hour. Change at Llandudno Junction for the Conwy Valley line, which connects Llanrwst, Betws-y-Coed, Pont-y-Pant and Blaenau Ffestiniog.

There's also an InterCity service from London via Birmingham to Shrewsbury, where you can take the line to Machynlleth for the scenic Cambrian Coast Railway via Harlech to Pwllheli.

For all train inquiries phone ☎ 0345-484950.

GETTING AROUND

Despite the reorganisation of county boundaries, bus and train information for the area continues to be produced in the useful *Gwynedd Public Transport Maps and Timetables*, available from TICs. Phone ☎ 01286-679535 for information.

Many bus companies operate services in the area and several share a route, often with one company operating during the week and another at weekends. Red Rover passes allow unlimited travel for a day on routes within the park as well as from access points, such as Wrexham and Aberystwyth, for £4.40.

The Snowdon Sherpa bus service operates in the area – these buses are particularly good for walkers and for people staying in youth hostels. The buses will stop on request at any safe place in the park, and they follow a round-the-mountain route so that walkers can go up one path and down another. Route 95 goes from Caernarfon to

Beddgelert five times a day, and once a day on to Llanberis throughout the year (daily except Sunday). Route 19 goes from Llandudno via Llanrwst, Betws-y-Coed and Pen-y-Pass Youth Hostel to Llanberis. The service operates three times daily (six times a day from Llandudno to Llanrwst) from Easter to October.

Apart from the narrow-gauge railways, there are three lines within the park that are useful for travellers – the Conwy Valley line, the Cambrian Coast line and the Ffestiniog Railway (see Getting There & Away).

If you plan to do a lot of travelling in one day, the North & Mid Wales Day Ranger allows travel on most bus services (except the 701), and most trains, including the Ffestiniog Railway, with discounts on many of the private railways. Only available for travel after 9 am, the ticket costs £16.90 for one day's travel. There's also the North & Mid Wales Rover, with the same bus and train coverage and restrictions. This costs £39.90 for seven days travel, or £25.70 for three days within a seven-day period. Family tickets for two adults and up to four children are available and offer good value.

BETWS-Y-COED
- pop 700   ☎ 01690

Betus (as it's known and pronounced) is a tourist village that styles itself as the eastern gateway to the park. The name means Chapel (or Prayer House) in the Wood, because of the 14th century church here, and the village is still in an attractive woodland setting in the Gwydyr Forest.

Betws-y-Coed has been Wales' most popular inland resort since the Victorian days, and it gets very crowded in summer. There are walks to Swallow and Conwy Falls nearby, and pleasant hikes in the surrounding hills. It can make a reasonable base for walking in the Snowdon range, particularly if you have your own transport, but you may wish to stay in one of the villages closer to the mountains.

Orientation & Information
There are only two streets of note, so it's easy to find your way around.

The National Park Information Centre (☎ 710426) is in Royal Oak Stables, at the far end of the playing fields past the train station.

On High St, Climber & Rambler (☎ 710555) is an outdoor shop that also sells books and has information on walking, climbing and scrambling in the area.

Things to See & Do
There's little to do here except walk and take tea, which in this case is enough. There are two museums, neither of very great interest. Betws-y-Coed Motor Museum (☎ 710760) is a small collection near the information centre; entry is £1.30/80p. There's also the Conwy Valley Railway Museum (☎ 710568), which is adjacent to the train station.

There's pony trekking at Ty Coch Farm (☎ 760248), Penmachno, 6 miles from Betws-y-Coed. Rides through the Gwydyr Forest cost from £9 for an hour. The farm also does a popular pub ride for £22.50, lasting around four hours.

Walks & Cycle Routes
The information centre has details of a number of walks in the surrounding area.

The popular Bridges & Rivers walk is an easy hike that takes two to three hours and starts from outside the information centre. You pass the meeting point of the Rivers Llugwy and Conwy, the Waterloo Bridge, built in 1815 (of course) and decorated with leek, rose, shamrock and thistle. The next bridge is Pont-y-Pair – the Bridge of the Cauldron – which was built in the 15th century, and finally there's the Miners' Bridge.

Mountain bikes can be hired from Beics Betws (☎ 710766), Tan Lan, behind the post office. The charge is a hefty £16 a day but you can also receive advice on routes.

Places to Stay
Betus has the largest number of beds in the park, and there are B&Bs and hotels to suit all budgets.

There are two youth hostels, both about 5 miles away. *Ledr Valley Youth Hostel* (☎ 01690-750202, *Pont-y-Pant*) is on the A470, and there's also the *Capel Curig Youth Hostel* (see Capel Curig later in this chapter).

In High St, *Cross Keys Hotel & Restaurant* (☎ 710334) charges £30/40 for single/double rooms with bath. Next door is *Glan Llugwy* (☎ 710592), which is non-smoking. The charge is £16 per person.

Closer to the centre, and also on High St, the *Pont-y-Pair Hotel* (☎ 710407) charges £19 to £22 per person. In the centre of town, on High St near the green, is the *Plas Dderwen Hotel & Restaurant* (☎ 710388). B&B is £17 to £20 per person.

There are several places on Llanrwst Rd, which is off the A470 heading to Llandudno and half a mile from Waterloo Bridge. The excellent *Bron Celyn Guest House* (☎ 710333) charges £44 for a double room with bath. *Bryn Bella Guest House* (☎ 710627), also on Llanrwst Rd, charges from £18/38. The proprietors of both guesthouses will pick you up from the train station.

East of Betws-y-Coed in Capel Garmon is *Tan-y-Foes Country House* (☎ 710507). In a 16th century stone building, it's a very comfortable non-smoking hotel. There are nine rooms, some with four-poster beds. B&B is from £45 to £75 per person but there are also short-stay options.

Ty Gwyn (☎ 710383), south of the bridge in the village, is a 17th century coaching inn, where B&B costs from £17.50 per person, rising to £28 for a room with bathroom or £37 per person for a four-poster bed. There's a good restaurant.

Places to Eat

On one side of the train station entrance is *Dil's Diner* (☎ 710346), open from 8.30 am until around 8 pm. It does cheap filling meals such as fish and chips (£4). On the other side of the station entrance is the excellent *Alpine Coffee Shop*. Good sandwiches are available on a range of breads including ciabatta (£2.25), full meals, and a range of traditionally British warming drinks such as Bovril, Horlicks or Ovaltine.

There are several teashops along High St. The *Pont-y-Pair Hotel* does good bar food.

The top restaurant is at the *Ty Gwyn* (see Places to Stay). Most dishes are £10.95 to £13.95 (eg rosettes of juniper-marinated venison with apricot).

Getting There & Away

Betws-y-Coed is served by rail and bus from Llandudno Junction. There are eight trains a day, Monday to Saturday, on the Conwy Valley line from Llandudno (25 minutes, £3.10).

Buses take about 10 minutes longer from Llandudno Junction to Betus. Snowdon Sherpa buses run from Llandudno to Conwy, Betws-y-Coed, Capel Curig and Pen-y-Pass (for the youth hostels), then on to Llanberis and Caernarfon.

CAPEL CURIG

Six miles west of Betws-y-Coed is a small village that is one of the oldest resorts in the area. It's a popular place with walkers, climbers and outdoor enthusiasts of all types.

The Plas Y Brenin National Mountain Centre (☎ 01690-720214) is on the edge of the village and has a bar and climbing wall. It runs two-day courses in canoeing and abseiling, and most evenings at 8 pm there are lectures that are open to all. You can rent equipment and some accommodation is offered.

The *Capel Curig Youth Hostel* (☎ 01690-720225) is open daily from mid-February to mid-December. It's in the village, next to the garage. The nightly charge is £8.80/5.95 for adults/juniors.

In the evenings, everyone meets at the *Bryn Tyrch* (☎ 720223), a hotel (B&B from £20.50 per person) with a busy pub, or at the bar at Plas Y Brenin.

The Snowdon Sherpa bus passes this way between Betws and Llanberis.

LLANBERIS

- **pop 2000** ☎ 01286

This tourist village lies at the foot of Mt Snowdon and becomes packed with walkers and climbers. It makes an excellent base, although accommodation can be booked out in July and August.

Orientation & Information

Llanberis is bypassed by the A4086, which also separates the village from its two lakes, Llyn Padarn and Llyn Peris. The TIC (☎ 870765) is on High St, opposite the post office. Almost all the accommodation and places to eat are strung out along this street – you can't get lost.

Snowdon Mountain Railway

Snowdon Mountain Railway (☎ 870223), Britain's only public rack-and-pinion railway, opened in 1896 and climbs more than 900m from Llanberis to the summit of Snowdon, a 5 mile journey that takes an hour.

Seven vintage steam locomotives and four modern diesel locomotives haul carriages up and down between mid-March and the end of October. Schedules are subject to the weather but trains usually start running at 9 am. The queues can be long during the main part of the season. If you can't be bothered walking to the top of Snowdon, you're made to pay for your laziness – a return ride is £14.80/10.70. It's sometimes also possible to buy a stand-by ticket down from the top for £6/5.

Other Things to See & Do

Across the bypass, the **Snowdonia Museum** adopts the Disney approach to Welsh history, with talking trees and a brief scattering of historical facts. The **Electric Mountain Dinorwig Discovery** tour also starts here. Visits to this underground power station built deep inside the mountain are quite interesting. Dinorwig is a quick-response power station, constructed to deal with power surges on the national grid when half the population of Britain simultaneously puts the kettle on during the commercial breaks on TV. Combined tickets for the museum and power station are £5/2.50; they're both open daily from March to November.

The **Llanberis Lake Railway** (☎ 870549) runs beside Llyn Padarn between March and

October. The round trip takes 45 minutes and costs £4.10/1.50. The **Welsh Slate Museum** (☎ 870630) is on the site of the old Dinorwic Quarry, on the shore of Llyn Padarn. Visits to the old quarry workshops and demonstrations of the skills involved in splitting slate into tiles are interesting. The museum is open April to September from 9.30 am to 5.30 pm; entry is £3.50/2.

Dolbadarn Castle (Cadw) is a 13th century ruin that was built to guard Llanberis Pass. It's a pleasant walk south-east of the town.

Activities

Apart from hiking up Snowdon, there are numerous other outdoor activities in the area. The **Dolbadarn Pony Trekking Centre** (☎ 870277) operates from the Dolbadarn Hotel. It charges £10 per hour, hard hat included.

The **Padarn Watersports Centre** (☎ 870556), Llyn Padarn, offers a wide range of activities (kayaking, canoeing, raft building, climbing, abseiling and mountain walking) for groups of two to four people (or more). The charge for a group of five for half a day is £18 per person – whatever the activity.

Places to Stay

Camping Just past Llanberis Youth Hostel is *Hafodlydan Campsite*. The charge is £2 a night per person. *Cae Gwyn Camp Site* (☎ 870718), at Nant Peris, 2 miles from Llanberis, charges £2.50.

Hostels There's dormitory accommodation at *The Heights Hotel* (☎ 871179, 74 High St) for £9.

Surrounded by Welsh Black cattle, and with a good view over the top of the slate quarry, *Llanberis Youth Hostel* (☎ 870280) was originally a quarry manager's dwelling. It's half a mile south-west of the town and is open from April to August, daily. For the rest of the year it's open for most of the week – phone for opening days. The nightly charge is £8/5.40 for adults/juniors. *Pen-y-Pass Youth Hostel* (☎ 870428) is superbly situated at the top of Llanberis Pass, 5½ miles from Llanberis. It was once a hotel popular with Victorian mountaineers. The hostel is open daily from January through October, and over the New Year; a bed with a view costs £8.80/5.95.

Gwastadnant Bunkhouse (☎ 870356) is at Nant Peris, 2 miles out of Llanberis on the way to Pen-y-Pass. There's bunkhouse accommodation from £4 per person, camping for £2.50 and B&B for £15. Facilities include a coin-operated drying room, showers and cooker.

About 3 miles from Llanberis on the Bangor road, *Jesse James Bunkhouse* (☎ 870521, *Penisarwaun*) has been going since 1966 and is a popular walkers' base – non-smokers only. JJ is a mountain guide who offers accommodation from £7 to £15.

B&Bs & Hotels *Beech Bank Guest House* (☎ 870414), at the far end of High St from the station, overlooking the lake, charges £15 per person. Also at the Caernarfon end of Llanberis is the *Alpine Lodge Hotel* (☎ 870294, *1 High St*), which has doubles/triples from £35/45 and a small single for £14.

Padarn Lake Hotel (☎ 870260), at the other end of High St, also charges £31/52 for singles/doubles. *Dolbadarn Hotel* (☎ 870277), opposite, has rooms for £17/34 (£40 for a double with bath). The hotel has a restaurant and bar, and there's a pony trekking centre (see Activities) beside it. Nearby, *Y Gwynedd Hotel* (☎ 870203) charges £24/48 for rooms with bath.

Pen-y-Gwyrd Hotel (☎ 870211) is 7 miles from Llanberis, just beyond Pen-y-Pass on the junction of the A498 and A4086. B&B is from £21 per person. The 1953 Everest team used the inn as a training base – you can see their signatures on the ceiling. The residents sit down together for the evening meal in the dining room, and bar food is also available.

At Llanrug, 5 miles north-west of Llanberis along the A4086, *Lakeside* (☎ 870065) offers B&B from £20 to £24 per person. It's set in delightful surroundings with peacocks and ornamental fowl in the grounds. You can even watch a pair of barn owls from a hide near the lake.

In Llanberis, the top place to stay is the *Royal Victoria Hotel* (☎ 870253), near the Snowdon Mountain Railway station. It has rooms with bathroom at £46 per person, including breakfast, or £52 for dinner, bed and breakfast. There may be reduced rates when business is slow. In the restaurant, there are two three-course set menus, one at £11.50 and the other at £16.75.

Places to Eat

Pete's Eats (☎ 870358, *40 High St*) is a warm café where hikers swap information over large portions of healthy food. For walking fodder, try their Big Jim – a mixed grill with bacon, sausages, liver, chips etc for £8.50. There are good vegetarian choices and the place is open Easter to October from 9 am to 9 pm on weekdays and from 8 am to 8 pm at weekends. For the rest of the year, it's open from 9 am to 6.30 pm during the week and from 8 am to 8 pm at weekends. There's a useful notice board here.

In the evenings, climbers hang out in *The Heights* (☎ 871179), a hotel (see Places to Stay) with a pub that even has its own climbing wall.

Y Bistro (☎ 871278, *45 High St*) is the place to go for a splurge – Welsh produce with a French twist. Char from Llyn Padarn is served when available. It's open only in the evening, with set dinners from £19 to £22.50.

Getting There & Away

Llanberis is 13 miles from Bangor. From Bangor, take the No 77 bus that runs nine times a day (at irregular intervals) from Monday to Saturday (45 minutes, £1.40). From Caernarfon, take bus No 88, which runs about twice-hourly from Monday to Saturday (25 minutes, £1.10). This service continues to Nant Peris.

There are five No 95 Sherpa buses a day from Caernarfon (1¼ hours), Monday to Saturday, and about three daily in the high season from Llandudno (two hours).

BEDDGELERT

This is one of the most attractive of the Snowdon villages, situated on the banks of the River Gwynant. The name means Gelert's Grave; and comes from a local legend that tells of Prince Llewlyn's dog Gelert, killed by its owner after he thought it had savaged his baby son, when the dog had in fact killed a wolf that was attacking the baby.

Just outside the village is the **Sygun Copper Mine** (☎ 01766-510100), mined from Roman times until it was turned into a tourist attraction. It's open daily and entry is £4.50/3.

Places to Stay

The *Snowdon Ranger Youth Hostel* (☎ 01286-650391) is 5 miles north of the village. Fully open from April to August (phone for other opening days), the nightly charge is £8.80/5.95 for adults/juniors.

The *Bryn Gwynant Youth Hostel* (☎ 01766-890251) is 4 miles from Beddgelert on the A498, in an idyllic location beside Llyn Gwynant. It's open daily from March through October; a bed costs £8.80/5.95.

For B&B, *Ael-y-Bryn* (☎ 01766-890310), in the centre of the village, charges £16.50 per person in summer. The *Sygun Fawr Hotel* (☎ 01766-890258) is about a mile from Beddgelert, in an old house. Rooms have a bathroom and the charge is £30/54 for a single/double.

Getting There & Away

Beddgelert is on the route of the Snowdon Sherpa bus. There are several services a day to Caernarfon and Llanberis.

BLAENAU FFESTINIOG

- pop 5500   ☎ 01766

Slate was the basis of the wealth in Snowdonia in the 19th century and Blaenau Ffestiniog was the centre of the industry. Although slate mining continues here on a small scale, it's now a tourist town. The history of the slate industry, the Ffestiniog Railway (which has its northern terminus

here) and the hydroelectric power station are the main tourist attractions.

Despite being in the centre of the park, the grey slate waste tips that surround Blaenau Ffestiniog prevented it from being officially included in the national park. The two main mines in the area are in the town – nearby is the smaller village of Ffestiniog.

The National Park Information Centre (☎ 830360) is in the High St, in the same building as the Ffestiniog Railway Office.

Ffestiniog Railway

A means of access as well as an attraction, the Ffestiniog Railway (☎ 512340) is a 13½ mile narrow-gauge line extending from Porthmadog on the coast.

Construction of the line began in 1832. In 1836, horse-drawn wagons started to take the slate from the mine down to Porthmadog, from where it was shipped to Europe and America. In the 1860s, steam locomotives were introduced and the line was opened up as a passenger service.

The railway is open daily March to October from 9.15 am to 5 pm. A return trip is £12.80 on a steam train. A 1st class ticket allowing you to sit in the observation car or in a traditional vintage coach is £5 extra for a return ticket.

Slate Mines

The **Llechwedd Slate Caverns** (☎ 830306) are open all year from 10 am to 6 pm (shorter hours in winter). You can ride into the tunnels on the miners' tramway, dating from 1846, or descend into the Deep Mine on the steepest passenger railway in Britain. As you walk through vast underground chambers, a commentary explains what it was like to work down here. Tickets cost £6.50/4.50 for a single tour and £9.95/6.75 for both tours.

Places to Stay & Eat

Most of the people who visit Blaenau Ffestiniog do so on day trips on the train. If you want to stay, there's a small choice of accommodation.

Afallon (☎ 830468, *Manod Rd*) is a friendly place with three rooms; B&B is

£15 per person. It's only half a mile from the station but they will meet you. Similarly priced and right by the train station is *Dolawel* (☎ 830511).

The excellent *Ty Clwb* (☎ 762658) is a modernised 18th century stone guesthouse in the square, offering B&B from £18 per person.

Tyddyn Du Farm (☎ 590281) is about 6 miles outside the town at Gellilydan. There are three rooms in the 17th century farmhouse, where B&B is from £18 to £25 per person. There are jacuzzis in some suites.

Five miles south of Blaenau in the village of Maentwrog is the *Old Rectory* (☎ 590305), where upmarket B&B costs £45/55 for a single/double in the house, £30/45 in the annexe. All rooms have a bathroom. Also in Maentwrog is *Grapes* (☎ 590208), a pub and restaurant that does excellent meals. As well as soup and sandwiches there are good main courses from £5.50.

Getting There & Away

From Monday to Saturday there are hourly buses from Caernarfon to Blaenau Ffestiniog (1½ hours, £3.20). There are also services to Harlech, Barmouth and Pwllheli. Bus No 35 goes to Dolgellau three times a day, Monday to Saturday.

The Conwy Valley line goes from Llandudno or Llandudno Junction via Betwsy-Coed to Blaenau Ffestiniog, six times a day, Monday to Saturday (35 minutes, £4). From Porthmadog there's the Ffestiniog Railway.

HARLECH

• pop 1300   ☎ 01766

Dramatically positioned above the plains, the ruins of Harlech Castle dominate this sleepy little town. There are superb views out to sea and some good beaches nearby.

The TIC (☎ 780658) is in High St and is open daily from April to October. The train station is on the plain below the castle.

Harlech Castle

The castle (☎ 780552, Cadw) is a World Heritage site, and rightly so. Another creation of Edward I, it was built between 1283 and 1289. The castle is rectangular with two concentric sets of walls, and is constructed of local grey sandstone.

Harlech is sometimes called the Castle of Lost Causes because it has been defended so many times to no avail. It was taken in 1404 by Owain Glyndŵr and became his stronghold until 1409. He was in turn besieged here by the future Henry V. It was the last castle to fall in the Wars of the Roses – attacks on the Lancastrians by the Yorkists continued from 1461 until 1468. By Elizabethan times, the castle was in ruins except for the massive twin-towered gatehouse and the outer walls, which are still intact. They make the place seem impregnable even now.

When it was built, the sea covered the plain below, and ships could sail right to the foot of the castle stairway that is still in use today. The castle is open daily; entry is £3/2.

Places to Stay & Eat

Llanbedr Youth Hostel (☎ 01341-241287, *Plas Newydd, Llanbedr*) is 3 miles south of Harlech. It's fully open from mid-April through August; phone for other opening times. The nightly charge is £8/5.40 for adults/juniors.

You can camp at *Min-y-Don Caravan & Camping Site* (☎ 780286), by the beach below Harlech, for £2 per person.

Godre'r Graig (☎ 780905) in Morfa Rd, called 'the bottom road' because it's under the castle, charges £15 per person for B&B. In the upper part of the town, in High St next to the church, *Byrdir Hotel* (☎ 780316) does B&B from £15 per person, or £20 in a room with bath.

The *Lion Hotel* (☎ 780731), near the castle, charges £19 per person. There's cheap pub grub in the bar.

The *Castle Hotel* (☎ 780529, Castle Square) has some rooms with great views – Nos 3 and 4 are the best, and it's £48 for two people.

Nearby *Castle Cottage* (☎ 780479) is a very comfortable place to stay, with singles/doubles with bathroom from £38/56. It also has two singles without bath for £26. This is also the top place to eat in Harlech, with set dinners at £21.50.

Plas Café (☎ *780204, High St*) boasts the finest view of any restaurant in Harlech – across to the castle and down to the sea. You can also sit outside. A variety of dishes is served from £3.95, and there are good vegetarian choices.

Getting There & Away

Trains run from Machynlleth to Harlech seven times a day (1¼ hours, £8). Bus No 38 operates from Barmouth to Harlech (25 minutes) nine times a day and continues to Blaenau Ffestiniog five times a day.

BARMOUTH
* **pop 2200**   ☎ **01341**

Barmouth is a popular seaside resort with a long sandy beach, and there are some pleasant walks in the area. You can hike up on the cliffs of Dinas Oleu above the town or across the estuary to Fairbourne.

The TIC (☎ 280787) is on Station Rd. There are numerous hotels and B&Bs. Non-smoking *Just Beds* (☎ *281165, Bryn Teify, King Edward St*) offers accommodation at £9 per person. *Wavecrest Hotel* (☎ *280330, 8 Marine Parade*) is a friendly sea-front hotel with comfortable accommodation from £17 to £25 per person. It's also noted for its food. The Fairbourne & Barmouth Railway (☎ 250362) runs 2½ miles from Fairbourne train station to Penrhyn Point, from April to October.

TYWYN

This little seaside town is best known for the **Talyllyn Railway** (☎ 01654-710472), which runs 7 miles inland to Abergynol-wyn. Trains run daily in summer and are all steam-hauled; tickets are £8/2. There's a small **railway museum** containing narrow-gauge locomotives by the station in Tywyn.

The Tywyn TIC (☎ 01654-710070) is in High St.

DOLGELLAU
* **pop 2300**   ☎ **01341**

Dolgellau (pronounced doll-geth-lie) is a market town that makes a good base for walks on Cadair Idris, the second-highest mountain in Snowdonia National Park.

In the 15th century the town was Owain Glyndŵr's capital and his parliament was held here. The town has historical links with the Quaker movement, which established a community in the area. The TIC offers theme walks round the various Quaker sites in the summer. In the 18th century, Dolgellau was the centre of the prosperous Welsh wool industry; it's now the administrative centre for the region.

The National Park Information Centre (☎ 422888) is in Ty Meirion, Eldon Square. The centre is open daily in summer from 10 am to 6 pm; shorter hours in winter. Upstairs, the **Quaker Heritage Centre** has an interesting exhibition; entry is free.

Walks

The information centre has leaflets (30 to 40p) on local walks, including National Park descriptions of the trails up Cadair Idris. The standard route up Cadair Idris is the Pony Track from Ty Nant, a return trip of four to five hours. It can be wild up here if the weather comes down. Francis Kilvert wrote of his 1871 trip in *Kilvert's Diary*, describing it as 'the stoniest, dreariest, most desolate mountain I was ever on … It is an awful place in a storm. I thought of Moses on Sinai'. On a sunny summer's day, however, it's glorious.

The least energetic walk is the town trail. The Precipice Walk, which sounds rather more lethal than it actually is, starts near Llanfachreth and takes in wonderful views of the Mawddach Estuary.

Places to Stay

According to local legend, anyone who spends the night on top of Cadair Idris will wake either as a poet or go mad. Luckily there's a wide range of accommodation in the area. There's a camping barn, camping ground and tearoom at *Ty Nant* (☎ *423433,*

Ffordd y Gader). The stone barn sleeps 12 (£4 per person) – all you need is a foam mat and sleeping bag. Gas cookers and cooking utensils are available.

Caban Cader Idris (☎ 01248-600478) is in a secluded valley at Islawrdref, about 3 miles south-west of Dolgellau. The nightly charge is £6 per person. It's usually let to groups at £30 for six people.

One mile out of Dolgellau, on the old Fairbourne Rd, is *Glynn Farm (☎ 422286)* with lovely views of the Mawddach Estuary. B&B is £15 per person, or £18 with bath. There's a small single for £14.

Non-smoking *Tanyfron (☎ 422638, Arran Rd)* is half a mile from Dolgellau and an excellent place to stay. B&B is £19 per person.

Clifton House Hotel (☎ 422554, Smithfield Square) has double rooms for £35, or £45 with bath. *Ivy House (☎ 422535)* is centrally located in Finsbury Square. B&B is from £18.50 per person; there's a bar and the restaurant serves good Welsh food.

Dolserau Hall Hotel (☎ 422522) is 1½ miles east of Dolgellau. The hotel is open all year and charges from £45 per person for B&B. It's in a peaceful location and there are excellent views from the rooms.

Penmaenuchaf Hall Hotel (☎ 422129), 2 miles from Dolgellau at Penmaenpool, is the most luxurious hotel in the area; a peaceful retreat in 9-hectare grounds. Singles/doubles are from £70/100 to £110/155.

Places to Eat

Dylanwad Da Restaurant (☎ 422870, 2 Ffos-y-Felin) is a good place for dinner with main dishes from about £8 to £13. Roast loin of lamb with Madeira sauce is £10.60. There are several vegetarian choices. The *Old Country Gaol Restaurant* in the Clifton House Hotel serves good Welsh food.

Outside Dolgellau, in Penmaenpool, is the *George III (☎ 422525)*, a pub that offers a wide range of reasonable food.

Getting There & Away

Arriva Cymru operates several services to Dolgellau. Bus No 2 from Caernarfon (1½

hours, £3.65) operates six times a day, Monday to Saturday, and twice a day on Sunday; the No 94 from Barmouth (22 minutes) operates six times a day, Monday to Saturday, and continues to Llangollen and Wrexham; and the No 34 from Aberystwyth/Machynlleth (35 minutes) operates six times a day from Monday to Saturday, twice a day on Sunday. Bus No 35 goes to Blaenau Ffestiniog three times a day, Monday to Saturday.

BALA
* **pop 2000** ☎ **01678**

Bala is a small market town situated at the eastern end of Llyn Tegid, the largest natural lake in Wales. The lake is 4 miles long and almost three-quarters of a mile wide, and it's now the centre for a wide variety of water-based activities.

The Bala Adventure & Water Sports Centre (☎ 521059) offers introductory sessions in mountain biking, canoeing, raft building, windsurfing, sailing, rock climbing and abseiling. Sessions cost from around £19 per person. It will also rent equipment for all the above sports.

Canolfan Tryweryn (☎ 521083) offers a 20 minute white-water rafting trip for £10.

There's a TIC (☎ 521021) on Pensarn Rd. *Cynwyd Youth Hostel (☎ 01490-412814, The Old Mill, Cynwyd)* is the nearest HI hostel, 10 miles from the lake. At least it's cheap – £6.50/4.45 for adults/juniors.

The Bala Lake Railway (☎ 540666) runs the 4½ miles from Bala station to Llanuwchllyn along the lake, from April to early October.

North-Western Wales

This section includes all of north-western Wales lying outside the Snowdonia National Park. Llandudno is a traditional seaside resort, Conwy and Caernarfon are dominated by spectacular castles, and the particularly Welsh areas of Anglesey and the Llŷn Peninsula see far fewer tourists than other parts of the country.

LLANDUDNO
- **pop 13,500** ☎ **01492**

As the largest seaside resort in Wales, Llandudno seethes with tourists, which in this instance seems entirely fitting. It was developed as an upmarket Victorian holiday town and it has retained its beautiful architecture and 19th century atmosphere. There's a wonderful pier and promenade – and donkeys on the beach.

Llandudno is on its own peninsula, situated between two sweeping beaches, and is dominated by the spectacular limestone headland – the Great Orme – with the mountains of Snowdonia as a backdrop. The Great Orme, with its Bronze Age mine, tramway, chair lift and superb views, is quite fascinating.

In its 19th century heyday, Llandudno's visitors included many of the famous people of the day, such as Gladstone and Disraeli. In 1861, the Liddell family, whose daughter was Lewis Carroll's model for *Alice in Wonderland*, spent the summer in the house that is now the St Tudno Hotel. The Liddells later built a house on the other side of the town, which has since become the Gogarth Abbey Hotel.

Orientation & Information
The town fills the central section of the peninsula, with the Llandudno Bay beach to the north and the West Shore to the southwest. Mostyn St is the main shopping street. The tip of the peninsula is the Great Orme; the Little Orme is to the east.

The TIC (☎ 876413), 1-2 Chapel St, is open all year, daily from April to October, from 9.30 am to 6 pm.

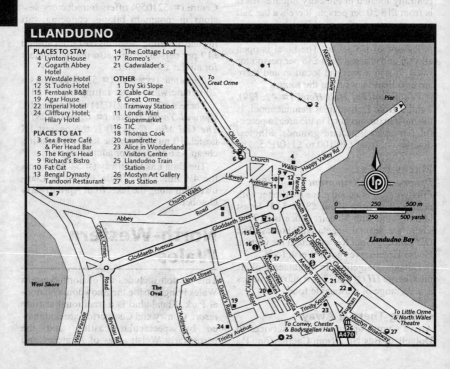

LLANDUDNO

PLACES TO STAY
4 Lynton House
7 Gogarth Abbey Hotel
8 Westdale Hotel
12 St Tudno Hotel
15 Fernbank B&B
19 Agar House
22 Imperial Hotel
24 Cliffbury Hotel; Hilary Hotel

PLACES TO EAT
3 Sea Breeze Café & Pier Head Bar
5 The King's Head
9 Richard's Bistro
10 Fat Cat
13 Bengal Dynasty Tandoori Restaurant

14 The Cottage Loaf
17 Romeo's
21 Cadwalader's

OTHER
1 Dry Ski Slope
2 Cable Car
6 Great Orme Tramway Station
11 Londis Mini Supermarket
16 TIC
18 Thomas Cook
20 Laundrette
23 Alice in Wonderland Visitors Centre
25 Llandudno Train Station
26 Mostyn Art Gallery
27 Bus Station

There's a laundrette at 25 Brookes St, and a Londis Mini Supermarket near the Fat Cat café bar on Mostyn St.

Things to See & Do

There are superb views from the Great Orme and the headland is home to many species of flowers, butterflies and birds. Guided walks are offered from May to September, and there's a café and gift-shop complex at the top.

The **Great Orme Tramway** (☎ 876749), at the top of Church Walks, takes you up in original 1902 tramcars. It operates daily, Easter to October, from 10 am to 6 pm; tickets cost £3.80/2.60 return. The **Great Orme Mine** is a Bronze Age copper mine halfway along the tramline; it's open at the same time as the tram. A combined ticket for the tramway and the mine is £7.25/5. There's also a **cable car** (☎ 877205) that operates, subject to the weather, from Happy Valley, above the pier. Tickets are £4.80/2.50 return.

Elegant Victorian **Llandudno Pier** reaches 670m into the sea. The pier was first built in 1857 but it collapsed in a storm two years later. The current pier was started in 1877, and its main use was as a disembarkation point for passengers from the Isle of Man steamers. There's jazz on Sunday afternoons, and you can rent fishing tackle from the Victoria Angling Centre (☎ 530663) at the pier entrance, and fish from the pier.

The **Alice in Wonderland Visitors Centre**, alias The Rabbit Hole (☎ 860087), 3 Trinity Square, makes the most of the town's Alice connection with amateurish tableaux that will excite only the most ardent fans. It's open daily in summer and from Monday to Saturday in winter; entry is £2.95/1.95.

The **Mostyn Art Gallery** (☎ 879201), 12 Vaughan St, is the leading gallery for contemporary art in North Wales; open Monday to Saturday; entry is free. The **North Wales Theatre** (☎ 872000), on the promenade, is one of the largest in Britain and opened in 1996.

If none of these interests you, there's always the **dry ski slope** above the town.

Places to Stay

There are 700 hotels and guesthouses here, so finding a bed is rarely a problem.

St David's Rd is a good place to start looking. *Cliffbury Hotel* (☎ 877224), at No 34, charges from £16 per person. At No 32, the *Hilary Hotel* (☎ 875623) does B&B from £19 per person in rooms with bath. *Agar House* (☎ 875572), at No 17, charges £17 per person.

There are many places in the £14 to £20 bracket along St Mary's Rd, one block towards the Promenade.

Fernbank (☎ 877251) is a few doors down from the TIC at 9 Chapel St. B&B is good value at around £13 per person.

Westdale Hotel (☎ 877996, 37 Abbey Rd) is a very comfortable place. B&B costs from £16.50 to £19 per person, and there is also a package that includes dinner from £22. *Lynton House* (☎ 875057, 80 Church Walks) is well-placed for the pier and the tramway, and charges £22 per person; all rooms have a bathroom.

At the top end of the accommodation scale are some of the hotels along the Promenade, such as the *Imperial Hotel* (☎ 877466), an elegant Victorian building where B&B is £65/95 for a single/double. Discounts may be offered when business is slack.

The *St Tudno Hotel* (☎ 874411, North Parade) is a luxurious hotel that charges from £45 to £125 per person. It's notable in that out of the many awards it has won, it has several times received the accolade 'Best Hotel Loos in Great Britain'!

The other hotel with *Alice in Wonderland* connections is *Gogarth Abbey Hotel* (☎ 876211, West Shore). B&B is around £40 per person; there are 40 rooms, all with bathroom. One of the top hotels in Wales, *Bodysgallen Hall* (☎ 584466), is 3 miles from the town, just off the A470. It's a luxurious country-house hotel where rooms cost from £100/145. It does off-season two-day breaks for around £99 per person.

Places to Eat

Many of the B&Bs and guesthouses will provide evening meals if arranged in advance. They're used to serving them early, so expect to eat between 6 and 7 pm.

Along Mostyn St are fast-food restaurants, cafés and fish and chip places. *Cadwalader's* is an ice-cream parlour that's part of the Welsh chain named after the brother of Owain Glyndŵr. *The Fat Cat (☎ 871844, 149 Mostyn St)* is an excellent café bar where you can get anything from a drink to a full meal. The baguette filled with melted gruyère cheese (£3.45) is excellent.

Romeo's (☎ 877777, St Georges Place) does pizzas from £4.50 and steaks from £9.90 to £11.90. The best Indian place is the *Bengal Dynasty Tandoori Restaurant*, Prince Edward Square.

On Church Walks, *Richard's Bistro (☎ 877924)* is open every night but is very popular: you may need to book. Main dishes range from £11.95 to £18.95.

The Cottage Loaf, just off Gloddaeth St, and *The King's Head*, by the tramway station, are good places for a drink. Both also do food.

The restaurant at the *St Tudno Hotel (☎ 874411)* is regarded as the best place to eat in town. A five course dinner costs £29.50.

Getting There & Away

There are two National Express (☎ 0990-808080) buses a day from London. Bus No 5 runs frequently between Llandudno, Bangor and Caernarfon.

The train station at Llandudno Junction is on the main line from London's Euston, a 3½ hour journey. On average, there are three direct services a day. Services from Crewe (1¼ hours, £11.50) and Chester (50 minutes, £8.30) are fairly frequent throughout the year. Trains run on the Conwy Valley line to Betws-y-Coed and Blaenau Ffestiniog.

Llandudno itself is a short train journey (10 minutes, £1.10) from Llandudno Junction. Trains run frequently only from May to the end of September. At other times of the year you may have to take a bus – Nos 14, 15, 16 and 100 – for the 8 mile journey.

CONWY
- **pop 3800   ☎ 01492**

Conwy has been revitalised since the through traffic on the busy A55 was consigned to a tunnel that burrows under the estuary of the River Conwy and the town. It's now a picturesque and interesting little place, dominated by the superb Conwy Castle, one of the grandest of Edward I's castles and a medieval masterpiece.

The TIC (☎ 592248) is in the Conwy Castle Visitors Centre, not to be confused with the Conwy Visitors Centre by the train station. It's open March to October, daily from 9.30 am to 6.30 pm, and Monday to Saturday for the rest of the year.

Things to See

Conwy Castle (☎ 592358, Cadw) looks every bit a castle, with eight massive crenellated towers. Its construction took just five years, from 1282 to 1287, and its shape was largely dictated by the rock on which it's built. The best view of the castle is from across the river, with the Snowdonia Mountains providing a dramatic backdrop – on the rare occasion when they're not veiled in cloud.

Inside, the castle is largely a ruin, although there are some rooms that contain tableaux and exhibitions. The great hall is impressive, and the royal apartments and chapel are interesting. From the battlements there are good views across town and of Telford's suspension bridge, built in 1826. Reached by a bridge, the castle is open the same hours as the TIC; entry is £3.50/2.50.

Conwy's **town walls** make this one of the best examples of a medieval walled town in Europe. Still enclosing the town, they are three-quarters of a mile long, with 22 towers and three original gateways. You can walk along part of the walls.

Aberconwy House (☎ 592246) is a 14th century timber-and-plaster house that has been restored by the NT. There are rooms furnished in period style and an interesting audiovisual presentation. The house is open daily except Tuesday, April to October, from 10 am to 5 pm; entry is £2/1.

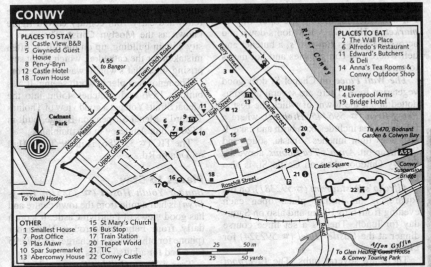

CONWY

PLACES TO STAY
3 Castle View B&B
5 Gwynedd Guest House
8 Pen-y-Bryn
12 Castle Hotel
18 Town House

A 55
to Bangor

Bangor Road
Town Ditch Road
Chapel Street
Crown St.
Berry Street
High Street
Castle Street

Cadnant Park

Mount Pleasant

Upper Gate Street

Rosehill Street

Castle Square

River Conwy

PLACES TO EAT
2 The Wall Place
6 Alfredo's Restaurant
11 Edward's Butchers & Deli
14 Anna's Tea Rooms & Conwy Outdoor Shop

PUBS
4 Liverpool Arms
19 Bridge Hotel

To A470, Bodnant Garden & Colwyn Bay

A55

Conwy Suspension Bridge

Llanrwst Road

Afon Gyffin
To Glen Heulog Guest House & Conwy Touring Park

To Youth Hostel

OTHER
1 Smallest House
7 Post Office
9 Plas Mawr
10 Spar Supermarket
13 Aberconwy House
15 St Mary's Church
16 Bus Stop
17 Train Station
20 Teapot World
21 TIC
22 Conwy Castle

0   25   50 m
0   25   50 yards

NORTH WALES

Plas Mawr (☎ 580167, Cadw) is a newly restored Tudor house that's well worth visiting. Entry is £4/3 and includes a headphone tour. It's open daily except Monday from 9.30 am to 6 pm.

The **Smallest House**, a tiny building that claims to be the smallest house in Britain, is down on the quay, but not surprisingly there's little to see for your 50/30p. There's also a **Teapot Museum** on Castle St.

A popular excursion from Conwy is to **Bodnant Garden** (☎ 650460, NT), 8 miles south, off the A470, one of the finest gardens in Britain. Entry is £4.60/2.30 and it's open Easter to October, daily from 10 am to 5 pm. Bus No 25 passes close by.

Places to Stay

Conwy Youth Hostel (☎ 593571, *Larkhill, Sychnant Pass Rd*) is in a converted hotel. Dorms are small and all have shower rooms. Open daily from mid-February to mid-December, the hostel is a 10 minute walk from the town centre. The nightly charge is £9.75/6.55 for adults/juniors.

Camping is possible at *Conwy Touring Park* (☎ 592856), 1½ miles south of Conwy on the B5106; tent sites cost from £7 for two people in summer.

Within the town walls there's the *Town House* (☎ 596454, *Rosehill St*) with B&B from £13.50 per person in a room with shared bath, £17.50 with private bathroom. *Castle View B&B* (☎ 596888, *3 Berry St*) charges from £13 per person.

Pen-y-Bryn (☎ 596445) is an excellent guesthouse above the tearooms on High St. B&B costs £17 per person (£19.50 with bath).

Glan Heulog Guest House (☎ 593845) is a good place on Llanrwst Rd, to the south of the town but within walking distance. B&B is around £15 per person.

Gwynedd Guest House (☎ 596537, *10 Upper Gate St*) has five rooms and charges £16 per person.

The *Castle Hotel* (☎ 592324, *High St*) is dead central and rooms are from £65/75 for a single/double. It also has two-day leisure breaks, including dinner, for £55 per person per night.

Places to Eat

For self-caterers, there's the *Spar Supermarket* on High St. A few doors down and across the road is *Edward's*, a butcher and deli where you can get pies and hot meals to take away.

The Wall Place on Chapel St does good vegetarian food. There are several tearooms dotted around the town, of which the best is *Pen-y-Bryn* (☎ 596445, High St), where a full cream tea includes bara brith and cake. It also does light lunches – pasta, soups and Welsh rarebit. *Anna's Tea Rooms*, above the Conwy Outdoor shop on Castle St, is also good.

Alfredo's Restaurant (☎ 592381), on the square, is an Italian place open each evening from 6 to 10 pm and also on Saturday for lunch. There's a set three course dinner at the *Castle Hotel* (☎ 592324) for £15.95.

There are several pubs. The *Liverpool Arms*, down on the quay, is where the fishing crowd drinks. The *Bridge Hotel* does good-value lunches, particularly on Sunday.

Getting There & Away

Situated 5 miles west of Llandudno, and a mile from Llandudno Junction, Conwy is linked to both places by several buses an hour. There are frequent buses to Bangor (40 minutes, £2.20).

Conwy's train station is now used only by regional trains. Llandudno Junction, a 15 minute walk from Conwy is the mainline station. There are only a few trains a day between Llandudno Junction and Conwy (three minutes, £1.10).

BANGOR

- **pop 12,000** ☎ **01248**

The town of Bangor is at its liveliest during the university terms. It's home to the University College of North Wales, which attracts students from all over Britain.

The first settlement here was probably the Celtic monastery established in 525 by St Deiniol, which would make Bangor the oldest diocese in Britain. The present **cathedral** was built in the 13th century, though much of it has been restored. Inside is the renowned early 16th century carved figure known as the **Mostyn Christ**. The university's main building, up on the hill, is often mistaken for the cathedral, which is not surprising since that's what it was modelled on.

The renovated **pier** is worth seeing. It was built in 1896 and stretches 450m into the Menai Strait. You get a good view of Thomas Telford's Menai Suspension Bridge, built in 1826 to link Anglesey to the mainland.

The TIC (☎ 352786) is in the Town Hall on Deniol Rd.

Places to Stay

Bangor Youth Hostel (☎ 353516, Tan-y-Bryn) is half a mile from the town centre and has good views of Penrhyn Castle. It's open daily from February through November (phone for other times); it charges £8.80/5.95 for a bed for adults/juniors.

Tros-y-Waen Holiday Farm (☎ 364448, Pentir) is 5 miles south of Bangor on the road to Caernarfon. You can camp here for £4 per tent.

The *University of Bangor* (☎ 371057) lets out student rooms on a B&B basis in July and August for £14.50 per person. It has special deals for longer stays.

Y Garreg Wen (☎ 353836, 8 Deiniol Rd) offers B&B for £12.50 per person. There are only a few rooms but it's convenient for the station, and a very friendly place.

The British Hotel (☎ 364911, High St) offers B&B from £22.50/45 for singles/doubles with a bath. A three course dinner is £10.50 and it also serves bar meals.

The excellent *Eryl Môr Hotel* (☎ 353789, 2 Upper Garth Rd), overlooking the pier and the Menai Strait, costs from £18 per person, or £32/46 for a room with bath.

The best place to stay is the comfortable *Menai Court Hotel* (☎ 354200, Craig-y-Don), which has rooms for £49.50/78, all with bathroom, and many with views.

Places to Eat

There are several cheap restaurants and takeaways along Holyhead Rd, the main student area, and on High St. The *Royal*

Tandoori (☎ 364664, 111 High St) does restaurant meals and takeaway.

The *Fat Cat* (☎ 370445, 161 High St) has long been a popular place with students for its home-made burgers (£4.95), filled baguettes (£2.95) and steaks (£9.95). Vegetarian choices include broccoli and stilton bake (£4.95), and wine, beer and cocktails are available.

The best place to eat is the *Menai Court Hotel* (see Places to Stay). The excellent set dinner is £21.95.

There's a bar at the university's *Students' Union* on Deiniol Rd, although it's supposed to be for students only. The best place in the area for live music is the *Victoria Hotel*, just across the bridge on Anglesey.

Getting There & Away

National Express (☎ 0990-808080) has two services a day from London to Bangor (£18).

Arriva Cymru (☎ 351879) operates bus services from Bangor to most places in the area. Most buses leave from Garth Rd. Services from Bangor operate to the following: Caernarfon (Bus Nos 5, 5A) every 20 minutes from Monday to Saturday and hourly on Sunday; Beaumaris (No 57) hourly and five (No 53) on Sunday; and Llanberis (No 77), from Bangor Plaza, about five times a day.

Bangor is on the InterCity line from London's Euston (£20). There are three trains a day direct to Bangor (4¼ hours), and many more services from Crewe to Bangor (1½ hours, £13.70). It's also on the North Wales coast line from Chester (1¼ hours, £10.30).

AROUND BANGOR
Penrhyn Castle

One and a half miles east of Bangor is Penrhyn Castle (☎ 01248-353084, NT). Unlike most other castles in the area it was not built by Edward I, nor is it a genuine Norman castle. It was constructed between 1820 and 1837 in the neo-Norman style, using a lot of local slate, by Thomas Hopper for Lord Penrhyn. It's certainly an impressive place, with the great hall modelled on Durham Cathedral and containing mock Norman furniture.

The castle is in a lovely setting and is worth a visit. It's open daily except Tuesday from April to the end of October, from 11 am to 5 pm during July and August, and from noon to 5 pm for the other months. Entry is £4.80/2.40.

CAERNARFON
• pop 9400   ☎ 01286

In 1301, Edward made his son the first Prince of Wales and installed him in the mighty castle that still dominates this town. In 1911, in a bid to involve the crown more closely with his constituency in this part of Wales, Prime Minister David Lloyd George had the investiture ceremony for the heir to the throne transferred to the castle. It was an action that did not curry favour with the local people, for Caernarfon is at the heart of Welsh nationalist Wales, and a very depressed area that the royal link has done little to help. When Prince Charles was ceremonially invested here by his mother in 1969, there was an attempt to blow up his train.

Like Conwy, Caernarfon has a magnificent attraction in its castle and comparisons between the two towns are often drawn. While both are spectacular, Caernarfon is probably even more impressive from the outside, but perhaps a little too neat and tidy within.

Caernarfon was important for the Romans, who established a fort, Segontium, in the 1st century.

Orientation & Information

The castle stands by the river and there's a large car park below it. The TIC and the market square are immediately to the north and the town walls enclose a small area four blocks wide and two deep.

The friendly TIC (☎ 672232) is at Castle Pitch, Oriel Pendeitsh, Castle St. It's open daily from 10 am to 6 pm.

Caernarfon Castle

Edward I wanted Caernarfon to be the most impressive of his Welsh fortresses, and it was modelled on the 5th century walls of Constantinople. The castle was built between 1283 and 1301 as part of Edward's series of monumental forts constructed to keep the Welsh under control. It's particularly attractive at night, when the walls are floodlit.

Caernarfon was also designed to be a palace, and Edward's son was born here. Living quarters were contained in the towers, one of which is the Queen's Tower, named after Edward's wife Eleanor. This tower contains the regimental museum of the Royal Welsh Fusiliers, a regiment that seems to have produced quite a few poets and writers – Robert Graves and Siegfried Sassoon among them. The other towers contain exhibitions on the royal investiture in 1969, and on Edward I's campaigns.

The castle (☎ 677617, Cadw) is open Easter to October, daily from 9.30 am to 6.30 pm, and until 4 pm for the rest of the year (from 11 am on Sunday). Entry is £4/3.

Other Things to See

The castle is very much the main attraction, but there's also a small **Maritime Museum** at Victoria Dock. The museum is open daily from June to September.

The foundations of the Roman fort **Segontium** are three-quarters of a mile east of the castle; there's also a museum. In the care of Cadw, it's open April to October, daily from 9.30 am to 6 pm (to 4 pm in April and October); afternoon only on Sunday. Entry is £1.25/75p.

Places to Stay

Totters (☎ 672963, Plas Porth Yr Aur, 2 High St) offers cheap, friendly accommodation in the centre of town by the yacht club. A bed in a four or six-bed dorm costs £9.50 including bedding and breakfast.

Cadnant Valley Camping & Caravan Park (☎ 673196) is half a mile from the castle on Llanberis Rd. It's open March to October; for a small tent it's between £4.50 and £8.

Cartref B&B (☎ 677392, 23 Market St) is only a couple of blocks north of the castle. It charges around £15 per person. One block east of the castle at 4 Church St

is *Tegfan* (☎ 673703), which costs from £16/28 for a single/double.

The *Black Boy Inn* (☎ 673604, Northgate St) is an attractive old pub, centrally located. There are rooms without bathroom at £20/34 and with bath for £23/40.

There are several guesthouses and hotels along North Rd, the road to Bangor. The *Menai Bank Hotel* (☎ 673297) is good and charges from £20/35. At No 21 North Rd, there's *Gorffwysfa Guest House* (☎ 678981); B&B is from £15.

Closer to the centre, North Rd becomes Bangor St. Here, the *Prince of Wales Hotel* (☎ 673367) is a former coaching inn. There are 21 bedrooms and B&B is from £25.50 per person in a room with bath.

Places to Eat

The main places to eat are down Hole in the Wall St. *Stone's Bistro* is a reasonable place with main dishes at around £9, including vegetarian choices.

Near Stone's Bistro is a good pub, *Y Goron Fach* (☎ 673338), where bar meals are available every day, and evening meals from Monday to Thursday. At the restaurant at the *Black Boy Inn* (see Places to Stay), there's a set three course dinner for £10.50. There's also good pub grub in the bar here.

The top place to eat is *Courtenay's Bistro* (☎ 677290, 9 Segontium Terrace), close to the castle. It's also surprisingly inexpensive, with most main dishes in the £7 to £10 range. Rack of lamb is £9. Local produce is used as much as possible – mussels, sea trout, lamb and Welsh cheeses. It's closed on Sunday and Monday.

Getting There & Away

There are no train services to Caernarfon, nor are there direct coach services from London. It's best to go to Bangor and pick up a bus from there. Bus Nos 5, 5A and 5B run several times an hour (hourly on Sunday) from Bangor to Caernarfon (20 minutes, £1.40).

Caernarfon is a focal point for bus services to Snowdonia and the Llŷn Peninsula.

ANGLESEY (YNYS MÔN)

Covering 276 square miles, Anglesey is the largest island in Wales and England, with a population of around 71,000. It has been connected with the mainland since 1826, when Thomas Telford built the Menai Bridge, the first heavy-duty suspension bridge to be constructed.

It's the flattest part of Wales, though there are some rugged cliffs around the coast. It has an interesting coastline with some good sandy beaches. Most visitors, however, see little more than the countryside that surrounds the A5 on the route through to Holyhead and the ferries to Ireland.

Anglesey was a holy place to the ancient Celts and there are still many remains of ancient settlements. Inhabitants since then have relied on farming, smuggling, copper and coal mining and quarrying, as well as the sea, for their income. The land is very fertile and the island is referred to as Môn Mam Cymru – Mother of Wales – because it provides wheat, cattle and other farm produce for North Wales.

Llanfairpwllgwyngyllgogerych-wyrndrobwllllantysiliogogogoch

The tour buses pour in to this little village simply because it's in the record books as having the longest name of any place in Britain, a sum total of 58 letters that are generally shortened to Llanfair PG or Llanfairpwll. The name means 'St Mary's Church in the hollow of the White Hazel near a rapid whirlpool and the Church of St Tysilio near the Red Cave', and was dreamt up in the 19th century to get the tourists in. It's a stop on the main line between Bangor and Holyhead and if you so wish you can buy a large platform ticket as a souvenir. At the TIC (☎ 01248-713177) in the knitwear shop next door, they'll teach you how to pronounce it.

Plas Newydd

This is one of the most interesting stately homes in North Wales, an 18th century house designed in the Gothic style for the marquess of Anglesey. There are superb views across to Snowdonia from the grounds. The house contains a celebrated mural by Rex Whistler. In the cavalry museum at the house is the state-of-the-art wooden leg designed for the marquess, who was field marshal at Waterloo.

Plas Newydd (☎ 01248-714795, NT) is open from April to October, phone to check opening days as they plan to close on Thursday and Friday in 1999; entry is £4.20/2.10. It's 1¾ miles from Llanfair PG train station.

Beaumaris

• pop 1500   ☎ 01248

Beaumaris used to be the principal town and chief port of Anglesey. It's now known for the castle that James of St George built here for Edward I, and as a sailing and watersports centre.

Beaumaris Castle (☎ 810361, Cadw) is the last and largest of the castles built by Edward I. Construction started in 1295 on a site overlooking the Menai Strait. The flatness of the site meant the castle could be designed and built with geometrical symmetry – it's truly impressive and it's clear why it's a World Heritage site.

The castle is surrounded by a water-filled moat, then the outer walls, then evenly spaced towers, then more walls and towers, so it seems impregnable – though Owain Glyndŵr did manage to conquer it. The castle last saw action in 1646 during the Civil War. Entry is £2.20/1.70.

Other things to see here include **Beaumaris Gaol** (☎ 810921), a model prison when it opened in 1829; the **Courthouse**, which can only be visited in summer when it's not being used as a magistrates' court; and the **Museum of Childhood** (☎ 810448), opposite the castle.

Cruises Several operators run summer cruises from Beaumaris pier to Puffin Island for the seabirds or along the Menai Strait. Try Beaumaris Marine Services (☎ 810746), which has a kiosk on the pier. Cruises are operated from April to October, from 12.30 pm. It costs £3.50/2 for an hour's cruise to Puffin Island.

Places to Stay There's little in the way of cheap accommodation in Beaumaris. *Swn-y-Don* (☎ *810794, 7 Bulkley Terrace*) is open from April to November, and offers B&B for £19 per person. Some rooms overlook the Menai Strait; all have a bath.

Ye Olde Bulls Head Inn (☎ *810329, Castle St*) is the best place to stay. It has 11 rooms, all with bath, from £38 per person. The inn dates back to 1472 – it was originally the posting house of the borough. The bedrooms are named after several of Dickens' characters, in honour of the author who once stayed in the hotel.

Getting There & Away Beaumaris is 10 miles from Bangor. Bus No 57 runs almost hourly Monday to Saturday from Bangor to Beaumaris (25 minutes, £1.50). On Sunday there are five services (No 53).

Holyhead
- **pop 12,700**   ☎ **01407**

Holyhead is a particularly grey and daunting ferry port. The only reason to come here would be to get to Ireland. The town is on Holy Island, which is separated by sandbanks and a narrow channel from the main island. If you're killing time waiting for a ferry, there's an RSPB **Nature Reserve** at South Stack, not far from the town.

The TIC (☎ 762622) is by the ferry terminal.

Places to Stay B&Bs are used to dealing with late ferry arrivals. Closest to the terminal is *Min-y-don* (☎ *762718*). It's pleasant and has rooms for £15 per person.

An excellent place, though it only has three rooms, is *Hendre* (☎ *762929, Porth-y-Felin Rd*). B&B is from £30/40 for a single/double. The *Boathouse Hotel* (☎ *762094, Newry Beach*) has B&B from £30 per person. *Tan-y-Cytiau Guest House* (☎ *762763, South Stack Rd*) has seven rooms, at £17.50.

About 5 miles south of Holyhead at Rhoscolyn, there's bunkhouse accommoda-

tion for £9.50 at *Outdoor Alternative* (☎ *860469, Cerrig-yr-Adar*). It's beautifully situated, 300m from the beach.

Getting There & Away Both Irish Ferries (☎ 0990-171717) and Stena Line (☎ 0990-707070) run ferries to Ireland. See Getting There & Away at the start of this book. If you fancy a day-trip to Dublin, Irish Ferries sometimes has special offers from as little as £10 return.

There are hourly trains east to Llandudno, Chester, Birmingham and London, via Bangor (40 minutes, £5.20).

Arriva Cymru (☎ 01248-370295) operates bus service No 4 from Bangor to Holyhead (1¼ hours, £2.70) twice-hourly from Monday to Saturday.

LLŶN PENINSULA

This isolated peninsula is the most staunchly Welsh part of the country – in the villages you rarely hear a word of English spoken. It's a peaceful, largely undeveloped place with 70 miles of coastline, a few small fishing villages, some beautiful beaches, good walks and quiet lanes for cycling.

The best beaches are at Abersoch, 7 miles from Pwllheli, Aberdaron, from where you can catch a boat to Bardsey Island, and Nefyn, on the north coast.

Criccieth

This busy seaside town is the gateway to the Llŷn. **Criccieth Castle** dates from the early 13th century. Open standard Cadw hours, it's worth a visit and there are good views over the bay; entry is £2.20/1.70.

Criccieth is on the train line between Porthmadog and Pwllheli and there are lots of B&Bs and hotels here. Just over a mile from Criccieth on the B4411 Caernarfon road, there's bunkhouse accommodation for £5 at *Stone Barn* (☎ *01766-522115, Tyddyn Morthwyl*). Book in advance.

Pwllheli
- **pop 5000**   ☎ **01758**

The only place of any size on the peninsula is the market town of Pwllheli, of greatest

The Bardsey Pilgrimage

A tiny island off the tip of the Llŷn peninsula, Bardsey was once known as the Isle of Twenty Thousand Saints. In the sixth century the obscure Saint Cadfan created a monastery here. At a time when journeys from Britain to Italy were long, perilous and beyond the means of most people, three pilgrimages to Bardsey came to have the same value as one to Rome. The twenty thousand were probably not so much saints as pilgrims who came here to die.

Most modern pilgrims to Bardsey are more prosaic seabird-watchers, although there are remains of a 13th century abbey to mull over. The Bardsey Island Trust is in charge of visitor arrangements; phone ☎ 01758-730740 for more information.

interest to the visitor for its Welshness. It was here in 1925 that Plaid Cymru, the Welsh nationalist party, was formed. In the minds of many British people, however, the town is synonymous with the Butlins Holiday Camp, which is several miles from Pwllheli and has been renamed Starcoast World.

The TIC (☎ 613000), opposite the train station, has useful information on the Llŷn Peninsula.

Places to Stay *Mrs Jones* (☎ *613172, 26 High St*) does B&B from £14. *Gwynfryn Farm* (☎ *612536*) is a working organic dairy farm a mile from Pwllheli, where B&B costs from £17. It also has flats for weekly rental.

Getting There & Away Pwllheli is the last stop on the train line from Shrewsbury (four hours, £12.90).

It's also accessible by bus route No 12, operated by Clynnog & Trefor (☎ 01286-660208) from Caernarfon. The other operator is Berwyn Buses (☎ 01286-

660315). The service runs hourly from Monday to Saturday (one hour, £1.50).

PORTHMADOG
- **pop 2000**   ☎ 01766

People come to this former slate port today for two reasons – to catch the Ffestiniog Railway to Blaenau Ffestiniog (see the Snowdonia National Park section) and to visit the nearby village of Portmeirion. The town makes a reasonable base for both.

The TIC (☎ 512981) is on High St.

Places to Stay & Eat
Mrs Jones (☎ *513087, 57 East Avenue*), offers B&B for £14 per person, though none of her rooms have bath. The B&B at *35 Madog St* (☎ *512843*) is similarly priced, and *5 Glaslyn St* (☎ *514461*) charges £17.

Tyddyn Llwyn Hotel (☎ *513903, Morfa Bychan Rd*) is on the edge of Porthmadog in open countryside. It's a comfortable place with singles/doubles for £30/45, all with bath.

A good place to eat is the *Harbour Restaurant* (☎ *512471, 3 High St*). Its set-price lunches (£7.25) are good value and sometimes include roast beef or lamb. There's an à la carte menu in the evening – Dover sole is £11.75. Alternatively, there's the *Cantonese Restaurant* above the *Ship Inn* on Lombard St. The Ship is the best place in Porthmadog for a pint.

The top place to stay, *Hotel Portmeirion* (☎ *770228*), is 2 miles from Porthmadog in the fantasy village of the same name (see Portmeirion). Charges are £120.90 for a double room in the main building, or £100 to £150 for a room in one of the cottages in the village. Prices are based on two people sharing and breakfast is extra. The restaurant does set lunches from £9.50, set dinners at £30.

Getting There & Away
From Caernarfon, Express Motors (☎ 01286-674570) operates an hourly service (No 1), Monday to Saturday, to Porthmadog (45 minutes, £2). The service continues to Blaenau Ffestiniog. On Sunday the service is operated by Arriva.

NORTH WALES

Porthmadog is on the train line from Shrewsbury (3½ hours, £12.90). You usually have to change at Machynlleth. The service is not frequent but there's at least one train a day throughout the year.

PORTMEIRION

Two miles from Porthmadog, Portmeirion is a private Italianate village (even the scenery is Mediterranean) created by the Welsh architect Sir Clough Williams-Ellis. It was built between 1925 and 1927 on a secluded peninsula 5 miles from his ancestral home. Sir Clough wanted to show that architecture could be fun, intriguing and interesting, and a visit to the village certainly fulfils all of these requirements, although in summer the crowds can detract from the pleasure.

There are 50 buildings around a central piazza; some of the buildings were brought to the site to save them from destruction elsewhere. Apart from the buildings, there's a restaurant, an ice-cream parlour, a hotel and seven shops, one of which sells seconds of the popular Portmeirion pottery line.

The perfect film set, Portmeirion was where the cult TV series *The Prisoner* was made in the 1960s. It still draws the fans and there's even a **Prisoner Information Centre**.

The village (**☎** 01766-770228) is open daily from 9.30 am to 5.30 pm; entry costs £3.70/1.90, and the charge is lower between November and March. There's a very good restaurant in the hotel here (see Porthmadog).

CHANNEL ISLANDS

The Channel Islands

'Little bits of France dropped into the sea and picked up by Britain' was how the exiled French writer Victor Hugo described this small group of islands in the English Channel just off the coast of France's Normandy.

There are five main islands in the group – Jersey, Guernsey, Alderney, Sark and Herm. Their separation from mainland Britain is not merely geographical. Although British since 1066, the islands are not part of the UK and are administered locally. Entry formalities are as for the UK: if you're visiting via Britain you don't need to show your passport.

Low rates of tax have made them something of a tax haven, and Jersey's capital, St Helier, is part buckets-and-spades beach-holiday resort, part international finance centre. The islands issue their own currency (exchangeable at par with the British pound) and postage stamps. There's no VAT on goods.

With reliable, sunny weather, sandy beaches and very low rates of crime, the Channel Islands are a good place for families with young children to holiday. The islands are also popular with the yachting crowd and the marinas at St Helier and Guernsey's capital, St Peter Port, are packed with some of the world's most technically advanced sailing hardware – plus attendant beautiful people. Catering to this clientele are some excellent, though very pricey, seafood restaurants. Local specialities include oysters, crabs and lobsters.

Although there are pleasant beaches, good walks and cycle rides on the islands and the famous conservation zoo started by Gerald Durrell on Jersey, compared to mainland Britain or the Scottish islands there's really not a lot to see and do. For the budget traveller there are no youth hostels but there are several camping grounds.

HIGHLIGHTS

- Gerald Durrell's conservation zoo, Jersey
- The German Underground Hospital, Jersey
- Cycling on the Alderney
- Sark – Europe's last feudal state

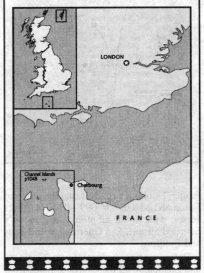

GETTING THERE & AWAY

Air

Jersey & Guernsey There are numerous daily flights between Britain, Jersey and Guernsey. British Airways/City Flyer Express (☎ 0345-222111) has seven flights each day from Jersey and/or Guernsey to London's Gatwick. British Midland (☎ 0345-554554) services the Midlands – mainly East Midlands airport. Jersey European (☎ 0990-676676) links Jersey and Guernsey with Gatwick, Birmingham,

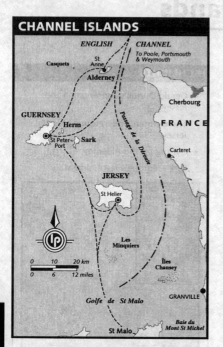

CHANNEL ISLANDS

ENGLISH   CHANNEL
To Poole, Portsmouth
& Weymouth
Casquets   St
              Anne
        Alderney
                        Cherbourg
GUERNSEY   FRANCE
      Herm
St Peter   Sark
  Port
                        Carteret
        JERSEY
      St Helier
                        Les
                      Minquiers
                              Îles
                            Chausey
0   10   20 km
0   6   12 miles
                            GRANVILLE
        Golfe de St Malo
                        Baie du
              St Malo   Mont St Michel

Passage de la Déroute

Exeter, Dublin, Cork, Belfast, Glasgow and Luton. KLM UK (☎ 0990-074074) links Jersey with South-ampton and London's Stansted airport, and Guernsey with Leeds and Bradford.

Return air fares between Jersey/Guernsey and London on all these airlines range from around £70 up to £250. The cheaper deals usually require you to spend at least Saturday night in the Channel Islands. Theoretically tickets don't need to be bought in advance but the earlier you book your flight, the greater the chance of cheaper tickets being available.

Alderney All Alderney flights are operated by Aurigny Air Services (☎ 01481- 822886) using tiny Trislanders painted an unmissable banana yellow. There are up to 10 flights a day to and from Southampton (40 minutes, £65.50 one-way, £88 budget

return). To France, it also operates flights between Jersey or Guernsey and Cherbourg or Dinard.

Boat

Condor (☎ 01534-601000) operates two fast ferries a day in each direction between Poole in Dorset and Jersey via Guernsey. Return fares between Britain and Jersey (four hours) start at around £74 for a foot passenger, £201 for a car and driver. A day return costs £29.90 for a foot passenger, or £79 for a car and driver.

Condor's daily ferry to St Malo in Brittany from Weymouth also stops in Guernsey. There's a day-trip fare of £29.90.

Channel Hoppers (☎ 01534-639111) runs a daily catamaran between Portsmouth and Jersey, Guernsey, Sark (except Sunday) and Alderney (Sunday only). The fare from Portsmouth to any of the islands is £34.50 each way. There's a cheaper excursion fare for £39.50 return, and a day-return fare of £25.

Ferry links to France are run by Emeraude (☎ 01481-711414) with services between Guernsey or Jersey and St Malo; and also to Granville, Carteret and Diélette in Normandy.

JERSEY

• pop 75,000   ☎ 01534

Jersey is the largest of the Channel Islands, and the most popular destination for visitors. There are lots of safe, clean, sandy beaches, the best in the region. The main surf break, Watersplash, is at St Ouen's Bay.

Orientation & Information

Covering 45 sq miles, the island is roughly rectangular in shape; St Helier is on the south coast.

Jersey Tourism (☎ 500777) is on Liberation Square, a short walk from the ferry terminal and opposite the bus station. It's open from 8.30 am to 8 pm daily in summer.

Landscapes of Jersey is a good pocket guide to walks and tours of the island.

Things to See

Of universal interest, the **Jersey Zoo** (☎ 864666), Les Augres Manor, Trinity, was started by writer and naturalist Durrell as a conservation and breeding centre for endangered species. It's a fascinating place to visit and is open daily from 9.30 am to 6 pm; entry is £5.50/3.50. Other things to see around the island include several castles, and the **German Underground Hospital**, dating from WWII when the Germans occupied the island. There are also lots of attractions that appeal to families with young children such as a shell garden, lavender farm, steam museum, bowling centre and several potteries.

St Helier, the capital, is not particularly attractive; it's an international finance centre that even boasts a few multistorey buildings. **Jersey Museum**, near the TIC, has an interesting display on Jersey's history.

Places to Stay

Jersey Tourism publishes a brochure listing over 300 places to stay and operates a free booking service, Jerseylink (☎ 500888).

There are camping grounds at St Martin, St Brelade and St Ouen. *Rose Farm Camping* (☎ 875236) at St Aubin is a very friendly place that's popular with backpackers. The charge is £4.50 to £6.50 for two people and a small tent.

Cheap B&Bs in St Helier, charging around £15 per person, include *Corinthian* (☎ 878655), *Elysia* (☎ 33918) and *Woodford Guest House* (☎ 21372).

The *Golden Sands Hotel* (☎ 41241) is a modern hotel right on the beach at St Brelade's Bay. Rates range from £26 to £45 per person. The island's top hotel is the *Longueville Manor* (☎ 25501, St Saviour) where double rooms start at £175.

Places to Eat

There's a wide choice – everything from fish and chip shops to excellent seafood restaurants. In St Helier there's reasonable Thai food near the TIC at *Rodees* (☎ 32548) – £7 for all you can eat at lunch time. The *Typsy Toad Town House* (New St) is an interesting

pub that has its own microbrewery and excellent pub grub.

For a special occasion, the *Longueville Manor* (☎ 25501, St Saviour) is one of the best places to eat on the island. Main dishes are around £20 and there are set menus from £35 to £55.

Getting There & Away

For services to Britain and France, see Getting There & Away at the start of this chapter. Aurigny Air Services (☎ 43568) has 18 flights a day each way between Jersey and Guernsey (15 minutes, £29), and flights to Alderney.

Emeraude (☎ 66566) runs one ferry in each direction between Jersey and Guernsey (one hour, £21). Condor ferries to Britain also link the two islands.

Getting Around

Between the airport and St Helier there's a choice of taxi (£6) or bus (£1.20). The journey takes 15 to 45 minutes depending on traffic.

Car hire is cheap – from £13 per day – but there are said to be around 55,000 cars on the island so you may find yourself sitting in a traffic jam. Try Holiday Autos (☎ 888700). It also rents motorcycles and bicycles.

GUERNSEY
- **pop 56,000**　☎ 01481

More easy-going and peaceful than Jersey, Guernsey is, however, the most highly populated of the Channel Islands. It's popular both with young families and elderly holiday-makers.

Orientation & Information

Guernsey is two-thirds the size of Jersey: roughly 9 miles long by 4 miles wide. There are TICs at the airport and ferry terminal but the main office of Guernsey Tourism (☎ 723552) is on the waterfront in St Peter Port, opposite the Crown Pier.

Things to See

There are numerous beaches. **St Peter Port**, the capital, is one of the most attractive towns in the Channel Islands, looking out across the busy harbour to Sark and Herm. Hugo was exiled here in 1855 and lived in St Peter Port until 1870. His home, Hauteville House (entry £3.50/1.50) is a popular tourist attraction.

The Germans occupied Guernsey during WWII and their **underground hospital** and the **military museum** can be visited. Fortifications around the island bear witness to the fact that Guernsey has been of strategic importance from as long ago as Neolithic times.

Places to Stay

There are several camping grounds. *Fauxquets Valley Farm Campsite* (☎ 55460, Castel) has a heated pool, cycle hire and restaurant. Charges are £4.90 for one person and a small tent.

There are about 100 hotels and B&Bs. The *Friends Vegetarian* (☎ 721146, 20 Hauteville) is a friendly place in St Peter Port with B&B for £16 per person. The *Midhurst House* (☎ 724391, Candie Rd) is an excellent small hotel in St Peter Port, with a quiet garden and good food. Rates are £35 per person. The *Old Government Hotel* (☎ 724921), formerly the official residence of the Guernsey governors, is a large old hotel with good views over St Peter Port and the harbour. Accommodation ranges from £55 to £105 per person.

Places to Eat

For good vegetarian food visit *Mrs P's Kitchen*, up the side alley opposite Victoria Marina in St Peter Port. There's good pub grub at the *Yacht Inn* (South Esplanade, St Peter Port). One of the top restaurants on the island is the *Café du Moulin* (☎ 65944, Rue de Quanteraine, St Peter Port). It has set lunches from £10.95, set dinners from £16.95 and separate menus for vegetarians.

Getting There & Away

See Getting There & Away at the start of this chapter for services to Britain and France. For inter-island services see the other islands.

Getting Around

From the airport to St Peter Port there's a choice of taxi (10 minutes, £6) or bus (20 minutes, £1.10). With outlets at the airport and harbour, Value (☎ 43547) rents cars from £18 per day. Quay Cycle Hire (☎ 714146) is on the New Jetty in St Peter Port. It rents out bikes from £6 per day and has cycling maps of the island for 90p.

ALDERNEY

- **pop 2500   ☎ 01481**

Although it's the third largest of the Channel Islands, Alderney is just 3½ miles by 1½ miles at its widest points. It's the quietest of all the Channel Islands – the day-trippers tend to head for Sark and Herm.

There are white-sand beaches, cliff walks, and coastal forts dating from the 19th century and from the 1940s when the Germans occupied the island. There's a small museum in St Anne, the capital. The Alderney Railway operates in the tourist season, using old carriages from the London underground.

The majority of the population lives in St Anne, in the centre of the island less than a mile from the airport. Alderney Tourism (☎ 823737) is on Victoria St in St Anne.

Places to Stay & Eat

The only place where camping is permitted is *Saye Campsite* (☎ 822556) on Saye Bay.

Accommodation is not cheap. There are about eight guesthouses on the island, with B&B generally around £20 per person. Try *St Anne's Guest House* (☎ 823145, 10 Le Heuret, St Anne).

There are more than a dozen hotels. The *Sea View* (☎ 822738) is by the beach in Braye, with B&B accommodation from £23 to £36 per person. *Hotel Chez André* (☎ 822777, Victoria St, St Anne) charges from £30 to £35 per person for B&B.

The *Georgian House* (☎ 822471, Victoria St, St Anne) does B&B for £30 per person, and is known for its seafood specialities. The *Divers Inn* at Braye Harbour is a popular pub.

Getting There & Away
Aurigny Air Services (☎ 822886) has two flights a day each way between Alderney and Jersey (15 minutes, £29), and eight a day each way to Guernsey (15 minutes, £29). See Getting There & Away at the start of this chapter for details of other flights. There are only one or two ferry links per week to Jersey or Guernsey in summer: contact the TIC for details.

Getting Around
For hire cars phone ☎ 822848, mopeds ☎ 823352, and bicycles ☎ 822294.

SARK
• pop 550   ☎ 01481

Traffic-free Sark is probably best known as Europe's only feudal state. The Seigneur, currently Michael Beaumont, rules through a feudal constitution that dates back to Elizabethan times. Sark levies no income tax, and maintains its own government and a collection of laws that includes such anomalies as the fact that no woman is entitled to divorce.

Three miles by 1½ miles but with a jagged coastline of over 30 miles, the island has beautiful scenery best appreciated after the crowds of day-trippers have departed. Sark is ideal for walkers who enjoy an unhurried pint – the pubs seem to remain open all hours, Monday to Saturday.

Contact Sark Tourism (☎ 832345) for its island guide which gives details and prices of places to stay.

Places to Stay & Eat
There are camp sites (both charging £4 per person) at La Vallette (☎ 832066) and Pomme de Chien (☎ 832316).

There are about 20 hotels and B&Bs. The cheapest is *Le Pellon* (☎ 832289), from £14 per person. *La Sablonnerie* (☎ 832061) is a very comfortable hotel in the south of the island across the isthmus on Little Sark. Charges per person range from £40 to £56.

On the west coast, the *Barn Bar* is known for its home-made sloe gin (note that Sark pubs are closed on Sunday).

Founiais Restaurant (☎ 832626) on Harbour Hill is a good fish restaurant. Main dishes are £8.95 to £11.50. There are several cafés and the larger hotels all have restaurants.

Getting There & Away
Isle of Sark Shipping (☎ 832450) has up to five sailings each way every day between St Peter Port in Guernsey and Sark (50 minutes, £18.50/9.25 return). The company also offers cheaper half-day excursions. Emeraude (☎ 01534-66566) operates a catamaran service to Jersey (45 minutes, £21/13 day return), daily except Sunday.

Getting Around
There are no cars on the island, a tractor and trailer being the only motorised form of transport. There are horse-drawn carriage rides for £5 to £7.50 per hour. For cycle hire (£4/5 per day for a standard/mountain bike), purchase a voucher from Isle of Sark Shipping's Guernsey office to exchange for a bike on Sark.

HERM
• pop 40   ☎ 01481

A 20 minute boat trip across the bay from Guernsey, Herm is a pretty island half a mile wide by 1½ miles long. No cars, motorcycles or even bicycles are allowed, making this a walkers' mini-paradise, but it's one that's very popular with day-trippers from the larger Channel Islands.

Herm had been deserted for years when Major Wood bought a 99 year lease on the island in 1949. The island is now run by his daughter Pennie Hayworth and her family. It's an undeniably attractive place with white-sand beaches famous for their variety of shells, clear sea and pleasant walks.

Places to Stay & Eat
Accommodation is booked through the administration office (☎ 722377). There's a choice between just one hotel – the upmarket *White House Hotel* (☎ 722159) from £52 to £62.50 per person for dinner, bed and breakfast – and 18 self-catering

cottages, and a camping ground (£5 site fee plus £4.15 per person).

For places to eat there's the *Mermaid Tavern*, the *Ship Restaurant* at the White House Hotel and two cafés.

Getting There & Away

Trident Travel (☎ 721379) runs up to eight trips in each direction between St Peter Port

and Herm (20 minutes). Beat the crowds in summer and take the Milk Boat (£5/2.50 return) at 8.30 am. Other departures cost £6.50/3.50 return.

Getting Around

The only way to get around is on foot. It takes about two hours to walk right around the island.

Language

Scottish Gaelic

Scottish Gaelic (*Gàidhlig* – pronounced *gallic* in Scotland) is spoken by about 80,000 people in Scotland, mainly in the Highlands and Islands, and by many native speakers and learners overseas. It is a member of the Celtic branch of the Indo-European family of languages which has given us Gaelic, Irish, Manx, Welsh, Cornish and Breton.

After two centuries of decline, the language is now being encouraged through financial help from government agencies and the EU. Gaelic education is flourishing from playgroups to tertiary levels. This renaissance flows out into the field of music, literature, cultural events, and broadcasting.

Grammar

The usual word order in Gaelic is verb-subject-object; English, by comparison, has a subject-verb-object word order, eg The girl (subject) reads (verb) the book (object). There are two forms of the pronoun 'you' in Gaelic: the singular *thu*, and the plural form *sibh* which is also used as a formal (ie polite) singular. We use the informal *thu* in the following phraselist.

Pronunciation

Stress usually falls on the first syllable of a word. The Gaelic alphabet has only 18 letters:

Vowels

There are five vowels: **a**, **e**, **i**, **o** and **u** – **a**, **o**, **u** are known as broad vowels, **e**, **i** are known as slender vowels. A grave accent indicates that a vowel sound is lengthened, eg *bata* (a stick), *bàta* (a boat).

Consonants

There are 12 consonants: **b**, **c**, **d**, **f**, **g**, **l**, **m**, **n**, **p**, **r**, **s**, **t**, and the letter **h** (only used to change other sounds).

c	always a hard 'k' sound; never an 's' sound
d	when broad, thicker than English 'd'; when slender, as the 'j' in 'jet'
l, ll	when slender, as in 'value'
n, nn	when slender, as in 'new'
s	when slender, as 'sh'
t	when broad, thicker than English 't'; when slender, as the 'ch' in 'chin'

When consonants are followed by 'h', a change of sound occurs:

bh mh	as 'v'
ch	when broad, as in *loch* (not 'lock'!); when slender, as the German *ich*
dh gh	when broad, voiced at the back of the throat; when slender, as 'y' – there's no English equivalent
fh	silent
ph	as 'f'
sh	as 'h' if before a broad vowel
th	as 'h'

Greetings & Civilities

Good morning.
 madding va
 Madainn mhath.
Good afternoon/Good evening.
 fesskurr ma
 Feasgar math.
Good night.
 uh eech uh va
 Oidhche mhath.
Goodbye. (lit: Blessings go with you)
 B yan achd let
 Beannachd leat.
Goodbye. (The same with you)
 mar shin let
 Mar sin leat.
How are you?
 kimmer uh ha oo?
 Ciamar a tha thu?
Very well, thank you.
 gley va, tappuh let
 Glè mhath, tapadh leat.

Please.
mahs eh doh hawl eh
Mas e do thoil e.
Thank you.
tappuh let
Tapadh leat.
Many thanks.
moe ran ta eeng
Mòran taing.
You're welcome.
sheh doh veh huh
'Se do bheatha.
I beg you pardon.
baaluv
B'àill leibh.
Excuse me.
gav mo lishk yal
Gabh mo leisgeul.
I'm sorry.
ha mee dooleech
Tha mi duilich.

Useful Words & Phrases

Do you speak (have) Gaelic?
uh vil ga lick ackut?
A bheil Gàidhlig agad?
Yes, a little.
ha, beg an
Tha, beagan.
Not much.
chan yil moe ran
Chan eil mòran.
What's your name?
jae an tannam uh ha orsht?
De an t ainm a tha ort?
I'm ...
is meeshuh ...
Is mise ...
Can you tell me ...?
un yee ish oo ghoe ...?
An innis thu dhomh ...?
I want to go to ...
ha mee ug ee urry uh gholl goo ...
Tha mi ag iarraidh a dhol gu ...
How do I get to ...?
kimmer uh yaev mee goo ...?
Ciamar a gheibh mi gu ...?

by bus
ir uh vuss   air a' bhus

by train
ir un tren   air an trean
by car
a woon un car   ann an car

a hotel
tuh ee awstu   taigh òsda
a bedroom
roowm caddil   rùm cadail
a toilet
tuh ee beck   taigh beag

a cup of coffee
coopa cawfee   cupa cofaidh
a cup of tea
coopa tee   cupa tì
a glass of water
glahnyuh ooshkuy glainne uisge

Cheers!
slahntchuh va!   Slàinte mhath!
beer
lyawn   leann
whisky
ooshkuy beh huh   uisge beatha
a glass of wine
glahnyuh feeuhn   glainne fìon
red wine
feeuhn jerrack   fìon dearg
white wine
feeuhn gyahl   fìon geal

Welsh

For newcomers, Welsh is not the easiest language to master. The following is a brief guide to the pronunciation.

Vowels

The Welsh vowels are **a**, **e**, **i**, **o**, **u**, **w** and **y**. All except **y** have short and long versions.

a	long, as in 'car', *tad* (father)	
a	short, as in 'ham', *mam* (mother)	
e	long, as in 'sane', *hen* (old)	
e	short, as in 'ten', *pen* (head)	
i	long, as in 'marine', *mis* (month)	
i	short, as in 'tin', *prin* (scarce)	
o	long, as in 'or', *môr* (sea)	

o	short, as in 'on' *ffon* (walking stick)	women	*merched*
w	long, as in the 'oo' in 'moon', *swn* (sound)	men	*dynion*
		exit	*allan*
w	short, as the 'oo' in 'look', *gwn* (gun)	open	*ar agor*
y	three possible pronunciations: as the 'ee' in 'geese', *dyn* (man); as the 'i' in 'tin', *cyn* (before); as the 'u' in 'run', *dynion* (men)	hotel	*gwesty*
		bus	*bws*
		pub	*tafarn*
oe	as the 'oy', in 'annoy', *coed* (wood)		
u	as the 'i' in 'imp', *pump* (five)	1	*un*

Word stress usually falls on the second-last syllable in Welsh pronunciation.

2	*dau*
3	*tri*
4	*pedwar*
5	*pump*
6	*chwech*
7	*saith*

Consonants

c	as in 'cat', *cath* (cat)	8	*wyth*
ch	as in Scottish 'loch', *fach* (small)	9	*naw*
dd	as 'th' in 'them', *mynydd* (mountain)	10	*deg*
f	as in 'of', *fach* (small)	11	*un-deg-un*
ff	as in 'off', *ffenestr* (window)	12	*un-deg-dau*
g	as in 'go', *gardd* (garden)	13	*un-deg-tri*
h	as in 'hat', *het* (hat)	20	*dau-ddeg*
ll	no equivalent sound in English; try putting your tongue on the roof of your mouth, near the teeth, as if to pronounce 'l', and then blow the 'l'!	21	*dau-ddeg-un*
		30	*tri-deg*
		40	*pedwar-deg*
		50	*pum-deg*
th	as in 'three' *byth* (ever)	60	*chwe-deg*
		70	*saith-deg*

Words & Phrases

If you're feeling brave, here are a few expressions you might like to try out in the Welsh speaking parts of the country.

80	*wyth-deg*
90	*naw-deg*
100	*cant*
200	*dau cant*
500	*pum cant*
1000	*mil*

Good morning.	*Bore da.*
Good afternoon.	*Prynhawn da.*
Good night.	*Nos da.*
How are you?	*Sut mae?*
Thanks.	*Diolch.*
Cheers!	*Hwyl!*
What's your name?	*Beth ydy'ch enw chi?*
How much?	*Faint?*
good	*da*
very good	*da iawn*

Wales is famous for having the longest place name in the world – Llanfairpwllgwyngyllgogerychwyrndrobwllllantysiliogogogoch – which, translated, means 'St Mary's church in the hollow of the White Hazel near a rapid whirlpool and the church of St Tysilio near the Red cave'. It can be tricky to say after a pint of Brains.

Glossary

abe – estuary (Wales)
afon – river (Wales)
agister – someone paid to care for stock
auld – old (Scotland)
aye – yes/always

BABA – Book-A-Bed-Ahead scheme
bach – small (Wales)
bailey – outermost wall of a castle
bairn – baby (Newcastle & Scotland)
banger – old, cheap car
bangers – sausages
bap – bun (northern England)
bar – gate (York)
ben – mountain (Scotland)
bent – not altogether legal
bevvied – drunk
bevvy – a drink (originally northern England)
bevvying – drinking
billion – a million million, not a thousand million
biscuit – cookie
bitter – beer
black pudding – a type of sausage made from dried blood (Scotland)
blatherskite – boastful or talkative person (northern England)
bloke – man
bodge job – poor-quality repairs
bothy – hut or mountain shelter (Scotland)
brae – hill (Scotland)
bridleway – path that can be used by walkers, horse riders and cyclists
broch – defensive tower (Scotland)
Brummie – Birmingham accent
bryn – hill (Wales)
BTA – British Tourist Authority
burgh – town (Scotland)
burn – creek (Scotland)
bus – local bus; *see also* coach
byob – bring your own bottle

cadair – stronghold/chair (Wales)
caer – fort (Wales)
caff – cheap café
canny – good, great (Newcastle)
capel – chapel (Wales)

car bonnet – hood
car boot – trunk
carreg – stone (Wales)
ceilidh – pronounced kaylee, informal evening entertainment and dance (Scotland)
cheers – goodbye
chine – valleylike fissure leading to the sea
chips – French fries
circus – a junction of several streets, usually circular
close – entrance
clun – meadow (Wales)
coach – long-distance bus; *see also* bus
coaching inn – inn along a coaching route at which horses were changed
coch – red (Wales)
coed – forest/wood (Wales)
Corbett – mountain of between 2500 feet (762m) and 2999 feet (914m) in height
couchette – sleeping berth in a train or ferry
courgette – zucchini
courts – courtyards
crack – good conversation (originally Ireland)
crannogh – artificial island settlement
crisps – potato chips
croft – plot of land with adjoining house worked by the occupiers
cromlech – burial chamber (Wales)
cwm – valley (Wales)

de – south (Wales)
dear – expensive
din (dinas) – fort (Wales)
DIY – do-it-yourself, as in handyman shop
dolmen – chartered tomb
donkey – engine
dosh/dough – money
downs – rolling upland, characterised by lack of trees
du – black (Wales)
duvet – doona

EH – English Heritage
eisteddfod – festival in which competitions are held in music, poetry, drama and the fine arts (Wales)

Essex – derogatory adjective, as in Essex girl, meaning tarty, and identified with '80s consumerism
EU – European Union
evensong – daily evening service (Church of England)

fag – cigarette; *also* a boring task
fagged – exhausted
fanny – female genitals, not backside
fawr – big (Wales)
fen – drained or marshy low-lying flat land
ffordd – road (Wales)
firth – estuary (Scotland)
fiver – five-pound note
flat – apartment
flip-flops – thongs
footpath – sidewalk
fussock – irritating woman (Yorkshire)

gaffer – boss or foreman
gate – street (York)
ginnel – alleyway (Yorkshire)
glan – shore (Wales)
glas – blue (Wales)
glen – valley (Scotland)
glyn – valley (Wales)
gobslutch – slovenly person (northern England)
grand – one thousand
greasy spoon – cheap café
gutted – very disappointed
guv, guvner – from governor, a respectful term of address for owner or boss, can be used ironically
gwrydd – green (Wales)
gwyn – white (Wales)

haar – fog off the North Sea (Scotland)
hammered – drunk (northern England)
Hogmanay – New Year's Eve (Scotland)
hosepipe – garden hose
hotel – accommodation with food and bar, not always open to passing trade
HS – Historic Scotland
Huguenots – French Protestants

inn – pub with accommodation

jam – jelly
jelly – jello

jumper – sweater

ken – know (Scotland)
kirk – church (Scotland)
kyle – narrow strait

lager lout – *see* yob
laird – estate owner (Scotland)
lands – multistorey apartment buildings (Scotland)
lass – young woman (northern England)
ley – clearing
lift – elevator
linn – waterfall (Scotland)
llan – enclosed place or church (Wales)
llyn – lake (Wales)
lock – part of a canal or river that can be closed off and the water levels changed to raise or lower boats
lolly – money; *also* candy on a stick (possibly frozen)
lorry – truck
love – term of address, not necessarily to someone likeable

mad – insane, not angry
manky – low quality (southern England)
Martello tower – small, circular tower used for coastal defence
mate – a friend of any sex, or term of address for males
mawr – great (Wales)
merthyr – burial place of a saint (Wales)
midge – a mosquito-like insect
motorway – freeway
motte – mound on which a castle was built
Munro – mountain of 3000 feet (914m) or higher (Scotland)
mynydd – mountain (Wales)

nant – valley/stream (Wales)
nappies – diapers
newydd – new (Wales)
NT – National Trust
NTS – National Trust for Scotland
NYMR – North Yorkshire Moors Railway

oast house – building containing a kiln for drying hops
off-license (offie) – carry-out alcoholic drinks shop

ogof – cave (Wales)
OS – Ordnance Survey
owlers – smugglers

pee – pence
pen – headland (Wales)
pend – arched gateway (Scotland)
pete – fortified houses
pint – beer
pissed – drunk (not angry)
pistyll – waterfall (Wales)
pitch – playing field
plas – hall/mansion (Wales)
ponce – ostentatious or effeminate male; *also* to borrow (usually permanently)
pont – bridge (Wales)
pop – fizzy drink (northern England)
postbuses – minibuses that follow postal delivery routes
pub – short for public house, a bar usually with food, sometimes with accommodation
punter – customer
pwll – pool (Wales)

quid – pound

ramble – to go for a short walk
reiver – warrior
rhiw – slope (Wales)
rhos – moor/marsh (Wales)
roll-up – roll-your-own cigarette
rood – alternative word for cross
RSPB – Royal Society for the Protection of Birds
rubber – eraser
rubbish bin – garbage can
rugger – rugby

sacked – fired
Sassenach – an English person or a lowland Scot (Scotland)
sett – tartan pattern
shout – to buy a group of people drinks, usually reciprocated
shut – partially covered passage
Sloane Ranger – wealthy, superficial, but well-connected young person
snicket – alleyway (York)
snogging – kissing

spondoolicks – money
sporran – purse (Scotland)
SSSI – Site of Special Scientific Interest
steaming – drunk (Scotland)
strath – valley (Scotland)
subway – underpass
sweet – candy

ta – thanks
thwaite – clearing in a forest
TICs – Tourist Information Centres
ton – one hundred
tor – Celtic word describing a hill shaped like a triangular wedge of cheese
torch – flashlight
towpath – a path running beside a river or canal
traveller – nomadic, new-age hippy
tre – town (Wales)
tron – public weighbridge
twitchers – birdwatchers
twitten – passage, small lane
twr – tower (Wales)
tube – London's underground railway (subway)
ty – house (Wales)

underground – subway
uisge-bha – the water of life: whisky (Scotland)

VAT – value-added tax, levied on most goods and services, currently 17.5%
verderer – officer upholding law and order in the royal forests

way – a long-distance trail
wellied – drunk (originally Scotland)
wide boy – ostentatious go-getter, usually on the make
wold – open, rolling country
WTB – Wales Tourist Board
wynd – lane (Scotland)

yaya – plumby, upper-class twit
ynys – island (Wales)
yob – hooligan
ystwyth – winding (Wales)

Glossary of Religious Architecture

Abbey

A monastery of monks or nuns or the buildings they used. When Henry VIII dissolved the monasteries between 1536 and 1540, many English and Irish abbeys were destroyed or converted into private homes, although some survived as churches. Thus an abbey today may be a church or a home.

Aisle

Passageway or open space along either side of the nave and/or down the centre.

Alignment

Even if this doesn't conform with geography, churches are always assumed to be aligned east-west, with the altar, chancel and choir towards the east end and the nave towards the west.

Ambulatory

Processional aisle at the east end of a cathedral, behind the altar.

Apse

Semicircular or rectangular area for clergy, at east end of church in traditional design.

Baptistry

Separate area of a church used for baptisms.

Barrel Vault

Semicircular arched roof.

Boss

Covering for the meeting point of the ribs in a vaulted roof (often colourfully decorated, so bring binoculars).

Brass

Type of memorial common in medieval churches consisting of a brass plate set into the floor or a tomb, usually with a depiction of the deceased but sometimes simply with text.

Buttress

Vertical support for a wall; see Flying Buttress.

Campanile

Free-standing belfry or bell tower; Westminster Cathedral and Chester Cathedral have modern ones.

Chancel

Eastern end of the church, usually reserved for choir and clergy. The name comes from the Latin word for lattice because of the screen which once separated the two parts of the church.

Chantry

Chapel established by a donor for use in his or her name after death.

Chapel

Small, more private shrine or area of worship off the main body of the church. In some British cathedrals, chapels were established by different crafts guilds.

Chapel of Ease

Chapel built for those who lived too far away from the parish church.

Chapter House

Building in a cathedral close where the dean meets with the chapter, the clergy who run the cathedral.

Chevet

Chapels radiating out in a semicircular sweep, common in France but also found at Westminster and Canterbury.

Choir

Area in the church where the choir is seated, usually to the east of the transepts and nave; sometimes used interchangeably with chancel or presbytery.

Clerestory

Also clearstory; wall of windows above the triforium.

Cloister

Covered walkway linking the church with adjacent monastic buildings.

Close

Buildings grouped around a cathedral, also known as the precincts.

Collegiate

Church with a chapter of canons and prebendaries, but not a cathedral.

Corbel
Stone or wooden projection from a wall supporting a beam or arch.

Crossing
Intersection of the nave and transepts.

Flying Buttress
Supporting buttress in the form of one side of an open arch.

Font
Basin used for baptisms, usually towards the west end of the building, often in a separate baptistry.

Frater
Common room or dining area in a medieval monastery.

Lady Chapel
Chapel, usually at the east end of a cathedral, dedicated to the Virgin Mary.

Lancet
Pointed window in Early English style.

Minster
A church connected to a monastery.

Misericord
Hinged choir seat with a bracket (often elaborately carved) that can be leant against.

Nave
Main body of the church at the western end, where the congregation gather.

Piscina
Basin for priests to wash their hands.

Presbytery
Eastern area of the chancel beyond the choir, where the clergy operate.

Priory
Religious house governed by a prior, inferior to an abbey.

Pulpit
Raised box where priest gives sermon.

Quire
Medieval term for choir.

Refectory
Monastic dining room.

Reredos
Literally 'behind the back'; backdrop to an altar.

Rood Screen
A screen carrying a rood or crucifix, which separated the nave from the chancel.

Squint
Angled opening in a wall or pillar to allow a view of the altar.

Transepts
North-south projections from the nave, often added at a later date and giving the whole church a cruciform cross-shaped plan. Some medieval English cathedrals (Canterbury, Lincoln, Salisbury) feature smaller second transepts.

Triforium
Internal wall passage above the arcade and below the clerestory; behind it is the 'blind' space above the side aisle.

Undercroft
Vaulted underground room or cellar.

Vault
Roof with arched ribs, usually in a decorative pattern.

Vestry
Robing room, where the parson's clerical robes are kept, and where they put them on.

Acknowledgments

THANKS

Many thanks to the travellers who used the last edition and wrote to us with helpful hints, useful advice and interesting anecdotes:

Z Abrahams, Oscar Abrahamsson, Jeff Adams, Graeme Aitken, Altan Akat, Kirsten & Mils Ake-Anderson, Peter H Allan, Trevor Allcott, Graydon Allen, Jennifer Allore, Richard Althoff, Kate Amos, Joe & Alma Gaskill, Dick Anderson, Lynn Andrews, Elwin Arens, J & M Armstrong, Chris Arundel, Newell Augur, Barbara Axon, Pam Baker, Lisa Barresi, Bonnie Baskin, G A Battrun, Philip Baum, N P Baykov, Carmen Bekker, Graeme Bell, Richard & Jinapon Bell, Jennifer Bennett, David Benson, Maxine Beresford, Linda Berg, Jason Berry, Lisette Billard, L Birnie, M Blackie, James Blakley, J Bly, John & Marilyn Boatman, Bert Bodecker, Barbara Bodenschatz, Billie Bonevski, Bernd B Bongartz, I D Booth, Shannon Boothman, David Bounds, Rosemary & Barry Breed, E M Bremmer, Stephen & Louise Broughton, Rosemary Brown, Melanie Brown, Hannah Brown, Joanna Brown, Ron Browne, Mike Brycefound, Klaus Bryn, K A Burnett, Laura Burr, Elvira Burster, Nicholas Burton, Dana Byerley, Joe Campbell, Lisa Cantonwine, Jessie & Gary Carlson, Fo Carmichael-Jones, Maxine Caws, Simon Chambers, Jane Chandler, Wilma Chappill, Ted Charlton, Jonathan Chatfield, Simon Chegg, Fei Chiao Liao, Lynn R Chong, M & M Clark, Alan Clark, Bill Coker, Sandy Colburn, Marie & Daniel Cole, Robyne Collings, Tracey Collins, Margaret Combo, Dee Cooper, Nicola Coppola, Jodie Cordell, Dominic Coughlin, Sallt Craiborne, J Craig, C Croke, Joseph Cultice, Pam Currie, H Daddona, Mark Daker, Tamsin Davidson, Jean Davidson Sinclair, Norma Davies, Richard Davies, Sue Davis, Kara Davis, Andre Delfos, Garry Denke, Robin De Wan, S Dorn, Dennis Dorney, Jennifer Doyle, B Doyle, Barbara Dunn, Phil Dunnington, Anneli Dyall, Alison East, Robert Egg, Renevan Eijk, Tiffany Ellis, Toby Ellison, I Famum, Adrian Ferre-D' Amare, Maggie Fifoot, Jan Howard Finder, Jody Finver, F B Fogarty, Belinda Fogg, Roberta For, Terry Forkwit, Paola Formenti, Louise Foster, S Fotini, Meg Francis, Melissa Freeland, Richard & Patricia Fryett, Peter Fulop, Peter Gainsford, Paul Garrett, Valerie Garrett, Chris Gibb, Andrew Gnoza, David Godley, Arron & Kirsten Goodwin, Matthew Gore, Ruth Goreham, Louise Gorrie, Denise Gow, John Green, Paul Greening, Edith Gregoire, Cath Gurlick, Andrew Haas, Jimmy Patrick Haffenrichter, Pam Hainsworth, Samantha Halewood, Denis Halliwell, R Hammersley, Graham Hannaford, Charles Harmer, C Harris, Jenny Harwood, Jim Hendrickson, Alex Hendry, Mike Hergert, Denise Highton, Indra Hildebrandt, N Hill, Gloria Hiscock, Fiona Hodson, Judith Holbrook, R Honeyman, Mark Hudson, David Hugh Smith, Christine Hughes, Nick Humphrey, Rod & Jill Hunter, Mike Huntington, Heather Hutton, Christiane Hyde Citron, Suzanne Ingram Armstrong, Takayoshi Ito, Stephan Jacobi, Marian Jago, Diana James, Tanya Janzen, Jill Jarvis, Willan T Jenkins, Ann Johns, Leah Judd, A V Julian, Ellen & Robert Kavash, Peter & Yvonne Kerr, Hans-Dieter Kers.holt, Roslyn Kinett, Andrea King, Christine Kirton, Simon Kretschmer, D J Lake, Rich Lamuru, Lucie Laplante, Gareth Lawton, Cecilia Leishman, Andrew & Gaye Leverton, Jenny Leviston, Mike Lima, J P Logan, Peter Lommer Kristensen, R T Loomes, Charlotte Luongo, Clare Lynam, Bruce & Trina MacAder, Shelley MacGregor, Hilda MacLean, Ofra Magidor, Robyn Mainsbridge, Pete & Mitzi Margetts, James Marshall, Tanya Martion, Ron Matson, Pat Matsumoto, Jory F Mattison, Sandra Mayo, Paula Mazzocato, Frank McCready, Tim McFarlane, Kenneth Mcfarlane, Jane & Richard McGowan, Sharon McGrath, Ross McGregor, Donny McLean, Helen McWilliam, Katie Mecke, Caroline Mecklem, John Meehan, Jillian & Jihn Meredith, Kathleen Millea, Edward Mills, Susan Moore, Deidre Morrow, David Murray, Sarah Musts, Anand Narasimhan, Jeff Newcomer, Stuart B Nicol, Stewart Nicolson, Dorothy Nielsen, Mil Niepold, Dave O'Brien, David O'Regan, John Palgan, Chris Parker, Simone Parkinson, Deborah Pascoe, Carolina Patane, Leigh Patterson, Kim Pavlak, Robert Pearl, John Peck, Robin Percy, Rok & Monica Perkavac, Geraldine Perriam, Cathrin Petersen, Katriu Petzer, Karen Phillips, Alison Pickard, Lance Pierce, M N Plant, Martin Platt, William Plummer, Susan Pogue, N C Pollack, R Porter, Stephen Porter, Dee Poujade, Jason Prisley, Heather Pruiksma, Joan Pryse, Stefan Punkenhofer, Mark Rainsley, L B Rapke, Megan Rapp, R Rees, Valerie Reichel Moberg, David Reid, Anja Renner, Peter Richardson, Evan Roberts, Kate Robertson, Alicia Robinson, Raul Rodriguez, Eva Romano, W Rosenboom, Judith Rowell, Francis M Russell, Kim Ryder, Andy Ryland, Marcin Sadurski, Jeff Sandvig, Peter Sarrett, Cheng Hin Saw, Bernhard Schoene, Katherine Scott, Marre Sebastian, Deepak Sharma, A Shepherd, Ruth Sherwin, Laura Shevchenko, Phyl Shimeld, Mark Shuttleworth, Mary Siddall, Lloyd & Margie Simes, Pete Simonson, Alex Sky, Sue Slogrove, Marnie Smedley, R A Smith, Dale Smith, A Smith, Jean Smith, Ceri Smith, Vaclav

1062 Acknowledgments

Sochor, Knut Albert Solem, Gary Spinks, Emily Stead, Helen Stephen, W G Stockman, Charlotte Stockwell, Elaine Sutton, Ray Swenson, Dorothy E Synnot, Mohit Tandon, Simon Taskunas, Peter Taylor, A R Teesdale, Jean Thio, Nigel Thomas, Elizabeth Thomas, Carol A Thomas, Nils Andreas Thommesen, J & P Thompson, Peter B Thompson, Carmel Tobin, Heike Trauschies, Yvonne Trevaskis, Lisa Tyndall, Beryl & Bruce Tyrie, Masumi Ubukata, Austin Bell, Jerry Varner, Sabrina A Varsi, B Vazda, Suzanne Veletta, Simon Wake, Leo & Jean Walker, Richard Walker, R Wallis, Rosie Ward, Barry Ward, Phil Waring, Louis Warwick, R J Washington, V A Waters, Genevieve Webb, Sally Webb, Adrian Wedgewood, Bernard Wellings, Sandra Wells, Kevin Wenlock, WL West III, Simonede Wet, Dennis Whittle, Elizabeth Wilder, D R Williamson, Ian Willis, Dom Wilson, Royce Wilson, Paul Wilson, Sandra Winter, Yvonne Wolff, Margaret Wood, Stewart Wright, JM Yeo, Rod York, Jason Young, Morris Zwi.

LONELY PLANET

Phrasebooks

Lonely Planet phrasebooks are packed with essential words and phrases to help travellers communicate with the locals. With colour tabs for quick reference, an extensive vocabulary and use of script, these handy pocket-sized language guides cover day-to-day travel situations.

- handy pocket-sized books
- easy to understand Pronunciation chapter
- clear & comprehensive Grammar chapter
- romanisation alongside script to allow ease of pronunciation
- script throughout so users can point to phrases for every situation
- full of cultural information and tips for the traveller

'...vital for a real DIY spirit and attitude in language learning'
– *Backpacker*

'the phrasebooks have good cultural backgrounders and offer solid advice for challenging situations in remote locations'
– *San Francisco Examiner*

Arabic (Egyptian) ● Arabic (Moroccan) ● Australian *(Australian English, Aboriginal and Torres Strait languages)* ● Baltic States *(Estonian, Latvian, Lithuanian)* ● Bengali ● Brazilian ● Burmese ● Cantonese ● Central Asia ● Central Europe *(Czech, French, German, Hungarian, Italian, Slovak)* ● Eastern Europe *(Bulgarian, Czech, Hungarian, Polish, Romanian, Slovak)* ● Ethiopian (Amharic) ● Fijian ● French ● German ● Greek ● Hill Tribes ● Hindi/Urdu ● Indonesian ● Italian ● Japanese ● Korean ● Lao ● Latin American Spanish ● Malay ● Mandarin ● Mediterranean Europe *(Albanian, Croatian, Greek, Italian, Macedonian, Maltese, Serbian, Slovene)* ● Mongolian ● Nepali ● Papua New Guinea ● Pilipino (Tagálog) ● Quechua ● Russian ● Scandinavian Europe *(Danish, Finnish, Icelandic, Norwegian, Swedish)* ● South-East Asia *(Burmese, Indonesian, Khmer, Lao, Malay, Tagalog Pilipino, Thai, Vietnamese)* ● Spanish (Castilian) *(also includes Catalan, Galician and Basque)* ● Sri Lanka ● Swahili ● Thai ● Tibetan ● Turkish ● Ukrainian ● USA *(US English, Vernacular, Native American languages, Hawaiian)* ● Vietnamese ● Western Europe *(Basque, Catalan, Dutch, French, German, Greek, Irish)*

Lonely Planet Journeys

JOURNEYS is a unique collection of travel writing – published by the company that understands travel better than anyone else. It is a series for anyone who has ever experienced – or dreamed of – the magical moment when they encountered a strange culture or saw a place for the first time. They are tales to read while you're planning a trip, while you're on the road or while you're in an armchair in front of a fire.

These outstanding titles explore our planet through the eyes of a diverse group of international writers. JOURNEYS books catch the spirit of a place, illuminate a culture, recount a crazy adventure or introduce a fascinating way of life. They always entertain, and always enrich the experience of travel.

MALI BLUES
Traveling to an African Beat
Lieve Joris (translated by Sam Garrett)

Drought, rebel uprisings, ethnic conflict: these are the predominant images of West Africa. But as Lieve Joris travels in Senegal, Mauritania and Mali, she meets survivors, fascinating individuals charting new ways of living between tradition and modernity. With her remarkable gift for drawing out people's stories, Joris brilliantly captures the rhythms of a world that refuses to give in.

THE GATES OF DAMASCUS
Lieve Joris (translated by Sam Garrett)

This best-selling book is a beautifully drawn portrait of day-to-day life in modern Syria. Through her intimate contact with local people, Lieve Joris draws us into the fascinating world that lies behind the gates of Damascus. Hala's husband is a political prisoner, jailed for his opposition to the Assad regime; through the author's friendship with Hala we see how Syrian politics impacts on the lives of ordinary people.

THE OLIVE GROVE
Travels in Greece
Katherine Kizilos

Katherine Kizilos travels to fabled islands, troubled border zones and her family's village deep in the mountains. She vividly evokes breathtaking landscapes, generous people and passionate politics, capturing the complexities of a country she loves.

'beautifully captures the real tensions of Greece' – *Sunday Times*

KINGDOM OF THE FILM STARS
Journey into Jordan
Annie Caulfield

Kingdom of the Film Stars is a travel book and a love story. With honesty and humour, Annie Caulfield writes of travelling in Jordan and falling in love with a Bedouin with film-star looks.

She offers fascinating insights into the country – from the tent life of traditional women to the hustle of downtown Amman – and unpicks tight-woven western myths about the Arab world.

LONELY PLANET

Guides by Region

Lonely Planet is known worldwide for publishing practical, reliable and no-nonsense travel information in our guides and on our Web site. The Lonely Planet list covers just about every accessible part of the world. Currently there are nine series: travel guides, shoestring guides, walking guides, city guides, phrasebooks, audio packs, travel atlases, diving and snorkeling guides and travel literature.

AFRICA Africa – the South • Africa on a shoestring • Arabic (Egyptian) phrasebook • Arabic (Moroccan) phrasebook • Cairo • Cape Town • Central Africa • East Africa • Egypt • Egypt travel atlas • Ethiopian (Amharic) phrasebook • The Gambia & Senegal • Kenya • Kenya travel atlas • Malawi, Mozambique & Zambia • Morocco • North Africa • South Africa, Lesotho & Swaziland • South Africa, Lesotho & Swaziland travel atlas • Swahili phrasebook • Trekking in East Africa • Tunisia • West Africa • Zimbabwe, Botswana & Namibia • Zimbabwe, Botswana & Namibia travel atlas
Travel Literature: The Rainbird: A Central African Journey • Songs to an African Sunset: A Zimbabwean Story • Mali Blues: Traveling to an African Beat

AUSTRALIA & THE PACIFIC Australia • Australian phrasebook • Bushwalking in Australia • Bushwalking in Papua New Guinea • Fiji • Fijian phrasebook • Islands of Australia's Great Barrier Reef • Melbourne • Micronesia • New Caledonia • New South Wales & the ACT • New Zealand • Northern Territory • Outback Australia • Papua New Guinea • Papua New Guinea (Pidgin) phrasebook • Queensland • Rarotonga & the Cook Islands • Samoa • Solomon Islands • South Australia • Sydney • Tahiti & French Polynesia • Tasmania • Tonga • Tramping in New Zealand • Vanuatu • Victoria • Western Australia
Travel Literature: Islands in the Clouds • Sean & David's Long Drive

CENTRAL AMERICA & THE CARIBBEAN Bahamas and Turks & Caicos • Bermuda • Central America on a shoestring • Costa Rica • Cuba • Eastern Caribbean • Guatemala, Belize & Yucatán: La Ruta Maya • Jamaica • Mexico • Mexico City • Panama
Travel Literature: Green Dreams: Travels in Central America

EUROPE Amsterdam • Andalucía • Austria • Baltic States phrasebook • Berlin • Britain • Central Europe • Central Europe phrasebook • Czech & Slovak Republics • Denmark • Dublin • Eastern Europe • Eastern Europe phrasebook • Edinburgh • Estonia, Latvia & Lithuania • Europe • Finland • France • French phrasebook • Germany • German phrasebook • Greece • Greek phrasebook • Hungary • Iceland, Greenland & the Faroe Islands • Ireland • Italian phrasebook • Italy • Lisbon • London • Mediterranean Europe • Mediterranean Europe phrasebook • Paris • Poland • Portugal • Portugal travel atlas • Prague • Romania & Moldova • Russia, Ukraine & Belarus • Russian phrasebook • Scandinavian & Baltic Europe • Scandinavian Europe phrasebook • Scotland • Slovenia • Spain • Spanish phrasebook • St Petersburg • Switzerland • Trekking in Spain • Ukrainian phrasebook • Vienna • Walking in Britain • Walking in Italy • Walking in Switzerland • Western Europe • Western Europe phrasebook
Travel Literature: The Olive Grove: Travels in Greece

INDIAN SUBCONTINENT Bangladesh • Bengali phrasebook • Bhutan • Delhi • Goa • Hindi/Urdu phrasebook • India • India & Bangladesh travel atlas • Indian Himalaya • Karakoram Highway • Nepal • Nepali phrasebook • Pakistan • Rajasthan • South India • Sri Lanka • Sri Lanka phrasebook • Trekking in the Indian Himalaya • Trekking in the Karakoram & Hindukush • Trekking in the Nepal Himalaya
Travel Literature: In Rajasthan • Shopping for Buddhas

Index

Text

A

á Becket, Thomas 126
A la Ronde 388
Abbotsbury 327-8
Aberdeen 854-60, **855**
Aberdeenshire & Moray 853-64
Aberdour 833
Aberfoyle 830
Abergavenny 1004-5
Aberystwyth 1013-16, **1014**
Abingdon 438
accommodation 49-53, see
   also individual countries
Ailsa Craig 799
air travel 83-90, **86**
   around Britain 98-9
   around Scotland 732
   buying tickets 84-5
   excess baggage 85-8
   special needs 85
   to/from Africa 89-90
   to/from Asia 90
   to/from Australia 89
   to/from Canada 88-9
   to/from Continental Europe 89
   to/from Ireland 89
   to/from New Zealand 89
   to/from Scotland 730
   to/from USA 88-9
   to/from Wales 958
Aldeburgh 540
Alderney 1050-1
Alexander Keiller Museum 348
Alfred the Great of Wessex 125
Alloway 797-8
Alnwick 688-9
Althorp 485
Alton Towers 511
Alum Bay 311
Ambleside 614
American Museum 365
American War Cemetery 560
ancestors, tracing your 75-7
Anglesey 1041-2
Anglo-Saxons 125
animals, treatment of 152

Anne of Cleves House
   Museum 285
Anstruther 840
Applecross 900
Appledore 396
Apsley House 204-5
Arbroath 853
Ardrossan 792
Argyll & Bute 810-23
Armadale 904
architecture 144-50, 715-16, 948
arts 141-4, 714-15, 947-8
arts and crafts movement 481
Arundel 291
Ashby-del-la-Zouch 496
Ashford 272
Assizes, bloody 322
Attingham Park 502
Auchterarder 845
Audley End House 535
Austen, Jane 36, 297, 301, 360
Avebury 346-8, **347**
Aviemore 870-3
Axbridge 370-1
Aylesbury 487
Ayr 796
Ayrshire 792-9

B

Bakewell 516-18, **517**
Bala 1033
Ballater 860
Balmoral Castle 860
Bamburgh 689-90
Banff 863
Bangor 1038-9
Bannockburn 827
Barbara Hepworth Museum
   416-17
Barmouth 1032
Barnard Castle 682-3
Barnstaple 395
Barra 916
Barry 971
Bath 357-65, **359**
Battle 277-8
Battle of Hastings 277
Beamish Open Air Mu
Beatles, the 591-2, **59**
Beauly 888

Beaumaris 1041-2
Beddgelert 1030
Bedford 488-90
Bedfordshire 488-90
Bellingham 698
Belvoir Castle 496
Ben Nevis 876
Benbecula 915
Berkeley 447-8
Berkshire 251-6
Berwick-upon-Tweed 690-2,
   691
Bess of Hardwick 512, 518
Bethnal Green Museum of
   Childhood 200
Betws-y-Coed 1026-7
Beverley 637-8
Bibury 441-2
Biddulph Gardens 510
Bideford 395-6
Birdoswald Roman Fort 696
Birmingham 479-85, **480**
Birnam 845
Birsay 923-4
Bishop's Castle 506
Black Isle 888-9
Black Mountains 999
Blackpool 599-601
Blackpool Tower 599-600
Blaenau Ffestiniog 1030-1
Blaenavon 1005-6
Blair Castle 846-7
Blair, Tony 133, 138
Blantyre 791
Blenheim Palace 436-7
Blickling H
Bloo

Bold indicates maps.
Italics indicates boxed text.

Bodmin Moor 421-2
bog snorkelling 1010
Bonnie Prince Charlie 602
books 35-6
Boscastle 421
Boston 569
Boswell, James 508
Bosworth Battlefield 496
Bournemouth 317-18
Bourton-on-the-Water 442
Bovington Camp 321
Bowness 610-14, **611**
Bradford 630
Bradford-on-Avon 343-4, **343**
Braemar 860-1
Brampton 696
Brantwood 616
brass rubbing 76
Brecon 1001-4, **1002**
Brecon Beacons National Park
    996-1009, **998**
Brighton 286-90, 287
Bristol 350-7, **352**
British Museum 191-3
Broad Haven 988-9
Broadford 904-5
Broadstairs 265-6
Broadway 444-5
Brodie Castle 889-90
Brontës, the 630
    Brontë Parsonage 631
Brora 891-8
Brown, Capability 294, 342,
    365, 437, 470, 487, 518,
    535, 539, 546, 629
Bryher 424
Buckfastleigh 402
Buckingham Palace 190
Buckinghamshire 486-8
Bude 422
Bunyan, John 489
Burford 437-8
Burghley House 569
Burns House 800
rns, Robert 800
    924-5
    ollection 778-9
    n-Trent 511
    ds 537-9
    -102

C
Cadbury World 484
Caerlaverock Castle 801
Caerleon Roman Fortress 971-2
Caernarfon 1039-40
Caernarfon Castle 1039-40
Caerphilly Castle 970
Caesar, Julius 124
Cairngorms, the 869-76, **869**
Caldey Island 985
Calke Abbey 512
Callander 830-1
Callanish 913
Cambridge 549-60, **551**, *553*
Cambridgeshire 549-63
canal travel 79-81
Canterbury 257-65, **259**
Canterbury Cathedral 260-2
Canterbury Tales 126, 141,
    258, *262*
Cape Wrath 897
Capel Curig 1027
Capel-y-Ffin 1006
car & motorcycle travel 93-4
    around Britain 110-16
    around Scotland 734
    around Wales 959
    to/from Scotland 730
    to/from Wales 958
Cardiff 963-70, **964**
    entertainment 968-9
    getting around 970
    getting there & away 969-70
    history 963-5
    information 965
    orientation 965
    places to eat 967-8
    places to stay 967
Cardiff Bay 966
Cardigan 1012-16
Carew Castle 986
Carisbrooke Castle 309
Carlisle 601-5, **603**
Carloway 913
Carlyle's House 202
Carmarthen 979
Carrbridge 873-4
Castell Coch 970
Castell Henllys 994-5
Castle Combe 345
Castle Drogo 403
Castle Howard 649-50
Castle Kennedy Gardens 806
Castle Rising Castle 549
Castlerigg Stone Circle 618-19
Castleton 519-21, **521**
stletown 597

Cawdor 889
Celts 124
Ceredigion 1012-16
Cerne Abbas 324
Cerne Giant 324
Chagford 403
Chalice Well 373
Chamberlain, Neville 130
Channel Islands 1047-52, **1048**
Charlecote Park 478
Charles I 128-9
Charles II 129
Charles, Prince 323
Charleston Farmhouse 282
Charlestown 409
Chartwell 273
Chatsworth 518
Cheddar Gorge 369-70
Cheltenham 453-7, **455**
Chepstow 973-4
Cheshire 571-8
Chesil Beach 327
Chester 571-8, **574**
Chesterfield 512
Chesters Roman Fort 695
Chichester 291-4, **292**
Chichester Cathedral 291-2
Chiltern Hills 487-8
Chippenham 344-5
Chipping Campden 444
Christchurch 318
Church Stretton 505-6
Churchill, Sir Winston 130, 189
cinema 142
Cinque ports *267*
Cirencester 448-50
Claudius 124
Clava Cairns 889
Claydon House 487
Cley Marshes 546
Clifton 353
Clifton Suspension Bridge 353
Clouds Hill 321
Clovelly 396
Clun 506
Cockermouth 605-7, **606**
Colchester 533-4
Coldstream 766-7
Coldstream Guards 767
Commonwealth, the 128-9
Coniston 616-7
Conwy 1036-8, **1037**
Cook, Captain James 391, 656,
    657, 659, 661
Corbridge 694
Corfe Castle 321
Cornish language 408

Cornwall 405-25
Corsham Court 345
Cotehele 407
Cotswolds 437, 441, **443**
Covent Garden 185
Coventry 468-70
Cowes 309
Crail 840
Cregneash 597
Crianlarich 831
Criccieth 1042
cricket 58-9
Crickhowell 1004
Crieff 844
crofting 891
Cromarty 888-9
Cromer 546
Cromwell, Oliver 128-9, 572
Crowcombe 375
Cuillins, the 905
Culloden 889
Culross 832
Culzean Castle 798-9
Cumbria 601-7
Cupar 834
currency see money
customs regulations 30
Cutty Sark 207
cycling 69-74

D

Danby 655-6
Dartmoor National Park 396-405, **397**
Dartmouth 389-90
Darwin, Charles 497
Dedham Vale 534-5
Deeside 860-2
Derby 511
Derbyshire 511-13
Devil's Bridge 1016
Devizes 346
Devon 382-96
Diana, Princess of Wales 150-1, *151*
Dickens' House 193
Dolgellau 1032-3
Dollar 829
Domesday Book 126
Donington Park 496
Dorchester 322-3
Dorchester-on-Thames 438

Dornoch 890
Dorset 317-31
Douglas 596
Doune 829
Dove Cottage 614
Dovedale 518
Dover 268-71, **269**
Dover Castle 269-70
Downing St 188-9
Dr Johnson's House 195
Drake, Sir Francis 391, 405
Drumnadrochit 883-4
Dryburgh Abbey 770
du Maurier, Daphne 422
Dufftown 862
Dulverton 378-9
Dumfries 800-1
Dunblane 829
Duncombe Park 653-4
Dundee 847-52, **850**
Dundee & Angus 847-53
Dunfermline 832-3
Dunkeld 845
Dunnet Head 894
Dunrobin Castle 890-1
Dunster 379
Dunster Castle 379
Durham 678-82, **679**
Durham Cathedral 678-81, **680**
Durness 896-7
Duxford Aircraft Museum 560
Dyrham Park 365

E

East Mainland 924-5
East Sussex 274-90
Edale 521-2, **521**
Eday 928
Edinburgh 735-761, **738**, **758**
  bus tours 750
  entertainment 755-7
  getting around 757-61
  getting there & away 757
  history 735-6
  information 737
  orientation 736-7
  places to eat 753-5
  places to stay 750-3
  Royal Mile 737-46
  special events 750
Edinburgh Castle 740-2
Edward I 126, 942
Edward II 126
Edward III 126
Edward IV 127
Edward the Confessor 125

Edward the Elder 125
Edward V 127-8
Edward VI 128
Edward VII 130
Edward VIII 130
Egilsay 927
Elgar, Sir Edward 463, 467
Elgin 863
Elgin marbles 192
Elizabeth I 128, 518
Elizabeth II 132
Ellesmere Port 578
Elterwater 615
Ely 561-3, **562**
email service 35
embassies 29
England 121-698
  architecture 144-50
  arts 141-4
  climate 134
  ecology 134-5
  economy 138-40
  environment 134-5
  fauna 135-7
  flora 135-7
  geography 133-4
  government 138
  language 153
  national parks 137
  population 140
  religion 152-3
English Heritage 44
Erddig 1018
Essex 533-5
Eton 251-7, **252**
Eton College 255
Evesham 467
Evie 924
Exeter 382-7, **383**
Exeter Cathedral 384
Exford 380
Exmoor National Park 376-82, **376**
Eyam 519

F

Fairford 448
Falkland 833-4
Falls of Measach 899
Falmouth 410
Farne Islands 689
Fawkes, Guy *285*
fax service 35
Ffestiniog Railway 1030
Fforest Fawr 1000
Fife 831-41

films 36
Findhorn 863-4
Firth of Clyde 790
Fishbourne Roman Palace &
    Museum 294
Fishguard 992-3, **992**
fishing 78
Fleet Street 194
Flemish weavers 579
Folkestone 272
food 54-6
football 58
Forde Abbey 329-30
Forest of Dean 458-9
Fort Augustus 882-3
Fort George 889
Fort William 876-80, **877**
Fortnum & Mason 242
Fountains Abbey 674-5
Fowey 407-8
Fox Talbot Museum of
    Photography 345-6
Freud's House 206

G

Gainsborough, Thomas 537
Gairloch 899-900
Galashiels 771
Gardens of the Rose 491
Gatehouse of Fleet 803
George VI 130
Gipsy Moth IV 207
Glamis Castle 852-3
Glasgow 773-90, **774**
Glastonbury 371-4, **371**
Glastonbury Abbey 372
Glen Coe 880-2
Glen Shiel 901
Glencoe massacre 707, 881
Glenelg 901
Glenshee 861-2
Gloucester 450-3, **450**
Gloucester Cathedral 451-2
Glyndebourne 282
Glyndŵr, Owain 942-3
golf 59-60, 75
Goodrich 463
Gourock 790
Gower Peninsula 978-9
Granada Studios 582
Grantchester 560
Grantham 568
Grantown-on-Spey 874
Grassholm Islands 988
Grassington 670
Great Glen, the 876-90

Great Malvern 463-4
Great Yarmouth 545-6
Greenock 790
Greenwich 206-8
Guernsey 1049-50
Gunpowder Plot 128

H

Haddon Hall 518
Hadrian 124-5, 692-3, 704
Hadrian's Wall 692-3
haggis 726
Hailes 445
Haltwhistle 696
Hampshire 294-309
Hampstead 205
Hampton Court Palace 211
Handa Island 897
Hardie, Keir 709
Hardwick Hall 512-13
Hardy's Cottage 323-4
Harewood House 629-30
Harlech 1031-2
Harris 913-5
Harrods 242
Harrogate 675-8, **676**
Harvey Nichols 242
Harwich 534
Hastings 278-82, **280**
Hatfield House 492
Haverfordwest 987-8
Hawksmoor, Nicholas 186,
    203, 437, 649-50
Hawkstone Historic Park 502
Haworth 630-2, **631**
Hayfield 522
Hay-on-Wye 1006-9, **1008**
Headingley 627
health 39-41
Hebden Bridge 632-4
Helmsdale 891-2
Helmsley 652-4, **653**
Henley-on-Thames 439-40
Henry I 126
Henry II 126
Henry III 126
Henry IV 127
Henry V 127
Henry VI 127, 552
Henry VII 128
Henry VIII 128, 552, 563
Heptonstall 632-4
Hereford 460-2
Herefordshire & Worcestershire
    459-68
Herm 1051-2

Hermitage Castle 773
Herriot, James 655
Hertfordshire 490-2
Hever 273
Hexham 694-5
Highland clearances 708-9
Hill Top 615-16
hitching 116-117
    around Scotland 730, 734
    around Wales 958, 960
Hitler, Adolf 130
Holford 374-5
Holy Island 690
Holyhead 1042
Hood, Robin 527
horse racing 60
horse riding 78-9
    Brecon Beacons National
        Park 1000-1
    Dartmoor 399
    Exmoor 377
    Snowdonia 1024-5
Houghton Hall 549
House of York 127-8
Houses of Lancaster 127-8
Houses of Parliament 188
Housesteads Roman Fort 695
Howmore 916
Hoy 925-6
Hundred Years' War 126
Huntly 862
Hyde Park 204

I

Ickworth House & Park 539
Ightham Mote 274
Ilfracombe 395
Industrial Revolution 479, 497,
    502, 511
Inns of Court 193-4
Internet resources 35
Inveraray 813-14
Inverewe Gardens 899
Inverey 861
Inverness 884-8, **885**
Inverpolly Nature Reserve 898-
    902
Ipswich 535-6
Ironbridge Gorge 502-5, **503**
Isle of Arran 792-6, **793**
Isle of Bute 811
Isle of Coll 823, **822**
Isle of Colonsay 817
Isle of Great Cumbrae 792
Isle of Iona 822-3
Isle of Islay 815-16, **816**
Isle of Jura 816-17, **816**

LONELY PLANET

Mail Order

Lonely Planet products are distributed worldwide. They are also available by mail order from Lonely Planet, so if you have difficulty finding a title please write to us. North and South American residents should write to 150 Linden St, Oakland, CA 94607, USA; European and African residents should write to 10a Spring Place, London NW5 3BH, UK; and residents of other countries to PO Box 617, Hawthorn, Victoria 3122, Australia.

ISLANDS OF THE INDIAN OCEAN Madagascar & Comoros • Maldives • Mauritius, Réunion & Seychelles

MIDDLE EAST & CENTRAL ASIA Arab Gulf States • Central Asia • Central Asia phrasebook • Iran • Israel & the Palestinian Territories • Israel & the Palestinian Territories travel atlas • Istanbul • Jerusalem • Jordan & Syria • Jordan, Syria & Lebanon travel atlas • Lebanon • Middle East on a shoestring • Turkey • Turkish phrasebook • Turkey travel atlas • Yemen
Travel Literature: The Gates of Damascus • Kingdom of the Film Stars: Journey into Jordan

NORTH AMERICA Alaska • Backpacking in Alaska • Baja California • California & Nevada • Canada • Florida • Hawaii • Honolulu • Los Angeles • Miami • New England USA • New Orleans • New York City • New York, New Jersey & Pennsylvania • Pacific Northwest USA • Rocky Mountain States • San Francisco • Seattle • Southwest USA • USA phrasebook • Washington, DC & the Capital Region
Travel Literature: Drive Thru America

NORTH-EAST ASIA Beijing • Cantonese phrasebook • China • Hong Kong • Hong Kong, Macau & Guangzhou • Japan • Japanese phrasebook • Japanese audio pack • Korea • Korean phrasebook • Kyoto • Mandarin phrasebook • Mongolia • Mongolian phrasebook • North-East Asia on a shoestring • Seoul • South-West China • Taiwan • Tibet • Tibetan phrasebook • Tokyo
Travel Literature: Lost Japan

SOUTH AMERICA Argentina, Uruguay & Paraguay • Bolivia • Brazil • Brazilian phrasebook • Buenos Aires • Chile & Easter Island • Chile & Easter Island travel atlas • Colombia • Ecuador & the Galapagos Islands • Latin American Spanish phrasebook • Peru • Quechua phrasebook • Rio de Janeiro • South America on a shoestring • Trekking in the Patagonian Andes • Venezuela
Travel Literature: Full Circle: A South American Journey

SOUTH-EAST ASIA Bali & Lombok • Bangkok • Burmese phrasebook • Cambodia • Hill Tribes phrasebook • Ho Chi Minh City • Indonesia • Indonesian phrasebook • Indonesian audio pack • Jakarta • Java • Laos • Lao phrasebook • Laos travel atlas • Malay phrasebook • Malaysia, Singapore & Brunei • Myanmar (Burma) • Philippines • Pilipino (Tagalog) phrasebook • Singapore • South-East Asia on a shoestring • South-East Asia phrasebook • Thailand • Thailand's Islands & Beaches • Thailand travel atlas • Thai phrasebook • Thai audio pack • Vietnam • Vietnamese phrasebook • Vietnam travel atlas

---

ALSO AVAILABLE: Antarctica • Brief Encounters: Stories of Love, Sex & Travel • Chasing Rickshaws • Not the Only Planet: Travel Stories from Science Fiction • Travel with Children • Traveller's Tales

LONELY PLANET

Lonely Planet On-line
www.lonelyplanet.com *or* AOL keyword: lp

Whether you've just begun planning your next trip, or you're chasing down specific info on currency regulations or visa requirements, check out Lonely Planet On-line for up-to-the minute travel information.

As well as mini guides to more than 250 destinations, you'll find maps, photos, travel news, health and visa updates, travel advisories, and discussion of the ecological and political issues you need to be aware of as you travel. You'll also find timely upgrades to popular guidebooks which you can print out and stick in the back of your book.

There's also an on-line travellers' forum where you can share your experience of life on the road, meet travel companions and ask other travellers for their recommendations and advice.

And of course we have a complete and up-to-date list of all Lonely Planet travel products including travel guides, diving and snorkeling guides, phrasebooks, atlases, travel literature and videos, and a simple on-line ordering facility if you can't find the book you want elsewhere.

Lonely Planet Diving & Snorkeling Guides

Known for indispensible guidebooks to destinations all over the world, Lonely Planet's Pisces Books are the most popular series of diving and snorkeling titles available.

There are three series: **Diving & Snorkeling Guides**, **Shipwreck Diving** series and **Dive Into History**. Full colour throughout, the **Diving & Snorkeling Guides** combine quality photographs with detailed descriptions of the best dive sites for each location, giving divers a glimpse of what they can expect both on land and in water. The **Dive Into History** series is perfect for the adventure diver or armchair traveller. The **Shipwreck Diving** series provides all the details for exploring the most interesting wrecks in the Atlantic and Pacific oceans. The list also includes underwater nature and technical guides.

FREE Lonely Planet Newsletters

We love hearing from you and think you'd like to hear from us.

Planet Talk

Our FREE quarterly printed newsletter is full of tips from travellers and anecdotes from Lonely Planet guidebook authors. Every issue is packed with up-to-date travel news and advice, and includes:

- a postcard from Lonely Planet co-founder Tony Wheeler
- a swag of mail from travellers
- a look at life on the road through the eyes of a Lonely Planet author
- topical health advice
- prizes for the best travel yarn
- news about forthcoming Lonely Planet events
- a complete list of Lonely Planet books and other titles

To join our mailing list, residents of the UK, Europe and Africa can email us at go@lonelyplanet.co.uk; residents of North and South America can email us at info@lonelyplanet.com; the rest of the world can email us at talk2us@lonelyplanet.com.au, or contact any Lonely Planet office.

Comet

Our FREE monthly email newsletter brings you all the latest travel news, features, interviews, competitions, destination ideas, travellers' tips & tales, Q&As, raging debates and related links. Find out what's new on the Lonely Planet Web site and which books are about to hit the shelves.

Subscribe from your desktop: www.lonelyplanet.com/comet

Isle of Man 596-8, **597**
Isle of Mull 820-2, **822**
Isle of Raasay 906
Isle of Skye 902-6, **907**
Isle of Staffa 823
Isle of Tiree 823, **822**
Isle of Whithorn 804
Isle of Wight 309-12, **310**
Isles of Scilly 422-5, **423**
Ivinghoe Beacon 488

J

Jacobite rebellions 707-8
James I 128
James II 129
James IV 706
Jane Austen House 301
Jedburgh 771-2
Jersey 1048-9
John o'Groats 893-4
Johnson, Samuel 508
Jorvik Viking Centre 644

K

Keats House 205-6
Kedleston Hall 511-12
Kellie Castle 839-40
Kelso 767-9, **768**
Kendal 607
Kenilworth 472-3
Kenneth MacAlpin 704
Kensington Palace 203
Kent 257-74
Keswick 618-21, **619**
Kew Garden 210-11
Keynes 132
Killin 831
Kilmartin Glen 814
Kincraig 873
King Arthur 673, 941
King Egbert of Wessex 125
King's College Chapel 552-3
King's Lynn 546-9, **547**
Kingston Lacy 319
Kingston-upon-Hull 636-7
Kingussie 874-5
Kinlochewe 900
Kintyre 814-15
Kirby Lonsdale 671
Kirkby Stephen 671-2
Kirkcaldy 833
Kirkcudbright 802-3

Kirkwall 918-21, **919**
Knebworth House 492
Knighton 1010
Knockan 898-902
Knole House 273-4
Kyle of Lochalsh 901
Kyleakin 904
Kylerhea 904
Kylesku 897

L

Lacock 345-6
Lake District National Park
    608-21, **609**
Lanark 791-2
Lanarkshire 790-2
Lancashire 598-601
Lancaster 598-9
Land's End 414-15
Lanhydrock House 408
Latheron 892
Laugharne 980
Lavenham 537
Lawrence, TE 320
Lawrence, DH 530
Leamington Spa 472
Lechlade 448
Leeds 625-9, **626**
Leeds Castle 274
Legoland Windsor 255
Leicester 493-6, **494**
Leicester Square 183
Leicestershire 493-6
Lerwick 932-5, **933**
Lewes 283-6, **284**
Lewis 911
Liberty 242
Lichfield 508
Lincoln 564-8, **565**
Lincolnshire 563-70
literature 141-2, 714-5, 947-8,
    see also books
Little Moreton Hall 510
Liverpool 587-95, **588**
Lizard, the 410-11
Llanberis 1027-9
Llandaff Cathedral 966-7
Llandrindod Wells 1010
Llandudno 1034-6, **1034**
Llanfairpwllgwyngyllgogerych-
    wyrndrobwllllantysiliogo-
    gogoch 1041
Llanfihangel Crucorney 1006
Llangollen 1018-21, **1019**, *1020*
Llanthony 1006
Llanwrtyd Wells 1009-10

Llŷn Peninsula 1042-3
Loch Carron 900
Loch Glencoul 897
Loch Leven 841-2
Loch Lomond 812-13
Loch Maree 900
Loch Ness 883
Loch Ness monster 883
Lochboisdale 916
Lochinver 897-8
Lochmaddy 915
London 154-248, **161-176**
    Docklands 200-2
    entertainment 233-40
    getting around 247-8
    getting there & away 245-7
    history 155
    information 158-78
    markets 242-5
    orientaion 155-8
    places to eat 222-32
    places to stay 211-21
    shopping 241-5
    spectator sports 240-1
    walking tour 178-80
London Zoo 196
Long Melford 536
Long Mynd, the 505-6
Longleat 342-3
Looe, East & West 407
lovespoons 956
Ludlow 506-7
Lulworth Cove 321-2
Lundy Island 395
Lydford 404
Lyme Park 524
Lyme Regis 328-9, **329**
Lyndhurst 308
Lynmouth 381-2
Lynton 381-2

M

MacDonald, Flora 708, *906*
Macduff 863
Machynlleth 1011-12
Mackintosh, Charles Rennie
    779-81
Madame Tussaud's 195-6
Magna Carta 126, 538
Maiden Castle 323
Mallaig 901-2
Malmesbury 349-50
Manchester 578-87, **580**
Manorbier 985-6
maps 25
Margate 265

Bold indicates maps.
Italics indicates boxed text.

Marlborough 349
Mary I 128
Mary II 129
Mary Queen of Scots 518, 563, 706
Mary Queen of Scots House 771
Matlock & Matlock Bath 524
Mealista 913
media
  magazines 37
  newspapers 36-7
  radio 37
  TV 37-8
Melford Hall 536
Mellerstain House 769
Melrose 769-70
Mendip Hills 369-71
Merseyside 587-96
Millennium Dome 159, 206, 207
Minack Theatre 414
Minehead 379-80
Minginish Peninsula 905
money 30-3
  ATMs 31-2
  credit cards 31-2
  exchange rates 30
  exchanging money 30-2
  taxes 33
  tipping 33
  travellers cheques 31-2
Monmouth 972-3
Montacute House 375
Moretonhampstead 403
Moreton-in-Marsh 442-4
motorcycle travel, see car & motorcycle travel
Mount Edgcumbe 394-5
Mousehole 413-14
Munro bagging *870*
music 142-3, 947-8

N

Nash, Sir John 190, 196, 288, 354
National Gallery 183
National Portrait Gallery 183
National Trust 44
Natural History Museum 203
Needles, The 311
Nether Stowey 374-5
Nevern 994
Neville, Richard 470
New Forest 306-8, **307**
New Galloway 801
New Lanark 791-2

Newcastle upon Tyne 683-8, **684**
Newent 459
Newgale 989
Newhaven 282-3
Newport (Isle of Wight) 309
Newport (Pembrokeshire) 993-4
Newport (South Wales) 971
Newquay 419-20, **420**
Newstead Abbey 529
Newton Stewart 803
Norfolk 540-9
Norfolk Broads 544-5
Normans 126-7
North Ronaldsay 929
North Uist 915
North York Moors National Park 650-66, **651**
Northampton 485
Northamptonshire 485-6
Northleach 441
Northumberland 688-92
Northumberland National Park 697-8, **697**
Norwich 540-4, **541**
Nottingham 525-9, **526**
Nottinghamshire 524-30
Nunnington Hall 655

O

Oban 817-20
Okehampton 403-4
Old Sarum 338
Old Trafford 583
Orford 540
organised tours 117
Orkney Islands 916-29, **917**
Osborne House 309
Outer Hebrides 906-16, **907**
Oxford 427-36, **429**
Oxfordshire 427-40

P

Padstow 421
Painswick 446-7
painting 143, 948
Paisley 790
Papa Westray 929
Parnham 329
Pass of Killiecrankie 846
Peak District 513-24, **514**
Peebles 772
Peel 597-8
Pembroke 986-7
Pembrokeshire Coast National Park 980-95, **981**

Penarth 971
Pendennis Castle 410
Penrhyn Castle 1039
Pentre Ifan 995
Penzance 411-13, **412**
Pershore 467-8
Perth 842-4, **842**
Perthshire & Kinross 841-7
Peterborough 563
Petworth House 294
Peveril Castle 520
Piccadilly Circus 183
Pickering 665
Pitlochry 845-6
Pittenweem 841
Plantagenets 126-7
Plas Newydd 1019, 1041
Plockton 900
Plymouth 390-4, **392**
Polperro 407
Poole 317-18
Porlock 380-1
Port Sunlight 595
Porthmadog 1043-4
Portland 327
Portmeirion 1044
Portpatrick 804
Portree 903-4, **903**
Portsmouth 301-6, **303**
postal service 33
Postbridge 401-2
Potter, Beatrix *452*
Powderham Castle 388
Powys 1009-12
Princetown 400-1
Prior Park 365
public holidays 46
Pwllheli 1042-3

Q

Quantock Hills 374-5
Quarry Bank Mill 586
Queen Victoria 129, 708

R

Raby Castle 683
Raglan Castle 973
Ragley Hall 478
Ramsgate 266
Regent's Park 195-6
Rhondda Valley 971
Richard I 126
Richard III 127-8
Richard the Lion-Heart 126
Richmond 672-4, **673**
Rievaulx Abbey 654-5

Robert the Bruce 705
Robin Hood's Bay 661-2
Roman Baths Museum 360-1
Romans 124-5, 602, 941
Romney Marsh 272
Roseland Peninsula 410
Ross-on-Wye 462-3
Rousay 927
Royal Academy of Arts 184
Royal Pavilion 288
Royal Shakespeare Company 477-8
rugby 59
Ruskin, John 616, 634
Rydal Mount 615
Ryde 309-11
Rye 275-7, **276**

S

Saffron Walden 535
Salisbury 331-8, **333**
Salisbury Cathedral 332-6
Sanday 928
Sandringham 549
Sandwich 266-8
Sandwick 935
Sark 1051
Saundersfoot 985
Scarborough 662-5, **663**
Scone Palace 843
Scotland 701-936, **702**
   accommodation 724-5
   architecture 715-16
   climate 710
   ecology 710-11
   economy 713
   entertainment 727-8
   environment 710-11
   fauna 711-12
   flora 711-12
   food 725-7
   geography 709-10
   government & politics 712-13
   history 703-9
   Internet resources 722-3
   language 719
   media 723
   money 721
   religion 719
   shopping 728-9
   tourist offices 720-1
   visas 721

Scottish Borders 766-73
Scourie 897
Scrabster 894-6
Selkirk 771
Settle 670-1
Shaftesbury 331
Shakespeare Globe Centre 209
Shakespeare, William 473-6, **475**
Shapinsay 926-7
Shaw's Corner 492
Sheffield 634-6, **635**
Sherborne Abbey 330
Sherborne Castle 330
Sherbourne 330-1
Sherwood Forest 530
Shetland Islands 929-36, **930**
shopping 60, see also individual countries
Shrewsbury 497-502, **498**
Shropshire 497-507
Sidmouth 388
Silbury Hill 349
Silverstone 485-6
Sissinghurst Castle Gardens 272-3
Skara Brae 923
Skegness 569-70
skiing 81-2
Skipton 669-70
Skokholm 988
Skomer 988
Slaughters, the 442
Slimbridge 447
Smailholm Tower 769
smuggling 283
Snowdon Mountain Railway 1028
Snowdonia National Park 1021-33, **1022**
Snowshill 445
Somerset 365-75
South Ronaldsay 924-5
South Uist 916
Southampton 306
Southwell Minster 530
special events 46-7
St Agnes 424
St Albans 490-2
St Andrews 834-9, **835**
St Brides Bay 988-9
St David's 989-91
St Ives 416-19, **417**
St Ives Tate 416
St Just-in-Penwith 415
St Martin's 424
St Martin-in-the-Fields 183
St Mary's 423

St Michael's Mount 411
St Paul's Cathedral 196-7
Staffordshire 508-11
Staithes 656
Stamford 568-9
steam railways 82
Stenness 923
Steps Bridge 403
Stirling 823-31, **825**
Stoke-on-Trent 509-10
Stokesay Castle 507
stone of destiny 742
Stonehaven 862-3
Stonehenge 338-41, **339**, **341**
Stonor Park 440
Stornoway 911-12
Stour Valley 536
Stourhead 341-2
Stowe Landscape Gardens 487
Stow-on-the-Wold 442
Stranraer 804-6, **805**
Stratford-upon-Avon 473-8, **474**
Stromness 921-3, **922**
Stronsay 927-8
Stuarts 128-9
Sudbury 536-7
Sumburgh 935
surfing 77-8
Surrey 256-7
Swanage 321
Swansea 974-8, **975**
swimming 77-8
Symonds Yat 463
Syon House 211

T

Taff Trail 999
Tarbert 914
Tate Gallery 191
Tatton Park 586-7
Taunton 375
Tavistock 405
taxi 117
tea 223
telephone service 33-4
Tenby 984-5
Tetbury 448
Tewkesbury 457-8
Thatcher 132-3
Thatcher, Margaret 568
Thaxted 535
theatre 142
Thirlestane Castle 770-1
Thirsk 655
Thurso 894-6, **895**

Bold indicates maps.
Italics indicates boxed text.

Tideswell 519
Tintagel 421
Tintern Abbey 973
Tolpuddle 319
Torbay Resorts 388-9
Torridon 900
Totnes 390
tourist offices 25-6
Tower Bridge 199
Tower of London 198-9
Trafalgar Square 182
train travel 91-3
    around Britain 102-10
    around Scotland 733-4
    around Wales 959
    Channel Tunnel 92
    European rail passes 92
    Eurostar 93
    Eurotunnel 92-3
    Great Central Railway 495-6
    Leeds-Settle-Carlisle Line 669
    North Yorkshire Moors
        Railway 665
    tickets 92, 108-10
    to/from Scotland 730
    to/from Wales 958
    trans-Siberian railway 90-1
    West Somerset Railway 375
Traquair House 772-3
Tresco 424
Trossachs, the 829-31
Trotternish Peninsula 905
Truro 409-10
Tudors 128
Turnberry 799
Tyndrum 831
Tywyn 1032

U

Uig 905-6
Ullapool 898-9, **898**
Ulverston 617-18
Unst 936
Urquhart Castle 884
Usk Valley 999

V

Vanbrugh, Sir John 203, 206,
    437, 649-50
Ventnor 309-11
Verulamium Museum 491
Victoria and Albert Museum
    202-2
Victoria Falls 900
Vikings 125
visas 26-9

W

Waddesdon Manor 487
Wales 939-1044, **940**
    accommodation 955
    architecture 948
    arts 947-8
    climate 944
    ecology 944-5
    economy 946-7
    environment 944-5
    entertainment 956-7
    flora & fauna 945-6
    food 955-6
    geography 944
    government & politics
        946
    history 939-44
    Internet resources 952
    language 950
    media 952-3
    money 952
    religion 949-50
    shopping 957
    tourist offices 951
    visas 952
Walker, William, 299
walks 61-9
    Cleveland Way 64-5
    Coast to Coast 68
    Cornwall 406
    Cotswold Way 64
    Cumbria Way 65
    Dales Way 67-8
    Dartmoor 398-9
    Hadrian's Wall 65-6
    Peddars Way & Norfolk
        Coast Path 66
    Pembrokeshire Coast Path
        69
    Pennine Way 66
    Ridgeway, The 66-7
    South Downs Way 67
    South West Coast Path
        63-4
    Thames Path 67
    West Highland Way 68-9
Wallace Collection 184
Wallace, William 602, 705,
    826-7
Walpole 129
Wantage 438-9
War of the Roses 127
Wareham 319-21
Warkworth 688
Warwick 470-2, **471**
Warwick Castle 470
Warwickshire & Coventry 468-

78
waterways 93-4
Wedgwood, Josiah 509
Wells 366-9, **366**
Wells Cathedral 367
Wells-Next-The-Sea 546
Welshpool 1010-11
Wendover 487-8
Wenlock Gorge 505
West Kennet Long Barrow
    349
West Somerset Railway 375
West Sussex 290-4
Westminster 185-91
Westminster Abbey 186-8
Westray 928-9
Weymouth 324-7
Whipsnade 490
whisky 728
Whitby 656-61
White Horse 439
Whitehall 188
Whithorn 803-4
Wick 892-3
Widecombe-in-the-Moor
    402
Wigan Pier Heritage Centre
    586
Wigtown 803
William II 126
William of Orange 129
William the Conqueror 126,
    565, 665, 942
Wilton House 338
Wiltshire 331-50
Wimborne 318-19
Wimpole Hall 561
Winchcombe 445-6
Winchester 295-301, **295**
Winchester Cathedral 296-8
Windermere 610-14, **611**
Windsor 251-7, **252**
Windsor Castle 251-4
Witney 438
Woburn Abbey & Safari Park
    490
Wollaton Hall 527
Wolvesey Castle 299
Woodstock 436-7
Wookey Hole 369
Worcester 464-7
Worcester Cathedral 464-5
Wordsworth House 605
Wordsworth Museum 614
work 47-9
Wren, Sir Christopher 155,
    181, 186, 195, 196, 202,

206, 207, 208, 334, 430,
432, 556, 650
Wrexham 1018
Wroxeter Roman City 502
Wye Valley 972-3
Wyre 927

Y
Yell 936
Yesnaby 923
York 639-49, **640**
York Castle 644
York Minster 641-3, **642**

Yorkshire Dales National
Park 666-77, **668**

Z
Zennor 415-419

Boxed Text

1066 Country Walk 278
Air Travel Glossary 86
Bardsey Pilgrimage 1043
Battle for Stonehenge 341
Birdwatching in the Shetlands 931
Bloody Assizes 322
Bonfire Night 285
Border Reivers 602
Brass Rubbing 76
Brave New World of the
Privatised Railways 109
Britain's First Fast Food 268
British Interior Design 52
Bus Lane to a Fortune 99
Cambridge – A University
Town 553
Centre for Alternative
Technology 1011
Chain Cuisine 54
Chalk Figures 332
Charles Rennie Mackintosh 780
Charlieville 323
Chaucer's Canterbury Tales 262
Cheddar Cheese 370
Christianity & the Synod of
Whitby 658
Cinque Ports 267
Climbers' Friend 607
Coldstream Guards 767
Crofting & the Clearances 891
Daphne du Maurier Trail 422
Decline & Fall of the British Car
Industry 139
Dianamania 151
Doing the Beatles to Death 592
Dracula 659
End to End Records 416
Fens, the 560
Flodden Wall 736
Flora Macdonald 906
Garden of Eden 409

Gay & Lesbian London 235
Gay & Lesbian Manchester 585
Glen Coe Massacre 881
Great Little Trains Of Wales 961
Guess the Theme? 236
Haggis – Scotland's National
Dish 726
Heather & Grouse 650
How to Punt 557
Is It Just For You, Then? 50
John Bunyan & Pilgrim's
Progress 489
Josiah Wedgwood 509
Kings & Queens 131
Ladies of Llangollen 1020
Lawrence Of Arabia 320
Legend of Robin Hood 527
Leicester's Weightiest Citizen 495
Letterboxing 405
Loch Ness Monster 883
London in a Hurry 181
London's Millennium
Attractions 159
Lovespoons 956
Male Voice Choirs 949
Malt Whisky Trail 728
Medieval Guilds 644
Miners of the Forest Of Dean
459
Monarch of the Glen 712
Munros & Munro Bagging 870
No Kilos Please, We're British
39
Old Bard, William Shakespeare
475
On the Elgar Trail 463
Origin of the Broads 545
Over the Bridge to Skye 902
Pictish Symbol Stones 848
Playing the Old Course 837
Pre-Raphaelites and the Arts

and Crafts Movement 481
Puffin Pence 396
Radical Politics 713
Rain, Floods & Divers 299
Return of Rutland 518
Rising of the North 683
Robert Burns 797
Scaling Snowdon 1024
Scapa Flow Wrecks 925
Scotland on Film 722
Scots Abroad 714
Scottish Inventions &
Discoveries 717
Sianel Pedwar Cymru's Success
953
Smuggling on the South Coast
283
Stone of Destiny, the 742
Surfing the Severn Bore 451
Sustrans & the National Cycle
Network 73
Tailor of Gloucester 452
Tanistry: Finding a King 705
Time For Tea? 223
Town of Books, the 1007
Wars – A Hundred Years &
The Roses 127
Wee Frees & other Island
Creeds 909
Wells Cathedral Clock 367
Welsh Rugby 969
What's in A (Pub) Name? 57
What's in a Name? 24
When did Cornish Die? 408
Which Bakewell Pudding? 516
Whither the Weather? 24
Whose Marbles are they
Anyway? 192
World Bog Snorkelling
Championships 1010

MAP LEGEND

BOUNDARIES

——————··············International
——————··············State
— — — — —··············Disputed

HYDROGRAPHY

··············Coastline
··············River, Creek
··············Lake
··············Intermittent Lake
··············Salt Lake
··············Canal
⊚ →》→ ··············Spring, Rapids
→》→ ··············Waterfalls

○ **CAPITAL** ··············National Capital
◉ **CAPITAL** ··············State Capital
● **CITY** ··············City
● Town ··············Town
● Village ··············Village
○ ··············Point of Interest

■ ··············Place to Stay
▲ ··············Camping Ground
⊞ ··············Caravan Park
⌂ ··············Hut or Chalet

▼ ··············Place to Eat
▮ ··············Pub or Bar

ROUTES & TRANSPORT

··············Freeway
··············Highway
··············Major Road
··············Minor Road
══════··············Unsealed Road
··············City Highway
··············City Road
··············City Street, Lane

⇥═══════··············Tunnel
├──┼──●──····Train Route & Station
──────Ⓜ──··············Metro & Station
───────··············Tramway
├═╫═╫═╫═┤··············Cable Car or Chairlift
─────────···Walking Track
─────────··············Ferry Route
··············Pedestrian Mall

AREA FEATURES

··············Building
❀ ··············Park, Gardens
+ + × × ··············Cemetery
··············Market
··············Pedestrian Mall
··············Urban Area

MAP SYMBOLS

✈ ··············Airport
⌒⌒ ··············Ancient or City Wall
∴ ··············Archaeological Site
❸ ··············Bank
🐪 ··············Beach
⚲ ··············Border Crossing
🅰 ··············Castle or Fort
⌒ ··············Cave
⊞ 🅵 ··············Church
⌢⌢ ··············Cliff or Escarpment
○ ··············Embassy
⊕ ··············Hospital
❄ ··············Lookout
☪ ··············Mosque
▲ ··············Mountain or Hill

🏛 ··············Museum
← ··············One Way Street
)(··············Pass
★ ··············Police Station
✉ ··············Post Office
❖ ··············Shopping Centre
⚶ ··············Ski field
🏛 ··············Stately Home
▦ ··············Swimming Pool
✡ ··············Synagogue
☎ ··············Telephone
🎋 ··············Temple
❶ ··············Tourist Information
● ··············Transport
🐾 ··············Zoo

Note: not all symbols displayed above appear in this book

LONELY PLANET OFFICES

Australia
PO Box 617, Hawthorn 3122, Victoria
tel: (03) 9819 1877 fax: (03) 9819 6459
e-mail: talk2us@lonelyplanet.com.au

USA
150 Linden St, Oakland, CA 94607
tel: (510) 893 8555 TOLL FREE: 800 275-8555
fax: (510) 893 8572
e-mail: info@lonelyplanet.com

UK
10a Spring Place, London, NW5 3BH
tel: (0171) 428 4800 fax: (0170) 428 4828
e-mail: go@lonelyplanet.co.uk

France
1 rue du Dahomey, 75011 Paris
tel: 01 55 25 33 00 fax: 01 55 25 33 01
e-mail: bip@lonelyplanet.fr

World Wide Web: www.lonelyplanet.com *or* AOL keyword: lp
Lonely Planet Images: lpi@lonelyplanet.com.au